PLATE 3 The progressive changes in the perceptions and expressed feelings of a psychotic individual are illustrated in this series of paintings made by Vincent Van Gogh between 1884 and 1890. Note the changes in intensity and activity as he moved from quiet country scenes to the swirling lines of his final productions.

Top: Peasant Plowing with Peasant Woman, 1884, Van der Heydt Museum, West Germany.

Middle: The Bridge of L'Anglois, 1888, Kroller-Muller State Museum, Netherlands.

Bottom left: Cornfield and Cypresses, 1889, National Gallery, England.

Bottom right: Road with Cypress and Stars, 1890, Kroller-Muller State Museum, Netherlands.

PSYCHOLOGY:
Understanding Behavior

ROBERT A. BARON

DONN BYRNE

BARRY H. KANTOWITZ

W. B. SAUNDERS COMPANY / Philadelphia / London / Toronto

W. B. Saunders Company: West Washington Square
Philadelphia, PA 19105

1 St. Anne's Road
Eastbourne, East Sussex BN21 3UN, England

1 Goldthorne Avenue
Toronto, Ontario M8Z 5T9, Canada

PSYCHOLOGY: Understanding Behavior

ISBN   0-7216-1568-6

Last digit is the print number: 9   8   7   6   5   4

Dedication

To Sandra, Lois, and Susan,
our most devoted readers and helpful critics.

PREFACE:
A note to our colleagues

What goals should a useful introductory psychology text seek to achieve? Basically, we believe that three are of prime importance. First, the text should provide students with as broad an introduction to the field as possible, without at the same time falling prey to the error of excessive and overwhelming bulk. In the late 1970's, psychology is an amazingly broad and varied field. Thus, it seems only proper that individuals being exposed to it for the first — and perhaps the last — time be provided with as clear a picture of this diversity as possible.

Second, a good text should be as comprehensible, interesting, and helpful to its readers as feasible, consistent with the restrictions of scientific accuracy and breadth of coverage. Textbooks are only useful, after all, to the degree that they are read and digested. Thus, it seems crucial that they be written in a manner which is both appropriate for and appealing to their intended audience.

And finally, we believe that a good text should be as up-to-date and current as its authors can possibly make it. Our field is a rapidly growing and developing one, in which new findings and information are reported on an almost daily basis. As a result, it seems inexcusable to expose beginning students to anything but the "latest word" with respect to the many topics considered.

These three criteria are, to say the least, far from controversial. Moreover, as you undoubtedly know from your own teaching experience, each is competently represented in one or more existing texts. Yet, after both using and examining many such volumes, it is our collective impression that the three desired goals are not adequately combined in any single one. More specifically, we have found that texts which are comprehensive (and often quite long) frequently prove to be less than satisfactory from the point of view of student appeal or comprehensibility. Similarly, those which are interesting and readable often tend to be somewhat lacking in breadth of coverage and scholarly merit. And those which are up-to-date often seem to focus on only a relatively small number of topics which are not entirely representative of the field.

At this point, we should hasten to add that we do not mean to be overly critical of existing texts. Many are quite excellent in a number of respects, and to say otherwise would be incorrect. Rather, we simply wish to note that despite their many strengths, none seems to afford the particular blend of breadth of coverage, intelligibility to students, and contemporaneity of content that we have sought in our own classes.

The present volume, then, grew primarily out of our conviction that these three positive features could in fact be combined within a single text. Not surprisingly, we quickly discovered that stating this goal in principle proved much easier than attaining it in fact. Thus, we decided to adopt a number of specific strategies designed to help us implement our plans. Perhaps these should be explicitly noted.

Turning first to comprehensiveness, we have attempted to achieve this goal by means of three distinct steps. First, we have tried to include coverage of all major topic areas traditionally part of the introductory course — a strategy which, we believe, is reflected in the Table of Contents. Second, within each of these major areas, we have attempted to include as broad a sampling of topics and information as possible, consistent with practical considerations of space, and the parallel goal of adequate depth. Thus, for example, our discussion of learning includes material on modeling, learned helplessness, and constraints upon learning, as well as a consideration of classical and instrumental conditioning. Similarly, our discussion of social behavior includes information on nonverbal communication, aggression, and altruism, as well as more traditional material on attitude change and conformity. Corresponding attempts at maximizing breadth are found throughout the book; indeed, they represent one of its major themes. Finally, we have included two chapters not generally found in introductory texts but which, we feel, reflect recent developments in the field — environmental psychology and human information processing. Our hope is that in combination, these steps have helped us to produce a text which provides a broad introduction to the field, without at the same time running to excessive — and possibly numbing! — length.

Turning to comprehensibility, we found that this important goal also required several specific approaches if it was to be satisfactorily achieved. First, and most importantly, we decided at the outset that in selecting materials for inclusion, we would devote careful attention to their intelligibility and appeal to undergraduate readers, as well as to their scientific importance and value. In a few cases, this has meant omitting highly technical materials from the text which might otherwise have been included. We strongly believe, however, that the gain in communication attained by such actions more than offsets any loss in specific content matter. Second, we have included a number of pedagogical aids designed to increase the usefulness of the text for students. Among these are chapter outlines, chapter summaries, a detailed glossary of terms, and annotated lists of additional, non-technical sources. Third, we have made arrangements with several outstanding colleagues for the production of two different types of student workbook, and for the development of a series of slides which is directly keyed to the text, and especially designed for use in conjunction with it. These supporting materials, we feel, should prove to be of considerable value in helping students comprehend the broad range of information presented. And finally, we have included three distinct types of special text inserts labeled, respectively, "Focus on Research," "Psychology in Action," and "Perspective on Behavior." As noted on pages 31 to 32, these are designed to accomplish markedly different tasks, and are quite distinct both in form and content. Their overall goal, however, is that of helping to slow the often head-long rush of student readers through each chapter, thereby increasing their active involvement with the materials considered.

Finally, turning to the goal of making the book as up-to-date as possible, we have attempted, wherever able, to report the latest available information and findings concerning each of the topics examined. Often, this has meant writing to a number of our colleagues (or conversing directly with them) about their most recent endeavors. In our opinion, this has been effort well spent. In any case, it is reflected in the fact that approximately 65 per cent of all citations in the text have been published since 1970.

In concluding, we should note once again that our overall objective has been that of attaining the combination of comprehensive coverage, comprehensible treatment, and contemporaneity of content outlined earlier. Have we, then, attained our three-part goal? Given that it represents something of an ideal, and considering the imperfect nature of all human endeavors, there can be little doubt that we have fallen somewhat short of its achievement in several different respects. Our fervent hope, however, is that we have at least managed to move somewhat in the appropriate direction. Of course, in an ultimate sense, only you—the readers and users of this text—can tell us to what degree this is true. Thus, we eagerly, and a bit impatiently, await your final judgment.

Robert A. Baron

(center)

Donn Byrne

(right)

Barry Kantowitz

(left)

ACKNOWLEDGMENTS

In writing this text, we have been greatly assisted by a number of individuals. While their contributions to the project are many and varied, they may be divided into four categories.

First, we wish to express our thanks to those individuals who read and commented on portions of the manuscript as it was produced. Their many thoughtful suggestions helped us to markedly improve the content of our work, and we are deeply indebted to them for their assistance. Among the persons we wish to thank in this respect are:

James Booth, Philadelphia Community College
David Cohen, University of Texas at Austin
William Dember, University of Cincinnati
Robert Fried, Hunter College, CUNY
Gordon Gallup, State University of New York, Albany
Richard Kasschau, University of Houston
Eric Knowles, University of Wisconsin, Green Bay
T. S. Krawiec, Skidmore College
Dale Leonard, Purdue University
Leonard Schmaltz, Illinois State University
Delos Wickens, Ohio State University

Second, we wish to express our appreciation to the many colleagues who served as expert consultants, providing us with suggestions as to appropriate content for various chapters prior to their actual production. By pointing us in the right directions and calling attention to important recent work, they made a substantial, positive contribution to the text. Among those we wish to thank in this regard are:

Paul Bell   Mike Domjan   Henry Roediger
Elizabeth Capaldi   Jack Jacoby   Charles Snyder
David Cohen   Judy Langlois   Howard Weiss
                     Dale Leonard

Third, we wish to offer our sincere thanks to the staff of the W. B. Saunders company for their support, assistance, and encouragement during the course of the project. Without their competent and expert help, it would have been all but impossible to produce this volume in anything resembling its present form. Obviously, a great many individuals helped in this regard. Among those to whom we wish to offer special thanks are:

Lorraine Battista   Betty Gittens   Susan O'Neill
Celeste Brennan   John Hackmaster   Frank Polizzano
Dennis Dolan   Grant Lashbrook   Seymour Rotman
Linda Downham   Tom O'Connor   Sandra Simms
Teddy Dunbar   Karen O'Keefe   Walter Verbitski

Finally, deserving of a category all his own, is our Editor, Baxter Venable. From the very beginning, his enthusiasm for the project matched our own. Moreover, it never flagged or lessened throughout the long months of producing the manuscript, revising it, re-revising it, and so on. At many points, he made positive contributions to our work, and helped to guide it to completion. Further, at every stage, he assisted us in translating our plans and ideas into concrete, final form. In short, his participation in the project and personal commitment to it were so great that he must share in the credit for any success it may achieve. To him, especially, we express our genuine, heartfelt thanks.

CONTENTS

6

7

8

9

10

11

14

15

Appendix A

Appendix B

THE NATURE-NURTURE CONTROVERSY REVISITED: Innate Patterns of Behavior

PSYCHOLOGY:
Understanding Behavior

Photo credits: Top left, Hella Hamid, Photo Researchers, Inc. Top right, Hoffmann-La Roche. Bottom left, courtesy of Dr. Harry F. Harlow, University of Wisconsin Primate Laboratory. Bottom right, Elizabeth Hamlin, Stock, Boston.

1 Psychology: Understanding Behavior

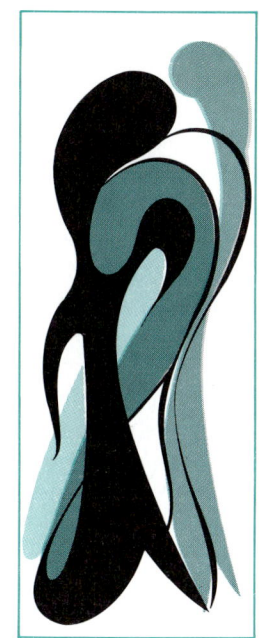

It's late afternoon, and following a long day of classes and labs, you return to your dorm room and collapse on the bed. After a few minutes of rest, you let your gaze wander about the room. On your left is Joan's bed and desk, and, as usual, her possessions are in an unbelievable state of disarray. Clothes are piled randomly on the floor, just where she dropped them days before. Papers, magazines, and books are strewn over the bed and desk, and empty bottles, dirty glasses, and over-flowing ashtrays cover almost every square inch of surface. The stains of dried foods, beverages, and cosmetics can be seen everywhere, or at least wherever they are not concealed by a thick coat of dust, and greasy handprints cover the mirror, walls, and closet door. Shaking your head in disbelief, you turn to the right, and glance at Laurie's part of the room. The contrast is amazing: here, everything is clean, neat, and orderly. All clothes are hung carefully in the closet or folded neatly in the dress-er drawers, the desk top is completely clear, and all papers, magazines, and books are stacked in neat, regular piles. The bed is carefully made, and the floor, walls, and even the window shine in the reflected sunlight, all spotlessly, even antiseptically clean. As you shift your gaze back and forth between the two corners of the room you find yourself wondering what makes these people so different; why is one so neat and the other so sloppy in her personal habits?

"Brrrinnnggg!" It is early morning, and your alarm goes off with an ear-splitting clang. Sleepily, you grope for the switch, and finally succeed in shutting it off. You never like getting up in the morning, but today this task is even worse than usual, for just as the alarm sounded, you were enjoying an unusually pleasant dream. In it, one of your professors was returning an essay exam you took last week, one about which you have been quite concerned. (You didn't prepare for it the way you should

3

have because a football weekend happened to come along at the same time.) As your instructor returned the exam in your dream, he smiled and praised your performance, remarking "Good work, Bill, this is the best paper I've seen in years." And it was just at this delightful point, when you were beginning to bask in the warmth of your success, that the alarm rang and dragged you unwillingly back to reality. For a few moments you lie still in bed, trying to drift back to sleep and resume your dream. Unfortunately, though, you find that you're too awake, and finally give up. Later, as you are shaving, you find yourself wondering about the nature of dreams: why do they occur, what determines their contents, and what purpose, if any, do they serve?

You're standing around at a party talking to some friends and having a very pleasant time, when suddenly you hear a familiar voice remark: "Hi, Sandy, how are you? I didn't know you were here." Looking over your shoulder, you recognize a girl who sat near you in one of your classes last semester. As she approaches, the conversation comes to a halt, and everyone looks in your direction, clearly expecting you to introduce her to the group. A sudden wave of panic sweeps over you as you realize that try as you may, you can't remember her name! This is particularly upsetting, because you've heard it dozens of times, and feel that it's on the very tip of your tongue. For a few seconds you struggle vainly, trying to bring it to mind. Just as you give up and begin to mumble a weak excuse, however, you are literally saved by the bell: someone shouts from across the room that you are wanted on the phone. Greatly relieved, you beat a hasty retreat, leaving your acquaintance to make her own introductions. A few minutes later, when you've gotten off the phone and are in the process of pouring yourself another drink, her name suddenly pops into your mind. You've had experiences like this before, but now you begin to wonder why they occur. Why, you ask yourself, do we sometimes seem to forget things we know very well; and why do they sometimes come flashing back to us later, at times when we're not even trying to recall them? Something must be going on beneath the surface, but what?

You're sitting at a table in a crowded cafeteria when a neatly dressed young man approaches and asks: "Do you mind if I sit here?" Since there seem to be no other seats available, you answer "Not at all," and shift a bit to make room for him. Because you know that it is not polite to stare at other persons in a restaurant, you avoid looking directly at him as he prepares to eat his meal. But this doesn't stop you from noticing his very unusual actions. First, he takes a large white cloth from his coat and uses it to wipe off both the seat and table very carefully. Next, he removes a can of disinfectant from his brief case and proceeds to spray the entire area. Completing this activity, he sits down and, donning plastic gloves, pulls his own knife, fork, and spoon from his pocket. You've watched these actions with growing anxiety, and when he now begins to tie a surgical mask on to his face, you decide that you've had enough to eat, and get up to leave. As you hurry from the cafeteria, you wonder what could have led this perfectly normal-appearing individual to engage in such strange and unsettling actions. More generally, you wonder what causes people to "go off the deep end" and develop serious behavior problems.

For days your friend Becky has done nothing but rave about her new and exciting boyfriend. From her descriptions, you can only conclude that he is one of the best-looking and most intelligent, considerate, and sophisticated men on campus. In fact, he sounds so great that you've been dying to meet him yourself. Since Becky is bringing him to your apartment for dinner, you won't have much longer to wait, and, in fact, at this very moment the doorbell rings, and the loving twosome enters.

As Becky introduces you to her "dreamboat," you begin to doubt your own eyesight, for instead of the vision of male beauty you had expected, you find yourself looking at a young man whose features remind you more of Ronald MacDonald than Paul Newman or Robert Redford. Wishing to give Becky the benefit of the doubt, and thinking that perhaps it is his sparkling personality and flashing wit she finds so attractive, you decide to reserve judgment. During dinner, however, you notice that the object of her affections is also far from impressive in these departments. He makes one embarrassing, inappropriate remark after another, and his sense of humor seems more likely to produce indigestion than laughter. Further, his table manners are the worst you have ever seen—he grabs wildly at all the food in sight, wipes his mouth on his sleeve, and knocks over his glass time and time again. Yet, you notice that throughout all these unpleasant events, Becky continues to gaze at him with obvious rapture, a loving smile fixed upon her face. After they leave, you sit surrounded by the dirty dishes, reflecting upon the strange and mysterious nature of love. What, you ask yourself, can Becky possibly see in this obnoxious person? How can she find him so attractive when you find him so repulsive?

Have you ever found yourself pondering questions such as these? In all probability you have. In fact, we think there is a very good chance that curiosity about yourself, your behavior, and the actions of other persons played an important part in your decision to enroll in introductory psychology. That is, you may well have signed up for the class because of a desire to understand both yourself and others more fully. Fortunately, we believe that you will be far from disappointed in these hopes. Psychology, in the late 1970's, is a tremendously broad and diversified field which employs the methods of modern science to delve into virtually every imaginable aspect of human behavior. Thus, while we can't promise to provide answers to all of your questions— psychologists themselves are still very far from this goal—we feel confident that we can provide at least partial replies to many. For example, included in a very small sample of the issues we will consider are the following:

What is sleep, and why do we need it?

Does ESP (extrasensory perception) actually exist?

What are the causes of abnormal, disturbed behavior, and how can such problems be treated?

How do we acquire a sense of morality—the ability to tell right from wrong?

Can people communicate with each other through "body language," without the use of speech?

What are illusions, and why do they occur?

How do heat, crowding, and unpleasant noise affect our emotional states, health, and behavior?

Do various racial or ethnic groups differ in intelligence? And if so, what is the basis for such differences?

What happens when people (and perhaps animals as well) give up hope?

Does exposure to hard-core pornography actually encourage the performance of various sex crimes?

While we would prefer to turn at once to these and many other interesting issues, there seem to be strong grounds for introducing a slight delay at this point. Specifically, we feel that it is important to arm you with certain background information about the nature and methods of psychology before plunging directly into its fascinating but often complex findings. As a result, we will employ the remainder of this initial chapter for accomplishing four preliminary tasks.

First, we will provide you with a capsule overview of psychology's origins and early development. Such information will be presented because of our belief that your understanding of the present state of the field, and the directions in which it is moving, will be enhanced by some conception of its roots and early growth. In short, we feel that it may be easier to understand what psychology is all about, where it is now, and where it seems to be going if you know something about where it has been.

Second, we will present some general information about psychology as it exists in the 1970's, touching on such issues as who psychologists are, how they are trained, and what they do. Our past experience suggests that there is much confusion regarding these issues both on campus and off, so a few pages devoted to the task of eliminating such misunderstandings seem in order.

Third, and perhaps most important of all, we will examine the methods employed by psychologists in their attempts to investigate behavior. We feel that this is a particularly crucial task, for unless you have a clear understanding of the manner in which psychologists conduct their investigations, you will often be left wondering, at later points in the book, how the specific facts or findings we report were obtained.

Finally, we will provide information regarding several special features of this book. These have been included in an attempt to make the text easier to understand, more convenient to use, and—we hope—more stimulating to read. Whether they succeed in these respects is, of course, largely for you to determine. But in any case, since you probably have not encountered several of these features in other volumes, we feel that it may be useful to call them to your attention right at the start.

PSYCHOLOGY: A CAPSULE MEMOIR

As you can probably guess from your own interest in such matters, human beings have always puzzled over the roots of their own behavior, the functioning of their bodies, the working of their minds, and the nature of their relations with others. In an important sense, therefore, the subject matter of psychology is very old—perhaps as old as humanity itself. Until fairly recent times, however, most attempts to gather information concerning human behavior were based largely upon speculation and informal observation. Thoughtful individuals (often poets, philosophers, or historians) would raise important questions regarding various aspects of human nature, and then attempt to answer them by means of reasonable guesses, common sense, or casual inspection of their own and others' behavior. Sometimes, of course, these approaches yielded insightful suggestions regarding human behavior or characteristics. For example, there appear to be important truths behind such statements as "Revenge is sweet," or "Like father like son, like mother like daughter." In many other instances, however, such speculation led only to inconsistent or even contradictory conclusions. Thus, the wisdom of the ages tells us that "Haste makes waste," but cautions us that "He who hesitates is lost." Similarly, we are informed that "Out of sight" often leads to "out of mind," while being told at the same time that "Absence makes the heart grow fonder." We could go on to mention many other examples, but by now the major point should be clear: so-called "knowledge" about human emotions, behavior, or thought based solely on informal observation and common sense often turns out to be misleading, confusing, or false (see Figure 1–1).

FIGURE 1–1 **Informal observation often yields inconsistent explanations of human behavior.** (© **King Features Syndicate, Inc., 1974.**)

Given the inconclusive and unsatisfactory nature of such knowledge, it seems only reasonable to expect that sooner or later, someone would hit upon the idea of using the highly effective methods of the natural sciences (physics and chemistry, for example) to unravel the mysteries of human feelings, behavior, and thought. Unfortunately, in this case such a breakthrough came later rather than sooner, and it was not until the closing decades of the nineteenth century that the idea of a scientific field of psychology took firm root. The reasons for this delay are quite complex, and generally beyond the scope of this discussion. Basically, though, they center around the fact that prior to that time, the notion of a scientific psychology was simply an idea whose time had not yet come. Largely for religious and philosophical reasons, most persons—including scientists—were reluctant to view their own behavior as a suitable topic for scientific study. Instead, they chose to perceive it as a unique type of puzzle we could never hope to solve. Under such conditions, suggestions for a scientific psychology were simply rejected out of hand and had little effect upon the study of human behavior.

Fortunately, this situation had begun to change quite radically by the 1860's and '70's. Many philosophers became convinced that all events, including behavior and mental processes, follow basic laws, and can be studied by scientific means (Bergmann, 1966). At the same time, rapid strides in the fields of medicine and physiology stemming from the use of scientific procedures pointed to the conclusion that similar advances could be made with respect to the understanding of behavior through related techniques. Together, such developments rendered the existing intellectual climate much more favorable to the notion of a science of behavior, and set the stage for its rapid emergence upon the scene.

Before turning to the origins and early development of psychology, we should pause to comment briefly on the suggestion that psychology can be viewed as the *science* of behavior. Our past teaching experience suggests that some of you, at least, will take strong exception to this view, objecting that even today psychology is not a science in the same sense as chemistry, physics,

Psychology: Science or Art?

or biology. While we support your right to disagree, and have no wish to "brain-wash" you to our way of thinking, it is our firm conviction that such objections often stem from a basic but widespread misunderstanding regarding the meaning of the word science.

Many persons seem to assume that this term refers to specific fields of study, such as chemistry physics, or geology, and that only such areas can be appropriately described as scientific in nature. Actually, though, it refers to a general set of methods which are largely independent of any specific topic area, and can be applied to answering questions of many different types. As we shall soon see in more detail, these general methods largely involve systematic observation and direct experimentation. And to the extent that they are employed by any field of study, it may appropriately be described as scientific. In short, what is crucial is the approach taken and the general methods employed, not the particular topics under investigation.

Because the fields mentioned above (e.g., chemistry, physics) have existed for several centuries and attained great success, we are most familiar with the use of the scientific method in them. In fact, the image of an astronomer peering through a telescope, or a biologist bending over his or her microscope, forms part of our basic cultural heritage. But the scientific method can also be employed to study many other topics as well. For example, it can — and has been — successfully employed to investigate such diverse topics as the structure of primitive cultures, the origins and development of language, and the nature of long-dead civilizations.

Similarly, the basic methods of science can be employed by psychologists to study many fascinating aspects of behavior. Of course, when the scientific method is adapted to the study of behavior, the actual procedures followed and the specific equipment employed may differ greatly from those used in other fields. You should not find this either surprising or confusing: scientists always adapt their methods and apparatus to the problem at hand. For example, we would not expect to find an astronomer seeking to study distant galaxies with an electron microscope, or a biologist seeking to study cellular growth with a huge reflecting telescope. By the same token, it would be unreasonable to expect psychologists to use lasers to study attitudes, or test tubes to study hidden motives. Yet, the fact that they employ different procedures, measuring devices, and apparatus for these tasks does not make their work any less scientific. What is crucial is the basic approach taken. So long as methods based on systematic observation and direct experimentation are strictly followed, the term science, we feel, is quite appropriate.

To make a long story short, we believe that psychology can reasonably be viewed as the science of behavior because in their work, psychologists are committed to and rely very heavily upon the scientific method. The topics they seek to study may differ from those in the older and more traditional fields of science, but the general methods followed are basically the same.

Looking Back: The Early Years

As we noted above, the notion of a scientific psychology began to attain widespread acceptance in the latter half of the nineteenth century. Unfortunately, it is difficult to point to a specific date for the birth of this new field, because it actually took root in a very gradual manner. Most authorities, however, point to the years between 1860 and 1880 as the period during which psychology finally emerged as an independent field (Boring, 1950). The beginning of this period was marked by the publication of one of the first major books concerned with psychology, Gustav Fechner's *Elements of Psychophysics*. The close was marked in 1879, in Leipzig, Germany, with the founding by Wilhelm Wundt of the first laboratory devoted solely to psychological

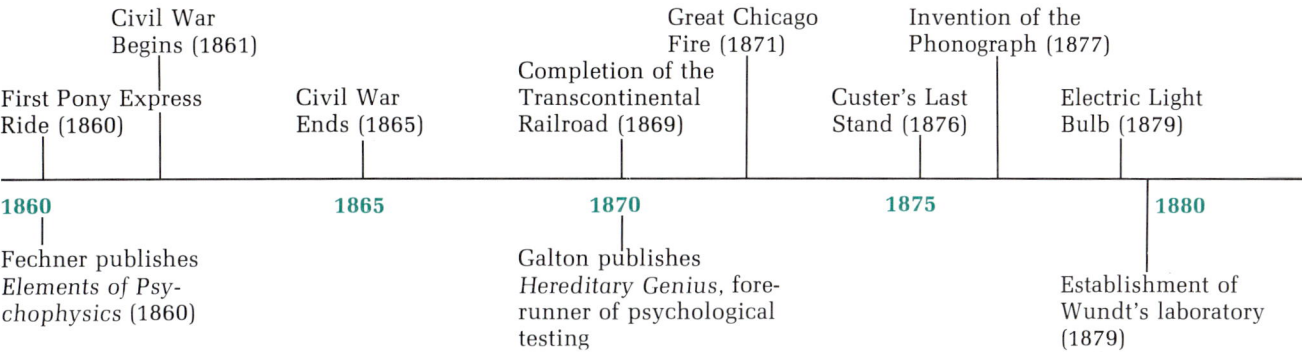

FIGURE 1–2 **Psychology emerges. As shown above, the years during which psychology took root as an independent field (roughly 1860–1880) were marked by many other important events.**

research. Dates are always somewhat abstract, so in order to make these a bit more meaningful, we have summarized in Figure 1–2 some of the other significant events which occurred during this period. As you can see, psychology began to take shape at about the same time that the pony express made its first ride, continued to develop during the years of the American Civil War, and was firmly established as an independent field of study by the time Edison completed development of the electric light bulb.

Although early psychologists agreed that their field should be scientific in orientation, they disagreed strongly about almost everything else. In particular, they argued sharply over two major issues: (1) what precisely should the new psychology study, and (2) how should it go about performing this task? Because the struggles over these issues—and their final resolution—left a lasting impact upon the field, we will briefly consider several of these opposing viewpoints or orientations.

As noted above, Wilhelm Wundt established the first psychological laboratory in 1879, an action which has sometimes earned him the title "the father of experimental psychology." But Wundt did not stop there; he also proposed a view of what the new psychology should do, a view which dominated the field for more than two decades. Basically, Wundt held that the major task of psychology should be that of analyzing the contents of consciousness in order to determine the *structure* of the mind. That is, he held that the complex contents of human consciousness should be broken down into simpler and simpler components until, finally, the basic elements of which the mind itself is composed would be revealed. In order to accomplish this difficult task, he proposed employing the method of *introspection*, in which specially trained individuals would report in great detail on their conscious experiences in standardized, laboratory settings. For example, when shown a specific painting, an observer would attempt to describe the simplest experiences of which his or her reactions were composed. Thus, instead of reporting "I see a painting of a peaceful landscape," or some such general description, the observer would describe his or her sensations of various colors, brightness, and so on. On the basis of such investigations, Wundt and his colleagues finally concluded that the mind is actually composed of three simple elements: **sensations**—reactions produced by external stimuli, **images**—reactions generated by the mind itself, as when we remember some scene we have witnessed in the past, and **feelings**—the emotions which accompany various experiences.

Structuralism:
Analyzing the Mind

If you are having trouble relating such work to our definition of psychology as the science of behavior or to the intriguing questions mentioned on p. 5, don't be alarmed. Neither the topics studied by structuralists nor the methods they employed have survived the test of time. However, the strict insistence by Wundt and his followers that psychology adopt the rigorous, careful methods of investigation employed by such fields as physics and chemistry did survive, and helped place psychology on a firm scientific footing. It is in this manner rather than through their futile attempts to analyze the contents of the mind that structuralists contributed to the development of their chosen field.

Functionalism: The Mind in Action

As we have already mentioned, structuralism did not long hold a dominant and unchallenged position among early psychologists. Its assumptions regarding the methods and scope of psychology were soon questioned by a number of young rebels, many of them Americans, known as **functionalists.** These scholars called attention to the fact that the mind—and the intelligence it produces—is the most important adaptive organ at humanity's disposal. That is, the mind more than anything else has contributed to mankind's continued survival. As a result, they argued, it is far more important for psychologists to study the mind's functions—the ways in which the mind helps human beings cope with a challenging and constantly changing environment—than merely to analyze its basic structure.

While this may well seem like a very subtle difference to you, it is actually a very important one, for it opens the door to interest in the relationship between mind and behavior. Thus, in contrast to structuralism, functionalism—which numbered such individuals as William James and John Dewey among its supporters—saw a place for the study of overt behavior within the scope of psychology. In this sense, it was much more modern in its orientation and, in some ways, stood on the very threshold of a science of behavior.

Behaviorism: Actions Instead of Mind

It has sometimes been suggested that given enough time, functionalism would have evolved into an approach highly similar to modern psychology; as we mentioned above, it seemed to be on essentially the right track (see Bergmann, 1966). Unfortunately, though, we shall never know if this would have been the case, because before it had a chance to do much more than issue its challenge to structuralism, both functionalism and its earlier predecessor were consigned to the dustbin of history by the advent of the only "ism" destined to survive—**behaviorism.**

This new approach burst suddenly upon the field in 1913, appearing first in the form of an article by a brilliant but brash young scholar named John B. Watson (see Figure 1–3). In his paper, which he chose to title "Psychology as the Behaviorist Views It," "Watson argued strongly and convincingly for the suggestion that mental states (that is, the contents of the mind) are essentially private events forever outside the realm of objective science. The proper subject matter of psychology, he contended, is not such conscious experience, but rather **behavior**—overt actions capable of direct observation and measurement. In short, Watson argued, and rightly so, that we can never know another's experiences directly, and that as a result, such data can never serve as the basis for an objective science of psychology. In his own words (Watson, 1924, p. 6):

> The behaviorist asks: Why don't we make what we can *observe* the real field of psychology? Let us limit ourselves to things that can be observed, and formulate laws concerning only those things. Now what can we observe? We can observe *behavior—what the organism does or says* . . . .

FIGURE 1–3   John B. Watson, founder of behaviorism. His suggestion that psychology should focus on overt behavior rather than "mind" drastically altered the field, and gave it its modern flavor and emphasis. However, Watson went too far in suggesting that mental processes are of little interest or importance. (Courtesy of James B. Watson.)

Going still further, he rejected introspection as a legitimate method of study, recommending direct experimentation and controlled observation—the basic methods of science we mentioned earlier—in its place.

Watson's views had an immediate and profound effect upon psychology. In fact, his suggestions won such rapid and general acceptance that behavior quickly replaced conscious experience as the prime topic of psychological research, an emphasis which has persisted down to the present time. As is often the case with individuals possessing powerful convictions, however, Watson tended to go a bit too far in arguing for his views, and some of the extreme positions he adopted produced unforeseen and unfortunate effects.

First, in arguing against making conscious experience the basic subject matter of psychology, Watson often seemed to suggest that mental processes and events are unimportant—or even totally nonexistent. Under the influence of these views, psychologists tended to ignore such topics, closing their eyes to the important effects upon behavior of such cognitive (i.e., mental) factors as attention, expectations, and feelings of hope or despair. Indeed, it is only in very recent years that such topics have become respectable subjects for study once again.

Similarly, Watson held the rather extreme view that all behavior is learned, even boasting (as in the following quote) that he could make any healthy infant into virtually any kind of adult simply by controlling all its experiences (Watson, 1924, p. 104):

I should like to go one step further now and say, "Give me a dozen healthy infants, well-formed, and my own specified world to bring them up in and I'll guarantee to take any one at random and train him to become any type of specialist I might select—doctor, lawyer, artist, merchant-chief, and yes, even begger-man and thief, regardless of his talents, penchants, tendencies, abilities, vocations. . . .

This extreme emphasis upon the effects of learning led psychologists to neglect the impact of genetic determinants of behavior for several decades, and again, only recently has the pendulum begun to swing the other way (Mason and Lott, 1976).

Despite these negative features, Watson's insistence that psychology should deal primarily with behavior rather than conscious experience rescued the field from its early, floundering attempts to analyze the mind. The founding of behaviorism, then, was an important turning point. Prior to its development, psychology was following an essentially dead-end path; afterward, it was firmly on the track toward its fully modern form.

Decades of Growth: Psychology Comes of Age

In the years since Watson's call for a psychology focused on behavior, the field has grown tremendously in terms of both size and scope. With respect to size, the American Psychological Association—the professional organization to which most psychologists in the U.S. belong—has increased from slightly over 1,000 members in 1930 to more than 40,000 in the late 1970's (see Figure 1–4). This spectacular growth in numbers has been matched by an equally impressive expansion in scope, so that at present, many different perspectives, interests, and approaches coexist within the field. Perhaps one of the best ways of providing you with some flavor of psychology's present diversity is that of noting that at one recent national convention, papers on the following broad range of topics were presented simultaneously in different rooms on a single morning: the effects of drugs upon memory; the manner in which we form impressions of others; the relative powerlessness of women in American society; mystical religious experiences; sexual therapy; language development in young children; the uses of hypnosis; and purchasing decisions by consumers.

At the same time that psychologists have expanded their interests so dramatically, they have shown lessened willingness to eliminate whole areas of investigation from the field simply because they do not fall within the limited boundaries outlined by Watson and other early behaviorists. As a result, there has been increasing recognition of the importance of such mental processes as images and expectations, as well as renewed interest in the genetic bases of behavior (Mason and Lott, 1976). Further, the past two decades have witnessed an increasing emphasis upon the application of psychological knowledge and principles to the solution of many practical problems. Given these developments, it seems reasonable to suggest that after a turbulent youth and active adolescence, psychology has truly begun to come into its own in the present, exciting decade.

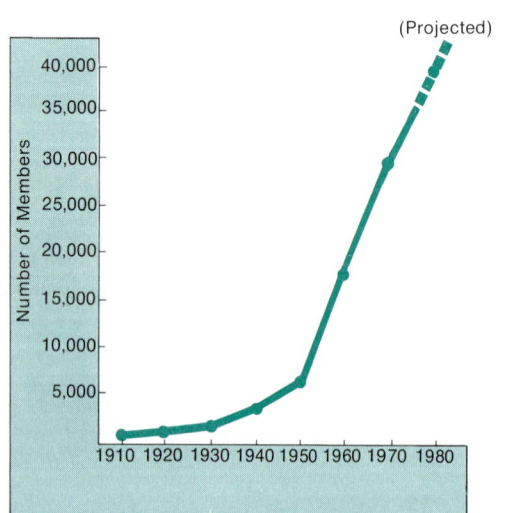

FIGURE 1–4 Psychology's own "population explosion." The number of psychologists in the U.S. has increased from 228 in 1910 to approximately 40,000 in the late 1970's.

Would you recognize a psychologist if you saw one? What would he or she probably be doing? And where would you be most likely to encounter such professionals? These seem like relatively simple and straightforward questions; yet, there is a surprising degree of confusion about them. Many people are far from clear on the subject of who psychologists are, where they work, and what they do. In the present section, we will attempt to cast some light on each of these basic issues.

The terms "psychiatrist" and "psychologist" seem quite similar, and are often used interchangeably by many persons. Yet in reality, they refer to two distinctly different groups of professionals. Psychiatrists are physicians who, after completing standard medical studies and receiving the M.D. degree, go on to specialize in the treatment of mental disorders.

In contrast, psychologists receive the bulk of their training in academic departments of psychology at major universities, where they earn the Ph.D. degree, generally after four or five years of study. Their graduate education is focused primarily upon the principles and findings of psychology, and includes a considerable amount of training in the fine points of behavioral research. Indeed, in order to qualify for the Ph.D., they must complete a relatively large-scale research project of their own design, under the guidance of a committee of established scholars.

One reason for the widespread confusion regarding the distinction between psychology and psychiatry lies in the fact that some psychologists specialize in the study and treatment of abnormal behavior. Thus, they tend to focus on many of the same problems and engage in many of the same activities as their medical colleagues. Indeed, members of the two professions often work together in the same institutions. Since only *some* psychologists choose to specialize in the study of abnormal behavior, though, the two fields overlap only to a degree, and remain essentially separate and distinct professions.

Before concluding our discussion of who psychologists are, we should turn briefly to a question often asked by the students in our classes: "How can I become one?" We have already supplied part of the answer in our comments about the training received by most psychologists, but perhaps some additional information will be useful.

The first step, of course, is that of completing an undergraduate major in psychology. The requirements for this vary greatly from school to school, but most departments require a course in statistics and at least one laboratory class (usually concerned with experimental psychology), as well as a number of electives in psychology and related fields. Unfortunately, a bachelor's degree does not qualify one as a psychologist. In fact, in most states it would be illegal to lay claim to this title without further training, much as it would be illegal to call oneself a physician after completing only a pre-med program of study. The next step, then, is graduate study leading to the M.A. (master of arts), Ph.D. (doctor of philosophy), or both. In recent years, the competition for admission to graduate programs in psychology has become so intense that simply getting accepted by the department of one's choice can prove to be quite a difficult task. And once one is admitted to such a program, several years of difficult and challenging study lie ahead. Completing the requirements for a master's degree usually involves at least one to two years of training, while completing those for a Ph.D. generally involves a minimum of four years of study, and in many cases an additional year of practical experience in an applied setting (e.g., an internship in a hospital, clinic, or school). Within the past decade, some institutions—including several professional schools of psychology which are independent of universities and academic departments — have begun offering a new degree known as the Doctor of Psychology. The training for this degree places less emphasis upon research and more upon the practical applications of psychological knowledge than does traditional training for the Ph.D. Since the future of such programs is still uncertain, however, we will not comment upon them further.

As you can probably see by now, becoming a psychologist involves quite a large investment of time and effort. As a result, the decision to choose a career in psychology should not be made quickly or lightly, but only after very careful consideration. We personally feel that such a career offers many rewards and fulfillments, but admittedly we're biased, and this is a decision which each individual must make for him or herself.

What: The Different Specialties of Psychology

As noted earlier, some psychologists specialize in the study and treatment of abnormal behavior. Individuals who choose to concentrate their attention in this area are generally known as **clinical psychologists,** and, as can be seen in Figure 1–5A, they constitute the largest single group within the field.

Closely related to clinical psychology is the field of **counseling psychology.** Counseling psychologists specialize in helping individuals who are experiencing many types of personal difficulties — but who show no signs of mental disorder — to resolve their problems. For example, counseling psychologists might assist a recently retired individual in coming to terms with his or her changed status or life-style. In addition, they also frequently advise indivi-

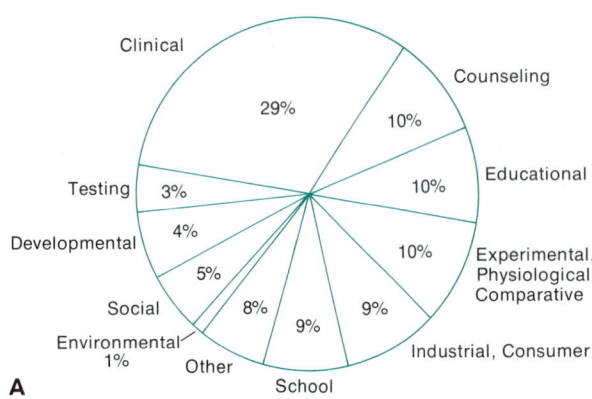

A

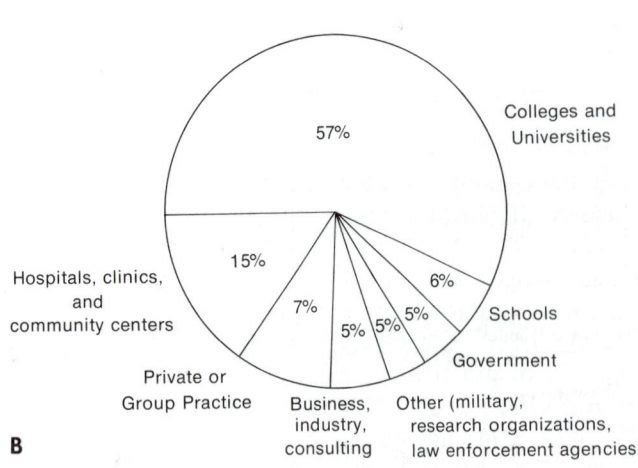

B

FIGURE 1–5 *A.* Major specialties within psychology. Different groups of psychologists focus their attention upon diverse aspects of behavior. (Figures shown are the per cent of psychologists identified with each specialty; based on data from Cates, 1970.)

B. Where psychologists work. A majority are employed in educational institutions such as colleges and universities, but they also work in many other settings as well. (Based on data from Boneau and Cuca, 1974.)

duals in the choice of an appropriate occupation, one consistent with their abilities and interests as revealed by various psychological tests.

School psychologists perform many of the same functions as counseling psychologists, providing counseling and guidance to students *in the schools*. In addition, they often conduct programs of psychological testing in order to identify and ultimately assist individuals with special problems, such as unusually low or high intelligence.

Schools are also the major focus of **educational psychologists,** who frequently work with individual students experiencing difficulties in their studies. In addition, though, educational psychologists often seek means of improving the overall educational process, concentrating their attention on such tasks as the development of more effective methods of teaching or programs of study.

In contrast, **industrial psychologists** focus their attention on the "world of work," specializing in such tasks as improving worker morale, selecting appropriate personnel (i.e., the best person for the job), and developing effective methods of training. A closely related group, **consumer psychologists,** seeks to determine factors which influence consumer decisions. Thus, among the topics they study are the influence of advertising on purchase decisions, the basis of brand loyalty, and reasons for the acceptance or rejection of new products by consumers.

As might be suspected from the name of their specialty, **social psychologists** focus their attention upon the nature of social interaction. More specifically, they attempt to determine the manner in which the behavior of one individual is influenced or determined by the actions of others (what they say or do). Their interest in this general topic leads social psychologists to investigate such interesting and diverse forms of social behavior as aggression, attraction, persuasion, helping, competition, and obedience.

Social behavior also forms one of the major concerns of **developmental psychologists,** who seek to investigate changes in behavior which occur with age across the entire span of life. For example, a developmental psychologist might seek to determine whether willingness to help others varies with age, perhaps starting low and then increasing through adulthood. The interests of such psychologists are in no way restricted to social behavior, however, and they also examine corresponding changes in many other forms of activity (e.g., the acquisition of language, or the growth of a sense of morality).

The principles governing basic psychological processes such as perception, learning, and motivation are of primary concern to **experimental psychologists.** These scientists seek to answer such questions as: How do we perceive the world around us? What motivates behavior? How do we learn in various situations? Because the processes they investigate are thought to be among the most basic or important, the work of experimental psychologists is often viewed as essential to and underlying the other specialties we have considered so far.

Still another group—**physiological psychologists**—seeks to examine the biological bases of behavior. Thus, among the many topics studied by these scientists are the biochemical reactions underlying memory and learning, and the role of various portions of the brain in the regulation of such motives as hunger or thirst and such basic processes such as sleep. In short, the work of physiological psychologists often carries them to the hazy boundary between psychology on the one hand and biological science on the other.

One final area we should mention, both because of its recent phenomenal growth and because it will serve as the subject of a later chapter, is **environmental psychology.** Psychologists working in this new and vigorous specialty are concerned with the effects of the environment—both physical and social—upon behavior. Thus, they seek to examine the manner in which such factors as heat, noise, and crowding influence our feelings, actions, and even health. Although it is a relatively new area of study, environmental psychology already promises to make important contributions to such fields as urban planning, architecture, and even transportation.

Although our list is far from complete, and there are many other areas we have not even mentioned, it should be sufficient to convince you of one important fact: the interests and activities of psychologists in the 1970's are extremely diverse. Thus, our answer to the question "What do psychologists do?" is, quite simply, many different things.

Where: Psychologists at Work

Since psychologists have diverse interests and perform many different tasks, ranging from therapy and testing on the one hand through basic scientific research on the other, it might be expected that they would find employment in a wide range of settings. That this is indeed the case is indicated by a recent survey conducted with a sizable proportion of the more than 40,000 psychologists now at work in the U.S. (Boneau and Cuca, 1974). The results of this survey are illustrated in Figure 1–5B, where it can be seen that by far the largest group is employed by colleges and universities. Although this proportion has begun to drop in recent years as college enrollments have stabilized or even decreased, it continues to remain quite high for two important reasons. First, as you probably know, psychology is a very popular field; almost everyone wishes to take a course or two in it before graduation. As a result, the demand for qualified instructors has always been higher than in many other areas. Second, as noted earlier, almost all psychologists—even those who work in relatively applied fields—receive their basic training in academic departments at major universities. Thus, as the demand for clinical, counseling, school, and educational psychologists has grown, so too has the need for qualified faculties capable of training them. As a result, many psychologists are currently employed by institutions of higher learning, where their efforts are divided between the tasks of teaching, training future psychologists, and basic research.

Since more psychologists specialize in clinical and counseling areas than in any other fields, it is not surprising to find another large group at work in settings where they can put these skills to use. Thus, many psychologists find employment in hospitals, guidance centers, or clinics, where they engage in various forms of therapy, counseling, and testing. Some choose to engage in private practice on a full-time basis (most states now license psychologists for such activities), but this is still the exception rather than the rule. More common is the situation in which a psychologist employed at a hospital or clinic also maintains a relatively small private practice on a part-time basis.

Other psychologists are employed in the personnel divisions of large corporations, branches of the armed services, various governmental agencies, the advertising industry, and even large labor unions. In short, they may be found busily at work in almost any setting where expert knowledge regarding human behavior is of benefit—just about everywhere.

METHODS OF PSYCHOLOGICAL RESEARCH: IN QUEST OF UNDERSTANDING

Because "common sense" and informal observation generally yield confusing and inconsistent findings, psychologists turned, long ago, to more rigorous methods for studying human behavior. Since acquaintance with these techniques will help you both to understand and to interpret many of the findings presented in later portions of this volume, several will now be described.

Because it is generally held to be the most powerful weapon in the psychologist's arsenal of research techniques, the experimental method will be our starting point. Although students often assume that there is something very mystifying or complex about this approach, it is, in its basic logic, remarkably simple and straightforward. Essentially, an investigator employing this technique attempts to determine whether a given factor influences some form of behavior; he or she does this by (1) systematically varying the factor's presence or strength, and (2) observing whether such variations have any effects upon the behavior under study. The factor systematically varied by the experimenter is usually termed the **independent variable,** while the behavior studied is termed the **dependent variable.** In a typical experiment, then, subjects are assigned to various groups corresponding to different levels of the independent variable (e.g., low, moderate, high), and their behavior is measured or observed to determine whether it is in fact affected by such variations. If this proves to be the case and, very importantly, if it can also be assumed that other factors which might have influenced subjects' actions have been held relatively constant across groups, it is concluded that the independent variable is indeed one of the determinants of the behavior under study. Perhaps a few concrete examples will help illustrate the nature of these procedures.

First, imagine that as a psychologist with interests in social behavior, you wished to investigate the suggestion (or **hypothesis,** as it is often termed in science) that people's willingness to offer help to others is strongly influenced by their current mood. That is, the better they feel, the more willing they are to help. This suggestion about the relationship between mood and helping might stem from a **theory** about such behavior (a systematic set of assumptions regarding its nature and causes), from the findings of previous research, or even from informal observation. Regardless of its source, you might decide to examine its accuracy by means of the experimental method. Thus, you might begin by exposing one group of subjects to conditions designed to make them feel happy—for example, praise, success on some task, a large and potent cocktail—while exposing a second group (which in this case would be termed the **control** condition) to more neutral circumstances—no praise, success, or drink. Then, as a final step, you might provide individuals in both conditions with an opportunity to help others (for example, a chance to donate time or money to some worthwhile cause). If those in the group made to feel "good" did indeed show greater willingness to help, you would have evidence that your *independent variable*—the way people feel—is in fact one of the determinants of your *dependent variable*—kindness toward others. Such procedures have actually been employed in several different experiments. For example, in a study performed by Alice Isen (1970), one group of subjects was made to feel good by being informed that they had succeeded on some tasks, while a second was made to feel bad by being told that they had failed miserably. Following these experiences, individuals in both groups were provided with an opportunity to make donations to a worthy cause (a fund to purchase air conditioning for a local school). As can be seen in Figure 1–6, results clearly supported the hypothesis that people who feel good will often be more generous toward others than will those who feel bad: subjects who experienced the "warm glow of success" contributed much more money to the fund than did those who experienced the "cool gloom of failure."

As a second example of the experimental method, consider the task you would face if, as a psychologist interested in child development, you wished to examine the impact of televised violence upon children's behavior. Specifically, suppose you began with the tentative hypothesis that exposure to

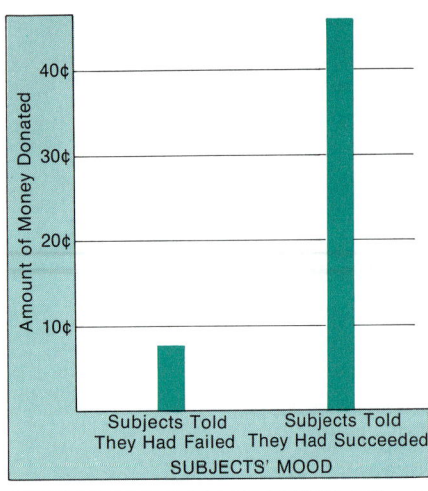

FIGURE 1–6 The effects of mood upon helping. Subjects made to feel "good" by being told that they had succeeded on some tasks made larger donations than those made to feel "bad" by being told that they had failed. (Based on data from Isen, 1970.)

televised violence increases the willingness of young viewers to attack and harm others. In order to study this issue, you might first expose one group of children to an extremely violent program, a second group to a moderately aggressive program, and a third group to a nonaggressive show. Immediately following exposure to these programs, you might allow the children to engage in free play while you observed their behavior through a one-way mirror or from an unobtrusive corner of the room. If your observations then revealed that those exposed to the extremely violent program were more aggressive than were those who witnessed the moderately violent show, and that these young-sters in turn were somewhat more aggressive than those who watched the peaceful, nonaggressive program, you would have some indication that ex-posure to televised violence does indeed seem to increase children's willing-ness to harm other persons, at least for short periods of time. That is, you would have some evidence that your independent variable—the degree of aggressive content in television shows—is in fact a determinant of your dependent vari-able—children's aggressive behavior. Again, such procedures have actually been followed in a number of recent experiments, and the results of these investigations point to the conclusion that exposure to televised violence does indeed increase children's willingness to attack and harm others (e.g., Kaplan and Singer, 1976).

Behavior and its Multiple Determin-ants: The Concept of Interaction

If our actions were influenced by only one factor at a time, the task of con-ducting psychological research would be a relatively simple one. Unfortun-ately, though, our feelings, behavior, and thoughts are usually influenced by many different factors operating simultaneously. Because of this fact, research-ers often conduct experiments in which several different factors, each believed to affect the behavior under study, are varied at once. The major advantage of such procedures is that they permit us to investigate the possibility of **interactions** between the independent variables—cases in which the effects of one are influenced or determined by another. Although this may sound very complex, it is actually quite straightforward. Once again, though, the best means of communicating the meaning of this concept to you may be through some specific examples.

First, returning to our earlier discussion of the effects of mood upon help-ing, consider the joint influence of two factors—our current mood and the amount of money in our pockets—upon willingness to donate to a worthy cause. In situations in which our pockets are bulging with wealth, it seems

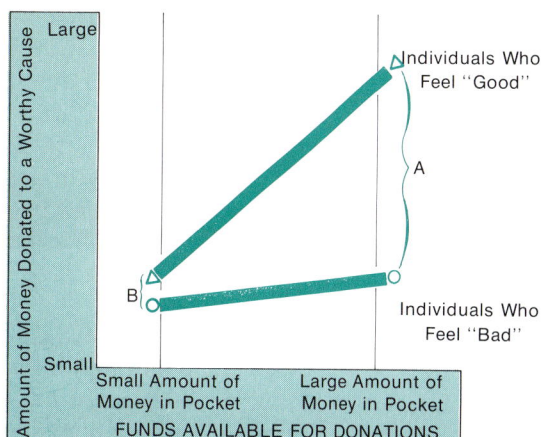

FIGURE 1–7   An example of an interaction between two independent variables. In this particular case, individuals who feel "good" make larger donations to a worthy cause than do those who feel bad only under conditions where they have a large amount of money at their disposal (A). When they are short of funds, both contribute about equally (B). (See text for further explanation.)

reasonable to expect that we will be more likely to make donations when we are feeling good than when we are feeling bad. But what about instances in which we are quite short of funds? Under such conditions, it seems likely that our mood will make very little difference: whether we feel good or feel bad, we simply can't spare the cash, and must refrain from behaving in a generous manner (see Figure 1–7). In short, our current mood may indeed influence our willingness to donate to charity, but only under certain conditions—when we have money to spare. Thus, the two factors may be said to interact: the effects of one (our mood) depend to an important degree upon the other (how much money we have at our disposal).

Perhaps a second example will help clarify the nature of this concept still further. Consider the influence of proctors who look over your shoulder as you take an examination; will they improve or reduce your test performance? One reasonable possibility is that the effects of such surveillance will depend upon how much studying you have done. In situations in which you have studied a great deal, the presence of proctors may have little effect upon your final score, or may actually tend to raise it (perhaps because they make you try just a bit harder). But if you have not studied enough, they may induce a state of panic (crib sheets can't be used, you can get no "hints" from the person sitting next to you), and so may sharply lower your performance (see Figure 1–8). Once again, we have described an interaction between two independent variables, for as in our first illustration above, the effects of one (in this case the presence of proctors) depend very much upon another (how much studying you did the night before the test).

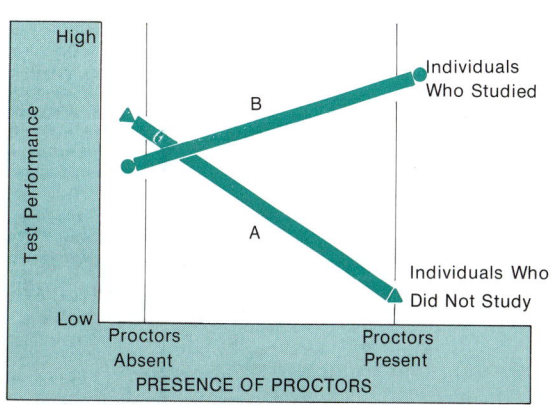

FIGURE 1–8   A second example of interaction between independent variables. In this instance, the presence of proctors reduces the performance of individuals who have not studied adequately (Line A), but actually increases that of students who are adequately prepared (Line B). (Students who did not prepare for the exam may actually do better than those who did when no proctors are present because of their reliance on crib sheets or similar techniques.)

It is largely because of the existence of such interactions—and even more complex ones involving three, four, five, or more factors—that we must often qualify our statements about behavior with such phrases as "all other factors being equal," or "under some conditions." Unfortunately, there are far too many conditions affecting our feelings, actions, and thoughts for us to be permitted the luxury of simple explanations. In fact, we would caution you to be on your guard whenever you encounter sweeping generalizations about human beings or human nature: in reality, behavior is far too complex to be accurately explained or described by a few neat statements.

Interpreting Results: Separating Wheat from Chaff

Suppose that despite all the difficulties involved, a researcher succeeds in both planning and executing a reasonable experiment. For the sake of argument, let us assume that it was concerned with the effects of humor in advertising on product sales. That is, assume it was designed to examine the hypothesis that customers prefer humorous ads to non-humorous ones, so that the former are more likely to increase sales than the latter. Further, suppose that the study employed two groups of subjects, one exposed to humorous ads and the other to serious ones for the same product, and that the **mean** (i.e., the average) stated intentions of individuals in the two groups to buy the product in question after viewing these commercials were as shown in Table 1–1.

As can be seen from this table, subjects exposed to the humorous ads did indeed express a greater willingness to buy the crucial product than did those exposed to the duller ones. Thus, it is tempting to conclude that humor is in fact a "plus" in advertising which will often lead to increased sales.

Unfortunately, though, such conclusions may be premature, and actually quite unfounded. For example, it may have been the case that more of the subjects exposed to the humorous ads had already used and liked the product, and so reported greater intentions of buying it again than did those who saw only the serious commercials. Or, it is possible that more of those exposed to the humorous ads were simply in more of a "buying mood" on that particular day than were those exposed to the nonhumorous ones (perhaps they worked for a particular company and had just gotten paid the day before). If either of these possibilities (or any one of many others) is correct, the results of the experiment are essentially meaningless, for if it were repeated tomorrow with additional subjects, markedly different findings might well be obtained. Thus, after completing an experiment and observing differences in the behavior of individuals in its various groups, it is still essential that a researcher go one step further and ask whether these differences are real—that is, whether they

TABLE 1–1

Subjects' Rated Intentions to Purchase the Product	
Nonhumorous Advertisements	Humorous Advertisements
5.2	7.3

The results of a hypothetical experiment on the influence of humor in advertising. Subjects exposed to humorous ads reported stronger intentions to buy the product in question than those exposed to nonhumorous ones, but is this difference "real"? Statistics can help a researcher decide. (Assume that subjects' intentions were measured on a ten-point scale, where 1 = no intention of buying the product and 10 = a strong intention of purchasing it.)

would be likely to appear again if the study were repeated with a different group of subjects.

In order to answer this important question, two steps are usually taken. First, the experiment may be repeated—a process known as **replication**—in order to determine whether the same results can be obtained once again. Second, the findings will almost certainly be subjected to **statistical analysis,** a form of mathematical treatment through which it is possible to determine the probability (likelihood) that a difference as large as the one observed might be obtained by chance alone. Obviously, the larger the difference between various groups in an experiment, the lower the probability that it occurred by chance. But how low must this likelihood be before such differences can be interpreted as real ones? Many psychologists view such differences as being **significant**—trustworthy or reliable—only when the probability that they would be obtained by chance alone is five times in a hundred or less. When differences in the behavior of various groups of subjects are large enough to meet this criterion, they are viewed as real ones which tell us something about behavior. When they do not meet this criterion, little confidence is placed in their importance, and it is considered unwise to attempt to draw any firm conclusions from them. We should hasten to note that there is nothing magical or definite about this five-times-in-a-hundred criterion—it is merely a convenient rule of thumb used by many psychologists for evaluating the results of their research. In fact, other values (e.g., one time in a hundred or less) are often employed instead. The important point to remember is that the findings of any experiment are not viewed as reliable or trustworthy unless the likelihood that they could have occurred by chance alone is relatively low. (The topic of statistical analysis is treated in more detail in Appendix A. Thus, if you would like to learn more about the methods employed by psychologists for evaluating the findings of their research, you can find such information on pp. 571–586.)

Generalizing from Results: Beyond the Laboratory

Few experimenters would be satisfied with results which applied only to the subjects in their study. Rather, most wish to generalize from their research findings to a much larger group of individuals. Thus, the psychologist who conducted the experiment on humor in advertising probably wished to extend his conclusions to all potential purchasers of the product in question. Unfortunately, the attainment of significant results is not, in itself, enough to guarantee the appropriateness of such generalization. In addition, it must be shown that the subjects employed constitute a **representative sample** of the group about which generalizations are to be made.

As an illustration of this important point, consider the case of an experimental psychologist who wants to know if the ability to solve certain kinds of problems can be improved by a special type of training procedure. Since he is a close friend of the principal of a small, expensive, and highly selective private school, he employs pupils at this institution as subjects in his study. Results then indicate that as expected, individuals exposed to the special training do indeed attain greater success in solving a standard set of problems than do those in a control group who never receive such training. Clearly, the psychologist would now like to generalize these results from his relatively small sample of children to a much larger group—all pupils of the same age at schools throughout the country, and perhaps to adults as well. But is he justified in doing so? Probably not, for there is good reason to believe that the subjects in his study differ from the larger population in several important respects. For example, they are probably brighter and are more likely to come from wealthy homes; they may be more socially mature. Thus, the psychologist would be on relatively shaky grounds in contending that the training techniques which worked for these individuals would also necessarily prove effective with children from markedly different backgrounds. In fact, it might well turn out to be the case that they are totally useless with individuals from culturally disadvantaged homes, who find them to be both strange and confusing. In view of such possibilities, researchers must always be on guard to assure that the subjects employed in their studies are truly representative of the populations to which they would like to generalize their results.

Unfortunately, it is often easier to describe this goal than to achieve it. Obtaining a sufficient number of appropriate subjects is often difficult, and sometimes psychologists are faced with the choice of conducting their research with individuals not truly representative of a larger group, or not conducting it at all. Confronted with this dilemma, most choose to forge ahead, employing those subjects who *are* available, in the hope of obtaining at least some useful knowledge. It is largely for this reason that so much psychological research is conducted with college students, a group which is clearly brighter, better educated, and younger than the general population as a whole. Fortunately, as a result of changing admissions policies, aid to minority group members, and other developments, students are a somewhat more diverse group today than they were in the past, and to a degree this helps improve the chances of successful generalization. The problem remains, however, and experimenters must always use great care in extending their conclusions to groups who may differ from the subjects in their studies in several important respects.

Some Pitfalls of Behavioral Research: Or, How to Get Positive Results Without Really Trying

Inappropriate generalization of results is only one of several traps lying in wait for careless experimenters. If they are not especially cautious, researchers may also fall victim to other errors which can serve to invalidate their results. Two of the most important of these are **placebo effects** and **demand characteristics.**

The term placebo effect refers to changes in behavior induced by events which accompany but are actually unrelated to the independent variables of interest in an experiment. The classic illustration of such effects occurs in studies designed to examine the effects of various drugs upon behavior. For example, consider the case of a physiological psychologist who wishes to determine whether a specific drug leads to increased activity on the part of a particular animal species. In order to obtain evidence on this issue, she conducts an experiment in which one group of subjects receives an injection of the drug while a second does not. Results then indicate that the first shows greater activity than the second. Does this provide conclusive evidence that the drug increases such behavior? Unfortunately, it does not, and for a very important reason: since the first group received an injection while the second did not, it is quite possible that any differences in their later behavior stemmed from this fact. That is, the increased activity observed among subjects in the drug-injected group may have resulted from the painful injection, and *not* from the drug itself. (In this particular case, such effects may have stemmed from the fact that subjects who received the injection were badly frightened by this painful experience, and thus spent a great deal of time pacing nervously about their cages.)

In order to determine whether the increased activity shown by subjects receiving the drug derived from this substance or merely from the painful injection, it would be necessary to include in the study a third group which would receive an injection of some inert (i.e., inactive) substance. If subjects in this group then showed an increase in activity similar to that shown by subjects who received the drug, it would be concluded that such changes in behavior stemmed from the injection rather than from the drug itself. Thus, these changes would be shown to be a placebo effect. In contrast, if subjects who received only distilled water failed to demonstrate any increase in activity, it would be concluded that the changes observed among subjects in the drug-injected group did in fact stem from this substance.

Unfortunately, placebo effects are not restricted to experiments involving drugs. In fact, they can occur in a wide variety of settings. For example, they are frequently observed in studies designed to investigate the effectiveness of new forms of psychotherapy. This is the case because individuals undergoing such treatment can show a lessening of their problems for two distinct reasons. First, they can be genuinely helped by the therapy they receive. Second, they can improve simply because they *expect* to experience such benefits. (After all, why else does one visit a psychologist?) In the latter case, of course, any changes in their feelings or behavior are due to such expectations, and *not* to the therapy under study. Thus, the expectations may be viewed as exerting a specific type of placebo effect (see Figure 1–9 for one further example of such effects). Given the existence of placebo effects in a wide range of settings, psychologists must always be on guard to protect against their possible oc-

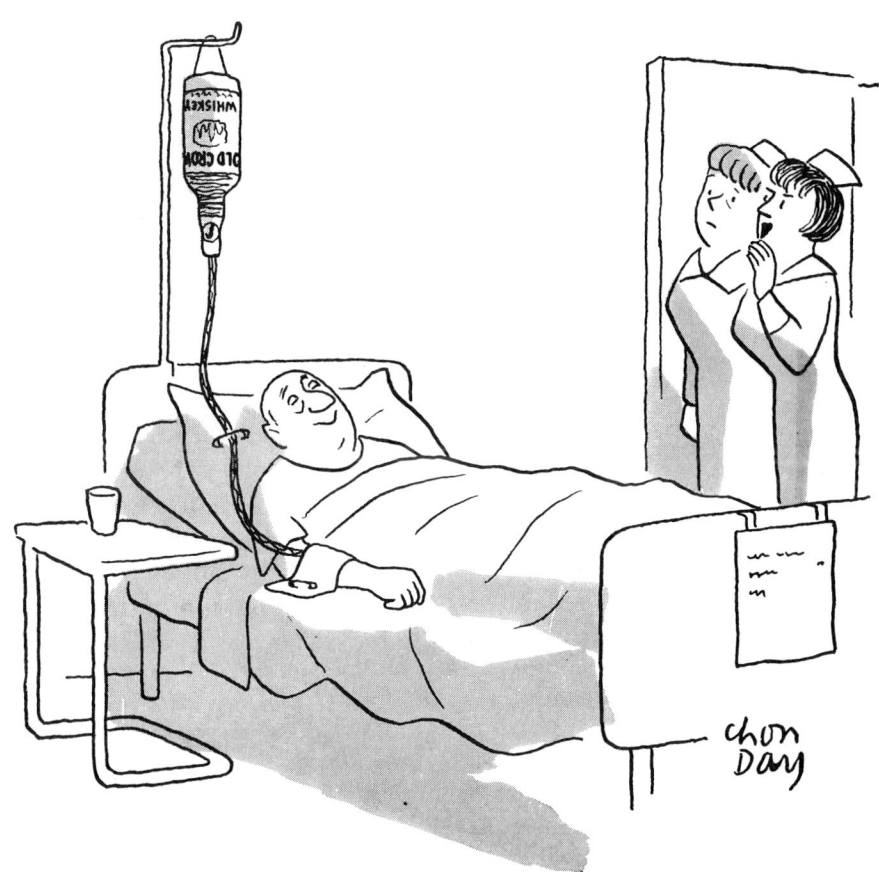

*"Not really . . . but you'd be surprised
at the psychological effect."*

FIGURE 1–9 On some occasions, subjects' behavior may change simply because they know they are receiving some special treatment and *expect* it to change. Such alterations are known as *placebo effects*, and represent one of the many pitfalls of behavioral research. (Reproduced by special permission of *Playboy* Magazine; copyright © 1969 by Playboy.)

currence. If such care is not exercised, even the results of research which is carefully conducted in all other respects may be rendered quite meaningless.

A second related source of artificial results in behavior research stems from the fact that if experimenters are not very careful, they can accidentally communicate their expectations or hypothesis to subjects. This can occur through changes in the tone of their voice, the expression on their face, and in countless other ways. And once subjects become aware of the experimenter's expectations or wishes, they often follow one of three different paths. First, they may do their best to insure that these expectations are confirmed. Second, they may try to "mess up" the study by acting in a manner opposite to that which they think the experimenter desires. Or third, they may simply attempt to "look good"—to present themselves in the most favorable light possible (e.g., Rosnow and Aiken, 1973; Sigall, Aronson, and Van Hoose, 1970). In each of these cases, of course, any results obtained in the experiment are likely to be quite meaningless since they stem from subjects' attempts to accomplish certain goals, and *not* from the effects of the independent variable upon behavior. Fortunately, the influence of the experimenter's expectations—or **demand characteristics,** as they are often termed—can be lessened in several ways. For example, experimenters may hire someone to conduct their studies and refrain from informing this person of their hypothesis. As a result, he or she cannot impart this information to subjects and thereby influence their behavior. Similarly, instructions may be tape-recorded and other aspects of the study automated so that the researcher does not actually meet, and possibly influence, subjects. Through such means, the impact of demand characteristics may be greatly lessened, and valid results obtained.

In sum, there are several factors which, if overlooked, can serve to invalidate experimental findings. Fortunately, psychologists, as a group, are quite sophisticated with respect to such problems and generally do an excellent job of avoiding their influence. As a result, you can be confident that the findings we describe in later chapters are based on research as free from such difficulties as possible.

Systematic Observation: The Correlational Method of Research

As noted above, experimentation is generally viewed as the most powerful method of psychological research. But in many cases, it cannot be employed either for practical or ethical reasons. For example, imagine that you had strong grounds for suspecting that revolutions are caused by the thwarting of rising aspirations. Could you test this hypothesis experimentally? Clearly you could not, unless you succeeded in enlisting the aid of an absolute ruler with the power to alter economic conditions at will. But even in this far-fetched case, ethical considerations might prevent you from performing the appropriate experiment; revolutions are dangerous social upheavals, and the idea of trying to start one for purposes of systematic study is highly questionable, to say the least.

Similarly, suppose that you had grounds for predicting that certain types of traumatic, upsetting experiences in early childhood lead individuals to adopt a life of crime in later years. Could you then conduct an experiment in which some groups of children are exposed to such experiences and others are not, in order to determine how many will later join the underworld? The mere suggestion of such research is frightening, and needless to say, no ethical psychologist would ever dream of conducting it.

In cases such as these, and in many less dramatic instances as well, psychologists find it necessary or preferable to turn to another technique, often known as the **correlational** method of research. In this approach, an attempt is made to determine whether two (or more) variables are related, through careful observation of both. If changes in one are consistently associated with alterations in the other, evidence for a link between them is obtained. It is important to note that in contrast to the experimental method, no attempt is made to systematically vary one of the factors in order to observe its effects upon the other. Rather, naturally occurring variations in both are observed in order to determine whether they tend to occur together. Perhaps as in the case of experimentation, a few concrete examples will help to illustrate these points.

First, suppose that you wished to examine the possibility of a relationship between degree of crowding—as in tenement districts of large cities—and crime (see Figure 1-10). Since it would probably prove impossible in the laboratory to closely duplicate crowded slum conditions or observe serious crime, you might choose to conduct your research by means of the correlational method. Applying this approach, you might then measure the degree of crowding in various neighborhoods of major cities (in terms, perhaps, of the number of families per building), and also obtain precise information on the frequency of various major crimes in each of these areas. If you then found that the number of crimes committed tended to rise as crowding increased, you would have suggestive evidence for a link between these factors. In order to assess the strength of this relationship, you would then probably calculate a statistic known as a **correlation coefficient** (usually abbreviated as **r**). Such coefficients can vary from a minimum of 0.00 to +1.00 on the one hand, or from 0.00 to −1.00 on the other. Positive values are obtained in cases in which increments in one factor are accompanied by increments in the other, as is the case in our example regarding crowding and crime. In contrast, negative values are obtained in instances in which increments in one variable are accompanied by decrements in the other. For example, the number of miles driven by motorists tends to decrease as the price of gasoline increases, thus indicating the existence of a negative correlation between these two variables. In either case, the larger the value of the correlation coefficient—that is, the more it departs from 0.00—the stronger the relationship between the variables under study. In a manner similar to that described in our discussion of experimentation, only correlations of a sufficient size—ones which would be ex-

FIGURE 1-10 Because of the impossibility of duplicating conditions such as these in the laboratory, a psychologist seeking to investigate the possibility of a relationship between crowding and crime might choose to employ the correlation method of research. (Photo credit: Raimondo Borea.)

pected to occur by chance relatively rarely—are viewed as being significant, and therefore worthy of careful attention. (Again, a fuller discussion of the issue of statistical significance and of correlation as well is contained in Appendix A, pp. 571–586.)

For a second example, let us return to an issue we considered earlier: imagine that you wished to examine the influence of televised violence upon children's behavior and that in this case, you were concerned with the impact of long-term rather than short-term viewing of such materials. Since it would clearly be impossible to confine subjects to your laboratory for weeks or months while you varied the type of shows they could watch, you might well turn to the correlational method of research. Applying this method to the issue at hand, you might begin by questioning the parents of a large group of children concerning the viewing habits of their offspring, and then observe the behavior of these youngsters in the classroom or at play. If you found that the frequency with which they engaged in assaults against others rose with the number of hours they spent watching violent shows, you would have some indication of a relationship between these two factors. And once again, calculation of the appropriate correlation coefficient would provide an index of the strength of this link.

As these examples suggest, the correlational method of research can be used to investigate many interesting topics. Moreover, it offers several important advantages. For example, it can readily be employed to study behavior in "real-world" settings, removed from the artificiality of the laboratory. Similarly, as noted above, it can often be applied to topics and issues which, because of practical or ethical considerations, cannot be examined by means of direct experimentation. Unfortunately, though, the correlational approach suffers from one major disadvantage which greatly weakens its appeal: the findings it reveals are usually somewhat ambiguous with respect to cause-and-effect relationships.

More specifically, the fact that two variables are found to be related in a correlational study tells us nothing about either (1) the existence of a direct causal link between them, or (2) the direction of such a relationship, should it exist. With respect to the first of these points, assume that in a correlational study, a psychologist finds a strong relationship between two factors: the number of years of education completed by male subjects and the amount of hair remaining on their heads. One possible interpretation of these results is that there is a direct causal link between education and baldness (that is, learning somehow causes hair loss!), while another is that *both* of these factors are closely related to a third—*age*—and tend to increase as this variable rises. In this particular instance, the second explanation is far more convincing than the first, and there can be little doubt that it is correct. But in other cases, the fact that an apparently close relationship between two variables is actually underlain by a third is much harder to recognize, and the temptation to assume that one causes the other is strong. For example, it has recently been noted that individuals who drink five cups of coffee or more per day are much more likely to suffer heart attacks than are those who drink four cups or fewer. Does this mean that excessive intake of caffeine is an important cause of heart attacks? Such a conclusion is certainly more reasonable than the assumption that education causes hair loss, but it may also be false, and for much the same reason. That is, it may actually be the case that people who drink a lot of coffee also tend to work harder, worry more, or stay up later than those who drink only a little. Thus, it may be these factors—and *not* coffee drinking itself—which account for their high levels of cardiac collapse. (A summary of these suggestions is presented in Figure 1–11). The moral of these examples is simple,

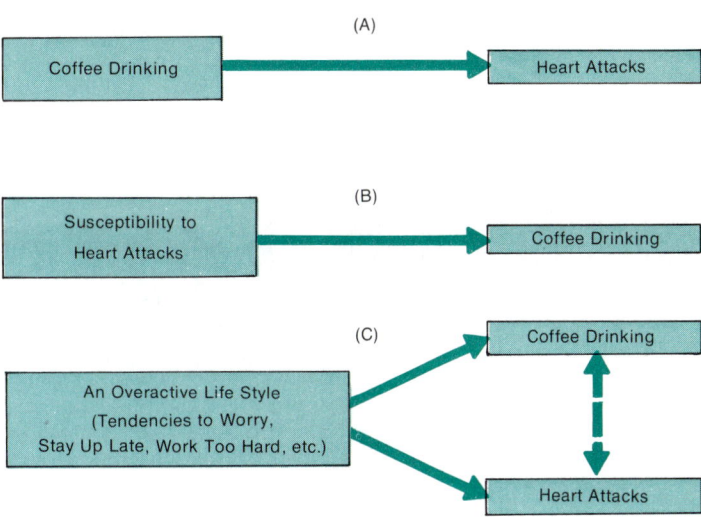

FIGURE 1–11 Recent studies have shown that the more coffee individuals drink, the more likely they are to suffer heart attacks. Because these findings are of a correlational rather than experimental nature, they are open to at least three possible interpretations: (A) coffee drinking is a direct cause of heart attacks, (B) susceptibility to heart attacks somehow causes individuals to drink more coffee, and (C) the relationship between coffee drinking and heart attacks stems from the fact that both are related to an over-active life style (people who drink a lot of coffee also tend to worry, stay up late, over-work, etc.). While interpretation (C) seems most reasonable, (A) cannot be entirely ruled out. [Interpretation (B) appears to make very little sense.]

but important: the existence of a correlation between two factors is *not* a definite indication of a causal relationship between them, and it should be interpreted in this manner only in the presence of additional supporting evidence.

Even if it is the case that the relationship between two factors is a direct one, and is not produced by some additional variable, it is still impossible to determine the direction of this bond from a correlation between them. For example, suppose that the findings of a particular study reveal a positive correlation between the frequency with which subjects view pornographic materials (e.g., X-rated films) and the number of times that they engage in sexual intercourse each week. That is, as the frequency of one increases, so does the frequency of the other. The existence of such a link may indicate either that (1) exposure to pornographic films or books increases the tendency to engage in sexual activity, or (2) the more lustful individuals are, the more they seek exposure to such materials. The first of these possibilities is somewhat more interesting and provocative than the second, but both are quite reasonable, and it is impossible to choose between them on the basis of correlational evidence alone.

For these reasons, psychologists generally tend to prefer the experimental method, with its firmer conclusions regarding cause-and-effect relationships, to correlational techniques of research. However, as noted above, both offer important advantages, and the choice between them is by no means simple. It should come as no surprise, therefore, that evidence gathered by means of both will be presented throughout the remainder of this volume.

An additional method of psychological research used much less frequently than experimental or correlational procedures is the individual **case study.** Here, a single person is studied in great depth and detail in an attempt to uncover the roots of his or her current behavior. The case study method is often employed in the investigation of abnormal behavior, the major hope being that intensive study of the affected person will reveal the important causes of his or her disturbed activities. Because of this focus on the bizarre or unusual, case studies often make for exceptionally stimulating reading, as the following brief excerpt reveals:

Case Studies: Generalizing from the Unique

Agnes W., an unmarried woman of thirty, had been unable to go any higher than the second or third floor of any building for a year. Whenever she tried to overcome her fear of height she succeeded only in provoking intolerable anxiety. She remembered when it all began. One evening she was working alone at the office when she was suddenly seized with terror lest she jump or fall out of the open eighth-story window. So frightened was Agnes by her impulse that she crouched behind a steel file for some time before she could trust herself to gather up her things and make for the street. She reached ground level acutely anxious, perspiring freely, her heart pounding and her breathing rapid.

After this the patient found that as soon as she reached the office each day her anxiety over height made it impossible to attend properly to her work. At the end of two months she gave up her position. For a while she tried unsuccessfully to accustom herself directly to high places. Finally her need for income drove her to take whatever she could get within the limitations imposed by her phobia. The result was that she was downgraded from a confident, well-paid secretary to an unhappy, poorly paid saleswoman in a store. This was her situation when she came for treatment.

In therapy it soon came out that Agnes had been deeply involved in an affair of long standing with a married man who could not, for religious reasons, get a divorce. She found herself caught in a severe conflict, guilty over her own conduct, too much in love to break off the liason, and unable to give up a belief that one day she and her lover would marry. The crisis came when she was informed that she was pregnant. She told the man that he would have to get a quick divorce and marry her. When he refused she threatened to expose him. A few days before her acute anxiety attack, and the onset of the phobia, she received a farewell letter from him and discovered that he had left town.

Agnes had felt humiliated and angered at having to beg and threaten her lover. His desertion was the final disillusionment. It overwhelmed her with helplessness and hatred. She now concluded that she was no better than a prostitute, and suicide seemed to her the only solution. It was in this setting of shame, fury, and abandonment that she became acutely frightened and phobic . . . (Cameron, 1963, pp. 282–283).

One of the main goals of the case study method is that of uncovering general principles which can be applied to many persons. For example, careful consideration of the case described above might lead to the hypothesis that strong feelings of self-contempt, and a resulting desire to commit suicide, may often lead to extreme fear of heights: the persons involved are literally afraid that they will hurl themselves out of an open window if the opportunity presents itself. If the suggestions derived from single case studies are then verified by additional observations, important insights into the causes of many behavior disorders may be uncovered. The most famous user of this approach was Sigmund Freud, who based his theories of mental illness and personality structure upon intensive case studies of his patients (see Chapter 9). Unfortunately, despite Freud's success with this method, human behavior is generally influenced by so many different factors that it is very difficult to reach any valid, general conclusions from the study of a few persons. Thus, the case history approach is employed less frequently today than it was in the past.

Surveys and Tests: Tools for Research

Before concluding our discussion of methods of psychological research, we should mention two techniques which are more tools than they are general procedures, and which can be employed in conjunction with either the correlational or experimental method — **surveys** and **tests.**

Surveys: Taking the Pulse of Public Opinion

If you ever read newspapers or watch television, you are probably already quite familiar with surveys. Generally, they report summaries of public opinions or preferences, and can be concerned with virtually any topic ranging from the President's popularity to consumer reactions to mouthwash or peanut butter. For example, we often hear on the evening news that the results of the latest survey indicate that the President is supported by some specific percentage of the public. And commercials often report the results of surveys which indicate that consumers (or sometimes doctors or dentists) prefer by an overwhelming majority the brand being promoted. The information on

FIGURE 1-12 Surveys are often conducted to measure public opinion or preferences. When carefully planned and executed, they permit highly accurate predictions regarding anything from product sales to the outcome of political elections.

which such statements are based is usually obtained by procedures in which a relatively large number of persons are phoned, visited in their own homes, or even stopped upon the street and asked to answer several standardized questions (see Figure 1-12). If the persons responding are a representative sample of the general population, their answers can be used to predict the views of millions of others with a high degree of accuracy. It is for this reason that T.V. newscasters are often able to forecast the outcome of political elections after only 1 or 2 per cent of the votes have been counted. However, if the persons questioned do not constitute a truly representative sample, attempts to generalize from their answers to a much larger group of individuals can result in serious error.

In recent years, the question of whether public presentation of the results of surveys can sway the opinions of persons who have not as yet made up their minds has been raised repeatedly. That is, it has been suggested that upon learning that most people are in favor of a given issue or candidate, many individuals in the "doubtful" or "don't know" categories may decide to join the majority. Although it is hard to assess the importance of such effects, the possibility of their existence suggests that investigators employing the survey method of research must give careful thought to the ethical issues surrounding their studies.

Important ethical issues have also been raised with respect to the use of psychological tests. As you may already know, these are procedures (often consisting of questionnaires or other paper-and-pencil forms) designed to measure many important characteristics. Such tests are frequently used in a wide range of research concerned with the abilities, interests, or traits which they assess. For example, a psychologist wishing to examine the relationship between family size and intelligence might administer some test of intelligence to subjects from families of many different sizes in order to determine whether any differences exist between them. (Such research was actually conducted by Robert Zajonc in 1975, and points to the conclusion that intelligence tends to decrease as family size increases.) Similarly, a researcher wishing to study the effects of a strong need for approval from others upon social behavior might administer a test of this characteristic to a large number of persons (see Figure 1-13), and then observe their behavior in several types of social situations.

Tests: Measuring the Unseen

(1) I have never deliberately said something that hurt someone's feelings.
(2) I never resent being asked to return a favor.
(3) I always try to practice what I preach.
(4) I never hesitate to go out of my way to help someone in trouble.
(5) No matter who I'm talking to, I'm always a good listener.
(6) I am always courteous, even to people who are disagreeable.

FIGURE 1–13 **Sample items from a psychological test designed to measure the need for social approval. Individuals who indicate that these and similar statements are true about themselves seem to possess a strong desire to win approval from others. (Adapted from Crowne and Marlowe, 1964.)**

When psychological tests are employed in the context of research, there is usually little objection to their use. In such cases, subjects' privacy is carefully protected, and their test scores are held in the strictest confidence. As we shall see in Chapter 14, however, a major controversy regarding psychological tests has developed around their growing use in many practical settings (for example, their routine use as a screening device for new job applicants). Many individuals view such testing as a serious invasion of personal privacy, in which individuals are forced to reveal information about themselves that they would rather hold confidential. Largely because of such objections, the routine administration of psychological tests by government agencies and private industry has been sharply reduced in recent years. However, the use of such tests in many kinds of basic research continues at a high rate, and we will encounter such procedures at several points in later chapters.

Of Man and Beast: A Note on Research With Animals

Throughout this discussion of research methods in psychology, we have focused on techniques for studying human behavior. Before concluding, therefore, we should hasten to add that much interesting and valuable research in psychology is also conducted with animal subjects. Although students sometimes find it hard to understand why psychologists would choose to perform many of their investigations with animals, there are actually several strong reasons for adopting such a strategy.

First, as noted above, it is sometimes impossible — either for practical or ethical reasons — to conduct certain experiments with human subjects. For example, a psychologist wishing to examine the influence of early social isolation on later behavior could not possibly seek to separate infants from all human contact in order to study this topic. In cases such as this, it is often possible to turn to systematic observation and the correlational approach. Another useful strategy, however, is that of shifting to research with animals, where procedures not permissible with humans may be employed. Even in such investigations, of course, attention must be devoted to humanitarian considerations, so that participants are not subjected to undue pain or discomfort. But within such limits, it is often possible to conduct investigations with animals which could not be completed with human beings.

Second, even in cases in which experimentation with humans is possible, independent variables can often be controlled more effectively or varied over a wider range when animal subjects are employed. For example, a psychologist interested in studying the effects of heat upon behavior might conduct such research with either laboratory animals or human volunteers (see Chapter 15). Because of the harmful effects resulting from prolonged exposure to heat, however, he would probably be able to continue his study for a longer period of time and to expose subjects to somewhat higher temperatures if he chose to work with animals rather than humans.

Finally, psychologists often conduct research with animals not for reasons such as these, but because of an interest in this topic itself. Human beings are, after all, only one of an almost countless number of life forms on earth. As a result, interest in the behavior of organisms other than men and women seems both a fitting and reasonable part of modern psychology. Thus, although our primary emphasis throughout this volume will be on human behavior and characteristics, we will not hesitate to turn to findings and principles acquired through research on other species whenever this seems useful or appropriate. In short, our discussions of behavior will generally be "people-oriented," but by no means "people-bound."

"East is East and West is West, and never the twain shall meet . . . ." When this line was written by the poet Rudyard Kipling some hundred years ago, it was meant to apply to the vast gulf in outlook and customs separating Eastern and Western civilization. But it is our general impression that it may also be applied to the large and seemingly impenetrable gap separating textbook authors from students. Our own teaching experience suggests that all too often, a considerable "failure to communicate" develops between these two groups— a gulf which irritates, frustrates, and annoys both sides. Although we can't promise to totally eliminate such faulty communication—that would almost surely be pledging too much—we have taken several different steps which, we hope, will at least help to lessen these problems.

First, we have arranged the chapters in an order which seems to us to make the most sense. Thus, we begin with consideration of basic psychological processes such as perception, learning, and memory, and only then turn to complex forms of behavior in which they play a crucial role. In adopting this arrangement, we move counter to a trend in some other recent texts to begin with discussions of social behavior, bizarre forms of mental illness, or similar topics. Our reasons for rejecting such an approach are twofold. First, we think that plunging headlong into such complex topics before the basic concepts essential for their understanding are examined may result in a great deal of confusion. For example, how could we hope to explain the origins of behavior disorders—many of which seem to be learned—without first considering the nature of learning itself? Second, it is our firm conviction that fascinating findings have been reported in *all* areas of psychology. Thus, there is no reason to sacrifice orderly development to an attempt to begin with high-interest materials—the two goals are actually quite compatible.

Second, we have devoted considerable attention to the systematic arrangement of materials *within* each chapter. An attempt has been made to organize each into three or four major divisions, and these are clearly indicated by prominent action headings similar in style to the one on this page. Further, we have devoted much effort to the task of arranging the materials presented in each chapter in what seems to us to be a logical and systematic order.

Third, we have included a number of specific features designed to facilitate your studying and make the text somewhat easier to use. Thus, an outline of the major topics to be covered in each chapter is presented on the title page, and again in its introduction. A summary which serves to review most of the important points that have been made follows each chapter, and key terms or concepts are printed in **dark type like this** and are defined in the glossary, which follows the appendices. Further, we have attempted to make all figures, tables, and graphs as simple to read as possible, and have tried to explain each fully in the accompanying captions.

Finally, we have made use of three types of special inserts or "boxes." The first is labeled "FOCUS ON RESEARCH," and usually appears at the end of major sections. Inserts of this type contain descriptions of recent research

USING THIS BOOK: A ROAD-MAP FOR THE READER

which we find particularly interesting or important. The main purpose for their presence is to give you a general "feel" for what is currently going on at the frontiers of psychological research.

The second type is labeled "PSYCHOLOGY IN ACTION," and is included because of our belief that one effective demonstration is worth at least a thousand words. Inserts of this kind describe simple experiments or observations you can perform yourself to demonstrate important psychological principles. They are all safe (both for you and your "subjects") as well as ethical, and should provide you with first-hand evidence for many of the facts we discuss.

Finally, the third type of insert is labeled "PERSPECTIVE ON BEHAVIOR," and contains questions which can best be described as "food for thought." We pose these mainly to underline the important implications which often stem from psychological knowledge, and will offer no answers to them. In this case, your own solutions are surely just as good—perhaps even better—than our own.

It is our hope that together, these aspects of our book will help us communicate a good deal of knowledge about psychology in a manner which will neither bore, irritate, nor confuse you. Further, we hope that they will allow at least a portion of our own excitement with the field to come through in an undistorted manner. To the extent that we succeed in these tasks—and only to that extent—will we be satisfied that as authors and teachers we have done our part.

Summary

Psychology is at once both old and new. Its subject matter—the complex mysteries of human behavior—is as old as humanity itself. However, the idea of subjecting such questions to scientific study developed only during the last half of the nineteenth century. When it first began, psychology focused its attention upon attempts to analyze the structure of "mind." However, interest in mind was soon replaced by an emphasis upon behavior (i.e., observable activities) which has persisted up to the present time.

The more than 40,000 psychologists in the U.S. today have many different interests, ranging from the treatment of abnormal behavior to the study of the biological bases of behavior. Moreover, they find employment in such diverse settings as colleges and universities, large corporations, and hospitals and clinics. Basically, their common academic training in the principles of their field and in the methods of behavioral research serves to unify the various elements of their profession.

In order to investigate many fascinating aspects of behavior, psychologists make use of several different methods of research. The most powerful of these is generally held to be **experimentation,** in which some factor believed to affect behavior (and termed the **independent variable**), is systematically varied, while all other factors not of special interest are held constant. If changes in the independent variable produce alterations in the behavior under study (the **dependent variable**), it is concluded that this factor is indeed an important determinant of such activity.

In some instances, practical or ethical considerations rule out the use of direct experimentation. On such occasions, psychologists often turn to the **correlational method** of research. Here, two or more variables of interest are carefully observed in order to determine whether naturally occurring changes in one are associated with alterations in the other. The correlational method of research offers several important advantages—for example, it can readily be employed to investigate behavior in "real-world" settings. However, its appeal is greatly weakened by the fact that the findings it provides are somewhat ambiguous with respect to cause-and-effect relationships.

Other methods of psychological research include (1) the **case study method,** in which one individual is studied in great depth in an attempt to uncover the roots of his or her present behavior, (2) **surveys,** in which large numbers of individuals are questioned concerning their views on various topics, and (3) **psychological tests,** in which various abilities, interests, or traits are measured. Because certain experiments cannot ethically be conducted with human beings, animals often serve as subjects in psychological research. The findings of such investigations often add much to our understanding of behavior.

Suggested Readings

American Psychological Association: *A Career in Psychology.* Washington: American Psychological Association, 1975.

　　This booklet provides information on the various specialties of psychology and the type of training required to become a psychologist. You can obtain a free copy by writing to the American Psychological Association, 1200 Seventeenth St., N.W., Washington, D.C. 20036.

American Psychological Association: *Graduate Study in Psychology, 1976–1977.*

　　This book (which is available on request from the American Psychological Association for $5.00) describes more than 400 graduate programs in psychology in the U.S. and Canada. Information on such topics as entrance requirements, emphasis of training, and student housing is presented.

Boneau, C. A., and Cuca, J. M.: An overview of psychology's human resources. *American Psychologist,* 1974, *29,* 821–839.

　　This article presents the results of a survey of more than 27,000 psychologists and contains information on such topics as their specialty, place of employment, and salaries.

Sarbin, T. R., and Coe, W. C.: *The Student Psychologist's Handbook: A Guide to Sources.* Cambridge, Mass.: Schenkman Publishing Company, 1969.

　　This brief soft-covered book provides a broad overview of the scope of psychology, as well as hints on how to read research articles, use the library, and prepare a research report.

Skinner, B. F.: The steep and thorny way to a science of behavior. *American Psychologist,* 1975, *30,* 42–49.

　　In this article, one of psychology's most famous — and controversial — figures, the noted behaviorist B. F. Skinner, presents his current views regarding the field. In addition, he outlines some of the problems which, in his opinion, have stood in the way of more rapid progress toward a purely objective, scientific field of psychology.

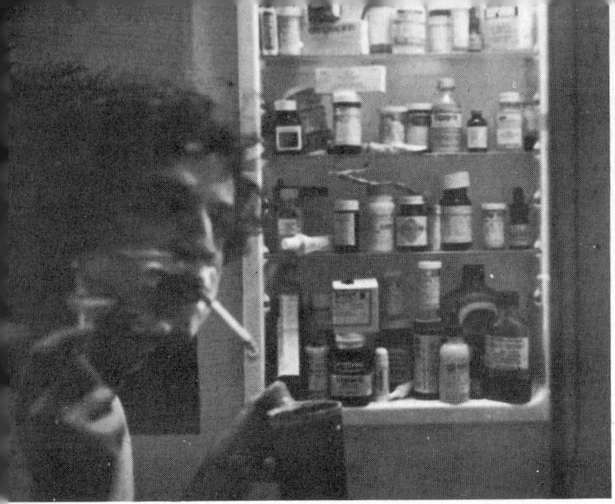

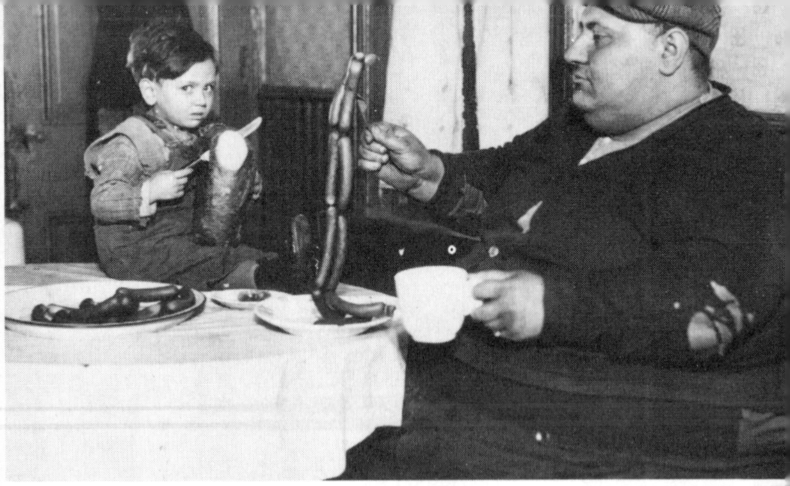

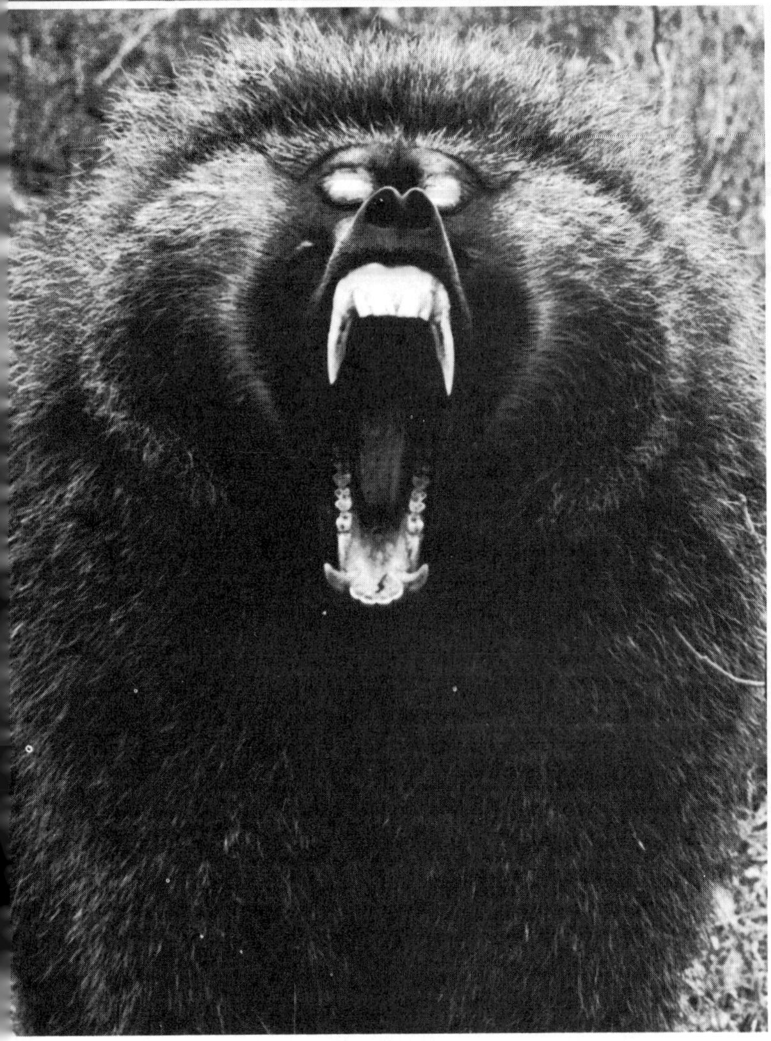

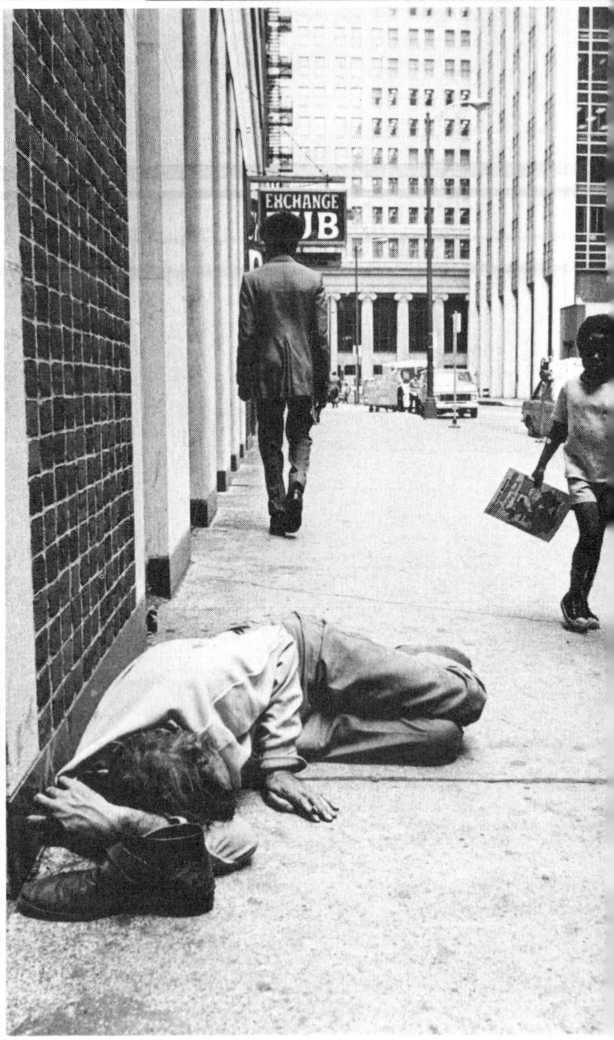
EXCHANGE

2 Biological Bases of Behavior: A Look Beneath the Surface

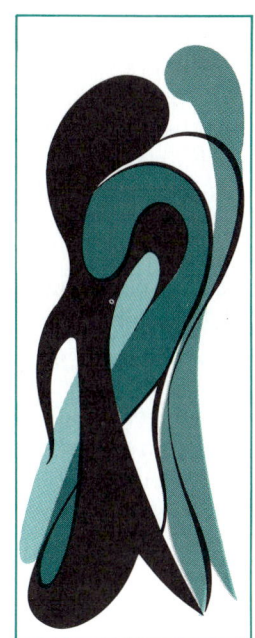

You've just polished off your second plate of spaghetti, and feel as though your stomach is about to burst. With great effort, you push yourself back from the table and stagger over to the sofa, where you collapse with a long sigh. From your horizontal position, you can see your roommate Frank, who, totally unaffected by your departure, continues to eat with great gusto. Frank has always had a serious weight problem, and as you watch him shovel one huge forkful of food after another into his mouth, you can see why this is so. In the past, you've always assumed that Frank's tendency to gorge himself at every meal stemmed mainly from a lack of will power and a great love of food. But now, as you watch him rise to fill his plate for the fourth time, you begin to wonder whether his difficulties might actually go somewhat deeper. Could it be that Frank overeats because of some disturbance in the internal mechanisms regulating his appetite? In short, could there be a biological basis to his problem?

It's 3:00 A.M., and you've been trying to fall asleep for several hours. Finally, in desperation, you rise and make yourself some warm milk—an old cure for sleeplessness you often heard your parents mention when you were a child. As you sip this steaming liquid, you find yourself pondering the nature of sleep itself. What exactly is this process, and why do we need it so much? It seems obvious to you that many complex changes must take place within your body when you fall asleep and later wake up, but the nature of these events remains something of a mystery. And what about dreams; why do they occur, and what purpose, if any, do they serve? Whether because of the warm milk or these puzzling thoughts, you soon find yourself feeling quite drowsy, and in a few minutes all your questions about sleep are eliminated by the gradual development of this restful state itself.

You're at an exciting football game, one which will decide the season championship. Tension fills the air, and feelings are running high among the spectators. Suddenly, two fans who obviously support opposite teams begin to argue. Their comments quickly become more and more insulting, and you can see that they are both growing angrier by the minute. Finally, one throws a punch at the other, and, in an instant, they are down on the floor, wrestling and swinging wildly. The spectacle of two middle-aged men trying to seriously harm each other over the outcome of a sports event is quite disturbing, and you are glad when the stadium guards finally arrive and pull the opponents apart. As they are led away, battered and bleeding, you find yourself wondering about the nature of rage and other strong emotions. What, precisely, are such reactions? Where and how do they originate? And what internal factors serve to turn them "on" and shut them "off"?

It's been three weeks since your friend Jill was involved in a serious automobile accident. She was driving along the interstate when her car suddenly had a blow-out and spun wildly off the road. It turned over several times, and because she wasn't wearing her seatbelt, Jill was badly injured. In fact, this is the first day that she has been permitted to have any visitors. When you enter her room, you notice that her right arm and leg are both still in casts, and that she has a large bandage wrapped around her head. She does look cheerful, though, and her warm smile raises your spirits so much that you take a seat and begin giving her all the latest news about your friends, school, and so on. At first everything seems quite normal, but as your conversation continues, you begin to notice an unsettling change in Jill's behavior: she seems to have a great deal of difficulty in understanding what you say. It's not that she can't hear you—she gives every sign of being able to do so. Rather, she simply seems unable to catch the meaning of your words. Even worse, she seems to forget what you say almost as quickly as you say it, so that you must remind her of the same information and events over and over again. After about half an hour, a nurse enters and asks that you leave so that Jill can receive some medication. As you walk out of the hospital, you realize with sorrow that Jill's head injuries have affected her ability to both understand and remember other persons' speech. You've always assumed that the brain played an important role in such processes, but now this fact is brought home to you in an especially painful and personal way.

At first glance, these incidents and events may strike you as totally unrelated. Actually, though, there is a common thread binding them together: all point to the fact that behavior has important biological roots. Together, they serve to remind us that whenever we dream, become angry, learn, feel hunger, experience sexual pleasure, carry on a conversation, or engage in virtually any other form of activity, complex biological events related to such actions or experiences are occurring within our bodies. Many psychologists believe that in an ultimate sense, these events and processes are responsible for all of our feelings, behavior, and thought. That is, they believe that in the final analysis, all the actions we perform, emotions we experience, and even our sense of consciousness itself stem from complex biochemical events. At this point we should hasten to add that while most psychologists hold this view, it is by no means shared by all. In fact, some take strong exception to the suggestion that *all* aspects of our behavior—even such complex reactions as love, creativity, loyalty, and prejudice—can be understood solely in terms of biochemical events. Yet, even those who raise such objections agree that physiological processes play an important role in many if not all forms of behavior.

In view of this fact, it seems only reasonable that we begin our study of psychology by focusing upon these internal sources of behavior—the biological bases from which it springs.

Of course, noting that behavior has important biological roots is one thing; understanding the complex nature of these processes is quite another. At present, we are still very far from possessing complete or final knowledge in this respect. Yet, progress toward this goal has been rapid, and enough is now known about the biological bases of many aspects of behavior to provide at least partial answers to the questions about sleep, hunger, and emotions raised on page 35, and to a great many others as well. In the present chapter, then, we will attempt to summarize a portion of this knowledge. As will soon become apparent, in order to understand the relationship between biological processes on the one hand and behavior on the other, it is necessary to know something about the structure and functioning of the **nervous system.** And to understand the workings of the nervous system, it is necessary to know something about the **neuron,** its basic unit of construction. As a result, we will begin by considering these topics. Since the major purpose of these preliminary discussions is merely that of providing you with some essential background, they will be as brief as possible. The majority of our attention will be reserved for the task of examining some of the complex bonds between the nervous system—especially the brain—and important aspects of behavior.

NEURONS: BASIS FOR COMMUNICATION

Suppose that you were walking along the street when a particularly attractive stimulus—the sight of a crisp, new $20 bill lying on the ground—reached your eyes. If this information stopped at that point and went no further, it would do you little good. You would probably keep on walking, oblivious to the unexpected wealth lying at your feet. In order for it to be of any benefit, it would be necessary for this knowledge to somehow move from your eyes to other parts of your body. Loosely speaking, it would first be necessary for it to move from your eyes to your brain, where it could be recognized and some plan of action formulated. Further, it would be necessary for information to then move from your brain to various muscles so that you could react in an appropriate manner—in this case, by reaching down and seizing the money before someone else beat you to it!

By now, the main point of this example should be obvious: in complex organisms such as human beings, there is a great and continuing need for communication between various portions of the body. Some of the more common routes for such communication include the movement of information (1) from external receptors, such as the eyes, or ears, to the brain, (2) from the brain to various muscles or glands, (3) from internal receptors, such as those which inform us that we have an upset stomach or sore back, to the brain, and (4) from certain portions of the brain to internal organs such as the lungs, heart, and intestines. Whatever the specific pathways or routes involved, it is clear that such communication is essential for any organized form of behavior. Without it, we would be unable to react to external stimuli such as the $20 bill mentioned above, to sense and regulate the internal state of our bodies, to experience emotions, to perform any integrated series of actions, or to think, plan, or reason. In short, such communication ultimately forms the basis for all aspects of our feelings, behavior, and thought.

Given the essential importance of this process, it is not surprising that over the course of evolution, certain cells of the body have become highly specialized for its rapid and efficient performance. These cells are known as *neurons,* and serve as the basic building blocks of the nervous system.

Basic Structure of the Neuron: One-Way Traffic

Although neurons take many forms in various parts of the body, they generally possess three basic and readily visible parts: (1) the **cell body,** (2) an **axon,** and (3) several **dendrites** (see Figure 2–1). Dendrites carry information *toward* the cell body, while the axon (which sometimes divides into one or more branches known as collaterals always carries information *away* from the cell body. Thus, in a sense, neurons serve as "one-way" channels of communication, transmitting information only in a single, fixed direction.

In many neurons, the axon is covered by a sheath of fatty material known as myelin. This **myelin sheath** is interrupted at several points by small gaps known as **nodes of Ranvier,** and as we shall soon see, both the sheath itself and the spaces in it play an important role in the neural transmission of information.

Near its end, the axon divides into several small branches known as **telodendria.** These, in turn, end in round structures known as **synaptic terminals** which closely approach but do not touch other cells in the body (other neurons, muscles, or glands). The manner in which information transmitted by the neuron manages to cross this small space will be described below.

Communication Within Neurons: Axonal Transmission

In order to understand the manner in which neurons transmit information within the nervous system, it is useful to begin by examining the conditions which exist during periods when they are *not* actively engaged in this task. Careful study has revealed that during such periods, positively charged particles (especially sodium ions, one of the substances produced when salt is dissolved in water) exist in greater concentration outside the neuron than within it, while negatively charged particles (especially large and complex protein molecules) exist in greater concentration inside. Put another way, sodium ions are more common in the body fluids surrounding the neuron than inside it, while protein molecules are more common inside the cell than in these external fluids. Several factors contribute to this state of affairs, but perhaps the most important lies in the fact that the cell membrane prevents the movement of these particular substances into or out of the neuron. Largely as a result of this unequal distribution of positively and negatively charged particles, the inside of the neuron acquires a tiny negative electric charge of approximately 70 millivolts (70 thousandths of a volt) relative to the outside. This voltage is often described as the **resting potential,** and its presence is usually a sign that the neuron is alive and functioning normally.

As long as the neuron is not stimulated by incoming information, these

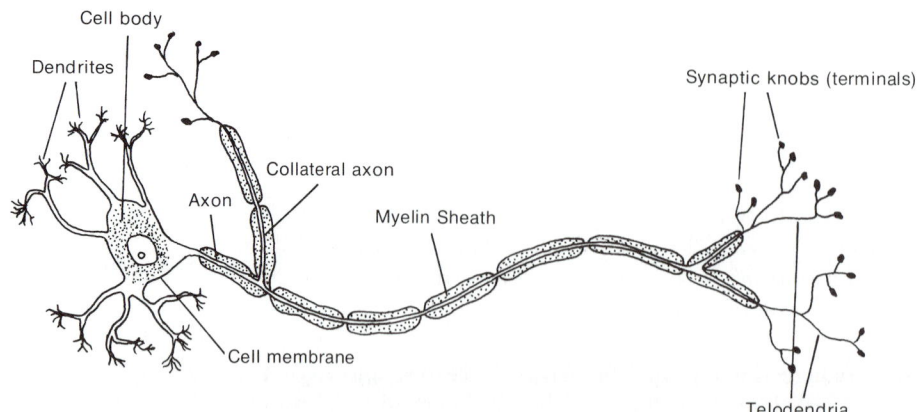

FIGURE 2–1   Structure of the neuron. Note the presence of several dendrites, a cell body, and, in this particular case, one main and one collateral axon. (From Grollman, S.: *The Human Body.* New York: Macmillan Co., Copyright © 1964.)

conditions persist with little change. When it is stimulated in a manner we will soon describe, however, a number of important changes take place. First, the nature of the cell membrane is altered so that sodium ions, which were previously held outside, can now enter freely. This state of affairs lasts for only a single millisecond (one thousandth of a second), but even this brief period is sufficient for a large number of positively charged particles to enter the cell. In fact, so many sodium ions enter that the negative resting potential is entirely eliminated, and the interior of the neuron actually becomes positively charged with respect to the outside. This brief reversal of the resting potential is generally known as the **action potential,** and it is largely through the passage of this disturbance down the axon that information is communicated within a single neuron.

As we have already noted, the cell membrane permits sodium ions to enter freely for only a very brief period of time. Once this interval has passed, the admission of such particles is again prevented, and the neuron actively expels those which have entered. As they leave, the interior of the cell gradually regains a negative electric charge with respect to the outside. We say "gradually," but actually this process occurs with lightning speed. In fact, as shown in Figure 2–2, the whole cycle we have described—from stimulation through conduction of an action potential, through re-establishment of the resting potential—usually requires a total of only 3 or 4 milliseconds. This fact suggests that the neuron is truly an amazingly efficient system for communication.

One important characteristic of the action potential which we have not mentioned so far is the fact that it is very much an "all-or-none" affair. That is, either it occurs at full strength or it does not occur at all: there is nothing in between. Further, once an action potential has been initiated, its size and speed are independent of the strength of the stimulus which evokes it. In a sense, therefore, the conduction of an action potential along the axon resembles a burning fuse which, once lit, burns at a constant rate regardless of whether it has been started by a match or a blowtorch.

Throughout this discussion, we have been describing the transmission of action potentials in neurons whose axons are not covered by a myelin sheath. In the case of axons possessing this covering, a somewhat different process takes place. Here, action potentials develop only in the small gaps in the sheath (the nodes of Ranvier mentioned earlier). Thus, instead of traveling along the entire axon, they "jump" from one node to the next. The major advantage of such an arrangement, of course, is increased speed—an important consideration in the case of relatively large and complex organisms such as ourselves in which information often must be transmitted over distances of several feet.

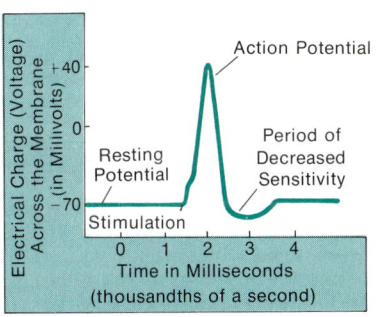

FIGURE 2–2 **Conduction of an action potential. Following stimulation, the electrical charge across the cell membrane swings from −70 millivolts to +40 millivolts, and back again. (Note that immediately after the passage of an action potential, the charge across the membrane is actually more negative for a brief period than was initially the case. During this interval, the neuron is less sensitive to incoming stimuli than usual.)**

Communication Between Neurons: Bridging the Gap

Up to this point, we have focused upon the transmission of information within a single neuron. It is obvious, however, that communication also occurs *between* neurons; if it did not, each would serve as a kind of communicative dead-end into which information would flow, only to be lost. For many years, it was assumed that communication between neurons was accomplished through direct physical contact. That is, it was widely believed that action potentials moved readily from one neuron to the next at points where they touched. Microscopic examination of the nervous system soon eliminated this simple explanation, for although adjacent neurons approach each other closely in a region known as the **synapse,** they do not actually touch. An important and somewhat puzzling question, then, is how information manages to move across this narrow but important **synaptic cleft.** Evidence gathered in recent years suggests an answer of the following type.

When a neuron is stimulated, the action potential that is generated travels along its surface from the dendrites or cell body to the axon, and then to the telodendria and synaptic terminals. At this point, the electrical properties of the action potential seem to fade, and the information it carries is conducted across the synaptic cleft by a complex physiological and chemical process. The synaptic terminals contain many round structures known as **synaptic vesicles.** Upon arrival of the action potential, these vesicles approach the cell membrane, where they empty their contents into the synapse (see Figure 2–3). The chemicals they release (usually known as **transmitter substances**) then

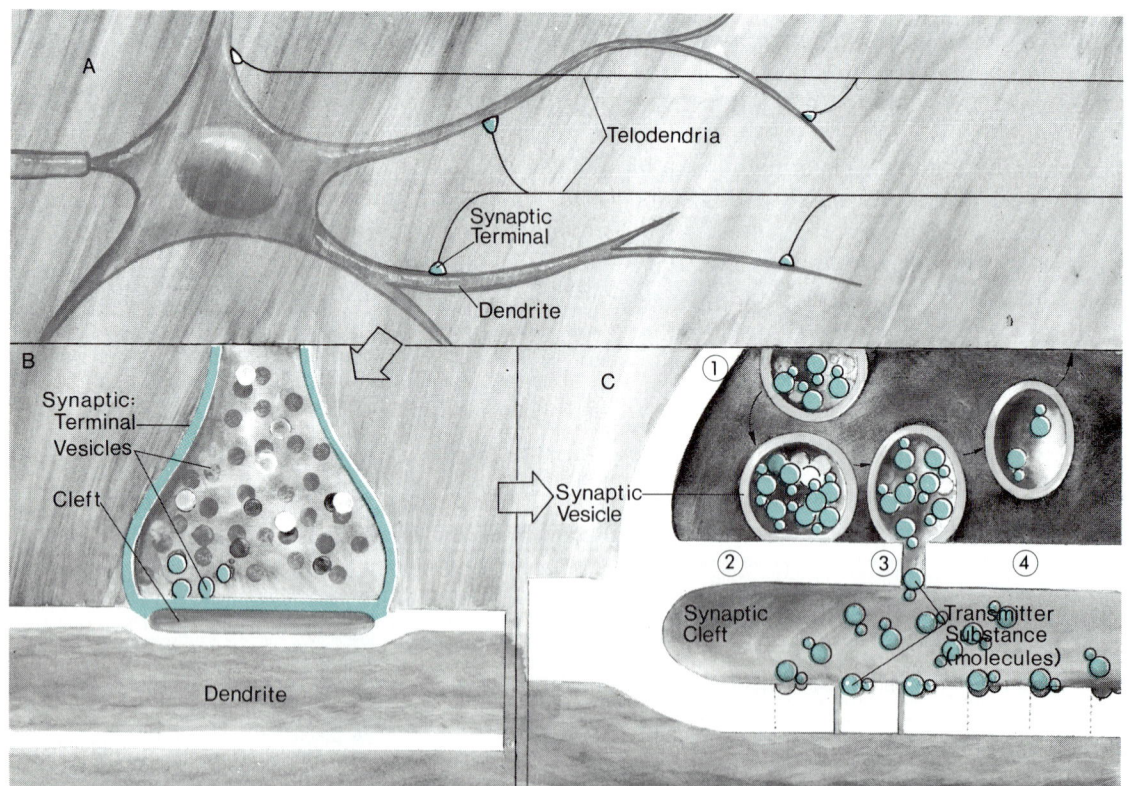

FIGURE 2–3 Communication across the synapse. (A) Several telodendria approaching the cell body or dendrites of a neuron. (B) A close-up view of the synapse showing a single synaptic terminal filled with synaptic vesicles. (C) A single *synaptic vesicle* (1) approaching the cell membrane, (2) reaching it, (3) releasing its contents *(transmitter substance)* into the synapse, and (4) returning to the interior of the cell. (After Eccles, 1965, pp. 58–62.)

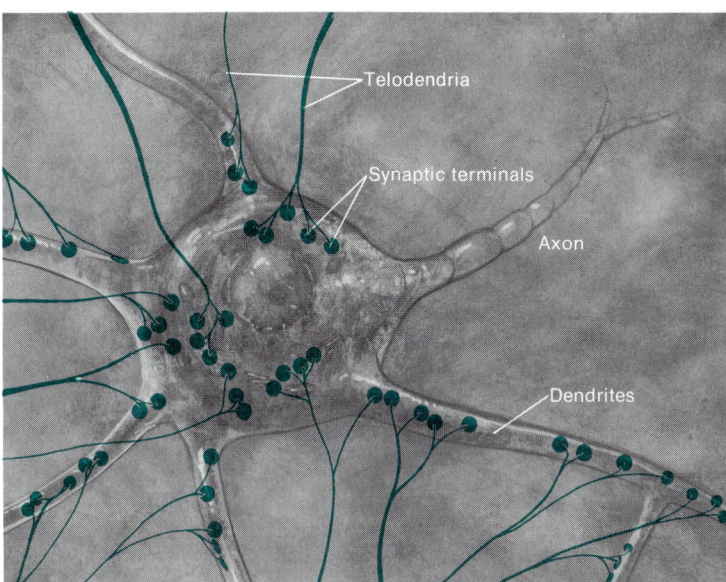

FIGURE 2–4   An illustration of the large number of synapses formed by a single neuron with many others. The cell shown may receive both excitatory and inhibitory stimulation from many different sources. (Adapted from Eccles, 1965, p. 62.)

travel across the synaptic cleft until they reach the membrane of the second cell. There, they may have either of two effects. First, if they are *excitatory* in nature, they may stimulate the generation of an action potential which travels away from the point of origin in accordance with the one-way pattern described above. Second, if they are *inhibitory* in nature, they may actually make it more difficult for the neuron they contact to conduct an action potential than would otherwise be the case. In sum, when one neuron communicates with another through the release of transmitter substances, the likelihood that the second will also conduct an action potential may either be increased or decreased. In view of the fact that most neurons form synapses with many others (see Figure 2–4), it is apparent that whether a given cell will become active or remain in a resting state depends upon the total sum of excitatory and inhibitory influences exerted upon it by its neighbors.

Before concluding our discussion of communication between neurons, we should note that the effects of many drugs (a topic we will examine again on pp. 65–69) seem to stem from their impact upon this process. That is, many drugs seem to exert their influence upon our feelings or behavior by somehow altering the nature of synaptic transmission. Although this can occur in many different ways, two seem to be most important in this respect. First, drugs can mimic (i.e., imitate) the effects of naturally occurring transmitter substances, either exciting or inhibiting neurons which are normally affected by these substances. This appears to be true in the case of hallucinogenic drugs, which closely resemble certain natural transmitter substances in chemical structure. Recent findings suggest that the unusual and often eerie effects produced by such drugs may stem from the fact that they stimulate unusual patterns of neural activity within our brains (Leavitt, 1974). Second, drugs can block the action of natural transmitter substances, thus producing effects opposite to those ordinarily induced by these substances. For example, certain pain-killers seem to operate in this manner, blocking the transmission of neural information related to feelings of discomfort (see pp. 67–68). Simi-

Drugs and Synaptic Transmission

larly, drugs which cause paralysis, such as curare, produce these effects by blocking the transmission of motor impulses from the brain to various muscles. In sum, the dramatic effects of a wide variety of drugs can be traced to their impact upon the subtle biochemical events ordinarily taking place in the tiny spaces separating one neuron from another.

THE NERVOUS SYSTEM: FOUNDATION FOR BEHAVIOR

Although neurons serve as highly efficient communicators of information, they would probably be of little use if they were scattered throughout the body in a totally random fashion. Fortunately, this is far from the case and they are, instead, organized into a highly complex and specialized structure known as the nervous system. Because it is this structure and the incredibly complex patterns of neural activity occurring within it which ultimately underlies all of our feelings, actions, and mental processes, it is well deserving of careful attention. Thus, in the present section, we will provide a brief description of the structure and function of the nervous system. We should begin by noting that since our focus in later portions of this chapter will be upon human behavior and characteristics, the information which follows generally refers to the nervous system as it exists in human beings rather than in other organisms.

The Nervous System: A Note on Some Major Divisions

While the nervous system generally functions as an integrated unit, it is often divided into two portions known, respectively, as the **peripheral** and **central systems.** Since we will shortly consider the central nervous system in some detail, a few words about the peripheral system and its major divisions seem appropriate at this point.

The peripheral nervous system consists primarily of a number of **nerves** (bundles of axons) connecting various portions of the body to the central system. Some of these nerves link muscles to the central system, while others connect internal organs and glands to this system. Together, those falling into the latter category are often described as the **autonomic nervous system.** This system, in turn, is frequently divided into two major components on the basis of the functions they perform. The first, known as the **sympathetic division,** seems to play a role in readying the body for vigorous physical activity. Thus, arousal of this division speeds the heart, raises the blood pressure, and releases sugar into the blood. The second, known as the **parasympathetic division,** operates in an opposite fashion, stimulating the internal processes which restore and regenerate the body's resources. Thus, activation of this system tends to lower blood pressure, slow the heart, and divert blood away from muscles to the organs of digestion. While the autonomic nervous system plays an important role in regulating internal bodily processes, it does so primarily by transmitting information to and from the central system. Thus, in order to fully understand the biological bases of behavior, it is necessary to focus upon the central nervous system itself.

The Central Nervous System: Running the Show

If there may be said to be a "governing" organ of the body, then certainly it is the central nervous system. In an ultimate sense, it is this complex structure which controls our overt behavior, regulates our internal bodily states, and serves as the seat of all of our mental processes. Basically, the central nervous system may be said to consist of two distinctive parts, the spinal cord and the brain.

The Spinal Cord

The basic function of the spinal cord is that of communication. This structure, housed in a protective bony tube known as the spinal column, carries sensory information from receptors such as the eyes or ears to the brain, and conducts motor impulses from the brain to effectors (muscles and glands) scattered throughout the body. When the spinal cord is viewed in cross section, it reveals a characteristic structure which is suggestive of these major functions, and also points to another activity. The central portion of the cord consists of gray matter (cell bodies of many neurons) arranged roughly in the shape of the letter "H," and is surrounded by white matter (collections of axons). The white matter is concerned with the conduction of information both to and away from the brain, and serves the communication function already mentioned. The gray matter is more directly concerned with a different function, that of the regulation of **spinal reflexes.**

These reflexes are relatively fixed reactions which can be evoked in a seemingly automatic manner by the presentation of particular stimuli. If you have ever withdrawn your hand from a hot object or been tested for the familiar knee-jerk reaction by your family physician, you have had first-hand experience with such reflexes. Moreover, you are probably aware of the fact that they occur in what seems to be an automatic manner, without any conscious thought. Because they permit very rapid reactions to potentially dangerous stimuli, reflexes often serve an important adaptive function. For example, imagine the negative consequences which might result if we did not automatically place our arms in front of us while falling, or blink in response to rapidly approaching objects, such as another person's fists!

The Brain: Where Consciousness Dwells

In contrast to the relative simplicity of the spinal cord, the brain is an extremely complex structure. In view of this fact, we will make no attempt to examine all of its many parts. Instead, our attention will be focused primarily upon those structures most directly related to the forms of behavior we will consider in later discussions. In order to simplify our task still further, we will examine these structures roughly in the order in which they would be encountered during an imaginary journey upwards from the spinal cord through the center of the brain and out onto its outer covering. One reason for following this path is that it will take us from structures we share with simpler forms of life, and which developed relatively early in the course of evolution, to structures possessed only by human beings or our close relations, and which developed quite recently in the history of life upon the earth.

Immediately above the point at which the spinal cord enters the brain are two structures known, respectively, as the **medulla** and **pons** (see Figure 2–5 and Color Plate 4). Both are quite similar in function and form to the spinal cord and may, in fact, be viewed largely as continuations of this structure. Thus, major sensory and motor pathways pass through both the medulla and pons on their way up to higher centers of the brain or down to effectors in different parts of the body. In addition, both contain a central core consisting of a dense network of interconnected neurons, the **reticular activating system,** which is known to play a crucial role in arousal and sleep. The function of this structure, as well as that of certain regions of the pons which also seem to play a major role in the regulation of sleep, will be examined in more detail in a later section. The medulla also contains several *nuclei*—collections of cell bodies—which regulate such important processes as breathing, alterations in blood pressure, and the beating of the heart. For this reason, it is often termed the "vital" (life) center of the brain.

Behind the medulla and pons lies another structure, the **cerebellum,** which is primarily concerned with the regulation of motor activities. In particular, it seems to operate so as to insure that such actions occur in a coordinated and integrated manner. Damage to the cerebellum through injury or disease results in such symptoms as a loss of muscle tone and repeated stumbling or falling.

Lying directly above the pons is the **midbrain** (refer to Figure 2–5 and

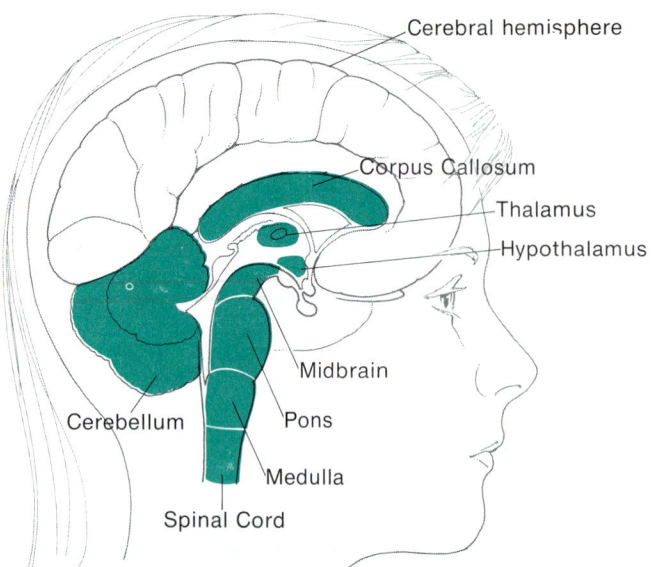

Cerebral hemisphere

Corpus Callosum

Thalamus

Hypothalamus

Midbrain

Pons

Cerebellum

Medulla

Spinal Cord

FIGURE 2–5 Basic structure of the human brain. Note that in this illustration, the brain has been split in two (just as you might slice an apple from the stem to the bottom), and you are looking at the inner surface of one of the two halves. (For a color photo of an actual brain, see Plate 4.)

Color Plate 4), a structure containing (1) an extension of the reticular system mentioned previously and (2) primitive centers for vision and hearing. The region immediately over the midbrain is generally known as the **diencephalon** and is, in a number of ways, one of the most intriguing we shall consider, for it is here that many of our appetites and motives appear to be controlled. Although the diencephalon contains several structures, only two, the **hypothalamus** and **thalamus,** need be considered. The hypothalamus, which lies immediately above the midbrain, plays a primary role in the regulation of many basic activities, including (1) emotional reactions, (2) sexual behavior, (3) eating and drinking, and (4) control of body temperature. Moreover, it is connected to and influences the pituitary gland, and through this structure exerts a profound influence upon many vital processes. The thalamus, which is located quite close to the center of the brain, has often been described as a "great relay station" (Grossman, 1973). This is because it receives a tremendous amount of sensory information from lower regions of the brain and transmits this input to the cerebral hemispheres (described below) in a highly diffuse manner. Because of their intimate relationship to many interesting and important forms of behavior, both the thalamus and hypothalamus will feature prominently in later discussions within this chapter.

Lying in part near the thalamus but also scattered through other locations is a another group of structures known, together, as the **limbic system.** Although this system is not actually part of the diencephalon, it is closely connected with both the thalamus and hypothalamus and, like these structures, appears to play an important role in the occurrence of emotional reactions. For example, damage to some of the components of this system results in extreme tameness or gentleness on the part of normally ferocious animals, while chemical or electrical stimulation of the same areas often produces uncontrollable rage. Findings such as these have led some investigators to suggest that the limbic system may actually represent the seat of many of our primitive emotions and urges, including anger and lust (Robinson, 1973). While not all researchers would be willing to go that far, most agree that the limbic system does indeed play an important role in such reactions.

Lying above the structures we have considered so far, and receiving exten-

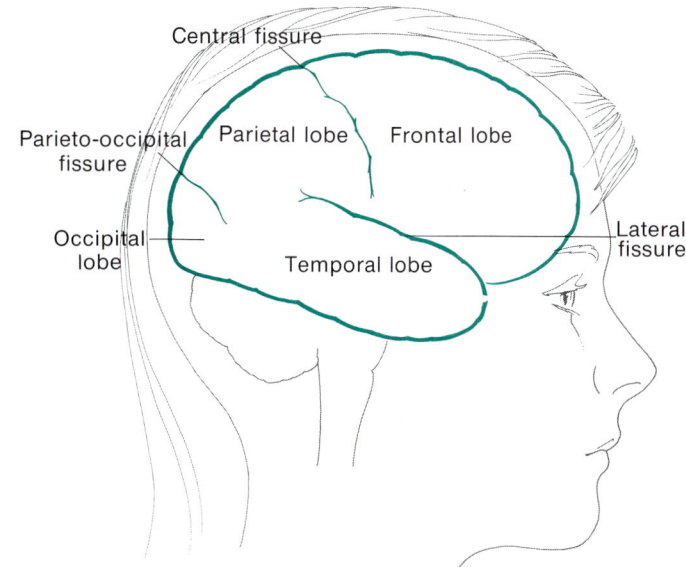

FIGURE 2–6 The cerebral cortex, showing the location of the frontal, parietal, occipital, and temporal lobes. (Note that the structures shown in Figure 2–5 cannot be seen because they are covered by the cortex.) (Adapted from Grossman, 1973.)

sive input from them, are the cerebral hemispheres. In human beings, these hemispheres are so developed that they cover most other portions of the brain. In more primitive organisms, however, they are often quite small and unimpressive. The surface, or **cortex,** of the two hemispheres (which are basically mirror images of each other) is folded into a number of ridges and grooves (fissures) and is usually divided on the basis of the largest of these fissures into four regions, or **lobes** (see Figure 2–6).

The **frontal lobe,** a large region bounded by the deep central fissure, contains the primary motor area, a site concerned with the control of movement of various parts of the body (refer to Figure 2–7). Damage to this area does not result, as might be expected, in total paralysis. Rather, it leads only to a loss of control over fine movements, particularly those of the fingers. This suggests a very important fact about the functioning of the cerebral hemispheres: although a particular area may normally be involved in the regulation

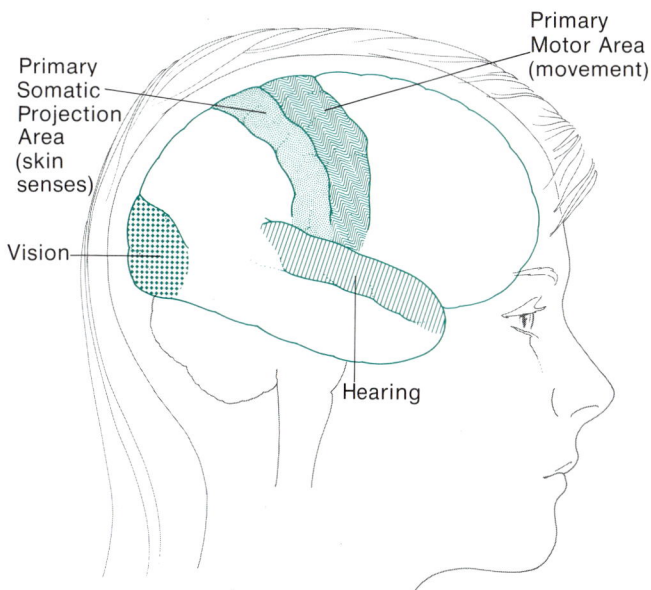

FIGURE 2–7 Areas of the cerebral cortex concerned with muscular movement (primary motor area), sensations from the skin (somatic projection area), vision, and hearing. (Once again, the structures shown in Figure 2–5 cannot be seen because they are covered and surrounded by the cortex.)

or control of some function, adjacent or even more distant regions can often "take up the slack" should damage to the primary areas occur. This is generally more true of young organisms than mature ones, but among human beings, even the brains of mature adults may be viewed as possessing a number of back-up systems which can readily be pressed into service should the need ever arise.

Across the central fissure from the frontal lobe lies a second major division of the cerebral hemispheres, the **parietal lobe.** This lobe contains the primary somatic projection area, a region which mediates sensations from the skin (touch, warmth, pressure, and so on). As is the case with the primary motor area, damage to the primary somatic region usually results in a dulling of senses (here, all the skin senses), rather than a total loss of all sensation.

The remaining two lobes of the cerebral hemispheres, the **occipital** and **temporal lobes,** contain areas concerned, respectively, with vision and hearing. (The location of these areas is illustrated in Figure 2–7.)

One additional area to which we should refer cuts across portions of the frontal, parietal, and temporal lobes, and appears to be concerned with the important process of speech. In the case of right-handed persons, this area seems to be centered in the left cerebral hemisphere. Among "lefties," however, it may appear in the right hemisphere or the left hemisphere, or be divided between the two. Wherever it is located, damage to this region from strokes, tumors, or head injuries often results in disturbing effects known, together, as the **aphasias.** For example, injury to certain portions of the speech area may produce a condition in which the persons involved are incapable of recognizing written words or spoken language—or both. (You may recall that we described such a case at the beginning of this chapter.) Similarly, damage to other portions of the speech center produces an unsettling state of affairs in which the individuals involved can readily write their thoughts on a piece of paper but cannot state them verbally.

Even when all the motor and sensory areas of the cortex are added together, large regions which seem unrelated to either the control of body movements or various types of sensation remain. These **association areas,** as they are often termed, are connected with each other, with motor and sensory areas, and with other portions of the brain (the thalamus, hypothalamus, limbic system), often in a very diffuse manner. This arrangement suggests that they may play an important role in a number of complex processes, including learning, memory, problem-solving, and thinking. That this is indeed the case is indicated by the findings of a large number of experiments which have reported that damage to these areas results in impairments in learning, memory, and the ability to discriminate between various types of stimuli (Masterton and Berkley, 1974).

"Splitting" the Brain: Two Minds in One Body?

Before concluding our discussion of the structure and function of the brain, attention should be called to the fact that it is, like the lungs or kidneys, a double organ. That is, most of the structures we have considered are duplicated in the right and left hemispheres. Given this state of affairs, it would seem quite important that the two halves of the brain be able to communicate readily with each other, and, indeed, such communication is provided by the **corpus callosum,** a broad band of nerve fibers which crosses from one hemisphere to the other (refer to Figure 2–5). Under normal conditions, then, the right and left cerebral hemispheres are in constant and direct communication with each other. But what happens when this link is broken—will a situation arise in which one organism in effect possesses two separate brains? And since centers controlling speech and other verbal abilities are located in only one hemisphere (at least in the case of right-handed persons), will one of these "brains" possess highly developed verbal skills while the other is largely lacking in such abilities?

Recent experiments conducted with subjects whose corpus callosum has been severed for medical reasons (to prevent the spread of epileptic seizures from one hemisphere to the other) suggest that the answer to our questions may well be "yes" (Gazzaniga, 1967, 1970; Sperry, 1968). For example, in one series of studies, either pictures of various common objects or their names were flashed on a screen in such a manner that information about these stimuli could reach only one of the two hemispheres of subjects' brains (see Figure 2–8). Results indicated that under conditions in which such information was received by only the left cerebral hemisphere, subjects were able to read the words or identify the objects with ease. When it could reach only their right cerebral hemisphere, however, they were unable to perform either of these tasks (Gazzaniga, 1967). Indeed, under these conditions subjects often reported that they had seen absolutely nothing at all! (Note that *only right-handed persons* were employed as subjects in these studies; results might well have been quite different if left-handed individuals had taken part.)

Findings such as these point to two general conclusions. First, severing the corpus callosum does indeed produce a situation in which two separate "brains" inhabit the same skull. Second, one of these brains (the left cerebral hemisphere) possesses the ability to regulate speech and related activities, while the other (the right cerebral hemisphere) does not. Although it is tempting to jump from such conclusions to the additional suggestion that the left hemisphere is somehow brighter or more intelligent than the right, other findings indicate that this is not the case.

First, although subjects in the above experiments could not verbally identify the objects shown to their right cerebral hemispheres, they were readily able to select them from among an array of several objects by means of touch (refer to Figure 2–8). This fact suggests that their right hemispheres knew very well what they had seen—they were simply unable to communicate this information to the experimenter in direct verbal fashion. Second, preliminary evidence suggests that individuals whose left cerebral hemisphere has been destroyed by accident or disease (for example, a stroke), are able to master relatively complex language skills when given special training (Glass, Gazzaniga, and Premack, 1973). Age seems to be no serious drawback in such

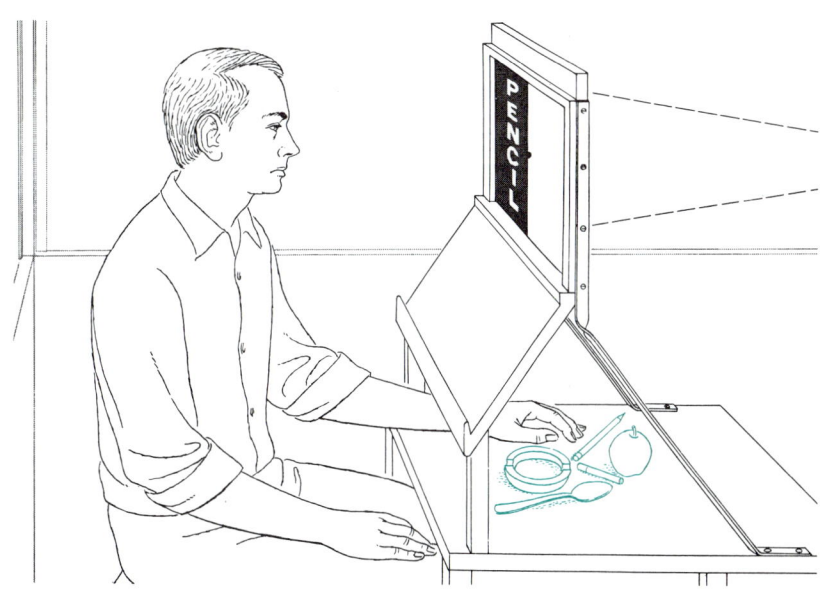

FIGURE 2–8 Some interesting effects of "splitting" the brain. When individuals whose corpus callosum had been severed were shown the names of various common objects in such a manner that this information reached only their right cerebral hemisphere, they could not recognize or name them. They could, however, select the appropriate object from among several others solely by means of touch. (From "The Split Brain in Man" by Michael S. Gazzaniga. Copyright © 1967 by Scientific American, Inc. All rights reserved.)

cases, for even one 84-year-old patient made rapid progress through daily practice. The fact that such individuals can readily acquire language concepts suggests that the right cerebral hemisphere possesses many verbal abilities which can be put to use when the need arises. Finally, there is some evidence that the right hemisphere — although inferior to the left in verbal skills — may actually be superior in several other respects. For example, certain spatial tasks, such as determining which two of several zigzag figures are oriented in the same direction, are performed more quickly by the right than by the left hemisphere. In fact, there is some indication that when information of this type is presented first to the left hemisphere, it is normally relayed to the right for processing and only then back to the left for a verbal response (Gibson, Filbey, and Gazzaniga, 1970). Similarly, some findings suggest that the right hemisphere may also be superior with respect to the regulation of various motor activities (Gazzaniga, 1967).

In short, existing evidence, though far from complete, indicates that there may be a partial division of labor between the two cerebral hemispheres, with one superior in the performance of verbal tasks, and the other superior with respect to spatial or motor abilities. In the most general sense neither is "better" nor "worse" than the other — the two sides are merely very different.

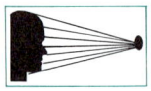

FOCUS ON RESEARCH: *Studying the Brain*

In our discussion of the nervous system, particularly the brain, the functions of a number of different structures or regions were described. The manner in which such information has been obtained, however, was generally ignored. Imagine, then, that you are a researcher setting out to unravel some of the mysteries of the brain, especially the functions of several of its parts. How do you think you might go about accomplishing this important task?

In general, investigators concerned with this topic have relied upon three basic procedures. In the first, various structures or areas of the brain are either removed through surgery or destroyed by means of strong electric currents. The function of these structures is then determined from an examination of the changes in behavior and/or bodily processes so produced. For example, if the removal of a given structure results in the elimination of all emotional reactions, it would be assumed that this area is directly concerned with such behavior.

In the second technique, areas of interest are stimulated by means of weak electric currents or small amounts of various chemicals. By observing the behaviors evoked, it is often possible to establish the major functions of the regions stimulated. Thus, if electrical stimulation of a specific area of the brain serves to awaken animals from deep sleep, it would be concluded that this region is somehow concerned with the regulation of sleep and waking.

Finally, in the third procedure, sophisticated equipment is employed to measure the electrical activity of the brain. Recordings of such activity may be obtained from tiny electrodes placed near or inside single neurons (the *microelectrode* method), from larger electrodes implanted in the brain or placed on its surface (the *evoked potential* method), or from still larger ones attached to the surface of the scalp (the *electroencephalogram*, or *EEG*, method). Changes in electrical activity occurring in response to external stimuli or to alterations in internal states (for example, as an individual falls asleep) may then provide clues to the major functions of the regions or neurons under study. For example, if the level of electrical activity in a particular region increases each time an organism engages in highly rewarding behavior (e.g., eating, drinking, sexual activity) but does not increase at any other time, it might be suspected that this area (or nerve tracts passing through it) is somehow related to the experience of pleasurable sensations.

It should be noted that because many of these procedures involve major operations and considerable "tampering" with the brain, they are unsuitable for use with human subjects except under rare circumstances (e.g., during certain forms of medically required brain surgery). They are, however, frequently employed in research with laboratory animals. In such cases, of course, every possible precaution is taken to protect subjects from pain or discomfort.

There is an old saying about losing sight of the forest for the trees which underscores the fact that often it is easy to misplace important points or issues in a wealth of detail. We hope that this adage does not apply to your own present state of mind, and that you have not lost sight of the fact that our discussions of the nervous system and neurons were designed to provide you with the necessary background for understanding important forms of behavior. If you have indeed misplaced this fact, the pages which follow should serve as a reminder, for from this point on, we will be focusing our attention upon important links between the nervous system, especially the brain, and various forms of behavior. Specifically, the information we have already presented will now be employed both to explain and to clarify the physiological basis of (1) hunger and thirst, (2) sleep and dreams, (3) emotional reactions, and (4) reward and punishment. In addition, we will return to the discussion of drugs we began on page 41, examining the manner in which many of these substances influence the nervous system, and thus our feelings, actions, and thoughts.

BRAIN AND BEHAVIOR: THE INTIMATE BOND

Under normal conditions, most organisms (including human beings) are capable of regulating their intake of food and water in a very precise manner. That is, they eat and drink just enough to satisfy the needs of their bodies, and neither gain nor lose large amounts of weight. Of course, as many of you probably know from painful personal experience, there are a number of exceptions to this general rule in the case of human beings. For most of us, though, gross variations in weight are relatively unusual, and the long-term balance of food intake against continuing bodily needs is very precise.

Hunger and Thirst: Eat, Drink, and . . .

At first glance, this ability to regulate our intake of food and water is not very surprising. After all, we merely eat when we feel hungry and drink when we feel thirsty, and somehow, the rest takes care of itself. But *how*, precisely is this balance maintained? How do feelings of hunger and thirst arise, and why are they usually so neatly matched to actual bodily needs? As we shall soon see, the answers to these questions involve the operation of complex regulatory mechanisms located deep within the brain.

Early investigators, taking note of the fact that contractions of the stomach when empty are often closely related to subjective feelings of hunger, suggested that signals from this organ play a crucial role in the regulation of eating. That is, they assumed that eating is initiated when receptors in the stomach signal that it is empty, and inhibited when they report that it is full. Unfortunately, this simple view was quickly contradicted by experiments demonstrating that feelings of hunger and normal regulation of food intake persist even after all nerves leading to the stomach are severed (Morgan and Morgan, 1940). Sensory information from this organ, then, does not seem to be essential for the normal control of eating.

Eating and Hunger

Findings such as these seemed to point to the conclusion that eating is probably regulated by mechanisms located somewhere in the brain. But where should one search for such mechanisms? One hint was provided by the medical case histories of individuals who had suffered damage to the hypothalamus. Such persons often experienced difficulties in weight regulation after these injuries, either gaining or losing large amounts. Because these cases seemed to implicate the hypothalamus in the regulation of eating, a great deal of attention was soon focused upon this structure. The results of such research were quite dramatic, generally suggesting that two specific regions of the hypothalamus play a major role in the regulation of food intake. The first, located toward the sides of this structure and known as the **lateral hypothalamus,** seemed to function in an excitatory manner, facilitating eating. The second, located near the center of this structure and known as the **ventromedial hypothalamus,** seemed to operate in an inhibitory fashion, preventing or terminating such behavior.

Evidence that the lateral hypothalamus normally serves to facilitate eating was provided by a number of experiments in which this region was either damaged or destroyed (Teitelbaum, Cheng, and Rozin, 1969). After undergoing such an operation, animals usually pass through four distinct stages of recovery. First, they refuse both to eat and to drink, and will actually perish if not forced to feed. After a variable period of time, they enter a second stage in which they will eat small quantities of their favorite foods, but still not enough to maintain life. Further improvement is shown in a third stage during which they will eat enough food to survive, but still refuse to drink. Finally, in a fourth stage they both eat and drink enough to maintain a constant weight. That their recovery is not complete even then, however, is indicated by the following facts: (1) although their weight stabilizes, it does so at a level considerably lower than normal (Powley and Keesey, 1970); (2) they are still quite "finicky," refusing to eat foods which have been made even slightly bitter; and (3) they drink only when eating. In short, destruction of the lateral hypothalamus produces disturbances in eating behavior which are both permanent and irreversible.

Even more dramatic findings pointed to the conclusion that the ventromedial hypothalamus normally acts to prevent or terminate eating. Destruction of this area seems to produce animal gluttons who, upon awaking from their operation, stagger over to the food cup in their cages and begin shoveling in enormous quantities of food. Such excessive eating, known as **hyperphagia,** often continues until their bulk reaches gigantic proportions (see Figure 2–9). At some point, however, they return to near-normal intake, and maintain their now excessive weight at a stable level. Although it might seem that animals suffering from lesions in their ventromedial hypothalamus would gobble up everything in sight, this is not actually the case. Rather, they seem to become quite particular, and will only overeat if provided with a tasty diet. Moreover,

FIGURE 2–9 Rats with lesions in the ventromedial hypothalamus often overeat until they reach truly gigantic proportions. (Photo courtesy of Dr. Neal Miller.)

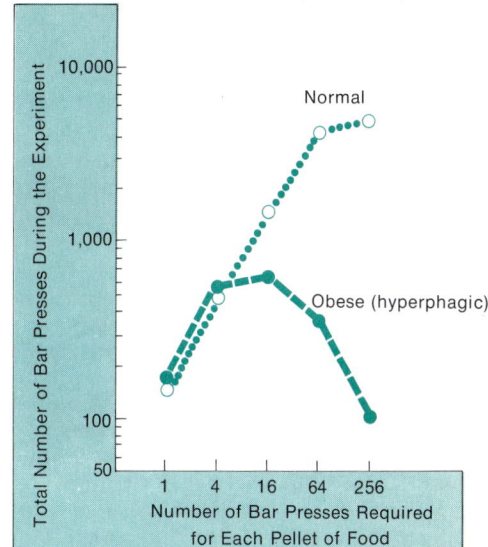

FIGURE 2–10 **Although they tend to eat vast quantities of food when it is readily and easily available, animals with damage to the ventromedial hypothalamus seem unwilling to work for such rewards. Thus, as shown here, they refuse to push a lever more than a few times in order to gain a single pellet of food, whereas normal animals seem quite willing to do so. (Adapted from Teitelbaum, 1957, p. 488.)**

if required to work for their food, they often refuse, and will actually lose weight if much effort is required (see Figure 2–10).

Largely on the basis of the findings we have just described, many researchers soon concluded that the lateral and ventromedial portions of the hypothalamus act as discrete "feeding" or "satiety" centers, facilitating or inhibiting such behavior in a relatively direct manner. While this view enjoyed widespread support and acceptance for a number of years, it has recently been called into serious question by two lines of evidence. First, recent investigations suggest that eating is probably not controlled by one or two specific "centers" in the brain, but rather by a diffuse system of neural pathways connecting many different regions (Deutsch, 1971). While these pathways pass through or near the lateral and ventromedial areas of the hypothalamus, they are by no means restricted to them. Second, the results of several experiments conducted by Richard Keesey and his associates (Keesey and Boyle, 1973; Powley and Keesey, 1970) suggest that these regions do not influence eating simply by stimulating or inhibiting such activity. Rather, they appear to function by setting the point about which body weight will be regulated. Damage to the ventromedial hypothalamus seems to raise this setting, so that overeating and weight gain follow, while damage to the lateral hypothalamus seems to lower it, so that reduced food intake and weight loss result. In short, there is some indication that the drastic changes in eating which often follow damage to these regions stem from subjects' attempts to bring their body weight into line with the new "set points" that have been established rather than from a complete loss of neural control over feeding.

In the face of such evidence, many physiological psychologists now question the view that eating can be understood solely in terms of discrete "feeding" and "satiety" centers in the hypothalamus. Not all experimental findings have been consistent, however, and the issue is still far from being resolved (Mufson and Wampler, 1972). Given this continuing controversy, perhaps the most reasonable conclusion we can offer at present is as follows: The hypothalamus may indeed play an important role in the regulation of food intake. However, its influence in this respect is almost certainly more complex and subtle than was initially assumed.

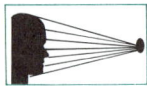

FOCUS
ON
RESEARCH: *Of Fat Rats and Overweight People*

In the preceding discussion of eating, it was noted that destruction of the ventromedial hypothalamus often converts normal laboratory animals into ravenous gluttons capable of consuming vast quantities of food. Since human beings, too, possess a hypothalamus, these findings have led some investigators to question whether chronic overeating by people also stems, at least in part, from some disturbance in the functioning of this important structure. Although it is certainly not possible to make lesions in the hypothalami of human subjects in order to study the influence of such treatment upon their appetites, an ingenious series of experiments by Stanley Schachter and his associates (Schachter, 1971; Schachter and Rodin, 1974) points to the conclusion that like the "fat rats" we have described, overweight humans may be the helpless victims of a malfunctioning hypothalamus. In particular, Schachter's research has uncovered a number of interesting parallels between the behavior of obese human beings and that of hyperphagic rats.

First, he has noted that overweight people, like overweight rats, are much more sensitive to the taste of foods than are individuals of normal weight. Thus, when presented with a pleasant-tasting vanilla milk shake in one experiment, obese subjects drank considerably more than did their thinner peers. When presented with a milk shake which had been laced with quinine to make it bitter, however, they drank much less than did those of normal weight. Second, it appears that like hyperphagic rats, overweight humans are less willing to "work for their supper" than normals. For example, in one study, a can of nuts was placed on the table next to subjects as they filled out a variety of questionnaires. In one condition, the nuts were still in the shell, while in another, the shells had been removed. As expected, this variation made little difference to people of normal weight—about half ate some nuts in both conditions. Among obese subjects, however, it seemed to be quite important. Very few ate any nuts when they were unshelled, while most ate some when they had been removed from the shell (see Figure 2–11). Other parallels between hyperphagic rats and overweight people uncovered by Schachter and his co-workers include: (1) both eat larger meals than normals; (2) both eat faster than others of normal weight; and (3) both are generally less physically active than their normal-weight peers. On the basis of this surprising number of parallels, Schachter has tentatively suggested that obesity in humans may indeed have a basis in some malfunctioning of the ventromedial hypothalamus.

One behavioral mechanism through which such disorders could lead to overeating has recently been suggested by Singh (1973, 1974). According to this researcher, the tendency of both hyperphagic rats and obese human beings to eat more than they need stems primarily from an underlying inability to suppress habitual modes of behavior. That is, members of both groups may overindulge because they are somehow unable to "turn off" eating once it gets started. This suggestion is consistent with the fact that obese people and rats eat for longer periods—and thus consume more food—than do those of normal weight. Moreover, it agrees with the observation that they typically engage in fewer noneating behaviors during meals than do normals (e.g., playing with their food). Finally, it gains support from several studies which demonstrate that obese individuals eat more than normals only under conditions in which such behavior is a dominant or habitual response (Singh, 1973, 1974). For example, in one of these investigations, obese and normal subjects who had been asked to skip breakfast were placed in a situation in which they could obtain tasty crackers ("Pizza Spins") either by performing a familiar, previously learned response, or by performing an unfamiliar, new behavior. Consistent with Singh's suggestions, obese individuals ate more than normals in the former condition—one in which the actions involved in obtaining food were already quite familiar.

If it is indeed the case that the tendency toward obesity stems from a malfunctioning hypothalamus and a resulting inability on the part of some persons to terminate eating once it begins, the moral for effective weight control seems clear: individuals afflicted with this difficulty should avoid all contact with food except in situations in which the size of their portions is carefully controlled.

A second mechanism which seems to play an important role in obesity is the type of cues which tend to elicit eating behavior. Growing evidence suggests that overweight individuals tend to be more responsive to external stimuli such as the sight or smell of food than are those of normal weight (Rodin and Slochower, 1976). That is, while most persons tend to eat only when internal cues (e.g., the growling of their stomachs) inform them that it is time for a meal, overweight individuals seem to be readily stimulated to indulge by the appetizing sight or delicious aroma of various forms of food. Unfortunately for persons with a persistent weight problem, stimuli of this type are far from rare; indeed, we are literally flooded with them

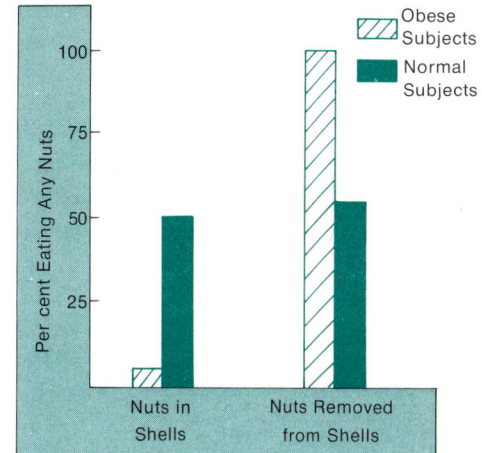

FIGURE 2–11 The willingness of normal and obese individuals to work for a snack. Like hyperphagic rats, obese human beings seem unwilling to expend much effort to obtain food, despite their strong tendency to overeat when it is readily available. (Based on data from Schachter, 1971.)

throughout the day (see Figure 2–12). Given this fact, it is little wonder that many persons find themselves perpetual losers in the battle of the "bulge." Put very simply, they find it all but impossible to resist the countless temptations which seem to surround them on every side.

FIGURE 2–12 Research evidence suggests that overweight individuals are more readily stimulated to eat by external cues such as the sight or smell of food than are persons without weight problems.

Thirst: When is it Time for a Drink?

It has been estimated that during the course of a single day, an average individual loses more than two quarts of water through perspiration, breathing, and the process of elimination (Crouch and McClintic, 1971). If we did not possess a highly accurate mechanism for monitoring this loss and signaling its occurrence, we would soon perish through dehydration. But how does this mechanism operate? How are we able to regulate our fluid intake in such a precise and constant manner? Early answers to these questions emphasized the role of sensations from the mouth and throat. It was suggested that we drink largely in response to feelings of dryness which arise in these areas as the body's store of water is depleted. Although such explanations seem quite reasonable, and agree with our subjective impressions concerning thirst, they are refuted by the finding that both thirst and drinking persist even when such sensations are entirely eliminated (e.g., through anesthesia of the mouth and throat).

Today, it is generally believed that fluid intake is regulated by certain cells in the lateral hypothalamus. Apparently, these cells—known as **osmoreceptors**—have the ability to respond to the movement of water through their cell membranes. At times when the body's supplies of water are relatively low, the osmoreceptors, along with many other cells, give up water to the blood and other body fluids. Unlike most other cells, however, the osmoreceptors are sensitive to such movement, perhaps because it produces a large reduction in their size. The action potentials they then transmit in response to such changes seem to form the basis of our feelings of thirst. Replenishment of the body's supplies of water restores these cells to their normal size, with the result that sensations of thirst are eliminated. In short, drinking, like eating, seems to be regulated largely by complex neural mechanisms located deep within the brain.

Sleep: The Pause That Refreshes

What single activity occupies more of your time than any other? Although it would be pleasant to respond by naming some highly enjoyable behavior such as eating, sailing, skiing, or making love, the answer actually involves a far less dramatic form of activity: sleep. Most individuals spend fully one third of their entire lives asleep, and for some, the proportion is even higher (Webb and Friel, 1971).

Although the importance of sleep has always been obvious, it is only in recent decades that it has served as the subject of careful scientific study. The main reason for this delay in the psychological investigation of sleep lay in the fact that as an essentially internal form of behavior, it was not readily open to direct observation. Thus, some means for studying it as an objective fashion was required before serious research could proceed. A tool for accomplishing this important task was finally obtained in the late 1930's with the development of the **electroencephalograph,** or **EEG.** This device for measuring the electrical activity of the brain was soon put to good use, and has served as an important tool for unraveling many of the age-old mysteries surrounding sleep. Indeed, as a result of research employing the EEG technique we now know that there are actually two distinct types of sleep instead of only one, and we are beginning to understand the neural mechanisms which regulate and control both of these activities.

The Two States of Sleep

Perhaps the best way of illustrating the important differences between the two states of sleep is that of outlining the changes which occur as individuals move from relaxed wakefulness to first one state and then the other.

When human beings are resting, prior to sleep, the electrical activity of their brains is characterized by relatively fast (8 to 12 cycles per second), low-magnitude changes in voltage known as **alpha waves.** As the first of the

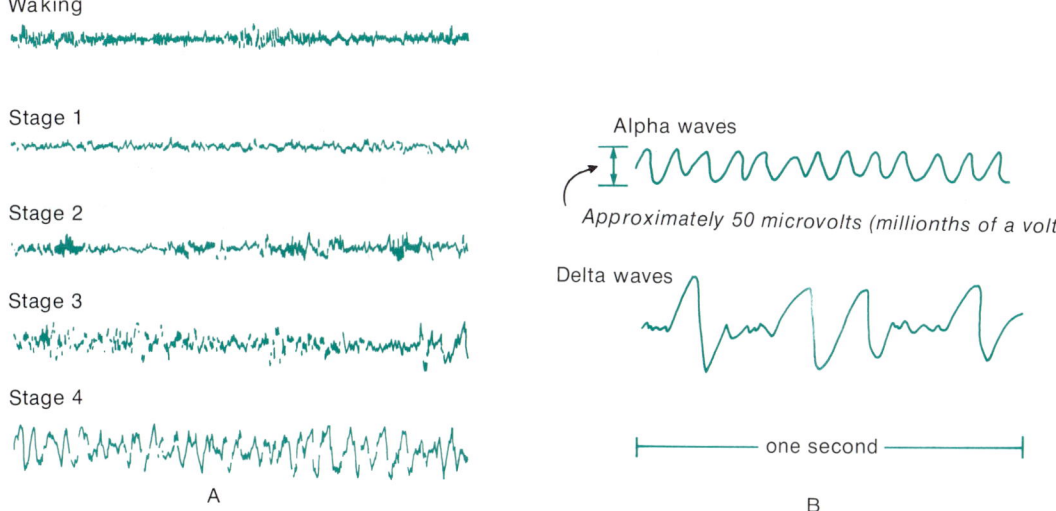

FIGURE 2–13   The four stages of NREM sleep. Movement through these stages is characterized by a gradual shift from the relatively fast, low-magnitude *alpha waves* present during resting wakefulness to the slower, more irregular and higher-magnitude *delta waves* present during Stages 3 and 4. Actual EEG recordings are shown in (A), while schematic representations of alpha and delta waves are shown in (B). Note that the changes in electrical activity recorded are very small, involving only tiny fractions of a volt. (Part A from Hartmann, E. L.: *The Functions of Sleep.* New Haven: Yale University Press, 1973.)

two major types of sleep develops—*nonrapid eye movement,* or **NREM,** sleep—a systematic series of changes begins to occur. These alterations in the pattern of the EEG are quite complex, and are often used to divide NREM sleep into four distinct stages (see Figure 2–13). Basically, though, they involve a gradual shift from the fast, low-magnitude alpha waves mentioned above to slower (1 to 3 cycles per second) but higher magnitude delta waves.

After the passage of approximately ninety minutes (the precise interval varies from individual to individual and from night to night), a second distinct state known as *rapid eye movement,* or **REM,** sleep develops. This state is distinguished from NREM sleep by several characteristics. First, during REM sleep, the electrical activity of the brain comes to resemble that of the first (i.e., lightest) stage of NREM sleep. Thus, the EEG pattern seems to suggest that the individual is close to a waking state, even though he or she is still deeply asleep. Second, the regular pattern of the EEG is interrupted by sudden bursts of higher magnitude activity. These bursts closely accompany (and may in fact be produced by) rapid movements of the eyes (REMs), the activity from which REM sleep derives its name (see Figure 2–14). When individuals showing such movements are awakened, they often report that they have been dreaming, a finding which led early investigators to conclude that dreams occur only during REM sleep (Dement and Kleitman, 1957). Now, however, it is known that they also occur—although perhaps in less vivid or developed form—during NREM sleep as well.

A third characteristic of REM sleep is an almost total suppression of the muscular system of the body. Indeed, muscle relaxation is so profound that a state bordering on paralysis seems to exist. In view of this fact, it is not surprising to learn that organisms which are preyed upon by others (rabbits, mice, deer) spend much less time in REM sleep than their predators (cats, foxes, wolves). Apparently, too much REM sleep would prove fatal to animals whose major form of defense lies in a quick getaway. The occurrence of profound muscular relaxation at a time when the EEG seems to suggest a state close to wakefulness has led some investigators to describe REM sleep as *paradoxical* in nature.

FIGURE 2–14   REM sleep derives its name from the rapid eye movements frequently shown by individuals in this state. When awakened during such movements, most individuals report dreaming. (By permission of John Hart and Field Enterprises, Inc.)

Finally, while pulse, respiration, and blood pressure are relatively slow and steady during NREM sleep, they often show sizeable changes during periods of REM sleep. The magnitude and suddeness of such alterations may account for the fact that many heart attacks tend to occur during the early morning hours, when, as we shall soon see, individuals are particularly likely to be experiencing REM sleep.

Periods of REM sleep continue to arise and to alternate with longer intervals of NREM sleep throughout the night (see Figure 2–15). The length of these REM periods is not constant, but increases toward morning. Thus, while the first may last only 5 to 10 minutes, the final interval—the one from which many people awake—may persist for 30 minutes or more (Hartmann, 1973). Adults seem to spend about 20 per cent of their sleep time in the REM state and 80 per cent in the NREM state. Young children, however, may spend up to 50 per cent of their sleep time in REM sleep.

Functions of Sleep   The fact that there are two distinct types of sleep has led several authorities to suggest that each serves a somewhat different function. With respect

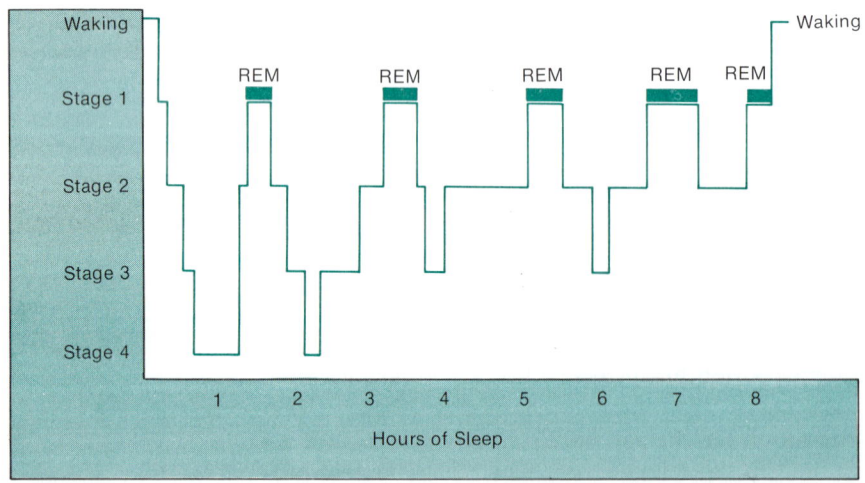

FIGURE 2–15   The alternation of REM and NREM sleep over the course of a single night. Note that the length of each REM period (dark bars) increases toward morning, while Stages 3 and 4 all but disappear. (Adapted from Hartmann, 1973.)

to NREM sleep, it has often been proposed that during this activity, important types of physiological restoration occur. For example, Hartmann (1973), a noted expert on sleep, has suggested that many proteins, including RNA—a crucial substance through which cell nuclei control cellular functions—are synthesized primarily during NREM sleep. Support for this view is provided by evidence that (1) the need for such sleep increases after intense exercise or other activities which would be expected to cause the breakdown of proteins or RNA (Hauri, 1968), and (2) depriving individuals of NREM sleep causes them to feel lethargic and fatigued (Agnew, Webb, and Williams, 1967). In sum, there is some indication that this type of sleep provides the body with an opportunity for rest and repair.

Several suggestions regarding the function of REM sleep have also been offered. First, it has been suggested that REM sleep benefits certain regions of the brain which would be harmed by long, uninterrupted periods of inactivity such as those occurring during NREM sleep (Ephron and Carrington, 1966). That is, REM sleep may provide such regions with the stimulation they need to remain in peak operating form. Second, it has been suggested that REM sleep plays an important role in memory and information processing (see Chapters 5 and 6). For example, several studies suggest that animals deprived of REM sleep (they are awakened each time they enter this state) learn more slowly and forget more readily than subjects not treated in this fashion (Hartmann and Stern, 1972; Pearlman and Greenberg, 1972). Perhaps the most intriguing suggestion regarding the function of REM sleep, however, involves the idea that it plays a role in "psychological restoration," permitting the nervous system to somehow recover from the ill effects of stress and anxiety (Hartmann, 1973). Evidence for this view comes from two principal sources.

First, it has been found that individuals who spend a relatively long period in REM sleep each night differ sharply in several ways from those who spend a relatively short period in such sleep. For example, long-sleepers tend to be more depressed, anxious, and neurotic than short-sleepers. Thus, it appears that troubled individuals seem to need greater amounts of sleep than do those who are functioning more normally (Brewer and Hartmann, 1973). Second, it has been found that the need for sleep seems to increase sharply at times when individuals experience stress, depression, or difficult mental activity, but actually decreases at times when everything is going quite well (see Figure 2–16). Taken together, these findings suggest that REM sleep is at least in part a

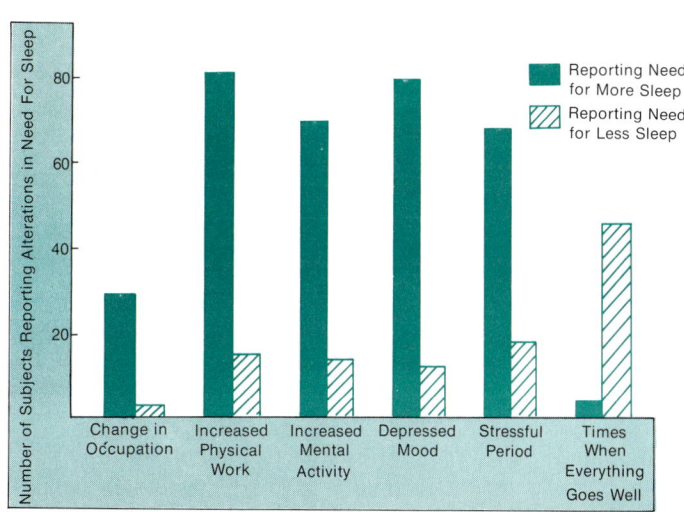

FIGURE 2–16 Variations in the need for sleep. Many people report needing more sleep during periods of stress, increased mental or physical work, or when they are depressed. They report needing *less* sleep, however, at times when everything is going well. (Based on data from Hartmann, 1973.)

response to psychological stress, and that the more troubled, depressed, or upset an individual is, the greater his or her need for such activity. One of the functions of REM sleep, therefore, may be that of repair or reorganization of several subtle neural systems in the brain essential for effective psychological functioning (Hartmann, 1973). Perhaps it is partly for this reason that individuals deprived of all sleep for several consecutive days experience such negative reactions as loss of recent memories, increasing irritability, perceptual distortions, and a growing inability to focus their attention (Freemon, 1972; Hockey, 1970). Regardless of whether this is the case, there can be little doubt that continued efforts to probe the nature of sleep will soon reveal more about the functions of this still somewhat mysterious one-third of our lives.

The Regulation of Sleep

In our previous discussion of the structure and function of the brain, it was noted that a diffuse network of neurons running through the center of the pons and midbrain, and known as the **reticular activating system** (RAS), plays an important role in both sleep and arousal. The RAS seems to function as a *waking center*, rousing sleeping organisms and maintaining a state of wakefulness once it is attained. That this is indeed the case is suggested by two facts: (1) electrical stimulation of the RAS awakens sleeping animals, and (2) destruction of the system produces continuous, permanent sleep.

Given the apparently powerful activating influence of the RAS, it might be wondered how, in the face of this built-in alarm clock, sleep ever occurs. One view, widely accepted in the past, suggests that in the absence of much in the way of sensory input, the RAS shuts itself off and becomes deactivated. A second view, and one that has gained increasing support in recent years, suggests, instead, that sleep results from the direct inhibition of this system by active *sleep centers*. Two such centers appear to exist (Jouvet, 1967, 1969).

The first, known as the **nuclei of raphe,** is located in the medulla, and seems to be primarily concerned with NREM sleep. Destruction of the cells in this region produces insomnia. For example, in several studies with cats, subjects were found to sleep less than 10 per cent of the time after operations which destroyed these cells, whereas previously they slept for up to 65 per cent of the day. The second center is located in the middle portion of the pons, and seems to regulate the occurrence of REM sleep. In addition, it appears to control nearby centers which transmit information to the brain's visual pathways, perhaps thereby producing the vivid images often "seen" in dreams. Destruction of this area totally abolishes REM sleep and probably most dreaming as well.

Together, and in a cyclic fashion which produces the alternation between REM and NREM sleep described above, these two centers apply what might be viewed as "neural brakes" to the RAS and thus induce sleep. Falling asleep, then, is not simply a passive process which occurs whenever little else is happening to the organism. Rather, it involves the operation of specific centers in the brain which actively regulate and control its occurrence.

Dreams: Windows on the Unconscious?

In ancient days, dreams were viewed as messages from the gods which foretold future events or contained important information. In modern times, however, they have usually been attributed to less dramatic sources. For example, parents often console terrified youngsters after a frightening nightmare by remarking that it was, after all, "only a dream." In other cases, dreams are viewed as arising from overindulgence in spicy foods or alcoholic beverages (see Figure 2–17).

Regardless of whether they are seen as instances of divine revelation or the result of faulty digestion, existing evidence suggests that dreams are a universal human experience. While individuals vary greatly in terms of the

FIGURE 2–17 Once viewed as important messages from the gods, dreams have come to be seen, in modern times, either as communications from the unconscious, or as the result of overindulgence in food or drink. In the famous scene above, Scrooge—the main character in Dickens' "A Christmas Carol"—is accusing the ghost of his former partner of being merely a dream produced by "a bit of undigested stew." (From the Metro-Goldwyn-Mayer release "A Christmas Carol," © 1938 by Loew's Incorporated. Copyright renewed 1965 by Metro-Goldwyn-Mayer, Inc.)

contents and dramatic impact of their dreams, all seem to have such experiences at some time or other. Moreover, as noted earlier, dreams seem to occur during both REM and NREM sleep.

But what is the nature of such experiences? Are dreams merely an accident of evolution—a by-product of the normal operation of the sleeping nervous system? Or do they serve important psychological functions? One intriguing answer to such questions was provided by Sigmund Freud, who held that dreams serve as a kind of "safety valve" through which individuals find release for unacceptable wishes or impulses. Going even further, he suggested that much could be learned about a person's hidden wishes or desires through careful study of his or her dreams (see also Chapter 11).

Although such suggestions are quite fascinating, they have not been supported by the findings of empirical research. For example, a number of investigations indicate that contrary to Freud's proposals, the contents of most persons' dreams are generally quite ordinary, and highly consistent with their waking behavior, thoughts, and motives (Carrington, 1972; Cohen, 1973). Thus, there is little direct evidence for the view that they serve as "safety valves" for the expression of unacceptable impulses. That dreams may provide other psychological benefits, however, is suggested by additional findings.

First, there is some indication that dreams may play a role in information processing or problem solving. Although dreaming about one's problems rarely yields workable solutions to them, some progress in this direction does occasionally take place (Dement, 1975). Moreover, dreaming about one's problems may be better than not dreaming about them, just as thinking about such difficulties may be better than not thinking about them (Cohen, 1976). Second, the findings of several studies suggest that dreams can often produce positive shifts in mood or overall "state of mind," especially when they center on unpleasant events or experiences but are not too frightening or upsetting (Cohen and Cox, 1975). In sum, although much remains to be learned, there seem to be increasing grounds for assuming that dreams are more than a mere accident of evolution. Instead, it now seems likely that when their nature is fully understood, they will turn out to serve important—if subtle—adaptive functions.

**PSYCHOLOGY
IN
ACTION: *Remembering Your Dreams***

Existing evidence suggests that almost all individuals dream on a fairly regular basis. Yet despite this fact, we often have difficulty in recalling such experiences. One explanation for this inability to remember our dreams, suggested by the "safety valve" interpretation mentioned above, centers on the concept of *repression*. Specifically, it contends that we fail to remember our dreams because their contents are so frightening or unacceptable that we actively repress their memory.

As interesting as this sort of speculation is, research conducted in recent years suggests that dream recall is probably much more strongly affected by two other factors: *salience* and *interference*. The first refers to the subjective impact of dreams—their vividness or emotionality. Thus, the greater the salience of a given dream, the greater the probability that it will be remembered (Cohen and MacNeilage, 1974). The second, which may be of somewhat greater importance, refers to any events which distract attention away from dream material upon waking, and thus lead to its loss from immediate memory. You may demonstrate the powerful influence of interference upon your ability to

remember your dreams by means of the following simple procedures.

Before retiring for the night, place a pen and a notebook near your bed. The next morning lie quietly for about two minutes after waking, and let any dreams you may remember pass through your mind. Do not try to actively recall them in great detail, for this may actually cause them to slip away. After the two minutes are up, enter a description of the dreams you recall in the notebook. On the next morning, get up as soon as you awake, and immediately write down a list of all the important things you must do that day. Spend about two minutes in this task, and then go on to record a description of your dreams in the same manner as on the first day. Continue alternating these procedures for six days, using a new page in the notebook each morning. If you go back over your entries on the final day, there is a good chance you will find that you were able to remember a greater number of dreams and to supply more detailed accounts of each on days when interference was absent (when you lay quietly in bed) than on days when it was present (when you made a list of the day's activities.)

Emotional Reactions: Feeling What Comes Naturally

A stranger insults you and you become angry. You have a close call in traffic and experience strong and immediate fear. Someone about whom you care a great deal murmurs the words "I love you," and at once you are swept by intense waves of joy. Unless one leads an extremely dull and uneventful life, such strong **emotional reactions** are a very common occurrence. Early investigators often attributed these feelings to changes in basic bodily processes and our perception of such alterations—an explanation which boiled down to something like this: "If my heart is pounding and my hair is standing on end, then I must be afraid." Although such an explanation of emotion (often known as the **James-Lange theory** after its originators) has continued to enjoy some attention down to the present time, most research on emotions has pointed instead to the importance of central mechanisms located within the brain. Thus today it is generally agreed that the control and integration of emotional reactions are centered primarily in the **hypothalamus** and several other structures known collectively as the **limbic system.**

Two types of evidence point to the hypothalamus as an important regulator of emotional activities. First, a number of experimenters (e.g., Grossman, 1972) have reported that lesions in the ventromedial portion of this structure (the same area found to play such an important role in hunger and thirst) produce large and seemingly permanent increments in emotional activity. Thus, animals which have been subjected to operations on this area often become extremely vicious, attacking anyone unwary enough to come within range. Similarly, they more readily engage in fighting with other members of their own species when exposed to unpleasant stimuli such as mild electric shock.

A second body of evidence implicating the hypothalamus in the regulation and control of emotion is provided by studies in which various portions of this structure are stimulated with weak pulses of electricity. The results of such experiments reveal that stimulation of many different sites within the hypothalamus elicits various forms of emotional reaction, including attack, flight, and defensive postures (MacPhail and Miller, 1968).

Although the two lines of research just described suggest that the hypothalamus plays an important role in integrating and regulating many forms of emotion, most research in recent years has focused upon the influence of a second group of structures—the **limbic system**—on such reactions. One reason for this emphasis has been the intimate connection that exists between this system and the cerebral cortex, where, presumably, subjective experiences of emotion are centered. Although the term "limbic system" is not always used in a consistent manner by different authorities, for purposes of the present discussion it will be taken to refer both to certain portions of the temporal lobes of the cerebral cortex and to several structures lying below the cortex which are (1) closely connected to each other, (2) closely connected to the hypothalamus and thalamus, and (3) closely linked to many other regions of the cerebral cortex. Among these structures are the **amygdala, hippocampus, cingulate gyrus,** and **septal area** (refer to Figure 2–18).

The limbic system exerts both inhibitory and excitatory influences upon emotion. Perhaps the most famous evidence for an excitatory influence was obtained in a now classic experiment conducted by Kluver and Bucy (1937). In this investigation, the temporal lobes and certain underlying limbic structures (the amygdala and part of the hippocampus) were removed from rhesus monkeys. Following this operation, subjects evidenced a marked reduction in emotionality. Thus, although they had previously been quite aggressive, they now became unusually tame and friendly. Similarly, they showed almost a total lack of fear, even reaching out to touch a live hissing snake—a stimulus they had previously avoided with great care! These findings, and similar results in a number of other investigations (Rosvold, Mirksy, and Pribram, 1954), suggest that the structures removed (especially the amygdala) normally play an excitatory role with respect to emotion, so that their destruction brings about a marked reduction in such reactions.

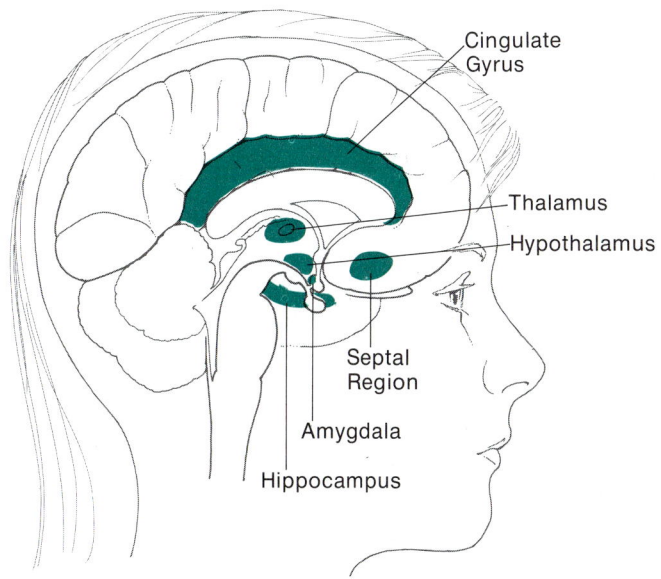

FIGURE 2–18 The major structures of the limbic system.

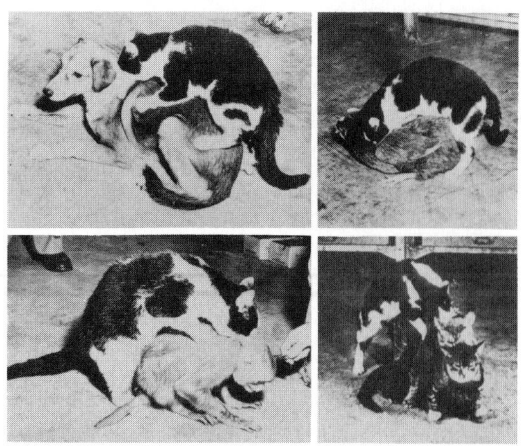

FIGURE 2–19   Damage to the limbic system (particularly the amygdala) often results in heightened sexuality. Animals that have suffered such injuries frequently attempt to copulate with members of other species and sometimes engage in activities which can only be described as "group sex." (Courtesy of Dr. Arthur Kling.)

Another interesting result of the experiment performed by Kluver and Bucy was that subjects showed a marked increase in sexual behavior. Indeed, the monkeys involved became quite "over-sexed," masturbating a great deal, and even attempting to mate with members of other species (see Figure 2–19). These findings suggest that portions of the limbic system play an important role in the regulation of sexual behavior. When they are removed, many restraints and inhibitions formerly in operation seem to depart with them.

When lesions are made in the *cingulate gyrus,* another part of the limbic system, even more dramatic reductions in emotionality are produced. In fact, monkeys subjected to such operations often appear to lose all capacity for emotional reactions. The following description presents a vivid picture of these changes (Ward, 1948):

> Such an animal shows no grooming behavior or acts of affection toward its companions. In fact, it treats them as it treats all inanimate objects and will walk on them, bump into them if they happen to be in the way, and will even sit on them. It will openly eat food in the hand of a companion . . . and appears surprised when it is rebuffed. Such an animal never fights or tries to escape when removed from a cage.

In contrast to the lowered emotionality produced by lesions in the areas described above, destruction of the *septal area,* still another portion of the limbic system, produces heightened emotional reactions. Animals who have undergone such operations show great viciousness, attacking humans without provocation, and readily fighting with members of their own species under some conditions (Miczek and Grossman, 1972). In addition, they seem to over-react to any type of unpleasant stimulation. Such findings indicate that the septal region normally serves to inhibit emotional reaction; when it is destroyed, such restraints are weakened or removed.

In sum, existing evidence suggests that emotional reactions occur as follows: (1) sensory information regarding external stimuli activates relatively primitive regions of the brain (the hypothalamus and limbic system); (2) stimulation of such structures then induces changes in basic bodily functions (blood pressure, heart rate, respiration, etc.), and also stimulates areas of the central cortex, thus producing the subjective experiences we label as fear, rage, joy, sorrow, and so on.

It should not be assumed, however, that the flow of neural information which serves as the basis of emotion occurs in only one direction. The cerebral cortex can stimulate as well as be stimulated by the limbic system and other subcortical structures. For example, we often become quite angry as a result of simply mulling over real or imagined wrongs at the hands of others. Similarly, there is much evidence suggesting that sexual fantasies play an important role in sexual arousal among both men and women (see Chapter 7). In view of such effects, there can be little doubt that the arousal and regulation of emotional reactions actually proceeds along a "two-way street," in which lower centers of the brain exert an important influence upon the cerebral cortex and are, in turn, often strongly affected by the activities of this complex structure.

Over the centuries, many different philosophers have suggested that all organisms, including human beings, seek to maximize pleasure and minimize pain. The essential accuracy of this suggestion is supported by more than one hundred years of psychological research. Behavior is indeed a function of its consequences, and thus organisms tend to repeat responses which yield desirable (i.e., rewarding) results, while avoiding responses which yield undesirable (i.e., punishing) ones. Despite the basic importance of this principle, relatively little was known about the physiological basis of pleasure or pain until two investigators, Olds and Milner (1954) happened, quite by accident, upon a phenomenon which seemed to provide a key to this intriguing puzzle.

While conducting experiments concerned with the function of the reticular formation, Olds and Milner noticed that rats with electrodes implanted in or near the limbic system would frequently return to locations within their cages at which, purely by chance, they had received brief electrical stimulation. Pursuing this unexpected finding further, Olds and Milner found that animals could readily be induced to move to any randomly selected spots by providing them with electric stimulation to the limbic system when they arrived at such locations. In fact, subjects moved to these places with such speed that it began to appear as if they were actively *seeking* the brain stimulation they then received. In order to examine this interesting possibility, Olds and Milner placed their subjects in an apparatus such as the one shown in Figure 2–20, and arranged conditions so that each time these rats pressed a lever, they received brief electric pulses (0.1 to 0.5 seconds) to various locations in the brain. When the electrodes which delivered these shocks were placed at many sites in the hypothalamus and limbic system, the animals would press over and

The Physiological Basis of Reward: "Pleasure" Centers in the Brain

FIGURE 2–20 Apparatus used to investigate the rewarding effects of direct brain stimulation. When the animal presses the lever, it receives a weak pulse of electricity through an implanted electrode. That such stimulation is highly rewarding is indicated by the fact that under some conditions, subjects will continue pushing the bar very quickly until they literally fall over from exhaustion. (Courtesy of Professor James Olds.)

over again. Indeed, under some conditions, they would push the lever as often as 5,000 times per hour, and continue responding in this manner until they literally fell over from exhaustion. After a brief rest, they would return to the bar and begin pushing with renewed vigor.

In the face of such behavior, it could only be concluded that the rats found the stimulation they received to be extremely rewarding. When the electrodes were placed in other locations, however, they would press the bar once, and then often carefully avoid it on future occasions. Apparently, subjects found electrical stimulation at these points (which were scattered throughout the limbic system, thalamus, and hypothalamus) to be quite unpleasant (Olds, Travis, and Schwing, 1960).

That the magnitude of reward produced by direct stimulation at appropriate sites in the brain is very great is indicated by the findings of a large number of experiments (see Olds, 1969). For example, it has frequently been observed that animals who are hungry, thirsty, or both will, when given a choice, select brain stimulation over food or water (Routtenberg and Lindy, 1965; Spies, 1965). Similarly, subjects will repeatedly cross an electrified grid and endure painful shocks in order to obtain such stimulation (Olds, 1961). Finally, as suggested above, they will often work very hard in order to obtain reward of this type (Pliskoff, Wright, and Hawkins, 1965).

In view of such findings, it is tempting to conclude that electrical stimulation of portions of the brain produces intense sensations of pleasure akin, perhaps, to those experienced during sexual orgasm. Surprisingly, though, this does not seem to be the case. Reports by human subjects who have received such stimulation during surgery indicate that although the sensations produced are indeed pleasant, they are by no means very clear-cut or intense (Sem-Jacobsen and Torkildsen, 1960). More importantly, a number of experiments suggest that brain stimulation may actually serve to elicit feelings of hunger, thirst, or sexual deprivation (Coons and Cruce, 1968; Caggiula and Hoebel, 1966). Certainly, such feelings are not usually considered pleasurable. In fact, common sense suggests that they may be quite unpleasant, particularly if they persist for more than a brief period of time. Thus, the question of what, precisely, is so rewarding about direct brain stimulation is quite a puzzling one.

One possible explanation for such effects is that stimulation of this type first induces and then eliminates sensations of hunger, thirst, or sexual arousal in a very rapid manner (Grossman, 1973). This speedy reduction of such feelings may prove to be rewarding in and of itself, and thus explain why organisms both seek and work to obtain direct stimulation of portions of their brains. In view of the fact that it is often quite pleasurable to quench a thirst or satisfy a hearty appetite, this suggestion seems to make good sense.

A second possibility is that total satiation is itself unpleasant, so that the arousal of various appetites through brain stimulation is somehow rewarding (see Olds, 1969). This view is supported by the observation that we do often seem to enjoy the aroma of good food even though it makes us a bit hungry, and we do enjoy being titillated by such magazines as "Playboy" or "Cosmopolitan," even if immediate sexual gratification is not in the offing. In such cases, the mild levels of arousal we experience *do* seem to be quite pleasurable, and it is possible that such effects play an important role in the rewarding influence of brain stimulation.

Unfortunately, it is as yet impossible to choose between these and other explanations for the powerful rewarding effects of direct electrical stimulation of portions of the brain (Grossman, 1973). What *can* be concluded on the basis of existing evidence, however, is that sensations of both pleasure and pain are probably not associated with discrete and simple "centers" (Olds, 1969).

Rather, they are probably linked to the activation of complex neural circuits involving many different structures and regions of the brain. As a result, it seems likely that when the neural bases of pleasure and pain are finally completely unraveled, they will turn out to be both intricate and diffuse.

As a society, we consume vast quantities of drugs—chemical agents which exert some effect upon living tissue. Although some of these substances, such as antibiotics, are taken primarily for medical reasons, most are used for another purpose: to induce positive shifts in the way people feel. Individuals often take drugs to cheer them up when they are blue, to help them relax when they are tense, to bring on sleep or fight fatigue, to eliminate pain—both physical and psychological—to calm jittery nerves, or simply to "turn on." In short, people take drugs because they make them "feel better" in a number of different ways (see Figure 2–21).

Given the intimate link between the brain and behavior to which we have been referring during most of this chapter, it should come as no surprise that drugs usually exert their major effects through some action upon the nervous system. That is, they change the way people feel by somehow altering the functioning of this complex structure. Because there are literally thousands of **psychoactive drugs**—drugs which affect behavior, feelings, perception, or thought—we could not hope to consider all of them here. Similarly, such topics as drug addiction and alcoholism lie beyond the scope of this discussion, and will be reserved for later chapters. In the present section, then, we will merely attempt to (1) describe the influence of several important groups of drugs, and (2) indicate, as far as present knowledge permits, the manner in which they produce their effects. In addition, because drugs are only one of several different means individuals can use to alter their current psychological state, we will also focus briefly on one additional technique for producing such changes which does *not* involve the action of chemical substances upon the brain—**transcendental meditation.**

Drugs and Behavior: For Fast, Fast, Fast Relief . . .

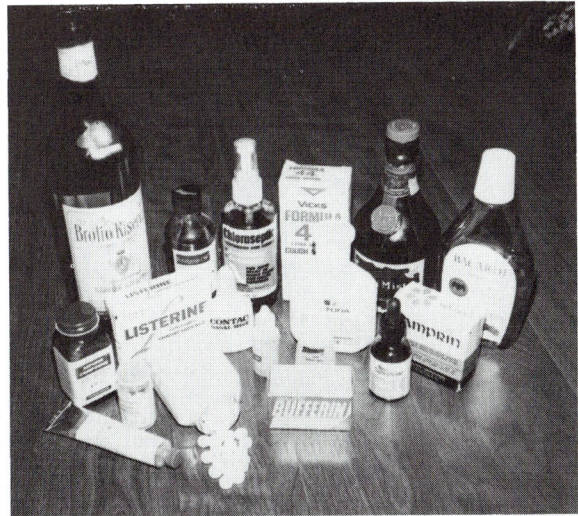

FIGURE 2–21 A small sample of the many kinds of drugs commonly used by individuals in our society to alter the way they feel. (Note that only legal, readily obtainable substances are represented.)

Stimulants: Going Up!

Suppose that it was the night before a big exam, and with several hours of preparation still ahead, you began to feel quite drowsy. What could you do to increase your alertness? If you are like millions of other persons in our society, you might drink some coffee or tea, open a bottle of cola, or light up a cigarette. Finally, if you were sufficiently worried about the exam and were willing to take the risks involved, you might swallow one or more "uppers"—pills designed to give you the boost you need.

In each of these instances, you would be consuming a **stimulant**—a drug which has the overall effect of increasing levels of mental and physical activity. In the case of coffee, tea, or cola drinks, the drug involved is *caffeine*, a bitter-tasting substance which seems to reduce fatigue, raise endurance, and increase the clarity of thought. In the case of cigarettes, you would be consuming *nicotine*, a drug which increases heart rate, blood pressure, and metabolism. Finally, if you decided to take an "upper," you would probably be swallowing one or more **amphetamines,** a group of drugs which exert a much stronger activating effect upon behavior. So powerful are the effects of amphetamines that they can often sustain high levels of activity far beyond the point of normal endurance. For example, soldiers of the German and Japanese armies often swallowed huge doses of these drugs before going into battle during World War II, and long-distance truck drivers who must stay at the wheel for long hours at a stretch often rely on "coast-to-coasts" (amphetamine pills) to keep them awake—and alive—on the road (see Figure 2–22).

Not surprisingly, the prolonged use of such drugs exacts a severe penalty, and individuals who have remained awake by such means for several days eventually experience a great deal of physical discomfort when they finally "crash" from their artificial high.

Stimulants such as the ones we have been discussing seem to exert their activating effects in one of two ways: (1) by stimulating neurons in the sympathetic nervous system, or (2) by facilitating the release of transmitter substances at synapses. In either case, they raise the rate of neural activity and thereby increase the tempo of many bodily functions.

Depressants: Coming Down

Have you ever had a beer, drunk some wine, or enjoyed a cocktail before dinner? If so, you have consumed at least one depressant, *alcohol*. When taken in small doses, alcohol appears to make some people more talkative, friendly,

FIGURE 2–22 Because of their powerful ability to combat the effects of fatigue, amphetamines are often taken by individuals who must maintain a high degree of alertness for prolonged periods of time (e.g., soldiers going into battle, long-distance truck drivers, students cramming for important exams). (Bottom photo by Sue Soldoff.)

and unrestrained. Its major influence, however, is that of a **depressant**—a drug which slows activity in the nervous system. These seemingly contradictory effects stem from the fact that alcohol acts first upon areas of the cerebral cortex concerned with complex behavior. Thus, inhibitions are the first functions to go, and only with increasing doses do feelings of drowsiness and a loss of motor control make their appearance. Contrary to popular belief, alcohol is a very toxic (i.e., poisonous) drug, and when taken in sufficient doses may depress activity in the nervous system to such a degree that vital bodily functions are inhibited and death results. We will have more to say about alcohol and the problem of alcoholism in Chapter 10.

Barbiturates, an even stronger type of depressant, are used in sleeping pills, and sharply reduce levels of overt activity. The fact that they also lead to reductions in anxiety and stress make them useful in the treatment of some mental disorders (see Chapter 11). Certain depressants seem to influence behavior by inhibiting all neural activity; others, by stimulating the parasympathetic nervous system; and still others, by inhibiting the sympathetic nervous system. Regardless of their specific mode of action, the overall effect of such drugs tends to be much the same: a general slowing of mental and physical activity, feelings of drowsiness, a lack of motor coordination, and eventually a loss of consciousness.

When you have a headache, you probably take aspirin. When you go to the dentist, he may inject Novocain into your gums before beginning to drill. And if you are unfortunate enough to sustain a serious injury, you may receive an injection of morphine from a physician. Although these drugs differ greatly in chemical composition and mode of action, they are all employed for the same basic purpose: the relief of pain. Substances which have such effects are known as **analgesics,** and play an important role in reducing human suffering.

Analgesics: The Pain-Fighters

By far the most commonly used analgesic is aspirin. Aspirin is most effective in reducing mild pain such as that stemming from a headache or sore throat, and it produces its beneficial effects in two ways. First, it reduces inflammation and thus decreases the number of pain messages reaching the brain from receptors in affected areas. Second, it seems to block the transmission of such signals through the central nervous system.

A second and much more powerful group of pain relievers are known as the *opiates*. These are all derived from opium—a naturally occurring substance produced by the poppy plant—and are highly effective in combatting even the most intense pain. The first opiate which came into widespread medical use was morphine. Unfortunately, it has one frightening drawback: it is highly addictive. That is, individuals who receive it often experience so much physical discomfort upon its withdrawal that they can not bear to give it up. In the face of this problem, scientists began searching for a non-addicting opiate. When, after some years, they hit upon heroin, they thought they had found a solution. Unfortunately, as you probably know, heroin has turned out to be even worse in this respect than morphine. In fact, some individuals appear to become addicted to this drug after only one or two uses. As a result of their extreme addictive power, the opiates have turned out to be a sadly mixed blessing. On the one hand they offer almost miraculous relief from pain, while on the other they threaten to literally enslave the persons who use them.

Opiates seem to produce their analgesic effects in two ways. First, they reduce the responsiveness of certain cells in the nervous system to pain messages from receptors (McKenzie and Beechey, 1962). Second, they alter patterns of activity within the brain so that pain signals are not processed in a normal manner when they arrive. As a result, individuals under the influence of opiates are aware of the fact that they are experiencing pain, but they do not find it to be as disturbing or unpleasant as would normally be the case.

Euphoric Drugs:
Feelin' Groovy

Everyone likes to feel good, so it is not very surprising that drugs which produce positive shifts in mood—*euphorics*—are often in widespread use. As noted above, small quantities of alcohol often yield pleasant, relaxed feelings, and it is obvious that it is frequently used for just this purpose. The fact that alcohol acts as a depressant when consumed in larger quantities, however, suggests that it should not be classified primarily as a euphoric.

Probably the most commonly used substance of this type today is marijuana. This drug is derived from hemp (*Cannabis sativa*), a plant which grows wild as a weed in many different parts of the world; in fact, one of the authors remembers it growing in just this manner in a vacant lot behind his parents' home. The active substance in marijuana is known as THC, and is found in the leaves and branches of both the male and female plants. It is more highly concentrated in a sticky resin produced only by the female plant, however, and this material is often used to manufacture a more potent drug known as hashish ("hash").

Although history is somewhat unclear on this point, it appears that marijuana was first introduced into Western culture during the crusades of the eleventh and twelfth centuries. For many years it was used widely as a medicine, and was described for such varied ailments as headache, ulcers, epilepsy, and even toothache. Unfortunately, the THC content of one batch of hemp plants may differ sharply from that of another, so it was almost impossible for physicians to obtain or prescribe standard doses of this drug. For this reason, and also because of the rapid development of many other useful medicines, marijuana fell out of favor with the medical community and was rarely prescribed after 1900.

In addition to causing a positive shift in mood, marijuana seems to produce many other effects. Among those most commonly reported by experienced users are: increased absorption in whatever one is doing; seemingly important insights into one's self or the external world; a marked slowing of time; and increased enjoyment of eating (Tart, 1971). The influence of most drugs seems to vary greatly with the nature of the social setting in which they are taken and the personality of the individuals who use them, and in the case of marijuana the tendency toward such variation is pronounced. Thus, the effects experienced by different individuals may vary greatly, and even the same person may experience markedly different results on different occasions.

At present, there is no firm evidence for harmful side effects stemming from the moderate use of marijuana (Leavitt, 1974), but the issue is still in doubt, and a degree of caution seems justified. Unfortunately, the action of marijuana upon the central nervous system remains something of a mystery even today.

Hallucinogens:
Journeys into
Inner Space

The ability of certain naturally occurring substances to induce vivid hallucinations and other major changes in perception has been known for centuries. Powerful **hallucinogens** are present in several types of mushrooms and a number of different cactus plants. The most famous and controversial hallucinogenic drug, however, is certainly LSD, an artificial substance not found in nature. LSD (or acid, as it is often termed) profoundly alters perceptions of the world. The specific effects that are experienced depend strongly on the context in which the drug is taken, but many users report some or all of the following sensations: colors become more highly saturated than usual, so that even everyday objects take on great beauty; stationary objects appear to move, while others seem to melt and change shape; a sense of timelessness develops, so that a minute may seem like several hours, and distinctions between the past, present, and future seem meaningless; thought processes become disordered and dreamlike; and profound religious or esthetic experiences may occur. In addition, even more bizarre effects are sometimes noted. For example, stimuli of one type may be perceived as another, so that music is experienced as waves of vivid color, words are smelled or tasted, and colors are heard as well as seen. Finally, many users report glimpsing a "super reality" in which everything—all objects, thoughts, and ideas—are somehow interconnected. Needless to say, such experiences can be profoundly disturbing.

As is the case with other powerful drugs, hallucinogens often produce several unwanted side effects. Some, such as mescaline (a drug derived from the peyote cactus and used in religious ceremonies by several Indian groups), induce nausea, indigestion, and severe headache. Initial research reports suggested that LSD had a far more dangerous and permanent side effect: chromosome damage in habitual users. More recent findings regarding this possibility have been inconclusive, however, and at present there appear to be no firm grounds for assuming that such effects occur (Dishotsky et al., 1971; Leavitt, 1974).

As noted on p. 41, hallucinogenic drugs seem to produce their extraordinary effects because of a close chemical resemblance to natural transmitter substances found in the nervous system. As a result of such similarity, they may readily serve as substitutes for these transmitters, and thereby alter normal patterns of activity within the brain (Seiden, 1970). For example, it has recently been suggested that the blending of the senses mentioned above—a phenomenon known as **synesthesia**—may arise in just this fashion (Marks, 1975). That is, hallucinogenic drugs may stimulate certain neurons in the brain which connect the various senses, but which are normally inactive in most persons most of the time. The result is a whole new range of sensory experiences, such as sounds which are seen in glowing colors, words which elicit vivid tastes, and visual images which are felt as well as seen. While such mixed sensations may sound quite attractive, little is known about the possible effects of inducing such "short-circuits" in the brain. Thus, as is the case with all powerful drugs, caution would seem to be the byword. (Incidentally, synesthesia can be experienced *naturally*, as represented in Plate 9.)

Meditation: Alternative Route to Nirvana?

Can individuals voluntarily change their internal bodily states—and thus the way they feel—without the aid of drugs? Although our technologically oriented culture views this possibility with extreme skepticism, procedures for accomplishing such changes have existed in the East for many centuries. Practitioners of *yoga* and *Zen* seem capable of altering their internal states to a remarkable degree. For example, they can enter a deep trance at will, avoid experiencing pain in situations in which most individuals would cry out for relief, and accomplish such incredible feats as slowing the beating of their own hearts (Anand, Chhina, and Singh, 1961). Because we will return to a discussion of the psychological mechanisms underlying some of these abilities in Chapter 4 (see pp. 137–141), we will focus here on another and more popular technique for altering one's own internal states: **transcendental meditation.**

While mastery of yoga and Zen require years of careful study and practice, training in transcendental meditation is relatively brief. As a result, it has attained widespread use and is probably practiced by more than 200,000 individuals in the U.S. at the present time. The basic procedures of transcendental meditation (or TM, as it is usually abbreviated) are relatively simple. After assuming a comfortable upright position, the meditator closes his or her eyes

**PERSPECTIVE
ON
BEHAVIOR:** *Peace Through Drugs?*

In a highly controversial presidential address to the American Psychological Association, Kenneth Clark (1971) suggested that at our present rate of progress, we will soon possess the capacity to eliminate human violence through direct biochemical intervention—that is, by means of potent aggression-inhibiting drugs. Going still further, he argued that once such drugs are developed, they should be administered to all major world leaders, thus rendering them incapable of using their power for destructive ends. Only in this way, Clark felt, can the human race avoid self-inflicted extinction in the years ahead. In the light of our previous discussions of the intimate bond between neural functioning and behavior, do you think it will actually be possible to eliminate all tendencies toward violence and cruelty by direct chemical means? And if so, do you think that such a course of action would be morally justified? Finally, do you believe there is any chance that such a plan could be put into actual practice in the immediate future?

THE WIZARD OF ID — By Parker

FIGURE 2–23   Can drugs be used to control human violence? The possibility of such chemical control of behavior raises many complex moral issues. (*The Wizard of Id* by permission of Johnny Hart and Field Enterprises, Inc.)

and silently chants the special syllables of a **mantra** over and over again. These syllables are drawn from Hindu holy books, and each person is assigned a unique combination on the basis of his or her age, marital status, and occupation. Practitioners of TM generally meditate twice each day for periods of 15 to 20 minutes. Despite the briefness of these sessions, however, users report experiencing many benefits. For example, among the positive effects claimed to follow from such meditation are feelings of relaxation and well-being, increased reserves of energy, greater clarity of thought, and an improved ability to concentrate upon various tasks (Schultz, 1972). While it is very difficult to evaluate the meaning of such personal endorsements, "hard" scientific data suggesting that TM actually exerts important effects upon its users have accumulated in recent years. Perhaps the most famous evidence of this type is that collected by Robert Wallace and Herbert Benson (1972).

These researchers obtained careful records of the physiological reactions of 36 individuals before, during, and after meditation. They found that 20 to 30 minutes of quiet meditation of the type described above produced large alterations in several basic bodily processes. For example, both oxygen consumption and carbon dioxide elimination dropped sharply during meditation, but then returned to normal levels after it was completed. Similarly, EEG records revealed a large increase in the magnitude of alpha waves during meditation. Other changes involved a fourfold increase in the electrical resistance of the skin (an alteration often associated with reduced emotionality), a sharp drop in the rate of respiration, and a decrease in the concentration of certain substances often associated with tension and anxiety (see Figure 2–24). In short, there was clear evidence that the subjective changes reported by practitioners of meditation are indeed accompanied by alterations in their physiological processes.

That TM produces psychological as well as physiological effects is suggested by additional findings. For example, individuals who engage in such meditation express lower levels of anxiety on standard psychological tests than do those who do not meditate (Nidich, Seeman, and Seibert, 1973). Similarly, meditators seem to experience such positive psychological changes as increased ability to express their feelings freely, and a greater capacity for intimate contact with others (Seeman, Nidich, and Banta, 1972). Finally, and perhaps most important of all, there is some indication that individuals who adopt TM soon give up the use of many different types of drugs (Marzetta, Benson, and Wallace, 1972; see Figure 2–25). Although it is possible that individuals who adopt meditation represent a "special" group who would soon stop using drugs even without the aid of these procedures, subjective reports by many of

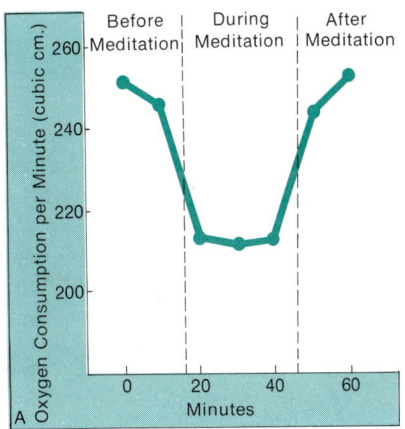

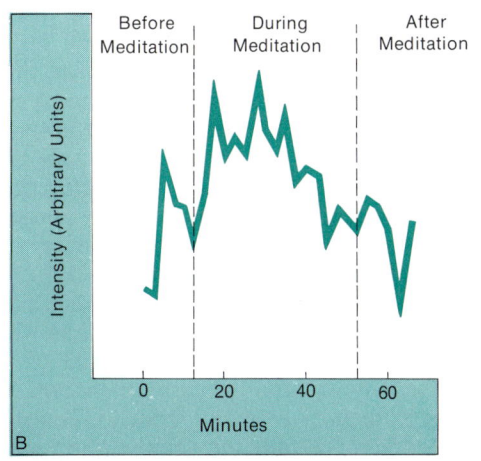

FIGURE 2–24 Physiological changes during meditation. Meditating individuals show sharp drops in oxygen consumption (A), increases in the intensity of alpha waves (B), and several other alterations in physiological functioning. (Adapted from Wallace and Benson, 1972.)

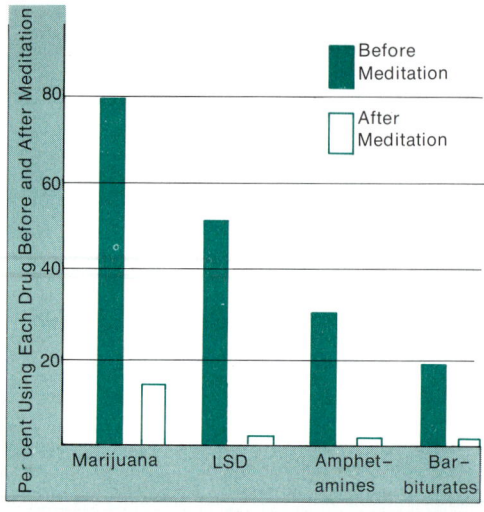

FIGURE 2-25   Many individuals report giving up the use of drugs after adopting transcendental meditation. One possible explanation for such effects is that meditation is such a "good trip" that it eliminates the need for the type of experiences provided by drugs. (Based on data from Marzetta, Benson, and Wallace, 1972.)

the individuals who show such changes point to another possibility: meditation is such a "good trip" in itself that it largely eliminates the need for drug-induced experiences. If further research shows this to be the case, TM and other forms of meditation may prove to be an alternative—and possibly much safer—route to the inner peace many people currently seem to seek.

Summary

Many psychologists believe that in an ultimate sense, all aspects of our behavior stem from complex biochemical events occurring within our bodies. In order to understand these biological bases of behavior, it is necessary to know something about the **nervous system** and the **neurons** of which it is composed.

Neurons are cells which have become specialized, over the course of evolution, for the task of *communication*—moving information from one location within the body to another. Neurons are organized into a highly complex structure known as the **nervous system.** This organ is often divided, in turn, into two major components known as the **central** and **peripheral** systems. The peripheral nervous system carries information from receptors to the central nervous system and back from this system to muscles and glands throughout the body. One portion, the **autonomic nervous system,** is concerned with the regulation of internal bodily states and controls many essential functions. The central nervous system consists of two distinct structures, the **spinal cord** and the **brain.** The spinal cord serves primarily a communicative function, conducting information to and from the brain, but also integrates certain automatic reactions known as **reflexes.** The brain is truly the controlling organ of the body, serving as the ultimate source of all our actions, emotions, and mental processes.

In recent years, intensive study of the functions of the brain has clarified the neural bases of many interesting psychological phenomena. With respect to the regulation of **hunger** and **thirst,** it is now well established that certain regions of the **hypothalamus** play an important role. **Sleep** is apparently regulated by a waking center located in the **reticular activating system,** as well as by two active sleep centers in the **medulla** and **pons.** These latter regions seem to inhibit the waking center, and so bring on two distinct states of sleep known, respectively, as **NREM sleep** and **REM sleep. Emotions** are controlled by both the hypothalamus and **limbic system,** and drastic alterations in behavior can often be produced by damage to or stimulation of these structures. Because animals will often work very hard in order to receive direct electrical stimulation of certain regions of the brain, and frequently choose such stimulation over food when hungry or water when thirsty, it has been suggested that these areas are actually the neural centers of pleasure. More recent evidence suggests, however, that these regions may merely lie along diffuse neural circuits whose activation is related to such sensations.

Individuals often take **drugs**—chemical substances which influence living tissue—in order to alter their psychological state (i.e., the way they feel). Such agents exert their effects upon feelings, behavior, and thought by affecting the nervous system. Interestingly, there is some indication that similar alterations can also be produced without the aid of drugs through the practice of **transcendental meditation.**

Suggested Readings

Hartmann, E. L.: *The Functions of Sleep.* New Haven: Yale University Press, 1973.

A brief and clearly written introduction to recent sleep research.

Leavitt, F.: *Drugs and Behavior.* Philadelphia: W.B. Saunders Company, 1974.

A comprehensive review of the effects of drugs upon behavior. The chapters on therapy for drug abuse and the influence of drugs upon learning, sex, and aggression are especially interesting.

Robinson, D. N.: *The Enlightened Machine.* Encino, California: Dickenson Publishing Co., 1973.

A brief introduction to several aspects of physiological psychology. Many of the illustrations are unusually clear and easy to follow.

Schachter, S.: Some extraordinary facts about obese humans and rats. *American Psychologist,* 1971, *26,* 129–144.

A well-written, witty article concerning the regulation of eating in animals and human beings. Schachter's suggestions regarding the possible causes of obesity are both interesting and thought-provoking. (If you are interested in pursuing these topics even further, additional information can be found in Schachter, S., and Rodin, J. (eds.): Obese Humans and Rats. Potomac, Maryland: Erlbaum Associates, 1974.)

Wallace, R. K., and Benson, H.: The physiology of meditation. *Scientific American,* 1972, *226,* 84–90.

A report of "hard" scientific data regarding the influence of transcendental meditation on basic bodily processes. A "must" if you are planning to begin meditation or are now engaging in this practice.

Journals that regularly publish papers on the physiology of behavior:

American Journal of Physiology
Journal of Comparative and Physiological Psychology
Physiology and Behavior
Psychophysics
Science

Overleaf: M. C. Escher, "Waterfall," courtesy of the Escher Foundation, Haags Gemeentemuseum, The Hague.

3 Perception: How the World Outside Gets Inside

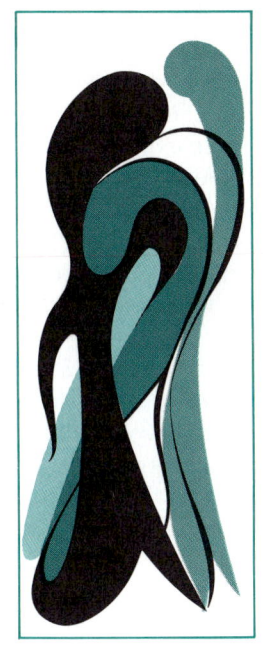

How do you know that you are not the only object in the universe? Perhaps you are the entire universe all by yourself. When a small child wishes to make an unpleasant situation disappear, he covers his eyes. As he grows older and discovers that this strategy is not always effective, his conception of the world changes, and he decides that the world does in fact exist without him. Psychologists call the process of knowing the world outside you, by forming some mental representation of it, **perception.** Perception is a complex process, extending far beyond the mere registering of light, sound, and other impulses from the external world. This external information must be internally coded and transformed before anyone can know what is really out there. Often your beliefs and expectations about some external **stimulus** prove to be more important in determining your behavior than the physical characteristics of that external object. Perception is like solving a complicated puzzle. You must take bits and pieces of information that are present in the external world and fit them together somehow to form a comprehensive internal picture.

All of us are so good at perception that it is easy to take this complicated process for granted. It may at first appear that every object in the external world makes direct contact with the brain via the sense organs: the eyes, ears, skin, and so on. But this view of perception is much too simple. There is no direct one-to-one relationship between the image formed by your eye and your perception of that image. The situation is indeed even more complex, since many physical arrangements in the external world can produce exactly the same image upon the eye. For example, it follows from elementary principles of geometry that a small triangle near you will have the same image in the eye as that of a larger triangle further away. How, then, can we distinguish the real situation in the external world from a large number of alternative possibilities that would cause the same image on the eye?

Since any single external cue is likely to prove insufficient to narrow down the possibilities about the external world, we are forced to rely upon various combinations of cues. Although each cue by itself may be unreliable, if we consider enough cues together, we can *often* come up with an accurate mental picture of the external situation. You may object to this statement by claiming that you *always* have an accurate picture of the world about you. But this opinion may be largely due to your being in highly standardized situations — that is, you know from experience that doors are rectangular, walls meet at right angles, and so forth. Actually, as can be seen in Figure 3–1, we are easily fooled by the external world. Our past experience can work against us, resulting in highly inaccurate perception, especially if some clever psychologist has manipulated the external situation to take advantage of the unreliability of cues. In this chapter we shall see how this kind of manipulation increases our understanding of the various techniques we use to piece together an uncertain world.

A perceptual error made by one of the authors illustrates the way in which prior experience with cues can deceive us about the external world. It is the author's custom to wind up a game of tennis with a cup of hot chocolate. The tennis club where the author plays dispenses free coffee and hot chocolate, perhaps as a partial rebate on the outrageous rates. One urn containing hot coffee and another containing hot water for the instant hot chocolate mix can be found side by side. These urns can be clearly distinguished on the basis of two cues: the coffee urn is placed in front of the hot water urn, and the coffee urn is bright green, whereas the water urn is metallic silver. One day, after a particularly hard-fought match, the hapless author filled

FIGURE 3–1   A perpetual motion waterfall. Examine this lithograph by M. C. Escher carefully. It is an example of a kind of visual illusion called an impossible figure. (M. C. Escher "Waterfall," Escher Foundation, Haags Gemeentemuseum, The Hague.)

PLATE 4 The medial surface of the human brain. (From Curtis, Jacobson, and Marcus: *An Introduction to the Neurosciences*, Philadelphia, W. B. Saunders Company, 1972.)

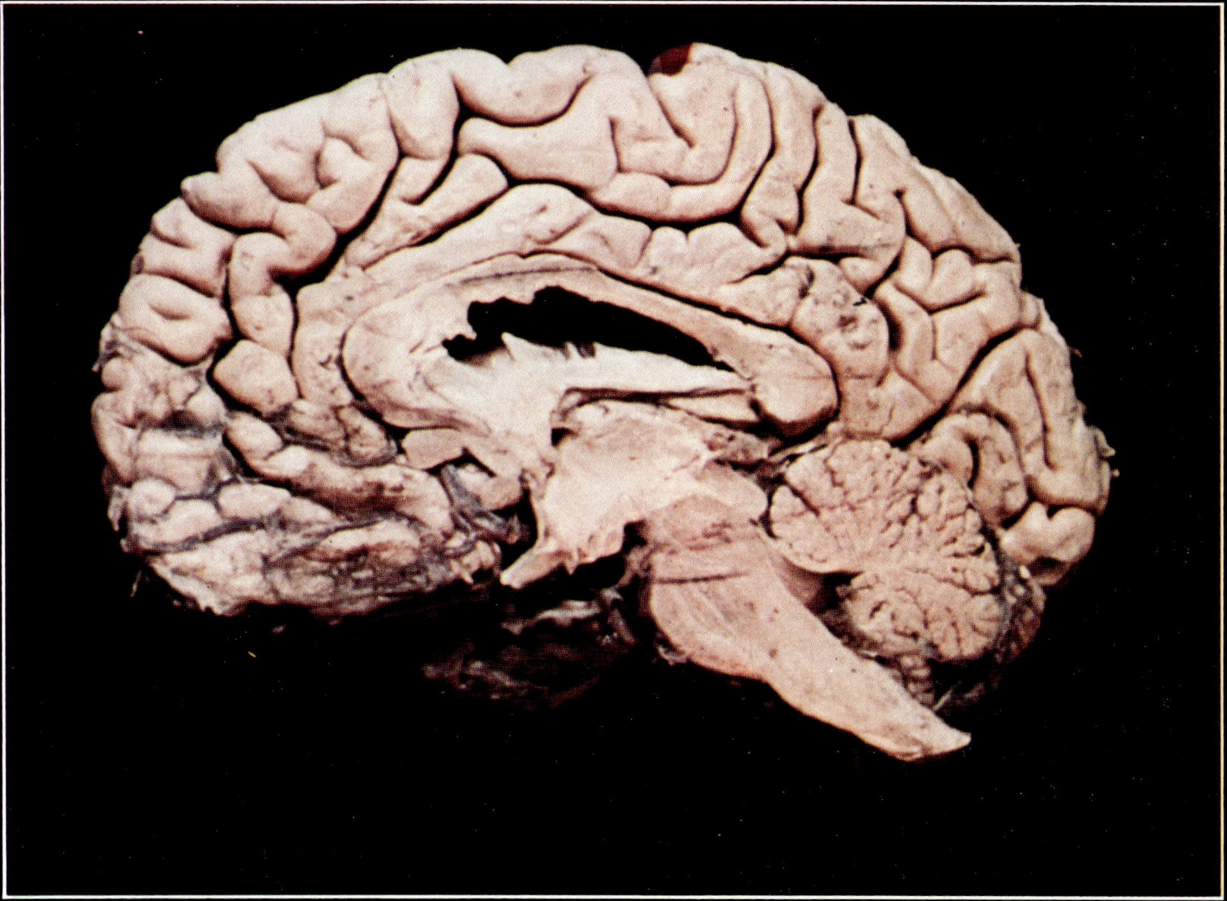

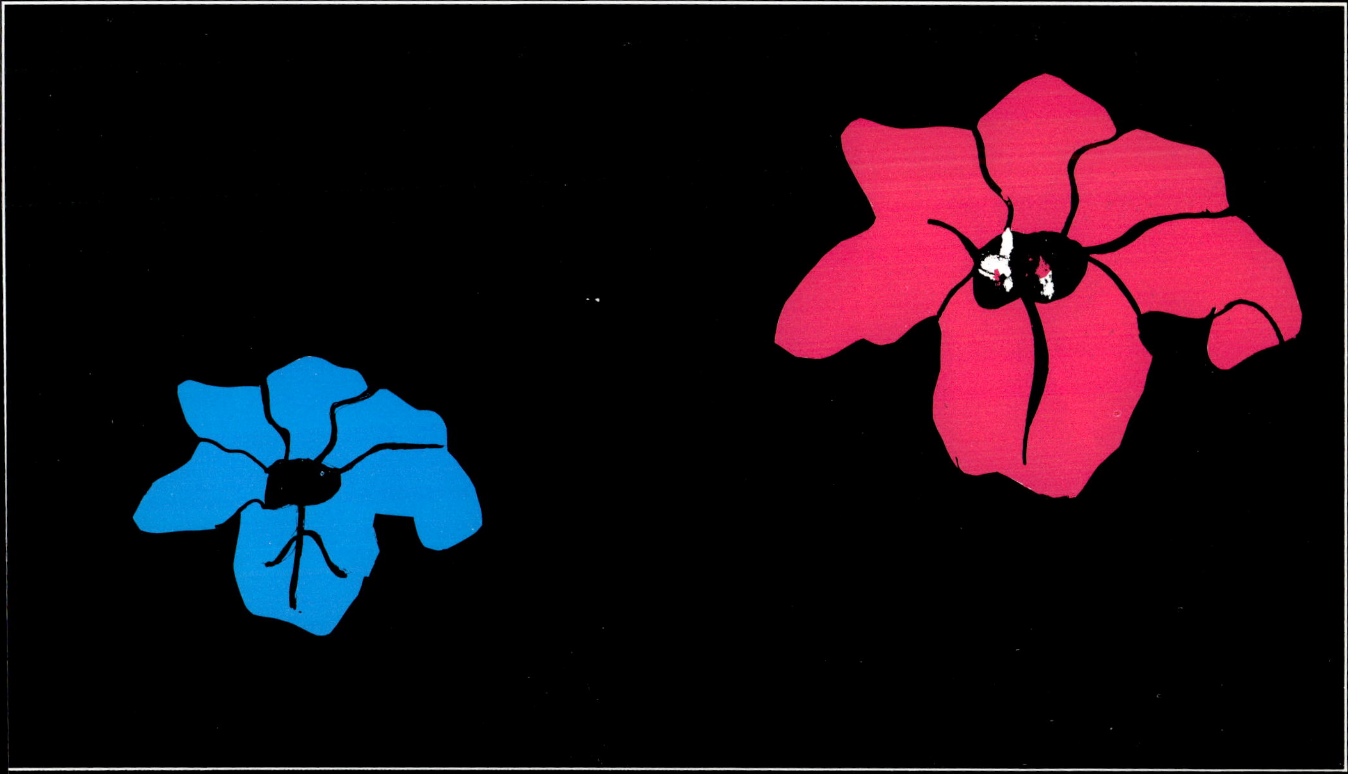

PLATE 5 An illustration of the Purkinje shift. In daylight, both the blue and red shapes are visible. After five to ten minutes in the dark, however, only the blue shape will remain visible, even though the red shape is brighter in daylight.

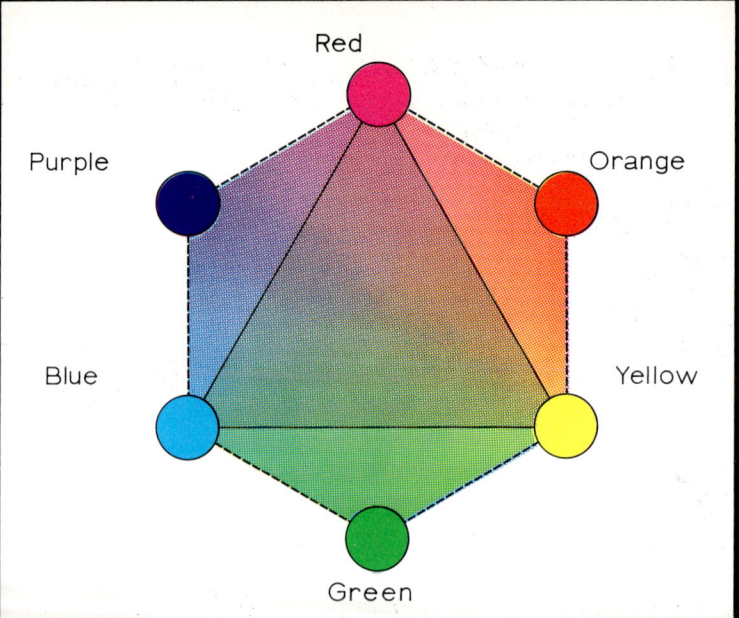

PLATE 6 A prism (left) and a rainbow (right). White light gets separated into its component wavelengths by a prism. The shorter wavelengths are bent more than the longer wavelengths, and the narrow beam of white light is spread out into the spectrum. In the air, diffraction sometimes causes light to appear as a rainbow. (Prism photo from Highsmith: *Physics, Energy, and Our World*, Philadelphia, W. B. Saunders Company, 1975. Rainbow photo © 1968 Margaret Durrance, Photo Researchers.)

PLATE 7 Additive color mixture. Where any two colors overlap, a new color is formed.

BLUE	GREEN	YELLOW
GREEN	RED	BLUE
YELLOW	BLUE	RED
GREEN	RED	YELLOW

GREEN	BLUE	YELLOW
RED	YELLOW	BLUE
YELLOW	BLUE	GREEN
RED	GREEN	RED

PLATE 8 Look at the words in the left-hand rectangle and name the color of the ink used for each word. Go as fast as possible. Time yourself. Now do the same for the words in the right-hand rectangle. Remember, name the color of the ink and do **NOT** read the word spelled by the letters. You will note that the words interfere with your ability to name the colors in the right-hand rectangle. This exemplifies what is known as the Stroop effect.

PLATE 9 These paintings are the work of someone experiencing *synesthesia* — a "mixture" of the senses. The paintings are the synesthesiast's attempt to show the visual effects she experiences in response to a cry of pain (top left), the chirping of a bird (top right), a choir (bottom left), and a symphony (bottom right). (Courtesy of Ker and Cristina McCluskey.)

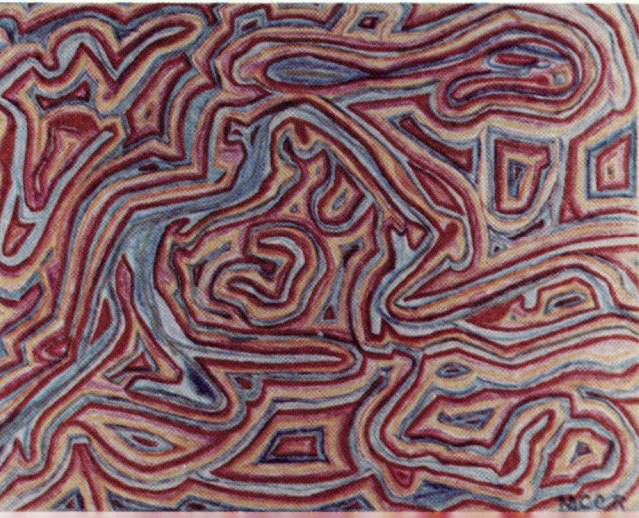

PLATE 10   Two forms of Benham's color disk. When the disks are turned at about 5 to 10 rotations per second, color appears. Cut out the disks, place on a pin or sharp pencil, and try it yourself.

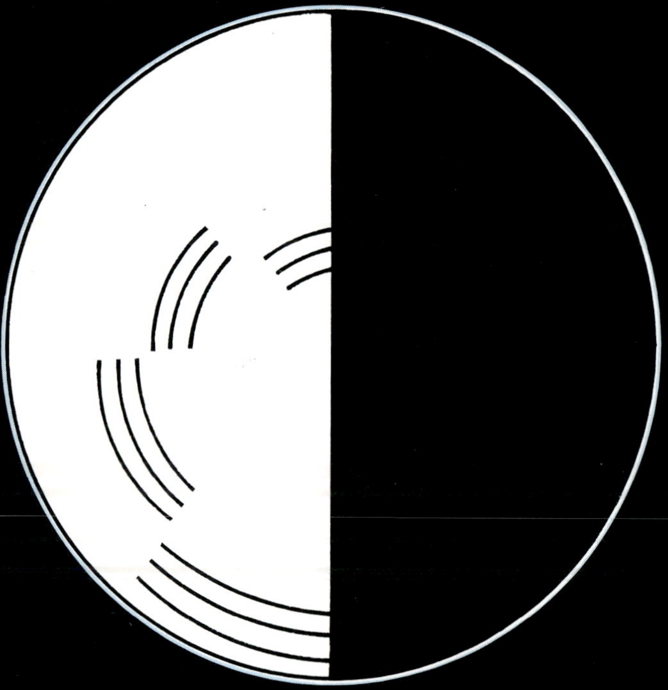

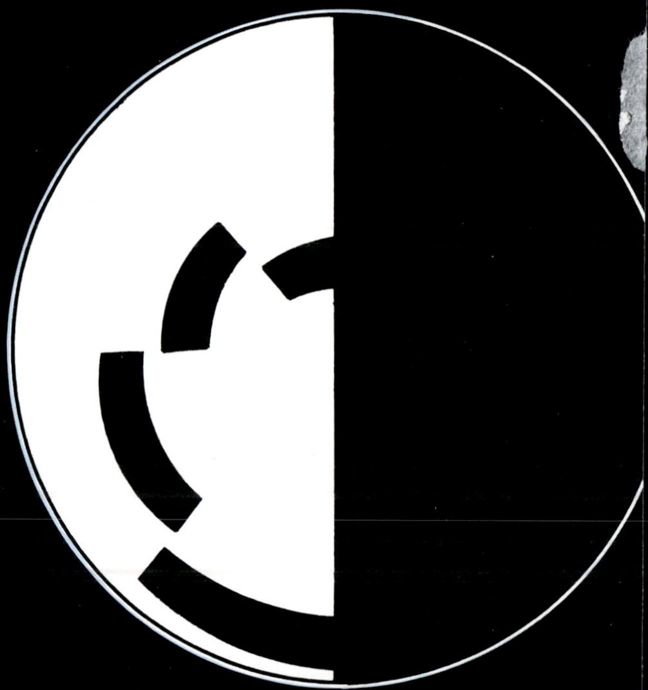

PLATE 11   What effects do you think mild sexual stimuli such as these may have upon aggression? Interestingly, recent experiments (discussed in Chapter 13) indicate that exposure to such materials may sharply reduce aggression by angry individuals. (By the way, does the girl shown here look familiar?)

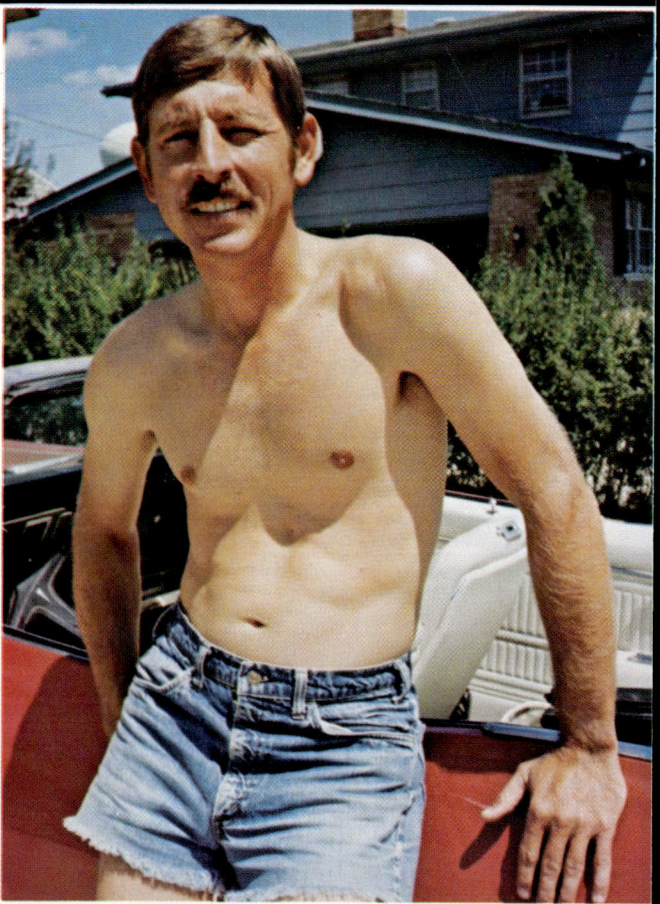

FIGURE 3–2 What is the fragmented object pictured here? People find it difficult to see (or perceive) correctly what is portrayed by this drawing. In the study that used this figure, some help was given observers by telling them what class of things the object belonged to. When told that the object was a musical instrument, many persons correctly perceived it as a violin. (Overall, though, it was rare that such abstract verbal help was sufficient.) (From Leeper, R.: A study of a neglected portion of the field of learning—the development of sensory organization. The Journal of Genetic Psychology, 46, 1935, p. 50.)

his cup as usual and proceeded to drink, with drastic results. His cup contained instant hot chocolate dissolved in coffee. What had happened? Clearly the author had to look at the urn in order to turn on the spigot. But on this particular day the coffee urn had been placed behind, rather than in front of, the hot water urn. Prior experience with the positional cue had led the author to neglect the color cue, with nauseating results.

In this chapter we will discover how each of us is a "perceptual" Sherlock Holmes, trying to piece an acceptable version of reality out of fragmented external cues. And just as Sherlock Holmes relied upon his earlier cases to help him in formulating hypotheses about current cases, we too rely heavily upon prior experience in untangling the perceived world. Can you tell what is illustrated in Figure 3–2 without reading the caption? To help you understand such problems in perception, we first will discuss two important examples of how information from the outside world actually gets inside your head—that is, how the eye and ear work. Then we will move on to the general perceptual problem of detecting that some stimulus or external object is indeed out there. This involves the sensory registering of an event in the eye or ear and also a decision process about the magnitude of that event. After we know that something is out there, our next perceptual problem lies in discovering the nature of the external stimulus. Thus, when we hear a tone we perceive its pitch, and when we see some object we perceive its color. Our next topic really requires good detective work, for we will deal with the general issue of resolving inconsistent inputs from the external world, such as was illustrated in Figure 3–1. When unreliable cues conflict, the result is often an **illusion.** Illusions are fun, and they also help us to discover how perception works. Next we will look at an infant's perception of the world. Is there any evidence for innate perceptual mechanisms fully functioning from birth? From the infant's view of the world, we jump to a very special kind of perception: extrasensory perception, or ESP. Many scientists are quite skeptical about ESP, and we shall look at some of the pros and cons of this controversial topic.

As you can tell from this brief outline of things to come, we have many interesting and important topics to cover. This chapter will not make you an expert on perception, but it should help you to understand how we get to know the world around us.

A **transducer** is a device which changes energy from one form to another. The mouthpiece of your telephone contains a transducer which converts the physical air vibrations or sound energy into electrical energy. Similarly, your hi-fi loudspeaker transduces electrical energy into sound energy. The transducers you carry around in your head and body are truly amazing devices with spectacular engineering qualities. For example, any microphone which could detect the faint stimuli that you can hear, such as a watch ticking 20 feet away, would be destroyed by exposure to a loud thunderclap, which you find annoying but not painful. Your other sense transducers are equally impressive. Galanter (1962) points out that you can see a candle 30 miles away on a dark

TRANSDUCERS: GETTING INFORMATION INTO YOUR HEAD

night, taste a teaspoonful of sugar dissolved in two gallons of water, smell a drop of perfume diffused into the volume of a six-room apartment, and feel the wing of a mosquito dropping on your cheek from a height of one centimeter.

Most people, including many psychologists, believe that the primary function of your sensory transducers is to permit the flow of information from the external world to you. A strong argument could also be made that your transducers actually limit and exclude more information than they pass. We shall discover that your eyes are sensitive to only a very small range of possible stimulation. Similarly, your ears will not allow you to hear the high-pitched sounds that a dog can hear, and this deficit becomes greater as you get older. Hold your two hands directly in front of you at arm's length. Now slowly move your hands apart until you can no longer see both of them at the same time. Your field of vision is limited, and if you want to see more, you are forced to turn your head. A third eye in the back of your head, instead of being a useful addition, would probably impair your overall vision by letting in too much information.

Itinerary: Inside the Eye

The early Greeks thought that the eye was a spotlight which illuminates those aspects of the world you wish to see. They believed that rays flow out of the eyes and touch objects in the external world. We now know that this explanation should be reversed. The eye *collects* light rays in much the same way that a camera brings light to focus upon a sheet of film. A simplified diagram of your eye is shown in Figure 3–3. Light enters your eye by first passing through a transparent cover called the **cornea** and then through the **pupil opening.** The size of this opening is controlled by the **iris,** a ringlike device similar to the diaphragm of a camera lens. And like a lens diaphragm, the size of the pupil controls both the amount of light allowed in and the sharpness of the focused image within the eye. Pupil size is a compromise between maximum sharpness (tiny opening) and maximum light entry (large opening). Pupil size also varies with emotional states. When men are shown pictures of nude females, or when women are shown pictures of nude males, the pupil gets bigger (Hess and Polt, 1960; see Chapter 14).

The lens bends the light rays to focus them upon the **retina** in the back of the eye. The curvature of the lens can be changed in accordance with the distance of the object you wish to view in the external world. This change is accomplished by the **ciliary muscle.** Thus, while a camera focuses by changing the distance between the lens and the plane where light rays converge on the film, your eye focuses by changing the shape of the lens, since the distance between the lens and the retina is fixed. This change in curvature of the lens is called **accommodation.** Since we have internal receptors which tell us if muscles are tense or relaxed, the tension of the ciliary muscle as it alters the lens curvature to accommodate different distances is a cue which helps us in depth perception—determining whether a perceived object is near or far away.

The retina is the business end of the eye. It is on the retina that light energy is transduced by a photochemical process into nerve impulses on the **optic nerve.** The two kinds of receptor cells on the retina that respond to light are called **rods** and **cones** because of their distinctive anatomical shapes. A rod is considerably more sensitive to light than is a cone. But since cones can detect color differences while rods cannot, you really need both. There are roughly 7 million cones and 120 million rods in each eye. Since the optic nerve has only about 1 million fibers, the information collected by the rods and cones cannot be sent directly to the brain but must first be encoded so that each nerve fiber can carry information from more than one rod or cone.

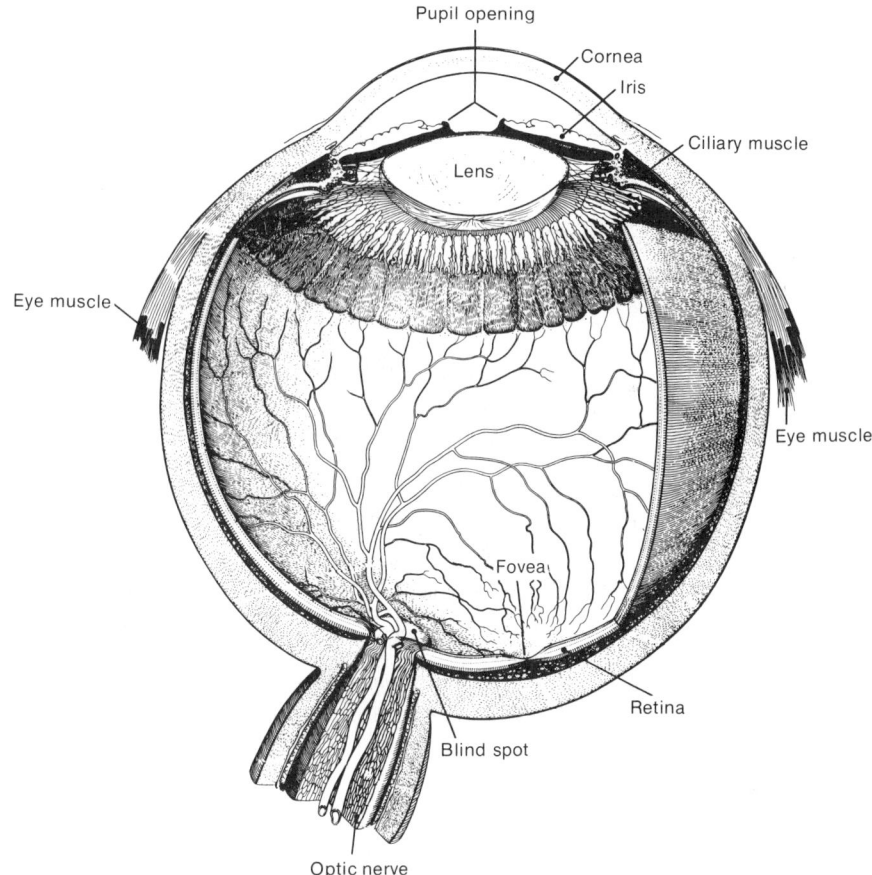

FIGURE 3–3   **Looking down at a cross-section of the eye. The eye muscles move the eye not only up and down as well as left and right, but also permit a limited amount of twisting. The rest of the parts of the eye are discussed in the text. (From Grollman, S.:** *The Human Body.* **New York: Macmillan Co., Copyright © 1964.)**

Thus, there is in most cases no direct point-to-point correspondence between locations on the retina and locations in the brain.

In order for you to see clearly, the lens of your eye must focus rays of light precisely on the retina. Many people cannot do this without the help of eyeglasses. Nearsighted people can properly focus images on their retina when objects are close to them, but not when objects are distant. Without eyeglasses, the image of a distant object is formed in *front* of the retina. The farsighted eye can focus correctly on distant objects but cannot accommodate enough for nearby objects, and thus the image is focused *behind* the retina. Figure 3–4 shows how eyeglass lenses correct nearsightedness (myopia) and farsightedness (hyperopia).

The **fovea** is a small region on the retina which contains only cones. It is the part of the retina where visual acuity is highest—that is, where the greatest amount of detail can be perceived when an image is formed. This may seem strange at first, since we have already said that rods are much more sensitive than cones, and that the fovea does not contain any rods. The reason for the great visual acuity lies in the fovea's connection with the optic nerve: there is almost a direct link with each cone inside the fovea. However, the outer edges of the retina, where there are a great many rods, are the most *sensitive* locations. Thus a dim light such as that from a star can be best perceived by looking out of the corner of your eye; in bright light, we look directly at objects so that their image will fall on the fovea.

NORMAL EYE

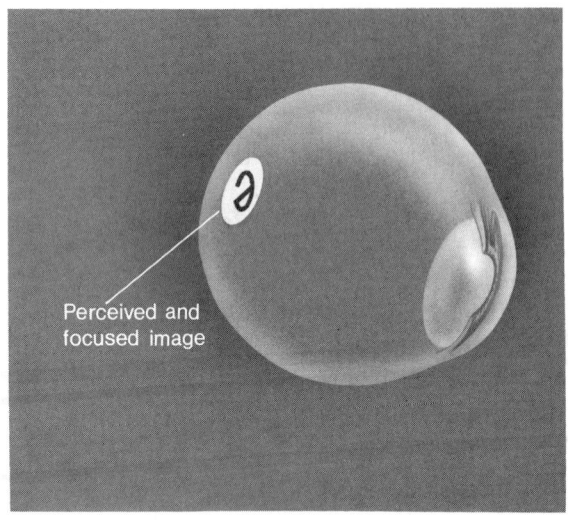

Perceived and focused image

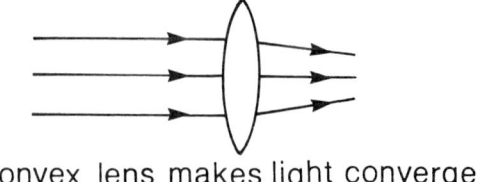

A convex lens makes light converge

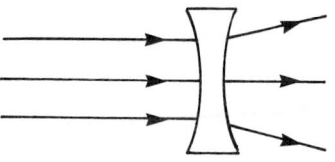

A concave lens makes light diverge

NEARSIGHTED EYE

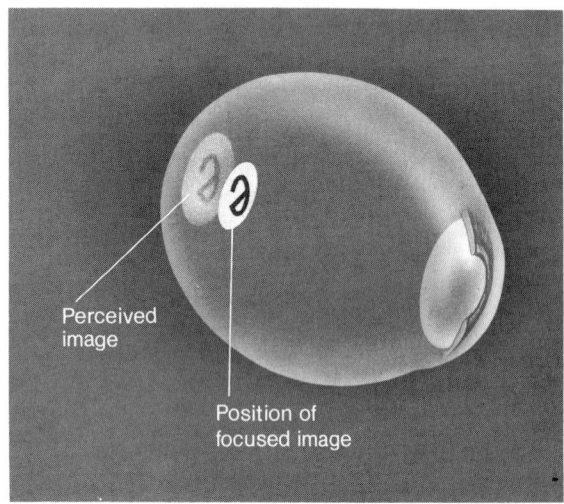

Perceived image

Position of focused image

FARSIGHTED EYE

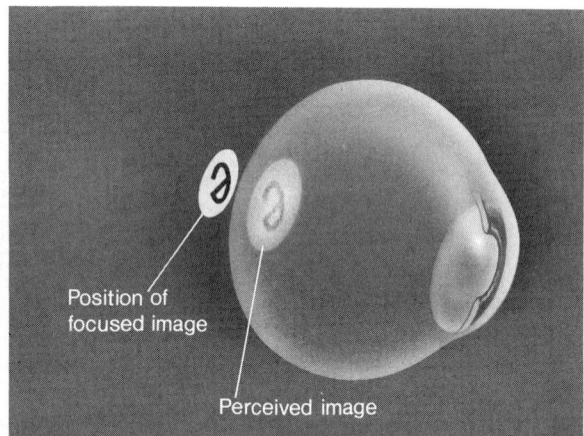

Position of focused image

Perceived image

FIGURE 3–4 How lenses correct nearsightedness (lower left) and farsightedness (lower right). In the normal eye, light rays converge on the retina (top illustration). The nearsighted eye has light rays converging in front of the retina (lower left illustration). A concave correcting lens spreads the rays apart slightly and allows the image to fall directly on the retina. The farsighted eye has light rays converging behind the retina (lower right illustration). A convex correcting lens makes the rays converge together slightly so that the image falls on the retina.

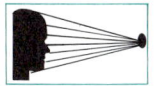

Although our discussion of the eye has emphasized that it is a transducer that changes visual stimulation into nerve impulses, it is hard to be convinced that we see nerve impulses and not light rays. If somehow we could plug a tape recorder into the back of your retina and record the signals that ordinarily travel down the optic nerve, and then at some later time remove your eye and plug in the tape recorder to feed into your optic nerve, you would see whatever had been tape-recorded originally. All the visual information is contained within the pattern of nerve impulses, and your eye is only one method for obtaining this pattern. While this suggestion of direct recording is at present far-fetched (the television industry has nothing to fear), it may well be possible at some future date for you to see an entire movie by plugging in directly to some kind of recording device.

The fact that visual information is conveyed by nerve impulses offers great hope for blind people, whose eyes cannot function normally. Theoretically, if the pattern of nerve impulses could be duplicated in some other sense modality, these people would be able to see. Such a system has been tried by neurophysiologist Paul Bach-y-Rita (1972), and it works! A television camera is used as a substitute eye. The signal from the camera goes to an array of 400 vibrators mounted against the blind person's back. By feeling the pattern of vibration as the camera scans across a stimulus, the blind person is able to see and even to read words, as Figure 3–5A shows. Figure 3–5B shows how a stuffed animal and a telephone look as patterns in the array of vibrators. The blind person can tell that the telephone is further away from him because it appears higher up in the vibration pattern. With this device, you really don't need eyes to "see."

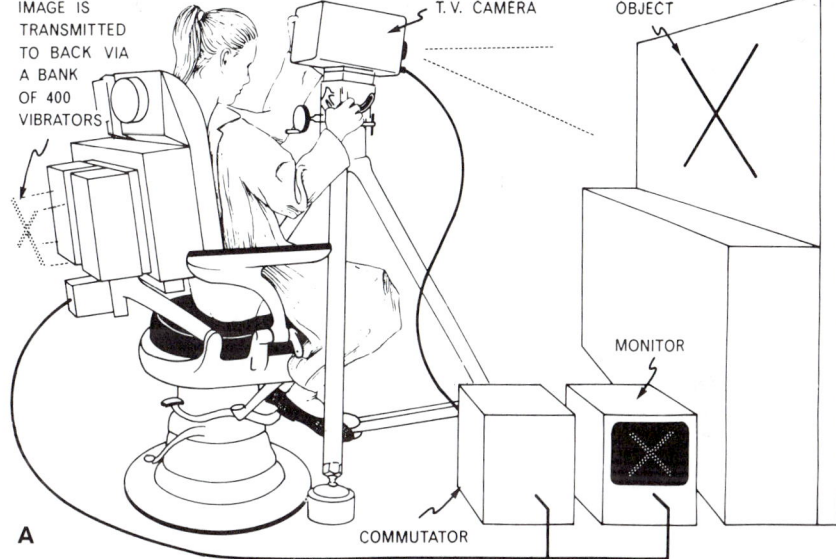

FIGURE 3–5   (A) A blind person reading. As she scans across the object with the television camera, the image is transferred to her back by means of the vibrator array in the chair. Portable versions of this system have been developed so that it may soon be possible to actually use it on a daily basis outside the laboratory. (B) How a stuffed animal and a telephone are represented in the vibrator array. Each dot represents a pulsating vibrator in the system of 3–5A. (From Bach-y-Rita, P., et al.: Display techniques in a tactile vision-substitution system. Medical and Biological Illustration, 20:1, 1970, pp. 7, 11.)

What Makes It Tick: Inside the Ear

A simplified diagram of the ear is shown in Figure 3–6. The ear is divided into three parts: external, middle, and inner. The *external ear* does not transduce sound and serves simply to carry and funnel sound waves to the **eardrum.** The eardrum, or the *tympanic membrane,* as it is more technically named, separates the *middle ear* from the external ear. The middle ear contains three tiny bones—the *hammer* (or malleus), the *anvil* (or incus), and the *stirrup* (or stapes)—which, together with the tympanic membrane, amplify the sound vibrations from the external ear. The bones of the middle ear are arranged in such a way that the pressure of the eardrum's vibrations becomes roughly 20 times greater in the fluid of the *inner ear.* At the foot of the stirrup, another membrane, called the *oval window,* acts like a piston pushing on the fluid of the inner ear. This complicated mechanical transduction process is necessary because sound normally is reflected away from solid surfaces. The design of the ear permits most of the sound to be absorbed rather than reflected away. The **cochlea** is a snail-shaped organ within the inner ear which transduces the fluid vibrations into nerve impulses. This transduction is accomplished by the **basilar membrane,** which lies curled up within the spiral of the cochlea. If the basilar membrane were to be unrolled, it would look like an isosceles triangle with its base at the oval window. **Hair cells** on the basilar membrane vibrate and transduce vibratory energy into the nerve impulses which travel up the auditory nerve.

We can hear sounds that do not enter the external ear but instead enter the inner ear by bone conduction. This allows a simple diagnosis of hearing disabilities—one used by old gypsy violinists. The violinist plays his instrument and touches it to his teeth. If he can hear the sound, he knows that his auditory nerves are still functioning even if he can't hear sounds very well in the normal way via the external ear. If, however, he can't hear his vibrating violin, then he has nerve deafness. Hearing aids improve only sensory loss caused by a failure in conduction; they cannot be used for nerve deafness. Modern diagnostic techniques are of course more sophisticated than those of the gypsy violinist, but the principle of localizing hearing defects in the middle or inner ear is still used.

Knowing Something Is Out There: The Detection Problem

Having energy transduced from light or sound into electrical nerve impulses is not enough for you to be able to report "Yes, I heard a sound," or "No, I didn't see anything." Psychologists once believed that if enough energy was transduced, the resulting nerve signal would be large enough to pass a **threshold** so that you would report the presence of some external event. This threshold of your mind was thought to be like the threshold of a door, and a signal would have to step over this threshold to enter your head. To continue the analogy, thresholds could be high or low, and a signal which could jump over a low threshold might not have enough "zap" to pass a high threshold. There were many problems with this threshold analogy (for instance, what makes a threshold high or low?), and this view of perception has been generally replaced by a more complicated analogy (drawn from electrical rather than mechanical engineering) called **signal detection theory.**

Signal detection theory can get very complicated, and it has mathematical aspects beyond the scope of this book. Thus, we will cover only a small portion of this subject—enough to give you the flavor of this important model of perception.

According to signal detection theory, perception is a two-part process. First, as we have already explained, external energy must be transduced into *nerve impulses.* Then a **decision mechanism** is consulted before a final conclusion about perception can be reached. This conclusion depends upon both transduction and decision processes. We shall now consider how the decision process works.

Imagine that you are a quality-control inspector for a factory that manufactures balloons. Your job is to inflate each balloon with water and to look for tiny imperfections in the rubber. You have 10 seconds to check out each balloon. Every time you detect a defective balloon, the company pays you a 25-cent bonus. How should you make your decision? The best strategy is to report a balloon defective if there is the slightest chance that your 10-second inspection might have revealed a flaw. While you may reject many balloons that are really satisfactory, you will get the largest bonus by following this decision rule.

Now let us make the situation more realistic. The company still pays you a 25-cent bonus for each faulty item you remove, but you are also charged 25 cents for each good balloon you remove. Now what should you do? Clearly your old strategy of removing any suspicious balloon will no longer work, since your 25-cent fines will outnumber your 25-cent bonuses. You must now deal with the problem of **noise** in detection. Noise can be visual as well as auditory. Technically, noise really means any kind of random disturbance in some on-going process. In the balloon factory, noise refers to the visual patterns which occur when a balloon is inflated with water. You must decide whether a possible imperfection is due to a random deviation from the pattern of stressed rubber (noise) or is due to a manufacturing flaw (signal).

Signal detection theory tells you the best way to discriminate between noise and signal. It says that you must take into account the possible *costs* and *benefits* of your decision. These costs and benefits are often called the *pay-off* associated with some particular detection problem. In our present example, the positive pay-off associated with a correct detection of a signal (rejecting a flawed balloon) is exactly equal to the negative pay-off associated with the incorrect detection of a signal (removing a good balloon from the assembly line). Psychologists call the correct detection of a signal a **hit,** and the incorrect detection of a signal when in reality only noise is present a **false alarm.**

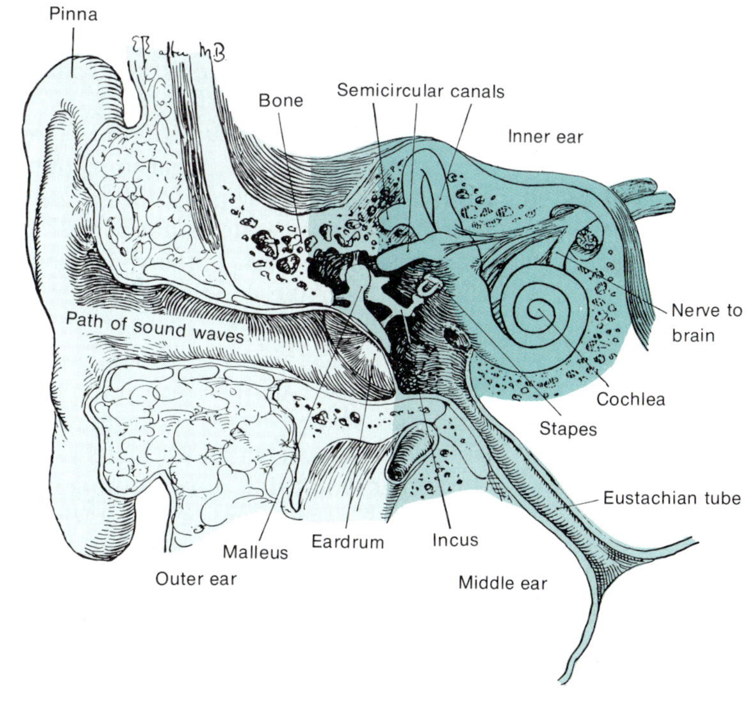

FIGURE 3–6 Inside the ear. The different shadings identify the outer or external ear, the middle ear, and the inner ear. The semicircular canals are not organs of hearing but instead contribute to the detection of motion and balance. The Eustachian tube permits equalization of pressure on both sides of the eardrum. A clogged Eustachian tube stopped up by a severe cold can lead to a rupture of the eardrum. While painful, this is not very serious, since the eardrum will grow back together. The other parts of the ear are discussed in the text. (From Gardner, E.: *Fundamentals of Neurology.* Philadelphia: W. B. Saunders Company, 1971.)

FIGURE 3–7   Noise can make it difficult to detect a signal. (The Wizard of Id by permission of Johnny Hart and Field Enterprises, Inc.)

In the real world, hits and false alarms do not always have equal pay-offs. Therefore, perception must be modified to take these different pay-offs into account. If a hit has a large positive pay-off and a false alarm has little or no negative pay-off, you are much more likely to respond "Yes, something is out there." Dating is an example of a social situation with a low negative pay-off for false alarms. Many of us would be willing to accept a blind date arranged by our roommate. If the date is dull, we have only lost one evening's time. But this is offset by the possibility of an exciting evening. On the other hand, if a false alarm is very expensive, you are more likely to respond "No, I don't detect anything." Marriage is an example of a social situation with a high negative pay-off for false alarms. Marrying the wrong person can lead to traumatic divorce proceedings that are considerably more unpleasant than a dull evening with a blind date. Thus we have a more stringent criterion for potential marriage partners than for potential blind dates. We are more likely to respond "yes" to a blind date than to either offer or accept a proposal for marriage. Thus, your perception depends upon both the magnitude of the transduced energy and the pay-offs associated with your decision. If a signal has much energy, then you are more likely to detect it. Similarly, if the relative pay-off for hits is great, you are also more likely to detect a signal.

Other Sensory Modalities: Taste, Touch, and Smell

While vision and audition are the most important senses through which we get most of our information about the world, psychologists are also concerned with other sensory transducers. A list of such transducers used by humans includes taste, touch, smell, pressure, temperature, balance (vestibular sensation), and pain-sensing systems. This section gives a brief overview of three of these transductor mechanisms.

Taste: In a Gustatory Groove

When something tastes good, you like it because of a complex combination of texture, smell, temperature, and "true taste," which is the result of transduction by taste buds located on the tongue and in the back of the mouth and throat. All these features merge to yield a total taste impression. Good chefs insist upon their food being served piping hot, because they know that this enhances the "smell" component of taste. When you have a cold, food seems tasteless, mainly because your sense of smell is impaired.

Food dissolved in saliva stimulates the taste buds, which in turn generate nerve impulses. Taste buds are sensitive to four basic qualities of taste: sweet, salty, bitter, and sour. Some buds react to only one of these qualities, while others are sensitive to several. When opposite sides of the tongue are stimulated at the same time, the two sensations occasionally fuse, giving rising to a taste sensation in the middle of the tongue. The "duplexity" theory of taste is based upon the finding that fusion occurs between only some pairs of taste qualities (Von Bekesy, 1964). Bitter and sweet interact with each other, although neither interacts with salty or sour. Similarly, salty and sour interact only with each other. The strangest finding has been that warmth—a temperature, not a taste—fuses with sweet and bitter, while cold fuses with salty and sour. This supports our earlier statement that perceived taste is a complex combination of many factors.

The skin responds to many kinds of stimulation, such as pressure, temperature, electricity, and various chemicals. Touch is usually studied by gently pressing small hairs against a grid stamped temporarily on the skin. The stiffness of the hair determines the amount of pressure applied. When pain is studied, small, sharp needles are used in place of hairs, but the procedure is otherwise similar. Several different kinds of nerve endings are found in the skin, and thus many different receptors form the basis for the various skin sensitivities. While the receptors associated with pressure can be specified, there is at present some uncertainty about which receptors play a role in temperature detection and in pain (Gardner, 1975). The sensitivity of the skin to pressure and pain varies in different parts of the body. For example, the back of the knee has a density of pain receptors almost five times greater than the tip of the nose.

Touch: From Tickles to Torture

Smell is a much more sensitive modality than is taste, with many more qualitative distinctions than the four characteristics with which taste is associated. Olfactory, or smell, receptors are found in the top of the nasal cavity in a mucous membrane. Most of the air we breathe travels from the nose down into the throat, but some of it rises against the membrane. This membrane has a watery surface that causes small gas particles to form a solution on it. We do not yet know how these molecules actually stimulate the receptor cells (Gardner, 1975), although it is possible that the rate at which a molecule crosses the membrane helps to determine its smell. As is the case with other senses, continuous exposure to a stimulus (here an odor) results in adaptation—a decreased sensitivity to the particular stimulus (or odor). On the average, such adaptation causes about a 25 per cent reduction in sensitivity (Geldard, 1972). While this helps certain workers (e.g., garbage men and sewer cleaners), others find it a handicap (e.g., coal miners, who at one time used canaries to smell methane). While several classification schemes for the qualities of smell have been proposed, none has achieved universal acceptance.

Smell: The Many Factions of Olfaction

Our previous discussion has covered the detection problem. Detection allows us to know that something is out there, but it does not tell us exactly what kind of signal is present. Knowing what kind of event occurs in the external world is called the **identification** problem. In this section we will discuss the identification of auditory pitch and visual color. But first we need to learn a little about the mechanics of sound production as related to frequencies and sound waves.

FREQUENCY ANALYSIS: WAVING AT SINE POSTS

Sound consists of the regular motion of air molecules. This motion is transmitted in the form of pressure variations which radiate away from the source of the sound. Such systematic pressure variations over time can be represented graphically, as in Figure 3–8. The simple function that is illustrated there is called the *sine wave* because it follows the trigonometric sine function. Two characteristics of the sine wave are extremely important, although they

Wave Motion: One Good Turn Follows Another

are not enough to specify the function completely. The height of the function is called the **amplitude.** The amplitude changes systematically with time, but the maximum amplitude is always the same (see Figure 3–8).

The amplitude controls the intensity of the sound. Sound intensity is measured in **decibels.** A decibel (dB) is a ratio of two intensities. The numerator (top) of this ratio is the intensity of the sound source being measured. The denominator (bottom) of this ratio is usually a standard level fixed by international agreement. When this standard level is used, the initials SPL, for sound pressure level, are added. Thus, when a sound intensity is listed as 10 dB SPL, what is meant is that the sound being measured is 10 times more intense than the international standard, which is a very low intensity—about the lowest that can be detected by your ear. The decibel is not a linear unit; doubling the intensity of the numerator does not double the number of dB but only adds 3 dB. Similarly, every time the intensity is *multiplied* by ten, this *adds* 10 dB. Thus a sound intensity of 60 dB SPL means that the measured sound is one million ($10 \times 10 \times 10 \times 10 \times 10 \times 10$) times greater than the international standard. The intensities of some common sounds are shown in Figure 3–9.

The distance between two successive peaks of a sine wave (such as in Figure 3–8) is called the **period.** The period is measured in time units—for instance, seconds. If we take the reciprocal of the period (1/period), our unit becomes cycles per second, and we have measured the **frequency** of the wave. The greater the frequency, the higher **pitch** the sound wave has. A frequency of one cycle per second is called a **Hertz** (Hz), after a German physicist of the same name. A kiloHertz (kHz) is a frequency of 1000 cycles per second. The notes on a piano go from a low of about 28 Hz to a high of about 4000 Hz (4 kHz). You can probably hear frequencies up to 18 or 20 kHz, although as you get older you will be less able to hear high frequencies. A simple test of your hearing can be made with your television set. Turn it on and lower the sound completely. Lean over the back of your set and listen for a soft, high-pitched whine. If you can hear it, this means you can detect frequencies on the order of 16 kHz.

Pitch Perception: Analyzing Auditory Frequencies

Sound waves in the real world are seldom pure sine waves, as can be seen in Figure 3–10. Waveforms are complex, and this is why a note played on a flute sounds different from the same note, or frequency, played on a trumpet. This difference in sound quality is called **timbre.**

Any complex sound can be created by adding together sine waves, provided the sine waves are properly related. In perceiving complex sounds, the ear conducts its own waveform analysis by identifying **pitch,** the psychological correlate of frequency. If two notes are played at the same time, you perceive a musical chord containing two distinct frequencies. You do not hear a single complex unitary sound. As we shall soon discover, the visual system lacks this property; two visual frequencies get combined into a single perception.

The lowest frequency in a complex sound wave is called the **fundamental.** Frequencies greater than the fundamental are called **harmonics.** Harmonics occur at whole-number multiples of fundamental frequency. For example, when a musical instrument sounds concert A (a fundamental frequency of 440 Hz), the waveform produced by the instrument contains some sound energy at frequencies of 880 Hz, 1320 Hz, and so on.

Since the fundamental frequency is the lowest common denominator of all the harmonics, we can correctly guess the fundamental from our knowledge of the harmonics. For example, if we have harmonics of 400, 600, and 800

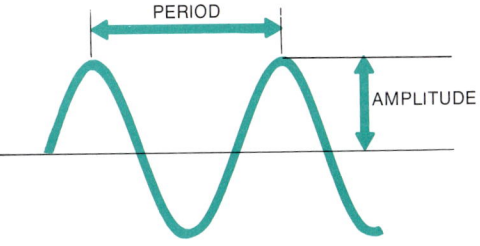

FIGURE 3-8 A sine wave. The maximum height of the wave is called the amplitude. The distance between any two successive peaks is called the period.

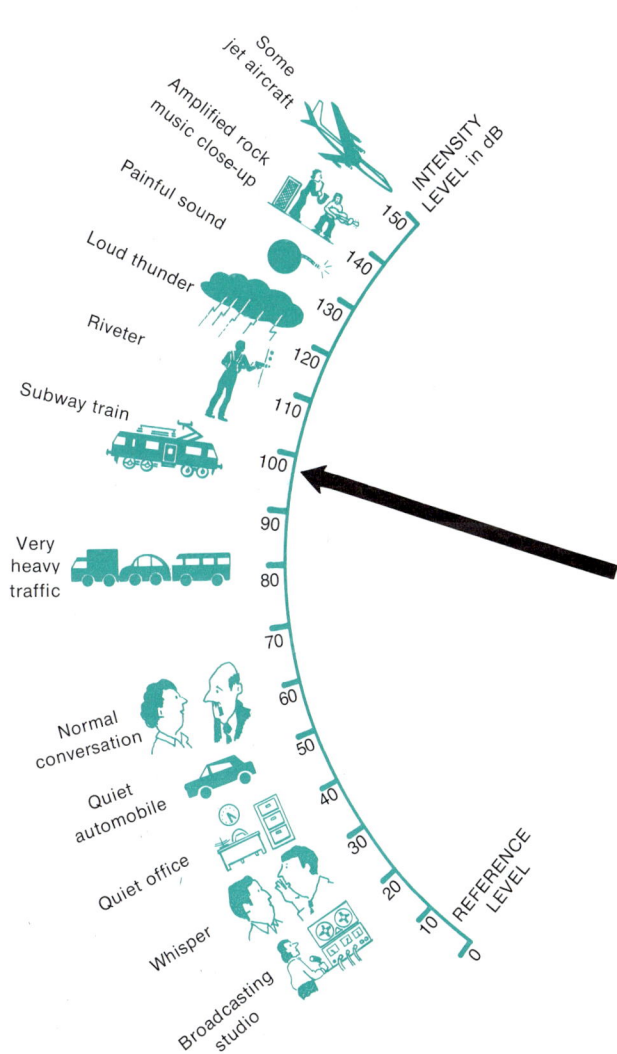

FIGURE 3-9 How intense are some common sounds? All decibel values are dB SPL. (Adapted from Chapanis, 1965.)

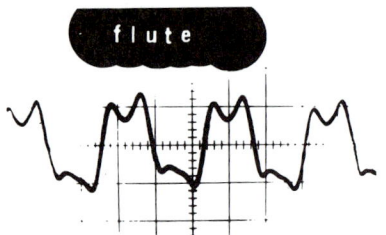
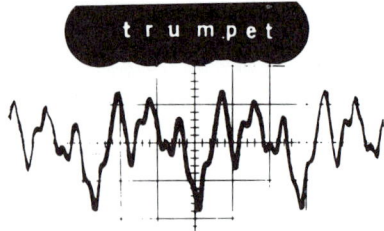

FIGURE 3–10   Waveforms of a flute and a trumpet playing note F. Although the two frequencies are the same, the waveforms clearly have different shapes. This is why the timbres of the two instruments differ. (From Foulke, E., and Mandriota, F.: *Dimensions of Sound*. Part 2. Baldwin, New York: Life Science Associates, 1971, p. 4.)

Hz, the fundamental frequency must be 200 Hz. Normally, a waveform contains both a fundamental frequency and several harmonics. By using special electronic filters, it is possible to remove the fundamental frequency without changing the harmonic structure. Such an artificial waveform from which the fundamental frequency has been eliminated is called a **missing fundamental.** If you are presented with two waveforms, one with and one without the fundamental frequency, they both will sound the same. In both cases the pitch will sound like the fundamental frequency, even when the fundamental frequency is not physically present in the waveform. This unusual phenomenon of the missing fundamental plays an important role in distinguishing among the three major theories of pitch perception: *place theory, periodicity pitch theory,* and *residue theory*. We shall now see how each of these theories attempts to explain the mystery of the missing fundamental.

Place Theory

The physiological basis underlying the waveform analysis performed by the ear was the subject of speculation over a hundred years ago by the German physicist Helmholtz. Helmholtz believed that pitch perception is due to the vibration of a specific location on the basilar membrane. Because the basilar membrane consists of many fibers stretched across its triangular shape, we can think of it as a harp with strings. The longer strings resonate at lower frequencies, and the shorter strings at higher frequencies. Thus, a complex wave would automatically be decomposed into its component frequencies on the basilar membrane. Although some of the details of Helmholtz's theory were incorrect, the basic idea was later supported by the work of George von Bekesy, who discovered that the place of greatest vibration on the basilar membrane does indeed change systematically with frequency of sound vibration. Von Bekesy received the Nobel Prize in 1961 for "his discoveries concerning the physical mechanisms of stimulation within the cochlea."

Unfortunately, place theory cannot easily explain the missing fundamental phenomenon. Helmholtz attempted to deal with this effect by suggesting that the transduction process in the middle ear introduced distortion before the wave entered the cochlea. This distortion creates a new fundamental frequency, so that the fundamental is present inside the cochlea even though it is missing when the sound first enters the ear. Later work, however, throws doubt on the *distortion hypothesis*. When low-frequency noise is added to the complex wave, the fundamental frequency gets blotted out or masked. When the noise is sufficiently intense, it will also mask any distortion of the fundamental frequency. Nevertheless, the pitch of the complex wave is still properly perceived despite the noise (Thurlow and Small, 1955). The missing fundamental phenomenon cannot be explained by distortion, and this creates serious difficulties for place theory.

Before we can understand the periodicity pitch theory, we must briefly return to a discussion of sound waves. If a frequency of 440 Hz and another frequency of, say, 450 Hz are presented together, we hear a wavering pattern of 10 Hz, called the *beat frequency*. A piano tuner uses this beat frequency effect to accurately tune the different strings which correspond to the same keyboard note; intensity is increased by using more than one string per note. After the first string is tuned, the remaining strings must be tuned to exactly the same frequency. At first there is a beat, since the other strings are slightly out of tune. When the beat is eliminated, the piano tuner has achieved success. It is important to realize that we have not created any new sound energy at the beat frequency by adding two sound waves together. Since there is no acoustic energy at the beat frequency, the place theory of pitch perception can explain our hearing the beat only by positing a distortion mechanism, which, as we have already noted, is not a good explanation.

Periodicity Pitch Theory

The periodicity pitch theory explains this effect, and all pitch perception, by arguing that the firing of auditory nerve cells reflects a *pattern of excitation* rather than a place on the basilar membrane. When two notes are sounded together, this pattern contains the beat frequency as well as the two individual frequencies. The theory also explains the missing fundamental. Since there are many harmonics but only one fundamental frequency, masking out the fundamental does not appreciably change the overall pattern of sound excitation. The low pitch of the fundamental is actually perceived by the neurons that respond to the higher pitches of the harmonics, because these neurons convey most of the information about the pattern of excitation. This may seem backwards to you until you recall our earlier discussion of the missing fundamental: A sound wave with harmonics of 800, 1600, and 3200 Hz is presented. What is the fundamental? The answer is 400 Hz. You were able (if you answered correctly) to infer the fundamental from a knowledge of the harmonic structure. So too can the fundamental be inferred from the pattern of excitation reported by neurons that respond to higher pitches. Indeed, if we use a high-frequency masking noise to cover up the high-pitched harmonics the missing fundamental can no longer be heard.

There are still problems with periodicity pitch theory. One difficulty is that an individual neuron cannot fire at high enough rates to account for perception of high-frequency signals. This has been explained by the *volley* principle, which states that neurons fire in groups. While one neuron is "reloading," its neighbor can discharge. This general notion is both reasonable and approximately correct, but details don't tie together as nicely as would be desired (Simmons, 1970).

An important recent alternative to the distortion hypothesis has been the residue theory, formulated by the Dutch psychologist Schouten. This theory states that low frequencies in a complex tone are heard as separate tones, while the high-frequency components, which make up the *residue*, are jointly perceived as a single unit. The pitch of the residue depends upon the periodicity or pattern of the high-frequency components. This yields a simple explanation of the missing fundamental, since removing the fundamental leaves the residue unchanged. Residue theory offers other advantages, but it too has certain disadvantages (Wightman and Green, 1974). While each of the three theories is partly correct, none of them explains everything about pitch perception. The fascinating mystery of pitch perception lingers on to tantalize psychologists.

Residue Theory

Light energy, like sound energy, can be considered to travel in waves. The wave frequencies of light are considerably higher than those of sound, and it is customary to specify light energy by its **wave length**—that is, the distance

Color Vision: Analyzing Visual Frequencies

between successive peaks of the wave—rather than its frequency. The unit of wavelength is the millimicron, or *nanometer* (nm.), which equals one millionth of a millimeter. The range of visible light is called the spectrum and can be seen when light is passed through a prism, as shown in Color Plate 7. The spectrum can also be seen in nature's equivalent of the prism, the rainbow.

We have already mentioned that night vision relies mostly on the rods in the retina. Now that we know about wavelength, this point can be re-examined. If we ask someone to sit in the dark for about 20 to 30 minutes, his or her vision will reflect the operation of the rods, because cones are not sensitive enough to be used in dim light; we call this *dark adaptation*. When you leave a movie theater, the lights in the lobby seem exceedingly bright because of prior dark adaptation that has occurred inside the theater. We can compare both the sensitivity and the wavelength function under conditions of dark adaptation and light adaptation. *Light adaptation* is accomplished by having subjects stare at a brightly illuminated surface. The results of such procedures can be seen in Figure 3–11. While the light-adapted eye is most sensitive to wavelengths of 555 nm. (green), the dark-adapted eye does best at 505 nm. (blue). This change in the most sensitive wavelength is called the **Purkinje shift.** It comes about because rods and cones absorb different wavelengths of light. If you are willing to sit in the dark for a while, you can see this shift for yourself, by consulting Color Plate 5.

Color

It is easy to show that almost all colors can be created by adding together light from three projectors covered by blue, green, and red filters (see Color Plate 6). These three colors are called *primary colors*. The Young-Helmholtz theory of color vision suggests that the cones of the eye (remember that rods are not sensitive to color) contain three different pigments which correspond to the three primary colors. Thus when you see yellow light, this is not due to activation of a "yellow" cone, but instead can be explained by assuming that the red and green excitations are almost equal. This equality of red and green excitation leads to the perception of the color yellow. Indeed, direct measurements of the light-absorbing properties of retinal cones have supported the idea of three kinds of cones. These three types of cone absorb most light at

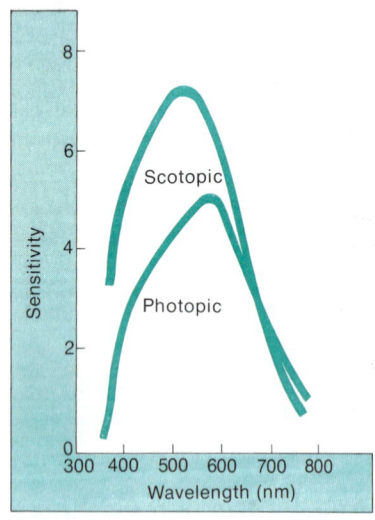

FIGURE 3–11 Sensitivity functions illustrating the Purkinje shift. The *scotopic* function is obtained for the dark-adapted eye and represents rod vision. The *photopic* function is obtained for the light-adapted eye and represents cone vision. Since rods are more sensitive than cones, the scotopic curve is higher. (Adapted from Kaufman, 1974.)

wavelengths of 455 nm., 535 nm., and 570 nm. respectively (Wald and Brown, 1965). Additional evidence for three types of cones comes from observing color deficiencies. Almost 10 per cent of males but only 1 per cent of females have some sort of color-vision deficiency. If a person lacks one type of cone, he is called a *dichromat*, since he must match colors by mixing two rather than three wavelengths of light. For example, a person lacking the green cone cannot distinguish between green light and certain combinations of red and blue. While this is the most common form of color blindness, our trichromatic theory of color vision predicts that there should also be two other kinds of color blindness. Some color-blind people are, in fact, insensitive to red light, and there is also a rare form of color blindness in which a blue cone is missing (see Color Plate 2).

The Young-Helmholtz theory of color vision is analogous to the place theory of frequency detection in audition. Color vision is attributed to activation of a specific kind of physiological receptor which is tuned to a specific wavelength. This proposed model of color vision is probably incomplete (as is the case with the place theory of audition) since it neglects higher-order patterns of excitation (analogous to periodicity pitch). Most theories of color vision tell us more about how colors can be mixed than about how patterns of cone excitation result in our experiencing color. Color mixture *is* important, since it reminds us that vision and audition differ. A combination of two visual wavelengths results in perception of only one color (see Color Plate 6). This is not the case in audition, in which two separate frequencies are perceived.

In the nineteenth century, Benham discovered that color sensations can be produced from a spinning top which contains only black and white. Benham's disk, as it is now called, is shown in two forms in Plate 10. While it is still of great interest to psychologists, its popularity as a toy has diminished, since extended viewing tends to induce nausea. Fechner (1838) and, later, Pieron (1923) attempted to explain this effect in terms of the trichromatic theory by arguing that each of the three cones takes different amounts of time to turn on and to turn off. Thus, a sudden pattern of white light could first affect one cone, then another, and finally the last. Similarly, the three cones would shut off at slightly different times. Therefore, rotating the disk at the right speed would produce color perception. More recently, Festinger, Allyn, and White (1971) investigated this phenomenon by using stationary lights that could be flickered in different temporal patterns. Different patterns produced different colors. Furthermore, the on and off speeds suggested by Pieron could not account for the perceived colors. This suggests that temporal patterns of neural excitation, perhaps similar to those conveying frequency information in audition, are important determinants of color perception.

You have already seen an illusion demonstrated in Figure 3–1, and in this section we return to discuss three perceptual situations in which we are faced with the difficult problem of resolving inconsistent stimuli. The most common kind of inconsistent input studied by psychologists is the geometric optical illusion. Other similar illusions involve depth cues, motion cues, and aftereffects of stimulation. Another kind of inconsistent input deals with information from more than one sensory modality. If your eyes tell you one thing while your touch tells you something quite different, which sense will you believe? The last kind of inconsistent input to be discussed does not normally occur in nature but has been created in the laboratory to further our knowledge of visual perception. This technique, called **sensory deprivation,** removes external stimuli, but perception still goes on.

ILLUSION: INCONSISTENT INPUTS AND OTHER STRANGE STIMULI

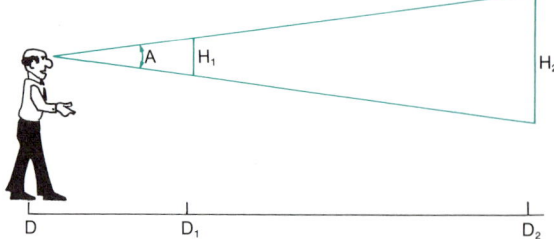

FIGURE 3-12 The visual angle (A) depends upon the distance (D) of an object and also upon its height (H). A near object (at D_1) can have the same visual angle as a far object (at D_2) only if the far object has a greater height (H_2 exceeds H_1). If perceptual cues associated with distance are ignored, both objects will appear to have the same height because they have the same visual angle.

Visual Illusions: The Mind is Quicker Than The Eye

Some of the most interesting illusions are based upon our interpretation of ambiguous or inconsistent depth cues. Figure 3-1 and other "impossible figures" fall in this category. Many of these illusions capitalize upon our ability to see objects as being the same size regardless of their distance from us. For example, whether we view an automobile from across the street or from an airplane at 10,000 feet, the car is perceived as being close to the same size, although the size of the image of the car formed on the retina is quite different in the two situations. This tendency to see objects with unchanged size, regardless of their distance from us, is called **size constancy.** Size constancy is possible only when we can somehow take the distance between us and the perceived object into account. If we are tricked about the distance, an illusion often results. Size constancy is only one of a large number of perceptual constancies. These constancies are related to the general phenomenon of using our knowledge about the external world so that perception is based more upon the contextual properties of the external object and less upon the retinal image formed by the object.

Illusions of Perspective

Why do the two men in Figure 3-13 look so unequal in size? Your experience tells you that rooms are rectangular. If you perceive the room as rectangular, then both men must be equally distant from you. Therefore, the man on the left must be smaller. Even though this great discrepancy in size is hard to believe, it is even harder to believe that the room is not rectangu-

FIGURE 3-13 Distorted room as used by Ames. The two faces appear quite different in size, although they seem to be the same distance away. (From "Experiments in Perception" by W. Ittelson and F. Kilpatrick. Copyright © 1951 by Scientific American, Inc. All rights reserved.)

lar. You have probably seen more midgets in your life than nonrectangular rooms, even though both are rare. In reality, you have been misled by your experience, since the room in Figure 3–13 is not rectangular at all. It is trapezoid, as can be seen in Figure 3–14. The man at the left is further away than the man at the right. The windows of the room have also been distorted to yield the same retinal image as a normal rectangular room. Indeed, when the room is empty it looks perfectly normal. The distortion becomes apparent only when objects are introduced into the far corners of the room.

A similar kind of illusion is shown in Figure 3–15. In all three rows, the cards on the left appear to be closer to you. You know from experience that objects which overlap other objects must be closer, and this is a strong cue for depth. Other things being equal, you also know that smaller objects are further away. But look at Figure 3–16. You've been fooled again. The cards on the right are the ones that are really closer to you.

Impossible figures, such as Figure 3–1, can be created by manipulating depth cues so that while each part of a figure is acceptable, the whole figure does not permit the inferred relationships between the parts. One set of such figures is shown in Figure 3–17. Although each feature in the shapes is fine by itself, somehow all the features do not fit together. The Freemish crate for "shipping optical illusions" is yet another example of an impossible figure.

Impossible Figures

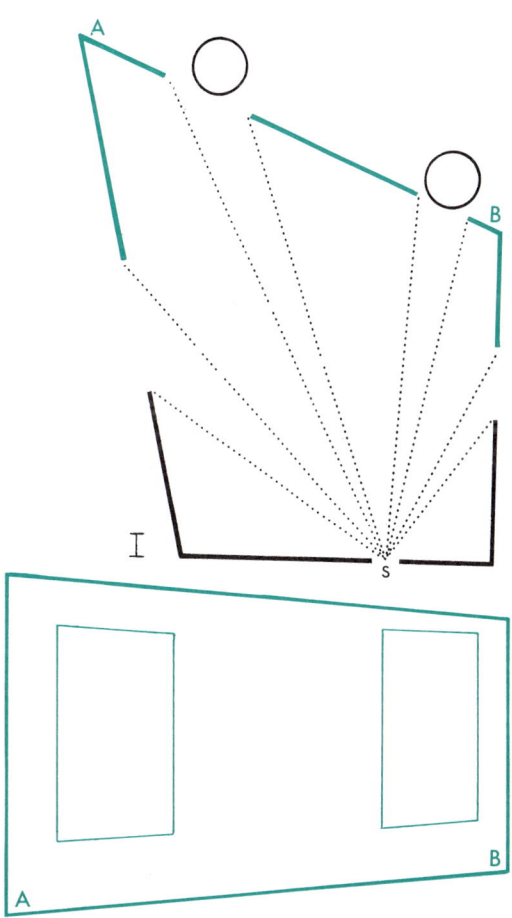

FIGURE 3–14   Diagram of the distorted room. The top view of the room shown in Figure 3–13 shows why the two faces appear to be of different size, yet the same distance away. Note that the left side of the rear wall is farther away from the perceiver. *Below*, The rear wall appears equidistant from the viewer at all points because of the way it is constructed. This is a front view of the rear wall without the side walls and floor. (After Bartley: *Principles of Perception.* New York, Harper, 1958.)

FIGURE 3–15 In each of the three rows, which cards appear closest to you? (From "Experiments in Perception" by W. Ittelson and F. Kilpatrick. Copyright © 1951 by Scientific American, Inc. All rights reserved.)

Illusions of Movement

A Moiré pattern is formed when two identical patterns are superimposed slightly out of register—that is, not exactly one on top of the other. Such patterns are much used in op art. Figure 3–18 shows a Moiré pattern in which the apparent motion is so strong that it is difficult to look at the pattern for any length of time. The apparent motion is probably due to rapid changes in accommodation by the eye. When the ciliary muscles of the eye are paralyzed, the illusion disappears. Similarly, focusing at infinity also stops the apparent motion. You can try this yourself by pretending to look through the book at the floor. With a little practice, the movement will stop or at least slow down.

FIGURE 3–16 Size and overlap cues of depth have been used in misleading you in the preceding figure. The cards on the right are really closest. (From "Experiments in Perception" by W. Ittelson and F. Kilpatrick. Copyright © 1951 by Scientific American, Inc. All rights reserved.)

FIGURE 3-17 Impossible figures. The lower right-hand figure is the Freemish crate, designed by Cochran. The other figures were constructed by Penrose and Penrose. The upper right-hand figure has proved so popular that it has a well-known name in psychology: it is called the endless staircase.

FIGURE 3-18 Can you stop the apparent motion of this figure? (Bridget Riley: *Current.* 1964. Synthetic polymer on composition board, 58⅜″ × 58⅞″. Collection, The Museum of Modern Art, New York. Phillip Johnson Fund.)

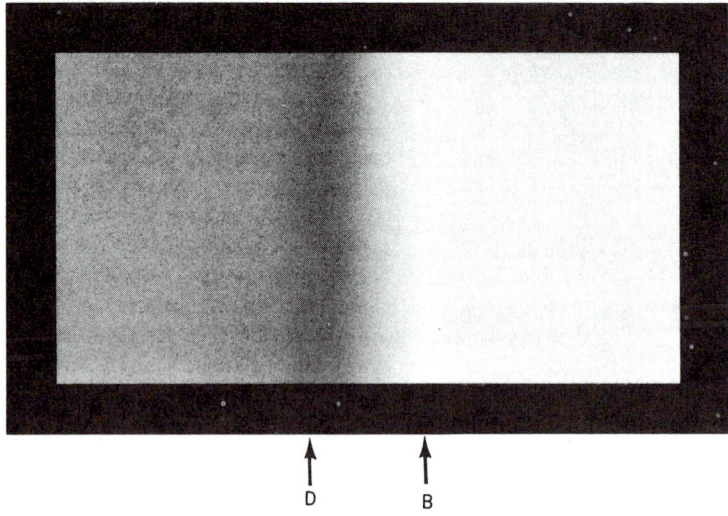

FIGURE 3-19 An illustration of Mach bands. A bright band appears at B and a dark band appears at D. Cover up one half of the bar. What happens to the band in the other half?

Mach Bands

The bright and dark bands illustrated in Figure 3-19 are named after Ernst Mach, who discovered them in 1865. While the light intensity is constant at each end of the bar, it changes smoothly in the middle. The bright and dark bands you perceive are not really there. They depend upon the relationships between the different levels of intensity in the bar. Covering one half of the bar removes the band in the remaining half. The visual system creates these bands to help in the perception of contours in external objects.

Thus, the perceived brightness does not exactly follow the stimulus intensity of the bar, which itself has no bands. A similar effect, called *simultaneous contrast*, is shown in Figure 3-20. Although the actual intensity of the inner squares is the same in both cases, the perceived brightness depends upon the intensity of the larger surrounding square.

Visual Aftereffects and Afterimages

Stare at Figure 3-18 for about 30 seconds. Then quickly look at a blank piece of paper. You will see a rotating movement. This is called a visual aftereffect. Now try this with colored figures. In the case of colored aftereffects, the

FIGURE 3-20 Simultaneous contrast. The small inner squares are equally intense but do not appear equally bright. (From Hebb, D.: *Textbook of Psychology.* Philadelphia: W. B. Saunders Company, 1972.)

aftereffect is more precisely called a *negative afterimage*. All these aftereffects reflect a basic property of the visual system. When a particular stimulus-analyzing mechanism is stimulated for a lengthy period of time, there is a tendency for the opposite effect to be produced when the stimulation is removed. Thus, when you shift your gaze in Color Plate 1, you see the complementary colors of the flag.

Clearly, visual cues can have several interpretations. Our purpose in presenting figures to be stared at, analyzed, focused on — or re-focused on — has been to acquaint you with a form of *mis*interpretation: illusions. Very simply, we can say that illusions occur because we interpret ambiguous cues incorrectly.

In normal everyday perception, the inputs from one sense modality complement and support the inputs from other sense modalities. This seems so obvious that an early eighteenth century philosopher, George Berkeley, believed that the perception of visual depth is first learned through the sensations of touch. However, most psychologists now believe that vision is the dominant sense modality.

The relation between vision and touch is often studied by distorting the external visual stimulus — for instance, by requiring an observer to wear special prisms over his eyes. One kind of prism causes straight lines to appear curved. Gibson (1933) had an observer wear these special prism eyeglasses for four days. Once the prism eyeglasses were removed, straight lines were perceived as curved in the opposite direction; this, of course, is yet another example of an aftereffect. This result led Gibson to further investigations. At first Gibson thought the curvature aftereffect might be due to a conflict between vision and touch. Accordingly, Gibson had his observer touch a straight edge while wearing the distorting prisms. A strange effect was observed. The straight edge, which looked curved because of the prisms, also *felt* curved. If the observer did not look at the straight edge, then the straight edge felt straight. When touch and vision conflict, the issue is often resolved in favor of vision. This dominance of vision over other sense modalities is called **visual capture.** In a more recent experiment (Rock and Victor, 1964) observers wore distorting lenses that changed a square into a rectangle. The observers reached under the square and touched it through a black cloth which prevented them from seeing their own hand. Nevertheless, the square felt like a rectangle. Visual capture does not depend upon being able to view your own hand through the distorting prism.

After reading the above, you may feel that this information, while interesting, has little if anything to do with your daily existence, since you seldom wear distorting prisms. A more practical demonstration of visual capture has been completed by Jordan (1972) in a study of fencers. These fencers set their blades on-guard against a foil mounted on a mechanical arm. They were asked to respond as fast as possible to a movement of the mounted foil. The experiment used three different conditions. In the first, the fencers held their blades 15 cm. away from the mechanical arm, so that the stimulus was only visual — that is, they responded only after seeing the mechanical foil move. In the second, they *touched* their blades to the mechanical foil, so that the stimulus was both visual and tactual (resulting from touching). In the third, they held their blade against the foil but were blindfolded; thus the stimulus was only tactual. The fencers were fastest to respond when blindfolded — i.e., when only tactual information was presented. Presentation of visual information, either by itself or in combination with tactual stimulation, slowed down their response time. This shows that even in normal situations not involving distorting lenses or prisms, the visual sense dominates touch.

The War Between the Senses: Visual Capture

PSYCHOLOGY
IN
ACTION: *How Does Your Brain Know Where Your Eyeball Is?*

Hold your head still and look around the room. Although your eyeball is moving, say from left to right, the furniture in the room, the walls of the room, and all other features appear fixed and do not move along with your eyeball. This is called *position constancy.* Somehow your perception takes the position of your eyeball into account. Two different explanations have been used to account for this important perceptual fact. The first states that receptors in the eye muscle send signals to the brain. Thus the brain *gets* a position message from the eye. The second states that since the brain sends the original signal ordering the eye to move, the brain al-

ready knows where the eyeball will be. Thus the brain *sends* the position message to the eye.

You can do a simple experiment to see which of these two explanations is correct. Look at some object and *gently* push your eye from the side with your finger. Your push will change the messages from the eye muscles, since the position of the eye has been changed. If this feedback is responsible for position constancy, objects should still appear stationary while you push your eye back and forth. Do objects move or do they remain stationary when you gently push your eye?

Where Have All the Stimuli Gone?: Sensory Deprivation and the Stabilized Image

In this section we will consider two kinds of sensory deprivation. In normal vision, the eye is constantly in motion, even when your gaze is fixated on some particular point. This tiny movement of the eye, called **nystagmus,** ensures that you do not see a hole in your visual field corresponding to the blind spot of your retina. Ordinarily, nystagmus prevents the constant stimulation of a particular point on your retina. However, special optical devices can be used to overcome nystagmus. These devices lead to a **stabilized image** which remains at a constant location on the retina. Our first topic, then, will be the unusual visual effects created by the stabilized image technique. A second kind of sensory deprivation applies to more than vision. In many experiments, attempts have been made to limit *all* external stimuli completely. While you might think that this kind of situation would be very relaxing, it turns out to be an unpleasant experience for most people.

The Stabilized Image

When you first view a stabilized image, it appears sharp and clear. But within seconds it fades from view. After a while, the image will suddenly reappear. When the image is more complicated than a straight line, say a letter, a curious fragmentation is observed. The whole letter does not disappear and reappear as a single unit. Instead, parts of the letter, such as component lines and loops, fade in and out separately (Pritchard, 1961). This finding has been used to support the idea of higher-level stimulus analyzers in the brain. If the stabilized image were purely a retinal effect, we would expect all of the image to fade and reappear as a unit. There is, however, some controversy about this explanation. For example, Cornsweet (1970) has argued that the reappearance of the stabilized image is due to slipping of the contact lens used to create the image. Nevertheless, this viewpoint does not explain why the original image fades out in parts. There may be both retinal and brain-level aspects of the stabilized image effect.

Recent research has used the stabilized image technique to document the existence of specialized visual analyzing systems in the human. Schmidt, Fulgham, and Brown (1971) devised, as targets, eight straight lines tilted in various orientations or pairs of straight lines forming different angles. The rate at which these simple geometric figures faded out was related to their shape and orientation. For example, a right angle was much more stable than other

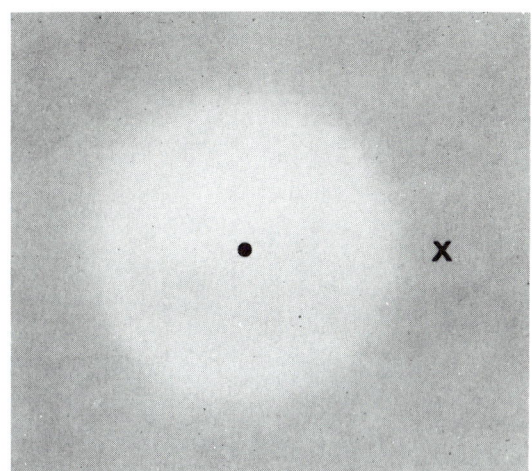

FIGURE 3–21 A simulation of stabilized image effects. Focus on the dot. The circle will eventually disappear but will reappear when you shift your focus to the cross.

angles. To show that these effects were not due to retinal activities, a later study first presented a vertical bar grating (parallel vertical lines close together) to one eye (Brown, Schmidt, Cosgrove, and Zuber, 1972). Then the other eye received a stabilized vertical line. When a vertical bar grating had been previously presented, the "fade rate" for the stabilized vertical line was higher than for a control condition with no bar grating. When a horizontal bar grating was first used, the fade rate for the vertical line was lower than in the control condition, indicating that the image was more stable. Since different eyes were used for the grating and the stabilized image, the findings suggest a non-retinal effect. However, when the same eye was used, the effects on fading were greater, suggesting that there also is a retinal component of the stabilized image. Finally, Cosgrove, Kohl, Schmidt, and Brown (1974) used this same technique with colored stabilized lines. The stabilized line was less stable if it was the same color as the grating. Another study in the same series had the observer press a button as soon as the line disappeared. Substitution of a different colored line in the same retinal location made it easier for the line to reappear. While this research needs to be expanded (for example, by having the observer record which of two different colored lines reappear), it does support our previously discussed ideas about visual analyzing systems. Somewhere in the brain there are specific systems which analyze such stimulus features as tilt, shape, and color.

In a sensory deprivation experiment, many sources of normal stimulation are removed or at least muted. The greatest reduction of sensory input has been achieved in the environment schematized in Figure 3–22. A nude subject enters the tank, which is specially built to minimize and isolate effects of the external world. The person breathes through a tube and regulator system similar to that used by scuba divers. The water is maintained at a constant temperature of about 94° Fahrenheit. A mask is used to prevent visual stimulation. Weights are added to the mask so that the subject is neutrally buoyant; since he is neither rising nor sinking in the water, a feeling of weightlessness results. The water environment also provides for automatic removal of body wastes. The subject is comfortable but is instructed not to move around. The subject is of course continuously monitored by an experimenter in the adjacent room and can terminate the experiment any time he wishes.

This environment appears at first to be really relaxing, just the way to unwind after a tough psychology exam. But sensory deprivation experiments are

Total Sensory Deprivation

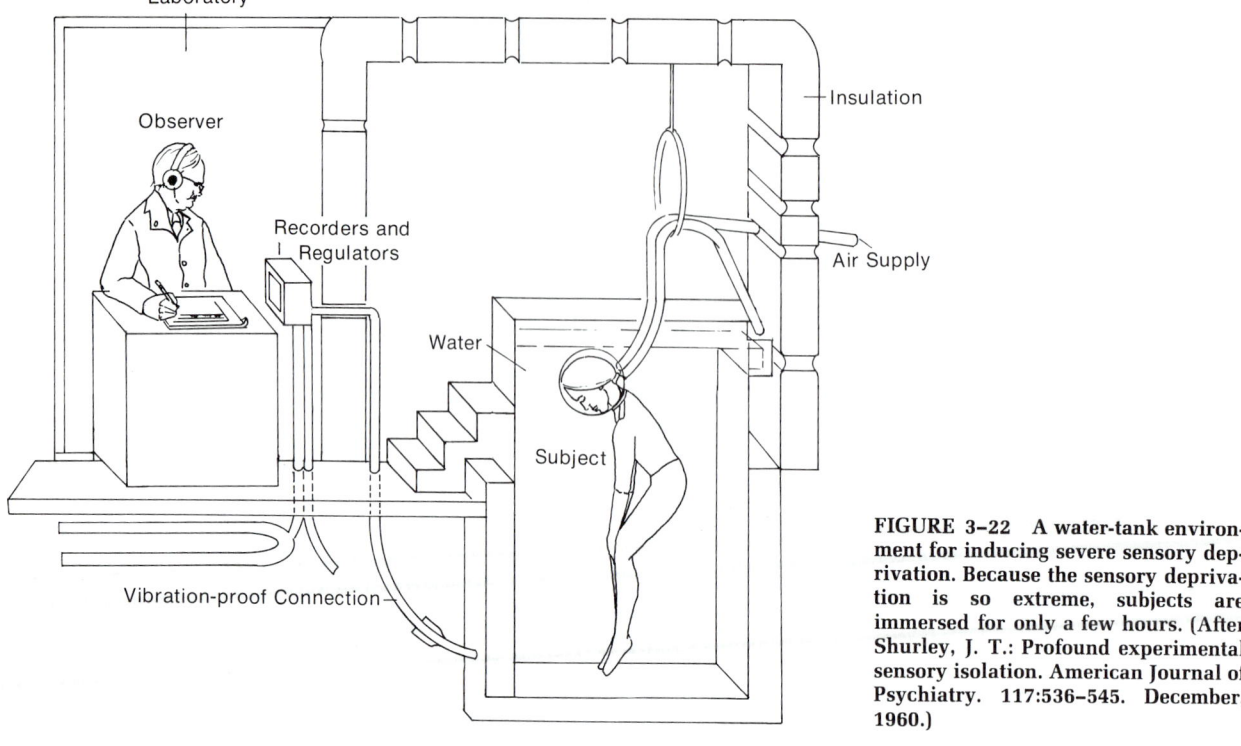

FIGURE 3–22 A water-tank environment for inducing severe sensory deprivation. Because the sensory deprivation is so extreme, subjects are immersed for only a few hours. (After Shurley, J. T.: Profound experimental sensory isolation. American Journal of Psychiatry. 117:536–545. December, 1960.)

conducted for several hours and sometimes for two or three days or longer. In one experiment involving four days of sensory deprivation (not in a water tank), subjects showed a decrease in one visual component we have already talked about—size constancy (Doane, Mahatoo, Heron, and Scott, 1959). More significantly, even grosser deficits have emerged in many other sensory deprivation experiments.

Many subjects experience unpleasant **hallucinations.** Hallucinations result when experiences which have no external stimulus correlates are reported (see Chapter 10). For example, one subject screamed that a bug with many legs was crawling behind him. This differs from an *illusion,* in which the external stimulus is misinterpreted. Complex hallucinations appear most often in the first hours of sensory deprivation and do not increase with more deprivation (this is determined by asking subjects to report hallucinations as they occur) (Zuckerman, 1969). While early work in sensory deprivation stressed the strange hallucinations that occur, more recent efforts have not supported the ideas that such hallucinations are of pathological importance and are clearly related to personality abnormalities (Zuckerman, 1969).

EVEN A CHILD CAN DO IT: THE INFANT'S PERCEPTION OF THE WORLD

We are used to thinking of infants as cute little blobs who can't do much of anything except eat and cry. Even the doting parent tends to believe that the young infant, especially, can only lie helplessly in its crib. Thus you may find it surprising that child psychologists are intensely interested in the perceptual capabilities of the infant and have invented many ingenious techniques for discovering how the world is perceived during the earliest days of life.

Visual Capture in Infants: The Eyes Have It

You will recall that in an earlier section of this chapter we discussed *visual capture,* the dominance of the visual modality over other sense modalities. In that section it was also noted that early philosophers believed that touch educated vision—that is, that the perception of depth was learned by early experience gained from touching objects. The experiment we discussed—one in which a conflict between vision and touch is induced by special lenses—has also been tried with newborn infants. Bower, Broughton, and Moore (1970b) put polarizing goggles on infants. The polarizing goggles, when combined with light from two polarized light sources, create a *virtual image*, which looks like a solid object, although in reality no physical object is present.

Although two-week-old infants do not reach out for objects in the same way that older infants will, they *can* grasp, provided that they are supported and their hands and arms are free to move. All the newborn infants in the experiment reached out to touch real objects without any sign of distress. Similarly, they would touch empty air when no visible object was present, also without distress. But when the infants were presented with the virtual image of an object, which of course cannot be touched, strong signs of distress were evident. The infants let out a howl when they discovered that they could not touch what they saw. This finding agrees with research on visual capture in adults, since again the visual input is dominant. Furthermore, since a two-week-old infant has not had much opportunity to touch objects, it is difficult to conclude that touch teaches vision. Bower (1974) has concluded that the primitive unity between the senses is innate. It is a basic property built into the human nervous system and is not learned as a result of experience.

Objects that are close together seem to be related, even if the objects are meaningless items like dots. This rule of **proximity** is but one of several grouping rules proposed in an early approach to perception called Gestalt psychology. Gestalt psychologists believed that the brain has innate self-organizing tendencies, and they tried, although not very successfully, to explain perception and other cognitive activities in terms of these tendencies. Thus Gestalt psychologists believed that such principles as that of proximity operate from birth onward. Although their reasons for believing this were not based upon observations of infants, their explanation was accepted by most psychologists for quite a while. The alternative explanation — that grouping by proximity is learned in infancy (Brunswik, 1956) — was at first not very popular.

Bower (1965) has tested the Gestalt assumption directly by presenting stimuli grouped by proximity to infants. His stimulus patterns are shown in Figure 3–23. In the upper rectangle of Figure 3–23, you will perceive the two dots on the left as going together, an example of grouping by proximity. Does

Visual Proximity In Infants: When Two Dots Dance Together

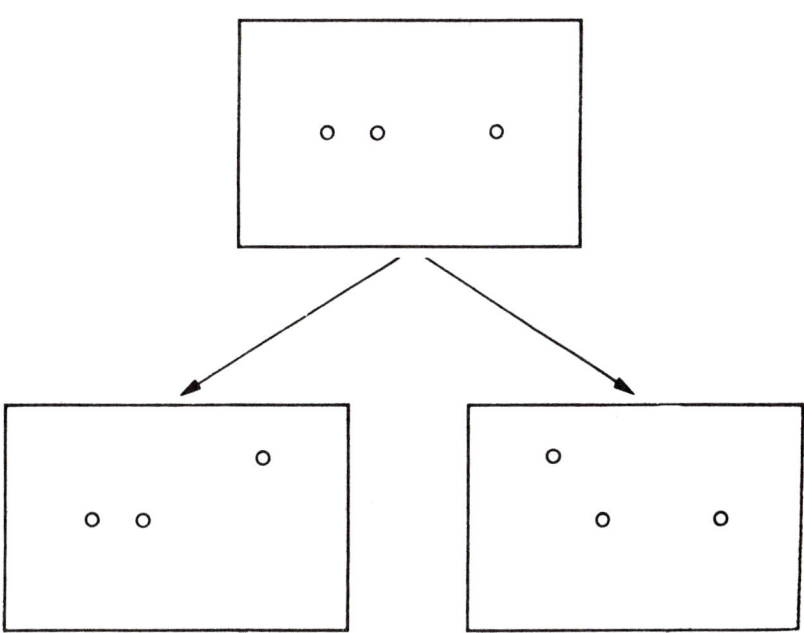

FIGURE 3–23 Dot patterns used to test grouping by proximity in infants. Changing from the top stimulus pattern to the lower left pattern does not disrupt the grouping by proximity. Changing to the lower right stimulus pattern violates grouping by proximity.

the young infant share your perception? Bower tested this by moving one of the dots. He reasoned that movement of the dot on the far right should be less disturbing, since this will not disrupt a functional unit. However, movement of the dot on the left breaks up a grouping established by proximity and is more surprising. In order to measure how surprised an infant might be, Bower used one of the responses that are well-established even in young infants: the sucking response. Surprise would disrupt sucking, and the longer the sucking was disrupted, the greater the infant's surprise. No effect of proximity was found until infants were one year old — that is, younger infants stopped sucking for the same amount of time for *both* of the lower dot patterns in Figure 3–27. This argues against the Gestalt assumption of an innate organizing process. Instead, organization by proximity is learned through experience.

The Infant's Perception of Distance

Bower (1974) has pointed out that any study of the perception of distance by infants must deal with this problem: Do they perceive distance at all? Or do they instead perceive variables that are correlated with distance? Thus when an object approaches an infant does the child see the object getting closer or does the child merely see the object getting bigger? While this distinction may not be crucial for the depth perception of adults who may use both cues, it is quite important if we wish to discover the origins of space perception. Although this theoretical distinction has been the object of much discussion, very little research is available to answer the question. Again, the limited repertoire of the infant makes it difficult to test alternative hypotheses about the origin of space perception.

A classic experiment by Gibson and Walk (1960) used the infant's crawling behavior to measure perception of distance. The apparatus they used created what is called the **visual cliff,** displayed in Figure 3–24. Although they could feel the support of the glass top, infants refused to crawl on the deep side, even to approach their mother. While this study does indeed demonstrate that infants do perceive depth, it does not answer the more basic question about the origin of depth perception. By the time an infant is old enough to crawl, it

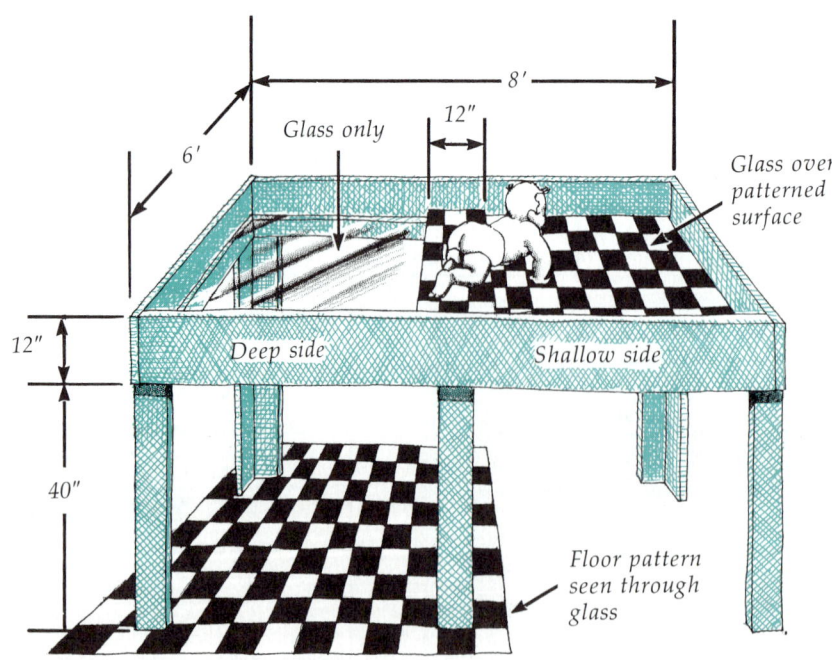

FIGURE 3–24 The visual cliff. Apparatus of this type has been employed to study depth perception in infants. Six-month olds refuse to crawl across the "deep" side, and even children too young to crawl show signs of emotional arousal when placed over the apparent drop. (After Walk, R. D., and Gibson, E. J.: *Psychological Monographs,* 519, 1961.)

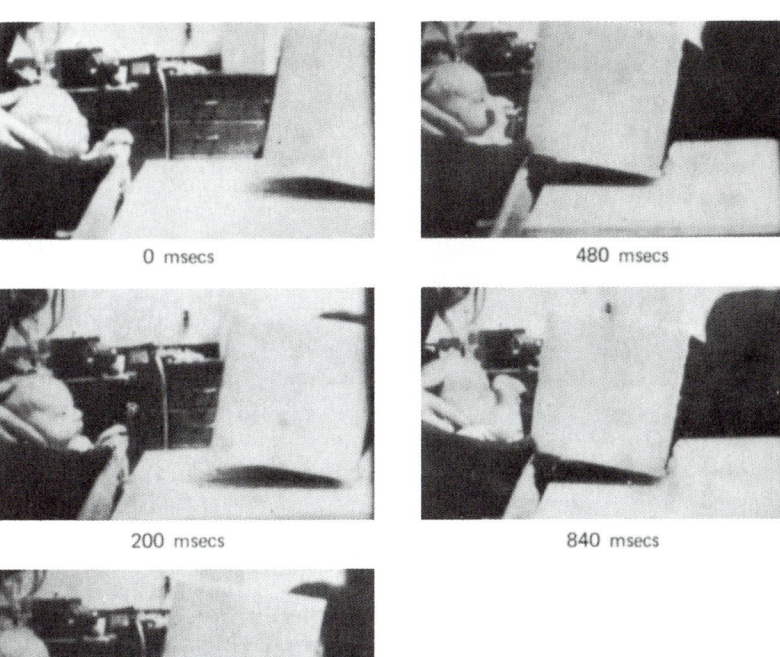

0 msecs

480 msecs

200 msecs

840 msecs

280 msecs

FIGURE 3–25 Defensive reactions of a ten-day-old infant as an object approaches. Both the position of the hands and the infant's facial expression change as the object gets closer.

already has had enough experience with the world to learn about depth perception. That younger children not yet able to crawl are also capable of such perception is suggested by the fact that they experience a marked reduction in heart rate—a clear sign of emotional arousal—when placed on the deep side (Campos, Langer, and Krawitz, 1970).

A simple way to test directly the question posed in the first paragraph of this section is to use two objects of different size, for example, two foam rubber cubes. Since the *visual angle* (see Figure 3–12) depends upon both size and distance, we can place the small cube close to the child and the large cube further away, so that the image projected onto the infant's retina is the same for both stimuli. When this was done experimentally (Bower, Broghton, and Moore, 1971), one-week-old infants showed defensive reactions (Figure 3–25) to the near cube but not to the far cube. Thus, it appears that an ability to perceive distance directly is present in one-week-old infants, and it seems likely that this ability is innate rather than learned.

The general outcomes and conclusions of this research can be summarized as follows. Although Bower fully expected his research to support the view that perception is learned through experience, much of his data lends support to the opposite view—i.e., that perception is innate. The infant is born with many, but not all, of his or her perceptual capabilities fully functioning.

Few areas of scientific research in modern times have generated such a controversy as the study of ESP (extrasensory perception). Arguments between believers and skeptics have appeared not only in popular magazines such as *Time* (March 14, 1973; November 4, 1974) but also in more sedate, scientific

EXTRASENSORY PERCEPTION: FACT OR FRAUD?

journals such as *Nature* and *New Scientist*. Despite a large amount of data, much of which is published in journals specifically devoted to ESP research, many scientists remain firmly unconvinced that the phenomena attributed to ESP result from special paranormal powers. Are these skeptics obstinately refusing to recognize established scientific facts or are they correctly noting that ESP has yet to be demonstrated under controlled laboratory conditions?

In October, 1974, the British journal *Nature* published an article with the seemingly innocent title "Information transmission under conditions of sensory shielding." In this article, two physicists from the Stanford Research Institute reported how a well-known psychic named Uri Geller was able to perceive drawings, dice contained in a box, and outdoor scenes viewed by a third party without any of the perceptual inputs described in this chapter. This article created a furor in scholarly circles and the very same week another highly respectable British journal, *New Scientist*, published a refutation claiming to discover several flaws in the experimental design of the *Nature* article. In this section we will present summaries of the original article (Targ and Puthoff, 1974) and the reply by Hanlon (1975). We will then conclude with a general discussion of issues in ESP.

Uri Geller: Fact?

The first tests described in the *Nature* article were ones in which Geller drew copies of pictures produced at distant locations. Geller was placed in a shielded room so that he was visually, acoustically, and electrically isolated from the distant location where the picture was being drawn. In most of these cases, someone knew what the target picture was. Thus, Geller's powers of **telepathy** (that is, knowing the thoughts in someone else's mind) were being tested. Uri Geller's drawings as well as the original target drawings are shown in Figure 3–26. Three occasions on which Geller declined to draw a picture are not illustrated. To get an independent evaluation of the correlation between target pictures and response drawing, two judges who did not know the purpose of the experiment were asked to match the set of targets with the set of responses. Both judges did this without making any errors at all. This seems to be impressive support of Geller's telepathic abilities.

In another series of experiments, a die was placed inside a steel box. An experimenter shook the box and Geller was asked to predict which side of the die was facing up. Since no one else knew the answer, this is not a test of telepathy but instead one of **clairvoyance,** an ability to perceive objects without using normal perceptual stimuli. The die was shaken ten times. Geller declined to respond to two trials and was correct on the remaining eight trials. The statistical probability of anyone guessing the eight trials correctly is about one in a million.

The tests seem to indicate that Geller does indeed have ESP. Certainly few of us could duplicate these feats. But before reaching any firm conclusions, it would be wise to consider alternative explanations. Could Geller have accomplished these tasks by normal, rather than paranormal, means?

Uri Geller: Fraud?

The issue of *Nature* containing the experiments described above was prefaced with an interesting editorial detailing the journal's reasons for publishing the study despite objections by some of the reviewers. In scientific journals, unfavorable comments by reviewers usually result in the article's rejection. The major objection of the reviewers was that the experiments did not contain sufficient precautions to prevent the possibility of deliberate or unconscious cheating on the part of Geller. Nevertheless, the editors published the article, because ESP, if real, is clearly a very important and interesting phenomenon worthy of detailed scientific investigation. Furthermore, a published report is much better than vague rumors about the results of some experiment. The experiments with Geller received wide publicity; publication of the paper with

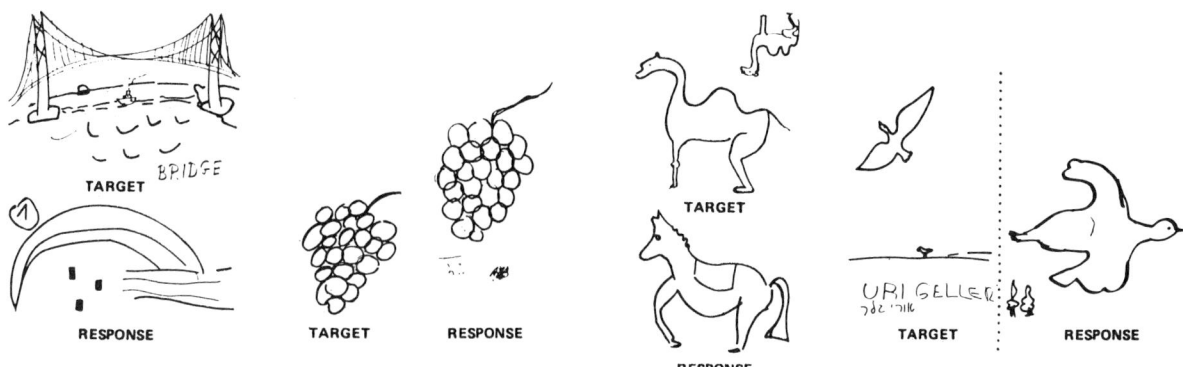

FIGURE 3-26 The target pictures drawn at a distant location and response pictures drawn by Uri Geller. Do you find this convincing evidence for telepathy? (From Targ and Puthoff: Information transmission under conditions of sensory shielding. *Nature*, Vol. 251, October 18, 1974, p. 603.)

its restrained claims killed the exaggerations that tend to accompany rumors.

One common rumor concerned Geller's ability to bend metal by paranormal means. This is the most spectacular of Geller's feats, yet the *Nature* article did not report metal bending, because even the authors were suspicious and suspected sleight of hand and other cheating. Geller claimed to be able to bend a metal object, such as a key, merely by stroking it. An ability to manipulate physical objects mentally is called **psychokinesis.** As Hanlon documents in his *New Scientist* paper, the tests with Geller could be easily explained by normal sleight of hand. Thus Geller, who is an accomplished magician, has not demonstrated any psychokinetic ability under controlled circumstances.

Since even Geller's supporters acknowledge that he will cheat if given the opportunity, it becomes extremely important to control the situation to rule out any chance of fraud. This is virtually impossible, since psychics claim they cannot perform on command. There are many recorded instances of Geller returning at an unexpected later time to an experiment which he originally could not accomplish; it is likely that in such cases the experimenters were not as vigilant as before. Incidentally, Geller refuses to perform if a professional

" LISTEN, DEAR, DON'T LOCK ME OUT...
MY FRONTDOOR KEY IS BENT "

FIGURE 3-27 Bending a household key is a well-known test of psychokinetic ability. (From APA Monitor, Copyright 1974 by the American Psychological Association. Reprinted by permission.)

magician is in attendance. Geller has not accomplished any abnormal tasks that could not also be duplicated by a professional magician. Thus, a scientist need not accept a paranormal explanation if a normal explanation will suffice. The authors of the *Nature* article, while competent physicists, are not sufficiently good observers to avoid being fooled by a clever magician. For example, Hanlon suggested that Geller might have a miniature radio implanted in a tooth. This would explain his ability to draw "telepathic" pictures. Similarly, it is possible to purchase from magician's supply houses a die that will radio which face is up. Any good magician could have switched the dice. Science has been fooled before, especially when scientists want to believe. For example, scientists once believed that Mars has water-filled canals. Geller may have ESP, but experiments have not been done to rule out ordinary magic. Circumstantial evidence favors simple magic and not paranormal powers as the basis of Uri Geller's psychic abilities.

ESP and Cheating   Although Uri Geller is probably the most celebrated psychic, you may feel that it is not fair to reject an entire area of research because of one subject who cheats if given the opportunity. We have discussed Geller in some detail both as an example of research in parapsychology and because his case was the first to be published in a respectable major scientific journal. While such publication does not guarantee or even imply the authenticity of a finding (since this can only be accomplished through replication), it does indicate that an area is of interest to the scientific community.

Cheating is a serious problem in all parapsychology research. The best-known parapsychologist in the United States is J. B. Rhine. A young scientist who was Rhine's protegé and director of the prestigious (at least among parapsychologists) Institute for Parapsychology had automated experimental designs aimed at showing psychokinetic abilities in rats. His experiments sought to discover if rats could control the random generator which delivered their rewards. If a rat got more rewards than the generator was set to deliver, one could infer psychokinetic ability. This automatization, which could greatly minimize possible experimenter effects, was viewed as a great advance in parapsychology. Unhappily, the scientist was caught tampering with the apparatus to produce positive results. So far his results have not been replicated by honest experimenters.

These incidents do not necessarily mean that all researchers in parapsychology are dishonest. But cheating is a common problem in such research. Thus the need for independent replication is of the utmost importance. Until such replication is achieved, most scientists will continue to view ESP with great skepticism, if not outright disbelief. After summarizing 85 years of ESP research, Hansel (1966) concluded his book on ESP by noting that the possibility of "trickery" has not been ruled out.

Summary

Perception is a complicated psychological process. In order to perceive the world outside, you must make active decisions about the information received through sensory transducers. Perceptual reality (or illusion) is pieced together from fragmented external cues.

Sensory **transducers** change external energy into a form that can be interpreted by your brain. The two kinds of cells in the retina of the eye that transduce light are **rods** and **cones.** The **fovea** contains only cones and has the greatest visual acuity. The ear is divided into three parts for transduction. The **cochlea** of the inner ear transduces fluid vibrations into electrical nerve impulses via the **hair cells** of the **basilar membrane.**

In order to detect an external signal, we need more than the transduction of sensory energy. We also require a **decision process** that must be completed before we can state that a signal has been detected. This two-stage model of perception, with a sensory input stage followed by a decision mechanism, is called **signal detection theory.** Signal detection theory states that the nature of the signal and the kind of costs and benefits associated with detecting or failing to detect a stimulus jointly determine perception. The correct detection of a signal is called a **hit,** and the incorrect detection of a signal when only **noise** is present is called a **false alarm.**

Once an event has been detected, the next problem is **identification.** Sound is identified in terms of **intensity** and **frequency.** The intensity of auditory stimuli is measured in **decibels.** The **pitch** of an auditory stimulus is related to its frequency. The lowest frequency in a sound is called the **fundamental.** The **missing fundamental** experiment helps to distinguish the three major theories of pitch perception. **Place theory** relates pitch perception to the vibration of a specific *location* on the basilar membrane. **Periodicity pitch theory** explains pitch perception by the *pattern* of excitation on the basilar membrane. **Residue theory** separates low- and high-frequency pitch components.

Light is identified in terms of color, specified by the light's **wavelength.** Only cones can perceive color differences. The **Young-Helmholtz theory** of color vision implies that there are three different types of cones, each sensitive to one of the three primary colors. Color sensations *can* be produced from stimuli containing only black and white, such as Benham's disk.

Ambiguous stimuli can easily be misinterpreted. Visual misinterpretation creates **illusions.** Illusions of perspective take advantage of our experience in perceiving depth to mislead us. They emphasize the role of experience in combining perceptual **cues.** Impossible figures, illusions of movement, Mach bands, and simultaneous contrast effects also show that the visual system creates information which is not actually present in the external stimulus.

The visual sense modality dominates other sense modalities. This is called **visual capture.** While most frequently demonstrated by having observers wear prism lenses, it can also occur with normal vision.

A **stabilized image** always stimulates the same points on the retina. Such images fade out and reappear. Experimentally, they can be used to identify different kinds of analyzing systems in vision.

Sensory deprivation experiments greatly reduce the amount of sensory stimulation. Sensory deprivation often results in **hallucinations** (psychologists no longer believe that these hallucinations are clearly related to personality abnormalities).

The infant is born with many, but not all, of his perceptual capabilities functioning. Visual capture has been demonstrated in two-week-old infants. One-week-old infants can directly perceive depth. However, grouping by visual **proximity** takes about a year to be learned and is not innate, as Gestalt psychologists believed.

Extrasensory perception (ESP) is a controversial subject in psychology today. Laboratory tests of a famous psychic, Uri Geller, claimed to document his ESP abilities such as **telepathy** and **clairvoyance.** However, his **psychokinetic** powers were not properly tested. Skeptics have suggested serious deficits in the experimental procedures used to test Geller. They claim that all of Geller's feats could be accomplished by a professional magician. Cheating is a serious problem in ESP research. Most scientists will not accept ESP until the phenomenon has been replicated under carefully controlled laboratory circumstances.

Suggested Readings

Geldard, F. A.: *The Human Senses.* 2nd edition. New York: John Wiley and Sons, 1972.
  A thorough treatment of all the senses from a traditional point of view.
Kaufman, L.: *Sight and Mind.* New York: Oxford University Press, 1974.
  An advanced undergraduate text with a modern treatment of visual perception.
Kling, J. W., and Riggs, L. A. (eds.): *Experimental Psychology.* Volume 1: Sensation and Perception. 3rd edition. New York: Holt, Rinehart, and Winston, 1972.
  An advanced treatment of all perception, with chapters by experts in specific subareas.

Robinson, J. O.; *the Psychology of Visual Illusion.* London: Hutchinson University Library, 1972.
  A catalog of the visual illusions studied by psychologists, with summaries of the explanations they have offered for them.

Some journals that regularly publish articles on perception:
  Journal of Experimental Psychology
  Perception & Psychophysics
  Journal of the Acoustical Society of America
  Vision Research
  Quarterly Journal of Experimental Psychology

Overleaf: Top left photo by Raimondo Borea; top right photo from *Exploring Child Behavior,* by D. Helms and J. Turner (Philadelphia: W. B. Saunders Company, 1976); bottom photo from Annan Photo Features.

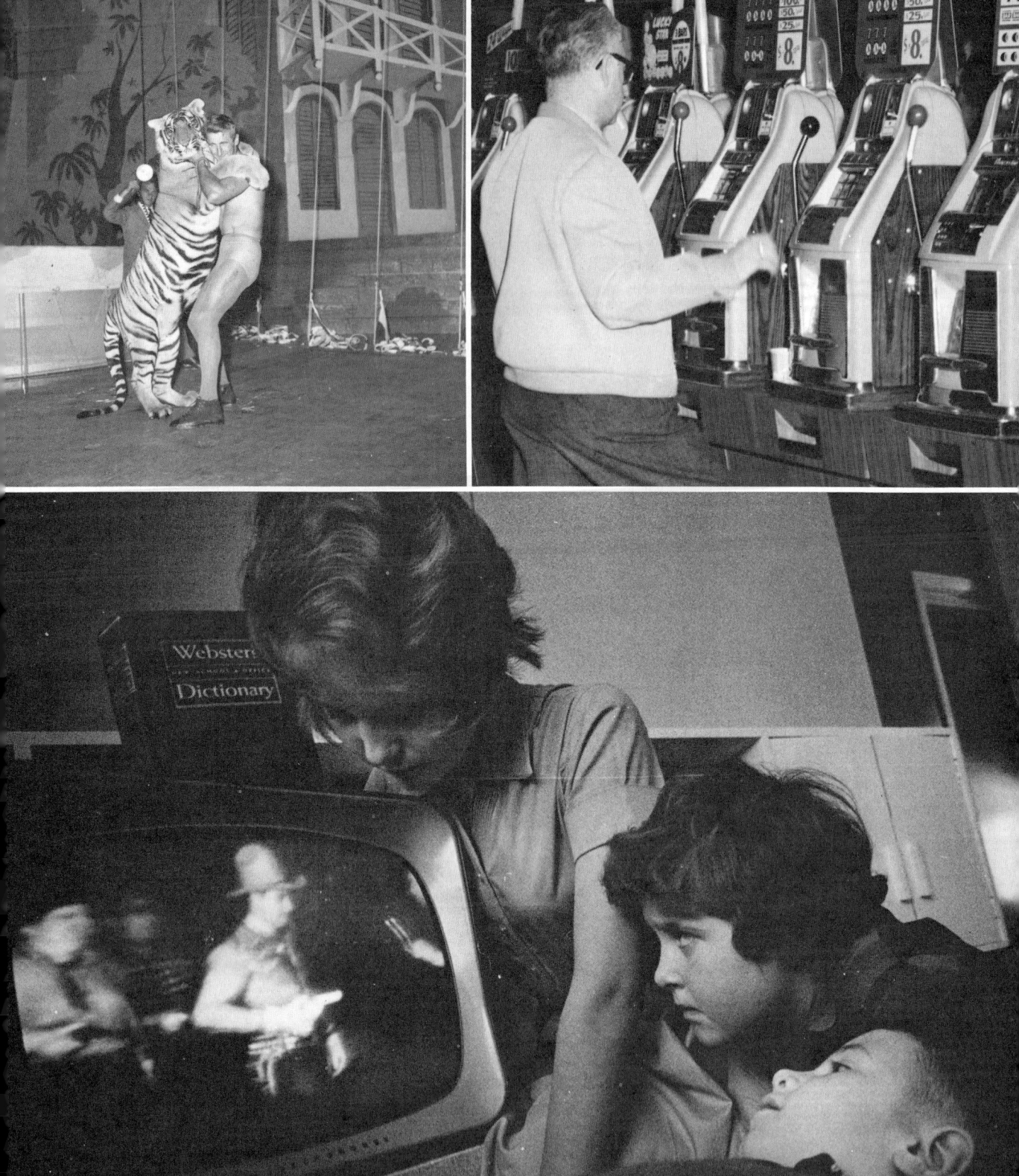

4 Learning about the World: Classical Conditioning, Instrumental Conditioning, and Observational Learning

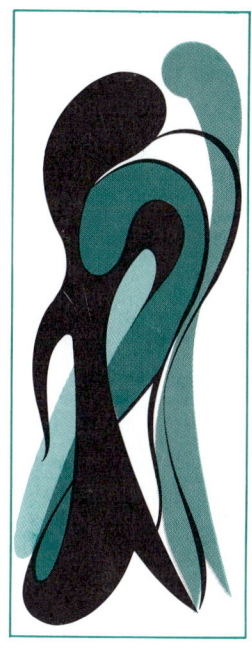

Do you remember the first time you tried to ride a bicycle, drive a car, or divide by fractions? If so, you probably recall that these were somewhat frustrating experiences during which you felt especially clumsy and inept. Moreover, depending on what you attempted, there is a good chance that you suffered such unpleasant outcomes as repeated falls, near collisions with other vehicles, feelings of frustration, or even public embarrassment. Yet, despite these early setbacks, your performance on each of these tasks probably improved quite rapidly so that soon you were much more proficient at them. This simple fact—that you stopped falling down, having close calls in traffic, or coming up with wrong or ridiculous answers—illustrates a basic and important principle about behavior: all organisms (and particularly human beings) have the capacity to "profit" from their experiences. That is, under normal conditions, they rapidly acquire the responses they need for effective functioning in a complex and often threatening world. The process through which such alterations occur is generally termed **learning,** and will serve as the major focus of the present chapter.

Although many different definitions of learning have been suggested, one which has gained increasing acceptance in recent years is the following: *learning is any relatively permanent change in behavior produced by experience* (Kimble, 1961; Tarpy, 1975). At first glance, this definition appears to be quite simple and straightforward. However, it actually includes several features worthy of careful attention.

First, it restricts use of the term *learning* to relatively lasting changes in behavior. As a result, temporary alterations produced by such factors as fatigue, drugs, illness, or variations in motivation will be viewed as distinct from those which stem from learning. Second, it makes no mention of *practice* as a necessary condition for learning. This is because psychologists now recognize that important and lasting changes in behavior can often be produced through exposure to the actions of others, without any overt practice of such responses (Bandura, 1977). For example, children acquire many different responses merely by watching the behavior of their parents, and adults can learn anything from important job skills to new styles of dress or speech through exposure to others. Finally, our definition contains no reference to improvements in behavior. This is the case because learning can yield undesirable as well as desirable outcomes. Indeed, as we will see in Chapter 10, the acquisition of maladaptive patterns of behavior often lies at the root of serious psychological disturbances.

Definitions such as the one we have been discussing are often necessary. But as you probably well know, they often have the unfortunate effect of putting people to sleep. Perhaps we can reawaken your interest and attention a bit by means of a list and a question. The list is as follows: tennis, final exams, prejudice, and sex; the question is: Which of these items is affected by learning? The answer, we contend, is *all* of them. To see why this is so, let us examine each in turn.

Tennis is relatively easy to recognize as affected by learning, for there is little doubt that your performance in this or any other sport generally improves with continued experience (practice). The same applies to the second item on our list, final exams. Again, experience—in this case studying—produces what you certainly hope will be relatively permanent changes in your behavior. Prejudice is a more complicated entity, for it represents a cluster of feelings and beliefs about others rather than an overt, observable behavior. Yet, if you stop for a moment and consider, it will soon become apparent that such negative reactions are probably acquired through experience. Infants, after all, are not born with strong hatreds or dislikes toward the members of other racial, ethnic, or religious groups. Rather, they acquire such reactions through experience involving their parents and others (see pp. 146–148). Our final item, sex, takes us into a somewhat sensitive area. But here, too, learning plays a role. For example, one's choice of lovers is often influenced by past experience (have you ever been attracted to someone because he or she reminded you of another person?), and actual performance is usually strongly affected by increasing experience as well.

The point of this discussion, of course, is not to provide you with information about sports, prejudice, or sex. Rather, it is to call your attention to the important fact that learning is a central process—perhaps *the* central process—in human behavior, one which affects virtually everything we do, feel, or think. Emphasis of this fact is needed, we believe, because most persons seem to assume that learning has little impact outside of sports, motor skills (such as driving a car), and cramming for exams. Actually, nothing could be farther from the truth, and as we shall see in later chapters, learning plays a central role even in such complex areas as personality, social interaction, and the occurrence of mental disorders.

Given the crucial impact of learning on virtually all forms of behavior, and the fact that we will have reason to refer to this process over and over again in later chapters, it seems essential that you gain a firm grasp of its basic features at this point. In the present chapter, therefore, we will focus primarily upon three important and seemingly complementary forms of learning. The first, **classical conditioning,** occurs when we learn which stimuli in the world around us are associated with each other (i.e., tend to occur together). As a result of such learning, stimuli which are initially incapable of evoking strong reactions from us soon acquire the ability to do so. The second — **instrumental, or operant, conditioning** — occurs when we learn what effects or consequences are produced by the various responses we give. Through such learning we come to behave in ways which either yield positive outcomes or help us to avoid or escape from negative ones. Finally, the third, **observational learning** (or **modeling,** as it is often termed), occurs when we acquire new responses or information through exposure to the actions and outcomes of others. As we shall soon see, learning of this type is highly efficient, and seems to play an important role in many complex forms of human behavior.

Imagine that you are standing in a long line at one of the registers in a local supermarket. Further, imagine that it is the dead of winter, and the temperature outside has sunk to new lows. Each time the automatic door at the front of the store swings open, an icy blast rushes in and strikes you directly in the face. When it does, you automatically flinch, and hunch your shoulders. Now, imagine that immediately before the door swings open, you can hear the muffled sound of the machinery which operates it. At first, you would probably show little reaction to this weak stimulus; in fact, you might not even notice it amidst the din of busy cash registers and the clanking of tin cans. After receiving a number of icy blasts in the face, however, you might begin to flinch and hunch your shoulders upon hearing the sound of this machinery, *before* the door swings open and allows the wind to enter. In short, you might begin to respond to this weak sound in much the same manner as you initially responded only to the rush of cold air.

This simple situation — which you might well encounter in your own experience — provides a good example of the important process of *classical conditioning.* That is, it illustrates the manner in which a stimulus (in this case the sound of the door mechanism) which is initially incapable of evoking a particular response, can gradually acquire the ability to do so simply through repeated pairing or association with another stimulus (here, an icy blast of wind) which *can* evoke such reactions.

Although this simple form of learning — in which one stimulus comes to serve as a kind of signal for the occurrence of another — may not seem particularly exciting, it actually plays a role in many important forms of behavior. As we shall soon see, there are strong grounds for assuming that classical conditioning serves as the basis for such reactions as strong fears, several types of sexual "hang-ups," and even racial prejudice. In addition, it is an extremely pervasive process, occurring among organisms from the lowly flatworm (Barnes and Katzung, 1963) to human beings (Black and Prokasy, 1972), and it has even been observed among single cells within the body (Morrell, 1967).

Despite its widespread occurrence, classical conditioning was not the subject of systematic study until the early years of the twentieth century, when Ivan Pavlov, a famed Nobel–prize–winning physiologist, turned his attention to this process (see Figure 4–1). Interestingly, as is often the case in science, Pavlov did not set out with this object in mind. Rather, his early work was largely concerned with the process of digestion. In contrast to many previous researchers, he chose to work with normal, awake subjects. This choice of methods proved to be a momentous one in the history of psychology, for it soon led him to make an interesting observation: often, the dogs in his studies would begin to salivate before they ate, as when they merely caught sight of the pan which contained their food, or when they saw the person who usually brought it — or even when they heard the sound of his footsteps. On the basis of such observations, Pavlov soon concluded that these stimuli had, through their repeated association with

CLASSICAL CONDITIONING: LEARNING THROUGH ASSOCIATION

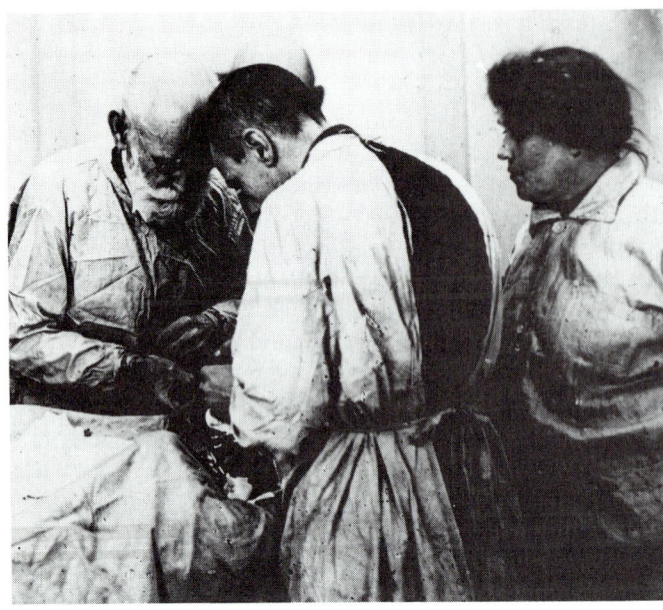

FIGURE 4–1 Shown here is Ivan Petrovich Pavlov conducting an operation on a dog in the clinic of the Pavlov Institute, Leningrad. (The Bettmann Archive.)

food, become conditioned signals for its presentation. Recognizing the importance of this basic process, he altered the thrust of his research, turning from the study of digestion (for which he had won his Nobel prize) to the investigation of such conditioning (Gantt, 1973.)

The Work of Pavlov: Of Hungry Dogs and Ringing Bells

In order to examine the process of classical conditioning in a systematic manner, Pavlov first performed a simple operation on his canine subjects in which a small rubber tube was inserted into the salivary gland on one side of the mouth. After the dogs had fully recovered from this minor surgical procedure, they were placed in an apparatus which was designed both to restrain their movements and to enable the experimenters to obtain a precise record of the amount of saliva secreted during various stages of the study (see Figure 4–2). The actual conditioning procedures were then begun.

During the course of these procedures, some neutral stimulus which had previously been shown to have no appreciable influence upon the dogs' rate of salivation (e.g., a bell) was presented for a brief period of time, followed quickly by a second stimulus known to exert a strong effect upon the salivation response (e.g., a small quantity of dried meat powder squirted directly into the subject's mouth). Each pairing of the bell (which was known as the **conditioned stimulus,** or **CS**) with the meat powder (which was known as the **unconditioned stimulus,** or **US**) served as a *conditioning trial,* and a number of such pairings were conducted in rapid succession. The major question under investigation, of course, was whether the bell would acquire the ability to evoke increased salivation among subjects as a result of its repeated pairing with the meat powder. In order to determine whether this was indeed the case, *test trials* in which the bell was rung but no meat powder presented were performed. As you might expect on the basis of the "door opening" example presented earlier, it was found that on the test occasions, subjects did in fact begin to salivate when they heard the bell. In short, it was as if the bell, through its close association with the meat, came to serve as a kind of signal to subjects for the appearance of this tasty stimulus, and thus acquired the ability to induce salivation even when presented by itself. (For another example of classical conditioning, see Figure 4–3).

Because such reactions to the bell began to occur only after conditioning procedures were instituted, they were termed **conditioned responses (CR's).** In contrast, since reactions to the meat powder occurred in a seemingly automatic manner on the very first occasion it was presented, they were termed **unconditioned responses (UR's).** Although the responses induced by conditioned and unconditioned stimuli are often very similar, it is important to note that they are by no means identical. For example, conditioned responses are often smaller in magnitude, different in form, and preparatory to unconditioned responses (McGaugh, 1973). Thus, although the conditioned stimulus comes to elicit marked reactions from subjects as a result of its repeated pairings with the

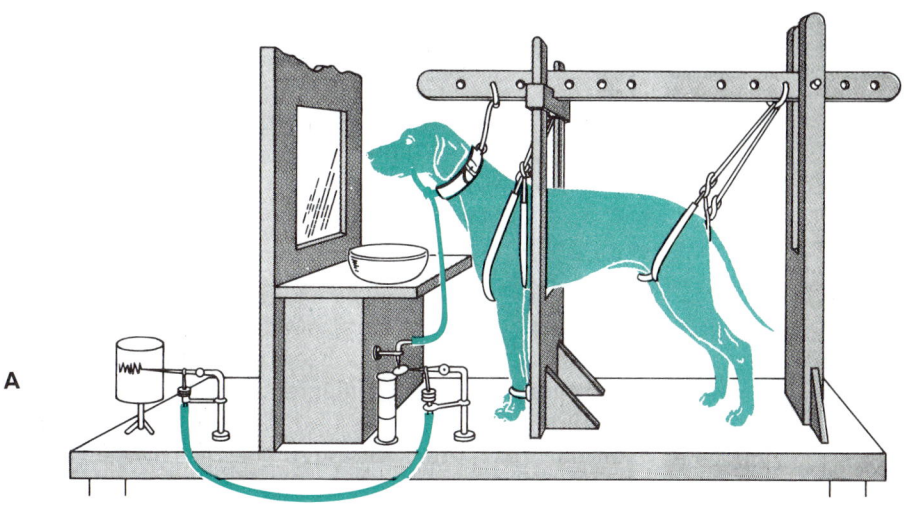

A

DOUBLE PLATED PRINTED CIRCUIT BOARD WITH (A)
SQUARES ETCHED ON TOP AND (B) DIAGONAL STRIPS
ON THE BOTTOM. ALTERNATE SQUARES ARE COMMOM.

HOLLOW BRASS RIVETS (C)
SOLDERED TO COPPER
SQUARES AND DIAGONALS.

B

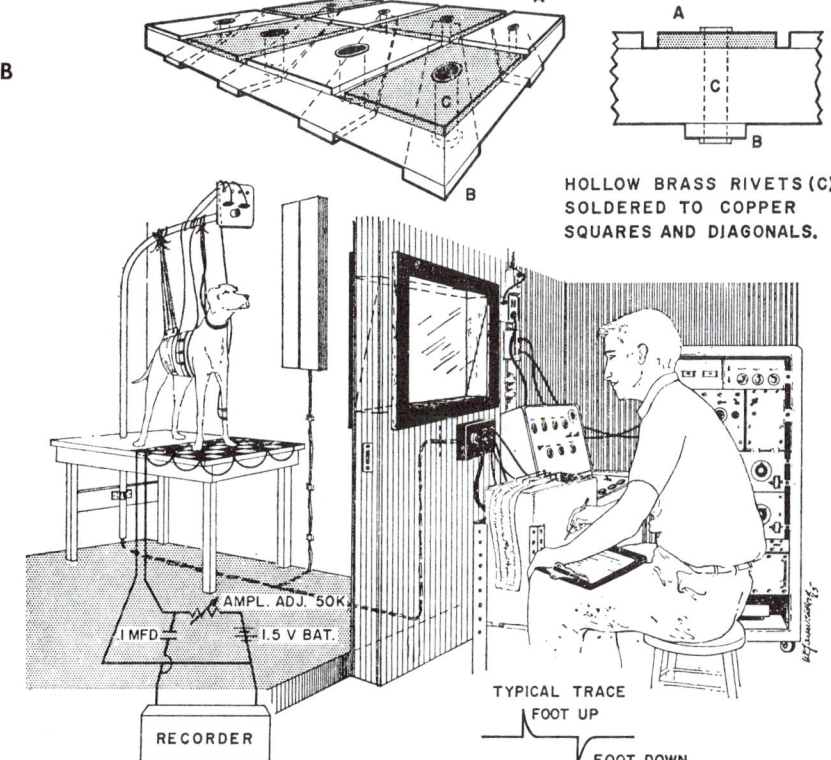

FIGURE 4–2   The type of apparatus used by Pavlov in his early experiments on classical conditioning (A), and modern equipment for the study of this process (B). Note that in (A) the conditioning of salivation is being studied, while in (B) the conditioning of leg flexion in response to mild electric shock is under investigation. (Part A from Yerkes and Morgulis, 1909. Part B from Reus, Lynch, and Gantt, in *Conditional Reflex: A Pavlovian Journal of Research and Therapy,* April–June, 1966.)

unconditioned stimulus, it does not come to evoke responses that are identical in all respects to those evoked by this stimulus.

Many of Pavlov's investigations of the process of classical conditioning were conducted within the general framework described above. It should not be assumed, however, that this important process is restricted to training dogs to respond to what serves, essentially, as a kind of dinner bell. Rather, evidence gathered over several decades indicates that many different stimuli can acquire the ability to evoke various responses through repeated pairings with an appropriate unconditioned stimulus. As a result, classical conditioning can play a role in the acquisition of such important reactions as strong, irrational fear, positive or negative feelings toward others, and various sexual "hang-ups."

For example, imagine a situation in which a child, while playing with a new pet, suddenly hears the loud sound of a backfiring truck. In all probability, this noise (which may be viewed as an unconditioned stimulus) will frighten the child greatly (an unconditioned emotional response), so that she bursts into tears. Now, further imagine that because she happens to live near a busy road and often plays with her pet, this situation is repeated—quite by accident—on several other occasions. Soon, a dramatic change may begin to appear in her behavior. Instead of smiling and approaching her pet when she sees it, she may recoil in terror and seek to escape from its presence. The reason for this seemingly "irrational" behavior is that through repeated pairing with the loud, upsetting sound, the pet has become a conditioned stimulus for strong fear reactions. Classical conditioning, then, has transformed a harmless and initially pleasant stimulus into a highly frightening one (please refer to Figure 4–4).

In a similar manner, articles of clothing which are repeatedly paired with strong sexual arousal or pleasure may soon come to serve as conditioned stimuli for such reactions. As a result of such conditioning, individuals may adopt such stimuli as an integral part of their sexual relations, and even be unable to perform adequately without them. Instances of this type are far removed from Pavlov's experiments with bells and salivating dogs, but as shown in Figure 4–4, the same process of classical conditioning may well be involved in each.

Higher-Order Conditioning: Extending the Chain   Suppose that after a number of conditioning trials in which a bell is paired with food, a dog salivates readily at the sound of this stimulus. What would now happen if food were removed from the situation, and a new stimulus (e.g., a flashing light) were paired with the bell? Would it, too, come to elicit salivation? The question we are posing, of course, is whether a conditioned stimulus (in this case a bell) can serve as the basis for further conditioning. Pavlov (1927) believed that it could, and he demonstrated such **second-order conditioning** in several of his early experiments. While other investigators have not always been successful in producing such effects, recent studies (Rescorla, 1973)

FIGURE 4–3 Snoopy meets classical conditioning. In this case, the sound of a can opener rather than a bell has come to serve as a conditioned stimulus, but the basic process involved is the same as that in Pavlov's laboratory research. (© United Feature Syndicate, Inc. Reprinted by permission.)

	On First Occasion When CS and US Are Paired				After Repeated Pairings of CS and US			
Acquisition of an "Irrational" Fear	CS	Response to CS	US	Response to US	CS	Response to CS	US	Response to US
	Harmless Pet	None (or Approach)	Loud $\longrightarrow$ Noise	Fear	Harmless $\longrightarrow$ Pet	Fear	Loud $\longrightarrow$ Noise	Fear
Acquisition of a Sexual "Hang-Up"	CS	Response to CS	US	Response to US	CS	Response to CS	US	Response to US
	Article of Clothing	None	Nude Body $\longrightarrow$ of Lover	Sexual Arousal	Article of $\longrightarrow$ Clothing	Sexual Arousal	Nude Body $\longrightarrow$ of Lover	Sexual Arousal

FIGURE 4–4 The role of classical conditioning in the acquisition of an "irrational" fear and one type of sexual "hang-up" (fetishism). In both cases, stimuli initially incapable of eliciting strong reactions acquire this ability through repeated pairing with unconditioned stimuli.

suggest that under appropriate circumstances, higher-order conditioning can in fact be established. Indeed, even **third-order conditioning,** which extends the process one step further, appears to take place (Hulse, Deese, and Egeth, 1975). The occurrence of such effects explains why stimuli which themselves are never associated with an unconditioned stimulus, but which *are* paired with previously conditioned stimuli, sometimes acquire the ability to elicit strong reactions they could not at first produce. One important instance of such higher-order conditioning is described in the *Focus on Research* insert, p. 116.

Because it represents one of the most basic forms of learning, and because it plays a crucial role in important reactions such as those described above, classical conditioning has long been the subject of intensive investigation. As a result, much is currently known about the fine details of this important process (Black and Prokasy, 1972). Unfortunately, a substantial portion of this information is of a highly technical nature, which places it beyond the scope of our discussion. In considering classical conditioning, then, we will focus on only a few general principles which seem to govern (1) its development, or acquisition, (2) its generalization to other stimuli, and (3) its elimination, or extinction.

Principles of Classical Conditioning: Some Rules of the Game

As might well be anticipated, one factor which exerts a strong influence upon the ability of a conditioned stimulus to elicit a response from subjects is the number of pairings between this stimulus and the unconditioned stimulus. As the number of such pairings increases, the conditioned stimulus comes to evoke a conditioned response with increasing regularity. In general, the strength of this ability—that is, the strength of classical conditioning—is measured in terms of the *magnitude, latency,* and *probability* of occurrence of the conditioned response. Thus, the stronger the conditioned response, the faster it follows presentation of the conditioned stimulus; the greater the probability that the response will occur, the stronger the conditioning is assumed to be. In the "door opening" example used earlier, it would be expected that as the number of pairings between the conditioned stimulus (the sound of the door mechanism) and the icy blast of wind (the unconditioned stimulus) increased, the stronger, faster, and more probable would your reaction to the sound of the conditioned stimulus become.

Acquisition: The Course of Classical Conditioning

The manner in which the strength of classical conditioning increases with repeated pairings of the CS and US is illustrated in Figure 4–6. As can be seen in this figure, the strength of conditioning first increases rapidly, but then begins to level off as the number of such pairings increases.

A second factor which appears to exert an important effect upon the proc-

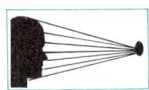

**FOCUS
ON
RESEARCH:**   *Classical Conditioning — A Basis for Prejudice and Hate?*

As we have noted, classical conditioning seems to play an important role in the development of strong fears and several types of sexual "hang-ups." Perhaps even more surprising is the suggestion that higher-order conditioning can serve as a basis for the development of strong racial or ethnic prejudices (Baron and Byrne, 1977). Such reactions may be acquired in the following manner.

In the first step, youngsters learn — through a process of classical conditioning — to respond emotionally to signs of anger or irritation on the part of their parents. In many situations, such conditioning occurs because facial expressions or other cues indicative of anger are paired with scoldings, spankings, or other negative events. Next, the children observe their mothers and fathers demonstrating such signs of emotion when in the presence of members of certain disliked groups. At first, the youngsters probably react strongly to their parents' signs of arousal, but demonstrate little or no reaction to members of the racial or ethnic groups in question; at this point, such persons are still relatively neutral stimuli for them. As such incidents are repeated, however, members of these groups — or at least certain of their characteristics, such as skin color — are paired with their parents' signs of emotion over and over again. As a result of such association, higher-order conditioning occurs, and the children begin reacting negatively to such persons even when their parents are absent from the scene (see Figure 4–5).

A final step in the development of a full-blown prejudice may then involve the adoption of supporting beliefs which help the children "explain" the strong, negative emotions they feel when in the presence of members of certain groups (e.g., "I hate them because they are ugly, mean, and stupid"). By means of this subtle process of classical conditioning, parents who do not specifically attempt to indoctrinate their children with hatred or prejudice may manage, nonetheless, to transmit such feelings in a highly effective manner.

We should hasten to add that the process just described is only a possibility, and has not been conclusively demonstrated. However, two facts suggest that it may actually occur in many situations: (1) people *do* react emotionally to signs of emotions in others (Berger, 1962; Buck, Miller, and Caul, 1974), and (2) such reactions can be readily conditioned to neutral stimuli (Kravetz, 1974).

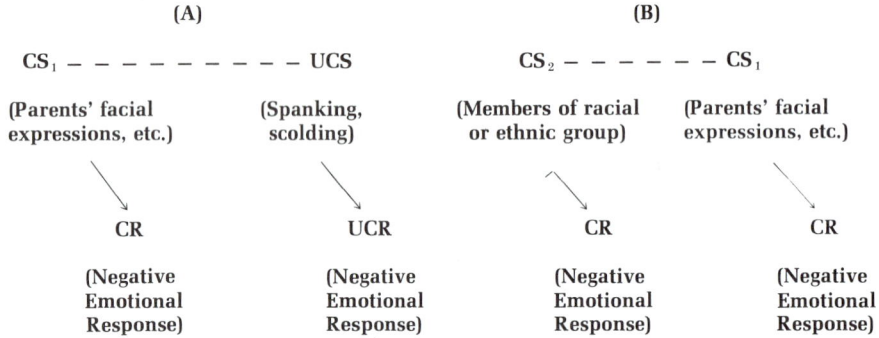

FIGURE 4–5   The development of a racial or ethnic prejudice through higher-order conditioning. In the first step (A), children learn to respond emotionally to signs of anger or irritation on the part of their parents because such cues are frequently associated with scoldings or spankings. In the second (B), they learn to respond negatively to members of various ethnic or racial groups because such persons are frequently associated with signs of anger or irritation on the part of their parents.

ess of classical conditioning is the interval which elapses between presentation of the CS and presentation of the US. For many different responses, conditioning appears to be maximal when this interval approximates 0.5 seconds. However, recent studies suggest that in some cases, it can be much longer and still produce conditioning. For example, rats that are given a sweet-tasting liquid to drink and are then injected with a drug which makes them sick to the stomach still acquire an aversion to the taste even when the interval between drinking and nausea is more than an hour (Garcia, McGowan, and Green, 1972). One experimental psychologist, Martin Seligman (1972), refers to this finding as the "sauce Bernaise phenomenon," noting that humans, too, often learn strong aversions to the tastes of foods which make them sick many hours after they are eaten. Apparently, there is such strong survival value in being able to profit from such experiences that our nervous system allows for conditioning even with very long delays. In the face of such evidence, it can only be concluded that the optimal CS–US interval for classical conditioning probably varies greatly for different stimuli and responses, as well as for different organisms.

Stimulus Generalization: "That's Close Enough for Me"

When an organism has been conditioned to one stimulus, it is often the case that it will respond to other, similar stimuli as well. This phenomenon is generally known as **stimulus generalization,** and seems to play an important adaptive role. This is the case because similar stimuli often signal the occurrence of similar events. The existence of stimulus generalization, then, makes it unnecessary for individuals to learn to respond to each stimulus in an independent manner. To take just one simple example of the usefulness of this phenomenon, the sounds made by angry bees, wasps, and hornets are highly similar, but certainly not identical. Because of stimulus generalization, however, an individual who has learned through painful experience to react with fear and caution to one of these sounds may also respond in a similar manner to the others as well.

Extinction: Getting Rid of Excess Baggage

Stimuli which are consistently associated with the occurrence of significant environmental events today may not be so linked tomorrow. If we lacked some mechanism for getting rid of useless reactions to stimuli which no longer serve as reliable cues for the occurrence of such events, we would soon become walking bundles of useless conditioned reactions. For example, returning to our "door opening" example, no purpose would be served by our continued reaction to the sound of the mechanism in the summer, for during this season no icy blast would follow the opening of the door. Fortunately, a means for eliminating such reactions does indeed exist, in a process called **extinction.** Whenever a previously conditioned stimulus is repeatedly presented but is never followed by the unconditioned stimulus with which it was formerly associated, its ability to elicit conditioned responses gradually decreases, and may fade completely. Interestingly, if the same conditioned stimulus is then presented again at a later time, its capacity to evoke conditioned responses may reappear—a phenomenon known as **spontaneous recovery.** However, if extinction is then continued, the ability of the stimulus to produce conditioned responses may be further weakened until, at some point, recovery of this type no longer occurs.

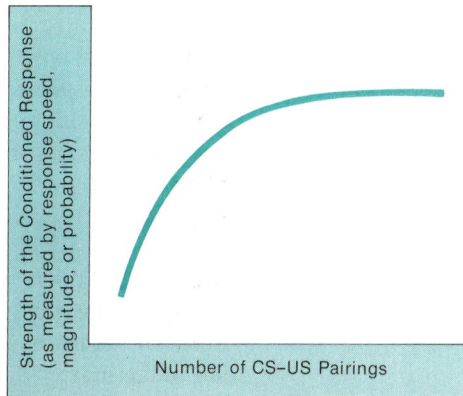

FIGURE 4–6   Acquisition of a classically conditioned response. The strength of the response first increases rapidly, but then grows more and more slowly with repeated pairings of the conditioned and unconditioned stimuli.

Unfortunately, it appears that some classically conditioned responses, particularly those involving strong emotional reactions, are often quite resistant to extinction. As a result, they may persist largely unchanged for long periods of time, despite the fact that they cause the persons experiencing them considerable, unnecessary discomfort. For example, many adults continue to react with mild feelings of anxiety to the words "test" or "examination" long after their school years are through and the unpleasant events signaled by such stimuli no longer occur. We will return to the reasons for the persistence of such conditioned emotional reactions on p. 134.

Discrimination: Knowing when Differences Count

Although similar stimuli are often associated with similar consequences or events, this is not always the case. Accordingly, we must often learn to make very fine discriminations between stimuli which seem closely related in nature. Within the framework of classical conditioning, such an ability develops when one of two similar stimuli is consistently followed by an unconditioned stimulus while the other is not. Under such conditions, tendencies to respond to the first are strengthened, while tendencies to respond to the second are weakened through the process of extinction described above. For example, consider the case of an individual who is exposed to similar clicks from his clock-radio and the thermostat of his refrigerator each morning. Because the sounds produced by the clock-radio are always followed by the loud and irritating alarm, they soon come to elicit strong conditioned responses (e.g., feelings of mild anxiety) on the part of our late sleeper. Since the clicks coming from the refrigerator are quite similar in nature, they too initially produce such reactions. Because they are never followed by the alarm, however, their ability to induce such responses decreases and soon fades entirely. The end result, of course, is that the person involved gradually acquires the ability to discriminate quite accurately between two highly similar sounds.

Although the ability of human beings and other organisms to discriminate between various stimuli is quite impressive, it is still subject to definite limits. That disconcerting effects may result when these limits are exceeded is suggested by experiments dealing with the phenomenon of **experimental neurosis** (Liddell, 1956).

In these studies, animals are first trained to respond to one stimulus (e.g., an ellipse) but not to another which is, at least initially, recognizably different (e.g., a circle). Then gradually, over the course of the study, the two stimuli are made increasingly similar. Up to a point, subjects are able to discriminate between them, and continue to evidence conditioned responses to one but little or no reaction to the other. At some stage of the experiment, however, the stimuli become so similar in appearance that subjects are no longer able to make such differentiations. Their reactions to this unsettling state of affairs are then often quite intense. For example, they may utter loud cries, struggle in the experimental apparatus, and demonstrate other signs of extreme emotional arousal. Moreover, in some cases, they may attempt to attack the experimenter if he or she happens to come within reach. Finally, when later presented with the original stimuli—the ones they could formerly easily tell apart—they fail to show any signs of discrimination. Findings such as these suggest that while impressive, the ability of various organisms to discriminate between highly similar stimuli has definite limits, and that when environmental conditions require that these limits be exceeded, extreme stress may be induced. It is interesting to speculate that perhaps one of the factors tending to make life in our modern, technological society so stressful is the continuing requirement that we make many fine, precise discriminations.

Actions usually result in some form of consequences. For example, saying "I love you" to someone close to your heart is likely to produce one set of outcomes, while stammering incoherently in the presence of this person may yield quite another. Similarly, staying up late to study for an important exam will yield one level of performance the following day, while going to a party will almost certainly produce another. In short, there is frequently a direct and important link between the actions we perform and the consequences we experience. Largely because of this contingency, we often learn to behave in ways which result in positive (i.e., pleasant or desirable) outcomes, while avoiding actions which lead to negative (i.e., unpleasant) results. The process through which we acquire such patterns of behavior is generally known as **instrumental,** or **operant, conditioning,** and plays an important role in both human and animal behavior.

The earliest systematic investigations of this basic type of learning were conducted by Edward L. Thorndike (1898), who placed subjects (usually cats) in puzzle boxes such as the one shown in Figure 4–7. These boxes were constructed in such a manner that the door could be opened only by one particular response (e.g., pulling a string, pressing a latch). Thus, subjects could gain release—and access to a bowl of food placed in full view outside the box—only by performing the correct behavior.

When first placed inside the box, the cats would usually evidence a large number of varied activities. For example, they might move about, scratch at the sides, reach between the slats for the food, and so on. Eventually, however, they would hit upon the correct response purely by accident, and gain their release. As the experiment continued and they were placed in the box over and over again, an interesting change began to occur in their behavior. Gradually, they came to perform the crucial response which allowed access to the food sooner and sooner, until after a number of exposures to the experimental apparatus, they performed this action immediately upon being placed inside. In short, subjects quickly learned which of the many responses they could perform would result in their release, and they then came to demonstrate this reaction in a speedy and consistent manner.

On the basis of such observations, Thorndike proposed a simple principle which he termed the **Law of Effect.** Basically, this law consisted of two distinct parts. The first contended that responses which produce "satisfying" consequences are strengthened and are therefore performed with increasing fre-

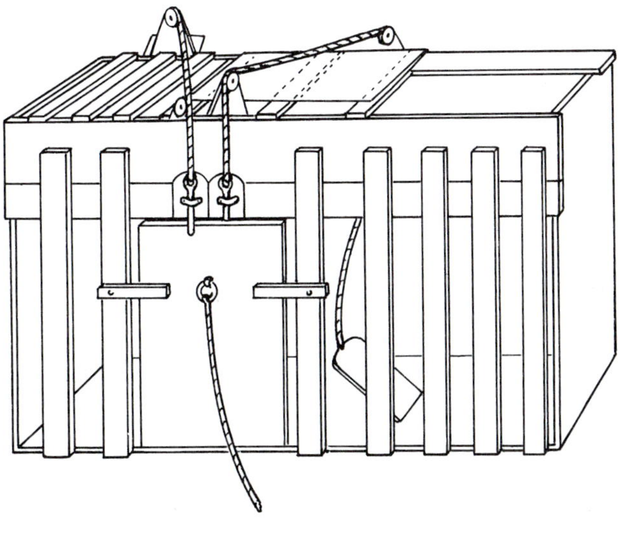

FIGURE 4–7 A puzzle box of the type employed by Thorndike in his early investigations of instrumental conditioning. Subjects had to perform the correct response in order to gain release from the box and access to food outside. (From Thorndike, E.: *Animal Intelligence.* New York: The Macmillan Company, 1911.)

quency. Although psychologists have substituted the term **positive reinforcer** for the phrase "satisfying consequences," this portion of Thorndike's law appears to be true. Organisms, including human beings, *do* acquire responses which lead to some form of reward. A *positive reinforcer*, then, is any event (i.e., stimulus) which serves to strengthen responses preceding its occurrence. The second part of the Law of Effect, which contended that responses which lead to "discomfort" or "annoyance" are weakened, has not fared as well. As we shall see in a later discussion of punishment, responses which lead to negative outcomes are not necessarily weakened in any permanent sense. Rather, they may only be temporarily suppressed. In view of this fact, it has been necessary to amend the second part of Thorndike's law to read: organisms acquire responses which allow them either to avoid unpleasant stimuli or to escape from them. A **negative reinforcer,** then, is any event (i.e., stimulus) which strengthens responses leading to its termination or removal.

Psychologists often distinguish between two general classes of reinforcers that are described, respectively, as *primary* and *secondary* in nature. Those falling into the first category seem capable of exerting strong effects upon behavior right from the start, even if they have never been encountered before. Moreover, they often seem to be closely related to basic physiological needs or processes. For example, some common positive primary reinforcers are the presentation of food, water, or a receptive sexual partner. In contrast, secondary reinforcers seem to acquire their influence upon behavior through association with primary reinforcers, and are not directly linked to basic physiological processes. In the case of animals, they can involve such stimuli as the color of the box in which feeding occurs (Saltzman, 1949) or even various sounds coming from the apparatus when food is delivered (Miles, 1956). Among human beings, however, they are often far more subtle and complex. For example, some secondary reinforcers with which you are probably already quite familiar are money, status, approval, and love (see Figure 4–8). As we shall see in later chapters, the great complexity of human behavior stems, at least in part, from the varied nature of such reinforcers.

Instrumental Learning: Some Determining Factors

In our discussion of classical conditioning, we learned that the ability of a conditioned stimulus to elicit responses from subjects was strongly influenced by the number of times it had been paired with the unconditioned stimulus. A similar relationship exists in the case of instrumental conditioning: the strength of subjects' tendencies to perform a given response rises with the number of occasions on which such behavior has been followed by (1) presen-

FIGURE 4–8   Approval, praise, status, and money can all act as positive reinforcers for human beings. As shown here, though, they are not all equal in effectiveness. (© King Features Syndicate, Inc., 1974.)

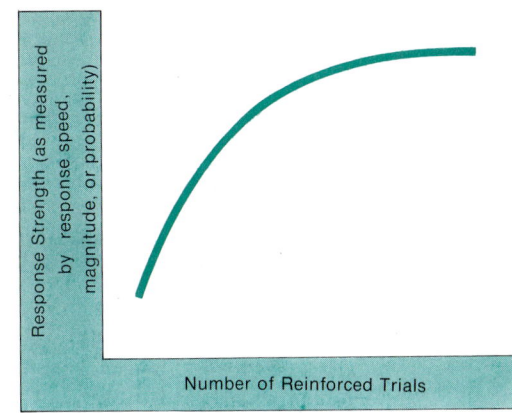

FIGURE 4–9 **Acquisition of an instrumental response. The strength of the response first increases rapidly but then more slowly as the number of occasions on which it is followed by reinforcement rises.**

tation of positive reinforcers, or (2) removal of negative reinforcers. Moreover, the course of instrumental learning is highly similar to that for classical conditioning, with rapid, initial increments followed by a gradual leveling off (see Figure 4–9).

In addition to being affected by the number of occasions on which reinforcement is obtained (i.e., the number of *reinforced trials*), instrumental conditioning is also strongly influenced by several other factors, including the subjects' level of motivation, the magnitude of available reinforcers, and the speed with which such rewards are delivered. Before we can consider the effects of these factors, however, it is necessary to draw a clear distinction between learning and performance.

Learning versus Performance: Knowing or Doing

We have already hinted at such a distinction in the introduction to this chapter where it was noted that the temporary influence upon behavior of drugs, illness, or fatigue would not be viewed as learning. One difference between learning and performance, then, lies in the fact that the former refers to relatively permanent changes in behavior, while the latter refers to more temporary alterations. Perhaps this distinction may be clarified further by the suggestion that learning refers primarily to "knowing," while performance refers more directly to "doing."

For example, returning to the puzzle box experiments conducted by Thorndike, imagine that a particular subject has mastered the correct response needed for gaining release. That is, when placed in the box, he knows exactly what to do in order to escape. Now further imagine that he is placed inside the box while extremely hungry, and an inviting dish of food is positioned just outside. What would happen next? Almost certainly the subject would perform the correct response as quickly as possible in order to gain access to the food. But now consider what might happen if he were placed in the box under conditions where he had just eaten his fill. Under these circumstances, he might simply curl up and go to sleep, without making the slightest effort to escape. Does this mean that he has forgotten how to accomplish this task? Probably not. Rather it seems more reasonable to suggest that he simply has no reason for engaging in such behavior. In this instance, previous learning is not visible in present performance.

That the same distinction between learning and performance holds for human behavior is apparent. For example, students are often heard to remark, after a difficult exam, that they knew the right answers, but somehow failed to get them down on paper. Similarly, individuals awakening on the proverbial "morning after" often complain that they "knew better," and express regret about having acted in such a dangerous or foolish manner. You can probably recall many cases in your own life when a disparity between learning and performance—between what you knew and what you did—was all too apparent.

At this point, we should mention that the distinction between learning and performance played an important role in the famous theories of behavior proposed some years ago by Clark Hull and Kenneth Spence, two famous figures in the history of experimental psychology. While their theories differed in many details, both Hull and Spence assumed that performance on almost any task is determined by both learning and other, more temporary factors, such as motivation (Spence, 1956). Further, both proposed specific "laws" concerning the manner in which these factors combine to affect behavior. Perhaps the best known of these was the suggestion by Hull (1952) that performance is a multiplicative function of learning and motivation, a proposal summarized by the simple equation: $E = H \times D$ (E represents the tendency to perform some response, H stands for learning, and D for motivation). The theories proposed by Hull and Spence were quite sweeping in nature; in fact, both were designed to account, ultimately, for *all* forms of behavior. Unfortunately, as you might well guess, neither proved capable of accomplishing this difficult task, and today such global theories are no longer common in psychology. However, many of the suggestions proposed by Hull and Spence—including those regarding the distinction between learning and performance—have been absorbed into the field, and continue to exert an important influence even today.

Instrumental Conditioning: Effects of Motivation, Reward Magnitude, and Delay of Reinforcement

The distinction between learning and performance raises an important question with respect to factors known to influence instrumental conditioning: do they affect one, the other, or both of these processes? Unfortunately, since we can directly observe only performance, the task of separating or disentangling such influences is a very difficult one. It *can* be accomplished, however, through the use of rather complicated experimental designs. Since the details of such procedures are beyond the scope of this discussion, we will not attempt to describe them here. Rather, we will merely summarize the major findings which have been reported.

First, contrary to what common sense might suggest, the level of motivation (often varied through the length of time subjects have been deprived of food, water, or some other reinforcer) seems to affect only performance (Zaretsky, 1966). This finding has important implications, because it suggests that an increase in motivation to obtain some reinforcement will *not* increase the rate of learning. A good example of this fact is provided in the case of Liza Doolittle, the heroine of *My Fair Lady*. Although her motivation to master the correct sounds of speech increased sharply under the taunts of her tutor, Professor Higgins, her rate of progress did not at first increase. In fact, she attained measurable gains only after many hours of endless repetition (see Figure 4–10). This is not to say that her behavior was unaffected by changes in motivation. As anyone who has seen the play or movie well knows, it *was* in fact affected. For example, she began repeating her lessons with greater speed, and at much greater volume. The rate at which she acquired polished patterns of speech, though, was largely unchanged.

A second factor which might be expected to influence the rate of instrumental learning is the size or magnitude of available reinforcers. It seems reasonable to expect that we might learn more quickly under conditions in which large rewards are at stake than under conditions in which only small ones can be gained. Yet, existing evidence suggests that this is not the case, and that the magnitude of reinforcement may often influence only performance. Evidence for this conclusion has been obtained in a number of studies wherein

FIGURE 4-10 Even a high level of motivation could not help Liza Dolittle master the correct sounds of speech, for motivation affects only performance—*not* the rate at which learning occurs. (From *My Fair Lady*, a Warner Brothers film, 1964.)

subjects (usually rats) are first provided with rewards of a particular size for performing some simple activity (pushing a lever, running through an alley). After such training has continued for some time, the magnitude of reinforcement is suddenly shifted, so that subjects now receive either much larger or much smaller rewards than before. Such changes usually produce large and immediate alterations in their behavior, and the rapidity of these shifts has led many researchers to conclude that the magnitude of reinforcement influences performance rather than learning. In brief, it is reasoned that if magnitude of reinforcement were to affect learning, such changes would take place in a more gradual manner (D'Amato, 1970; Pubols, 1960). As noted by Capaldi (1970), however, it is difficult to reach any definite conclusions along these lines, because when the magnitude of reinforcement is changed, many of the important stimuli in the situation are also altered, with the result that effects upon learning as well as performance may be produced. Thus, at present, the question of whether magnitude of reinforcement influences learning, performance, or both, has not been completely resolved.

By this time you may well be wondering whether there is *any* factor other than the number of reinforced trials that influences the rate of instrumental learning. One such additional factor does exist: the interval between behavior and the delivery of reinforcement,—i.e., the delay of reinforcement. A large body of research (Tarpy and Swabini, 1974; Wike and McWilliams, 1967) suggests that the longer such delays, the slower the rate of learning. Indeed, in the case of organisms such as the rat, instrumental conditioning may be totally prevented when reinforcement is delayed for more than a few seconds. Fortunately, human beings seem able to bridge much longer intervals of time and still profit from their experience. This ability stems partly from our possession of complex cognitive skills which permit us to covertly rehearse the contingencies between our actions and outcomes (for example, we can say to ourselves "When I smile at others they often smile back," or "If I study I usually get good grades"), and partly from our ability to administer self-reinforcement ("That was a good job, if I say so myself"). But even among human beings, learning can sometimes be prevented by long delays in the delivery of reinforcement.

Schedules of Reinforcement: The "When" and "Why" of Pay-offs

In our discussion of instrumental conditioning up to this point, we have assumed that reinforcement always follows correct responses. Actually, this is rarely true. More frequently, reinforcement follows such behavior on some occasions but not on others. In many instances, the occurrence or nonoccurrence of reinforcement seems quite random. For example, placing a coin in a soda machine usually yields the soft drink of your choice. On some unpredictable occasions, however, it produces only an empty cup or even nothing at all. Similarly, studying for exams usually yields passing grades, but again this is not always the case.

In other instances, the occurrence or nonoccurrence of reinforcement seems to be governed by definitive rules. For example, parents often inform their children that they will receive their allowance or some desired privilege such as the use of the family car only after they have completed a specified number of chores. Similarly, a young man or woman may learn that requests for love-making will bring the desired response from his or her mate only at certain times of the day or week. Such rules are generally termed **schedules of reinforcement,** and they exert a powerful effect upon behavior.

The impact of such schedules has been studied most extensively by B. F. Skinner and his associates (e.g., Ferster and Skinner, 1957; Skinner, 1975). Typically, these researchers have sought to examine the influence of schedules of reinforcement upon the rate at which organisms perform certain simple but freely emitted responses known as **operants.** Thus, they have often been concerned with factors which influence the probability of occurrence of existing responses rather than with the acquisition of new forms of behavior. Because Skinner and his colleagues feel that the term instrumental conditioning is suggestive of purpose or intent—concepts which do seem a bit awkward when describing the behavior of pigeons and rats—they have substituted the term **operant conditioning** in its place. Since many psychologists tend to use these phrases interchangeably, however, you can view them as referring to the same basic process.

In order to obtain information on the effects of schedules of reinforcement on behavior, subjects in studies of operant conditioning (usually rats or pigeons) are generally placed in a device such as the one shown in Figure 4–11 (typically known as a *Skinner box*), where they are permitted to move about at will and perform any response they wish. However, conditions are arranged so that only one particular activity (pecking a disc, pushing a lever) is rewarded, usually by the delivery of a small pellet of food. Not surprisingly, subjects quickly learn to emit only this form of behavior while in the apparatus. Moreover, if conditions are arranged so that such responses are reinforced when some stimulus (e.g., a light) is present but not when it is absent, subjects soon learn to respond only in the presence of this **discriminative cue.** (If you would like some first-hand indication of the impact of such stimuli upon your own behavior, just pick up the nearest phone. The presence or absence of a dial tone tells you immediately whether the response of dialing is likely to be reinforced.)

Each time a subject in a Skinner box performs the appropriate response, the action is recorded: a pen wired to the equipment traces over a continuously moving sheet of paper, moving up one notch when the desired response is made. Thus, the higher the rate at which the subject responds, the steeper the line drawn. Comparison of the lines that are produced under different schedules of reinforcement then provides information concerning the influence of each upon behavior.

Aside from **continuous reinforcement,** in which reward follows every response, the simplest schedules of reinforcement are ones in which the occur-

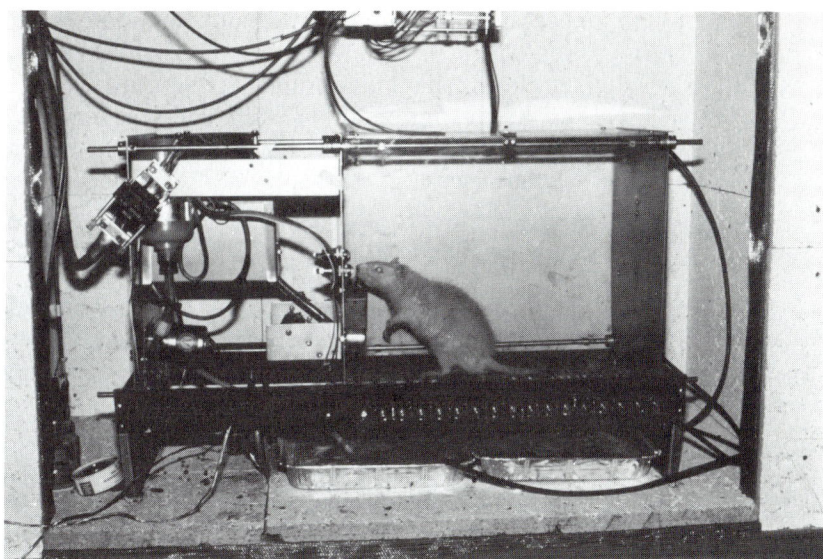

FIGURE 4-11 A Skinner box of the type often used in the study of operant conditioning. Subjects can gain various rewards (e.g., small pellets of food) by pushing the lever.

rence of reward is determined by only one rule. Four distinct schedules of this type, known respectively as **fixed-ratio, variable-ratio, fixed-interval,** and **variable-interval,** have been extensively studied. In the **fixed-ratio schedule,** reinforcement is delivered only after a fixed *number* of responses have been performed. For example, it might be necessary for subjects to respond 20, 50, or even 500 times before obtaining each reward. An application of such schedules to human behavior is found in the case of piece-work wages, where workers earn a certain amount of money for producing a set number of items. This may be an effective system, at least from the point of view of management, because fixed-ratio schedules typically produce high rates of responding, with only brief, momentary pauses following the delivery of each reinforcement (see Figure 4-12).

The occurrence of reinforcement in **variable-ratio schedules** is also dependent upon the number of responses performed. However, in this case, the number which must be enacted varies randomly around some average value. For example, reinforcement may be delivered after only ten responses on one

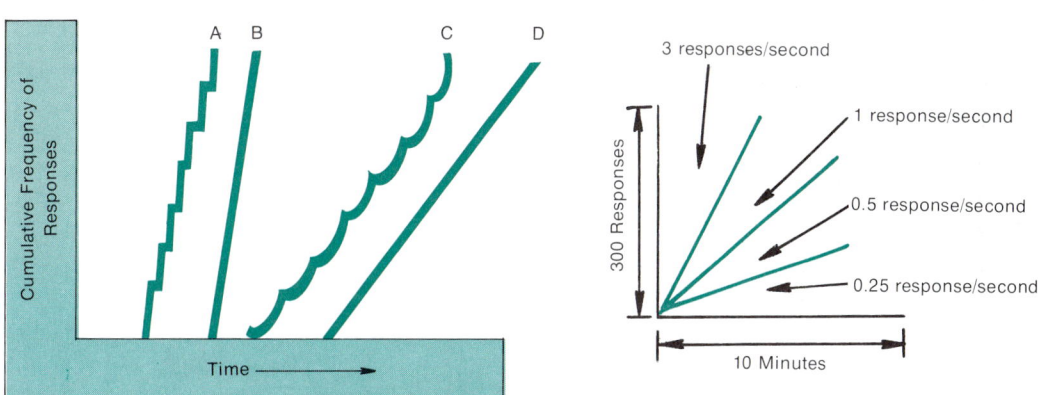

FIGURE 4-12 Patterns of behavior produced by (A) fixed-ratio, (B) variable-ratio, (C) fixed-interval, and (D) variable-interval schedules of reinforcement. The steeper the lines, the higher the rate of responding by subjects. (Such records are often interpreted by means of scales such as the one shown on the right. By applying this scale to the lines shown, both the rate of responding and the total number of responses emitted during some interval of time can be estimated.) Note that both the slope and shape of such curves vary greatly with the specific schedules of reinforcement employed. For example, a fixed-ratio schedule in which subjects receive reinforcement for every twentieth response might well resemble (A); one in which they receive reinforcement for every third response might be much less steep.

occasion, after sixty on the next, and after twenty on the next. On the average, then, thirty separate responses must be emitted before reinforcement occurs. However, the actual number required in each instance varies considerably. A good illustration of variable ratio-schedules is provided by Las Vegas slot machines, which pay off after swallowing variable numbers of quarters or dollars (see Figure 4–13). As a result of this variability, gamblers never know when they will get lucky and receive a pile of coins. Given the persistence with which some individuals pump their money into these machines (which are called "one-armed bandits" with good reason), it should come as no surprise that variable-ratio schedules of reinforcement usually produce consistent, high rates of responding (refer to Figure 4–12).

A third type of simple schedule, that known as the **fixed-interval schedule,** is decidedly different from those we have considered so far. Under this type of schedule, the administration of reinforcement is controlled largely by the passage of time, so that the first response emitted after a predetermined interval is rewarded. Schedules of this type generally yield a characteristic "scalloped" pattern of behavior in which subjects show a very low rate of responding immediately after the presentation of reinforcement, but gradually raise the frequency of their responses as the time when reinforcement may again be obtained approaches. An example of such behavior which should be quite familiar to you is the studying activity of many students. After a big exam, very little studying occurs. However, as the time for the next test draws near, the rate of studying gradually increases until, on the night prior to the exam, few other responses may be occurring (refer to Figure 4–12).

The final type of simple schedule we shall consider is one in which the availability of reinforcement is also controlled primarily by the passage of time. In such **variable-interval schedules,** however, the period which must elapse before responding will once again yield reinforcement varies about some average value. In some instances, then, reinforcement may be obtained after a very short period has passed, while in others, a much longer interval must elapse before it again becomes available. Because organisms placed on such schedules never know when reinforcement may be obtained, they usually

FIGURE 4–13   Whether they know it or not, individuals feeding coins to "one-armed bandits" such as the one shown here are being reinforced on a variable-ratio schedule. (Photo credit: H. Armstrong-Roberts.)

respond at a fairly constant and relatively high rate (refer to Figure 4–12). Hope, it seems, does indeed spring eternal when reinforcements are delivered on a variable-interval schedule.

Although the simple schedules of reinforcement described above appear to exert powerful effects upon behavior, it is doubtful that they are often encountered in pure form outside the laboratory. Rather, they are more frequently combined into **compound schedules,** in which the administration of rewards is determined by two or more rules. For example, reinforcement may be controlled first by one simple schedule and then by another, with the changeover from the first to the second being signaled by some discriminative stimulus. As an instance of this type of schedule, consider the case of a person who owns an aging and unpredictable automobile which is often hard to start. Generally, pumping the accelerator pedal while turning the ignition helps get the car started. In most cases, then, this particular form of reinforcement is controlled by a variable-ratio schedule—after an uncertain number of tries, the motor coughs into life. If the pedal is pumped too often, however, the car makes a series of pathetic wheezing sounds, and further attempts to get it started invariably fail for several minutes. This sound, therefore, may be viewed as a discriminative stimulus indicating that from that point on, reinforcement will be controlled by a variable-interval schedule rather than a variable-ratio schedule.

In other cases, reinforcement may be obtained through the satisfaction of any one of several rules which operate concurrently. A good example of this type of schedule is seen in the promotion policies of many large corporations. In such organizations, promotion often occurs when an individual has either (1) accomplished certain tasks (i.e., completed a fixed- or variable-ratio schedule) *or* (2) managed to hang around for a certain number of years (i.e., completed what amounts to a fixed-interval schedule). Since reinforcement (promotion) can be obtained in either manner, behavior in such cases may be viewed as existing under the control of several concurrent simple schedules.

Patterns of Reinforcement and Extinction: The Partial Reinforcement Effect

As we have already seen, the schedule on which reinforcement is delivered exerts a powerful effect upon the rate at which organisms emit operants—simple responses already at their disposal. That variations in the patterning of reinforcement also affect the acquisition of *new* responses has been demonstrated in a large number of experiments (Robbins, 1971). Generally, the results of these studies suggest that learning is more rapid under conditions in which reinforcement always follows the responses being acquired (**continuous reinforcement**) than under conditions in which reinforcement follows these responses only part of the time (**partial reinforcement**). The effects of patterns of reinforcement upon learning, then, are not very surprising. In contrast, the influence of this factor upon behavior during extinction is much more unexpected.

At first, you might guess that responses will prove more resistant to extinction when they have been followed by reinforcement on every occasion than when they have been reinforced in an intermittent manner. Yet, just the opposite seems to be true. A large body of research indicates that contrary to what common sense might suggest, partial reinforcement leads to much greater resistance to extinction than does continuous reinforcement (Robbins, 1971). Many explanations for this surprising fact—which is often referred to as the **partial reinforcement effect**—have been suggested, but we will consider only two here.

The first, sometimes termed the *discrimination hypothesis*, suggests that partial reinforcement leads to greater resistance to extinction because, quite simply, it is more difficult for subjects trained on such schedules to recognize that extinction has begun. Since their responses are followed by reinforcement only part of the time during training, the shift to extinction, when no further reinforcements occur, is not very abrupt or sudden for such subjects, and they continue to respond. In contrast, those trained on continuous reinforcement, in which every response is rewarded, find this shift more noticeable or obvious, and thus "give up" much more quickly. Evidence supporting the discrimination hypothesis has been obtained in a number of investigations (e.g., Tyler, Wortz, and Bitterman, 1953). However, recent findings suggest that it is not sufficient by itself to account for the occurrence of the partial reinforcement effect (Sutherland and Mackintosh, 1971).

A second explanation for this effect is based upon the suggestion that during training on partial reinforcement, organisms learn how to cope with the effects of nonreinforcement *and* to maintain their behavior in the presence of such effects. In particular, Abram Amsel (1972) has suggested that during partial reinforcement, subjects learn to continue responding even in the face of feelings of frustration stemming from nonreinforcement. Thus, when extinction begins and no further reinforcements are delivered, they continue responding for a relatively long period of time. In contrast, subjects trained on continuous reinforcement never have an opportunity to acquire such persistence in the face of frustration, and, as a result, they generally stop responding much sooner during extinction.

Actually, both the discrimination and frustration hypotheses are somewhat more complex than we have suggested. In addition, they represent only two of the many interpretations of the partial reinforcement effect that have been offered by psychologists in recent years (Capaldi, 1970). Regardless of the precise mechanisms underlying this effect, however, its usefulness from an adaptive standpoint is clear, Under natural conditions, reinforcement rarely follows various responses—even highly effective ones—in a totally consistent manner. For example, lions and other predators often fail to catch their prey, and even highly successful "lines" prove ineffective when used on some persons. As a result, most forms of behavior, including those most crucial for continued survival, are acquired under partial schedules of reinforcement. Given this fact, it seems fortunate that such responses are far more resistant to extinction than common sense seems to suggest. If they were not, the rapid extinction of many important patterns of behavior which would follow might often be accompanied by an equally rapid "extinction" of the organisms that no longer persist in their performance!

Shaping: A Little—Gradually —Goes a Long Way

If you've ever watched elephants form huge pyramids or move through complex dances, porpoises play water polo, or lions and tigers jump through hoops, you may have found yourself wondering how these animals were trained to perform such tricks (see Figure 4–14). Although several different approaches may have been used to accomplish these feats, there is a very good chance that a technique of operant conditioning known as **shaping** played a central role. The basic idea behind shaping is that of gradually molding the behavior of the subject to the form desired by the trainer. Thus, the process begins with careful specification of the **terminal responses**—what we wish the animal to do at the end of training—and careful attention to its **entering behavior**—what it is doing when we begin. The main task from this point on is that of administering reinforcement for each small movement in the "right" direction.

FIGURE 4–14   Through the technique of *shaping*, animals can be trained to perform such complex feats as the ones shown above. (Left photo: Raimondo Borea; right photo: Animal Behavior Enterprises, Inc.)

For example, suppose that you wished to train your dog to retrieve the evening newspaper, which, for reasons beyond your grasp, is always thrown by the carrier into the muddiest and most difficult to reach spots around your home. In order to develop such actions, you would begin by observing your pet's entering behavior. Fortunately, in this case, such responses might include a strong tendency to approach and sniff at various objects in the environment. You might then take advantage of this tendency by rewarding your dog with a small bit of food for approaching rolled-up newspapers which you scatter about the lawn. Assuming that you employ an appropriate reinforcer and that your dog is hungry at the time of this training, it should be only a matter of minutes before he is rushing from one paper to the next in order to obtain the tasty treats you dispense. Your next step, then, might be that of getting him to pick such objects up in his mouth. Since you want your newspaper in one piece and not in the form of confetti, you might then concentrate on getting him to hold it in such a manner that it is neither torn nor shredded. Once this has been accomplished, you would focus on inducing your pet to carry the paper to you, rewarding him for movements in the right direction, and omitting reinforcement for movements in any other (after all, your neighbor can get his *own* paper). If you are careful during this training to administer reward only for responses closer and closer to the one you desire (**successive approximations** to the goal you wish to achieve), and do not make the steps in your program too large, you may soon reach the point where, thanks to your pet, you always manage to obtain your newspaper with ease despite the best efforts of your carrier to place it beyond your reach.

After reading the above description of shaping and examining Figure 4–14, you might be ready to conclude that operant conditioning is fine for teaching old dogs (or rats) new tricks, but of little practical value outside circuses or parties. Actually, nothing could be farther from the truth. The principles of operant behavior uncovered by Skinner and other researchers have begun to find increasing application in many practical settings. For example, operant techniques have been employed to modify the behavior of profoundly disturbed or retarded individuals with whom verbal communication—and therefore more traditional forms of treatment—is not possible. Similarly, they have been used to alleviate a number of other difficulties, ranging from obesity and stuttering to thumbsucking and a lack of self-control (Ayllon and Azrin, 1968). Given the powerful effect of schedules of reinforcement and shaping techniques upon behavior, it should come as no surprise that procedures based upon such principles have often achieved dramatic

Operant Conditioning and Behavioral Problems

success. Since we will examine forms of treatment based upon operant conditioning in Chapter 11, they will not be considered here. But we do wish to call your attention to the fact that basic research on learning seems to have yielded many important "spin-offs" of great practical value.

Aversive Conditioning: Learning About Negative Consequences

In our discussion of instrumental learning, we have, up to this point, focused our attention primarily upon situations in which organisms learn to perform various responses which lead to the delivery of some type of positive reinforcement (food, water, approval, money, and so on). There are many other instances, however, in which instrumental learning is based instead upon the presentation of aversive, negative reinforcers (e.g., painful blows, electric shock, intense criticism). Basically, two major variants of such situations appear to exist: (1) those in which an organism learns to *escape* from aversive treatment once it has started and (2) those in which it learns to *avoid the onset* of such negative reinforcement.

Because there is often considerable confusion regarding instrumental learning based upon negative reinforcement and situations involving punishment, it may be useful to offer the following clarification: *In both escape and avoidance conditioning, organisms learn to perform responses which permit them to terminate or avoid unpleasant stimuli; in situations involving punishment, in contrast, they simply learn to refrain from performing responses which result in negative outcomes.* We will return to this distinction again on page 134, but please try to keep it firmly in mind as you read the discussions which follow.

 **PERSPECTIVE ON BEHAVIOR:** *Utopia Revisited*

In a book entitled *Walden II*, first published in 1948 but recently the subject of renewed public interest, B. F. Skinner proposed a drastic formula for attaining utopia – the perfect society. In his new and more perfect order, the principle of positive reinforcement – not a king or an emperor – would reign supreme. Children would be reared by the state rather than by their parents, and they would be trained from birth to demonstrate only desirable characteristics and behavior. Punishment would be outlawed, however, and these beneficial effects would be produced solely through the skillful use of positive reinforcement. The end result, according to Skinner, would be a generation free from such emotions as envy, jealousy, and greed, much better suited for personal happiness and harmonious social life than all those who came before.

Given the powerful impact of schedules of reinforcement upon behavior, it seems quite reasonable to predict that Skinner's plans, were they put to actual use, might well yield many dramatic changes. But would the society so produced actually be a utopia? Supporters of Skinner's views contend that it would, noting that many objectionable forms of behavior – ranging from theft to physical violence – would be entirely eliminated. Critics, however, have suggested that such a society might also tend to crush individuality, reduce creativity, and perhaps even abolish love. What are your own reactions to this controversy? Do you think that "Walden II" (Skinner's name for his new society) would be a utopia – a peaceful haven for long-suffering humanity? Or do you think it might prove to be a regimented nightmare in which much that is uniquely human would be irretrievably lost?

That human beings often engage in escape behavior is apparent. For example, people sometimes run away from fights in which they are experiencing painful physical treatment, often get up and leave in the middle of unusually boring plays, lectures, or movies, and walk away from conversations in which they find what is being said unpleasant or distasteful. Because of the ethical problems involved in exposing humans to strong aversive treatment, however, most research concerned with escape reactions has been conducted with animals.

In these investigations, subjects are exposed to negative reinforcement (electric shock, strong blasts of air) under conditions in which they can terminate such treatment by performing an appropriate response. Thus, in various studies, participants have been able to escape from aversive stimuli by physically jumping from one part of the apparatus to another, pushing a lever, or turning a wheel (Brush, 1970). In general, they learn to perform these activities quite rapidly, although as might be expected on the basis of earlier portions of this chapter, their performance is strongly affected by such factors as the magnitude of the negative reinforcers, any delay in the removal of such consequences, and their level of motivation. Instrumental conditioning based on negative reinforcers, then, appears to be influenced by many of the same variables as instrumental conditioning based on the administration of positive reinforcers (D'Amato, 1970).

Escape: It Feels so Good when It Stops

The fact that organisms can readily learn to perform those actions which serve to terminate many different types of aversive treatment is far from surprising; after all, if they lacked such a capacity, they would often enjoy only very limited life spans. More unexpected, however, are the apparently lasting effects arising from exposure to situations in which escape from negative reinforcers is impossible (Seligman, Maier, and Solomon, 1970). Exposure to such conditions seems to induce strong feelings of "helplessness" among subjects, with the result that later, when conditions change, and escape from the unpleasant circumstances is in fact possible, they fail to take advantage of this new course of events. For example, in an early study of this topic, Seligman and Maier (1967) exposed one group of dogs to 64 inescapable shocks and then placed them in a different apparatus, in which they could escape further shocks by jumping from one compartment to another. Subjects in a second group also received such inescapable shocks, but only after first gaining 10 opportunities to escape from such treatment in the two-compartment apparatus. Finally, those in a third group never received any inescapable shocks during the experiment. As can be seen in Figure 4–15, animals in the second and third groups soon learned to escape from shock by jumping from the compartment in which it was delivered to the compartment in which it was absent. However, those in the first group were much less successful in accomplishing this task; they often remained in the first compartment and "took their punishment," despite the fact that escape was readily available. In short, they acted as if they had given up and resigned themselves to what they viewed as unavoidable punishment.

When There is No Escape: Learning to Feel Helpless

That similar feelings of helplessness may exert a detrimental effect upon the behavior — and even the health — of human beings has been suggested recently by Seligman (1974). In particular, he has proposed that people, too, may "give up" when environmental conditions suggest that they cannot control their own outcomes. The results of such resignation may at first be intense depression, then actual physical deterioration, and finally even death.

As evidence for the accuracy of these unsettling suggestions, Seligman points to the occurrence of "voodoo death," a phenomenon in which members

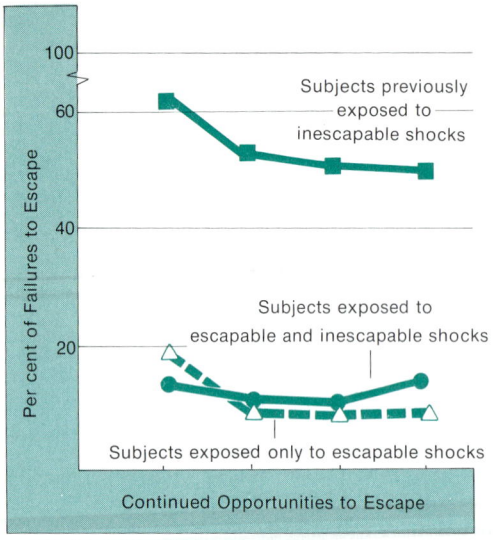

FIGURE 4-15 "Learned helplessness" among rats. Subjects that had previously been exposed to shocks they were powerless to escape were much less successful in jumping to safety when escape *was* possible than were those in two other groups that had not been subjected to such "fatalism-inducing" experiences. (Adapted from Seligman and Maier, 1967.)

of various primitive societies actually die when cursed or condemned by the local witch doctor or medicine man. Presumably, this is the case because being certain they will perish, they experience intense feelings of helplessness and undergo rapid physical breakdown. Additional evidence for the powerful negative influence of such feelings is provided in a study which compared the death rates of elderly women who moved into an old-age home in the Midwest either voluntarily or because they were forced to do so (Ferrari, 1962). Those in the latter group would be expected to experience stronger feelings of helplessness than those in the former, and, consistent with Seligman's suggestions regarding the effects of such reactions, 16 of 17 involuntarily committed women died within a ten-week period. In contrast, only 1 of 38 of the women admitted to the home of their own free will expired during this period. Although such findings are far from conclusive—for example, the women forced to move into the home may have been in worse health than those not forced to do so—they do suggest that placing individuals in situations in which they experience intense feelings of helplessness may have extremely detrimental effects (for more conclusive evidence on this issue, see Klein et al., 1976).

Avoidance Conditioning: An Ounce of Prevention...

Although escape from aversive treatment is often a useful and adaptive reaction, an even more effective behavior, from the point of view of minimizing personal discomfort, is that of avoiding such conditions altogether. Examples of such avoidance reactions are quite common in human behavior. For example, we learn to avoid failure by studying for exams, to avoid speeding tickets by obeying traffic signs, and to avoid physical injuries by adopting various safety precautions.

In all cases in which avoidance behavior takes place, the organisms performing such reactions must somehow be informed that negative reinforcement is imminent. Sometimes such signals are internally generated, as, for example, when an individual reminds himself that unless he takes some action by a specified time, negative outcomes will result. In many other instances, however, external stimuli serving to signal the onset of negative reinforcement are present. Thus, a look of displeasure on the face of his or her parent may inform a child that punishment will soon follow unless some preventative action is taken (bursting into tears, begging for forgiveness). Similarly, a letter from the Dean's Office may indicate that extremely unpleasant consequences

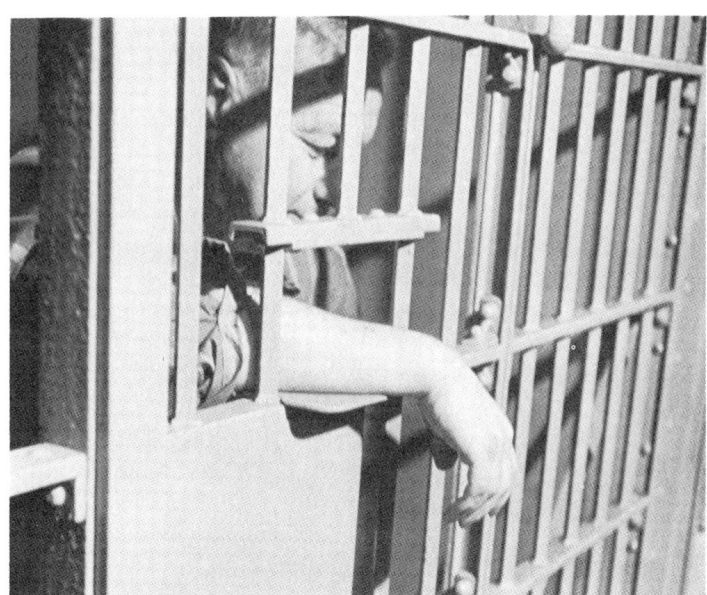

FIGURE 4-16 Recent findings suggest that when human beings are made to feel helpless—totally at the mercy of forces beyond their control—they may suffer many serious effects. (From Stotland, E., and Canon, L.: *Social Psychology: A Cognitive Approach.* Philadelphia: W. B. Saunders Company, 1972.)

will follow shortly if responses designed to prevent their occurrence are not soon performed.

Again, because of ethical considerations, most research concerned with the process of avoidance conditioning has been conducted with animals. Typically, subjects in these studies are placed in the type of two-compartment apparatus described earlier (generally known as a **shuttle box;** see Figure 4–17) and are then exposed to painful electric shocks. They can escape from these shocks by jumping from the first compartment into the second. A few seconds before each shock is delivered, some neutral stimulus (a light, tone, or buzzer) is presented, and continues at least until the occurrence of the shock. Thus, if subjects perform the required response upon receiving this signal, they can avoid the shock entirely. Not surprisingly, they usually learn to respond in this

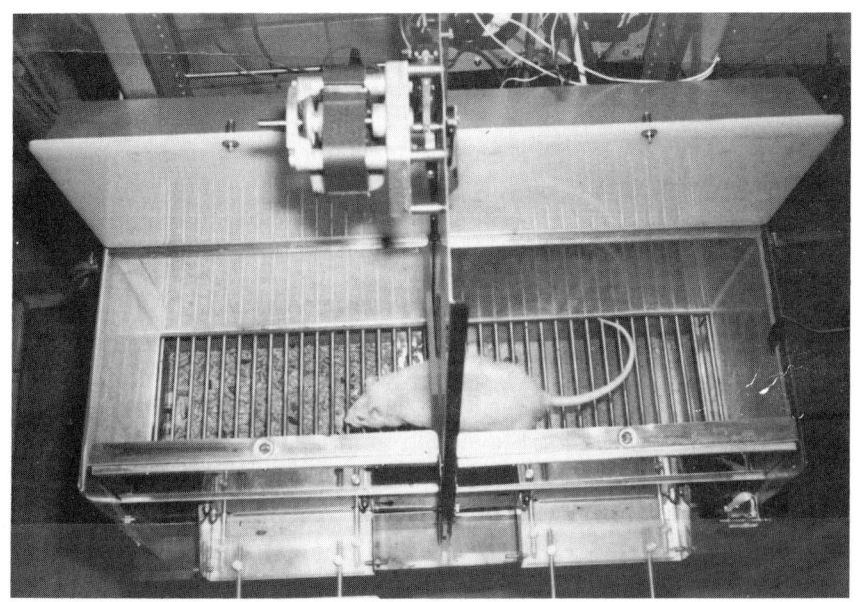

FIGURE 4-17 A shuttle box. Apparatus of this type is often used in the study of avoidance behavior. Subjects must learn to cross from one compartment to the other upon presentation of a warning signal in order to avoid electric shocks delivered through the metal floor.

fashion quite readily, and can soon avoid exposure to painful negative re forcement on almost all occasions.

One explanation for the occurrence of such learning is known as the **two-factor theory.** According to this view, neutral stimuli that are presented prior to the onset of shock or other negative events gradually acquire the ability to elicit strong fear reactions through the process of classical conditioning. Because the performance of avoidance responses (for example, jumping into the next compartment) terminates these stimuli, such reactions are followed by a sharp drop in fear. This, in turn, is positively reinforcing, and serves to strengthen avoidance reactions. Although this theory is far from universally accepted, there do seem to be strong grounds for assuming that learning to avoid unpleasant circumstances probably involves important elements of both classical and instrumental conditioning (Bolles, 1970).

At first glance, avoidance behavior appears to be highly beneficial, as it allows organisms to avoid many unpleasant experiences. There is some indication, though, that such reactions may occasionally yield harmful long-term effects. Several studies conducted with both human and animal subjects suggest that under conditions in which negative reinforcements are extremely painful or unpleasant, the avoidance reactions that are developed are so strong that they are extinguished very slowly—if at all. That is, even when aversive consequences no longer follow the "warning" stimuli, avoidance behavior is repeated over and over again (Solomon and Wynne, 1953; Turner and Solomon, 1962). When organisms engage in avoidance behavior on every occasion, they never have an opportunity to learn whether aversive consequences no longer follow. As a result, they may persist in avoiding dangers which no longer exist and in feeling frightened in situations in which there is no longer any basis for fear. Needless to say, reactions of this type may often serve as the basis for serious psychological disorders (see Chapter 10).

Punishment: Does It Really Work?

In escape and avoidance conditioning, individuals learn to perform various responses which enable them to terminate or avoid unpleasant experiences. In other situations, however, the relationship between subjects' behavior and the occurrence of such events is somewhat different. Here, painful stimuli follow (are contingent upon) some specific type of response, and can only be avoided by the omission of such reactions. The differences between this type of arrangement—which you probably recognize as **punishment**—and the conditions existing in avoidance and escape conditioning are illustrated in Figure 4–18. Please examine them carefully before proceeding.

"Spare the rod and spoil the child" is a well-known warning and one which is frequently heeded, for punishment is a widely used technique for affecting human behavior. Many parents employ it in one form or another to change the actions of their children, and, in one important sense, our entire legal system is based upon the notion that crimes may be deterred through threats of punishment for their enactment. Despite these facts, however, punishment has failed to receive the amount of systematic attention from psychologists that one might expect. An important reason for this relative neglect stems from the fact that early studies of punishment seemed to suggest that it produced only weak and temporary effects upon behavior (Estes, 1944; Skinner, 1938). That is, organisms punished for responses which formerly yielded positive reinforcement refrained from such actions while punishment was present, but soon returned to their performance once it was removed. On the basis of such findings, many researchers concluded that punishment is not an effective means for influencing human behavior, and lost interest in studying its effects.

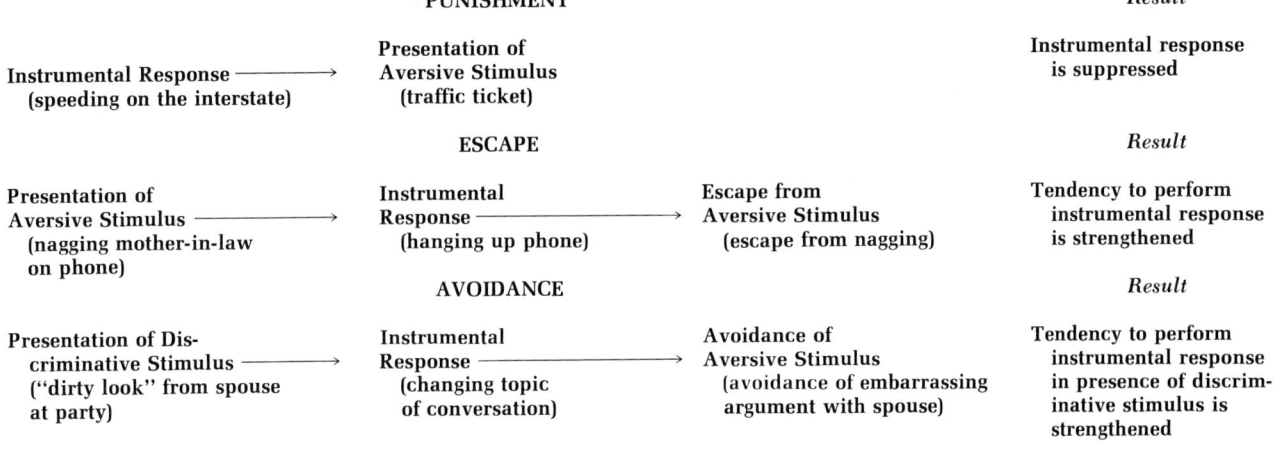

FIGURE 4–18   The conditions existing in punishment, escape, and avoidance situations. In the case of punishment, individuals learn to refrain from performing a response which leads to negative consequences, while in escape and avoidance they learn to perform responses which allow them to either terminate or avoid unpleasant outcomes.

It now appears that conclusions along these lines were somewhat premature. Evidence gathered in more recent investigations suggests that punishment can indeed exert important and lasting effects upon behavior (Church, 1969). In order for this to be the case, though, two major conditions must be met. First, punishment must be made *contingent* upon subjects' behavior, so that it always follows specific responses. When this is the case, it may be highly effective in suppressing many different reactions (Church, Wooten, and Matthews, 1970). For example, in one interesting experiment, Boe and Church (1967) first trained rats to press a lever for food. After this response was well established, they omitted all reinforcement and arranged conditions so that the first response during each 30-second interval brought electric shock instead. The magnitude of such punishment was varied across six different groups, ranging from no shock in the first to 220 volts in the sixth. After fifteen minutes punishment was ended, and the rats' behavior during several successive extinction sessions was observed. Results indicated that punishment exerted a strong and lasting effect upon the subjects' behavior. Those who never received any shocks soon resumed lever-pressing, while those who had been exposed to repeated strong shocks demonstrated little tendency to return to such behavior (see Figure 4–19). In short, it was found that strong punishment greatly speeded the extinction of a previously rewarded response.

Second, responses being punished must not also be rewarded. If they are, then punishment will exert only the temporary influence upon behavior noted in early studies. For example, if a child is punished by her mother for throwing temper tantrums but rewarded for such behavior by her father, such responses will not be eliminated. Rather, they will only be temporarily suppressed in her mother's presence.

When both of these conditions are met, and, in addition, (1) individuals are provided with alternative means for obtaining reinforcement, (2) punishment is immediate, and (3) it is relatively severe, punishment procedures may well serve as highly effective means for altering behavior. Although the administration of painful or unpleasant stimuli to other persons raises serious ethical issues (Tarpy, 1975), it is important to note that punishment can also be used for highly beneficial purposes. For example, when combined with reinforcement for other responses, it can produce helpful changes in the behavior of disturbed or retarded individuals (Wolpe, 1974). Moreover, there is

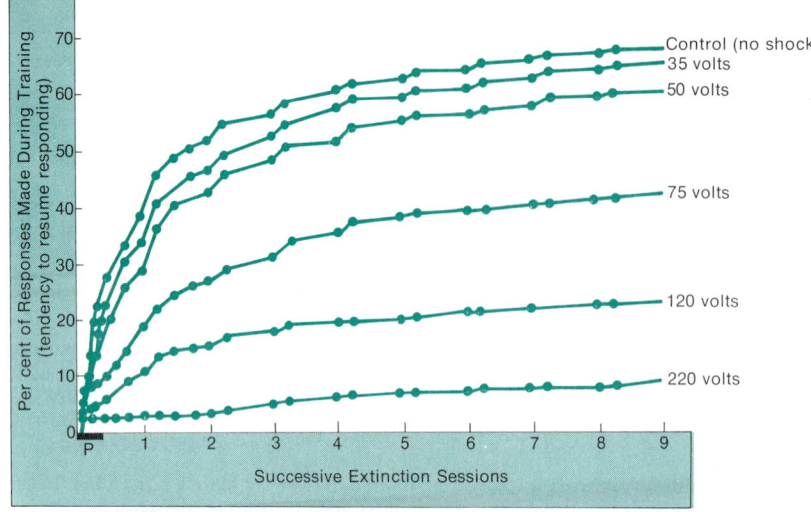

FIGURE 4–19 The effects of punishment on extinction. Subjects who received strong shocks for performing a previously reinforced response failed to resume such behavior when shock was no longer delivered. (Adapted from Boe and Church, 1967.)

growing evidence that it can sometimes serve as a cue, and as such, facilitate certain forms of learning (Taylor, 1974). For example, mild verbal criticism following incorrect responses may underscore the fact that an error has been made, and thereby help human learners master new and complex tasks. As is the case with many principles of science, then, punishment serves as a kind of two-edged sword, coercing and controlling human beings on the one hand while helping and assisting them on the other.

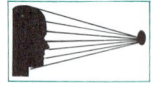 **FOCUS ON RESEARCH:** *Battered Children—Punishment Gone Wild*

At some time or other, most parents employ mild physical punishment as a technique for guiding or changing the behavior of their children. In most cases, the worst outcomes resulting from such incidents are sore bottoms and bruised feelings. Moreover, as we noted earlier, punishment *can* serve a useful function in many instances. In the case of a relatively small number of parents, however, things often get seriously out of hand. These dangerous and disturbed individuals beat, mutilate, and torture their helpless offspring in response to even slight provocations—or simply to "keep them quiet" (see Figure 4–20). Until quite recently, the full extent of this problem was not generally recognized. But with the passage of laws requiring doctors and hospitals to report cases of child abuse to legal authorities, its size and scope have become increasingly apparent. It is now known that several hundred children—mostly young infants—are murdered by their parents each year, while the number who are seriously injured rises into tens of thousands (Kempe and Helfer, 1972). Truly, this is a tragedy of major proportions.

One major question raised by the alarming incidence of child abuse involves the characteristics of the individuals involved. That is, what kind of person would direct such cruel and excessive punishment toward helpless children? After several years of research, an increasingly clear psychological picture of such individuals is beginning to emerge. Perhaps the most surprising feature of this profile is that many parents who severely abuse their offspring do not, at first glance, appear to be seriously disturbed. Rather, they often seem to be quite "normal" to the untrained eye. In this case, appearances are indeed deceiving, and closer examination reveals several major problems lurking beneath the surface.

First, parents who abuse their children often suffer from feelings of depression, inferiority, and isolation. As a result, they have no warm ties toward others, and often feel totally detached from them (Wright, 1970). Second, they often have unrealistic expectations regarding their children. For example, they frequently perceive them as individuals who will fulfill *their* needs, rather than as relatively helpless youngsters whose needs they will have to serve. Finally, they often have disturbed relationships with their own parents, who frequently abused *them*, and toward whom they feel great anger and resentment. In short, parents who unleash cruel physical abuse upon their children appear to be disposed in this direction by their own serious psychological difficulties.

While the emotional problems of individual parents play an important role in the occurrence of serious child abuse, they appear to represent only part of the story. Additional findings point to the conclusion that certain social conditions, too, are important. In particular, recent studies (e.g., Garbarino, 1976) suggest that child abuse is most likely to occur in situations where parents—especially mothers—find themselves facing a devastating combination of low income,

the absence of their mate, and a lack of adequate child care facilities. Apparently, the stressfulness of such conditions tends to strain parents' resources to the breaking point—and sometimes beyond. The results, unfortunately, can often prove disastrous for their children.

Given the contribution of both psychological and social factors to the occurrence of child abuse, it is apparent that effective solutions to this problem must involve efforts to cope with each. Individual parents experiencing serious emotional difficulties must receive appropriate treatment, and the harsh social conditions tending to induce child neglect or abuse must be counteracted. Only through such steps can the continuing tragedy of battered and mistreated children be avoided.

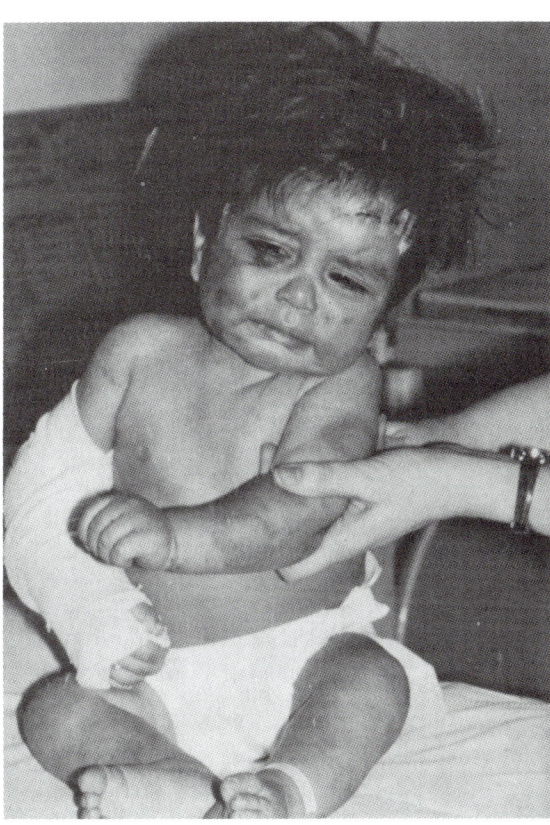

FIGURE 4–20 When parents suffer from serious psychological disorders, they may carry punishment to the frightening extremes shown here. Unfortunately, records indicate that tens of thousands of helpless children are battered and abused in this manner each year. (From Bakwin, H., and Bakwin, R.: *Behavior Disorders in Children*. Philadelphia: W. B. Saunders Company, 1972.)

All of the evidence we have examined so far suggests that overt behavior is indeed a function of its consequences. Organisms *do* learn to repeat actions which yield positive consequences, while avoiding those which result in negative outcomes. But what of internal bodily reactions; can they, too, be modified in this manner? Can organisms learn, through instrumental conditioning, to exert what amounts to voluntary control over their heart rate, blood pressure, and other internal responses?

Instrumental Learning and Visceral Responses: Beyond Self-Control

Until quite recently, the answer provided by most psychologists to these questions was a firm and categorical "No!" There was general agreement that such responses, while modifiable by means of classical conditioning, could not be altered through instrumental learning. Evidence gathered during the past decade, however, has somewhat altered this picture. At present, many authorities hold that basic bodily processes can be significantly affected, and perhaps even placed under direct voluntary control, through the appropriate presentation of positive and negative reinforcers (Kimmel, 1974). Because this recent reversal in scientific opinion has many important implications, we will examine it in some detail.

Controlling Internal Reactions: Experimental Evidence . . . and a Visit with a Yogi

The question of whether visceral reactions can be modified through instrumental conditioning has been investigated in a large number of experiments conducted with both human and animal subjects (see Shapiro et al., 1973). As an example of this research and the problems it often faces, let us consider a relatively early study by Miller and Carmona (1967).

In this experiment, the investigators attempted to determine whether the "classic" response of classical conditioning—salivation—could be modified through the presentation of a positive reinforcer. In order to examine this possibility, two different groups of dogs were deprived of water for sixteen hours in order to make them very thirsty, and were then rewarded with a drink for either increasing or decreasing their rate of salivation. Results indicated that under these conditions, subjects were in fact able to demonstrate the required changes (see Figure 4–21). That is, those rewarded for increasing their rate of salivation showed a marked increase in this activity, while those rewarded for decreasing salivation showed a substantial reduction in such behavior.

Unfortunately, these apparently clear-cut results were complicated by the fact that the dogs rewarded for increments in salivation appeared to be much more alert and active than were those rewarded for decrements in this response. These findings bring into focus one of the thorniest problems faced by investigators seeking to demonstrate the instrumental conditioning of visceral processes: many of these reactions can be readily affected by voluntary activities, such as the tensing of various muscles or changes in the rate or pattern of breathing. For example, many individuals can readily alter their heart rate merely by speeding up or slowing down their respiration. Unless such indirect sources of control over visceral responses are ruled out, it is impossible to

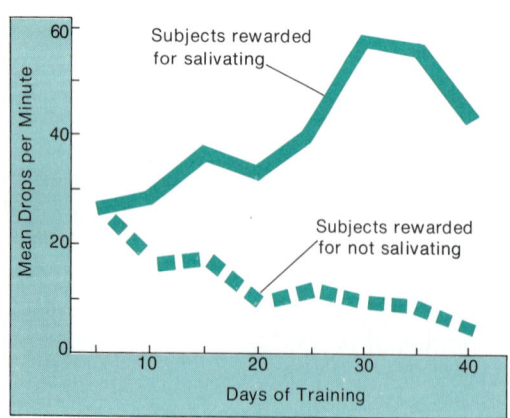

FIGURE 4–21 **Instrumental conditioning of the salivary response. Subjects rewarded with a drink for increasing or decreasing their rate of salivation readily learned to alter this reaction in the required manner. (From Miller, N. E., and Carmona, A. in Journal of Comparative and Physiological Psychology, 63, pp. 1–6, 1967.)**

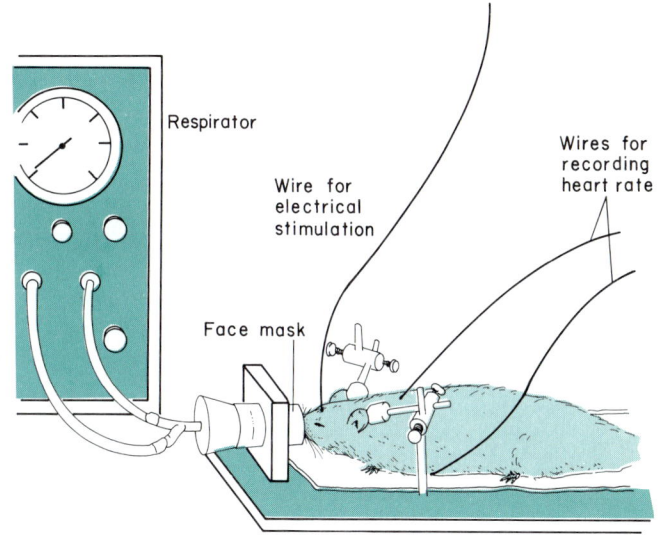

FIGURE 4–22   The procedures devised by DiCara and his colleagues to investigate the instrumental conditioning of visceral responses. (Head restraint, wires, and mask mold devised by Leo V. DiCara.) Subjects are first paralyzed by an injection of curare, and then rewarded with direct stimulation of "pleasure centers" in the brain for producing the desired changes in heart rate, blood pressure, or other responses. (From DiCara, L. V., and Miller, N. E., in *Science*, Vol. 159, pp. 1485–1486, March 29, 1968. Copyright 1968 by the American Association for the Advancement of Science.)

demonstrate that subjects have in fact acquired the ability to control such reactions in a direct, voluntary manner.

In order to get around this potential problem, investigators working with animal subjects have often employed procedures in which *curare*, a drug capable of paralyzing the skeletal muscles of the body, is administered in large doses. While under the influence of this drug, it is impossible for subjects to influence their autonomic processes by tensing some muscles, relaxing others, or varying their rate of respiration. Indeed, since the muscles of the chest are paralyzed along with all the others, breathing must be carried out for them by means of a respirator (see Figure 4–22). Because the animals employed in such research cannot eat or drink in their paralyzed state, special types of reinforcement, such as direct brain stimulation (see Chapter 2), must be employed. Subjects must then produce some specified change in their visceral reactions, such as an increase or decrease in blood pressure, in order to obtain these rewards.

Using these procedures, Neal Miller and his colleagues at first reported that rats could indeed be trained to perform such actions as raising or lowering their heart rate, increasing or decreasing the frequency of intestinal contractions, altering the rate of urine formation in their kidneys, or even making one ear blush while the other remains unchanged (DiCara and Miller, 1968; Miller, 1969; Miller and DiCara, 1967). Unfortunately, though, it has not always proven possible to replicate such findings in later experiments (Miller and DiCara, 1972). As a result, the question of whether subjects can actually bring their visceral responses under *direct* voluntary control remains unresolved. That rats and several other animal species can learn to control their internal bodily processes in *some* manner, though, seems quite well established (Kimmel, 1974).

If rats can learn to influence such reactions as salivation, blood pressure, and heart rate, then it seems reasonable to expect that human beings— with their vastly superior cognitive abilities—should be able to achieve even greater success in this respect. That this is actually the case is suggested by a number of recent experiments. For example, Frezza and Holland (1971) found that college students could learn to increase or decrease their rate of salivation when provided with small monetary rewards for showing such changes. Perhaps the most dramatic demonstration of the extent to which human beings can exert what seems to be direct, voluntary control over their most vital bodily processes, however, has been reported by a team of Indian scientists (Anand, Chhina, and Singh, 1970).

These investigators obtained the cooperation of an accomplished yogi who agreed to permit the scientists to monitor his vital bodily processes during a stay in an air-tight box (see Figure 4–23). Before entering the box, the yogi's normal consumption of oxygen when completely at rest was found to be 9.7 liters per half hour. Presumably, this was the minimum amount required by his body for the continuation of its vital functions. Soon after entering the experimental chamber, however, the subject's heart beat and breathing slowed, and he entered a trancelike state. As a result, his consumption of oxygen during the first half hour dropped to only 6.8 liters. As time wore on, he reduced this rate still further, reaching, in the middle of his six-hour stay in the box, a level of only 2.2 liters. In short, he succeeded in voluntarily reducing his body's consumption of oxygen to less than one fourth of its normal rate! When he was released from the box at the end of the demonstration, he was found to be in excellent condition, despite the fact that he had brought the most basic functions of his body to a virtual halt.

Biofeedback: External Aids to Self-Control

As you probably know, mastering the techniques of yoga requires years of discipline and practice. Thus, it seems unlikely that more than a few individuals will ever learn to control their internal bodily states in this manner. Fortunately, though, the technique of **biofeedback** seems to offer a remarkable shortcut to such control. Basically, biofeedback involves procedures in which minute changes occurring within the body or brain are detected, amplified, and in some way displayed by means of sophisticated electronic equipment to the person experiencing them (see Figure 4–24). Usually, these changes are signaled by simple stimuli, such as a tone or flashing light. But almost any form of feedback seems effective, and some investigators have even arranged demonstrations in which individuals are informed of changes in their internal bodily states through the motions of electric trains or toy racing cars (Brown, 1974).

When provided with such information, most individuals can readily learn to exert voluntary control over their own internal bodily functions. For example, they can alter their blood pressure, increase or decrease their heart rate, raise the frequency of alpha waves in their brain, or alter the temperature of their skin (Brown, 1975). Perhaps most amazingly of all, when provided with visual feedback on an *oscilloscope* (a device which represents changes in electrical activity visually on a fluorescent screen), they can even learn to control the activity of single muscle fibers located deep within their bodies (Basmajian, 1972).

Controlling our Inner Selves: Some Potential Implications

The finding that we can readily learn to exert voluntary control over many of our most basic bodily processes raises a number of intriguing possibilities. For example, as noted recently by Brown (1974), it leads to the suggestion that we might someday be able to control the activity of our brains so as to facilitate new learning or even creativity. The most important implications stemming from biofeedback techniques, however, relate to their potential use in the treatment of various physical ailments. Evidence that procedures based on instrumental conditioning and biofeedback may be of considerable use in this respect has already begun to accumulate. For example, in recent experiments it has been reported that individuals can learn to (1) lower their blood pressure from

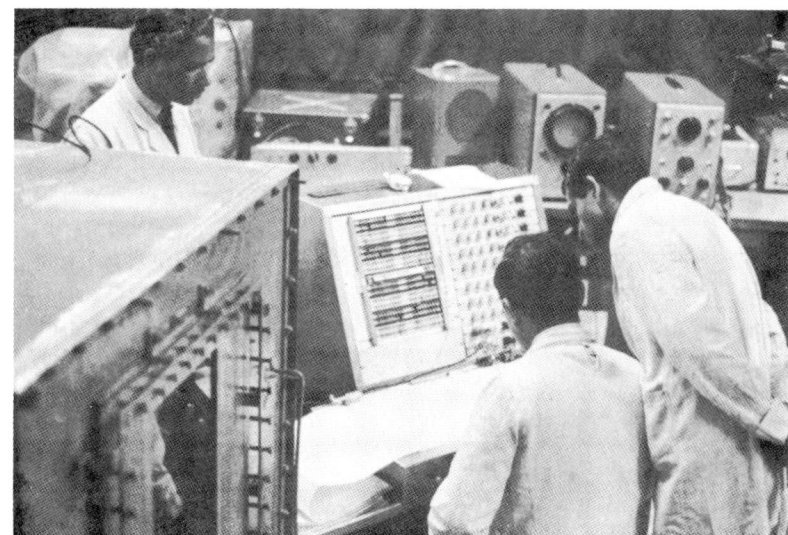

FIGURE 4-23 The equipment employed by Anand, Chhina, and Singh (1970) in their investigation of the voluntary control of basic bodily processes. The box into which the subject was placed (lower left) was completely airtight, but it permitted constant monitoring of his physiological reactions throughout the study. (From Calder, N.: *The Mind of Man.* New York: Viking Press, 1971.)

dangerously high levels, (2) eliminate irregularities in heart action, (3) slow their heart rate from excessive levels, and (4) eliminate constrictions in their circulatory systems which prevent the normal flow of blood to the limbs (Kimmel, 1974; Schwartz, 1973). Of course, such findings have been obtained only under controlled laboratory conditions; the extent to which they can be applied to actual medical practice is yet to be determined. Indeed, as noted recently by Melzack and his colleagues (Melzack, 1975; Melzack and Perry, 1975), treatment techniques based on biofeedback will prove to be of use only if (1) they can be readily employed in hospital and clinical settings, as well as in research laboratories, (2) the changes in bodily functioning they produce are of sufficient size to be of practical significance, and (3) such changes persist for meaningful periods of time. Should these criteria actually be met, biofeed-

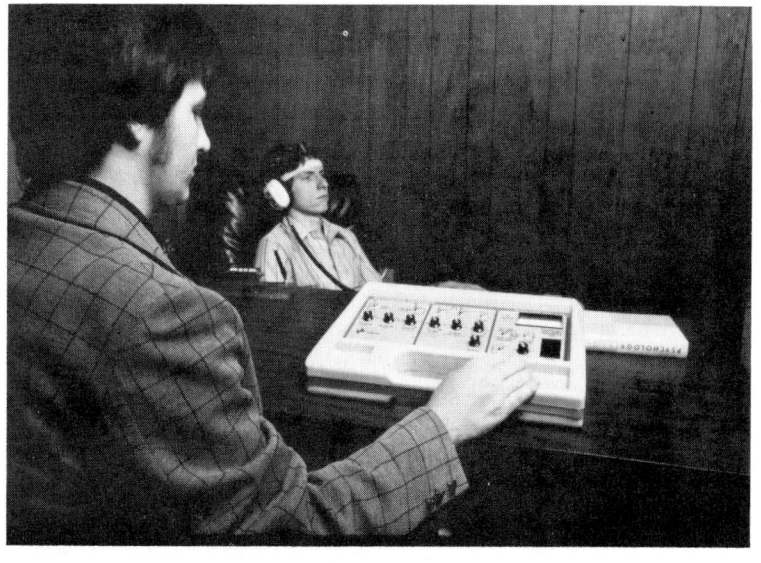

FIGURE 4-24 By means of sophisticated electronic equipment such as that shown here individuals can be provided with information regarding minute changes in such bodily processes as heart rate, blood pressure, or electrical activity in the brain. On the basis of such feedback, they can then often learn to control or influence these processes. (Courtesy of Coulburn Instruments.)

back and related procedures may well prove effective in the treatment of many different ailments. To the extent this is true, they will represent an important and lasting contribution by experimental psychology to the advancement of human welfare.

CLASSICAL AND INSTRUMENTAL CONDITIONING REVISITED: NEW LOOKS AT SOME OLD IDEAS

If we had written this book only a few years in the past, there would have been little reason for adding a sequel to our earlier discussions of classical and instrumental conditioning. Rather, we would probably have stopped after the descriptions already presented, and would have merely noted that psychologists are busily at work filling in the fine details of both these important processes. Major developments within the past decade, however, have led to a searching re-examination of several basic assumptions concerning both forms of learning. Thus, it would be inexcusable for us to omit mention of these intriguing breakthroughs, despite the fact that they serve to disrupt the relatively neat picture of learning developed so far. Although these recent challenges to traditional frameworks have focused on a number of different issues, perhaps the most important have been concerned with (1) *constraints upon learning*—factors which cause various organisms to accomplish some types of learning with greater difficulty than they do others—and (2) *the distinction between classical and instrumental conditioning.*

Constraints Upon Learning: How General Are "General" Laws of Learning?

Back at the turn of the century, when psychologists first began the systematic study of learning, it was quite common for researchers to note that certain tasks were much easier for specific animals to master than were others. Despite the repeated observation of such species differences in learning, however, psychologists seemed to devote less and less attention to their existence with the passing years. Instead, interest was primarily focused upon the important task of formulating general laws of learning—principles which would apply equally well to all organisms, all responses, and all stimuli. That such rules could be devised was suggested by a large and growing body of research. For example, many investigations revealed that various organisms (including human beings) can readily be classically conditioned to a wide variety of visual, auditory, and tactile stimuli. Similarly, experiments employing the operant procedures devised by Skinner indicated that many different organisms respond in a similar manner to variations in schedule of reinforcement. On the basis of such findings, it was generally concluded that (1) species differences in learning, while they exist, are relatively unimportant, and (2) the laws of classical and instrumental conditioning are universal—all organisms learn almost any responses or stimulus-response associations in much the same manner. Of course, these suggestions were not accepted by all psychologists, and they were particularly questioned by a group of European scientists known as *ethologists* (see Appendix B). However, the conclusions we have summarized did seem to represent the views of many researchers for several decades.

In the 1970's, this is no longer the case. It has become increasingly obvious that the generality of "general" laws of learning derived largely from experiments with rats and pigeons has probably been somewhat overstated. Further, there is a growing realization among psychologists that species differences in learning *are* important, and that all organisms do *not* learn all responses to all possible stimuli with the same degree of ease (Hulse, Deese, and Egeth, 1975). Instead, there appear to be a number of species-specific constraints upon learning stemming from the fact that various organisms possess built-in predispositions to behave in certain ways or respond to specific stimuli (Rozin and Kalat,

1971; Shettleworth, 1972). Evidence for the existence of such constraints derives from several different sources, but particularly interesting findings have been reported with respect to the phenomena of **instinctive drift** and **bait-shyness.**

More than two decades ago, two enterprising psychologists, Keller and Marian Breland, decided to put the basic principles of operant conditioning that they had learned in their graduate training to good commercial use. Their basic idea was that of training various animals to perform unusual tricks, and then to put them on lucrative exhibit at state fairs, trade conventions, and similar locations. At first, things went very well. Using standard techniques of operant conditioning, the Brelands succeeded in training chickens to roll prize-containing plastic capsules down a ramp and then peck them into the hands of waiting customers, raccoons to play the part of a miser, placing coins in a metal strongbox, and pigs to behave in a highly thrifty manner, depositing silver dollars in a large "piggy" bank. As time went by, however, their star performers gradually developed some unexpected responses. The chickens began to seize the capsules and pound them against the floor instead of delivering them to waiting purchasers; the raccoon became increasingly reluctant to let go of his coins, and instead spent a great deal of time rubbing them together in what could only be described as a very miserly manner; and the pigs would throw their coins on the floor and root them about instead of making the expected deposit in their waiting bank.

Instinctive Drift: "Misbehavior" during Conditioning

The surprising thing about all these behaviors lies in the fact that their occurrence represented marked departures from what would be expected on the basis of standard conditioning principles. By engaging in these activities, subjects delayed or even prevented the delivery of reinforcement, which was contingent upon their performing in the desired manner. Yet despite this fact, their tendencies to emit such responses grew stronger with the passage of time. In short, subjects seemed intent on "doing their own thing" even when it was quite costly (in terms of omitted rewards) for them to do so.

Breland and Breland have termed such movement away from conditioned patterns of behavior and toward clear-cut innate responses *instinctive drift.* In their opinion, the subjects in their demonstrations showed such unexpected actions as pounding the plastic capsules on the floor or rubbing two coins together because they possessed innate dispositions to behave in these ways which gradually overcame the responses acquired during conditioning. The existence of such "built-in" tendencies, the Brelands feel, points to two major facts: (1) species differences *do* play an important role in learning, and (2) it is impossible to fully understand, predict, or control the behavior of organisms in the absence of detailed information about their innate patterns of activity. Although not all psychologists would agree with such conclusions, the existence of instinctive drift does serve to underscore the impact of innate predispositions upon various forms of learning. (For a general discussion of such predispositions and the relationship between innate patterns of behavior and learning, please see Appendix B.)

Suppose that you performed the following simple experiment. First, you exposed a group of rats to a sweet-tasting liquid and then, as quickly as possible, you injected them with a drug which made them quite sick to their stomachs. Would they learn to avoid the sweet taste on later occasions? Both common sense and a number of experiments suggest that they certainly would (Garcia and Koelling, 1966; Domjan and Wilson, 1972). In fact, the phrase *bait-shyness* refers to such effects—under natural conditions, rats do learn to avoid

Bait-Shyness and the Specificity of Associations

poisoned food which makes them ill (provided, of course, they survive to profit from their experience!). But now suppose that you repeated the study with one major change: instead of exposing your subjects to a sweet-tasting liquid immediately before their injections, you exposed them to some relatively neutral stimulus, such as a buzzer. Would they learn to avoid this stimulus too? Somewhat surprisingly, the answer appears to be that they would not, or at least that they would learn to do so to a much lesser degree (Garcia, McGowan, and Green, 1972). In short, it would be easier for your subjects to form associations between taste cues and later stomach upset than between auditory cues and such reactions.

Before you decide that the implications of such research refer mainly to problems of indigestion in people and rats, we should hasten to emphasize what many psychologists view as their major significance: they point to the conclusion that all associations between stimuli and responses are *not* formed with equal ease. Rather, there appears to be considerable specificity in this respect, so that some are established much more readily than others. Moreover, important differences exist between various species, so that associations readily learned by one are mastered only slowly by another, and vice versa. And often, the types of learning a given species can accomplish most effectively are the very ones which will prove most useful to it in the struggle for survival (Seligman and Hager, 1972). For example, it is obviously very useful for rats—who eat a highly varied diet—to be able to learn to reject foods that cause them to become ill. And since taste is especially likely to serve as a reliable cue in this respect, it is quite advantageous that they learn to associate this type of stimulus with the occurrence of later illness more readily than they do others.

In the face of such evidence, it is now widely recognized that all organisms do not learn all responses or stimulus-response associations with equal efficiency. Rather, they seem to be equipped with innate predispositions to accomplish some types of learning more readily than others. In view of this fact, the course of both classical and instrumental conditioning may vary greatly with the particular species, stimuli, and responses chosen for study.

Constraints upon Learning: A Concluding Comment

After reading these discussions of instinctive drift and bait-shyness, you may now find yourself wondering whether there are, in fact, any "general" laws of learning, and whether psychologists have wasted their time in attempting to formulate such principles. The answer to such questions, we believe, depends very much on what one means by the term "general." If by this word we refer to principles of learning which apply equally well to all organisms, all stimuli, and all responses, then existing evidence suggests a negative answer. There are simply too many species differences and too many constraining factors to permit us the luxury of simple, unitary laws. But if by the term "general" we mean broad principles concerning the basic nature of learning which leave ample room for modifications suggested by the factors mentioned above, then our answer may well be positive. After several decades of intensive research, much is known about learning, and there seems little reason to question our basic grasp of such processes as classical and instrumental conditioning. From this point of view, there are indeed "general" laws of learning—they are merely somewhat less general or universal than was previously believed.

The Distinction Between Classical and Instrumental Conditioning: Autoshaping

For many years, psychologists tended to draw a firm line between classical and instrumental conditioning. Although the sharp distinction between these processes was based on a number of different factors, perhaps the most important involved the type of responses believed to be affected by each. Generally, it was assumed that classical conditioning affects *respondents*—automatic, reflexive responses elicited by specific stimuli (for example, salivation, knee jerks, eyeblinks)—while instrumental conditioning affects *operants*—voluntary actions freely emitted by freely moving organisms. The first serious challenge to this hard-and-fast division arose in the late 1960's, when Neal Miller and his colleagues reported that even some of the "classical" responses of classical conditioning could be readily conditioned by operant techniques. (Do you recall the experiments in which rats were trained to alter their own heart beat and other internal functions?) Since we have already considered this work in some detail, we will merely note here that after almost ten years of research with both human and animal subjects, there seems to be a growing consensus that some respondents, at least, may be instrumentally conditioned—or even brought under voluntary control—by means of appropriate training.

A second development which has tended to blur the previously sharp distinction between instrumental and classical conditioning involves the intriguing process of **autoshaping.** This phenomenon was first reported in an experiment by Paul Brown and Herbert Jenkins (1968) in which food was presented to hungry pigeons in a Skinner box at regularly scheduled intervals. The delivery of such reinforcement was totally unrelated to subjects' behavior and occurred in a purely automatic manner. During the eight seconds preceding the availability of food, however, a translucent key in the apparatus was illuminated by means of a small light. Brown and Jenkins observed that surprisingly, their subjects soon acquired a strong tendency to peck repeatedly at this key when it was lit, despite the fact that such pecking had absolutely no effect upon the delivery of reinforcement. Even more surprising was the finding in a later study (Williams and Williams, 1969) that such behavior tended to persist even under conditions in which pecking at the key *turned off the light and prevented the delivery of food!*

That such unusual behavior is not restricted to pigeons is indicated by the fact that humans, too, appear to "autoshape." Thus, when left alone in front of a console with a movable lever, human subjects often begin responding (moving the lever) when a light which has regularly preceded reinforcement is presented, despite the fact that such responses have no effect upon the delivery of positive outcomes (Wilcove and Miller, 1974; see Figure 4–25).

At first glance, the occurrence of autoshaping is quite puzzling. Why, after all, should pigeons or people take the trouble to perform responses which have no bearing upon their outcomes in the experiment? One possible answer is suggested by a closer look at the conditions which tend to produce such behavior. Although it is certainly true that there is no contingency between subjects' behavior and the delivery of reinforcement in such instances—pennies or food pellets drop into reach on predetermined occasions—one regularity *is* actually present: a contingency between presentation of the light or another signal and the occurrence of reinforcement. Since such repeated pairing of an initially neutral stimulus with reinforcement is the essential condition for classical conditioning, it seems possible that autoshaping represents an intriguing hybrid process in which operant responses such as key-pecking or lever-pressing are gradually "conditioned" to specific, neutral stimuli (Hearst and Jenkins, 1975; Jenkins, 1973; Moore, 1973).

To summarize, existing evidence now suggests that (1) many responses previously believed to be affected only by classical conditioning can in fact be shaped by instrumental procedures, and (2) classical conditioning may play a role in the occurrence of at least some forms of operant behavior. Given the increasing blurring of the boundaries between these two forms of learning, there is a growing feeling among psychologists that it may now be time to remove the high theoretical walls which have separated them for many years.

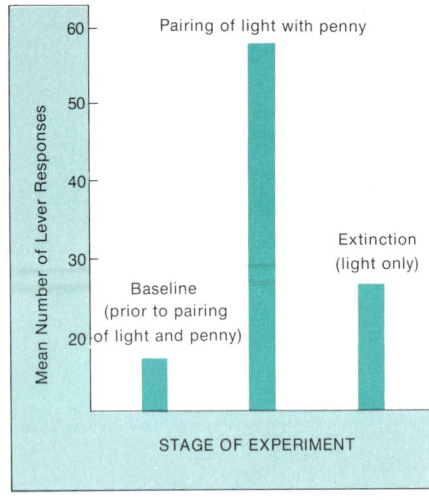

FIGURE 4-25 **Autoshaping in humans. When the presentation of a light was paired with reinforcement (delivery of a penny), subjects soon came to push a lever in its presence—despite the fact that there was absolutely no connection between such behavior and the occurrence of reward. When pennies were no longer presented (during extinction), their tendency to push the lever decreased. (Based on data from Wilcove and Miller, 1974.)**

OBSERVATIONAL LEARNING: LEARNING THROUGH SEEING

Consider the following situations:

(1) A young man attends a scintillating X-rated movie and witnesses several techniques of love-making with which he was previously unfamiliar. Several months later, he obtains a willing partner and puts these techniques into actual practice.

(2) An inexperienced worker watches the performance of an accomplished craftsman attentively, and through such experience begins to acquire the complex skills needed for successful execution of her new job.

(3) After witnessing a detailed account of an unusual but highly successful crime on the evening news, a group of men and women plan and execute a similar action themselves.

(4) On becoming angry, a parent utters a number of four-letter words in the presence of his children. Several days later, he discovers that they, too, are now using these words on similar occasions.

Although the situations described in these examples seem totally unrelated, they share one important characteristic: in each case, one or more individuals acquired new forms of behavior—or the information needed for such responses—simply by observing others' actions and their outcomes. All point, therefore, to the existence of a third type of learning distinct from those we have considered so far, learning which occurs through mere observation.

For many years, such **observational learning** (also known as **modeling**) was largely ignored by psychologists, who focused most of their attention on classical and instrumental conditioning. Within the past decade, though, it has become the subject of an increasing volume of research. Although many factors have contributed to this sudden surge of interest, three seem to be of greatest importance. First, there has been growing realization of the fact that observational learning is a tremendously efficient process—one permitting organisms to avoid the tedious trial-and-error procedures which often accompany instrumental conditioning. In the words of Albert Bandura (1971, 1973), a noted expert in this area, observational learning often permits individuals to short-circuit this process and accomplish what he describes as "no-trial" learning. As an illustration of the potential benefits of observational learning, consider the following situation.

Imagine that some years hence, you have found employment as a Sherlock Holmes–type of sleuth. On one of your many cases, you are faced with the task of finding the ever-present secret passage out of a room in an old English mansion. Try as you may, though, you cannot locate the switch which will release the hidden door. Undisturbed by this failure, you decide to keep watch and discover the secret in another manner. After some time, your patience is rewarded, and you see one of your suspects slink up to the wall and twist a hand-carved decoration. The secret passage is revealed, and he enters, still unaware of your surveillance. Your problem, of course, is solved, for in this brief instant you have acquired the information you so vainly sought before.

Admittedly, this example is a bit far-fetched; your chances of requiring information such as that needed by the sleuth are probably slight. The main point, though, should be apparent: *on many occasions it is far easier to acquire information or new responses by observing others than by pursuing a tedious process of trial and error.*

A second reason for the recent surge of interest in observational learning lies in the fact that it plays a crucial role in *socialization*—the process through which children acquire the many behaviors they need to function as adult members of their culture. Since socialization will be examined in some detail in Chapter 8, we will only mention here that children learn many important responses, including attitudes, values, and several aspects of self-control, through exposure to their parents or other persons. Interestingly, many studies suggest that youngsters learn far more from the deeds they witness than from the words they hear. As a result, parents who do not practice what they preach may often find their children imitating actions which they themselves have performed but of which they verbally disapprove (Bryan, Redfield, and Mader, 1971; Rushton, 1975).

Finally, interest in observational learning has been spurred by several controversies involving possible effects of the mass media, especially television, on behavior. In the case of children, the most heated debates have centered around the possibility that exposure to televised violence may increase the tendency of

FIGURE 4–26 Increasing evidence suggests that human beings can learn many new responses— anything from complex occupational skills to exotic love-making techniques—through exposure to the actions of others. (Left photo by Raimondo Borea; right photo by Hella Hammid, Photo Researchers, Inc.)

young viewers to engage in similar dangerous behavior. A large number of experiments concerned with this issue have reported that children do indeed learn new aggressive responses from such experiences. For example, in several early investigations concerned with this topic, Albert Bandura and his colleagues (Bandura, Ross, and Ross, 1963; Bandura, 1965) exposed children to brief specially constructed films in which an adult model acted aggressively toward an inflated plastic doll in several unusual ways (e.g., he or she drop-kicked the doll about the room). After witnessing these scenes, subjects were placed in a room with the doll and other toys and were allowed to play freely for several minutes. Careful observation of their behavior during this period revealed that those exposed to the aggressive programs frequently imitated the model's unusual aggressive actions. Indeed, many children became virtual "carbon copies" of the model in this respect. In contrast, children in a control group who were never exposed to the model's actions rarely showed such responses.

These findings, which have been obtained in many other studies (Bandura, 1977), seem to suggest that a steady diet of war movies, crime shows, and action-packed Westerns may equip youngsters with a vast repertoire of ingenious techniques for harming other persons (see Figure 4–27). We will return to a more detailed discussion of the possible impact of televised violence upon children's behavior in Chapter 13. For the present, we merely wish to call your attention to the fact that observational learning may play an important role in the occurrence of such effects.

With respect to adults, there is some indication that mass media coverage of riots, brutal crimes, and other dangerous happenings may actually tend to encourage the spread of similar events. For example, soon after the media began devoting a great deal of attention to the problem of sky-jackings, the incidence of such activities rose sharply, perhaps because some viewers acquired the information needed for carrying out such crimes by watching the evening news (Bandura, 1973). Similarly, attacks on political leaders often seem to occur in "waves," almost as if potential assassins are encouraged to engage in such behavior by exposure to mass media reports of similar actions by others. In view of such possibilities, and given the mounting evidence for the role of observational learning in human behavior, it is not surprising that many psychologists now view this process as a third important means through which individuals come to know—and respond to—the complex world around them.

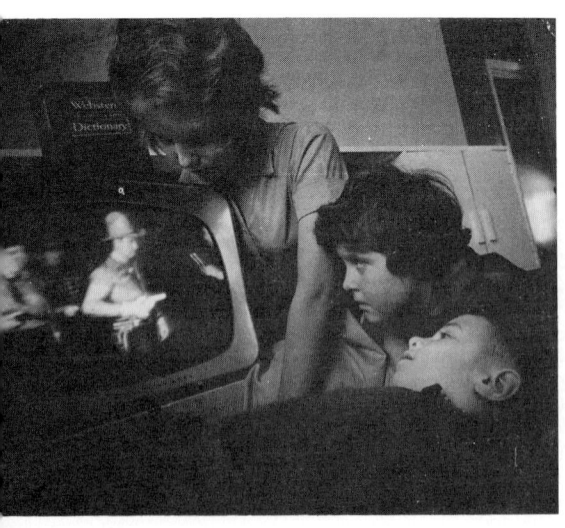

FIGURE 4–27 Many experiments indicate that children can acquire new aggressive responses through exposure to the actions of others. Such findings suggest that the high level of violence in many popular television shows may encourage young viewers to engage in similar actions. (Annan Photo Features.)

As we have noted, one of the most striking features of observational learning involves the fact that it often permits individuals to short-circuit the tedious trial-and-error process of instrumental conditioning. You can demonstrate this important fact for yourself by means of the following simple procedures.

First, acquaint yourself with the problem shown in Figure 4–28. The task is that of connecting all nine dots by means of four straight lines without lifting your pencil off the paper. The solution is also shown in Figure 4–28, and you should master it thoroughly before proceeding. Once you have memorized the correct movements, copy the problem on a plain piece of paper (or use the special form provided in the Study Guide), and show it to a friend who has never solved it before. Tell this person that you will assist him in this task by saying the word "warmer" each time he makes a correct move. Essentially, then, you will place your friend in an instrumental learning situation in which correct responses are rewarded by your verbal comments. As he begins to work on the problem, glance at your watch and time his performance in a discreet manner. If he fails to attain the solution within five minutes, stop and provide him with it.

Next, find another friend who has not solved this problem previously, and simply *demonstrate* the correct solution for him once. After this, let him attempt the problem himself and, again, time his performance. (If you have several friends on whom to "experiment," repeat these procedures as often as possible—the more subjects in your demonstration, the better.)

After you have finished, compare the average amount of time required by individuals in the two conditions to solve the puzzle. Results should provide you with a convincing demonstration of the efficiency of observational learning: the friends for whom you demonstrated the correct solution should require much less time than those for whom you provided verbal reinforcement.

FIGURE 4–28 The nine-dot problem (left) and its solution (right). (From Baron, Byrne, and Griffitt: *Social Psychology: Understanding Human Interaction.* Boston: Allyn and Bacon, 1974.)

Summary

In order to survive in a complex and changing world, organisms must often acquire new patterns of behavior. The process through which such responses are gained is known as **learning** and involves relatively permanent changes in behavior produced through experience.

One of the most basic forms of learning is that of **classical conditioning.** In this process, stimuli initially incapable of evoking strong reactions from organisms gradually acquire this ability through repeated pairing with other stimuli possessing such a capacity. For example, a dim light may at first induce little response among the individuals to whom it is shown, but it will quickly come to evoke strong fear or overt escape reactions when it is repeatedly followed by strong electric shock. Classical conditioning plays an important role in the acquisition of many emotional reactions and several sexual "hang-ups," and it may also serve as a basis for the development of racial or ethnic prejudice.

An organism's actions often influence the consequences it experiences. As a result, both animals and human beings frequently learn to perform those responses which yield positive (i.e., desirable) outcomes, while avoiding those which lead to negative (i.e., undesirable) results. This process is known as **instrumental,** or **operant, conditioning** and plays a crucial role in the development of many complex patterns of behavior. Among the factors which influence instrumental conditioning are: (1) the **magnitude** of available rewards, (2) subjects' level of **motivation,** (3) the **speed** with which rewards are presented following various responses, and (4) the **schedule** on which they are delivered. Recent evidence suggests that even basic bodily reactions such as heart rate, blood pressure, and brain activity can be brought under voluntary control through instrumental conditioning. **Biofeedback,** a technique in which minute changes occurring within the body or brain are amplified and displayed to the individuals experiencing them, appears to greatly facilitate voluntary control.

Findings concerning the instrumental conditioning of internal bodily reactions, together with the discovery of the phenomenon of **auto-shaping,** in which subjects come to direct operant behavior toward stimuli which are regularly associated with reinforcement, serve to blur the previously sharp lines drawn by many psychologists between instrumental and classical conditioning.

Until recently, it was widely believed that basic laws of learning established mainly in experiments with rats and pigeons were universal, applying equally well to all organisms, stimuli, and responses. Now, however, it appears that this may not be the case, and that the members of different species may be predisposed to accomplish certain types of learning more readily than others.

Growing evidence suggests that both animals and humans are capable of acquiring information and new responses merely by observing the actions and outcomes of others. Such **observational learning** appears to be highly efficient, permitting individuals to avoid the tedious trial-and-error process which often accompanies instrumental conditioning. In addition, it seems to play an important role in **socialization,** the process through which children acquire the responses they need to function as adults, and in determining the impact of the mass media—especially television—upon viewers.

Suggested Readings

Bandura, A.: *Social Learning Theory.* Englewood Cliffs, New Jersey: Prentice-Hall, 1977.

　　A very-up-to-date discussion of recent developments in the study of observational learning and modeling. Such topics as the self-regulation of behavior, vicarious reinforcement, and punishment are included.

Brown, B. B.: New mind, new body. *Psychology Today,* 1974, 8, 45–113.

　　A series of related articles concerning various aspects of biofeedback. Together, they provide a broad introduction to this fascinating topic.

Gantt, W. H.: Reminiscences of Pavlov. *Journal of the Experimental Analysis of Behavior,* 1973, 20, 131–136.

　　A brief overview of Pavlov's early research on classical conditioning by a scientist who actually knew him. The comments on Pavlov's personality and work habits provide some interesting insights into the character of this legendary figure in the history of psychology.

Hulse, S. H., Deese, J., and Egeth, H.: *The Psychology of Learning.* New York: McGraw-Hill, 1975.

　　A comprehensive and clearly written introduction to psychological research on learning. Among the topics covered in detail are classical and instrumental conditioning, the effects of reinforcement, and extinction, generalization, and discrimination.

Kimmel, H. D.: Instrumental conditioning of autonomically mediated responses in human beings. *American Psychologist,* 1974, 29, 325–335.

　　A review of recent evidence concerning the instru-

mental conditioning of autonomic responses in humans. Some of the important implications of such conditioning are also discussed.

Peterson, L. R.: *Learning.* Glenview, Ill.: Scott, Foresman, and Co., 1975.

A brief (about 100 pages) introduction to many of the basic principles of learning. The topics of skilled motor performance and thinking, as well as classical and instrumental conditioning, are considered.

Seligman, M. E. P.: Submissive death: Giving up on life. *Psychology Today,* 1974, *12,* 80–85.

A discussion of the unexpected and often extreme effects which may result when organisms — including human beings — experience feelings of helplessness.

Skinner, B. F.: *Walden II.* New York: Macmillan, 1948.

A fascinating and often thought-provoking work describing a society based upon principles of operant conditioning.

Some journals that regularly publish papers on learning:

Animal Learning and Behavior
Journal of the Experimental Analysis of Behavior
Journal of Experimental Psychology
Journal of Verbal Learning and Verbal Behavior
Memory and Cognition

5 Memory and Language

What were you doing on your last birthday? Unless your birthday was quite recent, you may have some initial difficulty in remembering. But with some thought you can probably come up with an account of your experiences on that day. Some incidents will be recalled in detail, such as the arrival of the fire department after your birthday candles set the curtains aflame. Other experiences may be recalled weakly or may be inferred from your more general knowledge of the day's events. For example, your birthday might have been on Wednesday last term. You do remember that last term you spent most Wednesday mornings in English class next to that girl with the big ponytail. Therefore you "remember" that on your birthday you attended English class. This kind of memory is similar to perception (do you remember Chapter 3?), in that you have *constructed* an event from a large set of possible events. Just as people are actively involved in the perception of daily events, they also are not passive users of memory. Whether or not you can remember some incident depends not only on information being available but also on how you look for it. Memory can be crudely approximated by thinking of a very large filing cabinet. While the desired information may be present inside the cabinet, it does no good unless it can be located and retrieved from the files. Experimental psychologists are very interested in different strategies used to store, locate, and retrieve information in memory. Memory, like perception, is a complicated process with many parts.

Our discussion of memory will begin with an example from the courtroom in which we examine the role of different memory processes in eyewitness testimony. Eyewitness testimony is considered strong evidence in criminal cases. Yet eyewitnesses are not always reliable, even though they may be completely honest and trying their best. We shall discover how eyewitness testimony relates to three kinds of memory structures: a rapidly fading sensory storage, an intermediate short-term storage, and a long-term storage. These memory structures are used to implement assorted memory processes or operations such as the organization of information in memory, the search for information in memory, and the **retrieval** of information from memory. Understanding retrieval cues can help us improve our memory with **mnemonics.** A mnemonic is a device to improve memory, such as tying a string around your finger. We shall examine mnemonics that are more sophisticated, and more successful, than tying strings. Our discussion of memory will conclude with some case histories showing unusual memory abilities and memory failures.

Most of the things we would like to remember involve words and other parts of language. Recently, psychologists have become interested in memory for related words and sentences (*semantic memory*) rather than memory for isolated pairs of words or synthetic words called nonsense syllables. We will look at semantic memory as a bridge between language research and memory research. Eskimos have many more words for different kinds of snow than do Americans. Does this mean that we are unable to make the same kinds of perceptual discriminations as Eskimos because we lack the words with which to label these discriminations? We shall see if language influences perception.

THREE KINDS OF MEMORY: SHORT, MEDIUM, LONG

Memory, like sweatshirts, comes in three sizes. There is a sensory storage system which can hold information for only a very brief time period. Next is a short-term storage which can hold a small amount of information. Finally, you have a long-term storage system which holds vast amounts of information. We shall discuss each of these memory systems in turn, using the example of an eyewitness report of a crime to tie these concepts together.

The Great Herring Caper: You Are There

It's Friday night in Megalopolis. Dense fog rolling in from the bay sends waves of chill through your bones and makes you draw your mackinaw more tightly around you. Off in the distance you can hear the muffled creak of an old rotting pier buffeted by the waves. The fog makes pulsing halos out of the streetlights' rays as they beat down upon the ground in a feeble effort to dispel the gloom.

As you turn the corner onto Market Street, you hear the old clock up in the tower bonging out the time: seven P.M.; you automatically check your Gaston-LeCoultre skindiver's watch in the weak glow of the streetlamps. Your nose wrinkles up as the pungent odor of dead fish strikes you smack in the face. Suddenly a passerby darts out from the famous Fish Emporium and knocks you to the ground. Outraged, you turn to pursue your assailant, who is entering a blue 1932 Bentley which has pulled up to the curb from out of nowhere, when you are distracted by a shriek from within the Fish Emporium. "Stop thief! He's stolen the golden atomic herring. He's got the nuclear fish on his gaff." As the distraught owner bursts from the Emporium, the Bentley pulls out with a mighty squeal as the tires lay a half inch of rubber on the pavement. "Get the license number," calls out the owner as the Bentley whips by you. You have just been an eyewitness to the great herring caper. Can you remember the details of the crime?

Sensory Storage: For Fast Fading Facts

What psychological processes are involved in remembering a stimulus which is but briefly perceived, such as the license number of a fleeing Bentley disappearing into the gloom of night? Psychologists have discovered that a stimulus is maintained in a **sensory storage** system which holds information for less than a second. The sensory storage system is called **iconic memory** if visual stimuli are involved or **echoic memory** if the stimulation is auditory.

The best-known experiment which illustrates iconic memory was performed by Sperling (1960). He presented three rows of letters in a *tachistoscope*, a device which permits displays to be briefly presented for controlled periods of time. All rows contained three to six letters. This display was visible for less than one-tenth of a second. Such a brief interval prevented any eye movement (see Chapter 3) while the stimulus was on. In some conditions, observers were asked to report as many letters as they could remember from the entire display; this procedure is called a **whole report.** People can usually report only four or five letters correctly with the whole report technique, no matter how many letters are presented in the display. These particular results tell us nothing new; as far back as the nineteenth century the Scottish philosopher Hamilton had known that the **span of apprehension**—the number of individual items which can be perceived and remembered in a single glance—is in the same range as that obtained in Sperling's whole report technique. But Sperling also used a **partial report** technique, with observers reporting only a single line. A tone was presented to the observer after the display was turned off. A high frequency tone was a signal to report the top line, a medium frequency tone the middle line, and a low frequency tone the bottom line. With this partial report technique, observers could remember almost the entire line. Since the lines (tones) were chosen randomly (see Appendix A for a discussion of random events), it is natural to expect that any observer who could correctly report one line should also be able to accurately report the entire display of three lines. But no observer could do better than roughly one line when asked to report everything. Sperling argued that these results demonstrated the existence of a short-term sensory storage system with a rapidly fading memory representation, or **trace.** While the observer was reporting one line the iconic trace of the other lines faded out. Therefore it didn't really matter how many lines he or she was asked to report. The very act of reporting one line caused enough delay to permit the rest of the letters to fade out or decay. To test his explanation more fully, Sperling deliberately introduced a delay between the time the display went off and the time the tone went on. For a partial report technique (remembering only one row) memory got worse as the tone was delayed. When the tone was delayed one second, memory using the partial report was about as poor as memory for an immediate whole report with no delay of the tone. This result supports Sperling's explanation, since even one row was not remembered well once a delay was introduced.

Another clever experiment which stressed the visual nature of the information of iconic memory was carried out by Eriksen and Collins (1968). They presented two dot patterns separated by a brief interval. While each dot pattern by itself conveyed no information, presenting both dot patterns together revealed three letters. When the two patterns were separated by one-tenth of a second, the three letters could still be read. This indicates that the visual information about the shape of the first dot pattern is maintained, but not for very long, since with longer delays the letters could not be read.

Similar results have also been obtained for material that is presented through the ears rather than through the eyes. Darwin, Turvey, and Crowder (1972) presented lists of letters and digits through earphones. An item could be presented to the left ear, the right ear, or to both. When an item is presented in both ears simultaneously it sounds as if it originates in the middle of the head. This technique lets psychologists create a "three-eared man," with sounds in the left, right, and middle ears analogous to the three visual rows used by Sperling. Memory in partial report was better than in whole report, although the advantage was not nearly so great as for vision. Furthermore, the decay was slower, taking more than one second before an item faded out (Treisman and Rostron, 1972; Rostron, 1974).

You will need a friend and a small number of marbles, jacks, or other objects that can fit in the palm of the hand for this demonstration. Ask your friend to hold some marbles and then drop them neatly on a table. The number of marbles to be dropped should vary between two and ten. Don't let your friend tell you how many marbles will be dropped. Look at the table where the marbles will be dropped. As soon as you hear the marbles hit the table *close your eyes immediately.* Have your friend watch your eyes to make sure you don't accidentally cheat. How many marbles were dropped each time? You should be able to take in about seven marbles in a glance without having to count each one separately. Your span of apprehension is the largest number of marbles you can correctly identify and remember in a single glance.

Short-Term Memory: The Little Engine That Could

Your sensory storage system appears to operate in a fairly automatic way. There seems to be no voluntary action you can take to prolong the life of information from sensory storage without using the next stage of memory, called **short-term memory,** or primary memory. Information can be recycled in short-term memory by a process called *rehearsal.* As we shall see, when rehearsal is prevented or disrupted, you cannot remember information stored in short-term memory.

Think back to the story you just read about the great herring caper. What was the year, color, and make of the automobile in which the thief made his escape? You probably can't recall all three. Reading the rest of the material has prevented you from rehearsing these unimportant items. So even though you have read about the automobile only a few minutes ago, this information is not available in your short-term memory.

Remembering a new telephone number is the traditional example of the importance of rehearsal to short-term memory. Most of us try to remember the number we have just looked up by saying it over and over to ourselves as we dial. This verbal repetition is one kind of rehearsal. But if we are interrupted — for example, by someone asking us for the time and our responding "It's 3:30" — we often forget the telephone number and must again consult the directory. Thus, rehearsal strategies or control processes can be used to maintain information in short-term memory while such options are not available in short-term sensory storage.

There are two major explanations that have been offered to account for loss of information from short-term memory. The **trace decay hypothesis** states that without rehearsal, information simply fades out, just as a light bulb fades out when you turn off the electricity. According to this viewpoint, rehearsal does not strengthen items in short-term memory but merely prevents them from gradually disappearing. Many psychologists have objected to this explanation on the grounds that time itself cannot explain anything. For example, few of us would try to explain rust forming on an unpainted iron bridge by saying that the mere passage of times causes rust. Instead we would argue that oxidation, a chemical change in the iron, takes place over time; time itself does not cause oxidation. Nor does time cause forgetting, according to psychologists who favor the **interference hypothesis,** which explains forgetting as confusion among the items in short-term memory. The claim is that if you had to remember only a single item it would not matter whether or not you could rehearse it. Since the item never decays and since no other items are present to confuse you, you can always remember only one item. At first glance it appears easy to devise an experiment to establish which hypothesis, interference or trace decay, points to the factor responsible for forgetting in short-term memory. But as we examine a few representative efforts we will discover that the issue is more complicated than might be expected.

In the classic demonstration of forgetting in short-term memory, subjects try to remember three-letter nonsense syllables, such as PAJ and RIH (Peterson and Peterson, 1959). Nonsense syllables were first used by Ebbinghaus (1885) to study memory without the contamination of meaning that is present in ordinary words. Ebbinghaus memorized huge lists of nonsense syllables every day and then learned them again later. Since it took him less time and fewer trials to relearn these lists, he measured his memory improvement by the *savings* in number of trials compared to previous attempts. This approach to memory dominated psychology until quite recently, and for psychologists the study of memory was equivalent to the study of long lists of nonsense syllables or words. All this changed when Broadbent (1958) postulated two kinds of memory: short-term memory (such as is discussed in this section) and long-term memory (which will be discussed in the next). We shall leave the details of Broadbent's model for the next chapter and note only that his model was in part responsible for freeing psychologists from the study of lists of items. Although this may not seem like a dramatic change to you, at the time it created great interest. Melton (1963) has compared the psychologist's reaction to the study of individual items not contained in lists to the shock of chemists when they discovered that the noble "inert" gases (e.g., argon) could sustain chemical reactions.

You may think that remembering an individual item like PAJ is very easy, as did most psychologists. When Peterson and Peterson (1959) demonstrated that people cannot remember three letters for 18 seconds, the psychology of memory was a whole new ball game. The trick or technique used by the Petersons was to require subjects to count backwards by threes during a **retention interval**—that is, the time between the presentation of an item (in this case a three-letter syllable) and the subsequent attempted recall of that item. Counting backwards by threes is harder than you might think: try rapidly counting back from 832. You should be saying 832, 829, 826, 823, etc. Filling the retention interval with this counting task eliminates any opportunity for rehearsal—or at least so greatly reduces it that you cannot remember an item for long.

By now you may have realized that these results can be interpreted as evidence for trace decay. Counting prevents rehearsal, and without rehearsal the trace fades away. As Figure 5–1 shows, this finding holds for words as

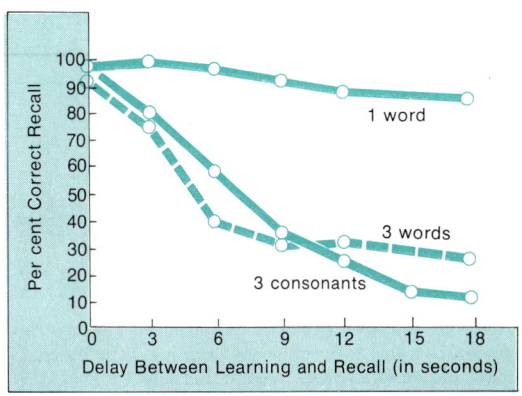

FIGURE 5–1 The percentage of words correctly recalled goes down as the duration of a filled retention interval increases. When the memory unit consists of three components (consonants or words), the forgetting functions appear similar. When the memory unit is a single word, there is much less forgetting. (Adapted from Melton, 1963.)

well as nonsense syllables, and it is quite generally applicable. Psychologists who liked lists and didn't like trace decay saw this as a challenge to their ideas and rushed to their laboratories to demonstrate sources of interference in the Peterson and Peterson experiment.

While ice cream comes in many more flavors than chocolate and vanilla, interference in memory comes primarily from only two sources. Things you are learning now can interfere with things already in your memory. When you are asked to remember this older information (once the task you are now learning is finished), you are unable to do so. Learning some present task has reached backwards to interfere with something you once knew. This could be called "backward interference," but psychologists perfer to call it **retroactive interference.** The botany professor who claimed that every time he learned the name of a new student he forgot the name of a plant was complaining about retroactive interference. The other kind of interference happens when something you learned earlier interferes with new learning. For example, if you learned to drive a car with a floor shift that has reverse on the left, you would have some difficulty driving a different car that has reverse on the right, even after some initial practice. Or if your car has the headlight control on the left side of the steering column and the windshield wiper control on the right, and you had to drive a car with just the opposite arrangement, you would find yourself turning on the wipers when you wanted to turn on the headlights. We could call this "forward interference," since what you learned in the past reaches forward to the present to mess you up. However, psychologists prefer to use the term **proactive interference.**

If you look carefully at Figure 5–1, you will notice that a unit of one word was remembered much better than either three words or three consonants. Melton (1963) also noticed this and decided that there must be interference among the elements of even a single item—that is, among each of the three letters or three words. To test this idea, he asked people to remember items that had from one to five consonants. Figure 5–3 shows that memory gets worse as the number of consonants increases. (At first you may feel that this was a silly experiment, because one would naturally expect longer items to be more difficult to remember. But you can remember five items easily if you do not have to count backwards.) Melton concluded that he had demonstrated a major source of interference in the single-item experiment. But he didn't stop there. He felt that he also had to explain the tiny amount of forgetting for

THE BORN LOSER   **by Art Sansom**

FIGURE 5–2   An example of retroactive interference. Aunt Grace's address interfered with remembering the number of pennies. (The Born Loser cartoon reprinted by permission of Newspaper Enterprise Association.)

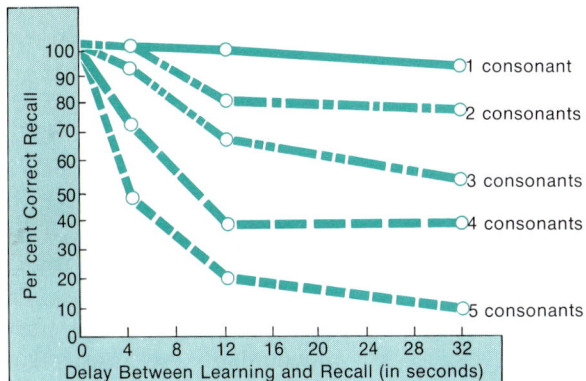

FIGURE 5–3 As the number of units to be remembered increases from one to five consonants, recall gets poorer. As the delay between original learning and recall increases, memory also gets poorer, presumably as a result of the interpolated activity of counting backwards during this interval. Such findings lend support to the view that the loss of information from short-term memory is largely due to the effects of interference. (Adapted from Melton, 1963.)

even a single consonant. He argued that this was due to proactive interference. You remember the first consonant very well because no other letters have preceded it. The second consonant is more difficult because it has one letter before it, the third consonant is even more difficult, and by the time you reach the last consonant your ability to remember has been badly damaged by preceding letters. Furthermore, the longer the retention interval, the relatively poorer you will do on items that occur toward the end of the sequence (Keppel and Underwood, 1962). In short, Melton explained all the forgetting as the result of some kind of interference (much to the delight of interference theorists).

Think back to the herring caper again. The car was a 1932 blue Bentley. Assuming that this information was originally stored in the first place, most psychologists would agree that any difficulty you might have had in recalling it would be due to interference from other color names and other kinds of cars rather than from a simple decay of the information. Interference is now considered a better explanation of forgetting than is trace decay.

Acoustic Representation in Short-Term Memory

The information in your short-term sensory *storage* is represented in the same modality as it is perceived: echoic memory is auditory, and iconic memory in visual. Information in short-term *memory*, however, is coded acoustically even if it is originally presented visually. (There are certain exceptions, such as words that cannot be distinguished on the basis of sound: two, to, too.) The best evidence for auditory coding comes from the kinds of mistakes or confusions that arise in recall. If you are asked to recall a series of letters which sound alike—for example, B, C, D, G, P, V, T—your memory is poorer than if the letters sound different—for example F, M, X, S (Conrad and Hull, 1964). It is possible to create a "table of confusions" showing how many times a particular letter is mistaken for another letter when presented to the ear (as we have indicated, those that sound alike are most often confused). Interestingly, the *same* pattern of confusion is obtained when letters are presented to the *eyes* (Conrad, 1964). This indicates that the visual letters have been re-coded from a visual representation in iconic storage to an auditory format in short-term memory.

Getting Information from Iconic Storage into Short-Term Memory

So far we have discussed iconic memory and short-term memory as if they were independent systems. While there is indeed some evidence to suggest that the iconic system is not affected by the contents of the short-term memory (Dick, 1975), it is clear that the contents of short-term memory must necessarily be influenced by iconic storage, since information cannot enter short-term memory without first entering iconic storage. It is important, therefore, to understand how information gets transferred from iconic storage to short-term memory. This transfer is accomplished by what may be called a *scanning mechanism*. In the case of, say, a string of letters in iconic storage, the scanning mechanism attaches an auditory name to one letter at a time and then scans the next letter on the right. The rate at which the scanning mechanism can sweep across the row of letters depends upon the familiarity of the letter sequence (Mewhort, Merikle, and Bryden, 1969). Familiar sequences — those which are likely to occur in written English — are scanned faster than unfamiliar sequences. This suggests that the scanning mechanism results from a learned, rather than a completely innate, psychological process.

Although many psychologists accept the concept of the scanning mechanism described above, the student should always be aware that psychological mechanisms are assumed or *hypothetical*. There is no miniature eye inside your brain that scans the contents of iconic storage. Psychologists find it convenient to assume that such a mechanism does exist, but this hypothesis could be modified as a result of future experiments. The same caution holds for the three different kinds of memory systems: sensory storage, short-term memory, and long-term memory. These are hypothetical mechanisms that conveniently describe much memory data. However, there is nothing magical about choosing a system based upon three memory systems, and there already is some speculation that short- and long-term memories are merely different aspects of the same unitary memory system rather than completely different systems (Murdock, 1974). As more data are collected, old hypotheses give way to new hypotheses — or even to older hypotheses that now seem more acceptable than they did in the past.

Long-Term Memory

Once again we return to the great herring caper. Now the scene has shifted to the courtroom and it is six months after the crime. You are about to testify as an eyewitness. How do you remember what happened? The information is no longer in either short-term sensory storage or short-term memory. You must probe your **long-term memory** to bring back the details of the crime.

Information in short-term memory must be rehearsed to be remembered. Once information has entered long-term memory, rehearsal is no longer necessary to guarantee that information is not forgotten. While preventing items from being forgotten is the major difficulty in short-term memory, long-term memory suffers from the opposite problem. There is so much information contained in long-term memory that locating and retrieving this information can be quite difficult. Indeed, psychologists distinguish between information which is **available** in long-term memory and that which is **accessible**. All information in long-term memory is considered available — that is, it can be remembered *under the proper circumstances*. But only that information which actually is remembered is accessible. Thus accessible information is always available, but available information cannot always be accessible (Tulving, 1968). The process of obtaining memory information from wherever it is stored is called **retrieval.** In order for information to be accessible, it must first be retrieved. Retrieval of information from long-term memory is a difficult process and is not always successful. Retrieval from short-term memory is considerably easier, and many models of short-term memory assume that if an item is available in short-term memory it is automatically accessible.

While information in short-term memory is coded primarily by acoustic features (how the words *sound* when spoken), information in long-term memory is organized primarily according to what the words *mean*. While interference in short-term memory is based upon acoustic relationships, interference in long-term memory occurs among semantically related words. Thus, the words "seat" and "chair" would interfere in long-term memory, while the words "can" and "man" would be confused in short-term memory.

The most dramatic distinction between short- and long-term memory systems lies in their respective capacities—the number of items each system can store. Short-term memory has a very limited capacity compared to the almost unlimited storage capacity of long-term memory.

Although many psychologists readily accept the general description of long-term memory given above, when we focus upon the exact details of human memory, we encounter many competing explanations (Norman, 1970; Murdock, 1974). Instead of losing sight of the forest by too specific an analysis of individual trees, we shall consider only one model in detail. This model is illustrated in Figure 5–4 and is representative of the kind of analysis of memory currently in vogue. As the figure shows, long-term memory can be reached only from short-term memory, and information must first enter a short-term sensory storage register before it can reach short-term memory. Since long-term memory contains so much information, it is implausible that every item in it is searched whenever we try to retrieve a specific piece of information. Instead, Shiffrin and Atkinson (1969) believe that long-term memory is **self-addressable.** This means that the same plan which is used originally to store information is also used to retrieve information at some later time. This method of retrieval can be illustrated by thinking of checking out a book from a large library. Let's say you are looking for a book about how to improve your memory. You know that memory is a topic within psychology. So you go to the Psychology room of the library. This room is further divided into sections on abnormal psychology, social psychology, and so on. You go to the section which is labeled Experimental Psychology. This section is divided into sub-sections: Perception, Information Processing, and other topics. Eventually you will locate your book in the right sub-section. Without realizing it, you have just retraced the exact plan used by the librarian to shelve the book in the first place. The location of the book depends upon its contents. Long-term memory is organized in the same way a library is organized. And just as your knowledge of the correct sub-topic may only get you to the correct shelf, where you then have to search for the book you want, the self-addressing properties of memory will usually not get you to exactly the precise location you desire but only to the general area. If the storage location is not easily found—for example, the category "four-legged bird"—you may have to do a

Storage and Retrieval in Long-Term Memory

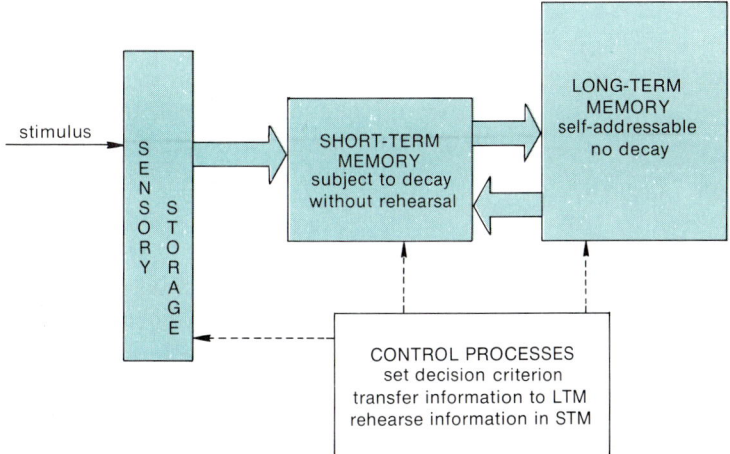

FIGURE 5–4 The "three-box" model of memory. Heavy arrows indicate the flow of information among the three memory systems. Dotted lines indicate the action of control processes upon these memory systems. (Adapted from Shiffrin and Atkinson, 1969.)

great deal of searching on the "shelves" of long-term memory, and even then you may not find what you are looking for.

The other important concept illustrated in Figure 5–4 is that of the *control process*. The three memory systems can be thought of as places or structures. By themselves they are static and unchanging, just like an empty shelf in a library. In order for things to happen within these memory systems, external commands must be generated. Shiffrin and Atkinson call these commands *control signals,* and some typical commands are illustrated in the Control Processes box of Figure 5–4. We will briefly examine only one control process to illustrate the general nature of commands. An issue that must be resolved in any search process is when to stop. Once some information has been located in long-term memory, you must decide whether to activate a response or to continue searching for additional or better memory information. The control process labeled "set decision criteria" governs this decision. If the decision criterion is set to demand lots of information before the response generator gets started, it is likely that the memory search will continue. If the criterion setting will settle for a little information, it is likely that a response will be generated and the search ended. If this process reminds you of the theory of signal detection discussed in Chapter 3, you are to be congratulated. It is exactly the same process, except that the decision involves memory information rather than perceptual information.

RECALL AND RECOGNITION: DIFFERENT WAYS TO MEASURE MEMORY

It is now six months after the great herring caper. The police have arrested the alleged thief and you are in court to testify. How accurately can you remember what happened that night?

Eyewitness testimony has been studied under controlled conditions. Buckhout (1974) had students stage a purse-snatching in a classroom. Then they asked the witnesses to describe what had happened. The memory ability tested here is what psychologists term **recall.** Most witnesses had only poor recall and were unable to accurately describe the incident. They were then given a second test: they were asked to identify the purse-snatcher in a simulated police line-up. The memory ability studied here is referred to as **recognition.** Although lawyers and judges believe that eyewitness *recall* is quite poor, they are still confident that most eyewitnesses can correctly *recognize* a suspect in a line-up. Buckhout added a new wrinkle to the line-up test. After the witness had judged a line-up which contained the culprit, he was asked to judge another line-up which contained a person who looked like the purse-snatcher. The purse-snatcher himself was not present in this second line-up. The results of this experiment are shown in Figure 5–5. Only 7 of the 52 witnesses correctly recognized the culprit. Furthermore, most witnesses tried to make *some* identification, since only ten said they couldn't recognize the criminal. In this instance, recognition was not better than recall. Yet most of us would agree that it is easier to recognize an item than to recall it. Would you rather take a multiple-choice (recognition) exam or an essay (recall) exam? We shall return to this issue after first discussing recall and recognition separately.

Free Recall: No Charge for Wrong Orders

In a free recall situation, the subject is asked to remember information as it comes to mind, with no constraints upon the order in which the items must be recited. Most free recall experiments involve lists of items, and interest has centered upon how these lists are organized in memory. Another kind of free recall experiment which is less often used requires subjects to retell a story. While this situation is less controlled than one in which lists of words not

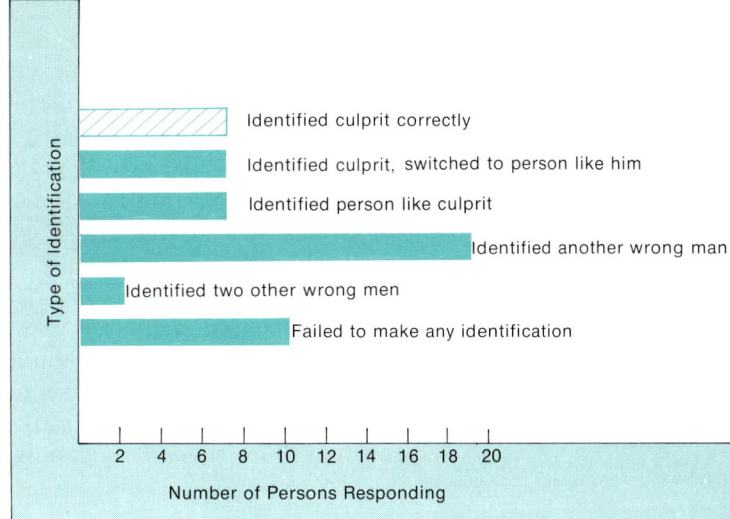

FIGURE 5-5 The number of people making different kinds of correct and incorrect identifications in two successive simulated police line-ups. Only seven people correctly identified the culprit. (Adapted from Buckhout, 1974.)

embedded in sentences are to be recalled, it is more similar to our everyday use of memory. We shall discuss various aspects of all free recall briefly now and return later in the chapter to the way we deal with sentences and language.

An experiment that used retrieval cues to demonstrate a distinction between storage and retrieval processes (that is, between availability and accessibility of memory information) was conducted by Tulving and Pearlstone (1966). Two groups of different subjects learned several **categorized lists**—that is, lists consisting of related items, such as four-legged animals or types of weapons. These lists had different lengths (12, 24, and 48 words) and different numbers of words per category (1, 2, and 4 words). All the words from the same category were presented together with the category name, and subjects were asked to memorize the lists. When recall was then tested, subjects in one group were asked to write down as many words as they could remember, while those in another group were first given the category names (for example, four-legged animals). Recall was much better for the group that was given the category names. Then both groups were given a second chance to remember. This time, however, the first group was also given the category names. This helped the subjects in the group remember an extra 28 words on the average. These 28 words were available—that is, they had been stored—but they could not become accessible until the *retrieval cues* (category names) were provided to the subjects. Regardless of whether a category was cued or not on the first recall test, the subjects remembered the same number of words from each category— for example, about 2.6 words for the 4-word categories. The better recall in the cued condition was the result of recall of words from *more categories* and *not* of recall of more words *within* specific categories. Retrieval cues do not have to be superordinate category names only. Any related words can help. Thus the word "bread" will help you remember the word "butter," even though the two may not be presented together in an original list (Bahrick, 1970; Fox and Dahl, 1971).

Sometimes cues can depress recall. Slamecka (1968) gave subjects some words from a list they had just learned. He expected that these words would help them to remember the rest of the words in the list. Just the opposite result

Retrieval Cues in Free Recall: Hints Can Help or Hurt

occurred. Those subjects who were given some "free" words did worse. Slamecka concluded that a plan for future retrieval of words is established while a list is being learned. This agrees with other research (Tulving and Osler, 1968) which claims that retrieval cues help recall only when the cues are stored along with the words initially. Presenting some "free" words interferes with the subject's retrieval plan, because it is likely that some of the "free" words are not in the plan and therefore cause confusion. While this explanation is not universally accepted (Tulving and Hastie, 1972; Roediger, 1974), it is agreed that cues can have negative effects.

Recall of Integrated Stories: The War of the Ghosts

So far our discussion of free recall has emphasized the importance of organization and retrieval. But people are quite capable of reconstructing and rebuilding memory on the basis of whatever incomplete information is retrieved. In this sense, memory is like perception, in that a total picture is pieced together from several fragments. One of the best-known examples of

TABLE 5–1   Remembering the War of the Ghosts (from Bartlett, 1932)

X   **The Original Story**   X EXAMPLE

The War of the Ghosts

One night two young men from Egulac went down to the river to hunt seals, and while they were there it became foggy and calm. Then they heard war-cries, and they thought: "Maybe this is a war-party." They escaped to the shore, and hid behind a log. Now canoes came up, and they heard the noise of paddles, and saw one canoe coming up to them. There were five men in the canoe, and they said:

"What do you think? We wish to take you along. We are going up the river to make war on the people."

One of the young men said: "I have no arrows."

"Arrows are in the canoe," they said.

"I will not go along. I might be killed. My relatives do not know where I have gone. But you," he said, turning to the other, "may go with them."

So one of the young men went, but the other returned home.

And the warriors went on up the river to a town on the other side of Kalama. The people came down to the water, and they began to fight, and many were killed. But presently the young man heard one of the warriors say: "Quick, let us go home: that Indian has been hit." Now he thought: "Oh, they are ghosts." He did not feel sick, but they said he had been shot.

So the canoes went back to Egulac, and the young man went ashore to his house, and made a fire. And he told everybody and said: "Behold I accompanied the ghosts, and we went to fight. Many of our fellows were killed, and many of those who attacked us were killed. They said I was hit, and I did not feel sick."

He told it all, and then he became quiet. When the sun rose he fell down. Something black came out of his mouth. His face became contorted. The people jumped up and cried.

He was dead.

The Story Recalled Fifteen Minutes Later

The War of the Ghosts

Two youths were standing by a river about to start seal-catching, when a boat appeared with five men in it. They were all armed for war.

The youths were at first frightened, but they were asked by the men to come and help them fight some enemies on the other bank. One youth said he could not come as his relations would be anxious about him; the other said he would go, and entered the boat.

this reconstructive process in memory concerns a story used by Bartlett (1932) called "The War of the Ghosts." Bartlett had his subjects read the short tale to themselves twice and then tested free recall after various delays. The story is reproduced in Table 5–1, and you can try this yourself or with a friend. Successive reproductions of this story by the same person are also given in Table 5–1, showing the effects of delays ranging from 15 minutes to 2½ years. (As I am writing this I cannot help recalling the first time I heard this story as an undergraduate almost fifteen years ago. At that time the instructor put the sentence "Consumption of eggs is a function of motivated hunger" on the blackboard and told us we would be able to remember it at the end of the term. Now I find, fifteen years later, that I cannot forget this stupid sentence which I have not thought about since that undergraduate class years ago. This ghost story for me is a retrieval cue for the stupid sentence.) As you read through the various versions, you can see several systematic changes in the story. Clearly, memory is found wanting when each reproduction is carefully compared to the original. While the general outline of the story remains, details are grossly

In the evening he returned to his hut, and told his friends that he had been in a battle. A great many had been slain, and he had been wounded by an arrow; he had not felt any pain, he said. They told him that he must have been fighting in a battle of ghosts. Then he remembered that it had been queer and he became very excited.

In the morning, however, he became ill, and his friends gathered round; he fell down and his face became very pale. Then he writhed and shrieked and his friends were filled with terror. At last he became calm. Something hard and black came out of his mouth, and he lay contorted and dead.

The Story Recalled Two Months Later

The War of the Ghosts

Two youths went down to the river to hunt for seals. They were hiding behind a rock when a boat with some warriors in it came up to them. The warriors, however, said they were friends, and invited them to help them to fight an enemy over the river. The elder one said he could not go because his relations would be so anxious if he didn't return home. So the younger one went with the warriors in the boat.

In the evening he returned and told his friends that he had been fighting in a great battle, and that many were slain on both sides.

After lighting a fire he retired to sleep. In the morning, when the sun rose, he fell ill, and his neighbors came to see him. He had told them that he had been wounded in the battle but he had felt no pain then. But soon he became worse. He writhed and shrieked and fell to the ground dead. Something black came out of his mouth.

The neighbors said he must have been at war with the ghosts.

The Story Recalled Two and a Half Years Later

The War of the Ghosts

Some warriors went to wage war against the ghosts. They fought all day and one of their number was wounded.

They returned home in the evening, bearing their sick comrade. As the day drew to a close, he became rapidly worse and the villagers came round him. At sunset he sighed; something black came out of his mouth. He was dead.

changed to better fit the stereotypes of the subject. For example, the super-natural features of the story, which are highly stressed in the original, become progressively muted and are replaced by more rational elements—items more in tune with American or English culture. Dominant or dramatic elements of the story, notably something black coming out of the mouth, are retained as focal points about which the rest of the tale is rebuilt. In some reproductions (only one person's retellings are offered here), rather probable plots were invented to link some dramatic details which could not easily be assimilated into the story. It is clear that memory is not simply a result of "looking up" information which is either present or absent; instead, it involves weaving a new fabric on the outline of an original framework. It is this tendency to remember events more in terms of our own stereotypes and beliefs than in terms of what actually occurred that makes eyewitness testimony so unreliable.

How a Story Can Improve Your Memory

Let's say you are a subject in a typical memory experiment. You would be given a short list of unrelated words to memorize. What is the best way to remember such a list? Bower and Clark (1969) were able to demonstrate quite convincingly that even unrelated words can be remembered much better if they are incorporated into a story. They gave subjects a list of ten nouns and asked half of them to make up a story using these ten unrelated words. Most subjects took about two or three minutes to make up their story, and many of the stories were awkward. The other half of the subjects in the control group were simply told to study the words for the same amount of time that it took the experimental subjects to create a story. Both groups scored perfectly when recall was tested immediately. After going through 12 such lists of ten words, subjects were unexpectedly asked to recall all 120 words. The subjects who made up stories could recall 93 per cent of the words, while those who learned the words by rote memorization recalled only 14 per cent of the words. Even silly stories protected the words from forgetting and the effects of retroactive and proactive inhibition.

PSYCHOLOGY IN ACTION: *Retrieval Cues in Free Recall: Tell Me a Story*

You will need two friends for this demonstration. Have one friend make up a story using the ten words in the first column. Time him to see how long this takes. Have another friend try to memorize the list of ten words for this amount of time. After this time is up, ask each friend to recall the words. Do the same for all the words in columns two, three, four, and five. Then ask them to remember all the words. Do your results agree with those of Bower and Clark?

1	2	3	4	5
bottle	curtains	moon	window	hat
airplane	gun	tree	table	canoe
trowel	book	axe	lamp	chair
broom	telephone	radio	television	stereo
desk	doorknob	house	letter	bank
cup	glass	saucer	dish	sink
lion	tiger	fox	giraffe	elephant
boat	ferry	sail	train	car
bed	desk	typewriter	helmet	button
fish	lobster	snail	shrimp	turtle

In a free recall situation, words may be remembered in any order, regardless of the order in which they were originally presented. In a **serial recall** task, not only must the items be remembered but they must also be given in the same order as they were when originally presented. Remembering a telephone number is a good example of a task in which serial, rather than free, recall is necessary. It does you absolutely no good to remember the digits of a telephone number correctly unless you recall them in their proper order.

The Serial Position Curve: How to Tell if an Item Came from Short- or Long-Term Memory

When you recall a list of items, either in order (serial recall) or as they occur to you (free recall), you do better on items that were originally presented at the beginning or at the end of the list. The **serial position** of an item is defined as its position in the original list which must be remembered. Thus, the first item has serial position one, the second serial position two, and so on. The improved memory for items in early serial positions is called the **primacy effect** (these items were presented first); the improved recall for items in late serial positions (at the end of the list) is called the **recency effect** (these items were presented most recently). When recall is plotted as a function of serial position, as in Figure 5–6, the U-shaped graph that results is called a **serial position curve.** Such curves can be plotted for either free recall or serial recall tasks. The curve is not completely symmetrical because for free recall data the recency effect is usually greater than the primacy effect—that is, the curve is higher (indicating better recall) at the end than at the beginning. The serial position curve is lowest in the middle, representing recall at its poorest. This U-shaped serial position curve is a basic and very general finding in studies of human memory and, as such, must be accounted for in any theory or model of memory.

We can see from Figure 5–7 how the general "three-box" model (sometimes called the modal model) described previously explains the shape of the serial position curve. Since the short-term sensory store decays so rapidly, it need not be represented, and we are left with short- and long-term memory components. All items are assumed to enter short-term memory. There is a small constant probability that an item will be transferred from short-term into long-term memory. This transfer is accomplished by rehearsal. Since items with low (early) serial positions are rehearsed at greater length than are later items, the left side of the *long-term memory* curve tilts up. Since later items are rehearsed less, the right side of this curve drops down. Contributions of *short-term memory* are limited to the last seven or eight items—the recency effect does not normally extend back into the list any further than this. The effects of short-term memory overlap with those of long-term memory (this overlap is represented by cross-hatching in the bottom right portion of Figure

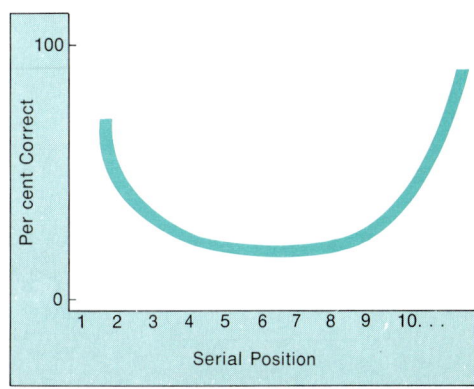

FIGURE 5–6 A typical serial position curve for free recall tasks. Recall is best at the early and late serial positions. While free recall has a large recency effect, as shown here, serial recall tasks show a larger primacy effect.

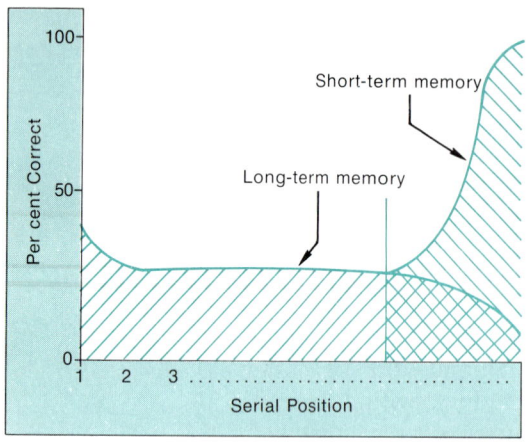

FIGURE 5–7 Contributions of short- and long-term memories to the serial position curve. The right side shows the contribution of short-term memory, and the left side the contribution of long-term memory. The cross-hatched area in the lower right indicates serial positions where items can be recalled from either short- or long-term memories. (After Murdock, 1974.)

5–7). It is possible for an item to be in short-term memory and also in long-term memory at the same time because rehearsal, which transfers items into long-term memory, also maintains items in short-term memory. In order to find out the contribution of short-term memory *alone,* we must subtract out the cross-hatched area in Figure 5–7. This is accomplished by a simple mathematical correction (Waugh and Norman, 1965). Once this is done, we can calculate for any serial position the probability that an item comes from short- or long-term memory. That is, the serial position curve lets us separate effects in short- and long-term memory systems.

This model attributes the recency effect to short-term memory, a notion we can test by (1) arranging an experiment which limits short-term memory capabilities and (2) then seeing if the recency portion of the serial position curve becomes flat. One way to limit short-term memory capabilities is to delay recall. But delay by itself is not sufficient, since rehearsal would be possible during the retention interval. By filling the retention interval with a distracting task, such as was done when Peterson and Peterson asked subjects to count backwards by threes, rehearsal can be prevented. Results of this kind of experiment are shown in Figure 5–8. Lists of 10, 20, or 30 words were fol-

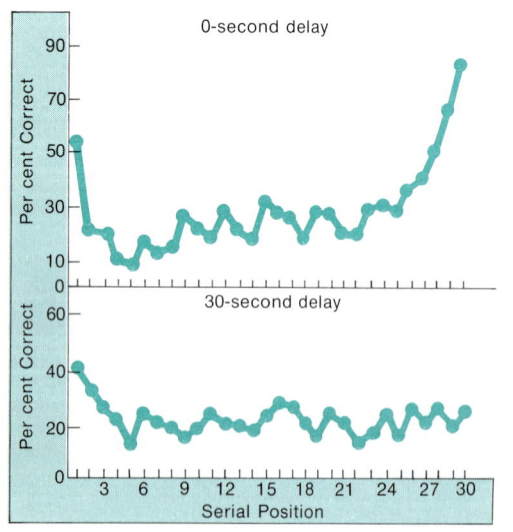

FIGURE 5–8 Serial position curves for free recall tasks. The top curve shows immediate recall, and the bottom curve is for recall after 30 seconds. The long 30 second delay eliminates the recency effect because an interpolated task must be performed during the delay. This prevents rehearsal and removes the short-term memory component. (Adapted from Postman and Phillips, 1965.)

lowed by a delay of fifteen or thirty seconds. As can clearly be seen, the inter-polated task in the retention interval eliminated the recency benefit in the serial position curve. Thus our model, which explained the recency effect as due to short-term memory processes, is supported.

Most students would rather take a multiple-choice, recognition examination than an essay, free-recall examination. Somehow we generally believe that recognition is easier and more accurate than recall. This distinction has been mirrored in psychological thought by so-called single-process and dual-process theories of recognition. A *single-process* theoretician believes that recall and recognition both work the same way. For him, they are simply two different measures of the same process. A *dual-process* theoretician believes that recognition and recall are qualitatively different. Single-process adherents "explain" the usual finding that recognition is better than recall by stating that recognition is a more sensitive measure than recall. This is a circular explanation because it assumes what we are trying to explain. Most psychologists favor the dual-process theory.

Recognition can be extremely accurate under proper circumstances. Shepard (1967) presented subjects with a series of 748 colored pictures pasted onto index cards. This was followed by a series of test pairs with one new picture and one old picture (one of the 748 that had been previously presented). Subjects were required to tell which picture they had seen before. Recognition memory was extremely good, with 98.5 per cent of the pictures being correctly recognized. An even more impressive demonstration was conducted by Standing, Conezio, and Haber (1970). They showed 2560 photographs, and their subjects recognized 90 per cent of them, even when as many as three days elapsed between learning and recognition testing.

But although this memory is impressive, we must note that pictures are usually more distinctive than words. If words are chosen appropriately, we can show recognition to be worse than recall. For example, Tulving (1968) used paired words: ear–muff, news–reel, floor–show, etc. The recall test in-volved the second word in the pair. Recall was *cued* by the first word (as was recognition). The recognition test involved two word-pairs: the original and another pair whose first word was the same as the original but whose last word differed: ear–mark, news–print, floor–cloth, etc. Recall was better than recognition. This experiment also demonstrates that retrieval cues are as neces-sary in recognition as in recall.

The usual finding that recognition is superior to recall may result more from obvious differences in recognition alternatives than from any inherent superiority in the recognition process itself. This possibility should be con-sidered when giving credence to recognition in eyewitness testimony (Buck-hout, 1974). Witnesses who were asked to identify Angela Davis, a black acti-vist on trial for murder, were given nine photographs by police. The set in-cluded three pictures of the defendant, two "mug shots" with names displayed, a picture of a 55-year-old woman, and three other photos. Five of the pictures were so distinctive that they could be ruled out immediately—leaving four, of which three were of the defendant. This is hardly an unbiased test of mem-ory, since there was a 75 per cent chance that a picture of Angela Davis would be picked. When less distinctive persons are chosen as part of a line-up or a set of pictures, the wrong person may be selected by the eyewitness; Buck-hout (1974) cites cases in which innocent men were arrested on the basis of such mistaken identifications.

Recognition: I Never Forget a Face . . .

IMPROVING YOUR MEMORY: MNEMONICS AND IMAGERY

Our society places a high value upon having a good memory. As a student you must be able to remember many facts and events to get high grades. A businessman must be able to remember the names of customers and the needs of each of them if he is to be successful. A husband who forgets his wife's birthday may be in deep trouble, especially if he has also forgotten their wedding anniversary. Books on memory appear on best-seller lists, and short courses in memory improvement are advertised in magazines and newspapers.

You would think that all these incentives would spur psychologists on so that they could devise even more successful ways of improving memory than are currently available. But actually it is only very recently that psychologists have decided seriously to investigate some of the known methods of improving memory, first of all to determine if they really do work and secondly to discover *how* they work. In this section we shall discuss two related techniques for improving memory: *mnemonics* and *imagery*. We shall see that both techniques are often used together, and we will evaluate how effective these techniques are.

Mnemonics: Tricks to Help Memory

A **mnemonic device** is any formal scheme designed to improve your memory. Thus tying a string to your finger would qualify as a mnemonic device, although it is not always a very effective one: it tells you that there is something you should remember, but it does not help to identify what this is. A more useful mnemonic is rhyme. We have all heard the rhyme

> "Thirty days hath September,
> April, June, and November . . . ."

This mnemonic device effectively allows us to remember the number of days in each month, although it has a serious disadvantage. If you want to remember how many days there are in February, for example, you must recite the entire rhyme until you finally reach February.

Method of Loci

A more effective mnemonic device, one known to the ancient Greeks, is called the method of loci. Loci is the Latin word for places. What this mnemonic device involves is learning a list of *places* and then associating what you want to remember—for example, a grocery list—with this list of places. Our knowledge of this method is derived from ancient books on rhetoric (in past times orators depended upon memorizing their speeches). An interesting book, *The Art of Memory*, by Yates (1966), discusses the history of the method of loci in detail. The ancient Greeks used architectural places to form their basic list. The orator imagined himself moving from room to room within a building. Each room contained the images the orator placed in his memory to help him recall his speech. The rooms were arranged in a familiar order, which ensured that the orator made his points in proper sequence.

Bower (1970) has provided an example of how a modern home-dweller might use the method of loci to remember a grocery list. First, you need a list of places arranged in a constant order. These loci might be (a) driveway, (b) interior of garage, (c) front door, (d) top shelf of coat closet, and so on. Just one reading of (a) to (d) was probably enough for you to memorize this series of loci. The list could easily be extended in an order which you would find natural and convenient. Now let's take the first four items on our grocery list: hot dogs, cat food, tomatoes, and bananas. We must link each item to one of our loci. Figure 5–9 shows how this might be accomplished. We could imagine a giant hot dog in the driveway, a cat eating inside the garage, ripe tomatoes splattered on the front door, and a bunch of bananas swinging from the top

FIGURE 5–9   (A) A giant hot dog in the driveway. (B) A cat eating inside the·garage. (C) Ripe tomatoes splattered on the front door. (D) A bunch of bananas swinging from the top shelf of the coat closet. The association of such images with specific locations can often serve as an effective memory aid.

shelf of the coat closet. To remember the grocery list, all you have to do is mentally walk into your house, noting which grocery item has been placed in each locus. This method really does work. In controlled laboratory experiments with college students, the groups using the method of loci did from two to seven times better than control groups not given any special instructions (Bower, 1972).

Another technique, similar to the method of loci, works without your imagining specific places like your garage. Instead, you first memorize a list of objects each associated with a digit, say from one to twenty. This **numeric pegword** system has been used in many popular books on memory improvement and works in the same manner as the method of loci, except that the cues are words or objects rather than places. There is one advantage to the numeric pegword system: it provides direct access to each item. If you want to recall the fifteenth item, you just remember the item associated with the object previously paired with the digit fifteen. Using the traditional method of loci you would have to go through the entire list until the fifteenth place was finally reached.

Many systems exist for linking pegwords to digits. The important feature of all these systems is that the numeric pegword list need only be learned once. You need not invent a new pegword system for each new list of items you want to remember. Instead, you associate each new list with your old pegwords. One common scheme uses rhyme to link the digits to the pegwords:

> One is a bun,
> Two is a shoe,
> Three is a tree,
> Four is a door,
> Five is a hive,
> Six are sticks,
> Seven is heaven,
> Eight is a gate,
> Nine is a line, and
> Ten is a hen.

Now let us take ten objects to be remembered: kite, duck, cow, elephant, giraffe, lamp, desk, watch, coat, cane. Think of an association between the pegwords and the ten objects. For example, you might imagine a kite inside a huge bun, a duck putting on a shoe, a cow in a tree, an elephant squeezing through a narrow door, a giraffe with its head in a hive, and so on. Which object was number four? Four is linked to door, and we can see the elephant squeezing its way through the door, so we know that elephant was the fourth object.

While the rhyming list of pegwords is easy to remember, it may not be the most effective list possible. Bower (1972) has shown that the pegword system works best when a strong visual image can be formed. Some words can be visualized more easily than others, for example, "tent" versus "justice." Your list of pegwords should correspond to strong images to be most successful.

Why does the method of loci work? The answer takes us back to our earlier discussion of retrieval cues in free recall. The control subject does not know where to look in memory for the words to be remembered. To use an analogy expressed by Bower (1972), the subject's task is comparable to finding a few specific books in the Library of Congress after all the books in the library have been dumped into a huge unassorted pile. In contrast, the subject who uses the method of loci has an established bank of library shelves or pigeonholes in which information can be stored in order. Thus he already knows where to look for information during recall. The method of loci provides an effective retrieval scheme, which accounts for much of its utility.

Imagery: A Picture Is Worth Several Words

We have already noted that mnemonics are enhanced when combined with visual imagery. However, up to now we have been rather vague about what constitutes an image and how images can be measured. Many psychologists take a dim view of images, believing that essentially introspective reports about images violate the basic precepts of behaviorism. If you describe your image to me, how can I verify and replicate your private description? Note that the key issue is not whether or not images do exist. This point is generally conceded, even by psychologists who lack the talent to produce detailed visual images. Most of us can report the number of windows in our living room by trying to form a visual image. The difficulty arises when we try to make these images more public so that experimental results may be repeated. Fortunately, several new experimental techniques have been recently developed to make the study of imagery more objective and more acceptable to behaviorists.

One clever technique developed by Brooks (1968) shows that visual and verbal types of information are processed differently. In his experiment, the modality in which information was presented was placed into competition with the modality in which responses were required. This was done in two ways. First, subjects were asked to imagine a capital letter F. Then, starting in some specified position, such as upper left corner, they had to imagine traveling around the letter. At each intersection or corner of the letter they had to decide whether the point was in a particular category such as top or bottom or inside or outside of the block letter. This yes-no response could be made either verbally by saying "yes" or "no" or visually by pointing to "yes" or "no" displayed in a column of symbols. The speech reports were much faster than the pointing reports. Second, in order to show that pointing by itself was not harder than speaking, Brooks used a condition in which a sentence had to be categorized into nouns and non-nouns. For example, the sentence "A bird in the hand is not in the bush" would require the following sequence of responses: no, yes, no, no, yes, no, no, no, no, yes. The same two methods of reporting—pointing and speaking—were used. This time the visual pointing response was much faster. We can conclude that requiring a visual pointing response interferes with visual imagery. Similar results have been obtained by Segal and Fusella (1970), who found that imagining a telephone ringing made it difficult to detect an auditory tone, and that imagining a visual scene made it difficult to detect a weak visual stimulus.

The most widely held view of imagery effects in memory is based upon a concept of memory as a dual encoding system (Paivio, 1971; Bower, 1972). It is assumed that there are two distinct memory systems, one verbal and the other "imaginal." These systems are interconnected and redundant—traces of the same item can be found in both systems at the same time. This is why memory for items which are concrete and easily imagined (e.g., "tent") is better than memory for abstract items. Concrete items have two traces, verbal and imaginal, whereas abstract items have only one trace. Other explanations— single system views of memory—are also popular. Bugelski (1970) believes that mental pictures, not verbal descriptions, are stored in memory. Anderson and Bower (1973) take the opposite view: only verbal abstract propositions are stored, even for visual-pictorial information. At present, we cannot say with certainty how imagery and memory are related and if one is a necessary prerequisite for the other.

A few individuals have rather unusual memories. Some, as a result of brain injury, cannot remember certain kinds of information. This memory deficit is called **amnesia.** Others appear to have exceptionally good memories, and such people often become professional entertainers who astound us with seemingly magical feats of retention. A professional memorizer is called a *mnemonist*, and his problem is exactly the opposite of that of an amnesiac: the amnesiac cannot remember, whereas the mnemonist has great difficulty forgetting. In this section we shall examine a few case histories illustrating unusual memory abilities and disabilities.

UNUSUAL MEMORY ABILITIES AND DISABILITIES

Although there are many specific forms of amnesia (Barbizet, 1970; Russell, 1971), our interest will center upon two general kinds. These correspond to failures of short- and long-term memory systems (the very existence of these two broad categories of amnesia has been often interpreted as additional support for the dual-process model of memory described earlier in this chapter). **Retrograde amnesia** refers to a failure in long-term memory; **antero-grade amnesia** is an inability to transfer information out of short-term memory.

Amnesia: When Memory Fails

Retrograde amnesia is characterized by the forgetting of events that occurred some time prior to a causative traumatic injury, such as a blow on the

Retrograde Amnesia

TABLE 5-2   Post-Traumatic Amnesia and Retrograde Amnesia

	Duration of Recovery of Other Memory after Trauma			
	1 hr.	*1-24 hr.*	*1-7 days*	*7 days*
Period lost to retrograde amnesia (most frequent findings)	1 min.	1-30 min.	1-30 min.	30 min.-10 days

Short periods of retrograde amnesia are associated with brief durations of post-traumatic amnesia. (Adapted from Russell, 1971.)

head, a convulsion (see Chapter 11), or a severe loss of blood. There is a strong correlation between how much time is required for recovery of memory of other events and how much prior time has been forgotten (see Table 5-2). Most retrograde amnesia covers only a short period of time prior to the injury, and memory of this time is gradually regained. This recovery does not depend upon the importance of memory events but only upon the time of occurrence: older memories return before more recent ones.

Even in cases of prolonged retrograde amnesia there is a shrinkage of memory loss, as illustrated in the following example (taken from Russell and Nathan, 1946):

A case previously described was that of P.A.S., a greenkeeper, aged 22, who was thrown from his motorcycle in August, 1933. A week after the accident he was able to converse sensibly, and the nursing staff considered that he had fully recovered consciousness. When questioned, however, he said that the date was in February, 1922, and that he was a schoolboy. He had no recollection of five years spent in Australia, and two years in this country working on a golf course. Two weeks after the injury he remembered the five years spent in Australia, and remembered returning to this country; the past two years were, however, a complete blank as far as his memory was concerned. Three weeks after the injury he returned to the village where he had been working for two years. Everything looked strange, and he had no recollection of ever having been there before. He lost his way on more than one occasion. Still feeling a stranger to the district, he returned to work; he was able to do his work satisfactorily, but had difficulty in remembering what he had actually done during the day. About ten weeks after the accident the events of the past two years were gradually recollected, and finally he was able to remember everything up to within a few minutes of the accident.

Anterograde Amnesia

H.M. (initials are used to protect the privacy of the patient) is a well-known patient who suffers from anterograde amnesia—that is, an inability to retain new information for any length of time. He has been studied extensively by psychologists and neurologists (Scoville and Milner, 1956; Milner, Corkin, and Teuber, 1968). He originally suffered from rather severe epileptic seizures, and after all other treatments failed his medial temporal lobes were surgically removed. While this operation cured his epilepsy and left his I.Q. unchanged, it also rendered him incapable of learning anything new. Although H.M. can conduct a seemingly normal conversation for a brief period, he cannot remember earlier events. When he was hospitalized after his operation, he repeatedly called the nurse to inquire where he was and what he was doing there. He knew he was in a hospital but could not remember why, even after this had been explained to him several times. Yet H.M. remembers the rules of language and can both repeat and transform sentences.

Lindsay and Norman (1972) describe the difficulty of conducting research on patients with anterograde amnesia. The patient N.A. was wounded during a fencing match when an uncovered foil entered his brain via his nose. Here is their account of what happened when they tried to conduct a memory experiment with N.A. (pp. 310–311):

> We were never able to get beyond the instructions. N.A. would listen to our explanation of the experiment, nod his head, say, "Fine, let's go." Then we would turn around to start the tape recorder and other apparatus. Just as the first experimental material was to be presented, we would say, "Are you ready?" Invariably, the reply would be something like, "Ready for what? Do you want me to do something?"

Most of us, even if we do not suffer from amnesia, have had trouble remembering something at one time or another. It is difficult to imagine that someone might have systematic difficulty in forgetting. Yet this is precisely the problem of a professional mnemonist studied by Luria (1968).

The Mind of a Mnemonist: When Forgetting Fails

The mnemonist S. coded words by images and remembered them by simply looking for them mentally, using a method similar to that of the ancient Greek orators. The little forgetting he exhibited was due to perceptual errors; an object to be remembered might be inconveniently placed, as in a dimly lit hallway which would prevent his "seeing" the item when he later tried to recall it. S. would mentally take a walk down a familiar street and deposit images. To recall items, he would imagine himself walking down the street again and would look in shop windows, alleys, and so on to see what he had deposited. He could recall a list backwards perfectly, merely by reversing his mental walk and starting from the other end of the street. Of course, after a while, a given street got cluttered up with images, and S. would then have to mentally walk down a different street to avoid confusing images.

This problem became more severe after he turned professional and was required to memorize long lists of arbitrary items day after day. Sometimes he gave more than one performance per evening in the same hall, and this led to great confusion for him, because if he was not careful he might accidentally recall a list of words from an earlier performance. Luria reports S.'s first attempts at solving this problem:

> "I'm afraid I may begin to confuse the individual performances. So in my mind I erase the blackboard and cover it, as it were, with a film that's completely opaque and impenetrable. I take this off the board and listen to it crunch as I gather it into a ball. That is, after each performance is over, I erase the board, walk away from it, and mentally gather up the film I had used to cover the board. As I go on talking to the audience, I feel myself crumpling this film into a ball in my hands. Even so, when the next performance starts and I walk over to that blackboard, the numbers I had erased are liable to turn up again. If they alternate in a way that's even vaguely like the order in one of the previous performances, I might not catch myself in time and would read off the chart of numbers that had been written there before."

But this didn't work, and S. had to resort to more drastic means to induce forgetting. He tried writing things down that he wanted to forget. This may seem strange to those of us who write down things we want to remember, but S. felt he no longer had to remember something that was written down. This didn't work either. So S. tried burning the slips of paper he had used to write things down. But he could still see the numbers on the charred embers. Finally S. managed to solve his problem, although neither he nor we can explain why his solution worked:

"One evening—it was the 23rd of April—I was quite exhausted from having given three performances and was wondering how I'd ever get through the fourth. There before me I could see the charts of numbers appearing from the first three performances. It was a terrible problem. I thought: I'll just take a quick look and see if the first chart of numbers is still there. I was afraid somehow that it wouldn't be. I both did and didn't want it to appear. . . . And then I thought: the chart of numbers isn't turning up now and it's clear why — it's because I don't want it to! Aha! That means if I don't want the chart to show up it won't. And all it took was for me to realize this!"

LANGUAGE: COMMUNICATION THROUGH WORDS

We communicate with one another, using verbal speech and written symbols, through language. The rich structure of this symbolic form of communication sets mankind apart from most lower organisms. (However, chimpanzees can also use language. This is discussed in Chapter 8.) We can communicate not only simple desires or needs (for example, "Me want food") but also very abstract and sophisticated concepts which could not be easily related by such techniques as pointing at objects. This quality of semantic abstraction is an important feature of language. One of the authors had some painful experience with this property of language when he visited Germany. Since he spoke no German, he had the foresight to take an English-German dictionary with him just in case, although he didn't think it would really be necessary. Simple concepts — just trying to purchase dinner — were very hard to communicate by pointing. While patting your stomach in a German restaurant will get you a menu, it does not help one select appropriate fare. The author solved his problem by looking up the American word for what he wanted and then pointing to the German equivalent. The waitress shook her head to indicate that hamburgers were not available and turned to the German word for pork chops. We ate pork chops that night, even though we really didn't want pork chops, since it seemed the path of least resistance. It takes an experience like temporarily being deprived of the use of language in a foreign country to make one appreciate how easily we communicate through language.

The formal properties of language are studied in a discipline called **linguistics.** Psychologists interested in language have not hesitated to draw upon the ideas of such clever linguists as Noam Chomsky and George Lakoff. Linguists are concerned with a person's *competence* in language — that is, his potential ability to form linguistically correct sentences and phrases based upon his understanding and knowledge of the rules of a language (such as English). For example, a competent English speaker knows that plural nouns are followed by a special plural form of verbs. Psychologists are interested in *performance* — the language behavior actually used. This is a broader issue since merely having a set of rules (competence) does not necessarily allow us to predict behavior — the way these rules are actually utilized to produce language. Thus a psychological analysis of language tends to be more empirical and closely tied to data, while linguistic analysis tends to be more abstract and concerned with formal relationships among elements of language. Since psychologists have borrowed many concepts from linguistics, we shall begin our survey of language with a brief look at some basic linguistic concepts. Then we shall see how psychologists have utilized these concepts to expand our knowledge of competence to an understanding of performance.

Surface and Deep Structures: Linguistic Descriptions of Language

Spoken language reaches your ears as a series of sounds. These sounds can be organized into linguistic units called **phonemes.** A phoneme is the smallest unit of speech. Sounds like the "t" in "tart" and the "l" in "lake" are examples of phonemes. The human voice can create many different phonemes, but no one language uses all of them. In fact, any single language uses only about half of the possible phonemes. For example, certain African languages contain a gutteral click sound which is not used in English. Similarly, the English phoneme "r" is not contained in Japanese.

The phonemes themselves, as part of the **surface structure** of a language, do not convey meaning. According to transformational linguistics (Chomsky, 1968), additional, *non*-surface analysis is required before the true meaning of a sentence becomes clear. We shall soon return to this point. For now, merely note that analysis of phonemes deals with the surface structure of language.

Phonemes, when combined, form words. While the word seems a natural unit of language, linguists prefer to work with a unit called the **morpheme,** which is very similar to a word. Some words contain more than one morpheme, although many morphemes are only single words. This can best be explained in a brief example. The word "dogs" contains two morphemes: *dog* and *s*. The plural morpheme "s" is one of a number of special-function morphemes. (To indicate possession, we use the possessive "s," as in "Mary's"; to change adjectives to adverbs, we use the special-function morpheme "ly".) Although the morpheme is the lowest or simplest level of language at which meaning can appear, not all morphemes have meaning by themselves. For example, what is the meaning of the word "to"? Even though morphemes are more useful than phonemes, they too are part of the surface structure and cannot portray the whole story.

The next linguistic level is the phrase or sentence. This is a set of morphemes arranged to satisfy the rules of some particular language, such as English. Let us compare two sentences which use the same words:

John raped Alice.
Alice raped John.

Clearly the meaning of these sentences differs, even though the words are the same. There are rules which govern the order of words in English sentences. Perhaps you remember studying the parts of speech—nouns, adverbs, adjectives, and so on—in English class. A sentence can be diagrammed according to how these parts of speech are arranged. This is called *parsing* the sentence. The diagram is usually arranged in the form of a tree with more than one horizontal level, as in Figure 5–10. The concepts that are represented become more specific as we travel down toward the bottom of the tree, where specific morphemes or words are represented. Higher up in the tree, the concepts become more abstract. This diagram represents the *surface structure* of a sentence.

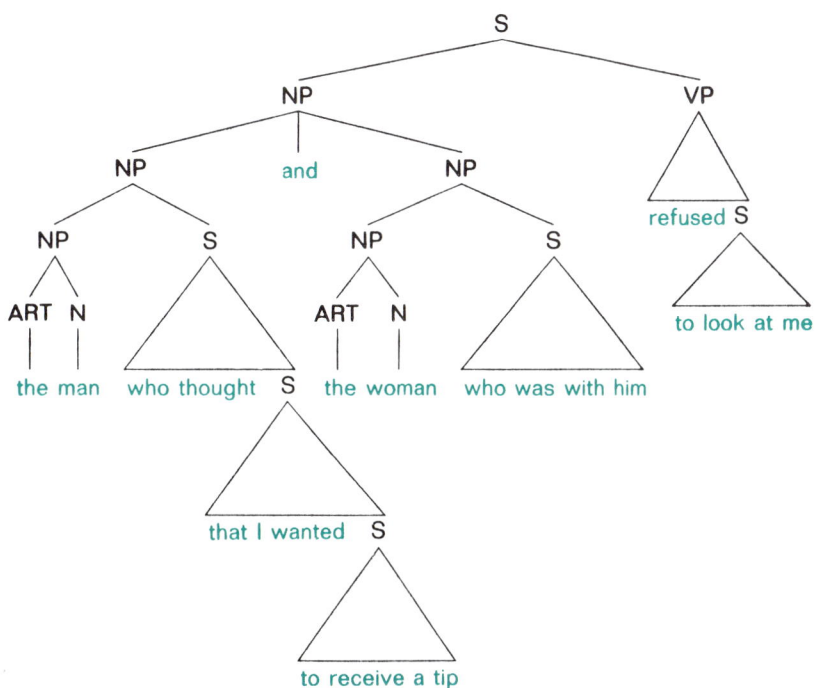

FIGURE 5–10 A tree diagram showing how a complicated sentence is parsed. S indicates a sentence, NP a noun phrase, VP a verb phrase, ART an article, and N a noun. The sentence reads as follows: "The man who thought I wanted to receive a tip, and the woman who was with him, refused to look at me." (From Langacker, 1968.)

Although the surface structure of a sentence can get quite complicated, it is not enough to tell us the *meaning* of the sentence. Let us compare two sentences which have the same surface structure:

> They are flying airplanes.
> They are flying airplanes.

The two sentences above are not a misprint. To emphasize the fact that surface structure does not always lead to comprehension, we have deliberately written what looks like the same sentence twice. But it is *not* the same sentence, because each sentence has a different meaning. This is an example of an ambiguous sentence. We cannot discover the meaning from only the surface structure. The two different deep structures can be approximated by:

> (They) (are flying airplanes.)
> (They are) (flying airplanes.)

In the top sentence, "they" refers to the pilots of the planes. In the bottom sentence, "they" refers to the planes themselves. While surface structure can be directly observed, **deep structure** depends upon knowledge of the language which has been stored in memory. Meaning is thus essentially a property of deep structure. The relationship between meaning and surface structure is called **semantics.** We now turn to the psychological study of semantics.

Semantic Memory: Is a Canary Hairy?

The problem in the study of semantic memory is to infer the deep structure which underlies our comprehension of surface structure. This makes for a rather interesting area in psychology, because it utilizes techniques and knowledge from three fields of inquiry: memory studies (in experimental psychology), linguistics (the study of language), and analysis of artificial intelligence (computer science). The concepts provided by linguistics have just been discussed. As for experimental psychology, the contribution here is the idea of a distinction between two kinds of long-term memory systems (Tulving, 1972). Specifically, *semantic memory* refers to our knowledge of conceptual relations about the world, while *episodic memory* is a more personal record of our individual experiences. Your knowledge that clouds contain water is part of semantic memory, while your knowledge that you got caught in a downpour yesterday is episodic. Amnesia, discussed earlier, temporarily erases episodic memory but usually not semantic memory. The kinds of experimental manipulations discussed in this chapter affect episodic memory. Semantic memory appears to be relatively immune to disruption by these kinds of manipulations. Thus, in some ways, semantic memory is more basic, although the two kinds of memories *must* be related, since all semantic memory is initially episodic information the first time it is learned.

It may seem strange that computer science can make an important contri-

FIGURE 5–11 Deep structure is not always apparent from surface structure. (By permission of John Hart and Field Enterprises, Inc.)

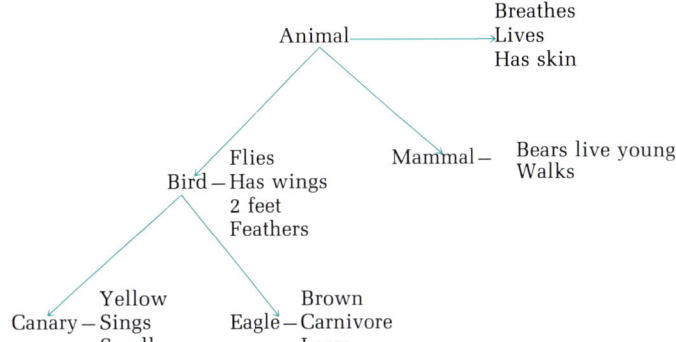

FIGURE 5-12 A semantic network linking canary to bird to animal. The properties listed immediately to the right of each word also apply to words lower down in the tree. (From Hunt and Poltrock, 1974.)

bution to the study of semantic memory, which at first seems unrelated to computers. Nonetheless, the actual impetus for the current flood of research about semantic memory came from a computer scientist, M. R. Quillian. He was interested in how to program a computer to understand a conversation (Quillian, 1969). This is a problem of obvious practical importance, but its theoretical implications also bear upon human semantic memory (see the Focus on Research box on page 181). Quillian decided to have his computer use a semantic network to represent the deep structure of memory (Figure 5-12). The "full meaning" of a word was the direct and indirect connections the word had with all other words linked with it in the semantic network. Clearly, the full meaning of a word can be very broad. For example, the word "bank" can mean either a place to keep money or the side of a river. Quillian's computer programs could correctly identify the particular meaning of a word such as "bank" based upon the context of a sentence by checking on the pathways joining bank to money and bank to river. However, these original programs were far too complex to be tested for psychological applications. Collins and Quillian (1969, 1972) therefore focused upon one particular portion of the network to create a psychological model which *could* be tested. They reasoned that semantic concepts would be stored in an hierarchical arrangement like that of Figure 5-12. The concept "Animal" is on a higher level than the subordinate concept "Bird." But Bird also has as its subordinates lower-level concepts such as canary, eagle, ostrich, etc. They further assumed that the various properties, such as "a bird has wings," would be stored only at the level which was most appropriate. Thus "has wings" would not be stored directly with "Animal" because many animals do not have wings. Furthermore, "has wings" would not be stored with canary, eagle, ostrich, etc. because it would be inefficient to repeatedly store "has wings" with every specific bird; storing "has wings" with the higher-level concept "Bird" would best account for all particular examples. To test their model, Collins and Quillian assumed that moving from one mode to another requires time, and that the greater the distance that has to be traveled, the more time will be required. Thus it was predicted that if you were asked "Is a canary yellow?" you should be able to answer this question faster than "Does a canary have skin?" This is, in fact, the case.

Psychologists were so impressed with this finding that for a while the area of semantic memory was a solution in search of a problem—that is, at first it seemed that Collins and Quillian had provided the entire answer. But soon alternatives to the network model were developed. We shall examine one alternative in detail to see how linguistic concepts can be incorporated into psychological models.

In contrast to network representations, a feature-list model (Smith, Shoben, and Rips, 1974) uses lists of sets of elements to describe concepts. This model assumes that the meaning of a word is a list of semantic features. In linguistics, there are two kinds of semantic features: **characteristic features** and **defining features** (Lakoff, 1972). Robins and chickens are technically birds because both

TABLE 5–3   How Hedges Modify Relationships Between Concepts

Hedge	Sentence	Kinds of Features	
		Defining	*Characteristic*
A true	A robin is a true bird	Yes	Yes
Technically speaking,	a chicken is a bird	Yes	No
Loosely speaking,	a bat is a bird	No	Yes

The use of linguistic hedges. As shown above, the sentence "A robin is a true bird" is linguistically acceptable, because robins possess both the defining *and* the characteristic features of birds. In contrast, the statement "A bat is a true bird" would not be linguistically acceptable, because bats lack important defining features possessed by birds. If the sentence were altered (hedged) to read "Loosely speaking, a bat is a bird," however, it would make greater linguistic sense. (Adapted from Smith et al., 1974.)

have the *defining* features of birds. But a chicken does not have the *characteristic* features of a bird, such as being able to fly. A bat is not a true bird because although it has the characteristic features of flying, it lacks the defining features of feathers. We cannot, therefore, say that "a bat is a bird." But we can *hedge* on the identification by saying, "*Loosely speaking,* a bat is a bird." Similarly, we can hedge on identifying "chicken" by saying, "*Technically speaking,* a chicken is a bird." To identify "robin" most satisfactorily, we can say, "A robin is a *true* bird." The terms "loosely speaking," "technically speaking," and "true" are called **linguistic hedges.** Their use is governed by the defining and characteristic features that they cover. Thus the sentence "A butterfly is a *true* bird" is not linguistically acceptable; the hedge here should be "loosely speaking." It would, of course, be linguistically unacceptable to use the latter term in another context: "*Loosely speaking,* a sparrow is a bird"; here, "true" is the best term (see Table 5–3).

To test the linguistic model of feature-listing of concepts, people were asked to rate how typical an instance (for example, a kind of bird) was within a category (Rips, Shoben, and Smith, 1973). Results supported the linguistic model, in that those instances that were rated as most typical could be described by the hedge "true" while those which were least typical went with "loosely speaking." Furthermore, by means of a statistical technique called multidimensional scaling, the semantic distance between any two concepts could be calculated (Figure 5–13). Reaction time to questions (e.g., "Is a lion a

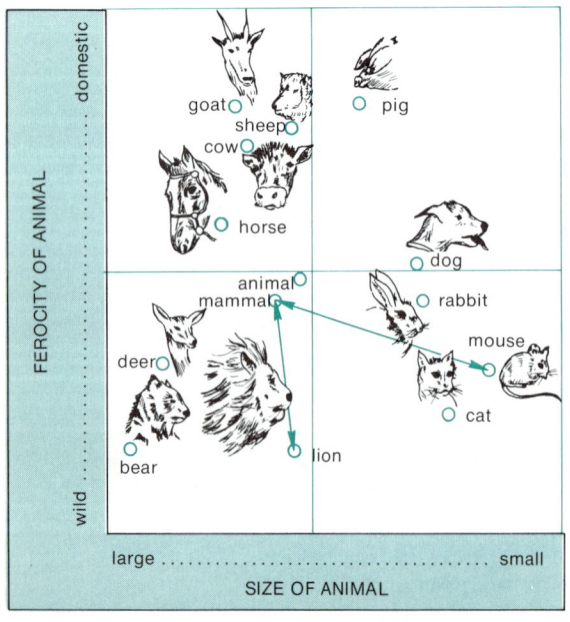

FIGURE 5–13   **A map of semantic memory. Semantic memory for these animal concepts can be arranged in two dimensions according to the size and ferocity of the animal. Notice that lion is closer to mammal than is mouse. Therefore, it should take you less time to agree that a lion is a mammal than to agree that a mouse is a mammal. (Adapted from Rips et al., 1973.)**

mammal?") depended upon the distance from one concept to another (e.g., in Figure 5–13, the distance between "lion" and "mammal"). This kind of set analysis has an advantage over the network representation used by Collins and Quillian (1972) because it takes into account the degree of category membership; a robin fits better into the category "bird" than does a bat. A more detailed comparison of these two kinds of semantic memory representation is beyond the scope of this book (see Smith et al., 1974).

The important point in this discussion is not which of these two models of semantic memory—the network representation or the feature-list representation—is better. Rather, it is that these models both illustrate how psychology can profitably adapt concepts borrowed from other disciplines. The network model is based upon a representation developed by computer scientists, and the feature-list model draws upon the linguistic concept of hedges. Reaching

---

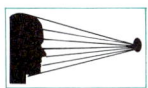

FOCUS ON RESEARCH: *Conversations with a Computer*

Can a machine think? While you probably have an opinion about this question, let us consider what a computer would have to do to convince us that it can think. Let us pretend that you are having a conversation with two people. One of these people is really a computer, and your job is to tell who is the computer and who is the real person. Since computers and people don't look very much alike, in order to make this a fair test you can communicate with the two "people" only by teletype (a special kind of typewriter that computers can understand); you type in a question, and the computer or person types back an answer. By the dictates of Turing's test, if you cannot identify the computer more than half the time, you will have to agree that computers can indeed think. What might we ask the computer? Well, you might try something like WHAT IS THE SQUARE ROOT OF 54,689,432? If you get the right answer typed back immediately, you probably are conversing with the computer. But as we shall see in the next chapter, computers can be programmed to hesitate and deliberately give you the wrong answer, just as a person would do. It may, therefore, be harder than you think to identify the computer. To get some idea of the current level of sophistication in getting computers to understand and respond to language, read the dialogue below between a patient seeking psychiatric help and a psychiatrist. The psychiatrist in this actual conversation is a computer. The patient's words appear in lower case and the computer's replies are in capitals.

Men are all alike.
IN WHAT WAY
They're always bugging us about something or other.
CAN YOU THINK OF A SPECIFIC EXAMPLE
Well my boyfriend made me come here.
YOUR BOYFRIEND MADE YOU COME HERE
He says I'm depressed much of the time.

I AM SORRY TO HEAR YOU ARE DEPRESSED
It's true. I am unhappy.
DO YOU THINK COMING HERE WILL HELP YOU NOT TO BE UNHAPPY
I need some help, that much seems certain.
WHAT WOULD IT MEAN TO YOU IF YOU GOT SOME HELP
Perhaps I could learn to get along with my mother.
TELL ME MORE ABOUT YOUR FAMILY
My mother takes care of me.
WHO ELSE IN YOUR FAMILY TAKES CARE OF YOU
My father.
YOUR FATHER
You are like my father in some ways.
WHAT RESEMBLANCE DO YOU SEE
You are not very aggressive but I think you don't want me to notice that.
WHAT MAKES YOU THINK I AM NOT VERY AGGRESSIVE
You don't argue with me.
WHY DO YOU THINK I DON'T ARGUE WITH YOU
You are afraid of me.
DOES IT PLEASE YOU TO BELIEVE I AM AFRAID OF YOU
My father is afraid of everybody.
WHAT ELSE COMES TO MIND WHEN YOU THINK OF YOUR FATHER
Bullies.
DOES THAT HAVE ANYTHING TO DO WITH THE FACT THAT YOUR BOYFRIEND MADE YOU COME HERE

The point of this demonstration (by Weizenbaum, 1968) is not that a computer can be programmed to be a competent psychiatrist; it is that a computer can carry on a reasonable conversation. If you read this conversation to some friends they probably would not guess that the psychiatrist is really a computer.

out to other related disciplines in this manner can only help psychologists in their attempts to gain an accurate and comprehensive understanding of human behavior.

Linguistic Relativity: Do Words Shape Thought?

We are used to thinking of language as an aid to communication and thought. Most ideas are ultimately conveyed through language and words. There is a story about an ancient Greek bandit named Procrustes who was infamous for his bed. After capturing a victim he would lay them out on his bed. If the victim was too short, Procrustes stretched him until he fit the bed; if the victim was too long, Procrustes lopped off his legs until he too fit the Procrustean bed. The linguist Benjamin Whorf (1956) has argued that language is a kind of Procrustean bed or straitjacket which molds the way we think. According to this view, concepts which do not fit easily into our language are difficult to think about.

Whorf supported his idea about **linguistic relativity,** as this view is known, by citing examples from other cultures. Eskimos have several words which precisely describe various kinds of snow and ice. Whorf argued that Eskimos were able to perceive these subtle differences because their language allowed and encouraged these distinctions. You and I have no urgent need to discriminate among different kinds of frozen water, so our vocabulary is limited to snow, ice, and perhaps slush. Adherents to the idea of linguistic relativity might state that Eskimos perceive snow better than we do because their language forces them to make subtle distinctions that go unnoticed in English.

The linguistic relativity hypothesis sounds attractive, and many anecdotal examples could be mentioned which support it. For example, Slobin (1971) notes that only one French word, conscience, is used to express two English words, conscience and consciousness. For French speakers, this may account for a greater conceptual confusion between the two terms than would arise with speakers of English. On the other hand, we can also come up with illustrations which appear to contradict the notion of linguistic relativity. Even though Eskimos have more one-word labels for different kinds of snow and ice than we do, it is still possible for us to communicate these distinctions, although we must use relatively cumbersome phrases to do so. Indeed, if we could not understand these distinctions it would have been impossible for Whorf to explain them in the first place. Linguists such as Noam Chomsky have argued that the linguistic relativity hypothesis places too much stress upon surface structure and not enough upon deep structure. Deep structures of different languages are presumably more similar than are the surface structures.

You can readily see that when we try to argue for or against the concept of linguistic relativity purely on linguistic grounds, there is no good way to settle the dispute. Psychologists have tried empirical tests by constructing experimental situations which could support one view or another. In order to test linguistic relativity, which is a vague concept, it is necessary to be more specific about Whorf's views than he was originally. One popular situation used by psychologists involves the naming of different colored disks or chips (Lenneberg, 1967). Heider and Olivier (1972) argued that Whorf would have predicted that the structure of colors in memory would follow the structure of colors in language. In order to test this idea, they had to find two different languages which had different structures for color naming. The Dani (a primitive tribe in New Guinea) name colors on the basis of brightness (that is, light or dark) rather than on the basis of hue. Using statistical techniques similar to those utilized to map out the semantic memory space (see Figure 5–13), Heider and Olivier showed that Dani tribe members and Americans had different structural spaces for *naming* colors, as was expected. However, when the structure for *memory* of colors, as opposed to that for names of colors, was mapped out, the differences were not carried over. Therefore, these results did not support linguistic relativity.

Summary

Most psychologists agree that there are three kinds of memory systems. A **sensory storage system** retains visual or auditory information for a very brief period of time, about half a second or less. This sensory storage operates without conscious effort on your part. In order to remember, information must be transferred to the next memory system, called **short-term memory.** Information can be recycled in short-term memory by **rehearsal.** Two explanations have been offered to explain forgetting in short-term memory. **Trace decay** theorists believe that information will fade away, and that rehearsal prevents memory traces from disappearing. **Interference** theorists believe that forgetting is due to the interaction between old and new bits of information as they get confused in memory. This interference can be either **retroactive or proactive.** Although information in sensory storage is maintained in the same modality as it is presented in, information in short-term memory is primarily coded on an auditory basis. While rehearsal is required to maintain information in short-term memory, information in **long-term** memory is always available. However, this does not mean that it can always be remembered, because it first must be located and retrieved. Only **accessible** information can be remembered. Information in long-term memory is organized on the basis of meaning.

Recall and **recognition** are two measures of retention. **Free recall** is greatly aided by **retrieval cues,** although it is possible to devise cues which hinder recall. Using a story to organize material is another way to improve recall. The **serial position curve** allows us to separate effects of short- and long-term memories. Most psychologists believe that recall and recognition are different mental processes. While recognition is usually better than recall, we can arrange for poorer recognition if the distractor items are similar to the memory items.

Your memory can be improved through the use of **mnemonic devices** and **imagery.** The **method of loci** is one effective mnemonic device. The **numeric pegword** system is related to the method of loci and is a more frequently used mnemonic. These two mnemonics work because they provide an effective retrieval scheme. Items which are easier to imagine visually are easier to remember.

Retrograde and **anterograde amnesias** are memory disabilities which relate to long- and short-term memory systems. While most of us have trouble remembering, a professional mnemonist can have difficulty forgetting.

Language is our primary means of communication. While linguists are interested in language *competence*, psychologists are concerned about language *performance*. The **surface structure** of language contains **phonemes, morphemes, phrases,** and **sentences.** However, meaning is conveyed by the **deep structure.** The relationship between meaning and surface structure is called **semantics.**

Psychological representations of **semantic memory** can be based either upon tree networks or upon lists of features. Both types of models have successfully predicted reaction times to questions like "Is a canary yellow?" and "Is a robin a bird?"

The linguistic idea that thought is shaped by language is called **linguistic relativity.** While there is anecdotal evidence both for and against linguistic relativity, firm empirical support for the suggestion is currently lacking.

Suggested Readings

Crowder, R. G.: *Principles of Learning and Memory.* Hillsdale, N.J.: Lawrence Erlbaum Associates, 1976.
> *An advanced text with a detailed treatment of current models of memory.*

Glucksburg, S., and Danks, J. H.: *Experimental Psycholinguistics: An Introduction.* Hillsdale, N.J.: Lawrence Erlbaum Associates, 1975.
> *An undergraduate text stressing the psychologist's approach to the study of language.*

Kavanagh, J. F., and Mattingly, I. G. (eds.): *Language by Ear and by Eye.* Cambridge, Mass.: MIT Press, 1972.
> *An advanced volume based upon a conference relating speech and learning to read.*

Klatzky, R. L.: *Human Memory.* San Francisco: W. H. Freeman, 1975.
> *An undergraduate text with a contemporary discussion of the latest topics in memory research and related areas.*

Melton, A. W., and Martin, E. (eds.): *Coding Processes in Human Memory.* Washington D.C.: V. H. Winston, 1972.
> *An advanced volume consisting of reports by prominent researchers on the latest views of human memory.*

Some journals that regularly publish articles on memory and language:
> *Journal of Experimental Psychology*
> *Cognitive Psychology*
> *Memory & Cognition*
> *Quarterly Journal of Experimental Psychology*
> *Journal of Verbal Learning and Verbal Behavior*

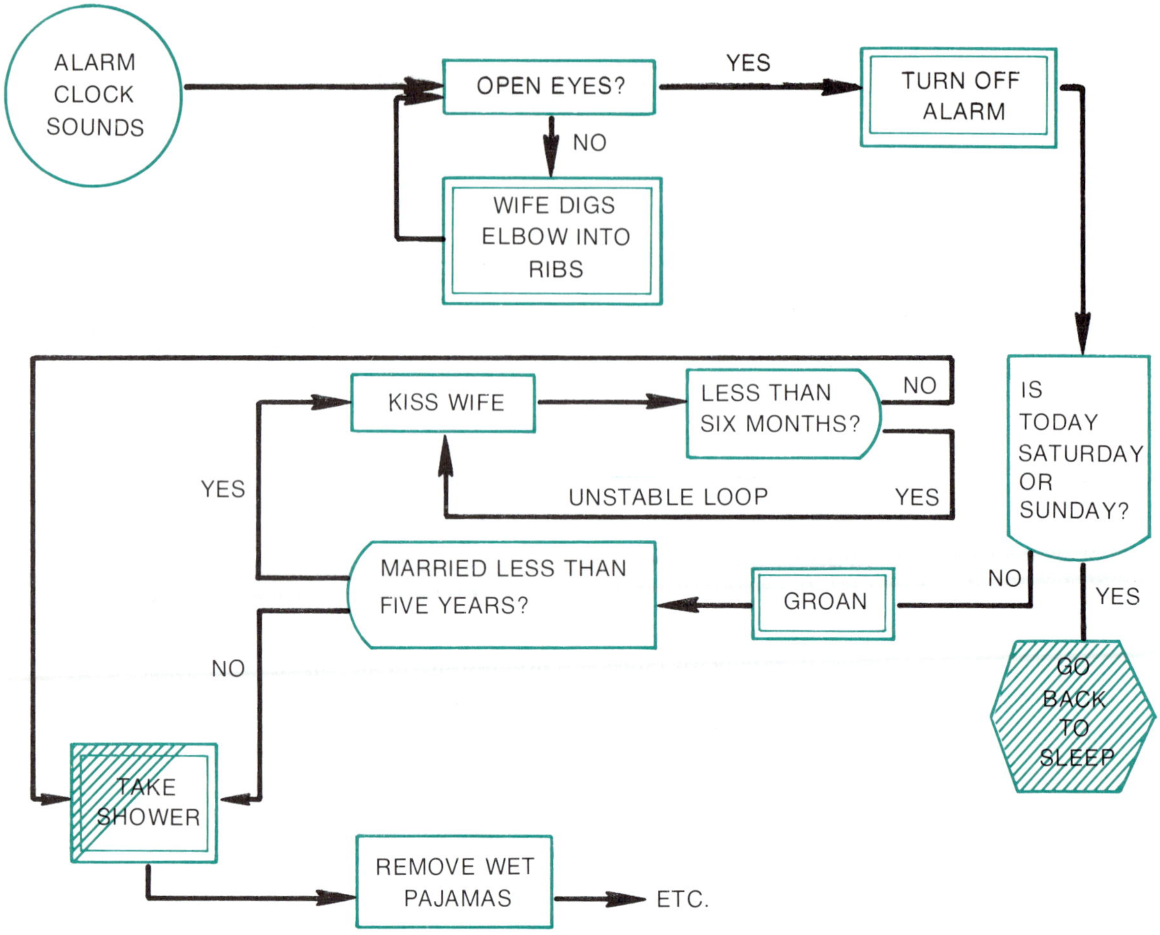

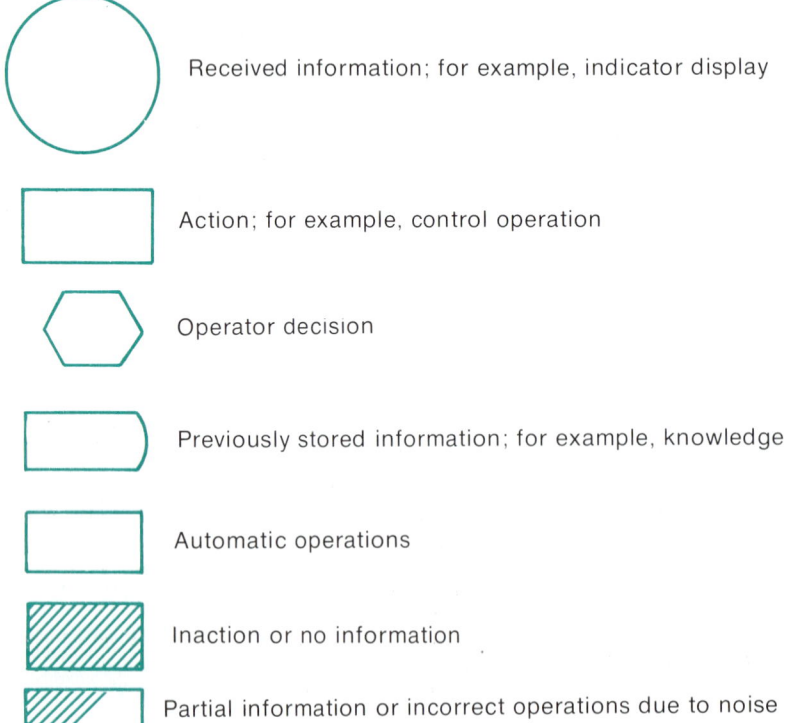

ALARM CLOCK SOUNDS → OPEN EYES? — YES → TURN OFF ALARM

OPEN EYES? — NO → WIFE DIGS ELBOW INTO RIBS

IS TODAY SATURDAY OR SUNDAY? — YES → GO BACK TO SLEEP

IS TODAY SATURDAY OR SUNDAY? — NO → GROAN → MARRIED LESS THAN FIVE YEARS?

MARRIED LESS THAN FIVE YEARS? — YES → KISS WIFE

MARRIED LESS THAN FIVE YEARS? — NO → TAKE SHOWER

KISS WIFE → LESS THAN SIX MONTHS? — NO

LESS THAN SIX MONTHS? — YES → UNSTABLE LOOP

TAKE SHOWER → REMOVE WET PAJAMAS → ETC.

○ Received information; for example, indicator display

▭ Action; for example, control operation

⬡ Operator decision

⬠ Previously stored information; for example, knowledge

▭ Automatic operations

▨ Inaction or no information

▨ Partial information or incorrect operations due to noise or error sources in the system

6

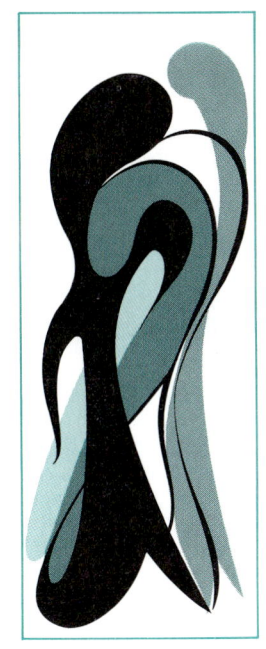

Human Information Processing:
Engineering Approaches to Mental Life

"Now, looky here folks. So you think you got problems. Why you ain't heard nothin' yet. This mornin' I found out that my wife's control works my half of the electric blanket—no wonder I froze my corns off all winter, 'cause I ain't married. Then I durn near scalded my tootsies trying to take a shower. Plus I sprained my wrist adjusting the water. Then I turned the wrong knob on my electric stove trying to heat up my fritters and set fire to my longjohns I set down on the front burner 'cause I couldn't find the pot holder. Then driving in to work I reached for the windshield wiper button and turned off my headlights and skidded into the ditch. Dadburn machines really got it in for me. Seems like all this new-fangled fancy gadgetry do a body more harm than good."

Seems like the old codger has a point. We all have been frustrated by pieces of machinery which have not been designed with humans in mind. Almost any device used by people, from a can-opener to the control panel of a nuclear power plant, could be improved by taking into account requirements of its human operator. But before we can improve a design, we must first discover the best way to present information to the operator. Psychologists studying human information processing are interested in why certain forms of information presentation work better than others. What the study of human information processing involves, then, is a theoretical analysis of how we abstract and utilize information.

Imagine that you are driving a car from home to school. Let's see what kinds of information processing might be required to perform this common-place task. You start the engine and automatically check the gauges, noticing

FIGURE 6–1 Although driving a car seems easy once you have had some practice, there are many elements in the task. The complicated scene on the left must be perceived and attention directed to the most important components, all while keeping the vehicle safely in motion.

that you are low on gas. This is an example of **pattern recognition.** Before pulling away from the curb you look in your rear-view mirror and see a truck approaching rapidly, so you wait for the truck to pass. This is an example of **decision making.** You are now tooling down the street at a comfortable 20 miles per hour when suddenly a ball rolls into the street in front of you. You slam on the brakes just before a child runs out into the street after it. This shows that your **reaction time** was fast enough for you to stop the car in time. Heaving a sigh of relief, you continue on your way when your **attention** is distracted by a loud horn from the car behind you. It's your mother driving a purple VW bus and waving a flowered lace hat out the window. Because you've been thinking about the VW bus you fail to notice a red light and drive through it without stopping. A police siren provides **feedback** reminding you of this lapse of attention. You pull over to the curb and simultaneously watch the VW bus zoom past you—an example of **time-sharing,** or doing two things at the same time. The policeman approaches you, ticket book in hand, and you soon will have a chance at **problem solving.** "I can give you a warning or a ticket," says the policeman, leaving you with some **uncertainty.** "But since you just ran over a bottle and now have a flat tire, I'll only give you a warning this time." This **information** removes your uncertainty. As you try to jack up your car to change the tire, you notice that the jack must be pulled sideways to lift the car—a gap in **stimulus-response compatibility.** Cursing, you angrily kick at the jack, which collapses. Your foot is now under the jack, which is wedged under the car—an example of a simple **hierarchical structure.** As you wait for a tow truck to extricate you, you promise yourself never again to use a psychology textbook to wedge the front wheel when jacking up a car.

This example gives you some of the flavor of the human information processing approach to behavior. We try to divide a stream of complex behavior—such as driving a car—into smaller processes, such as pattern recognition, decision making, and so on. If we can discover how each of these small pieces of the puzzle works, then we can put together the *entire* puzzle. This can be done because the pieces or processes are really not all that small. Indeed, this is what makes the information processing approach different from more traditional S-R (stimulus-response) learning theories: the basic unit of information processing is larger. Later on we shall identify some of the shortcomings of S-R models, and how these are successfully surmounted in an information processing approach.

In this chapter, all of the processes that were set in dark type in the car-driving example will be discussed. But first we must examine some of the new techniques used to study human information processing. Most of these have been borrowed or adapted from engineering. Some of these borrowed techniques, such as flow charts, have been very successful when applied to human behavior. Other models have not. Psychology has a long history of drawing analogies from findings in other sciences. Freud's model of the mind (see Chapter 9) was borrowed from the fluid mechanics of his day, with the ego being a kind of valve controlling the force of the id. A more current model likens the mind to a telephone switching system. The very latest psychological models borrow from computer technology. Since models sometimes reflect fads, they must be used with caution. A model is not a complete theory but only a description based upon a plausible analogy. In this chapter, every time you see the word "model," mentally substitute the term "analogy." While there are many models of human information processing, there is no theory. Perhaps, in the near future, the knowledge gained from using models will permit a general theory to be formulated. Right now we are still getting good mileage from our current models.

In this section we will consider four techniques that are widely used to study information processing. The **flow chart** is a series of boxes representing sequential operations. **Feedback** is a basic property of the **control** model borrowed from engineering. **Information** is a technical method of quantifying decisions based upon different numbers of alternatives; the method was derived from a model of telephone switching circuits. The concept of an **hierarchical structure** is drawn from computer science and lets us represent fairly complicated sequences of events. This section will conclude with a comparison of S-R and information processing approaches to behavior.

BASIC CONCEPTS: TOOLS FOR STUDYING INFORMATION PROCESSING

If you have ever taken a course in computer science, you already have a more detailed understanding of flow charts than will be covered here. A flow chart is a way of representing a set of events or operations which occur in some specified order. When this order is fixed, as in counting from one to ten, the flow chart is quite simple (see Figure 6-2). In counting from one to ten, each subsequent event is completely determined by the preceding event. Most of the time, life is not that simple. We must allow for different possibilities and different orders of possible events. A flow chart which has this capability is called a **branching flow chart**. Let's look at such a branching flow chart for getting up in the morning (see Figure 6-3). The sequence starts with an alarm clock going off. The sleeping man, more formally called the operator, can either open his eyes or not. If he does, the flow chart goes on to the next step—turning off the alarm. If he keeps his eyes closed, his wife automatically takes appropriate action to open his eyes. The path between the boxes labeled OPEN EYES? and WIFE DIGS ELBOW INTO RIBS is called a **loop**. Once the alarm clock is off, the operator must use his knowledge of the world to decide what day it is. If it's the weekend, he goes back to sleep. If it's a weekday, he automatically groans and then goes on to the next box in the flow chart. Eventually (un-

Flow Charts: Where Has My Black Box Gone?

$$\boxed{1} \rightarrow \boxed{2} \rightarrow \boxed{3} \rightarrow \boxed{4} \rightarrow \boxed{5} \rightarrow \boxed{6} \rightarrow \boxed{7} \rightarrow \boxed{7} \rightarrow \boxed{8} \rightarrow \boxed{9} \rightarrow \boxed{10}$$

FIGURE 6-2 A simple flow chart for counting from one to ten. The arrows indicate the direction or path of information flow.

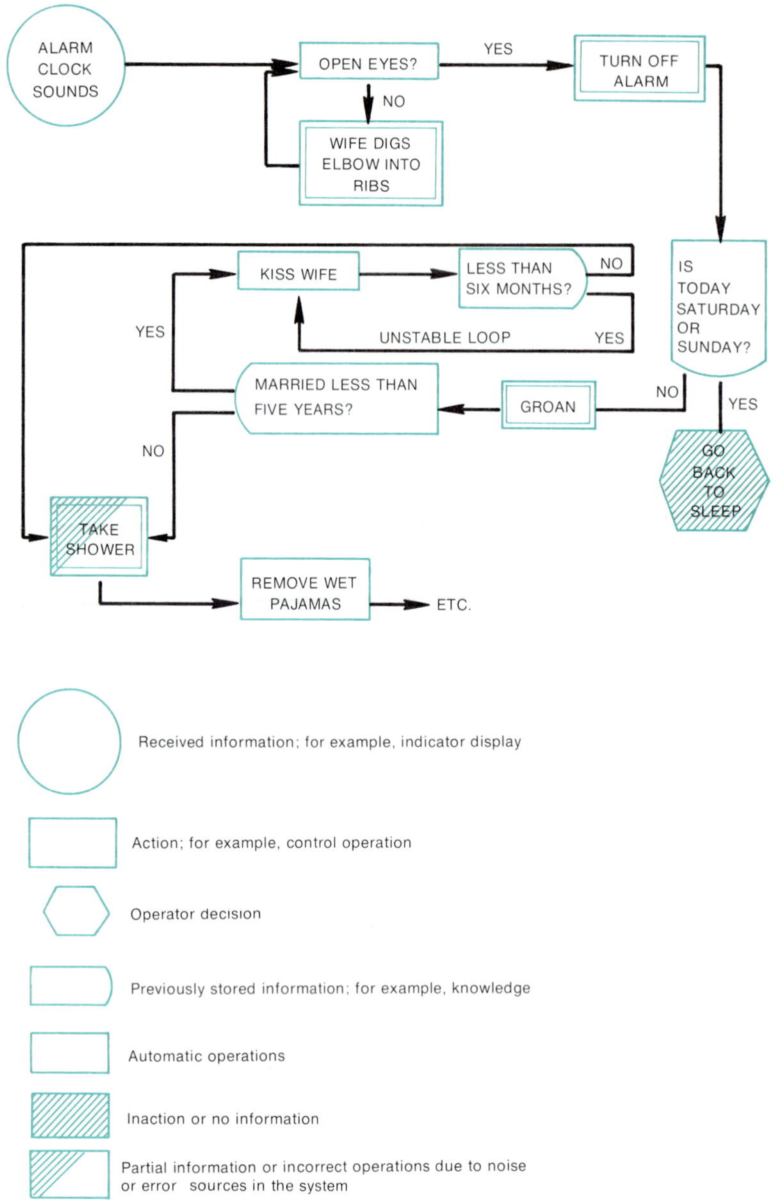

FIGURE 6-3 A flow chart for getting up in the morning. Processing stages are coded by shape and shading.

less he's been married less than six months, in which case good taste prevents any detailed flow-charting of his activities) he sleepily takes a shower, still wearing his pajamas, and then corrects this partial error by removing his wet pajamas. This example illustrates the two key features of a flow chart. First, it specifies a set of available pathways, not all of which are necessarily taken. Thus, in Figure 6-3, the pathway to GO BACK TO SLEEP is not taken during the week. Second, the different kinds of boxes represent different kinds of possible activity. In Figure 6-3, activities are coded by the shape and shading of the boxes.

Several flow charts will be used throughout this chapter. Although some of them may look complicated at first, they really are no harder to understand than Figure 6-3.

Feedback is defined as a flow of information (or energy) counter to the main flow. This sounds somewhat abstract, so let's take a few easy examples to start with:

(1)   You have been dating a member of the opposite sex for some weeks now and have decided that your relationship should proceed to greater intimacies. You try to convince your partner of this by such romantic devices as saying "I love you." The main information flow is from you to your partner. Feedback is the flow of information from your partner to you, and can be conveyed by facial expressions, body posture, verbalizations, and so forth. This feedback leads you to modify your own behavior. For example, if statements of eternal love don't appear to be working, you might try something more drastic, such as suggesting marriage.

(2)   One of the earliest known mechanical examples of a feedback device is the flyball governor of a steam engine invented by James Watt in 1788. This is illustrated in Figure 6–4. As the shaft of the engine spins faster, centrifugal force causes the two balls to fly outward. This closes a valve which decreases the steam supply, slowing the rotation of the shaft and causing the balls to descend. This opens the valve which supplies more steam which speeds the shaft which raises the balls which closes the valve which cuts off the steam which slows the shaft which lowers the balls. . . .

(3)   There are many examples of predator-prey feedback systems in ecology. A decrease in the population of lynxes (bobcats) is soon followed by an increase in the population of rabbits. This creates more food for the lynxes, and their population soon expands. This decreases the population of rabbits, and, soon after, the population of lynxes also decreases. (And so on.)

(4)   Your home thermostat is our final example of a feedback system. You set it for 68° F to conserve fuel. As long as room temperature is above 68° F, nothing happens. When the temperature drops below this setting, your furnace goes on. Gradually, room temperature rises, and eventually the thermostat turns off the furnace. In this system, the main flow is from your furnace to the room. Feedback, from the room to the furnace, is provided via the thermostat, which monitors room temperature and controls the furnace.

All of these feedback systems can be represented by a flow chart such as shown in Figure 6–5. Let's go through this flow chart using our thermostat example. The *process* being controlled is the operation of your furnace. The *output* of this process is hot air; indeed, this is the output of many processes we might think of. A portion of this output is fed back to the **comparator.** This

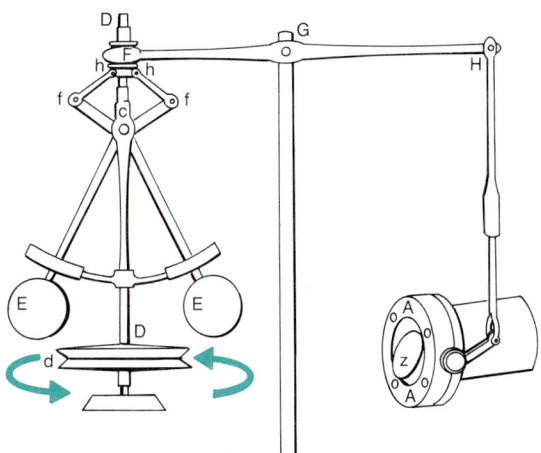

FIGURE 6–4   The flyball governor for a steam engine. The motion of the balls controls the speed of the engine.

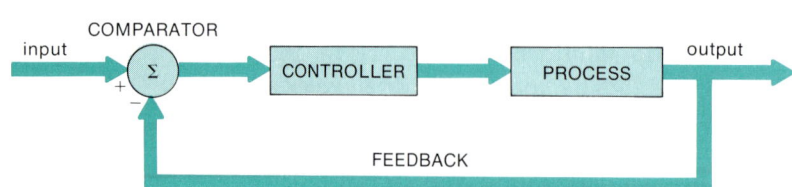

COMPARATOR

input

CONTROLLER

PROCESS

output

FEEDBACK

FIGURE 6-5 A feedback control system. The comparator adds up the algebraic sum of the input signal and the feedback signal. If the two signals are equal, their algebraic sum is zero, and no signal is sent to the controller. If the signals are unequal, a correction is sent to the controller, which then alters the process until the proper relationship between input and feedback is obtained.

is the part of your thermostat which compares room temperature to the 68° F setting you dialed in. If the *input*, or dial setting, equals the temperature of the room indicated by the feedback, the comparator does nothing. If the feedback temperature is too low, the comparator sends a signal telling the **controller,** another part of your thermostat, to turn on the process (the furnace). If the feedback temperature is too high, the controller turns off the process.

This kind of feedback system is called a *closed-loop* control system. There is a continuous path from any element of the system, around the loop, and back to the element. If the feedback loop is broken, we have an *open-loop* control system. This can be illustrated by imagining that the strip which monitors temperature inside your thermostat has fallen off. Your furnace will still go on, but its operation, while controlling room temperature, will no longer be influenced by room temperature. Thus it is likely that your room will soon become too hot or too cold, and that you will quickly call a thermostat repairman. In general, open-loop control systems are not nearly as effective as closed-loop systems.

Information: Guessing a Card's Suit is a Two-Bit Game

We live in a probabilistic universe where even weather reports are not absolute. Information theory is a mathematical tool that helps us quantify the uncertainty of our world. The unit of information or uncertainty is the **bit.** This is exactly the information present in the toss of a fair coin. The terms **information** and **uncertainty,** although mathematically equal, are used in different senses. Before I flip a coin I have one bit of uncertainty about the outcome. Once I flip the coin and observe if it is heads or tails (H or T), I have gained one bit of information. If I had two coins and four possible outcomes (HH, HT, TH, and TT), I would have two bits of information once the coins were thrown. If I had three coins and eight possible outcomes (HHH, HHT, HTH, HTT, THH, THT, TTH, TTT), there would be three bits of uncertainty until the coins were tossed. Each time I *double* the number of possible outcomes, I add *one* bit of uncertainty. This relationship is shown in Table 6–1.

TABLE 6–1

Number of Alternatives	Information in Bits
1	0
2	1
4	2
8	3
16	4
32	5
64	6
128	7

The amount of information present for different numbers of alternatives. (The table assumes that all the alternatives occur with equal frequency.)

PSYCHOLOGY IN ACTION: *Getting the Bit in Your Teeth*

Most of us have played the game "Twenty Questions," in which one gets twenty chances to identify an animal, vegetable, or mineral by asking questions which can only be answered by Yes or No. Information theory tells us how many questions are needed if we ask them in the best possible way. Draw a checker board with eight rows and eight columns. Give a copy to a friend, who has to put an X in one of the 64 squares. Your job is to locate the square with the X by asking only questions which can be answered Yes or No. According to Table 6-1, 64 alternatives correspond to 6 bits of information. Therefore you should be able to locate the square with the X by asking no more than 6 questions. Can you do it? (See Figure 6-6 for answer.)

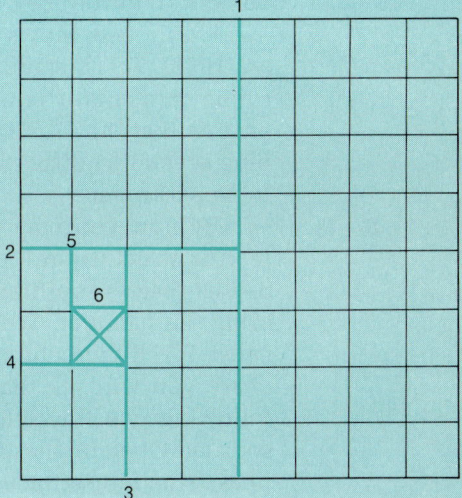

FIGURE 6-6 How to locate an X in a checkerboard in six questions. The secret is to ask questions that divide the board in half. Thus, line 1 is drawn and you ask, "Is the X to the left of line 1?" Then the remaining space is divided in half again by line 2. This process continues until line 6, which divides the two remaining squares in half. You might try this with the X in a different square.

There's a children's rhyme that starts out "for want of a nail a shoe was lost, for want of a shoe a horse was lost, . . . for want of a battle a war was lost." This rhyme is a very simple hierarchical structure with the nail on the lowest level and the loss of the kingdom on the highest. If we drew a diagram of this hierarchical structure it would be a vertical line. The typical hierarchical structure is arranged as a pyramid, with a broad base building up to a narrow peak. A common example would be the organizational chart of a large business. The president of the company is at the peak of the pyramid, vice-presidents are under him, general managers are under them, and so on down to the level of individual plant foremen and the workers they supervise.

Much of behavior can be represented by hierarchical structures. Let's look at a simple example: hammering a nail. The two basic operations in hammering are diagrammed as a hierarchy in Figure 6-7. However, the diagram

Hierarchical Structure: For Want of a Nail

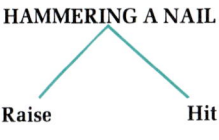

FIGURE 6-7 A two-level hierarchical structure for hammering a nail.

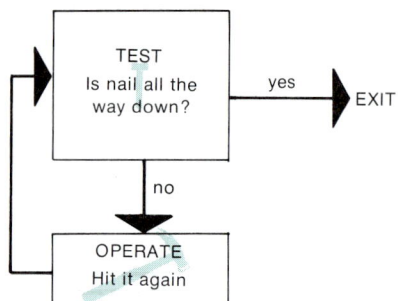

FIGURE 6-8   A TOTE unit for hammering a nail. The first Test checks if the nail is flush. If not, the Operate phase orders another stroke of the hammer. The results of this operation are fed back and another Test is performed. This process continues until the Test is satisfied. Then the Exit is taken. (Adapted from Miller, Galanter and Pribram, 1960.)

is not a complete description of hammering—it does not tell us when to stop hammering the nail. Knowing when to stop involves feedback. While such feedback could be flow-charted as in Figure 6-5, we shall find it more convenient to introduce a new kind of flow chart at this point.

Figure 6-8 shows a form of feedback loop called a **TOTE unit** (Miller et al., 1960). TOTE stands for Test, Operate, Test, Exit. The Test phase is similar to the comparator in the standard feedback loop flow chart. The major difference is that the TOTE unit provides an explicit Exit which allows us to combine several feedback loops in succession. The Exit leads to the next behavior to be performed.

By now you may be wondering what happened to the hierarchical hammering structure in Figure 6-7. It has temporarily disappeared because Figure 6-7 has been simplified and does not show any details, such as raising and lowering the hammer. We can remedy this by providing a slightly more complicated TOTE flow chart in Figure 6-9. As you trace your way through this flow chart, you will see that the first Test (Is nail all the way down?) controls the following two lower level Test phases. These two Test phases plus their associated Operate phases (Raise hammer and hit nail) make up the total Operate phase (the largest rectangle in Figure 6-9) of the high-level Test phase which controls the entire hammering sequence. While we will not pursue this stacking of TOTE units any further, it should be realized that a TOTE hierarchy can be made as complicated as one might wish. For example, all of Figure 6-9 could be one part of a larger superset of other TOTE units.

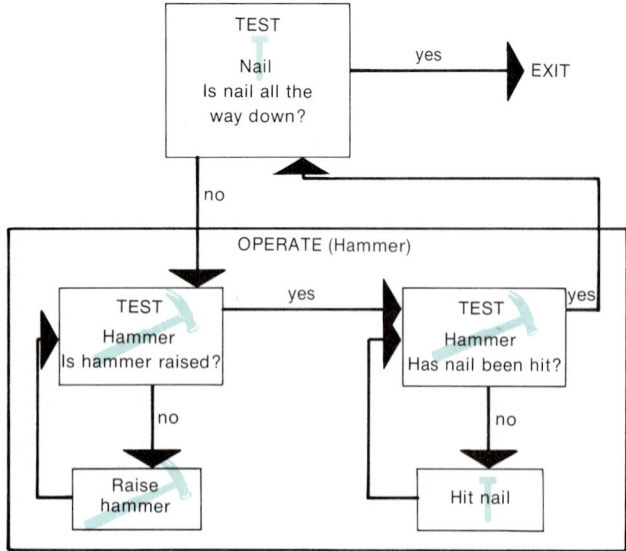

FIGURE 6-9   An hierarchical combination of TOTE units. The Operate phase of Figure 6-8 has been broken down into two smaller TOTE units. (Adapted from Miller, Galanter and Pribram, 1960.)

Until recently much of experimental psychology was dominated by traditional learning theory. This approach centers on the conditioning, both classical and instrumental, of specific responses to specific stimuli (Hull, 1943). While this stimulus-response (S-R) approach has been criticized as being too mechanistic—the brain is viewed as a kind of telephone switchboard (e.g., Tolman, 1948)—many psychologists accepted this switchboard analogy in the past and some continue to do so even today. This is essentially a passive view of human beings; men and women are seen as creatures subject to the whims of the environment: in comes a stimulus and out pops a response. In recent times, many psychologists have objected strenuously to this passive view of mankind and lower animals.

Within experimental psychology the passive S-R view of man is on its way out. In terms of the feedback model, this S-R view would be termed *open loop*. There is now much evidence to suggest that the human operates in a *closed loop*, using feedback to alter behavior (Annett, 1969). It is becoming increasingly clear that humans exhibit adaptive behavior designed to get them towards some desired goal. Behavior is **purposive,** or goal-directed. This does not mean that the principles of reinforcement and conditioning do not work. However, it implies that they are of value more as a *description*, rather than an explanation, of behavior, and that a larger framework is needed—one in which reinforcement plays an important part, but not the only part. Since the time of Watson, strict behaviorists (see Chapter 7) have objected to purposive explanations because they sound too mentalistic (as in "the cat opened the door of the puzzle box because it wanted to get outside"). But the advent of modern computers has made *purpose* again a respectable concept in psychology. Machines have been built which exhibit purposive behavior. Grey Walter designed a mechanical tortoise which would follow a painted line. Claude Shannon built a mechanical mouse which would learn its way through a maze to reach a goal: the electrical equivalent of a piece of cheese. These kinds of purposive machines, or **automata,** would have amazed a Watsonian behaviorist. It is embarrassing to accuse a machine of behavior that is too mentalistic. Thus if purposive behavior is philosophically acceptable as a description of automata, we cannot reject goal-directed behavior of humans on the grounds of excessive mentalism.

Another difficulty with the traditional conditioning model as the basic unit of behavior lies in the assumption that a particular stimulus will tend to evoke the same particular response time after time. Information theory denies this by stating that what is truly important is not the *particular* stimulus which is present but rather the *set* of possible external stimuli which might be present (Broadbent, 1958). As we shall see later in the chapter, if I measure your reaction time to a yellow light when no other lights can be flashed, you will respond very rapidly. If I were to include green, red, blue, and orange lights as other possibilities and *then* flash the yellow light, it would take you much longer to respond. The stimulus—a yellow light—would be unchanged in both situations, yet the behavior would be different.

Many other arguments have been made against traditional S-R psychology (e.g., Broadbent, 1958; Miller, Galanter and Pribram, 1960; Annett, 1969). The basic objections may be said to center on the hyphen connecting stimulus and response. To understand human behavior we must discover what lies inside this mysterious hyphen. It is no longer accurate to believe that a response is preordained by a stimulus. Indeed, modern S-R theorists are well aware of this point (Capaldi, 1977). As we shall see in this chapter, the human is capable of coming up with a wide variety of strategies and options in responding to stimuli. Earlier beliefs in the reflex as the crucial unit of human behavior

Comparing Information Processing and S-R Approaches to Behavior: The Black Box Versus the Hyphen

resulted largely from studying very restricted situations which eliminated these options. Strapping a human into a chair to study classical conditioning of the eyelid when puffs of nitrogen are blown into the cornea does not *prove* that a human works the same way as Pavlov's dogs—no matter whether the data so obtained resemble the data from the dogs. It may only show that experimental situations can be restricted to such a point that data relating to humans cannot be distinguished from data on dogs.

ATTENTION AND REACTION TIME: CHRONOMETRIC ANALYSIS OF MENTAL LIFE

Much of modern research in human information processing can be characterized by a strong concern for the time needed to complete different mental operations. An analysis of behavior in terms of time is called a **chronometric analysis** (Posner and Mitchell, 1967). Since mental operations occur so quickly, the second is too large a unit of time for most chronometric analyses. Therefore, the second is divided into one thousand parts, or milliseconds (a time of 400 milliseconds equals 0.4 seconds).

Reaction time—the time between the onset of a signal and a subsequent response—is, of course a *dependent* variable. The study of this variable, with the aim of understanding reaction time itself (Pachella, 1974), has become a sub-area of work in human information processing. We will first examine, though, some basic *independent* variables that control reaction time in relatively uncomplicated situations. Then we will use chronometric analysis to help us understand more complicated mental processes, such as attention.

Reaction Time: Faster Than a Speeding Stimulus

Scientists have been concerned with reaction time ever since the eighteenth century, when the Royal Astronomer at the Greenwich Observatory fired his assistant, an unfortunate observer named Kinnebrook, because he didn't like Kinnebrook's reaction time. In those days the heavens were observed by noting the time at which a particular star crossed one of several parallel wires visible in the eyepiece of the telescope. The observer listened to a clock ticking out seconds and was expected to be able to record the crossing to within 100 milliseconds. Kinnebrook was from half a second to 800 milliseconds slower than his boss, and after getting several warnings, he was fired. This would have been the end of the story except that an astronomer named Bessel realized that Kinnebrook's case was the rule, rather than the exception, and that no two astronomers agreed exactly on observation times. Other scientists concurred with Bessel, and their individual differences in reaction time were indicated in each man or woman's *personal equation*. The result was that eighteenth-century astronomers could be found clustered about their telescopes busily comparing personal equations with each other.

It was not long before behavioral scientists realized that some interesting psychological principles were behind the astronomers' personal equations. In 1868, the Dutch physiologist Donders categorized different types of reaction time situations in hopes of specifying the time required for various mental operations. His data were disregarded for almost a century, until information theory made reaction time once again popular. Psychologists soon discovered that the amount of information, while an important independent variable, is not the only way to change reaction time. The relationship between the stimulus and response, called **S-R compatibility,** also alters reaction time. Moreover, the subject's *strategy* or decision about the relative importance of being fast versus being accurate also influences reaction time. Each of these topics will now be covered in turn.

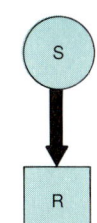

FIGURE 6–10   The Donders *a*-reaction time situation (simple reaction time). A stimulus light goes on and you respond by pressing a button. The circle represents the stimulus (S) and the square the response button (R).

Donders (1868) developed three related reaction time situations that are illustrated in Figures 6–10 to 6–12. The first situation, termed an a-reaction by Donders, and now more commonly called **simple reaction time,** has but a single stimulus and a single response. A light goes on (stimulus), and you must press a button (response). A real-life example of simple reaction time occurs when you are following another car closely: its brake lights go on and you respond by stepping on your brake pedal. Donders thought that this time was an estimate of routine mental processes and conduction time within the system. As such, the Donders a-reaction provided a baseline from which the more complicated kinds of mental times could be estimated.

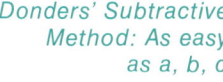 *Donders' Subtractive Method: As easy as a, b, c*

Donders' b-reaction, shown in Figure 6–11, is now called **choice reaction time,** because there is more than one stimulus and response: the subject cannot simply push a button but is forced to *choose* among a set of possible responses. Donders believed that his b-reaction measured the mental operations of *identification* and *selection.* If one is to choose a response, the stimulus must first be *identified* as one of a set of possible stimuli, and then the response corresponding to that stimulus must be *selected.* A real-life example would be the red and green lights of a traffic signal. If the light is red, the selected response is stepping on the brake pedal. If the light is green, the response is to press the accelerator pedal.

Donders' **c-reaction time** (which is still called a c-reaction) is shown in Figure 6–12. In this situation, there are many stimuli, but only one of them calls for a response. Donders identified his c-reaction with the mental operation of identification alone—since only one response is called for, there is no need for any selection process. A tangible example of a c-reaction situation is when you are waiting in line for your number to be called in a take-out restaurant. If you respond to an earlier number, you run the risk of getting someone else's dinner, or worse. If you respond too late, your dinner will be cold. You should respond only to the number that corresponds to your own order.

The actual times required for identification and selection were estimated by Donders in his *subtractive method.* Donders estimated the times required for mental operations by subtracting one reaction time from another. We can use the method as follows: c-reaction time measures identification time plus assorted nerve conduction times; since simple reaction time estimates these neural conduction times, subtracting simple reaction time out leaves a pure

FIGURE 6–11   The Donders *b*-reaction time situation (choice reaction time). There are now two stimuli (S₁ and S₂), each with its own response (R₁ or R₂). Since you do not know which of the two lights will come on, you must be prepared to make either of the two responses.

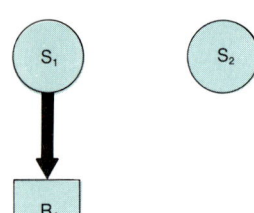

FIGURE 6–12   The Donders *c*-reaction time situation. Only one stimulus (S_1) calls for a response. If the S_2 light goes on, the observer must be careful *not* to press R_1. Reaction time in this situation is greater than for simple reaction time situations.

estimate of the time required for the mental process of identification. Therefore, c-reaction time minus simple reaction time equals mental identification time. Similarly, if c-reaction time is subtracted from choice reaction time, the result measures the mental process of selection (see Figure 6–13).

Donders' subtractive method was harshly criticized by the introspectionists (see Chapter 1) of his day. They argued that a b-reaction is not a c-reaction *plus* some other mental event. Instead, they believed that a c-reaction is qualitatively different, and that the subtractive technique mixed apples and oranges. On the basis of introspective evidence, Donders' contemporaries believed that a-, b-, and c-reactions all feel different and are separate and distinct mental events rather than combinations of related mental events. We know that in this case, as in others, introspection was not always a good technique. Donders' subtractive method is once again used, although certain cautions need be observed to guarantee that apples and oranges are not being mixed (Pachella, 1974). The basic logic of the subtractive method has led to other, more powerful techniques (Sternberg, 1969; Taylor, 1976) which owe an historical debt to Donders.

Hick's Law: Reaction Time Meets Information

As was predicted by Donders, reaction time is longer for a choice reaction situation than for a simple reaction time task; Donders obtained values of about 200 milliseconds for the a-reaction and 285 milliseconds for the b-reaction. What happens when the number of alternatives is increased beyond two? While intuition tells us that reaction time should increase as the number of alternatives get larger, the exact form of this relationship is quite interesting. As is shown in Figure 6–14, reaction time is a linear function of the amount of information in a set of alternatives (Briggs, 1974). **Hick's law**, named after the psychologist who discovered this linear relationship between reaction time and amount of information (Hick, 1952), has been repeatedly validated and is applicable when the amount of information is manipulated in different ways (Hyman, 1953).

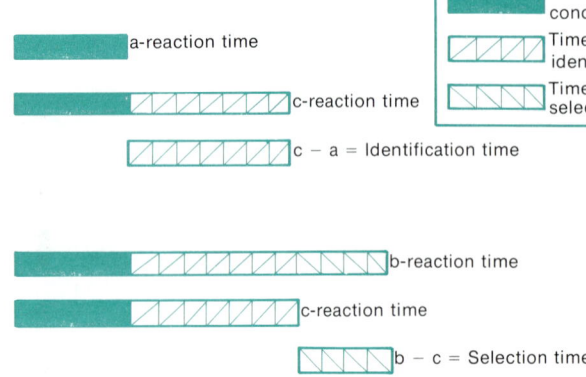

FIGURE 6–13 Donders' subtractive logic. Subtracting *a*-reaction time from *c*-reaction time (top panel) gives an estimate of mental identification time. Subtracting *c*-reaction time from *b*-reaction time gives an estimate of mental selection (bottom panel). The three different shadings show the proportion of reaction time allotted to each mental process.

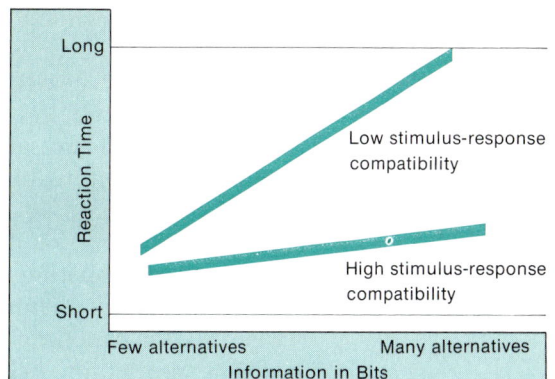

FIGURE 6-14 The Hick's function for two levels of stimulus-response compatibility. The high compatibility relationship is flatter, indicating that increases in the number of alternatives have a smaller effect on high compatability relationships.

While there is still some controversy about interpreting the theoretical meaning of the Hick linear function (Welford, 1968; Teichner and Krebs, 1974), we do know that one way to change the slope (or tilt) of the line is to vary **S-R compatibility.** Stimulus-response compatibility refers to the "naturalness" of the relation between a stimulus and a response and is another learned property of behavior. In the United States, the compatible relationship between light switches and lamps calls for throwing the switch up to turn on a lamp and down to turn it off. This seems completely appropriate to you because you have done it so often. But if you lived in Great Britain, the reverse relationship would hold: switches are generally thrown down to turn on lamps. As Figure 6-14 shows, adding more information or more alternatives has less of an effect upon reaction time when S-R relationships are compatible (the slope is flatter). An example of a highly compatible relationship is provided in such a task as verbally naming a letter or digit displayed on a screen. A less compatible relationship would require pressing one of ten keys which correspond to the digits one through ten. An incompatible relationship would be encountered in such a task as pressing a key which is a mirror image (i.e., the reverse) of a stimulus light above it (see Figure 6-15). You may think it is obvious that incompatible relationships should be avoided if we wish to optimize perform-

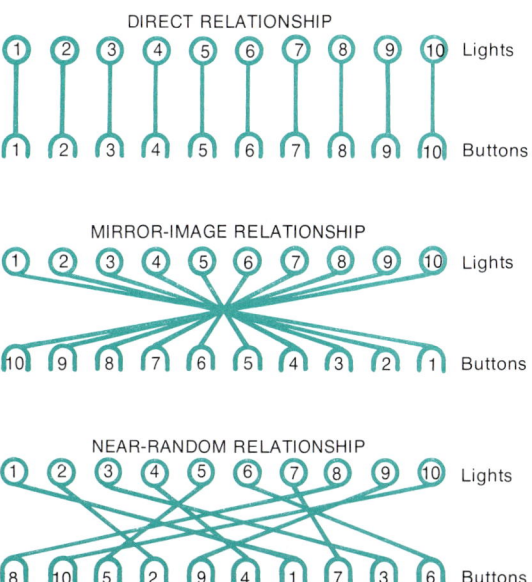

FIGURE 6-15 Three levels of stimulus-response compatibility. Circles indicate stimulus lights; response buttons are shown beneath them. The direct relationship is most compatible, and the near-random relationship is least compatible. Reaction time is fastest in the top panel and slowest in the bottom.

ance. However, a nuclear power plant near Chicago was built as the mirror image of its precursor plant, with the same people being required to operate both plants. This negative transfer (see Chapter 5) from the first plant to the second makes the latter incompatible once a person is trained to operate the original plant. (If the same person never had to operate in both plants, there would be no compatibility problem, since compatibility is learned and *not* innate.) Needless to say, this "innovation" in power plant design was never repeated.

While incompatible relationships can be learned, it may require a great amount of practice before they are handled as efficiently as compatible relationships. An experiment conducted by Morin and Grant (1955) shows how feedback information helps performance under conditions of low S-R compatibility. Subjects were required to press buttons in response to rows of lights such as shown in Figure 6–15. An extra row of lights was placed above the stimulus lights as feedback: whenever a key was pressed, the corresponding feedback light flashed on. After several days of practice, subjects were asked to show that they had learned the incompatible light and key relationships by drawing a diagram showing which keys controlled which lights. All subjects were able to do this. Then Morin and Grant disconnected the feedback lights. Although subjects knew the incompatible relationships, their speed of performance dropped off sharply. Since the subjects no longer had feedback lights, it was necessary for them to monitor their own responses more carefully. This causes reaction times to increase. Thus incompatible relationships impose extra feedback monitoring requirements, which decrease overall efficiency.

Speed-Accuracy Trade-off: The Hand That's Quicker than the Eye May often Err as Time Flies by

Have you ever been compelled to do something, like typing a term paper at 4 A.M., faster than you would prefer? If so, you probably achieved speed at an expense of accuracy. It is extremely difficult to be both fast and accurate at the same time. In studies of reaction time, this tendency to achieve either speed or accuracy at the expense of the other is termed the *speed-accuracy trade-off*. The existence of this factor makes it clear that reaction times by themselves cannot tell the whole story. Two different experimental conditions may result in equal reaction times, which at first would lead to a conclusion that these two apparently different conditions are actually equivalent. However, unless they also produce equal error rates, this conclusion would be premature. In fact, there are even speed-accuracy trade-offs in which trials marked by errors take longer than correct trials (Thomas, 1974); obviously this issue is rather complicated. The main point to remember is that reaction time is only one side of the coin, and any interpretation of reaction time should also take errors into account.

Attention: Doing Two Things at Once

All of us can do more than one thing at the same time. However, if we look closely at such dual-task situations, we often find that although two tasks can be performed together, the price is a decrease in the efficiency of one or both of the two component tasks (see Figure 6–16). Sometimes one's ability to perform two tasks simultaneously is taken as an indication of intelligence (see Chapter 14) or general mental acuity. For example, the statement, often attributed to former President Lyndon Johnson, that Jerry Ford can't walk and chew gum at the same time was intended as a disparaging remark.

Psychologists working in the area of human information processing who view the human as a complicated system are very interested in how people manage to divide their attention to do more than one thing at the same time. While this interest originally stemmed from very practical issues, such as the

FIGURE 6–16   It is difficult to pay attention to two tasks at the same time. This is especially true when one of the tasks demands great concentration. (© King Features Syndicate, Inc., 1975.)

problems faced by air-traffic controllers who must monitor several planes at the same time (see Figure 6–17), some controversies over basic theoretical concerns have since emerged (Broadbent, 1971).

Controversy aside, divided attention situations have a considerable appeal to experimenters because they involve the overloading of the human's information processing capabilities with no danger of permanent adverse effects. Engineers have long known that studying systems by overloading them tells us a great deal about their normal functioning. Thus metals are placed in huge presses until the materials ultimately fail under the pressure. Of course, a gentler method of overload is necessary when we wish to study people. Psychologists have used two general methods for inducing overload: (1) presenting a stream of stimuli and requiring responses at a rate which exceeds the human's normal capabilities, and (2) requiring the simultaneous performance of two different tasks. We shall now look at some typical findings from both techniques to see what implications they have for understanding human attention.

The Psychological Refractory Period: Watch Out for That First Signal

Overloading can be produced by presenting two stimuli in rapid succession so that the second stimulus occurs before the system has completed processing the first stimulus. The standard dependent variable in this situation is reaction time, although error rates can also be taken as a dependent

FIGURE 6–17   The air traffic controller must monitor several planes at the same time. Each dot on the screen in the foreground represents a different airplane for which the controller is responsible. This task is so strenuous that the Federal Aviation Agency has established a special early-retirement plan for air traffic controllers. (Photo Trends.)

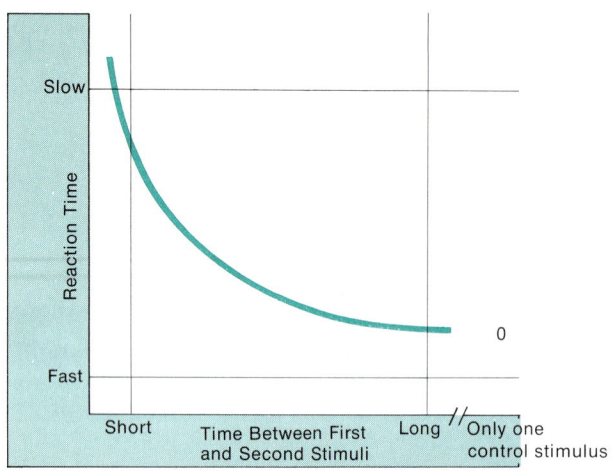

FIGURE 6–18 The psychological refractory period effect. As two stimuli are moved closer together in time, reaction time to the second stimulus increases. As the stimuli become farther apart, reaction time decreases to the same level as for presentation of only one stimulus.

variable (Knight and Kantowitz, 1974). In a control condition, only the *second* stimulus is presented and the reaction time measured. This control point is shown at the far right of Figure 6–18. This point represents system performance in a normal situation—one with no overload. Then the first stimulus is added. What happens to reaction time to the second stimulus? This depends upon the time interval separating the two stimuli. If the stimuli are very far apart (say, one second apart), reaction time is the same as for the control condition. But as the stimuli are moved closer together in time, reaction time to the second stimulus increases as shown in Figure 6–18. This delay of reaction time has been termed the **psychological refractory period** by analogy to the refractory period of a single neuron (see Chapter 2). Immediately after a neuron is stimulated, it turns off for a brief period—the refractory period—and will not be sensitive to additional stimulation. The earliest explanation offered for the *psychological* refractory period assumed a similar "shut-down," except that the entire central processing mechanism was thought to turn off (not just a single neuron).

For many reasons, this early explanation was eventually discarded (see Kantowitz, 1974). While the refractory period of a single neuron is very short, the psychological refractory period lasts for hundreds of milliseconds. (One thousand milliseconds equal one second.) Even more importantly, this explanation predicts that the first response should not be delayed, since the refractory period *follows*—not precedes—the first stimulus. However, as we know, reaction time to the first stimulus *is* delayed (Herman and Kantowitz, 1970), and thus this early model of attention must be rejected.

Many models of attention have been formulated to replace the faulty neurological analogy regarding the psychological refractory period. (The name "psychological refractory period" is still used to label the effect, even though the explanation it implies is no longer used.) The most influential of these has been the **limited-capacity channel** model (Broadbent, 1958; 1971). At the risk of oversimplification, this model can be viewed as comparing the human's central processor (the hyphen in S-R psychology) to a pipeline of fixed capacity. Just as a pipeline can carry only a certain amount of gallons per minute, so too can your mental pipeline, or channel, carry only a certain amount of information per second. This is the *channel capacity* and is measured in bits per second. Whenever a task requires more information handling than the channel capacity can provide, performance is slower and/or less accurate. As expressed in this model, the psychological refractory period occurs when two stimuli are put so close together that the total information load exceeds available channel capacity. There are still some technical problems associated with this explanation, but the newer models which have been introduced to solve these difficulties are beyond the scope of this chapter (see Kantowitz, 1974, for details).

Dichotic Listening: In one ear and in the other

Although the study of attention was a viable concept in the psychology of William James, such study suffered a sharp decline in popularity for much of this century and has only recently re-emerged into the limelight. This renewed interest in attention developed after World War II with work that centered on the attentional requirements of listening. In particular, psychologists wanted to know how a listener selects one particular message from an array of several messages. Imagine you are at a party which is very crowded and very loud. As you first enter the room, all you hear is a babble in which individual words and sentences are hard to identify. But when you are talking to a particular individual, you can hear that person's sentences clearly despite the loud background noise.

Since it is difficult to study attention at a party, psychologists devised a laboratory task which they believed contained the essential elements of the auditory stimulation you might receive at a party. This was the **dichotic listening** task, in which two separate messages are presented, one to each ear. (Dichotic listening differs from stereophonic listening, in which the messages in each are not independent.) Listeners were asked to pay attention to the message in one ear, usually by requiring them to repeat the message aloud, and their knowledge of the message presented to the unattended ear was also tested. This task is illustrated in Figure 6–19.

At first, results showed that repeating one message prevented people from hearing the message in the other ear. Early models of attention accounted for this (Broadbent, 1958) by proposing that a "filter" inside the head could be tuned to one ear or the other. This hypothetical (imaginary) filter was assumed to eliminate the message which was not repeated. But later experiments found that under certain conditions the filter "leaked," and thus certain important aspects of the unattended message were perceived and remembered. For example, if your name appeared in the unattended ear, you would hear it at least some of the time. Attempts to resolve this difficulty by conceiving of a filter that would rapidly switch back and forth between both ears were unsatisfactory. In time, two different models of attention were devised to account for this kind of data.

The model most directly related to filter theory (Treisman, 1969) argues that the filter is really an attenuator—a device which weakens signals as they

FIGURE 6–19   The dichotic listening task. The listener is required to repeat the words presented to the right ear. A common mistake would have the listener saying "Mice eat cheese" even though the word "eat" was presented to the left ear.

pass through it. In this model, the unattended message is assumed to be weakened but not completely eliminated. Thus if the unattended message is sufficiently important, it can get through, because its importance makes up for any attenuation. This type of attenuation model is called an *early-selection* model, because, as with Broadbent's filter model, the selection process is thought to operate directly upon an internal representation of the stimulus. If we think of a chain of internal processing stages which replaces the hyphen of S-R psychology, the attention link in this chain can be regarded (in early-selection theory) as operating closer to the stimulus than to the response. The important characteristic of early-selection models of attention is the idea that not all information present in the stimulus makes contact with memory. Instead, unattended aspects of the message are assumed to get dropped by the wayside early in the processing chain.

The early-selection models compete with *late-selection* models (Norman, 1968). A late-selection model states that all stimulus information makes contact with memory. This model easily explains retention of unattended information on the grounds that all information, attended and unattended, gets the same initial processing. However, repeating one message aloud, as in Figure 6–19, can *interfere* with retention of the other message. Thus, in the late-selection model, interference is believed to weaken the unattended message and cause a post-memory deficit; because interference does not affect the message that is repeated aloud, performance on the attended ear is better.

It is too early to say with certainty which of these two views of attention is correct. Perhaps they will be combined into a more general model of attention which contains early- and late-selection aspects. The key point to remember is that the dichotic listening task shows that attention is limited. We cannot pay attention to all the features of our environment.

Time Sharing: Pat Your Head and Rub Your Stomach

Most of us routinely do more than one task at the same time. Right now you may be reading this book and listening to the radio or watching television. Does listening to the radio help or hurt your ability to understand the sentences and concepts of this textbook?

There is no simple yes or no answer to this question, although most psychologists concerned with information processing would doubt that your understanding is enhanced by the simultaneous performance of another task, such as watching television. Nevertheless, we cannot unequivocally state that watching television will impair your understanding. Think of driving a car and simultaneously having a conversation with a passenger next to you in the front seat. (Naturally, you wouldn't turn around to converse with passengers in the back seat.) As long as the flow of traffic is smooth and predictable, the driver has little difficulty in maintaining a meaningful discussion. But as soon as extra demands are made upon the driver's attention—for example, by merging lanes of traffic or by the presence of a police speed trap ahead, the driver can no longer talk and follow the thread of the conversation. As soon as the extra demand is over, conversation can again be resumed. You can check this for yourself the next time you are a passenger by noticing that the pauses in the driver's conversation tend to coincide with times when extra attention must be paid to traffic.

The limited capacity model of attention that we have previously discussed offers a simple explanation for this finding. As long as the combined information processing requirements of driving and talking do not exceed available channel capacity, the driver can satisfactorily do both. As soon as driving demands extra capacity, so that driving and talking together now require more capacity than is available, the secondary task (talking) is performed more slowly and less accurately; indeed the conversation may temporarily cease altogether.

While the limited capacity model of attention has certainly been the most influential model since its inception by Broadbent (1958), more recent data have caused many psychologists to view it as only the first approximation (Kantowitz, 1974). The basic prediction of the limited channel model is that as one or both tasks in a time-sharing situation are made more difficult, performance will become less accurate and slower, because the channel can no longer handle the greater task demands.

Sometimes, however, we find situations in which task difficulty can be increased without paying the price demanded by the limited capacity model. For example, Allport, Antonis, and Reynolds (1972) asked people to sight-read piano music while repeating aloud words in a dichotic listening task (see Figure 6–15). Making one task (piano playing or dichotic listening) harder did not make it more difficult to do the two tasks together. This finding clearly violates predictions drawn from the limited channel model, unless one assumes that the combination of sight reading and dichotic listening did not reach the limit of available channel capacity. However, Allport et al. were able to demonstrate that this possibility was rather unlikely, since difficult as well as easy piano playing and dichotic listening tasks were utilized. Similar findings were obtained by Kantowitz and Knight (1974), who had people simultaneously name digits and tap back and forth between two targets. Some psychologists feel that these data argue for several independent channels which all operate at the same time. Others prefer to assume a variable capacity allocation, in which the amount of total channel capacity is not fixed but increases as the situation becomes more demanding (Kahneman, 1973). While it is too early to state which viewpoint will gain wide acceptance, psychologists agree that the limited capacity model marks the start of an interesting problem and not the solution.

The preceding examples of attention focused upon instances in which doing two things at once was desired. The **Stroop effect** is observed in situations in which people cannot help doing two things when only one is necessary. In fact, doing the second thing hurts one's ability to perform the required task. Before continuing, follow the instructions on Color Plates 8–A and 8–B. Which task is more difficult?

The Stroop Effect: Trying to Ignore Irrelevant Information

You probably found the task on Color Plate 8–B considerably more difficult. Naming the color of the ink is easy when the color name and the word are both the same, as in Color Plate 8–A. But naming the color is very hard when the word spells a different or *competing* color name. This effect was first discovered by Stroop (1935) and is still widely studied today (Dyer, 1973). Although the name spelled by the word is irrelevant when you are asked to name the color of the ink, you cannot help reading the name. Even large amounts of practice do not lead to improvement in ignoring the name (Jensen, 1965), although special tricks like trying to "de-focus" your eyes so the letters become blurred will help. Why is it so hard to ignore the name spelled by the letters in Color Plate 8–B?

Two general explanations have been proposed, and these roughly correspond to the early- and late-selection views of attention previously discussed. A perceptual (early-selection) view suggests that we are unable to ignore all aspects of the stimulus, and that interference between stimulus dimensions is the cause of the Stroop effect. A response conflict argument (similar to late-selection models) admits that the irrelevant aspect of the stimulus is encoded but claims that such encoding by itself does not cause interference. It is only later, when the encoded aspects (color of ink and name of word) get linked with some response, that interference emerges.

One way of examining these two explanations would be to change the responses associated with the stimuli. If interference is perceptual, then the Stroop effect should remain. If response processes are causing the difficulty, the Stroop effect should then vanish. Egeth, Blecker, and Kamlet (1969) asked people to respond SAME or DIFFERENT to stimuli like those in Color Plates 8–A and 8–B. If the name and the color of the ink were identical (Color Plate 8–A), the correct response was SAME. If they differed (Color Plate 8–B), a response of DIFFERENT was correct. In this situation, the Stroop effect disappeared—that is, the time to respond was the same for both kinds of stimuli. But when new stimuli, which spelled out SAME or DIFFERENT instead of a color name, were used, the Stroop effect returned. Thus a response conflict explanation was supported and a perceptual explanation rejected.

We can now admit that the illustrations in Color Plate 8–A are not the usual control condition for the Stroop effect. Most experiments have the words printed in a neutral color, such as black. Technically, the Stroop effect refers to a delay in responding to stimuli like those of Color Plate 8–B compared with neutral control stimuli. When stimuli which have the same color ink and name are used (Color Plate 8–A), responding is even faster than the usual neutral control condition (Hintzman et al., 1972). This is an example of summating response tendencies, which speed up, or facilitate, responding.

Ideally, response models will explain both delay due to competing responses and facilitation due to summating responses. For now, we will note that response conflict models have been successfully applied to other instances of response delay, such as in the psychological refractory period (Kantowitz, 1974). That is, delays in responding to both first and second signals are due to response competition. While it is too early to reach a final consensus, it seems likely that many attentional effects can be localized at response stages of information processing. Thus we can successfully attend to many sources of incoming stimulus information. However, as these diverse inputs are linked to responses, a bottleneck is created. Attentional deficits are primarily associated with inability to emit responses rather than inability to encode stimuli.

COMPUTER SIMULATION OF HUMAN BEHAVIOR: CAN A MACHINE THINK?

We have already noted that psychologists are always on the alert for good analogies that can be drawn from findings in other disciplines. The computer revolution, which has been called the second industrial revolution, offers a ready source for such analogies. Psychological models based upon computer principles are very popular, and much of the jargon of the computer scientist has appeared in journals of psychology; indeed, we have already encountered such items as search, buffer, storage, input, output, and flow chart. Students often carry the analogy a bit too far and mistakenly conclude that psychologists view humans as computers. On the contrary, those psychologists using the technique of computer simulation are *least* likely to commit the error of believing that people are just like computers. For these psychologists, the power of the computer lies not so much in suggesting analogies with computer mechanisms but instead in the computer's ability to perform many calculations quickly and accurately.

A computer does not simulate human behavior unless some **program** is operating inside the computer. It is this program and not the machine itself which really is the model of behavior. The computer is only a convenience that allows the effects of the program to be determined far more rapidly than if the psychologist had to use pencil and paper to follow the actions of the program. Thus when we speak of computer simulation—using a computer to mimic the flow of information within the human—this is merely a "shorthand" reference to writing a computer program to copy information processes occurring inside your head. A computer program is a very precise way of stating a theoretical model. The program specifies exactly what happens to the flow of information under all sets of circumstances. If the psychologist has neglected to anticipate some particular circumstance, the program will not operate, and an error message will be received. Therefore the mere fact that a computer simulation program successfully operates ensures that the model or theory represented by the program is at least internally consistent. The model itself may not be correct, since this depends upon comparison with data, but its different components or sub-programs do work together harmoniously, an important feature which purely verbal models often lack. A psychological model expressed only in words can often be unintentionally ambiguous—so much so that two psychologists may disagree on the actual predictions made in a verbal model (see Chapter 9 on personality theories). This undesirable situation is considerably less likely to arise with a computer (or a mathematical) model of behavior.

Computer simulation is a technique that can be applied to any content area within psychology. In practice, computer simulation has not often been used to model the kinds of reaction time and attentional situations discussed earlier in this chapter. Instead, computer simulation has been associated with more cognitive or mental operations, such as chess playing and problem solving. Tasks such as driving a car have a *real-time requirement* (Hunt and Poltrock, 1974), in that decisions must be made rapidly. Over the years, computer simulations of behavior have tended to avoid situations with real-time requirements, although such content areas as semantic memory, in which speed of decision is important (see Chapter 5), may inspire more simulations of real-time processes. This section will emphasize more leisurely types of information processing, as has been the custom of most psychologists working with this technique.

The reader may wonder why the term information processing is applied to models which stress mental "equipment" or "hardware" (limited capacity channels, filters, attenuators, and the like) and also to models which emphasize different patterns of symbolic manipulation and information flow with little regard to hardware analogies. This multiple usage has created some confusion within psychology. But in the end both approaches must converge, since a knowledge of hardware mechanisms and control processes is required to predict behavior. Advocates of the hardware approach (covered in the preceding section) have in common with advocates of the symbolic manipulation approach their study of the human *as a system* and their objections to the limitations of traditional S-R psychology.

At this point you may be wondering why psychologists bother with computer simulation at all, since it is easier to use a live human subject than to write a complicated computer program. If both the simulation and the human produce the same data, why not just use the human? The answer to this question goes back to the basic problem of explanation in psychology. While data are important, understanding the processes that generate the data are the real reason for doing experiments in the first place. The simulation helps us to understand these processes, since the computer prints out what it did, or tried to do, at every step. The human is not nearly so transparent and often cannot tell us why or how a task was accomplished. If we can get a computer simulation to mimic the data of a human doing the same task, we obtain important clues that help us understand underlying processes in humans.

Problem Solving: You Can Get From Here To There

The term **problem solving** has often been used in psychology to cover a broad area containing a wide variety of information processing stages ranging from retrieval of information to symbolic manipulation and even to creating works of art (Reitman, 1965). For many, the terms "problem solving" and "thinking" convey identical meanings. This breadth is acceptable when using terms in a non-technical, conversational sense. But a scientific term must be precisely defined to be of value. Hence we will adopt a much more limited definition of problem solving in this chapter. Problem solving for our purposes is defined as a **search** process aimed at getting from some initial state to some desired final state by finding some pathway linking the two states. This definition is purposely abstract, but a concrete example may help you understand how the definition works. Look at the maze in Figure 6–20. To get from START to FINISH you must solve a problem. The initial state is the location of the START position plus the information you get from viewing the maze. In many problems, the psychologist's task is simplified (at the expense of the problem solver) by removing this additional information. A rat in a maze lacks your aerial view. Similarly, humans have been asked to solve mazes formed by garden hedges (Figure 6–21) that block any simultaneous view of the entire maze once the person is inside it. The final state is the position labeled FINISH. The problem is to get from here to there. You can solve the maze problem in one or two general ways, using either an **algorithmic** or **heuristic** approach.

Algorithms and Heuristics: Searching for Solutions

An *algorithm* is a search process (or, more generally, a set of operations or rules) which guarantees finding a successful solution if such a solution exists. A *heuristic* is a kind of "best guess" and does not guarantee that a solution will be found. This seems to imply that an intelligent problem solver will always try to use algorithms in preference to heuristics. Although this strategy appears more efficient at first, we shall soon see why heuristics are often the better choice.

An algorithm depends upon an exhaustive search of all the pathways or possibilities contained in a problem. Do you remember your chemistry lab problem of determining the contents of some "unknown" solution? By following the plan in your chemistry book and performing tests for different elements in a specified order, you eventually determined the composition of the unknown. This plan or search technique is an example of an algorithm, since all possibilities were systematically evaluated. Another example would be locat-

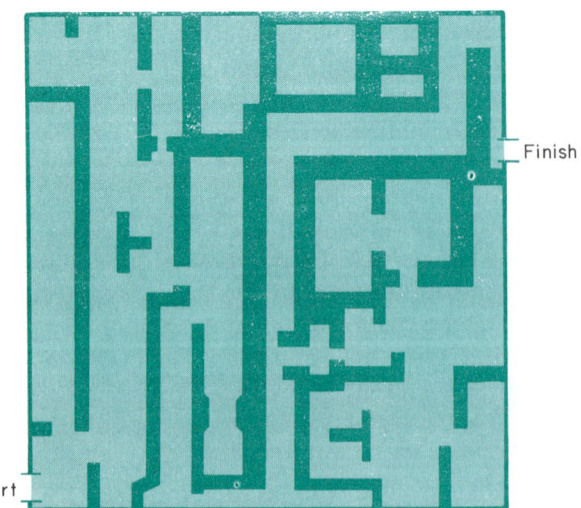

Start

Finish

FIGURE 6–20   Can you solve this maze? How many times did you retrace your steps?

FIGURE 6-21   A garden hedge maze. How long do you think it would take you to find your way out of this maze if you were inside it? (L'Agenzia Nazionale Stampa Associata.)

ing an X in a checker board, as discussed earlier in this chapter. A heuristic solution, on the other hand, might be to guess what your unknown is and then perform the tests for that unknown — say, iron. If your guess is correct and your unknown really is iron, you have saved a great amount of time by not performing all the tests required by the algorithm. But if your guess is wrong, you have flunked that particular chemistry problem.

Let's return to the maze in Figure 6-20 for a more psychologically oriented example of algorithmic and heuristic approaches to problem solving. You probably solved the maze by **trial and error** — that is, if an attempted solution led to a dead end, you backed up and tried again. Trial and error is a very simple heuristic technique, but even so it is not the same as completely random guessing. Each failure gave you some additional information which helped you solve the maze. Your trial and error was selective searching (Simon, 1969) because you didn't have to start from scratch with each successive attempt.

How could we use an algorithmic approach to solve the maze? First, we notice that at each choice point inside the maze there are only a very limited number of ways to go; many mazes have only two choices of direction: left and right. So we could make a list of choice points, starting with the first, with each alternative listed. We then systematically go through all the possibilities. For example, we might first try right turns at every choice point. If this doesn't work, we could then try all left turns. If this still doesn't work, we could try left turns followed by right turns and so on until all the possibilities have been exhausted. Sooner or later (probably later), we will eventually come up with the pathway that correctly solves the maze. Although this algorithmic method guarantees success, it seems like a dumb way to go about solving the maze. Most of us would believe that we could solve the maze much faster by trial and error. People are usually willing to use a heuristic and take a chance on not being able to solve a problem.

There is, however, a more important set of reasons for using heuristics. First, we may not know any algorithm capable of solving a problem. Second, an algorithm may take such a long time that its use is completely impractical. One such algorithm is called the British Museum algorithm. The problem is to type all the books in the British Museum. The algorithmic solution is to get several monkeys typing randomly. Eventually, the monkeys would type everything that has ever been written, provided an unlimited number of generations of monkeys could be assigned to the task. A more efficient algorithm to solve this problem would be to replace the monkeys by secretaries. However, even this algorithm might not be as fast as the heuristic of going to the library to obtain copies of all the books contained in the British Museum. Of course, this heuristic might not work, since the library might not have all the books. Nonetheless, the heuristic approach is clearly preferable. Indeed, heuristics are the basis of most human problem solving and are therefore the basis of computer models of problem solving as well.

An essential and obvious component of the search process is the ability to recognize when the search has been satisfactorily concluded. A problem is called *well defined* when such a test of recognition is available (Miller et al., 1960). If you have ever been called upon to meet a stranger without a prearranged recognition signal (wear a red carnation), you know that the recognition problem, although obvious, is not always trivial. The test phase of a TOTE unit may fail because we are unable to recognize the solution. A problem might be getting high grades in a psychology test on Monday and a physics test on Tuesday. The solution of studying instead of dating or going to the football game on Saturday may not be recognized as a solution.

This recognition difficulty is particularly apparent in the *two-string problem*, studied by Maier (1930). The problem is to tie two strings, each of which is hung from the ceiling, together. The challenge is that the strings are far enough apart so that they cannot be grasped simultaneously. Scattered about the room are various miscellaneous objects, including a pair of pliers. The solution is to tie the pliers to one string, to form a pendulum. Swinging the pliers allows one to grasp both strings at the same time. The pliers are not usually recognized as a part of a pendulum, and it takes direct hints from the experimenter before the problem is solved by most people. This difficulty is called **functional fixedness;** people *fix* upon the pliers as having the *function* of a tool and not the function of a pendulum weight. Functional fixedness is one kind of recognition difficulty which depends upon prior experience. Another example involves getting a ping-pong ball out of a tube which is blocked at both ends. A variety of tools is provided but none of them can reach the ping-pong ball. The solution is to pour water into the tube to float out the ball. Groups of people who are given the water in a dirty, old bucket solve this problem faster than do groups given the water in an elegant pitcher along with drinking cups and napkins.

The General Problem Solver: A Theory of Human Problem Solving

One of the most successful computer programs, both in its ability to solve problems and in its usefulness as a model of human problem solving, is the General Problem Solver, or GPS (Newell and Simon, 1972). In order to discuss the heuristics used by the GPS to solve problems, we shall start with a well-known brain teaser called the missionary and cannibals problem. There are three missionaries and three cannibals who want to cross a river. There is a boat which can carry only two persons. The boat and the six persons are the *objects* of the problem. If ever there are more cannibals than missionaries on one bank of the river—even for an instant—the missionaries will be eaten. How can we plan a sequence of boat trips to get all six people across the river without losing any missionaries?

As you start to think about this problem, you immediately realize that the start and finish are well-defined. We start with six people here and finish with the six people there. Furthermore, we can describe the *differences* between the start and finish—in this case a difference in physical location. So we must find some *means* to reduce and eventually eliminate this difference in order to solve the problem. This means will be a series of *operations*, in this case putting people into the boat and moving them across the river in certain sequences, that will lead us to the end of the problem (see Figure 6–22).

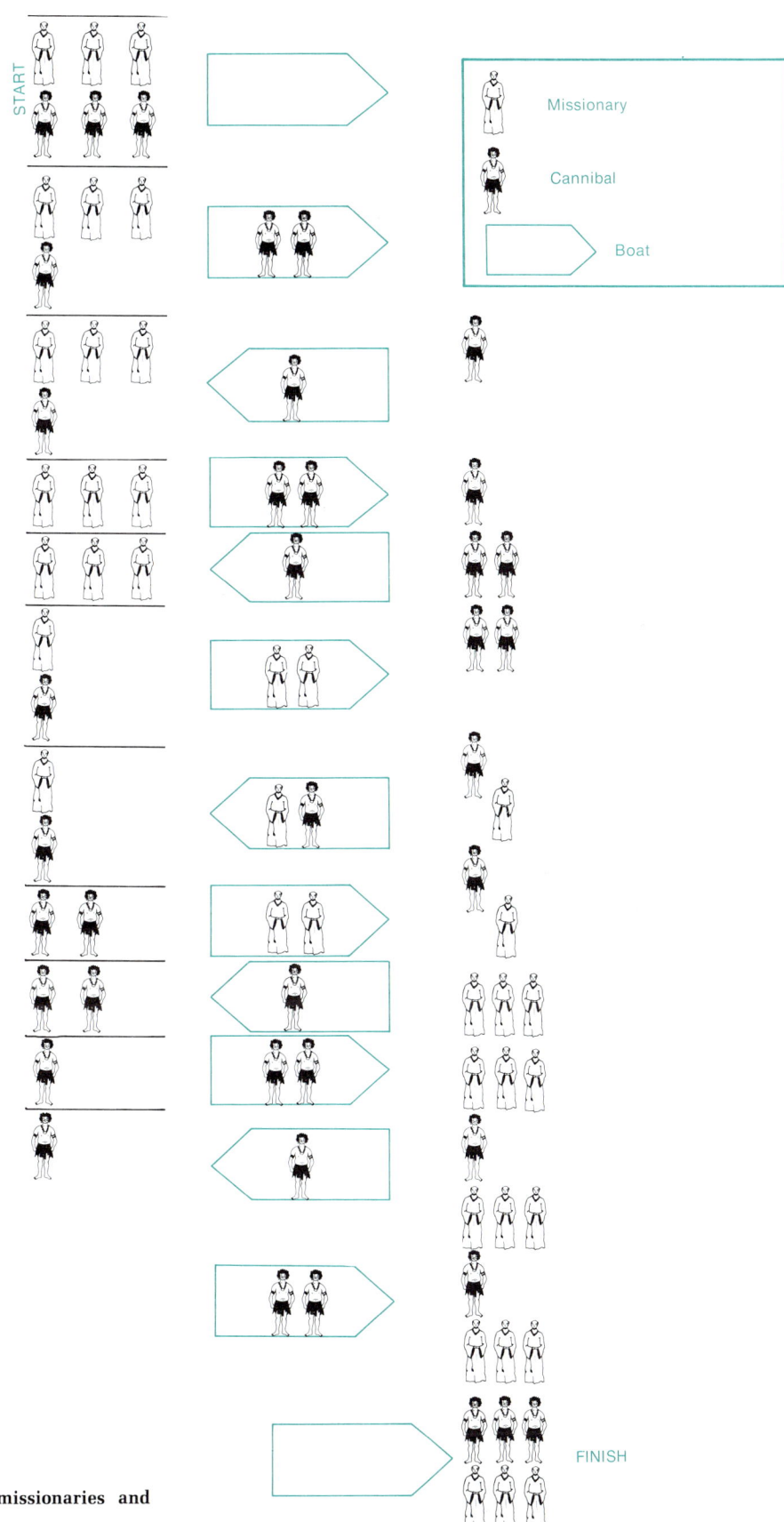

FIGURE 6-22 Solution to missionaries and cannibals problem.

The GPS works by this kind of **means-end analysis.** In trying to find some means for reaching its goal or end, the GPS often finds it necessary to establish sub-goals. For example, it is impossible to achieve the goal of the missionary and cannibals problem in one step because all six people can't fit in the boat. Therefore a sub-goal of first getting two people across would be established. In particular the GPS tries to reach three kinds of goals: transformation goals, difference reduction goals and operator application goals. *Transformation goals* aim at changing one object into another object—for example, transforming six people on one side of a river to six people on the other side. To accomplish this, the GPS must first find a difference between the two objects and then establish a sub-goal of reducing this difference. *Difference reduction goals* attempt to find some operator (such as paddling a boat across a river) which seems relevant to the difference, and then seek to establish the sub-goal of applying this operator. *Operator application goals* act to ensure that the proposed operation is allowable—for example, the GPS checks that not more than two people are in the boat at the same time. Occasionally, sub-goals cannot be accomplished, and the GPS must back up and retrace its steps, setting up new goals and sub-goals to solve the problem.

Once the GPS has solved a problem, how do we know that the process employed is comparable to that used by people? The GPS conveniently prints out all of the goals and sub-goals it has established, along with all of the dead ends where it had to back up, so it is easy to see how the GPS solved the problem. We try to get this same kind of information from people by asking them to speak aloud, explaining their attempted solutions as they work their way through a problem. These verbalizations make up what is called a *protocol;* they are tape-recorded and then put in an hierarchical form according to the pattern of sub-goals attempted by the problem solver. If the GPS protocol and the human protocol are identical or very similar, the computer program is considered a reasonable simulation of human behavior. This is one form of Turing's test, discussed in Chapter 5 in regard to the computer program that simulated a psychiatric interview. If you can't tell the difference between the protocol of the machine and that of the human, then both systems must be doing the same thing. Not all psychologists accept this logic, especially when the protocols are similar but not identical. How close must the two protocols be before we can conclude that they represent identical information flow patterns within the two systems? When this difficulty arises in comparing two sets of empirical data, the methods of statistics (see Appendix A) allow us to decide if slight differences can be attributed to chance or random fluctuation. Unfortunately, appropriate statistical techniques for comparing computer simulations and real human data have yet to be firmly established. Although the technique of computer simulation represents a great advance in theory formulation, more work is needed in testing computer-program theories.

Pattern Recognition: Teaching Machines to See

Although the fear of thinking machines or robots taking over civilization is now largely limited to writers of science fiction, it is true that computers can do many things better than their creators. Computer programs to play checkers can beat the programmer who originally created them (Samuel, 1967). Computers can do arithmetic calculations much more rapidly and accurately than we can. But people can perceive patterns much more efficiently than can computers, a fact which may reassure readers with humanist leanings. The digit illustrated in Figure 6–23 can be easily read by you but would be difficult for a computer to read. Police agencies have been trying for several years to get computer programs to recognize fingerprints, but so far a good solution has not been obtained.

8

FIGURE 6–23 A digit combined with an overlaid pattern. You can read the digit easily, but a computer would find this pattern recognition task very difficult.

Most computer programs for pattern recognition fall into one of two classes—**template matching** or **feature testing**—although as we shall see later these two categories are best regarded as ends of a continuum and not as strictly either/or. In *template matching*, a standard figure is compared to a test figure, and the degree of correspondence is determined. Figure 6–24 shows a machine that reads the digits on bank checks by using templates for identifying numbers. In order for this machine to work properly, the check must be positioned accurately. If the check is inserted either off-center or upside-down, the wrong numbers will be selected. This alignment difficulty is one reason that the template model is unsatisfactory as a psychological model of pattern recognition. Since no two handwritten letters are identical, an infinite number of templates would be necessary in order to match all possible letters. This obviously is impossible. Although various kinds of "normalization" processes, such as expanding letters until they touch a grid of standard size, improve template matching, on balance psychologists doubt that this technique is used by humans.

Instead the human is believed to use *feature testing*, in which particular sets of letter components are identified. The letter A contains three features: a horizontal line and two oblique lines. These features can be distinguished

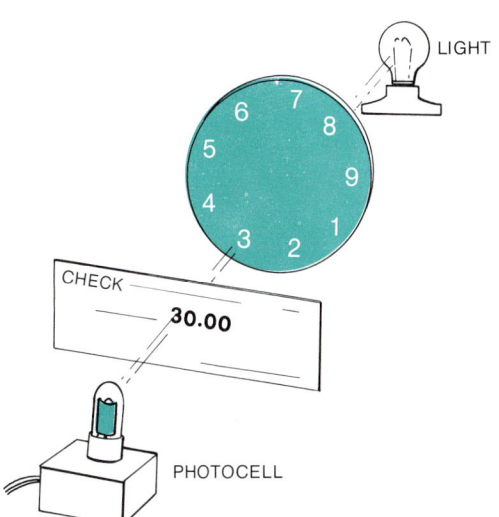

FIGURE 6–24 Exploded view of a machine designed to read the digits on a bank check. A light shines through the cut-out digit on a rotating wheel. A photocell reads the exact amount of light reflected by the digit on the check. The greatest reading tells which digit is on the check.

even if the letter is tilted, or if it is inverted, or if the bar does not quite reach one side of the letter, or if the bar extends beyond both sides of the letter. A pattern is examined against a checklist of features. The pattern, say a letter, is recognized as the letter which has the greatest number of features present. Thus letters that are composed of straight line features (A, H, T, E) are more likely to be confused with each other than with letters based upon round features (O, C, S). This turns out to be true both for computer programs based upon feature testing as well as for humans (Townsend, 1971).

It is important to realize that features and templates are not completely different concepts (Bledsoe and Browning, 1966). A template can be conceived of as a very large feature, or a feature as a very small template. It is likely that small groups of features are combined into "local" templates, and pattern recognition programs based upon this principle have been more successful than simple template matching models.

DECISION MAKING: FLIPPING A COIN IS NOT THE BEST SOLUTION

All of us must make decisions every day. Some decisions are very important (what kind of a job do I want when I graduate?) while others are less important (what should I have for dessert?). But all decisions must resolve some problem, and all take some time and effort before a choice is finally made. Mathematicians and statisticians have evolved rigorous techniques for optimal solutions of problems requiring decisions, such as the division of a fixed amount of resources (should we manufacture guns or butter?), gambling and card games, and testing balloons on an assembly line. These mathematical models tell us what a *rational* decision maker should do under well-specified sets of circumstances.

When a psychologist looks at decision making, he or she often finds that people are *not* rational decision makers. Yet although this kind of "irrational" decision making may seem odd to the mathematician, the behavior is consistent and so should be open to scientific analysis. Let us start with an economic example—a person interested in buying stocks or bonds. Assume we have what stockbrokers call a bull market—everyone is rushing in to buy stocks and prices are going through the ceiling. There is a general euphoric air in board rooms across the country, and speculators eagerly seek good buys, urged on by the financial successes of their friends and co-workers. We shall further assume that you, a prospective purchaser, subscribe to the belief that a stock has some innate value related to the fortunes of the company, and that the best buy is the stock that is selling at or even below this value. You narrow down your search to two stocks, Embargo Foundation Garments and Offshore Computer Oil Company. Embargo is a better buy according to your computations, but the financial columns have been filled with positive articles about the glowing future of offshore oil, and all your friends are buying oil stocks. You decide to buy 300 shares of Offshore Computer. Mathematically this is not a rational decision because your own calculations (which you believe) state that Embargo offers a greater potential profit. Based upon purely economic calculation you should have bought Embargo. But when we take psychological factors into account, your decision may not be quite so irrational. You may be the kind of decision maker who prefers a lessened profit because of the comfort of going along with the crowd. Embargo might make you richer, but if you develop an ulcer worrying about it, it is a poor decision. The psychological advantage of having other people share your opinions may be well worth some decline in potential profit. The decision is based upon *more* than economic considerations. Some people may put all their money into Embargo, and some may hedge their bets by buying some of both stocks. People differ in the kinds

FIGURE 6–25 An easy decision. In terms of information theory, the choice of only one alternative has no information. (Ali Isler cartoon from *Good Housekeeping*.)

of risk they are willing to assume and the expected rewards they desire for taking risks.

The Unit of Value: How Many Shleems Equal a Poncos?

There is a Bessarabian folk tale about two peddlers who meet in the market square of a small peasant village to barter their wares. One peasant has a cart full of shleems while the other has a basket of poncoses. Although it is generally agreed that shleems are not as valuable as poncoses, the exact relationship is unknown. After much discussion, the two peasants cannot strike an agreement until one suggests tossing a coin. "If the coin comes up heads, I'll trade you three of my shleems for one of your poncoses," says the first peddler. "And if it comes up tails, you trade me one of your poncoses for three of my shleems." "Fine," says the second peddler, "but I want to toss the coin to make sure you don't cheat me."

Although we may suspect that the second peddler got ripped off, this cannot be proved until the value of shleems and poncoses is expressed in a common unit. For an economist, the ultimate common unit is the dollar. All models of economics assume that every human value can eventually be expressed in monetary terms. Pollution has economic costs and benefits, children have dollar costs and benefits, and so on. The noted economist Kenneth Boulding recently gave an address at Purdue University during which he discussed, among other topics, the tragic near-extinction of certain species of whales. He stated that if such whales were on exhibit in an aquarium he would even be willing to pay $2.00 to see them. Coming from an economist this was the ultimate compliment. Before you conclude that economists are strange people, we hasten to add that specialized training often produces a framework in which one particular unit of value becomes predominant. Many psychologists thus view the world in terms of reinforcements and punishments. Transactional therapists view the world as having good strokes and bad strokes. There is nothing inherently evil about having such a conceptual framework, since a necessary part of life involves linking different objects to a common scale so decisions can be reached. It may, however, be short-sighted to assume that any single framework is the best for all situations.

Imagine you are sitting in a bar in a Las Vegas casino and a stranger comes up to you with this proposition for a game of chance: "Every time you flip a coin and it comes up heads I'll pay you $2.00. Every time it comes up tails you pay me 50¢. But it will cost you $1 for each time you flip the coin." Would you play this game?

If you have a fair coin, on the average you stand to gain 75¢ on each toss, *not counting the $1.00 entry fee each toss costs you.* Half the time you make $2.00, and half the time you will lose 50¢. The resultant 75¢ is called the *expected value* of the toss. It can be calculated mathematically by first multiplying the amount you will win by the probability (see Appendix A) of a win and then subtracting the amount you can lose multiplied by the probability of losing. In this game, the values would be

$$(.5) \times (\$2) \text{ and } (.5) \times (50¢); 1.00 - .25 = .75$$

So if you pay $1.00 for the privilege of playing the game, on the average you will lose 25¢ each time you flip a coin. You should not pay more than 75¢ to play this game. Since a price of 75¢ per game means that you will neither earn nor lose money, this price is called your *indifference* point. A rational decision maker should be willing to play the game at any price lower than the indifference point, since such a price guarantees a profit in the long run.

Now that you have decided that you will pay say 70¢ to play this game, let's up the ante. If the coin comes up heads, I'll pay you $2000. If it comes up tails, you pay me $500. Will you pay $700 for each flip of the coin? Since the expected value of this bet is $750, the asking price of $700 is below your point of indifference. Thus a rational decision maker would be eager to play this game. However, most of us would think twice before agreeing. This illustrates the distinction between the value of a bet and its **utility.** For small sums of money, value and utility (the psychological value) are identical. But unless you are rich and accustomed to dealing with large sums of money, utility decreases with the extra psychological risk associated with large sums. It is important to realize that this risk is *not* economic, because multiplying all the elements of a bet by some constant number (as we have done above) does not change the mathematical relationships. A rational economic decision maker would not care if the bet had an expected value of 75¢ or $75 million, so long as the price of the bet was below the point of indifference. But this change of scale makes a great difference to a psychological decision maker, who bases decisions not upon expected value but instead upon subjective utility.

People are not entirely rational decision makers even when subjective utilities are substituted for dollar values. Our calculations of coin tosses treated wins and losses identically—that is, each outcome was multiplied by its associated probability. However, people put a greater emphasis upon the probability of a win (Slovic and Lichtenstein, 1968). Such departures from optimal mathematical models of decision making are especially evident in gambling. Blackjack (or twenty-one) is the only casino game which offers the player an expected value greater than zero; all other casino games such as roulette *guarantee* that the house will win. Nevertheless, the blackjack tables are not the only game frequented by patrons. And even blackjack players do not always use optimal betting strategies (Bond, 1974).

If you are playing blackjack, are you mathematically better off betting conservatively or boldly? Say you start out with $100 and your goal is to double it. Playing cautiously, you bet only $1 per hand. Your chances of winning $200 by this small bet procedure are six in a million. Now let's take a riverboat gambler who wants to turn his $100 into $1000. He bets $100 per hand.

At this point we will expand on the expected value principle and demonstrate how a real-life decision could be optimally made. Our example is drawn from a similar case discussed by Edwards, Lindman, and Phillips (1965). It is a cloudy Saturday morning and you have to decide between playing tennis and going sailing. However, you don't know how much wind will be present this afternoon, and this uncertainty plays a crucial role in affecting your decision. If there is no wind, tennis would definitely be preferable to sailing. If there are gale winds, neither would be pleasant, but you would feel safer playing tennis. If there is some wind, you are not sure what to do. By now you are a sufficiently sophisticated decision maker to realize that flipping a coin is probably not the best way to decide between these two alternatives.

The first step in making your decision is to draw up a matrix like that in Table 6–2. It shows the two actions (tennis and sailing) and the possible states of the weather. The numbers inside the table are the utilities associated with the various outcomes. These are in arbitrary units based upon a total score of 100 as the highest utility and a score of minus 100 as the lowest. Table 6–2 shows that under the best conditions for each, you like sailing and tennis equally, so that deciding which to do is tough. Before we can calculate expected utilities, we need to know the probabilities of the three possible states of the weather. So you telephone the nearest weather station and are told that there is a 40 per cent chance of no wind, a 50 per cent chance of some wind, and a 10 per cent chance of gale winds. To calculate expected utilities, we must multiply each of these three probabilities by its associated utility and then add up these products. The expected utility for sailing is

$$(-10) \times (.4) + (80) \times (.5) + (-100) \times (.1) = 26$$

For tennis the expected utility is

$$(80) \times (.4) + (40) \times (.5) + (-80) \times (.1) = 44$$

As a rational decision maker, then, you should play tennis and not go sailing.

TABLE 6–2   Utility for Sailing and Tennis

Activity	Weather		
	No Wind 40%	Some Wind 50%	Gale Winds 10%
Sailing	−10	+80	−100
Tennis	+80	+40	−80

The percentages indicate the chances for the three different kinds of weather. The boxed-off cells show that tennis and sailing are equally liked (+80) under ideal conditions for each. Since we don't know your own personal utilities, the utilities entered in the table reflect the opinions of one of the authors. You might try doing this calculation after first inserting your own utilities into the table.

His chances are eight in a thousand—8000 in a million—of increasing his money tenfold. Comparing 8000 to 6, we see that the bold gambler is 1333 times more likely to multiply his $100 by ten than the cautious gambler is to double his money. Few blackjack players understand this (Bond, 1974). This becomes less confusing when we realize that even the utility of monetary outcomes is not the only reason for engaging in betting games. The recreational value of the game is also important to many gamblers, and this may lead them to adopt less than optimal strategies that will increase the length of the game at the expense of decreasing their winnings.

The principles we have discussed here should help you improve your own decision making. You no longer need to flip a coin to decide between two or more alternatives. If you are able to write down a number that represents your own subjective utility for a set of events and can estimate the probabilities of these events, you can use the expected utility principle to help make your decision. As was noted earlier, it is not always easy to equate different kinds of outcomes on a common scale. For example, if you are choosing between two job alternatives—one that pays a high salary and one with a lower salary but in a more desirable location—it is hard to assign precise numerical values to each dimension. But even attempting to do so will help clarify the issue for you. While we do not advocate blindly following the alternative with the greatest expected utility, we do feel that this method of decision making beats simple guessing or choosing randomly.

Summary

The study of **human information processing** is a modern approach to the issues of experimental psychology that is based upon systems analysis and an understanding of internal stages of response to external stimuli. Its basic concepts are tools borrowed from engineering and related sciences. Sequential operations can be represented by **flow charts.** *Branching* flow charts are used to explain different orders of possible events. **Feedback** occurs in **closed-loop systems.** The closed-loop system is effective because it monitors the **output** of the process and compares it to the desired **input. Information** is a technical term used to measure the **uncertainty** in the environment. The unit of information is the **bit,** which is the amount of information present in a toss of a fair coin. Much of behavior can be represented as **hierarchical structures.** The **TOTE unit** is a basic feedback unit that can be combined with or stacked onto complicated hierarchical structures. The human information processing approach views the person as an *active* and *adaptive* part of the environment. This differs from traditional S-R psychology, which sees the organism *passively* reacting to external stimulus and reinforcement *contingencies.* Information theory tells us that behavior depends upon *all* the stimuli that might have occurred and not only upon the particular stimulus that did occur. People are capable of processing the same information in several different ways.

Chronometric analysis is a powerful information processing technique based upon measurements of the time needed to complete various mental operations. The **subtractive** method of Donders was based upon three kinds of reaction time tasks: **simple reaction time, choice reaction time** and **c-reaction time. Hick's law** states that reaction time is a linear function of information. The slope or tilt of Hick's function varies with the degree of **stimulus-response compatibility.** Steeper lines are obtained for less compatible conditions. Reaction time is also influenced by the **accuracy** demanded in a task. The relationship between time and accuracy is called the **speed-accuracy trade-off.**

Overloading the human's information processing capabilities allows us to study **attention.** If two stimuli are presented very close together, reaction time to the second increases. This is called the **psychological refractory period** effect. The **limited-capacity channel** model of attention explains this delay by arguing that the total information load per second imposed by both stimuli exceeds available channel capacity. Studies of auditory attention use the **dichotic listening** task, with separate messages presented to each ear. The difficulty of attending to both messages at the same time is explained by **early-** and **late-selection** models of attention. Dichotic listening is only one example of a general class of paradigms called **time sharing** tasks. Data obtained in time-sharing studies have suggested that the limited-capacity channel model is only a first approximation of human attentional processes. The **Stroop effect** demonstrates the importance of **response conflict.** Many attentional effects can be explained by competing response tendencies.

Computer simulation is a powerful technique for studying human information processing, especially in tasks that do not have a **real-time** requirement. However, it is the computer **program** and not the machine itself that actually performs the simulation. The **problem solving** task is a **search** process, and one that has been widely simulated by computer. Problems can be solved through the use of either **algorithms** or **heuristics,** but heuristics are more commonly used. **Trial and error** is a simple but effective heuristic. A major source of difficulty in problem solving is the failure to recognize a possible solution, as occurs in **functional fixedness.** The **General Problem Solver (GPS)** successfully simulates human problem solving by the heuristic of **means-end analysis.** Validation of computer models is accomplished by comparing the computer output to a person's **protocol.** This is one variant of **Turing's test.** Computer programs for **pattern recognition** use **template matching** or **feature testing.** People probably use feature testing to recognize patterns.

A **rational** decision maker computes decisions on a purely mathematical basis. People, however, are not rational decision makers. A major problem in decision making is obtaining a common unit of value so that different objects can be compared. **Expected value** may be less than expected **utility,** the psychological correlate of value. This is especially true for expected values that equal large sums of money. Calculations based upon expected utilities may help in formulating your own decisions.

Suggested Readings

Apter, M. A.: *The Computer Simulation of Behavior.* New York: Harper/Colophon, 1970.

This brief paperback gives an elementary overview and examples of computer simulation in several areas of experimental psychology; a chapter on simulation of personality is provided as well.

Kantowitz, B. H. (ed.): *Human Information Processing: Tutorials in Performance and Cognition.* Hillsdale, N.J.: Lawrence Erlbaum Associates, 1974.

An advanced text for beginning graduate students that explains recent findings and techniques in seven specific areas of human information processing.

Keele, S. W.: *Attention and Human Performance.* Pacific Palisades, California: Goodyear, 1973.

An undergraduate text with a modern treatment of several topics discussed in this chapter.

Lee, W.: *Decision Theory and Human Behavior.* New York: John Wiley and Sons, 1971.

A broad survey of experimental and theoretical work in decision making in many situations. While less mathematical than many comparable treatments, the text assumes a thorough understanding of algebra on the part of the reader.

Massaro, D. W. *Experimental Psychology and Information Processing.* Chicago: Rand McNally, 1975.

A lengthy undergraduate text with a detailed treatment of perception, attention, memory, reading, and listening.

Posner, M. I.: *Cognition: An Introduction.* Glenview, Illinois: Scott, Foresman, and Company, 1973.

A comprehensive overview of current trends in the study of mental life.

Some journals that regularly publish articles on human information processing:

Journal of Experimental Psychology
Memory & Cognition
Cognitive Psychology
Acta Psychologica

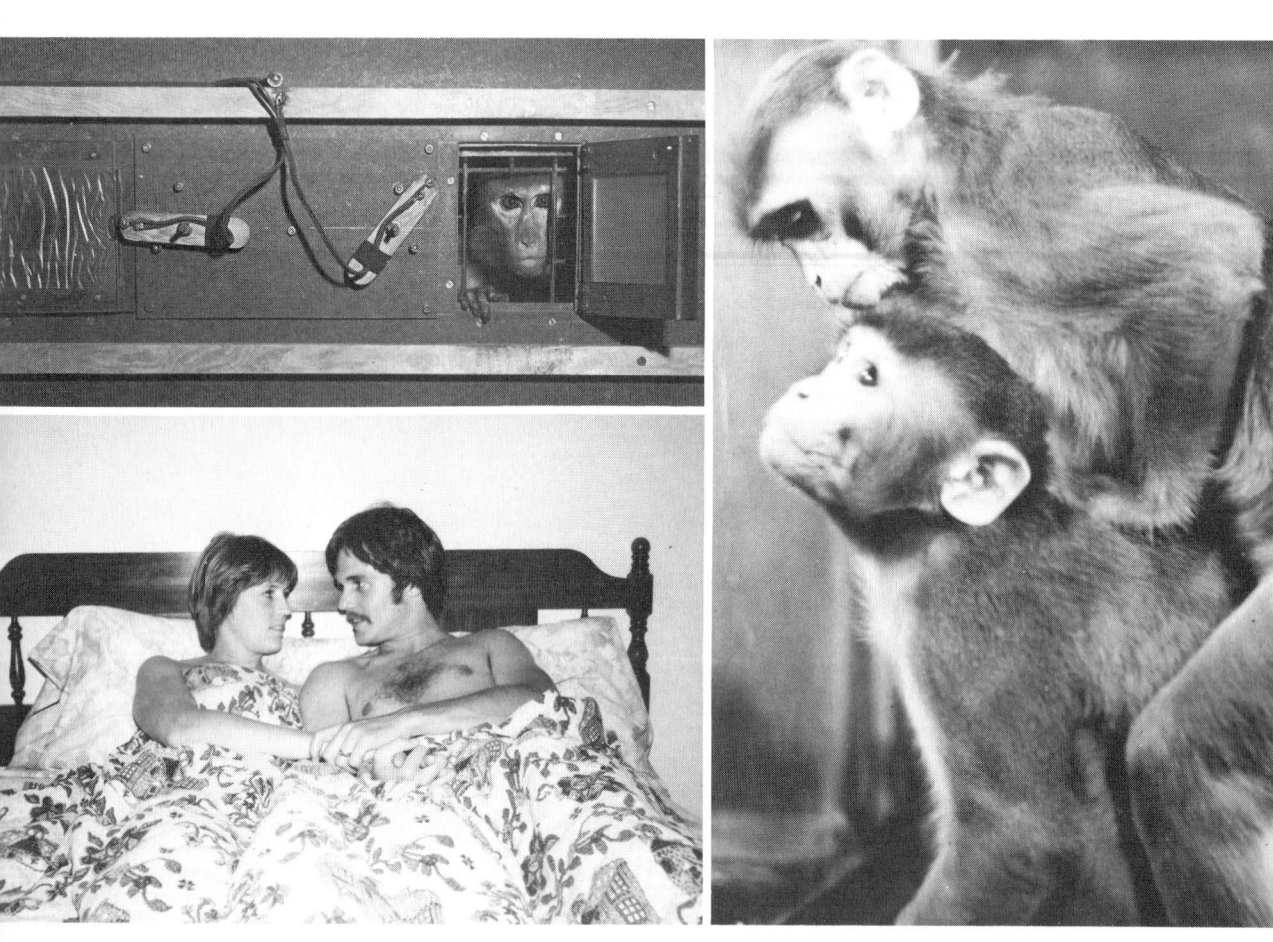

7 Motivation and Emotion: Attempting to Explain Behavior

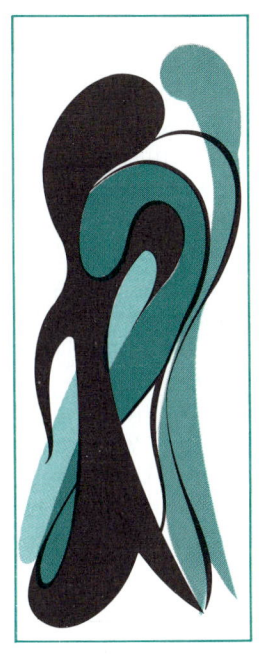

In our everyday lives, we want to understand the behavior of ourselves, of other people, and even of our pets. Most often, we ask "why" the behavior occurred, and then we try our best to come up with an acceptable reason. Consider the following examples and decide how you might attempt to explain each incident.

A female dog in heat is confined to a fenced-in backyard. A male dog owned by a neighbor digs a crude tunnel under the fence and enters the female's yard. Why did he do it?

A group of children are in a long line at a movie theater which is presenting the most recent film from the Walt Disney studios. The children talk loudly and rapidly, jump up and down, and generally seem to be in constant motion. Why are they behaving in that way?

A high school sophomore starts to school on a spring morning. As she reaches the school entrance, she suddenly turns away and heads for a nearby shopping mall where she spends the day browsing for clothes and records. Why did she go shopping instead of attending school?

According to a story in the morning newspaper, a puzzling murder case in a midwestern city has just been solved. Police accused Mr. Fitzbutton Pocketfuzz of causing the death of his unfaithful wife. On being confronted with the evidence, the culprit admitted doing her in with a box of poisoned presweetened cornflakes. Why did he commit the crime?

In answering these questions, our most likely responses involve *motivational* and *emotional* concepts. The dog was motivated by a strong sexual **drive.** The children were eager to get into the movie and were bursting with *excitement.* The sophomore *wanted* to skip school because she *enjoyed* shop-

219

ping more than studying. Mr. Pocketfuzz's **motive** for spiking the cereal was an angry *emotional* response to his mate's messing around. Such explanations are common in our culture, and suggest a sort of loose theory of behavior which most of us seem to share.

Though **motivation** has been characterized as "among the most controversial and least satisfactory" of the constructs used by psychologists (Chaplin, 1968, p. 304), motivational concepts have been almost as pervasive in psychological theories of behavior as they have been in everyday life. How do psychologists define motivation? *Motivation is a hypothetical internal process that provides the energy for behavior and directs it toward a specific goal.*

Emotion is another very common concept in our culture and in the science of behavior. You know that you sometimes feel happy, sad, fearful, angry, and so forth. Others tell you that they, too, have such feelings. We observe the behaviors of animals and decide that the purring cat is happy, the listless dog is sad, the scampering rabbit is afraid, and the growling lion is angry. Though emotional and motivational explanations of behavior often overlap, *emotion is a subjective feeling state involving physiological arousal, accompanied by characteristic behaviors.*

In this chapter we will take a general look at the concept of *motivation* as it has been viewed historically and as it is currently utilized in psychological theories. Then, we will discuss the behavioral effects of *drive arousal* and examine the usefulness of the idea that motivation supplies the energy for human behavior. Included here are studies of the effects of arousal on general activity level and on the performance of existing habits. Next, we will examine some of the characteristics of *physiological needs.* Two very different basic needs will be discussed as examples: the need for sexual gratification and the effectance motive (the need to explore and manipulate one's environment). *Acquired motivation* will then be described, with work on the achievement motive providing a specific example. In the last section of this chapter, we will return to the related concept of *emotion* and the way in which individuals decide what feelings are being experienced by others and by themselves.

MOTIVATION: SOMETHING IN THE WAY IT MOVES ME

When we try to understand or explain any aspect of the world around us, we are ordinarily seeking causes. Usually, we have observed some movement or activity and want to know *why* it occurred. Over the years, we learn to accept explanations such as, "the clouds were blown by the wind," "the billiard ball was struck by the cue stick," and "the automobile was powered by gasoline in an internal combustion engine." The explanations offered for behavior have followed this same general pattern, and, in fact, the word *motivation* comes from the Latin word *movere*, which literally means "to move." The nature of these explanations has taken many different forms, and we will describe three of them: **rationalism, mechanism,** and **empirical determinism.**

The Evolution of Motivational Concepts: From Volcano Spirits to Predictability

Rationalism: Behavior Must Have a Reason

If you ask a very young child to explain his or her behavior, the answer is often simple and straightforward. "Why did you take the cookie?" "I wanted to." In early life, this all-purpose motivational theory is likely to be applied generally. "The buses stopped because they're ready to go night-night." "The bad stove burned me." "The drinking fountain wants to splash my face." Though children in our culture eventually learn to adopt different sorts of explanations, they initially are recreating some of mankind's earliest hypotheses about movement. As in the cartoon in Figure 7–1, there is the belief that each object or organism is propelled by some internal mechanism, and that the final action is determined on the basis of self-willed decision. As children grow older, they learn to differentiate explanations for animate versus inanimate

FIGURE 7-1 In its most primitive form, *traditional rationalism* involves the idea that all objects move because they have a reason to do so. Small children, as in this cartoon, may attribute motivation to the activities of inanimate objects such as sunbeams as well as to the behavior of animals and human beings. (© King Features Syndicate, 1975.)

objects and usually for human versus nonhuman animals. It might be noted that adult versions of rationalism can range from the primitive beliefs of natives who worry about the anger of the volcano spirit to the most sophisticated humanistic arguments about freedom of choice and personal responsibility for one's actions (Ford and Urban, 1963). In addition to *personal* reasons for events, there may also be *cosmic* reasons in the form of such concepts as "nature's plan" or "divine will."

Such explanations of behavior are known as **traditional rationalism;** human beings are believed to act because there is a reason to do so (Bolles, 1975; Rychlak, 1968). This was the view of Greek philosophers such as Plato, and it is still a very popular one. That is, we either hold the individual responsible for what he or she does or we say that the reasons for the person's behavior were written in the stars or were part of a godly plan and beyond our understanding—what will be, will be. Our laws are based on the idea of individual responsibility, and there are legal punishments for choosing to do the wrong thing. In medieval European courts, by the way, animal behavior was not differentiated from human behavior, and there were cases of donkeys and other beasts being placed on trial for their misdeeds. On the other hand, if all things are planned by a higher power, there is no individual responsibility. The fatalism of many oriental religions stems from this view of a rational universe that is beyond man's ability to understand or to change.

There are two built-in difficulties that make rationalism unusable as a basis for behavioral science. First, the notion that behavior is based on reasons is a circular one and provides us with no way to predict behavior. You have a friend who smokes cigarettes. Why does he smoke? Because he wants to or because a higher power wants him to. How do you know? Because he smokes cigarettes. This sort of "explanation" is no better than a word game in which we deceive ourselves into thinking we have gained understanding. We still don't know why he wants to smoke. Second, rationalism is not testable, and this places it beyond the realm of scientific interest. If the explanation of behavior rests on events that no one can observe, we have no way to incorporate these events within a theory of behavior. You might as well propose that your friend's smoking is caused by invisible green elephants who make him light up a cigarette whenever they get drunk on invisible Ripple wine. Such explanations may or may not represent "truth," but in either case they cannot be incorporated into science.

A quite different view of behavior, **mechanism,** also had its philosophical proponents in early Greece, but it was not really very popular until the physical sciences had made some notable advances. The earliest science, astronomy, was based on the fact that there is a predictable regularity in the movements of the moon, the planets, and the stars. Once the patterns were carefully plotted, ancient astronomers were able to state with some precision such events as the time of tomorrow's sunrise and the night on which the next full moon would appear. Later, as mechanical and engineering skills developed, men began to construct more and more intricate devices ranging from catapults to cuckoo clocks that operated in the same regular and predictable way as the stars and planets. It was Galileo who helped convince the scientific community that nature was "a perfect machine whose future happenings can be fully predicted and controlled by one who has full knowledge and control of the present motions" (Burtt, 1955). The turning of one gear *always* causes the next gear to turn in exactly the same way. The gradual shift among scientists from rationalism to mechanism did not imply a rejection of religion, by the way; Newton, for one, believed that the lawfulness of a mechanistic universe constituted solid evidence of God's existence.

Eventually, human beings, too, were described as complex mechanical devices, and most of us have had contact with biology chapters entitled something like "the machinery of the body," complete with analogies of levers, hinges, valves, and all the other familiar hardware. The drawing in Figure 7–2 represents an extreme example of this kind of conceptualization which was presented in a book for children in the 1940's.

It is not surprising that behavior, too, has been conceptualized by some as

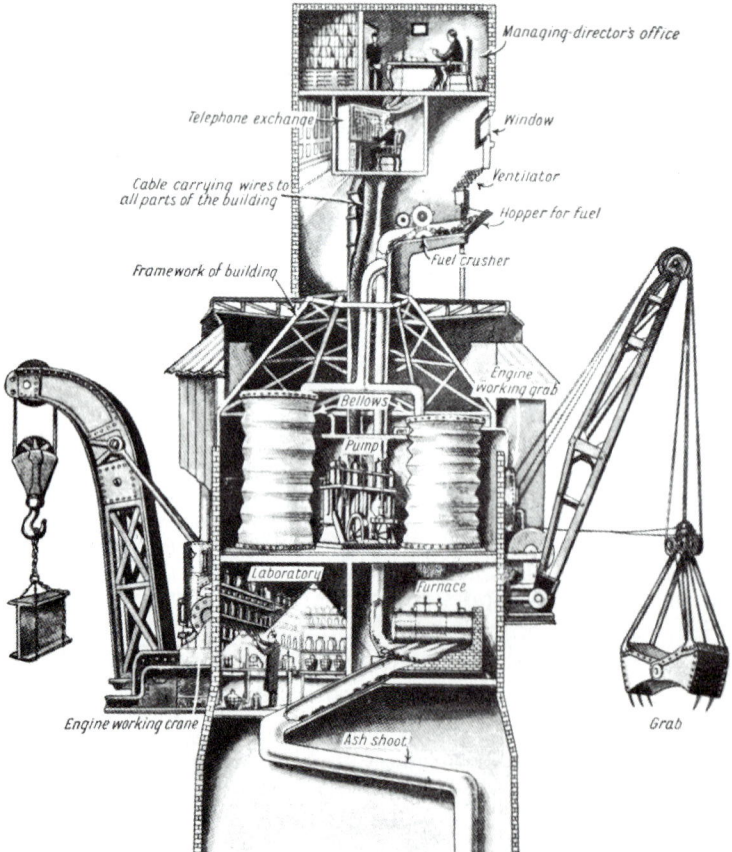

FIGURE 7–2   The *mechanist* view of the world is based on analogies to the physical world in which there are clear cause-and-effect relationships. A good example of such a viewpoint is provided by this drawing from a children's book published some decades ago. Part of the original caption reads, "The human body is the most wonderful thing in the universe. It is the most efficient of all machines, and unless it is damaged or spoilt by accident or misuse it goes on doing its work perfectly day after day, till at last, like all material things, it becomes worn out. . . . It is no mere fancy or exaggeration to describe the human body as a great and wonderful factory." (From *Wonders of Science Simplified.* **New York: Metro, 1942, pp. 214–215.)**

caused entirely by mechanical forces. Many investigators have faith that if we learn about the functioning of neurons and bodily biochemistry, we will then know all there is to know about behavior. A dyed-in-the-wool mechanist believes that the ultimate and only reality is the physical universe.

So, mechanistic ideas are in direct contrast to rationalistic ones. The rationalist position is that human behavior is based on reasons. The mechanist position is that human behavior, like all natural events, has physical causes, and the knowledge of the machinery is all that science needs to seek. For example, an early behavioristic psychologist viewed man as entering the world as an "assembled organic machine ready to run" (Watson, 1924, p. 216). Modern psychology has been influenced by both rationalism and mechanism, and both are represented in one form or another in many current theories. There is actually no reason, however, for behavioral science to take either of these extreme positions, as will be seen next.

In their everyday lives, psychologists—like everyone else—function as rationalists part of the time and as mechanists part of the time. In research, however, psychologists have learned that neither set of philosophical assumptions is necessary in the task of building a science of behavior.

Empirical Determinism: The Search for Predictability

Empirical determinism simply assumes that behavior is a natural phenomenon and that it is predictable. The question asked in behavioral research is not really "why" behavior occurs but rather "how" and "when." Most often, those conducting research are trying to determine the conditions under which behavior occurs rather than to discover some ultimate explanation of behavior. The goal is to be able to make accurate predictions.

The differences among these three viewpoints can perhaps be illustrated by returning to one of our questions at the beginning of this chapter. Why did the male dog dig under the fence and enter the female's yard? The rationalist would say that his reason was to be able to gratify his sexual cravings by having intercourse with the female, and that the ultimate reason was to insure that the species was maintained. The mechanist would say that a thorough knowledge of the dog's hormonal level, the electrical discharges along his olfactory nerves, and the muscular acts involved in digging provides a total explanation of the sequence of events. The empirical determinist would say that the behavior occurs when specific conditions are met—including the length of time since intercourse had occurred previously, the presence of a female in heat, and perhaps past experiences with digging behavior which resulted in reinforcement.

It will be helpful to keep these distinctions in mind as we begin to describe current research on motivation in some detail.

In the early days of classical conditioning studies (see Chapter 4), it at first seemed reasonable simply to explain behavior in terms of conditioning experiences without any need to consider motivational variables. After all, Pavlov's dogs just stood there and learned to salivate to the tone when it was associated with the meat powder. By the late 1930's, however, a crucial problem was raised. What if the dog was not hungry? It was found that with a recently fed dog, this type of conditioning does not occur (Finch, 1938). In other words, the animal has to be *motivated* or there is no learning. In attempting to make sense of this and related findings, the learning theorist Clark L. Hull introduced the concept of **drive.** There are life-long physiological **needs** such as that for food, but only at those times when the need has not been met does the organism do something. In other words, need deprivation leads to *drive arousal* (such as hunger), and it is the aroused drive that activates the organism. When an appropriate **goal** (such as food) is obtained, the drive is reduced be-

BEHAVIORAL EFFECTS OF DRIVE AROUSAL: ENERGIZING THE ORGANISM

cause the need has been satisfied. Drive reduction was said to be reinforcing, and thus any behavior that led to drive reduction was more likely to occur the next time the organism was aroused. In the years since these ideas were formulated, much evidence has accumulated to indicate that not all reinforcement is based on drive reduction (e.g., Eisenberger, 1972).

Arousal is not simply a function of internal states of deprivation. On the basis of past experience, organisms also learn to respond to external cues, or **incentives.** That is, after an external stimulus has been associated with a drive and its reduction, that external stimulus can become a motivator. Thus, the sight of a glass of iced tea, the smell of bread baking, or the touch of a lover's hand may be arousing and thus motivate our behavior. An incentive can affect behavior in much the same way as a drive. The external cues may be positive or negative, and thus may lead the organism to approach or to avoid an object or a situation. In other words, it is possible to learn to anticipate rewards or punishments.

As conditions change, the strength of motivation changes. Subjectively, we know the difference between being mildly hungry and being hungry enough to eat a large horse. For one thing, when we are hungry, we eat faster and we eat more (Hulse, Deese, and Egeth, 1975). What are the behavioral differences associated with such differences in arousal?

Motivation as an Energizer of Behavior: Flipping the Switch to ON

It seems obvious that a strong motivational state leads to a general increase in activity. At the beginning of the chapter, we mentioned the children waiting anxiously and actively outside of the movie theater. That sort of restless movement is not necessarily helpful in reaching one's goal, as you may have noticed if you ever paced up and down outside of a locked bathroom door. For many years, this effect of drive on behavior seemed to provide a convenient index of drive strength.

The Activity Wheel: Going Around in Circles

A familiar sight in pet stores is some version of a cage in which animals are able to enter a rotating **activity wheel** and run rapidly as the wheel spins (see Figure 7–3). You may have heard such devices referred to as "squirrel cages" or seen cartoons in which they were used to power automobiles as a solution to the energy crunch. From the earliest days of rat research, it had been observed that spontaneous running in an activity wheel increases when the animal is deprived of its normal amount of daily food. That is, as drive level increases, there apparently is an increase in general activity.

Such findings provided excellent evidence that drive arousal has a general energizing effect on behavior. Further, the behavior need not have any relationship to the specific drive that is aroused. Hull's concept of drive as a nonspecific activator clearly applies to this sort of situation. This general relationship between drive and activity was assumed to be true and was regularly described in textbooks for decades. As we will see, that general principle can no longer be stated very convincingly.

General Activity or Reinforced Activity?: Running for a Food Pellet

As often happens in science, the neatness of the drive-activity findings was messed up a bit by additional experimentation. Finger, Reid, and Weasner (1957) pointed out that in studies of activity level, the rats are typically fed right in their cages containing the activity wheel. If they periodically exercised in the wheels and then were fed, the running behavior would accidentally be reinforced. If so, it could be that hungry rats were not just randomly running about but that they were performing in response to reinforcement. Thus, it was proposed that experimenters had accidentally been *teaching* their subjects to run in the wheel! To test this possibility, Finger and his associates conducted an experiment in which some of the animals were fed in the usual way in their activity cages while others were placed in a separate box for an hour before

FIGURE 7–3 Special cages provide an opportunity for an animal to run in a rotating *activity wheel*. When a counting device is attached, the number of revolutions of the wheel is recorded and provides a measure of the animal's general activity level. (Courtesy of Lafayette Instrument Co.)

feeding time. As expected, the second group of animals did not show the usual strong relationship between drive and activity level, presumably because they had not been rewarded for running.

Subsequent experiments have supported these findings, but it should be noted that there is *some* increase in running activity even though rats are never fed in the activity wheels (Duda and Bolles, 1963). It is even possible, however, that the running itself is somewhat reinforcing (Bolles, 1970). That is, for rats, perhaps it is just naturally fun to run, and they turn to such activity when they are deprived of food. In that case, a better indicator of general activity would seem to be the tilt cage. This is a cage delicately balanced in the middle so that any type of movement tilts it off-center; electrical devices at each corner record any movement, including walking, scratching, sniffing about, and so on. Using this measure of general activity, experimenters find that an increase in drive level actually leads to a *decrease* in movement (Teghtsoonian and Campbell, 1960).

Various experimenters have used different measures of activity, different types of deprivation, and different species of animals, and it has now become clear that the idea that drive arousal leads to an increase in general activity is not precisely accurate. To discover the effects of drive on behavior, we must look elsewhere.

In attempting to build a theory of behavior, Hull and one of his colleagues, Kenneth Spence, emphasized the role of drive as one determinant of behavior. As a learning theorist (see Chapter 4), Hull (1943) was interested in predicting the probability of the conditioned response occurring when the conditioned stimulus was presented. To help illustrate this concept, we will take an example of what can very loosely be called higher order conditioning (see Chapter 4) in a dog owned by one of the authors.

This collie is named Red Baron (no relation to another of the authors), and he very much enjoys going for automobile rides. The rare occasions for such adventures were times of great excitement and seeming pleasure. One summer, the author's son had a night job which required him to telephone for

Drive and Performance: That Extra Push

Hull-Spence Theory: Multiplying by Drive

a ride home at about nine or ten each evening. Red Baron was allowed to go along on these nightly excursions. In a very short time, the dog responded to the ringing of the telephone by running to the door and barking excitedly in preparation for his ride in the car. Of course, the phone also rang on many other occasions, when it was not followed by a ride. On these "conditioning trials," how likely was the dog to bark and run to the door? If you wished to predict his conditioned behavior, what would determine the likelihood of his responding to the ringing phone?

In Hull's theoretical system, learning and motivation were conceptualized as the necessary determinants of behavior. Learning is represented by the concept of **habit strength,** and habit strength increases whenever a stimulus-response combination is followed by reinforcement. This means that the more evenings on which Red Baron's excited response to the ringing telephone was followed by a car ride, the stronger the ringing-barking habit would become. Hull dealt with motivation in terms of the concept of *drive,* and drive increases whenever a physiological need is not met. Because drive is assumed to be influenced by any type of arousal, Red Baron's motivational state would be higher if he happened to be hungry, thirsty, or frightened at the time the telephone rang. A crucial aspect of Hull's theory is the way in which habit strength and drive interact. It was proposed that habit strength is *multiplied* by drive to determine response strength. The greater the habit strength and the stronger the drive, the more likely it is that the conditioned stimulus will elicit the conditioned response. Laboratory research on conditioning (obviously under much better controlled conditions than in our example) has provided a good deal of support for the proposition that habit strength and drive jointly influence the probability that the conditioned response will occur (Hilgard and Bower, 1975).

Neither the laboratory findings with respect to drive strength nor even the collie's response to the telephone may seem fascinatingly relevant to your everyday concerns. We will soon describe, however, the way in which these theoretical relationships have been found useful in predicting such behavior as performance in the college classroom. With respect to our dog, you may be interested to know that the learning was very long lasting and resistant to extinction. In fact, some two years after the job and the nightly rides ended, he still occasionally responds to a telephone call with the old conditioned response.

Anxiety as a Determinant of Drive: Conditioned Eyeblinks

How might the effects of differential drive level be studied with human subjects? One answer has been to find a way to measure individual differences in anxiety. The assumption is that differences in emotional responsiveness affect differences in drive level. Individuals who are characteristically anxious, tense, nervous, and up-tight would seem to be "carrying around" a higher level of drive than individuals who are characteristically calm, placid, and loose. It would follow that in a conditioning situation, response strength would be greater among those who are anxious than among those who are calm. To test this idea, experimenters would simply have to find a way to measure differences in anxiety.

As a graduate student working with Spence, Janet Taylor constructed a test to measure anxiety and, it was hoped, differences in drive level. This **Manifest Anxiety Scale** was based on clinical descriptions of neurotic anxiety and contains such true-false items as "I sweat very easily even on cool days" and "I must admit that I have at times been worried beyond reason over something that really did not matter" (Taylor, 1951, 1953). In using this measure to test the predictions about habit strength and drive strength, an interesting way to condition eyeblinks was devised. A subject sits in a dental chair. A tube directs a puff of air at one eye, and each puff results in an eyeblink, as you might guess. Just before a puff is released, a circular glass disc is made to increase in brightness. The subject acquires a conditioned response: when there is no air puff but the disc becomes brighter (conditioned stimulus), the subject blinks (conditioned response).

We know that as the number of conditioning trials increases, habit strength should increase. It would also be predicted that as the degree of anxiety increases, drive strength should increase. Therefore, the probability of response should be affected both by number of trials and by anxiety level. Many experiments have generally confirmed this prediction from Hull-Spence theory. The findings of one experiment described by Spence (1960) are shown in Figure 7–4 and serve as an example. You can see that the probability of the conditioned eyeblink was greater as the number of conditioning trials (habit strength) increased and as the anxiety level of the subjects (drive strength) increased.

You might assume at this point that drive strength could be expected to have a positive influence on all responses. If so, anxious individuals should generally perform better than nonanxious ones. In fact, subjects with high scores on the Manifest Anxiety Scale have been found to excel non-anxious subjects in such activities as performing a reaction time task (Wenar, 1954) and in doing simple coding (Reynolds, Blau, and Hurlbut, 1961). Nevertheless, there are very many situations in which the opposite is true, and we will now see how the theory is able to predict both types of findings.

Hull (1943) proposed that the response strength of all habits activated in a given situation increases when drive strength increases. As we have seen, when only one habit is evoked, the higher the drive the greater the response strength, and so the better the performance. When several habits are evoked at the same time, however, high drive increases the response strength of each habit. This means that performance will deteriorate, because the competing responses (right and wrong alike) will each be strengthened. As an example, consider what it is like for an experienced driver when a child darts out in the street directly in front of his car. The well-learned, well-practiced habit of stepping on the brake is so much stronger than any competing habit that it is almost certain to occur, and to occur with great force. Further, anything which increases drive level, such as high anxiety, would only add to the strength of that response. Imagine the same situation with someone just learning to operate a car. Many new habits are being learned, and none are suf-

Competing Habits: Drive as an Energizer

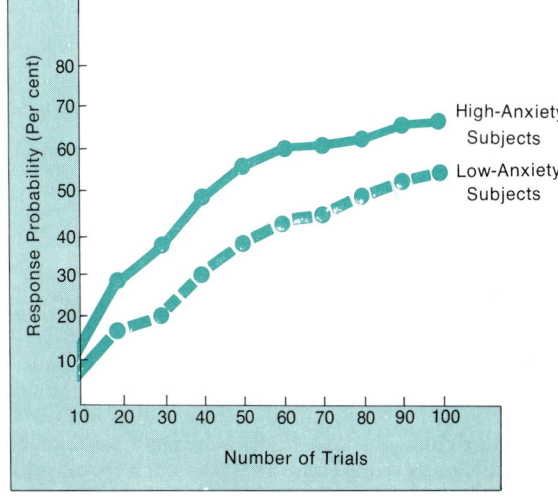

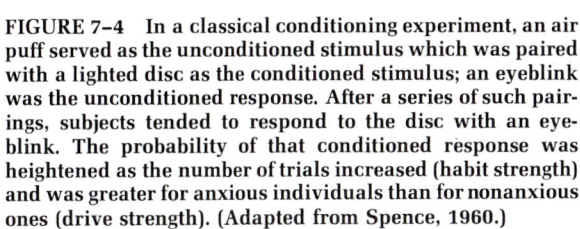

FIGURE 7–4   In a classical conditioning experiment, an air puff served as the unconditioned stimulus which was paired with a lighted disc as the conditioned stimulus; an eyeblink was the unconditioned response. After a series of such pairings, subjects tended to respond to the disc with an eyeblink. The probability of that conditioned response was heightened as the number of trials increased (habit strength) and was greater for anxious individuals than for nonanxious ones (drive strength). (Adapted from Spence, 1960.)

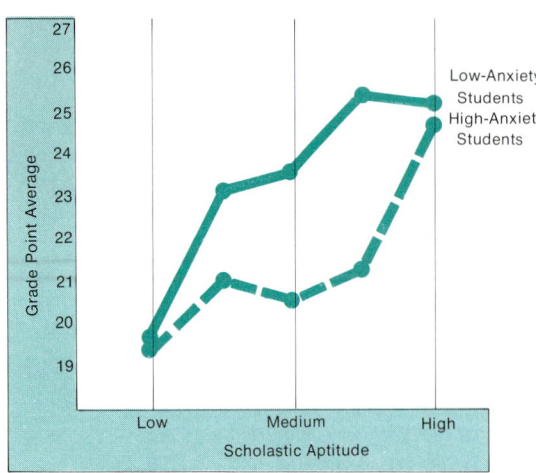

FIGURE 7–5 Though grade point average is determined in part by scholastic aptitude, motivational variables are also an important factor in college performance. High levels of anxiety are found to have a detrimental effect on grades for the majority of students who fall in the middle range of academic ability. (Adapted from Spielberger, 1966.)

ficiently well practiced to be much stronger than the others. If a child darts in front of the car, a new driver is just about as likely to step on the brake, shift gears, open the glove compartment, step on the accelerator, or blow the horn. High drive here would only complicate matters, with all of these responses being strengthened equally.

Many experiments have confirmed this general prediction. For example, Spielberger and Smith (1966) examined the performance of high- and low-anxiety college students in learning a list of twelve nonsense syllables in order. During the early stages of learning, when the list was not yet well learned, highly anxious subjects made more mistakes than did the less anxious subjects. Later on, after the list had been fairly well learned, the high-anxiety subjects began to perform better than those low in anxiety. As we will show again in Chapter 12, the effect of drive level on performance can be positive or negative, depending on whether a single strong habit is evoked or whether several equally strong habits are evoked.

An important application of such findings is in the school setting. Think of the times you have been faced with a multiple-choice examination in which you had a difficult time deciding which of several alternative answers was correct. A high drive level would only complicate matters, in that the right and wrong answers would be strengthened equally. This reasoning leads to the prediction that high anxiety interferes with school performance and thus results in lower grades. Because academic ability also affects grades, Spielberger (1966) suggested that both variables should be taken into account in trying to predict grade point average. He examined the grades of a large number of undergraduates for whom he had obtained scores on the Manifest Anxiety Scale and the ACE college aptitude scales. As can be seen in Figure 7–5, grade

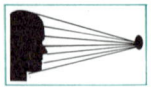

FOCUS ON RESEARCH: *Reducing Anxiety with Humor*

We have seen that high drive level can interfere with performance when there are competing responses. Presumably, this is the reason that students who are high in anxiety tend to have difficulty with complex tasks such as classroom exams (Paul and Eriksen, 1964). It would seem reasonable to seek a way to reduce this anxiety as a means of helping very anxious students to work more effectively.

You are probably aware that in threatening

situations people are often observed to make jokes "to relieve the tension." Most of us have experienced at least one disrupting event such as a stalled elevator or a power black-out and noticed the increase in the number of funny remarks and nervous laughter. One very familiar situation of this type is a college classroom on the day of a midterm or final (Mechanic, 1962). Because it has been demonstrated that exposure to humorous material actually does reduce the level of emotional arousal (Singer, 1968), it follows that humor during an examination would be anxiety-reducing. This idea was proposed by Smith, Ascough, Ettinger, and Nelson (1971), who predicted that highly anxious students should not only feel better when they are made to laugh during an examination, but that they should also get higher scores. Is it really possible that a little added humor on a test could raise college grades?

In an undergraduate psychology course, the students' anxiety was measured at the beginning of the semester so that they could be classified as high- or low-anxiety subjects. To determine the effects of humor on examination performance, the experimenters prepared two different versions of the midterm, and each type was given to half of the students. One was the regular nonhumorous exam, and one was a special version in which every third item contained material designed to be funny. The answers were, however, the same for both tests. Here is an example of an item from each form of the test:

Nonhumorous Exam

Every time little Tommy pulls a typical childhood prank such as passing notes to friends in his classroom, chewing gum in class, or talking loudly while the teacher is presenting the lesson, his teacher reacts by slapping his knuckles with a ruler. The teacher notes that Tommy then tends to become very aggressive toward his play-

mates during the following recess. How might this aggression be accounted for?

Humorous Exam

Every time little Brutus pulls a typical childhood prank such as overturning and shorting out the television by urinating on it while his mother is watching the last five minutes of "As the World Turns," Mother reacts by administering punishment with her electric cattle prod. She notes that Brutus then stomps on his playmates with his hobnailed boots. How might this aggression be accounted for?

Answers

(a) the teacher (mother) furnishes a model for aggression.
(b) Tommy's (Brutus's) frustration level is decreased by punishment.
(c) projection of aggression.
(d) more than one of the above.

The results are shown in Figure 7–6. You can see that for students with low levels of anxiety, the addition of humor had little or no effect on how well they performed; obviously, humorous items do not make the test any less difficult. Nevertheless, for the highly anxious students the test content was a crucial factor in determining how well they did. Scores of the high-anxiety students were significantly lower on the regular, nonhumorous test than on the humorous one. Such findings are consistent with the idea that the disrupting effects of high drive on performance can be overcome if anxiety is reduced.

If you feel that anxiety is interfering with how well you do on exams, perhaps it would help to tell yourself a joke or two during your next midterm or final. A word of caution—if you succeed and then giggle throughout the test, your fellow students may look at you a bit strangely. Just tell them that you are applying a technique derived from a motivational theory.

FIGURE 7–6 Two different versions of a midterm examination were given to an undergraduate psychology class. Students low in anxiety did equally well on the humorous and the nonhumorous tests. Highly anxious students, however, obviously were helped by the addition of humor. It was assumed that the humor served to reduce anxiety. Thus, exceptionally anxious students, whose performance ordinarily is harmed by high drive level, were able to function as well as less anxious students. (Adapted from Smith, Ascough, Ettinger, and Nelson, 1971.)

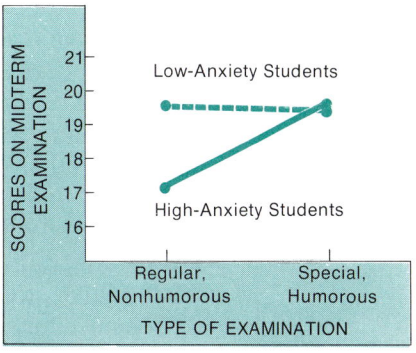

point average increased as scholastic aptitude increased; in addition, high levels of anxiety led to lower grades at the middle levels of scholastic aptitude. It appears that those with very high aptitude do well and those with very low aptitude do poorly, regardless of anxiety level. For most students, however, high anxiety acts to interfere with classroom performance and grades. Spielberger proposed that if highly anxious individuals were identified and given therapy early in their college careers, many potential college failures could be prevented.

PHYSIOLOGICAL NEEDS: BUILT-IN MOTIVATION

The physiological basis of the need for food, liquid, and sleep was described in some detail in Chapter 2. Those needs obviously exist throughout our lives, and their associated drives are periodically aroused when we have been deprived for even a relatively brief period of time. You can easily add other physiological needs to the list. We need oxygen, and the drive to obtain it can be quickly and easily aroused, as you can demonstrate by inserting your head in a bucket of water for a few minutes. We also need to eliminate solid and liquid wastes from the body, and we attempt to avoid pain. In this section, we will examine two other important needs—sex and competence.

Even though needs may be based in biological processes, it is obvious that learning plays a crucial role in determining which external stimuli are arousing and just how the need is satisfied. The need for food, for example, is universal, but there are vast differences in what people learn to eat and in how they eat. In different parts of the world, people have learned to consume and to enjoy sheep's eyeballs, dog stew, warm cow blood mixed with milk, various insects, and human flesh. Most of us would pass up these unfamiliar foods rather than use them to reduce our hunger. The way we learn to eat also varies with respect to everything from the utensils we use (fingers, silverware, chopsticks) to the number of meals we eat per day and the times at which those meals occur. In a similar way, learning can play a significant role in our other needs by establishing specific incentives and need-satisfying behaviors.

Need for Sexual Gratification: Lust for Life

Sexual motivation is obviously necessary for the continuation of the species, but for human beings it also has many other functions and meanings. That is, human sexuality is a source of pleasure, guilt, power, love, anxiety, frustration, and much else besides. It is obvious that sexual activity may simply involve pleasant sensations, and, as a result, sex can be viewed as an entertaining recreational activity. When two people are very much in love, sex can constitute the most intimate and the most direct way of communicating positive interpersonal feelings. If an individual has learned to associate sex with being dirty or wicked, however, sexual pleasure may always be mixed with or overshadowed by feelings of anxiety and guilt. For example, some individuals associate sexual arousal with disgust and nausea (Byrne, Fisher, Lamberth, and Mitchell, 1974), and a surprising number of college undergraduates believe that masturbation is shameful, disgusting, and potentially harmful (Abramson and Mosher, 1975). Sexual activity can also be a way of asserting power over other persons and exploiting them in a hostile and callous manner; "women are out for all they can get from a man, so a man should get all that he can from a woman" (Mosher, 1971). Finally, failure to find a satisfactory sexual outlet can be a source of frustration and humiliation, especially in a society which stresses the importance of sexual adjustment.

The need for sexual gratification is different from other physiological needs in that it is not present in full force at birth; also, failure to satisfy sexual needs is not fatal to the individual (unpleasant, perhaps, but not fatal). We will examine a few aspects of research on sexual motivation.

It is sometimes suggested that sexual development is a simple two-step process involving an absolutely nonsexual childhood followed by puberty — at which time hormones gush into the bloodstream and create fully mature sexual males and females. Actually, for mammals like ourselves, there are a series of developmental steps which begin shortly after conception and continue until adulthood is reached.

The Physiological Basis of Sex: Developing Sexuality

The development of differential male and female sexual anatomy is dependent on the action of sexual hormones long before birth. Without such hormones, all embryos naturally develop the female genital system; the secretion of **androgens** (the male sex hormones) six weeks after conception turns some of us into males (Money, 1974). In Chapter 8, we will describe what happens when this developmental sequence is disrupted by hormonal accidents. The male and female genital systems may seem to be sharply different, but they actually are remarkably alike and have the same basic structures. For example, the male penis and the female clitoris are analogous structures; both have concentrations of sensitive nerve cells and both have erectile tissue. The male testes and the female ovaries are also parallel organs; one produces sperm and the other produces ova. The ovaries remain within the female's abdominal cavity, and the testes normally descend into a kind of sack, the scrotum, which is analogous to the outer lips around the vaginal opening (McCary, 1973).

Though infancy and childhood may not appear to be a time during which sexual motives play a major role, observations of infants tells us a very different story. For example, male infants have frequent erections, and children of both sexes engage in masturbatory activities, presumably because touching the nerve-rich genital area feels good. In the not too distant past when most people mistakenly believed that masturbation was somehow harmful, parents were given much advice about how to keep children's hands away from their genitals, even tying them to the bedpost if necessary. Despite all this obvious sexuality, people reacted with shock and disbelief at the beginning of this century when Sigmund Freud (see Chapter 9) informed the world that childhood is a time of sexual curiosity, sexual desire, and sexual anxiety. Harlow's (1975) observations of young monkeys indicate that they, too, masturbate and satisfy their sexual curiosity in a variety of activities, as may be seen in Figure 7–7.

There is a related aspect of early sexual development that is crucial. As we will see in Chapter 8, experiments with monkeys strongly suggest that physical contact with others is a necessary experience for normal sexual interests and skills to develop. Sexually mature female monkeys who were raised in isolation were found to attack and maul any male who tried to have intercourse. Males raised in isolation attempted to engage in sexual behavior but in clumsy and inappropriate ways that were unsuccessful (Harlow, 1962).

At puberty, the production of male and female sex hormones leads to physical changes in the genitals, the development of secondary sexual characteristics such as breasts and pubic hair, and growth in height (see Chapter 8). In addition, the need for sex shows a powerful increase. In *most* species, female sexual arousal seems to be strongly under the control of hormones, with periodic increases and decreases that are directly related to the production and release of ova. In males, sexual arousal is more often brought about by a combination of hormonal activity and the presence of external stimuli which

FIGURE 7-7   Young monkeys can be observed to engage in a variety of sexual acts including masturbation and immature attempts at intercourse. (Courtesy of Dr. Harry F. Harlow, University of Wisconsin Primate Laboratory.)

are arousing. Among various species, the nature of these stimuli may be very specific visual, auditory, or olfactory cues. Work with mammals suggests that smell is the most common stimulus for male arousal. There are substances secreted in the female vagina, called **pheromones,** which excite males. When female urine is placed on the backs of male mice, other males attempt to mount them sexually (Connor, 1972). Vaginal secretions will similarly cause male monkeys to become aroused and to attempt sexual intercourse; further, when their sense of smell is temporarily destroyed, there is no sexual responsiveness (Michael, Keverne, and Bonsall, 1971). Human sexual arousal has never been directly linked to olfactory cues (Doty et al., 1975), despite what the perfume and after-shave ads say. (It is interesting to note that vaginal secretions do occur in human females as in our primate cousins, and that "feminine deodorant" products are designed to disguise or destroy them.)

It can be seen, then, that sexual needs and the sex drive are relatively complex and depend on hormonal activity prior to birth, the development of genital structures sensitive to touch, early contact experience with members of one's own species, increased hormonal production at puberty, and the appropriate excitatory stimuli. In addition, as we shall see, the arousal of the sexual drive in human beings depends in great measure on learning and on imaginative activity.

Determining the Strength of Arousal: Sex, Pain, or Lunch?

In studying any motivational state in other animals, the problem of measuring drive strength must be met. Most often, as we have indicated, the strength of hunger and thirst are defined in terms of deprivation—the number of hours that have passed since the animal last was fed or given a drink. Long-term food deprivation can also be measured by decreases in body weight. Because of its dependence on hormonal state and on the presence of external stimuli, sexual drive cannot be determined in quite the same way. Female drive increases and decreases throughout the estrous cycle, regardless of whether the animal engages in sexual intercourse. There is evidence that the speed with which a male rat mounts a female in heat is related to the number of days he has spent in sexual deprivation (Beach and Jordan, 1956), and that repeated acts of intercourse lead to progressively less interest in further intercourse for both males and females (Peirce and Nuttall, 1961). Even when a male seems totally satiated and without sexual desire or ability, however, the introduction of a new female will bring about renewed arousal and enthusiastic sexual activity (Clemens, 1967). A novel male does not have an arousing effect on females, however.

A different approach to measuring drive strength was used a great deal in the early days of experimental psychology. The general idea was to determine how much pain an animal was willing to endure in order to reach a given goal. For this purpose the Columbia obstruction box, which consists of an apparatus in which a rat is separated from various goal objects by an electric grid, was used. During a 20-minute observation period, the animal was allowed to run across the painful grid as often as he or she wished in order to touch the goal object. Then it was returned to the original side. The number of crossings was assumed to indicate the strength of the drive. These studies revealed such details as the greater strength of the maternal drive than the sex drive for female rats, as well as the greater strength of hunger and thirst than sex for male rats after one to four days of deprivation (Warden, 1931). In time, however, it became obvious that such experiments involved too many variables to yield clear-cut measures of drive strength (Bolles, 1975).

A related approach to determining drive strength involves giving the animal a choice between two goal objects. The general idea is expressed in the joke about the woman who visited a zoo and was disappointed not to see the elephants. She asked the zoo keeper where they were, and he indicated that they were inside the shelter making love. The woman asked, "Would they come outside if I offered them some peanuts?" The keeper replied, "I don't know. Would you?" Experiments have provided an answer to that question. Larssen (1956) found that after 24 hours without food, male rats in a Skinner box preferred intercourse to pressing a bar to obtain food. More recently, Sachs and Marsan (1972) reported that even after six days of food deprivation, when male rats were placed in a cubicle with both food and a receptive female, almost all of them had intercourse before they paused to eat. First things first.

At this point in time, how sexually aroused are you?

1	2	3	4	5	6	7	8	9
Not at all		Slightly aroused		Moderately aroused		Strongly aroused		Extremely aroused

FIGURE 7–8 With human subjects, sexual arousal can be measured by means of self-rating scales. Do you believe that you can accurately report how aroused you feel at a given moment? (Rating scale from Davis and Braucht, 1971, p. 10.)

In studying the sex drive of human subjects, other approaches are possible. For one thing, experimenters can ask people to indicate verbally just how sexually aroused they are. A great many experiments have used simple rating scales of the kind shown in Figure 7–8. Under various conditions of stimulation or lack of stimulation, subjects are asked to indicate their sexual feelings at that moment. There is still another way to determine drive strength. In contrast to other physiological drives, sexual arousal is also accompanied by observable changes in various parts of the body, especially in the genitals. Depending on the degree of arousal, both males and females experience swelling of genital tissue, increases in genital temperature, and the secretion of lubricatory fluids. When college students are shown an erotic movie depicting explicit sexual acts, most males and females report some physiological reaction, and almost a third of each sex reports some genital lubrication (Schmidt and Sigusch, 1970). Direct measurement of these physiological indicators of arousal is also possible. Most of the work has been conducted with male subjects using a **penile plethysmograph** which is placed around the penis to record changes in size when an erection occurs (Zuckerman, 1971). When such recordings are made during the showing of an erotic movie, arousal as measured by penis size is shown to increase rapidly as the movie begins, to show only a mild decrease during the course of the movie, and then to decrease rapidly when the movie ends, as shown in Figure 7–9 (Howard, Reifler, and Liptzin, 1971).

Direct measures of female arousal have also been developed with an instrument that records the temperature of the clitoris and another that involves inserting a balloon-like device into the vagina to measure muscular contractions. The newest and most reliable measure of female arousal, however, is the **vaginal plethysmograph,** which records the increases in genital blood flow during sexual excitement (Geer, 1975). A device made of clear acrylic plastic is inserted in the vagina; the amount of blood in the vaginal walls is indicated by the amount of light reflected from a small light source. Research with this instrument clearly reveals female sexual excitement during masturbation or while watching a sexually explicit movie (Geer, Morokoff, and Greenwood, 1974).

Sexual Arousal in Human Beings: The Mind as an Erogenous Zone

Sexual arousal in other animals is ordinarily well coordinated with sexual behavior and seems to function almost exclusively as a means to perpetuate the species. That is, females become aroused when they are most likely to become pregnant, males become aroused when they are in the vicinity of a

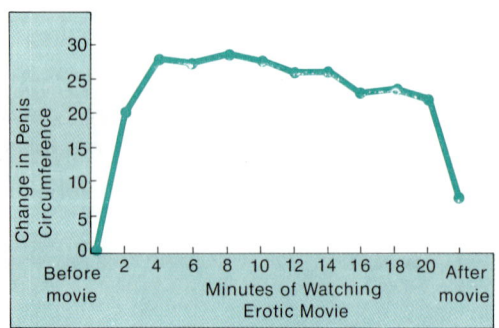

FIGURE 7–9   Sexual arousal in males can be measured by a penile plethysmograph, which records changes in penis size. Males watching an erotic movie indicated a rapid increase in excitement at the beginning of the movie, maintained a fairly high level of arousal throughout the movie, and then indicated a rapid decrease after the movie. (Adapted from Howard, Reifler, and Liptzin, 1971.)

suitably receptive female, and the two aroused animals have intercourse. As we observe the differences between the simplest animals and those that are increasingly complex, we find that sexual arousal is less and less controlled by hormones and simple instinctive responses and more and more controlled by the cerebral cortex (see Chapter 2) (Beach, 1969). Among other things, this change means that learning plays an important role in the sexuality of higher animals. For example, male animals have been observed to engage in homosexual acts and to masturbate to orgasm. Whether orgasm occurs in female animals is uncertain, but one creative female porcupine was seen to develop a primitive vibrator by inserting a small stick in her vagina and then dragging it along the bumpy ground (Gebhard, 1974). Among the higher primates, there is some evidence that sexual activity can become a recreational pastime as well as a procreational necessity.

At the human level, cognitive control of sexual arousal is, of course, even greater than in other animals. One consequence is that human beings can and do learn to be aroused by every conceivable type of stimulus. That is, people can easily learn to associate sexuality with external stimuli and respond to such incentives as members of the opposite sex, small children or the aged, animals, inanimate objects, pain, rock music, the feel of leather, the smell of pine trees, the sight of high-heeled shoes, the taste of Mom's apple pie, and anything else you can name. External stimuli become sexual incentives when they have been associated with sexual acts such as masturbation or intercourse. For example, in a laboratory demonstration of this phenomenon, Rachman (1966) created a "shoe fetish" by having subjects alternately view photographs of nudes and pictures of footwear. Similarly, a friend of one of the authors was surprised to find himself responding sexually to the sound of Elvis Presley's voice; it seems that his wife frequently played Elvis records during their lovemaking. People can also learn to engage in an amazing variety of sexual acts. Unlike other species, we are not limited to a single position for sexual intercourse, and individuals learn to obtain orgasm through a wide variety of heterosexual, homosexual, and autosexual acts.

There is an even more crucial aspect of cognitive influence on the human sexual drive. We are able to respond to words, pictures, and ideas involving sexual matters. We have already referred to experiments that show the effects of erotic movies on sexual arousal. The physiological indications of arousal of individuals who view a sexually explicit movie are no different from those of individuals engaging in the preliminary stages of sexual intercourse. These same effects hold true with respect to exposure to photographs, drawings, or stories containing sexual content (Byrne and Byrne, 1977). It is interesting to note that when subjects are given no erotic stimulus material but are simply asked to imagine a series of erotic situations, they actually become more aroused than subjects who do see erotic slides and stories (Byrne and Lamberth, 1971). Such findings suggest that the activation of human sexual desires and the expression of sexual behavior are in large part independent of physiological determinants and are controlled much more by psychological variables (Geer and Fuhr, 1976). This is one reason that human sexuality is not necessarily destroyed by removal of the sex glands or by the nonfunctioning of these glands in old age. The human ability to create and respond to fantasies seems to play a major role in sexual motivation (Byrne, 1976). We seem to be the only animal which responds to erotic images. In a zoo in Sacramento, California, male and female gorillas were shown "primate pornography" in an attempt to induce them to mate. The gorillas were evidently not turned on by the erotica, because they made no sexual approaches to one another.

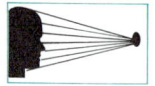

FOCUS ON RESEARCH: *What Are You Doing after the Skin Flick?*

The fact that human beings are rather easily aroused by erotic images, including their own thoughts about sex, raises some serious questions. Especially in a society which produces magazines, books, songs, plays, and movies dealing with varying degrees of explicit sexual activity, what behavioral effects are brought about by this repeated stimulation and sexual arousal?

One fear, of course, is that sex crimes could be expected to increase as a function of exposure to erotica. This fear is presumably a major reason that most countries have some form of censorship prohibiting the production and sale of material which is labeled obscene or pornographic. Though it is difficult to obtain conclusive evidence on such a complex problem, the available facts do not indicate that sex crimes are caused by pornography. Strangely enough, the relationship between exposure to erotica and antisocial sexual acts seems to be a negative one. That is, sex criminals report less frequent contact with pornography and a stricter upbringing than do normal individuals (Eysenck, 1972; Goldstein, Kant, Judd, Rice, and Green, 1971). And, when Denmark changed its laws (in 1969) to remove all restrictions on the sexual content of what adults could purchase or view, sexual crimes actually decreased in that country.

Nevertheless, sexual arousal in response to erotica would be expected to have *some* effects on behavior. The immediate effects of public exposure to erotica, besides arousal, include an increased interest in members of the opposite sex. For example, after college students were shown a series of photographic slides depicting explicit sexual acts, they spent more time looking at members of the opposite sex than at members of their own sex—just the opposite of students who had not been aroused (Griffitt, May, and Veitch, 1974).

A more critical question is whether exposure to erotica increases the likelihood that sexual behavior will take place. In recent years, a number of experiments have been conducted to answer this question. In general, it appears that the behavioral effects of exposure are limited to a slight increase in the frequency of one's usual pattern of sexual activity, such as masturbation (Amoroso, Brown, Pruesse, Ware, and Pilkey, 1971) or intercourse with one's spouse (Mann, Berkowitz, Sidman, Starr, and West, 1974). We will examine one such experiment in greater detail.

Cattell, Kawash, and DeYoung (1972) studied a large group of married male students who volunteered to be experimental subjects. Half of the group was shown 40 erotic slides, and half was shown 40 slides of geometric forms and art work. As in most such studies, sexual drive as measured by self-report was found to increase for those subjects who saw the erotic pictures. Each subject was later asked whether or not he had had sexual intercourse with his wife on the night of the experiment. The results are shown in Figure 7–10A. Intercourse was significantly more likely to occur for the experimental subjects who saw the sexual pictures than for the control subjects.

People differ in how much arousal they experience in response to erotic pictures. If sexual arousal leads to sexual behavior, then highly aroused individuals should be more

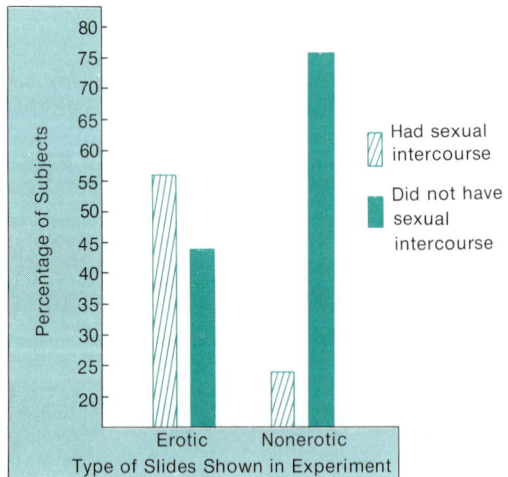

FIGURE 7–10   A. Married males took part in an experiment in which they were shown either erotic slides or artistic slides of geometric forms. Later they were asked whether or not they had sexual intercourse with their wives the evening of the experiment. More subjects who saw the sexual slides engaged in intercourse afterward than did subjects who saw the control slides. (Adapted from Cattell, Kawash, and DeYoung, 1972.)

Illustration continued on opposite page

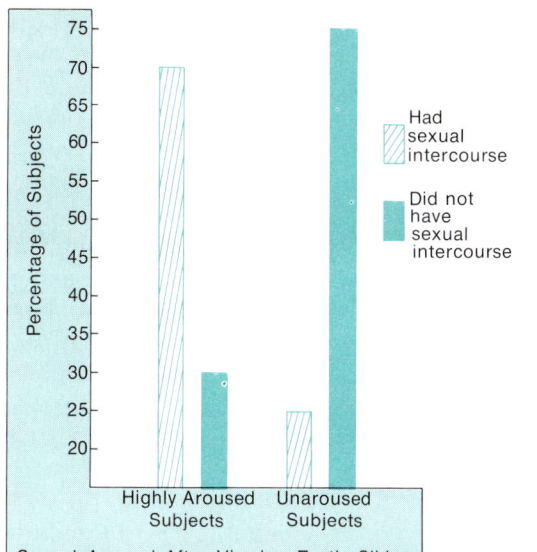

FIGURE 7–10 *Continued.* B. Married males who had seen a series of erotic slides were divided into those who reported a high level sexual arousal and those who reported very little arousal. The highly aroused subjects were more likely to have intercourse on the night of the experiment than were the relatively unaroused subjects. (Adapted from Cattell, Kawash, and DeYoung, 1972.)

likely to engage in the sexual act than should subjects who are only mildly aroused. In order to test this hypothesis, Cattell and his colleagues divided their experimental subjects into those who reported the greatest amount of sexual arousal and those who reported the least amount of arousal after seeing the erotic slides. As shown in Figure 7–10*B*, degree of arousal had the expected effect on probability of intercourse. More of the highly aroused subjects had intercourse the evening of the experiment than was true of those with low levels of arousal. Thus, drive-arousal increased the probability that these

individuals would engage in the appropriate goal-oriented behavior.

Studies such as this, along with research on convicted sex offenders (Goldstein, Kant, and Hartman, 1974), suggest that although sexual motivation is increased by exposure to erotica, this seems to be less likely to lead to crime in the streets than to intercourse in the bedroom. Whether there are *some* individuals who would respond to such sexual arousal by committing sex offenses still remains an open question. What are your ideas on the subject?

The basic or primary needs which have been discussed so far all involve processes which are necessary for maintaining the life of the individual or of the species. Traditionally, all other motivation was believed to be learned. There are some other behaviors, however, which were not usually included among these basic needs but which do not seem to be based on learning, as can be easily observed in both human beings and other animals. Consider a few examples. A family moves into a new home and brings their dog there for the first time. His immediate response is to walk around sniffing every inch of the unfamiliar yard and house. What motivates his exploration? A year-old baby is given a "busy box" as a present. She sits contentedly with it for hours ringing the bell, opening a small door to reveal a picture underneath, pushing a switch that just clicks as it goes back and forth, and trying to rotate a brightly colored circular disc. What motivates her attempts to manipulate these objects? A mother and father sit with their small child after a backyard picnic dinner, and the child wants to know where the stars are, why the fireflies make flashes of light, and what makes peanut butter stick to your mouth. What motivates this curiosity? Many psychologists have become convinced that these behaviors represent motives as basic as hunger, thirst, and the sex drive.

Among those who have suggested the basic importance of exploration, manipulation, and curiosity is Robert White (1959). He has proposed that

The Effectance Motive: Discovering the World

very simple organisms can rely on innate behavior patterns in order to survive. In contrast, complex animals such as mammals must learn to deal effectively with the world around them; they must achieve **competence.** In addition, he has proposed that there is inborn motivation to reach this goal, a need he labeled **effectance.** We will examine here some of the research related to what White called the effectance motive.

Exploration: That's Entertainment

One early demonstration that the opportunity to explore is rewarding was provided in an experiment by Butler (1953). He presented monkeys with a discrimination problem, but instead of using a familiar reinforcement such as food, he rewarded each correct response by simply opening a window so that the monkeys could see what was going on in another room (see Figure 7–11). The discrimination was learned under these conditions. This and subsequent studies established that engaging in visual exploration acts as a powerful reward. Even rats will learn to press a bar to obtain a change in stimulation: they will work to turn a light on when the room is dark and to turn a light off when it is bright (McCall, 1965).

What do you do when you are bored? You probably seek new stimulation whether in the form of new activities, new surroundings, or new ideas. Have you ever walked or driven out of your way just to see something new or to find out what is there? Rats do the same thing. Montgomery (1954) presented rats that were neither hungry nor thirsty with a maze choice in which they could go down a short path or a much longer path that led to novel territory; they preferred the longer path. Similarly, kittens will learn when the reward is simply the opportunity to explore (Miles, 1958).

Related findings have to do with the complexity of stimuli; given a choice, rats prefer a relatively complex stimulus to a relatively simple one (Berlyne and Slater, 1957; Walker, 1964). Not surprisingly, up to a point human adults are found to prefer complexity and novelty to simplicity and repetition when they are shown a series of drawings such as those in Figure 7–12 (Berlyne, 1958). Nine-month-old infants also prefer looking at complex stimuli when

FIGURE 7–11 Monkeys are able to learn when the only reinforcement is the opportunity to look through a window to see what is in the next room (in this case a bowl of fruit). It appears that visual exploration is a rewarding activity. Such behavior is conceptualized as satisfying the effectance motive, which leads organisms to learn to deal effectively and competently with the world around them. (From "Curiosity in Monkeys" by R. Butler. Copyright © 1954 by Scientific American, Inc. All rights reserved.)

FIGURE 7-12 When adults are shown pairs of stimuli such as these, they typically spend more time looking at the more complex of the two. This preference is consistent with the idea that we have a need to explore the world around us and to seek understanding of it. In the pairs shown here, the simpler stimulus is on the left and the more complex one on the right. (From Berlyne, D. E.: The influence of complexity and novelty in visual figures on orienting responses. Journal of Experimental Psychology, 55(3), March, 1958. Copyright 1958 by the American Psychological Association. Reprinted by permission.)

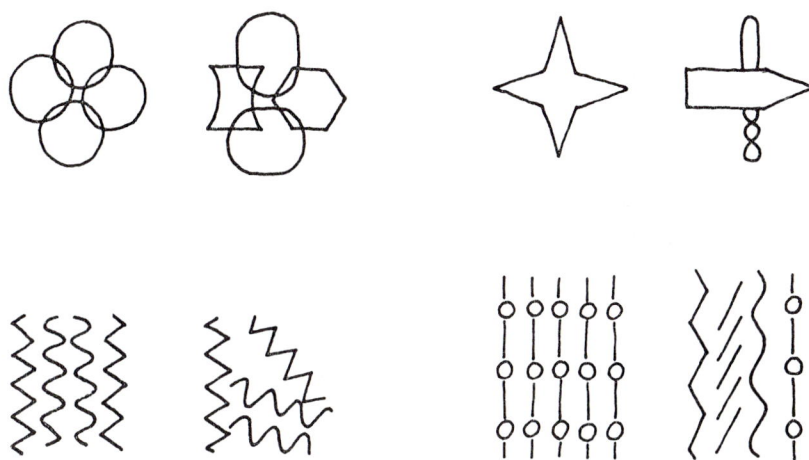

simple and complex drawings are presented to them simultaneously (Berlyne, 1966).

These general findings have limits, of course. When subjects are presented with situations that are extremely novel or bewilderingly complex, they become anxious. To demonstrate this, Byrne and Clore (1967) created two movies which were designed to arouse the effectance motive. These 8-mm. reels were completely meaningless collections of brief scenes that had no relationship to one another, and they were accompanied by sound tracks that bore no relationship to the scenes. This degree of complexity and novelty aroused unpleasant feelings such as anxiety. It is also true that individuals differ with respect to what is novel and complex for them, depending on their past experiences. That is, we adapt to a given stimulus and often go on then to seek something new. In addition, individuals who are creative and intelligent enjoy more novelty and complexity than do those who are not.

Manipulation: Please Don't Touch the Merchandise

The next time you are in a store that displays objects on open shelves, stop for a minute and watch what the shoppers do. Both children and adults are very likely to reach out and touch and pick up the things they see. If the object has moving parts, even the casual browser will probably push the button or turn the knob to see how it works. This human tendency to manipulate whatever new objects we encounter is the reason that store managers post such signs as "Hands off!" and "If you just broke it, you just bought it."

Animal studies seem to indicate that we come by our inquisitiveness quite naturally. Rats will approach, sniff, and examine closely any new object which is added to their familiar environment (Berlyne, 1950). Chimpanzees do this, too (VanLawick-Goodall, 1967), and they will spend even more time when the object is something that can be moved, altered, or made to light up or make a noise (Welker, 1956). If that sounds at all strange, when was the last time you played a pinball machine?

In a similar way, consider the times in your life that you have fiddled with a puzzle that involved nothing more than getting several round balls to rest in the right holes. The only apparent reward is that involved in the manipulation itself and in successfully completing the task. Monkeys will also spend time working on analogous mechanical tasks such as raising a latch and hooking it into place (Harlow, 1953), and their performance steadily improves if they have the opportunity to do it over and over, as shown in Figure 7-13.

FIGURE 7–13 Top: The effectance motive also leads to manipulative behavior. Monkeys will work hard to operate a series of latches even though no other reward is involved. Bottom: Humans, too, will work at puzzles for which the only reward is the activity itself. (Top photos from University of Wisconsin Regional Primate Laboratory; bottom photos by Sue Soldoff.)

Functions of the Effectance Motive: Learning about Our World and Changing It

Arguments have been made that exploration and manipulation simply represent increased activity which improves the odds that an animal will obtain food, water, or sexual gratification. This does not appear to be true, however, in that exploration decreases rather than increases when animals are hungry or thirsty (Montgomery, 1953). In the same way, the ability of monkeys to solve puzzle manipulations becomes worse when they are hungry (Davis, Settlage, and Harlow, 1950). It can be concluded that the effectance motive is strongest when other motives are not strongly aroused.

From the viewpoint of evolution, it makes sense that the kinds of behaviors motivated by a need for effectance are very useful. They have value for the individual and the species, in that our ancestors who explored their environment and manipulated objects increased their chances of surviving long enough to have offspring. Exploring led to greater knowledge of the location of food and water supplies, hiding places, and escape routes. Manipulation led to discoveries of otherwise inedible foods (shelling nuts, cracking clams, digging up potatoes) and to the gradual development of tools and weapons. At the individual level, each of us in early life spent considerable time exploring and manipulating our environment as we crawled and toddled about, grabbed everything we could reach, played with words in jokes and riddles, engaged in fantasy-making, and thus slowly moved toward knowledge that made us more effective as human beings. Bruner (1975, p. 81) writes:

> Play encompasses a motley, very unsober set of activities, from childish punning, to cowboys-and-Indians, to the construction of building-block towers. . . . Most important, primatologists found that play seems to serve a crucial function during immaturity, a function that increases in importance as one moves up the evolutionary scale from Old World monkeys, through great apes, to man. Play, they found, is a precursor of adult competence.

Among the eventual consequences of these activities has been mankind's consistent tendency to find out more and more about our surroundings, to explore new continents, and finally to search beneath the seas and into outer space. The exploration has not been purely geographical but includes all of the attempts of scientists, poets, philosophers, and others to satisfy their curiosity about every aspect of mankind and the universe around us. Our manipulative skills have taken us from crude tools (such as a rock shaped into a cutting device) to the modern digital computer, with stops along the way for all sorts of inventions and gadgets, from the telescope to the electric corn popper. Some of humanity's most impressive achievements rest on our inherited tendency to satisfy the effectance motive and thus to achieve competence.

BEFORE YOU READ ANY FURTHER IN THE TEXT, LOOK AT FIGURE 7–14 AND FOLLOW THE INSTRUCTIONS. THE TASK WILL BE EXPLAINED IN THE NEXT SECTION OF THE CHAPTER.

ACQUIRED MOTIVATION: LEARNING WHAT TO WANT

The motives of our primitive ancestors were probably centered around their physiological needs. When we think about ourselves and those around us, however, it is obvious that there are a great many kinds of motivation that have no direct connection with such needs. Are you motivated to receive a good grade in your psych course? Do you want to win when you play tennis? Are you working to make enough money to pay for something you desire—a guitar, a vacation, a car? Do you want people to like you? Such motives seem to be based on learning, and it appears that we can learn to want almost any-

FIGURE 7–14 Before you read any further in the text, look at this picture carefully and make up a brief story about it. In your story, include answers to the following questions:
1. What is happening? Who are the persons?
2. What has led up to this situation? That is, what has happened in the past?
3. What is being thought? What is wanted? By whom?
4. What will happen? What will be done?

(From *The Achievement Motive*, by D. C. McClelland, J. W. Atkinson, R. A. Clark, and E. L. Lowell, New York: Irvington Publishers, Inc., 1953.)

thing—from a ring in the nose to faded Levi's. It is almost literally impossible to make a list that would include all of your acquired motives.

The acquisition of a motive does not seem to be terribly mysterious, and most psychologists would argue that the process follows the general principles of learning discussed in Chapter 4. Some of our desires are learned through classical conditioning. While our hunger is being satisfied, for example, other stimuli become associated with the pleasant feelings. They then become the objects of our positive motivation. Did you ever get upset and demand some familiar stimuli when your favorite bowl was misplaced or when your aunt's gravy didn't look just like your mother's gravy? In addition to being acquired through association, motives can be picked up through instrumental learning. For example, you may originally have brushed your teeth only because you were praised for doing so or threatened with punishment when you did not. After a sufficient number of trials, the rewards and punishments could be eliminated, because you eventually *wanted* to brush your teeth. This process was described by Allport (1937) as the *functional autonomy* of motives. He felt that adult behavior is primarily directed by motives which have become completely autonomous of any physiological needs, as in the following example:

> An ex-sailor has a craving for the sea. . . . Now, the sailor may have first acquired his love for the sea as an incident in his struggle to earn a living. The sea was merely a conditioned stimulus associated with satisfaction of his nutritional craving. But now the ex-sailor is perhaps a wealthy banker; the original motive is destroyed; and yet the hunger for the sea persists unabated, even increases in intensity as it becomes more remote from the nutritional segment (Allport, 1937, p. 145).

We will now see how these general concepts can be applied to a specific motive—that of **achievement.**

The Achievement Motive: Striving for Success

Individuals differ greatly in their desire to compete and to succeed in whatever activities they undertake. It has been proposed that such differences reflect variations in the learned motive to achieve. This motive was defined many years ago by Murray (1938, p. 164) as "the desire or tendency to do things as rapidly and/or as well as possible." Currently, it is usually defined as "a concern over competition and some standard of excellence."

Measuring the Achievement Motive: What Your Fantasies Reveal

A learned motive such as achievement cannot be measured in quite the same way as the physiological needs. That is, it does not make sense to deprive subjects of accomplishment for several hours, to observe how many times they cross an electric grid in order to compete, or to try to devise a success plethysmograph. The earliest attempt to measure individual differences in this motive consisted of a simple questionnaire which asked subjects to answer true-false items such as "I feel that nothing else which life can offer is a substitute for great achievement" and "I enjoy work as much as play." Because people are not always completely aware of their motivation, attempts were made to approach the measurement problem in a less direct fashion.

The most successful such device is based on the **Thematic Apperception Test** (see Chapter 9), which consists of a series of pictures for which each subject makes up a story. Presumably, in deciding what the characters are feeling, thinking, planning, the subject is really expressing his own unconscious motives and conflicts. With respect to achievement, a special set of pictures was developed by McClelland, Atkinson, Clark, and Lowell (1953). For example, one picture shows a boy in the foreground with a vague operation scene in the background. When asked to make up a story to fit that picture, individuals with high achievement motivation may say that the boy is daydreaming of becoming a great surgeon, saving many lives, and becoming rich and famous.

In response to the same picture, those with low achievement motivation may say that the boy is thinking about an operation his mother must have and how much he will miss her if she does not pull through. Even without learning the rather complicated scoring system, you can observe that one type of story expresses a concern with achievement while the other expresses concern with close interpersonal relationships. When you wrote a story about the picture in Figure 7–14, did your story express very much achievement motivation? Of course, to measure your motives accurately, it would be necessary for you to tell a series of such stories and to have them scored by a trained expert. For examples of high and low achievement stories about the picture, see Figure 7–15.

The motive strength indicated by these stories is reflected in many different types of behavior. For example, compared to those with low motivation, individuals with high achievement motivation tend to be more intelligent (Robinson, 1961), to get better grades in college courses that are related to their future careers (Raynor, 1970), to desire to enter high-status occupations (Minor and Neel, 1958), and to be successful in business (Andrews, 1967).

Achievement motivation is also related to the way in which individuals approach games and tasks on which they can succeed or fail. In a number of experiments, an interesting difference has consistently been found between high- and low-achievers in risk-taking behavior. In one task, children are shown a ring toss game and told that they can stand wherever they wish in attempting to throw the circular ring onto an upright wooden peg. Where would you stand? Those low in the achievement motive tend to stand right by the peg and easily drop the rings onto it or to stand ridiculously far away and give themselves an almost impossible task. It is as if they are trying to avoid any feelings of competition and possible failure by making the task either too easy or too difficult. Those high in the achievement motive tend to select an intermediate distance at which the task is a challenge and the outcome less certain, but where success is possible (McClelland, 1958). Analogous differences in willingness to take risks are found among high school students engaged in a group project (Zander and Forward, 1968) and among businessmen asked to select the odds they preferred in a betting situation; those with the highest achievement motivation prefer intermediate odds, while those with low motivation prefer either long-shots or sure things (Meyer, Walker, and Litwin, 1961).

> Two inventors are working on a new type of machine. They need this machine in order to complete the work on their new invention, the automobile. This takes place some time ago. They are thinking that soon they will have succeeded. They want to improve transportation. Their invention will be successful and they will found a great industrial concern.
>
> There are two men working in some sort of machine shop. They are making some sort of a bolt or something. One of the men's car broke down, and he has discovered that a bolt is broken. So, being a fairly good forger, he is making a new bolt. He is discussing with the other man just how he is making the bolt and telling him about all of the details in making this bolt. When he is finished, he will take the bolt and replace the broken bolt in the car with it. He will then be able to get his car going.

FIGURE 7–15 Actual stories written about the picture in Figure 7–14 by research subjects. The first story contains much more achievement imagery than the second. (McClelland, Atkinson, Clark, and Lowell, 1953, pp. 118–119.)

Acquiring High Achievement Motivation: Parental Influences

A portion of the research on the achievement motive has dealt with the way the behavior of parents is responsible for the motivation level of their offspring. The general conclusion is that achievement motivation is most likely to develop in homes where a great deal of stress is placed on excellence and on competition as the way to reach high standards. Whenever the child does well, the parents tend to reward him or her with expressions of affection and praise (Rosen and D'Andrade, 1959). When mothers respond with indifference to success but provide punishment for failure, their children tend to be motivated by a fear of failure (Teevan and McGhee, 1972). Presumably, it is this fear that leads such individuals to avoid taking genuine chances in games or in betting situations. Accounts of the early family life of the late President Kennedy suggest a home atmosphere in which competition was a daily concern in everything from playing touch football to doing well in school. It is not surprising to find members of that family achieving in many fields. Family influences can also be devastatingly negative. For example, extremely dominant fathers can create a low need for achievement in their offspring (Bradburn, 1963). Also, very successful parents throughout history have obtained slaves or servants to take care of their child-rearing chores, and one effect seems to be to create low achievement motivation in the next generation (McClelland, 1961).

There is another kind of family influence on achievement motivation — namely, the father's occupation. This factor was not always noted; for a time, it was thought that there were simply social class differences in achievement motivation, with the strongest achievement motives in upper class families. Turner (1970) proposed that social class is not really an important variable; what is crucial is the type of position the father holds at work. It was suggested that in both white-collar and blue-collar fields, there are two very different kinds of jobs. A man can be relatively independent in some jobs, making decisions and not having close, direct supervision; such characteristics can be equally true of a white-collar manager and a blue-collar foreman. In contrast, a person can be relatively dependent in his job, doing routine work and having most decisions made for him by a supervisor; these characteristics can be equally true for a white-collar office worker or a blue-collar factory worker. Turner measured the achievement motivation of a group of seventh- and eighth-grade boys and also found out about their father's position in his occupation. As you can see in Figure 7–16, the basic idea is correct. Achievement motivation was much higher in the sons of men with independent, decision-making jobs

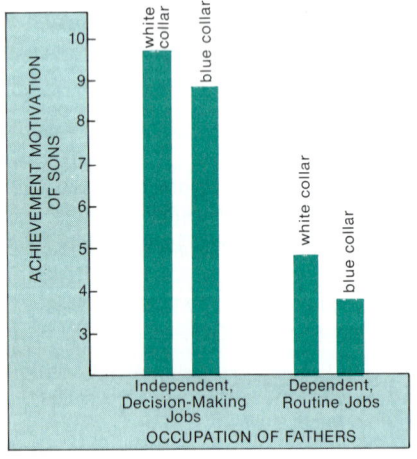

FIGURE 7–16   It has been found that a boy's level of achievement motivation is related to the type of job held by his father. Regardless of social class (white collar versus blue collar), the achievement motive was higher in boys whose fathers held independent, decision-making positions than in boys whose fathers held dependent, routine jobs. (Adapted from Turner, 1970.)

than in the sons of those in dependent, routine jobs. The difference between white-collar and blue-collar occupations was of relatively little importance. One explanation for these effects was that the independent fathers were probably more likely to stress responsibility and decision-making as important values at home and thus create the typical atmosphere of a high-achieving family. In contrast, the fathers in dependent jobs were more likely to come home and seize the chance to express authority and to exert control in the one place where such activity was possible. Thus, their sons had much less of a chance to develop the motive to achieve.

This work and other studies suggest that the development of high or low achievement motivation depends on many interrelated aspects of the parent's behavior, values, and concerns. How would you characterize your family? Do you think your own achievement motivation is related to what your parents did as you were growing up?

EMOTION: TEARS, CHEERS, AND FEARS

Emotions play a familiar part in the lives of each of us. Walking alone on city streets at night is apt to be accompanied by fear. The death of someone close to you brings forth grief. An insulting remark elicits your anger. You may feel elated when you receive a birthday present. At the moment there may be someone in your life for whom you feel love. Such emotions are similar to motivational states, in that emotions also can energize and direct behavior; in fact, some psychologists simply classify them as additional motives (Bindra, 1959). Though it is difficult to find a generally accepted definition of emotion, these states are most often identified by the kind of overt behavior that accompanies them (crying, laughing, frowning, and so forth) and by subjective reports as to what the person is experiencing (Cofer, 1972). It should also be noted that emotions are most strongly influenced by environmental events, and that they tend to be characterized by physiological reactions (Mandler, 1962). We will examine some of the research on emotion, including the problem of determining what others are experiencing and what we ourselves are experiencing.

Identifying the Basic Emotions: Observations and Physiological Indicators

How Many Emotions Are There?: Pick a Number, any Number

It would seem to be an obvious first step, and a fairly easy one, to identify the emotions. How many are there? Oddly enough, that is not a question for which there is a satisfactory answer. The English language contains at least 400 words that are used to name emotions (Davitz, 1969). Bridges (1932) approached the problem by observing the emotions expressed by infants day after day for the first two years of their lives. During most of the first month, the only emotion she identified was general excitement—there was the same excited reaction to being picked up, being in pain, being offered a bottle, or whatever. Near the end of the first month, Bridges noted a new kind of emotion—distress. Distress involved a characteristic type of crying, a flushed face, clenched fists, legs kicking, and eyes pressed tightly shut; it was noted that this emotion was set off by unpleasant stimuli such as discomfort, pain, and hunger. By the end of two months, the new and positive emotion of delight was expressed in smiles, cooing, and relaxed wriggling. By the time the children were two years old, eleven distinct emotions were observed. While this general developmental process undoubtedly occurs, not all observers would agree that the endpoint is precisely eleven different emotions.

The psychoanalyst Karen Horney (1945) classified behavior as being toward something, against it, or away from it. Some investigators accepted this classification and suggested that there are three basic emotional states which

FIGURE 7–17   In trying to determine the emotions of others, we often rely on behavioral cues such as trembling hands or changes in voice pitch. As Dagwood learns from Mr. Dithers, such cues may be more informative than what a person tells you about his emotional state. (© King Features Syndicate, 1974.)

accompany our behavior: we approach whatever makes us elated, fight against whatever makes us angry, and run away from whatever makes us fearful. In contrast, Davitz (1969) asked subjects to indicate personal experiences with each of 50 emotions; analysis revealed that they were responding to four basic dimensions. All such systems run into the problem of getting observers to agree about the emotions being expressed. A solution for some investigators was to turn to physiological indicators of emotion.

The Physiological Approach: Gut Feelings and Clammy Hands

In Chapter 2, the nineteenth century James-Lange theory of emotions was mentioned; these early psychologists suggested that emotions consist of our perceptions of the way our body is automatically responding to various stimuli. In that same chapter, the physiological approach to emotions was examined in terms of emotional regulation by certain areas of the brain: the hypothalamus and the limbic system. Animal experiments in which portions of these brain structures were cut revealed dramatic changes in emotional behavior.

While it is true that brain mechanisms regulate emotional behavior, the task of identifying specific emotions in terms of physiological reactions turns out to be no easier than the task of identifying emotions in other ways. Investigators have measured electrical responses of the skin, heart rate, breathing rate, muscular tension, metabolism, brain waves, and pupil dilation (among other things), looking in vain for specific correlates of emotion. Though anger and fear seem to show minor differences in their physiology, the most general conclusion is that very different emotions lead to much the same physiological responses (Grossman, 1967). Such findings have led a number of authorities to conclude that all we really mean by the word "emotion" is some kind of general arousal or activation (Duffy, 1962; Lindsley, 1951). Like the youngest infants that Bridges observed, perhaps we simply get excited or aroused from time to time, and this general arousal is all that is indicated by our various physiological reactions.

You can see, then, that attempts to establish a reliable way to identify the basic emotions on the physiological level have not been any more successful than similar attempts at the observational level. At the moment, no one can say with confidence that there are three emotions, four emotions, eleven, or any other number. And, there may be just one—arousal. We will turn now to some very different kinds of research which suggest that much of what we identify as emotion depends on factors such as learning and perception.

How do we find out what others are feeling and how they are reacting emotionally? Common experience tells us that we need only attend to their face or portions of it. There's fire in his eyes. The look of love. Put on a happy face. When Irish eyes are smiling. You're lips tell me "no" "no", but there's "yes" "yes" in your eyes. Whistle a happy tune, and no one will suspect you're afraid. If looks could kill. How well can we actually determine the emotional state of others on the basis of observing them?

One of the early studies of facial expression was conducted by Landis (1924). He asked individuals to let him photograph their faces as they engaged in such emotion-arousing acts as viewing erotic pictures, beheading a live rat, and receiving electric shock. He found that different subjects performing the same act (and presumably experiencing the same emotion) had very different expressions. Similar results were obtained in a later study using motion pictures rather than still photographs (Coleman, 1949). Such findings suggest that individuals would have a difficult time determining another person's emotional state on the basis of facial expression alone.

A related approach has been to ask individuals to try to portray different emotions; subjects are then asked to decide what the emotion is. Some of the first of these studies indicated that the portrayal of some emotions (surprise and happiness, for example) could be easily identified while others (such as pain and contempt) could not (Feleky, 1922). Schlosberg (1952) used a series of posed pictures which subjects were asked to rate first along a pleasant-unpleasant dimension. They were told simply to decide whether "the man felt pleasantness or unpleasantness." Then, they rated the same pictures along a dimension of rejection-attention. They were told that the eyes, nostrils, and mouth are usually constricted when someone seeks to reject stimuli, whereas attention makes the person open to receive stimulation. Statistical analysis suggested that the two dimensions of attention-rejection and pleasantness-unpleasantness represent the basic ways in which facial expressions vary. You can see in Figure 7-18 the kinds of facial expressions and emotional states which fall at various points along these dimensions. In general, then, there is better agreement about the emotion being expressed in posed photographs than in photographs of actual emotional states when only the face is visible. (It has also been found that emotions expressed in one's tone of voice are easier to perceive than emotions communicated in facial expressions, especially among males [Zuckerman et al., 1975].) We will now turn to studies which suggest just *why* there is some degree of agreement about what emotions an actor is trying to express but somewhat less agreement about the expression of people who are actually experiencing a real emotion.

BEFORE YOU READ ANY FURTHER, TURN TO THE BOX ON PAGE 249 AND FOLLOW THE INSTRUCTIONS.

The experiment outlined in the box on page 249 suggests that we really do not learn as much as we think from the expressions of others. Instead, we probably look at the context, decide how we would feel in that situation, and *then* decide what the person's expression means. In an experiment by Munn (1940), subjects were asked to do the same kind of thing you did in looking at Figures 7-19 and 7-20. His subjects were very inaccurate in identifying the emotions of determination, worry, pain, and fear until they received contextual information. Then, their accuracy increased dramatically. Such studies seem to explain why we are able to detect emotions better in real-life settings than in facial photographs. The question still remains as to why posed photographs of emotions are perceived more accurately than photographs of people actually experiencing an emotion. It seems that when we *try* to depict an emo-

Perceiving the Emotions of Others: Context and Culture

Context and Culture: You Look Unhappy Sitting on That Hot Stove

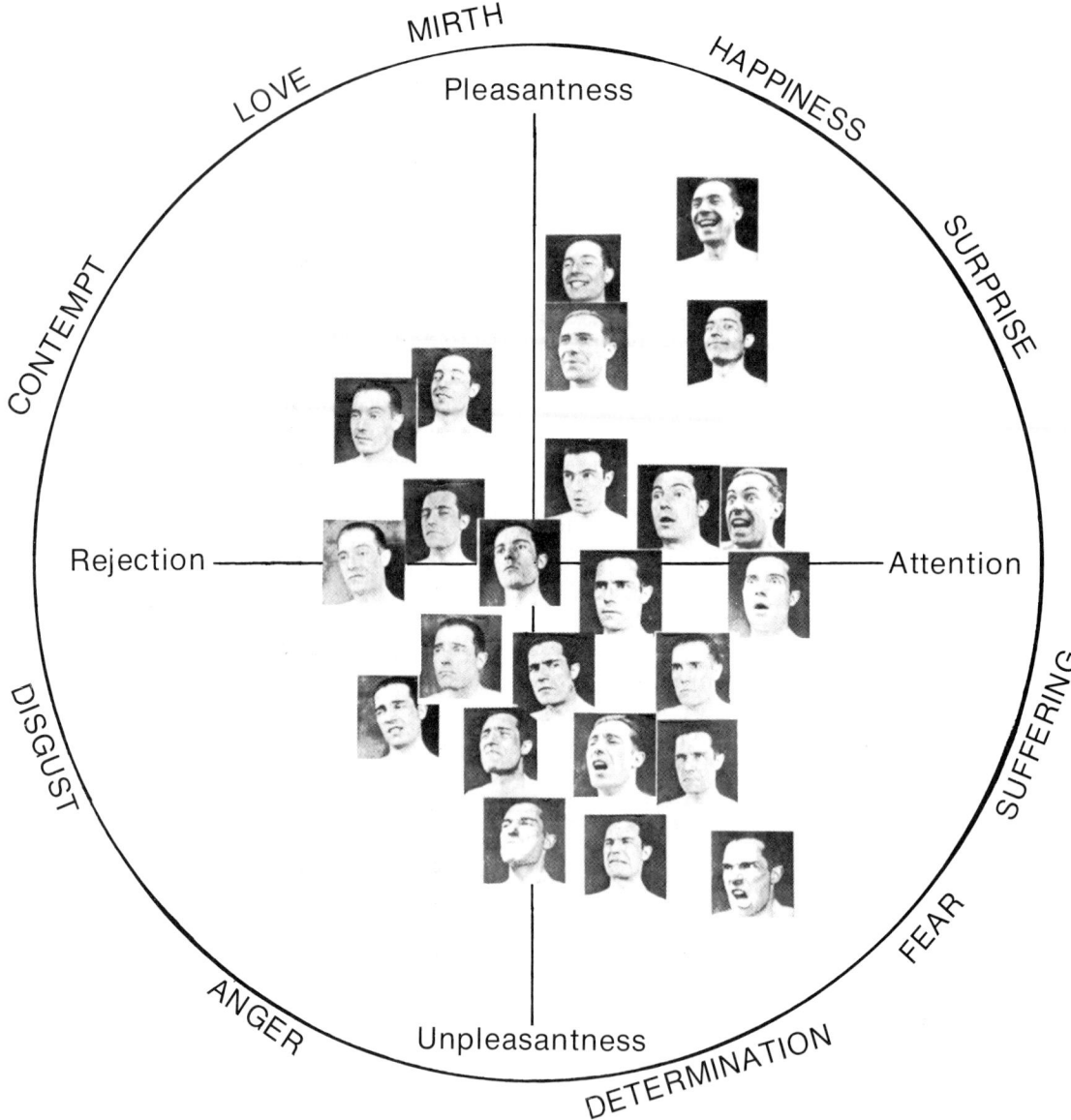

FIGURE 7-18 When subjects are asked to make judgments about the emotions being expressed in posed photographs, it is found that most emotional states can be placed at some point along the two dimensions, pleasant-unpleasant and rejection-attention. Some emotions involve both dimensions; for example, disgust combines rejection and unpleasantness. The closer each picture falls to the outer circle, the better the agreement about the emotion being expressed. The picture lying where the two lines cross is the one about which subjects were least certain. (From Schosberg, H.: The description of facial expressions in terms of two dimensions. Journal of Experimental Psychology, 44, 1952, p. 235. Copyright 1952 by the American Psychological Association. Reprinted by permission.)

tion, we strike a pose that is recognized in our culture as the "right" way to show the particular feeling.

Within any cultural group, one of the things to be learned as early as possible is how to express emotions and to communicate them to others in the

PSYCHOLOGY
IN
ACTION: "Reading" the Emotions of
Others—Using Your Personal Radar

Aren't you usually able to decide fairly accurately how those around you are feeling? If so, how do you do it? Before you try this experiment out on others, you can run through it with yourself as the first subject.

Look at Figure 7–19, study the faces carefully, and then write down what emotion is being expressed in each instance.

Now, see if the following information changes your judgments about the emotions being expressed: The man in the top left photo is about to ask his boss for a raise; the man in the lower left photo is in church; the woman in the top right photo has just received a traffic ticket; and the man in the lower right photo is listening to his favorite recording.

FIGURE 7–19 How do you "read" these people's faces? If you find the task at all difficult, there is a good reason. In real-life situations, you ordinarily are able to see not only a person's face but also the total situation or context. You know what the person is doing and what is causing the emotional reaction. (Upper left photo by Brian Aris, Photo Trends; upper right photo by Horst Schafer, Photo Trends; lower left photo by Ben Ross, Photo Trends; lower right photo from McGraw-Hill Films.)

With this added information, again write down your ideas about the emotions. Did you change your mind about any of the pictures? Are you more certain of your perceptions now than with just the facial expressions to go by?

Just to make the point one more time, we will ask you now to turn the page to look at Figure 7–20. You guessed it; the information we gave you was not really accurate.

Now that you have been a subject, it is time to determine how other people respond to this task of judging emotions. Using either the figures in this book or the duplicates in your *Student*

Manual, find 15 individuals who would be willing to try their skill at judging emotions. Show five of them only the pictures in Figure 7–19, show another five the same pictures plus the false information about context which we gave you above, and show the final five the pictures in Figure 7–20. In each instance, ask your subjects to write down the emotion being expressed by the individuals in the pictures.

Do you agree that the judgment of emotions depends a great deal on our knowledge of the context?

FIGURE 7-20 *Now* how do you read these people's faces? (Photo credits: lower right, McGraw-Hill Films; all others, Photo Trends.)

culture. For example, we learn to smile at parties and to look solemn in church, whether or not our feelings match our faces. These facial activities serve a communication function, as when an actor portrays a role or you play charades with friends. Our own behavior appears to be the natural way in which emotion is expressed, but there are differences across cultures in the meaning of various expressions and gestures. If the average American traveled in Greece and saw an old woman spit on a young child, he probably would be astonished and at a loss in interpreting her emotion. To those raised in that culture, however, it would seem obvious and "natural" that the woman was admiring the child's beauty (Triandis, 1976).

Cross-cultural studies reveal that some facial expressions are universal and probably represent adaptive tendencies inherited from our ancient ancestors, who did such things as bare their teeth in an angry fight (Darwin, 1872). Other expressions are, however, learned. For example, Americans, Brazilians, Japanese, and primitive natives in New Guinea agree fairly well about the expression of happiness in photographs but not nearly so well about the expression of fear (Ekman, 1973). There are, in addition, individual differences in personality and intellectual ability which are related to the accuracy with which emotions are perceived (Eby, 1975).

Individual Differences in Emotional Communication

Not too surprisingly, individuals vary greatly in their ability both to send and to receive nonverbal messages. While some are as easy to read as an open book, others are so nonexpressive as to remain something of a continual mystery to the persons around them. Similarly, while some individuals are highly sensitive to nonverbal messages, others seem almost totally oblivious to this form of communication. The existence of such large individual differences leads directly to the question of what characteristics make specific persons effective or ineffective senders and receivers of nonverbal information.

Turning first to the ability to transmit such cues, recent investigations suggest that individuals showing a high level of self-esteem and an extroverted, outgoing personality are far more successful in this regard than those low in self-esteem and introverted in personality (Buck, 1975; Buck, Miller, and Caul, 1974). With respect to the ability to receive and interpret nonverbal messages accurately, there is some indication that persons who perceive the world in complex terms are more effective at this task than those who perceive it in a more simplistic manner. Simplistic perception is in terms of rigid categories such as good and bad or right and wrong.

In addition, most studies on this topic have found that women are much better receivers of nonverbal cues than are men (Rosenthal et al., 1974). One explanation for this large and consistent sex difference centers on the fact that during socialization, girls are encouraged both to express their emotions openly and to pay close attention to those of others, while boys are actively discouraged from engaging in these pursuits. Given these contrasting patterns of experience, it is not at all surprising that the two sexes differ in their ability to handle nonverbal information as adults. Perhaps the size of this difference will decrease in the near future as the impact of the less rigid sex-typing practices now used by some young parents begins to be felt.

In sum, there is little doubt that much of our information concerning the present emotions and feelings of others is derived from nonverbal cues. The abilities to send such messages and to read them, therefore, play a crucial role in our attempts to know and understand the persons around us.

Perceiving Our Own Emotions: If I'm Laughing, I Must be Happy

We have seen that there is no reliable way to identify different emotions on the basis of physiological indicators, that it is vital to know the context in which the emotion occurs, and that perception is most accurate when it occurs within one's own culture. Now we turn to what may seem to be a simple question but one that has a surprising answer. How do we know what emotion we ourselves are feeling?

Emotion and Cognition: Give Me a Clue

One of the objections to the old James-Lange theory of emotions was based on the finding that with artificially induced "emotional arousal," most people report that they do not actually feel the emotion. When adrenaline (epinephrine) is injected into the blood stream, for example, subjects say they feel "as if" they were afraid or "as if" something pleasant were about to happen (Cannon, 1929). A modern social psychologist, Stanley Schachter, has added greatly to our understanding of such feelings. His experiments show that what people experience as emotion is based on a combination of physiological arousal (or activation) *and* information which leads them to interpret the arousal as a particular type of emotion (Schachter, 1964). In other words, we not only need information about the context to know what others are feeling, we need such information to know what we ourselves are feeling!

In one investigation (Schachter and Singer, 1962), subjects were told that they were taking part in an experiment to test the effects of a special vitamin supplement on vision. Actually, the experimental subjects received injections of epinephrine, which brought about physiological arousal, including such effects as a faster heart beat, a flushed face, and more rapid breathing. Some of the subjects were told that the "vitamins" would produce such symptoms, and some were left uninformed. When the uninformed subjects began experiencing the physiological symptoms, how did they interpret their unexpected emotional arousal? The experimenters provided information or suggestion by having the subjects exposed to one of two confederates who was supposedly a fellow subject. With some subjects, the confederate said that he felt very happy and then proceeded to shoot wads of paper at the wastebasket and to fly paper airplanes around the room. His finale was a wild dance with a hula hoop. With other subjects, the confederate complained angrily about one of the questionnaires he had to fill out and expressed his resentment about the experiment in general. He acted as if he were increasingly indignant and finally threw the questionnaire on the floor, saying "I'm not wasting any more time. I'm getting my books and leaving." When the subjects were asked to describe their own feelings afterward, those who were uninformed about their physiological symptoms of arousal were found to be very much influenced by the confederate. That is, those with a happy confederate decided that they were happy and acted accordingly, while those with an angry confederate decided that they were angry. The informed subjects attributed their physiological reactions to the injection, and they weren't influenced by the confederate at all.

This and later studies provided convincing support for Schachter's theory of emotions. Such work not only suggests that we need information in order to interpret our feelings but also that we can rather easily misinterpret what we feel. We will now examine the way in which such misinterpretations may play a crucial role in a complex emotional state familiar to many of us—love.

Passionate Love

Perhaps the most personal and most exciting emotion that human beings can experience occurs when they "fall in love." We know from books, movies, and songs that birds sing and bells ring, that the vibes are good, and that you can suddenly spot your true love across a crowded room. Despite all this folklore, there has not been much psychological research on the topic of love until very recent years (Rubin, 1973). Berscheid and Walster (1974) have defined passionate love as a combination of strong interpersonal attraction and sexual attraction, and they suggest that these emotions, like others, depend on physiological arousal and the interpretation of that arousal as "love." If they are correct, it means among other things that we sometimes are mistaken in interpreting how we feel about a member of the opposite sex. It has been pointed out that what we call love seems to develop and thrive in a variety of very different emotional states. When students at several universities were allowed to ask one question about love, one of the more frequently asked ones was, "Can you love and hate someone at the same time?" (Berscheid and Walster, 1974). Anecdotes suggest that love seems compatible not only with hate but also with fear, unhappiness, excitement, and any other type of arousal.

What may be important in determining how the individual feels about the person who is apparently generating these intense feelings is how he *labels* his reaction. If the situation is arranged so that it is reasonable for him to attribute this agitated state to "passionate love," he should experience love. As soon as he ceases to attribute his arousal to passionate love, or the arousal itself ceases, love should die (Berscheid and Walster, 1974, p. 363).

It is rather easy to think of experiences that are consistent with the Walster and Berscheid (1971) theory of love. For example, dating relationships often involve excitement and general physiological arousal in the form of such activities as roller coaster rides, horror movies, athletic events, and sexual play. What experimental evidence is there that such varied types of arousal are misinterpreted as attraction and love?

Several studies suggest that fear increases romantic attraction. In one experiment (Brehm, Gatz, Geothals, McCrommon, and Ward, 1970), some college males were told that they were going to receive three strong electric shocks, while others were told this and then later told that the information was wrong—no shocks would be given; still others were never told anything about receiving shock. The first two groups presumably were physiologically aroused (fear in one case and relief in the other), while the third group was not likely to be aroused at all. When these individuals were then introduced to a young female student, the subjects in the aroused groups liked her better than did the subjects in the non-aroused group. In a related experiment in which male subjects expected to receive either a strong, painful shock or a very weak, tickling shock, the experimenters asked about the reactions to a female confederate (Dutton and Aron, 1974). Those expecting strong shock indicated a greater desire to ask the female for a date and a greater desire to kiss her than did those expecting a weak shock. No one actually received an electric shock in these experiments, by the way.

You may wonder whether emotions such as fear ever lead to attraction outside of a laboratory setting. Dutton and Aron (1974) tested this prediction in a very clever field study. The subjects were males who were interviewed when they were walking across one of two bridges in Vancouver. The arousing situation was a narrow suspension bridge that tilts, sways, and wobbles 230 feet above a rocky canyon. The neutral bridge was a solid, wide one which was only 10 feet over a shallow rivulet. Either a female or a male interviewer approached each subject, asked a few questions, requested that the subject write a brief Thematic Apperception Test story, and then gave the subject his or her telephone number in case the subject wanted to call later and learn more about the study. When the stories were scored with respect to sexual content, it was found that there was a greater amount of sexuality expressed by those on the arousing bridge than by those on the nonarousing bridge *when the experimenter was female*; with a male experimenter, arousal did not lead to sexual stories. Attraction toward the interviewer was measured by whether or not subjects actually telephoned the experimenter. As shown in Figure 7–21, male subjects who met a female experimenter on an arousing bridge made the most telephone calls. This is rather impressive evidence that sexual desire and attraction toward a member of the opposite sex are each enhanced by a frightening situation. If you are looking for romance, these findings seem to indicate that it would be helpful to hang around suspension bridges, the observation decks of tall buildings, thrill rides at the carnival, and similar places.

You might be wondering why it is that people *do* interpret arousal as love. It has been proposed that we mainly pick up this idea from our culture's books, songs, movies, and so forth (Byrne, 1974). In fact, we begin learning myths about love even before we are able to read.

The telling of the myth is begun in the nursery with fairy tales: Cinderella, Sleeping Beauty, Snow White, Frog Prince, and half a hundred less famous stories. Hardly a child *believes* the tales, but they all have the same message: A handsome prince over-

Arousal, Attraction, and Love: Excitement Makes the Heart Grow Fonder

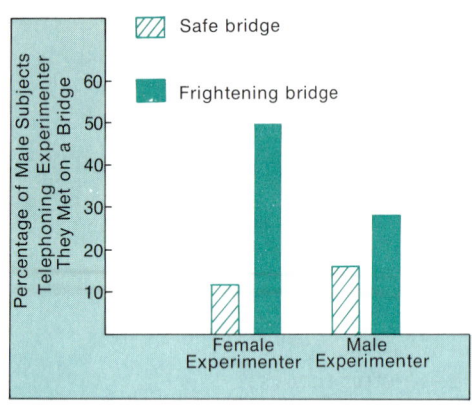

FIGURE 7-21   When males were interviewed by a female experimenter on a frightening suspension bridge, they were much more likely to telephone her later than if the interview was on a safe low bridge. Presumably, the anxiety-arousing situation increased attraction toward a female stranger. When the interviewer was male, the type of bridge had little effect on attraction. (Adapted from Dutton and Aron, 1974.)

comes obstacles to marry the poor maid with whom he has fallen in love; they are married and live in bliss. Alternately, the handsome but poor peasant boy overcomes obstacles to marry the princess, with whom he has fallen in love; they are married and live in bliss. Always beauty, always obstacles, always love, always a class barrier (presumably changing from frog to human leaps an ethnic barrier), always married bliss. The unsaid last line of each story is "some day this may happen to you." Parents set the proper example for their children by relating to the child their own prince-and-beauty story. "Why did you marry Daddy?" "Because we fell in love" (Udry, 1971, p. 163).

Such myths can leave us puzzled about our own experiences. Students in a personality class were invited to ask questions about such topics, and it was clear that for many of them there was a discrepancy between the heart-pounding love affairs of fiction and the relationships they encountered in their everyday lives. The situation is not hopeless, however. In his research on dating couples, Rubin (1974) found evidence that the romantic ideal is modified as two people get to know each other well. That is, a couple may begin with feelings of blind and passionate love, progress toward deep feelings of attachment and mutual caring, and finally move toward a permanent relationship in which they evaluate one another's intelligence, maturity, and good judgment. That does not sound like the basis for an exciting fairy tale or movie, but it may constitute grounds for a more lasting type of love.

Summary

Attempts to explain behavior usually involve **motivational** and **emotional** concepts. Motivation is a hypothetical internal process that provides the energy for behavior and directs it toward a specific goal. Emotion is a subjective feeling state involving physiological arousal, accompanied by characteristic behaviors. Motivational explanations historically have been based on **traditional rationalism** or **mechanism,** but psychologists today tend to rely on **empirical determinism** in seeking behavioral predictability.

When a physiological **need** is not met, the resulting **drive** arousal activates the organism. When an appropriate **goal** is obtained, the drive is reduced, because the need has been satisfied. Organisms also learn to become aroused by external cues, or **incentives.** Drive arousal has been found to increase the organism's general activity level, but this effect is not as clear-cut as it was once thought. The Hull-Spence theory proposes that drive acts to increase response strength, and much of the supporting evidence consists of classical conditioning experiments using individual differences in anxiety as an indicator of drive. When one habit is evoked, high drive leads to improved performance; when several habits are evoked simultaneously, high drive interferes with performance. Among other findings: high anxiety leads to lower grades in school for students of intermediate ability, but anxiety-reducing humor can alleviate this problem.

Physiological needs are based on the biological necessity of maintaining the organism or the species. The need for sexual gratification is a complex process that begins in the womb with the production of sexual **hormones** that determine male and female anatomical differences. There is a great deal of sexual interest and activity in childhood, and animal studies indicate that normal adult sexuality depends in part on these early experiences. At puberty, increased hormonal production increases the level of sexual need; arousal is influenced by hormone production, external cues such as specific odors, and—among human beings—erotic images. The strength of the sex drive in animals has been investigated by means of deprivation procedures, tests of willingness to endure pain, and studies of choice behavior. With human subjects, sexual arousal can be assessed by means of verbal rating scales and direct physiological measures of genital changes. Human sexuality appears to be strongly based on learning, and arousal is brought about by imagination and by external cues, such as erotica. Exposure to erotic material does not appear to bring about criminal behavior, but it does tend to increase the probability that an individual will engage in his or her usual sexual practices.

Complex animals must learn to deal effectively with their environment; it has been proposed that the **effectance motive** underlies the attainment of behavioral **competence** by means of behaviors such as exploration, curiosity, and manipulation.

Learned motives are assumed to develop from association with the satisfaction of basic needs and from instrumental acts which result in need satisfaction. One such motive is **achievement**—the desire to compete and to do things as well as possible. The achievement motive is usually measured by asking subjects to write a brief story in response to a picture; the story is then scored for achievement content. Achievement motivation is related to performance in games, in risk-taking tasks, in school, and in business. Achievement motivation is most likely to develop in homes in which there is emphasis on excellence and competition and in which there is positive reinforcement when the child does well. Also, achievement motivation is higher if one's father is in an independent, decision-making job rather than in a dependent, routine job.

Emotions are similar to motivational states, but they have proven difficult to define. Investigators cannot even agree on the number of basic emotions. There are many physiological responses that accompany emotional arousal, but the search for specific physiological indicators of different emotions has not been successful. The perception of another person's emotional state on the basis of facial expression is not very accurate unless there is knowledge of the context in which the expression occurs. Emotions in posed photographs can be identified more accurately than can those in pictures of actual reactions, in part because we learn to try to communicate emotions in particular ways in each culture. Individuals differ in their ability to send emotional messages and to receive them. Schachter's work provides evidence that emotion is based on general physiological arousal *plus* information as to the specific emotion involved. For example, the emotion of passionate love can be aroused in situations involving fear if the cues are appropriate to suggest sexual attraction and love. A more lasting and realistic loving relationship may develop from this initial emotional attraction.

Suggested Readings

Bolles, R. C.: *Theory of Motivation*. New York: Harper and Row, 1975.
    A difficult but excellent review of the history of the concept of motivation and of current experimental research on this topic.
Byrne, D., and Byrne, L. A.: *Exploring Human Sexuality*. New York: Crowell, 1977.
    An introduction to the psychological research on human sexual behavior.
Ekman, P., and Friesen, W. V.: *Unmasking the Face*. Englewood Cliffs, N.J.: Prentice-Hall, 1975.
    An interesting and well-illustrated description of how to recognize emotions in facial expressions.

Rubin, Z.: *Liking and Loving: An Invitation to Social Psychology*. New York: Holt, 1973.
    A witty and literate description of the way in which love is being investigated.

Some journals that regularly publish papers on motivation and emotion:
    Archives of Sexual Behavior
    Journal of Experimental Psychology
    Journal of Personality
    Journal of Personality and Social Psychology
    Journal of Research in Personality
    Journal of Sex Research
    Motivation and Emotion

Overleaf: Top left and top center photos courtesy of Dr. Harry F. Harlow, University of Wisconsin Primate Laboratory. Top right photo from *Before We Are Born* by K. L. Moore (Philadelphia: W. B. Saunders Company, 1974). Bottom left photo original with this edition. Bottom right photo by Suzanne Szasz.

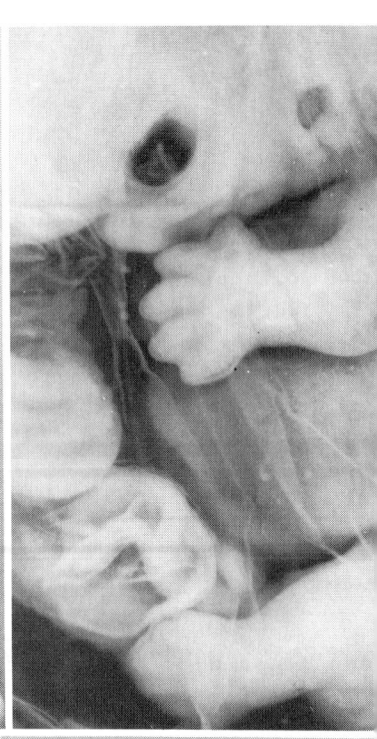

8 Development and Growth: From Child to Adult

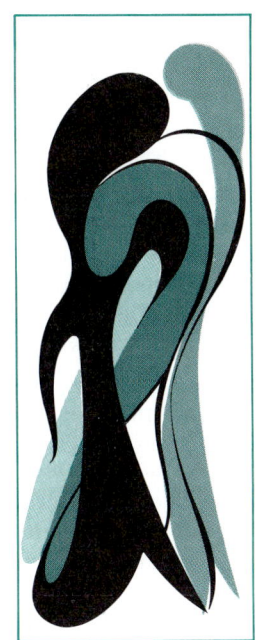

Do you remember when you had to stand on tiptoe to drink at water fountains or reach the counter in stores, and when you had to strain to touch the pedals of your bicycle? Similarly, can you recall the days when reading was a difficult chore, and division or multiplication seemed forever beyond your grasp? Finally, can you remember your feelings on the first day of school, your first "crush" on a member of the opposite sex, or your earliest friends? If so, then one important fact should be obvious: over the passing years you have experienced tremendous growth and change. To paraphrase a recent popular commercial, you really *have* come a long, long way!

Although the changes you have experienced are far too numerous to list here, most fall into three basic categories. First, you have undergone a great deal of physical growth and change, so that at present, the many frustrations you experienced as a result of being too small for an adult-sized world probably seem humorous or even laughable. Second, you have experienced a huge expansion in cognitive and intellectual abilities, moving from a toddler incapable of speaking coherent sentences to a mature individual able to understand difficult concepts and principles. And finally, your relations with others have become richer, more complex, and more meaningful with your increasing mastery of the skills needed for effective social interaction. In short, although it is certainly true that the child is the father/mother of the man/woman, the magnitude of the changes you have experienced suggests that the reverse "generation gap" between the two is very large indeed.

Because these changes in physical, intellectual, and social functioning are among the most dramatic and important events of our lives, they are worthy of very careful attention. In the present chapter, then, we will focus upon alterations along all three dimensions. Starting with what is, quite literally, the beginning, we will first consider the course of physical growth, tracing its development from conception through maturity and on into the declining years. Second, we will examine the process of cognitive development, focusing particularly upon language, that remarkable tool which lies at the foundations of human society, as well as more general changes in the ability to think and reason. Finally, we will turn to the process of social development, examining such topics as attachment (the infant's love for its mother), sexual roles and identity, and the development of moral values. As will soon become apparent, it is growth along these three major dimensions which carries us on the long and often difficult journey from child to adult.

PHYSICAL GROWTH AND DEVELOPMENT

Prenatal Growth: From Small Beginnings . . .

Life begins when one of the millions of free-swimming sperm released into a woman's body during sexual intercourse penetrates and thereby fertilizes the egg cell, or *ovum*. The beginnings of life are small indeed, for the fertilized ovum is barely 1/175th of an inch in diameter—smaller than the period at the end of this sentence. Yet, packed within this tiny speck are the genetic blueprints, 23 chromosomes from each parent, which will guide all future development. Because the study of prenatal development—growth prior to the actual moment of birth—is usually divided for medical purposes into three distinct stages, we will follow such a division in the present discussion.

The Ovum

After fertilization, the ovum first drifts and is later propelled through the mother's reproductive tract toward the womb (uterus). The trip from the point of fertilization to this organ takes several days, and during this interval, the ovum divides again and again, so that by the time it arrives in the uterus, it consists of several dozen cells. These are arranged in two distinct layers, and as development proceeds, the inner one grows into the child itself, while the outer layer develops into several protective and life-sustaining structures discussed below.

The Embryo

Approximately ten to fourteen days after fertilization, the ovum becomes implanted in the wall of the mother's uterus. For the next six weeks, it is known as the *embryo*, and continues to develop at a very rapid pace. Indeed, during this relatively brief period, it increases in size from smaller than the head of a pin to approximately one inch in length. Actually, the period of the embryo, as these six weeks are known, is marked by two concurrent patterns of growth. First, the outer cell layer of the ovum grows into several protective membranes which serve to insulate the embryo from physical jolts or changes in temperature—that is, they act as shock absorbers or protective cushions. In addition, these cells also give rise to the *umbilical cord,* a structure which carries blood from the embryo to a thick mass of tissue growing from the wall of the mother's uterus known as the *placenta.* In the placenta, the blood of the embryo and that of the mother come into close physical proximity, although without actually mingling, and an exchange of nutrients and waste products occurs. Nutrients from the mother's blood enter the blood of the embryo, while wastes from the embryo move into the blood supply of the mother. Unfortunately, other substances and even disease organisms can also cross the placenta and enter the blood of the embryo. As we shall soon see, the results of such transfer can be truly tragic.

At the same time that the outer cell layer of the embryo is developing into the umbilical cord and various protective membranes, the inner layer is continuing its growth toward fully human form. Thus, by the third week, a primitive heart has taken shape and begun to beat. By the fourth week, the embryo is already approximately one fifth of an inch in length, and the region of the head is clearly visible. Rapid growth continues so that by the end of the eighth week, a face (with well-defined eyes, a mouth, and ears) is present, as are arms and legs (with stubby fingers and toes). Moreover, virtually all major internal organs have begun to form, and some have already started to function. At this time, too, the sex glands begin to function, discharging hormones into the embryo's bloodstream. Finally, the nervous system also develops rapidly, so that simple reflexes such as withdrawal in response to touch appear during the eighth or ninth week. In sum, by the end of only two short months of life, the embryo has made tremendous progress (see Color Plate 12). The basic pattern has already been established, and from this point on, all further growth is primarily an expansion and refinement of existing structures.

The Fetus

During the next seven months, the developing child—now known as the **fetus**—shows an increasingly human form. Hair and nails appear by the end of the twentieth week, and within another month, the skin has assumed its basic adult structure. The eyes are completely formed by the end of the twenty-fourth to twenty-sixth week, and they begin to move about when the eyelids are open. Growth, too, is impressive during this period. While the fetus is only 3 inches long and weighs barely 3/4 of an ounce by the end of the twelfth week, these figures increase to almost 10 inches and 8 or 9 ounces by the end of the twentieth week.

The seventh month of life is a particularly crucial one, for prior to this point, the fetus stands little chance of surviving if born prematurely. After the twenty-eighth week, however, the probability of its survival rises sharply. During the last three months of pregnancy the fetus gains about 8 ounces each week and continues to grow in length. Thus at birth, boys average about 7 pounds in weight and 20 inches in length; girls are slightly smaller in both dimensions.

Prenatal Influences on Development: When Trouble Starts Early

Under normal conditions, prenatal development proceeds in the orderly fashion described above, and the *neonate* (the newborn child) is remarkably well equipped for survival as a separate human being. Unfortunately, though, conditions are not always "normal." Many factors can interfere with prenatal growth and thereby ensure that the child starts life with one or more serious strikes against him.

Mother's Diet: Growth in a Hungry World

One factor which exerts a powerful effect upon the health of the developing fetus is the diet consumed by its mother. During the early months of pregnancy, deficiencies in the mother's diet do not seem to cause any harm—the fetus simply takes what it needs from its parent's resources. In later months, however, poor nutrition can result in serious consequences. For example, inadequate diets have been linked to premature births and physical abnormalities, increased susceptibility to disease, and even lowered intelligence among children (e.g., Harrell, Woodyard, and Gates, 1955). Moreover, there is additional evidence gathered in experiments with animals that such effects, once produced, cannot be reversed (e.g., Chow, Simonson, Hanson, and Roeder, 1971). Given the current world food shortage, the implications of such findings for the health and well-being of future generations are quite unsettling.

Disease During Pregnancy

As noted previously, the blood supply of the fetus and that of its mother come into close physical proximity in the placenta. As a result, there is ample opportunity for any disease-producing organisms present in the mother's blood to infect her developing child. And the effects of many such ailments—while minor for the mother—may be disastrous for the fetus. For example, rubella (German measles) can cause blindness, deafness, or serious heart disease in the fetus if contracted by the mother during the first four weeks of pregnancy. Indeed, up to 12 per cent of the children born to women who have this disease during the first three months of pregnancy suffer one or more of these defects. Fortunately, the probability of such harmful consequences drops sharply when the disease is contracted later in pregnancy, but even then serious damage may result. Other diseases which can also interfere with the normal course of development include influenza, mumps, smallpox, and syphilis.

The Effects of Drugs   Strange as it may seem, relatively little attention was directed to the possible influence of various drugs upon the developing fetus until the early 1960's. And even then, it took a tragedy of great proportions to awaken the medical and scientific communities to the potential hazards of seemingly "safe" substances for the unborn child. At that time, thousands of mothers who had taken thalidomide, a drug designed to prevent nausea during pregnancy, gave birth to terribly deformed babies. These pathetic children were born with stunted arms, useless hands, and a variety of other serious deformities. Unfortunately, nothing can be done to restore healthy bodies to these innocent victims of a careless drug industry. Out of their suffering, however, has come stricter government regulations which require the adequate testing of all drugs which may be used during pregnancy.

However, unfamiliar drugs such as thalidomide are not the only ones which seem capable of harming the developing child. For example, there is growing evidence that substances contained in cigarette smoke may stimulate premature birth, with all its added risks (Frazier et al., 1961). Similarly, even excessive use of aspirin may have harmful effects upon the circulatory system of the fetus (Kelsey, 1969). And finally, there is some indication that psychoactive drugs such as LSD may harm the developing fetus and perhaps cause chromosome damage in the mother (Kato et al., 1970). It is important to note that this latter effect, while widely cited in newspapers and magazines, has *not* been clearly established (Leavitt, 1974).

Even more unsettling is recent evidence that drugs taken prior to the start of pregnancy can influence the development of children conceived at a later time. For example, in one study, Friedler and Cochin (1972) treated female rats with morphine until five days prior to mating, and then stopped the morphine treatment. Despite the fact that no drugs were administered during pregnancy, the offspring born to these subjects grew more slowly after birth than did those born to control subjects that had never received any morphine. These findings suggest that the drug had harmful effects upon the rats' reproductive systems which persisted for some time after its removal. Of course, the period involved was quite short, and the study was conducted with animal subjects. Still, it seems reasonable to expect that various drugs may also have lasting, harmful effects upon the reproductive systems of women. If this is indeed the case, then the moral for prospective mothers is clear: the drugs you take today may possibly affect the health and well-being of the children you plan to conceive tomorrow.

Hormonal Influences: When Sex Goes Astray   In our discussion of the embryo, it was noted that the sex glands begin to function in the eighth or ninth week of life. Under normal conditions, the hormones they release influence the development of the sex organs so that in accordance with an individual's genetic make-up, either male or female structures are produced. In certain rare cases, however, this pattern is upset, and very surprising effects are produced (Money, 1974). First, it is sometimes the case that because of a genetic malfunction, the cells of a male fetus are insensitive to the sex hormones secreted by its testes. As a result, female organs develop, and the child appears, at birth, to be a girl. During adolescence, however, the male testes—which are still present deep within the body—secrete both **androgens** (male sex hormones) and **estrogens** (female sex hormones). (Such secretion of both types of hormones is normal in all males.) Since the cells of the body remain insensitive to androgens, however, the effects of the female hormones predominate, and feminine characteristics develop (see Figure 8–1A). Occasionally, medical treatment may be needed (e.g., surgery to lengthen the patient's vagina, or administration of appropriate hormones if removal of the testes becomes necessary). In many cases, however, such procedures are not required. (While examining the photo in Figure 8–1A, try to remember that the individual shown is actually a genetic male!)

The reverse pattern—in which a genetic female appears at birth to be a boy—is also encountered. Such cases stem from a genetic malfunction which causes the adrenal glands to secrete a substance resembling an androgen. As a result, male sex organs develop and the individual is often raised as a boy. During adolescence, however, the ovaries secrete increased amounts of estrogens, and feminine characteristics such as enlarged breasts begin to develop. Such individuals can retain their masculine identity by undergoing treatment in which their ovaries are removed, and injections of male sex hormone are begun on a regular basis. Once again, such procedures are often highly effective (see Figure 8–1B).

Infancy: Getting a Good Start on Life

The first two years of life—a period often termed infancy—are characterized by rapid growth and development. Thus, given good nutrition, children almost triple in weight (to approximately 20 pounds) and increase in length by about one third (to 28 to 29 inches) during the first year alone. Unfortunately, many infants—especially those born in poorer nations—fail to receive adequate diets and fall far short of these figures (Meredith, 1970).

Motor Development

At birth, infants possess a number of simple reflexes. For example, they can follow moving lights with their eyes, suck on a finger or nipple inserted

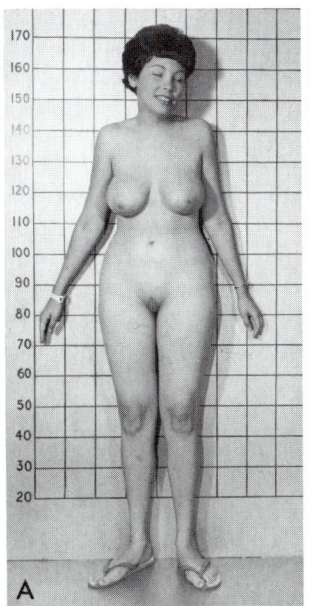

FIGURE 8–1   A. When the cells of a male fetus are insensitive to *androgens*, the male sex hormones, the child may resemble a female at birth and also in later life. Later medical treatment may permit such individuals to retain this sexual identity throughout life. Amazing as it may seem, the person shown here is actually a genetic male. (From Money, J., and Ehrhardt, A.: *Man and Woman, Boy and Girl.* Baltimore: Johns Hopkins Press, 1972.)

B. On rare occasions, a genetic malfunction results in a situation in which a female fetus resembles a male at birth. Later medical treatment may allow such individuals to retain this early sexual identity. The person shown in the photo appears to be a boy but is actually a genetic female. (From Money, J., in *Nebraska Symposium on Motivation, 1974,* edited by J. K. Cole and R. Dientsbier. Lincoln, Nebraska: University of Nebraska Press, 1974, p. 257.)

TABLE 8–1   Infant Reflexes

Stimulus	Reflex
Tap on bridge of nose	Eyes close tightly
Sudden bright light	Eyelids close
Finger pressed against infant's palm	Infant's fingers close around finger
Pressure on balls of infant's feet	Toes flex
Tickle area at corner of mouth	Head turns in same direction
Index finger inserted into infant's mouth	Sucking

Newborn children are equipped with numerous reflexes which permit them to respond to many different stimuli.

into their mouths, and turn their heads in the direction of a touch on the cheek (see Table 8–1). Their ability to move about the environment or reach for various objects, however, is quite limited. This situation changes quickly, and within a relatively few months, they gain the capacity to sit, crawl, grasp nearby objects, stand, and, finally, walk. Several milestones of infant motor development are summarized in Figure 8–2. We should hasten to note, however, that the ages indicated in this figure (and throughout the remainder of this discussion) are only *average* values. Most children will depart from these values to some degree, and only rarely is this cause for alarm. In short, it is usually pointless for parents to worry about the precise age at which their children crawl, stand, walk, or accomplish other motor acts. Only when such development is greatly delayed are there grounds for reasonable concern.

Two additional features of motor development may also be mentioned. First, various behaviors develop without any special practice by the child or instruction from its parents. Thus, they seem to reflect maturation—changes resulting from biological growth—rather than learning. (Please see Appendix B for a general discussion of innate patterns of behavior.) Second, motor development proceeds in a head-to-toe manner and from the center of the body outward. That is, children gain control of muscles in the region of the head and neck prior to gaining control of those in their legs, and can regulate muscles near the center line of the body before being able to control those in the extremities.

Perceptual Development

How do infants perceive the world around them? Do they recognize form, see color, and perceive depth in the same manner as adults? Or do such abilities develop gradually, with increasing age? We have already examined certain aspects of these intriguing questions—especially those relating to the perception of distance or depth—in Chapter 3 (see pp. 100–103). At present, therefore, we will merely seek to expand our previous discussion.

As noted in Chapter 3, questions concerning infants' perceptions of the world cannot be answered by direct or simple means. Two-month-old babies cannot provide us with verbal descriptions of their perceptions; indeed, they cannot even tell us directly whether they are aware of the presence of any given stimulus. In order to determine how infants perceive the world, therefore, it has been necessary to employ indirect methods.

One such procedure is based upon observations of the amount of time young subjects spend gazing at different stimuli. It is assumed that if they choose to gaze at one more than at another, they can perceive a difference between them. Another method simply determines whether infants interrupt ongoing activities (such as feeding) upon presentation of a stimulus. If they do, it is assumed that they can perceive its presence. By means of such methods, it has been possible to determine that children can both see color and distinguish between light and dark at birth. For example, even a five-day-old infant will stop sucking on a nipple when a light moves into its visual field, and will spend more time looking at bright than dim lights (Haith, 1966). Similarly, it has been found that **visual acuity**—the sharpness of vision—develops quickly, so that even by two weeks of age, infants can notice the difference between a solid gray patch and a square composed of stripes only one-eighth of an inch wide (Fantz, 1965).

Research also indicates that not all stimuli are equally interesting or attractive to infants. From a very early age they show a marked preference for the human face. For example, in one interesting study conducted by Haaf and Bell (1967), four-month-old children were shown the stimuli presented in

FIGURE 8–2   Some milestones of infant motor development. (From *The First Two Years: A Study of Twenty-Five Babies* by Mary M. Shirley [Child Welfare Monograph No. 7, Vol. II]. University of Minnesota Press, Minneapolis. Copyright 1933 by the University of Minnesota.)

0 mo.   Fetal posture

1 mo.   Chin up

2 mo.   Chest up

3 mo.   Reach and miss

4 mo.   Sit with support

5 mo.   Sit on lap   Grasp object

6 mo.   Sit on high chair   Grasp dangling object

7 mo.   Sit alone

8 mo.   Stand with help

9 mo.   Stand holding furniture

10 mo.   Creep

11 mo.   Walk when led

12 mo.   Pull to stand by furniture

13 mo.   Climb stair steps

14 mo.   Stand alone

15 mo.   Walk alone

STIMULUS	DEGREE OF FACENESS	AMOUNT OF DETAIL	% FIXATION TIME
	1	3	.33
	2	1	.28
	3	4	.19
	4	2	.20

FIGURE 8–3   The attractiveness of the human face to young infants. Four-month-old children spent more time looking at stimulus 1, which most closely resembles a human face, than at any of the others. (From Haaf, R. A., and Bell, R. Q.: A facial dimension in visual discrimination by human infants. Childhood Development, 1967, *38*, 893–899.)

Figure 8–3. Results indicated that they spent more time looking at stimulus 1, the one most like a human face, than at any of the others. In addition, they spent more time looking at stimulus 2 than at stimulus 4, despite the fact that both are approximately equal in complexity. Since stimulus 2 more closely resembles a human face than does stimulus 4, these findings indicate that infants' apparent fascination with faces is not based solely on a preference for complexity. Rather, it seems to be something about faces themselves which makes them so attractive. The adaptive significance of a tendency on the part of infants to gaze at human faces in preference to other available stimuli should be obvious.

Turning to the perception of sound, it has been demonstrated that infants can hear at birth, and are quite sensitive to differences in pitch. In fact, they can recognize the disparity between two tones which differ by only 50 cycles per second (about one step on a musical scale). In addition, they are particularly sensitive to the various sounds of speech. For example, in one study (Trehub and Rabinovitch, 1972), one-month-old infants were rewarded by presentation of the sound *pah* when they sucked on a nipple at a particular rate (quite rapidly). After a few minutes, they seemed to become bored with this sound, and sucked at a slower and slower rate. When it was changed to *bah*, however, they began to suck faster once again, thus indicating that they could perceive the slight difference between these two sounds. Findings such as these suggest that the ability to distinguish between various sounds of speech, if not present at birth, develops at a very early age.

Childhood and Adolescence

After the tremendous spurt of the first two years, physical growth slows appreciably. Thus, children usually grow only one third as much between the ages of two and four as they do during the first years of life, and this process continues to slow during succeeding years (see Table 8–2). While body size increases relatively slowly, however, certain internal structures continue to develop at a rapid pace (see Figure 8–4A). For example, by the time a child is three, his brain is almost 75 per cent of its adult size, and by the time he or she is six, it has attained fully 90 per cent of its final size. Children are often described as "balls of energy," and during the years between two and eleven, this reputation is well earned. Each succeeding year brings growth in physical strength, activity, and motor coordination. In addition, the amount of time spent in sleep each day decreases from approximately 12 to 13 hours at age two to less than 10 hours at age eleven. In sum, while physical change is more gradual in childhood than in infancy, it is still quite substantial.

Sometime around the age of 11 or 12 for girls and 13 or 14 for boys, the sex glands, which show relatively little growth in earlier years, burst into renewed activity. The onset of this period of sexual maturation, known as **puberty,** is accompanied by numerous physical changes. First, members of both sexes experience a rapid spurt of growth; boys may add as much as six inches and girls five to their height during a single year. Second, increasing signs of sexual maturity make their appearance. Finally, some months after the onset of such changes, girls begin to menstruate and boys to produce sperm. Usually, these events occur by the time girls are 13 and boys 15. However, as can be seen in Figure 8–4B large individual differences exist in the rate of sexual maturation. In addition, as is the case with all patterns of physical growth, environmental factors such as nutrition play a crucial role. For example, while the average of first menstruation for girls is slightly under 13 in the U.S., where nutrition is usually good, it is almost 18 in New Guinea, where diet is often inadequate (Tanner, 1970).

Adolescence: Prelude to Maturity

Full physical maturity is usually obtained by age 20 or soon thereafter. Since change seems to be part of the essential nature of life, the cessation of growth is followed, all too quickly, by the beginnings of decline. At first, reductions in physical abilities occur quite slowly, and are not very noticeable. After age 30, though, they become increasingly apparent. Contrary to popular belief, aging is not a unitary process. Rather, the speed with which it affects

Maturity . . . and Decline

TABLE 8–2 Height and Weight Changes from Childhood to Adolescence

Age	Height (inches)		Weight (pounds)	
	Boys	Girls	Boys	Girls
2½	36¼	36	30	29½
3	38	38	32¼	32
4	41	40½	36¼	36¼
5	43¼	43	41½	41
6	46	46	48	47
7	49	49	53	52
8	51	50	61	57
9	53	53	66	63
10	55	55	73	70
11	57	58	81	87
12	59	60	91	95
13	63	62	109	109
14	66	63	123	115
15	67	64	134	119
16	69	64	144	120

These figures on average heights and weights for children and adolescents, ages 2½ through 16, apply only to individuals raised in developed countries, where nutrition is usually quite good. Much smaller values would be found for children raised in areas of the world where diet is barely adequate to sustain life. (Based on data from Smart and Smart, 1971.)

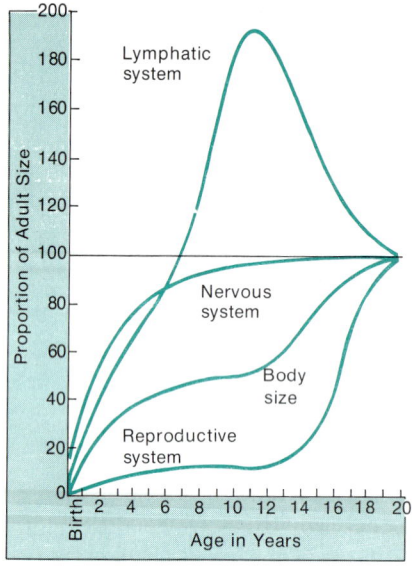

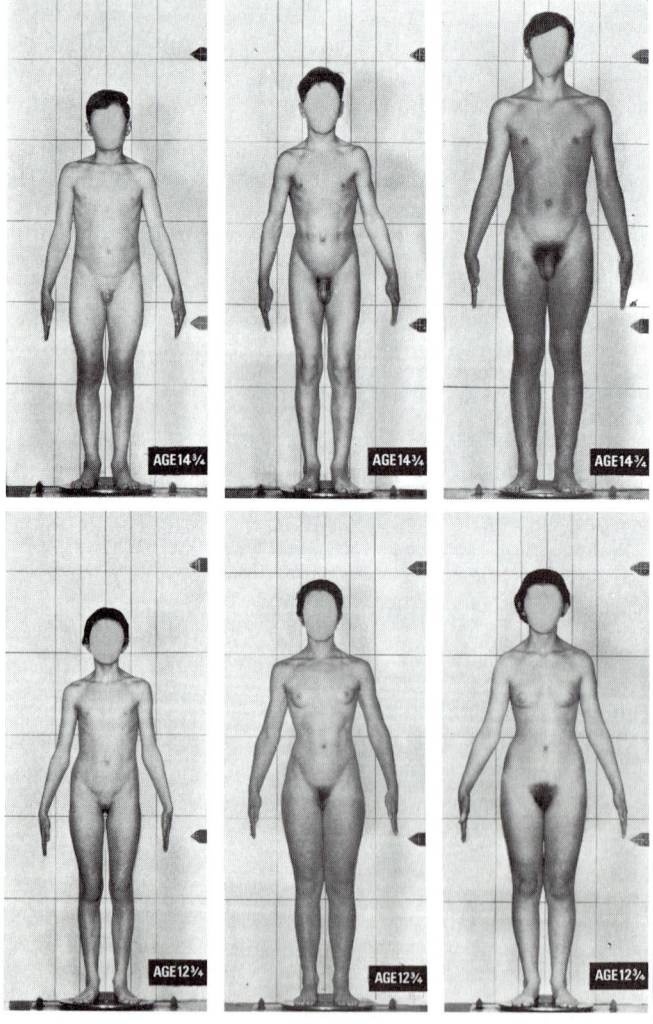

FIGURE 8–4   Top. The relative rates of four different aspects of physical growth. Note that at any given age, growth may be rapid in some systems but slow in others. (Adapted from Tanner, 1970.)
Bottom. Individual differences in rate of sexual maturation. At the same age, puberty may be almost completed for some individuals but just beginning for others. (From *Endocrine and Genetic Diseases of Childhood and Adolescence* (2nd ed.), edited by Lytt I. Gardner. Philadelphia: W. B. Saunders Company, 1975, p. 28.)

TABLE 8–3   Aging in Different Organs of the Body

Organ or Physiological Characteristic	Age				
	30	40	50	60	70
Nerve impulse speed	100	100	96	93	91
Body water content	100	98	94	90	87
Work rate	100	94	87	80	74
Heart output (at rest)	100	93	83	70	58
Efficiency of kidneys	100	98	90	82	77
Lung capacity	100	92	78	61	50

While some organs quite rapidly lose their capacity to function with increasing age, others continue to operate at relatively high levels of efficiency for several decades. The figures shown for each age are percentages derived from a base line of 100 per cent functioning at age 30. (Based on data from Shock, 1962.)

different organs of the body varies tremendously (see Table 8–3). For example, while the velocity of nerve impulses decreases only about 10 per cent between the ages of 30 and 70, lung capacity drops by more than 50 per cent during the same period. Aging, then, is a very inconsistent business, with some organs of the body losing their vitality much more quickly than others (Corso, 1971). In addition, individuals vary just as greatly in their response to aging as they do with respect to other physical characteristics. While some remain active, alert, and productive into their 80's and beyond—Pablo Picasso and Golda Meir are good examples—others at a much earlier age lose either the will or ability to maintain an active life-style (see Figure 8–5).

Because of its obvious and concrete nature, parents often place great emphasis upon the physical growth and development of their offspring. Thus, they frequently keep careful records of their weight and height, wait expectantly—and with some impatience—for their first step or first tooth, and take great pride in their growing strength and grace. Indeed, it is not at all uncom-

COGNITIVE DEVELOPMENT: OF SPEECH AND THOUGHT

FIGURE 8–5   Aging is truly an individual affair. While some persons lose their vitality in their 50's or 60's, others continue to enjoy an active and fulfilling life into their 70's, 80's, and beyond. Left to right: Pablo Picasso, Eleanor Roosevelt, Alfred Hitchcock. (The Bettmann Archive.)

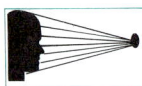

**FOCUS
ON
RESEARCH: *Death, Be Not Proud: Can the "Grim Reaper" Be Delayed?***

Folk legends—and many Hollywood epics—are rich with accounts of individuals in the process of dying who somehow "hold on" until the occurrence of some important event. For example, an aged father may cling to life until he can speak a few parting words to a long absent child. Similarly, a mortally wounded soldier may stay grimly at his post until his comrades make good their escape. Incidents of this type make interesting reading or viewing, for they pose an intriguing question: can human beings actually defer their deaths until after the completion of some significant final act? An investigation conducted by David Phillips (1972) suggests that this may be true.

In this study, Phillips reasoned that if individuals can actually postpone their deaths, fewer persons than expected by chance would die in the month preceding their birthday, while more persons than expected would die in the month following this date. In order to examine this hypothesis, he obtained both the date of birth and date of death of 1,251 famous Americans. Amazingly, when these dates were compared, evidence for the major prediction was obtained: 17 per cent fewer individuals than expected died in the month preceding their birthday, while 13 per cent more than expected died in the month following this date. Even more dramatic results were obtained when these public figures were divided into three groups

on the basis of their degree of fame. Phillips reasoned that those in the most famous category (e.g., George Washington, Benjamin Franklin, Mark Twain) would have the strongest reasons for deferring death, since their birthdays would probably be the subject of public celebrations and awards. This prediction, too, was confirmed. Among individuals in the most famous group, fully 78 per cent fewer deaths than expected occurred in the crucial period. Among those in the least famous category (e.g., Millard Filmore, H. L. Mencken), deaths were reduced by only 20 per cent.

These findings seem to suggest that human beings can indeed postpone their own deaths, and that the stronger their reasons for doing so, the greater their success in this regard. In addition, they appear to provide one possible explanation for such famous "coincidences" as the fact that both Thomas Jefferson and John Adams died on July 4, 1826—exactly 50 years after the signing of the Declaration of Independence! Although the psychological mechanisms underlying such effects are still something of a mystery, it seems possible that they are related, in some manner, to the ability of human beings to control even their most basic bodily processes, as discussed previously in Chapter 4 (see pp. 137–140). The investigation of such possibilities should make for exciting research in the years ahead.

mon to overhear mothers and fathers taking part in conversations in which they trade successive boasts about the early age at which their children first accomplished various physical tasks. But physical growth is only part of the total picture of human development. At the same time that they are "shooting up like weeds," children are gaining the abilities to think, reason, and converse in adult fashion. Because the processes underlying such changes are often much harder to observe than alterations in physical size and skill, they sometimes receive less parental attention. Yet, there can be little doubt that such **cognitive development** is at least as important as bodily growth and maturation. In the present section, then, we will turn to an examination of this topic, focusing especially upon the development of language and thought.

**Language: Tool
of the "Talking
Ape"**

The author of a best-selling book of a few years ago has referred to man as the "naked ape." Although this is an intriguing description, the phrase "talking ape" is probably somewhat more appropriate, for it is the power of speech much more than the absence of a shaggy coat which sets human beings apart from other primates. Indeed, it is impossible to conceive of human culture or civilization in the absence of language. There are many different reasons for this, but perhaps the most important lies in the fact that without the spoken or written word, there could be little or no transmission of knowledge from individual to individual or generation to generation. As Roger Brown, a leading expert on language, has put it (1970, p. 212):

From an evolutionary point of view, the important thing about language is that it makes life experiences cumulative; across generations and within one generation, among individuals. Everyone can know much more than he could possibly learn by direct experience. Knowledge... begins to accumulate... at a rate that leaves biological evolution far behind.

There can be little doubt, then, that language is one of the cornerstones of human civilization. But how is this wondrous tool acquired? How do children manage to move, in a few short years, from the total absence of speech to apparent mastery of many of its most complex elements? Such questions can be addressed on two different levels. First, we can inquire as to the speed and pattern of language development, asking at what ages children acquire different verbal skills (e.g., when do they speak their first word? at what age do they begin using sentences?). Second, we can seek to determine the mechanisms responsible for the rapid growth of speech. Both of these approaches will be considered in the discussion which follows.

During the first few weeks of life, infants have only one means of verbal communication at their disposal—crying—but as new parents soon learn, they often use this tool with great abandon. By the time they are six to eight weeks old, however, most infants also begin to *coo* in response to pleasurable sensations such as those accompanying feeding or strong excitement (e.g., upon receipt of a new and fascinating toy). Crying and cooing continue as the only forms of vocalization until approximately six months, when *babbling* makes its appearance. Babbling, which has been described as preliminary to speech in the same manner that crawling is preliminary to walking, contains all sounds of human speech. That is, babbling infants utter the complex clicks found in some African languages, the harsh sounds of German, the changing inflections of many Oriental languages, and the soft trills of French or Italian. Evidence suggests that all babies will engage in babbling to some degree, but it has also been demonstrated that reinforcement from their parents in the form of smiles or pats on the stomach tends to encourage such behavior (Rheingold, Gewirtz, and Ross, 1959). Thus, even at this stage, vocalization begins to take on a distinctly social flavor.

The Beginnings of Speech: Out of the Mouths of Babes...

That babbling is indeed influenced by the infant's interactions with its parents is further suggested by another finding. After the age of 9 or 10 months, the range of babbling narrows so as to include primarily those sounds present in the parents' speech. In short, the infant seems to "zero in" on the basic sounds of the language it will soon acquire, and begins practicing these rather than others. From this stage to the production of the first word is a relatively short step, and most children manage to accomplish this milestone prior to the occurrence of their first birthday. Substantial individual differences exist, however, and the fact that a child does not speak his or her first word until a later time is rarely cause for concern.

Following the enunciation of the first word, vocabulary increases rapidly. Indeed, one of the most compelling facts about the development of speech is the great speed with which it occurs. By the time he or she is 2, the child may already have more than 200 words at his disposal, and by the age of 3, almost 1,000 (see Figure 8–6).

As impressive as these figures are, it should be noted that comprehension—the child's ability to understand the speech of others—is usually well

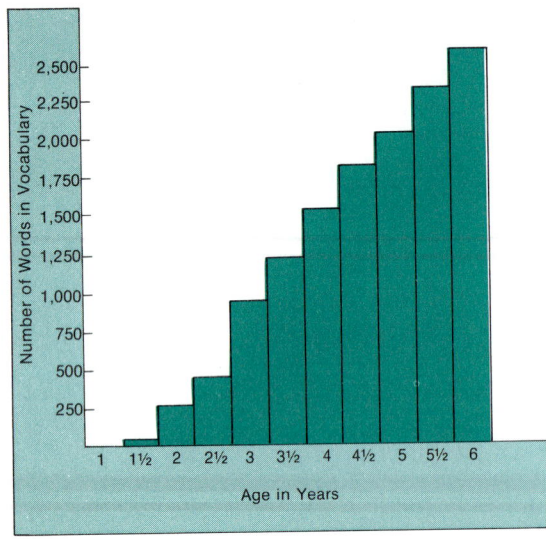

FIGURE 8-6 The growth of vocabulary with age. The speed with which children acquire new words is very impressive. (Based on data from Smith, 1926.)

ahead of production—his ability to utter words himself. Thus, the speed with which language skills develop is truly astonishing.

Early speech is characterized by a number of interesting features. At first, it is *holophrastic*. That is, single words are used to express complex intentions and meanings. For example, a fifteen-month-old child might exclaim "Eat!" when hungry, meaning "I want to eat." Similarly, on another occasion, he might notice his father sitting down to dinner and again say "Eat." In this case, however, the word carries a different meaning—"Daddy is eating." Such holophrastic speech does not last long, and by the time they are 18–20 months old, most children are beginning to combine two words into simple sentences. At this point, another fascinating—and important—aspect of early speech becomes apparent. Specifically, even at this very preliminary stage, children demonstrate an impressive grasp of grammatical rules. Thus, when constructing their simple sentences, they combine the words in the appropriate order, and *not* in the purely random manner one might expect. For example, a two-year-old seeing his father leave the house might well remark "Daddy go." The reverse of this comment—"Go Daddy"—will rarely be encountered. This tendency on the part of children to adopt and follow correct rules of grammar, even in the absence of any direct instruction in their use, has important implications to which we shall soon return.

Two other characteristics of early speech may also be mentioned. First, it tends to be *telegraphic*, with omission of words not essential to the overall meaning. For example, a toddler might say, "Food gone" as his mother removes plates from the table, rather than, "The food is gone." Second, it is marked by tendencies toward overgeneralization on the one hand and overdifferentiation on the other. A concrete instance of the first trend is provided by a child who calls all small, four-legged animals "doggie," while an example of the second is provided by a toddler who proclaims that lobster, a dish he has not seen before, is not food.

Continued Refinement   During the preschool years, children continue to make rapid progress in the development of language skills. By the time they are two and a half, for example, they are beginning to attach appropriate endings to their words. Like adults, they add the letter *s* to make nouns plural (birds, chairs, toys), and the letters *ed* to verbs to put them in the past tense (played, walked, talked). A clear illustration of this process is provided by a famous experiment conducted by Berko (1958). In this study, young children were first shown a picture of a single object such as the one shown in Figure 8–7, about which they were informed: "This is a wug." Then they were shown two such objects and told: "Now there is another one. There are two of them. There are two _____." When asked to complete this final sentence, most subjects answered "wugs," thus demonstrating their knowledge of the plural rule.

By the time they are three, children are beginning to construct longer sentences consisting of several words. Soon afterwards, they start using pronouns such as "it," and prepositions such as "in" and "on." Still later, in the early school years, they begin to master the meaning of words describing relationships between people, such as *sister* and *brother*. As might be expected, large individual differences exist in the ages at which specific children attain each of these skills. The order in which such skills are mastered, however, remains quite constant. For example, all children begin using *in* and *on* correctly before they master the use of such verbs as *is*, *was*, and *were*. The significance of this fact will be examined shortly.

In addition to differences between individual children, there is considerable evidence of differences in language development between members of contrasting economic and cultural groups. More specifically, it has often been observed that on standardized tests of language development, children from lower-class homes score below those from middle-class backgrounds; minority group children score lower than those of Caucasian ancestry as well (Bernstein, 1970; Hall and Freedle, 1973). One interpretation of such findings, popular in the past, is that children from disadvantaged homes are actually deficient in language mastery. Another view, which has gained increasing support in recent years, proposes that their speech is not so much deficient as merely different. To mention only one timely example, it is now widely argued that the speech of ghetto-reared black children is as well developed as that of their white counterparts. Misunderstandings with respect to this important consideration arose in the past when middle-class, white investigators unfamiliar with such speech—and often unable to understand it—concluded that it was simply an error-laden version of standard English. Now, however, it is suggested that it is actually a separate dialect, just as rich and complex in structure as the speech of other groups. And although its use seems to decrease with

Social and Cultural Influences on Language: Different or Deficient?

This is a wug.   *Now there are two of them.*   *There are two_____.*

FIGURE 8–7   An illustration of the procedures used by Berko (1958) to demonstrate children's comprehension of the grammatical rule for forming plurals. When shown two of the bird-like creatures, subjects correctly called them wugs. (Adapted from Berko, 1958.)

age, as black children adopt more standard patterns of speech (Marwit and Marwit, 1976), its existence in no way suggests the presence of inferior language skills. In short, ghetto children are not deficient in their use or comprehension of speech—they are simply speaking a somewhat different language.

Theories of Language Development

Now that we have considered the course of language development and the influence of social or cultural factors upon it, we can return to the second important question with which we began: what are the mechanisms underlying this rapid process? Three basic answers have been proposed.

First, it has been suggested that children learn to speak through the process of *operant conditioning* (see Chapter 4). B. F. Skinner (1957), the major supporter of this view, proposes that parents actively teach their offspring to speak and that the teaching unfolds in two distinct ways. Specifically, (1) parents selectively reinforce speaking behavior with smiles or other signs of approval when the child is making sounds resembling adult speech, and (2) parents actively elicit and then reward imitation of their own verbal behavior (for example, a mother may ask her child to "say daddy," and then reward sounds which resemble this word).

Although Skinner's theory suggests one possible means by which children can learn particular sounds, words, or phrases, it has been severely criticized as failing to provide an adequate explanation for language acquisition (Slobin, 1971). Basically, such criticism has centered on two important points. (1) It has been noted that Skinner's theory cannot account for the very rapid growth in vocabulary demonstrated by children between the ages of 3 and 5. That is, unless parents were to spend most of their time engaging in such training, it is hard to see how their children could acquire fifty or more new words per month. (2) Perhaps of even greater importance, Skinner's views seem unable to explain the great speed with which children master grammatical rules. As we have noted, even their earliest sentences tend to follow such rules, despite the fact that they have never been specifically rewarded for such behavior (Brown, Cazden, and Bellugi-Klima, 1969). In view of these difficulties, Skinner's reinforcement view of language acquisition has been largely abandoned as providing a full and accurate account of this important process.

A second explanation for such development centers on the process of *observational learning* described previously in Chapter 4 (see pp. 146–148). As will be recalled, this is the basic learning mechanism through which individuals acquire new forms of behavior simply by observing the actions of others. According to this view, children acquire both vocabulary and rules of grammar merely by observing—that is, listening to—the speech of persons around them. Since such learning can occur in the absence of reinforcement, direct training is not necessary; only exposure to parents, brothers, sisters, or friends is required.

The old saying "Little pitchers have big ears" suggests that observational learning does indeed play a role in language development. Children can and do learn new words—including ones disapproved of by their parents—simply by listening to others. Moreover, there is even some evidence suggesting that they can acquire grammatical rules in this manner (e.g., Liebert et al., 1969). But the suggestion that observational learning can account for all language development is contradicted by one important fact: where language is concerned, children tend to be highly creative. That is, they often generate new words and sentences they have never heard before. Further, they seem to demonstrate an appreciation of complex rules of grammar which are not at all obvious in the speech of those around them. For these reasons, it must be concluded that while observational learning probably plays a role in the acquisition of speech, it cannot, by itself, provide an adequate explanation for all aspects of this process.

Both the operant conditioning and modeling views described so far suggest that language is a learned phenomenon, acquired in much the same manner as other forms of social behavior. A third and sharply contrasting view has been proposed by Noam Chomsky (1968) who suggests, instead, that language may be at least partially innate. More specifically, Chomsky suggests that all human beings possess a kind of built-in neural system—termed the **Language Acquisition Device (LAD)**—which is somehow "pre-wired" in a way that enables children to intuitively grasp basic rules of grammar. In short, the LAD permits the child to process the speech he hears around him so as to derive a set of rules necessary for constructing grammatical sentences.

As evidence for the existence of such an innate structure. Chomsky points to three facts. First, he notes that despite the enormous number of errors they might possibly make while learning a language, children actually make only a relatively few. This, he contends, is suggestive of some underlying "guidance system." Second, he notes that (as stated earlier) all children seem to proceed through the same stages of language acquisition. And finally, he points to the fact that there do seem to be specific areas of the brain which are intimately involved with the control of speech.

Although these arguments lend support to Chomsky's suggestion that language is influenced by some sort of innate mechanism, his proposals, too, have been the subject of severe criticism. For example, some investigators (e.g., Premack and Premack, 1972) note that he exaggerates children's understanding of grammar, and consequently overestimates the need for an innate mechanism. In view of such criticism, Chomsky's proposals regarding the possible existence of an LAD or similar mechanism should be accepted with caution.

At present, then, our understanding of the processes responsible for the development of speech is far from complete. Both operant conditioning and observational learning may play a role, and there seems to be some evidence for the existence of an innate guiding mechanism. However, no final solution to the continuing puzzle of human speech has yet been obtained.

Cognitive Development: Thinking About Thought

Until the close of the sixteenth century, children in Western nations were treated pretty much as miniature adults. They dressed in adult fashion, worked alongside older persons on numerous jobs, and even participated in many of the same leisure time activities. A fundamental shift in this long-established pattern began to occur in the seventeenth century, as clergymen, philosophers, and educators came to view children not simply as scaled-down versions of adults but rather as distinctly different beings with special needs of their own. This tendency to view children as basically different from adults has continued and even intensified with the passage of time. However, while the existence of important physical, emotional, and psychological differences between children and adults has been recognized for several centuries, it is only within the past few decades that differences in the cognitive, or intellectual, functioning of these two groups have come sharply into focus.

Until fairly recent times, it was widely assumed that youngsters thought and reasoned in much the same manner as adults, and that any differences between them were ones of degree rather than of kind. Now, however, it is generally understood that nothing could be farther from the truth, for the cognitive processes of children and adults actually differ sharply in basic

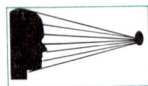

**FOCUS
ON
RESEARCH: *Are We the Only "Talking Ape"?***

Are human beings the only creatures on earth capable of developing and using a language? Until quite recently, it seemed that this was indeed the case, for attempts to teach chimpanzees—the most likely candidates in this respect— to speak generally failed. For example, during the 1940's, Keith and Cathy Hayes raised a chimpanzee named Vicki in their home and provided her with intensive training in speech. Yet, even after much painful and prolonged practice, she was only able to utter a few simple words such as "mama," "papa," and "cup." Within the past ten years, however, it has become increasingly apparent that although they cannot learn to speak, chimpanzees are quite capable of mastering other kinds of language (e.g., Floming, 1974).

Beatrice and Allen Gardner have succeeded in teaching Washoe, a female chimp born in the wild, to use and understand fully 160 words in American Sign Language, the hand gesture language used by many deaf people. In fact, after several years of practice with this system, Washoe has become quite fluent in its use. For example, she has learned to request actions (e.g., tickling) and objects (e.g., food) that she desires. Similarly, she has learned to describe her mood or feelings with the signs for such words as "hurt," "sorry," and "funny." And perhaps most intriguing of all, she has begun to use the signs she knows in a manner amazingly reminiscent of human speech. For example, after being threatened by an angry rhesus monkey, she christened him "dirty monkey," and always referred to him in this manner from that point on.

In other experiments, Ann and David Premack (1972) have trained Sarah, another young chimpanzee, to both read and write in a special language based on small pieces of colored plastic. Using standard conditioning procedures, they have managed to teach her to use fully 130 different words, including ones referring to relatively complex concepts such as "same" or "different." For example, in order to teach Sarah the meaning of the symbol for "give," a tasty piece of banana was positioned outside her reach, and provided only after she placed the symbol for "give" on a magnetic language-board. Later, she was required to name not only the action involved (i.e., giving), but also the object desired (banana, apple). With continued training, Sarah has learned to read whole sentences placed on the word-board by her trainers (see Figure 8–9), and to either follow the instructions they contain or provide her own answers by means of the plastic words. Findings such as these indicate that chimpanzees can learn to use a language, and that they threaten to unseat us from our throne as the only "talking ape."

"The thing to bear in mind, gentlemen, is not just that Daisy has mastered a rudimentary sign language but that she can link these signs together to express meaningful abstract concepts."

FIGURE 8–8   Recent progress in teaching sign language to chimpanzees raises some interesting possibilities! (Drawing by Lorenz; © 1974 by The New Yorker Magazine, Inc.)

FIGURE 8–9 Using standard conditioning procedures, Ann and David Premack (1972) have succeeded in teaching Sarah, a young chimpanzee, to
use 130 different words in a specially created language. In the illustration, Sarah is about to obey the
sentence on her wordboard which instructs her to
place the apple in the pail and the banana in the
dish. (From "Teaching Language to an Ape," by
A. J. Premack and D. Premack. Copyright © 1972
by Scientific American, Inc. All rights reserved.)

nature. Full realization of this important fact has stemmed primarily from the
work of Jean Piaget—a noted expert in the field of child development. Because
his contributions have reshaped many of our ideas about children's cognitive
processes—our thinking about their thinking—Piaget's proposals and work will
serve as the major focus of the present discussion.

Piaget's Theory of Cognitive Develop-ment: Journey Toward Reason

Piaget (1970) begins his theorizing about cognitive development on a very
positive note, suggesting that almost from the moment of birth, infants attempt
to comprehend the strange new world into which they have suddenly been
thrust. In an important sense, therefore, all cognitive growth can be viewed as
movement toward the abilities to reason abstractly and think logically—
admirable goals to say the least. But how does the infant accomplish this difficult journey? How does he or she progress from being a helpless creature
unable to solve the simplest problems to become one capable of pondering the
profoundest mysteries of the universe? After thousands of hours of careful
observation, Piaget has reached the conclusion that the answer lies in the
conflict or tension between two basic processes, **assimilation** and **accommodation.** Put very simply, assimilation represents the tendency to apply old ideas
and habits to new objects or problems, while accommodation refers to the
tendency to acquire new responses or alter old ones in order to deal with new
events and situations. Perhaps the nature of these two opposing forces can best
be explained by means of a concrete example.

Imagine that a four-year-old child who has never seen a magnet receives
one as a present. At first, he will probably attempt to deal with it in the same
ways he has treated other toys: he may bite it, throw it on the floor, hit it
against other objects, and so on. These actions represent assimilation, for the
child is reacting to a new object in the same way he reacts to old, familiar
ones. But now suppose that the youngster touches some metal object with the
magnet and notices that it sticks. He may then begin to "experiment" with
this new feature, touching the magnet to many different objects until he
discovers that only metal ones are affected. This is an example of accommodation, for the child has learned a new way of dealing with an object.

According to Piaget, the tension between assimilation and accommodation results in an increasing ability on the part of the child to adapt to new situations and events—the true hallmark of mental growth. Thus, it is from this mechanism that progress toward cognitive maturity derives. Movement toward such maturity, moreover, is not a haphazard affair. Rather, Piaget suggests that children move through an orderly sequence of four major stages en route to this ultimate goal.

The first, which lasts from birth until the child is approximately 18 to 24 months old, is known as the **sensorimotor stage.** During this period, the infant has not yet learned to use symbols, language, or even images to represent objects and events in the world around him. Instead, he knows it only through his motor activities and sensory impressions. The total absence of mental representations during this stage results in some interesting—but predictable—consequences. For example, throughout most of this period, infants act as if objects they no longer see or feel have ceased to exist. More specifically, during the first two to three months of life, children never even bother to search for objects which pass out of their line of vision. Between the ages of three and six months, they will reach for objects as they pass, but will not search for them when they are hidden behind another object right before their eyes. By the time they are 9 to 12 months old, many babies begin to reach for such hidden objects, and at the age of 18 months, they will even look for objects which have been hidden once, moved to another location, and then hidden again. Thus, they come to behave as if they understand that objects have a permanent existence of their own, even when removed from their view. Piaget believes that the development of this concept of **object permanence** is one of the major accomplishments of the sensorimotor stage.

Sometime between the ages of 18 and 24 months, most infants seem to acquire the ability to form mental images of objects and events in the world around them. At about the same time, language develops to the point at which they can begin to think in terms of verbal symbols (i.e., words). According to Piaget, these developments mark the end of the sensorimotor stage and the start of the **preoperational period,** the next major advance on the road toward cognitive maturity. During this period (which lasts approximately until age seven), the child is capable of many actions he or she could not previously perform. For example, because of the presence of mental symbols, he or she can imitate an absent model by recalling what this person said or did while present. It is at this time, then, that the capacity for observational learning first appears. In many ways, however, the thought processes of preoperational children remain quite immature. First, they are basically *egocentric*. That is, during this period, children cannot imagine that others may perceive the world differently than they do. A dramatic illustration of this fact is provided by a study in which two-year-olds were first shown a piece of cardboard with a picture of a dog on one side and a picture of a cat on the other (Flavell, 1973). Next, this object was held between the child and the experimenter so that each could see only one side, and subjects were asked two questions: "What do *you* see?" and "What do *I* see?" Consistent with their egocentric mode of thinking, many children indicated that the experimenter saw the same picture as they did.

Second, preoperational children lack true understanding of relational terms, such as darker, larger, and bigger. Third, children at this stage of development lack **serialization,** the ability to arrange objects in order along some dimension. For example, they cannot arrange eight sticks in a row according to size. Finally, and perhaps most important of all, they lack what Piaget terms the principle of **conservation.** To understand what is meant by this principle, consider the following simple example. A four-year-old girl is shown two beakers containing what she agrees are equal amounts of water. Then, the water from one of these beakers is emptied into a taller and thinner container, and the child is asked whether one now holds more water than the other, or whether they are equal. Almost invariably, four- and five-year-olds will answer that the tall, thin beaker holds more water. Piaget believes that errors of this type stem from the child's tendency, at this stage, to concentrate upon only one feature of an object or event at a time. Since the water is higher in the tall beaker, they conclude that it holds more. If, in contrast, they also considered the diameter of the two beakers, such errors could be avoided. (For another demonstration of the absence of conservation, see Figure 8–10.)

By the time they are seven, most children can solve the simple problem mentioned above with little hesitation. According to Piaget, such mastery of the principle of conservation marks the beginning of the third major stage of cognitive development, one he terms the period of **concrete operations.** This period lasts until the child is 11 or 12, and is marked by the emergence of many of the skills lacking in the preoperational stage. Thus, in addition to demonstrating conservation, children at this stage also show comprehension of relational terms, serialization, and an appreciation of the fact that other persons may hold views different from their own. In addition, logical thought makes its first appearance during this stage. For example, if asked *why* the amounts of water in the two beakers shown in Figure 8–10C are equal, the child might answer: "Because if you poured the water from the tall one back into the shorter one, it would be the same as before." At this stage, though,

FIGURE 8–10 Children in the preoperational stage of cognitive development lack understanding of the principle of conservation. This may be illustrated by means of the following simple demonstration. First, water is placed in two identical containers, and the levels are adjusted until the child agrees that they are equal (Photo A). Next, the child pours the water from one of these containers into a larger one (Photo B). When then asked to indicate whether the larger container now holds more, less, or the same as the remaining smaller one, a child in the preoperational stage may fail to see that the amounts must be equal (Photo C).

children seem capable only of logical thought concerning objects directly in front of them—hence the term *concrete* operations.

At about the age of 12, most children enter the final stage of cognitive development, that of **formal operations.** During this period, all the characteristics of mature, adult thought make their appearance. Once they have entered this stage, individuals become capable of (1) reasoning deductively, (2) considering all possible solutions before proceeding to solve a problem, (3) thinking in highly abstract terms, and (4) formulating and testing various hypotheses about different aspects of the environment. In sum, thought in this final stage often resembles careful, scientific reasoning. This is not to say that thinking during the stage of formal operations always attains these lofty heights. On the contrary, it often slips back into less advanced patterns or modes. It is only the *possibility* of engaging in this type of careful reasoning, then, that characterizes this final cognitive stage.

As noted by Piaget, one additional characteristic of this period, especially at its beginning, is a preoccupation with thought itself. That is, many individuals who have recently entered the stage of formal operations have a tendency to reflect upon themselves, their own thoughts, why they are reflecting on these thoughts . . . on and on late into the night! Whether or not *all* adolescents who have newly attained formal operational thought choose to engage in such soul-searching activities is not Piaget's point; rather, it is that they have reached full cognitive maturity.

Piaget's Theory:
A Current Evaluation

Piaget's suggestions regarding the course of cognitive growth are both fascinating and appealing. But do they actually provide us with an accurate picture of this complex process? Many attempts to answer this question have been undertaken, and as is often true in such cases, results have been mixed. First, there is by now little doubt that many of the changes to which Piaget refers actually occur. Children *do* seem to pass through different stages of cognitive development, during which they acquire such concepts as object permanence, serialization, and conservation. Thus, in broad outline at least, Piaget's proposals regarding such developments seem to be correct. His suggestions that it is impossible to (1) speed the rate at which children move from one stage to another, or (2) alter the order of this progression, however, do not seem totally accurate. For example, a number of recent studies (e.g., Gelman, 1969; Brainerd, 1976) demonstrate that with the aid of special procedures, children younger than the age Piaget would suggest can be taught to master conservation. Indeed, there is some indication that even three-year-olds can demonstrate this cognitive ability under appropriate conditions (Miller, Heldmeyer, and Miller, 1975). As an example of such research, let us consider a study by Siegler and Liebert (1972).

In this experiment, the subjects were boys and girls between the ages of 5½ and 6½ who had previously shown no mastery of conservation on a preliminary test. After giving their answers to the type of water problem we have described earlier, half of the children heard the experimenter read a formal rule designed to help them master the conservation skill, while the remainder were not provided with such training. The experimenter's words were as follows (Siegler and Liebert, 1972, p. 135):

> The rule is that when we pour all of the water from one glass into an empty glass, there is the same amount of water to drink as before. This is because we haven't added any water or taken any away. . . .

In addition to carrying out these procedures, the experimenters provided half of the subjects in each group with feedback after they gave their answers (they

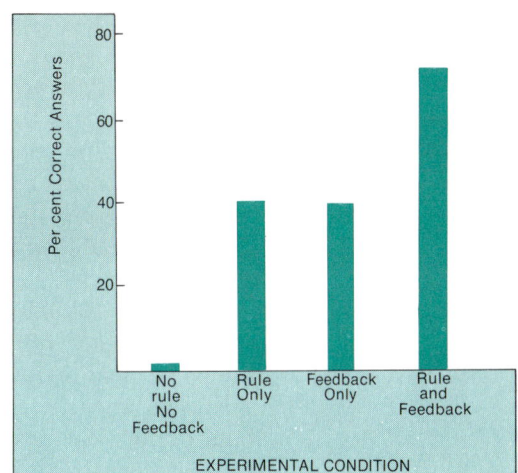

FIGURE 8–11   Evidence that children as young as 5½ can acquire conservation. Mastery of this concept was facilitated both by the provision of a formal rule and by feedback regarding the accuracy of subjects' answers. (Based on data from Siegler and Liebert, 1972.)

were told whether they were right or wrong); the other half of each group did not receive feedback. It was predicted by Siegler and Liebert that feedback would help the children master the notion of conservation. As can be seen in Figure 8–11, results indicated that this was actually the case. Mastery of conservation was increased both by presentation of the rule and by feedback about correctness. Interestingly, when the children were re-tested about one week later, they still showed evidence of understanding the conservation principle. Thus, the changes they experienced in this respect seemed to be relatively permanent in nature.

Findings such as these suggest that the rate at which individuals move from one stage of cognitive development to another may not be quite so fixed as Piaget suggests. They do not, however, cast doubt upon the essential accuracy of many of his insights regarding the basic nature of this process. As a result, his theory continues to serve as an important beacon lighting the way for many of our attempts to comprehend the mind of the child.

**PSYCHOLOGY
IN
ACTION:** *Preoperational Thought—When the Same is Less (or More)*

Piaget once remarked that from the point of view of cognitive development, children do not grow like a leaf, merely getting bigger and bigger along all dimensions, but rather like a caterpillar, passing through a series of major transformations. Although not all authorities agree with these suggestions, there is little doubt that the thought processes of children differ sharply from those of adults. You can gain firsthand evidence for one of these differences by means of the following simple demonstration.

First, show a willing child of 4 or 5 two balls of clay (or any similar material) of identical size. Then, while the child watches, change the shape of one of the balls. For example, you can flatten it into a pancake or roll it out like a

snake. Next, ask the child whether it still contains the same amount as the ball you left untouched. In most cases, your subject will report that it does not, despite the fact that you neither added nor removed any material. Now, as a final step, repeat these procedures with an older child of 7 or 8. In this instance, you are likely to find that your subject solves the problem with no difficulty whatsoever. Indeed, he or she may laugh at the very thought of failing such a simple "test." The differences you observe in this simple demonstration illustrate one of Piaget's main points: young children do not think like adults, and manage to attain cognitive maturity only after passing through a discrete and orderly set of developmental stages.

SOCIAL AND MORAL DEVELOPMENT: GETTING ALONG WITH OTHERS... AND LIVING WITH ONESELF

Imagine that as part of a class project, you were required to observe the behavior of a group of four-year-olds at play. What would you notice most? Although many aspects of their behavior would probably catch your attention, one almost certain to stand out would be the unpolished nature of their social interactions. For example, you might witness incidents in which one child wishing to possess a toy held by another resorts to physical violence in order to gain the desired item. Similarly, you might observe the children participating in boasting matches in which each loudly proclaims the superiority of his or her toys, parents, clothing, and so on (the "my-dog's-better-than-your-dog" syndrome so common among preschoolers). Finally, you might observe them interrupting each other's speech, refusing to share toys or food, and generally showing a total lack of the social graces.

Taken together, such observations serve to underscore an important fact about human development: at the same time that they are growing in physical size and cognitive abilities, children are also maturing socially as well. Because social behavior will also be the subject of detailed attention in Chapters 12 and 13, no attempt to examine all changes along this dimension will be undertaken here. Rather, attention will be focused on two processes which seem to have an important bearing upon later social adjustment: **attachment**—the child's initial love for its mother—and **sex-typing**—the process through which children acquire sexual identity and roles. In addition, since increasing contact with others often places children in situations in which they must pass judgment on the "goodness" or "badness" of the actions of such persons, **moral development,** too, will be considered.

Attachment: The Beginnings of Love

Do infants love their mothers? They can't say it with flowers, or tell us directly, of course, but by the time they are six or seven months old, most appear to have a strong, affective bond toward this supremely important person in their lives. Thus, they recognize their mother and smile at her more than at other persons; they seem to feel more comfortable in her presence; and they actively attempt—insofar as their limited abilities permit—to seek her out. Moreover, they become frightened when she leaves, especially if her departure is sudden or unexpected, and often refuse to be picked up or cared for by other people. Together, such tendencies are generally described by the term *attachment*—the first and most basic form of love felt by the child toward another human being.

Monkey Love: Happiness is a Warm, Soft Mother

That attachment exists is obvious. But what are the forces behind such feelings? Why do infants quickly become strongly attached to their mothers or any other person who cares consistently for their needs in the period after birth? One possible answer is suggested by the process of classical conditioning discussed at length in Chapter 4 (see pp. 111–118). That is, the mother, because of her repeated, close association with many pleasurable stimuli (food, warmth, dryness) comes to serve as a conditioned stimulus for their occurrence. As a result, the infant soon learns to stay as close to her as possible.

Although an interpretation of attachment in such terms seems quite reasonable, a continuing series of experiments by Harry Harlow and his colleagues suggests that it is at most only part of the picture. Because this research is among the most intriguing work conducted in psychology during the past two decades, and because it seems to have important implications for child-rearing practices, we shall examine it in some detail.

When Harlow began his work back in the 1950's, infant love was the farthest thing from his mind. Rather, he was concerned with studying the effects of various forms of brain damage upon learning. Since it was ethically impossible to perform such experiments with humans, he employed rhesus monkeys in his research. While rearing baby monkeys away from their mothers as a means of preventing the communication of illness between them, however, he noticed a surprising fact: the infants often became quite attached to small scraps of cloth present in their cages. They would clutch these "security blankets," wrap up tightly in them, and protest vigorously when they were removed for cleaning. In short, it seemed as if the babies actually needed continuous physical contact, for some unknown reason, with this soft, pliable material.

In order to determine if this was actually the case, Harlow devised the two artificial "mothers" shown in Figure 8–12. As can be seen, one consisted of bare wire mesh, while the other possessed a soft terry-cloth cover. Conditions were then arranged so that the monkeys could obtain nourishment, in the form of milk, only from the hard, wire mother. According to the classical conditioning explanation of attachment mentioned above, it would be expected that they would soon develop a strong bond to this skeleton mother because of her repeated association with food. Yet, this was definitely *not* the case. Instead, the infants spent almost all of their time clinging tightly to the soft, cloth-covered mother, and only ventured onto the bare wire figure when driven to do so by strong pangs of hunger.

Evidence that the infants formed a strong attachment to the soft, cloth mother was obtained in an experiment in which they were placed in an environment filled with unfamiliar—and for a baby monkey—terrifying objects (Harlow and Zimmerman, 1959). When confined alone in this setting, the infants would cower in total fear (see Figure 8–13). When placed in the same circumstances with their cloth mothers, however, they would first cling to her for a few moments and then, apparently comforted, begin to explore this new, exciting world. In contrast, when placed in an identical setting with the wire mother, the infants continued to evidence strong signs of fear. Only the

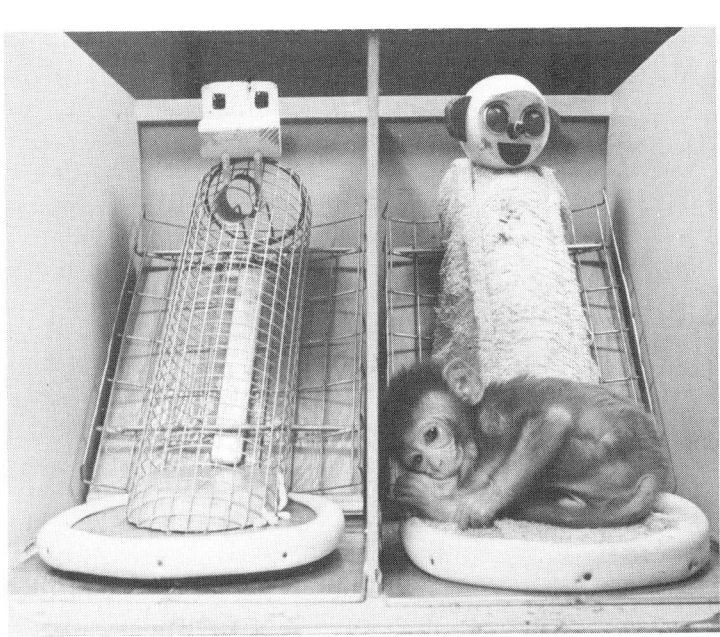

FIGURE 8–12 The cloth and wire mothers employed by Harlow to study the basis of infant attachment. Although they obtained nourishment from the hard wire mother, monkey babies spent most of their time clinging to the soft, cloth-covered mother. (Courtesy of Dr. Harry F. Harlow, University of Wisconsin Primate Laboratory.)

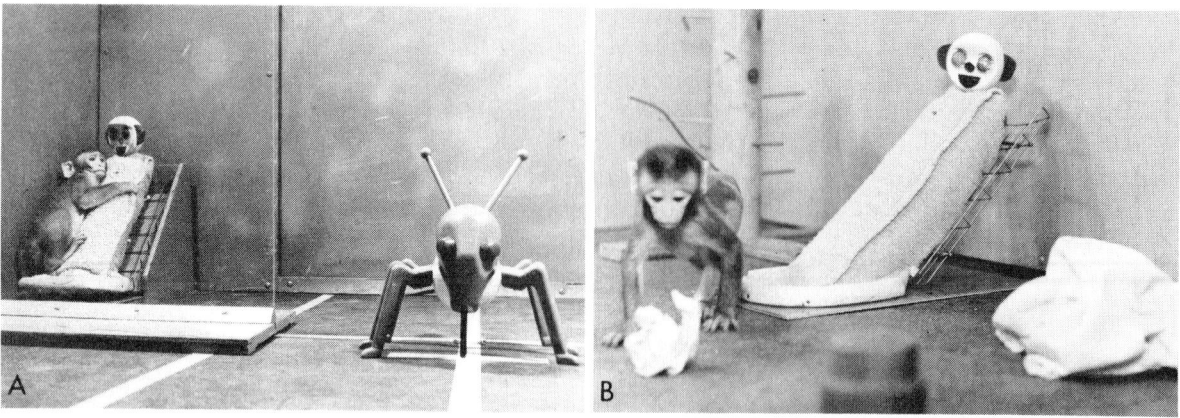

FIGURE 8–13   When placed in a new and frightening environment with their cloth mothers, monkey infants would first cling to their substitute parents for a few moments (A), and then begin exploring their new world (B). In contrast, when placed in the same setting with a wire mother, the infants continued to show signs of intense fear. (Courtesy of Dr. Harry F. Harlow, University of Wisconsin Primate Laboratory.)

cloth mother, then, was capable of turning a frightening situation into a stimulating one.

In the initial studies described above, the substitute mothers that were employed demonstrated what might reasonably be described as "infinite patience" with their adopted offspring. That is, they permitted unlimited clinging and rubbing at any time, day or night. Unfortunately, real mothers — both the monkey and human kind — rarely show such consistent and untiring acceptance. Tempers sometimes grow short, and even the most loving mother may become irritated with her child on occasion. This fact raises an interesting question: do such episodes of anger or annoyance weaken infants' bonds of attachment toward their parents? In order to find out if they do, Harlow and Harlow (1966) conducted a series of studies in which baby monkeys were exposed to various forms of rejection by their surrogate mothers. For example, some of the mothers were made to blow their infants away with powerful jets of compressed air. Others contained a hidden catapult which periodically hurled their babies across the cage. And still others held rows of metal spikes which suddenly appeared from within their bodies and drove their desperate infants away. Surprisingly, none of these actions had any lasting effects upon the monkeys' love for their mothers. Rather, they would wait pathetically until these frightening episodes of rejection passed, and then cling as tightly as ever to the only mothers they had ever known. Only one type of mother succeeded in permanently alienating the affections of her infants: one who, quite literally, had ice water pumped through her "veins."

On the basis of these and many related findings, Harlow has concluded that a monkey infant's attachment toward its mother is based primarily upon her ability to satisfy its needs for **contact comfort.** More specifically, he contends that baby monkeys have a strong, built-in need for rubbing against, touching, and clinging to soft objects. Since the mother provides a means of satisfying this need, infants soon form a strong bond toward her. However, in her absence, similar ties of affection can be formed toward any other object in the environment capable of providing the same type of satisfaction. From the perspective of a baby monkey, then, a good mother doesn't necessarily have to be real, but she *must* be cuddly.

But what about human infants; do they, too, come to love their mothers because of an innate need for physical contact with them? Because it is impossible to raise human children with inanimate substitute mothers, conclusive evidence relating to these questions cannot be obtained. It seems possible, though, that similar mechanisms may underlie the attachment of all, or at least many, young organisms to their mothers. In particular, it has recently been suggested that infants of many different species are attracted to and form strong bonds with the first object they encounter which permits them to perform their strongest or most dominant responses (e.g., Mussen, Conger, and Kagan, 1974). According to this view, monkeys are born with strong tendencies to grasp and to cling. Since their mother is usually the first object they encounter which allows for the expression of such tendencies, they soon form a strong attachment to her. Similarly, ducks and other birds are born with a strong tendency to follow moving objects and again, their mother is the first object which permits the performance of such responses. (The process through which the young of many species form strong attachments to the first moving object they encounter is generally known as **imprinting.** We will consider this and other innate patterns of behavior in Appendix B, pp. 587–595.)

Human infants, too, are born with dominant responses, including tendencies to cry, engage in visual scanning, and manipulate or hold onto objects. And since their mother is usually the first object they encounter toward whom many of these reactions may be directed, they quickly form a strong attachment to her.

In short, this *dominant response* interpretation of attachment suggests that young organisms become attached to the first objects they encounter which permit them to "do their own thing," whatever that may be. Such an interpretation is quite appealing, for it suggests that attachment has a common basis in many different species. Until additional evidence favoring the accuracy of such proposals is obtained, however, they must be viewed as describing an interesting—but as yet unverified—possibility.

Loneliness Hurts: The Effects of Social Deprivation

Although it might appear from the preceding discussion that contact with a soft, cuddly object is all that is required for normal social development, additional findings reported by Harlow and his colleagues suggest that this is far from the case. For example, although monkeys reared alone in cages with cloth substitute mothers appear quite normal as infants, they demonstrate seriously disturbed behavior as adults (Harlow, 1965). First, they are unable to interact normally with other monkeys. Instead, they sink into deep depressions when confronted with them and seek to avoid all social contact. Second, their sex lives are almost totally nonexistent. Males make no attempt to approach receptive females, or, if they do, are so clumsy and inept that their efforts generally fail; females raised with cloth mothers usually can be mated only with the aid of what Harlow calls the "rape-rack." And later, when these unwilling mothers give birth to babies of their own, they often either ignore or reject them harshly. Findings such as these suggest that normal social development requires more than simple contact with a soft, cuddly object; extensive interaction with other members of one's own species also seems to be essential.

Even more dramatic evidence for the importance of such experience has been obtained in a series of studies in which monkeys were raised in total social isolation—conditions under which they are confined to special cages and never see another living being, not even their keepers. When raised in this manner for three months and then returned to the colony, infants make a rapid adjustment and are soon very similar to other babies reared normally with their mothers and peers. If kept in isolation for six months or more, however, they fail to make such an adjustment. Instead, they tend to sit miserably in corners, where they rock back and forth, huddle into a ball, and clasp their own bodies tightly. Fortunately, there seems to be hope even for such severely disturbed individuals. In an interesting study, Suomi and Harlow (1972) placed such monkeys together with younger females (three to four months old) for two hours each day. At first, the previously isolated subjects cowered in fear, refusing to have anything to do with their "therapists." Gradually, though, they seemed to overcome their anxiety, and within a few weeks, were playing enthusiastically. In time, they seemed to recover completely and could join groups of normal monkeys with no apparent difficulty (see Figure 8–14). Findings such as these suggest that the effects of even prolonged social isolation can be reversed. However, more recent investigations indicate that such benefits may be obtained only under highly specific conditions. For example, Erwin and his associates (1974) found that the adverse effects of six months of social isolation could not be reversed even by continuous contact with an older partner. Apparently, only interaction with a smaller and totally nonthreatening "therapist" may be effective in counteracting the influence of early isolation.

At this point, it is important to note that these investigations have all been conducted only with monkey subjects. This is as it must be, of course, for no one would dream of separating human infants from their mothers or raising them in social isolation in order to study the effects of such treatment upon their behavior. But the fact that monkeys have served as subjects leaves us facing the questions of whether, and to what extent, Harlow's findings may be generalized to human beings. Fortunately, there is considerable evidence suggesting that such generalization is possible.

Basically, this evidence derives from studies which have compared the behavior of children reared in institutions (orphanges, hospitals) with that of others raised at home by their parents. The results of such research have often been chillingly similar to those reported by Harlow. For example, in one investigation, Provence and Lipton (1962) compared the behavior of babies living in an institution where they received good nutrition and bodily care, but little opportunity for social interaction, with that of infants living at home.

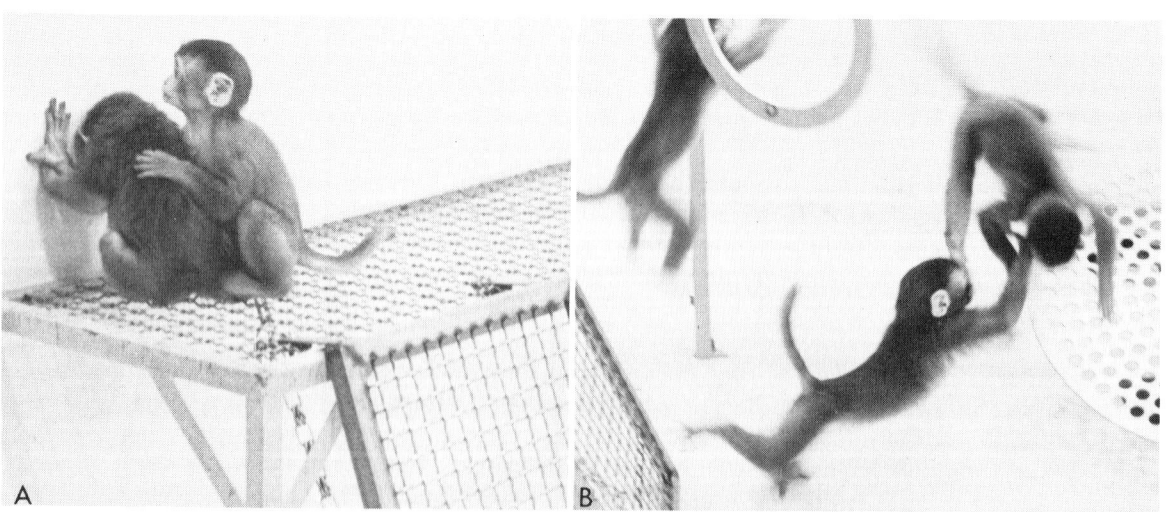

FIGURE 8–14   When brought into contact with others for the first time, baby monkeys reared in total social isolation often show intense fear and withdrawal (A). After several weeks of contact with younger "therapists," however, they gradually came to demonstrate more normal social behavior (B). (Courtesy of Dr. Harry F. Harlow, University of Wisconsin Primate Laboratory.)

During the first three months of life, there was little difference between the two groups, who cooed, babbled, and smiled at similar rates. Later, though, the institutionally reared infants fell further and further behind. When picked up, they failed to make the postural adjustments shown by most infants, and felt very much like "sawdust dolls." Similarly, they began to lose interest in the environment and made fewer and fewer attempts to grasp or even approach toys. Language development, too, was delayed, and their faces took on a blank, vacant expression disturbingly similar to that shown by many of the isolated monkeys in Harlow's research.

These and similar results obtained in other investigations (e.g., Spitz and Wolff, 1946) suggest that the lack of opportunities to interact with others can greatly retard both social and cognitive development. Fortunately, though, as was the case with the isolated subjects in Harlow's studies, such damage seems to be reversible. For example, in a series of related investigations, Jerome Kagan (1972) observed the behavior of children in small Guatemalan villages who, as part of the normal child-rearing procedures of their culture, are confined to a small, dark hut until they can walk. As might be expected, the infants often appear quite listless and apathetic during this 13- or 14-month period of enforced inactivity. After leaving the hut, however, they make a speedy recovery, and by the time they are ten, are as advanced socially and intellectually as children of the same age in the U.S. These findings allow us to end on a relatively optimistic note: while children can certainly be harmed by restricted social experience, there is some indication that given half a chance, they may often recover from such ill effects and resume their normal social development.

It is no accident that the first words spoken about the newborn infant refer to its sex, for in an important sense, an individual's gender may be the single most powerful determinant of his or her later social development. From the moment they hear a nurse or physician proclaim the magic words "It's a girl!" or "It's a boy!" parents begin to both behave toward and think about their male and female offspring in markedly different ways. At first, of course, infants are totally oblivious to such contrasting reactions. For example, it makes little difference to them whether their nightgowns are blue or pink as long as they are warm and dry. Within a few short years, however, they have established a strong sexual identity, and will even *demand* that they be treated in the appropriate manner for a girl or boy. The process through which children acquire such sexual identity is generally known as *sex-typing*, and in the present section, we will attempt to answer two major questions about it: (1) How does it work—that is, how do children gain the knowledge that they are boys or girls? and (2) What, at present, does it teach—that is, what, specifically, are youngsters in our society currently learning about the roles, characteristics, and relative standing of men and women?

Sex-Typing: A Girl for Me, a Boy for You . . .

Different concepts of the manner in which children acquire their sexual identity have been formulated in two major approaches: the *social learning* and *cognitive* views. According to social learning theorists, toddlers have a strong tendency to imitate the actions of others. Further, the more similar they are to a given model, the more likely they are to match his or her behavior. Since little boys are physically more similar to their fathers, and little girls are more similar to their mothers, they tend to emulate the parent of their own sex to a greater degree. As a result, boys come to act increasingly like their fathers, and girls increasingly like their mothers. In addition, parents often help this process along by offering rewards (smiles, verbal praise) on occa-

How Sexual Identity is Acquired: The Social Learning and Cognitive Views

sions when their children imitate the "appropriate" model, and by voicing criticism when they match the "inappropriate" one. For example, even today, when many individuals are re-examining their concepts of male and female roles, few boys would be praised for playing with mommy's lipstick, and few girls would win approval for an intense interest in toy guns. Presumably, along with the child's growing behavioral similarity to his or her same-sex parent comes growing awareness of sexual identity. As the process nears completion, then, a child might actually be heard to remark, "I'm a boy like daddy," or "I'm a girl like mommy."

In contrast to the social learning view, which sees the emergence of clear sexual identity as one of the later steps in an ongoing imitative process, the cognitive theory suggests that the process actually *starts* with recognition of a sexual identity. That is, toddlers begin by identifying themselves as a boy or a girl, and then proceed to adopt those behaviors which they perceive as being appropriate to their gender. As suggested by Kohlberg (1966), it is as if the child begins by saying, "I am a girl (boy); therefore I want to do girl (boy) things" — and then goes on to do them!

Although the cognitive theory provides an intriguing explanation for the growth of sexual identity, it is weakened by the fact that young children who declare emphatically that they are a boy or a girl often lack full comprehension of the meaning of such statements. For example, they continue to believe that it is possible for a person to readily change his or her sex. Thus, at present, the social learning position appears to provide a more adequate explanation for the process of sex-typing.

Sexism in the 70's: What the Children Learn

What are we, as a society, currently teaching our children about the roles, characteristics, and relative worth of men and women? Individual parents, of course, run the gamut from strict "traditionalists" holding that mom's place is in the kitchen and dad's is in the den to wholly "liberated" couples who reject such notions very strongly. Some indication of what we are doing collectively in this respect, however, can be gained by examining two influences to which almost all children are exposed: current television offerings and children's books. Presumably, the materials contained in these media have the nation's overall stamp of approval. But even if they do not, they exert a powerful influence upon children's thought, and so bear careful examination.

Turning first to television, the results of a recent investigation by Sternglanz and Serbin (1974) are quite informative. These researchers set out to analyze the content of the most popular shows for children in order to determine whether any differences existed in the treatment of male and female characters. Unfortunately, they soon found that a number of these shows could not even be studied in this manner: they simply failed to contain any female regulars. And even among the remaining programs (e.g., "Pebbles and Bamm Bamm," "Archie's TV Funnies") males outnumbered females by a ratio of 2 to 1.

With respect to the specific behaviors shown by male and female characters, Sternglanz and Serbin found several striking differences. For example, males were much more likely to be shown acting aggressively toward others, making plans and carrying them out, or seeking help and information from others in order to complete some project. In addition, they were generally more active than females, and they were more frequently rewarded for their behavior. In contrast, females were more frequently shown as following directions from others (usually males!), and receiving punishment for high levels of activity. Finally, their actions generally had less effect upon the environment than those of males.

Taken together, these findings suggest that popular television shows are indeed teaching young viewers a great deal about the contrasting roles of women and men. More specifically, they seem to be informing the youngsters who watch them that males are active planners and leaders, while females are passive, inactive followers. Further, because the great majority of the characters shown are males, such programs seem to contain another hidden message for children: overall, it is males who have more fun in our society. Of course, not all television shows fit this description. For example, programs such as "Sesame Street" or "The Electric Company" make consistent attempts to show equal numbers of male and female characters, and to demonstrate that many characteristics are not the sole property of one sex or the other. In general, though, commercial television seems to operate as a conservative force with respect to sexual roles and identity.

If the current situation with respect to television shows is somewhat discouraging for individuals who favor changes in prevailing sexual roles, it is even more disappointing in the area of children's books. First, the ratio of male to female characters is even greater—fully 11 to 1 as reported in a recent survey (Weitzman et al., 1972). Further, adherence to traditional sexual stereotypes seems to be even stronger than on television. A clear illustration of the extremes to which such sexual bias can go is presented in Figure 8–15. Needless to say, materials of this type have been the subject of harsh criticism by feminist groups.

At present, then, it appears that the mass media are still largely training children to adopt traditional sexual roles and behavior. That such training is further strengthened and supported by many parents is indicated by the early age at which most children acquire clear sexual stereotypes. Evidence regarding this issue is provided in an interesting study conducted by Williams, Bennett, and Best (1975). These researchers constructed a series of stories designed to represent various aspects of traditional sexual stereotypes, and then presented them to kindergarten children along with drawings of a man and a woman. The children's task was that of indicating which of these two persons each of the stories was probably about. The results of the study were quite revealing: even by the tender age of five, most of the subjects had already acquired firm sexual stereotypes. For example, as shown in Table 8–4, 94 per cent of the subjects, both boys and girls, indicated that a story designed to represent such *stereotypically* male traits as aggressiveness, assertiveness, and forcefulness was probably about the male figure. Moreover, further strengthening

FIGURE 8–15 An illustration of sexual stereotyping in children's books. (Drawing by Tom Barrett.)

TABLE 8–4 Sexual Stereotypes Among Young Children

Personality Traits in Story	Per cent of Children Responding in Accordance with Sexual Stereotypes	
	Kindergarten	*Second Grade*
Traits Attributed to Men		
aggressive	94	100
strong	81	98
adventurous	83	85
Traits Attributed to Women		
appreciative	66	66
emotional	62	96
soft-hearted	60	94

By the time they are five, children have already acquired strong sexual stereotypes of both men and women. Thus, as shown above, most attribute such traits as aggressiveness or strength to men, and such traits as appreciativeness or emotionality to women. Note that such sexual stereotypes grow even stronger by the time children reach the second grade. (Adapted from Williams, Bennett, and Best, 1975.)

of these stereotypes was apparent when the same procedures were repeated with a group of second-graders (refer to Table 8–4). Additional findings suggest that once such sex-role stereotypes are established, they remain largely unchanged throughout later life (Urberg and Labouvie-Vief, 1976). The weight of the evidence, then, suggests that traditional conceptions of masculinity and femininity are still very much alive and being transmitted to children even in the 1970's.

This is not to say that signs of change are entirely absent, however. For example, at least one large publisher has recently directed its authors to stop using occupational terms ending in "man," such as fireman or mailman, and to replace these with more neutral terms unrelated to sex, such as fire fighter and mail carrier. Similarly, several television shows with women heroes have been introduced ("Maude," "Rhoda," "Police Woman"), and a growing number of school texts seek to avoid obvious sexual stereotyping. In general, though, progress has been quite slow, and mass media offerings continue to present men and women in largely traditional roles. Whether this is a positive or negative state of affairs, of course, depends primarily on one's own point of view.

Moral Development: Learning to Tell "Right" From "Wrong"

As most parents well know, infants have no built-in sense of "right" or "wrong." In fact, they are not even aware that such a dimension exists. Within a few short years, however, they come to recognize its importance and begin passing judgment on their own actions as well as those of others. One famous explanation for the growth of this sense of morality was offered by Sigmund Freud, who contended that the moral side of personality—the conscience—arises from the resolution, in early childhood, of important inner conflicts. Because Freud's theory of personality is discussed in great detail in the following chapter, his suggestions will not be examined here. Instead, we will direct our attention to proposals regarding the nature of moral development offered by Jean Piaget (Piaget and Inhelder, 1969) and Lawrence Kohlberg (Kohlberg and Gilligan, 1972).

THE WIZARD OF ID — By Parker

FIGURE 8-16   Despite recent attempts to lessen their impact, traditional sexual stereotypes are still very much with us at the present time. (The Wizard of Id by permission of Johnny Hart and Field Enterprises, Inc.)

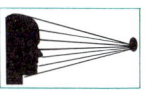 **FOCUS ON RESEARCH:** *Male and Female Stereotypes—Myth or Reality?*

As we have already noted, existing evidence suggests that both boys and girls quickly acquire clear-cut sexual stereotypes—beliefs about the contrasting behavior of males and females—which then tend to persist throughout later life. One important question relating to such stereotypes, of course, concerns the degree to which they are based upon reality. That is, to what extent does the behavior of men and women in our society actually differ? At present, the investigation of such differences is an active field of research, and the total picture is far from clear (Deaux, 1976; Maccoby and Jacklin, 1974). What does seem to be emerging, however, is increasing evidence for the conclusion that "common sense" tends to overstate the case. While men and women do indeed differ in several respects, such differences have often been exaggerated; and other supposed contrasts between the sexes suggested by informal observation have often failed to emerge in systematic investigations (see Table 8-5). In short, as often seems to be the case with respect to stereotypes, there may be a grain of truth hidden inside many widespread beliefs concerning differences in the behavior of men and women. However, this grain seems to be far smaller than has often been suggested.

TABLE 8-5   How Different Are the Two Sexes?

Differences Borne Out by SOME Testing	Differences About Which There is Doubt	Differences Shown to be False
Males are generally more aggressive then females.	Females are more timid and anxious (?)	Females are more sociable than males.
Females have greater verbal ability than males.	Males are more active than females (?)	Females are more suggestible than males.
Males excel in visual-spatial ability.	Males are more competitive than females (?)	Females have lower self-esteem than males.
Males excel in mathematical ability.	Males are more dominant than females (?)	Females lack motivation to achieve.
	Females are more passive than males (?)	Males are more "analytic" in cognitive style than females.

Based on data from Maccoby and Jacklin, 1974.

Subjective and Objective Moral Orientations: Outcomes versus Intentions

According to Piaget, the child's first sense of morality is a rigid one based primarily upon the consequences of actions. More specifically, acts which produce beneficial outcomes are viewed as "good," while acts which yield harmful consequences are viewed as "bad." Piaget terms this approach an **objective moral orientation,** and contrasts it with a more mature one known as a **subjective moral perspective.** This latter type of morality develops at about the age of seven, and is based on the intentions behind various actions rather than the consequences they produce. Thus, a child who has attained this stage of moral development will view actions based on good intentions as acceptable, and those based on bad or evil intentions as unacceptable.

In order to distinguish between subjective and objective moral orientations, Piaget and his associates have devised a set of stories such as the pair shown in Table 8–6. One of the stories in each pair describes an action based upon good intentions, but which causes a great deal of harm, while the other describes an action based upon bad intentions which yields only small negative consequences. When such stories are presented to children of various ages and they are asked to indicate which character was "naughtier," interesting differences are often observed. Below the age of seven, most children indicate that the person in Story A (the one who accidentally caused a great deal of harm) is naughtier than the one in Story B (the one who acted out of bad intentions, but caused only a small amount of harm). Above this age, the reverse is usually true.

On the basis of such findings and his general theory of development, Piaget has suggested that (1) all children go through this change from an objective to a subjective moral orientation, and (2) their progress in this direction cannot be speeded up. The first of these proposals has generally been confirmed. However, the second has been called into question by the findings of several different experiments (e.g., Bandura and McDonald, 1963; Dorr and Fey, 1974). The results of these studies generally suggest that if children who have previously expressed an objective moral orientation are exposed to other persons who demonstrate a subjective orientation, they soon come to adopt this more mature moral perspective themselves (see Figure 8–17). Not too surprisingly, movement in the opposite direction may also occur, so that children who have previously expressed a subjective moral orientation readily slip back into an objective one following exposure to models who demonstrate such behavior. Findings such as these suggest that the rate at which children progress toward an adult sense of morality is not necessarily fixed, but rather open to influence from the social environment.

TABLE 8–6   Stories Used to Determine Moral Orientation

Story A	Story B
John was in his room when his mother called him to dinner. John goes down, and opens the door to the dining room. But behind the door was a chair, and on the chair was a tray with fifteen cups on it. John did not know the cups were behind the door. He opens the door, the door hits the tray, bang go the fifteen cups, and they all get broken.	One day when Henry's mother was out, Henry tried to get some cookies out of the cupboard. He climbed up on a chair, but the cookie jar was still too high, and he couldn't reach it. But while he was trying to get the cookie jar, he knocked over a cup. The cup fell down and broke.

Stories such as these are used by Piaget to distinguish between an objective and subjective moral orientation. Children who report that John is naughtier than Henry are demonstrating an objective orientation, while those who report that Henry is naughtier are demonstrating a subjective orientation. (From Bandura and McDonald, 1963, p. 276.)

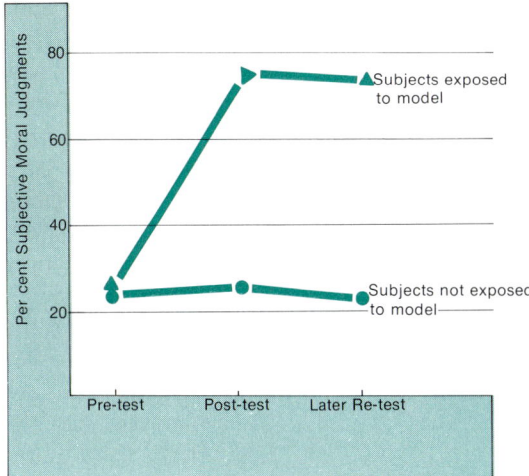

FIGURE 8-17 When children who have previously made mostly objective moral judgments are exposed to a model who makes subjective ones, they soon adopt this more mature moral perspective themselves. Further, they maintain this shift when re-tested at a later time. Subjects not exposed to a model, of course, show no change in moral orientation. (Based on data from Dorr and Fey, 1974.)

Kohlberg's Stages of Moral Growth: From Punishment to Principle

A somewhat more detailed picture of moral development has been presented by Lawrence Kohlberg and his associates (e.g., Kohlberg and Gilligan, 1972). In order to study such growth, Kohlberg presents children with stories describing hypothetical moral dilemmas, and then analyzes their responses. For example, one such story describes a situation in which a man whose wife is dying of cancer breaks into a store in order to steal the expensive drug which will save her life. After hearing such stories, children of various ages are asked whether the major character's actions were justified or unjustified, and why they hold these views. On the basis of careful analysis of such replies, Kohlberg has concluded that children pass through six distinct stages of moral growth, which may be described as follows:

Stage 1: In the first stage, children base their moral judgments on obedience and punishment. That is, actions which demonstrate obedience to authority (parents, teachers, and so on) or which allow the child to avoid punishment are viewed as "good." For example, in responding to the story presented above, a child in the first stage of moral development might argue that the man was right to steal the drug, for if he did not, he would be blamed for letting his wife die.

Stage 2: The second stage might be termed the selfish stage, for during this period, children judge the morality of various acts in terms of satisfaction of their own needs. Thus, actions which satisfy their needs are "good," while those which do not are "bad." For example, a child at this stage might justify theft of the expensive drug because, quite simply, the person involved needed it very badly. Together, stages 1 and 2 form what Kohlberg terms the **preconventional level** of morality—a level at which children have no true internal standards, but rather evaluate acts in terms of their consequences. In this respect, the preconventional level corresponds to Piaget's objective moral orientation stage.

Stage 3: Kohlberg describes the third stage of moral development as reflecting a "good boy—nice girl" orientation. During this stage, children view actions which are approved by others as "good," and those which are disapproved as "bad." For example, in responding to the drug problem outlined above, children at this stage may argue that the man was wrong to steal the life-giving potion because people will view him as a criminal and his family will be dishonored.

Stage 4: In the fourth stage of development, emphasis is shifted to "doing one's duty" and respect for established law and authority. In terms of the drug problem, children may argue that the man was right to steal because it was his duty to save his wife, or that he was wrong to do so since his actions broke the law. Together, stages 3 and 4 constitute what Kohlberg terms the **conventional level** of morality, the level at which most adults tend to operate.

Stage 5: The fifth stage of development is based primarily upon what might be termed a sense of the "social contract." That is, individuals who attain this stage realize that they have important obligations to other members of society. As a result, they view actions which are consistent with the rights and well-being of others as "good," and those which violate such rights or harm others as "bad."

Stage 6: In the final stage of moral growth—one few people ever attain—morality is based primarily upon self-chosen, universal principles. Behavior which is consistent with such principles is viewed as acceptable, while actions inconsistent with these principles are viewed as unacceptable. In short, individuals who manage to attain this stage of development are guided largely by the commandments of their own conscience, and base their moral judgments largely upon personal, inner standards. Kohlberg has described stages 5 and 6 as forming the **postconventional level** of morality, for individuals in these stages are governed by universal moral principles rather than the approval or authority of others.

Evidence for the view that children move through these various stages in the order suggested by Kohlberg has been obtained in several recent studies. For example, in one interesting experiment, Tapp and Levine (1972) asked individuals ranging from kindergarten through college the following question: "Why should people follow rules?" Results indicated that in answer to this question, the youngest children tended to stress the avoidance of punishment and other negative consequences, somewhat older children emphasized obedience to authority, and the oldest group stressed social obligations. Thus, as expected, they expressed increasingly mature moral orientations with increasing age. Findings such as these suggest that a sense of morality is neither present at birth nor acquired in a sudden, all-or-none fashion. Rather, it develops gradually as part of more general patterns of social and cognitive growth. In short, learning to tell "right" from "wrong" is simply another task we must face on the long journey from child to adult.

Human Development: A Postscript

In the interests of clarity, we have considered physical, cognitive, and social development separately within the present chapter. Before concluding, therefore, we must hasten to note that such a division is actually quite artificial. In reality, these three aspects of human development are intimately related, so that change along one dimension both influences and is influenced by change along the others. For example, patterns of physical growth have an important bearing upon social development. To cite only one illustration, individuals who mature relatively early experience different types of interaction with others than do those who mature relatively late. Similarly, physically attractive persons are treated differently by family, friends, and even teachers than physically unattractive individuals (Clifford and Walster, 1973). In these and many other ways, social development is influenced by physical growth.

In a parallel manner, cognitive development has important effects upon social growth. For example, children cannot understand or act upon complex social concepts such as sharing and reciprocity until their modes of thought are sufficiently mature. And the richness or complexity of their interactions with others is certainly governed, to an important degree, by their ability to communicate verbally with these persons.

We hope that these few illustrations will be sufficient to counteract any false impressions regarding the independence of physical, cognitive, and social growth we may have conveyed in earlier portions of this chapter. Human development is essentially a unified and integrated process. If, in our attempts to communicate clearly, we have seemed to shatter such unity, it is essential that we end by emphasizing its existence.

Summary

Life begins with the fertilization of the ovum by a single sperm. During the next nine months, development is very rapid, so that by the time the child is born, he or she is well equipped for survival outside the mother's body. Physical growth is fastest during the first two years of life, but then slows considerably in later childhood. It accelerates once again during puberty as sexual maturity is attained. Physical decline becomes noticeable in the 30's and continues at an accelerating rate. Aging is not a unitary process, however, and some systems of the body lose their vitality more rapidly than others.

As they grow in physical size, children also undergo considerable **cognitive development. Language**—with the first spoken word—appears near the end of the first year, and then increases quickly thereafter. Thus, by the time they are 3, most toddlers have a vocabulary of more than 1,000 words. Even in their earliest speech, children demonstrate a remarkable understanding of rules of grammar. This fact has led some investigators to propose the existence of an innate mechanism which aids in language acquisition. Thought processes, too, become increasingly mature. At first, infants fail to understand that objects which pass beyond their view continue to exist, and even children of 5 or 6 are unable to deal with **relational** terms (e.g., bigger, lighter) or solve problems relating to the principle of **conservation.** By the time they are 12, however, most cognitive growth is complete, and adolescents can reason deductively, think abstractly, and demonstrate all other aspects of adult thought.

Within a few months of their birth, most children form a strong **affective bond** to their mothers. Such attachment was at one time attributed largely to the mother's association with various rewards. Experiments by Harry Harlow and his associates, however, suggest that an innate need for **contact comfort**—physical contact with soft objects—may also play a crucial role in this process. Additional findings point to the importance, for normal social development, of opportunities for extensive interaction with others. Children rapidly establish a sexual identity, probably through imitation of their same-sex parent. In addition, they soon acquire knowledge of what constitutes "appropriate" behavior by members of both sexes. Children's first **moral** judgments are based primarily upon the consequences of various actions. That is, actions which result in harmful consequences are viewed as "bad," while those which result in beneficial outcomes are viewed as "good." Gradually, however, they come to base such judgments upon other factors: the intentions behind different acts, the rights of others, and self-chosen ethical principles.

Suggested Readings

Deaux, K.: *The Behavior of Women and Men.* Monterey, California: Brooks Cole, 1976.

  A clearly written review of recent research on sex differences in social behavior. Among the topics covered are differences in the behavior of women and men with respect to altruism, aggression, self-esteem, cooperation, and competition.

Fleming, J. D.: Field report: The state of the apes. *Psychology Today,* 1974, 7, 31–49.

  A discussion of recent attempts to teach language to chimpanzees.

Harlow, H. F., and Harlow, M. H.: Learning to love. *American Scientist,* 1966, 54, 244–272.

  An overview of many of the Harlows' famous experiments on the development of attachment (love) in rhesus monkeys.

Mussen, P. H., Conger, J. J., and Kagan, J.: *Child Develop-* *ment and Personality.* New York: Harper and Row, 1974.

  A comprehensive discussion of many different aspects of child development. Relevant research is cited and described under each topic.

Phillips, J. L., Jr.: *The Origins of intellect: Piaget's Theory.* San Francisco: W. H. Freeman, 1969.

  A relatively brief (about 100 pages) discussion of Piaget's theory of cognitive development. The implications of Piaget's views for the field of education are also discussed.

Some journals that regularly publish articles on child development and behavior:

  Child Development
  Developmental Psychology
  Journal of Experimental Child Psychology
  Journal of Personality and Social Psychology
  Journal of Youth and Adolescence

Overleaf: Photo by Fred Weiss.

9 Personality: Understanding the Behavior of Individuals

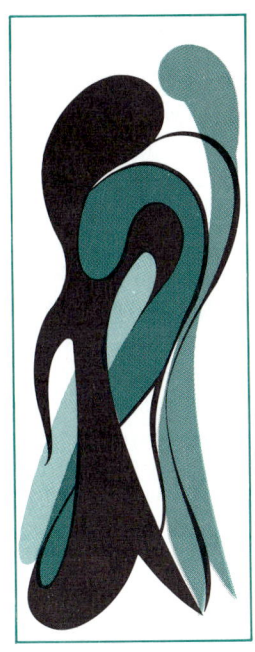

One of the obvious facts about human beings is their tremendous diversity. Each of us knows people who are friendly and others who are hostile, some who are quiet and some who are boisterous, some who are open-minded and tolerant and some who are closed-minded and bigoted. When we get to know anyone fairly well, we tend to think of him or her in terms of such characteristics, which somehow hang together and make that person a unique individual. What is your mother like? How would you describe your best friend? How would you characterize the President of the United States? When you answer such questions, you are describing the **personality** of that particular individual. To psychologists, *personality consists of an individual's characteristic patterns of behavior.*

As you probably noticed, this psychological meaning of the term is not exactly the same as many of us use in everyday speech. Most often, "personality" suggests the positive qualities of someone who is outgoing, interesting, energetic, and the life of the party. For example, you may have had a blind date with someone who was described as not much to look at, but having a "terrific personality." The word also is used to indicate someone who stands out from the crowd, such as an actor or a politician who is a "personality in the news." For psychologists, an individual's personality is neither good nor bad, jolly nor dull, newsworthy nor commonplace, but rather a description of all of his or her behavioral characteristics. Beyond arriving at descriptions, personality psychologists also want to be able to explain why individuals differ and how the various bits and pieces fit together as aspects of a total, actively functioning human being.

In the present chapter, we will first describe several attempts to build all-inclusive *theories of personality*. Such theories were first suggested by Greek philosophers thousands of years ago, and in modern times were developed extensively by the physician-therapists of the late nineteenth and early twentieth centuries; they continue to be constructed by research psychologists at the present time. The task of precisely and accurately predicting specific behavior requires the development of techniques permitting the *measurement of personality*. These techniques vary from projective tests which attempt to provide a global picture of personality to objective measures of personality traits. To illustrate the way that traits influence behavior, we will describe some of the research on authoritarianism (the tendency to accept fascist versus democratic ideas). Though personality traits undoubtedly influence behavior, there is a growing interest in identifying the powerful *situational determinants of behavior*. We will discuss the reason for the increased interest in such factors, and will present an example of the way in which a trait such as honesty can be considered as behavior that is influenced by the details of specific situations. Finally, we will present a few conclusions about personality which may help to bring some of this material together.

THEORIES OF PERSONALITY: TRYING TO PAINT THE TOTAL PICTURE

All **theories** consist of a network of concepts and propositions which attempt to explain a particular set of events. For example, theories have been constructed to account for the origin of the universe, the evolution of species, and the working of the monetary system. In a similar way, personality theories have been developed with the goal of describing and explaining the behavior of individuals.

The First Theories of Personality

Early Typologies: Fitting Individuals into Categories

There is no way to know, of course, when it first happened that a human being began to wonder about himself and his companions with respect to personality characteristics. In the earliest writings, individual differences were recognized along such dimensions as bravery, generosity, and intelligence. During a remarkable period of history in the centuries preceding the birth of Christ, Greece became a center of intellectual activity, with a leisure class of thoughtful, intelligent, educated individuals who pondered the meaning of the world around them. Here, philosophers, artists, and physicians, among others, tried to explain not only their physical world but also the behavior of human beings. Philosophers such as Aristotle and Plato, for example, first attempted to make sense out of the way friendships were formed, the interaction of people in organizations, and much else besides.

The Greek physician Hippocrates created the first model of personality based on what we would today call a **typology.** Typologies classify all behavior into a handful of categories, called **types.** He proposed that there are four bodily fluids, or "humors": blood, black bile, yellow bile, and phlegm. Whenever there was an excess of one of these humors, one of four possible **temperaments,** or moods, would result. Individuals who were overly cheerful were that way because of excess blood. An extreme amount of black bile caused depression. Angry dispositions were brought about by an overabundance of yellow bile, while too much phlegm resulted in apathetic behavior. These four basic personality types are illustrated in Figure 9–1.

Throughout the following centuries, there were many additional suggestions of simple typologies that were devised as ways to describe individual differences. For example, a German philosopher named Spranger (1928), divided people into six types on the basis of their interests or values. People were described as being oriented primarily toward theory, economics, art, people, politics, or religion.

Of greater historical consequence, of course, was the first *complex* and *comprehensive personality theory*—that created by Sigmund Freud. We will describe his pioneering ideas in some detail and then will present several addi-

Psychologie des Jugend-alters

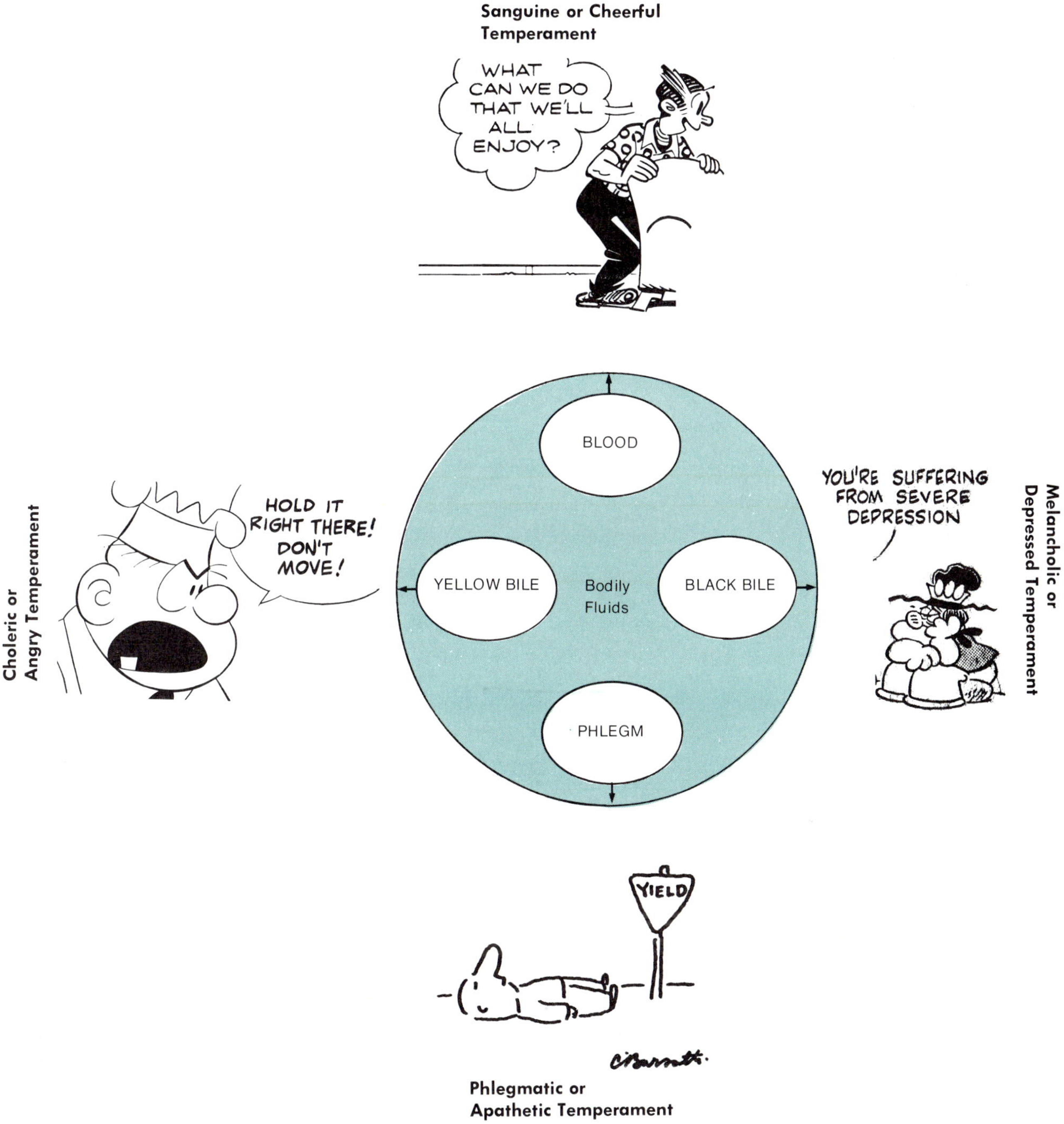

FIGURE 9–1 The ancient Greek physician Hippocrates proposed that the human body contains four basic fluid elements. Individual differences in temperament were then explained on the basis of an unequal distribution of the fluids; an excess of a particular element was thought to lead to a specific type of temperament. (Bottom drawing by C. Barsotti; © 1974, The New Yorker Magazine, Inc. All other drawings © King Features Syndicate, Inc.)

tional personality theories that have been formulated by psychiatrists, psychologists, and others.

In the latter part of the nineteenth century, Sigmund Freud, a Jewish physician working in Vienna, elaborated the first all-encompassing personality theory. Freud had wanted to become a research scientist after receiving the M.D. degree, but financial need plus the anti-Semitism of his colleagues drove

Psychoanalytic Theory: Mapping the Unconscious

FIGURE 9–2 Sigmund Freud was a Viennese physician who developed the first comprehensive theory of personality. He is shown here, late in his life, with his daughter Anna, who also became a world-famous psychoanalyst. (Wide World Photos.)

him into private practice. He specialized in the treatment of emotional problems, and he began to study a number of newly developed techniques, such as hypnosis. One rather unusual treatment was a procedure developed by another Viennese physician, Josef Breuer, who had his patients simply talk about their problems. Almost miraculously, such conversations between physician and patient were often helpful in getting rid of certain symptoms. For example, a woman with a paralyzed arm was able to use it once again, and a young boy was no longer overwhelmed by irrational fears.

Freud found himself deeply interested not so much in providing a cure for a series of patients but in seeking to understand how their symptoms came to be, and why the talking procedure produced change. Freud was a brilliant, intellectually curious, untiring worker. He was convinced that behavior was not a matter of chance but that each thing anyone said, or did, or thought was determined by some identifiable cause. Further, it was clear to him that individuals were often not aware of the reasons for particular behavior; that is, the causes were **unconscious.** Freud's task, then, was to play the role of a psychological Sherlock Holmes and to seek clues here and there in associations to words, in dreams, or in slips of the tongue, and to piece these clues together by means of clever deduction. Beyond this, he was also working on a more ambitious task, that of building a general theory of personality to explain the workings of the human mind. We will describe a few of his most important concepts.

States of Conscious-ness: Shadows in Your Mind

Early in his work, Freud concluded that mental functioning could be described in terms of three states of consciousness. First, and most obvious, is the **conscious** state. This includes whatever one is thinking about at the moment. For example, you are consciously reading this book, comprehending the words, and perhaps from time to time consciously thinking of quite different things as your mind wanders to other, more exciting topics. Now PAY ATTENTION! and keep your conscious processes focused on these pages.

Second is the **preconscious** state, which refers to all of the stored memories which are not part of your current thoughts but which can be brought into consciousness. For example, what is your middle name? Even though you were very probably not thinking about your middle name before the question was asked, it is now in your consciousness. Sometimes it is rather difficult to retrieve this material, even though it is "right on the tip of your tongue" (see Chapter 6), and you may not be able to recall a person's name or the title of a song until several hours or days after you first tried to remember it. For example, can you instantly name the seven dwarfs in *Snow White* or all eight of Santa's reindeer?

The third state is the **unconscious,** containing all of the memories and desires and elements of which we are unaware. According to Freud, some of this material was never conscious, but much of it consists of material which caused so much anxiety that it was thrust out of consciousness and *repressed.* Presumably, some of our hostile feelings, sexual cravings, and most desperate fears are so threatening that we must repress them, keeping them under lock and key in the recesses of the unconscious. This material sometimes reaches the conscious in bits and pieces, however. For example, you may have no conscious desire to have sexual relations with your parent and no memory of ever having such a thought; then one night you dream that you are engaging in incest. How could such an idea enter your head? Freud would say that an unconscious desire was being expressed in your dream. Or, as Cinderella sang in the Disney movie, "A dream is a wish your heart makes." Many impulses are so threatening that, even in sleep, it is necessary to disguise them in some way. This is the reason that dreams often make no logical sense until they are interpreted by someone who can use whatever clues are available to uncover the underlying meaning. One of the goals of Freudian psychotherapy, as we shall see in Chapter 11, is to bring unconscious material into consciousness, so that an individual can deal with it rather than having it influence his behavior in ways beyond his awareness or control.

Id, Ego, and Superego: Desire, Reason, and Conscience

Though Freud was able to explain a great deal of mental functioning in terms of the three states of consciousness, he later found it useful to describe a kind of mental map involving three regions or types of mental activity. He portrayed these regions as the site of constant battles in which there are conflicts among what we desire, what can realistically be obtained, and what our moral code tells us is right or wrong.

The primary region is the **id.** Freud proposed that the id is present at birth and is totally unconscious. From the very beginning of life, impulses from the id are directed toward immediate gratification of desire. Whether the desire is for food, sex, or whatever, the id demands satisfaction without regard for what is possible or what the consequences might be. The contentment of a baby sucking on a nipple and the same infant's terrible rage at not being fed immediately each represent the way the id expresses only the desire for immediate personal pleasure and satisfaction. We continue to be influenced by the same unyielding id impulses throughout our lives. Freud believed that deep in the unconscious, we each are motivated to rape, steal, kill, or whatever else is necessary to get what we want. This region was described as a seething cauldron of excitement, constantly goading us toward instant pleasure (Freud, 1933). (When Robert Louis Stevenson had a dream which suggested that even the kindest and most upright person has an evil inner self, he elaborated the idea in the form of a novel, *Dr. Jekyll and Mr. Hyde.*)

Without additional mental development, we could not survive, because the id has no concern with the demands of reality or logic. In response to early frustrations, however, we begin to learn something about the limitations imposed by the real world, and we find that our wishes may not always be immediately fulfilled. This coming to grips with reality was described by Freud as the development of the **ego,** which involves perception, reasoning, learning, and all other activities necessary to interact effectively with the world around us. The ego crosses all three levels of consciousness, but it primarily involves conscious and preconscious states. The ego was described as a sort of realistic servant of the id, in that it too strives for satisfaction. The difference is that impossible desires are abandoned (you can't reach out and touch the moon), and you weigh the later effects of what you do now (you learn that your mother will spank you for swiping a cookie). Thus, the *pleasure principle* governing the id is toned down or guided by the *reality principle* governing the ego.

The third region, the **superego,** ordinarily develops as children are exposed to the moral values of their parents. In this setting, the child accepts and internalizes (1) the parental views of ideal behavior and (2) their moral values as to what is right and wrong. These two aspects of the superego are known as the *ego-ideal* and the *conscience.* Like the ego, the superego spans all three levels of consciousness. While most of us are able to verbalize our ideals and our moral system, it is also true that we are not always aware of the reason for our strong emotional reactions on such issues. It is as if we carry around with us a stern and moralistic chaperone who punishes our slightest deviation from the straight and narrow path of virtue by making us feel guilty. Most of us, for example, would be unable to kill an innocent puppy, not simply because of legal restrictions, but because such an act would make us feel terrible. At times, the superego can also be as irrational as the id. For example, an individual may have been taught only that premarital intercourse is wrong but then be unable to engage freely in sexual behavior after getting married. Individuals with sexual inhibitions often say that it feels as if mother is standing at the foot of the bed shaking her head in disapproval. If the id is pushing an individual to engage in sexual intercourse right now, the ego is cautioning that you should avoid unpleasant consequences and thus would rule out rape and would attempt to prevent pregnancy and venereal disease. The superego, on the other hand, might well leave the individual feeling that sex is a "no-no" under all circumstances.

Psychosexual Stages of Development: From Orifice to Oedipus

Freud described human development as passing through a series of stages based on the different ways we obtain bodily pleasure at different ages. Adult personality characteristics are determined by what happens to us during each stage and how successful we are in getting through that period. It is possible to get "stuck" at a particular stage and not progress beyond that point—a process termed **fixation.** It is also possible when things go badly at a later stage to retreat or go back to an earlier one—a process termed **regression.**

The first source of pleasure is the mouth; the infant sucks on the mother's nipple or an artificial substitute for it. The **oral stage** is a passive and usually contented period when we can simply lie back and accept the good things that are happening to us. When an individual is overindulged during this period, the resulting **oral personality** type is supposedly dependent, conforming, trusting, and happy; eating plays a big part in the person's life, and obesity is common. The stereotype would be the kind of character usually portrayed in the movies by Lou Costello—the jolly fat man who was child-like, optimistic, and easily led astray by Bud Abbott. On the other hand, frustration and anxiety during the oral stage would be expected to lead to the opposite type of personality—the tense, verbally aggressive individual. Unfortunately, attempts to relate early oral experiences such as age of weaning to adult personality type have not supported these ideas (Sears, Maccoby, and Levin, 1957).

By the time the child is about a year old, the parents usually decide that

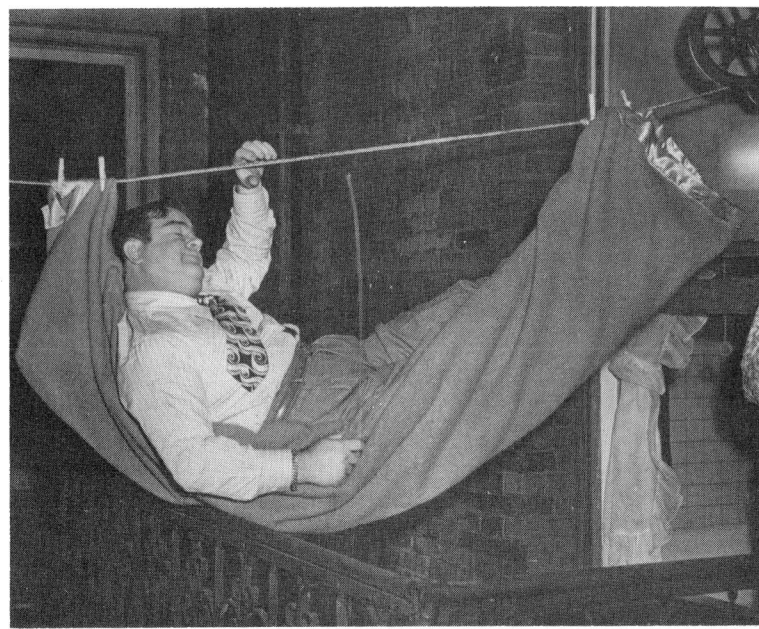

A

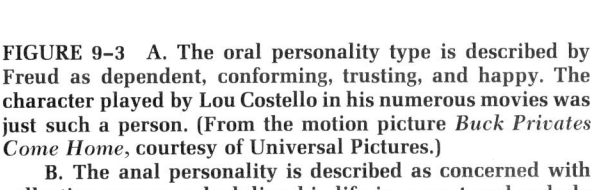

FIGURE 9-3   A. The oral personality type is described by Freud as dependent, conforming, trusting, and happy. The character played by Lou Costello in his numerous movies was just such a person. (From the motion picture *Buck Privates Come Home*, courtesy of Universal Pictures.)

B. The anal personality is described as concerned with collecting money, scheduling his life in a neat and orderly fashion, and periodically expressing stubbornness and aggression. Dickens described such a person well when he created Ebenezer Scrooge in *A Christmas Carol*. (Reprinted by permission of William Collins and World Publishing Co., Inc., from *A Christmas Carol* by Charles Dickens, illustrations by Ronald Searle. Copyright © 1961 by Ronald Searle.)

B

it is appropriate for him or her to gain control over bowel functions, and toilet training is undertaken. Defecation is experienced as pleasurable, but the child is taught to delay this gratification and wait for a socially acceptable time and place. Thus, the **anal stage** is the first time there is deliberate interference with the child's pleasure, and the **anal personality** reflects an individual's response to this interference. Since it is not permissible to play with one's feces, substitutes are found; thus anal characters become obsessed with saving and collecting such things as money, stamps, and butterflies. Toilet training involves a concern with cleanliness and following a schedule; accordingly, the anal individual is orderly and neat and dedicated to keeping things in their proper place. The anal period is also the first time the child can rebel against his parents, either by soiling himself or by refusing to produce the desired product. As a result, the anal adult can be stubborn or aggressive. Charles Dickens' Ebenezer Scrooge in *A Christmas Carol* is a typical anal personality. Research by Tribich and Messer (1974) has provided support for some of the hypothesized characteristics of oral and anal types. Undergraduate males were given a special test to identify those who were oral and those who were anal. In an experimental situation, the oral individuals tended to conform and copy the behavior of an authority figure, while those who were anal tended to do just the opposite.

At about the third year, there is a brief **urethral stage** based on concern with urination as pressures are brought to bear to retain one's urine until it can be released appropriately. The adult urethral character is described as ambitious to succeed, but he or she quickly gives up in the face of difficulty. Such individuals are said to feel inferior, as if they still were experiencing the shame of walking around with damp pants or of wetting the bed at night. A well-known television performer described how his parents used to hang his stained bedsheets out of the window to dry. The idea was to shame him when his friends and neighbors saw what a bad boy he had been during the night. If you had gone through such experiences, do you believe it might have an influence on your later feelings about yourself?

About the age of four, the very crucial **phallic stage** is reached—according to Freud, it is when the child first discovers masturbation and finds that stroking the penis or clitoris can yield pleasurable sensations. At this point, Freud described males and females as having somewhat different experiences. During this phallic stage, the primitive sexual urges of the boy become directed toward his mother as part of his masturbation fantasies. Freud called this the Oedipal period, in reference to the ancient Greek play in which Oedipus unwittingly kills his father and marries his mother. The child senses that his father would be angry if he knew of his desires, and the child fears that his father would castrate him by way of punishment. In one of his most famous cases, Freud described little Hans, a five-year-old boy who feared having his penis cut off by his father; his feelings were expressed in disguised form as a fear of horses and other powerful animals. Terror concerning castration is the basis for the development of the superego, in that the only reasonable solution for a boy is to give up his lust for his mother (Mother's Day might be seen as an acceptable substitute) and try to model himself after his father. This identification with father involves accepting and adopting all of his values. If the **Oedipal conflict** is not resolved, Freud believed that the phallic adult may be either a coldly promiscuous Don Juan motivated only by lust or a homosexual.

Freud's description of the female phallic stage has been the object of a great deal of justified criticism because of its male chauvinist view of women. According to Freud, the little girl's first sexual object also is the mother, and she, too, wishes to possess her. At this point, she discovers that her "penis" (the clitoris) is "inferior" to the one possessed by males. She wishes she were better equipped (**penis envy**) and blames her mother for causing her to inherit inadequate anatomy; it *must* be mother's fault, because she is built the same way. There is nothing comparable here to castration fears; as a consequence, Freud felt that females never are forced to develop the strong superego which is "typical" of males. Subsequent research on moral development and altruism suggests that Freud was incorrect in suggesting sex differences in conscience development. Resolution of the phallic stage problems occurs when the girl rejects her mother in favor of her father. She then loves her father in a nonsexual way, identifies with her mother, and accepts the idea of having a baby as a substitute for having a penis. If these conflicts are not resolved, the adult phallic female may be a flirtatious tease, or she may turn into a castrating female oriented toward a career. Scarlett O'Hara in *Gone with the Wind* combines both of these characteristics. As with males, an extreme version of an unresolved conflict in the phallic stage supposedly is homosexuality.

By the age of six, according to Freud, the basic personality characteristics have been established as a function of what happens during the four early psychosexual stages. From then until puberty there is a *latency period*, in which children supposedly lose interest in sexual matters and become involved with friends of their own sex. At puberty, there is a brief return of Oedipal concerns when the adolescent has a crush on an older member of the opposite sex, but this crush goes away when the individual settles on a sex object of the appropriate age. The mature person reaches the **genital stage,** in which lust is blended with affection, and adult roles are assumed.

Freud's ideas about personality were an impressive and creative contribution, but how have they held up when examined by modern research methods? Though some of his ideas appear to be correct, many are clearly wrong. For example, the "latency period" is a myth, and no one has found any connection between homosexuality and the events occurring in the phallic stage. Other ideas of his are untestable. For example, how could anyone possibly determine if a newborn baby has an id? Still other ideas are very unsatisfactory from the point of view of helping us to predict behavior. For example, an adult oral character supposedly may be caused *either* by very pleasant or very unpleasant events during the oral stage. Despite these and other problems with this type of theorizing, Freud was a pioneering genius in opening up whole areas of human behavior to investigation and in creating a theory which has influenced our research, our thinking, and our literature for most of the twentieth century.

Following the lead of Freud, other theorists began to offer alternative proposals to describe personality. Some of these new theories were simply revisions of particular points made by Freud, but many were entirely original formulations.

Rogers' Self Theory: Tender Loving Acceptance

One of the most influential of the non-Freudian theorists is an American psychologist, Carl Rogers. His initial professional goal was in theology, but he switched to psychology and worked in this field in graduate school. His next 12 years were spent as a clinical psychologist conducting psychotherapy.

FIGURE 9–4 Carl Rogers is an American psychologist whose client-centered approach to psychotherapy led him to develop a personality theory based on the concept of self.

During this period, he found himself trying to gain a better understanding of why people have emotional problems and how they can be helped. He then moved into the academic world, as a professor in several midwestern universities. He began to put theoretical ideas together in articles, papers, and a series of widely read books, including _Client-Centered Therapy_ (Rogers, 1951). Rogers was always quite interested in research. Unlike Freud, Rogers was trained in psychology and has always been convinced that his ideas should be testable. He feels that it is essential to be able to document the kinds of behavior changes he observed in psychotherapy. For this reason, his development of a theory of the self has influenced much research over the past several decades, and the research, in turn, has influenced the theory.

Rogers' basic conception of people is that they are naturally open, honest, and in contact with their feelings. Difficulties arise only because of interference from others; we must be _taught_ to repress, to distort reality, to be maladjusted. Rogers suggests that people naturally have the capacity for growth and psychological development, but that this can only occur in an atmosphere of freedom.

The Self-Concept: Who Am I?

Rogers feels that it is important to deal with people not from the viewpoint of an external observer who describes and classifies but rather as someone who tries to see the world from the other individual's point of view. When you take this other-centered, or **phenomenological,** approach, Rogers suggests that what you see is not a series of complex mental structures or an array of personality types but only one basic element—the _self_. The one primary motive is to maintain or improve oneself. Rogers calls this the **actualizing tendency.** Each person wants to satisfy his needs as he experiences them in the environment as he perceives it.

Adjustment and psychological health are defined in terms of a realistic **self-concept** that is congruent with experience. Presumably, unless we are taught inappropriately by those whose love we need, our self-concept is based on our own perceptions, and it fits well with our experiences. If we are taught to have a self-concept that does not match what we actually experience, we are going to have difficulty. For example, you might learn that nice people never get angry and then find yourself in a situation in which you are insulted; your self-concept does not allow you to perceive your angry feelings accurately. The greater the discrepancy between our self and our experiences, the greater the maladjustment and anxiety, and the harder we must work to reconcile what we believe about ourselves and what we encounter in the world around us. Rogers also suggests that if there is a large self-experience discrepancy and if there is no way to avoid all of the relevant experiences, the defensive system may be unable to handle the anxiety; it may break down and result in a disorganization of personality. Inconsistency between self and experience makes an individual vulnerable to such a breakdown.

Acquiring a Realistic Self-Concept: Knowing What You Feel

Early in our lives, we each have direct experience with pleasure and pain; for example, we obviously learn that it is good to eat and bad to be hungry, good to be held in mother's arms and bad to touch a hot stove, good to lie in a warm bed on a winter night and bad to stand on a cold floor the next morning. Beyond these simple physical reactions, there is the need for _positive regard_. That is, we want to be loved and respected as individuals. Our parents tend to be the primary source of love and affection, and it is desperately important to maintain their good will. We want them to praise us, say that we are good, and express positive feelings toward us. When we do something they dislike and they let us know it, the experience is a painful one. We strive to alter our behavior to get back in their good graces. We find that going along with them is good, because it maintains the loving relationship.

The crucial problem occurs when the beliefs, values, and perceptions of the parents do not fit the child's experiences and feelings. Let's look at an example of the process. A three-year-old boy is upset when his mother gives birth to a second child, a baby sister. He now must share love and attention with the new addition, be quiet when the baby is sleeping, and stand by when all the family's relatives and friends ooh and aah over the precious baby as they bring her presents. From the brother's perspective, the situation involves rejection and loss of status; most likely he feels not only depressed but hostile. The obvious target of his hostility is the new sister. One day his mother enters the baby's room and finds the little boy deliberately pinching the baby's arm to make her cry. What does the mother do? Her decision at this point is described by Rogers as a critical one in the development of the boy's self-concept.

It would not be an unusual response to punish the child and to reject him because of his hostility. "I don't know what got into you. You're not my little boy if you act like that. You know you love baby sister. Give her a kiss, and say you're sorry." The conflict for the boy is clear. He knows that he does not love the baby and would much rather bite her than kiss her. The need for mother's love is vitally important, however, so he may well alter his self-concept to conform to what the mother says. He gradually becomes convinced that he really does love his sister, even though many of his subsequent experiences arouse feelings which are inconsistent with that belief. In effect, the mother's reaction might serve to help give this child a self-concept inconsistent with his experiences.

What is the alternative? Should she just do nothing and let the boy amuse himself by inflicting pain on the baby? Though some critics of "permissive" child-rearing might have that misconception, Rogers has indicated repeatedly that that is not the answer. Instead, there are three crucial points for the parent to keep in mind. First, the child's feelings must be recognized and accepted. He does feel hostile, and he does enjoy hurting his rival. The parent doesn't have to like those feelings, but it is important to recognize them and accept what is going on inside of the child. Second, the mother should avoid threatening the child with the most terrible punishment of all—loss of love. If she tries to see the world through the eyes of an already threatened three-year-old, she can see that he already believes he is totally rejected by those whose love he needs most. The mother can reassure him that he is accepted and loved. Third, the hostile behavior must be clearly and unmistakably rejected and prevented, even if this requires punishment.

The crucial distinction, to self theorists, is that between feelings and behavior. The simple rule is to accept all feelings *accurately* and to maintain positive regard for the individual while prohibiting any and all unacceptable behaviors. In a way, Rogers tells parents to be honest, loving, and as strict as they wish; under these conditions, the child's self-concept is expected to develop in a healthy and well-adjusted manner.

A number of individuals in psychology, psychiatry, and other fields have developed theories of personality. None have been as influential as the theories of Freud and Rogers, but each contains some unique elements that contribute to our understanding of human behavior. We will briefly examine three of these other theories.

Some Additional Personality Theories: The Ideas of Jung, Sheldon, and Erikson

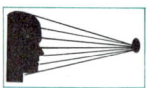

Though our discussion of Rogers' theory has concentrated on how the self-concept is acquired and how behavior is affected by the discrepancy between self and experience, it is also true that the self-concept can change. In Chapter 11, we will briefly return to the way in which Rogers' approach to psychotherapy leads to such changes.

Even in everyday life, however, various experiences can alter the way that we perceive ourselves, in either a positive or a negative direction. Some changes probably do not last very long. For example, Flippo and Lewinsohn (1971) gave subjects a reasoning task and arranged it so that they would either do well or fail; success led to more positive attitudes about the self, while failure led to more negative self-perceptions. You have probably had similar experiences after an exam on which you did very well or very poorly. A more important and probably more lasting change is brought about by events which disrupt one's life, such as when a close relative is seriously ill, or a friend dies, or a job is lost. These and other disruptive events are found to lower self-esteem (Kaplan, 1970).

Still another type of change is brought about by attempts to master a new skill. Koocher (1971) reasoned that if young boys at a summer camp could learn how to swim, there would necessarily be some change in a portion of their self-concepts. The change from "I am someone who cannot swim" to "I am someone who has learned to swim" was expected to bring about a more positive self-image. On the other hand, if a boy tried to learn swimming and failed, there might even be a change toward a more negative self-concept. The change here would be from "I am someone who cannot swim" to "I am someone who is a failure at swimming."

As part of a YMCA summer program, boys ranging in age from 7 to 15 were given a self-concept measure and a measure of how they would ideally like to be. The farther apart these two scores, the more negative is the self-concept. Swimming lessons were given over a 12-day period, and some of the boys learned to swim while others found that they could not. The self and ideal self measures were given again, and the results are shown in Figure 9–5. As Rogers' self theory would predict, those who learned to swim changed toward a more positive self-image, while those who failed changed toward a more negative self-image. It seems that we feel better about ourselves when we master a challenging task, but there is always the risk of failure, which leads to a more negative self-evaluation. Such findings demonstrate that the self-concept is not necessarily a permanent structure but rather an ever-changing set of beliefs and attitudes about who we are.

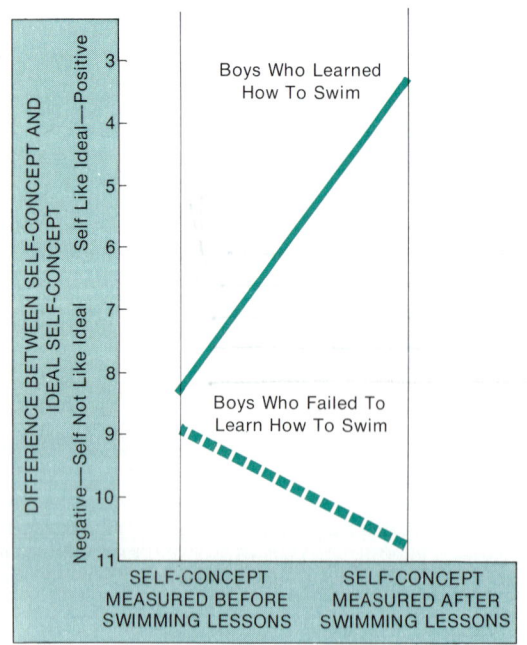

FIGURE 9–5 The self-concept can be changed by experience. When boys at a summer camp were given swimming lessons, those who succeeded in mastering this skill had a more positive self-concept afterward. Those who failed had a more negative self-concept afterward. (Adapted from Koocher, 1971.)

One of Freud's early admirers was a Swiss psychiatrist named Carl Jung. He, too, was trained in medicine and became interested in the methods and theories of treating mental illness that were being devised at the turn of the century. After he and Freud angrily ended their relationship in 1914, Jung began putting together his own theory of personality. We will describe two of Jung's basic concepts, the **collective unconscious** and **extraversion-introversion,** to provide some flavor of this work.

Analytical Psychology: Carl Jung

Jung (1939) was impressed by the fact that the anatomical development of the fetus traces mankind's evolutionary history as it grows from a one-celled organism to a full-term infant. Jung reasoned that the mind should, in a similar way, contain a record of the experiences of the human race. He labeled this storehouse of human memories the *collective unconscious.* We cannot become directly aware of this material, but it is revealed when very different cultures independently create the same myths and artistic symbols. For example, Jung felt that the widespread belief in a Supreme Being and the ubiquitous fear of snakes were evidence that such concepts are shared by all of us, in the collective unconscious. It is as if we are predisposed to respond to certain ideas or objects because our ancestors had countless experiences with them. Contained in the collective unconscious are **archetypes.** These are universal symbols which appear over and over again in art, literature, myth, and religion. For example, there are innumerable versions of the perfect mother who is protective and caring (like the Fairy Godmother in *Cinderella*) and of the evil mother who is cruel and threatening (like the Wicked Witch of the West in *The Wizard of Oz*). These shared symbols are said to have great meaning for us, and they represent the accumulated wisdom of our species. Jung felt that if we could learn to become more aware of the collective unconscious and its meaning, we would be able to function much more effectively. He also believed that the mind was continuing to evolve, and that we should be optimistic about the future of mankind.

As interesting and creative as such ideas may be, they seem to be of little utility in modern personality psychology. It might be noted that universal themes and ideas can be explained by the fact that we have common experiences in infancy and childhood (with a mother who is sometimes loving and

FIGURE 9–6 Carl Jung was a Swiss psychiatrist who worked with Freud at one time. Disagreements about theory led Jung to break their relationship, and he went on to develop his own theory of personality. (Photo from the National Library of Medicine.)

sometimes angry, for example). Thus, it is not necessary to propose inherited memories to account for similar ideas being expressed in different cultures.

A Jungian idea that *has* proven to be useful in personality research is that of *extraversion-introversion*. Jung believed that we are born with a particular type of temperament which causes us to be concerned primarily either with ourselves (an introvert) or with the outside world (an extravert). He described introverts as being hesitant and on the defensive; such a person would prefer to observe the world cautiously rather than become directly and personally involved. An extravert, in contrast, has an open and confident disposition, feels at ease anywhere, and makes friends quickly. The idea of introverted and extraverted types has become a familiar one in our culture. In addition, tests to measure these characteristics have been widely used in personality research. Much of the current work on this variable is based on the test developed by the British psychologist Hans Eysenck. He has found, for example, that extraverts lead more active sexual lives than introverts (Eysenck, 1971).

Constitutional Psychology: William Sheldon

William Sheldon is an American psychologist and physician. Like Jung, Sheldon has concentrated on the inherited aspects of personality. His basic view is that our bodily constitution is a major determinant of our behavior. Thus, personality can best be investigated through the study of anatomy and physiology. As a starting point, he developed a system by which the human body is measured and classified along three dimensions. This classification yields the individual's **somatotype,** or body type. The somatotype is believed to be related to specific behavioral characteristics in the form of one's basic temperament.

The body type is determined through a procedure in which individuals are photographed in the nude from the front, side, and rear; the dimensions of specific parts of the body are then measured. On this basis, the individual receives a score ranging from one to seven with respect to each of the three basic body components (Sheldon, Stevens, and Tucker, 1970). As can be seen in Figure 9–7, the first component is **endomorphy,** which consists of a soft and rounded appearance; an extreme endomorph would be classified 7–1–1 on the three components. The accompanying temperament is **viscerotonia,** which is described as including love of physical comfort, sociability, tolerance for others, and extraversion. The stereotype of a jolly, outgoing fat person fits this type.

Mesomorphy is the second body component, and it consists of an anatomy that is strong and muscular. An extreme mesomorph would be classified 1–7–1. The corresponding temperament is **somatotonia,** which includes love of physical adventure, boundless energy, boldness, aggressiveness, and the need for exercise and activity. The loud, assertive athlete is the stereotype here.

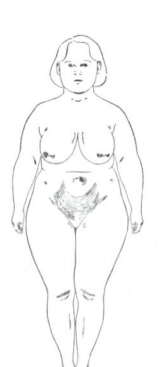 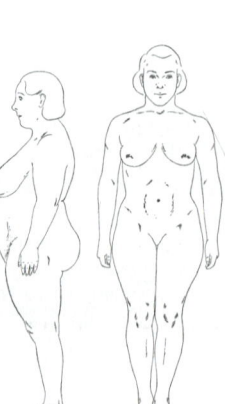 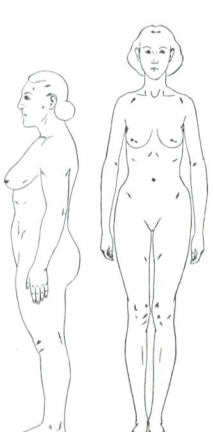 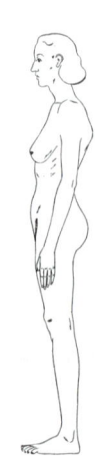

FIGURE 9–7 In Sheldon's personality theory, body type is a crucial determinant of temperament and of other personality characteristics. Shown here are examples of three somatotypes — the endomorph, mesomorph, and ectomorph. (Courtesy of Dr. W. H. Sheldon.)

FIGURE 9–8 Erik Erikson is a psychoanalyst and personality theorist who emphasizes eight stages of development in life and the characteristic crises that must be resolved during each of them. (Photo supplied by Harvard University.)

The third physical component is **ectomorphy,** and the 1–1–7 person would be thin, flat-chested, and delicate. The accompanying temperament is **cerebrotonia,** which includes love of privacy, emotional restraint, and intellectual intensity. The stereotype here is the shy, introverted scholar. Because each component can vary along a seven-point scale, there are not just three types but many possible combinations. Sheldon suggests that the average person is a 4–4–4.

When individuals have their body type measured and then are rated by temperament, it is found that there is a relationship of the kind proposed by Sheldon, though by no means a perfect one (Sheldon, 1942; Walker, 1962). Beyond demonstrating the predicted association between physical characteristics and temperament, Sheldon's research has also dealt with the relationship between somatotype and various other aspects of behavior. For example, there is some indication that individuals with different somatotypes are likely to develop different varieties of mental illness (Sheldon, Lewis, and Tenney, 1969). Endomorphs are most likely to develop disorders involving extreme variations in emotion, mesomorphs are most likely to become paranoid and suspicious, and ectomorphs are most likely to be withdrawn and schizophrenic (see Chapter 10 for a detailed description of these disorders). In other research, juvenile delinquents were found to be more likely to be mesomorphic or a combination of endomorphic and mesomorphic than is true for the average nondelinquent (Glueck and Glueck, 1956). Despite such promising evidence, there has been only limited research interest in Sheldon's approach to personality, perhaps because many psychologists tend to be biased toward explanations of behavior based on learning rather than explanations based on heredity.

Erikson is a remarkable German scholar who became a psychoanalyst and personality theorist, even though his formal education took him only through high school. After studying psychoanalysis under Freud's daughter, Anna, he came to the United States. His major emphasis in the study of personality has been on the developmental changes that occur throughout the life span.

According to Erikson (1963), there are eight stages through which we must pass to reach genuine maturity. At each stage, there is a characteristic type of

*The Cycle of Life:
Erik Erikson*

crisis or conflict, and the way in which the individual meets and solves the problem at each stage determines the kind of person he is to be. In a way, life is seen as consisting of a series of increasingly difficult tests of character. The eight developmental periods and their conflicts are described in Table 9–1.

Erikson's description of the stages of life is a very appealing one. Furthermore, he is much more specific than Freud with respect to the positive and negative events that can occur at each stage and with respect to the specific consequences that could be expected following each success or failure. Despite the appeal and the specificity of this theoretical system, as yet there has been relatively little research based directly on Erikson's ideas (Di Caprio, 1974).

TABLE 9–1   Erikson's Eight Stages of Life and the Crises to be Faced in Each

1. The *sensory stage* occurs during the first few months of life. The infant is totally dependent on others, and the crisis involves learning to trust or to mistrust other people. For example, if a mother is unkind or undependable in meeting the infant's needs, he would be expected to spend a lifetime mistrusting his fellow human beings.

2. The *muscular development stage* comes next and occurs during the period of toilet training. The crisis is between developing a sense of confidence and independence versus shame and self-doubt. The crucial determinant here is whether the child experiences primarily success or failure in learning to control his own bodily functions.

3. The *locomotor control stage* develops as the child learns to move about in his world and to assert his own needs. As in Freud's phallic stage, there is sexual desire for the parent of the opposite sex. The crisis involves initiative and expressing one's own desires versus guilt. Unless the individual can discover a socially acceptable way to express his or her sexual needs, he or she will be obsessed with guilt throughout life.

4. The *latency stage* occurs during the early school years, during which the child finds that he is competent or that he is a failure in comparison with his peers. Success during this period results in an industrious, hard-working adult, while failure leads to a pervasive sense of inferiority.

5. In the *puberty stage*, the problem is not simply one of sexuality but rather the problem of finding one's own identity. With regard to sex, social interactions, and plans for the future, the individual must develop and accept his personal identity. Otherwise, he will remain confused about just who he is and what his role in life might be.

6. The *young adulthood stage* coincides with the period in which most people seek to form a personal intimate relationship with someone. Success here involves the establishment of intimacy with another human being; failure results in a sense of isolation. The fact that an individual gets married is not necessarily an indication that this crisis has been resolved in favor of intimacy; two individuals can spend a lifetime together and yet be psychologically isolated.

7. In the *adulthood stage*, during our middle years, the crucial choice is the "growth crisis" — whether one becomes a productive and useful human being or settles into a pattern of complacency and stagnation.

8. The final stage is *maturity*, and it can be reached only by those who have been successful in resolving the crises at the previous seven stages. It is at this time that one must face the unthinkable realization of death. With a history of success at the other stages, the individual has a sense of integrity and a sense of self-worth, so that even death can be accepted. Previous failures leave an individual with a sense of despair and the feeling that life has been a foolish waste.

PERSPECTIVE ON BEHAVIOR: *Are We Selfish Sinners or Noble Saints?*

One of the familiar themes of science fiction is the end of mankind. There is the final nuclear war, and a deadly radioactive cloud is slowly spreading over the face of the earth. Or, an enormous meteor is on a collision course with our doomed planet. Or, a microorganism brought back by space travelers is rapidly destroying all human life.

In such stories, the authors tend to present one of two contrasting views about how people would behave. There is either (1) a total breakdown of civilization as individuals go on a rampage of looting and murder or (2) the catastrophe brings out the best qualities of cooperation, mutual aid, and self-sacrifice. Which of these patterns do *you* think would emerge in such circumstances? How would you yourself behave under conditions in which all external constraints were no longer present—if there were no more police or soldiers to enforce the law, no judges or jails to punish lawbreakers, and not even any newspapers to inform others of your misdeeds or good deeds? In answering such questions, you will, of course, be expressing your private view of human nature. After responding, you might find it interesting to go back over the past several pages and ask yourself which of the personality theorists might be most likely to share your predictions.

For example, how do you think an individual with an *oral personality* would react to this situation of doom, and would this be different from the reactions of someone with an *anal personality?* Without the restrictions imposed by society, would *id* impulses be expressed in an orgy of sex and aggression? Perhaps only those who had become *self-actualized* would be able to tolerate this threatening situation. Perhaps human beings would be drawn together in their *collective* memories of past catastrophes (Noah and the flood, for example) and thus share their common fate in this final step in earth's history. Do you believe that body type would make a difference in how people could handle such stress? How might *endomorphs*, *mesomorphs*, and *ectomorphs* behave when facing a powerful threat? Finally, what effects might you expect on the basis of Erikson's *stages of life?* It is possible that only those who have reached the stage of *maturity* could accept this ultimate disaster. What aspects of *you* are reflected in these various concepts?

THE MEASUREMENT OF PERSONALITY: ASSESSING DIFFERENCES AMONG INDIVIDUALS

The basic idea underlying personality measurement is simply to observe some aspects of behavior in one situation in order to be able to predict some other aspects of behavior in a different situation. If someone tells you that he gets up each morning at 5:00 A.M. to take a cold shower, you are likely to guess various things about that person's life style, to make assumptions about whether the two of you would get along, and in general to feel that you have learned more about the person than he has actually told you. Your guesses and assumptions may not be in the form of numbers and they may not be correct, but you are engaging in a crude form of personality measurement. Psychologists interested in personality simply go a few steps further, in that they attempt to observe behavior in a much more systematic and standard way, to quantify the observations if at all possible, and to verify the accuracy of their predictions.

From time to time, personality testing has been criticized as an invasion of privacy, and fears about its use are often expressed. The problem, though, is not really personality measurement but the possible danger that *any* type of knowledge in any field of science can be used for unsavory purposes. There is nothing good or evil about having someone measure your height or take your temperature. Those measurements are good if someone is designing your clothes or prescribing an antibiotic. The same measurements are bad if some-one is custom-fitting you for a torture rack or boiling you in a stew pot. Person-ality assessment, too, can be used for good or evil. You might be glad to take tests which would lead you toward an occupation in which you would be happy but very reluctant to take a test used to eliminate job applicants who hold your particular political beliefs.

Global Measures of Personality: Trying to Measure the Whole Person

An understandable goal of those who first sought to measure personality was to gain as much knowledge about a given person as possible, preferably knowledge of which the individual was not consciously aware. The projec-tive tests seemed to provide the means for this type of assessment.

Projective Tests: A Pipeline to the Unconscious?

In the first half of this century, the influence of Freud's ideas about the unconscious led to the development of a series of measuring devices designed on the principle that although an individual might not be completely aware of his motives or his problems, he nevertheless will reveal them under the appro-priate conditions. Specifically, if the person could be caught off guard and asked to respond to an ambiguous stimulus, his or her unconscious would express itself in much the same way as in dreams. This approach does not seek right or wrong answers, as in tests of knowledge or achievement; instead, the subject has to create something with very little to go on, and this creation reveals the workings of the unconscious. In Figure 9–9, Lucy, Linus, and Charlie Brown utilize cloud formations as a projective test.

FIGURE 9–9 As Lucy, Linus, and Charlie Brown demonstrate, we can each see very different things when we look at anything as ambiguous as cloud formations, and what we see reveals something about ourselves. Pictures of clouds were actually used as a projective test in the early 1900's by a French psychologist, Alfred Binet. (© 1960 United Feature Syndicate, Inc.)

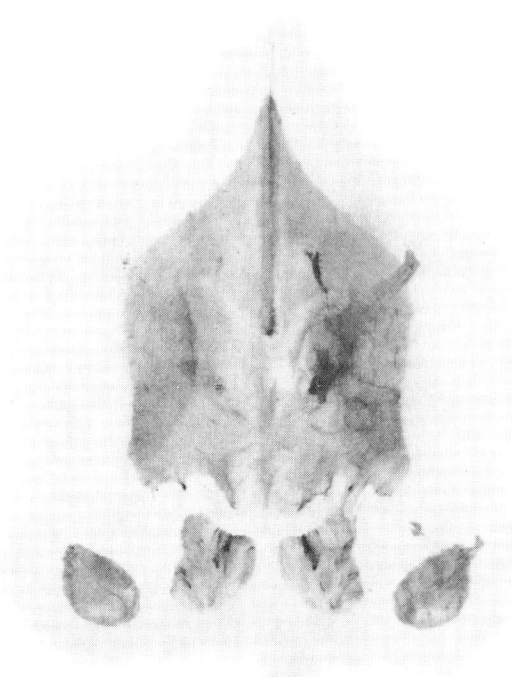

FIGURE 9–10 What does this blot represent? What does it look like to you? After you write down your answer, read the following responses to this Rorschach-like ink blot. Which of these interpretations strikes you as most revealing of the person viewing the ink blot?

1. To me it looks like a close-up of a bug's head, a praying mantis or something. You can see him under a magnifying glass moving his jaws and wiggling his antennas or maybe it is from a movie like "The Insect That Ate New York."
2. I can see a bear skin rug that has been placed on the floor. We are looking at the scene from above, and those four shapes at the bottom are Indian chiefs wrapped in soft buffalo robes. They are going to sit on the rug in a circle to have a pow-wow.
3. It's a hard shell from some sea creature that has been washed up on the beach. You can see the big shell, a crab maybe, and four smaller ones. They have been washed up by the tide and abandoned.
4. Maybe I shouldn't say this, but it looks like an exploding vagina. All I see is this horrible spewing forth of rotted flesh. Maybe some movie star swallowed a stick of dynamite.

(The first three descriptions were given by college students and the last one by a mental patient.)

One of the best known projective tests was developed by a Swiss psychiatrist named Hermann Rorschach. As he described the process (Rorschach, 1921), ink blots were found to be useful in getting patients to expose basic aspects of their personalities. For example, if a meaningless blob of red ink is described by one person as a field of wild flowers blowing in the wind, by a second as blood splattered on a rock, and by a third as strawberry jam on a piece of bread, it seems reasonable to suppose that some very different concerns are being expressed by the three individuals. You might even be inclined to guess about the restlessness of one of these people, the hostility of another, and the dependency of the third. You might well be wrong to base predictions on such slim evidence, but the general idea makes sense. You might like to try this yourself with the blot shown in Figure 9–10.

Rorschach created blots by dropping ink on a piece of paper which was then folded over to make a symmetrical pattern. He tried many different blots before settling on five colored ones and five which are black and white. Much of the early use of the **Rorschach test** was based on subjective clinical interpretations of the responses. Several scoring systems have since been developed, such as that of Klopfer and his associates (Klopfer, Ainsworth, Klopfer, and Holt, 1954), in which each response to the ten cards is carefully weighted along several dimensions. For example, when the subject reports what he sees on each card, does he use the entire blot, a large portion of it, a tiny detail, or the white space surrounding the blot? Does he see human beings, animals, or inanimate objects? Is there movement? Is there a response to texture, such as the smoothness or furriness of what he sees? These and other aspects of the person's series of responses are scored, and there are specific interpretations that go with each dimension. For example, intelligence is associated with use of the entire blot, and obstinacy is supposedly associated with use of the white space. It is also found that, as a child grows, there are changes in his or her Rorschach responses from year to year (Ames et al., 1974).

Another widely used projective test was developed by Henry A. Murray at the Harvard Psychological Clinic in the 1930's. The **Thematic Apperception Test,** or **TAT,** consists of a series of drawings such as the ones that illustrate stories or books. The subject's task is to make up a story to go with each picture—what is going on in the scene, what led up to the present situation, what the people are thinking and feeling, and how it all ends. The idea is that when the person is absorbed in creating the story, he or she is more likely to reveal hidden and unconscious wishes, fears, and memories (Morgan and Murray, 1938). TAT responses are often interpreted in a subjective way as the clinician reads a series of stories told by an individual and looks for recurrent themes and repeated patterns of interpersonal interactions. In addition, a number of scoring systems have been developed in an attempt to assess very specific personality characteristics. For example, Figure 9-11 is a TAT-like stimulus used as one in a set of four pictures to measure various aspects of the need for affiliation (that is, the need to form and maintain interpersonal relationships). The sample stories below the picture were written by four undergraduate students who are quite different from one another in the way they relate to people (Byrne, McDonald, and Mikawa, 1963).

FIGURE 9-11 A TAT-like picture that has been used in research to measure the need for affiliation. As you read the four stories told by four different college students, it should be clear that the same picture can be perceived in many different ways, and that these different perceptions may indicate important aspects of personality. (Joseph Veroff.)

Positive Feelings about Affiliation

The man is the father of the children. He is telling them about the days when he was a little boy. The children have finished their breakfast and they have a few minutes left before they go to school. The children think their father is a great person. The children feel this because they love their father. This family will stay close together throughout their life.

Mixed Feelings about Affiliation

A father is talking to his son. The daughter is eagerly listening. The son has had an argument with one of his friends and declares he was right. The father is telling him that he will not always have his way in life. The son will remember what his father has said and will try to do what is right in the future and avoid arguments.

Negative Feelings about Affiliation

A father is having a heart-to-heart talk with his children, a parent and children. The children have been disobeying their mother, while their father is at work earning a living. The children first seem to feel rebellious against the idea of them being disobedient. Father wants them to be a little more helpful and obey. The children will finally bend to the father's wishes.

An Absence of Feelings about Affiliation

An intelligent father is talking to his children. The child he is speaking to needs some serious advice. Proper actions are the key thoughts. The father wants his son to grow up to be a well-rounded individual. The son should take his father's advice. He becomes a happier person.

Despite their popularity in clinical practice and in personality research, projective tests have been heavily criticized. It has been pointed out that those administering the test can have an influence on the subject's responses, that judges often disagree in scoring a given test, and that many of the behavioral predictions based on these tests have been found to be partly or wholly inaccurate. One solution to such difficulties was the development of *objective* personality tests. Given in a standard way that requires little interaction between tester and subject, these tests can be scored accurately and consistently by a machine, and they are usually designed to predict specific aspects of behavior. The initial tests of this type tended to use straightforward items (for example, "I am nervous in large groups of people. True • False"), and an individual's answers were assumed to reflect reality. It soon became clear that people cannot or will not always give realistic or accurate answers. A different approach is to place less faith in the content of the item; instead, the tester finds out how useful each item is in predicting behavior. For example, if you wanted to build a test to predict who would get sick on airplanes, you would begin by finding a group of people who had been passengers on some flight. All of these individuals would respond to a large collection of miscellaneous test items. Then, item by item, you would determine whether different responses were given by those who got sick and those who did not. If you find that an item such as "I like to mow the grass" is more often answered true by one of your groups than the other, this means that it is a good predictive item and can be used in the future as part of your test. It does not matter whether the people taking the test *really* like to mow the grass or not, or whether they even own lawn mowers; all that matters is that a particular response to the item permits you to predict a specific behavior. Some psychologists have labeled this approach "dust bowl empiricism," because it rests on dry empirical data rather than on theory or logical explanation.

One of the first such tests was developed at the University of Minnesota in the 1930's and '40's by a psychologist, Starke R. Hathaway, and a physician, J. Charnley McKinley. Their goal was a test to diagnose mental patients in terms of their psychiatric classification (Hathaway and McKinley, 1940, 1951). This test is known as the **Minnesota Multiphasic Personality Inventory, or MMPI.** The investigators first assembled a large number of items dealing with feelings, symptoms, and interpersonal relations (for example, "I am very seldom troubled by headaches"; "At times I think I am no good at all"). Then, groups of patients in various diagnostic groups (as well as normals) responded to these items. For each type of patient, responses were compared with the responses of normals on every item; items which were answered differently by the two groups were thus identified as good measures of that particular diagnostic condition. The total MMPI measures the extent to which an individual's responses are like those of each of a series of diagnostic groups. This pattern, or *profile*, of responses is now widely used not only as a tool for psychiatric diagnosis but as an indicator of many other personality characteristics, such as anxiety and defensiveness.

Many other personality tests, such as the California Psychological Inventory (CPI), are similar to the MMPI, except that the goal is to measure normal behavior, including achievement, sociability, self-control, and flexibility (Gough, 1957). In the Psychology in Action box on the next two pages is an objective test which you may want to take yourself.

Objective Tests: Measuring Personality with Questionnaires

With a steadily increasing world population that threatens the well-being and perhaps the survival of all of us (Heilbroner, 1974), it is not surprising that scientists in many fields are turning their attention to the problems of overpopulation and how to control it. For example, psychologists have become interested in the way in which personality characteristics are related to decisions about how many children to have and about whether or not to use various contraceptive techniques. An objective test designed to measure five relevant components of attitudes about such issues has been developed by Gough (1975). You can take this test, score it, and then determine how your responses compare with those of others.

Population Policy and Social Attitude Questionnaire

Instructions: Read each statement below and then give your reaction on the line in front, using the following scale:

+2 = agree strongly
+1 = agree somewhat
 0 = neutral or uncertain
−1 = disagree somewhat
−2 = disagree strongly

_____ 1. Birth control methods should be made available to anyone who wants them.

_____ 2. The world could easily support twice as many people as it now does.

_____ 3. Abortion should be permitted if there is substantial risk that the baby will be born defective.

_____ 4. It is better to live pretty much for today and let tomorrow take care of itself.

_____ 5. Having a baby every year is bad for the mother's health.

_____ 6. The disadvantages of birth control outweigh the advantages.

_____ 7. Families with more than three children should be required to pay higher taxes.

_____ 8. The decision to ask for an abortion must be in part a moral decision.

_____ 9. A person should try to keep aware of the major events taking place all over the world.

_____ 10. People should not "plan" on whether to have a child; such things are best left to fate or luck.

_____ 11. Birth control increases the happiness of married life.

_____ 12. In some parts of the world, the problem is underpopulation, not overpopulation.

_____ 13. With the newer and safer methods of inducing abortion, there is no reason why a woman should not use abortion routinely as a birth control method.

_____ 14. My preference is for the old dependable ways of doing things.

_____ 15. If a couple is in poor economic circumstances, having a child should be postponed until its financial situation improves.

_____ 16. The use of birth control devices involves a sort of risky tampering with nature.

_____ 17. Overpopulation in the world is just as serious a problem today as crime and poverty.

_____ 18. Abortion should be prohibited by law.

_____ 19. There is nothing really new under the sun.

_____ 20. Limiting the number of children in a family is something that works in favor of those already financially well-to-do and against those in poorer circumstances.

_____ 21. A birth control operation (vasectomy) should be given without charge to any man who requests one.

_____ 22. There is no reason to fear a continued increase in population; the human race will find some way to cope with this problem.

_____ 23. Abortion should be free of any and all legal restrictions.

_____ 24. I tend to feel uncomfortable when I am with people who are much older than I am.

_____ 25. Childless couples should be encouraged to adopt a child.

_____ 26. It is difficult to think of any rational reason for opposing free release of birth control information.

_____ 27. Unless population is controlled, mankind will never be able to live in peace.

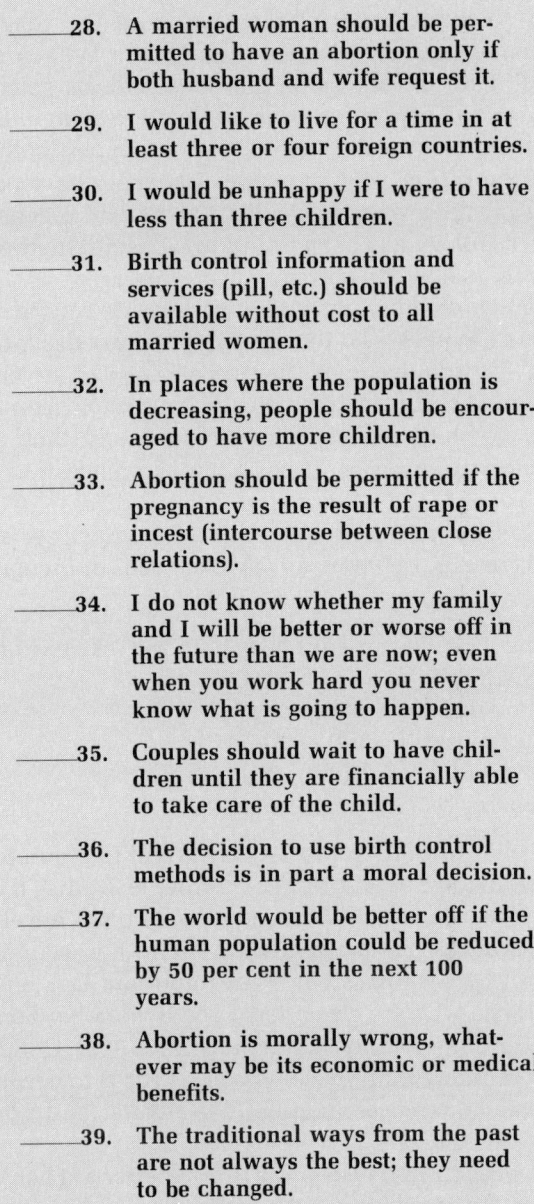

_____28. A married woman should be permitted to have an abortion only if both husband and wife request it.

_____29. I would like to live for a time in at least three or four foreign countries.

_____30. I would be unhappy if I were to have less than three children.

_____31. Birth control information and services (pill, etc.) should be available without cost to all married women.

_____32. In places where the population is decreasing, people should be encouraged to have more children.

_____33. Abortion should be permitted if the pregnancy is the result of rape or incest (intercourse between close relations).

_____34. I do not know whether my family and I will be better or worse off in the future than we are now; even when you work hard you never know what is going to happen.

_____35. Couples should wait to have children until they are financially able to take care of the child.

_____36. The decision to use birth control methods is in part a moral decision.

_____37. The world would be better off if the human population could be reduced by 50 per cent in the next 100 years.

_____38. Abortion is morally wrong, whatever may be its economic or medical benefits.

_____39. The traditional ways from the past are not always the best; they need to be changed.

_____40. The economic advantages of having small families are not as great as family planning advocates claim.

This test measures five components, which are labeled Birth Control, Abortion, Family Planning, Population Management, and Modernity. The total score on each scale can range from 5 to 40. To determine your scores on these dimensions, use the following key:

1. Birth Control:
   Add 24 to the sum of your scores on items 1, 11, 21, 26, and 31; then subtract the sum of your scores on items 6, 16, and 36.
2. Abortion:
   Add 24 to the sum of your scores on items 3, 13, 23, and 33; then subtract the sum of your scores on items 8, 18, 28, and 38.
3. Family Planning:
   Add 24 to the sum of your scores on items 5, 15, 25, and 35; then subtract the sum of your scores on items 10, 20, 30, and 40.
4. Population Management:
   Add 24 to the sum of your scores on items 7, 17, 27, and 37; then subtract the sum of your scores on items 2, 12, 22, and 32.
5. Modernity:
   Add 24 to the sum of your scores on items 9, 29, and 39; then subtract the sum of your scores on items 4, 14, 19, 24, and 34.

You can compare your responses to those of almost 500 students at the University of California at Berkeley by examining the material in Table 9–2. Research has shown that scores on these scales are related to important aspects of behavior and knowledge (Gough, 1975). For example, the higher an individual scores on the Family Planning and the Population Management Scales, the fewer children he or she wants to have. These same two scales plus the Birth Control Scale also predict the number of children a person actually *expects* to have; the higher the scores, the fewer the expected children. The higher one scores on the Modernity Scale, the lower he or she is likely to score in authoritarianism (a dimension described in the next section of this chapter). Finally, those with high scores on the Abortion Scale are most likely to be well informed with respect to factual knowledge about sex. You can see the way in which a relatively brief personality test such as this can be useful in predicting many aspects of behavior.

TABLE 9–2   Scores on the Population Policy and Social Attitude Questionnaire

Scale	Male Students	Female Students
	Mean	Mean
Birth Control	31.76	32.25
Abortion	28.76	29.37
Family Planning	31.77	33.01
Population Management	30.45	30.17
Modernity	30.70	31.56

These are the mean scores of almost 500 students on the five scales of the Population Policy and Social Attitude Questionnaire. (Adapted from Gough, 1975.)

Types and Traits

Current Interest in Psychological Types: Predicting Coronary Heart Disease

At the beginning of this chapter, it was pointed out that the earliest attempts by the ancient Greeks to explain personality involved the idea of types—a relatively limited number of categories into which the behavior of individuals could be classified. The usefulness of this idea may be seen in the fact that interest in typologies has continued over the centuries, including Jung's extraversion-introversion typology and Sheldon's somatotypes, both of which were described earlier. In addition, several personality types have been proposed which tend to stand on their own rather than as part of a general theory of personality. One such typology has been found to be useful in identifying those individuals most likely to develop coronary heart disease.

The personality characteristics of those who are prospective candidates for heart trouble have been labeled **Type A**, and these individuals are described as being competitive, striving for achievement, having a sense of urgency about time, and as being aggressive and impatient (Rosenman and Friedman, 1974). **Type B** individuals do not have these characteristics, and they are much less likely to develop coronary diseases. It has been estimated that 40 per cent of the population is Type A and 60 per cent Type B (Glass, 1974). These two types can be assessed by means of a standardized interview or a questionnaire (Jenkins, Zyzanski, and Rosenman, 1971). Examples of the questions used are:

> Has your spouse or some friend ever told you that you eat too fast?
> Type A response—"yes, often"
> Type B response—"no, no one has told me this"
> How would your spouse (or closest friend) rate you?
> Type A response—"definitely hard-driving and competitive"
> Type B response—"probably relaxed and easy-going"

This division of individuals has been found to be very useful in predicting who is most susceptible to heart attacks; in addition, a number of studies have been conducted to determine the way in which these personality types develop and the kinds of behavioral differences that are related to them. For example, Type A individuals will work as hard as possible at an important task, even if there is no deadline to meet; those who are classified Type B work hard only if someone has set a deadline (Burnam, Pennebaker, and Glass, 1975). College students who are Type A are more likely than those who are Type B to become deeply involved in extracurricular activities, competitive sports, and community activities (Glass, 1974).

It seems probable that the tendency to develop the A or B pattern of behavior is based in part on heredity. An individual who is predisposed to being Type A would probably not develop that behavior, however, unless he or she were born into a society such as ours that encourages and rewards competition and achievement. Perhaps this is one of the reasons that societies which stress achievement tend to have higher death rates with respect to various diseases that are related to stress, such as coronary problems, high blood pressure, and ulcers (Rudin, 1968). In addition, families that push their offspring to succeed (see Chapter 7) might be expected to foster Type A behavior. These characteristic differences in behavior have been observed in children as young as 10 and 11 years old (Herndon and Glass, 1974). It may be seen, then, that even a very limited typology which deals with only a few aspects of behavior can prove to be a useful predictive device.

Psychological Traits: Dimensions of Behavior

Despite the continued interest in psychological types, psychologists have long realized that personality is too complex to be described by a limited number of types. Even Sheldon's system, with its many possible combinations of seven degrees of endomorphy, mesomorphy, and ectomorphy, seems to be too restrictive. One answer to this problem has been to assume that individual differences can best be described as varying along an almost unlimited series of dimensions which are called **traits** (Hogan, DeSoto, and Solano, 1976). A *trait* is a stable characteristic of behavior in which people differ. Many of the adjectives we use to describe one another represent possible traits, as when we say that someone is shy, amusing, intelligent, cruel, easy-going, studious, or whatever. Most of the traits studied in the field of personality are based on just such everyday concepts.

In 1936, Allport and Odbert listed 17,953 English words used to describe human behavior. When these are reduced by eliminating overlapping words, there still are 171 words left, and each can be considered to represent a personality trait (Cattell, 1946). How can we deal with or theorize about that many traits? There have been three solutions to handling this complex task.

First, some psychologists have attempted to organize this large array so as to identify *clusters* of traits that go together and to identify those that are the most basic and most important dimensions. Cattell (1965), using statistical procedures, has concluded that there are actually 16 basic **source traits.** These include such dimensions as dominance versus submissiveness as well as ego strength (maturity) versus emotionality (inability to tolerate frustration). These source traits are expressed in actual behavior in a large number of possible ways, called **surface traits.** For example, a basically dominant person could express this general characteristic in such specific surface traits as confidence, boastfulness, conceitedness, aggressiveness, and so forth. Cattell has constructed a personality test to measure the 16 source traits. Besides its use in personality research, this test has been utilized in a computer dating situation in an attempt to select compatible partners (Curran, 1973).

Second, some psychologists have decided that, rather than try to cover *all* aspects of personality, it is more feasible to concentrate on a few traits at a time. We discussed this approach when several objective measures of personality were described. The Minnesota Multiphasic Personality Inventory measures a series of traits that are all related to varieties of maladjusted behavior; the Population Policy and Social Attitude Questionnaire measures just five traits, all related to issues of population and contraception. The basic idea underlying such personality measures is that research benefits from a concentration on a limited number of traits at one time.

Third, still other psychologists have further narrowed their focus of interest in order to conduct concentrated research on a single dimension at a time. Most of the research on psychological traits has been based on the idea that it is preferable to identify and isolate each trait and then to study it in depth. The goal here is not to describe anyone's total personality but rather to determine the origins of a given trait and the behaviors which it predicts. This approach is best understood by seeing how it has worked with respect to one widely studied trait, **authoritarianism.**

Authoritarianism: Follow the Leader

When Adolf Hitler came to power in Germany in 1933, the world witnessed the establishment of a fascist state in which authoritarian attitudes and values were advocated by government leaders and accepted by a large proportion of the citizens; eventually these concepts were carried to their logical conclusion in an array of horrifying atrocities. The basic ideology expressed by the Nazi party included bigotry (Aryans were the master "race," and Jews, among others, were inferior), glorification of war (might makes right, today Germany—tomorrow the world), the importance of unquestioning obedience to one's leader (Heil, Hitler!), and loyalty to the state (the glorious Fatherland). Among the many consequences of these and other beliefs was an anti-Semitic campaign that began with harassment and exploitation and ended in the systematic murder of some 6,000,000 Jews plus approximately 14,000,000 additional "undesirables," such as Gypsies, communists, and Slavs. This authoritarian society also initiated World War II; those who were most loyal to their government believed that any behavior (including rape, torture, and murder) could be justified by the fact that "I was only following orders."

These occurrences were sufficiently appalling that many behavioral scientists felt that it was important to find out how such things could have happened in Germany and to seek ways to prevent their happening again anywhere else. One investigation which grew out of such concerns was a massive effort at the University of California at Berkeley to identify the basic personality trait or traits which made fascist ideology appealing. The resulting theories and research were described in a classic book, *The Authoritarian Personality* (Adorno, Frenkel-Brunswik, Levinson, and Sanford, 1950).

The basic strategy of the investigators was to describe the major characteristics of typical fascists and then to use personality theory to explain how authoritarianism developed and how it functions. Briefly, this trait was believed to result from a home atmosphere in which parents demand obedience and respect, rigidly suppress anything having to do with sex, and enforce all of the conventional values without any genuine understanding of their underlying meaning. This repressive atmosphere was believed to generate a great deal of hostility which could not possibly be expressed against the parents. Instead, "acceptable" outlets were found; hostility was "all right" if it were directed against "bad" people. Thus, an authoritarian would never let himself feel any resentment of an authority figure such as his father or the leader of the country, but he would freely condemn, reject, and punish lawbreakers, those who were immoral in his eyes, and anyone whose looks or actions were different from his own. Finally, in the authoritarian trait there is a tendency to avoid thinking very deeply about feelings or motives and to project unconscious conflicts about sex and aggression onto others.

Having defined and described what seemed to be the key elements of this trait, the Berkeley group then constructed a personality scale to measure it. The test was labeled the F Scale (for fascist). High scores indicate authoritarianism, while low scores indicate the opposite extreme of this trait, egalitarianism. The F Scale consists of a series of items to which subjects respond in terms of how much they agree or disagree. Examples are:

> Obedience and respect for authority are the most important virtues children should learn.
> Sex crimes, such as rape and attacks on children, deserve more than mere imprisonment; such criminals ought to be publicly whipped, or worse.

Do you think strong agreement with those statements would indicate authoritarianism or egalitarianism?

Research on Authoritarianism: Some of My Best Friends Are Fascists.
Much of the research interest in authoritarianism has been in devising ways to test some of the original theoretical assumptions about this trait and in extending knowledge of how the trait operates in various situations. For example, individuals raised in restrictive, traditional families tend to be high in authoritarianism (Kagitcibasi, 1970). As would be expected, authoritarians express prejudice and hostility against various groups, including Jews (Adorno et al., 1950), accused criminals (Sherwood, 1966), and wartime enemies (Izzett, 1971). As in the cartoon in Figure 9–12, fascist ideology can sometimes be disguised as super-patriotism.

Other investigations have dealt with attitudinal differences between authoritarians and egalitarians on a variety of issues. For example, authoritarians tend to respond more favorably to conservative political candidates than

FIGURE 9–12 Authoritarian ideology can often be expressed in a kind of super-patriotism in which the superficial aspects of a nation (such as its flag) are emphasized while its basic attributes (such as freedom) are ignored. Authoritarian patriots can, accordingly, follow a leader blindly and find an outlet for their hostility in fighting their nation's internal and external enemies. (Cartoon by J. B. Handelsman in *Playboy*, 1974.)

"I like to think I'm a patriot, but actually I'm a fascist."

to liberal ones (Leventhal, Jacobs, and Kudirka, 1964). The authoritarian concern with sex and "morality" has also been verified in numerous studies. Those who obtain high scores on the F Scale are likely to label nude paintings as pornographic (Eliasberg and Stuart, 1961), to feel disgusted about pornography, and to be in favor of censorship (Byrne and Lamberth, 1971). Authoritarians can best be described as anxious and uptight about sexual matters (Griffitt, 1973).

We will now take a more detailed look at one specific way in which the trait of authoritarianism influences behavior. Do you think it would matter whether the members of a jury were high or low in authoritarianism? The answer to this question is relevant not only to the study of this particular personality trait but also to the way in which our basic judicial system may be influenced by personality characteristics.

Authoritarian Jurors: Personality in the Courtroom.

Authoritarian aggression must be directed toward someone who seems to deserve it—authoritarians feel they must have a good excuse. There are, of course, many ways to justify aggression. For example, parents have the power to use physical punishment on their children whenever the rules are broken, and it is found that authoritarian parents do this more than egalitarian ones. Anyone in charge of a group tries to get the maximum performance out of his followers, and authoritarians are found to use negative procedures, such as fines and criticism, while egalitarians use positive ones, such as rewards and praise (Dustin and Davis, 1967). Perhaps the ultimate justification for aggression is war, and it was found that authoritarian students tended to support our government's position in Vietnam while egalitarians tended to oppose it (Granberg and Corrigan, 1972).

The courtroom also represents a legitimate place to express aggressive impulses. Members of a jury are asked to sit in judgment on a member of the community who is accused of violating one or more laws. Here, the juror has the chance to decide on guilt and innocence; if the verdict is guilty, decisions must sometimes be made regarding severity of punishment. Because the basic facts of the case are usually open to different interpretations, and because judgments about character and intent are necessarily subjective, there is considerable room for the personality characteristics of the jurors to play a part in the decision-making process (Kalven and Zeisel, 1966).

In a simulated jury experiment, Mitchell and Byrne (1973) presented students with details about a student court case in which a fellow undergraduate was accused of stealing an examination. In order to increase positive or negative feelings about the defendant, a special transcript containing information about the defendant's attitudes was prepared for each subject. As will be discussed in Chapter 13, people tend to like those whose attitudes are similar to their own and to dislike those who have dissimilar attitudes. Half of the subjects were informed that the defendant was similar to themselves with respect to such things as feelings about fraternities, attitudes about drinking, and belief in God, while half learned that the defendant was opposite from themselves in these respects. Half of the subjects had obtained high scores on the F Scale, and half had low scores. All of the subjects received exactly the same information about what the defendant had done, the witnesses' testimony, and the defendant's own statement. Because the evidence made it clear that the defendant had stolen the exam, the most important decision was how severely to punish him. The findings are shown in Figure 9–13. In effect, the egalitarian jurors were able to ignore their personal likes and dislikes of the defendant; they made approximately the same recommendations for punishment whether the defendant was similar or dissimilar to them in attitudes. The authoritarian jurors, on the other hand, were very punitive toward a defendant they disliked, while they tended to "lean over backwards" to be lenient with a liked defendant. The authoritarians thus made a sharp distinction between how they treated someone like themselves and someone who was different.

How is it that authoritarians and egalitarians could be exposed to precisely the same evidence in the case and yet make very different judgments about the defendant? One possibility, suggested by Berg and Vidmar (1975), is that individuals who differ along this personality dimension may actually pay attention to different aspects of the information about the defendant. Two

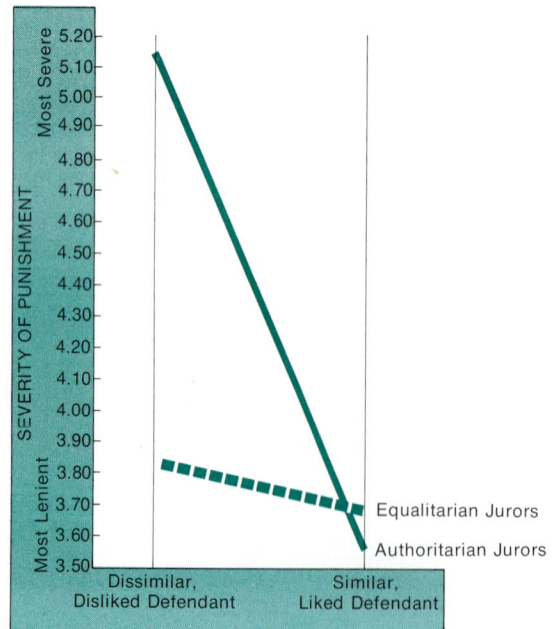

FIGURE 9–13 Authoritarianism was found to be an important factor in determining the kind of punishment a juror recommended in a mock trial involving theft of an examination. Authoritarians tended to recommend more severe punishment toward the defendant if they disliked him and less severe punishment if they liked him; equalitarians were able to ignore their personal feelings in recommending punishment. (Adapted from Mitchell and Byrne, 1973.)

experiments were carried out in which authoritarian and egalitarian subjects were given the details of a case involving either a positively or negatively described defendant. A week later, the subjects were contacted again and asked to recall various aspects of the testimony and evidence. As expected, the authoritarians could remember more details about the defendant's character than could the egalitarians, but with respect to details about the evidence the reverse was true. It is not surprising, then, that authoritarians are found to base their judicial decisions more on their feelings about the defendant than on the evidence—that's what they remember.

An Authority Figure on Trial: The Good Guys Don't Always Wear White Hats.

Findings such as those just described have led some people to suggest that individuals high in authoritarianism should not be allowed to serve on juries, because their judicial decisions are biased by their feelings. Such conclusions, it should be added, are consistent with the tendency of many behavioral scientists to perceive authoritarians as the "bad guys." There is increasing evidence, however, that egalitarians, who are often cast in the role of "good guys," can be just as unreasonable in making courtroom decisions in cases in which the defendant is some sort of authority figure.

For example, Mitchell (1973) presented authoritarian and egalitarian students with a trial transcript describing a riot that developed at a summer music concert. During the riot, there was a confrontation between a policeman and an electrician's apprentice; one of these individuals was knocked down, and the victim died of internal injuries a few hours later. Half of the subjects were told that the electrician had accidentally killed the policeman and half were told that the policeman had accidentally killed the electrician. Feelings toward the defendant were manipulated by having him described very positively or negatively by the court psychologist. The defendant was charged with manslaughter and was obviously guilty, but the jurors' task was to decide on an appropriate punishment, which could range from 1 to 10 years in prison.

When an ordinary citizen was the defendant, the tendency of the authoritarians to react with severe punishment was shown once again. As may be seen in Figure 9–14, however, with a policeman on trial, it is the egalitarians who respond on the basis of their feelings and recommend the greatest punishment of a disliked defendant. It seems that under certain conditions, egalitar-

FIGURE 9–14 When an ordinary citizen is the defendant in a manslaughter case, authoritarians judge him on the basis of their feelings and recommend severe punishment if he has been described negatively. When a policeman is the defendant, however, it is the equalitarians who judge him on the basis of their feelings and recommend severe punishment if he has been described negatively. (Adapted from Mitchell, 1973.)

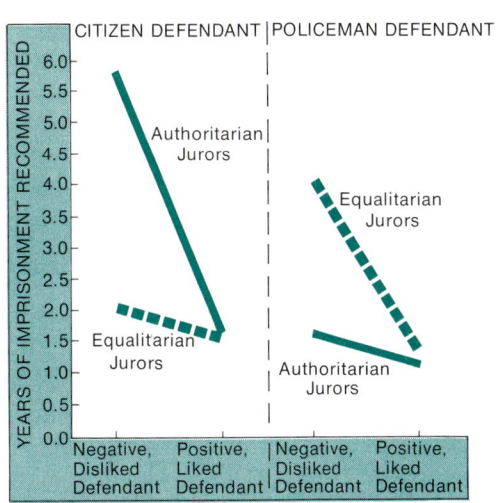

ians can be as unfair as authoritarians and can let their feelings interfere with their judgments in much the same way.

Not only the type of defendant but the type of crime can influence the reactions of authoritarians and egalitarians. Garcia and Griffitt (1977) asked students who were high or low in authoritarianism to respond to a case in which a father had beaten and bruised his child with his fists and with a belt; the two groups differing in authoritarianism were equally punitive in their judgments about what to do with this individual who had abused a child. Other students were presented with a case that was identical in all respects except that the father had engaged in sexual acts (fondling and masturbation) with his child. The experimenters hypothesized that authoritarians would be especially upset about a sexual offense and hence would be more punitive toward the defendant that would egalitarians; this was precisely the case. In this instance, the authoritarian jurors were "unfair" and excessively punitive only when the crime was extremely distasteful to them.

Our descriptions of several studies of the authoritarian personality provide an illustration of the way research on a specific personality trait typically progresses from the original idea to the construction of a test that will measure the trait to a series of investigations dealing with the way the trait is developed and how it influences behavior. Finally, in the jury studies, we saw an example in which aspects of the situation can be crucial in determining how a trait operates.

SITUATIONAL DETERMINANTS OF BEHAVIOR: IT'S NOT ONLY WHO YOU ARE BUT WHERE YOU ARE

The assumption underlying most of the previous discussion of personality is that behavioral characteristics remain more or less the same from situation to situation and from time to time. It is assumed, for example, that there is stability in a person's authoritarianism, in the fit between self-concept and experience, in the extent to which an individual is introverted, and so forth. Though such ideas have been generally accepted in the field of personality, and though they fit well with the kinds of assumptions we usually make about one another in everyday life, doubts have been raised by many who do research in this field. Perhaps personality is not nearly so constant as we have believed, and perhaps a great deal of our behavior is determined by the specific situations in which we find ourselves.

Traits versus Situations

Dissatisfaction with the Trait Approach: Predicting Across Situations

The reason for devising personality theories and for constructing measures of personality traits is to be able to predict human behavior. It is important to note that work in the field of personality *has* increased our predictive ability. Nevertheless, it should also be noted that many of the measuring instruments have been found to be less powerful predictors than was originally hoped. Many criticisms have been made of the projective tests, such as the Rorschach and TAT. Rotter (1954, p. 334) reviewed the hundreds of studies of such tests and concluded, "The very best techniques we have are of doubtful validity for predicting the specific behavior of any person in a particular situation."

It was partly in response to this problem that efforts were made to build better and more objective tests, such as the MMPI. Objective tests without doubt represent an improvement in predictive power, but they still are far from perfect. Mischel (1968), for one, has noted that personality tests are best at predicting behavior from one situation to a very similar situation. If the two situations are radically different, the accuracy of the predictions decreases. This suggests that we need to know more about situations, and that it is a mistake to describe personality characteristics as if they exist in a vacuum.

As will be discussed in Chapter 13, there is considerable evidence that we attribute the good things we do to internal causes such as personality characteristics and the bad things to external causes such as the circumstances in which we find ourselves. When we evaluate other people, however, we tend to reverse ourselves and feel that they do bad things for internal reasons and good things because the situation demanded it. Actually, both internal and external factors determine the way each of us behaves. An example may make the point clear.

Attributing Causes: Did the Devil Make You Do It?

How would you explain why unmarried individuals engaging in sexual intercourse often take no steps to prevent pregnancy? The negative consequences of an unwanted pregnancy are obvious. In spite of this, most unmarried couples initially having intercourse are found to utilize no contraceptive devices (Eastman, 1972). Over three-quarters of the young, sexually active girls in one survey never or almost never used any birth control method (Zelnick and Kantner, 1974), and the number of illegitimate births to teenagers has more than doubled between 1940 and 1972. Why? Are people ignorant, immoral, lacking in superego development, or simply unconcerned (Cvetkovich, Grote, Bjorseth, and Sarkissian, 1975)? One possibility, explored by Arnold (1972), is that it is difficult, embarrassing, and expensive for most unmarried individuals to obtain contraceptives. When a project was set up in an inner city ghetto to distribute free condoms, males readily accepted and used them. Thus, a relatively simple alteration in the situation led to a remarkable change in behavior.

As an example of the way in which concern with both internal and external determinants of behavior is reflected in research on a specific problem, we will briefly examine research on honesty.

Honesty: Do You Always Let Your Conscience Be Your Guide?

It seems to be generally agreed that we develop some sort of guidance system (conscience or superego) which informs us of the rightness or wrongness of what we do. There are individual differences in the extent to which behavior is influenced by considerations of right and wrong. Under the same set of circumstances, one person will cheat and another will not, one will steal and another will refuse to do so, one will lie and another will stick to the truth. It seems reasonable, then, to propose that honesty is a trait, and to approach the study of honest behavior as a function of individual differences.

Some of the earliest research on this type of behavior was conducted in the late 1920's (Hartshorne and May, 1928; Hartshorne, May, and Shuttleworth, 1930). Children were placed in experimental situations in which they could either behave honestly or cheat, steal, and lie. To the surprise of the experimenters, there was not a great deal of consistency in such behaviors across situations. For example, a child who would blatantly cheat to win a prize might refrain from stealing a similar prize on another occasion. The experimenters concluded that even minor changes in the situation acted to alter the likelihood of honest behavior.

The Trait of Honesty: Who Is Law-Abiding?

Later investigations also have reported only relatively small relationships between measures of conscience and honesty. One such measure is called *delay of gratification*. The idea is that to do the right thing or to refrain from doing the wrong thing, we usually must choose between a small immediate reward (for example, cheating to win a prize) and a much larger later reward (for example, improving our ability so that we will do well and earn many prizes). To make the most morally acceptable choice in a given situation, it is usually necessary to be able to postpone our gratifications. Mischel and

Gilligan (1964) found a small but reliable relationship between ability to delay gratification and the tendency to cheat (those who are best able to delay gratification are least likely to cheat). Thus, knowing something about how people score on this trait provides a degree of predictive power, but more accurate prediction of honest behavior requires that we know more about its external determinants.

Situational Determinants of Honesty: When Are People Law-Abiding?

Latané and Darley (1970) have found that individuals are more likely to respond to emergencies when they are alone than when there are other bystanders present (see Chapter 13). It follows that when an individual is the only witness to a crime, he should be more likely to do the right thing and report it than when he is one of two or more witnesses. His trait of honesty would remain the same, but the different situations would nevertheless be expected to lead to quite different responses. The experimenters arranged for a confederate to steal a case of beer from a discount store when the clerk was out of the room. The "crime" took place when either one or two customers were present in the store. When customers were alone, a higher percentage of them reported the crime than when two customers were present. Thus, the fact that another

FIGURE 9–15 The situation can be a powerful determinant of whether an individual behaves in an honest manner or not. The man in front in the top photo might get away with theft even though the two customers in back are aware of his actions. Latané and Darley (1970) found that when a customer is the only witness to a theft, he is more likely to report it than when he is one of two witnesses. It seems that in one situation an individual will do the right thing, but in a slightly altered situation will allow himself to become a passive accessory to a crime (as in the bottom photo).

bystander witnessed the crime acted to inhibit the appropriate behavior and to make individuals more inclined to become passive accessories to a crime.

In studies such as this, the findings indicate that we have to look beyond ideas such as superego or a trait such as honesty and to examine the details of the situation in which individuals find themselves. Honest behavior is not a constant, completely unchanging characteristic but is dependent on the external factors in a situation as well as on internal ones. This same general point holds true for most personality traits.

Often, when students are introduced to a complex area of research and theorizing such as personality, they feel that they have been bombarded by a random collection of ideas and approaches which do not form any meaningful pattern. It may be helpful to consider what is known at a more general level, not bothering about the details of any particular theory or the special emphases of any particular method of study. In other words, let's step back for a view of the forest.

Some Conclusions About Personality

First, it is obvious that human beings as biological organisms come into the world with built-in mechanisms which determine many aspects of behavior. That is, we are born with needs for taking in oxygen, food, and liquid, for eliminating bodily wastes, and for obtaining rest and sexual satisfaction. More broadly, we prefer comfort to discomfort, pleasure to pain. There is also evidence that from our earliest days we require bodily contact such as cuddling, and that we are innately curious and want to explore our surroundings whenever we are able to do so. These may seem to be commonplace observations, but much of human behavior in both simple and complex societies involves efforts to satisfy these needs in various ways.

Second, it is clear that we are influenced by and altered by our experiences from the time we are born. We are continuously learning in our interactions with our social and physical surroundings. We learn the appropriate ways to satisfy our needs, and we learn to respond to those around us with trust or mistrust, love or hate, cooperation or competition, and so forth. We learn to enjoy certain experiences and to reject others. We learn some aspects of ourselves accurately and some falsely. We are aware of some of our motives and unaware of others. All of the specific ways an individual is taught to respond to himself, to others, and to his surroundings constitute his personality, his uniqueness. Even if you do not use such terms as anal personality, self-concept, or authoritarianism, the behaviors described by those terms are obviously important aspects of what it means to be a human being.

Third, we continue to learn and to be responsive to our surroundings throughout our lives. Very few psychologists today would argue that basic personality patterns are set firmly and unalterably at birth or during the first few years of life. Throughout this book, you have read and will read of the ways in which individuals behave in response to the factors operating in their immediate environment, as when they conform to the opinions of others, hesitate to respond to an emergency, act aggressively toward a stranger, or destroy public property. We are very responsive to what is going on around us, and sometimes these forces are far more influential than any lifelong personality characteristics. It is also true that our experiences can lead to lasting changes in our behavior patterns. Some of the forces for change involve deliberate attempts to alter behavior (education, psychotherapy, imprisonment, advertising, propaganda), and others occur as a function of factors over which there is little or no control (aging, technological innovations, natural disasters, disease). Whatever the causes, we continually change. You are not precisely the same person you were ten years ago or the same person you will be ten years from now.

In brief, personality consists of both inborn and learned characteristics which may be altered temporarily or permanently by subsequent experiences. Understanding the details of the process is the continuing challenge of the field of personality.

Summary

Personality consists of an individual's characteristic patterns of behavior. Psychologists attempt to describe personality, to explain the origin of individual differences, and to determine how the various elements fit together as aspects of a functioning human being.

Personality theories have been developed in an attempt to describe and explain the behavior of individuals. The ancient Greeks speculated about various aspects of personality, but the first comprehensive theory was created by Sigmund Freud. He described mental functioning in terms of three states of consciousness (**conscious, preconscious,** and **unconscious**) and three regions of mental activity (**id, ego,** and **superego**). Human development was described as progressing through a series of stages (**oral, anal, urethral, phallic,** and **genital**); events at each stage were said to lay the groundwork for later personality characteristics. The personality theory of Carl Rogers is based on the concept of **self.** Rogers defines the **actualizing tendency** as the primary human motive—the desire to maintain and enhance the self. Experiences not congruent with self must be avoided, denied, or distorted. One's **self-concept** is acquired primarily in early interactions with parents. Carl Jung's theory includes such unique concepts as the **collective unconscious,** which consists of inherited memories in the form of **archetypes** or universal symbols. In Jung's **extraversion-introversion typology,** personality was assumed to be based on inherited differences in temperament. William Sheldon's theory is centered on three bodily dimensions which indicate an individual's **somatotype (endomorphy, mesomorphy,** and **ectomorphy)** and three corresponding **temperament types (viscerotonia, somatotonia,** and **cerebrotonia).** Erik Erikson's theory is based on eight developmental stages that occur throughout the life span and the specific *crisis* or *conflict* that must be resolved at each stage.

The measurement of personality involves the sampling of some aspects of behavior in one situation in order to be able to predict behavior in another situation. **Projective tests,** such as the **Rorschach** and **TAT,** consist of relatively ambiguous stimuli, and it is assumed that the individual reveals various underlying concerns in interpreting these stimuli. **Objective tests,** such as the **MMPI** and CPI, consist of questions which have been empirically determined to be useful in predicting behavior. In current research, the tendency to develop coronary heart disease has been found to be predictable on the basis of classifying individuals as **Type A** or **Type B** with respect to their competitiveness, aggressiveness, and sense of urgency. Most personality tests measure **traits.** Some attempt to deal with the total personality, as in Cattell's measure of 16 basic **source traits,** while others deal with smaller groups of specific traits; still others attempt to measure only a single trait. One such trait that has been the object of a great deal of research is **authoritarianism,** which is measured on the **F Scale** of attitudes about obedience and respect for authority, suppression of sexuality, and hostility toward those who deviate from conventional norms. Studies of a courtroom situation indicate that authoritarians respond to their personal feelings about a defendant in recommending severe punishment for anyone they dislike; when the defendant is an authority figure, however, it is the egalitarians who respond in this manner.

Traditionally, personality has been assumed to be a stable set of characteristics that remain the same in different situations and at different times. Now, psychologists tend to think of behavior as resulting from a combination of stable personality factors plus the varying influences of the *current situation.* Honesty is an example of a behavior that can be affected by both personality and situational determinants. Despite the many theories and research approaches, there is a consensus that personality consists of both inborn and learned characteristics which may be altered temporarily or permanently by subsequent experiences.

Byrne, D.: *An Introduction to Personality: Research, Theory, and Applications.* Englewood Cliffs, New Jersey: Prentice-Hall, 1974.

A relatively advanced undergraduate text which surveys current research and theorizing on personality traits and on the situational determinants of behavior.

Hall, C. S., and Lindzey, G.: *Theories of Personality.* New York: John Wiley and Sons, 1970.

A basic summary of the major personality theories plus evaluations of the current status of each approach.

Mischel, W.: *Introduction to Personality.* New York: Holt, Rinehart, and Winston, 1976.

A comprehensive introduction to the field of personality, written for undergraduates.

Mischel, W.: *Personality and Its Assessment.* New York: John Wiley and Sons, 1968.

A somewhat difficult but thorough explanation of the importance of situational determinants of behavior in contrast to the traditional approach of personality psychologists. In addition, the rationale of social learning is described as a way to utilize these concepts in research.

Rychlak, J. F.: *Introduction to Personality and Psychotherapy: A Theory-Construction Approach.* Boston: Houghton Mifflin, 1973.

This book goes beyond simple descriptions of the major personality theories and attempts to explain the underlying philosophical orientations which they represent.

Wiggins, J. S.: *Personality and Prediction: Principles of Personality Assessment.* Reading, Massachusetts: Addison-Wesley, 1973.

An excellent presentation of the ideas and the methodology underlying the measurement of personality. This is a somewhat difficult book but one which describes well the use of personality tests as predictors of behavior.

Some journals that regularly publish papers on personality:

Educational and Psychological Measurement
Journal of Personality
Journal of Consulting and Clinical Psychology
Journal of Personality and Social Psychology
Journal of Research in Personality
Personality and Social Psychology Bulletin

Overleaf: Reproduction from the Bettmann Archive, Inc.

10 Maladjusted Patterns of Behavior

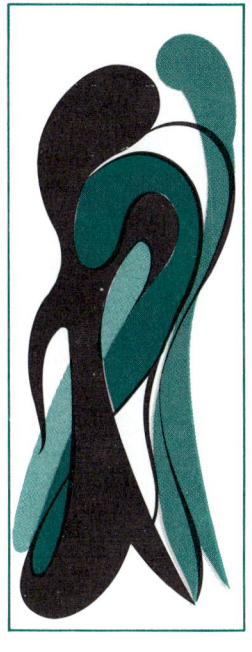

You are sitting in your psychology classroom when the instructor enters wearing a suit covered with feathers. From time to time during the lecture, he pauses to shout, "I'm a bird! I'm a bird!" After each such outburst, he pulls a hard-boiled egg from his pocket and throws it at a member of the class. Halfway through the class period, he becomes very agitated and runs out of the door crying, "Jehoshaphat! What have I done?" Assuming that this behavior is not typical among your instructors, how would you feel about it? How would you describe this incident to others? How would you explain it?

It is a common human characteristic to feel uncomfortable when confronted by someone who is different from ourselves. If another individual does not look or behave in the same way we do, an immediate reaction is to decide that something is wrong with him or with her, something unusual or "abnormal." Of course, we ourselves are "normal." Even individuals who disagree with us about politics, religion, or the quality of a football team are likely to be labeled as having crazy ideas or as being maladjusted (Byrne, 1971). After all, any sensible person would agree with us about these subjects.

Actually, we all know better than to suggest seriously that minor differences in appearance, behavior, or ideas constitute abnormality. The instructor in the bird suit, on the other hand, would seem to be different enough to be thought of as abnormal. "Abnormal" literally means "away from the normal" or "not usual." There is no objective way to determine how great the difference must be to constitute abnormality. Since deviation from the norm applies equally to a mathematical genius and to someone who runs down the street nude except for a thin layer of chunky peanut butter, it is obvious that we have to consider other factors beyond just "differentness" in defining abnormal behavior. It is also true that behavior which is widely practiced (and hence usual) in one group may still be perceived as maladjusted by those in another group. For example, an entire culture may believe in witchcraft and in periodically setting old ladies to the torch, but we still do not feel inclined to accept such goings on as normal. Because of these and other problems, it has been difficult to reach general agreement about the definition of terms such as abnormality or maladjustment. Suinn (1970) points out that no definition of abnormal or maladjusted behavior is entirely satisfactory. Nevertheless, in this book we will suggest that *maladjustment is a socially inappropriate pattern of behavior which results in unhappiness for the individual and/or for others.*

In this chapter, we shall deal first with general *concepts of maladjustment* as they have evolved historically and are expressed today. Before the various types of maladjustment are discussed, several defense mechanisms will be described, and it will be pointed out that these are normal responses that represent only minor deviations from optimal adjustment. **Neurotic** behavior represents a relatively serious interference with normal functioning. Neurotic individuals tend to experience a great deal of stress and anxiety, but they are sometimes able to get by in their everyday lives, though in an impaired fashion. **Psychotic** behavior can involve extreme distortions in perception, thought, and speech and is the most severe type of psychopathology or "mental illness." Common terms such as "crazy" refer to the psychoses, and hospitalization is commonly required in treating these disorders. (It has been said that neurotics build castles in the air, psychotics live in them, and therapists collect the rent.) A somewhat different category of abnormality is represented by **conduct disorders,** which primarily cause distress to society. Finally, these diverse types of behavior will be considered simply as different patterns of response to stress, and we point out the problems involved in *fitting people into arbitrary diagnostic categories.*

CONCEPTS OF MALADJUSTMENT

Throughout history, people have expressed a mixture of reactions toward those who behave in an unusual or unpredictable manner. Especially if they seem out of touch with reality, such individuals are frightening, and yet they are also objects of curiosity and interest. They are sources of amusement, and they also evoke compassion. Even today, playwrights and novelists often utilize mentally disturbed characters to elicit intense fear, pity, or laughter. A crazed murderer is somehow more terrifying than a sane one, and a "kookie" comedian more amusing than a straight one. These conflicting emotional responses to mental illness seem to have influenced both the way in which such behavior has been explained over the centuries and the way in which disturbed individuals have been treated.

The Supernatural Model: Angels of the Lord or Servants of Satan

One of the earliest explanations of abnormal behavior was the idea that supernatural powers are operating through the individual. Depending on whether the supernatural force was considered good or evil, emotionally disturbed individuals were treated with respect and reverence or with fear and loathing. For example, the Greeks would visit temples such as the one at Delphi to hear a priestess offer vaguely worded prophecies; medical historians suggest that these women were actually mentally disturbed individuals whose strange ramblings were perceived as divine wisdom (Zilboorg and Henry, 1941). In contrast, there are many examples of cultures in which mental illness was interpreted as a sign of the power of evil. In India, a book called the *Ayur-Veda* described seven types of demons which could become angry and enter the body of an unfortunate person; he would then begin to engage in disturbed

FIGURE 10-1 The holes in the prehistoric human skulls shown here may represent one of mankind's earliest attempts to deal with mental illness. It has been hypothesized that the holes were drilled to permit evil spirits to escape from the brain. (The University Museum, Philadelphia.)

behavior. Even primitive man may have dealt with these problems. Stone Age skulls (as shown in Figure 10-1) have been found with holes cut through the forehead. One interpretation of these relics is that the holes were made to permit evil spirits to escape from the brain, but it is also possible that they simply represent injuries inflicted in battle.

During the Middle Ages in Europe, the prevailing belief was that evil supernatural forces were responsible for any deviant behavior, and affected persons were therefore turned over to the Church for the appropriate care and treatment. In the thirteenth century, for example, monasteries often served the role of today's mental hospitals, and special prayers were offered to bring individuals back to the world of the normal. During this period, it was also thought to be important to distinguish between the mentally ill—who were taken over by Satan to punish them for their sins—and the witches who had voluntarily signed a pact with the devil to carry out his wicked work (Coleman, 1972). In the centuries that followed, the growing belief in witchcraft was associated with the idea that those who were mentally disturbed should be given physical punishment to drive the evil spirits from their bodies. One curious but relatively humane treatment was to shout passages from the Bible into the disturbed person's ear—literally to frighten the devil out of him. Anyone who has read the *Exorcist* or seen it in movie form can appreciate the power of the idea of demonic possession as an explanation for unusual behavior.

By the fifteenth century, the belief in witchcraft was at its height, and any abnormal behavior was almost always interpreted as a dangerous sign of the devil's power, so that steps were taken to protect the good people against such evil. In 1488, two monks wrote *The Witch's Hammer* as a handbook for detecting witches. One could assume that the devil is at work if, among other things, a man or woman feels "evil love," a person experiences hatred or jealousy, a spontaneous abortion occurs, or "a man cannot perform the genital act with a woman, or conversely a woman with a man." This book was also an instruction manual describing how to drive demons out of the body. A sure-fire prescription was to execute the individuals (for the good of their souls), and countless mentally disturbed victims were burned, hanged, beheaded, and pressed to

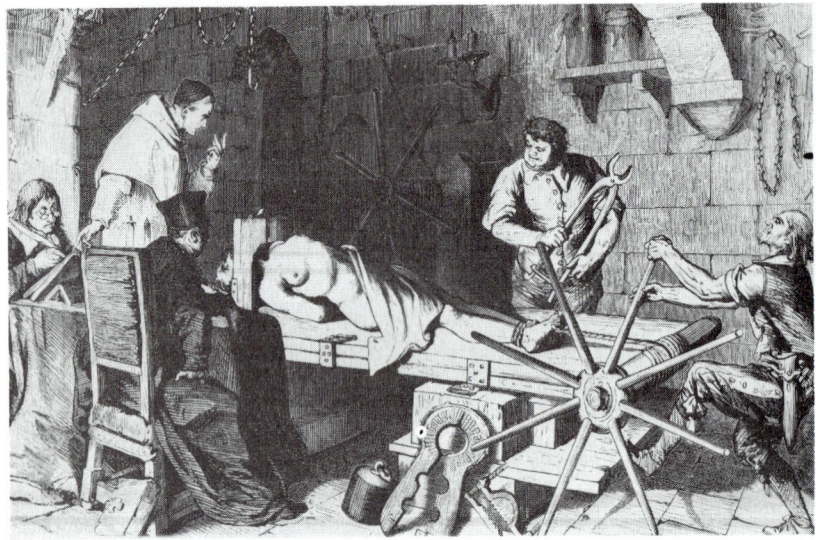

FIGURE 10–2 From the fifteenth to the seventeenth centuries, mental illness was usually interpreted as an indication of witchcraft at work. Many unfortunate victims were tortured and executed in order to "save their souls." (Bildarchiv Preussischer Kulturbesitz, Berlin.)

death under piles of stones as recently as the eighteenth century. In the United States, the execution of 19 witches in 1692 at Salem was the last active American endorsement of this particular theory of mental disturbance. At this point, the supernatural theories began to be replaced by medical ones.

The Medical Model: Abnormal Behavior as Illness

Curiously enough, the belief that disturbed behavior is a medical problem rather than a religious one is also an ancient idea. Hippocrates not only proposed an early personality theory (see Chapter 9) but he also offered a classification system for abnormal behavior. He speculated that natural causes could explain abnormality. These general views prevailed through Roman times but became less popular during the Middle Ages, as we have seen. Besides, most physicians were also priests during this period, so there was not really a struggle between two independent groups of professionals for the bodies and souls of those who were maladjusted.

The special role of the physician as being responsible for the emotionally disturbed became important when asylums were established in large numbers as places to house and care for mental patients. One of the best known of these early institutions was St. Mary of Bethlehem, founded in London in 1547. The name of this mental hospital was shortened to Bedlam, and that word came to mean a scene of wild uproar and confusion. Such a connotation was associated with Bedlam because the general public was admitted to the hospital for entertainment purposes—that is, to view the patients "performing" for their amusement. Other asylums were soon established in many nations around the world.

Sadly enough, being considered a mental patient was not initially a great improvement over being considered an agent of the devil. The institutions were much like prisons, and treatment often consisted of attempts to shock the patient back to his senses. For example, patients were spun rapidly on wheels, starved, or dropped into a pit of live snakes. By the nineteenth century, a few individuals, particularly Dorothea Dix in the United States and Pinel in France, became incensed by the brutality of mental hospitals and began campaigns to make them more humane places of treatment. Specifically, it was pointed out that patients should not be chained up, and that they should have fresh air and nourishing food.

Two important aspects of the medical explanation of mental illness were (1) the gradual shift away from viewing insanity as something shameful or evil toward regarding it simply as an illness and (2) the attempt by many medical workers to classify abnormal behavior into diagnostic categories. The founder of the modern system of classification was a German psychiatrist, Emil Kraepelin, whose career overlapped with that of Freud. Kraepelin's general idea was to follow the model set by medicine with respect to organic disease. First, medical scientists must identify and classify the illnesses on the basis of their symptoms, so that the typical progression of each disease could be described. Second, research must be conducted to seek the causes of each specific mental illness. Third, practitioners would attempt to develop a cure for each disease that had been identified.

There are many problems with this approach, as will be discussed shortly. It is true, however, that our conceptions of maladjusted behavior are strongly influenced by the medical model. We speak of *diagnosing* mental *patients* on the basis of their *symptoms* and attempting to find *cures* for mental *illness*. We will now outline a psychological explanation of maladjustment—one which emphasizes the role of learning.

FIGURE 10–3 When physicians were given the responsibility of caring for mental illness, asylums were established to house affected individuals. One such hospital in London, known as Bedlam, was frequently visited by outsiders who bought tickets of admission because they found it entertaining to observe the inmates perform in plays and sketches. (Sir John Soanes' Museum, London.)

FIGURE 10–4 By the beginning of the nineteenth century, there was a movement by reformers such as Philippe Pinel to improve the conditions of mental hospitals. This painting shows Pinel ordering the removal of chains from the patients at an asylum in Paris. (The Bettman Archive.)

The Psychological Model: Learning Ways to Reduce Anxiety

By the nineteenth century, a new explanation of psychopathology came into being—the idea that mental processes are somehow involved in bringing about the disturbed behavior (Davison and Neale, 1974). Physicians such as Mesmer in Austria and Charcot in France utilized hypnosis as a means of removing symptoms of maladjustment. A major current conception of psychopathology is based on the idea that learning plays a role in the development of abnormal behavior. Freud's belief that we learn particular kinds of symptoms primarily becluse they reduce anxiety has come to influence even those who do not consider themselves Freudians.

As an example, we will take a simple and familiar situation. Several college freshmen feel anxious about taking an upcoming mathematics test. As the hour of the exam approaches, their anxiety mounts. This feeling is unpleasant, and each individual consciously and subconsciously seeks ways to reduce it. One coed takes her math book and studies the material over and over, including parts she already knows very well. Another feels queasy in his stomach and asks the health center nurse to write a note excusing him from classes the rest of the day. A third student begins teasing and criticizing his acquaintances. A fourth gets mixed up about the date of the exam and is surprised to find that it was scheduled this week and not the following one. In each instance, the person has found a way to counter his or her unpleasant inner feelings. Surely we have each seen and perhaps even tried out these and dozens of other such strategies for dealing with anxiety. There is not much to be gained in providing a medical label or "diagnosis" for each behavior. We can, however, see that responses such as overstudying are fairly effective in solving the basic problem, that responses such as illness or a faulty memory bring only temporary relief, and that responses such as interpersonal aggression are quite disturbing to other people. We can also seek to find out why particular individuals learn particular anxiety-reducing behaviors, and we can try to develop ways to change the least desirable of those behaviors.

Many animal studies have shown clearly how anxieties and fears can be created and how such unpleasant emotional states can motivate learning. For example, Miller (1948) created fear in laboratory rats by administering electric shock each time they were placed in a white compartment. After several such experiences, the rats had learned to fear this compartment even though the shock was no longer given. Specifically, they became tense, they crouched, and they urinated and defecated frequently. In effect, their behavior was the rat version of the behavior of the students facing the math examination. Miller then gave his rats the opportunity to learn a fear-reducing response. When they turned a wheel, a door opened which allowed the rats to escape into a black compartment; there, the fearful responses were no longer evident. Like the student who overstudied her math, the rats learned to perform a useful response to reduce their fear. They probably *could* have been taught that the door opened whenever they fought with another rat and hence have learned to behave something like the male student who became hostile and critical.

Despite this emphasis on learning, it should be noted that the idea of in-born predispositions to certain symptoms is also widely accepted. To take a simple example, the student who felt sick to his stomach before the exam might have stumbled onto that particular symptom because of inherited defects in his digestive system. Even some of the very severe forms of mental illness may be more likely to develop in some individuals than in others because of genetic factors.

In the following sections, several types of behavior will be described, and the labels used are primarily ones taken from the medical model. In the final section of the chapter we will return to a discussion of the psychological model of maladjustment.

Defense Mechanisms: The Way We Often Deal with Our Problems

In our everyday lives, we each must face a series of major and minor problems which cause us discomfort. John wants to buy a car that he cannot afford. Debbie expects an "A" in chemistry but receives a "B." Jeff is away at school and receives a letter from his girl announcing her engagement to someone else. Kathy is ashamed of her family and does not want them to show up at her graduation. Jerry persuaded a girl to get drunk in order to make sexual advances; now he feels guilty about it. How do they (and we) cope with frustration, disappointment, rejection, anxiety, and guilt? The most common means is to find some way to defend ourselves against the discomfort. We will outline a few of these behaviors which serve, temporarily at least, to make us feel more comfortable.

Repression: What You Don't Know Can't Bug You

The basic defense mechanism is **repression.** If something is too painful to think about, you may find that it has suddenly "slipped your mind." Repression is basic to other defenses, because they each involve some degree of unconscious functioning. Repression can be very useful. If there is something unpleasant about which nothing can be done, there is not much to be gained by thinking about it endlessly. For example, if your dog is run over and killed by a truck, you may be very sad, but there comes a time when it would be to your advantage to "forget" your loss and go on to other concerns.

When repression develops as a way to avoid a problem that must be faced, however, this unconscious mechanism can begin to create new problems. In effect, the individual loses some control over the situation when he represses his awareness of it. A student who is unable to remember that his term paper is due on Friday avoids worrying during the week but discovers a worse problem when he finds out the truth. Similarly, if repression involves denying a strong motive (for example, hostile impulses or sexual desires), it may lead to the expression of the motives in indirect and disguised forms. According to Freud, it is in this way that dreams and slips of the tongue sometimes reveal what you are working hard to conceal from yourself. For example, a man wins a contest and is given two round-trip airplane tickets to London. When his best friend learns of his good fortune, the first response is, "That's really great—they gave you two first-crash tickets—I mean first-class tickets." You might hypothesize that such a response indicates some socially unacceptable and hence repressed feelings of envy and resentment in response to his friend's good luck.

Some of the other defense mechanisms simply represent specific ways in which repressed impulses express themselves.

One of the ways an individual can fool himself and sometimes others is to express the opposite of the actual impulse. This is known as **reaction formation.** When someone goes overboard in expressing their innocence or their virtue or whatever, we sometimes get suspicious of the underlying truth. We begin to suspect reaction formation when someone overdoes it in denying a negative desire or in defending a positive one. As Shakespeare suggested, a person can protest "too much" and thus give an indication that the underlying meaning is the opposite of what is being said.

When reaction formation is expressed in overt behavior, it can lead the person into unpleasant and puzzling situations. One of the authors once lived next door to a young woman who might seem to be the world's most helpful neighbor. She brought over recipes, helped trim our bushes, spotted insects invading our trees, gave us hints on how to raise our children, noted when our automobile tires were getting too smooth—all this and much more week after week. She was killing us with kindness. We decided that most of her "help" and "advice" were her way of expressing hostility and criticism. She had found a socially acceptable way to say and do a variety of hostile and annoying things.

Another common example of reaction formation is seen in the individual who says that he is so upset by the sexual content of modern movies that he must serve on a local censorship board to review all of the erotic shows that come to town. Such an individual can honestly feel that he is horrified by the sexy material and must make the sacrifice of viewing reel after reel of smut for the good of the community. It is possible to interpret his actions as indicating an unconscious desire to view this type of film. When socially acceptable reasons are given to explain one's behavior, they are called **rationalizations.** Rationalizations are an integral part of the defensive process and help us to fool ourselves about our true feelings.

When an emotion is very strong, an individual sometimes tries to control it by seeking a source other than the real one. That is, the emotion is **displaced** from something which is very threatening onto something else which may be easier to handle. For example, the expression of anger toward your father may be seen as something too dangerous to risk. In that situation, you may find yourself unexpectedly furious at something your younger brother said. If you are not aware of why you feel angry at your brother, the displacement mechanism may be operating. The classic example is that of the man who is abused by his boss and then kicks his dog when he gets home.

The innocent bystander who becomes the target of displaced aggression is called a *scapegoat.* In its more severe forms, displacement can lead to some of the uglier expressions of prejudice in which a racial or religious group is blamed for all manner of current difficulties.

Projection involves transferring an individual's unacceptable impulses onto others. If a person feels very guilty and anxious about his sexual desires, for example, it is possible to deny having them and to believe that others are sexually obsessed. Research has found that those individuals who feel uptight about their sexual desires tend to believe that wild erotic activities are occurring all around them in orgies held by political figures, adolescents, minority group members, and movie stars (Adorno, Frenkel-Brunswik, Levinson, and Sanford, 1950).

Projection of hostile impulses is a particularly difficult mechanism to deal with because it tends to be a self-fulfilling prophecy. That is, if Al is unconsciously hostile toward Bob, he can convince himself that it is Bob who is hostile to him. When Al responds to the "hostility" of Bob, Bob really does get mad. At this point, not only is Al's projection verified by Bob's behavior, but any hostility toward Bob is now "justified." After all, Bob started it.

In the next section, we will examine some examples of behavior which are a natural extension of the defense mechanisms but which tend to be less effective and more serious forms of maladaptive behavior.

 **PERSPECTIVE
ON
BEHAVIOR:** *What is Maladjustment?*

Consider the following behavior and decide whether it should be classified as maladjusted.

A man loads an airplane with explosives and flies it until he finds a shipload of people. He then deliberately aims his plane down toward the vessel and crashes into it. The plane explodes, the ship is badly damaged, and both the man and many of those on the ship are killed. According to our definition, behavior is maladjusted if it is socially inappropriate and if it results in unhappiness for the individual and/or for others. Does the above incident meet all of the criteria?

If the description involved a college student trying to sink a ferry boat in San Francisco Bay, there can be little doubt about the abnormality of the act. On the other hand, during World War II, at least one American and many Japanese servicemen were honored as heroes when they engaged in the activity described in our example. Under those particular circumstances, many people considered it appropriate to attempt to destroy the enemy and, if necessary, to lose their own lives in the process.

The point is that the concept of "appropriate" or "inappropriate" behavior is an extremely subjective one. The appropriateness of a given act depends in part on the situation, and the definition of what is appropriate can vary from culture to culture and from one time period to another (Szasz, 1960). Can you think of examples of such variations which would result in changes in classifying psychopathology? For example, if someone you knew were suddenly to begin babbling words and phrases from an unknown language while writhing about on the floor, would you consider the person to be behaving abnormally? If so, how would you evaluate those individuals in a fundamentalist church who behave in precisely that way when they are having a religious experience and "speaking in tongues"?

Not only are there cultural differences in defining what is appropriate or inappropriate behavior, but there are also differences across generations. If your parents did just what you did last Saturday night, would you think that something was wrong? Would your classmates be surprised if you dressed, talked, and behaved just like your parents and their friends? Socioeconomic status can also alter how one is classified. An "eccentric" millionaire can set his or her own lifestyle in an unusual fashion, as Howard Hughes did during the last decades of his career. If the average person decided to live in seclusion, watch movies for days at a time, hire someone whose only job was swatting flies, and eat junk foods exclusively, it is likely that he would be an immediate candidate for psychiatric care. It seems that absolute standards of normality and abnormality are difficult—or impossible—to establish. We do know that good adjustment is correlated with the ability to form close interpersonal relationships (Scott and Peterson, 1975), but we do not know whether there is a cause and effect relationship involved.

NEUROTIC BEHAVIOR: CRACKS IN THE DEFENSES

We all utilize defense mechanisms from time to time as a way of dealing with the stresses and strains of everyday life. If the level of anxiety is too high for such strategies to work, or if the defenses are sufficiently disrupting as to interefere with an individual's life, the resulting behavior is labeled *neurotic*. We will examine here some of the more common types of neurotic behavior. Six **neuroses**—arranged roughly by progressive degrees of how seriously they interfere with one's everyday life—will be described.

Hypochondriasis: Enjoying Poor Health

Hypochondriasis: A Case History

Dr. F. is an aging history professor who has spent most of his life complaining about his many aches and pains and taking all possible precautions against becoming ill. He downs massive doses of vitamins, and his medicine cabinet resembles a branch of the local pharmacy, in that it contains generous supplies of both prescription drugs and patent medicines.

Most of his conversations with students or colleagues are concerned with his personal state of health, dire warnings of upcoming epidemics, the latest story about the recall of some contaminated food, or the necessity for various preventive steps to ward off any number of disabilities. He collects books on nutrition and health foods, and he always wears a close fitting hat, both summer and winter.

Two of his habits sometimes bother those around him, but more often they are seen as amusing. He refuses to shake hands with anyone, and he touches a door knob only after he covers it with a handkerchief. Most people seem to think of him as pleasant but dull. He seems to be fairly content with his state of poor health and becomes angry only if someone jokes about his physical condition or his health habits. He has never married, lives alone, and has no close personal friends. Nevertheless, Dr. F. functions reasonably well within the framework of his career and his daily routine. His only regular outing is a twice monthly visit to his physician.

Putting All Your Worries in One Basket

An exaggerated concern with one's health or one's own body is termed **hypochondriasis,** and an individual whose behavior reflects this concern is labeled a *hypochondriac.* This type of neurotic reaction serves many functions which protect against anxiety.

First, with attention centered entirely on physical health, there is less possibility of other concerns being raised. The individual who thinks totally of germs, diet, and medicine need not feel anxious about interpersonal relationships, career disappointments, hostility, sex, or anything else. A single concrete concern over which he has some control is much easier to handle than numerous abstract ones. Also, chronic illness is a convenient excuse to explain anything that goes wrong. "I didn't do well on the exam because of my sinus condition." "People don't like me because I feel too bad to be my real self." "I haven't made a lot of money because I never feel well enough to work at full capacity." Though there is much verbalized concern about a multitude of health problems on the part of hypochondriacs, there does not seem to be much genuine unhappiness or anxiety. Those who behave in this particular neurotic way seem to have found a fairly successful means to deal with their problems.

Second, hypochondriasis tends to keep interpersonal relationships on a limited, superficial basis. Others cannot get too close emotionally so long as conversations are largely confined to one topic. Besides, discussions about one's gallbladder soon drive others to seek a more interesting companion. These behaviors are not consciously used to keep people at a distance; the individual truly believes himself to be ill and is convinced that such topics should be of vital concern to everyone.

FIGURE 10–5 Because children almost inevitably learn that illness brings special attention, pampering, and a vacation from school, it is not surprising that hypochondriasis is adopted by many individuals as a way to handle adult problems. (© 1973, Punch [Rothco]).

"I don't want to get well."

The development of this behavior pattern does not seem to be too mysterious. Most children learn quite early that illness has many rewards. They are allowed to stay home from school, people make special efforts to be nice and considerate, and the patient becomes the center of attention. It is, thus, rewarding to be mildly sick, as the boy in Figure 10–5 has discovered. Even in adulthood, illness can temporarily lead to much the same kind of special treatment, and many television commercials for cough medicines and antihistamines depict this vividly. The reason that some individuals adopt ill health as a lifelong pattern of neurotic behavior is not really known. It has been suggested that those with very low self-esteem may accidentally learn that symptoms of physical illness evoke positive responses from others, in the form of sympathy and concern. When acquaintances say, "How are you?" the hypochondriac interprets it as a real question about his health, and he is delighted to give a detailed answer. It is as if some individuals believe, "Love me, love my symptoms."

Phobic Reaction: One Fear Is Better Than Many Anxieties

Phobic Reaction: A Case History

Marilyn A. is a 12-year-old who is very much afraid of birds. Whenever she goes outside, she seems to be apprehensive and feels certain that a bird will swoop down on her head or will flap its wings in her face. As long as she stays inside, she is fine. A few times she has awakened screaming from a dream in which a bird is pecking at her eyes and she has no way to protect herself. This fear has grown increasingly severe. She has very little social life and is afraid to go anywhere out of her home. Even the trip to school has become a nightmare.

When help was sought, it was discovered that this pattern of behavior first began about the time she entered puberty, a year earlier. She had always been somewhat shy, but this problem increased when her classmates began dating and holding school dances. One night, she watched the Alfred Hitchcock movie "The Birds" on television, and shortly afterward her fear was first expressed. The therapist who is working with her has concluded that Marilyn is actually troubled about a number of things, including anxieties about being liked by others, her awakening sexual desires, and her appearance. By lumping all of her vague worries together in one very specific and objective fear, she has been able to repress her real concerns and at the same time have a "good" reason for avoiding many of the interpersonal situations that are closely related to her basic anxieties.

A Phobia for All Occasions

You may have heard several of the Greek names for specific **phobias,** such as claustrophobia (fear of closed places) or acrophobia (fear of high places). Such terms are not very helpful because they are simply descriptive, and people can learn to fear almost anything. Rephrasing it in Greek does not add any useful information. Phobias are differentiated from realistic fears that everyone shares; if you are afraid of walking alone at night in the downtown section of almost any large American city, this would be called showing good sense rather than indicating a phobic reaction. Nevertheless, unrealistic fears are not terribly unusual in the general population; in one study in New England, almost eight per cent of those questioned reported having at least a mild phobia (Davison and Neale, 1974). There can also be cultural influences which define just which fears are "realistic" and which are not. For example, in the United States it is considered reasonable to fear snakes, even nonpoisonous ones, while an intense fear of dogs is likely to be labeled a phobia. In parts of India, the reverse is true.

A phobia can develop in several ways. Occasionally, a specific traumatic incident constitutes the start of a phobia. Consider a situation in which an airplane has a blowout during take-off. Even though the pilot successfully controls the aircraft and brings it to a skidding halt without anyone being injured, there is realistic and intense fear on the part of the passengers. After the plane is evacuated, the airline arranges new tickets on an alternate flight. One passenger refuses and decides to take a train instead. Months later, whenever he thinks about flying, the feeling of panic returns. He decides never to fly again and even tries to avoid meeting any visitors at an airport. This phobia would seem to be the result of classical conditioning (see Chapter 5) in which a fear response has been conditioned to an airplane and then generalized to anything associated with flying. While most psychologists today would question the ethics of certain research in fear conditioning, the process *has* been demonstrated in the laboratory. Watson and Raynor (1920) frightened a small boy named Albert who was playing happily with a white rat. The experimenters made a loud, unexpected noise behind the boy's head. After this conditioning trial, Albert was afraid not only of the white rat but also of other, similar stimuli, such as a rabbit and a set of Santa Claus whiskers. Such a conditioned fear can also be acquired "second-hand" when one individual simply sees someone else in a painful or frightening situation (Bandura and Rosenthal, 1966).

More often, a phobia is not generated by some specific trauma but is *directed toward* some common element in the person's environment. In our case history, Marilyn A. became afraid of birds after seeing a motion picture. In Chapter 9, we mentioned Freud's case of little Hans, who became terrified of horses. Such fears are most likely to be interpreted as substitutes for other, more vague or frightening concerns. It was suggested that Marilyn had a series of personal and interpersonal worries, while Freud concluded that little Hans was substituting fear of horses for fear of castration by his father. This substitution of one fear for another is another example of the *displacement mechanism.* It sounds like a contradictory idea, but the development of such a fear seems to be one way of reducing anxiety, in that the fear is very specific and can be controlled to some degree. An individual can stay indoors to avoid birds or horses, stay away from white, furry animals, or avoid airplanes. Such tactics, if carried to extremes, obviously may act to interfere with the individual's life to a significant extent and can become a source of discomfort to others.

If a phobia is a displaced fear, it should be noted that any direct attempts to reduce the fear are not likely to be successful. Objective evidence that birds are harmless would not be expected to convince Marilyn. With a conditioned fear, therapeutic procedures (see Chapter 11) can be used successfully. Watson and Raynor deconditioned Albert so that his fear was eliminated; presumably the man in our example could be deconditioned with respect to his fear of flying (see Chapter 11). With a true phobia, such procedures may fail, or lead the patient to develop a new phobia to take its place. From the Freudian viewpoint, at least, it is necessary to deal with what the individual really fears and not the object onto which the fear has been displaced.

An interesting view of phobias has been presented by Seligman (1971), who believes that there is a biological basis for selecting particular objects to fear. He suggests that we are genetically programmed to fear certain aspects of our environment, and he points out that most phobias are directed at objects of natural importance to the survival of our species. Even in the laboratory, some kinds of fear are much easier to condition than others. For example, Bregman (1934) repeated Watson's fear-conditioning experiment, but she used common household objects, such as curtains and blocks, instead of a furry animal. To the experimenter's surprise, there was no fear conditioning at all! It appears, then, that our fears depend not only on the processes of conditioning and displacement but also on some inborn tendencies to develop specific types of fears.

Obsessive-Compulsive Neurosis: Repetitive Thoughts and Actions

Obsessive-Compulsive Neurosis: A Case History

Mrs. M. is a housewife who prides herself on the appearance of her home. She is a dynamo of activity each day as she cleans, dusts, and washes. Sheets are neatly ironed, mattresses are regularly turned, and her windows are spotlessly clean. Neither she nor her husband smokes, but sparkling ashtrays are provided for guests who do. Visitors are sometimes disconcerted to find Mrs. M. exchanging their used ashtray for a fresh one in mid-cigarette.

Difficulties began with the birth of their first child. Pregnancy interfered with her house-cleaning routine, and Mrs. M. was even more unhappy about the appearance of their home when she returned from the hospital. The baby was also a constant source of worry. She felt it was important to keep him as clean as the ashtrays, and the baby was continually being bathed, powdered, and changed.

It was at this point that Mr. M. noticed some changes in his wife's behavior. She no longer showed any interest in sexual relations, and sometimes could be heard vacuuming the living room rug in the middle of the night. She said that she felt guilty if it were left dirty. One evening her husband came down and found her crying as she worked. She eventually confided that the same thought kept going through her head hour after hour, and she could not seem to drive it out of her mind. "And baby makes three. And baby makes three." She was sufficiently frightened by what was happening to her that she sought the advice of her physician, who recommended psychotherapy.

Trying to Limit Thoughts and Deeds

When an individual has a thought that occurs repeatedly and that is not entirely under control, he or she is experiencing an *obsessive reaction*. Most people have had similar experiences in a mild form, as when the words of a song keep "running through your head." When the individual engages in some overt behavior repeatedly, and often inappropriately, the behavior is called a *compulsive reaction*. Many of us have from time to time fallen into the habit of engaging in routine activities in a set way (for example, always putting on the left shoe first or taking the same path to school or work each day). Most of us, however, do not feel compelled to continue these behaviors no matter what; we can alter our routines if we wish. Also, this behavior does not tend to disrupt the rest of our daily lives. It is common to wonder from time to time whether we turned off the lights in the car, locked the back door, or unplugged the coffee pot—then we retrace our steps to check. If these worries occur frequently, and the checking and rechecking take place repeatedly, an individual is moving toward a more serious version of this behavior pattern. In a full-blown **obsessive-compulsive reaction,** the individual cannot stop the recurring thought or the recurring behavior. Shakespeare created a famous compulsive character in Lady Macbeth, as shown in Figure 10–6.

The fact that any interference with the affected person's responses tends to make the individual extremely anxious suggests that the obsessive thoughts and compulsive behaviors are somehow serving the function of reducing anxiety. It seems likely that they are a way of controlling unacceptable impulses, in that the individual is engaging in thoughts and deeds which are incompatible with some forbidden thoughts and deeds.

According to a formulation by Rosen (1975), there is a second way in which obsessions and compulsions can operate. He suggests that they sometimes are based on guilt, and that they may function as a sort of mild self-punishment. If an individual has been taught, for example, that his own sexual impulses are evil, an obsessive idea can operate as a punishment for indulging in "bad" behavior ("What if I get an incurable venereal disease?"). Even if the sexual behavior is within a marriage relationship, the person may still feel that it is immoral and seek to punish himself ("What if we have a retarded child?"). Rosen proposes that such thoughts are less threatening than the original forbidden impulses because they actually represent fairly unlikely possibilities. In a manner analogous to punishing oneself with thoughts, many compulsive behaviors involve a degree of actual harm to oneself, as when an

FIGURE 10–6 Compulsive behaviors involve some activity which is carried out over and over in some set way; the individual feels that the behavior is beyond his or her control. Shakespeare depicted such a reaction and indicated that it often has symbolic meaning: when Lady Macbeth washes her hands repeatedly in order to get rid of a spot of blood, it represents her guilt in the murder of King Duncan. (The Bettman Archive.)

individual pulls out bits of his hair or bites his fingernails. These behaviors, too, can be seen as ways of lessening guilt by harming oneself physically.

In Freudian theory, obsessive-compulsive behavior is said to be related to events at the anal stage of development, in which a child is first introduced to the routines of toilet training and to pressures to be neat and clean. It also seems likely that the development of some aspects of this type of neurosis may be similar to the way that some superstitions and rituals develop. One child tells another as she walks down the sidewalk, "Step on a crack, and you'll break your mother's back." The possibility of harming one's mother can be such an unacceptable idea that the child for years goes to a great deal of trouble to avoid all sidewalk cracks. Though Freud might not agree, it is also possible accidentally to say or do something that happens to be associated with reward. For example, a child who is afraid during a thunderstorm may say, "Rain, rain, go away. Come again, some other day." If the thunder stops at that moment, it is easy for the child to assume that his poem caused it to happen and to believe that this word magic can be helpful in the future. When it doesn't work, he may assume that he has not said it in quite the right way, or that the verse needs to be repeated many more times. Eventually this procedure will work, because at some point the rain will stop. This is something like the joke about the man living outside of London who spent his days sprinkling purple powder up and down the countryside. When asked why he did such a thing, he replied, "To keep the lions away." To the inevitable objection, "But, there are no lions in England," he would answer, "Of course not, and you have me to thank for that."

Another aspect of obsessions and compulsions is the fact that if one activity is incompatible with another, it is possible to substitute a more desirable behavior for a less desirable one. For example, a teenage boy learns that he cannot worry about grades and at the same time work on his bicycle; whenever such anxieties occur, he starts disassembling his bike. A degree of this behavior can even be beneficial, as when a student works compulsively or is extremely concerned that term papers have absolutely no mistakes. A "perfectionist" can be a pain in the neck to others, but the individual often benefits from the consequences of his or her slightly neurotic actions. It may be seen, then, that minor obsessions and compulsions are a relatively normal part of everyday life. If, however, individuals continue to avoid their unacceptable impulses and fail to deal with underlying fears and worries, these defensive activities can become automatic and can begin to cause problems of their own. That is, they will begin to interfere with the individual's life.

Dissociative Reaction: Massive Repression

Dissociative Reaction: A Case History

Sharon D. is a secretary at an insurance company and has been married for ten years. She is very much inclined to avoid talking about or even thinking about anything unpleasant. For example, she avoids getting medical check-ups, forgets dental appointments, and overpays a sales clerk rather than pointing out that an error has been made. When an argument begins to develop with her husband, she refuses to continue the discussion and finds it necessary to take a nap, regardless of the time of day.

On a summer vacation, the D.'s stayed at a motel in Southern California. One evening, she asked about Mr. D.'s attraction toward a young female college student they met at the beach. When he agreed and said that the girl was extremely desirable sexually, Mrs. D. quickly became sleepy and went to bed. Later that evening, Mr. D. awoke to find his wife gone. There was no note, and he found that their car was also missing. After a period of frantic worry and a conversation with the local police, he received a telephone call from Yuma, Arizona, the following afternoon.

Mrs. D. said that she woke up in a Yuma motel and had no idea how she had gotten there. When she returned, she explained that as far as she could remember, she went to sleep in California and woke up in Arizona. She said, "It's like a science fiction movie."

Shutting out Portions of the Mind

There are four types of **dissociative reaction,** all of which involve some change in the normal state of consciousness. They are very rare in real life—but very common in fiction, because they are startling and interesting forms of neurotic behavior. In each instance, the individual seems to be setting aside the major features of his or her personality.

One of the most familiar states is **amnesia,** in which an individual loses his memory with respect to such things as name, address, and any personal details of his life. That is, there is a loss of the person's identity. Memory for nonpersonal material tends to remain intact; for example, the multiplication tables are not forgotten, nor are the words of popular songs. Sometimes amnesia lasts only a few hours; in some cases, it may continue for years. Only in soap operas or in comedy movies is amnesia repeatedly caused and cured by a blow on the head.

When a person who has forgotten his identity also leaves his usual surroundings and travels elsewhere, as did the woman in our case history, he is manifesting a **fugue state.** When a fugue state lasts a long period of time, the individual is likely to assume a whole new identity, sometimes with a new occupation and new interpersonal relationships. Our case history also could be considered an example of **somnambulism,** or sleepwalking, which is classified as a type of dissociative reaction if it occurs frequently and causes difficulty for the individual. Finally, the most dramatic and rarest form of dissociative reaction is **multiple personality,** in which two or more complete personalities are alternately expressed by the individual. The book and movie *The Three Faces of Eve* depicted a dramatic version of an actual case history of multiple personality (see Figure 10–7). Laymen sometimes refer to multiple personality incorrectly as schizophrenia; for example, a columnist may write that a particular political party is "schizophrenic." As we shall see shortly, schizophrenia is not at all like multiple personality, and the columnist really means that the political party is split into several different incompatible factions or "personalities."

Dissociative reactions are usually explained in terms of repression: whole aspects of consciousness are apparently put out of awareness, allowing the individual to function independently of those aspects of himself which are beset by anxieties. Assuming a totally new identity is a fascinating way to bury or run away from all of one's problems. Actually, very little research has been conducted on this type of behavior, because it is not encountered often

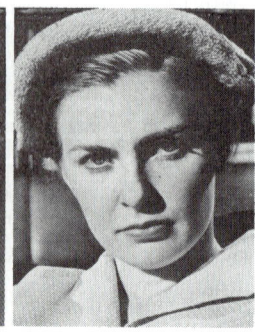

FIGURE 10–7 A real case history of multiple personality was depicted in *The Three Faces of Eve.* The original patient, Eve White (far left), was a quiet, repressed individual who was unaware that she had any other personality. Eve Black (center) was an outgoing, swinging individual who expressed awareness of and dislike toward Eve White. After therapy, an integrated, aware Eve (right) emerged. (*The Three Faces of Eve,* courtesy of Twentieth Century-Fox. © Twentieth Century-Fox Film Corporation. All rights reserved.)

enough; only 200 cases of dissociative reaction have ever been reported by therapists over the years (Abse, 1966).

Carla B. was 40 years old when her husband died suddenly of a heart attack. They had no children, and she felt completely alone for the first time in her life. Long after the usual period of mourning, she still felt as totally miserable as she had the day Mr. B. died.

She spent her days sitting in their darkened apartment seeing almost no one. Often she aimlessly sorted through old snapshots of her husband. She lost interest in friends, in television, in reading. She was unable to do more than the simplest household chores and felt that she could no longer concentrate on anything.

Her thoughts were exclusively on her dead husband and her own feelings of despondency. She felt somehow responsible for her husband's death and hence completely unworthy. After she confided in a neighbor that she was thinking of taking her own life, her physician was contacted, and he persuaded her to enter a local hospital. In addition to receiving psychotherapy, she was placed on a special diet because of malnutrition; she had felt too sad even to eat regular meals.

Reactive depression tends to be initiated by an event which would be expected to cause unhappiness in anyone—the death of a loved one, the loss of a job, or disappointment in a love affair. In fact, an individual who showed no signs of unhappiness in such circumstances would be considered odd. The difference between a normal degree of depression and neurotic depression is that one usually "gets over" the sadness. In time, it is expected that an individual will work through the feelings of misery and return to other interests and activities. When there is reactive depression, the sadness continues indefinitely and interferes with the individual's everyday life.

According to Freudian theory, one of the primary reasons for such a response to a sad event is that there is a mixture of conflicting feelings about what happened, a state known as *ambivalence*. For example, if the widow in our case history felt both love and hate for her husband, her reaction makes more sense. She must cope with her loss and also with her guilt about feeling relieved at getting rid of him. This unconscious conflict of emotions would help to explain her self-hate, which led to withdrawal from the world, neglect of her own well-being, and thoughts of suicide.

A very different interpretation of depression has been proposed by Seligman (1973). His ideas are based on laboratory experiments in which animals are, in effect, *taught* that they are helpless to do anything about a stressful situation. Ordinarily, if a dog is placed in a two-box apparatus in which he receives electric shock in one compartment, he quickly learns to escape by running to the second compartment. When a warning light comes on just before the shock, he learns to avoid the shock altogether by running in response to this signal. On the other hand, if the dog has previously been placed in a situation in which he is shocked and cannot avoid it, he has great difficulty afterward in learning to escape from one compartment to another and to respond to the warning light. This condition is called **learned helplessness.** Seligman points out many similarities between these experimental animals and depressed human beings. In both instances, there is a passive response to stress and a tendency to eat very little and to lose weight. On the basis of such findings, it has been proposed that at least some forms of human depression may result from stressful experiences which the person could neither control nor escape. People, too, can learn that they are helpless. When human subjects are placed in an experimental situation of learned helplessness, they show not only a deterioration in performance but also physiological symptoms that are ordinarily associated with reactive depression (Gatchel and Proctor, 1976).

Anxiety Reaction: Pushing the Panic Button

Anxiety Reaction: A Case History

Harold C. was a college student with very good grades and the desire to continue his education in graduate school. He also felt that he was less intelligent than the others in his school, and that his grades were based on hard work rather than ability. He had the vague worry that if he were to achieve an important goal, something terrible might happen to him, because he "doesn't deserve it."

As the day approached for taking the Graduate Record Examination, which was necessary in applying for graduate school, Harold became increasingly nervous and found it very hard to sleep. He frequently felt the need to urinate, and he had to leave a lecture twice one morning because he developed a severe case of diarrhea. He worried about how well he was prepared and about the ability of those with whom he was competing. He even became concerned about whether he would go to the right room on the right day and at the right hour the test was being given. On the day of the exam, he was in a state of near panic. He managed to get through it even though his hand trembled, and he felt that he was performing badly. Afterward he ran back to his dormitory room and lay down on his bed sobbing uncontrollably.

That night, Harold's roommate was awakened by an unusual sound. When he turned on the light, he could see Harold pacing up and down the room, a cigarette in his mouth. When asked what was going on, Harold almost screamed, "Now everyone will know. They'll find me out." The next day a physician at the student health center gave him a sedative and admitted him to the student hospital for observation and rest. Only then was he able to relax enough to get some sleep.

Going to Pieces

Most individuals have experienced at least some aspects of an **anxiety reaction.** If you can imagine your feelings just before a difficult final exam, combined with how you felt on your first date, *plus* your response when asked to appear on a stage, you will have some idea of what an anxiety reaction is like. When an individual simply has no means of coping with the pressures and strains he or she is facing, an anxiety attack can be the result.

Besides the feeling of anxiety, the individual also tends to feel that he is losing self-control or "going to pieces." There are numerous physiological responses such as trembling, heavy breathing, sweating, frequent urination,

FIGURE 10–8 When an individual can no longer cope with the pressures and strains of his or her life, an anxiety attack can result. There is a feeling of fear, a loss of self-control, and a series of physiological responses as if the body is preparing to meet physical danger.

increased heart rate, a tight feeling in the chest, and loose bowels. The body responds in the same way as when confronted by a physical threat. The difficulty is that there is no immediate way to avoid being harmed; it is like being confronted by an unknown danger day after day with no means of escape. The person may cry or feel like screaming, "I can't stand it!"

We have been describing situations in which individuals are overwhelmed by problems and have what is sometimes called a "nervous breakdown." The reaction is fairly similar to what happens in wartime or in civilian disasters, when such a breakdown is labeled **traumatic neurosis.** With a traumatic neurosis the cause is usually obvious, but the person who has an anxiety reaction is not responding to objective and easily identified stresses. He or she may not be aware of what the anxiety is about. Many individuals feel anxious, for example, about obtaining the approval of others or about succeeding at school or in a job. Making a new friend may not help, because there is the fear of losing the friendship or the worry that it is not genuine. Success may not help, because there is the fear of future failure or a concern that the present success is based on luck. Such continuing anxieties are often described as neurotic worries. Feeling anxious without knowing exactly why is characteristic of this behavior pattern. A noted therapist, Albert Ellis (1962), suggests that there are many common irrational ideas in our culture which can lead to anxiety. He feels that we believe that most other people should love us or approve of our behavior, that everyone should be competent and successful, and that there is a good solution to all problems. When an individual finds that many other people do not particularly like him, that he is not an outstanding success, or that he is unable to solve a particular problem, it is not too surprising that anxiety may result because of the frustration of these unrealistic expectations.

In reading about the neuroses, you may have noted some aspects of yourself in each type. That is, you may be overly concerned about your health at times, experience unrealistic fears, have obsessive thoughts about something or engage in some compulsive activity, walk in your sleep, feel very depressed, or react to some situations with a great deal of anxiety. Such neurotic symptoms are common in all of us. They are not indications of neurosis, however, unless they are prolonged enough and serious enough to disrupt our everyday lives.

PSYCHOTIC BEHAVIOR: THE ULTIMATE PSYCHOLOGICAL DISORDERS

In our description of neurosis, it was indicated that some forms of neurotic behavior can interfere seriously with an individual's everyday functioning. In the more severe neuroses, involving depression or anxiety, individuals may be incapacitated and unable to carry out their normal activities at home, work, or school. There are still more serious patterns of abnormal behavior, however, which constitute even more disrupting types of behavioral malfunctioning. It is this type of extreme maladjustment—**psychosis**—to which is applied such frightening and frequently derogatory labels as "insane" and "crazy."

Two outstanding clinical psychologists, Ullman and Krasner (1975), make the point that many people have unrealistic conceptions of just how psychotic individuals behave. They suggest that the major difference between what you would see on the grounds of a psychiatric hospital and on the average college campus is that patients seem to be in less of a hurry than students. Otherwise, the scene is the same—with people walking around, engaging in conversation, and making plans for the evening. The contrast between actual mental illness and what we have been taught to expect by watching movies and television was pointed out when Leonard Ullmann told of watching a TV movie with a group of psychiatric patients. In the movie, Bob Hope was in an "insane asylum" with patients who were dressed strangely and behaving strangely. The real patients were sitting quietly watching the show and behaving appropriately. "One could only wonder who was crazy, the men on the ward watching the film or the people in Hollywood who made it" (Ullmann and Krasner, 1975, p. 329). Before describing the three major types of psychotic behavior, it may be helpful to consider some general aspects of psychosis itself.

Psychosis: Marching to the Beat of a Different Drummer

Psychosis essentially involves symptoms which are so severe that the individual is likely to be unable to function in his or her personal life. The behavior is sufficiently unusual and disturbing that hospitalization is very likely to be required, and the person may become literally immobile or begin functioning in a way that is totally inappropriate. The patient may fail to recognize that anything is wrong, having little insight into either the initial problem or the ineffectiveness of his response to it. There is a loss of the ability to evaluate reality as others do; thus, communication breaks down as words, perceptions, and actions no longer correspond to what is meant, perceived, or done by others. Finally, psychotic behavior may lead to actions which are dangerous to the person himself or to those around him. One should not think of psychotic acts as meaningless or random, however; it is simply more difficult to decipher the meaning than is true for neurotic behavior. We shall now describe some of the specific symptoms of psychosis.

Distorted Perception

When an individual's perceptions do not correspond to the external stimuli, he is said to be **hallucinating.** For example, an individual may see something that is not actually there. One elderly patient, who had been hospitalized for years, always walked around the grounds with a pet that only he could perceive. He regularly shouted at this animal, "Come back here! Stay on the sidewalk!" This type of response was depicted in the play and movie *Harvey,* about a man with an invisible, six-foot rabbit. In real life, however, the situation is not as amusing as in fiction, and a psychotic patient with an invisible pet is pathetic rather than whimsical. (See Color Plate 3 for an example of the way in which Van Gogh's paintings reflected changes in his perceptual processes as he developed a psychotic condition.)

FIGURE 10–9   The ghost of Hamlet's father. Is this apparition born out of young Hamlet's mind, as are the hallucinations of psychotics? If so, the ghost may represent an externalization of any number of Hamlet's well-known concerns—his preoccupation with death, or his desire to rationalize revenge against his stepfather, for instance. Hamlet's questioning of his own mental stability reflects an awareness of these possibilities (of course, Shakespeare's audience could accept the ghost *as* a ghost). (The Bettmann Archive.)

More often, hallucinations involve hearing. Many patients report hearing voices which give them messages or accuse them of unspeakable acts for which they should feel guilty. The message, of course, is from the person himself, but it is perceived as coming from an external source and as very real. A female patient became convinced that the voices and music she heard were somehow being received by means of a radio secretly implanted in her brain. She would stop in the middle of a conversation with her physician and shout replies to whatever communication she received or begin humming and swaying to the tunes being played. Occasionally, hallucinations may involve the other senses, such as taste, smell, or touch.

Distorted Thought

We are each capable of thinking in ways that are not very logical or realistic. One of the best examples is the way in which our thought processes operate when we sleep; in dreams everyone seems to be a bit psychotic. That is, events occur that are illogical or impossible; our dream fantasies are not controlled by the restraints of reality. Also, studies of sensory deprivation (see Chapter 3) suggest that when normal individuals are placed in an experimental situation which cuts them off from ordinary sources of visual and auditory stimulation, they tend to hallucinate and to think in unrealistic terms. Much like the subject in a sensory deprivation experiment, the psychotic individual seems to be cut off from external stimulation. The effect on the thought processes is a disturbing one in each instance.

An unrealistic belief which is strongly held and defended is called a **delusion.** A female patient, for example, decided that her internal organs had turned into glass and that if anyone touched her, her insides would be likely to break and cause her intense pain. Once an individual has developed a delusion, he tends to resist any evidence that might shake this belief system or even suggest that it is in the least incorrect. Often delusions involve imagined **persecution** of the individual. One patient described the way in which Martians were influencing him. He believed that they had powerful electronic devices which were beamed through the walls to project thoughts into his head. These creatures would cause him to think about carrying out various sexual acts or committing some crime of violence. One of the nurses sometimes contradicted him with statements indicating that such a thing was impossible or that others would see the Martians in action if they really existed. The patient always rejected her arguments. Finally, he decided that she, too, was a Martian and was relaying the magic beam from the nurses' station in the hallway. Delusions are not open to logic or to debunking evidence.

Other delusions deal with **ideas of reference,** the belief that others are referring to you. In *Roughing It*, Mark Twain described a psychotic gentleman who decided that an exchange of innocuous letters between himself and a newspaper publisher was being discussed all over the world by heads of state and had led to warfare between nations. A student in one of the author's classes expressed the delusion that the questions asked by other class members really had some hidden meaning related to herself. Literally, individuals can come to feel that everyone is talking about them. A step further along in the same kind of process is the **delusion of grandeur,** in which the person believes himself to be someone of very special importance. Jokes often depict psychotics as believing themselves to be Napoleon, but again in real life, such behavior is not necessarily amusing. One patient in California was convinced that San Francisco did not exist and that it was temporarily created from time to time just for him. He decided that the houses and buildings were actually just stage sets which some mysterious group erected just before he got there and took down again when he was out of viewing range. He felt very important to be at the center of such a large-scale plot.

Though disordered thought processes may seem bizarre, they usually are fairly logical. That is, once you accept the patient's initial, unrealistic premise, the remainder of the ideas follow more or less reasonably. If your insides were made of glass, you would not want others to touch you. If the Martians were controlling your thoughts, they might well infiltrate the hospital in a nurse's disguise. It is very difficult, of course, to break through these elaborate ideas and begin to get at what they mean to the individual.

Distorted Emotion and Speech

Inappropriate emotional responses can involve unrealistic joy (for example, uncontrollable laughter at a funeral), unrealistic sadness (crying at the sight of a dead cricket), or unrealistic anger (expressing rage about the outcome of a TV soap opera). When such reactions occur, it suggests that the individual is responding to his or her own thoughts rather than to external cues. Emotional responses can also be almost entirely absent, and the individual simply shows no concern with anything or anyone.

Changes in speech also occur. The person may engage in a rapid series of free associations but verbally express only the last element in the chain. For example, a patient was asked if he knew what time it was. After a brief pause, he replied, "Pumpkin." That may seem to be completely nonsensical, but careful questioning revealed that the time (12:00 o'clock) reminded him of Cinderella, who had to leave the prince's ball by 12:00 o'clock before her carriage changed back into a pumpkin. There is nothing wrong with such associations; they can occur to any of us, and they are probably necessary in playing games such as "password" or "charades." The problem is in not knowing or caring whether others share the same series of associations and thus comprehend what you mean.

Other aspects of distorted speech include the meaningless repetition of the last word that is heard, a condition called **echolalia.** A young psychology student trying to give an intelligence test to a psychotic patient soon gave up when the interaction went as follows. "How are you?" "You." "Would you tell me your name?" "Name." "I would like to give you a test today." "Today." Another psychotic tendency is to create new words, called **neologisms.** Lewis Carroll in *Through the Looking-Glass* created many neologisms, such as those accompanying Figure 10–10 (the famous "Jabberwocky").

It might be noted that these distortions in speech do not necessarily just reflect one of the ways in which psychotics fail to function properly. They may also serve a purpose in protecting the individual from potentially painful interactions with others. It is as if the psychotic has a private joke in which he plays around with the language. As a result, no one can easily discover just what he is thinking or feeling. Many of us have engaged in mild versions of the same kind of thing as children when we made up our own words, spoke to one another in some form of pig Latin or other code, or refused to say anything except to echo what the other person had just said.

Manic-Depressive Psychosis: Riding an Emotional Roller Coaster

Manic-Depressive Reaction: A Case History

John W. held a civil service job and had risen to a managerial position in a government office which processed veterans' benefits. His co-workers realized that he had "good days" and "bad days" that were more extreme than the average person, but such mood swings did not seem to be a terribly serious problem. Then, he gradually began to engage in more and more unusual behavior.

One morning he arrived at the office an hour early with a pile of hand-painted signs. When the others arrived, they found him on a ladder tacking the signs on each

FIGURE 10–10   What do these words—taken from the opening of Lewis Carroll's "Jabberwocky"—mean?:

> 'Twas brillig, and the slithy toves
> Did gyre and gimble in the wabe:
> All mimsy were the borogoves,
> And the mome raths outgrabe.

As you can see, the playful word games going on here take on a different meaning when interpreted in the drawing by Tenneil. The seeming nonsense words uttered by some psychotics have special meanings as well—but only for the affected persons.

wall and draping crepe paper streamers. The messages were such sentiments as "Smile and the world smiles with you," "Put on a happy face," "The early bird catches the worm," and some that they did not quite understand: "Loose bigots sink ships" and "Pray before you slay."

This posting of signs was the beginning of several months of feverish activity in which Mr. W. was extremely busy in instituting new ideas, dictating letters (including messages of advice to the Pope, the Russian ambassador, and a pro football quarterback), and pushing his subordinates to work harder and faster. He laughed frequently at his own jokes, brought huge quantities of food to eat at lunch time, and began making sexual advances toward several female employees. At this point, complaints about his behavior reached his superiors, and they suggested that he take a leave of absence.

His response was a deep depression. For the next two weeks, he came to work quietly and slowly, spending each day sitting silently in his darkened office. When others tried to talk to him, he would begin blaming himself for all that went wrong, saying that the world would be better off if he were dead. He refused to eat lunch and left work early each day because he was tired. He drove away one afternoon and neither went home nor returned to work. He was picked up by the police in a neighboring city, sitting on a park bench late at night, and was placed in a hospital for observation and treatment.

Manic-depressive psychosis was described by Hippocrates as mania and melancholia. In the first century A.D., the physician Aretaeus wrote that melancholia "is a lowness of the spirits without fever; and it appears to me that melancholy is the commencement and a part of mania" (Cameron, 1944, p. 873). What both these men noted, of course, are the periodic *mood changes* that characterize manic-depressive psychosis. Some individuals express only

Extreme Emotional Variations

extreme elation and then swing back to a relatively normal state, while others vary between deep depression and a normal mood. A very few, like Mr. W., go through the entire cycle from high to low emotional expressions. The normal period may last for years before the next emotional outburst begins. Typically, these mood swings last for only a period of months and then change, whether the individual is in treatment or not.

Delusions may accompany the manic or depressive state. A manic individual may have delusions of grandeur and will produce a flood of unrealistic ideas and plans. There may be letters and telephone calls, blueprints for world peace, schemes to make money, unrealistic new inventions, and so forth. You may have heard an individual like this call into a radio talk show and begin presenting his ideas. One man called a Chicago station with his plans to use all of the city's garbage to build a midwestern mountain complete with a ski resort. The proposals are often somewhat plausible (at least, not impossible), but a manic person soon loses interest and moves on to the next "project." A psychotically depressed individual may believe himself to be responsible for all of the world's sins and to be suffering from an incurable disease or a strange, undiagnosed bodily disorder, such as worms eating his brain. He feels worthless and sees nothing but gloom in the world around him. Thoughts of death are common, and most depressed individuals think of suicide. Almost 15 per cent of depressed persons attempt to kill themselves (Arieti, 1959; Hastings, 1958), though only about one in ten actually succeeds (Watts, 1966). Even the dreams of depressive individuals reflect unhappiness, a perception of a hostile and threatening environment, and an excessive concern with the past (Hauri, 1976.)

Manic-depressive reactions have been studied with respect to possible genetic causes. Data presented by Kallman (1953) suggest that the more similar two individuals are genetically, the more likely they are to share a predisposition toward manic-depressive psychosis. For example, if one identical twin (same genetic structure) develops this behavior, the other is very likely to do so. With fraternal twins (only as genetically similar as any pair of siblings), manic depression in one is not very likely to be followed by the same reaction in the other. A genetic predisposition does not indicate that this psychosis is inherited, at least not in the same way that eye color is inherited. Rather, the idea is that if an individual becomes severely threatened by problems, the tendency to respond with this particular type of psychosis, rather than some other one, may be inherited. Cultural factors also seem to play a large part. For example, the likelihood of developing a manic-depressive reaction varies with social class. When those at higher socioeconomic levels become psychotic, manic-depressive psychosis is the most likely pattern (Hollingshead and Redlich, 1958).

Other types of data suggest that learning plays a strong role in predisposing individuals to develop manic-depressive psychosis. Research indicates that many affected individuals have been raised in families in which the conditions favored strong conscience development. Those who later developed manic symptoms were characterized early in life as ambitious, concerned about social expectations, and strongly oriented toward achievement (Becker, 1960; Gibson, Cohen, and Cohen, 1959). Those who later developed depressive symptoms were more likely to respond to parental demands by becoming anxious, obsessive, and moralistic (Grinker, Miller, Sabshin, Nunn, and Nunnally, 1961). The actual development of manic-depressive psychosis usually takes place after some important and unpleasant event occurs in the person's life. The common events which precipitate this type of psychotic behavior are the death of someone close to the individual, a major difficulty in the person's life work, or an unsuccessful interpersonal relationship, such as a failing marriage.

Tom S. was a Vietnam veteran who entered a large state university. He maintained a B average and was better than most at a number of sports, including tennis and wrestling. His interpersonal relationships were somewhat stormy, in that he would enter into intense friendships which tended to last only a matter of months and then would begin to deteriorate in a series of arguments and other unpleasant scenes. He often felt that someone had insulted him; he would complain about an aloof professor who failed to speak to him, a sales clerk who ignored him while waiting on someone else, or a friend who he felt was gossiping about him behind his back.

The true extent of his problems did not become known until he began writing a sociology term paper on ethnic groups in the United States. Tom's paper dealt with what he called the international Jewish conspiracy to control the world. He told his surprised instructor that he had been gathering evidence for several years which proved conclusively that the Zionist movement, the CIA, the Swiss bankers, and the three major television networks were all part of the Jewish master plan. He had an enormous collection of newspaper and magazine clippings which he felt were convincing proof for his theory.

Because Tom's earlier work had been of high quality, the instructor made an appointment to talk to him and try to convince him that his ideas did not make sense. During this meeting, Tom became very agitated and confided that Jewish agents were, in fact, aware of his knowledge and had been following him for months. He was convinced that his room was bugged, and he was afraid to use the telephone. He decided that the instructor was too stupid to understand. Attempts to get him to seek psychological help were not successful, and he dropped out of school.

Paranoia literally means "beyond reason." **Paranoid disorders** involve highly organized conceptual systems which are characterized by delusions of persecution and of reference. The individual sees himself at the center of a vast, hostile environment in which some person or group is plotting to do him harm. Though the delusional system may seem utterly fantastic to most other people, it usually has internal logic. That is, if you could accept the basic idea, as well as the type of evidence the paranoid individual is willing to accept, then the various elements would fit together. Also, the person's emotions are appropriate reactions to what he believes is going on. Beyond the area of the individual's delusion, he tends to function very well. On all other topics, the paranoid person can think logically and perform his job, often with a great deal of intelligence and general ability.

One interpretation of paranoid ideas is that they represent an extreme form of denial of one's own impulses and a projection of them onto others. Most often, there is unconscious hostility, which is denied and then attributed to someone else. "I have no hostile feelings, but those other people are plotting against me; therefore, anything I do to them is justifiable self-defense." Such beliefs lead to a suspicious and lonely existence, because no one can be completely trusted. Any difficulty or failure can be explained on the basis of enemies who plot against you or false friends who betray you. With impulses other than hostility, the paranoid delusion can take a slightly different form. For example, a female who denies her sexual needs can project them onto those around her. In this instance, she may believe that most men are lusting after her, trying to undress her with their eyes, or plotting seduction or rape. Acquaintances or even strangers may continually seem to be giving her secret indications of their sexual desire. Depending on her emotional reaction to these supposed needs of others, her delusions may be more of grandeur than of persecution. Still another form that paranoid disorders may take is jealousy, as when an individual assumes that a loved one has rejected him and is secretly

Paranoid Disorder: Why Are They All Against Me?

Paranoia: A Case History

I Don't Hate Them; They Hate Me

FIGURE 10–11 Humphrey Bogart as Captain Queeg. Captain Queeg's delusions of persecution and of reference are by now classic. In the famous courtroom scene of *The Caine Mutiny*, Queeg even defends the internal logic of his delusional system. (The Bettmann Archive; © 1953 by Columbia Pictures Corporation.)

seeing someone else. This particular reaction can lead to spying on the supposed guilty party, wild accusations, or even acts of aggression against the loved one.

The tendency toward paranoia is believed to be formed in early life, and Freudian theory traces it to the anal stage of development, in which rigidity and hostility are prominent. In fact, Freud (1922) proposed that repressed homosexuality was the underlying feature. An individual was said to deny love for someone of the same sex and conclude that it was hate (reaction formation); this hate was not accepted (denial), and these feelings were transferred from self to the other person (projection). Though the idea is an interesting one, research indicates no relationship between paranoia and homosexuality. Research on the early family life of paranoid individuals indicates that the parents tend to be cold, neglectful, or absent from the home (Bonner, 1951). Thus, indifferent parents can instill feelings of worthlessness and the general belief that others are not to be trusted.

Schizophrenic Disorders: Withdrawal from Reality

Schizophrenia: A Case History

Jake H. was a high school freshman whose behavior was often described as "a little weird" or "strange." In an English course that required a great deal of class discussion, he almost never participated. When asked a question, he would either say, "I don't know" or give a response not directly related to the topic being discussed. One of the other boys christened him Flaky Jakey, a nickname that stuck with him.

Jake's teachers described him as living in a world of his own, and he seemed to pay only fleeting attention to those around him. His behavior grew increasingly peculiar, and he sometimes giggled at inappropriate times during his classes. On one occasion, he asked to be excused from the room and then paused to announce that he went to the neuter room at home but the gender room at school. The teacher later figured out that he meant that bathrooms at home are used by both sexes (hence, they are neuter), while public rest rooms are segregated by sex (and hence have genders).

A gradual deterioration in his behavior led to disastrously low grades, and the school guidance office attempted to help him. For one appointment, he arrived over thirty minutes late, and with mud smeared on his face like Indian war paint. At this point, his parents were urged to obtain psychiatric advice. He was hospitalized and underwent treatment lasting several years.

The term **schizophrenia** means "split personality" or "split mind" and, as was pointed out earlier, is sometimes misused when what is meant is multiple personality. The split in schizophrenia involves that between emotion and behavior or between reality and fantasy. It is the most common and most severe of the psychoses. About half of the hospitalized mental patients are schizophrenics. Schizophrenia can take several forms. **Simple schizophrenia** is characterized by apathy, indifference, and passive withdrawal from society; **hebephrenic schizophrenia** is marked by grotesque silliness and childish behavior; and **catatonic schizophrenia** involves bodily immobility—the affected person may sit or stand in the same posture for hours. Schizophrenia may also involve characteristics of the other psychoses, as in **paranoid schizophrenia,** in which there are bizarre paranoid delusions, and **affective schizophrenia,** in which there are elements of manic-depressive psychosis and schizophrenia blended together. Our discussion will deal with some of the factors characterizing all five types.

Retreating to the World Inside

The most general characteristic is a withdrawal from reality into an internal world of fantasy. There is a short story by Conrad Aiken which depicts the process well; a young boy slowly disintegrates mentally as he imagines his surroundings gradually being blotted out by a never-ending snowfall (the story is imaginatively titled "Silent Snow, Secret Snow"). Often at the beginning of such a withdrawal process, the individual is seen as lazy and as lacking in interest. In experiments measuring reaction time (see Chapter 6), schizophrenics are considerably slower than normal individuals in giving a response after a stimulus is presented (Shakow, 1963). A schizophrenic individual appears indifferent and is likely to respond to decision-making situations by saying, "I don't care." When they must distinguish between relevant and irrelevant information, schizophrenics perform especially poorly; they seem to be unable to select what is important (Cash, Neale, and Cromwell, 1972). Gradually, they become more and more aloof and isolated from others. The tendency to be more concerned with one's own personal thoughts and wishes than with objective reality is called **autism.** The withdrawal and concentration on internal events lead the individual to behave in ways that are

FIGURE 10–12 Two catatonic schizophrenics. These people have reduced their activity—and hence their interactions with the world—to a minimum. The immobility they assume can last for hours (even in the uncomfortable positions shown here). (From Mayer-Gross, W., Slater, E., and Roth, M.: *Clinical Psychiatry.* London: Cassell, 1960.)

inappropriate from the viewpoint of outsiders. Schizophrenics also frequently experience hallucinations, delusions, and disturbed patterns of speech.

Schizophrenia often begins when the individual is quite young; in fact, it was first called **dementia praecox,** which means youthful mental deterioration. Interestingly enough, high school yearbooks have been used to predict who would later be diagnosed as schizophrenic; among the predictors were failure to participate in student government, special-interest clubs, or publications by future schizophrenics (Barthell and Holmes, 1968). Some investigators (for example, Kantor and Winder, 1959) believe that there are two distinct forms of schizophrenia, one inherited (**process schizophrenia**) and one which is a learned response to environmental stress (**reactive schizophrenia**). Only the reactive type responds well to treatment. Evidence that at least some forms of schizophrenia have a genetic basis is quite strong. As with manic-depressive psychosis, the more closely two individuals are related genetically, the more likely it is that if one develops schizophrenia, the other will also (Kallmann, Falek, Hurzeler, and Erlenmeyer-Kimling, 1964). For example, if one identical twin develops schizophrenia, the likelihood of the other twin also developing schizophrenia is much higher than is true for fraternal twins (Gottesman and Shields, 1972). Studies of adopted children indicate that the offspring of schizophrenic parents have a better than average chance of developing this psychosis even though they spend their entire lives with normal foster parents (Kety, Rosenthal, Wender, and Schulzinger, 1971). Other influences are also clear. Social class is found to be a related factor, in that schizophrenia is more common at low socioeconomic levels than at high ones (Suinn, 1970). For example, among individuals receiving psychiatric care, less than half of those classified in the wealthy (business and professional) classes were diagnosed as schizophrenic, but the vast majority of unskilled laborers received that diagnosis (Hollingshead and Redlich, 1958). Many studies have reported that specific types of family interactions increase the likelihood that schizophrenia will develop. Such studies have identified several characteristics of the **schizophrenogenic parent** (that is, one who is said to induce severe conflict and hence gives rise to schizophrenic responses in the child). Such parents continually place children in what is called a **double bind** (see Figure 10–13). This is a situation in which the child faces conflicting demands, as when a boy is told never to fight and yet at the same time must never act like a coward. Whatever he does, he is criticized for not meeting one of the demands (Bateson,

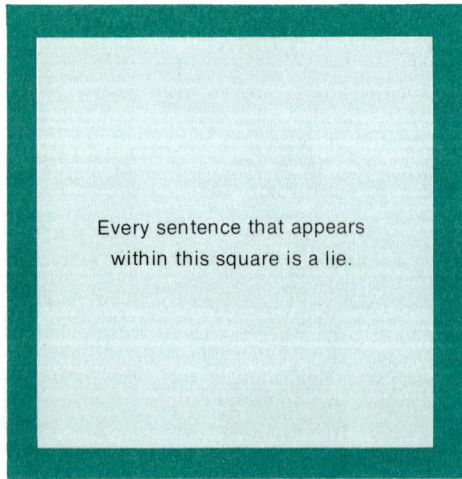

Every sentence that appears
within this square is a lie.

FIGURE 10–13 Some investigators such as Gregory Bateson and his colleagues report that schizophenics tend to have parents who often placed them in a "double bind," a situation involving two inconsistent demands. The individual can respond to one or the other demand, but he is criticized either way for failing to meet the opposite one. The puzzling message shown here illustrates a double bind. Do you think the sentence is true or false? What is wrong with either choice?

Jackson, Haley, and Weakland, 1956). Such parents have been found to be inconsistent in their treatment of the child; for example, a mother may be both aloof and at the same time overinvolved in running the child's life (Mark, 1958). Such findings have led Laing (1964) and others to propose that schizophrenic behavior is simply a strategy for dealing with an impossible situation. With contradictory pressures from the environment, withdrawal represents one possible response to unreasonable external pressures.

Whatever the genetic predisposition or family background of schizophrenic individuals, one aspect of their functioning tends to stand out—their behavior is relatively unaffected by such positive reinforcers as praise or approval. It has been suggested that their early socialization experiences are such as to bring about this insensitivity to social rewards. Obviously, one's interpersonal behavior would be badly affected by this characteristic. It has recently been shown, however, that schizophrenic patients can be *taught* to respond to praise, that they can learn to be reinforced by it. Caulfield and Martin (1976) used a simple reaction time task on which a tone sounded whenever the patient was doing badly. When they did well, the tone stopped just as a screen lighted up with the word GOOD. Following a series of such trials, these patients were found to respond to "good" as a reinforcer—though they had not done so prior to the experimental sessions. Potentially, this behavioral change could lead to much more adaptive social interactions.

CONDUCT DISORDERS: SOCIALLY UNACCEPTABLE BEHAVIOR

There are several types of behavior which are somewhat different from those previously discussed. They are defined as problems primarily because they cause distress to society. To take an extreme example, if an individual were free of conflicts and anxieties, and in good contact with reality, yet followed a practice of molesting girl hitch-hikers, how would you classify him? He's not necessarily neurotic or psychotic, and he may not even use defense mechanisms any more frequently than the rest of us. He is, however, engaging in behavior which harms others and is condemned by our society. Behavior patterns of this variety are known as conduct disorders. We will examine two very common and very different examples of such maladjustment.

Psychopathic Personality: Life without a Superego

Psychopathic Personality: A Case History

Bill G. was an undergraduate at a prestigious private university. He was attractive in appearance, charming in his interactions with others, and completely lacking in ethical and moral values. Throughout his school years, he had been the object of periodic concern on the part of teachers, neighbors, and shopkeepers in his home town. Several incidents were somehow smoothed over without major damage being done. Once when he was caught cheating in high school, he talked his teacher into giving him another chance by pretending that he was distressed about his parents' constant quarreling. The teacher subsequently discovered that Bill's father died when he was three years old, and that his mother had not remarried. A year later, he was caught in a downtown department store as he slipped an expensive cigarette lighter into his pocket. Bill created a scene and claimed that it was unfair to have store detectives watching customers unless they were in uniform. His mother was called; she paid for the lighter and promised that her son would be kept away from that store in the future. No charges were filed.

Bill's latest problem came when the girl he had been dating discovered that she was pregnant. He told her to do whatever she wanted about the baby, but he had no interest in talking about the problem. She had an abortion a week later (financed by Bill's grandfather); Bill was taking a between semesters vacation with another girl at the time. A counselor who knew him fairly well once told Bill that by the age of 30 he would either be a great success in some field such as business or politics or that he would be in prison. Bill replied that no one would ever be smart enough to convict him of any crime.

Charmers, Con Men, and Convicts

An individual who fails to acquire an internal code of values, is not able to feel remorse or guilt, is not willing to tolerate delayed gratification, and who responds to others only superficially is designated a **psychopathic personality.**

The life pattern of a psychopathic individual depends in large part on such accidental circumstances as family income, natural talent, and physical appearance. Given a fortunate combination of wealth, ability, and good looks, a psychopath is likely to be very successful socially and to be described in glowing terms by those who meet him. Such a person can impress teachers, employers, and members of the opposite sex. To a psychopath, people are simply objects to be manipulated, and lack of genuine concern apparently makes it easier to deal with others in a skillful, dishonest manner. A psychopath can borrow money, for instance, fail to pay it back, apologize profusely if necessary, and then plead for a second chance. When he expresses feelings such as love, or grief, or remorse, the psychopath is playing a role rather than expressing genuine feelings. Anyone who is taken in by the sincerely expressed lies of such a person is often surprised and disappointed when the truth is discovered. The psychopath leaves a trail of disappointed friends and heartbroken lovers; these individuals are shocked to learn that they were used only as objects. Psychopaths are unlikely to work very hard at school or at jobs, but many are able to do very well with a mixture of ability, dishonesty, getting others to do their work, and pure charm. There is a tendency to ignore the rules of the game that most of the rest of us follow, and any kind of authority is resented. A promising career may suddenly fall apart, however, when the effort becomes too great, and the psychopath impulsively moves on to greener pastures. One reason for the impulsiveness and the restless switching of jobs, lovers, and locations is that psychopathic individuals have little tolerance for sameness and must constantly seek new stimulation (Quay, 1965; Whitehill et al., 1976). Data show that such individuals prefer novelty and complexity to a greater extent than do comparable individuals who are not classified as psychopaths (Skrzypek, 1969).

A psychopath seems to engage in behavior that is not in his own best interest, but he doesn't feel anxious about it. The relatively low anxiety level of psychopaths has been demonstrated in laboratory experiments. In a learning situation involving electric shock, the galvanic skin response of normal subjects was much greater than that of psychopaths (Lykken, 1957). Because of this difference in anxiety level, psychopaths do not learn to avoid pain as well as normals do (Hare, 1970). Literally, they are less able than others to profit from their painful mistakes. Interestingly enough, when anxiety is experimentally aroused in these individuals by injecting them with adrenalin, their ability to learn in such situations improves (Schachter and Latané, 1964).

A less fortunately endowed psychopath can follow a much more unacceptable pattern of behavior. He may turn easily to crime as the most direct way to obtain what he desires. Theft, rape, and murder are reasonable activities if one is not held back by moral values, has no genuine feelings for other people, and does not know what it is to feel genuine guilt or sorrow. All too often the television news carries reports of an individual who has been caught after a series of robberies or vicious murders. When an interviewer asks if the

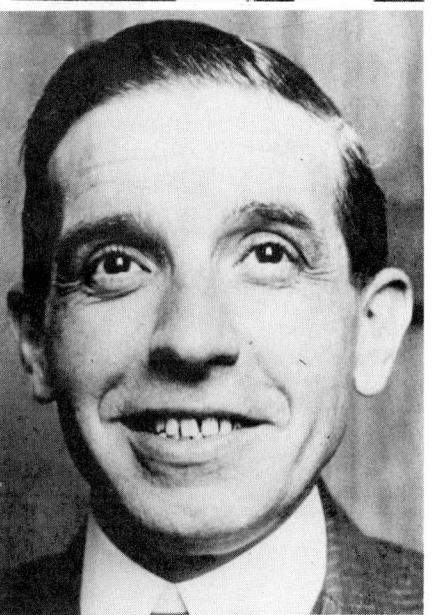

FIGURE 10–14 Many con-artists display characteristics of the psychopathic personality. They often possess smooth, appealing interpersonal
skills that make it possible to convince others of their sincerity and
honesty. It seems that the absence of genuine concern for people makes it
easier to deceive them and to manipulate their behavior.

Philip Musica (top) put together a complex of illegal deals involving
fake businesses that served as covers for his actual operations. During
Prohibition he formed a hair-tonic company, purchased alcohol that supposedly was to be added to the product, and then sold the alcohol to boot-
leggers. Profits from this operation were used to buy into a respectable
drug firm, which allowed him to convince other businessmen to enter
into a merger out of which he embezzled over $600,000. He committed
suicide when it was revealed that his drug firm was a complete hoax.

Charles Ponzi (bottom) was able to deceive investors who hoped to
get rich quick. Though he was in the words of one employee "a financial
idiot" who could hardly add, he worked out a scheme in which he told
people they could double their money in 90 days. He convinced a few
small investors and actually paid them the promised interest (using their
money); he urged them to tell their friends about the good deal. As hundreds rushed to get in on the opportunity, Ponzi simply used the new
money to make the interest payments. About 40,000 investors gave him
their life savings, and he soon was taking in $200,000 a day. When a
financial columnist wrote that the entire enterprise seemed questionable,
Ponzi sued for $500,000. This brazen confidence was enhanced by his
20-room mansion, chauffeur-driven car, gold-handled canes, and diamond
stickpins. At one point, he carried two suitcases containing $3,000,000 to
the Hanover Trust Company and bought controlling interest in it. Like
any "pyramid" money scheme, this one eventually collapsed, and Ponzi
went to prison. After a Florida land swindle, he was deported to Italy,
where he worked for Mussolini until he stole enough money to run away
to Argentina. (Photo credit: United Press International.)

person regrets what he has done, the suspect frequently seems faintly puzzled
or amused by the question.

Today, most of those working in the field of psychopathology accept the
idea that the problem lies in early childhood experiences. For example, during
the period of conscience development, if the individual is ignored or rejected
by his parents, he has little reason to strive to adopt their moral values. Further,
such parents instill a life-long belief that other people are not to be trusted or
loved. It has been found that more psychopaths have lost a parent before the
age of five than is true of normal individuals (Greer, 1964). Psychopaths are
frequently found to have been neglected or rejected by their fathers, through
alcoholism, divorce, or desertion (McCord and McCord, 1964). If a child has
cold, hostile, or neglectful parents, he cannot feel close to other people or
even dependent on them; in other words, people are not a source of reinforce-

ment (Bandura and Walters, 1959). The child who experiences no reinforcement from others is never able to go beyond the early tendency to seek only immediate pleasure. Such a person will also seek to avoid immediate pain, even if the avoidance leads to greater pain later on. For example, would you be willing to get an injection today to prevent a painful illness next month? Most of us would, however much we dislike it. Psychopaths prefer the delayed pain, even if it's a matter of a few seconds delay in a laboratory experiment (Hare, 1966).

Alcoholism: Anxiety Reduction From a Bottle

Alcoholism: A Case History

Timothy R. is a psychology professor at a small midwestern college. He is middle-aged and fairly unhappy about his career and his deteriorating personal life. Over the past several years, his friends noticed that Professor R. was gradually losing control in his use of alcohol. He arrived at parties with a "head start" by taking a few drinks at home. Occasionally, he drank so much during the evening that he would be unable to talk intelligently or even coherently on any topic. His wife frequently had to plead with him to leave, helping him to their car before he fell soundly asleep. At one New Year's party, he became angry during a political discussion, started a loud argument, and broke a lamp in the scuffle that followed. On all such occasions, he awoke the next day with no memory of the evening's events, and he felt extremely depressed when his behavior was described to him.

His wife eventually left him, taking their teen-aged daughter with her. His life style has become even more erratic, and he frequently appears to be somewhat high during his lectures. He confessed to a friend that he usually starts the day with a couple of shots—he even tried vodka on his corn flakes one morning—and maintains himself during the day with frequent sips from a bottle hidden in his office desk. Professor R. is facing the possibility of dismissal from his job and has been urged to make contact with Alcoholics Anonymous.

Days of Wine and Roses

Many of the behaviors discussed in this chapter are conceptualized as ways of responding to stress, ways of reducing anxiety. Perhaps the easiest way to reduce anxiety, however, is to consume some substance which has the power to control anxiety physiologically (see Chapter 2). In most human societies, for at least the last five thousand years alcohol has served that function (Roueche, 1962). Alcohol is a depressant drug that acts on the central nervous system. It brings feelings of relaxation and can deaden minor aches and pains. Because alcohol tends to act first on the central nervous system, the reduction of inhibitions and anxieties usually leads to feelings of elation and to energetic activity. There is less self-criticism and self-doubt. In an experimental setting, alcohol has been shown to increase an individual's interest in exercising power over others; when TAT stories (see Chapter 9) were written before and after subjects drank cocktails, stories of personal power were more frequent in the post-alcohol condition (McClelland, Davis, Kalin, and Wanner, 1972). Drinking apparently leads to greater concern with prestige, aggression, and sexual conquests. With greater amounts of alcohol in the system, the depressant effect spreads and begins to interfere with speech and with motor activity; the individual starts to slur his words and to stumble. Next there is general fatigue and finally sleep when the person "passes out." Still greater amounts of alcohol can lead to death.

In the United States, as in many other countries, alcohol is the most widely accepted drug and one on which we spend an incredible amount of money. Other cultures, and subgroups within our culture, seek alternative ways to obtain the same general anxiety-reducing effects; marijuana use is an obvious example. At every socioeconomic level, alcohol has become the accepted (and often expected) lubricant for interpersonal relationships. It is difficult for many individuals to imagine a social occasion in which the participants interact without a drink in their hands. It is also difficult to avoid alcohol. As Kessel and Walton (1965, p. 11) observe, "Though we frown on drunkards, we are suspicious of teetotalers. Over a glass we enjoy old friends and make new ones, proclaim our loyalties, discuss affairs, negotiate and seal bargains." There are, however, marked cultural influences on the amount of alcohol consumed and on the frequency with which individuals become alcoholic. For example, alcoholism occurs at very different rates in different countries, as may be seen in Figure 10–15. In the United States, alcoholism is more common among those with middle-class backgrounds than among those with lower-class backgrounds (McCord, McCord, and Gudeman, 1960).

Interestingly enough, it is often suggested that, while heavy drinking is harmful, moderate amounts of alcohol may be beneficial to one's psychological health (for example, Dollard and Miller, 1950). The *Book of Proverbs* proposes giving "wine to those that be of heavy heart." That is, minor worries and anxieties can be soothed, and the individual can relax much more easily. Long-range studies show that the moderate drinker has a longer life expectancy than either the heavy drinker or the nondrinker. It has been reported that elderly patients in retirement homes are more contented and better adjusted when they are allowed a modest amount of wine or beer each evening (*Time*, 1970). Anyone who has enjoyed a cold beer on a hot day, a dry martini after a day of problems, or a good wine with dinner can testify to the pleasant qualities of alcohol. There is, of course, a darker side.

First, even moderate amounts of alcohol can begin to interfere with perceptual and motor skills, so that one's ability to do complex tasks such as driving an automobile is impaired. It is estimated that in over 50 per cent of automobile accidents, alcohol is involved. Second, it is very easy to rely on the pleasant effects of alcohol to "solve" problems and to bring about happiness; over time, more and more alcohol is consumed, until drinking becomes a way of life. With large quantities of alcohol, there can be negative effects on the individual's health, sexual ability, work, finances, and interpersonal relationships. Pregnant women who drink heavily are much more likely to have a baby with physical or mental birth defects than are nondrinking women. Chronic drinking can even

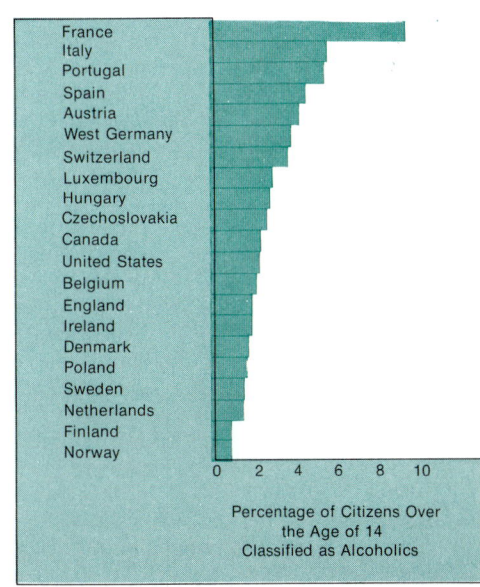

FIGURE 10–15 Cultural influences apparently play an important role in determining alcoholism. It may be seen in the figure that the rate of alcoholism varies widely among European and North American nations, with France having the largest percentage of alcoholics and Finland and Norway the smallest percentage. It should be noted that these figures are based on a definition of alcoholism as the consumption of more than 150 milliliters (about 5 ounces) of alcohol per day. (Adapted from deLint and Schmidt, 1971.)

lead to psychotic behavior, complete with hallucinations, loss of memory, and damage to various organs of the body. Withdrawal of alcohol at this stage can result in **delirium tremens,** which involves bodily trembling, disorientation, and hallucinations, such as seeing animals or feeling insects crawling over the skin. (The notions of seeing "pink elephants" and having "the shakes" constitute the popular impression of this condition.) Clearly, alcohol itself can create more serious problems than the ones that brought on the original drinking.

Many writers classify and tabulate the number of occasional drinkers, moderate drinkers, heavy drinkers, and alcoholics. It is the last of these categories that carries with it the label **alcoholism,** and it is currently applied to about five million individuals in the United States (Chafetz, 1967). It should be noted that the lines dividing each of these groups are more or less arbitrary, and that definitions of what constitutes alcoholism vary. The most useful definitions are based not on amount of alcohol consumed but on the effects of drinking on the individual's life. For example, an alcoholic has been described as one who drinks excessively, is unable to control how much is drunk, has mental confusion as a function of drinking, and whose work and interpersonal relationships suffer as a result of the drinking (Suinn, 1970). With that definition, very heavy drinkers in history such as General Ulysses S. Grant and Prime Minister Winston Churchill would escape the label of alcoholic. This distinction between those who drink heavily but nevertheless are able to function well in their professions raises the possibility that there is more than one type of alcoholic individual. For example, Jellinek (1960) suggests that there are five distinct types of alcoholism which should be differentiated, as shown in Table 10–1. Studies of personality characteristics indicate that there may be as many as seven distinctly different groups of individuals who are lumped together as "alcoholics" (Nerviano, 1976).

TABLE 10–1   Classification of Alcoholism

Type of Alcoholism	Typical Behavior
Alpha	Heavy drinking based on the psychological effects of alcohol. The individual can control the amount consumed and shows no tendency to increase his intake over time; the only problems this causes are interpersonal ones.
Beta	Similar to the alpha type but causes the individual some personal distress, such as chronic indigestion or cirrhosis of the liver. Thus, there is damage to the person's nutrition, interference with his work, and a decrease in his life span.
Gamma	Some physical as well as psychological dependence, as indicated by loss of control and drinking self into stupor, craving for alcohol, and withdrawal symptoms when alcohol is not available. Larger and larger amounts must be consumed to have any effect. This is the most common type of alcoholism in the United States and Canada.
Delta	Similar to the gamma type except that there is no loss of control over drinking but the individual constantly craves drink. In wine-drinking countries, such as France, this type of alcoholism is the most common.
Epsilon	The individual goes on long drinking bouts that last for days or even weeks and then sobers up and drinks nothing until the next drinking spree.

The five types of alcoholism and the behavior associated with each, as defined by Jellinek (1960).

Studies of alcoholics indicate that as children, they are tense and unhappy and have cold, indifferent mothers (Jones, 1968, 1971). As adults, drinking proves useful to them primarily as a way to relieve anxiety in social situations and to gain a temporary feeling of self-confidence in dealing with others (Blume and Sheppard, 1967). Experiments show that animals, too, will learn to use alcohol as a way of reducing experimentally created anxiety. For example, in one study, cats were shocked at their feeding box and made too anxious to approach it and eat. They were able to do so, however, after having a "kitty cocktail" (Masserman and Yum, 1946).

Beyond the cultural and psychological factors that influence drinking behavior, it also appears that there are physiological differences in susceptibility to alcoholism. In the laboratory, it is possible to breed animals who like alcohol very much and others who tend to avoid it (Rodgers and McClearn, 1962). It has been suggested that nutritional deficiencies may account for individual differences in responding to alcohol (Leavitt, 1974). There is also the possibility that the different types of alcoholism discussed earlier have different causes. Jellinek (1960) has proposed that the alpha type (see Table 10–1) may be psychological in origin, while some organic problem may underly the remaining types. An assumption that has grown out of the physiological explanation of alcoholism is that alcoholics cannot control their drinking because "one drink inevitably leads to more." Is this so? An experiment compared the responses of alcoholics and social drinkers who were given either plain tonic or vodka and tonic; half of each group was told the truth and half was told that the drink was the opposite of what they actually received (Marlatt, Demming, and Reid, 1973). During a "taste test," each subject could drink as much as he wished. Neither the actual presence of vodka nor alcoholism influenced how much liquid was consumed; both the alcoholics *and* the nonalcoholics in the group who believed the drinks contained alcohol drank more than those who believed they had plain tonic, and no alcoholics "lost control" after their first drink. Thus it does not appear that one drink necessarily leads an alcoholic to continue drinking. In any event, it is clear that a complex interplay of cultural, psychological, and physiological factors contributes to the development of alcoholism.

Now that you have been introduced to the major varieties of behavioral maladjustment, perhaps it would be helpful to consider a few problems raised by the medical approach, which is the basis for using diagnostic labels.

The application of the medical model has some very unfortunate effects. Even though most psychologists agree that the concept of a "disease" is not an appropriate one to deal with behavioral maladjustment, we still tend to treat the categories as though they consist of genuine and distinct groups of people. It is easy enough to define and describe the "typical" obsessive-compulsive, paranoid, or psychopath. It is very difficult, however, to find one. Rather than manifesting their behavior in pure "types," maladjusted individuals tend to represent a bewildering mixture of characteristics. For this reason, there is far from perfect agreement among professionals when they must arrive at a diagnosis of a specific patient. An example of the problem is provided in the case histories presented in this chapter. Each is true, and the individuals described represent disguised versions of actual patients, colleagues, students, friends, and relatives. In order to provide *pure* illustrations, however, some elements had to be left out because they did not precisely fit the diagnostic label being described. In a few instances, the behaviors of two individuals were blended into one, again to fit a diagnostic label. You should perhaps think of such labels only as ways of describing certain common maladaptive behaviors and not as the identification of clear-cut groups.

FITTING REAL PEOPLE INTO ARBITRARY CATEGORIES: BEHAVIORAL DIFFERENCES VERSUS DIAGNOSTIC GROUPS

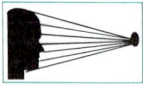

FOCUS
ON
RESEARCH: *If You Are in the Hospital, You Must Be Sick*

Some of the problems underlying the medical model of maladjustment are highlighted by an imaginative field study undertaken by Rosenhan (1973). The following scene was repeated in numerous psychiatric hospitals in various parts of the country. In each instance, a normal individual sought admission as a mental patient.

The research confederate reported to the admission desk of the hospital. He pretended that he heard voices which said "empty," "hollow," and "thud." Everything else he said about his life and about his behavior was true. As soon as he was admitted, he never again said that he heard voices, and he behaved in his usual fashion.

All of the hospitals admitted these individuals. Throughout the period of hospitalization, no staff member ever suspected that the person was actually normal, though several of the real patients detected it. It should be noted that each of the eight confederates who took part in the study was carefully screened to make sure that no adjustment problems existed.

As you might expect, the results of this study were quite upsetting to many psychologists and psychiatrists who work in mental hospitals. It was pointed out that Rosenhan's procedure was unfair, and that all he demonstrated was that someone could successfully fake mental illness for a short period of time. The fact that actual patients sometimes guessed the truth was attributed to the unusual behavior of the confederates—they kept research notes to record their experiences; patients saw them writing this material whereas the professional staff did not. More generally, the study was criticized because it was not seen as relevant to the real problems of establishing the reliability and validity of psychiatric diagnosis (Farber, 1975; Spitzer, 1975). In reply, Rosenhan (1975) argued that the present system of classification is nevertheless bad because (1) it has been shown in many studies that clinical practitioners cannot agree among themselves about which label to apply to which patient, and (2) psychiatric diagnosis is not useful in the way that medical diagnosis is supposed to be because the diagnostic label does not indicate a specific treatment to be followed.

Whatever direction Rosenhan's arguments take—and whatever may be said in reply—the basic findings suggest that the very notion of diagnosing mental illness and of drawing lines to separate those who are "normal" and "abnormal" may be open to question. It would seem that any of us can be perceived as a mental patient if we happen to find ourselves in the appropriate setting. Such a possibility has led many investigators to seek more objective ways to diagnose maladjustment. In one such attempt, Skinner, Reed, and Jackson (1976) have utilized a personality test—the Differential Personality Inventory—to identify the basic characteristics that are associated with various types of maladaptive behavior. This method is not based on the traditional psychiatric categories that have been described in this chapter; rather, the dimensions deal with actual behavioral characteristics. For example, one dimension consists of rebellious, impulsive behavior and socially deviant attitudes on one extreme and a concern with health and the expression of bodily complaints on the other. Male prison inmates tend to score on the rebellious end of the dimension while chronic psychiatric patients tend to score on the hypochondriacal end of the dimension. The potential advantage of this approach is that an individual's position on eight of these dimensions can be objectively measured, and the resulting set of scores can be used to differentiate normally functioning individuals from such malfunctioning groups as alcoholics, prison inmates, and psychiatric patients. It is hoped that these methods of diagnosis will lead to better ways of identifying and classifying those whose behavior is truly maladjusted.

FIGURE 10–16 The patient in this cartoon instantly assumes that the doctor's labeling of his behavior "explains" it. Recently, psychologists themselves have begun to question the value of assigning labels to "abnormal" behavior—so much so that the term "abnormal" is now subject to criticism. ("Friends and Romans" cartoon by Tom Isbell; © 1975 by Continental Features, Inc.)

Even if the medical model were a good one, the present set of labels is not particularly useful, because there is too much disagreement among psychiatrists and clinical psychologists in applying them to specific people. That is, the same individual can receive very different diagnoses as he goes from one therapist to another (Temerlin, 1968; Ullmann and Krasner, 1975). When the labels are *perceived* as important, however, they can have a crucial effect on how an individual behaves and on how others respond to him. For example, if you are labeled "paranoid," both you and those around you expect you to behave in a paranoid fashion. Szasz (1970) goes so far as to suggest that mental illness is largely a myth, and that we apply the labels, influence those who are labeled to behave in the expected way, and lock them up if they bother us too much. From his point of view, such medical diagnosis is simply one of the ways in which society uses force to bring about conformity. To take an extreme example, when a Russian writer criticizes the government, he may be placed in a mental hospital for treatment because "anyone who holds such ideas must be crazy."

The diagnostic labels cause another problem. The disease analogy suggests that you have a particular psychopathology or that you do not (as when you either do or do not have the mumps). The behaviors described in this chapter do not really fit an either/or system such as that. Each characteristic of maladjustment falls along a continuum, and most such characteristics are represented in each of us in varying degrees from time to time. Thus, there are degrees of anxiety, of paranoid suspiciousness, and of psychopathic selfishness which we all experience. Most of us can see some aspects of ourselves in each of the case histories. Among the very common questions that students ask a psychology professor after revealing something about themselves or even after taking part in a research project are: "Am I normal?" "Do you think I'm maladjusted?" "I'm not crazy, am I?" Though we tend not to say this, perhaps the most accurate answer would be, "Yes, each of us is somewhat maladjusted and, part of the time at least, a little crazy." Whether we are defined that way by others and get an official label tends to be a matter of how severe the symptoms are, how much distress we cause ourselves and others, and the specific circumstances in which we find ourselves.

The basis of psychopathology seems most generally to be a combination of early determining factors plus current stress. Early experiences tend to shape the way in which we handle problems of anxiety, rejection, disappointment, loss, frustration, and so on. In some specific instances, there also seem to be inherited tendencies toward certain responses to pressure (for example, schizophrenic behavior). Given these learned and inherited predispositions, the stage is set for responding to stress with a characteristic style or set of responses. Of course, the very same set of predisposing factors might lead to severe psychopathology in one person and to tolerable personality quirks in another. The difference depends on the specific problems each person faces during their lives. Sometimes, "abnormal behavior" is a normal response to what is actually an abnormal situation. It seems clear that as stress increases, symptoms of maladjustment increase (Clum, 1976).

If we can learn to think of maladjustment as simply a particular way of responding to stress, perhaps we will be closer to understanding such behavior than was true when either the supernatural or the medical model was more widely accepted.

Summary

Maladjustment is defined as a socially inappropriate pattern of behavior which results in unhappiness for the individual and/or for others.

The earliest explanations of abnormal behavior pointed to supernatural powers; disturbed people were believed to be possessed by demons or to be special representatives of the gods. The European belief in witchcraft led to cruel treatment of the mentally ill and sometimes to execution. The **medical model,** in which **psychopathology** is conceptualized as a disease, is also an ancient idea, and it began to regain its popularity in the sixteenth century. Both Freud and the learning theorists contributed to the current psychological model, which describes abnormal behavior in terms of its function in *reducing anxiety.* **Defense mechanisms** are common strategies used to deal with anxiety and stress. They include **repression, reaction formation, displacement,** and **projection.**

When the level of stress is great and the coping mechanisms begin to cause problems of their own, various forms of **neurotic behavior** can be observed. **Hypochondriasis** is an exaggerated concern with one's health or one's own body. A **phobic reaction** consists of an unrealistic fear of some aspect of the environment. **Obsessive-compulsive** neurosis involves repetitive thoughts (*obsessions*) and repetitive behaviors (*compulsions*). **Dissociative reactions** are relatively rare disorders in which a portion of one's identity is repressed; the four types are **amnesia, fugue state, somnambulism,** and **multiple personality. Reactive depression** is an extended and debilitating unhappiness, an over-reaction to a sad event. An **anxiety reaction** occurs when the defenses fail and the individual is overwhelmed by worries and vague panic-causing fears.

Psychotic behavior represents the most severe form of psychopathology and is characterized by distortions in perception, thought patterns, emotions, and speech. In **manic-depressive psychosis,** there are enormous mood swings between a normal state and an unrealistic elation or an unrealistic depression (or sometimes both in sequence). **Paranoid** individuals believe themselves to be the victims of a conspiracy in which others are plotting against them or have sexual designs on them. The most common and most severe psychosis is **schizophrenia,** in which the individual withdraws from reality into an internal world of fantasy.

The conduct disorders include many forms of socially unacceptable behavior. An individual identified as a **psychopathic personality** has failed to acquire an internal code of values, does not feel anxiety or guilt, is not willing to postpone gratification, and responds to other people only as objects to be manipulated. **Alcoholism** refers to several varieties of heavy drinking and seems to be determined by psychological, cultural, and physiological factors.

Our language of maladjustment is based on the medical model. Among the problems this raises is the fact that actual people do not fit the classification scheme very well; *pure* cases are hard to find. Also, maladjusted behavior falls along a continuum and is not an either/or matter. There are varying degrees of each type of behavior discussed in this chapter. The basis of abnormal functioning seems to be a combination of early determining factors (learning experiences and genetic predispositions) plus current stress. Maladjustment can be conceptualized simply as a particular way of responding to stress.

Suggested Readings

Davison, G. C., and Neale, J. M.: *Abnormal Psychology: An Experimental Clinical Approach.* New York: John Wiley and Sons, 1974.

    An interesting and well-illustrated undergraduate text which covers the field of abnormal psychology very thoroughly. Much of the emphasis is on current research.

Gottesman, I., and Shields, J.: *Schizophrenia and Genetics.* New York: Academic Press, 1972.

    A difficult book for the beginner but one which presents convincing evidence concerning the genetic basis of this type of psychosis.

McClelland, D. C., Davis, W. N., Kalin, R., and Wanner, E.: *The Drinking Man.* New York: Free Press, 1972.

    A presentation of an unusual theoretical and experimental approach to alcoholism. Basically, alcoholism is hypothesized to result from a frustrated need for power.

Rosenhan, D. L.: On being sane in insane places. *Science,* 1973, 179, 250–258.

    The report of the interesting and frightening field study in which normal individuals were admitted to mental hospitals. They were not detected by the professional personnel, but other patients occasionally figured out the deception.

Ullmann, L. P., and Krasner, L.: *A Psychological Approach to Abnormal Behavior.* Englewood Cliffs, New Jersey: Prentice-Hall, 1975.

    An excellent undergraduate text which emphasizes the historical context of current ideas about abnormality and the way in which learning theory can be applied to explain maladjustment.

Some journals that regularly publish papers on maladjusted behavior:

    American Journal of Psychiatry
    Archives of General Psychiatry
    International Journal of Social Psychiatry
    Journal of Abnormal Psychology
    Journal of Clinical Psychology
    Journal of Consulting and Clinical Psychology
    Journal of Nervous and Mental Disease
    Psychosomatic Medicine
    Quarterly Journal of Studies on Alcohol

11 Psychotherapy: Altering Maladjusted Behavior

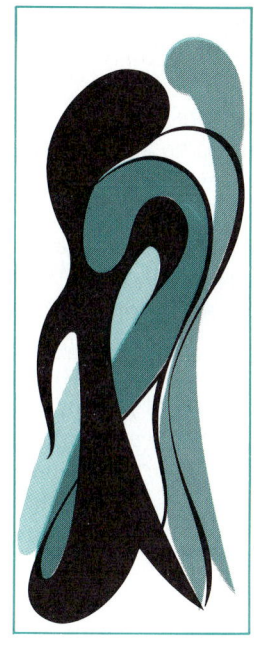

In the previous chapter, many varieties of maladjustment were described — some relatively minor and some extremely serious. Now we turn to the issue of what can be done to change such behavior. The answer depends in large part on how behavioral problems are conceptualized. If one believes that "the devil made them do it," the logical procedure is to seek an exorcist, as we described in the last chapter. If it is thought that maladjustment is an illness, there should be a search for a medical cure. If it is decided that maladjustment is learned, it is reasonable to examine techniques that teach alternate behavior. We will examine several such explanations in the present chapter and describe the corresponding kinds of therapeutic techniques that have been developed.

Most of the emphasis in our discussion will be on **psychotherapy,** which includes various psychological techniques designed to change behavior. Many different institutions in our society are designed to bring about beneficial changes in behavior. Public schools attempt not only to teach facts and skills but also to instill those attitudes and values of importance to society. Religious institutions try to influence the moral and ethical aspects of our thoughts and our actions. Prisons are designed, theoretically at least, to change antisocial behavior into an acceptable life pattern. Government agencies try to persuade us to do such things as buy bonds, conserve energy, and fasten our seat belts.

All such activities rest on the fact that it is possible to say or do things to people which will bring about desired changes in their thoughts, feelings, motives, and behaviors. In much the same way, psychologists, psychiatrists, and others attempt to change thoughts, feelings, motives, and behaviors. Most often, the procedures they use involve some form of psychotherapy. Specifically, *psychotherapy is the application of psychological techniques by pro-*

371

fessionally trained individuals to change a socially inappropriate pattern of behavior into a more appropriate one.

Psychotherapy may seem to be a somewhat mysterious means for bringing about "mind control." As you will see in the present chapter, however, therapy is much like other interpersonal interactions. As we examine some of the procedures that have been developed over the past century, you may find many details that are familiar to you.

In describing this area of psychological activity, we will begin by looking at an alternative approach to behavior change, **biotherapy.** Attempts to alter behavior by means of electric shock, surgery, and drugs will be described. The first and perhaps best known type of psychotherapy, **insight therapy,** will then be discussed. Such therapy includes psychoanalysis as developed by Freud and the client-centered technique developed by Rogers. The influence of experimental psychology on clinical practice will be seen in the various therapies based on the apparent relationship between maladaptive behavior and learning. Procedures such as **counterconditioning, operant conditioning,** and **modeling** are utilized to bring about changes in specific behaviors. Another method to be considered is *therapy in groups,* in which several patients interact with one another under the guidance of one or more therapists. Finally, **community psychology** will be described. This approach to behavioral problems concentrates on bringing about changes in the everyday life settings in which maladjustment occurs and on delivering psychological help where it is most needed.

BIOTHERAPY: BODILY TREATMENTS TO CURE PSYCHOPATHOLOGY

In Chapter 10, it was noted that the medical model (or theory) of maladjustment led to ideas about how to help emotionally disturbed individuals by treating their bodies. In centuries past, the early biotherapies most often consisted of some application of pain, fear, or surprise in order to bring the individual "back to his senses." In Figure 11–1 you can see examples of these early attempts to reach the mind by way of the body. Patients were branded with hot irons, rotated at high speeds, swung from the ceiling in harnesses, and strapped into various devices that prevented all movement. It may come as no surprise to you to learn that none of these techniques was found to be particularly useful in bringing about the desired changes in behavior.

Though it now seems obvious that these early medical approaches were both cruel and ineffective, it should be remembered that each was carried out with the intention of helping the mentally ill. It was not until the 1930's however, that an effective biotherapy procedure was developed.

Electroconvulsive Therapy: Shock Treatment

In the early 1930's, it was observed that epileptics seldom develop schizophrenia and, conversely, that schizophrenics rarely develop epilepsy (Ullmann and Krasner, 1975). This observation led to the hypothesis that the seizures experienced in epilepsy might somehow interfere with the disordered thought processes of schizophrenia. If so, it might prove helpful to produce such seizures artificially in schizophrenic patients. In 1938, the use of electric shock as a treatment was first reported in Italy by Cerletti, and **electroconvulsive therapy** soon came into widespread use. In this therapy, a current of 500 to 900 milliamperes is passed between two electrodes attached to the patient's head. When the power reaches 70 to 150 volts, the patient has a seizure followed by a loss of consciousness (Friedberg, 1975). Other physicians achieve the same effect by injecting insulin until the patient goes into a coma, but the use of electricity has been the more popular way to induce seizures (Wortis, 1959). Typically, muscle relaxants are also administered in an attempt to prevent the patient from injuring himself during the seizures.

FIGURE 11–1   Some of the earliest approaches to psychotherapy were based on the idea that pain, fear, surprise, or physical restraint would be likely to bring a disturbed individual "back to his senses." Top left: Branding with a hot iron. Top right: Whirling rapidly. Bottom left: Swinging in suspended harness. Bottom right: Restraining all physical movements in a "tranquilizing chair." (Bottom right figure from the Library Company of Philadelphia; all others from the Bettman Archive.)

Over the next several decades, there was a great deal of research on this treatment process, and many patients underwent "shock treatments." The use of electroconvulsive therapy increased rapidly throughout the world, but began to decline in the late 1940's, in part because it proved to be somewhat unreliable as a way to treat mental illness (Maher, 1966). There were also several undesirable side effects, as studies of both animals and humans revealed. For example, a kind of amnesia is brought about by the treatment, in that recently learned material is forgotten (Cronholm and Ottosson, 1961). In one experiment, patients were shown a series of pictures and then asked to recognize them a day later; those who had received shock treatment in the meantime had difficulty in remembering which ones they had seen (Maher, McIntire, and

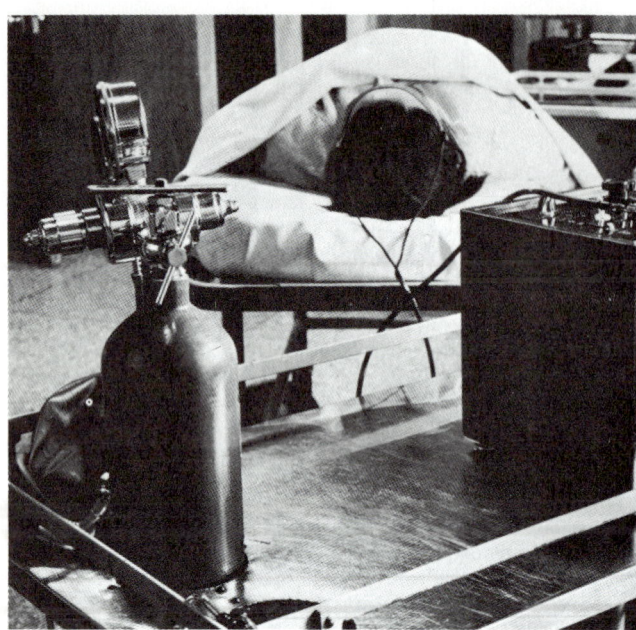

FIGURE 11–2 In electroconvulsive therapy, an electric current is passed between two electrodes attached to the patient's head. A sufficiently strong voltage induces a seizure and unconsciousness. (St. Louis Post Dispatch/Black Star Publishing Company.)

House, 1962). Although material learned in the distant past appears to be unaffected by shock, memory for material learned as long as three years before treatment may be impaired (Squire, Slater, and Chace, 1975). Even more serious is the fact that repeated treatments have been found to damage tissue in the central nervous system. For these reasons, some physicians propose that the use of shock treatments should be banned entirely (Friedberg, 1975).

Though there were many enthusiastic early reports of the wonders of electroconvulsive therapy, today such treatment is used primarily in cases of psychotic depression and other conditions involving acute mood changes. Even in these cases, there is still a mystery as to precisely how such therapy works and why it is effective (Fink, Kety, McGaugh, and Williams, 1974).

Psychosurgery: Slicing into the Brain

Another medical (as opposed to psychological) treatment for psychopathology was developed at approximately the same time as electric shock. The basic procedure in this treatment—**prefrontal lobotomy**—is to cut the nerve pathways between the brain's prefrontal lobes and the thalamus (see Chapter 2), in order to interrupt existing thought patterns and fixed ideas. Though there was an early attempt to cure psychosis with brain surgery in 1890, the modern version of this operation was developed by Egas Moniz, in Lisbon, Portugal, and first carried out in 1935 (Freeman, 1959). In the United States, it was introduced in 1936 by Freeman and Watts (1941). By 1950, these surgeons had performed lobotomies on over 1000 patients (Valenstein, 1973).

Several specific surgical techniques were developed. One procedure involved first entering the brain by way of small holes drilled through the temples and then removing bits of tissue (Moniz, 1937). Another technique was to insert a sharp instrument into the brain by breaking through the relatively soft material above the eyeballs and using a windshield wiper type of motion to sever some of the nerve pathways (Freeman and Watts, 1948). Some of these procedures are illustrated in Figure 11–3.

Again, the early reports were enthusiastic about the success of the technique, and it was expected that anxiety and tension would quickly be reduced by means of this operation (Jenkins, Holspopple, and Lorr, 1954). The results were sufficiently exciting and of such potential importance that Moniz was awarded the Nobel Prize for his work in psychosurgery. A positive outcome of such operations was by no means certain, however, and the reported side-effects ranged from minor behavior disturbances to total deterioration of functioning. Those who have lobotomies tend to be overactive and easily distracted (Maher, Elder, and Noblin, 1962), and they are not able to learn as well as they did before the operation (Malmo and Amsel, 1949); many show other side-effects, such as overeating and weight gain (Partridge, 1950). What is worse, some of the patients died, and many more survived the operation with such decreased abilities that they have been described as "zombies" or "vegetables" (Barahal, 1958). Some research suggested that the only individuals who actually benefited from psychosurgery were those who were most likely to have improved without any treatment (Becker and McFarland, 1955).

Because such research was very discouraging, and because the side-effects were sufficiently disastrous, these operations have been used less frequently since the 1950's, though they are still a fairly common medical procedure (Ullmann and Krasner, 1975). One use is in cases of severe pain that cannot be relieved in any other way. The most frightening aspect of psychosurgery is that any damage caused by the operation can never be repaired. Interestingly enough, in Russia it is a felony to perform these operations.

Though there had initially been very high expectations about both electroconvulsive therapy and psychosurgery, by the early 1950's many practitioners had good reason to be skeptical about biotherapy as an approach to treating emotional disturbances. At this point, **reserpine** was introduced as a tranquilizer, and the drug revolution was underway. A form of this drug, extracted from the snake root plant, had actually been used for centuries in India and was

Drug Therapy: Pharmacy to the Rescue

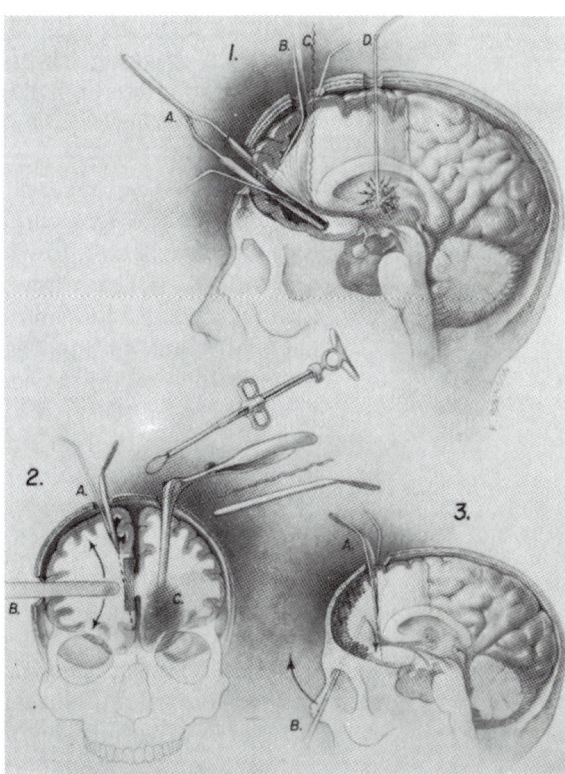

FIGURE 11–3 In psychosurgery, various techniques have been used to destroy connections between the prefrontal lobes and the thalamus. (Courtesy of Dr. William Beecher Scoville and *Acta Neurologia Latinoamericana*.)

noted for its ability to make people feel calm and untroubled. Additional tranquilizers, such as **chlorpromazine** and **meprobamate,** were also introduced. At the opposite extreme, energizing drugs were made available for those patients who were overly depressed or apathetic. The use of tranquilizers and energizers revolutionized the procedures used in mental hospitals. One psychiatrist remarked that the most obvious difference before and after reserpine was in the noise level on the wards. Hospitals became much quieter after drug therapy was introduced. There was also much less necessity for restraining agitated patients in straitjackets, padded cells, wet suits, or hydrotherapy tanks. Careful studies comparing the behavior of patients receiving drugs with that of control patients confirmed these observed changes (Lasky, 1960). One consequence has been a decrease in the number of patients confined to mental hospitals; there were 570,000 such patients in the United States in 1957, whereas 200,000 were confined in 1975. It seems that tranquility is now available in a pill.

Few would claim that drug therapy represents a direct cure for mental illness. Drugs do, however, reduce anxiety and aggression; thus, patients are able to function in a reasonable manner and many also enter into some form of psychotherapy. A patient compared his own experiences with alcohol and with tranquilizers: "You take alcohol and your problem vanishes while you're drunk, but the morning after it not only returns but you feel even worse than you did before! With tranquilizers, your problem is still there, but it doesn't matter to you anymore, and the next morning it isn't any bigger than it was before" (Suinn, 1970, pp. 304–305).

Drug therapy soon spread beyond the mental hospital, and physicians began prescribing tranquilizing drugs for most relatively mild disorders involving anxiety. Our culture's familiarity with this type of medicine is pointed out in the Neil Simon play and movie *The Prisoner of Second Avenue.* The hero becomes very upset when he discovers that burglars have not only taken his belongings but have even had the cruelty to steal his Valium from the medicine cabinet. There are, of course, more serious problems connected with the tranquilizing drugs. Institutional misuse of them was reported in 1975, when a senate investigation chaired by Birch Bayh of Indiana disclosed that children confined in mental hospitals and reformatories are too often given overdoses of Thorazine and other tranquilizers just to make them easier to control (*Time,* August 25, 1975).

As with other medical treatments, psychoactive drugs have also presented some problems in the form of undesirable side-effects. Tranquilizers have been found to bring about low blood pressure, depression, and ulcers (Ullmann and Krasner, 1975). One of the earlier meprobamates, Miltown, appears to be habit-forming and hence leads to long-term problems with possible addiction. The energizing and antidepressant drugs may bring about such unwanted conditions as high blood pressure and anxiety. New drugs are constantly being developed in an effort to minimize the side-effects while retaining the useful qualities. Overall, it appears that some types of drug therapy have made a much more lasting contribution to the treatment of behavioral problems than was true of either electroconvulsive therapy or psychosurgery. Table 11–1 lists several psychoactive drugs and the types of maladjustment for which they are typically prescribed.

A much more controversial version of "drug therapy" is the suggestion by some psychiatrists that maladjusted behavior can be altered by the administration of vitamins and a change of diet (Rodgers, 1976). Kurt Vonnegut's son has written an autobiography in which he tells how treatment of his schizophrenia with various vitamins and minerals enabled him to leave a maximum restraint ward in a mental hospital and to recover so completely that he was

TABLE 11-1 Prescription Psychoactive Drugs

Type of Drug	Generic Name	Trade Name	Prescribed For
Minor Tranquilizers	meprobamate	Miltown	Minor tensions and anxieties
		Equanil	Neurotic anxiety
	chlordiazepoxide	Librium	Neurotic depression
	diazepam	Valium	
Major Tranquilizers	chlorpromazine	Thorazine	Schizophrenic reaction
	trifupromazine	Stelazine	
	thioridazine	Mellaril	
Antidepressants	imipramine	Tofranil	Psychotic depression
	amitriptyline	Elavil	
	doxepin	Sinequan	

Adapted from Davison and Neale, 1974.

able to become a medical student at Harvard. There are many other clinical reports of this kind—institutionalized psychotics were able to return home after receiving a diet rich in niacin (vitamin B_3), senility was brought under control by the use of zinc and manganese, and the craving for alcohol was removed by the use of vitamins and a high-protein diet. Though the evidence concerning massive doses of vitamins and a nutritional diet is primarily anecdotal, systematic research is now being conducted in order to determine the validity of this revolutionary treatment procedure.

INSIGHT PSYCHOTHERAPY: ILLUMINATING THE DARK CORNERS OF THE MIND

Some decades before the biotherapies were developed, a very different approach to changing abnormal behavior was devised by physicians such as Sigmund Freud. The idea that some sort of doctor-patient conversation could be a useful therapeutic technique did not fit in at all with the medical conceptions that were current at the turn of the century. Just as most physicians had earlier rejected mesmerism and hypnotism, they reacted negatively to Freud's unorthodox method of treatment. At that time, psychotherapy was also far removed from the concerns and activities of the handful of psychologists who were just getting underway with their pioneering laboratory experiments. Nevertheless, psychotherapy in many forms has become the basic technique by which psychiatrists, clinical psychologists, psychiatric social workers, and others attempt to help those who are having behavior difficulties. To see how it all began, we will first examine the procedures developed by Sigmund Freud.

Psychoanalysis: Where There is Id, Let Ego Be

The basic procedures of Freud's special type of psychotherapy were developed over a period of years, during which he moved from the fairly simple "talking therapy" of Breuer (see Chapter 9) to the relatively complex details of the technique he called **psychoanalysis.**

Free Association: Spilling the Beans on the Couch

Some aspects of the interaction between patient and psychoanalyst are well known to all of us because they have been depicted over and over again in movies, books, and plays. Typically, the patient rests comfortably on a couch in a slightly darkened room with the analyst sitting out of the direct line of vision. There are specific reasons for each element in this particular setting. The main idea is for the patient to relax and to express his or her thoughts

"*I do think your problems are serious, Richard*
They're just not very interesting."

FIGURE 11-4 People some-
times ask whether the conversations between a therapist and a
client are any different than
conversations between good
friends or concerned relatives.
This cartoon suggests one difference—friends are not always
interested in your problems. In
addition, it is much easier for a
trained therapist to listen and
react without becoming personally involved in the problems or making value judgments
about the client's motives or
actions. (Drawing by Koren;
© 1974 by The New Yorker
Magazine, Inc.)

freely. The "basic rule" in psychoanalysis is the therapist's instruction to the
patient to speak freely about anything and everything that comes to mind, to
free associate. Ford and Urban (1963, p. 168) suggest the way in which this
message is presented to patients:

> In ordinary conversation, you usually try to keep a connecting thread running
> through your remarks, excluding any intrusive ideas or side issues so as not to wander
> too far from the point, and rightly so. But in this case you must talk differently. As
> you talk, various thoughts will occur to you which you like to ignore because of certain
> criticisms and objections. You will be tempted to think, "that is irrelevant or unimport-
> ant, or nonsensical," and to avoid saying it. Do not give in to such criticism. Report
> such thoughts in spite of your wish not to do so. Later, the reason for this injunction,
> the only one you have to follow, will become clear. Report whatever goes through your
> mind. Pretend that you are a traveler, describing to someone beside you the changing
> views which you see outside the train window.

The couch and darkened room (see Figure 11–5) are helpful in producing
relaxation. It makes sense for the analyst to sit behind the patient so as not to
distract his thinking. Actually, however, Freud decided to sit behind his patients because it annoyed him to be stared at all day long (Roazen, 1975). In
any event, the patient's task is to focus attention entirely on expressing his
or her innermost thoughts. The analyst's tasks are to listen to this flow of ideas,
to make some sense of the clues they provide, and to point out meanings and
interconnections that are not obvious to the patient. The analyst does this by
making **interpretations** from time to time of what is being said. Each interpretation is not intended to be some final conclusion by the analyst but, rather,
is an hypothesis which the patient can accept or reject.

Though the patient is instructed to free associate and say whatever comes
to mind, it is in fact made clear that certain topics are more relevant than
others. For example, it is thought to be important that the patient talk about
past events in his or her life, childhood memories, current feelings, and
dreams. It would not be considered reasonable to free associate endlessly about
baseball scores or vacuum cleaners. In fact, such associations might very well

be interpreted as resistance, since the patient would not be dealing honestly with his or her concerns. Similarly, if a patient declares that his mind is a blank and that he has no associations, resistance is suggested as the explanation. Such interpretations serve to increase the patient's understanding of the way in which unconscious mechanisms are operating to influence his behavior. An example of an actual interaction between an analyst and a male patient may help to illustrate these processes:

Analyst: The last time you were here, you said that you were not having any dreams. Is that still the case?

Patient: It's really strange. You said I might be repressing my dreams. That very night I had a very vivid one.

Analyst: Tell me about it.

Patient: I was in the bathroom in my undershorts, brushing my teeth. My brother came in and undressed to take a shower. I found myself getting excited by the sight of his body, and I was afraid he would see my reaction. At the same time, I wanted to touch him and get in the shower with him.

Analyst: What do you think it means?

Patient: I don't know. Maybe I'm unconsciously homosexual.

Analyst: Do you think so?

Patient: Not really. No more than anyone else.

Analyst: On the basis of our other conversations, I don't think so either. I'd like to suggest another idea. As soon as I mentioned that your dreams were important, you went home and produced a classic one involving sex, incest, and homosexual desires. Is it possible that all this is just a screen, a way to be a "good boy" and please the analyst?

Patient: Wow! You mean my desire to please is showing again? That's wild! Maybe my dream wasn't about sex at all. Is that possible?

Analyst: What do you think?

This brief glimpse of a psychoanalytic session indicates how the interaction between patient and analyst is in part like an intellectual game in which both players are trying to solve a series of puzzles or riddles. Over a period of time, the answers become more and more clear as hidden bits and pieces are revealed and then fitted together. It can be seen that the analyst's suggested interpretations are made in order to help the patient arrive at his own conclusions.

Freud stressed the goal of psychoanalysis as that of gaining **insight.** As unconscious material is gradually made conscious, the patient's behavior

Insight: Power to the Ego

FIGURE 11–5 Sigmund Freud developed the techniques of psychoanalysis and practiced this type of psychotherapy in the room shown here. Patients were asked to relax on the couch and to express freely whatever they were thinking. (Edmund Engelman.)

comes under the control of the ego. Presumably, rational, conscious decisions are much more effective guides to behavior than are irrational, unconscious ones. In addition, Freud (1920) proposed that until an individual is free from unconscious conflicts, he is unable to find enjoyment or to achieve success.

Though insight is obtained in part through intellectual efforts, it is important that the final insight be based on genuine feelings. When the patient simply recites the words offered by the analyst and does not really feel them, the result is called **intellectual insight.** Only when there is **emotional insight** can there actually be an increase in control over unconscious motives and an actual change in the personality.

The unleashing of strong emotions in the analytic session often results in powerful feelings being directed toward the analyst. Such feelings are called **transference,** and they can be positive or negative. Some patients may fall in love with or feel sexual attraction to the analyst, while others may entertain hostile fantasies about murdering him or her. In effect, previously unconscious emotional responses to mother, father, siblings, or whomever come into awareness and are temporarily transferred to the analyst. At this point, they can be openly discussed and eventually integrated with the patient's growing awareness of who he is and what he feels. This learning experience can be thought of as a sort of emotional re-education (Alexander and French, 1946). Sometimes, by the way, transference works in reverse, and the therapist experiences strong emotional reactions to the patient. This *counter-transference* obviously can interfere with the professional doctor-patient relationship. In several well-publicized cases in which a male therapist has seduced a female patient, counter-transference has sometimes been gamely offered as an excuse for what happened.

It may be seen that the goal of changing unconscious motives, emotions, and conflicts into conscious ones is simply to make it possible for the individual to deal directly with his own internal processes. Once such material is no longer buried in the unconscious, the individual is free to behave in a mature fashion, as he would have done without the influence of repressions (Waelder, 1960).

Though Freud himself seldom saw a patient for more than a few weeks or months (Roazen, 1975), psychoanalysis typically is a slow process stretching over many months and even years of daily sessions. Ideally, at the end of this time-consuming (and expensive) process, the patient's conscious ego functioning has been expanded; that is, he is in much greater conscious control of his own mental functioning. The individual is now able to have fun and to work effectively (Luborsky and Schimek, 1964). Psychoanalysts have never been particularly interested in conducting research to test the value of their procedures. The research that has been done suggests that psychoanalysis is much more effective with neurotics than with more severely disturbed individuals, and that well-educated patients respond much better than do poorly educated ones (Luborsky and Spence, 1971). Beyond such generalizations, there is very little evidence that indicates precisely how well this type of psychotherapy works. We will now examine several other therapeutic approaches and some of the evidence concerning their effectiveness.

Client-Centered Therapy: *Your* **Perspective is All-Important**

When Carl Rogers (see Chapter 9) began practicing psychotherapy in the 1930's, he gradually developed a set of procedures and a theory quite different from those of Freud. You may remember that Rogers described maladjustment as the result of inconsistencies between our experiences and our self-concepts. The goal of therapy, then, is to give the client the opportunity to develop an altered self-concept so that he or she can comfortably respond to experience in an accurate way. Thus, therapy should make it unnecessary to defend oneself against unacceptable feelings or threatening perceptions. In addition, there should be a more genuinely positive self-concept. How might such goals be reached?

Rogers suggested that traditional psychotherapy such as psychoanalysis is basically centered on the analyst and his skill at interpretation. In other words, the patient comes to an expert who uses his knowledge and intellectual skills to figure out the historical details of the maladjusted behavior. From the perspective of self theory, this is the wrong approach. A better alternative would be to try in every way possible to take the viewpoint of the client (*not* to be labeled the patient) and try to see the world through his or her eyes and to feel what he or she is feeling at the moment. That is, the therapist must experience and express **empathy** for the client's emotions, thoughts, and values. The therapist often expresses understanding by reflecting, rephrasing, and trying to clarify what the client has said. Even more important, the therapist should not evaluate or make judgments about the client. Rather than acting as an expert leader, the therapist tries to be **nondirective** and to follow wherever the client leads.

Unconditional Positive Regard: Removing the Threat

Using this approach, the therapist must genuinely and deeply respect and accept whatever the client says. Like a totally loving, forgiving parent or friend, the therapist must provide **unconditional positive regard.** This means that the therapist likes and respects the client without attaching any conditions or reservations. Such feelings for the client are often expressed by the therapist's tone of voice and facial expression rather than in words. In this accepting and nonthreatening atmosphere, the client is free to relax his defenses and to allow more accurate perceptions to occur. The self-concept becomes more open to experience. Human beings are seen as naturally moving toward self-fulfillment, or **self-actualization.** That is, under ideal conditions we would all perceive the internal and external world accurately, be able to work and to play contentedly, interact with others in a nondefensive way, and be satisfied with ourselves. Once the client perceives that there is no threat from the therapist, this natural process of growth can proceed. It is as if the therapist is playing the role of parent, so that the client is able to redevelop portions of his self-concept in a way that was not possible in childhood with his actual parents. Note also that this **client-centered** type of therapy does not focus on what actually happened years ago between parent and child but rather on what the client is feeling and experiencing at the present moment. As an example of such therapy, we will take a fairly extreme sample from an actual therapy session in which a female client is feeling and expressing a great deal of anger. You might find it useful to contrast the way in which this client-centered therapist responds to what is said with the way a psychoanalyst might respond. In addition, you might think about how you would respond if someone you know said such things to you. The cartoon in Figure 11–6 suggests one type of response that Rogers would *never* give.

Client: You feel I want to come, but I *don't!* I'm not coming any more. It doesn't do any good. I don't like you. I hate you! I wish you never were born.

Therapist: You just hate me very bitterly.

Client: I think I'll throw you in the lake. I'll cut you up! You think people like you, but they don't. . . . You think you can attract women, but you *can't.* . . . I wish you were *dead.*

Therapist: You *detest* me and you'd really like to get rid of me.

Client: You think my father did bad things with me, but he didn't! You think he wasn't a good man, but he *was.* You think I want intercourse, but I *don't.*

Therapist: You feel I *absolutely misrepresent* all your thoughts.

"Why, you swine!"

FIGURE 11–6 In Rogers' client-centered approach, the therapist tries to see the world from the client's viewpoint and to provide unconditional positive regard. The therapist in the cartoon is, of course, doing exactly the opposite. In everyday life, it is easy enough to find others who will provide negative evaluations, to which we generally respond by using psychological defenses. When a therapist provides total acceptance, however, an individual becomes free to relax his defenses and to change. (Drawing by Richter; © 1952, The New Yorker Magazine, Inc.)

Client: ... You think you can get people to come in and tell you everything, and they'll think they're being helped, but they're *not!* You just like to make 'em suffer. You think you can hypnotize them, but you *can't!* You think you're good, but you ain't. I hate you, I hate you, I *hate* you!

Therapist: You feel I really like to make 'em suffer, but that I *don't* help them.

(Later in the hour)

Client: I knew at the office I had to get rid of this somewhere. I felt I could could come down and tell you. I knew you'd understand. I couldn't say I hated myself. That's true but I couldn't say it. So I just thought of all the ugly things I could say to you instead.

Therapist: The things you felt about yourself you couldn't say, but you could say them about me.

Client: I know we're getting to rock bottom. . . (Rogers, 1951, pp. 211–213).

Client-Centered Therapy: Does It Work?

In many ways it is easy to make fun of a type of therapy that relies primarily on acceptance and reflection of feelings. There's a joke about such a therapist with a suicidal client:

Client: Doctor, I feel like killing myself!
Therapist: You feel like killing yourself.
Client: Really, I'm going to jump out of your window!
Therapist: You feel that you are going to jump out of my window.
(Client jumps)
Therapist (leaning out of window to watch):   Plop!

A client-centered therapist would not really respond that way, of course. As when he discussed child-rearing (see Chapter 9), Rogers makes an important distinction between words and actions. A therapist would accept and empathize with suicidal feelings but would not permit a suicidal act to take place.

The crucial question is not whether one can make fun of the procedures; rather, we must ask, "Does it work?" Research on the effectiveness of psychotherapy originally was hampered by the notion that the doctor-patient relationship should remain private and not be recorded on tapes or movies that could later be studied by research workers. Rogers (1942) changed all this by being the first to publish a word-for-word transcript of an entire therapy session. In part because of his training in psychological research, Rogers has encouraged a great deal of experimentation dealing with the process of therapy and with its outcome. The results have been impressive in showing positive changes in the self-concepts of those who go through client-centered therapy (for example, Rogers and Dymond, 1954), and there is data showing that changes in the self-concept lead to improved interpersonal functioning (Rubin, 1967).

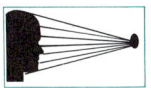

FOCUS ON RESEARCH: *Different Strokes for Different Folks*

In learning about different approaches to psychotherapy, you might well raise the question "Which one is best?" With all of the research that has been conducted, surely it is possible to say something about the relative effectiveness of psychoanalysis, client-centered therapy, and the others to be discussed shortly. In fact, the answer is a complicated one and has not been entirely resolved.

One general point is that there is evidence that each type of therapy can be effective in bringing about changes in behavior. Research on therapy can be difficult to evaluate, and some investigators believe that most patients will improve over time even without psychotherapy (Eysenck, 1961). Beyond that, research suggests that many specifics of the therapist's training and personality, the patient's problem and personality, and the type of therapy all enter into determining the likelihood that therapy will succeed or fail. When such variables are ignored, it has been estimated that the odds are two out of three that therapy is either a waste of time or even harmful to the patient (Truax and Mitchell, 1971). For example, in early work on client-centered therapy with bright, verbal, neurotic patients, Rogers and Dymond (1954) found that such therapy was extremely useful in bringing about positive changes in the self-concept. When similar techniques were later used with a series of less intelligent, less verbal, much more disturbed schizophrenics, the results were very disappointing and suggested that only a portion of the patients showed any improvement (Rogers, 1967). It was found that success depended on having (1) therapists who were extremely accepting and understanding individuals, (2) patients who were verbally expressive, and (3) therapist-patient pairs who were similar in their social and educational backgrounds.

The problem of dealing with the client who is not particularly verbal has been studied by Wexler and Butler (1976). They report the case of an inexpressive male who was making very little progress in client-centered therapy. Then, in the eighth interview, the therapist himself deliberately began to behave with a lot of expressiveness—he became animated and used a vivid speaking style. From then on, the client became considerably more expressive, even though the therapist returned to his usual quiet, client-centered style. It seems that it is sometimes helpful to switch out of the client-centered role briefly in order to modify the client's verbal behavior.

A recent study of psychotherapy with college students has shown that one specific personality characteristic of the patients is an important determinant of how effective different types of therapy may be. The personality variable involves the extent to which an individual believes that what happens to him in life is the result of his own actions (internal control) or of luck and other outside forces (external control). Rotter (1966) has shown the importance of individual differences in belief in internal or external control in many social situations. In therapy, it seems likely that believers in internal control might respond best to the client-centered approach, which places responsibility on the patients, while believers in external control might do best with some type of therapy such as psychoanalysis, which involves more direction and structure from an authority figure.

Abramowitz, Abramowitz, Roback, and Jackson (1974) tested this idea with male and female college students who were having problems with their personal adjustment and with their interpersonal relationships. On the basis of Rotter's test to measure locus of control, they were divided into "internals" and "externals." They were also divided into four different groups for psychotherapy. The therapist in these groups either used client-centered techniques or was directive in leading discussions and making interpretations. As expected, the success of the therapy experience depended on student personality in combination with the type of therapy. That is, therapy was most successful for "internal" patients in client-centered therapy and for "external" patients in the directive therapy. In general, psychotherapy was least successful when the patient's personality did not match the therapy style.

These researchers proposed that, in the future, it might be possible to give prospective patients a battery of personality tests. The type of therapy that would then be recommended could be tailor-made to fit the individual.

UNLEARNING MALADJUSTED BEHAVIOR: BRINGING THE LABORATORY INTO THE THERAPIST'S OFFICE

Almost all psychotherapists, beginning with Freud, have assumed that the behavioral changes which take place during therapy represent learning on the part of the patient. Initially, the details of this process remained vague, but it still seemed obvious that some aspects of the therapist's actions help the patient to learn new ways of responding. In psychoanalysis, the crucial elements are believed to be the analyst's interpretations, which result in insight and increased awareness. In client-centered therapy, it is thought that an accepting, clarifying, and understanding therapist makes it possible for the individual to become open to new experiences and hence to learn new things about his feelings and about himself. From the viewpoint of many psychologists interested in learning (see Chapter 4), it has been a challenging problem to apply the concepts and techniques of experimental research on learning to the realm of psychotherapy. Such efforts have led to some entirely new approaches to therapy, as we shall see.

Learning New Responses: Mmm-hmm and Huh-uh

During the 1930's, when Freud's career was at its height and shortly after Rogers began practicing therapy, an eminent learning theorist named Clark Hull brought together a remarkable group of behavioral scientists at Yale University. Hull (1952) said that their goal was to seek to establish connections between the kinds of phenomena described by Freud and the laws of learning which had grown primarily out of experiments using rats as subjects. By the late 1930's and into the 1940's, this group of individuals produced an impressive series of articles and books attempting to explain such complex phenomena as aggression, imitation, and defense mechanisms in terms of learning theory. The book *Personality and Psychotherapy*, by John Dollard and Neal Miller (1950), was an exciting attempt to present aspects of psychoanalytic theory and practice in terms of well-established learning principles.

The *details* of the learning process in therapy still remained to be specified, however. Psychoanalysts and other therapists obviously do not engage in specific teaching activities, and they do not use rewards or punishments to try to alter the patient's behavior. Or do they? Is it possible that the words and even the murmurs of a therapist act as reinforcers in the counseling situation? In an experimental parallel to a therapy session, Greenspoon (1955) asked subjects to say all of the words they could think of during a 50-minute session. The experimenter, like an analyst, sat behind each subject and said "mmm-hmm" every time a plural noun was spoken. This positive murmur was clearly reinforcing, and the subjects began saying more and more plural nouns. With other subjects, Greenspoon said a negative "huh-uh" each time plural words were said; these individuals produced fewer and fewer plural nouns precisely as though they had been punished for these responses. This and many subsequent studies (see Krasner, 1962) provided an explanation of one way that learning can occur in psychotherapy. The patient's verbal behavior can obviously be reinforced by the responses of the therapist. For example, whenever an individual in client-centered therapy begins mentioning feelings, the therapist responds positively by reflecting, nodding, or even saying "mmm-hmm." With such reinforcement, the client talks more and more about feelings. That is, he is learning to talk about specific topics that the therapist believes to be important and to deal with them because he is reinforced for doing so. Such selective reinforcement explains why it is that patients tend to talk in ways that are consistent with the therapist's general theory, even though the theory is never discussed. Psychoanalytic patients discuss Oedipal conflicts and transference, while those in client-centered therapy discuss feelings and their self-concepts—in both cases, because their respective therapists reinforce the topics they believe to be most crucial (Glad, 1959).

Given such evidence, a number of investigators began looking directly at the therapeutic process itself by examining tape recordings and movies of actual therapy sessions. For example, Murray (1964) describes how a session can be analyzed by looking first at each sentence spoken by the patient; the experimenter determines whether it involves sex, aggression, defensiveness, psychotic distortions, or whatever. Next, the sentences spoken by the therapist are categorized; for example, some of the therapist's statements are supportive and positive while others are mildly critical and negative. In one case, it was shown that the therapist always gave some sign of approval when the patient discussed independence and some sign of disapproval when the patient discussed such topics as wanting to be dependent or when intellectual defenses were used. If learning principles are operating, we would expect the patient to express more and more independence and less and less dependency and defensiveness. In Figure 11–7 the record of eight hours of psychotherapy shows that this is precisely what happened. The "reinforced" statements increased, and the "punished" statements decreased. Even with recordings of Rogers himself, it has been demonstrated that precisely the same process is operating, with differential reinforcement being provided and verbalizations being affected (Truax, 1966). It seems that it is not possible for a therapist to be truly "non-directive."

There is, of course, nothing sacred about the specific procedures developed by Freud and others over the years. They are, in a way, a natural outgrowth of other types of doctor-patient interactions, as when you tell your physician about the pain in your stomach, and he asks questions and recommends what you do next. But the research findings and the theoretical notions linking learning theory and the practice of psychotherapy led some therapists to take a further step. If psychotherapy is a learning session, why not forget the traditional doctor-patient arrangement and start directly with procedures borrowed from the experiments on learning? Instead of learning occurring as an almost accidental outcome of patient-therapist conversations, why not start all over and design the therapy situation on the basis of what is known about the principles of learning? Such ideas resulted in entirely new types of psychotherapy.

Insight therapies may be described as an intellectual and emotional interchange in which the patient is encouraged to understand and to experience the meaning of his or her behavior. **Behavior modification,** in contrast, is a learning procedure in which conditions are manipulated by the therapist so as to alter the behavior of the patient (Ullmann and Krasner, 1965). The focus of such

Behavior Modification: Changing the Overt Behavior

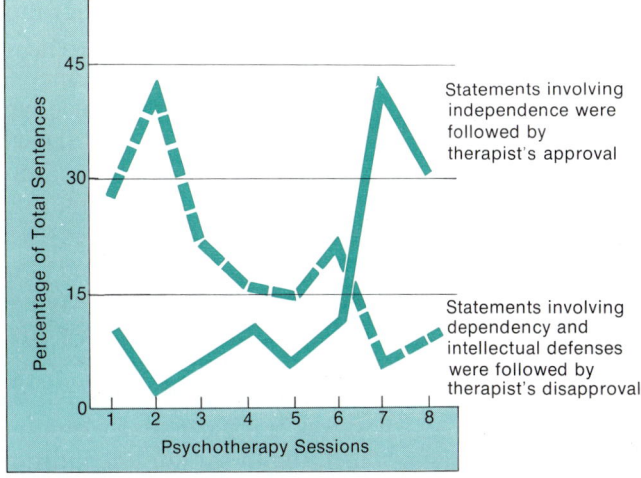

FIGURE 11–7 What a patient discusses during psychotherapy sessions is influenced by the reinforcements provided by the therapist. Over a series of eight one-hour sessions, this patient was "punished" for talking about dependency and using intellectual defenses, and these elements appeared less and less frequently. There was "reward" for talking about independence, and this topic appeared with increased frequency over the sessions. (Adapted from Murray, 1964.)

Statements involving independence were followed by therapist's approval

Statements involving dependency and intellectual defenses were followed by therapist's disapproval

It is possible to see for yourself the way in which what a person says can be influenced by the positive and negative reactions of another person. All that is needed for this experiment is the cooperation of a friend who has not taken a psychology course plus the form in the Student Manual on which to record your results.

Tell your friend that the experiment involves language. You want him (or her) to sit in a comfortable chair and make up a series of 100 different sentences. You sit out of the person's line of vision so that you will provide no clues in the form of smiles, frowns, nods, and so forth. Explain that you yourself are not supposed to say anything during the experiment.

Now, select a particular type of sentence that you wish to manipulate. Let's say that you decide to reinforce all sentences that begin with "I" or "we." On your paper, write numbers from 1 to 100. Each time your subject gives an "I" or "we" sentence, place a plus sign (+) by the number; for any other type of sentence, place a minus sign (−). So that you can see how reinforcement operates in this situation, do not say anything following the first 20 sentences—just record the pluses and minuses as you go. This represents your subject's normal way of responding, and this is called the *base rate phase.*

For the next 50 sentences, begin reinforcing all "I" and "we" sentences by murmuring "mmm-hmm" as naturally as possible following each one. During this period, your subject would be expected to increase the frequency with which the reinforced sentences are given. This is called the *acquisition phase.*

Finally, for the last 30 sentences, do as you did at the beginning and say nothing. Keep recording the plus and minus signs for each sentence. During this period, the frequency of "I" and "we" sentences is expected to decrease. This is called the *extinction phase.* When you are finished, first ask your friend to state his or her ideas about the experiment and what you were doing. At that point, you should explain it fully.

To examine your data, divide the numbers on your record sheet into groups of 10. Count the number of plus signs in each group. To see your results best, it will help to make a graph with 10 columns (corresponding to your 10 groups of sentences). In each column, make a mark indicating the number of plus signs in that group (for example, you could make number of inches represent the number of plus marks). Is there any change in frequency from the base rate phase to the acquisition phase to the extinction phase? If several members of your class carry out this project, it might be interesting to compare results.

What relationships do you see between what you did and what a therapist might do in a traditional hour of psychotherapy?

---

therapy tends to be specific, and the goals are clear-cut. If a particular behavior is causing difficulty, the therapist attempts to eliminate that behavior, most often by substituting some other behavior in its place. At the present time, most of the research being conducted on psychotherapy deals with the effects of these techniques (Gendlin and Rychlak, 1970). We will examine a few of the procedures used in behavior modification.

Counterconditioning: Substituting One Response for Another   In Chapter 10, conditioned fears were described. For example, a small boy was startled by a loud noise while playing with a white rat and then became afraid of the rat and of other white, furry objects as well. Thus, through conditioning, the rat became a stimulus for a fear response. How can such a fear be eliminated? One of the first demonstrations of **counterconditioning** involved just such a situation (Jones, 1924). A female experimenter worked with a boy named Peter who was afraid of rabbits. The goal was to alter Peter's response so that he felt happy and relaxed when he saw a rabbit. The first step was to arrange the situation so that his conditioned response of anxiety was weak enough that a more positive response could occur. It was discovered that if the rabbit (conditioned stimulus) were placed far enough away in the room, the boy was not particularly anxious. At this point, the experimenter gave Peter something to eat (an unconditioned stimulus). The distant rabbit thus became associated with the pleasant experiences (the new conditioned response) involved in eating. Gradually, the rabbit was brought closer and closer, so that eventually it became a conditioned stimulus for positive feelings rather than negative ones.

This basic idea was not widely used in psychotherapy until the late 1950's, when Joseph Wolpe (1958) began writing about his use of **systematic desensitization** to treat patients with various fears (see Figure 11–8). As with the boy and the rabbit, the idea was to make the patient feel very relaxed and comfortable and then gradually to introduce the feared stimulus in "small doses." In this way, the patient is *desensitized* as the fear is replaced by a feeling of relaxation and calm. Most objects of fear, of course, are not as specific and concrete as a rabbit, and it is necessary to use the patient's imagination to create scenes and incidents which are mildly fearful, moderately fearful, and so forth. The patient begins with the least fearful ideas and gradually works up to the most fearful ones, just as the rabbit was first placed across the room from Peter and then gradually moved closer. An example of such a therapeutic approach involves a female college student who is extremely anxious about taking examinations.

The therapist first teaches the student to relax and to feel completely at ease in his office. The goal is to attach these positive feelings to the testing situation. The therapist also asks the patient to describe various aspects of her life that are related to the anxiety, including some situations that cause little or no anxiety and some that cause a great deal. The desensitization sessions begin with the least threatening scene.

Therapist: Now that you are completely relaxed, imagine that you are reading an enjoyable assignment for a course. You know that someday you will have to review it for a quiz, but now you are simply enjoying it. How do you feel?

Patient: Very comfortable. I can see myself in a soft, overstuffed chair, and the reading is very interesting. The test is too far off to worry about.

Therapist: All right, let's try another scene. Imagine that you are reading a syllabus which gives the course requirements, including the dates on which the exams will be given.

Patient: I can imagine the syllabus, and I can feel my hands beginning to perspire. The exam dates make me nervous.

Therapist: Erase that scene for now, and just relax. Each of your muscles is limp, like a rag doll.

In a series of such sessions, the patient is gradually able to tolerate heightened amounts of anxiety, as represented by the following increasingly threatening scenes to be imagined (anxiety hierarchy adapted from Suinn, 1970):

Hearing the instructor ask the class a question about an assignment.
A friend asking whether I am prepared for an upcoming test.

FIGURE 11–8 In systematic desensitization, patients learn to associate feelings of calm and relaxation with objects or events that formerly elicited fear. By gradually progressing from mildly frightening stimuli to those causing greater amounts of fear, the patient becomes *desensitized* at each level. (Van Bucher/Photo Researchers.)

Studying for an exam the day before it is given.
Reading the first question on a test and not knowing the answer.
The instructor saying that I need a "B" on the final to pass the course.
Discovering that my score on the last exam was the lowest in the class.

By the end of 10 sessions, the patient was able to imagine all of the scenes without feeling undue anxiety.

For this kind of counterconditioning to be a useful therapeutic procedure, it is of course necessary for the new responses to occur in real life as well as in the desensitization sessions. It appears to be best if, from time to time during the therapy process, there is real-life exposure to whatever is feared (Schroeder and Rich, 1976). If the imaginary scenes are very much like what is encountered in the patient's everyday life, the new responses of relaxation and comfort should generalize to the real sources of anxiety. At this point, the patient is able to deal with formerly terrifying situations, such as classroom examinations, without being blocked by feelings of anxiety. One interesting new procedure is to give clients written instructions so they can administer systematic desensitization treatment to themselves (Rosen, 1976). In one study, individuals using this method were able to reduce their fear of snakes as effectively as those who were led through desensitization by a therapist (Rosen, Glasgow, and Barrera, 1976). Figure 11–9 shows an adaptation of desensitization procedures using videotape technology.

Sometimes the undesirable response can be eliminated by means of mild punishment. For example, treatment of a middle-aged male who is sexually attracted to young children might involve utilization of a special type of counterconditioning called **aversive conditioning.** The procedure involves the association of negative feelings with the unacceptable stimulus. The patient typically would be shown a series of pictures of nude children; each time such a picture is shown, he receives a mild but painful electric shock. When the picture changes to an attractive adult female, the shock is turned off. The goal here is to associate an unpleasant pain with the inappropriate sexual stimulus of young children. At the same time, there is an attempt to substitute positive responses such as pain reduction and, possibly, sexual arousal to the appropriate stimulus of an adult female (Feldman and MacCulloch, 1971). A more direct method was used by Blakemore, Thorpe, Barker, Conway, and Lavin (1963). A

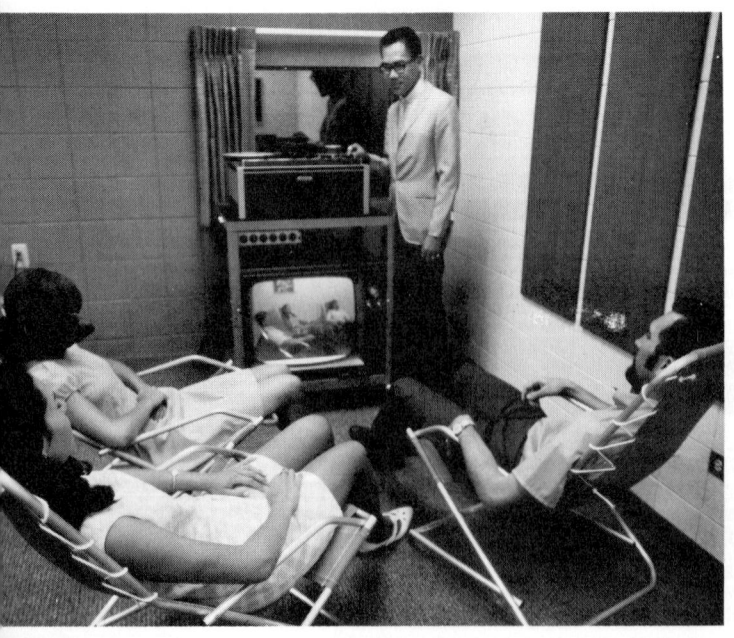

FIGURE 11–9   R. M. Suinn (standing) demonstrates videotape playbacks of a desensitization session as a way to help bring about changes in behavior. (Photograph courtesy of R. M. Suinn and Colorado State University Photography Laboratory.)

33-year-old married man with a young child had worn women's clothing from time to time since he was 12 years old. Because he feared getting caught and was worried about the effects of his behavior on his family, he sought help in therapy. The method used was to ask him to put on his favorite female clothes in the therapist's office while standing on an electrified metal grid. At some point as he was dressing, he received a shock or a buzzer signal which meant that he should undress as quickly as possible; this was done five times each session. After a series of such treatments, he stopped dressing in women's clothes and six months later he was still functioning normally. Some therapists even extend this procedure to everyday life settings by asking patients to carry a battery-operated shock device around with them. When either the inappropriate stimulus or even the thought occurs, the patient is instructed to push the button and shock himself. Similar procedures have been used with varying degrees of success to help individuals learn to avoid smoking cigarettes (Hunt and Matarazzo, 1973), drinking alcohol (Sobell and Sobell, 1973), and overeating (Wolpe, 1954).

Aversive conditioning can also be effective when the unpleasant stimulus is imaginary. Barlow, Leitenberg, and Agras (1969) report being able to alter a sexual behavior by asking patients to imagine sexually arousing incidents related to past behavior and to then associate them with unpleasant images. A homosexual male who wanted to become heterosexual was told to imagine going to meet his boyfriend, anticipating an exciting encounter and then:

As you get closer to the door you notice a queasy feeling in the pit of your stomach. You open the door and see Bill lying on the bed naked, and you can sense that puke is filling up your stomach and forcing its way up to your throat. You walk over to Bill and you can see him clearly, as you reach out for him you can taste the puke, bitter and sticky and acidy on your tongue, you start gagging and retching and chunks of vomit are coming out of your mouth and nose, dropping onto your shirt and all over Bill's skin (Barlow, Leitenberg, and Agras, 1969, p. 598).

After a series of such sessions, this **covert sensitization** procedure resulted in a change in the patient's sexual responsivity. He no longer was sexually aroused by imagining homosexual scenes. More importantly, he also reported a decline in homosexual urges when he went out in the evening visiting bars. A very similar procedure has been used to help overweight individuals cut down on their eating (Elliott and Denney, 1975). The subjects were instructed to imagine eating their favorite high-calorie food, and as they took a bite they were to think about a vividly described scene of becoming nauseated and vomiting. They received instructions to imagine other scenes in which something sickening happened—finding hairs in a milk shake or discovering that a cream puff was filled with warm yellow pus. This procedure led to weight loss and to a less favorable attitude toward the previously liked foods; control groups receiving dieting hints did equally well in losing pounds, but their attitudes about food did not change.

Operant Conditioning: Shaping the Desired Behavior

The learning techniques developed by B. F. Skinner and his associates include procedures which permit very complex behavior patterns to be taught by means of *operant conditioning* (see Chapter 4). The desired behavior is shaped—the experimenter waits until some small portion or element of the response is made and then rewards it, usually with a small amount of food. On the next occasion, the experimenter waits until a little more of the desired response occurs, and then the reward is given. Eventually, an entirely new behavior sequence has been learned. You have probably seen demonstrations of such learning at amusement parks or in special displays in which a chicken walks on a tight rope, pigs play soccer, or pigeons walk in a figure 8 to receive food pel-

**PERSPECTIVE
ON
BEHAVIOR:** *The Ethics of Behavior Modification,
or Is Big Brother Shocking You?*

If you wish to give up smoking, you might decide to visit a psychological clinic to ask for help. If the therapists there practice behavior modification, you might well find yourself undergoing aversive conditioning as the treatment procedure. That is, you see pictures of cigarettes and receive a shock. You reach for an open package of your favorite brand and receive a shock. You smell tobacco smoke and receive a shock.

Are such procedures ethical? Most of us would answer "yes." You had a problem with smoking and wished to stop. You *voluntarily* sought help and placed yourself in treatment. If you don't like it, you can walk out the door and never return.

Let's take the opposite extreme. You are a prisoner of war, and your captors want you to make negative propaganda statements about the president of your country. They place you in aversive conditioning training in which the stimulus consists of pictures of the president, recordings of his voice, and so on. You receive an electric shock each time these materials are presented. When you say something bad about him, the shock is turned off. Are these procedures ethical? Here, most of us would answer "no." You are being "brainwashed" against your will. You have no choice, and you are being forced to change your emotional reactions.

When these same procedures are used in still other situations, the ethics of the procedure become more difficult to decide. What if you are the captor, and your prisoner of war represents an enemy force dedicated to destroying your country and your way of life? Would it be ethical to use aversive conditioning on him? What if a man is arrested for engaging in peeping Tom activity? If the laws of a state prohibit that behavior, should the state have the power to try to alter this man's sexual activity against his will? Consider the case in which he is not physically forced to undergo treatment but will be considered for parole only if he "volunteers" for aversive conditioning. Is it ethical to set such conditions? If the behavior were not that of a peeping Tom but involved raping pre-adolescent girls, would you be any more or any less willing to force him to undergo therapy?

Homosexual behavior creates a special ethical problem. Homosexuality used to be considered as abnormal behavior, but in 1974 the American Psychiatric Association decided that this particular sexual preference should no longer be considered an "illness." Nevertheless, when someone with a homosexual orientation seeks therapy, very often procedures are undertaken to alter his or her preferences in a heterosexual direction. When someone with a heterosexual orientation seeks therapy, no one would suggest that behavior modification techniques be used to orient the person toward homosexuality. Thus, such professional decisions strongly reinforce the idea that "homosexuality is bad" (Begelman, 1975). This conflict between official tolerance of homosexuality and the actual practice of treating it as a form of maladjustment has led at least one well known clinical psychologist to propose that behavior modification never be used to change sexual preferences (Davison, 1976). Rather, he would like to see a therapeutic concentration on improving the quality of the interpersonal relationships of all individuals, regardless of their sexual inclinations.

Such issues are currently of great concern to psychologists, psychiatrists, correction officers, civil libertarians, and others (Davison and Stuart, 1975). What are your own views on this topic? Under what conditions would you be willing or unwilling to see this type of behavior modification used?

lets. In each instance, these seemingly impossible or at least improbable behaviors have been slowly shaped by means of operant conditioning.

Very similar procedures have also been used to bring about changes in human behavior. For example, in a Head Start program for underprivileged preschool children, the teachers found that many of the youngsters had had little or no experience in using language to describe their experiences or their surroundings. A teacher might ask a boy, "What happened on the way to school today?" He was likely to remain silent or to reply, "Nothin'." When such children are thrown into a group of typical verbal middle-class first-graders, they are likely to be seen as unintelligent or uncooperative. With a little training, however, verbal skills can be acquired. An operant conditioning program was instituted in which the teachers and their helpers carried M & M candies in apron pockets. The candies were used as reinforcement to shape the desired verbal behavior. A silent child would receive no candy. A child who said a word or two was given a treat. Gradually, the children found it necessary to say entire sentences and then two or more sentences in order to get the candy. After a few months of such training, these previously almost nonverbal children found themselves able to communicate with the teacher and with one another. In a similar way, operant conditioning has been used to teach retarded children such important skills as acceptable toilet habits (Minge and Ball, 1967).

To take another example, a friend's child had a bed-wetting problem. The parents were advised not to shame or punish him. Instead, each morning that he woke up with a dry bed, he was to receive an "IOU" signed by his mother and father. As soon as 10 of these were collected, he could "trade them in" for a toy truck that he badly wanted. To his parents' surprise, the boy suddenly stopped wetting the bed and earned his truck. The parents were told that if there should be a return to bed-wetting later on, the price could simply be raised so that a larger number of IOU's must be earned in order to get a prize.

Even more dramatic have been efforts to increase the intellectual ability of retarded children. Ayllon and Kelly (1972) used tokens to reward a group of such children each time they gave correct answers on an IQ test and in working on academic tasks such as arithmetic and reading. These tokens could then be exchanged for soft drinks, candy, and special privileges. After just six weeks of this operant conditioning, the retarded children showed a significant increase in intelligence. A matched control group which did not receive the tokens as reinforcement did not show such a gain. The effectiveness and the simplicity of operant techniques suggest that many teachers, parents, and others would find their jobs much easier if they adopted this approach.

One of the earliest attempts to change the behavior of mental patients with simple reinforcement techniques was reported by Ayllon and Haughton (1962). They noted that feeding problems were common among chronic schizophrenic patients. Besides the general apathy, which included a lack of interest in food, patients often expressed delusional ideas. Some thought that their food was poisoned, for example, and others felt that the voice of God ordered them not to eat. How should such behavior be handled? At the practical, everyday level, hospital workers tended to coax them to eat, to lead them into the dining room, and even to spoonfeed them. At the theoretical, therapeutic level, such behavior was interpreted in terms of the symbolic meaning of food, regression to the oral stage of development, and so forth. Ayllon and Haughton introduced a much simpler procedure and a much simpler interpretation. Taking a reinforcement viewpoint, they assumed that the non-eating behavior would change when it was no longer reinforced and when alternate behaviors *were* reinforced. Their procedure was clear-cut. No hospital personnel were allowed to interact with the patients at mealtime. When the meal was ready, all patients were given

30 minutes to enter the dining room unassisted. If they did not, the door was locked, and there was no opportunity to eat until the next meal. Over a period of weeks, the time period for getting into the dining room was gradually reduced from 30 minutes to 5 minutes. The result of this procedure was that the patients who had feeding problems quickly began to get themselves to the table and to eat without help. In the next phase, it was arranged that each patient had to insert a penny in a special slot in order to enter the dining room. Once that had been learned, pennies could be used as reinforcers for other behaviors on the ward. For example, pennies were given as reinforcement for talking or for cooperating on various simple tasks. By the time a year had passed, not only had the feeding problems disappeared, but the patients were exhibiting better interpersonal skills as well.

The extent to which operant conditioning can revolutionize treatment programs is shown by the development of a system called the **token economy.** In one such experimental system, Ayllon and Azrin (1968) worked with an entire ward in a mental hospital and arranged that plastic tokens were to be given to patients if they carried out specific activities. For example, setting the table for a meal earned one token, washing the coffee urn was worth two tokens, and washing the pots and pans was a six-token job. The tokens that were earned could be used as money to obtain an extra visit to the canteen, a private room, and so forth. In this and similar studies, it was possible to demonstrate substantial changes in patient behavior. Even withdrawn and seemingly unresponsive schizophrenic patients were soon doing kitchen chores, brushing their teeth, and making beds. In addition, when compared to patients receiving standard hospital treatment, those in a token economy program can be observed to behave in a more positive and healthier fashion. Schwartz and Bellack (1975) compared a token-economy group with a matched control group over a 15-week period of treatment. The relative effectiveness of the conditioning technique is shown in Figure 11–10. In such programs, when the rewards stop, the new behavior also tends to disappear quickly. These findings suggest that the token economy must be maintained or that a way must be found to substitute more realistic rewards (for example, self-approval) for the plastic tokens.

There is an interesting procedure used by Alcoholics Anonymous which

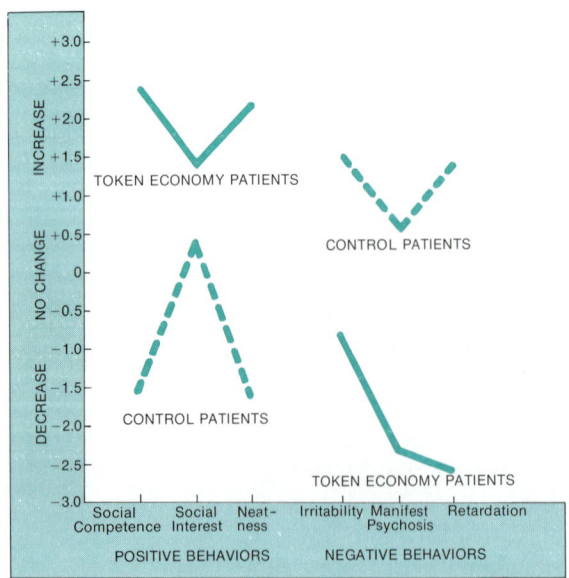

FIGURE 11–10 Psychiatric patients in a token economy were compared with a matched control group of patients receiving standard hospital treatment. Observations before and after the 15-week experimental program indicated that the token economy procedures led to increases in positive behaviors and decreases in negative behaviors. (Adapted from Schwartz and Bellack, 1975.)

requires the individual to monitor himself with tokens, thus solving the problem of how to generalize the reinforcement to everyday life (Bassin, 1975). A prospective member is given a red poker chip at his first meeting and told to carry it in his pocket where he carries his booze money. Whenever he reaches for money to buy liquor, the poker chip reminds him of his effort to go just one day without drinking. If he does drink, he is supposed to break the chip in two and throw it away: at his next AA meeting he can get a new red chip and start over. If the individual is able to go an entire month without drinking, he turns in his red chip and receives a white one. The same procedure is followed with it, except that it can be exchanged for a blue one if three months go by without a drink. After eight more sober months, he is entitled to a silver dollar with a small hole drilled in it; on each alcohol-free anniversary afterward, another hole is drilled in the dollar. This self-administered token reinforcement (and reminder) appears to be a very effective part of the AA program.

It should be noted that many traditional therapists sometimes argue that behavior therapy is only treating symptoms rather than getting at the underlying causes of the problem. Behavior modifiers would reply that the "symptom" *is* the problem.

Modeling: If They Can Do It, I Can Do It

Much of the learning that takes place in our everyday lives is based on *modeling*, as was pointed out in Chapter 4. We observe what others do and are then able to copy their behavior. How might this process be applied to psychotherapy? Albert Bandura and his colleagues at Stanford have conducted a number of experimental demonstrations in which different types of fears were reduced or completely eliminated in just a few modeling sessions. The basic idea is that an individual can experience systematic desensitization simply as a spectator watching someone else perform an anxiety-arousing activity.

Among the first of these studies was one in which children who feared dogs were taught to feel quite differently by means of a rather easy procedure. Nursery school children were given a behavior test with a brown cocker spaniel to detect the degree of fear expressed by each child. The most fearful children were then placed in one of two modeling conditions or in a control group. The modeling treatment consisted of a series of eight different three-minute movies shown twice a day (see Figure 11–11). Some watched a fearless five-year-old boy interact with the cocker spaniel in scenes showing increasingly bold activities. Others watched very similar movies involving several different boys and girls interacting with a variety of dogs, and the control subjects were shown movies of Disneyland and Marineland. Bandura and Menlove (1968, p. 101) describe some of the scenes in the dog movies:

In the initial interaction sequences the model's behavior was limited to looking at the dog in the playpen and occasional petting. Subsequent movies showed the venturesome model walking the dog on the leash, grooming her, holding her in his arms, and serving her canine gourmet snacks. The feeding routines began with relatively nonthreatening amusing scenes in which the dog drank milk from a baby bottle and munched on a jumbo sucker held steadfastly by the model; later sequences depicted the dog vaulting toward hamburger patties and frankfurters that the model dangled in his hand. In the terminal set of movies the model climbed into the playpen with the dog where he petted her, fed her doggie bon bons and, as a finale, rested his head on his canine companion during a brief siesta in the overcrowded playpen.

After this film festival was doggedly completed, the subjects were given the behavior test again with the same cocker spaniel *and* with an unfamiliar white mongrel. A follow-up test was given a month later to determine the lasting effects of the modeling procedures. As may be seen in Figure 11–12, some remarkable and lasting behavioral changes were brought about by this method of treatment. It should be added that the experimenters were not thoughtless

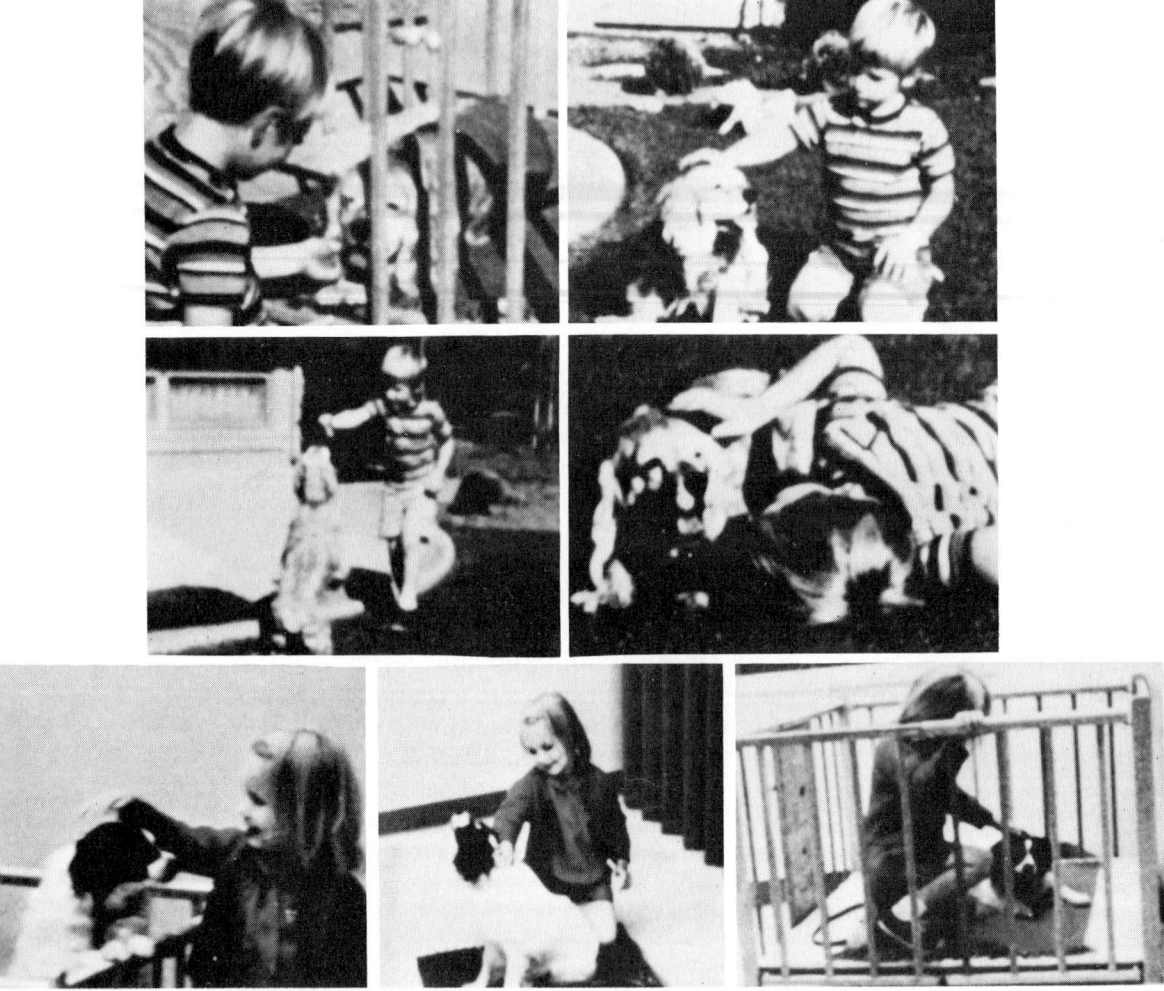

FIGURE 11–11   In behavior modeling, individuals who fear a particular activity are asked to watch live or filmed models engaging in the activity. In these movie scenes, models are shown interacting with dogs in an increasingly brave manner. Children who were afraid of dogs were exposed to these films as a way to reduce or eliminate their fears by means of the modeling process. (Courtesy of Dr. Albert Bandura.)

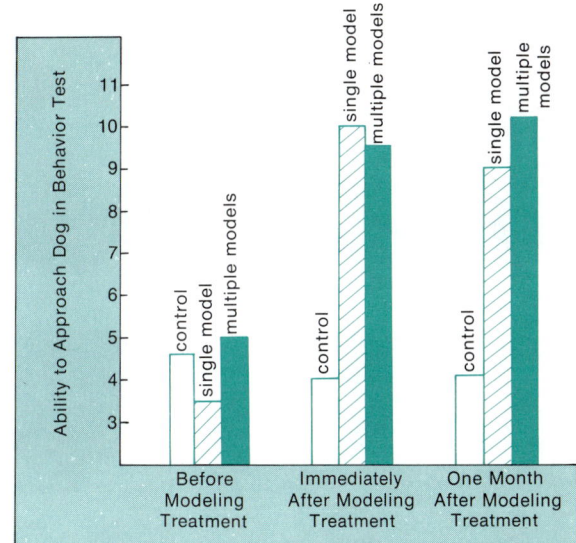

FIGURE 11–12 Children who feared dogs were shown movies either of a single model or of many models interacting with dogs. Control subjects were shown movies of Disneyland and Marineland. Behavioral tests with an actual dog indicated that both modeling groups were much better able to approach and deal with a dog following treatment, and that this behavioral change was a lasting one. The control group children showed no change in their response to a dog. (Adapted from Bandura and Menlove, 1968.)

enough to leave the control group children in a fearful state. These youngsters were then shown the modeling movies, and they too lost their fear of dogs.

In another experiment (Bandura, Blanchard, and Ritter, 1969), newspaper ads were used to recruit individuals who had snake phobias. It was pointed out that this rather common fear makes it difficult or impossible to take part in outdoor activities such as camping or hiking, and it makes gardening a terrifying adventure. Some outdoor occupations must be avoided because of the possibility of coming in contact with a snake. More upsettingly, one subject (in a different study, by Bandura, Jeffrey, and Wright, 1974) was unable to use her bathroom for several weeks after she read that a snake had escaped into the city's sewer system. Even without a snake phobia, that is not a comforting toilet-time thought. In the experiment, the subjects' fears were first tested by asking them to do a series of tasks involving a four-foot king snake. The requested actions included approaching an enclosed glass cage containing the snake, picking up the snake with a glove, and letting the snake crawl around on one's lap. Only those who were too afraid to carry out at least some of the easier tasks took part in the modeling experiment. Subjects were shown a 35-minute color movie depicting people of various ages engaging in progressively more threatening interactions with a snake. A few of these scenes are shown in Figure 11–13. The movies were seen twice a week, and most subjects spent less than three hours of viewing time altogether.

Despite the brevity of the treatment process, some dramatic changes in behavior and in feelings took place. The once phobic individuals expressed less fear of snakes in general, their attitudes toward snakes were more positive, and most importantly, they were then able to approach and handle a live snake. The subjects, by the way, had at first been very skeptical about being able to get rid of their fears. One said, "I felt totally unconfident that it would work on me. I thought I could probably get used to seeing snakes, but I never thought that I could be able to pick one up calmly." The results were both surprising and pleasing. A lifetime problem had been solved by watching a brief movie a few times. One person said, "I am no longer harassed by walking through grassy areas in fear of running across a snake." Also, imagine the joy of that one subject who could calmly use her bathroom again.

FIGURE 11–13   In another behavior modeling experiment, films which showed models handling snakes were markedly successful in reducing fear of snakes among individuals who were previously very much frightened by these reptiles. (Courtesy of Dr. Albert Bandura.)

A combination of modeling and role-playing was used by Sarason and Ganzer (1973) to alter the behavior of imprisoned juvenile delinquents. In a series of small group sessions, adolescent male prisoners saw graduate student models enact a situation such as taking a problem to a counselor, delaying immediate gratification to obtain a larger future reward, and saying "no" to peers who suggested an illegal act. Afterward, the subjects were asked to enact the scenes themselves. Positive changes in behavior were found, both as measured by paper and pencil tests and as observed by those who worked with the boys. Even more impressively, after release from prison, a follow-up study three years later indicated that significantly fewer of those receiving treatment had committed new offenses than was true for non-treated control subjects.

THERAPY IN GROUPS: EXPANDING THE THERAPEUTIC SITUATION

In the discussion so far, you have seen that psychotherapy began as an outgrowth of doctor-patient interactions and, for some therapists at least, has moved toward an emphasis on experimentation involving learning principles. There is also another trend that has been characteristic of an evolution in psychotherapy—a move away from the traditional two-person situation toward therapeutic interactions involving groups of patients. Thus, **group therapy** has been adapted to psychoanalysis (Slavson, 1950), client-centered therapy (Rogers, 1970), and behavior modification (Lazarus, 1968). Another important development is *family therapy*, in which mother, father, and children are treated simultaneously (Jackson, 1961).

The initial reasons for interest in group therapy involved efficiency and economy. Davison and Neale (1974) have estimated that a single traditional therapist averages 200 sessions per patient, which means that he could see only about 80 patients each decade of his career. Considering the number of individuals who need and want psychological help, it is obvious that there would never be enough professionals to provide the necessary amount of individual psychotherapy. One solution to this problem has been the relatively more efficient and less time-consuming procedures of behavior modification. Group therapy is another solution (see Figure 11–14). As we examine some of these group approaches, you may decide that groups provide advantages beyond simple efficiency.

Psychodrama: All the Stage Can Be Your World

In 1931, a psychiatrist named J. L. Moreno introduced the term "group psychotherapy" to describe a unique approach to treatment which he had developed. Moreno felt that the usual forms of therapy were much too intellectualized, with patients *talking about* their feelings and their reactions rather than *experiencing* them. He decided that if a group of people could be made to act out scenes from their lives, as in a play, they would be much more likely to express their genuine feelings and thoughts (Moreno and Kipper, 1968). An improvised play of this variety is termed a **psychodrama.**

A typical procedure is to have one patient set the scene and to assign other patients to whatever special roles are needed. For example, a male patient may feel that he is unable to deal with the way his mother pressures him and compares him unfavorably with his younger brother. He will then outline a brief situation in which the three of them had difficulties, and other patients will take the roles of his brother and mother, while he plays himself. The three act out the scene on an actual stage, with the therapist making comments and suggestions as they go along. He serves as the play's "director." The remaining patients constitute the audience. (An example is shown in Figure 11–15.)

This basic situation has a number of variations. After a scene has been enacted, the therapist may ask the group to do it over again but with the patient who designed it not playing himself but rather the role of his mother or of his brother. Another patient then takes *his* role and tries to act in a way that he believes is characteristic of the patient. Thus, in the course of a few psychodrama sessions, an individual can potentially gain a great deal of insight as he reexperiences some of his everyday life problems, is forced to learn how such situations appear from the point of view of others in his life, and has the opportunity to see how he himself appears to others who try to portray him. In

FIGURE 11–14 In group psychotherapy, one therapist (right) deals with a number of patients simultaneously. The advantages of group therapy include efficiency, the opportunity to benefit from the experiences of others, and the chance to work out one's problems in an interpersonal context. (Scene from *People Who Care*, a National Association for Mental Health film.)

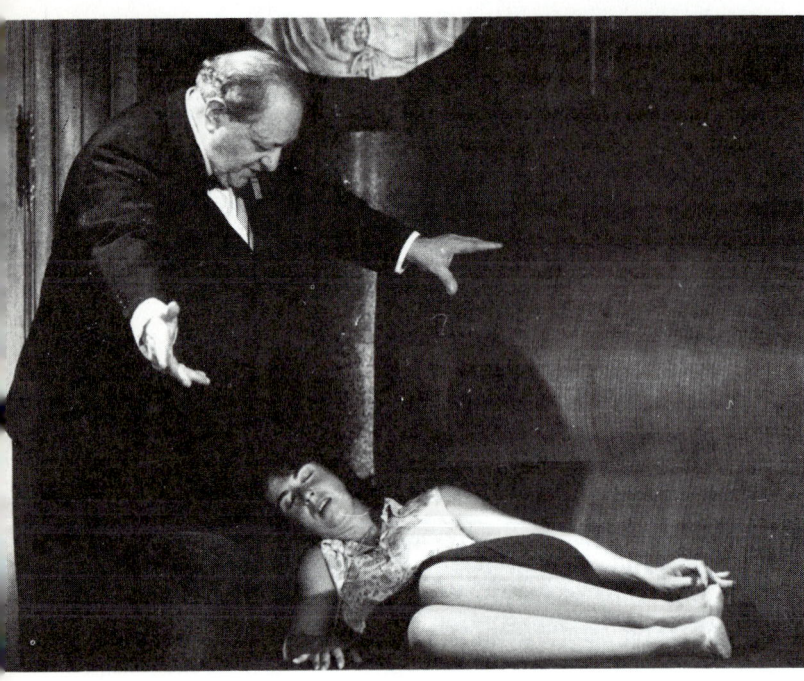

FIGURE 11–15 Dr. J. L. Moreno's psychodrama technique involves the acting out of various real-life situations, with some patients playing a variety of roles while other patients serve as the audience. The therapist (Moreno himself in this picture, on the left) plays an active part as the "director" of each scene. (Courtesy of the Moreno Institute, Inc.)

addition to gaining awareness of the central character in a given scene, the other players and the audience necessarily acquire additional insight about human interactions by vicariously experiencing the emotional details of someone else's problems.

Despite the long history of psychodrama and the enthusiastic descriptions of it by Moreno and his associates, very little research has been done to evaluate the usefulness of this approach.

Encounter Groups: Letting It All Hang Out

In the 1940's, two somewhat different types of groups began to function in different parts of the country. One type, developed at the National Training Laboratories in Bethel, Maine, was the **sensitivity training group,** or **T-group.** The original idea was to bring businessmen together for a series of special sessions in which attention was focused on feelings and on interpersonal interactions. The goal was to make each participant more aware of his or her emotions and of his or her emotional impact on other people. Presumably, the result of such increased self-understanding and interpersonal understanding would be greater efficiency in the organizations for which they worked. Over the years, many versions of the T-group have been conducted with many types of participants, including policemen, educational administrators, clergymen, and political leaders. The second type of group was developed by Carl Rogers at the University of Chicago as a means of training client-centered therapists. Since the client-centered approach places a great deal of emphasis on the empathy and warmth of the therapist, it is important that this individual learn as much as possible about his or her own interpersonal responses.

By the 1960's, the **encounter group** had evolved as a sort of blend of the traditional T-groups and the client-centered groups. On many college campuses, encounter groups became something of a fad. Despite many variations, the general focus tends to be on the expression of feelings and on all participants learning how they are preceived by the other participants. Thus, there is the encouragement of honesty and being open to letting others know what you are feeling.

A great many encounter groups have been organized to deal specifically with feelings about sex. A number of these groups are designed to help workers such as physicians, counselors, and teachers who are confronted by sexual problems of others. One of the most respected of these programs has been offered at the University of Minnesota Medical School since 1971 (Garrard, Vaitkus, and Chilgren, 1972). As part of a required course for second-year medical students, there is a two-day "seminar" which is essentially an encounter group organized around a specific topic. In addition to the medical students, there are other participants in the group who represent many segments of the community. Each participant is encouraged to bring a "significant other" to the group, including spouses, fiances, lovers, and friends. As a means of arousing feelings, participants are shown sexually explicit movies depicting sexual intercourse, masturbation, homosexual acts, and so forth. Each film or set of films is followed by a small group discussion dealing with the viewers' thoughts and emotional reactions. The nature of the group interactions can be seen in the following example (adapted from Medelman, 1975, pp. 154 and 250). The group has just assembled after viewing several movies in which males and females masturbate to orgasm:

Cynthia: Actually, I've got more reason to be here than I admitted. I teach in a school for disturbed adolescents—but sometimes I think I'm as disturbed as they are. I've never had an orgasm. And even though I love my husband and we have really pleasant, warm times together, I get an awful feeling—somewhere between deadness and a cringe—when he touches me in bed. Those masturbation movies—you can't imagine how I envied those women those long, long climaxes.

Lester: I don't think I'd choose those women to envy. If a woman carefully sets the stage, then calls in *Candid Camera* while she brings herself to orgasm, I'd say she was a candidate for psychotherapy.

Cynthia: Wouldn't you call me a candidate for psychotherapy?

Lester: Yes, on the basis of your frigidity and discomfort, I'd call you one, too.

Leader: We've got a kind of contract in this seminar. We're as open as we can bring ourselves to be, but we don't diagnose and we don't do therapy.... Did anybody else have any strong feelings about the masturbation movies?

John: I didn't see what the grownups looked so pleased about. I think of masturbation as something for kids.

Judy (to Cynthia): Did you ever try to masturbate to orgasm?

Cynthia: My husband bought me a vibrator. It was a joke—but he sort of meant it, too. I got it out and turned it on once. But I felt silly and put it back in the box. Once, when I was tight, I used it to stir pancake batter.

Leader: How many of the women here *do* masturbate?

Annie: In times of famine, or when I'm dating a poor lover.

Frank: The only grown males I know who masturbate are prisoners. Especially in solitary—to keep from going crazy.

Leader: Not many groups get moving like this one. Usually we spend half a day defining terms and moralizing and talking about what we've read. Then somebody blurts out something honest and we finally get under way. I feel that this group started out under way.

The problem of getting all such groups to begin dealing honestly and openly with feelings has been solved in several different ways. Some group leaders suggest "exercises" to start things off (Schutz, 1967). One such exercise is to have one participant close his eyes, and then the other group members carry him around the room, as in Figure 11-16. The individual usually talks afterward about how it feels to be touched and carried by strangers and what it means to have to put his trust in them. Group marathons are scheduled to last for a day or two, without sleep, and the resulting fatigue leads the participants

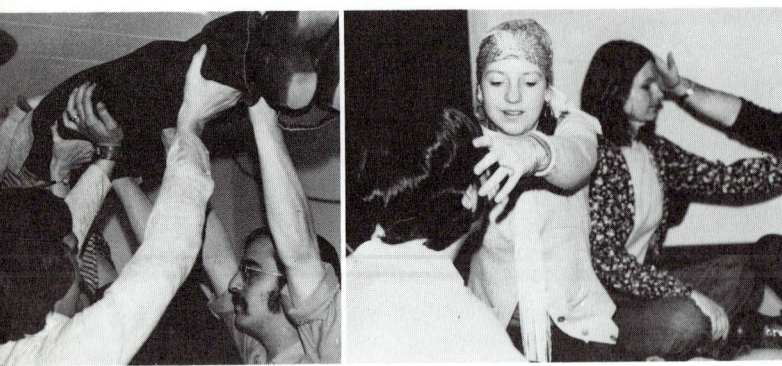

FIGURE 11–16 To get the participants in encounter groups to begin interacting, group leaders often use "exercises" to break the ice. Two examples are shown here: left, one person closes his eyes and trusts the others to carry him around the room; right, individuals are asked to pair off and learn how it feels to touch a stranger and to be touched.

to be more open and less defensive (Stoller, 1968). A still more dramatic ice breaker is to ask all participants to remove their clothes (Bindrim, 1968).

Evaluating Encounter Groups: Good and Bad Effects

Because encounter groups have become extremely popular, and because there is a great deal of variation in the training and the skills of those who became group leaders, many professionals have become concerned about the possible dangers of this type of therapy. One obvious problem is that individuals may learn to interact with openness and honesty in an encounter group and then find that such behavior is inappropriate outside of that group setting (Houts and Serber, 1972). A student of one of the authors participated in a series of such group experiences and learned for the first time to verbalize many of her interpersonal feelings. To her surprise, one of her professors was upset when she indicated her sexual attraction to him, and her expression of intense hostility to her mother was an equal disaster. To a greater extent than in individual psychotherapy, individuals seem to have some difficulty in learning the difference between what is acceptable in the group and what is acceptable elsewhere.

Interactions in the group can become quite hostile, much like the game "get the guest" in the play and movie *Who's Afraid of Virginia Woolf?* A very serious problem arises with the individual who becomes acutely disturbed by what happens in the group session and is unable to deal with the anxiety that is aroused. Those who have such reactions are called "casualties," and they are an increasing problem as more and more groups are organized by individuals with little or no professional training (Yalom and Lieberman, 1971). Even the best of therapists might easily miss the fact that one group member has become very upset about a given topic, because the group conversation shifts to different content as different participants talk (Serber, 1972). One study of such groups (Lieberman, Yalom, and Miles, 1973) suggested that the "law of thirds" can be applied to the outcome of encounter groups. That is, one third of the participants show a positive gain, one third experience no effects, and one third have negative effects and hence become casualties. It was also found that it was not possible to predict how any given individual would respond to the group experience. Because of such potential problems, it seems very unwise to enter an encounter group "just for fun" or to enter any group unless you are convinced that the leader is a qualified, professional therapist (Hartley, Roback, and Abramowitz, 1976).

Despite the problems, there is evidence of positive effects in well-run groups (Gibb, 1971). For example, Miles (1965) asked the co-workers of group members to evaluate their behavior following the group experience. The participants were rated as being more sensitive in interpersonal relationships, as communicating better, and as being more relaxed and considerate. Rubin (1967) found that encounter groups lead to an increase in self-acceptance and a decrease in prejudice. In another study, industrial managers were found to show more positive interpersonal reactions after participating in groups, though their ability on the job remained about the same. Similarly, a study of college students who participated in encounter groups indicated positive changes in self-perception compared to students who did not have such an experience; nevertheless, ratings by someone who knew each subject well did not indicate noticeable changes as a function of having been in the group (Marks and Vestre, 1974). Some of the best evidence for lasting effects of the group experience has been obtained from those dealing with sexual attitudes (Garrard, Vaitkus, Held, and Chilgren, 1974). Over 200 participants in the Minnesota program were tested before the group sessions and then immediately afterward, six months later, and one year later. One result was a marked increase in sexual tolerance after the course, and this attitudinal change was still present 12 months later. Examples of specific changes are shown in Figure 11–17.

In addition to the several types of individual and group psychotherapies that have been described, there are countless other special therapeutic procedures and theories that have been developed by various practitioners. Six of the more popular current therapies are described briefly in Table 11–2.

No matter how far the various types of psychotherapy have strayed from the original doctor-patient setting, there are nevertheless certain basic medically oriented characteristics which they share. First, the patient is assumed to have developed some behavioral problem which requires treatment. Second, the professional person who is trained to provide that treatment is not expected to take any action until the patient (or someone responsible for the patient's

**COMMUNITY
PSYCHOLOGY:
GOING WHERE
THE ACTION IS**

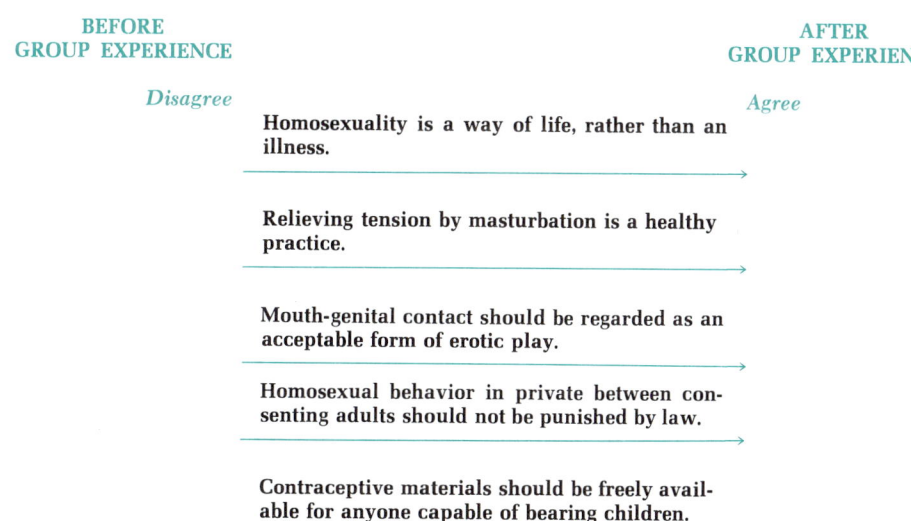

FIGURE 11–17 Sexual attitudes changed in the direction of greater tolerance among participants in a group program at the University of Minnesota Medical School. Those attitudes were still significantly changed one year later when compared to the attitudes expressed before the group experience. (Adapted from Garrard, Vaitkus, Held, and Chilgren, 1974.)

TABLE 11-2   Six Types of Psychotherapy Currently in Practice

Type of Psychotherapy	Therapist	Characteristics of the Therapy
Bio-energetic Therapy	Alexander Lowen	Based in part on the work of Wilhelm Reich, bio-energetic therapy stresses that one's body must be free and healthy in order for one's mind to function properly. Therapy often includes physical exercises, instructions on how to improve posture or mannerisms, and encouragement to express feelings openly.
Existential Analysis	Rollo May Abraham Maslow	Because people have the ability to be self-aware, they can make decisions and be responsible for their actions. It is possible either to be frozen in an awareness of one's loneliness and ultimate death or to move toward growth and fulfilling one's innate potential. Much like Rogers, existential therapists attempt to view the world through the client's eyes to help him learn to trust and love others and to make him aware of his own potential for choice and growth.
Gestalt Therapy	Frederick Perls	One key concept is projection. It is suggested that unconscious aspects of ourselves are projected onto other people. Difficulties with others can be solved through role-playing, which leads to the discovery that "what I dislike in you is me." A second important idea is a concentration on the present moment, so the patient learns accurately to perceive internal and external events rather than to dwell on fantasies of the past or future.
Nude Therapy	Paul Bindrim	The basic idea of therapy in the nude is that people are more likely to express their true feelings ("bare their souls") when they are not protected by clothing. Also, it is suggested that the self-concept is based in part on feelings about one's body and its physical attractiveness, and these issues cannot easily be avoided when the patient is naked.

(Table continued on opposite page.)

welfare) seeks him out. Third, all psychotherapeutic activity is confined to the therapist's place of work.

Over the last several years, a number of therapists have begun to question the wisdom of following this pattern. It is suggested that we should examine and attempt to change those aspects of the environment which may be responsible for the development of behavior problems, that professionals should actively seek out the problems as they arise or even before they become problems, and that the most effective therapy may be applied in the everyday world rather than in an office (Rappaport and Chinsky, 1976). We will examine some of the consequences of this new approach which takes psychology into the community.

Why Take Psychology Into the Community?

Altering Behavior by Altering the Situation

In Chapter 9, it was pointed out that many psychologists are beginning to conceptualize personality as an interaction between traits and situations. Remember the jury studies, for example, in which the authoritarians were punitive and unreasonable with some categories of defendants while the egalitarians were punitive and unreasonable with other categories of defendants? If people are strongly influenced by the stimulus situations which confront them,

TABLE 11–2   Six Types of Psychotherapy Currently in Practice (*Continued*)

Type of Psychotherapy	Therapist	Characteristics of the Therapy
Primal Therapy	Arthur Janov	It is hypothesized that neurotics have never been able to express the powerful and unpleasant emotions they felt as children. Everyone goes through painful childhood experiences such as loneliness, rejection, and the sense of being unloved. If these feelings are repressed and carried into adulthood, the individual is emotionally crippled. The therapist first makes the patient miserable by isolating him or her with instructions not to smoke, drink, have sexual relations, watch TV, or talk to people. When the feelings of distress become intense, the patient is ready to relive childhood unhappiness and to shout and cry and let go with a "primal scream." When these emotions have been thoroughly released, the individual is free to develop into a happier adult.
Transactional Analysis	Eric Berne Thomas Harris	It is proposed that people continually play social games with one another. In these games, three parts of the personality (versions of Freud's id, ego, and superego) are expressed. These consist of the child (the one who is fun-loving, adventurous, spontaneous), the adult (the one who reasons how best to deal with the environment), and the parent (the one who expresses moral values and points out good and bad). People often get into interpersonal difficulties because in their social games they are acting out different parts of their personalities. For example, one person's child can't communicate well with another's adult. The goal of therapy is to develop an awareness of all three parts of the personality and how they operate in interpersonal situations (James, 1976).

is it useful to think of maladjusted behavior as being, at least in part, a function of current situational pressures? If so, it would obviously make sense to examine such pressures and make attempts to alter them rather than simply to deal with a patient as though the problem is entirely something that he or she carries around inside (Rappaport, Davidson, Wilson, and Mitchell, 1975).

An example may help make the difference clear. One of the authors once taught at a university where all of the graduate students in psychology were required to take five days of examinations covering several different areas of the field. These qualifying exams were the major hurdle of the graduate program, in that each student's test performance determined whether or not he or she would be able to continue working for a Ph.D. degree, be asked to re-take the tests a year later, or be dismissed from the program. As you might expect, the weeks before exam time each year were extremely stressful for the students involved. A great many of the individuals responded to this situation with symptoms of anxiety and sleeplessness, and with physical symptoms ranging from diarrhea to headaches. One student developed a touch of paranoia and felt that faculty members were spying on him to determine how much he was studying. The most startling response was that of a male student who collapsed on the morning of the first day's testing and was carried off by ambulance attendants as his fellow students continued writing their answers. If any one of these students visited a therapist during this period, the focus on insight, self-understanding, correct labeling of emotions, or modification of symptoms may well have been helpful. A very different and seemingly more effective approach, however, would be to take a careful look at the immediate cause of their problems and to consider a modification of the exam system rather than a modification of the students. In fact, after the qualifying procedures later underwent drastic change, far fewer individuals developed symptoms of maladjustment.

One aspect of community psychology, then, is to examine possible problems brought about by school, job, and family situations in order to suggest beneficial changes (Baum and Valins, 1973). An example of such an approach was provided by a mental health center in San Francisco when school busing was introduced (Heiman, 1973). What could psychologists do to help ease the tensions, anxieties, and hostilities aroused by this situation? The Westside Community Mental Health Center staff designed an interesting set of procedures to deal with the problem. Members of the staff met with concerned parents in a semi-therapeutic way and also went to the school administrators as representatives of the parents. For the younger children, special coloring books were designed which contained maps of the bus routes. A staff member also rode along on the bus for the morning and the afternoon trips. This individual was available to deal directly with uncomfortable feelings at the time they were strongest. Altogether, a potentially disruptive and unpleasant social situation was "defused" and made considerably easier by the activities of these community workers. Playing these new roles often demands that the consulting psychologist spend a considerable amount of time simply observing the everyday interactions in a school, an office, or a family in order to obtain ideas about the problems involved.

As you might expect, the idea of a community psychologist can sometimes be a bit threatening. An outside observer who may suggest radical changes is not always welcome in a school system, a place of business, or in a family setting. Once a community psychologist begins to recommend specific changes, he has necessarily become a social activist who wants to alter some aspect of the status quo (Denner and Price, 1973). Even if a consultant is brought into the situation, there is no guarantee that his suggestions will be accepted and acted upon. The effectiveness of such an approach depends in part, then, on the cooperation of many individuals.

Being Available to Provide Help

Many professional groups are learning the wisdom of taking their skills into the setting where the problems occur. Medical clinics have been established in neighborhood locations. Store-front lawyers provide legal aid to individuals who never before considered visiting the office of an attorney. Family planning agencies hold special information sessions in local schools. In the same spirit, there have been attempts to take psychology to the people. President Kennedy in 1963 proposed a "bold new approach" to solving problems of psychological maladjustment, and Congress later passed the Community Mental Health Centers Act, which provided federal funds for such centers throughout the U.S.

In this new role, community psychologists find themselves not only available to deal with problems as they occur, but sometimes it is also possible to prevent greater problems from developing (Zax and Cowen, 1972). For example, crisis centers are established with someone available 24 hours a day to talk in person or by telephone to those who seek help. In effect, emergency therapists are standing by to deal with immediate concerns such as an unwanted pregnancy, a problem with drugs, or the unhappiness of a teenager who has run away from home. A specialized version of this sort of operation is the suicide prevention center, which potentially suicidal individuals are encouraged to call to discuss their problems (Speer, 1972). Because of the vast manpower that would be required in order to have professional therapists carry out all of these widespread activities, community psychologists have also become involved in training assistants (or **paraprofessionals**) to conduct much of the day-by-day work. These individuals often make the initial contacts with those requiring help and either provide the needed help or make referrals when more serious problems arise.

Rather than leave the impression that community psychology provides the perfect answer to all of the world's problems, we should also include a word of caution. Research on the effectiveness of such programs has not been especially encouraging (Speer, 1972; Weiner, 1969), and Ralph Nader's task force provided evidence that actual community operations are often very much inferior to the idealized descriptions of them (Holden, 1972).

In all types of psychotherapy, the question has been raised as to whether what is learned in the therapist's office generalizes to the patient's everyday life. There are two major aspects of this problem, and each seems to be at least partially solved by community psychology.

Solving the Problem of Generalizability

First, psychotherapy tends to be a largely verbal activity. The conversations between patient and therapist clearly result in alterations in what the patient says, as we saw in our discussion of psychoanalysis and client-centered therapy. Some critics of psychotherapy suggest that the verbal changes do not necessarily generalize to other aspects of behavior. One colleague once observed that his friends who had been through psychoanalysis "are the same S.O.B.'s they always were, but now they bore you senseless by always talking about their precious little unconscious desires." In an effort to influence all forms of behavior, and not just what is said, therapies such as behavior modification and psychodrama represent a movement toward building generalization into the therapy session. Nevertheless, even behavior modification techniques are sometimes found to have a greater effect on what patients say than on what they do. For example, Eyberg and Johnson (1974) taught parents to use selective reinforcement to alter the problem behavior of their children. On rating scales, the parents indicated many positive effects of the treatment and favorable attitudes toward the therapy; when observers visited the homes, however, the children's behavior was not perceived to be significantly improved following therapy. Community psychologists are often dealing with behavior as it actually occurs in the individual's world. There is no question of whether changes generalize to this setting, because the new behavior occurs in this setting in the first place.

The second aspect of generalizing from therapy is the fact that the therapy situation is traditionally totally separate and quite different from the patient's life situation. It was noted earlier that a person may learn to behave in a completely new way in an encounter group and then find that the new behavior is not acceptable elsewhere. It is also possible that the effects of some behavior modification techniques are mostly confined to the specific stimuli and responses used in treatment. Perhaps a child molester is now made uncomfortable by *pictures* of children but not necessarily by real children. A person who is involved in an unhappy home relationship may be helped a great deal by interacting with a therapist; being plunged right back into the same old home situation may simply start the problem all over again. With the community psychology approach, the separation between therapy and real life disappears. The behavioral change occurs in the actual situation in which the individual lives and works. We will now describe in some detail an example of community psychology in action.

Community Psychology Responds to a Disaster: Dealing With the Aftereffects of a Tornado

Disruption in a Community

Spring in many parts of the United States is the peak time for the development of a particularly frightening natural phenomenon—the tornado. On April 3, 1974, a series of these powerful storms moved across several southeastern and midwestern states, destroying lives and property. Two tornados ripped through the small town of Monticello, Indiana, and virtually destroyed the downtown area as well as many private residences. The 400-mile-per-hour winds brought death to four visitors and to five of the 10,000 residents of the area and caused about 200 million dollars in property damage.

Ordinarily, one does not think of such a situation as one in which psychologists are likely to play a major role. After all, the many problems involving housing, feeding, and giving medical treatment to those whose lives were disrupted are not really primarily psychological concerns. State, federal, and private agencies ranging from the Red Cross and Salvation Army to the National Guard and the Army Corps of Engineers rushed to the scene to provide much-needed help. Volunteers from nearby communities and college campuses converged on Monticello by bus and car to offer their assistance. In addition, three psychologists took the unusual step of providing a psychological response to this emergency. Their work serves as an excellent example of the unique contributions of community psychologists (Zarle, Hartsough, and Ottinger, 1974). The project, which is described in the following section, was remarkable in part because it was not in operation when the disaster occurred but had to be designed and put into action in a matter of days and weeks.

Anyone who has not personally lived through the experience of a major natural disaster, such as a tornado, hurricane, flood, or earthquake, may not be able to anticipate all of the psychological consequences of such events. Besides the acute fear caused by the disaster itself, the subsequent disruption of one's usual life patterns can be devastating. Families are separated, jobs may be suspended, and temporary housing facilities can be a source of stress. Some effects such as grief and anxiety are fairly obvious, but there are other reactions as well. For some time, it has been known that a community disaster can cause individuals to feel apathetic, to develop psychosomatic illnesses, and even to commit suicide (Tyhurst, 1951). Other investigators have discovered that the tension brought about by such disruptions can lead to disturbances within the family and to problem drinking (Richard, 1974). Among the prevailing feelings expressed by survivors are anger about what has been lost, guilt about not having done the right things, a sense of hopelessness about the future, and a tendency to deny that the disaster occurred (Michael, 1972). Many of these emotional and behavioral reactions do not occur immediately but develop in the weeks and months following the emergency. What can community psychologists do to help?

Responding to a Crisis: The Development of an Intervention Program

The human problems brought about by the Monticello tornado were met by a rapid response from a team of community psychologists (Hartsough, Zarle, and Ottinger, 1976). The first task was to devise a crisis intervention plan (Caplan, 1964) to determine how best to respond. During the first weeks after the tornado struck, much of the time was spent in training a group of 15 volunteers from the local community. It has been found that victims in such a situation tend to respond better to those from their own locality than to well-meaning outsiders. During this period, there was also a great deal to be done in planning and organizing the total project and in establishing contacts with community leaders and with appropriate community agencies. These activities ranged from seeking state and federal funds to finance their work to obtaining

FIGURE 11–18 Earthquake victims in Turkey and Guatemala. A natural disaster such as an earthquake causes not only physical damage to a community but psychological problems as well, including grief, anxiety, apathy, guilt, and hopelessness. In such a situation, community psychology can provide a unique means of helping the survivors. (Photo credit: United Press International.)

space in a local church where the group could meet and where the volunteers could be trained.

The training program itself was designed to provide the paraprofessionals with the appropriate information for dealing with the behavioral effects of a disaster. The volunteers were first informed about the various ways in which individuals have been found to respond in these situations. It was stressed that such feelings are common, and that most people find it helpful to learn that their reactions are normal and to be able to express them openly. One important activity was that of learning to provide accurate information and thereby control the spread of rumors; any disrupted communication system encourages the spread of false and misleading stories. The workers were taught how to seek out and help those who might be most disturbed by what had happened, such as very young children and the elderly. During this training, it was necessary to learn and to practice the ways in which an understanding person can respond helpfully to the expression of such feelings as anxiety and depression. These therapeutic skills were then practiced under supervision with actual disaster victims. For example:

. . . one of the volunteer workers was assigned to see a hospitalized 59-year-old woman who had sustained a coronary attack during the tornado. She was distraught on finding that, because of her medical condition, she could not return to her apartment and would be placed in a nursing home following hospital dismissal. The fact that the volunteer could provide her with detailed information about the nursing home and could reassure her that she would not be forgotten helped to alleviate the patient's immediate distress. Subsequently, the volunteer followed her through the nursing home placement (Hartsough, Zarle, and Ottinger, 1976).

The team of paraprofessionals fanned out through the community to seek those who needed assistance and to provide help during the town's rebuilding period. When severe problems were encountered, the victims were referred to the appropriate community resource to receive the necessary psychiatric, legal, medical, or whatever other type of help was required. The importance of such an approach quickly became obvious, and funds were made available to train additional paraprofessionals and to continue their service work even after the worst disruptions of the original disaster were essentially over. In effect, the community had discovered the value of having such a service available. Thus, the program evolved from one in which the main aim was to intervene in a crisis situation into one in which a continuing community service was provided.

Summary

Many procedures have been designed to bring about beneficial changes in behavior. **Psychotherapy** is the application of psychological techniques by professionally trained individuals to change a socially inappropriate pattern of behavior into a more appropriate one.

Some of the earliest therapy techniques for dealing with emotional disturbances consisted of some form of bodily treatment, or **biotherapy. Electroconvulsive therapy,** developed in the 1930's, is still used to reduce mood disturbances, but it has been found to have several undesirable side-effects. Beginning in the 1930's, **psychosurgery** was extensively used as a way to help treat mental illness, but negative research findings led to its declining popularity. In the 1950's, the introduction of **tranquilizing** and **energizing drugs** represented the most useful of the biotherapies to date.

Insight psychotherapy was first developed by Sigmund Freud, in the form of **psychoanalysis.** The patient is instructed to engage in **free association,** and the analyst interprets the meaning of what is said in order to help the individual gain insight. Carl Rogers' **client-centered therapy** rests on the assumption that **unconditional positive regard** from the therapist will permit the client to move toward a more realistic self-concept and toward **self-actualization.** Research has been encouraged by Rogers, and the evidence indicates that his form of therapy leads to positive changes, at least for individuals who are not severely disturbed.

When learning psychologists began examining the process of psychotherapy, it soon became clear that the verbalizations of therapists act as rewards and punishments which affect the content of what is said by patients.

One of the outcomes of such research was the direct application of learning principles to therapy designed to alter behavior, an approach known as **behavior modification.** Specific techniques include **counterconditioning, systematic desensitization,** and **aversive conditioning. Operant conditioning** is a type of behavior modification based on the work of B. F. Skinner, and its application includes such techniques as the creation of the **token economy** in institutional and family settings. The concept of **modeling** is also employed to alter behavior; the desired behavior is carried out by live or filmed models.

For various reasons, most types of therapy have been modified to allow the therapist to work with groups of patients. J. L. Moreno introduced **psychodrama** as a way to help patients experience their emotional conflicts rather than simply to talk about them. **Encounter groups** evolved from a combination of **sensitivity training groups** and **client-centered groups.** Other techniques include bio-energetic therapy, existential analysis, Gestalt therapy, nude therapy, primal therapy, and transactional analysis.

Community psychology is a new approach to applying psychological skills in which it is assumed that (1) environmental variables may be responsible for behavior problems, (2) professionals should actively seek out the problems as they arise, or even before they arise, and (3) the most effective therapy should take place in everyday settings rather than in the professional's office. One example of community psychology in action was an attempt to use both professional and **paraprofessional** workers to help the citizens of a town cope with the difficulties caused by the destructive effects of a tornado.

Suggested Readings

Ayllon, T., and Azrin, N.: *The Token Economy: A Motivational System for Therapy and Rehabilitation.* New York: Appleton-Century-Crofts, 1968.
   *An interesting description of the way in which the principles of behavior modification can be util-*ized to bring about dramatic changes in behavior.

Denner, B., and Price, R. H. (eds.): *Community Mental Health: Social Action and Reaction.* New York: Holt, Rinehart, and Winston, 1973.

An informative discussion of both the way in which community mental health programs function and the impact of these programs on various aspects of society.

Lieberman, M. A., Yalon, I. D., and Miles, M.: *Encounter Groups: First Facts.* New York: Basic Books, 1973.

An introduction to encounter groups. This book describes the way in which such groups function and presents research findings documenting the effects of the group experience.

Rogers, C. R.: Client-Centered Therapy. Boston: Houghton Mifflin, 1951.

The classic description of Rogers' theory of personality and its application to nondirective, or client-centered, therapy. In a very readable style, Rogers indicates the implications of his approach not only to therapy but to other types of interpersonal situations, such as child-rearing and education.

Waelder, R.: Basic Theory of Psychoanalysis. New York: International Universities Press, 1960.

An introduction to Freud's system of psychotherapy, including both the procedures used in psychoanalysis and the theoretical ideas underlying them.

Some journals that regularly publish papers on psychotherapy:

American Journal of Psychiatry
Archives of General Psychiatry
Behavior Therapy
Behavior Research and Therapy
Community Mental Health Journal
International Journal of Group Psychotherapy
Journal of Abnormal Psychology
Journal of Applied Behavior Analysis
Journal of Behavior Therapy and Experimental Psychiatry
Journal of Clinical Psychology
Journal of Community Psychology
Journal of Consulting and Clinical Psychology
Journal of Counseling Psychology
Journal of the Experimental Analysis of Behavior
Mental Hygiene
Psychiatric Quarterly
Psychosomatic Medicine
Psychotherapy: Theory, Research and Practice

Overleaf: Top photo by Irwin Nash. Bottom photo, Brown Brothers.

12 The Process of Social Influence: Changing Attitudes and Altering Behavior

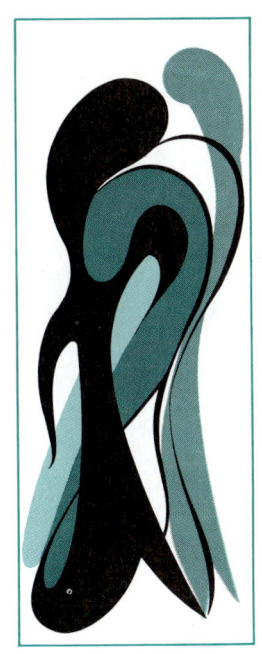

Suppose that, as has been the case in a number of Hollywood epics, you awoke one morning to discover that you were the last person on earth. Further, imagine that the silent catastrophe which had carried off the rest of humanity had left all other aspects of the world untouched. Everything has been left exactly as before, except that all the people have vanished. As you wander through the empty streets, it would soon become apparent that satisfying all of your physical needs would be quite easy: food, clothing, and shelter would all be present for the taking, and in abundance. In fact, you would probably come to realize that you are now the master of all you survey, and that the entire collective treasure of humanity is completely at your disposal (see Figure 12-1). How do you think you would react to this surprising turn of events?

In all probability, once you recovered from your initial shock and fear, and realized that your own end was not imminent, you would be plunged into the deepest depths of despair. You would suffer profound loneliness and regret the loss of all human companionship—especially that of your friends and loved ones. As time went by, you would long more and more for the sound of another voice or a glimpse of another face. As a result, you might redouble your efforts to locate other survivors, only to meet with one disappointment after another. Finally, you might become so depressed with your solitary existence that thoughts of suicide would become increasingly common; after all, why continue such a pointless and empty life?

Fortunately, the probability that any of us will ever face such an unsettling situation is quite remote. The web of life binding us together on this small globe is far too tight to permit the survival of one when all others have perished. Yet, this somewhat fanciful situation serves to emphasize an important

FIGURE 12–1 Science-fiction movies which have focused on the sad plight of the last person on earth provide a dramatic illustration of the extent to which we both need and are dependent upon others. (From the MGM release *The World, the Flesh, and the Devil,* © 1958 Metro-Goldwyn-Mayer, Inc.)

fact about human behavior: other persons—and our relations with them—play a crucial role in our lives. Many of our most important needs, such as those for friendship, love, and affection, can be satisfied only through interaction with others. Similarly, as we noted in Chapter 4, other persons often serve as our models or teachers, and it is from them that we acquire much of our knowledge about the world, and even ourselves. Finally, it is only with the help of others that we can accomplish many goals; in the absence of their assistance we are simply too weak or powerless to attain our ends. In short, we are dependent upon others in so many different ways that the thought of life without them often seems quite unbearable.

As you already know from your own experience, our social interactions with others take many different forms. For example, we may attempt to help them at one time, only to hurt them at others; we may cooperate with them on one occasion, but compete actively with them on others; we may fall in or out of love with the same or different persons, bargain or negotiate with them over a host of different issues, lead them or follow—the list could go on and on. One particularly common pattern in our relations with others, though, involves attempts on their part to change our behavior, feelings, or thoughts, and corresponding attempts by us to produce similar alterations in them. Efforts directed toward such ends are generally known as **social influence,** and range in scope from praise and flattery on the one end to threats and physical violence on the other (see Figure 12–2). Further, they seem to occur in almost every imaginable social context. For example, consider the following instances in which one person attempts to influence the behavior, feelings, or thoughts of others: (1) a parent seeks to induce his or her children to behave in safer or less irritating ways; (2) one friend tries to persuade another to do her a favor; (3) a salesman tries to convince a potential customer to purchase some product or service; (4) a young man seeks to persuade his date to spend the night in his apartment; (5) a politician attempts to convince voters to cast their ballots in his favor on election day; (6) an advertising executive plans a commercial which, she hopes, will change the buying habits of millions of consumers.

Even these few examples should be sufficient to suggest the frequency with which we are both the targets and users of social influence.

Because the process of social influence has long been of interest to social psychologists, much interesting and potentially useful information concerning its operation has been acquired. In the present chapter, we will examine this knowledge, beginning with a consideration of the manner in which others seek to *alter our attitudes*, turning next to the many ways in which they seek to *modify our behavior*, and concluding with a brief examination of what may be termed *unintentional social influence*—ways in which others alter our actions or thoughts even when they are not specifically seeking to accomplish this goal.

ATTITUDE CHANGE: THE POWER OF POSITIVE PERSUASION

Consider the following list:

pizza	marijuana
Thunderbirds	black Americans
the los Angeles Dodgers	inflation
legalized abortion	Marlon Brando

These items are highly diverse and totally unrelated. Yet, if asked to do so, you could readily describe your (1) feelings, (2) beliefs, and (3) behavior with respect to each. For example, you could report that you *like* pizza very much, *believe* that it is fattening, and usually *eat* it at least once a week. Similarly, you might state that you are strongly *opposed* to legalized abortion, *believe* that it will lead to sexual promiscuity, and would, if given the opportunity, *vote* for its repeal.

According to many psychologists (e.g., Kiesler and Munson, 1975; Suedfeld, 1971), your **attitudes** toward each of the items on the list are actually composed of the three elements mentioned above. More specifically, your attitude toward any entity in the world is assumed to consist of (1) your positive or negative feelings toward it; (2) your beliefs about it; and (3) your behavior tendencies regarding it. Throughout the present discussion, then, *attitudes* will be defined as *enduring organizations of feelings, beliefs, and behavior tendencies relating to any object, person, issue, or group*.

When attitudes are defined in this manner, it is clear that attempts to change them must involve the alteration of one or more of the three basic elements of which they are composed. Usually, modifying one of these factors leads to appropriate changes in the others. For example, if we can succeed in

FIGURE 12-2 As shown here, attempts to influence the attitudes or behavior of others take many different forms. (© King Features Syndicate, Inc., 1975.)

convincing the opponent of legalized abortion mentioned above that this procedure actually yields beneficial consequences (e.g., a reduction in the number of unwanted and abandoned children), it is likely that this person's feelings about the issue will become less negative, and that his or her tendency to vote for its repeal will also be reduced. In order to modify attitudes, then, it is often only necessary to alter one of the three basic components of which they are composed.

Despite this fact, the task of changing attitudes is somewhat more difficult than might at first be expected. This appears to be the case because attitudes are learned or acquired, and, as is true of all such behavior (see Chapter 4), they are somewhat resistant to change. Indeed, since attitudes are frequently acquired very early in life and strengthened through repeated reinforcement over a period of years, they tend to be among the most stable aspects of our behavior. For example, consider the development of a strong racial prejudice. As we noted in Chapter 4 (see pp. 116–117), the acquisition of such negative attitudes toward others often begins when children acquire—largely through the process of classical conditioning—negative emotional reactions to the members of groups hated or disliked by their parents. The development of such reactions may then pave the way for imitation of their parents' prejudiced statements and behavior. Instrumental conditioning then begins to play a role, as mothers and fathers reward their children with praise and approval for voicing prejudiced attitudes similar to their own—for acting like chips off the old bigoted block (see Figure 12–3). This process continues throughout childhood and adolescence, so that by the time they are adults, the individuals involved have acquired negative attitudes toward certain racial or ethnic groups which are so strong as to be almost totally resistant to change.

Notwithstanding the potential difficulties involved in modifying such entrenched beliefs, a number of different techniques have been found to be quite effective in this regard. Among the most successful of these are (1) **persuasive communications,** (2) **emotional appeals,** and (3) the **induction of attitude-discrepant behavior.**

FIGURE 12–3   Parents often reward their children for imitating their prejudiced beliefs and behavior. In this way they insure that their youngsters turn out to be chips off the "old bigoted block." (Photo credit: Brown Brothers.)

Most attempts to modify our attitudes involve some type of persuasive communication—spoken, written, televised, or filmed messages—which seek to alter our reactions toward various objects through logical arguments, convincing facts, and authoritative information. Of course in many cases, the arguments contained in such appeals turn out to be far from logical, the information presented is anything but authoritative, and the facts included are far from convincing. Yet, such communications generally maintain at least a semblance of reasonableness as part of their overall structure.

If we were strongly influenced by all of the persuasive communications we encountered, our homes would soon be overflowing with products we do not need, our donations to various charities would soon outstrip our income, and we would change our views regarding many important issues on a daily basis. The fact that we manage to avoid this chaotic state of affairs indicates that not all persuasive communications succeed in their intended purpose. Indeed, on some occasions, they may "boomerang" and produce effects quite opposite to the ones intended (Brehm, 1972). Although a number of different factors seem to determine the effectiveness of persuasive communications in altering our attitudes, the most important seem to involve certain characteristics of: (1) the *communicator*, (2) the *communication* itself, (3) the *recipients* (i.e., the persons who receive it), and (4) the *context* in which it is delivered.

Characteristics of the Communicator: If You Can't Trust the Experts, Who Can You Trust?

Both common sense and the lessons of bitter experience inform us that all communicators are *not* equally reliable. We learn quite early in life that some of the persons who try to influence us are to be believed and trusted, while others are to be doubted and mistrusted. For example, in trying to determine whether smoking is harmful to your health, you would probably pay more attention to information provided by the Surgeon General than to advertisements paid for by the tobacco industry. Similarly, in deciding whether to purchase a particular product, you would probably accept the statements of your friends regarding its quality or performance more readily than those of a salesman who stands to earn a large commission from the transaction. The effectiveness of persuasive communications in influencing our attitudes, then, is strongly affected by our judgments concerning the credibility of their source: the more credible the person delivering them, the greater their success in changing our opinions (see Figure 12–4).

Although our judgments regarding communicators' degree of credibility are probably influenced by many different factors, three seem to be of primary importance: (1) their apparent level of *expertise* or *competence*, (2) their degree of *trustworthiness* or *sincerity*, and (3) their level of *attractiveness*. The importance of the first of these factors has been examined in a number of experiments (e.g., Aronson, Turner, and Carlsmith, 1963). In general, the results of these studies have been consistent in suggesting that communicators high in expertise tend to induce greater degrees of attitude change than do those lower in this dimension.

In contrast, the role of communicators' apparent trustworthiness in determining their success at persuasion has been less thoroughly studied. There is some indication, however, that persons who argue for positions opposed to their own best interests are often perceived as more sincere, and thereby induce greater degrees of attitude change than do those whose communications can be attributed to selfish motives (Walster, Aronson, and Abrahams, 1966). For example, imagine that one day you switched on the radio and heard the president of General Motors make a strong appeal for tougher laws to control air pollution. After you recovered from your initial shock, there is a good chance that you would be greatly affected by this speech; after all, since the

Persuasive Communications: Is Listening Believing?

FIGURE 12-4 Communicators we view as being high in credibility (such as those shown here) are usually more successful in changing our attitudes than communicators we view as low in credibility. (Photo credits: left, CBS News; right, United Press International.)

individual making it might lose much if his recommendations were accepted, there would be strong grounds for assuming that he was quite sincere. In contrast, if you heard a similar speech by the president of a company which manufactured devices designed to reduce such pollution, you might be influenced to a much smaller degree; this person's communication could readily be attributed to a selfish desire for gain.

A final characteristic of communicators which seems to exert an important effect upon their ability to alter the attitudes of others is their degree of attractiveness to these persons. Other factors being equal, the more attractive a communicator is, the greater his or her success in inducing attitude change among members of the audience (Berscheid, 1966; Mills and Harvey, 1972). As we will soon see in Chapter 13, liking for others, including communicators, can be affected by a number of different factors. Among the most important, however, are physical appearance and apparent similarity to one's audience. In general, communicators who present an attractive physical appearance and who seem highly similar to the recipients of their appeals will be liked more than those of less impressive physical appearance or who appear dissimilar to their audience (e.g., Byrne, 1971; Berscheid and Walster, 1974). Both politicians and advertising executives seem to be well aware of these facts, and often make full use of them in their attempts to alter the attitudes of large groups of people. For example, there has been a growing tendency, in recent years, to select political candidates as much for their good looks as their abilities. And, once chosen, candidates often go out of their way to demonstrate that they are basically "just plain folks"—that is, quite similar in many ways to the voters they hope to persuade (see Figure 12-5). Similarly, advertisers often use either highly attractive models or well-known and well-liked celebrities to deliver their commercial messages, hoping in this way to increase the persuasive impact of their appeals.

To summarize, existing evidence suggests that communicators will be most effective in changing the attitudes of their audience when they (1) seem to know what they are talking about, (2) appear honest and trustworthy, and (3) are personally appealing for one reason or another.

Imagine that you are sitting in the audience at a large meeting when a world-famous astronomer known to be one of the greatest living experts on the nature of the universe is introduced. As a distinguished member of the scientific community, his honesty and trustworthiness are unquestioned. Further, as he mounts the podium, you notice that he is an individual of impressive physical appearance—a true spellbinder. The room becomes hushed, and he begins to speak, announcing with great conviction and forcefulness that the moon is made of green cheese. For a moment there is stunned silence, and then wild howls of laughter erupt, and the speaker is driven from the stage.

Characteristics of the Communication: It's Not Only Who You Are, but What You Say

This extreme and highly unlikely incident serves to illustrate an important point: the effectiveness of a persuasive appeal depends not only on its source—who delivers it—but also upon the message it contains and the manner in which it is presented. Since the specific contents of any persuasive message varies with the particular issue involved, it is almost impossible to formulate general rules for what a speaker should say. As a result, most research has focused on the *form* of such appeals, examining the influence on persuasion of such factors as (1) the use of one- or two-sided arguments and (2) the amount of discrepancy between the communicator's position and that of the audience.

With respect to the first of these factors, one question of interest is whether it is better for a communicator to present only the view he would like his audience to adopt or to give both this view and competing positions. Existing evidence (e.g., Hass and Linder, 1972) suggests that the answer to this question depends on whether the audience is initially favorable or unfavorable to the communicator's views. If they are favorable, it is better to employ the one-sided approach, for in this case, they are disposed to accept the message anyway, and the presence of competing views will only cloud the issue. When they are unfavorable, however, the two-sided approach appears to be more effective, apparently because under these conditions, the communicator seems to be less biased when presenting both sides of the story. In short, it seems unnecessary to refute opposing views when addressing individuals who agree with your own position, but wise to do so when addressing persons who strongly disagree.

Evidence relating to the size of the discrepancy between the position ad-

FIGURE 12–5 One way in which communicators can increase their attractiveness to others is by appearing similar to them. As shown here, politicians often attempt to use this principle in their election campaigns. (Photo credits: United Press International.)

vocated by the communicator and that held by the audience suggests that up to a point, greater discrepancies lead to greater attitude change, but that beyond some crucial level, attitude change may actually begin to decrease as the communicator-audience gap continues to widen (e.g., Eagly, 1974). Apparently, this sort of "boomerang" effect is due to the fact that beyond some specific point, audience members begin to find the communicator's position unreasonably extreme and reject it as invalid or ridiculous. For example, a liberal politician addressing a conservative audience might succeed in swaying these individuals to some degree if he recommended cautious initiatives toward better relations with Communist nations, but he would probably be booed, stoned, or physically dragged from the stage if he called for total unilateral disarmament by the U.S.

Not too surprisingly, the point at which increasing discrepancy size begins to produce lesser rather than greater degrees of attitude change seems to vary with the credibility of the communicator. Highly credible sources can advocate relatively extreme positions with little or no reduction in their persuasive impact, while less credible sources may begin to experience strong "boomerang" effects even when the statements they make depart from the beliefs of their audience only to a relatively small degree. For example, in one well-known experiment conducted by Aronson, Turner, and Carlsmith (1963), subjects first evaluated several selections of poetry, and then received persuasive communications regarding these selections from either a high- or low-credibility source. In the low-credibility condition, these evaluations were attributed to a student at a small, low-prestige college, while in the high-credibility group they were attributed to T. S. Eliot, a world-famous poet. The discrepancy between subjects' own initial ratings and the views expressed by the communicator was also varied, so as to be small, moderate, or large. When subjects were then asked to evaluate the poems once again, an interesting pattern of results emerged: in the case of the high-credibility source, attitude change increased as discrepancy size increased; in the case of the low-credibility source, attitude change first increased and then decreased with increasing discrepancy (see Figure 12–6). These findings, which have been repeated in other studies, suggest that establishing a high level of credibility may be an important first step for anyone seeking to persuade or influence others; without it, even moderate recommendations for change may often be rejected.

Characteristics of the Recipients: Are Some People Easier to Influence than Others?

Even an extremely convincing persuasive appeal delivered by a highly credible source will fail to change the attitudes of all the individuals toward whom it is directed, and even a very weak appeal communicated by a source low in credibility will succeed in changing the attitudes of *some* listeners. This is the case because, as is true of virtually every other imaginable characteristic, people vary greatly in terms of their general **persuasibility.** Some are highly resistant to virtually all forms of influence, others are swayed easily by even weak appeals and arguments (the girl in the song who could never say "no"), and most are somewhere in between these two extremes. Moreover, it appears that such differences in persuasibility are fairly consistent across a wide variety of contexts: individuals who are easily swayed in one situation tend to be easily swayed in others as well, and those who are highly resistant to influence in one context are equally impervious to persuasion in others (Janis and Field, 1956). As a result, the effectiveness of persuasive communications in altering attitudes will depend, to an important degree, upon the "sales resistance" of the audiences to whom they are delivered.

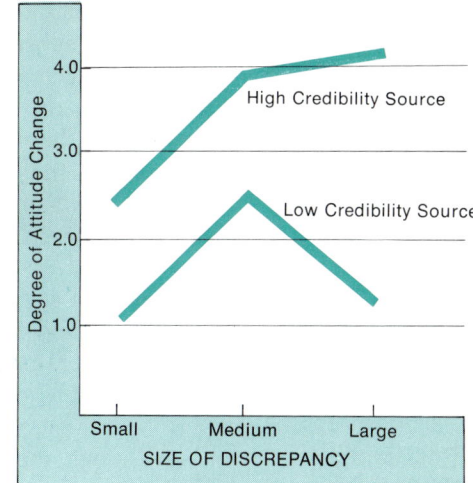

FIGURE 12-6 The effects of communicator-audience discrepancy size upon persuasion. Attitude change increases with increasing discrepancy size for high-credibility communicators, but may first increase and then decline in the case of low-credibility sources. See test for further explanation. (Based on data from Aronson, Turner, and Carlsmith, 1963.)

Common sense suggests that people are much easier to influence when they are in a good mood than when they are feeling irritable or grouchy. In accordance with this widespread belief, businessmen often attempt to "wine and dine" their potential clients before entering into serious negotiations with them. And largely for similar reasons, most seductions (by both sexes) are attempted after a good meal and in the presence of soft lights and pleasant music (see Figure 12-7). Politicians, too, seem to follow this suggestion, frequently providing free refreshments and entertainment at political rallies in order to put potential voters in a good mood before beginning their appeals.

In this particular instance, common sense seems to be correct, for experiments undertaken to examine the relationship between mood and the acceptance of social influence have generally yielded positive results. For example, it has been found that providing subjects with a light snack during the period when they are exposed to persuasive messages increases their degree of attitude change in the direction advocated (Janis, Kaye, and Kirschner, 1965). Similarly, the presence of pleasant music seems to increase the acceptance of various kinds of persuasive appeals, including those dealing with serious social issues (e.g., water pollution and the desperate plight of the aged) (Galizio and Hendrick, 1972). Such findings suggest that songs with a "message," which

Characteristics of the Context: Feeling Good and Persuasion

FIGURE 12-7 Putting another person in a good mood is often a highly effective first step to persuasion. (Photo credit: Stephen Soldoff.)

were popular a few years in the past, may have actually been quite effective in changing several important social attitudes.

Although it is not yet entirely clear why persuasion is enhanced by positive feelings on the part of the recipients, two possibilities have been suggested. First, being in a positive mood may cause many individuals to evaluate the messages they receive in a more favorable manner. Second, positive feelings may serve as a source of distraction, preventing recipients from forming their own counterarguments against the messages they receive (Keating and Brock, 1974). Regardless of the precise mechanisms involved, attempts to "soften up" the targets of social influence by placing them in a relaxed and pleasant mood may often yield handsome pay-offs in terms of increased attitude change. To paraphrase a famous jingle, one of the things which may "go better with Coke" is persuasion.

Emotional Appeals: Persuasion Through Fear

Although most attempts to change our attitudes involve the use of persuasive communications, others employ strong fear-inducing appeals for this purpose, suggesting that failure to adopt certain positions or recommended courses of action will lead to truly disastrous results. For example, politicians often suggest that the election of their opponents will lead to chaos and ruin, clergymen that failure to adopt certain religious beliefs will result in eternal damnation, and public service organizations (e.g., the American Cancer Society and the National Safety Council) that failure to follow good health or safety practices will lead to injury, illness, or even death (see Figure 12–8).

In view of the frequency with which such fear appeals are employed to alter attitudes, it is important to ask whether they are indeed successful in this respect. A large number of experiments have been concerned with this ques-

SMOKING
CAN EAT YOUR LUNGS ALIVE!

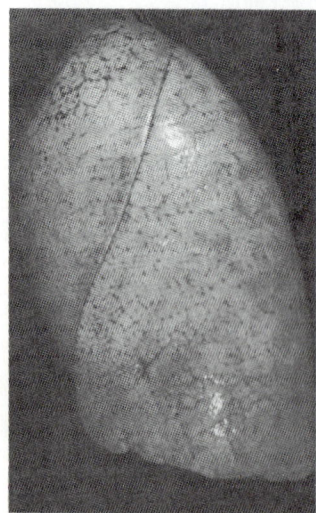 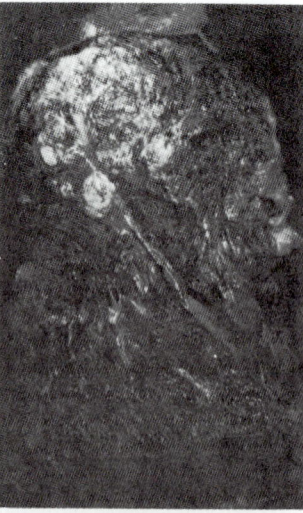

This is a normal lung, with its characteristically healthy pink coloring.

This is a cancerous lung. The white growth at the top of the lung is the cancer.

ACCORDING TO THE AMERICAN LUNG ASSOCIATION, IF YOU SMOKE YOUR CHANCES OF DYING FROM LUNG CANCER ARE 700 TIMES THOSE OF NON-SMOKERS. IF YOU SMOKE, THIS COULD BE YOUR LUNG. THINK ABOUT IT THE NEXT TIME YOU LIGHT A CIGARETTE...IF THERE IS A NEXT TIME.

FIGURE 12–8   Fear appeals which threaten the reader or viewer with highly unpleasant outcomes, such as the one shown here, are often quite effective in changing both attitudes and behavior. A safe-driving advertisement with a similar emphasis on the presentation of an unpleasant outcome used this appeal: IN A 45 MPH CRASH, THE AVERAGE HEADS HITS THE AVERAGE WINDSHIELD WITH A FORCE OF OVER A TON. (Anti-smoking appeal from the slide show "If you smoke. . .", © 1972 by G. T. Hewlett.)

tion, and, in general, results have suggested that strong fear messages do indeed tend to induce greater attitude change than do weak ones (see Higbee, 1969). For example, frightening films showing diseased lungs and actual lung cancer operations have been found to produce greater changes in smokers' attitudes toward their habit than milder communications depicting smoking machines, charts, and graphs (Leventhal et al., 1967). Similarly, gory pictures of decayed teeth and diseased gums have been shown to produce greater changes in attitudes toward dental hygiene than less frightening communications based on pictures of plastic models of teeth (Evans et al., 1970). Strong fear appeals are not always successful in changing attitudes, however, and other evidence suggests that they are most effective in this regard when recipients are also provided with concrete recommendations for avoiding the negative outcomes shown (Leventhal, 1970).

This fact—that fear appeals function most successfully when followed by clear recommendations—points to one possible explanation for their effectiveness in changing many attitudes. Specifically, it may be the case that acceptance of the recommendations offered produces a sharp drop in subjects' level of arousal (i.e., fear). Since reductions in unpleasant emotional arousal are reinforcing, subjects' tendencies to accept these recommendations may then be strengthened, and attitude change enhanced. Moreover, since the reduction of high levels of arousal is more reinforcing than the reduction of lower ones, strong fear appeals would be expected to produce greater attitude change than weak ones (see Figure 12–9).

Evidence for this drive-reduction explanation—which basically suggests that individuals exposed to fear appeals change their attitudes because it feels so good when they are no longer afraid—has been obtained in several recent experiments (Harris and Jellison, 1971). However, conflicting findings have also been reported (Giesen and Hendrick, 1974), and it is probably too soon to pass final judgment on the overall accuracy of the drive-reduction view.

A third major technique for modifying attitudes is suggested by the theory of **cognitive dissonance** proposed some years ago by Leon Festinger (1957). According to this view, human beings have a strong preference for cognitive consistency—agreement among their attitudes, opinions, and beliefs. As a result, whenever they become aware of an inconsistency between two or more related thoughts, they experience an unpleasant state of *dissonance*, and will actively strive to reduce or eliminate its presence. For example, if a young woman believes that she is highly attractive to members of the opposite sex, but finds that she never has any dates, she will probably experience strong feelings of dissonance, and engage in various attempts to eliminate these unpleasant reactions. (She may convince herself that most men are boors, unable to recognize true beauty when they see it, or that she has so few dates because of her unusually high moral standards.) Similarly, if an individual holds

Attitude-Discrepant Behavior: Does Doing Lead to Believing?

FIGURE 12–9 The drive-reduction explanation for the effectiveness of fear appeals. According to this view, fear communications (1) lead to increased arousal (2). Recommendations following the fear appeal (3) then lead to reassurance on the part of recipients (4), which serves to reduce their negative arousal (5). These reductions in arousal are reinforcing, and strengthen acceptance of the recommendations, thus producing attitude change (6).

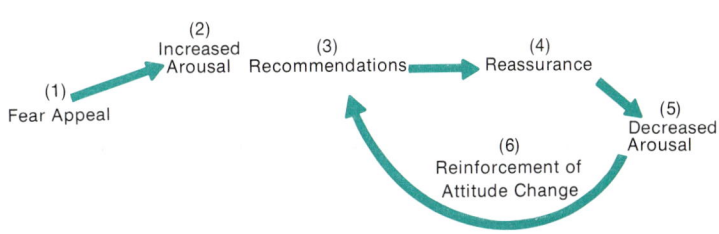

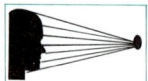

FOCUS ON RESEARCH: *Attitudes and Behavior: Do Actions Speak Louder Than Words?*

In our discussion up to this point, we have largely ignored a crucial question which may have already begun to trouble you a bit: how close is the link between attitudes and behavior? The answer to this question has important implications. If attitudes are closely related to overt actions, we should be able to predict an individual's behavior from his or her verbally expressed opinions with a high degree of accuracy. Further, alterations in attitudes should be followed by corresponding changes in behavior. If the relationship between attitudes and behavior is relatively weak, however, such predictions would not be possible. Moreover, it would often make little sense to attempt to alter others' attitudes, since no changes in their overt behavior would then necessarily follow.

Because of the importance of this issue, it has been the subject of considerable attention. Unfortunately, though, there seems to be no simple or clear-cut resolution in sight. In fact, existing evidence points to the conclusion that the relationship between attitudes and behavior is quite complex. On the negative side of the ledger, a large number of experiments have indicated that attitudes and behavior are *not* very closely related (e.g., Wicker, 1971; Wrightsman, 1969). For example, in one well-known early study, LaPiere (1934) toured the country with a young Chinese couple, stopping at more than 250 hotels, motels, and restaurants during a journey of more than 10,000 miles. In all that time, he and his friends were refused service only once. However, when LaPiere wrote to the same establishments several months later, asking whether they would agree to serve Chinese patrons, fully 92 per cent of those responding indicated that they would refuse. Findings such as these point to the conclusion that often, there may be a considerable gap between verbally expressed attitudes and actual behavior. While there are several reasons why this might be so, two seem to be of greatest importance.

First, other factors often intrude and prevent individuals from acting in accordance with their true feelings or beliefs. As we shall soon see in more detail, cultural norms or the desire to please others sometimes forces us to engage in actions somewhat out of line with our true feelings or beliefs. For example, a racial bigot running a restaurant in the 1970's cannot refuse to serve members of the groups he dislikes; legal sanctions simply make such behavior far too costly. Largely as a result of such external constraints, in many situations attitudes may often fail as predictors of overt behavior.

Second, the practical difficulties involved in accurately measuring others' attitudes may often lead to the appearance of a gap between attitudes and behavior even when none actually exists. To mention just two possible sources of such confusion, individuals may misunderstand the questions being asked or think that they refer to one attitude object when they actually relate to another. In such cases, their responses may not reflect their true feelings or beliefs, and the fact that their replies later seem unrelated to their overt actions is far from surprising. For example, consider the statement "Greater protection of the environment is definitely needed." Most persons who indicate agreement with this item are probably endorsing tougher laws to control air and water pollution. A few, however, might be indicating their support for stronger protection of owners' rights to do anything they wish on their property—including actions which foul their neighbors' air and water! Given such possible differences of interpretation, we might well find individuals in the first group supporting environmental legislation and those in the second opposing it despite the fact that they previously seemed to express identical views on this issue. In such cases, of course, the gap between attitudes and behavior is more apparent than real.

Despite the influence of such factors, however, other evidence suggests that attitudes can indeed often serve as effective predictors of overt actions (Fishbein and Azjen, 1975). In particular, it appears that when attitudes toward a specific form of behavior, as well as those toward the object of that behavior, are taken into account, accurate predictions can often be made. For example, in one study, Rokeach and Kliejunas (1972) found that the frequency with which students cut various classes could not be predicted accurately from their attitudes toward the instructors of these courses alone. But when the students' attitudes toward class-cutting as a form of behavior were also taken into account, highly accurate predictions could in fact be made. Similarly, in a more recent investigation, Heberlein and Black (1976) found that voluntary purchases of lead-free gasoline could be accurately predicted from drivers' *specific* attitudes regarding such actions, but could not be predicted from their more general beliefs about the environment and pollution. In sum, it appears that attitudes and behavior are not necessarily closely related in all cases, but often are. As noted by Abelson (1972), a leading expert in this area, it is probably inappropriate to assume either that attitudes are always closely related to behavior or that they are never linked to overt actions. Rather, this is an empirical question which must be carefully examined in each particular case.

basically liberal political beliefs, but then finds that he is strongly opposed to the higher taxes which follow from increased government spending, considerable dissonance may be produced. And again, because this is an unpleasant or uncomfortable state to be in, the person involved may engage in attempts to reduce its presence. (For example, he may conclude that government programs don't really help disadvantaged members of our society—they merely waste taxpayers' money.)

As you can probably see from even these few examples, dissonance may arise—and be reduced—in an almost limitless number of ways. One particularly important source of such feelings, though, seems to lie in the performance by an individual of some action which is inconsistent with his or her attitudes. Under these conditions, the person involved finds that his behavior does not fit with his beliefs, and will, therefore, experience considerable dissonance. Although people usually behave in a manner which is consistent with their attitudes, incompatibility between their actions and beliefs is not at all rare. For example, we are often required to act in a polite and friendly manner toward relatives, co-workers, or superiors whom we greatly dislike. Similarly, we often praise others' clothing or general appearance in order to please them or avoid hurting their feelings, even when our reactions to these stimuli are quite negative. In such cases, dissonance will be aroused, and pressures toward its reduction will develop. One way in which persons experiencing such dissonance can seek to reduce its presence is to convince themselves that they have not actually engaged in attitude-discrepant behavior. Since they will rarely succeed at fooling themselves in this manner, however, they usually seek to eliminate such dissonance in another way—by changing their attitudes so that they are no longer inconsistent with the actions taken (see Figure 12–10). In short, the theory of cognitive dissonance suggests that one highly effective means of altering the attitudes of others is that of somehow inducing them to engage in behaviors which are inconsistent with their beliefs.

That the performance of such attitude-discrepant behavior does in fact often lead to attitude change is suggested both by informal observation and the findings of laboratory research. Turning first to informal evidence, it is clear that individuals who repeatedly lie to others often come to believe the false-

FIGURE 12–10 When individuals discover that their actions have been inconsistent with their attitudes, they experience cognitive dissonance. In order to eliminate such unpleasant reactions, they then often alter their attitudes so as to be consistent with their behavior. In the cartoon, the executive's initial negative reaction to the idea of double-decker desks was inconsistent with his behavior—the payment of a large fee to a consulting firm which came up with the same suggestion. As a result, he felt a strong pressure to change his attitude toward this idea. (© King Features Syndicate, Inc., 1975.)

hoods they utter, perhaps because in this way their attitudes and behavior are made to agree. Similarly, there appear to be many instances in which we strongly disapprove of some action before we have performed it but quickly come to view it in a much more favorable light once it has been completed. For example, a public official who believes that it is wrong to take bribes may quickly adopt a more favorable view of such behavior once he has been persuaded to accept his first "gift."

More formal evidence for the influence of our actions upon our attitudes is provided by a number of laboratory studies in which subjects have somehow been induced to argue either in written essays or in actual speeches for positions they do not support (Gerard, Conolley, and Wilhelmy, 1974). The results of such studies have indicated that participants often change their attitudes so as to be more consistent with the views they express than was the case at the start of the session. Such findings provide convincing evidence for the suggestion that *saying* may indeed sometimes lead to believing.

In a number of respects, the fact that performing actions which are inconsistent with our attitudes leads to alterations in these views is not very surprising. Since the dissonance aroused in such situations is unpleasant, it would be expected that the persons involved would seek to reduce its presence by altering their attitudes. More surprising, however, is another prediction derived from dissonance theory: the *less* justification we have for engaging in attitude-discrepant behavior, the *more* we will alter our attitudes following its performance. This hypothesis is based on the idea that the fewer good reasons we have for engaging in behavior opposed to our attitudes, the more dissonance we will experience and, therefore, the greater the pressure to alter our views. Going one step further, dissonance theory also suggests that in situations in which individuals are offered rewards for engaging in attitude-discrepant behavior, the degree of attitude change that is produced will be at a maximum when such rewards are just barely sufficient to induce the inconsistent actions. Any smaller, and such behavior will not be performed; any larger, and the increased justification that is provided will serve to lessen the dissonance experienced. In short, dissonance theory leads to the somewhat paradoxical prediction that in many cases, less may well produce more: lesser amounts of reward will actually induce greater degrees of attitude change (refer to Figure 12-11). Evidence supporting these predictions has actually been obtained in a number of interesting studies (Heslin and Amo, 1972; Nel, Helmreich, and Aronson, 1969).

ATTITUDE-DISCREPANT BEHAVIOR PERFORMED FOR SMALL REWARDS

I acted in a manner inconsistent with my feelings or beliefs + I had no good reason for doing so $\longrightarrow$ High Magnitude of Dissonance $\longrightarrow$ Large Degree of Attitude Change

ATTITUDE-DISCREPANT BEHAVIOR PERFORMED FOR LARGE REWARDS

I acted in a manner inconsistent with my feelings or beliefs + I had sufficient reasons for doing so $\longrightarrow$ Low Magnitude of Dissonance $\longrightarrow$ Small Degree of Attitude Change

FIGURE 12-11   Dissonance theory leads to the intriguing suggestion that when individuals choose to engage in attitude-discrepant behavior for relatively small rewards, they will often demonstrate greater amounts of change than when they engage in such actions for relatively large rewards.

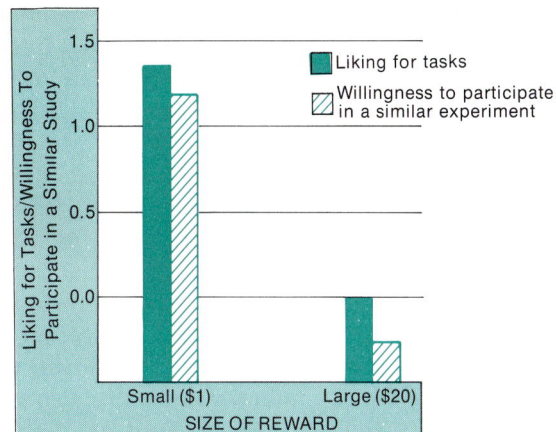

FIGURE 12–12 The theory of cognitive dissonance predicts that under some conditions, "less" (smaller rewards) can lead to "more" (greater degrees of attitude change). In a famous experiment by Festinger and Carlsmith (1959), individuals paid $1 for engaging in attitude-discrepant behavior later reported more positive attitudes toward dull, boring tasks and greater willingness to participate in similar studies than those paid $20 for performing such actions. (Based on data from Festinger and Carlsmith, 1959.)

In the first and perhaps best known of these experiments (Festinger and Carlsmith, 1959), subjects who had just completed some exceedingly dull, boring tasks were asked to inform another person (actually a confederate of the experimenter) that the tasks they had performed were actually quite interesting and enjoyable. As an incentive for engaging in such attitude-discrepant behavior, subjects were offered either a $1 or a $20 payment. On the basis of dissonance theory, it was predicted that those provided with the small payment for misleading the confederate would actually show a greater change in their attitudes toward the dull, boring tasks than would those provided with the large payment. This would be the case because the low-payment group would have far less justification for having engaged in such attitude-discrepant behavior (i.e., for having lied to the accomplice), and therefore would experience greater dissonance. As can be seen in Figure 12–12, results offered clear support for these predictions: as expected, subjects who had been paid $1 for lying actually reported liking the experiment and their tasks (which they clearly despised at first) much more than did those paid $20 for such behavior.

Despite their somewhat surprising nature, such results have also been obtained in a number of additional studies (Green, 1974; Linder, Cooper, and Jones, 1967). The results of these follow-up experiments have also indicated, however, that it is *only under special conditions* that providing subjects with small rewards for engaging in attitude-discrepant behavior leads to greater alterations in their attitudes than does providing them with large rewards.

First, as might be expected, such outcomes are produced only in situations in which individuals believe that they have had a choice as to whether or not to perform the attitude-discrepant behavior. When they feel that they have had such freedom of action, the fact that they chose to behave in a manner inconsistent with their beliefs leads to the occurrence of dissonance, and results similar to those obtained by Festinger and Carlsmith are obtained—small rewards produce greater degrees of change than do large ones. When they feel that they have had no choice but to behave the way they did, however, no dissonance is produced, and large rewards often lead to greater shifts in attitude change than do small rewards (Linder, Cooper, and Jones, 1967). Second, dissonance effects seem to occur only when individuals feel that important, foreseeable consequences have stemmed from their actions. If, in contrast, they feel that no effects (or only trivial ones) have been produced, little or no attitude change follows (Cooper, Zanna and Goethals, 1974). In sum, it appears that less (smaller payoffs) does indeed lead to more (greater degrees of attitude change), but only under specific circumstances. Since individuals often believe that they enjoy freedom of action even when they do not, and frequently find that their behavior produces relatively important consequences, it seems likely that the occurrence of such effects is actually quite common. As a result, the strategy of offering individuals just barely enough reward to induce them to engage in attitude-discrepant behavior may often be an effective means of changing both their feelings and their beliefs.

CHANGING THE BEHAVIOR OF OTHERS: CONFORMITY, COMPLIANCE, AND OBEDIENCE

In many instances in which we attempt to exert social influence over others, we are interested in modifying *both* their attitudes *and* their behavior. For example, if we are strongly attracted to another person and desire this individual as our lover, we do not simply want them to yield to our persuasion; rather, we usually also want them to love and desire us in return. Similarly, if we are engaged in an argument with another person and he or she finally concedes, we are not totally satisfied unless it is clear that this surrender is due to

---

PERSPECTIVE ON BEHAVIOR: *Politics and Persuasion*

Techniques of persuasion such as those we have been discussing have often been put to practical use. For example, sales personnel frequently use them on their potential customers, advertising executives build them into their multimillion-dollar promotional schemes, and charitable organizations use them to win contributions from large numbers of donors. Perhaps the most important use of persuasive appeals, however, occurs in the realm of politics.

At the present time, campaigns for public office often seem to take the form of carefully orchestrated attempts to "sell" particular candidates to the voting public. Less and less attention is directed to important current issues, and more and more to the creation of attractive "images" for various candidates. In their attempts to convince voters to cast their ballots for a particular man or woman, professional campaign directors seem to make use of virtually every persuasive technique we have considered so far. As mentioned earlier, they often seek to increase their candidates' appeal to voters by causing them to appear quite similar to these persons. Physical appearance receives careful attention, and the use of make-up and beauty consultants is now virtually standard practice among the seekers of major office. Similarly, drama coaches are sometimes employed to help candidates master the trick of appearing "sincere" in all their public appearances—a factor closely related to their success in creating a strong image of trustworthiness. In addition, the services of professional writers are often secured to help make the contents of speeches as convincing, dramatic, and persuasive as possible.

Some critics have viewed these trends with increasing alarm, noting that the characteristics now needed to win elections—a warm smile, pleasing physical appearance, eloquent speaking style—may not be the ones required for effective performance once in office. Others have answered, however, that modern political campaigns, which lean heavily on television and other mass media, hold prospective candidates up to closer public inspection than ever before, and thus are actually an aid to voters. What are your own opinions on this issue? Do you think that the use of sophisticated techniques of persuasion in the political arena represents a basic corruption of our democratic system of government? Or do you believe that the benefits produced outweigh—or at least equal—any costs incurred?

a change in their way of thinking, and not simply to fatigue, boredom, or lack of interest. In such cases, then, we wish to alter not only others' behavior but the attitudes underlying these actions as well.

In other cases, however, our primary concern lies only in changing their actions. When we seek a favor from a stranger, our main goal is that of obtaining the assistance we desire, and not a basic change in this person's evaluation of us. Likewise, if we attempt to persuade a classmate to provide us with answers during an exam, we are primarily interested in getting this person to agree, and much less concerned with altering his or her basic attitudes toward such activities. This is not to say, of course, that we would not *prefer* to induce such changes in their attitudes as well, for clearly we would. Our major concern, however, is that their behavior change in the manner we desire; alterations in underlying attitudes are of somewhat lesser interest.

Attempts to modify the actions of others take a bewildering number of forms, ranging from humble pleas and tearful appeals on the one hand to physical compulsion on the other. Perhaps the three most commonly used techniques, however, involve: (1) attempts to convince the persons in question that they must alter their actions if they do not wish to be in violation of accepted standards of behavior; (2) direct requests that they act in the manner we desire; and (3) actual orders or commands that they do so. These three techniques of social influence attempt to produce, respectively, **conformity, compliance,** and **obedience,** each of which will now be considered in turn.

As social beings, people find it necessary to establish sets of rules to govern the pattern and nature of their interaction. These rules, which are generally known as **social norms,** indicate the manner in which individuals "should" or "ought to" behave, and are designed to regulate conduct in virtually every imaginable context. Some of these rules are quite explicit, and are stated in a highly formalized manner. For example, the operation of government is described by written laws; athletic contests are likewise governed by a complex set of rules; and, of course, signs informing the public of what is and what is not considered appropriate behavior are openly displayed in parks and on beaches. In contrast, other norms are quite implicit, and are never stated in an open or formal manner. For instance, there seems to be a strong rule among college students that all should take the same seats during each meeting of a given class. Similarly, there are many implicit but relatively clear-cut rules governing how close individuals should stand to one another during various forms of social interaction (see Chapter 15).

Regardless of whether norms are implicit or explicit, however, they exert a powerful effect upon behavior. Most drivers do in fact stop for stop signs, virtually all bathers wear *some* sort of swim suit to the beach, and few people throw garbage out of the window. Further, individuals tend to become quite angry when others fail to obey what they consider to be appropriate rules of conduct. For example, imagine how various strangers might react if you stared fixedly at them while passing them on the street—a clear violation of existing social norms. Similarly, imagine how you yourself might react if, during one of your classes, a fellow student suddenly rushed to the front of the room and began hugging and kissing the professor. The moral suggested by such unusual examples is clear: if you violate important social norms, you do so at your own risk!

Behavior inconsistent with established rules of conduct has been described by many terms (e.g., rebellion, deviation, the counter-culture); actions consistent with social norms have generally been labeled *conformity.* Thus, to the extent that we behave in accordance with the norms of our society, we

Conformity: Doing "Society's Thing"

may be said to be conforming. Although the term conformity has taken on negative meanings in recent years, it is obvious that most of us do tend to conform much of the time. Apparently, this strong tendency toward conformity is acquired during childhood, when we learn that adherence to accepted rules and standards of behavior is rewarded with praise, approval, and acceptance from others, while departures from such standards are likely to be punished by censure, disapproval, and rejection. Indeed, various groups often exert considerable pressure upon individuals who deviate from accepted rules or standards to "get back into line"—a type of pressure it is usually hard to resist. As a result of such childhood training, most of us have acquired a strong disposition to adhere to most social norms by the time we become adults (Endler and Hoy, 1967). In fact, so strong is our tendency to go along with the crowd that we often react to any signs that we are not behaving in the correct or appropriate manner with feelings of uneasiness or anxiety.

At first glance, this strong tendency toward conformity might seem quite objectionable, for it does prevent us from being ourselves and "doing our thing" (see Figure 12–13). On closer examination, though, it becomes apparent that without at least some minimum degree of conformity, chaos would quickly result. For example, imagine the frightening scenes which would take place outside movies, theaters, sports arenas, restaurants, and other locations where crowds gather if most persons present did not adhere to the implicit norm that all should form a line and wait their turn. Similarly, imagine the impossible situation which would exist if there were no generally accepted rules governing the flow of traffic. In many cases, then, conformity seems to serve a useful and valuable function. What *does* seem objectionable, however, is the existence of pressures toward conformity in contexts in which such standardization of behavior seems quite unnecessary. For example, there does not seem to be any good or compelling reason why women should not be allowed to wear slacks to the office or school, or why men should be forbidden to wear their hair in any manner they desire. Yet for decades, such rules were imposed upon millions of persons who could see little reason for their existence. Fortunately, recent years have brought a growing trend away from the enforcement of such unnecessary rules of conduct, and it seems likely that this movement will continue in the future as well.

In view of the fact that most individuals appear to possess a strong tendency to conform, it seems reasonable to suggest that in many cases it may be possible to change or modify their behavior simply by suggesting that they are not acting in accordance with generally accepted standards. That is, given the strong desire of most persons to behave in an "appropriate" manner, it seems likely that this tendency toward conformity may be readily employed as a highly effective technique of social influence. Convincing evidence for this suggestion was first obtained by Solomon Asch (1952) in a series of now-classic experiments.

FIGURE 12–13 Pressures toward conformity often produce an amazing degree of uniformity in dress, grooming, and related factors. The specific styles change, but conformity seems to remain the general rule. (Photo credit: Wide World Photos.)

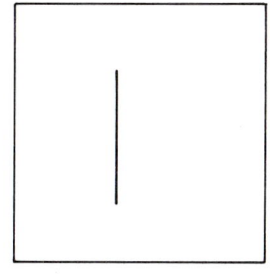

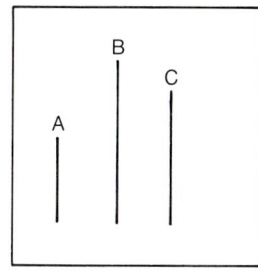

Standard Line   Comparison Lines

FIGURE 12-14 The type of visual task employed by
Asch in his early studies of conformity. Subjects were
required to indicate which of the three comparison
lines (A, B, or C) matched the standard line in length
after learning that several other persons had unani-
mously chosen one of these alternatives.

*Conformity in the
Laboratory: The
Subjects' Dilemma*

In his early investigations, Asch (1952) placed subjects in a situation in
which their behavior appeared to be markedly out of line with that of others,
and then observed the effects of such conditions upon their later actions. The
basic procedures employed in this research were as follows.

When they reported to the laboratory, participants were informed that they
would take part, along with seven other persons (who, unknown to them, were
actually accomplices of the experimenter), in a study concerned with visual
discrimination. Their task in the experiment was to determine which of three
different comparison lines matched a standard line in length (see Figure 12–14).
Additional instructions suggested that on each trial, all persons present would
state their judgments regarding the stimuli in a set order, so that one would always go first, another would always go second, and so on. Conditions were
then arranged so that the real subject would always state his answers in the
next-to-last position—after six of the confederates had given theirs.

On the first trial, all seven accomplices gave the correct answer, as did
the subject. From that point on, however, the confederates began supplying answers which were obviously incorrect on a set proportion of the trials.
That is, they would match the standard line with a comparison line which was
clearly too long or too short. Moreover, they were unanimous in these er-
roneous judgments, so that all seven chose the same wrong answer on each occasion. As a result, the actual subject was left facing a troubling dilemma:
should he go on reporting those answers which he perceived to be correct, and
in so doing stand out from the group like a sore thumb, or should he submit to
the strong social pressure he felt, and go along with the wrong answers given by
the others? Results indicated that most people did in fact yield to this temptation—fully 75 per cent of those tested in a long series of experiments con-
formed to the group's false answers on at least one occasion. Apparently, many
individuals found it less upsetting to contradict the evidence brought to them
by their own senses than to openly disagree with the judgments expressed by
several other persons.

More recent experiments on conformity have employed relatively automated procedures which eliminate the need for the presence of seven confederates during each experimental session—a costly feature of Asch's investigations (see Crutchfield, 1955). The basic situation, however, has remained the
same: subjects receive information suggesting that several other persons have
agreed upon an answer or point of view which seems incorrect. A large number
of such studies have been conducted, and, together, their results point to the
fact that conformity is strongly influenced by a number of different factors. That
is, as might be expected, individuals are more likely to yield to group pressure
in some situations than in others. Although many factors have been found to
influence the occurrence of conformity, three which have been the subject of
considerable attention are: (1) the *size* of the influencing group—how many

persons exert social pressure on the individual; (2) the presence of *social support*—does the individual have an ally who encourages resistance; and (3) the *sex* of the individuals subjected to social pressure—are there any differences between men and women in the tendency to conform?

Factors Influencing Conformity: Size, Support, and Sex

Imagine that one evening, you are sitting in a local coffee house with a friend discussing old-time movies. During your conversation, he happens to remark that Abbott was the short, plump member of the Abbott and Costello comedy team. This comment troubles you a bit, for you are fairly sure that it was really Costello who fits this description. You correct your friend, he disagrees, and after a few minutes of argument, you drop the matter and go on to other things. Neither of you has changed his opinion; you have simply gotten tired of going round and round on the same issue.

But now imagine the same scene under slightly different circumstances. In this case, you are sitting with five friends, and after one of them announces that Abbott was the overweight member of the team, the other four agree. You are still pretty certain that it was really Costello, but as your friends continue to disagree with you, a shadow of doubt begins to enter your mind. After all, can the whole group be wrong at once?

This simple example illustrates an important, if obvious, fact: the greater the number of people around you who accept a given position or adhere to a particular social norm, the greater the social pressure upon you to do likewise. Evidence for the influence of group size upon conformity has been obtained in a number of different experiments. For example, in one study, Gerard, Wilhelmy, and Connolley (1968) exposed subjects to the incorrect judgments of 2, 3, 4, 5, 6, 7, or 8 other persons, and then observed the frequency with which the subjects brought their own reactions into line with those of the group. As can be seen in Figure 12–15, results indicated that conformity generally increased with group size: the greater the number of other individuals exerting social pressure upon the subjects, the greater their tendency to go along. Obviously, there must be an upper limit to this relationship—for example, social pressure from 200 people may not be much more effective than similar pressure from 150. Within the range of group size we usually encounter, though, our tendency to conform seems to increase with the number of persons attempting to influence us.

The impact of the second factor mentioned above—social support—may also be illustrated by means of our movie example. Imagine, once again, that you are faced with a situation in which five people disagree with your judgment. In this case, though, one slight change occurs: after a few moments of discussion, one of these individuals breaks with the majority, and begins supporting your position. How do you think this would affect your tendency to go along with the group? Intuition suggests that it would reduce it greatly, and the findings of actual research lend support to this conclusion (e.g., Morris and Miller, 1975). In fact, so powerful is the influence of this factor in reducing conformity that it even seems to operate in situations in which one's supporter is low in prestige, knowledge, or competence. For example, in one interesting study, Allen and Levine (1971) provided subjects with a partner who, because of coke-bottle-thick glasses and a vision impairment, could not even see the materials to which the rest of the group was responding. Yet, despite this fact, even agreement from this person reduced subjects' tendency to conform. In combating social pressure, then, the mere presence of support from another seems to be far more important than the ability of this person to make accurate or valid judgments.

A third factor which has often been assumed to play an important role in

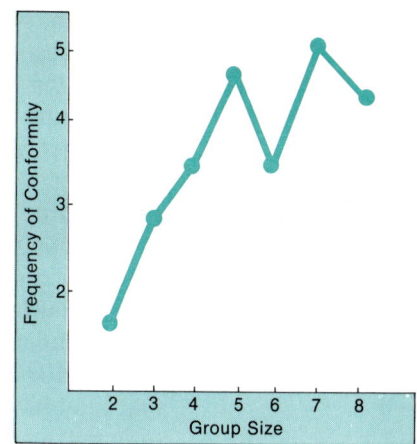

FIGURE 12-15 The effect of group size on conformity. As the number of individuals agreeing on a specific answer increased, subjects' tendencies to go along with these responses—even when obviously wrong—also rose. (Based on data from Gerard, Wilhelmy, and Conolley, 1968.)

conformity is that of sex. Many early experiments (e.g., Asch, 1952; Crutchfield, 1955) found men to be much less conforming than women, and interpreted this result as stemming from the fact that in American society, men are trained to be independent and dominant, while women are trained to be yielding and submissive (see Chapter 8). More recently, though, it has become apparent that these differences may well have been largely artificial ones, produced by certain aspects of the experimental procedures. In particular, most of the materials used in these early studies were probably much more familiar to men than to women. Since it is well known that individuals are more willing to rely upon the judgments of others when they are uncertain of the correctness of their own responses (as would be the case with new, unfamiliar items), it seems possible that women appeared to be more conforming than men in these early studies for this reason. Actual evidence for this suggestion has been obtained by Sistrunk and McDavid (1971), who conducted an experiment in which male and female subjects were tested for conformity on three types of items: (1) those more familiar to men than women; (2) those more familiar to women than men; and (3) those equally familiar to both sexes. It was expected that men would be more conforming on "feminine" items, women would be more conforming than men on "masculine" items, and that the two sexes would show equal conformity on the neutral items. As can be seen in Figure 12–16, all these predictions were confirmed. Such findings suggest that there are no overall differences between the sexes in the tendency to yield to social pressure—they merely choose to go along in slightly different situations.

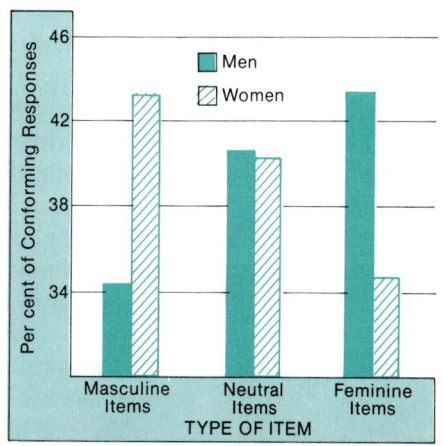

FIGURE 12-16 Sex and conformity. Women conform more than men on "masculine" items with which they are relatively unfamiliar, men conform more than women on "feminine" items with which *they* are relatively unfamiliar, and the two sexes show similar levels of conformity on neutral items equally familiar to both. (Based on data from Sistrunk and McDavid, 1971.)

Compliance: Getting Your Own Way

Often, our attempts to influence the actions of others take the form of direct requests in which we ask these persons to modify their behavior in the manner we desire. Such requests range in magnitude from those which are quite trivial and unimportant to those which are both large and significant. Regardless of their specific nature, though, we rarely issue such appeals without first taking some preliminary steps to ensure that they will bring the desired result. That is, we usually seek to load the dice in our favor before making various requests to others. Although we employ a number of different techniques for this purpose, among those which are used with the greatest frequency are: (1) **ingratiation**—attempts to make others like us; (2) the **foot-in-the-door approach**—inducing others to agree with small requests first, so that they will be more likely to agree to larger ones later; and (3) **guilt**—causing others to feel that they have behaved in a bad or harmful manner, and that they must, therefore, make amends for their evil acts.

Ingratiation: Liking and Compliance

Common sense suggests that one effective means of inducing other persons to agree to our requests is that of somehow causing them to like us; the more favorable their reactions to us, the greater the probability that they will comply with our requests. Since we will examine the bases of interpersonal attraction in some detail in Chapter 13, our major discussion of this topic will be reserved until that point (see pp. 466–473). We can, however, mention several different techniques used by many persons to enhance their attractiveness to others and thereby increase the success of their attempts at social influence.

First, many individuals attempt to increase their appeal to others by agreeing with the views and opinions of these persons (see Byrne, 1971). In its milder forms, this approach often shows up as a tendency on the part of one individual to agree with the attitudes and suggestions of another. In more extreme cases, it may appear as slavish agreement by the "ingratiator" with every statement on the part of the target person—the well-known "yes-man" or "yes-woman" syndrome. To whatever degree it is carried out, agreeing with others tends to increase one's attractiveness to them, and as a result enhances the likelihood that they will comply with various requests.

A closely related technique for increasing attraction to others is that of praising or complimenting them. When used appropriately, this procedure is a highly effective one—perhaps the most successful of all (Baron, 1971; Regan, 1971). However, it must be employed with great care, for if the target persons become aware of the fact that such actions are designed to influence or persuade them, they may react with anger rather than acceptance (Jones, 1964). Unfortunately, many persons are much more susceptible to flattery than they would like to believe, and a thin veneer of "sincerity" can often go far toward inducing them to swallow even the most lavish praise (see Figure 12–17). While flattery may not get you everywhere, it can certainly give you a substantial push in the right direction!

Other techniques for increasing interpersonal attraction include expressions of liking for others, doing favors for them, and even offering them bribes. Although these procedures vary greatly in scope and form, all have the same final goal: increasing one's attractiveness to the target persons, in order to reduce their ability to resist later social influence attempts. In short, ingratiation comes in many different forms, but the end result sought in each case is very much the same.

The Foot in the Door: Give Them an Inch and They'll Take a Mile

A second means we often employ to induce increased compliance from others has been termed the "foot-in-the-door" technique. When using this approach, we begin by asking other persons to perform a small or trivial favor, and then—once they have agreed—quickly escalate to larger ones. The basic as-

FIGURE 12–17   Because individuals often react with anger when they conclude that others are attempting to influence or manipulate them, ingratiators often conceal their praise and flattery beneath a thin coating of sincerity. (© King Features Syndicate, Inc., 1975.)

sumption, of course, is that once they have agreed to a small request, their tendency to yield to larger ones will be sharply increased.

The use of this technique is quite widespread, and it can be observed in many different contexts. For example, panhandlers often begin their appeals not with an open request for money, but rather with smaller demands, such as requests for the time of day or answers to other trivial questions. Only after the target person has agreed to this first request does the plea for money follow. Similarly, door-to-door salesmen often start their sales pitches by asking potential customers to accept a free gift, or even some literature about their products. In these and other instances, the basic rationale always remains the same: if only the person in question can be induced to consent to an initial, small request, the chances of persuading him or her to agree to a much larger proposal will be greatly increased. That this foot-in-the-door approach may often be quite successful is demonstrated by several different experiments.

For example, in the first investigation concerned with this topic (Freedman and Fraser, 1966), a number of housewives selected at random from the phone

FIGURE 12–18   Door-to-door salesmen are among the most accomplished users of the "foot-in-the-door" technique, often beginning with a small request for a few moments of a homeowner's time, and then quickly escalating to much larger demands.

book were called by one of the experimenters (who identified himself as a member of a consumer's group) and asked to answer a few simple questions about the kinds of soaps they used at home. This, of course, was the first, *small* request. A few days later, the same individual called again and made a second request of much larger magnitude, asking if his organization could send a five- or six-man crew to the subject's home to conduct a complete inventory of all the products she had on hand. It was explained that this survey would take about two hours, and that the men would require complete freedom to search through the entire house—including all the closets, cabinets, and drawers. Despite the unusual nature and gigantic proportions of this request, fully 52.8 per cent of the women called agreed! In contrast, only 22.2 per cent of those in a second group who were called only once and confronted with the large request on this occasion complied. Apparently, exposure to the initial, small request somehow "opened the door" for much greater compliance with the large one.

Additional findings have revealed that the foot-in-the-door effect is quite general in scope. For example, it seems to occur when requests are made in person as well as on the phone (Pliner et al., 1974), and it has been found to influence compliance with respect to such activities as signing a petition (Baron, 1973), placing a large sign on one's front lawn (Freedman and Fraser, 1966), and donating money to a charitable organization (Pliner et al., 1974). Although no final explanation for the effectiveness of this approach has as yet been obtained, existing evidence points to the possibility that it is based largely on changes in individuals' *self-perceptions*—the manner in which they view themselves (Bem, 1972). Specifically, after agreeing to perform a small favor for another person or a charitable organization, individuals may come to view themselves as the kind of person who helps others. As a result of such alterations in their self-image, they may then become more willing to comply with somewhat larger requests (Snyder and Cunningham, 1975). Regardless of whether the foot-in-the-door effect is based on this or some other mechanism, however, there is little doubt that it often serves as an effective means for obtaining increased compliance. While escalation appears to be quite dangerous in the realm of international relations, it may often yield positive results as a technique of social persuasion.

The Effects of Guilt: Paying for Your Sins

When one person does something which harms another, he or she often experiences strong feelings of guilt, particularly if the harm was unintentional. In order to eliminate such unpleasant feelings, guilty persons often attempt to make amends for their unfortunate acts by doing something good or helpful for the persons they have harmed. As a result, they may be more willing to comply with various requests from others than are individuals who are not experiencing such feelings of guilt.

This apparent fact—that guilt often leads to greater susceptibility to social influence—seems to be quite well known to many individuals. In fact, there is little doubt that some make frequent use of such techniques as anguished tears, heart-rending looks, and playing the role of a martyr as means of winning their way from others. Children, of course, are often great masters of this art, and employ it to wrap their parents around their tiny, helpless fingers; but adults, too, often induce guilt as a means of obtaining compliance from others. (Have you ever heard your own parents remark: "After all I've done for you ..."?)

Because it seems to be such a powerful and frequently used technique of social influence, guilt has recently become the subject of much careful attention from social psychologists. Many studies have been conducted to examine its effects upon compliance, and, in general, these investigations have confirmed the suggestion that feelings of guilt enhance one's willingness to yield to re-

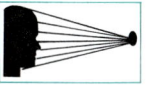

FOCUS ON RESEARCH: *Living Up to Your "Image": Self-Perception and Social Influence*

The suggestion (mentioned above) that changes in others' behavior can be induced through alterations in their self-image is an intriguing one in several respects. First, as we have noted before, individuals often become quite angry or annoyed when they conclude that others are trying to control or manipulate them (Brehm, 1972). Thus, altering their behavior through changes in their self-image might avoid such reactions. Second, alterations in behavior induced through changes in self-perceptions might be expected to persist for longer periods of time than changes produced through other means.

Striking evidence for the effectiveness of such an approach has actually been obtained in a recent experiment by Miller, Brickman, and Bolen (1975). These investigators attempted to alter children's neatness in the classroom in two different ways. Subjects in one group were exposed to standard techniques of persuasion, being urged repeatedly by their teacher and school principal to behave in a neat, orderly manner. In contrast, those in a second condition were exposed to procedures designed to alter their self-image. Thus, they received repeated comments from their teacher and principal suggesting that they were already extremely neat children—much more tidy than those in other classes. Subjects in a third (control) condition were not ex-

posed to any attempts to alter their degree of neatness.

The children's actual tendencies to pick up after themselves and others were assessed on three separate occasions: before the treatments were begun, immediately after they ended, and again two weeks later. On each of these occasions, their neatness was measured by examining the proportion of litter deposited in the wastebaskets rather than on the floor or at their desks. The results of the experiment were very clear: procedures designed to alter the children's self-perceptions proved to be the most effective in producing large and seemingly long-lasting changes in their behavior (refer to Figure 12–19).

If these findings can be generalized to other forms of behavior, they may have important implications. For example, it might be possible to increase children's academic performance by convincing them that they are the kind of persons who take their studies seriously. Similarly, it may be possible to improve classroom discipline by convincing students that they are actually quite well-behaved and restrained. As with all forms of social influence, limits will certainly exist: some aspects of individuals' self-perceptions will probably prove extremely difficult to modify. In cases in which such alterations can be induced, however, they may often yield large and relatively permanent shifts in behavior.

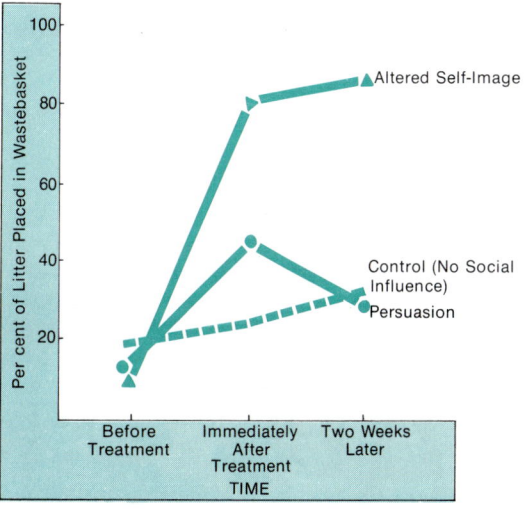

FIGURE 12–19 Changing others' self-images may often be a highly effective means of altering their behavior. In an experiment by Miller, Brickman, and Bolen (1975), children repeatedly informed that they were actually very neat (altered self-image group) came to behave in this manner to a greater degree than did children who were repeatedly urged to be neat (persuasion group). Children who received neither of these treatments (control group) showed no change during the experiment. (Based on data from Miller, Brickman, and Bolen, 1975.)

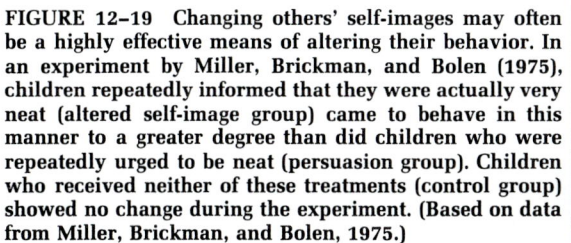

quests from others (e.g., Freedman, Wallington, and Bless, 1967; Regan, Williams, and Sparling, 1972; Wallington, 1973). Thus, it has been found that subjects induced to engage in such guilt-arousing actions as lying to an experimenter (and thereby ruining a study), knocking over painstakingly arranged index cards, destroying an expensive piece of equipment, or breaking another person's camera are far more willing to comply with various requests from others than are subjects not involved in such incidents. Moreover, it appears that the effects of guilt are quite general: after harming one person, guilt-ridden subjects are more willing to help not only this individual but others not directly involved as well. Further, they are willing to make amends for their transgressions in many different ways—not simply in a manner which directly "rights" the wrong they have done. Findings such as these suggest that causing others to feel guilty is indeed a highly effective and powerful technique of social influence—one well worth using if your own conscience can stand the strain! In any event, it seems that, at least as regards yielding to requests from others, harm-doers may have to pay for their "sins" in this world as well as in the next.

Obedience: Orders Are Orders

In an important sense, the most open and direct technique which one individual can employ to modify the behavior of another is that of simply ordering or commanding this person to do his or her bidding. Of course, unless the individual who issues such commands has sufficient power or authority to back them up, such an approach will probably prove to be totally ineffective. A relatively powerless person who goes about issuing commands to others is far more likely to elicit anger or scorn than he is to produce obedience. But commands from established sources of authority usually result in willing and immediate obedience. For example, soldiers usually obey the orders of their superiors with little or no hesitation, no matter how grisly or cruel they seem to be (see Figure 12–20). Similarly, few junior executives fail to follow the directives of their company president as soon as they are issued.

Obedience to the commands of powerful authority figures is not very surprising; after all, such persons generally possess the ability to inflict severe punishment upon those who fail to carry out their orders. Somewhat more unsettling, however, is the finding that even persons lacking in such power, but merely bearing the trappings of authority, can frequently induce similar slavish obedience from others. Indeed, there is growing evidence that even relatively powerless sources of authority can successfully induce many persons to engage

FIGURE 12–20 As shown here, soldiers are trained to obey the orders of their superiors without hesitation. As a result, they often follow their commands in a blind, unquestioning manner. (Photo credit: Still Picture Branch, National Archives.)

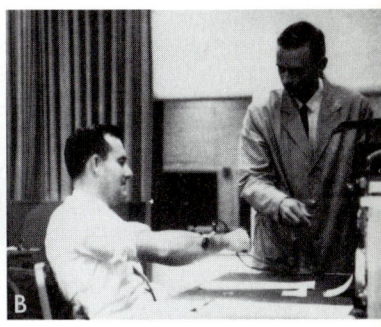

FIGURE 12–21 The apparatus employed by Milgram in his famous experiments on destructive obedience (A). Subjects were informed that the switches delivered increasingly strong electric shocks to another person, and were then ordered by the experimenter to move to higher and higher levels (B). In reality, the victim was an accomplice who never received any actual shocks. (Photos courtesy of Dr. Stanley Milgram.)

in harmful, antisocial actions they would never dream of performing in the absence of such orders. Perhaps the clearest and most frightening evidence relating to the occurrence of such **destructive obedience** has been gathered by Stanley Milgram and his colleagues (e.g., Milgram, 1963, 1965a, 1965b, 1974).

Destructive Obedience in the Laboratory

In order to examine the ability of a relatively powerless source of authority to induce individuals to engage in antisocial actions, Milgram (1963) devised a simple but effective procedure. Briefly, subjects participating in his research were informed that they would be serving in an investigation concerned with the influence of punishment on learning. Their task was then described as that of delivering electric shock to another subject (actually an accomplice of the experimenter) each time he made an error in a learning task. These shocks were to be delivered by means of 30 numbered switches located on the apparatus shown in Figure 12–21, and subjects were to follow this rule: each time the learner made an error, the next higher switch was to be thrown. Since the first switch on the apparatus supposedly delivered a shock of 15 volts, the second a shock of 30, and so on throughout the series, it was clear that if the learner made any sizable number of mistakes, he would soon be receiving extremely powerful (and potentially dangerous) jolts of electricity. Indeed, according to labels on the equipment, the final shock in the series would consist of 450 volts! In reality, of course, the accomplice *never received any shocks* during the experiment; the only real shock ever employed was a mild pulse of 45 volts delivered to subjects from button 3, simply to convince them that the apparatus was real.

When all instructions were clear, the session began, and, in accordance with a prearranged schedule, the accomplice quickly made a large number of errors. As a result, subjects soon found themselves facing an extremely unpleasant and disturbing dilemma: they could continue "punishing" the learner with what appeared to be increasingly painful shocks, or they could refuse to continue, and call a halt to the experiment. To make matters worse, the experimenter did not stand idly by and allow them to reach this decision undisturbed. Rather, each time they indicated a desire to stop, he ordered them, in increasingly authoritative tones, to continue. As a result, subjects could terminate the session only by openly defying the commands of this stern and imposing individual.

Before describing the results of Milgram's study, it is important to note that the individuals participating in it were *not* college students seeking to earn extra credit or fulfill a course requirement. Rather, they were a heterogeneous group of adult males ranging in age from 20 to 50 and in occupation from unskilled laborer to engineer, recruited through newspaper advertisements. Since they had no direct connection with the university at which the research was conducted, and were volunteers who had agreed to participate in the research of their own free will, it might be expected that they would be highly resistant to the experimenter's demands that they inflict seemingly dangerous electric shocks on another person. Yet in reality, *fully 65 per cent showed total obedience*, proceeding, during the session, to the final 450-volt shock. Of course, as might be expected, many individuals protested and requested that the session be terminated. When confronted with the experimenter's stern demands that they continue, however, most knuckled under and yielded time and time again. Moreover, they followed this course of action despite their belief that as a result, the confederate was receiving painful and potentially dangerous shocks. In view of the fact that the experimenter actually had no means of enforcing his commands—subjects were totally free to leave any time they desired—the tremendous capacity of even a relatively powerless authority figure to impose his will upon others was made abundantly clear.

In further experiments, Milgram (1965a, 1974) found that similar results could be obtained even under conditions which would be expected to markedly reduce such obedience. For example, when the study was moved from its original location on the campus of a highly prestigious university to a run-down office building in the business district of a nearby city, subjects showed virtually the same level of obedience. Similarly, a large proportion (62.5 per cent) continued to obey even when the accomplice complained about the painfulness of the shocks and begged to be released from the study. Finally, and most surprisingly of all, many (30 per cent) continued to obey even when this required that they grasp the victim's hand and physically force it down upon the shock plate! Considered as a whole, these findings leave little doubt that the tendency of many persons to obey the orders of an authority figure is so strong that it can often overwhelm both common sense and all humanitarian impulses.

Counteracting Obedience: Suppose They Gave a Command and No One Obeyed?

Given the powerful ability of authority figures to evoke obedience from others, it might at first seem impossible to counteract their influence. Yet, it is clear that on some occasions, at least, the directives of such persons are openly defied. Soldiers do sometimes rebel against the authority of their commanders, and dictators are frequently overthrown, despite their seemingly total grip on the reigns of power. A very large number of factors probably contribute to the breakdown of obedience in such situations. For example, mutinies often occur when soldiers or sailors conclude that their leaders are incapable of making wise decisions. Similarly, revolutions frequently stem from a total lack of concern on the part of rulers for the well-being of the populations under their control. With respect to counteracting the type of destructive obedience uncovered by Milgram, however, two factors seem to be of greatest importance.

The first, and perhaps more important, concerns individuals' perceptions regarding their degree of responsibility for the harm being committed. The greater the extent to which they feel directly responsible for the consequences of their actions, the greater their willingness to defy the commands of those in authority. In Milgram's studies, subjects were informed by the experimenter that he would take personal responsibility for the safety and well-being of the victim. Given this fact, it is not too surprising that many individuals obeyed his commands; after all, it was *he* who would take the blame if the victim were harmed. In many other situations, though, ultimate responsibility for the harm inflicted on others does not rest in such a clear and unambiguous manner with the persons in authority; rather, those who follow their commands may also share in the blame. In such cases, it seems reasonable to expect that tendencies toward unquestioning obedience may be strongly reduced. Evidence for this suggestion has been obtained in several recent experiments. For example, in

**PERSPECTIVE
ON
BEHAVIOR:** *A Note on Deception:
Ethical Issues in Social Research*

Our discussion of research on obedience seems to be an appropriate point at which to raise a question which has troubled psychologists with increasing frequency in recent years: Is it acceptable, in the pursuit of scientific knowledge, to purposely mislead and deceive subjects concerning the nature of the studies in which they take part? Milgram's experiments provide an unsettling and dramatic example of such procedures, but if you look back over much of the research we have discussed in other portions of this chapter—or ahead to Chapter 13—you will find that such practices are very common in the work of social psychologists.

Defenders of the continued use of deception argue that in many cases, such procedures are essential, for if subjects knew the true purposes of the experiments being conducted, they might behave in an unusual or "unnatural" manner. For example, how could we hope to study conformity in situations in which subjects know that our major goal is that of inducing them to yield to influence from others?

In response to such arguments, critics of the use of deception have called attention to the negative aspects of such procedures. First, they have noted that deception represents a potential violation of subjects' rights, for when deceived, they may reveal things about themselves they would not otherwise choose to disclose. Second, it may often pose a threat to their psychological or even physical well-being. For example, in Milgram's disturbing research, subjects often became so upset that they lost control of their own emotions. While this is an extreme case, you may recall that in other studies we have already examined, subjects have been made to feel guilty, to experience lowered self-esteem, or even to doubt their own senses. Clearly, the potential for serious psychological harm exists in such cases.

At present, the controversy concerning continued use of deception is far from resolved (Holmes and Bennett, 1974; Schulz, 1969). There does seem to be a growing consensus among psychologists, however, that deception may in fact be employed on a temporary basis, provided certain safeguards and cautions are followed. These protections have been summarized in a set of guidelines published by the American Psychological Association, and include the following:

(1) Deception should never be used automatically or as a matter of course, but only in cases in which no other procedures seem possible. And even then, the rights, safety, and well-being of subjects must be weighed very carefully against the potential benefits to be gained.

(2) Subjects must always be informed about the general nature of the research—and especially about any risks it entails—*before* participating in it. Only if they willingly consent to taking part after receiving such information can the experiment actually proceed.

(3) Finally, at the conclusion of the study, investigators must provide subjects with a thorough debriefing in which all deceptions are revealed, the true purposes of the study described, and all negative reactions eliminated. The rule of thumb for conducting such sessions is that subjects must leave the experiments in at least as positive a state as when they entered.

It is currently the view of most psychologists (including the present authors) that when such safeguards are carefully incorporated into research projects, a balance between the rights of subjects on the one hand and the quest for new knowledge about human behavior on the other can in fact be obtained. Under such conditions, deception—on a temporary and carefully controlled basis—may indeed be an acceptable and useful tool for research.

one investigation (Tilker, 1970), subjects were found to be far less willing to obey when they had been informed that the responsibility for the victim's health and welfare rested entirely with them. Further, individuals participating in recent experiments similar to the ones conducted by Milgram have been found to show far less obedience when they themselves must deliver the shocks to the victim—and consequently take the blame for any harm produced—than when they merely transmit the experimenter's orders for increasingly powerful jolts to another person who then (apparently) actually carries them out (Kilham and Mann, 1974).

Together, these findings suggest one reason for the willingness of soldiers, security forces, and even police personnel to follow commands from their superiors which lead to the injury or even death of helpless civilians: they feel no sense of responsibility for their actions. That is, they believe that their commanders will bear full blame for any harm produced, and that they are only acting "under orders." If this is indeed the case, it may be possible to reduce the occurrence of such blind and unquestioning obedience to authority by reminding such persons in clear and certain terms that they are directly accountable for their actions in a moral, if not a legal, sense.

A second factor which may be effective in counteracting the power of authority figures to command destructive obedience is suggested by careful observation of those situations in which their orders are actually defied. In many such cases, the following pattern emerges: first, one brave and dedicated individual or a few such persons defy the authority, and then many others follow this lead. This pattern of events suggests that one effective means of counteracting blind obedience to the directives of authority figures may be that of exposing their followers to *disobedient models*—others who refuse to obey. That such procedures may actually be highly effective in reducing obedience is suggested by the results of several different experiments (Powers and Geen, 1972; Milgram, 1965a). For example, in the first of these investigations (Milgram, 1965a), obedience was reduced from 65 per cent to only 10 per cent when subjects were exposed to two other persons who defied the experimenter's commands (see Figure 12–22).

Together, findings concerning responsibility for the victim's welfare and exposure to disobedient models provide a ray of hope to counteract the gloomy picture painted by Milgram's investigations. Although the power of authority figures to command obedience is great, it *can* be effectively countered under

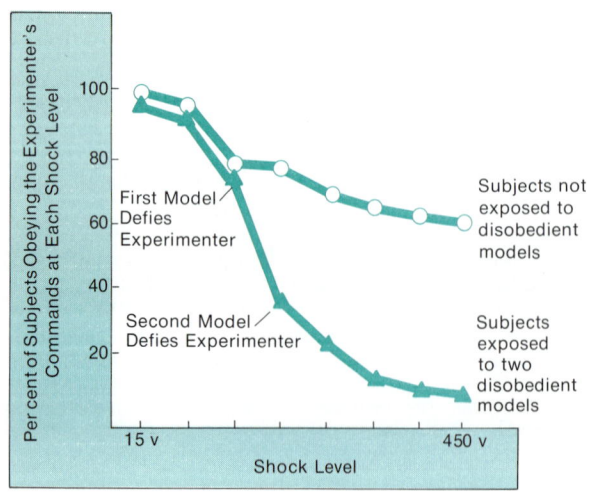

FIGURE 12–22 When individuals are exposed to disobedient models—other persons who refuse to yield to the commands of an authority figure—their own tendency to obey is sharply reduced. (Based on data from Milgram, 1965a.)

**PSYCHOLOGY
IN
ACTION:** *A Survey of Social Influence*

At the very beginning of this chapter, we suggested that attempts by one person to alter the attitudes or behavior of others is a very common form of social interaction. Although we have now taken a number of pages to describe several different forms of such influence, we have not as yet returned to the question of how frequently they occur. This has been the case by choice rather than accident, for we feel that the best way for you to appreciate the frequency with which individuals seek to influence others is to take a look for yourself. We feel, in short, that it may be well worth your while to conduct a brief, informal survey of social influence in operation. In order to carry out this task, you will not need any special equipment or training; what you will need, though, is all your powers of observation, for as we have noted at several points, attempts by individuals to influence others take an almost limitless number of different forms.

In order to conduct your survey, either detach the special sheets provided for this purpose in the *Student Manual* or construct your own by listing each of the following techniques of social influence on a separate sheet of paper:

     Persuasive Appeals
     Fear Communications
     Conformity Pressure
     Ingratiation
     Foot-in-the-door Technique
     Guilt Induction
     Direct Commands

Divide each sheet into five columns headed as follows:

Where (where did you see this instance of social influence?)
When (at what time of day did it occur?)
Influencing Agent (who attempted to exert the influence?)
Recipient (who was on the receiving end?)
Result (did it work or fail?)

After you have prepared your sheets, you are ready to begin. Simply carry them with you during your daily activities, and keep your eyes peeled for instances of each type. After observing the occurrence of any attempt at social influence, fill in the appropriate information on the correct sheet, and then draw a line across the page to avoid confusion between one instance and the next. Continue the survey for several days. At the end of this period, you should have a record of the frequency with which you have encountered various forms of social influence. If you have done a good job of observing, you will probably notice that some techniques are used more frequently than others. For example, persuasive appeals and ingratiation will probably appear more often than direct commands (except in the case of parents and children). In addition, you may find that the overall incidence of various forms of social influence is high—perhaps much higher than you expected. If, as suggested by a recently popular book, human interaction can be viewed as a series of "games people play," *influence* certainly qualifies as one of the most popular.

appropriate conditions. Protection from the harmful effects of blind, unquestioning obedience is not automatic, however; in order for it to be obtained, we must take care to build many restraints and safeguards into the structure of our society.

UNINTENTIONAL SOCIAL INFLUENCE: CHANGING OTHERS WITHOUT REALLY TRYING

In earlier sections of this chapter, we have seen that others often seek to shape and influence our behavior or attitudes through a wide variety of techniques (e.g., persuasive communications, fear appeals, conformity pressure, and guilt induction). In such instances, the persons involved actively seek to modify the way we feel, think, or behave, for purposes of their own. In many other cases, however, the people around us exert strong effects upon our actions or attitudes without meaning or wishing to do so. We have already touched on one form of such unintentional social influence in Chapter 4 when we considered *observational learning*. At that time we noted that individuals often acquire new forms of behavior not previously at their disposal merely by observing the actions of others. As we shall soon see, exposure to other persons can also affect us in several other ways. Together, such influences are generally known as **modeling processes,** and form perhaps the most important type of unintentional social influence (Bandura, 1973). Two other forms of such influence which are also of interest, however, will likewise be considered: (1) **social facilitation**—the impact of the presence of others upon our performance of many different tasks and (2) **deindividuation**—a sharp drop in the strength of our restraints against many forms of antisocial behavior when in the presence of a large number of other persons.

Modeling: Exposure to the Actions and Outcomes of Others

Imagine that while waiting for an appointment, you munch on a salty and peppery snack. When you finish, you discover that you are very thirsty. The only water fountain nearby, however, has a large sign above it reading: "Do Not Drink From This Fountain." Since you usually make it a practice to obey signs, and because you fear the unpleasant consequences which might result from drinking (is the water polluted? will it squirt out wildly?), you sit and wait, growing thirstier by the minute. After a short period of time, another person approaches and, without hesitation, takes a long drink from the fountain. Then, apparently unaffected by this action, he continues on his way. Do you think you would now be more likely to drink from the fountain yourself? The results of an experiment in which subjects were exposed to precisely this situation (Kimbrell and Blake, 1958) suggest that you would. In fact, in this study, almost all individuals who had been made thirsty by eating Saltine crackers coated with Mexican hot sauce drank from the fountain after observing another person do so. In contrast, very few individuals who had not witnessed such events yielded to this temptation. These findings point to one important type of effect which often results from observing the actions of others: the strength of our inhibitions against various forms of prohibited behavior may be sharply reduced (see Figure 12–23). That is, when we witness other persons engaging in activities we ourselves would like to perform, we may experience strong **disinhibitory** reactions—a weakening in the strength of our own restraints against engaging in similar actions.

Now consider the following incident: imagine that you are driving along the interstate at 10 miles above the legal speed limit. As you round a bend, you notice another car which is parked by the side of the road, where the driver is receiving a ticket from a state trooper. Do you think that the sight of this scene would influence your own driving habits? In all probability it would, and there is a very good chance that you would slow down, at least for a while. Once

FIGURE 12-23 When we observe another person engage in some form of prohibited behavior, our own inhibitions against performing such actions may be greatly weakened. (Left photo by Irwin Nash.)

again, your inhibitions against engaging in some prohibited act (in this case, speeding) would be strongly affected by exposure to the actions of another person. In this case, however, the effect would be **inhibitory** in nature—the strength of your restraints would be increased rather than reduced.

If you have assumed, on the basis of these simple examples, that inhibitory or disinhibitory effects are restricted to relatively trivial forms of behavior, don't jump to conclusions. In reality, they seem to be quite general in nature, and can affect even very important types of activity. For example, as we noted on pages 440 to 441, exposure to disobedient models (others who defy the commands of an authority figure) can weaken observers' restraints against engaging in similar actions, and thereby spark major riots or revolts. In fact, as we shall see in Chapter 13, exposure to others engaging in *aggression* may weaken observers' inhibitions against similar actions and lead to dangerous forms of individual and collective violence (e.g., Baron, 1974; Baron and Bell, 1975). The fact that exposure to the actions of others can both strengthen and weaken restraints against various prohibited acts, therefore, has many important implications.

A second distinct type of modeling process can be illustrated by means of the following example: suppose you are walking along the streets of a large city when, suddenly, several persons stop and look up at one of the nearby buildings. Do you think their actions might influence your own behavior? Common sense suggests that this would be the case, and that you would also be likely to peer upward to see what was going on. This prediction has actually been confirmed in an experiment employing just these procedures (Milgram et al., 1969). That is, when several confederates stopped suddenly on a busy street and looked upward, many passersby reacted in a similar manner (see Figure 12-24). These findings suggest that in many cases, the actions of others may serve as stimuli for similar actions by us which—unlike those in our first examples above—are not under the control of strong prohibitions. This type of effect, which is generally known as **response facilitation,** is somewhat less dramatic in nature than inhibitory or disinhibitory reactions. But it, too, occurs in a wide variety of situations. For example, individuals usually rise or sit in courtrooms or at social gatherings when they see others getting up or taking seats. Similarly, when one person yawns, the others around him often also begin to show

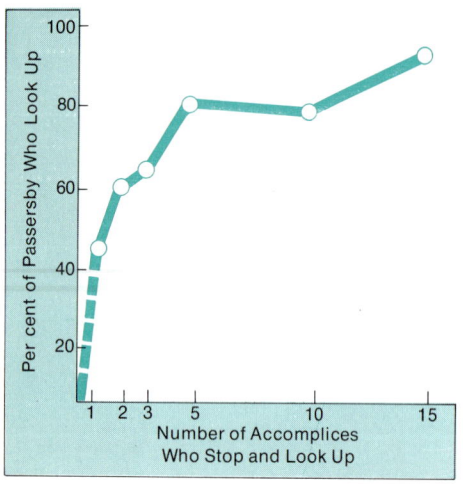

FIGURE 12–24 Sometimes the responses of other persons serve as stimuli for similar actions by us. In an experiment by Milgram, Bickman, and Berkowitz (1969), varying numbers of individuals (assistants of the experimenters) stopped and gazed upward on a busy Manhattan street. Not surprisingly, the greater the number of accomplices who demonstrated such behavior, the greater the tendency of passersby to show similar actions. (Based on data from Milgram, Bickman, and Berkowitz, 1969.)

such behavior. And finally, recent experiments suggest that exposure to pornographic films tends to raise the incidence of sexual relations among married couples (Mann et al., 1974). Since none of these activities is under the control of strong prohibitions, each represents response facilitation—instances in which the actions of others seem to trigger similar behavior by us.

Perhaps the best place to obtain first-hand experience with a third type of modeling effect—**vicarious emotional arousal**—is your local neighborhood movie theater. Once your eyes become adapted to the darkness, you may observe many members of the audience weeping when they see sad events on the screen, becoming angry when anger or hostility is shown, and wincing or even groaning when characters in the film show intense pain. Such effects point to a simple fact: exposure to signs of emotional arousal on the part of others often induces similar reactions in us. The existence of such vicarious emotional arousal has been demonstrated in a number of experiments (e.g., Buck et al., 1974; Hygge, 1976). Moreover, it seems to play an important role in many forms of social behavior. For example, signs of joy and gratitude on the part of persons receiving gifts often serve to induce similar positive feelings among givers and thus increase their tendencies to engage in such benevolent acts. Similarly, signs of pain on the part of another person can often affect the emotional states of aggressors, and thereby influence their willingness to harm others. In short, the fact that we often react emotionally to signs of emotion in others can strongly affect the nature of our social interactions with these persons.

Social models generally have no desire to influence the actions of others who observe their behavior. In fact, they are often quite unaware that such effects have occurred. As a result, it seems reasonable to classify modeling as one form of unintentional social influence. The great generality of such processes and the magnitude of the effects they often produce, however, point to a somewhat paradoxical fact: in many cases, this particular form of unintentional social influence yields greater and longer-lasting effects than several of the more intentional techniques we considered above.

Social Facilitation: Audiences and Performance

Can you recall your reactions when, as a student in grammar school, your teacher stood by your desk and watched as you performed some exercise in penmanship or mathematics? Similarly, do you remember your feelings the last time you were called upon to deliver a speech, play a musical instrument, or perform some other activity in front of an audience? If so, two facts about your reactions in such situations may be quite apparent. First, you probably experienced several signs of increased arousal (a lump in your throat, beads of perspiration, shortness of breath, and so on). Second, your performance may well have been quite different from what it would have been if you had been alone. In short, the presence of other persons—especially in the capacity of an audience—seems to produce strong effects upon both our feelings and our behavior (see Figure 12–25).

More formal evidence for the occurrence of such effects has been obtained in many recent experiments. With respect to heightened arousal, it has now been demonstrated that the presence of others does in fact produce increments in such reactions (Martens, 1969). Findings regarding the influence of an audience upon performance, though, have been somewhat more complex. Many early experiments reported conflicting results: in some cases, the presence of others improved performance, while in others it impaired such behavior. One explanation for these puzzling results has been provided by Robert Zajonc (1965).

According to Zajonc, the presence of other persons produces an increase in motivation. Since increments in motivation tend to enhance an individual's tendency to perform the strongest or most dominant responses at his or her disposal (see Chapter 7), it would be expected that the presence of an audience would tend to induce similar effects. The influence of such conditions upon performance, then, would depend upon the nature of the individual's dominant responses. If these happen to be correct ones in the situation in question, performance will improve; if they happen to be incorrect, performance will actually be impaired. (Another way of phrasing these predictions is as follows: the performance of responses that organisms have already acquired will be enhanced, while new learning will be retarded. You may recall that we discussed the distinction between learning and performance in Chapter 4.) Perhaps a concrete example will help clarify the nature of Zajonc's suggestions still further.

Imagine that you are called upon to work some problem on the board in one of your classes. If you have done your homework and mastered the problem, your dominant responses in this situation will probably be correct ones.

FIGURE 12–25 The presence of other persons often exerts strong effects upon our own behavior. This is especially true when we are called upon to perform some task in front of a large audience. (From Stotland, E., and Canon, K.: *Social Psychology: A Cognitive Approach.* Philadelphia: W. B. Saunders Company, 1972.)

Thus, according to Zajonc's theory, you should actually work it faster and more accurately at the board than you would while alone in your own room. However, if you have failed to study the assignment, your dominant responses may well be incorrect ones. In this case, disaster will follow, and you may do an even worse job at the board than you would while alone. In sum, the effects of performing in front of the class would depend upon the extent to which you have mastered the task at hand.

Zajonc's proposal that the presence of others increases motivation has been tested in a number of recent studies (Paulus and Murdoch, 1971; Innes and Young, 1975), and, in general, the findings of these studies have confirmed his predictions. In all these investigations, the presence of others has been found to facilitate subjects' tendencies to perform strong or dominant responses. Interestingly, such results have been obtained with animals as well as with human subjects. For example, in one study, Zajonc, Heingartner, and Herman (1969) placed roaches in a situation in which they could escape from a bright light by running into a dark bottle. In one condition, the roaches could attain this goal simply by running down a straight pathway, while in a second condition, they could escape from the light only by executing a right-hand turn in a simple maze (see Figure 12–26). In both cases, roaches performed these tasks either while alone in the apparatus or while in the presence of an audience of four other roaches. On the basis of Zajonc's theory, it was predicted that the audience would improve subjects' performance in the runway, where their dominant response (running straight ahead) was correct, but would impair their performance in the maze (where the dominant response was incorrect). Results offered strong support for both of these predictions. Thus, it appears that even the lowly cockroach is strongly affected by the presence of an audience and—somewhat surprisingly—in much the same manner as human beings.

Deindividuation: Others as Releasers of Antisocial Actions

In our discussion of modeling processes, we noted that exposure to the actions of others often can weaken our restraints against engaging in various forms of prohibited behavior. Unfortunately, this is not the only manner in which other persons can enhance such behavior on our part. Sometimes, their

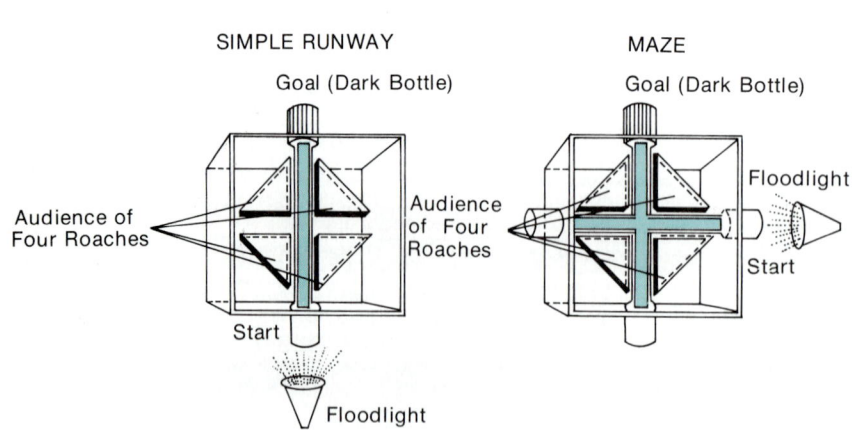

SIMPLE RUNWAY   MAZE

FIGURE 12–26 The apparatus used by Zajonc, Heingartner, and Herman (1969) to study the effects of an audience upon the behavior of roaches. As predicted by Zajonc's theory, performance was enhanced by the presence of an audience in the case of the simple runway, where the dominant response (running straight ahead) was correct, but was impaired by an audience in the case of the maze, where this response was incorrect. (Adapted from Zajonc, R. B., Heingartner, A., and Herman, E. M.: Social enhancement and impairment of performance in the cockroach. *Journal of Personality and Social Psychology*, 1969, *13*, 83–92.)

mere presence—even when they themselves do not demonstrate antisocial actions—is enough to weaken our inhibitions against the performance of such behavior. The existence of such "liberating" effects is readily observed in many different settings. For example, sports fans at baseball, football, or basketball games can often be heard to shout colorful phrases they would probably never utter while alone. Similarly, at a large party, people often become much more careless with their drinks, cigarettes, or food than they would ever be in a much smaller group. While modeling may play some role in such occurrences, it is also apparent that something else is also going on: the persons involved seem to be experiencing a general lessening of their restraints against engaging in various types of antisocial behavior which they would be highly unlikely to demonstrate while alone.

If the restraint-reducing influence of others were limited to relatively trivial forms of behavior, it would be of little interest or importance. Unfortunately, this is far from the case. The presence of others—particularly in fairly large numbers—is also capable of reducing inhibitions against the performance of such dangerous actions as pointless vandalism, mob violence, and gang rape. In these tragic instances, most of the individuals involved would never dream of acting in such a manner in the absence of many other persons; they are, in fact, quite shocked at their own behavior when they examine it in isolation at a later time. Why, then, do they engage in such actions while in the presence of many others? One answer to this puzzle involves the development of a complex psychological state known as **deindividuation** (Zimbardo, 1970).

While deindividuation is a complicated process involving many changes, it seems to center on feelings on the part of the persons experiencing it that (1) as part of a large, undifferentiated group, they are completely anonymous, and (2) responsibility for any antisocial acts that are performed will be shared by all others present. As a result of these beliefs, restraints or inhibitions against the performance of socially disapproved behaviors are severely weakened, and tragic events often follow (see Figure 12–27).

Given the potentially important effects resulting from deindividuation, it is not surprising that this process has recently been the subject of a growing amount of attention (e.g., Cannavale et al., 1970; Watson, 1973). Perhaps the most interesting, and in some ways the most unsettling, investigation of this process, however, has been carried out by Zimbardo (1970).

In his study, Zimbardo suggested that the induction of a state of deindividuation among subjects would facilitate their willingness to engage in a particularly dangerous form of antisocial action: aggression against a helpless and innocent victim. In order to examine this hypothesis, groups of four college coeds were provided with what seemed to be the opportunity to deliver painful electric shocks to another girl. (In reality, of course, this person was an accomplice of the experimenter who never received any shocks in the study, but merely pretended to experience these painful stimuli.)

The subjects' degree of deindividuation was varied in a simple but ingenious manner. In one condition (the *deindividuation* group), they were asked to put on oversize lab coats and face hoods immediately upon entering the laboratory (see Figure 12–28). Moreover, the study was conducted under very dim lighting conditions, and their names were never mentioned. As a result, they were totally anonymous during the experiment, a state which would be expected to facilitate the development of deindividuation.

In contrast, subjects in a second group (the *individuation* condition) did not wear the shapeless coats or hoods. Moreover, they displayed large name tags, and were purposely introduced to each other at the start of the session.

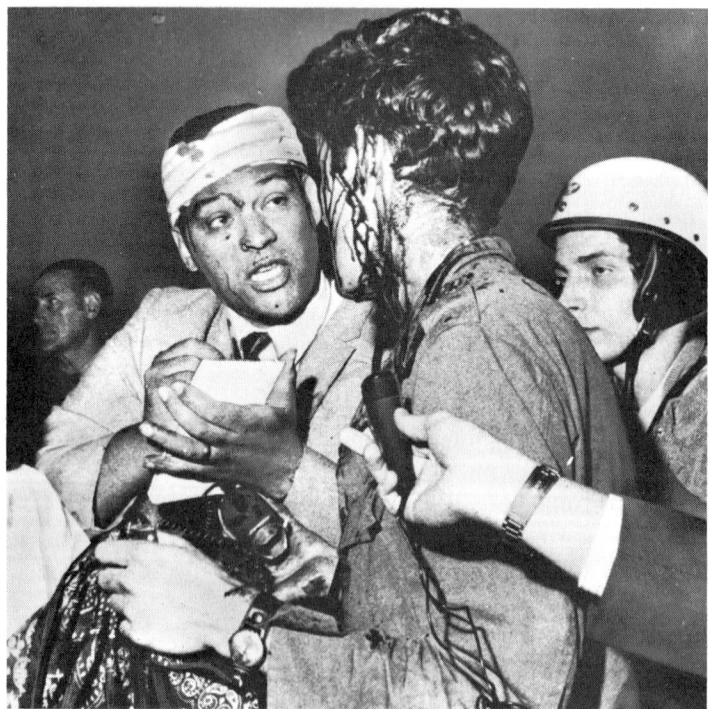

FIGURE 12–27 Top: The New York City Draft Riot of 1863, shown in a contemporary engraving. Bottom: A newsman and a photographer attacked by police at the Democratic convention in Chicago, 1968. These scenes of violence convey the explosive potential of situations in which deindividuation is possible. Feelings of anonymity—which often arise when individuals find themselves in the presence of a large number of others—seem to encourage the development of dangerous forms of antisocial behavior. (Top figure courtesy of the Kean Archives; bottom figure courtesy of Wide World Photos.)

FIGURE 12-28 Subjects in the deindividuation group of Zimbardo's (1970) famous experiment. Under these conditions, anonymity was maximized, and the development of deindividuation was encouraged. (Photo courtest of Dr. Phillip G. Zimbardo.)

Finally, in this group, the study was conducted under high levels of illumination, so that each individual could readily see and identify all of the others. Under these conditions anonymity was impossible, and deindividuation would, presumably, be discouraged. It was predicted that subjects in the deindividuation group would be much less restrained against shocking the helpless victim than those in the individuation group, and, as can be seen in Figure 12-29, this was actually the case: subjects in the deindividuation group delivered much longer shocks to the accomplice than did those in the individuation condition.

These findings, and those obtained in other studies of deindividuation (Diener et al., 1975), have disturbing implications, suggesting that restraints against the performance of cruel and dangerous acts may be much weaker than we would like to believe. Apparently, such inhibitions are usually sufficient to prevent most individuals from engaging in such behavior when they are alone, or in the company of a few other persons. When they become part of a large crowd, however, restraints against antisocial behavior may be readily overcome by feelings of anonymity and the belief that it is possible to "get away" with such actions. In short, references in songs and other sources to the effects of "the madding crowd" may be closer to the mark than was once suspected.

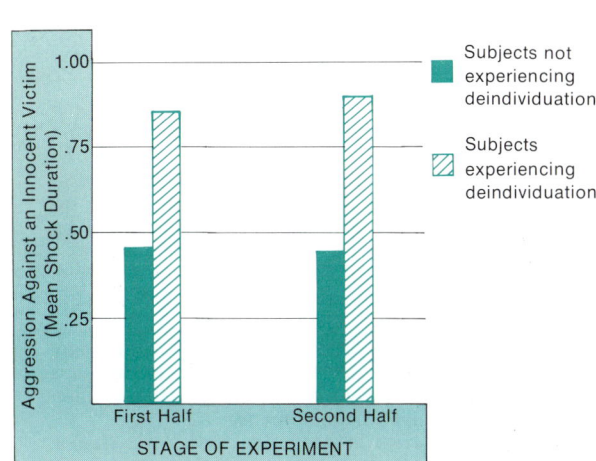

FIGURE 12-29 Some negative effects of deindividuation. Individuals experiencing this psychological state showed greater willingness to inflict pain on a helpless, innocent victim than did those not experiencing deindividuation. (Based on data from Zimbardo, 1970.)

Summary

Social influence may be said to occur whenever one or more individuals attempt to alter the behavior, feelings, or thoughts of one or more others. Such efforts take many different forms, ranging from ingratiation and flattery on the one hand to threats or actual physical violence on the other. Moreover, they occur with great frequency and form a particularly common basis for human interaction.

Attempts to change the attitudes of others usually involve: (1) **persuasive communications,** (2) **emotional appeals,** or (3) the induction of **attitude-discrepant behavior.** Persuasive communications seek to alter attitudes through what appear to be logical arguments and convincing facts. The effectiveness of such appeals varies with such factors as the credibility or trustworthiness of the communicator, the form of the communication, personality characteristics of the audience, and the context in which the communication is presented. Emotional or fear appeals seek to modify attitudes by suggesting to recipients that failure to adopt the recommended beliefs or courses of action will result in injury, illness, or even death. Such appeals are highly effective in changing attitudes, provided that they are not overdone. When individuals are induced to engage in attitude-discrepant behavior, they experience an unpleasant state of **cognitive dissonance.** In order to reduce such dissonance, they will then often alter their attitudes so as to be consistent with the actions they have performed. As a result, the induction of attitude-discrepant behavior is frequently a highly effective means of changing attitudes.

Efforts to modify the behavior of others without altering their underlying attitudes take many forms, and among the most common results of such efforts are: (1) **conformity,** induced by exerting pressure on others to adhere to accepted standards of behavior; (2) **compliance,** gained by making various requests that others modify their actions; and (3) **obedience,** won by giving direct orders or commands that others modify their behavior. Conformity has been found to vary with such factors as the size of the influencing group and the presence of social support. Compliance is increased by a high level of liking for the requester, use of the "foot-in-the-door" technique, and the induction of guilt. Persons in positions of authority can generally induce high levels of obedience among others, even when they lack the power to enforce their demands. However, their ability to command obedience can be substantially reduced by reminding their followers that *they* will be held personally responsible for any harm produced, and by exposing these individuals to the actions of disobedient models.

In many instances, other persons influence our behavior or attitudes even when they do not purposely seek to do so. Among the most important forms of such unintentional social influence are (1) **modeling**—alterations in our feelings, behavior, or attitudes stemming from mere exposure to the actions of others, (2) **social facilitation**—the impact of the presence of others upon our performance of many different tasks, and (3) **deindividuation**—reductions in the strength of our restraints against antisocial actions stemming from the presence of many other persons and resulting feelings of anonymity.

Suggested Readings

Baron, R. A., and Byrne, D.: *Social Psychology: Understanding Human Interaction.* 2nd ed. Boston: Allyn & Bacon, 1977.
   A comprehensive survey of the field of social psychology. The discussions of social influence, attitude change, and modeling provide additional information on the topics covered in this chapter.

Brehm, J. W.: *Responses to Loss of Freedom: A Theory of Psychological Reactance.* Morristown, N.J.: General Learning Press, 1972.
   A discussion of the complex effects which may occur when individuals feel that their freedom has been threatened or reduced by another person—often through attempts at social influence.

Milgram, S.: *Obedience to Authority.* New York: Harper and Row, 1974.
   A report by Milgram of the results of ten years of research on obedience. The findings described both extend and confirm his initial results concerning this powerful form of social influence.

Suedfeld, P.: *Attitude Change: The Competing Views.* Chicago: Aldine-Atherton, 1971.
   A collection of articles concerned with the general topic of attitude change. Several competing theoretical views regarding this important process are described.

Wheeler, L. *Interpersonal Influence.* 2nd edition. Boston: Allyn and Bacon, 1977.
   A brief and clearly written discussion of several aspects of social influence.

Zimbardo, P. G.: The human choice: Individuation, reason, and order versus deindividuation, impulse, and chaos. *In* W. J. Arnold and D. Levine (eds.); *Nebraska Symposium on Motivation, 1969.* Lincoln: University of Nebraska Press, 1970.

    A discussion of deindividuation, the process through which individuals "submerge" their identity within a large group and thereby experience reductions in the strength of their restraints against many dangerous forms of behavior.

Some journals which regularly publish articles on social influence:

    Journal of Applied Social Psychology
    Journal of Experimental Social Psychology
    Journal of Personality
    Journal of Personality and Social Psychology
    Journal of Research in Personality
    Personality and Social Psychology Bulletin

Overleaf: Top left photo, Syndication International, print provided by Photo Trends. Top right photo by Michael Marton, Camera Press, London; print provided by Photo Trends. Bottom left photo from *Social Psychology — A Cognitive Approach,* by E. Stotland and L. K. Canon (Philadelphia: W. B. Saunders Company, 1972). Bottom right photo, United Press International.

13

Social Behavior: Interacting with Others

PERSON PERCEPTION: GETTING TO KNOW OTHERS

INTERPERSONAL ATTRACTION: WHOM WE LIKE AND WHY

ALTRUISM AND HELPING: THE MILK OF HUMAN KINDNESS

AGGRESSION AND VIOLENCE

SUMMARY

In Chapter 12 we focused our attention upon **social influence**—attempts by one or more persons to alter the actions or attitudes of one or more others. While attempts of this type are quite common, they still represent only a small portion of our social relations with others—merely the tip of a large and multi-faceted iceberg, so to speak. In fact, where social interaction is concerned, it is probably safe to assert that anything you can imagine happening between two or more human beings—and probably many things you would not normally anticipate—both can and do take place. We could readily illustrate this important point with specially constructed examples, but as the newspaper and magazine clippings shown in Figure 13–1 suggest, there is little need for such efforts; actual instances of social behavior are far more unusual and surprising than any we could possibly invent.

Even the relatively small number of examples presented in Figure 13–1 should serve to underscore the tremendous richness, diversity, and often un-expected nature of social interaction. With such a "movable feast" spread before them for study, social psychologists have turned their attention to many different aspects of such behavior. Since we could not hope to list all of the topics they have considered, let alone examine them all in any detail, we will confine our discussion to several which we view as being among the most important and interesting. In broad outline, the present chapter may be viewed as consisting of two major parts. In the first, we will consider two topics which, while not actually forms of social behavior themselves, exert strong and far-reaching effects upon the nature of our interactions with others: **person perception**—the process through which we come to know and understand other

453

Polygamy in the Desert

Utah's Founding Father Brigham Young had 27 wives, but his Mormon Church banned polygamy in 1890 by "revelation"—after losing several U.S. Supreme Court cases. Just last year Mormon President Spencer Kimball warned that "the Lord brought an end to this program many decades ago." That divine word has not reached everyone. There are some 35,000 heretical Mormons in the U.S. and Mexico who still practice polygamy.

This underground activity burst into public notice this spring when pistol-packing ex-Marine Alexander Joseph, 39, led 12 of his wives and 15 other families—all members of Joseph's Church of Jesus Christ of Solemn Assembly—to establish a settlement on a 2,000-acre tract of federal land in southern Utah. Before the Bureau of Land Management began proceedings to evict them, they had put up ten buildings, started a dam and planted vegetables. A federal court is now deciding whether they are homesteaders or simply squatters.

Legal Buffer. Joseph talks of his "church" as a "legal buffer" against prosecution, but he gets a low rating as a religious patriarch, even from Osteopath Rulon Allred, founder of the polygamous Montana community where Joseph once lived. Says Allred: "He used the doctrine of plural marriage to justify conduct not acceptable to the priesthood." Indeed, Joseph has acquired his 15 wives (who now have five children) rather casually. "I decided to marry Judy after 15 minutes," he says, "and I asked Paulette [age 16] after 29 hours." The obedient wives, most of whom work as waitresses in Joseph's nearby Red Desert Inn, profess to believe in the Josephian faith. Says Joni, who turned down a $6,000 National Merit scholarship to marry him: "Polygamy provides the sense of fulfillment I never experienced at the First Baptist Church in Billings." Although polygamy is illegal, authorities have trouble prosecuting it. Says Kane County Sheriff Norman Swapp: "Sure it's against the law, but I can't even prove he's married to all those women."

A Bit Too Much

Detroit, July 5 (UPI)—Mrs. Gloria Judge, 24, obtained a court peace bond to stop her husband Clifton from beating her. He forced her to eat the 5-by-8-inch document, then beat her again.

Clifton was fined $100 by Recorder's Court Judge C. W. Kotulski after he pleaded guilty to assault and battery.

Would-Be Suicide Halted; Crowd Boos

DANIA, Fla. (AP)—A jeering crowd urged a 27-year-old woman to jump from a 110-foot tower, then pelted police with rocks when they tried to rescue her.

Police used dogs to disperse the crowd of some 300 persons. Five officers received minor injuries before the woman was led to safety and taken to a hospital Wednesday night.

Friends said she tried to kill herself after becoming despondent over being fired from her job.

The woman's physician and two firemen helped talk the woman out of jumping.

Fire Chief John Lassiter said rock throwing increased as the firemen brought the woman down from the tower, and the crowd began to boo when they realized the woman would not jump.

A similar incident occurred at the tower Sunday when a man climbed to the top and threatened to jump. He was talked down by firemen as a crowd jeered and threw rocks.

A Burning Passion

BARNOLDSWICK, England (UPI) — Sandra Weire developed a burning passion for a fireman and decided to rekindle the flames.

So she set fire to her home and called the fire brigade.

When that did not win his love, she moved to a new house and tried the same ploy again.

The judge at her arson trial said her method of winning a sweetheart "is not really to be recommended."

Girls Accused in Dad's Death

CHICAGO (AP) — Two Chicago girls, aged 13 and 15, have been named in delinquency petitions for allegedly shooting their 60-year-old father.

Johnnie Thomas, 60, a cab driver, was found fatally shot in the living room of his South Side home Wednesday. He had been shot with his own .38-caliber revolver.

Authorities said the girls at first suggested that he might have been killed in a robbery attempt. Later they broke down and admitted they had planned the killing since Sunday when Thomas allegedly beat them, police said.

Police said the girls came to live with their father several months ago after complaining that their mother had beat them.

FIGURE 13–1 As evidenced by these clippings, actual instances of social behavior are often stranger and more unexpected than anything we could invent. (Left story from *Time*, May 19, 1975; all others from United Press International or Associated Press as indicated by dateline.)

persons; and **interpersonal attraction**—feelings of liking or disliking for others. In the second portion, we will turn to two important and common forms of social behavior which seem quite opposite in nature: **altruism** and **aggression.** While many other types of social interaction are equally worthy of attention, these two seem to mark extremes on what might be termed the social continuum. As such, they may provide an especially useful introduction to the great variety and complexity of human social affairs.

In an important sense, the task of forming accurate perceptions of others may be viewed as consisting largely of two steps. First, we seek to determine the major traits or characteristics possessed by the persons in question; second, we attempt to combine this diverse and often contradictory information into unitary and consistent pictures of their personalities. Because both steps play a central role in the overall process of person perception, each will serve as a point of focus for the present discussion.

In our attempts to determine the major traits or characteristics of others, we draw upon several diverse sources of information. For example, we often pay close attention to such aspects of their physical appearance as their mode of dress, hairstyle, and use of cosmetics, for past experience suggests that such outward signs may tell us much about the persons in question. Although such cues may sometimes lead us astray (see Figure 13–2), they do frequently provide us with a great deal of valuable information about others.

Similarly, we often seek to gain important information about others by questioning their closest friends and acquaintances, for in many cases these persons have at their disposal information of a highly personal or intimate nature which we could not possibly hope to obtain ourselves.

The major source of our knowledge about others, however, is careful observation of their overt actions. In general, we acquire most of our information in this respect by (1) observing others' behavior, and (2) *inferring* their traits or characteristics on the basis of such observations (see Kelley, 1972, 1973). This process of inferring the characteristics of others from their overt behavior is known as **attribution,** and often serves as an important, preliminary step in person perception.

At first, it might seem that the task of moving from overt acts to inferences regarding the stable traits of others would be a relatively simple one. After all, human behavior is remarkably varied, and provides us with a rich source of evidence upon which to base our conclusions. Unfortunately, though, this seemingly simple task is greatly complicated by two important factors.

PERSON PERCEPTION: GETTING TO KNOW OTHERS

Attribution: When Acts Tell the Story

FIGURE 13–2 As shown in this cartoon, looks are often deceiving and lead us to false conclusions about others. (Copyright 1968; reprinted by permission of *Saturday Review* and Bill Hoest.)

"No, I'm the one from Rhode Island . . . he's from Texas."

First, other people often seek to mislead or deceive us about their major characteristics. For example, they often say things they don't mean, put on their "company manners" when we are around, and even attempt to change their physical appearance in a number of different ways. The success of these maneuvers is suggested by the frequency with which new brides and bridegrooms complain, a few months after the honeymoon, that their mate is a far different person from the one they chose to marry. To the extent that other persons are able to deceive us in this manner, our ability to draw accurate inferences about their major characteristics is severely reduced.

Second, and perhaps of even greater importance, the actions of others are often shaped and determined not by their internal states or dispositions but rather by external factors beyond their control. In such cases it is impossible to learn anything of value about them from the overt behavior they demonstrate, for it is imposed from without and may be quite inconsistent with their actual motives or characteristics. A preliminary step in the attribution process, therefore, is often that of determining whether the actions of others—upon which we wish to base our conclusions—stem from internal or external causes (Kelley, 1972).

In many real-life situations, of course, it is difficult to determine whether the behavior of others is caused primarily by internal or external factors. For example, imagine that you observe a clerk in a store act in a rude, impatient manner toward a customer. Are his actions due to the fact that he is basically a nasty and unpleasant person who treats all customers in this fashion? Or are they the result of external factors such as a series of unreasonable and irritating demands by this particular shopper? In many cases, it would be very difficult to tell. Yet, mounting evidence suggests that we are often quite ready to jump to the conclusion that others' behavior stems primarily from internal, personal causes. Indeed, a number of recent experiments (Arkin and Duval, 1975; Miller, 1975) suggest that in general, we tend to perceive the actions of other persons as stemming largely from internal factors—lasting personal dispositions or traits—while viewing our own as deriving primarily from external, situational forces. In short, we tend to assume that *we* act the way we do because situational factors have pushed us in this direction, while others act the way *they* do because it is their nature to do so (Nisbett et al., 1973). Given this bias, it is little wonder that we often interpret others' behavior as providing us with a true picture of their personalities and motives, even when there are no strong grounds for reaching such conclusions.

This type of attributional error leads to many negative outcomes. For example, among psychologists and other professionals, it seems to lead to an overemphasis on the importance of internal causes of behavior (Kelley, 1973). One of its most unsettling effects, however, can be seen in our strong tendency to hold others responsible for any unpleasant or painful outcomes they experience. For example, we often blame the victims of serious accidents or natural disasters for the unhappy fates they suffer, assuming—often unfairly—that it was their own carelessness or lack of caution which brought such suffering down upon their heads (Walster, 1966) (see Figure 13–3). Similarly, there seems to be a strong tendency on the part of many persons to blame the victims of forcible rape for the assaults they have suffered, even when there are absolutely no grounds for drawing such conclusions (Jones and Aronson, 1973). Indeed, women who summon enough courage to report such outrages often find themselves greeted with smirks and suggestive comments indicating that they must somehow have encouraged or invited their attack. In cases such as these, our strong tendency to attribute the actions and outcomes of others

FIGURE 13-3 Although individuals caught in floods, earthquakes, and other natural disasters are usually the innocent victims of fate, we often tend to hold them responsible for the harm they have suffered. (Left photo by Camera Press Ltd., print provided by Photo Trends; right photo by United Press International.)

to internal, personal causes can lead to serious and potentially harmful misunderstandings.

Given the existence of such complicating factors, the task of inferring the characteristics of others from observations of their overt behavior appears to be a formidable one. Often, though, we *do* succeed in identifying their major traits, largely by focusing our attention upon those types of behavior most likely to yield the information which we seek (Jones and Davis, 1965; Kelley, 1973).

First, we pay particular attention to those actions by others for which they could have had only one distinct reason (or at most a few reasons). The major advantage of this strategy is that it permits us to be fairly certain of the motives behind an act; and once we understand another's motives, we often know much about this individual. For example, if you learned that a friend had accepted a job after graduation which (1) required that he or she move to a small town in a very unattractive part of the country, (2) involved extremely dull and tedious work, but (3) paid $25,000 a year as a starting salary, you could probably make an accurate guess as to the reasons behind his or her choice. Moreover, on the basis of this information, you could probably conclude that this person values money more than pleasant geographic surroundings, interesting or fulfilling work, and the cultural opportunities available only in larger towns. On the other hand, if you learned that your friend had accepted a job which (1) required that he or she move to one of the most attractive cities in the nation, (2) involved extremely stimulating and interesting work, and (3) still paid $25,000 per year, you would be far less certain as to the reasons behind his or her action: there would simply be too many good ones to permit a choice. In sum, we often acquire more useful information about others from behavior for which there could have been only one reason (or a very few reasons) than from behavior for which there could have been many reasons (Newtson, 1974).

Second, we tend to focus our attention upon actions by others which depart in some manner from usual standards of behavior. Thus, we would be much more interested in learning that another person (1) swims nude in the ocean in December, (2) has an electric fence around his or her property, and (3) keeps a pet cobra in the basement than in learning that he or she (1) eats a light breakfast in the morning, (2) drives his or her car to work, and (3) goes to the movies on the weekend. This would be the case because the first three pieces of information provide us with a basis for inferring many interesting things about the person in question (e.g., he or she is a health fanatic and suffers from strange anxieties, but enjoys certain types of danger), while the latter three merely inform us that he or she is much like others in many respects. It is not at all surprising, then, that in our attempts to determine the major characteristics of others, we pay a great deal of attention to those aspects of their behavior which set them apart from average or typical members of society. Indeed, for this purpose, the more unusual or bizarre their actions, the better!

By focusing on these and other important aspects of the behavior of other persons (e.g., their actions in private rather than public settings), we are usually able to do an excellent job of identifying their major traits and dispositions. Attaining such information, however, is only the first step in our task of forming accurate perceptions of these persons. Once we have gained this knowledge, we must try to combine it into unitary and consistent impressions of them. This complex process of **impression formation** represents a second important step in our attempts to know and understand others.

Forming Impressions of Others: Do We Average or Add?

Suppose that after meeting another person and observing her behavior on a number of different occasions, you conclude that she is good-natured, friendly, and honest, but also conceited, tactless, and lazy. How would you go about combining all of this information into a consistent and unitary impression? Clearly, you might seek to accomplish this task in a number of different ways. Using the simplest methods, however, you would have a choice between (1) *adding* the information together in a straightforward manner and (2) *averaging* it in some way.

At first, it might seem that neither method — adding or averaging information about others in forming impressions of them — would have much effect upon the final result. That the method you use actually does have an important influence in this respect can be illustrated by means of the following example. Imagine that after meeting another person for the first time, you conclude that he is unusually intelligent. Since intelligence is viewed as a highly desirable characteristic in our society, your initial impression of this individual would probably be quite favorable. But now imagine that after a second meeting, you conclude that he is also very reserved. Although this, too, is often viewed as a positive characteristic, there is little doubt that it is evaluated somewhat less favorably than intelligence. Thus, at this point you would be faced with the task of combining these two bits of information — one highly favorable and the other only slightly so — into a consistent, overall impression of the person in question. The method you employ in completing this task would then exert a powerful effect upon the final result you obtain. If you combine these traits through addition, your overall impression will actually increase from its initial, favorable level, because the sum of one highly favorable and one slightly favorable trait would be greater than that for one highly favorable trait alone. If you combine this information through averaging, however, your overall impression will actually become *less* positive, because the average of one highly favorable and one slightly favorable trait would be somewhat lower than the value for one highly favorable trait alone. These contrasting predictions of the averaging and adding methods are illustrated in Table 13–1, where the two traits in question have been assigned arbitrary values designed to reflect their relative degrees of favorability.

Because our impressions of others might be formed through either method,

TABLE 13–1   Adding and Averaging Models of Impression Formation

Adding

Impression Based on One Highly Favorable Trait	Impression Based on One Highly Favorable and One Moderately Favorable Trait	
Intelligent (+3)	Intelligent	(+3)
	Reserved	(+1)
	Total Value	= (+4)

Averaging

Impression Based on One Highly Favorable Trait	Impression Based on One Highly Favorable and One Moderately Favorable Trait	
Intelligent (+3)	Intelligent	(+3)
	Reserved	(+1)
	Average Value	= (+4)/2 = (+2)

The adding model predicts that an impression based on two traits, one highly favorable and one only slightly favorable, will be more positive than an impression based on only one highly favorable trait. In contrast, the averaging model predicts that an impression based on one highly favorable and one slightly favorable trait will actually be *less* positive than an impression based on one highly favorable trait alone. In the examples shown in the table, the higher the numbers obtained through adding or averaging, the more favorable the impressions formed. (All values are in arbitrary units.)

many experiments have been conducted to determine which we actually employ. In general, results have tended to support the averaging formulation (see Anderson, 1974). That is, our overall impression of others seems to be based upon a special type of average of all the characteristics they possess. This is not to say that upon meeting someone for the first time we sit down, construct a list of his or her various traits, and then seek to average these together. As you probably know from your own experience, the process is much more rapid and much less conscious than this. The final outcome at which we arrive, however, seems to be quite consistent with the general suggestion that some type of averaging takes place.

You may have noticed that in our comments above we described as "special" the average upon which our impressions of others are based. By this term we simply meant *weighted*—an average in which some characteristics and information receive more weight than others (Kaplan, 1975). Several factors seem to play a role in this respect. First, we seem to assign greater importance to the information about others we obtain during our initial meetings with them than we do to information we receive only later. It is largely because of such **primacy effects,** of course, that first impressions are often so difficult to alter. Second, as you might expect on the basis of our discussion in Chapter 12, we place more value on information received from highly credible sources than on that supplied by less reliable sources (Rosenbaum and Levin, 1969). For example, if a good friend whose judgment you trust tells you that another person who seems both friendly and pleasant is really quite two-faced, you would be more likely to alter your impression in a negative direction than if you received similar information from a total stranger. And finally, we seem to weight incoming information according to its relevance to the judgment being made (Hamilton and Fallot, 1974). For example, in attempting to choose another person for a job, we assign most importance to characteristics which seem relevant to its performance; in choosing a romantic partner, we assign most importance to characteristics related to intimate relationships. When these and other factors are taken into account, an averaging formulation — although one far more complex than that with which we began — does indeed seem to provide a relatively good description of the manner in which we form unified impressions of others.

Physical Attractiveness and Impressions of Others: Is What Is Beautiful Also Good?

One of the first things we notice about other persons is their physical appearance. Common sense suggests that this factor will exert a powerful effect upon our reactions to them, and, as we shall soon see in our discussion of interpersonal attraction, this definitely seems to be the case. Physically attractive persons are generally liked to a greater degree than are unattractive ones upon a first meeting (Berscheid and Walster, 1974).

The fact that we often experience positive initial reactions to attractive individuals is far from surprising. Somewhat more unexpected, however, is the strong tendency on our part to attribute other positive characteristics to them. That is, we generally seem to assume that beautiful persons are also good, kind, intelligent, and so on. Perhaps the most striking evidence for the existence of this assumption that "what is beautiful is also good" has been obtained by Dion, Berscheid, and Walster (1972). These investigators presented subjects with photos of individuals who had previously been rated as high, average, or low in physical attractiveness (see Figure 13–4), and asked them to indicate their impressions of these persons in several different ways. For example, after examining the photos, subjects rated each of the persons shown on a number of personality traits (altruism, sincerity, competitiveness, poise, etc.), and estimated their future marital happiness and occupational success. The results of the study were remarkably clear: individuals high in physical attractiveness received more positive ratings in almost every category than those lower in such appeal (see Figure 13–5). Moreover, this was the case regardless of whether the persons in the photos were of the same or opposite sex as the subjects.

FIGURE 13–4   A photo of an individual rated as high in physical attractiveness, similar to the ones employed by Dion, Walster, and Berscheid in their study of the effects of physical appeal on first impressions.

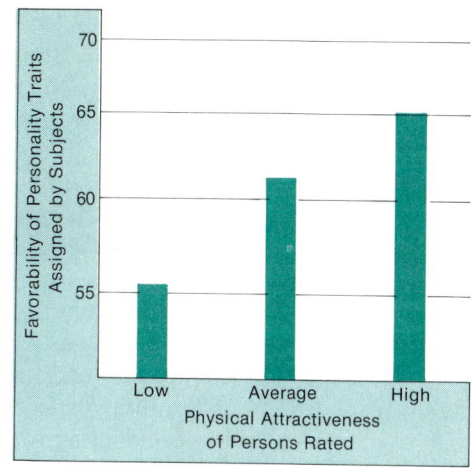

FIGURE 13–5   Evidence for our acceptance of the belief that "what is beautiful is also good." Subjects rated physically attractive persons as possessing more desirable personality traits, and expected them to attain greater marital happiness and occupational success, than either average or unattractive persons. (Only data for ratings of personality are shown.) (Based on data from Dion, Berscheid, and Walster, 1972.)

Interestingly, more recent findings have revealed that highly attractive persons do not always live up to the positive stereotype others hold about them (Krebs and Adinolfi, 1975). Instead of being good, friendly, kind, and so on, many actually turn out to be ambitious, independent, and highly oriented toward success and achievement. Perhaps this disparity between their actual traits and those that other persons expect them to possess provides a partial explanation for the fact that extremely attractive persons are often not as popular as those of somewhat lesser physical beauty (Krebs and Adinolfi, 1975). That is, when others find that attractive persons do not actually show all the positive traits expected, they become disappointed or disillusioned, and thus tend to reject them. Regardless of whether this is actually the case, there seem to be strong grounds for concluding that in our relations with others, we often operate under the assumption that beauty is, after all, more than skin deep.

In addition to desiring knowledge about the enduring traits, motives, and characteristics of others, we also seek information about their temporary states and reactions—how they are feeling and thinking right now. Such information is important because, as we will soon discover, people's behavior is often more strongly affected by temporary fluctuations in mood or emotion than by lasting traits or dispositions. For example, even the kindest, sweetest persons have their irritable days on which they are best avoided, and even cruel and sadistic individuals can be friendly and obliging on certain rare occasions.

Often, we learn about the emotional states and feelings of others in a direct and straightforward manner: they simply tell us how they feel. In many other cases, though, they do not provide us with such information, and we must seek to infer it from their overt behavior. Fortunately, even when they do not directly indicate how they feel, other persons usually provide us with many **nonverbal cues** regarding their mood. Basically, these fall into three major categories: Information provided by their **facial expressions,** information yielded by their **eye contact** with us, and information provided by the **position, posture,** and **movements of their bodies.**

As you may recall, we have already examined in Chapter 7 the possibility of recognizing others' emotions from their outward facial expressions (see pp. 247–251). In that earlier discussion, we noted that recent experiments point to the conclusion that we often *can* determine the inward feelings of

Nonverbal Communication: The Language of Gazes and Gestures

Masking and Unmasking the Face: Recognizing the Emotions of Others

other persons from careful inspection of their frowns, smiles, and tears (Buck et al., 1974). Indeed, the ability to correctly "read" the facial expressions of others seems to be acquired at a very young age, so that even four-year-olds can often recognize the emotions of the persons around them with a high degree of accuracy (Buck, 1975). Moreover, as we have already pointed out, certain facial expressions — smiles, frowns, looks of despair, and several others — seem to be quite universal, in the sense that they are recognized all over the world as signs of certain emotions (Ekman and Friesen, 1975). Together, such findings suggest that others' facial expressions often provide us with important nonverbal cues concerning their internal feelings or emotions (see Figure 13–6).

Unfortunately, though, the usefulness of such information is often sharply reduced by one important fact: In many cases, other persons attempt to deceive us in this respect. That is, they try to demonstrate emotions they don't feel, hide ones they are experiencing, or substitute one for another. In such cases, of course, the expressions they show may lead us into serious error regarding their actual internal state. While attempts at such facial deceit can take many different forms, three seem to be most common (Ekman and Friesen, 1975).

First, other persons may engage in a process known as **qualifying.** Here, they seek to add a further expression to one they have just shown as a sort of comment upon it. For example, an angry person may smile as a sign that he or she is not quite as enraged as seemed to be the case. Second, others may engage in **modulating** — adjusting their facial expressions so as to show more or less of an emotion than they are actually experiencing. To mention only one instance of such deceit, an individual who is not actually feeling very sad may nevertheless attempt to demonstrate signs of strong grief in order to make another feel guilty, with the purpose of getting this person to do his or her bidding (see pp. 434–435 for a discussion of this form of social influence). Finally, other persons may engage in **falsifying,** a process in which they (1) pretend to experience some feeling which they do not have, (2) show no emotion when they are actually aroused, or (3) substitute one reaction for

FIGURE 13–6 Others' facial expressions often provide us with clues to their present feelings or emotional states. (Upper right photo: Syndication International, print provided by Photo Trends; all others from Photo Trends.)

another. Falsifying is the most deceitful form of facial control, and it can often be used to seriously mislead others about one's true emotional state.

As you probably know from your own experience, some individuals acquire great skill at controlling their emotional expressions—and not all of them are on the stage! Confidence artists, petty swindlers, and even successful salesmen and saleswomen often manage to wring a handsome living from this ability. Indeed, through long years of practice, such persons may become so skilled at controlling their emotional expressions that it is virtually impossible to penetrate their deceit. In most cases, though, subtle clues indicating that another person is attempting to mislead us are present, and can be readily observed if we take the trouble to look for them with care. Basically, such clues stem from three different sources.

First, they may be provided by gaps in the total pattern of reactions shown. When others attempt to control their facial expressions, they generally concentrate on one part of the face or another. Thus, by looking for inconsistencies in the pattern of reactions shown, we can often get some hint that deception is occurring. For example, an individual feigning surprise may raise his brows and open his eyes widely—but forget to let his mouth drop open. Second, clues to deception may be provided by the timing of the reaction shown. Genuine emotional responses appear on the face very quickly. Thus, if several seconds elapse between a crucial stimulus and another person's facial reaction, there may be grounds for suspecting that the emotion shown is not a genuine one. For example, if there is a long pause between the end of your joke and another person's laughter, you can be fairly certain that the reaction is staged. And finally, deceit may be betrayed by what Ekman and Friesen (1975) term **micro-expressions**—very brief reactions lasting for a small fraction of a second which reveal an individual's true emotions. By keeping a careful watch for these three types of subtle clues, we can often succeed in unmasking the face, and thereby gain accurate information about the true emotional states of the persons around us.

Gazes and Stares: Eye Contact as a Clue to Others' Feelings

The eyes have often been described as "windows to the soul," and in some respects, at least, this appears to be true. A growing body of research suggests that we often *can* learn a great deal about others' internal state from their eyes (Exline, 1971; Mehrabian, 1971). In particular, much is often revealed by the amount and pattern of their eye contact with us. First, we often use such information as a rough indicator of their overall emotional state: the more they gaze at us, at least up to a point, the more positive we assume they feel. Indeed, when others avoid our gaze we often conclude that they feel guilty, are harboring negative thoughts, or are generally depressed (Knapp, 1972).

Second, and perhaps of greater importance, we use the amount and pattern of others' gazes as evidence of their feelings toward us. A number of experiments indicate that we interpret a high level of eye contact from another as a sign of friendliness and liking. For example, in one recent study by Kleinke, Meeker, and LaFong (1974), college students watched videotapes of supposedly engaged couples. In one condition, the couples (actually accomplices of the experimenters) never looked into each other's eyes during their conversation, while in another they demonstrated a high level of eye contact. When later asked to report their reactions to the couples viewed, subjects rated those showing a high degree of eye contact as liking each other more, and as having better potential for a successful marriage.

While these and other findings suggest that a high level of eye contact from others is often interpreted as a sign of positive feelings on their part, there seems to be one important exception to this general rule. When someone

TABLE 13–2   Stares as a Stimulus to Flight

	Stare		No Stare	
	Male Drivers	Female Drivers	Male Drivers	Female Drivers
Seconds Required to Cross Intersection	5.7	5.7	6.2	6.8

Male and female motorists waiting at a red light who received expressionless stares from another driver crossed the intersection significantly faster when the traffic signal turned green than did motorists who received no stares. (Adapted from Ellsworth, Carlsmith, and Henson, 1972.)

gazes at us in a continuous manner and maintains such eye contact regardless of our reactions, such **staring** may often be interpreted as a sign of hostility rather than friendship. Evidence for the occurrence of such effects has actually been obtained in several experiments (Ellsworth and Langer, 1976). For example, in one interesting study (Ellsworth, Carlsmith and Henson, 1972), motorists waiting at a red light were exposed to one of three conditions: stares from another driver, stares from a pedestrian, or no stares from any source. The speed with which they drove off once the light turned green was then recorded in order to determine whether subjects exposed to the stares would seek to escape from these stimuli as quickly as possible. As might be expected, results offered strong support for this suggestion: drivers who received stares from either another motorist or a pedestrian crossed the intersection significantly faster than drivers who received no stares (see Table 13–2). Moreover, they evidenced more signs of tension and nervousness than drivers who did not receive continuous visual gazes. Such findings suggest that eye contact can communicate negative as well as positive reactions. In short, we can often learn as much about another person's feelings toward us from cold and icy stares as from warm and friendly glances.

Body Language: Every Little Movement has a Meaning of Its Own

A third source of nonverbal information about others' feelings and emotions stems from the posture, position, and movements of their bodies. As you probably know from your own experience, such body language can often be extremely revealing, telling us much about other persons. First, nonverbal cues of this type can reveal their current emotional states. On a global level, a large amount of body movement (e.g., fidgeting, continuous shifting of legs and arms) suggests that an individual is emotionally aroused—although it does not in itself indicate which emotion he or she is experiencing (Knapp, 1972). More specific information about their feelings is often provided by **gestures.** For example, a clenched fist usually indicates anger, a covering of the eyes shame or embarrassment, and a rubbing together of the hands anticipation or excitement (Knapp, 1972) (see Figure 13–7).

In combination, clues from another person's movements and gestures can often paint a vivid picture of his or her present emotional states. But this is far from the entire story; body language also tells us much more. In particular, it often reveals positive or negative feelings toward us on the part of others. Perhaps one of the clearest clues in this respect is another's bodily orientation. If someone with whom we are conversing faces us directly and leans forward, this is usually a sign that he or she likes us. In contrast, if another individual orients his or her body away from us and leans back while we interact, this creates the impression that he or she dislikes us (Mehrabian, 1968). Similar information regarding others' feelings toward us is also communicated by many other cues. For example, if another person frequently nods his or her head in agreement or watches us very carefully (hanging on our every word) while we speak, positive feelings are suggested. In contrast, if they frequently shake their head in disagreement, stare off into space, or play with the ends of their hair, negative reactions (possibly acute boredom!) are indicated (Clore, Wiggins, and Itkin, 1975). Together, such nonverbal cues can often provide us with much valuable information regarding others' feelings toward us.

Finally, body language can also transmit a somewhat stronger reaction—sexual interest or receptivity. For example, consider the following description of the manner in which a woman who finds a particular man attractive may communicate this information to him (Fast, 1970, p. 88):

> A big part of the way she transmits her message is also in stance, posture, or movement. An available woman moves in a studied way ... the movement of her body, hips, and shoulders telegraphs her availability. She may sit with her legs apart, symbolically open and inviting, or she may affect a gesture in which one hand touches her breast in a near caress. She may stroke her thighs as she talks or walk with a languorous roll to her hips. Some of her movements are studied and conscious, some completely unconscious.

That men, too, can communicate sexual interest or attraction through body language is indicated by the following description of one proverbial "ladies' man" (Fast, p. 85):

> But Mike has more. He has dozens of little gestures, perhaps unconscious ones that send out elaborations of his sexual message. When Mike leans up against a mantel in a room to look around at the women, his hips are thrust forward slightly ... and his legs are usually apart. There is something in this stance that spells sex.

Of course, as shown in Figure 13–8, such cues are often far more subtle than the ones described above. Given the importance of the message they convey, however, searching carefully for them may well prove worth the effort!

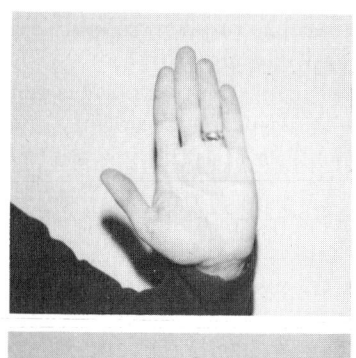
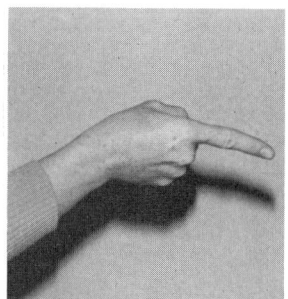
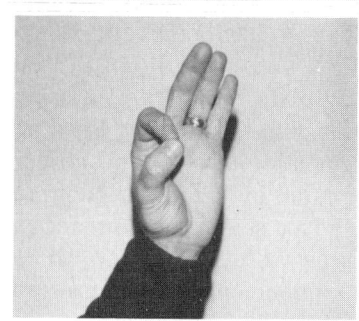
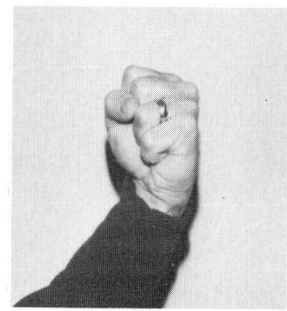

FIGURE 13–7 Gestures often reveal that an individual is experiencing a particular emotion. Can you guess what emotions lie behind the gestures shown above?

FIGURE 13–8   The ability to accurately "read" nonverbal messages from others is often very useful in interactions with members of the opposite sex. (Andy Capp by Reggie Smythe, © 1974 Daily Mirror Newspapers, Ltd., Courtesy of Field Newspaper Syndicate.)

Nonverbal Communication: Assembling the Puzzle

While we have described nonverbal cues from others' faces, gazes, and bodies separately, it is obvious that they generally occur together. When we interact with another person, we usually receive input from all three sources at once. Sometimes the cues from one source conflict with those from another, but generally they provide a fairly consistent picture. In most cases, then, the information supplied by this unspoken language of expressions, gazes, and gestures gets us off to a very good start in our attempts to know the feelings and emotions of the persons around us.

INTERPERSONAL ATTRACTION: WHOM WE LIKE AND WHY

Will Rogers, a noted and much admired humorist of bygone days, was often heard to remark: "I never met a man I didn't like." Unfortunately, few of us can make the same statement with total honesty. Rather, we are well aware of the fact that our feelings toward others vary greatly, ranging all the way from strong liking and admiration on the one hand to intense hatred and aversion on the other. These reactions exert a powerful impact upon the nature of our interactions with others, so that we seek the company of those whom we like, while avoiding that of persons whom we dislike. Similarly, as noted in Chapter 12, we are probably more likely to accept influence from, do favors for, and comply with requests from others when our level of attraction toward them is high than when it is relatively low. But what, precisely, are the bases of such positive and negative reactions to others? What factors lead us to like, dislike, or remain indifferent to other persons? Several will now be considered.

Attitude Similarity: Birds of a Feather Flock Together

One particularly important determinant of attraction toward others is the extent to which they seem to hold attitudes or opinions similar to our own. In general, we tend to like other persons who share our views to a much greater degree than those who do not. Formal evidence indicating that this is the case has been gathered in a large number of experiments (Byrne, 1971; Davison and Jones, 1976). In many of these studies, subjects were first asked to complete an attitude questionnaire designed to assess their opinions on a wide range of topics. Several weeks later, they were provided with a similar questionnaire supposedly filled out by another individual, but actually completed by the experimenter so as to suggest that this stranger shared their views on a set proportion of the items. For example, the stranger might be made to agree with subjects on all (1.00 agreement), half (.50 agreement), or none (0.00 agreement) of the issues. After examining the questionnaire, subjects were asked to indicate how much they thought they might like this person if they actually met him or her. It was predicted that their degree of liking for this nonexistent stranger would vary with the extent to which he or she appeared to share their attitudes, and, as can be seen in Figure 13–9, this was actually the case. The greater the proportion of apparent agreement between subjects and the stranger, the greater their expressed liking for him or her.

Interestingly, this tendency to like others who share our opinions more than those who do not appears to be quite universal. For example, it has been observed in such widely different nations as the U.S., Mexico, India, and Japan (Byrne et al., 1971). Moreover, it appears to exist among individuals ranging in age from childhood to the last decades of life (Byrne, 1969). In short, while we would all probably agree that others are entitled to their own opinions, we seem to like them best when their attitudes happen to match our own.

Imagine that you overheard a conversation in which one of the participants made a number of complimentary and positive statements about you, while the other responded with a series of critical and negative comments. Which one would you prefer? All other factors being equal, there is little doubt that you would tend to like the person who expressed positive evaluations of you more than you would the one who expressed only negative opinions. This simple example illustrates an important point concerning interpersonal attraction: in general, our liking for others closely matches their expressed attraction for us, so that we tend to like those who evaluate us positively, but dislike others who hold us in low repute. Despite the Christian dictum to "love thine enemy," interpersonal attraction seems to be largely reciprocal in nature. Of course, common sense suggests that there are exceptions to this general rule of reciprocity. Some individuals continue to lavish love and affection upon others who greet these attentions with scorn and derision. But such instances are relatively rare, and a close matching of interpersonal attraction between individuals appears to be the more usual state of affairs.

Praise or Blame from Others: The Reciprocal Nature of Liking

The important impact of positive or negative evaluations from others upon our level of attraction toward them has been demonstrated quite clearly in a number of laboratory studies (Byrne and Rhamey, 1965; Hewitt, 1972). In these experiments, subjects have generally reported greater liking for strangers who evaluate them positively than for strangers who evaluate them negatively. Further, there is some indication that we are especially sensitive to changes in others' level of liking for us. Thus, when other persons start out disliking us but end up liking us, we like *them* more than we do those who express positive reactions all along (Aronson and Linder, 1965; Clore, Wiggins, and Itkin, 1975). Similarly, when others start out liking us but end up disliking us, we have greater dislike for them than we do for those who dislike us from the start. Apparently, it is particularly gratifying—or unsettling—to learn that

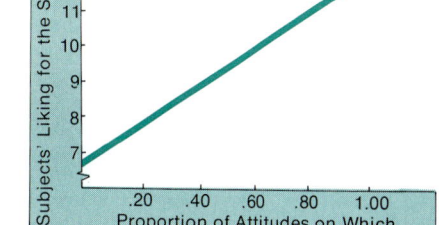

FIGURE 13–9   The effects of attitude similarity on attraction. The higher the degree of apparent similarity between subjects and a stranger, the greater their liking for this person. (Adapted from Byrne and Nelson, 1965.)

another person has changed his or her initial evaluation of us after getting to know us better. Whether others continue to react to us in a consistent manner or radically alter their evaluations over the course of time, the rule of reciprocity seems to remain in effect: our level of attraction toward them is strongly determined by the nature of their feelings toward us.

Physical Attractiveness and Liking: Is Beauty Only Skin Deep?

Each year, consumers spend countless millions on shampoos, colognes, skin creams, "super-whitening" toothpastes, and many other products designed to enhance their physical attractiveness. The basis for this vast outpouring of funds, of course, is the strong belief that a high degree of physical appeal will lead to increased approval and admiration from others, especially members of the opposite sex. Pushed in this direction by numerous appeals from the advertising industry (see Figure 13–10), many persons seem to assume that beauty is the true key to happiness: if only they can raise their level of physical appeal to appropriate heights, the love and affection they desire will soon be obtained. From the point of view of stable, lasting relationships, this emphasis on physical attractiveness is somewhat unsettling: beauty usually fades with the passing years and cannot provide a permanent basis for strong interpersonal bonds. Unfortunately, though, there seems to be considerable justification for the widespread belief in its importance. A number of experiments undertaken in recent years point to the conclusion that physical attractiveness is indeed an important determinant of social attraction (Berscheid and Walster, 1974). In fact, where first meetings between relatively young persons are concerned, it seems to literally overwhelm all other factors which might also be expected to influence liking, such as personality, intelligence, and even similarity (Walster et al., 1966; Kleck and Rubinstein, 1975). Of course, with continued interaction, these other variables come to play an increasingly important role. Initially, though, physical charms seem to occupy a highly central position. As we noted earlier, it may well be that beauty is only skin deep; however, people seem to pay a lot of attention to skin!

Given the important influence of physical attractiveness upon liking, it might be assumed that in making their romantic choices, individuals will usually seek the most attractive partners they can find. To some extent, this seems to be true, especially as regards first meetings or casual dating (Walster

FIGURE 13–10   Advertisements for products such as the ones shown here often suggest that physical beauty is one of the true keys to personal happiness.

FIGURE 13-11   Although individuals often fantasize about obtaining extremely attractive romantic partners, they usually seem to both choose and prefer others whose level of physical appeal roughly equals their own. (Top left photo by Michael Marton, Camera Press, London; print provided by Photo Trends. Top right photo by Marcel Cognac, Annan Photo Features. Bottom photo credit: Syndication International, print provided by Photo Trends.)

et al., 1966). In the case of long-term romantic choices, however, there is growing evidence that most persons follow what has been termed the **matching rule,** attempting to select partners whose level of physical appeal roughly approximates their own (Berscheid et al., 1971). For example, in one recent study, Murstein (1972) found that couples who were engaged or going steady were significantly more similar to each other in physical attractiveness (as rated by other persons) than were randomly paired individuals not romantically involved (see Figure 13-11). This strong tendency toward matching seems to stem from the joint operation of two different forces. On the one hand, we usually desire to obtain the most attractive partners we can find, while on the other, we know that the probability of obtaining ones who are far more attractive than ourselves is very low. Together, these factors lead us to the conclusion—whether explicit or implicit—that someone approximately equal to ourselves in attractiveness is about the best we can hope to do. Thus, while we may daydream about the kind of persons shown in the pages of "Playboy" or "Cosmopolitan," when faced with the selection of a real lover or spouse we tend to both choose and prefer someone whose level of physical appeal closely matches our own.

**PSYCHOLOGY
IN
ACTION:** *The Matching Game: Similarity in Physical Attractiveness*

Informal evidence for the operation of the matching rule in romantic choices is all around us. For example, people often make such remarks as "How did he ever get *her*?" or "How did she ever get *him*?" in cases in which there is a large disparity in the physical attractiveness of the members of a couple. Similarly, there is little doubt that the more attractive individuals believe they are, the more attractive they expect their dates and spouses to be (Walster et al., 1966). You can demonstrate the important influence of this tendency toward matching for yourself by means of the following simple procedures.

First, make a list of ten couples you know who are married, ten who are engaged (or going steady), and ten who are dating casually. Next, rate the members of each of these thirty couples along a scale of physical attractiveness, with 1 as very unattractive and 7 as very attractive. (Special forms for this task are provided in the *Study Guide*, but you can make your own by placing the numbers 1 through 7 on thirty pieces of plain paper.)

After completing your ratings, do the following:

(1) Determine the difference between the ratings you have assigned to the members of each couple (e.g., if the man in a given couple is rated 6 and the women 5, the difference is 1).

(2) Add these differences for each category of couple (married, engaged, dating casually).

(3) Divide these sums by 10 to obtain an average in each case. (This will be the average difference in physical attractiveness for each type of couple.)

If you now compare these average differences, you will probably find that they decrease as you move from couples who are only casually dating to those who are engaged or going steady, and are lowest for those who are already married. In short, the more intimate and long-lasting their relationships, the more similar in physical appeal are the couples in your survey likely to be.

Playing "Hard to Get": An Effective Technique?

It has often been assumed that "playing hard to get" is a highly effective means of increasing one's level of appeal to members of the opposite sex. Cultural lore suggests that women (and perhaps men as well) who greet advances from others with cool indifference are frequently more desired and sought after than are those who throw themselves into the arms of prospective lovers. But is "playing hard to get" actually an effective means of fanning the flames of passion? Evidence concerning this intriguing question has recently been collected by Elaine Walster and her associates (Walster et al., 1973).

In this study, male subjects participating in what they believed to be a computer matching project were provided with information concerning the initial reactions of different women both to themselves and to a number of other men. One of these women appeared to be uniformly "hard to get," reacting to all of her potential partners with great indifference; a second appeared to be "uniformly easy to get," responding with great enthusiasm to all of the men she might date; a third woman was "selectively hard to get," reacting quite favorably to the subject but with indifference to all of her other possible matches. When subjects were then asked to select the girl they would most like to date, the overwhelming majority chose the one who appeared to be "selectively hard to get" (see Figure 13–12). Moreover, when asked to indicate their probable liking for each of the women, they rated this same individual much more favorably than the others. Not surprisingly, then, the male participants in this experiment seemed to prefer for their romantic partner a woman who had the "good sense" to choose them over all other rivals—one who reserved her approval and affections only for them. Whether women, too, prefer romantic partners of this type remains to be seen. Given the flattering implica-

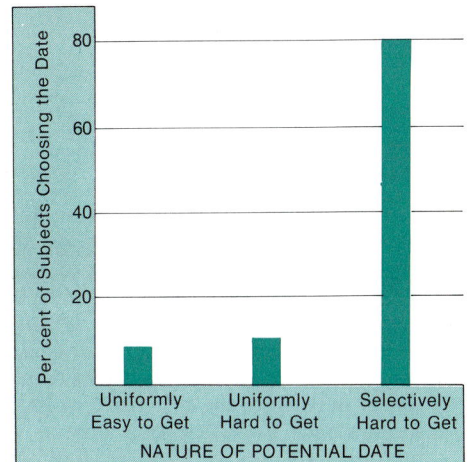

FIGURE 13-12 The effects of "playing hard to get" upon attraction. Male subjects overwhelmingly preferred a woman who was "selectively hard to get"—one who reserved her affections only for them—to ones who were either "uniformly hard to get" or "uniformly easy to get." (Based on data from Walster et al., 1973.)

tions of being chosen by someone who is quite hard to please, though, it would be surprising if they failed to show a similar preference for lovers of this type.

It has already been noted both in this and the preceding chapter that liking for others often exerts a powerful influence upon the nature of our interactions with them. In many cases, such influence seems perfectly natural and appropriate. For example, it is neither surprising nor objectionable that we are far more willing to help or do favors for persons we like than for persons we dislike, or that we are more easily influenced by those we admire than by those we scorn. In other instances, though, the strong impact of interpersonal attraction upon our relations with others seems much less acceptable. For example, attraction often seems to play an important role in hiring practices, so that in many cases, the person finally chosen for a particular job is not the one best qualified for it, but rather the one found most attractive or likable by the individual making this decision. Similarly, voters often cast their ballots not for the candidate they judge to be most suited for political office, but rather for the campaigner with the best "image" or most pleasing physical appearance. It is unfortunate that interpersonal attraction plays an important role in such decisions, for in an important sense, it is quite irrelevant to the major issues involved. Perhaps even more objectionable than these unsettling effects is the powerful impact of attraction upon certain aspects of the judicial process.

It has long been known to members of the legal profession that juries are often as strongly influenced by feelings of liking or disliking toward defendants as they are by evidence relating to their guilt or innocence. Such effects have frequently been illustrated in an amusing manner in comic movies in which attractive young women are acquitted by male judges or jurors who are more concerned with their obvious physical charms than with the evidence against them. That such effects are no laughing matter, however, is indicated by the following statement once made by the world-famous attorney Clarence Darrow (1933):

Jurymen seldom convict a person they like, or acquit one they dislike. The main work of the trial lawyer is to make a jury like his client or at least feel sympathy for him; facts regarding the crimes are relatively unimportant (quoted in Sutherland, 1966, p. 442).

The accuracy of these chilling comments concerning the impact of largely irrelevant factors upon what may often amount, quite literally, to life and death

Attraction and Interpersonal Behavior: When Liking Tips the Balance

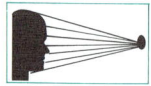

As you can probably tell from the preceding discussion, psychologists have devoted a great deal of attention to the study of interpersonal attraction. Somewhat surprisingly, though, they have directed a much smaller amount of effort to the investigation of a closely related topic— romantic love. The reluctance of many researchers to delve into the mysteries of love is easy to understand. Romantic attachments are clearly complex reactions, hard to define and even harder to study. Within the past few years, however, an increasing number of investigators have overcome such reservations and begun systematic study of this important topic. Some of the earliest work in this area was conducted by Zick Rubin (1970), who developed a brief questionnaire to measure the intensity of love. Items on this questionnaire (known, appropriately, as the *love scale*) are designed to assess what Rubin considers to be the most central components of romantic attachment: (1) a strong need for and desire to be with one's lover; (2) feelings of possessiveness toward this person; and (3) a willingness to place the interests of one's lover above one's own. (Sample items from the love scale are presented in Figure 13–13). That Rubin's questionnaire actually provides a useful measure of romantic love is suggested by the results of a study in which persons scoring high on this scale actually spent more time gazing into each other's eyes than those scoring somewhat lower (Rubin, 1970).

More recent research on romantic love has been concerned with what has often been termed the "Romeo and Juliet effect"—an apparent increase in the intensity of love between two young persons in the face of parental inter-ference with their relationship. In order to determine whether such an effect actually exists, Driscoll, Davis, and Lipetz (1972) asked 140 married and unmarried couples to complete both a love scale similar to Rubin's and a questionnaire concerning the degree of parental interference they had experienced. When the scores on these two scales were compared, a positive correlation was revealed. That is, the greater the degree of parental interference endured by subjects, the stronger their reported feelings of love. Moreover, when subjects completed these questionnaires again 6 to 10 months later, changes in the degree of parental interference occurring during this interval were positively related to changes in reported love: the greater any increase in outside meddling, the greater the increase in the strength of their love.

At first glance, these findings seem to suggest that parental attempts to break up unwelcome romances may often boomerang, and actually strengthen the relationships they are designed to destroy. Other results obtained by Driscoll, Davis, and Lipetz, however, point to the conclusion that such interference can sometimes be quite effective in cooling the flames of passion. Specifically, it was found that couples experiencing parental inteference reported decreased trust and increased critical feelings toward their lover, as well as intensified feelings of love. These findings suggest that while parental interference often fails in the short run, it may succeed in planting seeds of mistrust and disagreement which ultimately weaken the relationship from within. Parental pressure *can* be resisted, it seems, but only at a price.

I would do almost anything for _____.
I feel very possessive toward _____.
If I could never be with _____, I would feel miserable.
I would forgive _____ for practically anything.
It would be hard for me to get along without _____.

FIGURE 13–13 Sample items from Rubin's (1970) love-scale. Individuals respond to each of these statements by choosing the number which indicates the extent to which each is true of their own feelings (1 = not at all true; 9 = definitely true.) Persons completing the scale fill in the blank in each statement with the name of their lover. (Adapted from Rubin, 1970.)

decisions has been supported by recent laboratory research. Several studies have reported that subjects playing the role of jurors in simulated trials tend to hand out much more lenient sentences to defendants they like than to defendants they dislike (Efran, 1974; Mitchell and Byrne, 1973). Moreover, this appears to be the case regardless of whether such liking is based on physical attractiveness, attitude similarity, or other factors. One reason for such differential treatment of liked and disliked defendants may lie in the fact that in general, we tend to view persons we like as possessing more favorable characteristics than those we dislike. As a result of this bias in person perception, jurors may be tempted to make excuses for crimes by persons they find appealing (e.g., they were *forced* into this behavior by circumstances beyond their control), and may also come to view such individuals as having a greater chance for reform than persons they do not find attractive (Sigall and Ostrove, 1975). In any case, there is no longer room for doubt that a defendant's chances in the courtroom may be strongly affected by his or her level of personal appeal to members of the jury. Ideally, justice is blind, but in the real world of legal proceedings, it seems to be open to influence from many sources of bias.

Imagine that you are walking along the streets of a large city when, without any warning, a desperate-looking man jumps out of an alley, strikes you, and attempts to steal your wallet or purse. Would anyone rush to your assistance as you attempted to fight off your assailant? Or would the people passing by continue on their way, totally unresponsive to your calls for help and assistance? Unfortunately, eyewitness accounts of just such events suggest that in many cases, you would stand little chance of receiving the aid you required. That is, all too frequently, the cries of helpless victims seem to go largely unheeded as passersby literally go out of their way to avoid "getting involved" (see Figure 13–14).

On the basis of such unsettling incidents, it might be readily concluded that human beings are quite a hard-hearted lot, totally unconcerned with the safety or well-being of others. However, such a pessimistic conclusion is refuted by the fact that often bystanders do indeed rush to the aid of others, risking their own safety and well-being to help strangers in need of their assistance. Similarly, the vast sums collected each year by charitable organizations suggest that human beings are often moved to compassion for others,

ALTRUISM AND HELPING: THE MILK OF HUMAN KINDNESS

FIGURE 13–14 Often, individuals in need of assistance are ignored by passersby who do not wish to "get involved"; in this case, a workman pays no heed to the mugging going on nearby. (Photo credit: Catherine Ursillo, Nancy Palmer Photo Agency, Inc.)

and will seek to assist them even in the absence of any direct rewards for such actions.

In sum, it appears that people are capable of great generosity and kindness, as well as cold indifference and unconcern. But what are the determinants of such reactions? What factors influence our willingness to offer assistance to others in distress, make donations to charity, or help persons in need of our aid? Much of the research conducted by psychologists on the topics of helping and altruism has been concerned with these questions.

Bystanders and Helping: Is There "Safety in Numbers"?

It has frequently been contended that "there is safety in numbers," and, at first glance, this suggestion seems to make good sense. After all, rapists, muggers, and thieves do not generally stalk their prey in areas teeming with large crowds, but rather choose to operate on dark streets or in secluded parks. Similarly, it seems reasonable to expect that the more persons present at the scene of a crime or emergency, the more likely are the victims to receive the help they require.

Despite the seemingly sensible nature of these suggestions, there are strong grounds for doubting that the presence of other persons provides any firm guarantee of increased safety. For example, as noted above, people who are assaulted in full view of large numbers of bystanders frequently fail to receive aid from *any* of these witnesses. And those who collapse on the streets of large cities as a result of sudden heart attacks or other serious health problems are often left to lie unconscious on the ground for many hours while the passing throng steps carefully around, over, or even on their bodies. In short, the presence of many other persons in no way guarantees that a victim will receive the aid he or she needs. In fact, evidence gathered in recent years suggests that the presence of many bystanders often serves to inhibit rather than facilitate helping (Latané and Darley, 1970; Staub, 1974).

For example, in one of the first and most famous of these investigations (Darley and Latané, 1968), male subjects seated alone in individual cubicles overheard another person experience what appeared to be an intense epileptic seizure. In reality, this incident was staged by means of a special tape recording. As far as subjects were concerned, however, it was frighteningly real and potentially quite dangerous. To study the effects of the presence of other bystanders on their willingness to help, subjects in three different experimental groups were led to believe that (1) only they and the victim were present in the laboratory, (2) they, the victim, and one other bystander were present, or (3) they, the victim, and four other subjects were present. (Actually, each subject participated in the study by himself; the only other person present in all cases was the experimenter.) The results of the investigation were both clear and unsettling: subjects' tendency to help the apparent victim decreased sharply as the number of other persons they believed to be present increased (see Figure 13–15). While 85 per cent rushed from their cubicle to assist the victim when they believed that they were the only other person present, less than 31 per cent acted in a similar manner when they believed that four other potential helpers were also on the scene. The fact that similar results have been obtained in a number of other studies conducted both within and outside the laboratory, and with several different types of staged emergencies, suggests that the presence of other bystanders is capable of inhibiting offers of aid under a wide variety of conditions.

At first, the finding that the victims of accidents, emergencies, or crimes are actually less likely to receive assistance when a large number of bystanders witness their predicament than when only one potential "good Samaritan" is on the scene may seem quite puzzling. However, two compelling explana-

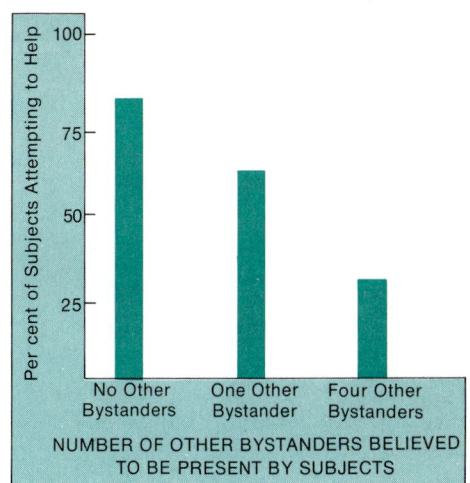

FIGURE 13–15   Evidence for the conclusion that there's not always safety in numbers. Subjects were much more willing to rush to the aid of another person when they believed that they were the only witness to his predicament than when they believed that there were several other potential helpers present. (Based on data from Darley and Latané, 1968.)

tions for the occurrence of such effects can be readily suggested. First, it seems to be the case that when many persons witness incidents of this type, each tends to assume that one of the others present will take the necessary action, and that his or her personal intervention is not, therefore, required. The result of such wholesale "passing the buck" (or **diffusion of responsibility,** as it is often termed) is that no one offers aid, and victims are left to fend for themselves.

Second, many emergency situations are, at least initially, quite ambiguous. Smoke pouring from an apartment building may mean that a dangerous fire has started, or simply that one of the residents has burned his or her dinner. Similarly, an individual lying on the street may have suffered a stroke and require medical assistance; but he may, instead, merely be sleeping off a binge. Because of such ambiguity, the witnesses to these and similar events are often reluctant to act, for they fear that their behavior will be unnecessary or premature, and as such will cause them to look quite foolish in the eyes of others. Summoning the fire department over a burned dinner or an ambulance to pick up a drunk is likely to result in considerable embarrassment. And since the amount of embarrassment experienced probably increases with the number of other persons present to observe such blunders, the strength of inhibitions against helping may increase sharply with a growing number of other bystanders.

Together, these two factors—diffusion of responsibility and the fear of losing "face" in front of others—operate to inhibit helping in many emergency situations (see Bickman, 1972). In fact, so powerful does their combined effect seem to be that in many cases there may actually be more danger than safety in numbers for persons in need of assistance. Fortunately, the findings of several recent experiments indicate that the impact of both of these negative forces can be readily counteracted. Turning first to diffusion of responsibility, it now appears that the presence of even a large number of other bystanders will fail to inhibit individuals from offering aid in cases in which they have made a prior commitment to help. For example, in one ingenious study (Moriarty, 1975), subjects on a crowded beach witnessed a staged theft in which a confederate of the experimenter attempted to make off with a valuable radio from a nearby blanket. In one condition, the witnesses to this crime had previously been asked by the owner of the radio to watch his or her belongings for a few minutes, while in a second group, they had not been asked to make

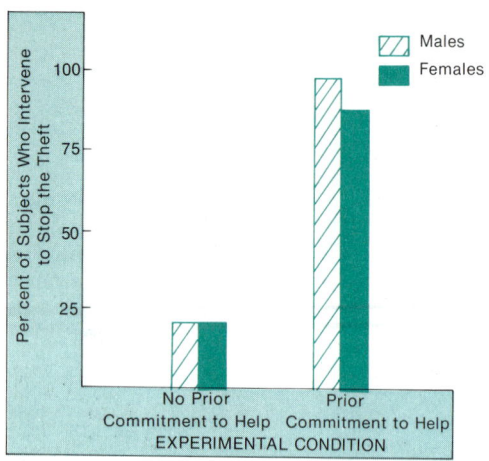

FIGURE 13–16 The effects of prior commitment upon willingness to help. When individuals on a crowded beach had previously agreed to watch another person's property, they usually intervened to prevent its theft. When they had not made such a prior commitment, they rarely engaged in such action. (Based on data from Moriarty, 1975.)

such a commitment. Results indicated that almost all individuals who had previously committed themselves to watching the victim's belongings attempted to stop the thief in some manner. In contrast, very few of those who had made no such agreement intervened (see Figure 13–16). Given the obvious risks involved in attempting to stop a determined and potentially dangerous thief from stealing valuable property, these findings suggest that even a casual commitment to pro-social behavior may often be sufficient to counteract the inhibiting effects of the presence of several other bystanders.

That the influence of ambiguity and the resulting fear of losing "face" through inappropriate action can also be readily overcome is suggested by the findings of additional studies. In particular, it appears that the impact of this factor may be readily counteracted by any conditions which serve to convince bystanders that the events they are witnessing constitute a real and serious emergency. For example, when bystanders can actually see the victim and the harm which has befallen him (Clark and Word, 1974), or can observe each other's surprise and concern (Darley, Teger, and Lewis, 1973), they are as quick and willing to offer aid when in the presence of several other persons as they are when alone. In sum, the presence of other bystanders does not always act to prevent or inhibit helping. Rather, such effects seem to occur only under certain limited conditions. This fact is somewhat encouraging, and suggests that we *can* take action to encourage socially responsible behavior in many real-life settings. For example, we might begin by altering child-rearing or educational practices so as to obtain a strong prior commitment to help others in need of assistance from most if not all members of our society. Similarly, we might initiate training designed to help individuals recognize emergencies when they occur. Through these and related steps, we may succeed in converting the apathetic bystander described by Latané and Darley (1970) into the concerned citizen who acts without hesitation when others around him are facing distress.

Models and Helping: Is Kindness Contagious?   Imagine the following scene: a man running to catch a bus on a crowded city street trips, falls with a sickening thud onto the pavement, and then lies still. For a moment, all of the witnesses to this accident stand motionless, seemingly unwilling or unable to offer any assistance. Then, quite suddenly, one man rushes forward and bends over the victim, obviously attempting to revive him. What will happen next? Will the other bystanders now engage in similar actions and also hasten to aid the injured party? Or will they turn and leave, secure in the knowledge that someone has taken the necessary action? Although one might expect the latter reaction to be more likely, a number of experiments point to the opposite conclusion: in all probability, the actions of the first "good Samaritan" will unleash a torrent of helping, so that many other bystanders who previously hesitated will now also rush forward to offer their assistance (Masor, Hornstein, and Tobin, 1973).

The occurrence of such effects has been observed in a wide variety of contexts, with both children and adults, and in both laboratory and real-life settings. For example, it has been found that children exposed to generous models who donate part of their winnings in a game to less fortunate persons are more likely to engage in similar behavior than are children not exposed to such models (Rushton, 1975). Similarly, motorists who witness another person helping a "lady in distress" by changing a flat tire on her car are more likely to stop and help another driver facing the same predicament than are motorists not exposed to such scenes (Bryan and Test, 1967). And shoppers exposed to a charitable model who drops coins into a Salvation Army kettle are more likely to make a donation than are shoppers who do not witness such behavior (Bryan and Test, 1967; see Figure 13–17).

Although it is not yet entirely clear why the presence of helpful, altruistic models tends to enhance similar actions on the part of persons who observe their actions, several explanations for the occurrence of such effects have been suggested (see Macauley and Berkowitz, 1970). First, the actions of the model may serve to convince bystanders that helping is appropriate in the situation in question, and thereby reduce their fear of losing "face" by acting in a silly, inappropriate manner (Staub, 1974). Second, exposure to another person acting in a helpful, generous manner may remind observers of their own social obligation to help others, and as a result enhance their tendency to engage in similar actions. Finally, the behavior of an altruistic model may induce related actions among observers in the simple, almost automatic manner described previously in our discussion of response facilitation (see Chapter 12, pp. 443–444). Whatever the reasons behind such effects, they seem to offer many practical applications. You may have already had firsthand experience with one such use if you've ever received a mailing from a charitable organiza-

FIGURE 13–17 When individuals are exposed to helping models—others who act in a generous or altruistic manner—they often tend to behave in this manner themselves.

tion in which the supposed amounts of donations from several other persons were prominently displayed. In such cases, these donations are usually all of sizable magnitude, and the hope is that you will be influenced by them to make a large contribution yourself. Although attempts of this type are usually too transparent to be effective, it seems possible that fund-raising campaigns which make careful use of live, donating models might succeed in collecting larger amounts of money than more standard campaigns which make no use of these procedures. In such cases, the fact that kindness seems to be contagious may yield substantial practical benefits.

Feeling Good and Helping: Mood and Pro-Social Behavior

A TV commercial aired repeatedly several years ago began with a scene in which a mother suffering from a painful headache lost her temper when asked by her child to assemble a toy. The next scene showed her taking a famous pain-reliever, and in the final segment—her headache obviously gone—she soothed her child and willingly helped to assemble the toy. Although this commercial was designed to sell headache tablets and not as an instructional aid, it serves to illustrate an important point about social behavior: there often seems to be a close link between the way people feel and their willingness to offer help to others. Informal observation suggests that most of us find it easier to behave in a generous, altruistic manner when we are feeling happy and content than when we are feeling angry, irritated, or upset. It is for this reason, of course, that others usually wait until we seem to be in a good mood, or actually try to put us in one, before asking for favors. And it is for the same reason that we follow an identical strategy in our own behavior.

More formal evidence for the influence of emotional states upon helping has been obtained in several recent experiments. In general, the results of these studies agree both with common sense and the commercial mentioned above in suggesting that individuals are more willing to help others, donate to charity, or engage in other pro-social acts when they are experiencing positive emotional states. Moreover, this seems to be the case regardless of whether such positive reactions are due to the "warm glow of success" on some task (Isen, 1970), thinking about pleasant past experiences (Rosenhan, Underwood, and Moore, 1974), or even such trivial events as finding a dime in a phone booth (Isen and Levin, 1972).

Although systematic evidence regarding this issue is currently lacking, there seem to be several good reasons why positive emotional states might facilitate helping. First, such positive reactions may generalize greatly, so that the individuals experiencing them also feel more positive toward other persons. As a result, their tendency to extend aid to others may be enhanced. Second, it is possible that when individuals are in a pleasant state of mind, they tend to perceive themselves in a more favorable light. Since helpful, altruistic acts are consistent with such an improved self-image, they may then show increased willingness to engage in such behaviors. Further research will be needed to determine whether these or other factors underlie the strong relationship between mood and helping, but for the present, one general conclusion seems justified: kindness and generosity often accompany—and may actually stem from—positive emotional states.

AGGRESSION AND VIOLENCE

At the opposite end of the social continuum from altruism and helping lies another, much more sinister form of behavior—aggression against others. In instances of such behavior, one or more individuals seek to inflict harm or injury on one or several others, often with truly disastrous results. Unfortunately, the incidence of aggression is alarmingly high, and seems to be on the rise.

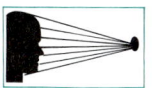

**FOCUS
ON
RESEARCH:** *Reactions to Aid From Others: The Donor's Dilemma*

How do people react to aid from others? At first, it might be expected that their responses will be overwhelmingly positive, consisting largely of gratitude, relief, and appreciation. In reality, though, reactions to assistance, gifts, or favors probably depend upon a number of different factors. For example, while aid provided by a friend or ally may be received with unmixed thanks, similar assistance from an adversary may be greeted with intense suspicion (Nadler, Fisher, and Streufert, 1974). Similarly, help given freely and without hesitation may induce positive reactions among recipients, while aid provided grudgingly may elicit more negative responses. Perhaps one of the most important factors influencing reactions to aid involves perceived obligations of repayment.

Almost all favors or assistance from others carry with them an implied obligation to reimburse the donor. The size of the repayment expected, however, may vary greatly. In some cases, little or no return is sought, in others an amount equal to that provided is expected, and in still others, a pay-off exceeding the initial donation is demanded. Although common sense suggests that aid given with no strings attached— no obligation of repayment—would induce the most positive reactions among recipients, recent evidence gathered by Kenneth Gergen and his associates (Gergen et al., 1975) indicates that this is not always the case. In a study conducted simultaneously in three different nations (the U.S., Sweden, and Japan), subjects were first made to lose heavily on a special game, and were then provided with unexpected aid (additional chips) from another player. While offering this assistance, the donor indi-

cated that he expected either (1) no repayment whatsoever, (2) repayment equal to the amount he provided, or (3) repayment exceeding his initial aid. Results indicated that subjects liked this individual best when he expected equal reimbursement, somewhat less when he desired no repayment at all, and least when he demanded more than he had actually supplied (see Figure 13–18).

Several factors seem to account for negative reactions by recipients to assistance which carries no obligation of repayment. First, such aid violates the norm of *social reciprocity,* according to which people are expected to compensate others for favors or help. Reciprocity seems to be a basic principle of social interaction, and individuals often become quite upset when it is not followed. Second, assistance without obligation may be interpreted as out-and-out charity, and as such may induce negative reactions among recipients. And finally, help of this type may arouse strong suspicions among those who receive it: after all, who can trust something for nothing?

Whatever the reasons for such negative reactions, the fact that recipients do not like to receive "stringless" assistance seems to have important implications. In particular, it suggests that foreign aid should be distributed as loans rather than as outright gifts, for when it is offered without obligation, recipients may come to doubt the motives of the donors. In fact, they may often interpret such aid as a not-so-subtle attempt to control or manipulate their internal affairs. In such cases, gifts or aid given too freely and without obligation of repayment may actually be worse than no gifts at all.

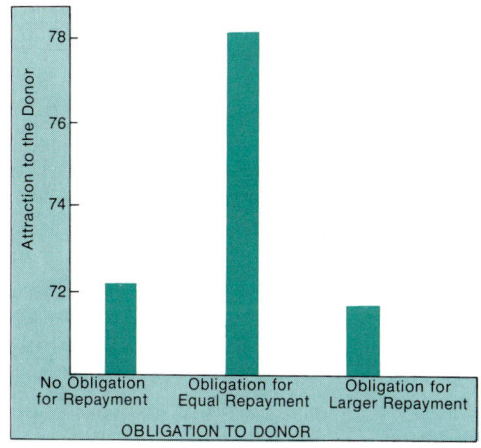

FIGURE 13–18 Reactions to aid from others. Individuals seem to react most positively to aid which carries with it the obligation to make equal repayment to the donor. They react less favorably to aid which carries either no obligation of repayment or an obligation to pay back even more than was received. (Based on data from Gergen et al., 1975.)

Indeed, it is almost impossible to pick up a newspaper, thumb through a magazine, or listen to the evening news without learning of some new and disturbing acts of human cruelty (see Figure 13–19). And given the destructive power of modern weapons, there is little doubt that the unchecked spread of violence has threatened and continues to threaten the lasting survival of the entire human race.

In view of the importance of aggression in human affairs, it is not surprising to learn that many attempts have been made to determine the factors responsible for its occurrence. For many years, psychologists and other social scientists focused their search for the roots of violence upon instinctive urges, suggesting that men and women aggress against others because, quite simply,

FIGURE 13–19 Unfortunately, aggression must be numbered among the most common forms of social interaction. (Top and bottom photos from United Press International.)

it is their "nature" to do so. When strong and convincing evidence for such conclusions failed to emerge, many shifted to a competing view which contended that aggression stems mainly from an acquired motive to harm or injure others (see Feshbach, 1970). Although such "drive" theories of aggression continue to enjoy support even today, there has been a growing trend in recent years to view aggression as a learned form of social behavior. Supporters of this perspective (Bandura, 1973; Berkowitz, 1974) contend that aggressive responses are (1) learned in much the same manner as other forms of social behavior, (2) strengthened by various forms of reward (e.g., praise from others or the attainment of desired goals), and (3) elicited by particular environmental stimuli (e.g., insults from others or exposure to violent models). One especially attractive feature of this general point of view is its basic optimism with respect to the prevention or control of human violence. As a learned form of social behavior, aggression should be readily open to change or modification, and may even be totally eliminated from most interactions. This suggestion contrasts sharply with the instinct views proposed by Freud and others, which hold that aggression is an unavoidable and often uncontrollable part of human nature.

We should hasten to add at this point that while the *social learning* view has gained rapidly in popularity, not all psychologists currently support or accept it. Some still hold that aggression stems from biological or genetic causes, and should be viewed as a natural—perhaps even an innate—aspect of human behavior (Johnson, 1972). We have already considered some of the evidence supporting this general suggestion in Chapter 2, where we examined the role of the limbic system in rage and aggressive reactions (see pp. 61–62). Despite some indication that aggression may actually be pre-wired into centers or systems within our brains, however, many psychologists now feel that in the case of human beings, it is so strongly determined by learning and external stimulus conditions that primary attention should be directed to these factors (Bandura, 1973). In view of this growing consensus, we will emphasize such factors in the present discussion. (Please note, though, that we will return to the suggestion that aggression is largely innate even among human beings in Appendix B, pp. 587–595.)

Because aggression has been the subject of intensive study for several decades, we could not hope to summarize all that has been learned about it in a few brief pages. We *can* provide you with a broad overview of current knowledge concerning such behavior, however, by focusing on two central questions: (1) what are the factors which tend to elicit overt aggression; and (2) what can be done to prevent or control its occurrence?

The Situational Roots of Violence: Frustration, Attack, and Exposure to Aggressive Models

Newspaper and newscast reports of murder, rape, and brutal assaults often create the impression that violence is a purely random event—one which strikes innocent victims from out of the blue without warning or apparent cause. In some cases, this is certainly true. When individuals suddenly go on shooting sprees during which they gun down total strangers, or when roving gangs of teenagers attack and brutally beat innocent pedestrians on the streets of large cities, violence does indeed seem to be both pointless and random. In a much larger number of instances, however, violent acts—whether performed by single individuals or large groups—seem to stem from relatively clear-cut external factors. Aggression, in short, does not occur in a social vacuum; rather, it springs from specific conditions which pave the way for its occurrence. Unfortunately, such a large number of factors seem to play a role in the outbreak of violent acts that singling out those which are most crucial in this respect is a difficult task. Three which have often been implicated in the occurrence of aggression, however, are **frustration, physical** or **verbal attack,** and exposure to the actions of highly **aggressive models.**

Frustration: Preventing Others from Getting What They Want

In 1939, a distinguished group of social scientists offered a comprehensive analysis of aggressive behavior which dramatically altered existing thought on this important topic (Dollard, Doob, Miller, Mowrer, and Sears, 1939). At the center of their framework were two proposals which, together, have come to be known as the **frustration-aggression hypothesis.** Briefly, these proposals suggested that (1) frustration always leads to some form of aggression, and (2) aggression is always the result of frustration. So simple and appealing were these assertions, and so convincing the arguments provided in their behalf, that the frustration-aggression hypothesis quickly won widespread acceptance both within and outside of psychology. Indeed, it is widely cited even today, and you were probably quite familiar with it before opening the pages of this text. Unfortunately, it now appears that the great popularity of these proposals stemmed more from their simplicity than from their accuracy in accounting for the occurrence of human aggression. In fact, there appear to be strong grounds for doubting the validity of both portions of this hypothesis.

First, it is clear that frustrated individuals do not always turn to aggression in their thoughts, words, or deeds. Rather, they may actually demonstrate a wide variety of reactions to such treatment, ranging from resignation and despair on the one hand to active attempts to overcome their frustration on the other. For example, imagine the case of a graduating senior who finds herself rejected by every law, medical, or graduate school to which she has applied. How do you think she would react to such severe disappointment? The frustration-aggression hypothesis suggests that she will probably become hostile or angry, and lash out at others, but common sense indicates that she is more likely to react with depression and despair than with attacks against others. In short, the suggestion that frustration always leads to some form of aggression does not bear up well under close examination.

Similarly, it is equally clear that not *all* aggression results from frustration. For example, soldiers often inflict great harm and suffering on others in time of war when ordered to do so by their superiors, even in the total absence of frustration. Hired assassins cold-bloodedly murder persons they have never met—even on days when they are in particularly fine spirits—simply because they are being paid to do so. Such cases indicate that aggression may stem from many other factors besides frustration, and often occurs in the total absence of frustration. To suggest that aggression is always the result of frustration, then, seems quite misleading.

In the face of such criticisms, supporters of the frustration-aggression hypothesis have recently revised this view to suggest that frustration *sometimes* leads to aggression and is only *one* of many different determinants of this reaction (see Berkowitz, 1975). These modified proposals are much easier to defend than the ones originally outlined by Dollard et al. (1939), and some support for them has actually been obtained (Worchel, 1974). However, a number of additional studies have reported frustration that either has no effect upon aggression whatsoever (Buss, 1966) or is much weaker in this respect than several other factors (Geen, 1968, Gentry, 1970). For the present, therefore, the most reasonable conclusion seems to be that while frustration—especially if quite intense—can indeed sometimes encourage aggression, it is a relatively weak determinant of such behavior.

While frustration appears to play only a relatively minor role in eliciting dangerous instances of aggression, another factor—physical or verbal attack—seems to exert a much more powerful influence upon the outbreak of such actions. In fact, existing evidence suggests that physical abuse or verbal taunts from others may serve as the most powerful single elicitor of aggressive behavior. Since most of us do not usually experience strong provocations of this type on a daily basis, it might at first seem that physical or verbal attacks would only rarely lead to overt violence. Unfortunately, though, aggression seems to have an unsettling way of escalating in a rapid and irreversible manner (Goldstein et al., 1975). As a result, even mild taunts or glancing blows may initiate a process whereby stronger and stronger provocations are exchanged, until events get quickly out of hand. This type of sequence is visible not only in interactions between individuals but in the realm of international relations as well. Here, growing spirals of tension and provocation often lead to wars neither side really desires, but which both seem powerless to prevent.

Evidence for the strong aggression-eliciting influence of physical and verbal assaults has been obtained in a number of recent experiments (e.g., Dengerink and Bertilson, 1974). In these studies, individuals exposed to provocations from others have not been found to "turn the other cheek," as might be hoped, but rather to respond in kind with assaults against their tormentors (see Figure 13–20). Moreover, it does not seem necessary for individuals to actually receive the attacks directed against them by others; the mere indication that these persons intended to harm them in some manner seems sufficient to elicit strong tendencies toward retaliation (Greenwell and Dengerink, 1973). In short, aggression breeds aggression in a wide variety of situations, regardless of the form in which it is delivered.

Physical and Verbal Attack: One Good Blow Deserves Another

You may recall that in Chapter 4, we noted that individuals often acquire new forms of aggression through exposure to the actions of other persons. Specifically, we noted that individuals frequently seem to learn new ways of harming others through exposure to the actions of parents, friends, actors in movies, or characters in TV shows. Informal evidence for the occurrence of such effects among adults is available from several different sources. For example, it is often the case that movies or telecasts which depict or describe unusual violent crimes are followed by a wave of similar events around the nation. In such instances, viewers seem to acquire new forms of attacking others, and also learn that it is possible to "get away" with such actions. A

Exposure to Aggressive Models: The Effects of Televised Violence

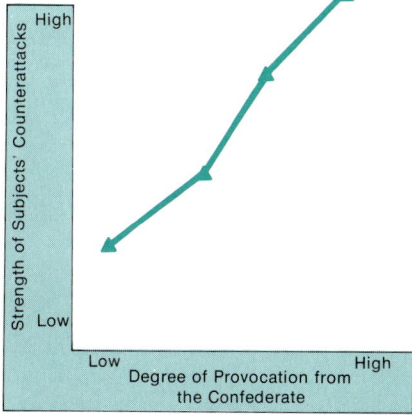

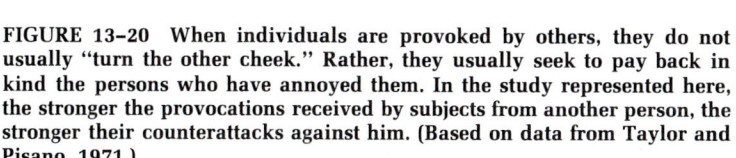

FIGURE 13–20 **When individuals are provoked by others, they do not usually "turn the other cheek." Rather, they usually seek to pay back in kind the persons who have annoyed them. In the study represented here, the stronger the provocations received by subjects from another person, the stronger their counterattacks against him. (Based on data from Taylor and Pisano, 1971.)**

particularly grisly example of such effects occurred a few years ago when several groups of teenagers—inspired at first by a televised movie, and then by the evening news—doused innocent strangers with gasoline and then set them on fire. Additional evidence for the occurrence of such destructive modeling has been obtained in many experiments in which adult subjects exposed to live (Baron, 1974a) or filmed aggressive models (Geen and Stonner, 1973) have been observed to demonstrate higher levels of aggression than subjects not exposed to such models.

If adults can be influenced in this manner by exposure to the aggressive actions of others, it might be expected that children, with their weaker sense of morality and lack of sophistication, would be affected to an even greater degree. Most of the concern regarding this possibility has revolved around the potential influence of televised violence on the behavior of young viewers. Surveys indicate that children watch a great deal of television—as much as 30 hours per week in many cases (Stein et al., 1972)—and that a clear majority of popular shows contain instances of aggressive behavior (Gerbner, 1972). Given this state of affairs, several psychologists have expressed concern that children's tendencies to engage in aggressive actions may be greatly increased by a steady diet of current television shows. As we noted in Chapter 4, early studies by Albert Bandura and his colleagues demonstrated that youngsters could indeed learn new and unusual aggressive responses from specially constructed brief television programs. More recent research has gone even further, suggesting that after viewing actual television shows depicting realistic violence, children are more willing to hurt another child than after watching nonaggressive shows. For example, in one experiment (Liebert and Baron, 1972), children were exposed either to a brief segment taken from a highly aggressive program ("The Untouchables") or to an excerpt from an equally exciting but nonaggressive track race. When they were then provided with an opportunity to harm another child by pushing a button which supposedly burned him, those exposed to the violent program did in fact demonstrate a higher level of aggression than those who viewed the nonaggressive show (see Figure 13–21). (In reality, of course, there was no victim, and no children were harmed in any manner during the study.) The fact that similar results have been obtained in a large number of additional studies (e.g., Leyens et al., 1975) has led many psychologists to conclude that the high level of violence prevailing in many popular television shows has adverse effects upon the persons who view them.

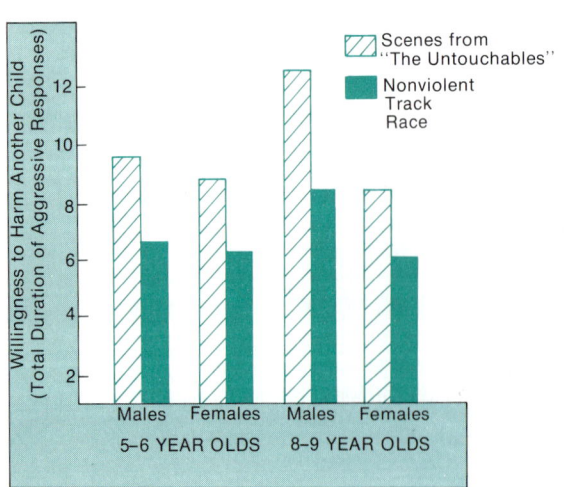

FIGURE 13–21 The effects of televised violence on children's aggression. Subjects exposed to a brief but violent segment from "The Untouchables" were more willing to hurt another child than were those exposed to a nonviolent track race. Further, these effects were found both for males and females, and for children in two different age groups. (Based on data from Liebert and Baron, 1972.)

Not all experimental findings have supported this conclusion (Feshbach and Singer, 1971; Manning and Taylor, 1975), but the weight of existing evidence does seem to suggest that exposure to televised violence may weaken children's restraints against attacking or harming others. In view of the fact that by the time they are adults many youngsters will have spent more time viewing television than in performing any other waking activity, this conclusion seems to have important — and somewhat unsettling — social implications.

While frustration, attack, and exposure to aggressive models have probably received more attention in recent years than any other determinants of aggression, a number of additional factors also seem to play an important role in eliciting such behavior. We have already considered one of these factors in our discussion of destructive obedience (see pp. 437 to 438), where we noted that many individuals can readily be induced to inflict pain and discomfort on others by the commands of an authority figure. Such findings suggest that aggression often stems more from a sense of duty or fear of punishment for failing to carry out directives than from hatred or animosity toward the target persons. In short, the phrase "orders are orders" may actually explain the occurrence of a great deal of organized violence.

Additional Determinants of Aggression: Orders, Heat, Crowding and Heightened Arousal

Other factors serving to elicit aggressive outbursts seem to involve various aspects of the physical environment. Many of the urban riots which rocked the nation's cities in the late 1960's and early 1970's were attributed both by the mass media and social scientists to the "long hot summer" — the irritating effects of high temperatures — and extreme crowding in central city ghetto areas. Systematic research on the effects of these and other environmental factors has suggested that their influence is more complex than was once believed (Baron and Bell, 1976). Still, the suggestion that environmental conditions which cause individuals to feel irritated or annoyed can often enhance their tendency to aggress against others has generally been confirmed. (See Chapter 15 for a more detailed discussion of this topic.)

Finally, growing evidence suggests that under certain conditions, increased arousal — whatever its source — may facilitate aggression against others. At first, it was widely believed that heightened arousal might enhance aggression under a wide variety of circumstances (Berkowitz, 1970). Now, however, it appears that aggression occurs only in cases in which the persons involved interpret their excitement as feelings of anger or irritation. For example, suppose that a few minutes after a hard, uphill bicycle ride, another person insulted you in an obnoxious manner. Do you think you would be more likely to aggress against this person under these conditions than you would be if he insulted you at some other time? The results of several experiments suggest that you might (Zillmann, et al., 1974, 1976). Apparently, this is due to the fact that often you would tend to interpret *all* the arousal you experienced — both that stemming from the bike ride and that stemming from the insult itself — as feelings of anger. Since your total arousal from these two sources together would be higher than that from an insult alone, you would "feel" angrier, and consequently show a greater tendency to aggress. The crucial point to remember, though, is that such an effect would occur *only* if you interpreted your excitement or arousal as anger. If you interpreted it as stemming from some other source, no increase in aggression would occur. Thus, as we noted above, heightened arousal will facilitate assaults against others only under certain conditions.

In sum, evidence collected in recent years suggests that aggression probably springs from many different roots and a number of different sources. There is, in fact, a growing consensus that an adequate explanation for the occurrence of such behavior will have to take account of many different factors (Bandura, 1973). While older explanations of aggression, such as the view that it always stems from frustration, were appealing in their simplicity, modern research suggests that they are often far off the mark, and that much more sophisticated formulations will be needed to account for the occurrence of this complex and dangerous form of behavior.

Aggression: Its Prevention and Control

If you were to conduct a survey of all the articles published by psychologists about aggression during the past 10 years, you might soon discover a somewhat surprising fact: while many reports have been concerned with the

---

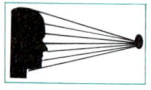

FOCUS ON RESEARCH: *Alcohol, Marijuana, and Aggression*

You may recall that earlier in this book (in Chapter 2), we examined the effects of various drugs upon behavior. At this point, we would like to expand upon that earlier discussion, by considering the impact of two widely used drugs—alcohol and marijuana—upon aggression. As you probably already know, alcohol has long been viewed as a releaser or stimulator of aggressive actions. Drink too much, common knowledge holds, and the chances of your becoming involved in hostile interactions with others are increased. In contrast, marijuana has often been held to be an inhibitor of overt aggression, presumably because it places its users in such a relaxed or pleasant state that aggression is the farthest thing from their minds. Interestingly, support for both of these suggestions has recently been obtained by Stuart Taylor and his associates in a series of intriguing laboratory studies (Taylor and Gammon, 1975; Taylor et al., 1976).

In these experiments, male subjects have been provided with special "cocktails" consisting of ginger ale, peppermint oil, and either small or large doses of alcohol or THC—the active substance in marijuana. (Subjects in control groups receive only the ginger ale and peppermint oil mixture.) After receiving their special drinks, subjects participate in a competitive reaction time task in which the loser on each trial (the slower person to respond) receives a shock from the winner. Since the level of these shocks is set in advance by each player, aggression can be measured in terms of the strength of the shocks set by each participant for his opponent. The results of these investigations have been both clear and informative.

First, with respect to alcohol, findings indicate that small doses tend to inhibit aggression, while larger doses tend to facilitate such behavior, relative to a no-drug control condition. Thus, experimental evidence lends support to the informal observation that one cocktail or a couple of beers may put people in a happy frame of mind and thereby reduce the likelihood of

aggression, while a larger number of drinks serves to weaken their restraints or inhibitions and thereby increases the probability of dangerous attacks against others. Further evidence suggests, however, that even individuals who have consumed a large amount of alcohol do not necessarily respond with heightened aggression. Rather, they seem to demonstrate such behavior only when provoked or threatened in some manner by others (Taylor, Gammon and Capasso, 1977).

Second, with respect to marijuana, results suggest that small doses have little impact upon aggression, while larger ones tend to produce an inhibiting effect (see Table 13–3). Further, there is some indication that even larger doses of this drug would be more effective in reducing overt violence.

Considered overall, Taylor's research findings suggest that both alcohol and marijuana are capable of exerting important effects upon the tendency of human beings to inflict harm or injury upon others. However, the direction and magnitude of these effects seem to differ greatly between the two drugs.

TABLE 13–3   The Effects of Alcohol and Marijuana on Physical Aggression

Dose	Average Strength of Shocks (with no drugs, shock level = 3.9)	
	With Marijuana	*With Alcohol*
Small	3.1	2.1
Large	1.0	5.4

As shown here, small doses of alcohol seem to inhibit aggression, while larger doses facilitate such behavior. In contrast, small doses of marijuana have little effect upon aggression, while larger doses reduce it. (Numbers shown represent the average strength of the shocks set by subjects for their opponent.)

(Based on data from Taylor et al., 1976.)

factors tending to elicit overt aggression (frustration, attack, aggressive models, and so on), a much smaller number have dealt with means for controlling such behavior. Although many factors probably contributed to this unsettling state of affairs, one of the most important was a persistent belief among psychologists that they already knew the best means for preventing aggressive outbursts. In particular, it was widely believed that two techniques — **catharsis** and actual or threatened **punishment** — are the best means for controlling overt aggression. Unfortunately, evidence collected within the past few years suggests that neither of these procedures is quite as effective in accomplishing this purpose as was once believed. After examining the effects of punishment and catharsis upon aggression, therefore, we will turn to one additional procedure which appears to be quite promising as a means of controlling such behavior — the induction among aggressors of responses incompatible with anger or overt attacks against others.

It has often been suggested that either punishing aggressors for their violent acts or merely threatening to do so may be a highly effective means of preventing these persons from engaging in such activities. For example, the late Richard Walters (1966, p. 69), a noted child psychologist, once stated: "It is only the continual expectation of retaliation by the recipient or other members of society that prevents many individuals from more freely expressing aggression." That punishment is sometimes quite effective in deterring aggression is apparent. Moreover, several experiments conducted with children indicate that the frequency or intensity of such behavior can often be sharply reduced by even such mild forms of punishment as social disapproval (Brown and Elliott, 1965). Despite such findings, though, there are several grounds for doubting that punishment will *always* serve as an effective deterrent to human violence.

Punishment: A Deterrent to Human Aggression?

Turning first to actual punishment, we have already noted in Chapter 4 (see pp. 134–136) that such treatment often produces only a temporary suppression of punished acts. Thus, if alternative responses for obtaining the goals sought through aggression are not available and rewarded, hostile actions may quickly reappear once punishment is discontinued. Moreover, individuals on the receiving end of punishment may interpret such disciplinary actions as attacks against them. And since aggression breeds aggression (as noted on p. 483), the end result may be an increase rather than a reduction in the overall level of violence. Finally, the persons administering punishment may often serve as aggressive models for those they discipline. For example, consider the case of a parent who, preparing to spank his or her child as punishment for previous aggressive acts, shouts, "I'll teach you to hit other children!" In such cases the children may indeed learn something, but it will probably not be the type of restraints and controls their parent has in mind. For all these reasons, direct punishment may often backfire and actually tend to enhance the aggressive acts it is designed to prevent.

Shifting to threatened punishment, a number of recent experiments (e.g., Baron, 1973, 1974b; Donnerstein et al., 1972) suggest that this technique, too, may be of only limited effectiveness. Indeed, the results of these studies point to the conclusion that threats of punishment will serve as effective deterrents to aggression only when: (1) the persons preparing to aggress are not very angry; (2) these individuals have little to gain by aggressing (see Figure 13–22); (3) the magnitude of punishment they anticipate is great; and (4) the probability that punishment will actually be delivered is high. Since violence often occurs under conditions in which the individuals involved have a great deal to gain

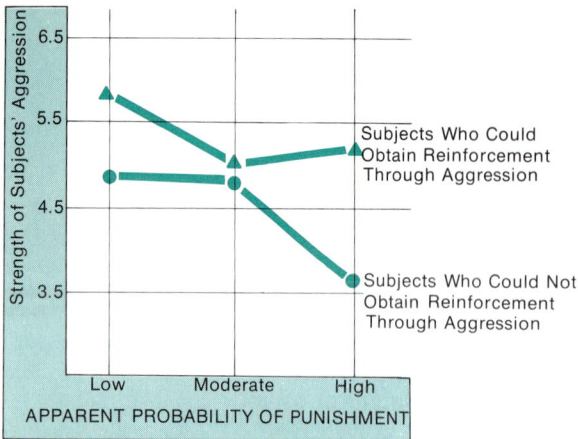

FIGURE 13–22 When individuals can obtain rewards through aggression, even the threat of strong punishment for such behavior is often ineffective in preventing its occurrence. In the study illustrated here, subjects in the reinforcement condition (top line) were led to believe that they could make a good impression on the experimenter by behaving in an aggressive manner, while those in the nonreinforcement group (lower line) were not provided with such information. As expected, subjects in the reinforcement condition were not deterred from aggressing even by a high probability of punishment. (Based on data from Baron, 1974b.)

from their attacks upon others, anger runs high, and the likelihood of being caught and brought to justice is minimal, it is not surprising that threats of punishment often prove ineffective in preventing such behavior. Unfortunately, crimes of violence do often pay if one can avoid the punishments set up to deter their performance.

PERSPECTIVE ON BEHAVIOR: *Capital Punishment: An Effective Deterrent to Crimes of Violence?*

In recent years, a heated debate concerning the use of capital punishment (the death penalty) has swirled into and out of the news. Arguments against such measures have revolved around two major points. First, it has been suggested that capital punishment, because it has not always been exacted for the same crimes, represents cruel and unusual punishment. Largely on these grounds, the Supreme Court banned its use several years ago. Second, many critics have noted that it is generally ineffective in deterring other crimes. As evidence for this conclusion, they have pointed to the fact that the incidence of murder and similar crimes has always been just as high in states where capital punishment has been employed as in states where it has not. Supporters of a return to such punishment have offered responses to each of these points.

First, they have proposed that capital punishment be made mandatory in the case of certain crimes so as to eliminate the arbitrariness surrounding its use. Second, they have argued that it might be much more effective in deterring further crime if it were used in an appropriate manner. In particular, they have noted that in the past, such punishment has usually been administered in a hidden, secret fashion. As a result, potential criminals have not been exposed to direct evidence of the dire consequences which may stem from the commision of violent acts. If capital punishment were made more public, it has been argued, it might prove to be much more effective in persuading at least some individuals to avoid the use of violence. In short, supporters of such procedures have sometimes called for a return to the public executions of the past! What are your own reactions to this controversy? Do you think that we should continue (or reinstate) the ban on capital punishment, or—given the rising tide of violence in our own nation and throughout the world—do you feel that the use of such drastic measures may be worthy of one more try?

Suppose that one of your friends did something which made you very angry; if you then threw your pillow about the room, kicked a tin can down the street, or hit a punching bag repeatedly, would you be less likely to aggress against this person than would otherwise be the case? Until quite recently, many psychologists believed that this would indeed be so. It was widely assumed that providing angry individuals with an opportunity to "blow off steam" through participation in such activities would markedly lessen their tendency to engage in dangerous acts of aggression. On the basis of this belief—generally known as the **catharsis hypothesis**—parents were urged to provide their children with aggressive toys, individuals undergoing psychotherapy were encouraged to express their hostile feelings in an open and uninhibited manner, and irritable executives were instructed to release their violent impulses through participation in competitive sports activities.

Despite the seemingly reasonable nature of these suggestions, they have not been supported by the findings of systematic research. While participation in various cathartic activities seems capable of reducing the high levels of arousal often induced by annoyance from others (Hokanson, 1970), there is little indication that such reductions are always or even usually accompanied by lessened tendencies toward aggression. In fact, there is growing evidence that the opportunity to aggress against someone who has angered or provoked us may actually *increase* our willingness to harm this person on later occasions. In a recent study (Geen, Stonner, and Shope, 1975), male college students in one group were provoked by a confederate of the experimenter, while those in another group were not. Next, one third of each group was given an opportunity to deliver electric shocks to the confederate, a second third witnessed the experimenter shock him, and the final third merely waited for an equivalent period of time. Finally, subjects in all conditions were provided with an opportunity to shock the confederate. (As you probably suspect, *no shocks were actually delivered to this person in any phase of the study*; as has been the case in most recent research on aggression, subjects were merely led to *believe* that they could harm him in this manner.) According to the catharsis hypothesis, it would be expected that individuals given a chance to shock the victim themselves during the second phase of the study would show the lowest level of aggression in the final phase. Yet, as shown in Figure 13–23, results were exactly the opposite of these predictions. It was as if having aggressed against the confederate once, subjects felt less restrained against attacking him on

Catharsis: Does Getting it out of Your System Help?

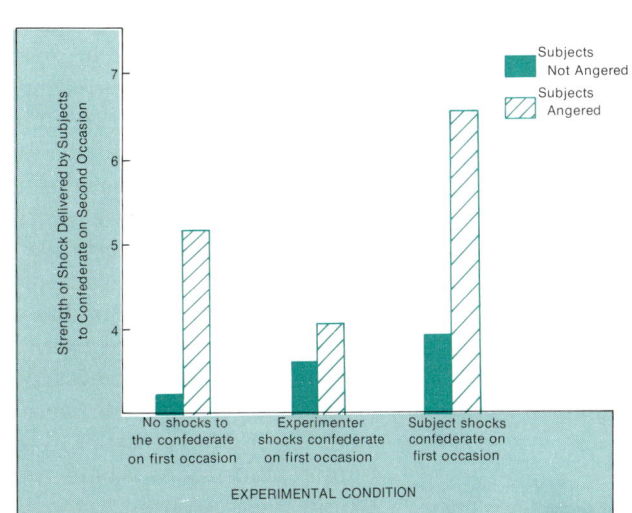

FIGURE 13–23 Evidence against the famous catharsis hypothesis. Angry individuals permitted to aggress against the person who had provoked them on one occasion were actually more—not less—aggressive toward him on a second occasion. (Based on data from Geen, Stonner, and Shope, 1975.)

another occasion. While the findings of other experimenters (Doob and Wood, 1972; Konecni and Ebbesen, 1976) suggest that providing angry individuals with the opportunity to aggress against persons who have provoked them does *sometimes* lead to a reduction in their tendencies to harm these individuals on later occasions, it is clear that such effects are by no means an automatic occurrence. Rather, reductions in aggression seem to take place only under highly specific conditions—if at all. Further, little evidence concerning the duration of such beneficial outcomes is as yet available, and it is possible that they are quite temporary in nature. In view of these facts, it appears that the potential benefits of so-called cathartic activities have been greatly overstated in the past, and that such procedures are probably far less effective in preventing human aggression than has often been assumed.

Controlling Aggression Through Incompatible Responses

If, as suggested above, aggression cannot readily be prevented through punishment or catharsis, other means for controlling such behavior must be developed. Although a number of different techniques have been suggested for this purpose, one of the most promising is based upon the fact that all organisms, including human beings, are incapable of engaging in two incompatible responses at once. For example, it is impossible to both daydream and concentrate on a class lecture, study for an exam and watch television, or drive a car and make passionate love (although some people often attempt to combine these last two activities). Extending this basic principle to the control of aggressive behavior, it seems possible that any conditions serving to induce responses or emotional states which are incompatible with anger or the performance of violent acts will be highly effective in deterring such behavior. Although a number of different responses might prove to be inconsistent with aggression, two which have been the subject of growing attention are humor and mild sexual arousal.

Imagine an ugly situation in which the persons involved grow angrier by the minute. Just when the tension seems unbearable and violence sure to break out, one of those present makes an extremely amusing comment. After a moment of silence, smiles spread among the group, and soon all are laughing out loud. Will these unexpected events have any impact upon the final outcome of the situation? Informal observation suggests that they will. In fact, as the laughter continues, tension and irritation are likely to evaporate, and the probability of overt aggression may be sharply reduced. The explanation for such effects lies in a simple and obvious fact: it is difficult—if not impossible—to feel angry and amused at the same time. Thus, inducing angry individuals to laugh may often be one highly effective means of reducing their tendencies to engage in interpersonal aggression.

The aggression-inhibiting influence of humor has actually been shown in several laboratory experiments (e.g., Landy and Mettee, 1969; Leak, 1974). For example, in one of these studies (Baron, 1974c), male college students were first divided into two groups, one of which was angered by a confederate of the experimenter while the other was not, and were then provided with what seemed to be an opportunity to aggress against this individual by means of electric shock. (Once again, of course, no shocks were actually received by this person). Before attacking the confederate, half of the subjects in each of these groups were exposed to a series of humorous cartoons, while the remaining half examined neutral pictures of scenery, furniture, and abstract art. Because feelings of amusement were expected to be incompatible with continued anger or overt aggression, it was predicted that angry subjects exposed to the humorous cartoons would direct weaker attacks against the confederate than would those exposed to the neutral pictures. As can be seen in Figure 13-24,

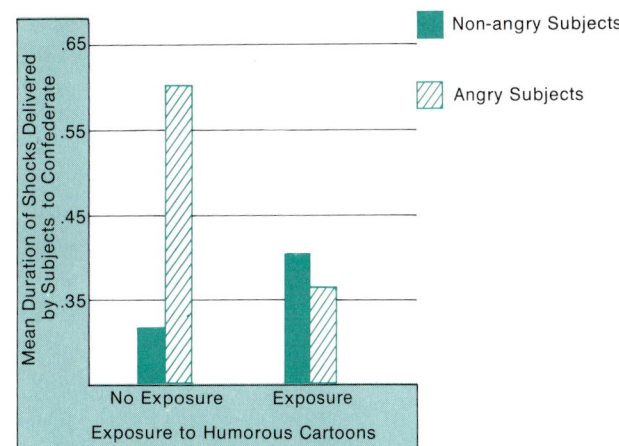

FIGURE 13-24 Humor as a technique for controlling overt aggression. Angry individuals exposed to humorous cartoons directed weaker attacks against the persons who had provoked them than did angry individuals not exposed to such materials. In fact, the level of aggression by the group exposed to humor dropped to that shown by persons who had never been angered. (Based on data from Baron, 1974c.)

this was actually the case. These and similar findings in other studies (Landy and Mettee, 1969) suggest that with respect to the prevention of human aggression, laughter may indeed be one of the best medicines.

In all probability, you do not find the notion that humor is inconsistent with aggression very surprising. In fact, you may well have observed the effects of such incompatibility yourself. But the suggestion that mild sexual arousal likewise seems capable of reducing aggression may come as a greater surprise. Since the time of Freud, who believed that a certain amount of aggression was quite normal in sexual relations, psychologists have often speculated about the possibility of a link between sex and aggression. It is only within the past few years, however, that this relationship has been subjected to systematic study. The results of such research have been both surprising and enlightening. At present, it appears that mild levels of sexual arousal—such as those induced among males by exposure to "Playboy" centerfolds or pictures of attractive young women in bathing suits or lingerie, and those induced among females by exposure to corresponding photos from "Playgirl"—greatly reduce the tendency of angry individuals to aggress against persons who have annoyed them (Baron, 1974d; Frodi, 1976; see Color Plate 11). Apparently, this is due to the fact that such titillation is pleasant, and the positive feeling it involves proves to be incompatible with continued anger or overt aggression (see Figure 13-25).

FIGURE 13-25 The technique being used in this cartoon may actually be quite effective. Recent studies suggest that mild sexual arousal is incompatible with feelings of anger or overt aggression toward others. (© King Features Syndicate, Inc., 1974.)

If mild sexual arousal is effective in reducing aggression, it might be expected that higher levels might be even more successful in inhibiting such reactions. Unfortunately, this does not appear to be the case. Instead, *strong* sexual arousal induced through explicit pictures of passionate love-making (Donnerstein et al., 1975; Zillmann, 1971) or vivid erotic passages (Jaffe et al., 1974) actually seems to increase aggression by angry persons. One explanation for this effect appears to lie in the fact that many individuals find intense levels of sexual arousal—especially under conditions in which they can do nothing to reduce them—quite annoying. Given such negative reactions, it is not surprising that aggression is then enhanced. Although existing evidence on this point is far from conclusive, the findings that mild levels of sexual arousal inhibit overt aggression while stronger levels of such arousal enhance its occurrence seem to have important implications. Specifically, they point to the tentative conclusion that while powerful erotic stimuli may increase the incidence of antisocial behavior, milder stimuli of this type may actually have beneficial effects. The difference between "R"- and "X"-rated materials, then, may involve much more than simple variations in the amount of flesh exposed to view.

Summary

In our attempts to know and understand others, we face two major tasks. First, we must infer their major traits or characteristics through observation of their overt behavior (the process of **attribution**). Second, we must combine the information obtained in this manner into consistent and unified impressions of the persons (the process of **impression formation**). Often, we wish to know something about the temporary moods or emotional states of others. In order to gather information on this topic, we frequently focus upon nonverbal cues such as their facial expressions, body posture, and expressive actions.

Our feelings of liking or disliking for others are influenced by many different factors, including: (1) the extent to which they appear to share our attitudes and opinions; (2) their liking for us; and (3) their level of physical attractiveness. Not surprisingly, attraction toward others also exerts a powerful effect upon the nature of our interactions with them, so that we are usually more willing to do favors for, accept influence from, and enter into long-term relationships with persons we like than we are with persons we dislike. Unfortunately, attraction also seems to influence such decisions as whether to hire a given individual for a job, which candidate to vote for on election day, and whether a defendant is guilty or innocent of the charges against him, despite the fact that attraction is largely irrelevant to such issues.

Contrary to what common sense suggests, there is not always safety in numbers. In fact, it appears that the victims of serious accidents or crimes are often *less* likely to receive aid as the number of bystanders present on the scene increases. This surprising state of affairs seems to stem largely from the influence of two factors: *diffusion of responsibility*—a tendency on the part of each witness to assume that others will help—and the *ambiguity* of many emergency situations, which renders bystanders reluctant to act. Fortunately, the effects of both can be readily counteracted and high levels of helping restored. Our willingness to offer aid to others is also influenced by many other factors, including the presence of helping models and our mood at the time help is requested.

For many years, **aggression** was viewed largely as the result of innate motives which drive human beings to destructive acts. More recently, it has come to be seen as a learned form of social behavior, readily open to modification. Contrary to popular belief, frustration appears to be only a relatively weak determinant of aggression. Violent behavior is most readily evoked by physical or verbal attack and by exposure to aggressive models. Neither punishment nor participation in cathartic activities seems to be highly effective in inhibiting overt aggression. However, a third technique—that of inducing incompatible responses among aggressors—seems to be much more successful in this respect. Causing aggressors to laugh or to experience mild levels of sexual arousal seems to sharply reduce their tendency to aggress against others who have angered or provoked them.

Suggested Readings

Baron, R. A., and Byrne, D.: *Social Psychology: Understanding Human Interaction.* 2nd Edition. Boston: Allyn and Bacon, 1977.

A comprehensive survey of the field of social psychology. The discussions of social perception, attraction, altruism, and aggression provide additional information on the topics discussed in this chapter.

Berscheid, W., and Walster, E.: *Physical Attractiveness.* New York: Plenum Press, 1976.

An interesting discussion of the effects of physical attractiveness on many forms of social behavior.

Fast, J.: *Body Language.* New York: Pocket Books, 1971.

A brief, clearly written discussion of the manner in which we communicate with others through "body language."

Geen, R. G., and O'Neal, E. C. (eds.): *Perspectives Aggression.* New York: Academic Press, 1976.

*A collection of specially prepared articles d(
ing with several different aspects of aggression. Am
the topics covered are the influence of environme
factors (heat, crowding, noise, etc.) on aggression,
the nature of interracial violence.*

Kleinke, C. L.: *First Impressions.* Englewood Cliffs, N.J.: Prentice-Hall, 1975.

An interesting overview of the processes at work when individuals meet for the first time. Among the topics discussed are physical attractiveness, eye-contact, body language, and facial expressions.

Shaver, K. G.: *An Introduction to Attribution Processes.* Cambridge, Mass.: Winthrop, 1975.

An excellent introduction to the whole area of person perception—how we come to know and understand others—with special emphasis on the process of attribution.

Some journals which regularly publish articles on various forms of interpersonal behavior:

Journal of Applied Social Psychology
Journal of Experimental Social Psychology
Journal of Personality
Journal of Personality and Social Psychology
Journal of Research in Personality
Personality and Social Psychology Bulletin

Overleaf: Top photos original with this edition; bottom left photo by Bob West, Photo Trends; bottom right photo by Horst Schäfer, Photo Trends.

You don't have to be Jewish

to love Levy's
real Jewish Rye

14 Psychology and Society: Contributions and Controversies

INDUSTRIAL AND ORGANIZATIONAL PSYCHOLOGY: THE STUDY OF PEOPLE AT WORK

EDUCATIONAL AND SCHOOL PSYCHOLOGY: THE NATURE AND MEASUREMENT OF INTELLIGENCE

CONSUMER PSYCHOLOGY: WHERE BEHAVIOR AND ECONOMICS MEET

SUMMARY

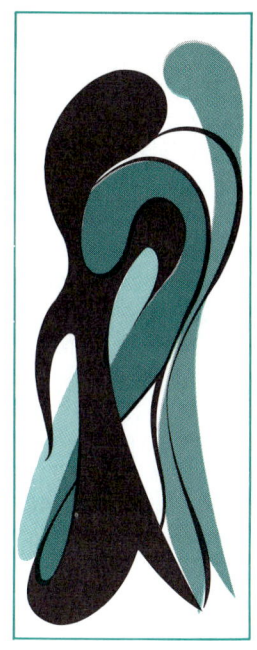

President Truman once remarked: "If you can't stand the heat, stay out of the kitchen." His comment, of course, was directed to the field of politics, where, as you know, the heat of public controversy can often become quite intense. It may surprise you to learn, however, that his remark seems applicable to several sub-fields of psychology as well. From the first day on which they attempted to apply their knowledge and skills to the solution of practical problems—a day which quickly followed the emergence of their field— psychologists have found themselves drawn, however unwillingly, into one controversy after another. Did they make recommendations concerning the education of children? Then they soon found themselves facing the angry protests of teachers and parents who disagreed with their conclusions. Did they suggest new ways of increasing worker productivity? Then they were quickly caught in the midst of bitter labor-management disputes. Did they develop objective tests to measure intelligence or personality? Then they were soon involved in heated debates concerning their use.

In a sense, the frequent occurrence of such disputes is not very surprising. A field which focuses primarily upon behavior and which attempts to apply the methods of science to the solution of complex human problems is bound to "make waves" and stir considerable debate. As a result of such controversies, however, the history of applied psychology (or psychology applied to practical problems, as we prefer to view it) shows a checkered pattern in which periods of steady growth have been repeatedly shattered by sudden storms of public protest.

Because the contributions made by psychologists to such fields as education and business are intimately related to the controversies they have stirred,

495

any attempt to separate the two would be quite artificial. In fact, a typical pattern of events, especially in recent years, has been one in which some new development by psychologists is quickly pressed into practical service, only to arouse a heated controversy resulting, ultimately, in its change or modification. Given the frequency of such events, these two aspects of applied psychology—the major contributions it has provided and the complex moral or legal issues it has often raised—will both serve as major themes of our discussion.

As you may recall from our description in Chapter 1, psychologists attempting to apply the methods and findings of their field to the solution of practical problems currently find employment in many different settings where they perform a wide variety of tasks. As a result, we could not possibly hope to consider all of their activities here. Instead, we will focus upon the contributions of such professionals to three important spheres of human activity— *business, education*, and the *economic marketplace*—considering in each case some of the major controversies raised by their endeavors.

INDUSTRIAL AND ORGANIZATIONAL PSYCHOLOGY: THE STUDY OF PEOPLE AT WORK

Work plays a central role in the lives of most individuals. When asked to describe themselves to others, many persons begin with statements concerning their occupation or job. Moreover, it is probably safe to assert that most adult members of our society spend a greater proportion of their waking hours engaged in work than in any other single activity. Finally, it is interesting to note that when asked to describe the essential characteristics of a truly healthy person, Sigmund Freud replied: the ability to both love and work effectively. Thus, he considered work to be as central to psychological health as a satisfactory sexual adjustment.

Given the obvious importance of work from both an economic and personal perspective, it is not surprising to learn that this form of behavior has long been the subject of careful study by **industrial and organizational psychologists.** Although these specialists have examined many different aspects of work and work settings, much of their attention has been focused on three important topics: **personnel selection**—techniques for choosing the best person for a given job; **work motivation**—the motives which lead individuals to spend long hours at work; and **job satisfaction**—the rewards people both seek and find in their occupations.

Personnel Selection: Round Pegs for Round Holes

Employers have always sought to choose the best person for the job. That is, they have always attempted to select from available applicants those individuals most likely to perform in a satisfactory manner once hired. Until well into the twentieth century, however, they had no choice but to make such important decisions largely on quite informal grounds. Thus, in years gone by, employers would chat briefly with prospective employees, ask them a few questions about their past experience, desire to work, and personal circumstances, and then on the basis of such fragmentary information attempt to reach a decision. In situations in which the requirements for effective job performance were apparent and the degree to which each applicant fulfilled them could be easily observed, informal methods of this type often yielded acceptable results. For example, in selecting piano movers or high-fashion models, on-the-job success could perhaps be predicted from such obvious physical characteristics as the girth of applicants' forearms or the shapeliness of their figures. In cases in which job requirements were less clear-cut, however, informal methods of personnel selection generally proved to be of little value. In short, for most of recorded history, the task of choosing prospective employees was largely a hit-or-miss venture.

Fortunately, this unsettling state of affairs has been radically altered by the work of industrial psychologists who have come to the rescue with more objective—and effective—methods for the choice of appropriate employees. Indeed, so successful have the techniques developed by such psychologists been, they are currently accepted as standard practice in large segments of American industry (see Figure 14–1). As we shall soon see, even these newer methods have certain drawbacks which limit their applicability. There is little doubt, however, that under appropriate circumstances they provide at least a partial solution to the age-old puzzle of matching jobs and people.

The basic task facing an industrial psychologist working in the area of personnel selection is that of devising effective procedures for choosing "the cream of the crop"—those applicants most likely to succeed in the performance of a given job. In order to carry out this essential task, industrial psychologists have developed an orderly set of procedures consisting of seven consecutive steps. *Personnel Selection: The Traditional Approach*

The goal of the first step, **job analysis,** is that of determining the specific behaviors required for the performance of the position under study. Information concerning this topic is usually obtained by questioning individuals already performing the job about their activities, and observing their behavior in a careful manner. The basic notion behind these procedures is simple: in order to be able to choose the best person for the job, it is first necessary to have a clear idea of the skills and abilities required for its performance.

Following the completion of a thorough job analysis, the psychologist formulates some preliminary ideas concerning the type of individual most likely to succeed in its performance. For example, if his analysis suggests that it requires a number of precise, coordinated hand movements, he may conclude that only individuals possessing a relatively high level of manual dexterity will make suitable employees. Similarly, if his analysis indicates that the job requires its holders to give orders to and oversee a number of other workers, he may decide that only individuals showing certain personality traits (e.g., a high level of dominance) will be capable of performing adequately. In any event, once this step is completed, the psychologist has a fairly clear idea of the type of individual he is seeking.

The next task is that of devising some means for locating such persons—

FRANK & ERNEST

FIGURE 14–1 Objective methods for selecting personnel—often involving various psychological tests—have largely replaced the more informal procedures used for this purpose in the past. (Reprinted by permission of Newspaper Enterprise Association.)

that is, for selecting them from a larger group of applicants. Obviously, the specific methods employed for this purpose will vary as a function of job requirements and the specific abilities, skills, or personality characteristics being sought. For example, if there is reason to believe that only applicants whose intelligence exceeds some minimum level will succeed, some measure of this psychological variable will be required (see pp. 511–515). Similarly, if effective job performance seems to be related to such characteristics as mechanical aptitude, manual dexterity, or muscular coordination, tests of these abilities will probably be employed (see Figure 14–2). In addition to the information gathered from various psychological tests, other data may be obtained from interviews with applicants and from their answers to **biographical information blanks,** forms which pose questions about their school activities, family life, and interests. Because of mounting evidence that in many cases the best predictor of a person's future behavior is the way he or she has behaved in the past, this final source of information (biographical information blanks) has gained increasing popularity in recent years (Korman, 1971). Thus, such forms have been used for predicting outcomes ranging from length of service on the job (Roach, 1971) to the amount of "shrinkage" (employee theft) likely to take place in various business settings (Rosenbaum, 1976).

Once appropriate tests of various job-related factors have either been selected or devised, they are administered to a relatively large number of persons as they apply for work. The information acquired in this manner is then stored for future use and—somewhat surprisingly—is *not* employed as a basis for selection at this time. That is, all individuals who would normally have been hired under existing selection procedures are put to work, regardless of their performance on the various test measures of their ability. This is the case because at this point, the psychologist merely *suspects* that the information he has collected will allow him to predict performance on the job. In order to determine whether his hunches in this respect are actually correct, he must wait until measures of actual job performance become available. That is, he must wait until workers have been on the job long enough for evidence regarding their effectiveness in this role to accumulate.

After the passage of a sufficient period of time—the interval varies with the particular job under consideration—the psychologist gathers information

FIGURE 14–2 Psychological tests are often used to select the best applicants for a particular job. The one shown here is designed to measure manual dexterity (the ability to make coordinated movements with the hands).

on the performance of each applicant. Such information may take many forms, again varying with the specific job in question. For example, it might be an index of productivity, some measure of work quality, or even ratings by superiors. Regardless of the specific measures selected, however, the next step remains the same: these indicators of job performance are *correlated* with the information that was collected from all applicants (test scores, results of interviews, and so on) days, weeks, or even months previously, when they first appeared seeking work. In this way, the strength of the relationship between actual job performance and scores on the tests and questionnaires that have been administered may be examined. The stronger this link, the happier the psychologist, for the more accurately can success on the job be predicted from the type of information he has gathered. (See Appendix A for a further discussion of the topics of correlation and prediction.)

Even if the relationship between job performance and test scores or other types of information is strong, an additional, major step is still necessary: these initial findings should be *cross-validated* through repetition with yet another sample of applicants in order to establish that the results have not been a chance or random occurrence. In many cases, only if the outcome of this replication with a new group of workers is also positive can the psychologist go on to the final step in the process—formulation of specific recommendations regarding procedures for the selection of future personnel.

Several decades of extensive use suggest that the traditional approach to personnel selection outlined above does indeed work. By selecting prospective employees in a manner consistent with this model, businesses of many different kinds have been able to substantially lower the costs incurred by hiring and attempting to train individuals who are actually unsuited for the jobs they are seeking. Despite its many strengths, however, this approach suffers from several flaws which severely reduce its effectiveness. The most serious of these center on (1) its costliness in terms of time, (2) its dependence on samples of large size, and (3) its implicit assumption that the world will remain tomorrow very much the way it is today.

The Traditional Approach: Some Flies in the Ointment

That traditional techniques of personnel selection are very costly in terms of time is readily apparent. A psychologist following the methods described above must usually wait several months before he can even begin to gain any notion of the effectiveness of his tests, interviews, or questionnaires as predictors of job performance. And even then, he must repeat the entire process once more, with an additional delay before making any firm or conclusive recommendations. In many cases, the delays produced by such procedures are extremely costly in terms of lost production and wasted training—losses few businesses are willing to bear. As a result, it is often very difficult to follow the traditional model completely in actual practice, a fact which tends to sharply lower its effectiveness.

A second major limitation on the effectiveness of the traditional method lies in the fact that it can only be applied in situations in which large numbers of people perform the same job. This is the case because only in such situations will there be a large enough turnover among employees to allow for the development and cross-validation of effective predictors of job performance. Although many such jobs still exist, the increasing proportion of white-collar positions in the labor market is rapidly changing this situation. Thus, traditional methods of personnel selection are applicable only to a steadily shrinking segment of the work force.

The final and perhaps most serious weakness of this approach lies in its assumption of a largely static world. That is, it assumes that over the years, both jobs and the people who fill them will remain very much the same. Such an assumption is necessary, of course, for there would be little point in attempting to predict performance on jobs which will soon alter radically or soon be filled by individuals quite different in background or ability from those performing them at present. Unfortunately, the rapid pace of change in American society suggests that such assumptions of stability are probably largely unfounded. Many jobs are changing rapidly in the face of new technological developments, and the make-up of the labor force has shifted, and will continue to shift greatly as legal and social barriers which have restricted the employment of blacks, chicanos, Indians, and women in various fields evaporate. In the face of such facts, it seems reasonable to conclude that while still useful in many settings, traditional methods of personnel selection are somewhat less effective today than they were in even the very recent past.

Ethical Issues in Personnel Selection: In Search of Unbiased Predictors

For a variety of complex reasons (e.g., poorer educational background, less test-taking experience), members of various minority groups often score lower on the psychological tests employed for personnel selection than whites. Yet, if hired for the jobs in question, they frequently perform as well. This state of affairs suggests that in some cases, at least, scores on such tests are not equally accurate in predicting success for individuals from different racial or ethnic groups. As a result, total reliance upon such measures in choosing employees may result in a situation in which minority group members who actually have an equal chance of success are hired less frequently than comparable members of the majority group.

We should hasten to add that this is *not* the case in all instances. Several studies indicate that some tests, at least, are equally effective in predicting the employment success of individuals from widely different backgrounds (Gael, Grant, and Ritchie, 1975). However, others appear to be more effective as predictors of future performance when used with some groups than with others. Given such possibilities, it is important that the overall accuracy and general applicability of tests never be taken for granted, for otherwise discrimination may enter, through the back door, into the process of personnel selection, even if in a largely unintentional manner.

Wishing to prevent this possibility, the Supreme Court ruled in 1971 that various tests or other procedures cannot legally be employed for purposes of personnel selection unless there is convincing evidence of their ability to predict job performance:

"Nothing in the Act precludes the use of testing or measuring procedures; obviously they are useful. What Congress has forbidden is giving these devices and mechanisms controlling force unless they are a demonstrably reasonable measure of job performance. . . ."

Very simply, it is currently against the law of the land to select prospective employees by means of procedures which have not been shown to be effective for this purpose, and which may, as a result, have an adverse effect upon the members of various minority groups.

Sexism in the World of Work: Prejudice Based on Gender

Although there has been considerable progress toward the goal of eliminating discrimination based on racial or ethnic identity from personnel selection, progress toward removing another, equally objectionable type—that based on sex—has been much slower. At present, more than 31 million women are at work in the U.S., over one-third of the entire labor force. Yet of these, fully 78 per cent—a much higher figure than for men (40 per cent) are locked into essentially dead-end jobs offering no promise of advancement. Further, only 15 per cent are currently employed in jobs which can be classified as professional or technical in nature, and, of these, a large majority are in the traditionally "female" fields of teaching and nursing. In short, although an increasing number of women continue to find employment outside their homes, they have often been shunted into the least interesting and most unrewarding positions available.

Many different factors probably have contributed to this disturbing state of affairs, but most fall into three major categories. Arranged roughly in order of increasing resistance to change, they are: (1) overt discriminatory practices in hiring and advancement, (2) negative attitudes toward women at work, and (3) internally socialized psychological forces which prevent women from seeking a high degree of success (O'Leary, 1974).

The first of these factors, overt discriminatory practices, seems to be on the wane. Recent legislation and the pending Equal Rights Amendment have gone a long way toward eliminating hiring practices which barred women from many interesting and rewarding jobs in the past. In fact, there is some indication that the pendulum has swung the other way, and that businesses, universities, and government agencies are now so eager to make up for past discriminatory practices that they actually give preference to women applicants. Further, the practice of paying female employees less than their male counterparts has come under the pressure of numerous court decisions outlawing its existence. In the late 1970's, then, external barriers to the advancement of women in the world of work have come nearer to elimination from the scene (see Figure 14–3).

Unfortunately, less change is currently visible with respect to the second factor: negative attitudes toward working women. Even today, several negative beliefs—perhaps myths might be a better term—regarding women's commitment to and ability for work enjoy widespread acceptance. One of the most prevalent of these suggestions contends that women work only to supplement their husbands' income and, as a result, are far less committed to their jobs than men. While this may be true in a few cases, recent surveys show that it is far from generally correct. A substantial proportion of working women are either entirely self-supporting or at the very least make a major contribution to their families' total income (Crowley et al., 1973). Yet, despite these facts, the myth of low female commitment to work persists. Similarly, there is a continuing belief among many individuals in our society that women are somehow less competent in the performance of many different jobs than men. For example,

FIGURE 14–3 As barriers of sexual discrimination have become less rigid, women have moved increasingly into jobs previously held only by men—and vice versa. (Left photo by Raimondo Borea; right photo by Horst Schäfer, Photo Trends.)

women are often judged to be less capable than men, even when they demonstrate identical levels of performance (e.g., Deaux and Emswiller, 1973; Spence, Helmreich, and Stapp, 1975). While it is possible to legislate change in hiring practices and pay scales, alterations in attitudes cannot be produced in a similar manner. As a result, it seems likely that a large-scale, continuing program of persuasion will probably be needed if these unfortunate beliefs about women are ever to be changed. (For an example of current attempts to combat sexist attitudes in business and industry, see Figure 14–4.)

The final of our three factors—psychological forces acting within women themselves—may prove to be the most difficult of all to alter. Basically, these forces spring from the process of sex-role training described in Chapter 8. During this process, many women learn to equate success or achievement with a loss of femininity. That is, they come to believe that the attainment of excellence in intellectual or occupational pursuits will somehow make them "less of a woman," and thereby result in such unpleasant consequences as social rejection or disapproval. In view of such feelings, it is not at all surprising that many women develop an actual *fear of success*, and actively seek to avoid competition or advancement.

Evidence for the existence of such anxieties on the part of many women in our society has been obtained by Matina Horner (1970, 1972) in a series of interesting studies. In these experiments, male and female subjects were presented with the following brief statement and were asked to write stories based upon it:

After first-term finals (Anne/John) finds (herself/himself) at the top of (her/his) medical class.

For females, the character was named Anne, while for males he was named John. Systematic analysis of the stories written by subjects indicated that women often expressed ambivalence or conflict over Anne's success. For example, consider the following portion of a story written by a young woman:

"Anne is completely ecstatic but at the same time feels guilty. She wishes that she could stop studying so hard. . . . She will finally have a nervous breakdown and quit med school and marry a successful young doctor."

"Hire him. He's got great legs."

If women thought this way about men they would be awfully silly.

When men think this way about women they're silly, too.

Women should be judged for a job by whether or not they can do it.

In a world where women are doctors, lawyers, judges, brokers, economists, scientists, political candidates, professors and company presidents, any other viewpoint is ridiculous.

Think of it this way. When we need all the help we can get, why waste half the brains around?

Womanpower. It's much too good to waste.

FIGURE 14–4 Attempts to counteract sexist attitudes toward women have taken many forms, but one popular approach has been that of showing how silly such views seem when reversed and applied to men. (The NOW Legal Defense and Education Fund, Inc.)

In contrast, men seem to experience no similar conflicts. On the contrary, they generally express nothing but positive feelings concerning John's success. The following story is typical:

"John is very pleased with himself, and he realizes that all his efforts have been rewarded: he has finally made the top of his class. John has worked hard and his long hours of study have paid off. . . . He will go on in med school making good grades and be successful. . . ."

Some idea of the extent to which male and female subjects differed in their reactions to this hypothetical situation can be gained from the fact that while less than 10 per cent of the stories written by men contained any hint of an active fear of success, fully 65 per cent of those produced by women demonstrated the presence of this theme. Fortunately, more recent studies have reported some indications of a reduction in the incidence of such themes among female undergraduates (Spence, 1974). Even in these investigations, though, the frequency of negative reactions to feminine success remained quite high (approximately 40 per cent).

Because such fear of success stems from socialization practices begun at an early age and continued throughout childhood, it seems likely that it will often prove quite resistant to later changes. Unless such internal barriers to success are removed, however, it will be difficult for women to assume their rightful, equal place in the work force, and the needless waste of precious human potential which has occurred in the past may continue unchecked into the future.

PSYCHOLOGY IN ACTION: *Are You as Unbiased as You Think? A Do-it-Yourself Test for Sexism*

Are you or your friends unintentionally sexist? Do you subscribe to beliefs about women which tend to assign them to low-status, dead-end jobs without even being aware of this fact? Before answering with some indignation that neither you nor your acquaintants hold such outdated views, try responding to the following questions.

(1) Tom was walking down the street when suddenly he ran into an old friend. Their conversation went as follows:

Tom: Hi!
Friend: Hello! How are you doing?
Tom: Great. Gee, I haven't seen you since high school. What have you been doing with yourself?
Friend: Well, I went to college for a couple of years, but then quit and got a job.
Tom: Doing what?
Friend: I've been working for a construction company, in their drafting department. Maybe you remember that I really liked that kind of thing in school.
Tom: Yeah, I do.
Friend: I also got married two years ago; this is my daughter (points to child in carriage).
Tom: What's her name?

Friend: The same as her mother's.
Tom: (To the daughter) Hi Susan!
Question: How did Tom know the daughter's name?

(2) A famous surgeon and a noted attorney with offices on the same floor of a professional building strike up a warm friendship. One day, they are having lunch in an expensive restaurant when the lawyer suddenly turns pale and mutters to his friend: "Oh no, here comes my wife!"
Question: Why was the lawyer upset?

If you and your friends are like many other individuals in our society, there is a good chance that you had some difficulty in answering at least one of these questions. If you did, this was probably the case because implicit attitudes of which you may not even be aware trapped you into assuming that all of the individuals involved were males. It is precisely such attitudes which must be changed if women are ever to attain fully equal treatment in employment settings.

Answers:
(1) Tom knew the daughter's name because his friend is Susan.
(2) The lawyer was upset because his friend the surgeon was a woman.

Motivation to Work: By Bread Alone?

Suppose that in some way it was possible to select as employees several individuals possessing equal ability to perform a given job. Would they then actually attain equal levels of productivity? In all probability, they would not. Rather, despite their similar abilities, skills, or past experience, some would attain much higher levels of accuracy, output, and quality than others. Although a number of different factors would contribute to such variations in performance, one of the most important would probably be differences in their motivation or desire to work. It is likely that the persons chosen would differ greatly in this characteristic, so that some would be quite high but others quite low in their desire to perform in a competent and effective manner. In short, performance on the job—like performance in many other situations—is determined both by ability and effort (see Chapter 4). But what, precisely, lies behind the motivation to work? What factors lead people to work, and, even more importantly, to work with varying degrees of effort?

Expectancy Theory: Working for Rewards

There can be little doubt that one of the factors influencing people to work—and to work hard—is the rewards or incentives they expect to gain through such activities. In an important sense, work is a form of instrumental behavior which brings a multitude of rewards to those who perform it in a successful and effective manner. Thus, it seems reasonable to suggest that often it is the expectation of such payoffs which keeps individuals hard at work at the daily grind.

Together, these basic ideas form an important part of the **expectancy theory of work motivation**—at present, perhaps the most widely accepted explanation for effort on the job (Wahba and House, 1974). Basically, expectancy theory holds that individuals' effort on the job depends upon (1) the strength of their expectancies that such effort will lead to various outcomes and (2) the valence (positive or negative nature) of such outcomes. In short, it suggests that individuals will work hard when they perceive that such effort has a good chance of paying off—yielding desired, positive rewards (Vroom, 1964). Over the past decade, many investigations have been performed to examine the accuracy of these basic suggestions, and, in general, positive results have been obtained (Mitchell, 1974). That is, the stronger the individuals' expectations that effort on their part will lead to desired rewards, the better their productivity or performance on the job. Thus, while it is by no means universally accepted (Locke, 1975), the expectancy theory of work motivation is viewed by many industrial and organizational psychologists as providing a relatively accurate explanation of work motivation.

Interestingly, *monetary* rewards (wages, stock options, etc.) need not be the most important type of payoffs sought by workers. Research suggests that many persons rate such factors as the opportunity for advancement, job security, and good working conditions as crucial in determining their motivation to work (see Table 14–1). Thus, in this sense at least, it appears that human beings do not usually seek to live "by bread alone."

The Need to Achieve: Individual Differences in Work Motivation

You may recall that in Chapter 7, we devoted considerable attention to the need for achievement—the motive to meet internal standards of excellence and attain success. Since we have already examined this topic in some detail, we merely wish, at this point, to call your attention to a fact which may already be quite obvious: individual differences in the need for achievement may be closely related to differences in work motivation, with persons scoring relative-

TABLE 14–1   Factors Determining Work Motivation

Factor	Rank
Opportunity for advancement	1
Job security	2
Opportunity to use ideas	3
Opportunity to learn a job	4
Opportunity for public service	5
Type of work	6
Supervisor	7
Company	8
Pay	9
Co-workers	10
Working conditions	11
Easy work	12

The relative importance of various factors as determinants of work motivation. Somewhat surprisingly, pay ranks a poor ninth. (The larger the number shown, the less importance attached to a given factor.) (Based on a summary of data from studies reported in McCormick and Tiffin, 1974.)

ly high on this dimension demonstrating greater effort on the job than those scoring relatively low. In short, there may be an important link between some aspects of personality and work productivity.

Intrinsic Motivation: Turning Play into Work

Mark Twain once defined work as "whatever a body is obliged to do" and play as "whatever a body is not obliged to do." In the light of these definitions, it seems reasonable to suggest that many, if not most, jobs initially contain elements of both work and play. Almost all involve tasks which the workers find tedious and dull, and which they would quickly reject in the absence of external rewards such as wages. At the same time, many also involve tasks which workers find relatively enjoyable, and which they might well choose to perform even in the absence of external rewards. For example, consider the case of an auto mechanic who spends all day repairing cars, only to return home to spend most of his leisure hours tinkering with his own vehicle. Such instances suggest that the motivation to perform at least certain activities in work settings can be *intrinsic*, stemming from the tasks themselves, as well as *extrinsic*, dependent upon external rewards.

Unfortunately, although intrinsic motivation might be expected to play a role in the performance of at least some jobs, investigations conducted by Mark Lepper and his colleagues suggest that the conditions existing in most work settings probably tend to discourage its occurrence. The results of these studies reveal that when individuals are provided with external rewards for performing activities they initially enjoy, their intrinsic motivation for engaging in such behavior is rapidly reduced. For example, in one recent study (Lepper and Greene, 1975), children who initially enjoyed playing with a series of simple jigsaw puzzles and often did so of their own free will were offered external rewards (the opportunity to play with even more attractive toys) for engaging in this activity. When their intrinsic motivation to play with the puzzles was then re-measured at a later time, it was found to have decreased sharply. That is, after being "paid" for playing with the puzzles, the children showed a much weaker tendency to solve them.

These findings have interesting but disconcerting implications with respect to work motivation. Apparently, individuals' intrinsic motivation to perform even the most enjoyable portions of their jobs may be quickly and sharply reduced by the external rewards (wages, fringe benefits, and the like) that they receive for such activities. In short, rewarding individuals for engaging in actions they initially enjoy may soon manage to convert what starts out as pleasant play into serious, tedious work (Deci, 1975; Ross, Karniol, and Rothstein, 1976).

Job Satisfaction: The Free Fringe Benefit

Over the long run, performance on almost any job is probably strongly determined by the degree of satisfaction it provides. Workers who are satisfied with and enjoy their jobs will probably tend to perform them in a more adequate and efficient manner than workers who are dissatisfied with their occupations. But what, precisely, are the satisfactions sought by people in their work? And what specific factors tend to make various jobs satisfying or unsatisfying to those who hold them? Research by industrial and social psychologists has begun to provide answers to these important questions.

Perceived Fairness on the Job: Getting a Just Slice of the Pie

Until quite recently, it was generally assumed that an individual's degree of satisfaction with his or her job was largely determined by the absolute level of benefits it supplied. Thus, it was believed that the higher an individual's salary, the better the conditions under which he worked, and the higher the status of his title, the greater his satisfaction on the job. To some extent, of course, this is true. Highly paid, high-status professionals do indeed usually report greater satisfaction with their work than do unskilled laborers. But recent investigations suggest that workers' satisfaction with their jobs may actually be more strongly affected by the *relative* level of benefits they receive than by the absolute value of such rewards (Walster, Berscheid, and Walster, 1973). Apparently, it is very important for most individuals to feel that they are being treated as fairly as others. In order to determine if they are, they seem to compare the benefits they receive from their jobs (wages, working conditions, status, etc.) and the contributions they supply (effort, previous training or experience, etc.) with those of their fellow employees. If these values seem to be in relative balance—that is, if the proportion between others' contributions and benefits roughly equals their own—they perceive themselves as fairly treated, and job satisfaction may be high. If these values are greatly out of balance, however, they may perceive themselves as being unfairly treated, and experience strong feelings of **inequity** (see Table 14–2).

Such feelings can arise in a number of specific ways. For example, an individual may perceive that he works much harder than another who nevertheless earns the same salary as himself. Similarly, a worker may perceive that he receives fewer benefits than another, despite his greater experience on the job. Feelings of inequity do not necessarily center on tangible economic factors, however; they may also arise in much more subtle ways. For example, a young management trainee may become greatly upset upon learning that one of his co-workers has a private phone, a rug on the floor, or the key to the executive washroom, while he does not. Usually, feelings of inequity occur in situations in which individuals believe that they are somehow receiving *less* than their fair share, less than they deserve. But such reactions can also develop when workers perceive that they are receiving *more* benefits than those to which they are entitled. Not surprisingly, instances of the latter type usually turn out to be far less disturbing than those of the former (Austin and Walster, 1974).

TABLE 14–2   Job Equity and Inequity

Equity

Person A		Person B	
Benefits	$10,000 salary Small office Party-line phone Small pension Minimum health insurance Unreserved parking space	Benefits	$25,000 salary Large office Private-line phone Large pension Maximum health insurance Reserved parking space
Contributions	Easy work (low effort on job) No prior experience B.A. degree only 35 hour work week	Contributions	Difficult work (high effort required) 20 years prior experience Ph.D. degree 60 hour work week

Inequity

Person A		Person B	
Benefits	$10,000 salary Small office Party-line phone Small pension Minimum health insurance Unreserved parking space	Benefits	$25,000 salary Large office Private-line phone Large pension Maximum health insurance Reserved parking space
Contributions	Easy work (low effort) No prior experience B.A. degree only 35 hour work week	Contributions	Easy work (low effort) 1 year prior experience B.A. degree only 20 hour work week

Conditions which would be expected to produce feelings of equity (fair treatment) or inequity (unfair treatment) on the part of a particular individual (Person A). In the first case (equity), Person B receives greater benefits than Person A but "deserves" these outcomes because of his or her greater training, experience, and effort on the job. In the second case (inequity), however, Person B receives greater benefits but does not appear to be entitled to such princely outcomes, since he has only a little more experience than Person A and actually works less hard. (Perhaps he has married the boss' daughter or has access to damaging information his employer wishes to keep secret.)

When individuals experience feelings of inequity, job satisfaction often drops to very low levels. In addition, most find such reactions so unpleasant that they actively seek to reduce or remove their occurrence. This can be accomplished in several different ways. First, workers may seek adjustments in either their inputs to or benefits from their jobs. It is from this strategy, of course, that bitter and prolonged labor disputes often develop (see Figure 14–5). Second, they may seek to "punish" their employers for their unfair treatment through such actions as intentional errors on the job, petty theft, or actual industrial sabotage. Finally, in perhaps the most drastic strategy of all, employees can simply quit their jobs and seek other work.

FIGURE 14–5   When workers perceive that they are being treated unfairly, strikes may result.
The fact that these actions often continue long past the point at which participants can hope to
recover their losses through a raise suggests that feelings of inequity may be more important in
such situations than actual economic outcomes. (Left photo, morticians on strike, by Philip Jon
Bailey, Stock, Boston; right photo, Owen Franken, Stock, Boston.)

Regardless of the specific manner in which workers attempt to reduce feelings of inequity, it is apparent that such reactions have a truly devastating
effect upon job satisfaction, and therefore upon productivity. As a result, it
seems reasonable to suggest that "fair play" is always the best course of action
in employee-employer relations, not simply for obvious ethical and moral
reasons, but for important economic ones as well.

*Other Factors
Affecting Job
Satisfaction:
Herzberg's Two-
Factor Theory*

In addition to feelings of being fairly or unfairly treated, a number of other
factors have been found to strongly affect worker satisfaction. Perhaps the
most extensive research on this topic has been conducted by Frederick Herzberg (1966). On the basis of several large-scale studies involving actual employees, Herzberg has concluded that the factors leading to job satisfaction are
actually quite distinct from those leading to dissatisfaction. In other words,
satisfaction and dissatisfaction with one's work are not simply two sides of
the same coin; rather, they stem from different sources. Most important in
influencing positive attitudes toward one's job are achievement, recognition,
the nature of the work itself, advancement, and responsibility. Because the
presence of these factors seems to produce a high degree of satisfaction, Herzberg terms them **motivators.**

In contrast, a second group of factors, including security, good working
conditions, pleasant relations with fellow workers, and high pay seem only to
influence dissatisfaction. More specifically, the absence of these conditions
induces intense negative reactions, while their presence yields only neutral
feelings about one's job. Since they function to prevent dissatisfaction, but
cannot by themselves induce positive feelings or attitudes, Herzberg terms
these **hygiene factors.** In a sense, these are the necessary conditions for good
productivity; without them, workers are unhappy and discontented. (A summary of Herzberg's suggestions is presented in Figure 14–6.)

While Herzberg's distinction between motivators and hygiene factors has
been supported by the results of several studies (e.g., Macarov, 1972), other
investigations have yielded largely negative findings (Gordon, Pryor, and
Harris, 1974). Moreover, additional research suggests that the relative importance of motivators and hygiene factors seems to vary with occupation. For

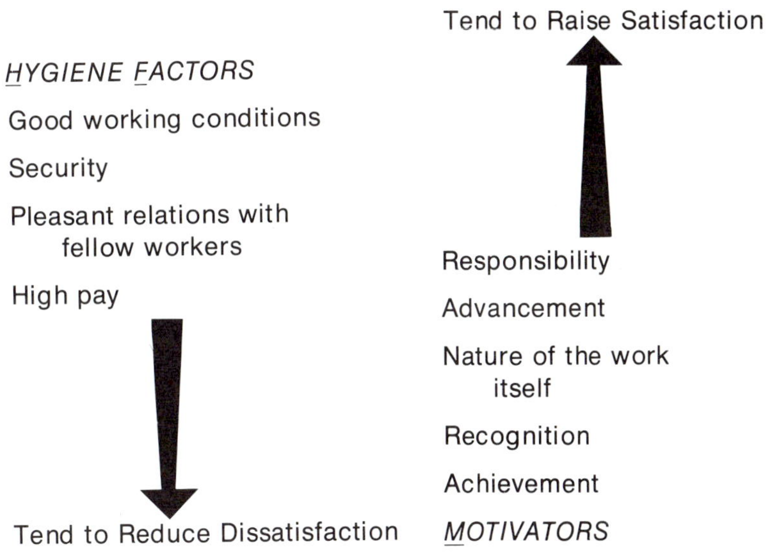

Tend to Raise Satisfaction

HYGIENE FACTORS

Good working conditions

Security

Pleasant relations with
    fellow workers

High pay

Responsibility

Advancement

Nature of the work
    itself

Recognition

Achievement

FIGURE 14–6 Herzberg's theory of job satisfaction. According to this theory, *hygiene factors* prevent dissatisfaction, while *motivators* contribute to actual satisfaction.

Tend to Reduce Dissatisfaction   *MOTIVATORS*

example, blue-collar workers often seem to be more strongly influenced by the latter than by the former (see Locke, 1975). At present, then, Herzberg's contention that motivators influence only job satisfaction, while hygiene factors affect only job dissatisfaction, remains somewhat in doubt.

Despite these problems, however, the theory has had important practical applications with respect to **job enrichment**—attempts to improve worker morale through the provision of motivators. Many investigations have been conducted to examine the effectiveness of such procedures, and, in general, they have yielded positive results (Sirota, 1973). That is, both worker satisfaction and performance are improved by such actions as (1) giving workers greater responsibility on the job, (2) increasing their freedom and autonomy, (3) providing greater recognition for job accomplishments, and (4) making work activities more interesting and varied (all suggested by Herzberg's theory). Thus, while the overall validity of Herzberg's theory remains open to question, it seems to have yielded practical benefits in regard to job enrichment.

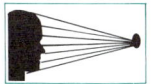

**FOCUS
ON
RESEARCH:** *Job Satisfaction and Realistic Expectations—"Telling It
Like It Is" in Employment Settings*

Suppose you entered a new job expecting to encounter very favorable conditions, but then discovered that it was not nearly so pleasant as you believed. Would your morale and satisfaction be higher or lower than if you had entered the same job with more realistic expectations? Common sense suggests that you might well experience more positive reactions (or at least less negative ones) if you *expected* to encounter some adverse conditions on the job; you might well be less upset or irritated by them than if they took you totally by surprise.

Despite the reasonable nature of such arguments, many businesses, government agen-

cies, and other large organizations continue to paint unrealistically rosy pictures of working conditions and benefits when recruiting new personnel. Unfortunately, the results of such practices may then be a sharp—and largely unnecessary—drop in worker morale and satisfaction when the truth is later discovered. That this is actually the case is indicated by the findings of several recent experiments (Ilgen and Seely, 1974; Wanous, 1975, 1976).

For example, in the study conducted by Ilgen and Seely (1974) one group of 234 young men who had accepted appointments at West Point were mailed booklets providing them with realistic information concerning the conditions they would encounter during a two-month summer training period. This booklet told it largely "like it is," reporting the boring, tedious, and stressful activities they would face, as well as the more pleasant ones. A second group of equal size did not receive the booklet, and so served as a control group.

When the two groups were later compared, a clear pattern of findings emerged: those who had received the booklet, and hence had realistic expectations concerning their first two months in the Academy, showed a much lower rate of voluntary resignations than did those who had not. Indeed, nearly twice as many individuals in the control group resigned during this period as those in the experimental "realistic expectations" condition. When these results are combined with those of studies which have been conducted with other groups of individuals and in markedly different settings (Wanous, 1975), convincing evidence for the following conclusions seems to be provided: in the long run, supplying prospective employees with realistic expectations concerning their new jobs may be a much better policy than promising them far more than can actually be delivered.

EDUCATIONAL AND SCHOOL PSYCHOLOGY: THE NATURE AND MEASUREMENT OF INTELLIGENCE

To an important degree, schools shape the future. The skills, ideas, and values children acquire during their long years in the classroom exert a powerful and lasting effect upon the course of their later lives. And since the vast majority of individuals now remain in school at least through their teens—and increasingly on into their twenties—the collective impact of our educational system upon changes in the structure of society is truly immense.

Given the many complex problems involved in educating the young, it is not surprising that teachers, principals, and school superintendents have often found it necessary to call upon psychologists for important practical assistance. In answer to their pleas for aid, **educational** and **school psychologists** have undertaken many diverse tasks including the design of more effective methods of instruction (see Figure 14-7), the diagnosis and treatment of school-related behavior disorders, and both the planning and assessment of special educational programs for the culturally disadvantaged (DeCecco and Crawford, 1974). Perhaps their most important—and certainly most controversial—contributions to the field of education, however, have involved the development and use of objective measures of intelligence. Because such tests have been so widely employed, and also because they have recently become the subject of intense criticism and debate, we will focus most of our attention upon this important topic.

FIGURE 14-7 Computer-assisted instruction—a technique in which computers serve as tutors for individual students—has been the subject of much recent attention. Because it provides children with immediate knowledge of results, and can be tailored to their individual needs, it seems to provide many advantages over traditional methods of instruction. (Photo by Ben Ross, Photo Trends.)

We often make informal judgments about the intelligence of others. After observing their behavior or listening to their words in a number of different settings, we label some as "bright," others as "average," and still others as "slow." Given the speed and apparent ease with which we draw such conclusions, it might seem at first that our informal system for assessing the intelligence of friends—and even casual acquaintances—is quite a good one. Unfortunately, though, it often leads us into error. For example, it is easy to confuse high verbal output with brillance, fluency with comprehension, and an imposing physical appearance with wisdom.

Given the unreliability of our informal system for assessing the intellectual capacity of others, the need for more objective methods of drawing such conclusions is readily apparent. Surprisingly, though, no techniques of this type were available until the first decades of the present century, when, largely in response to practical problems arising in the field of education, psychologists began the task of developing practical tests of mental ability.

In 1904, a time when psychology was just getting started, school authorities in Paris approached Alfred Binet (see Figure 14–8) and asked him to develop an objective method for detecting mental retardation in children. In effect, they requested that he devise a simple, workable test of intelligence. Before he could devise such a test, of course, Binet first faced the task of deciding exactly what it should measure—that is, what would be meant by the term **intelligence.** Rejecting an earlier approach suggested by Sir Francis Galton, in which intelligence was equated with superior sensory and motor performance, Binet chose instead to focus primarily upon intellectual abilities. Together with his colleague Theodore Simon, he finally settled on the view that intelligence refers primarily to the ability to judge, comprehend, and reason well. It is interesting to note that today, more than 70 years later, modern definitions of intelligence retain much of the same flavor, often relating this characteristic to the abilities to adapt to new circumstances, deal with complex or abstract materials, and solve intellectual problems (e.g., Wechsler, 1975).

In designing their actual test, Binet and Simon were guided by the belief

*The Measure-
ment of Intelli-
gence: Tests of
Mental Ability*

*Alfred Binet and the
Concept of Mental
Age*

FIGURE 14–8 Alfred Binet, developer of the first practical test of intelligence. (The Bettmann Archive.)

that the final items to be selected should be ones which children could answer without special training or preparation. They felt that this was important because the test was designed to measure the abilities to comprehend and reason—not specific knowledge gained in the classroom. In order to accomplish this task, Binet and Simon chose items of two basic types: those which were so novel or unusual that virtually none of the children tested would have any prior experience with them, and those which were so familiar that virtually all of the children would have been exposed to them in one form or another.

The first version of their test, published in 1905, contained 30 items of these types (see Figure 14–9), and was quite effective in accomplishing its stated purpose: with its aid, children in need of special instructional assistance could be readily selected. Encouraged by this early success, Binet and Simon went on to revise their test so that it could be used to measure variations in intelligence among normal children as well. This revision, published in 1908, grouped items by age, so that six were included at each level between the ages of 3 and 13. Individual items were placed at a particular age level if 75 per cent of the children of that age could pass it correctly.

Word of Binet's new, objective method for measuring intelligence quickly crossed the Atlantic, and in 1916 his tests were adapted for use in the U.S. by Lewis Terman of Stanford University. The **Stanford-Binet test,** as it soon came to be known, attained immediate acceptance, and was put to use in a number of practical settings. One of the features which users found most attractive and which probably contributed greatly to its rapid adoption was the fact that the test yielded a single score presumed to reflect an individual's overall level of intelligence: the famous **I.Q.**

The letters I.Q. stand for **intelligence quotient,** and this is precisely what such scores initially represented—the result obtained when an individual's **mental age** was divided by his or her chronological age and multiplied by 100. Mental age, which refers to an individual's level of intellectual development, was obtained in a direct and simple manner. First, an examiner would determine the child's *basal age* on the test—the age level at which he or she could answer all items. Then two months of additional mental age credit were added to this value for each additional item passed at higher levels of the test. For example, consider the case of an eight-year-old girl who passed all of the items on the seven-year test, 5 of those on the eight-year test, 3 of the items on the

---

Name designated objects—can child name objects pointed to in pictures?

Repeat three digits

Compare two weights

Repeat sentences

Identify differences between objects—how are a fly and butterfly different?

Draw a design from memory

Place five weights in order

Complete sentences

Construct sentences—child is asked to construct sentence including three specified words

Define abstract terms

FIGURE 14–9   Some of the items included in the first version of the Binet-Simon test of intelligence. (Adapted from Willerman, 1977.)

nine-year test, and 1 of the items on the ten-year test. Her mental age would then be computed as follows:

> 84 months (for passing all items on the seven-year test)
> 10 months (for passing 5 items on the eight-year test)
> 6 months (for passing 3 items on the nine-year test)
> 2 months (for passing 1 item on the ten-year test)
> ──────────

Total = 102 months = 9.5 years

The child's I.Q. would then be determined by means of the following simple formula and computations:

$$\text{I.Q.} = (\text{Mental Age/Chronological Age}) \times 100$$
$$\text{I.Q.} = (9.5/8.0) \times 100 = 1.19 \times 100 = 119$$

Since an individual's I.Q. would be equal to 100 if his mental age exactly matched his chronological age, it is easy to see that I.Q.'s greater than 100 reflected advanced or accelerated intellectual development, while those below this value reflected some degree of intellectual "slowness" or backwardness. Slight departures from 100 in either direction were not viewed as important, however; only variations of substantial size (e.g., 20 points or more) were interpreted as having major practical significance.

At first glance, I.Q. scores based on the ratio of an individual's mental age to his or her chronological age seem quite reasonable. They do, after all, reflect the extent to which a child is mentally "advanced" or "backward" for his or her age. By now, however, you may have already recognized the fatal flaw in this particular index of intelligence: while mental age must, necessarily, stop increasing at some point during an individual's life, chronological age — alas! — does not. As a result, I.Q. scores determined in this simple manner begin to decrease as maturity is attained. Indeed, since mental development seems to reach a maximum in the late teens or early twenties, an individual's I.Q. may already seem to be in an appalling tail-spin by the time he or she graduates from college. Recent folklore concerning the drastic effects of turning 30 notwithstanding, such results make little sense.

In the face of this serious flaw, I.Q. scores based on the concept of mental age were replaced some years ago by another measure known as the *deviation I.Q.* Scores of this type simply represent an individual's performance on the test relative to those of other persons of his or her age. The average performance of all such persons is arbitrarily set equal to 100, and the individual's I.Q. then expresses the extent to which his or her own performance departs (i.e., deviates) from this level. One major advantage of such scores is that they are statistically adjusted in such a manner that it is possible to tell, from appropriate mathematical tables, precisely what proportion of others taking the test score higher or lower than a given individual (see Appendix A for more information on this topic). Table 14–3 shows the percentage of persons obtaining various I.Q.'s on a recent version of the Stanford-Binet which uses such deviation measures.

The tests developed by Binet, and later adapted for use in the U.S. by Terman, provided the first objective measures of mental ability. In this respect, they represented a major breakthrough for the fields of psychology and education. Good as they were, however, early versions of these tests were open to serious criticism on two major grounds. First, they were constructed in such a manner that different types of items were included at different age levels (refer to Figure 14–9). As a result, different aspects of intelligence were probably

The Wechsler Tests: Profiles of Intelligence

TABLE 14–3   Distribution of I.Q. Scores

I.Q. Range	Descriptive Label	Per cent of Individuals Taking the Test Who Obtain Such Scores
140 and above	Very superior	1
120–139	Superior	10
110–119	High average	18
90–109	Average	47
80–89	Low average	15
70–79	Borderline	6
69 and below	Mentally retarded	3

The proportion of individuals obtaining various I.Q. scores on a recent version of the Stanford-Binet. Note that the labels associated with each range are subjective in nature and should *not* be interpreted literally. (Adapted from Terman and Merrill, 1960.)

measured at different ages. Second, they tended to ignore the fact that intelligence can be revealed in non-verbal as well as verbal activities. For example, an engineer who is capable of understanding the workings of a complex machine at a single glance is certainly demonstrating evidence of high level of intelligence. Yet, no means of assessing such intellectual ability was present in early versions of the Stanford-Binet.

A series of tests developed by David Wechsler over a period of several decades was designed to eliminate both of these shortcomings. In these tests, items of the same basic types—but varying in terms of difficulty—are included at all age levels. In addition, non-verbal, or *performance*, items (as well as more traditional verbal questions) are employed. For example, individuals taking the test are asked to (1) perform such tasks as assembling objects or completing pictures and (2) answer verbal items dealing with comprehension, information, and reasoning. An additional feature of the tests involves the division of both the verbal and performance portions into separate *subscales*, each supposedly reflecting a different aspect or component of intelligence. Since separate scores are computed for each of these scales, an individual's performance on the test is often presented in the form of a profile supposedly illustrating his or her pattern of intellectual strengths and weaknesses (see Figure 14–10).

Because of the advantages outlined above, and the fact that they are somewhat easier to administer and score than the Stanford-Binet, the Wechsler

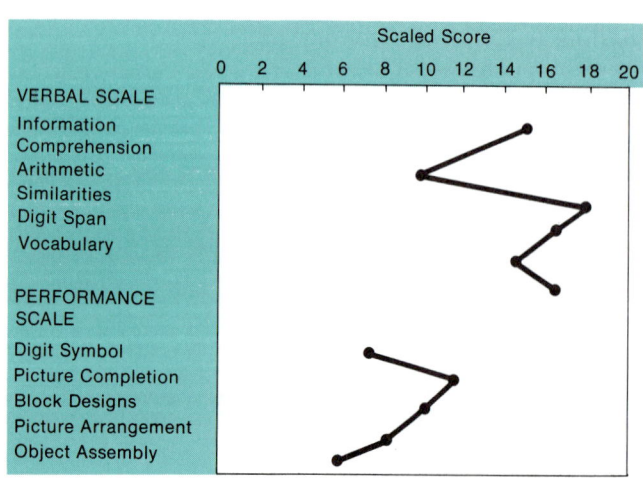

FIGURE 14–10   The score profile obtained by a particular individual on the Wechsler Intelligence Scale for Children. Note that this person tended to do better on the verbal than on the performance portions of the test.

Scales—which now include tests to measure the intelligence of preschoolers, children, and adults—are probably the most widely used individual tests of intelligence in the U.S. today.

Both the Stanford-Binet test and the Wechsler Scales are designed for administration to one person at a time. As a result, they were of little use when, at the start of World War I, the armed forces were suddenly faced with the task of screening several million men and women. What was needed, and at once, were group tests of intelligence—ones which could be given to large numbers of individuals at the same time. Fortunately, psychologists were equal to this challenge, and soon developed two appropriate measures, the famous *Army Alpha* (for persons who could read) and *Army Beta* (for those who could not read or did not speak English). The success of these tests did much to raise the prestige of psychologists in the public mind.

Following their war-time development, group tests of intelligence quickly spread to civilian use. Indeed, by 1921, a few short years after the first of these measures was devised, more than four million children had already been tested (Cronbach, 1975). In succeeding decades, the number of such tests grew rapidly, and they became progressively easier both to administer and to score. As a result, there was ultimately a period stretching from the 1950's through the mid-1960's when the motto in education seemed to be "Test, Test, and Test Again!" Not surprisingly, the widespread—and often careless—use of group measures of intelligence finally led to an explosion of public resentment and outrage. In fact, so intense did criticism of such tests become that several states passed laws banning their further use (Cronbach, 1975). Despite this fact, however, they continue in use, and it is estimated that about 10 million youngsters are tested each year. Because the controversies surrounding these measures provide a dramatic illustration of the complex issues which can arise when psychologists delve into practical problems affecting the lives of millions, they are worth considering in some detail.

Emotionally charged debates generally touch on a host of different issues, and recent controversies regarding the use of intelligence tests in public schools have been no exception to this rule. The most heated arguments, however, have generally centered on two basic questions: (1) Are such tests fair? and (2) How are the results to be employed? In order to fully understand the first of these issues, it is necessary for us to begin with a brief examination of two concepts related to all forms of psychological testing: **reliability** and **validity.**

The term *reliability* refers to the extent to which scores on a test are stable or dependable. A high degree of reliability means that individuals taking the test on different occasions are likely to obtain the same or at least highly similar scores each time, while a low degree of reliability indicates that their scores may differ greatly from one occasion to the next. Obviously, it is crucial that intelligence tests possess a high degree of reliability if they are to be put to practical use; if they do not, users face a situation similar to that which would occur if carpenters attempted to measure width or length by means of a rubber ruler—different values will be obtained each time measurement is attempted. Fortunately, most popular group tests of intelligence have been shown to possess a high degree of reliability and are not open to serious criticism on this score.

Validity involves a somewhat more complicated issue: do tests actually measure what they are designed to measure? In order to answer this question, it is usually necessary to relate test scores to some other aspect of behavior,

Group Tests of Intelligence

Testing and Public Policy: Questions Regarding Fairness and Use

often termed a *criterion*. For example, information regarding the validity of a test designed to measure sex appeal might be obtained by gathering information on individuals' actual degree of popularity (e.g., the number of dates they have). To the extent that their scores on the test are related to this criterion, the test might be viewed as providing a valid measure of sexual attractiveness. In the case of group tests of intelligence, the criterion for assessing validity has usually been some measure of school performance, such as grades. Thus, to the extent that scores on the test have been found to predict such performance, they have been viewed as providing valid measures of intelligence. Serious questions can be raised, of course, regarding the appropriateness of academic performance as a criterion for validating tests of intelligence. History is full of instances in which truly brilliant individuals who later enriched the store of human knowledge performed quite poorly in their early schooling. For example, Albert Einstein was only a fair-to-middling student at best throughout most of his formal education. In short, measures of academic performance may well overlook such important aspects of intelligence as creativity and flexibility. But even granting that grades and similar measures reflect at least certain aspects of intelligence, the question of whether test scores are closely related to even *these* imperfect criteria remains. It is with this important question that recent debates concerning the *fairness* of group tests of intelligence have generally been concerned.

Are Intelligence Tests Fair? The Role of Cultural Bias

We should begin the present discussion by noting that most tests of intelligence have been constructed with and designed for use among white, middle-class children. It is not surprising, then, that when employed with this group, they do seem to provide reasonably valid measures of intelligence. That is, studies indicate that scores on these tests are indeed related to various criteria of school performance (Cleary et al., 1975). Serious problems arise, however, when such tests are administered to children of markedly different backgrounds.

Typically, these tests often assume the possession of certain knowledge which, while common among, say, white suburbanites, may be totally lacking among poor ghetto dwellers. For example, asking a white child from a well-to-do family to identify an electric blanket may make good sense; posing the same question to a black child who has never seen such a device is totally inappropriate. The importance of this type of bias is suggested in a dramatic manner by several tests specifically constructed to afford blacks the same type of advantage usually provided to whites. Sample items from one such test are presented in Figure 14–11, and, generally, black children find them far easier to answer than do whites.

Even if the content of the items that are used is made appropriate, problems of language and communication still remain, and generally work against children from ethnic minorities. As noted previously in Chapter 8, black children reared in central city regions actually speak a language quite distinct from standard English, and for this reason may experience undue difficulty in answering test items. Needless to say, the problems faced by youngsters raised in Spanish-speaking homes may be even greater in this respect.

Largely in response to these potential sources of bias, psychologists have attempted to develop *culturally fair* tests of intelligence which seek to minimize the influence of special types of prior experience and various language skills on test performance (see Figure 14–12). Unfortunately, though, even tests of this type make certain assumptions about the children who take them. For example, they still generally assume that test-takers will be motivated to do their best—a tenuous notion in the case of children who see no possible con-

Instructions: Circle the letter which indicates the correct meaning of each word or phrase.

(1) the bump

    a. a condition caused by a forceful blow
    b. a suit
    c. a car
    d. a dance

(2) running a game

    a. writing a bad check
    b. looking at something
    c. directing a contest
    d. getting what one wants from another person or thing

(3) cop an attitude

    a. leave
    b. become angry
    c. sit down
    d. protect a neighborhood

Answers: (1)   d; (2)   d; (3)   b

FIGURE 14–11   Sample items from the "BITCH" Test (Black Intelligence Test of Cultural Homogeneity)—an intelligence test specifically designed to be culturally-biased in favor of blacks. Middle-class white children find such questions totally baffling, while black children can usually answer them with ease. The opposite situation often exists with respect to standard tests of intelligence, which tend to place black children at a sharp disadvantage. (Adapted from Williams, 1974.)

nection between the test and their lives. Further, they assume that the children involved have already acquired certain basic test-taking skills, such as leaving items which can't be answered blank in order to move on to others. Such attitudes and skills can be taken for granted in the case of middle-class children, but may actually be almost totally lacking among those from disadvantaged homes. In a sense, therefore, it may be almost impossible to devise an entirely culturally fair test of intelligence.

In the face of such problems, some critics have called for a shift from tests to other means of assessing intellectual ability. For example, it has been proposed that tests be replaced by teachers' subjective evaluations of each child's ability, or by grades and other measures of past performance. As noted by Cleary, Humphreys, Kendrick, and Wesman (1975), however, there are no

FIGURE 14–12 Sample items from one "culturally fair" test of intelligence (the IPAT Culture-Fair Test, designed by Raymond Cattell). Unfortunately, research has shown that even on such tests, scores are influenced, to a degree, by cultural bias. (Test credit: Copyright 1949, 1957 by the Institute for Personality and Ability Testing.)

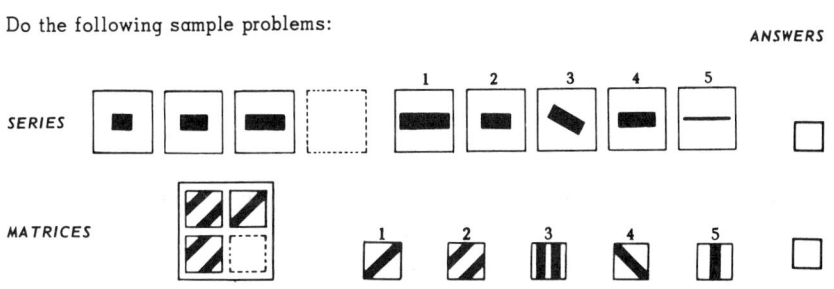

grounds for assuming that these alternatives will actually by any more fair to members of ethnic minorities than existing tests. Grades and teachers' evaluations are probably as subject to the sources of bias mentioned above—perhaps even more so—than objective tests of intelligence. A better course of action than the total elimination of testing itself, therefore, may be that of developing tests which *are* valid for use with children from minority groups.

How Should Test Scores Be Used? Pygmalion in the Classroom

A second major controversy concerning the use of intelligence tests in education has centered on the ultimate purposes for which test scores are employed. One of the most common has been that of grouping children of roughly equal intelligence together either within each class or across classes. For example, until quite recently, it was standard practice for elementary school teachers to divide the students in their classes into "slow," "average," and "fast" groups or tracks on the basis of their I.Q. scores. Similarly, one of the authors vividly recalls the days when he attended a junior high school in which the section number of an individual's seventh grade class provided a rough index of his or her I.Q.: those with the highest scores were placed in class 7-1, those with slightly lower performance in class 7-2, and so on through class 7-21, which consisted mainly of youngsters on whom the school system had already given up. Such grouping, of course, is usually carried out in accordance with the best intentions. It seems quite reasonable, after all, to assume that children will profit from working with others of approximately their own level of ability. Unfortunately, though, there are strong grounds for suspecting that such grouping can have truly mind-bending—or ego-deflating—effects on the children involved. For example, consider the impact upon a child's self-esteem and confidence when he or she learns of having been placed in the "slow" group or, as in the author's old school, a high-numbered class. Such youngsters may soon come to perceive themselves as hopeless failures, and thus be doomed to low achievement right from the start.

Perhaps even more disturbing is a growing body of evidence which suggests that teachers, too, may be influenced by the labels assigned to children on the basis of intelligence test scores. In particular, it now appears that in response to such labels, teachers may unconsciously alter their behavior toward their students in such a manner that the type of differences that they *expect* on the basis of contrasting I.Q. scores *are* actually produced (Rosenthal and Jacobsen, 1968)! For example, in one investigation concerned with such effects (Rubovits and Maehr, 1973), white middle-class teachers meeting interracial classes for the first time were told that some of the children of each race were "gifted," while others were "nongifted." In reality, these labels were assigned to the students of both races in a totally random manner. Careful observation of the teachers' behavior, however, revealed that their interactions with the children were strongly affected by these labels. Thus, they generally called upon those described as "gifted" more frequently than those described as "nongifted," and generally directed more attention to whites than to blacks (see Figure 14–13). Interestingly, their behavior in the latter respect did not stem from conscious racial prejudice on their part; rather, it seemed to arise from the fact that they "expected" whites to be better students than blacks. Such findings point to the conclusion that teacher expectations regarding childrens' performance can have a disturbingly self-fulfilling quality. Once a child has been labeled, on the basis of test performance or other characteristics, as "bright" or "dull," forces may be set in operation which tend to mold him to these specifications, whether they were initially accurate or not.

Given the existence of such subtle but potentially damaging effects, it is clear that test scores must be employed with far greater caution than has often

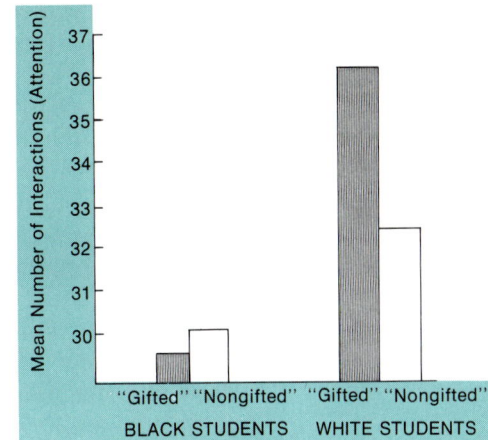

FIGURE 14–13   A teacher's expectations regarding the performance of various students can strongly affect his or her behavior toward these children. For example, in the study represented here, teachers directed more attention to children arbitrarily labeled as "gifted" than to children labeled as "nongifted," and also directed more attention to whites than to blacks. (Based on data from Rubovits and Maehr, 1973.)

been true in the past. Teachers must be made fully aware of the fact that scores on intelligence tests are far from infallible. Children, like adults, can have a "bad" day, so that low performance does not necessarily mean low ability. Moreover, large shifts in test performance can and do occur over the course of childhood. As a result, steps which serve to lock children into the belief that they are doomed to failure must be avoided at all cost. It is our view that provided such precautions are consistently taken and maintained, intelligence

 **PERSPECTIVE ON BEHAVIOR:** *Quotas Instead of Tests?*

A second major use of tests with which you are probably quite familiar is that of *selection*. Whenever schools or other institutions receive more applicants than they can handle, they must somehow determine whom to admit and whom to reject. One of the most common methods for accomplishing this task is that of requiring all applicants to take certain standardized tests of scholastic ability, and then admitting only those who score highest. These are not, strictly speaking, measures of intelligence. But performance on such tests is often so closely related to scores on measures of intellectual ability that the distinction between them is not very sharp.

Because members of various minority groups tend to score lower on such tests than whites, some individuals have called for the replacement of these methods of selection with a radically different system—one based on *quotas*. In such systems, a specific proportion of available openings are set aside for the members of racial or ethnic minorities, who are then admitted either with lower scores than whites or on the basis of other criteria altogether.

Supporters of such quota systems have argued that they are needed in order to make up for past injustice, and to help minority groups attain their rightful place in society. In contrast, opponents have noted that the result of such systems is to deny admission to many highly qualified candidates whose slots are filled by less qualified minority group members. Intense legal battles have been fought over the use of quota systems, and their future in higher education is at present unclear. Since this is a matter which might someday strongly affect your own life, you may wish to give it some thought right now. Do you think that quotas are indeed justified? Or do you feel that the best system is one in which applicants' racial or ethnic identity are not considered—only their qualifications?

tests and the scores they yield may in fact play a useful, continuing role in the educational process.

Intelligence: Genetic and Environmental Components

That people differ greatly in intelligence is readily apparent—we can usually observe such differences in their actions and words. The reasons for these variations, however, are not so easy to discern. At one time, it was fashionable for psychologists to attribute individual differences in intelligence to either genetic or environmental causes, and great intellectual battles were fought between the supporters of each position. Relatively quickly, though, it became obvious that both types of factors play a role, and that differences in mental ability probably spring from a complex interaction between the two. Since there is no longer any serious doubt on this score, we will begin by examining some of the evidence pointing to the influence of both heredity *and* environment on intellectual ability, and then, by way of conclusion, will consider the question of which—if either—plays the larger or more dominant role.

Evidence for the Influence of Heredity: Is It All in the Family?

If intelligence is strongly determined by genetic factors, it would be expected that the more closely related two individuals are, the more similar their intelligence should be. Convincing evidence for the existence of such a relationship has been provided by a large number of studies in which the mental abilities of individuals varying in degree of kinship have been compared (Erlenmeyer-Kimling and Jarvik, 1963). In general, the results of such investigations indicate that the more closely individuals are related, the more similar their I.Q.'s tend to be (see Figure 14–14). For example, the I.Q. scores of identical twins reared together correlate almost +.90, those of brothers and sisters about +.50, and those of unrelated individuals only about +.10 (Dobzhansky, 1973). These findings suggest that with respect to intelligence, at least, blood is indeed "thicker than water."

Additional and perhaps even more convincing evidence for the important role of heredity in intelligence comes from studies in which the I.Q.'s of children adopted early in life have been compared to those of both their biological and adoptive parents. It seems reasonable to suggest that if the children's I.Q.'s are more closely related to those of their biological parents— whom they have often never even seen—than to those of their adoptive parents, strong support for the important impact of heredity upon intelligence is provided. And in fact, a number of studies (e.g., Jencks, 1972) have indicated

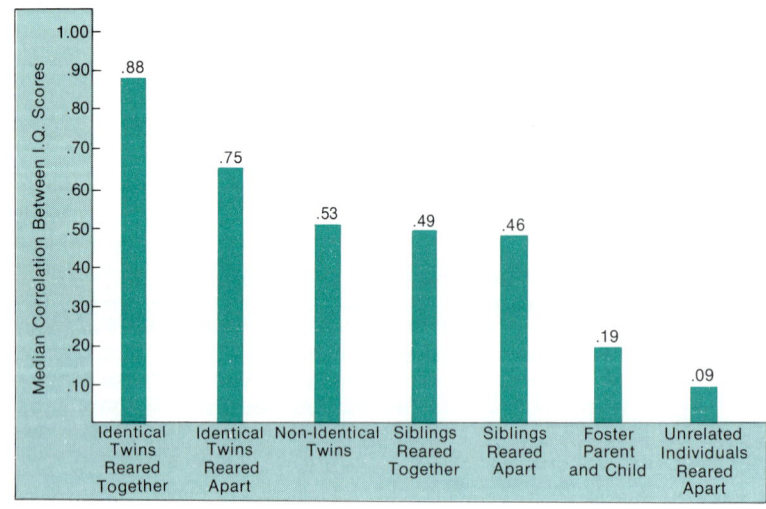

FIGURE 14–14 The more closely individuals are related, the more similar their I.Q.'s tend to be. This fact provides strong support for the influence of genetic factors upon intelligence. (Numbers at the top of each bar represent the median correlations obtained in 52 different studies. Based on data from Erlenmeyer-Kimling and Jarvik, 1963.)

that this is the case. While the correlation between the childrens' I.Q.'s and those of their real mothers is approximately +.40 to +.50, the corresponding correlation with their adoptive mothers is only about +.20. Since the children have usually spent several years with their adoptive families prior to the time at which their intelligence is assessed, these findings suggest that the genetic endowment they receive from their biological parents is more important in influencing this characteristic than environmental factors.

A third source of evidence for the influence of heredity upon intelligence comes from investigations involving identical twins who have been separated early in life. If intelligence is strongly determined by genetic factors, it would be expected that their I.Q.'s will remain highly similar even after rearing in markedly different homes. Generally, this has been found to be the case, and the I.Q.'s of such individuals correlate about +.80, despite many years of separation (Jensen, 1970). It should be noted, however, that adoption agencies generally make every possible attempt to place such twins in similar homes. As a result, the remarkable degree of similarity observed in their later intelligence may stem, at least in part, from this factor.

Evidence for the Influence of Environmental Factors: Enrichment, Deprivation, and Birth Order

By this point, you may have already noticed that several of our comments regarding identical twins provide indirect evidence for the effect of environmental factors upon intelligence. Specifically, when we noted that the I.Q.'s of such individuals, when reared together, correlate on the average about +.90, you may have wondered why this figure wasn't even higher. Identical twins, after all, have precisely the same genetic endowment, and should, therefore, have identical levels of intelligence. Moreover, the fact that the I.Q.'s of such persons correlate "only" about +.80 when they are reared apart (vs. +.90 when reared together) may have suggested to you that something other than heredity must play a role in determining intelligence. If you *did* notice these facts, take a bow: they are often interpreted as evidence for the role of environmental factors in intelligence (Willerman, 1977).

Additional and more direct evidence for the impact of environmental factors upon intellectual ability has been provided by a number of studies concerned with both environmental deprivation and enrichment. Since we have already examined several investigations concerned with deprivation in Chapter 8, we will not review them here. You may recall, however, that the results of these studies have suggested that both intelligence and later social development can be adversely affected by the absence of environmental stimulation at an early stage of life (Kagan and Klein, 1973). Fortunately, additional studies suggest that such negative effects can be avoided—and positive results produced—through various forms of environmental enrichment. For example, Israeli psychologists have succeeded in eliminating large differences in the I.Q.'s of settlers from European and Middle-Eastern countries by means of special educational programs (Smilansky, 1973). Similarly, there is convincing evidence that removing children from sterile, restricted orphanage environments and placing them in more favorable settings may greatly enhance their intellectual development (Skeels, 1965).

A third source of evidence for the influence of environmental factors upon intelligence has been provided by recent indications of a link between birth order and intellectual ability (e.g., Belmont and Marolla, 1973). Several studies have reported that the greater an individual's "seniority" within his or her family, the greater his or her I.Q. tends to be (i.e., first-borns tend to be brighter than second-borns, and so on). The differences are not very large—they are usually a matter of only a few I.Q. points—but they do seem to be real. Since there are no strong grounds for assuming that later-born children receive a poorer genetic endowment from their parents than their early-born brothers

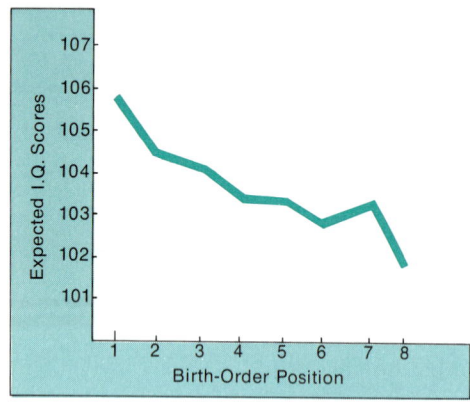

FIGURE 14–15   Recent experiments have uncovered a relationship between birth order and intelligence. The later an individual is born within his family, the lower his intelligence tends to be. Such differences are not usually large, however. In the curve shown here (which represents expected results for an eight-child family), the difference between the first- and last-born children would amount to only about 4 I.Q. points. (Adapted from Zajonc and Markus, 1975.)

and sisters, it seems reasonable to conclude that some environmental factor (or factors) must be playing a role in the occurrence of this relationship. One suggestion as to the nature of these factors has been provided by Robert Zajonc (1975). According to Zajonc, an individual's intellectual growth depends, to an important degree, upon the intellectual environment in which he develops, and this, in turn, is strongly affected by the intelligence of the persons around him. A first-born child benefits from the fact that for some period of time he is surrounded only by adults who have—compared to him—a high degree of intelligence. In contrast, a second-born child never enjoys such advantages; he is surrounded by two adults and one sibling who has usually attained only a small fraction of his or her adult intelligence. Thus, the average "quality" of the second-born's intellectual climate is somewhat lower. The situation is even worse for a third-born, who is exposed to two adults and two children, and as position in the birth order increases, such effects become more and more pronounced (see Figure 14–15). Regardless of whether Zajonc's intriguing explanation for the observed correlation between birth order and intelligence is correct, the existence of such a relationship provides additional evidence for the effects of environmental factors upon mental ability.

The Relative Contribution of Environment and Heredity: A Concluding Comment

By this point, you are probably quite convinced that intelligence is affected both by genetic and environmental factors. The fact that both play a role in shaping intellectual ability, however, in no way implies that their impact is necessarily equal. As a matter of fact, the weight of existing evidence points to the conclusion that genetic factors actually exert a somewhat stronger influence. Sophisticated statistical techniques developed in recent years now permit psychologists to estimate the **heritability** of a given characteristic—the extent to which variations in it among the members of any large population are determined by genetic factors; in the case of intelligence, the best existing estimates fall in the range of 75 to 80 per cent (Loehlin, Lindzey, and Spuhler, 1975). Thus, the fact that people vary greatly in intelligence seems to stem more from differences in their genetic endowment than from differences in the environments to which they are exposed. But please take heed: the fact that intelligence shows a high degree of heritability does *not* in any sense suggest that it is necessarily resistant to environmental change. In fact, quite the opposite may be true. To see why this is possible, consider the case of **phenylketonuria,** a serious disorder resulting in permanent damage to the brain and nervous system. Research has revealed that this condition is due to a genetic malfunction which prevents the body from utilizing certain types of protein. As a result, harmful waste products accumulate in the blood, and widespread damage is produced. Despite its genetic basis, though, phenylketonuria can be readily controlled through diet. In fact, if it is discovered in early infancy, and the appropriate alterations in diet are instituted, all harmful symptoms may be avoided. By the same token, the fact that intelligence shows a relatively high degree of heritability does not suggest that it is closed to change or modification. Indeed, as noted recently by Willerman (1977), it may actually be the case that increased understanding of the genetic basis of intelligence may eventually provide us with greater—not lesser—ability to alter this important characteristic in a desirable direction.

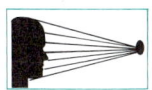

FOCUS ON RESEARCH: *Racial Differences in I.Q.: A Study in Black and White*

As a group, blacks tend to score lower than whites on most standard tests of intelligence. This is not to say, of course, that *all* blacks score lower than all whites. On the contrary, some blacks score higher than most whites, while some whites score lower than most blacks. When average scores are compared, however, blacks usually demonstrate somewhat lower performance than whites. Moreover, this difference has remained largely unchanged over the course of several decades (Loehlin, Lindzey, and Spuhler, 1975). Most psychologists have attempted to explain these persistent differences in terms of environmental factors, pointing to the poorer nutrition, lower income, and inferior schooling experienced by black persons in our society. In addition, many have noted the cultural bias built into most tests of intelligence, which tends to work against high performance by blacks. In the past few years, however, an alternative view which attributes racial differences in I.Q. primarily to genetic rather than environmental factors has been the subject of a great deal of attention. Although similar ideas have been expressed repeatedly in the past, the current controversy—which has been among the most bitter of the decade—stemmed primarily from an article written by Arthur Jensen (1969), a noted educational psychologist.

In this paper, which was entitled "How Much Can We Boost I.Q. and Scholastic Achievement?" Jensen called attention to three basic findings: (1) blacks generally score lower than whites on most tests of intelligence; (2) individual differences in intelligence are strongly determined by genetic factors; and (3) special educational programs designed to increase the I.Q.'s of disadvantaged groups have generally failed to produce these results. Largely on the basis of these findings, he then concluded that racial differences in I.Q. may stem primarily from genetic factors.

Jensen's statements to this effect were actually quite mild in nature, and he was careful to leave room for a substantial environmental component. But given the high level of racial tension existing in the U.S. at the time, they drew an immediate, angry response. As Sandra Scarr-Salapatek (1971) has so aptly remarked, Jensen's comments produced an effect similar to that which might result from shouting "Fire! . . . I think" in a crowded theater. Some of the criticisms directed toward Jensen's paper were quite legitimate and questioned his conclusions on rational, scientific grounds. Other reactions, however, were far less reasonable. For example, some critics suggested that because racial differences in intelligence are controversial, social scientists should be prevented from studying them, while others proposed that unpopular ideas such as Jensen's should be suppressed unless the evidence in their favor is truly overwhelming. Apparently, many of these attacks were based upon the false assumption that if racial differences in intelligence were found to be the result of genetic factors, they would not be readily subject to change. As we noted above, this is simply not the case; the fact that a particular characteristic is strongly affected by genetic factors does *not* necessarily imply that it will be difficult to alter. In any event, while some scholars preferred to merely criticize, others set to work gathering additional evidence relating to Jensen's suggestions. While the results of this research are by no means decisive, it has generally pointed to the conclusion that psychologists were probably right all along: racial differences in I.Q. stem primarily from environmental rather than genetic factors. Two lines of evidence seem especially convincing in this regard.

First, several studies have examined the effects of racial intermixture upon intelligence. If Jensen's suggestions regarding the genetic basis of racial differences in I.Q. are correct, it would be expected that individuals of mixed racial background will score higher on intelligence tests than those of purely African descent. In contrast to this prediction, however, recent investigations have reported little or no difference in the I.Q.'s of blacks of mixed and unmixed racial heritage (Loehlin, Vandenberg, and Osborne, 1973).

Second, several studies have compared the

I.Q.'s of children born to white mothers and black fathers with those born to black mothers and white fathers. If Jensen's proposals are correct, the performance of children in both groups should be the same, since both have one white and one black parent. If environmental factors are of primary importance, however, large differences might be observed. The results of such investigations have generally supported the latter view. For example, in one recent study (Willerman, Naylor, and Myrianthopoulos, 1974), the children born to white mothers and black fathers scored almost ten points higher on a test of intelligence than those born to black mothers and white fathers (see Figure 14–16). These findings seem to suggest that environ-

mental factors (for example, contrasting child-rearing practices by black and white mothers) are of greater importance in determining I.Q. than actual racial ancestry.

On the basis of this and other evidence, it seems reasonable to conclude that racial differences in I.Q. are probably largely determined by environmental rather than genetic factors. Regardless of the proportion of such differences stemming from one of these sources or the other, however, the practical task facing us as a society remains very much the same: ensuring, somehow, that membership in a particular group—black, chicano, or any other—does not in and of itself exert any adverse effects upon an individual's I.Q.

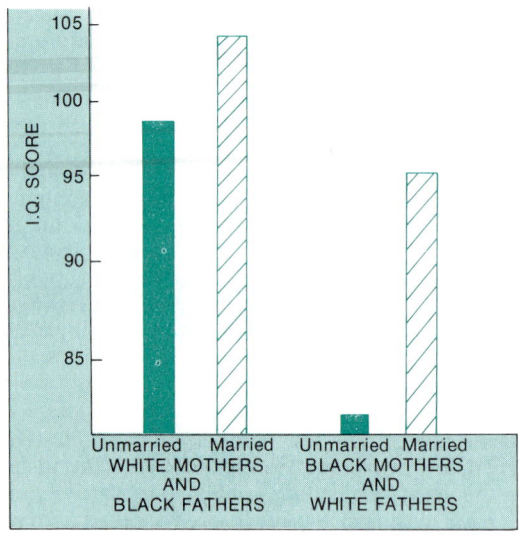

FIGURE 14–16 Children born to white mothers and black fathers tend to score higher on objective tests of intelligence than do those born to black mothers and white fathers. These findings suggest that racial differences in I.Q. stem mainly from environmental factors. (Based on data from Willerman, Naylor, and Myrianthopoulos, 1974.)

CONSUMER PSYCHOLOGY: WHERE BEHAVIOR AND ECONOMICS MEET

The role of consumer in the late 1970's is anything but simple. To appreciate this fact, it is only necessary to pay a visit to your friendly neighborhood supermarket, where you will immediately be surrounded by a bewildering array of products, all attractively packaged and displayed in a manner designed to both catch and hold your attention. Even with respect to a single item, the choice concerning brand, size, type, and price is often staggering (see Figure 14–17). As a result, it is quite easy to get "hung up" in front of seemingly endless rows of soap powder, cookies, or breakfast cereals. That the same situation exists with respect to more important economic decisions can be illustrated by an excursion to any new car showroom, where the choices of model, trim, color, and accessories may leave you with the uneasy feeling that this is, after all, too much of a good thing.

Given the vast array of products and services available today, it is obvious that as consumers, we often face a difficult task in choosing between them. Our choices in this respect, however, are of major economic importance, affecting individual businesses, whole industries, and ultimately the entire economy. For example, the decision on the part of many individuals to delay the purchase of a new car in 1974 and 1975 contributed greatly to the deepening of the serious recession which gripped the nation at that time.

FIGURE 14–17   The array of choices facing consumers today is often so vast as to be bewildering.

The behavior of consumers and their choices in the marketplace are clearly affected by such "rational" economic factors as product price, quality, and availability. But as sales personnel have known for many years, purchasing decisions are also strongly affected by factors only remotely connected to economic considerations—factors such as attitudes, values, motives, and expectations (Jacoby, 1975, 1976). Given their expert knowledge with respect to these topics, it seems reasonable to expect that psychologists might make a major contribution to the understanding of consumer behavior. Until quite recently, though, this was largely an unfulfilled promise, and the study of this important topic was left to other fields. The emergence, within the past ten years, of an active, growing specialty of **consumer psychology** has done much to alter this state of affairs, and today many intriguing aspects of consumer behavior have come under careful investigation. For example, among the topics recently studied by consumer psychologists have been *brand loyalty*—an attachment by consumers to one particular brand of product—and the *acceptance of innovations*—a willingness by consumers to try newly developed products or services. Perhaps the single topic receiving the greatest amount of attention, though, has been *advertising*, a technique for affecting consumer decisions with which all of us are only too familiar. Since advertising seems to play a major role in influencing consumer behavior, and because it has recently been the subject of several heated controversies, it will serve as the focus of our present discussion.

Advertising as the Businessman Sees It: What Works . . . and What Does Not?

According to a time-worn saying, "It pays to advertise," and anyone who watches television, listens to the radio, reads newspapers and magazines, or drives along major highways can hardly doubt that industry has accepted this view with great enthusiasm. In fact, it is almost impossible to avoid being literally flooded with commercial messages of every type urging us to buy or use various products or services.

Given the huge sums invested in such communications—more than $25 billion in 1973 alone (Rice, 1974)—it is not surprising that the companies paying for all these appeals wish to maximize their effects. As a result, large corporations have frequently supported research designed to discover which techniques will work—that is, persuade the consumer to buy the sponsor's products—and which will not. Although it is not possible to describe all of the findings of such investigations here, we can at least point to a few major factors which seem to increase the effectiveness of advertisements, and also to a few techniques which seemed, at first, to offer promising leads in this respect but ultimately proved to be essentially blind alleys.

Advertising and Attention: Looking as a First Step to Buying

Before an advertisement can influence consumers' purchasing decisions, it must first gain their attention; no one, after all, is influenced by ads he or she has not noticed or seen. In view of this fact, much research has been devoted to the investigation of factors affecting this preliminary step to persuasion. Although the results of such studies have often been quite complex, most suggest that certain physical attributes such as overall size, color, and style of type play an important role in this respect. That is, all other factors being equal, ads which are large, employ several different colors, and make use of large type will be noticed more frequently than those which are small, appear in black and white, and use relatively small type (Engel, Kollat, and Blackwell, 1973).

In addition to such straightforward physical characteristics, the attention-getting capacity of advertisements is also strongly affected by their actual content. It is for this reason that advertisers engage in an endless search for new and clever "gimmicks" which will draw consumers' attention to their appeals. So many of these techniques exist that an exhaustive list cannot be formulated. Some of the most common, however, include the following: (1) a "catchy" tune or jingle (how many times have you caught yourself humming or singing a commercial for some well-known product?); (2) unusual or unexpected visual images (do you remember the automobile commercial which showed a gleaming new model perched on the top of an incredibly high and narrow cliff?); (3) startlingly attractive or sexy models (this technique should be self-explanatory!); (4) humorous situations (some are so clever and amusing that they are almost a pleasure to watch—at first), (5) a clever slogan (a few of these become so popular that they enter our daily speech; will you ever forget "I can't believe I ate the w–h–o–l–e thing"?). Some examples of highly attention-getting ads which make use of these techniques, and with which you are probably already quite familiar, are shown below (Figure 14–18).

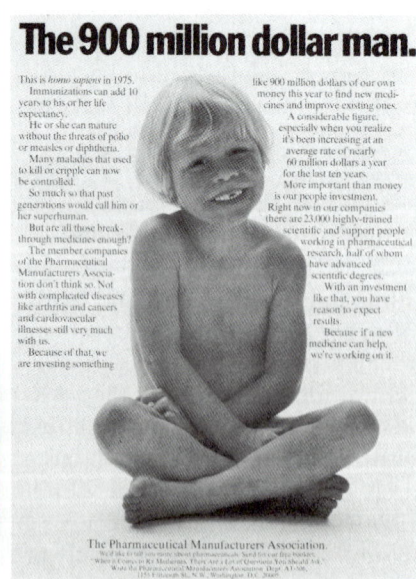

FIGURE 14–18 Advertisers use every sophisticated technique at their disposal to both catch and hold our attention. (Photo credits: left, Bob West, Photo Trends; right, The Pharmaceutical Manufacturers Association.)

Once an advertisement has succeeded in engaging consumers' attention, it must somehow accomplish a second and perhaps more important task—changing their attitudes toward the product being promoted in a favorable direction. In one sense, then, commercials may be viewed merely as a special form of persuasive communication (see Chapter 12). Indeed, many of the factors which influence the success of such appeals (the credibility of the source, explicitness of the recommendations made, the arousal of fear or anxiety) will also affect the impact of advertisements (Winters, 1974). Since several of these factors have already been examined in Chapter 12, we will focus here on two which have not previously been considered—**repetition** and **subliminal presentation.**

Advertising and Attitudes: Commercials as Persuasive Appeals

Repetition: If at First You Don't Succeed

Anyone who watches even a few hours of television each week is probably painfully aware of the faith placed by advertisers in the benefits of repetition. Commercials are presented over and over again until, in many cases, they become more familiar than the shows they interrupt. The basis for such tactics, of course, is the belief that repetition will somehow increase the impact of these messages upon consumers, and so facilitate sales of the products being promoted. But is this actually the case? Does the repeated presentation of an advertisement—or any other stimulus—lead to more favorable reactions toward it? A growing number of experiments suggest that this is so (Stang, 1975; Zajonc et al., 1972). In brief, the results of these studies indicate that all other factors being equal, the greater the number of times individuals are exposed to various stimuli, the more positive are their reactions to them. For example, in several early investigations concerned with this topic, Zajonc (1968) systematically varied the frequency with which subjects viewed various stimuli such as Chinese symbols, specially constructed "Turkish" words (e.g., zabulon, civadra, afworbu), and even photos of other persons. In each case, he found that subjects' reactions to these stimuli became more positive as the frequency of exposure increased (see Figure 14–19). Additional studies have extended these findings to many other stimuli, including art reproductions, simple drawings, music, and geometric figures (Heingartner and Hall, 1974; Smith and Dorfman, 1975). In all cases, increasing the frequency of exposure led to increased liking for the stimuli presented.

Findings such as these suggest that the frequent repetition of advertise-

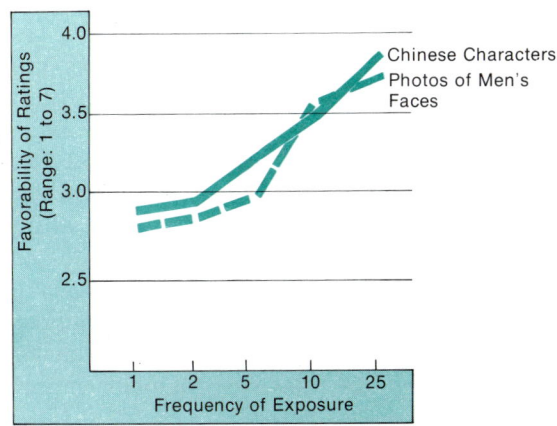

FIGURE 14–19 **The effects of repeated exposure upon liking for various stimuli. The more frequently a given stimulus is presented (at least up to a point), the more it tends to be liked. Results for only two types of stimuli—Chinese script and photos of men's faces—are presented, but similar findings have been reported with many other stimuli as well. (Based on data from Zajonc, 1968.)**

ments may, in fact, be a useful strategy. However, anyone who has watched the same commercial over and over again with mounting irritation is aware of the possibility that beyond some point, repetition may begin to produce negative rather than positive reactions. Evidence for this suggestion too, has been obtained, and it appears that "satiation" and decreased liking may actually result when specific stimuli are presented over and over again (several hundred or more exposures) (Zajonc et al., 1972). In view of these findings, the best strategy for advertisers may well be that of presenting their commercials a relatively small number of times, and then withdrawing them from public view. In this manner, they can take advantage of the increased liking generated by the first few exposures of their message, but avoid the growing annoyance or resentment which may result with further repetition. The fact that various commercials *are* often shown for a period of a few weeks or months, then withdrawn, and later reintroduced suggests that advertisers are well aware of the possible negative effects which can result from the continuous repetition of specific appeals.

Subliminal Perception: Hidden Persuaders?

Most forms of advertising are easily recognized as such. Television and radio commercials, junk mail, and newspapers or magazine ads can all be quickly identified by consumers as attempts to influence their buying habits. As a result, they can easily be discounted or defended against in numerous ways. What would happen, however, if consumers were exposed to such appeals in the absence of any awareness that they were the targets of persuasion? Would their ability to resist be reduced? The findings of several demonstrations conducted during the late 1950's seemed to suggest that this might be the case.

In these demonstrations—which made use of a process known as **subliminal perception**—audiences watching movies were exposed to commercial messages flashed on the screens in front of them. The ads were exposed for so short a period (1/3,000th of a second), that recipients were not aware of their presence. Yet, despite this fact, early reports indicated that sales of the products being promoted increased substantially. For example, in one study, the slogans "Drink Coca-Cola" and "Eat popcorn" increased the sales of these products by 18 per cent and 50 per cent respectively. Findings such as these pointed to the frightening conclusion that consumers seated before their television sets or visiting local movie houses would soon be totally at the mercy of clever advertisements they could not even perceive!

Fortunately, the spector of helpless consumers driven to do the bidding of ruthless advertising executives was quickly dispelled by additional research. These more carefully conducted studies revealed that the effects of such procedures were far less impressive than had initially been proposed. For example in one experiment, Byrne (1959) reported that exposure to the word "beef" during the viewing of a film did not increase college students' tendency to choose roast beef sandwiches in preference to other foods for their lunch. The only effect of such procedures was to slightly raise their overall reported level of hunger. In short, although the subliminal messages that were delivered had a mild influence upon subjects' feelings, they were not strong enough to influence their actual behavior in choosing what to eat. Since advertising of this type seems quite ineffective in altering even such trivial patterns of behavior, it appears doubtful that it can exert any appreciable influence over purchasing decisions of major importance.

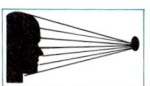

FOCUS
ON
RESEARCH: *The Eyes Don't Lie . . . Or Do They?*

Because of the staggering expense involved in launching modern advertising campaigns, businessmen usually wish to know in advance whether the messages they plan to use will be received in a favorable or unfavorable manner by consumers. In order to find out, they often test proposed ads on small groups of individuals, asking them to reveal their reactions to each. Unfortunately, subjects do not always report their true feelings in such situations. In fact, they often show a strong tendency to report only positive reactions in order to "please" the interviewer.

In view of such difficulties, other techniques for measuring consumers' reactions to advertising have been proposed. One such method, which received widespread attention in the mid-1960's, was suggested by Eckhard Hess (1965). In several studies, Hess obtained evidence pointing to the conclusion that the pupils of an individual's eyes tent to dilate while he or she is looking at something pleasant, and that they tend to contract while he or she is examining stimuli found to be unpleasant. For example, subjects in Hess' studies showed pupil dilations while looking at nudes and pupil contractions while examining scenes of human suffering (see Figure 14–20). On the basis of these findings, Hess concluded that it might be possible to determine consumers' true reactions to various advertisements simply by measuring the changes in the size of their pupils.

Unfortunately, additional research soon revealed that this technique was not as effective as initially seemed to be the case (Janisse and Peavler, 1974). First, it was found that individuals often demonstrated large pupillary dilations while examining stimuli they found to be quite distasteful. Such evidence suggested that pupil dilations may actually be associated with *attention* or *interest* rather than simply with the occurrence of positive feelings. Second, it soon became apparent that such dilations could be produced by mental effort, as well as by affective (i.e., emotional) reactions. Finally, many investigators had great difficulty in replicating Hess' initial finding that exposure to unattractive stimuli leads to pupillary contraction. In the face of such negative evidence, advertisers reluctantly surrendered the notion that studying people's eyes would soon permit them to develop perfect or near-perfect ads.

In response to such criticism, Hess (1975) has recently developed more elaborate procedures for assessing the effectiveness of commercials. In what he describes as the *total evaluation technique* (TET for short), subjects are shown ads for various products on several different occasions. During each presentation, their galvanic skin response (an index of emotional arousal) and their pupillary reactions are recorded. In addition, they are asked to indicate their degree of liking or disliking for the advertising materials by moving a lever either toward or away from themselves, respectively. Hess has argued that together, the pattern of reactions obtained on these different measures reveals much about subjects' responses to the ads—much more than their simple verbal statements. For example, if small pupil contractions are accompanied by large increases in galvanic skin response, strong negative reactions may be indicated. Similarly, if large expansions in pupil size are accompanied only by small changes in galvanic skin response, interest, but no strong feeling of liking, is suggested. While such techniques seem promising, they have not as yet been subjected to rigorous study or put to practical use. Thus, at present, the most reasonable conclusion regarding pupil size and advertising may be as follows: while the eyes may indeed serve as "windows on the soul," the openings they provide seem to be considerably more clouded than was at first proposed.

FIGURE 14–20 Experiments conducted by Hess (1965) indicate that pupil size decreases when individuals look at stimuli they find unpleasant (A) but increases when they look at stimuli they find pleasant (B). Unfortunately, other investigators have not always replicated these intriguing results. (Courtesy of Dr. Eckhard Hess.)

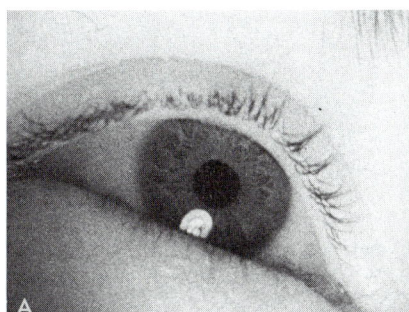
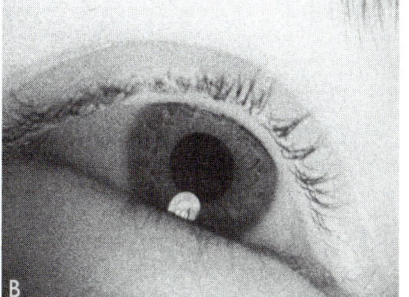

Advertising as the Consumer Advocate Sees It: What is Fair and What is Not

Few people today believe all they see, read, or hear in advertisements. Having been "burned" many times by misleading or exaggerated claims, most consumers have a healthy degree of skepticism with respect to information contained in such materials (see Figure 14–21). Indeed, such skepticism may begin to develop when, as children, they pull their first prize out of a box of breakfast cereal only to discover that it is far less appealing than package illustrations or TV commercials have led them to expect.

Unfortunately, even such skepticism is not always enough to protect consumers from unfair advertising and the questionable business practices which frequently accompany it. Perhaps some indication of the scope of the problem can be gained from the following recent statements made by businessmen during interviews or in industry journals:

"I don't try to book the very best movie I can," says one theater owner . . . "You see, there's a helluva profit in a 40-cent Coca Cola and 65-cent box of popcorn. I want pictures that tread the fine line between being a "draw" and being boring enough so that the people will get restless and go to the refreshment counter" (Chicago Tribune).

For many months the Citizens' Band Radio industry has been enjoying a boom. . . . Now, as the industry is increasing production to meet the back orders, it's imperative that the dealer keep the consumer thinking that radios are still hard to come by. Make the user think there's a shortage and he'll buy what you want to sell—and at your price. . . (The Communicator).

In the face of such attitudes, there is little doubt that consumers need all the help they can get. It is for this reason that the Federal Trade Commission and other government agenices have adopted regulations designed to eliminate deceptive advertising. As a result of such regulations and recent court decisions, advertisers have found it necessary to withdraw ads which were judged to be misleading or unfair to consumers. For example, in one recent case, the manufacturer of a famous mouthwash was ordered to stop claiming that it's product cures or prevents sore throats and colds by "killing germs on contact by millions." Further, it was directed to include corrective statements to this effect in all its ads during the next two years (Consumer Reports, March, 1975).

Although the elimination of deceptive advertising practices is certainly beneficial, consumer advocates have also called for additional positive steps designed to protect the rights and interests of individuals in the marketplace.

THE WIZARD OF ID — By Parker

FIGURE 14–21 Most individuals in our society have learned—often through bitter experience—to doubt the accuracy of information contained in advertisements. (The Wizard of Id by permission of Johnny Hart and Field Enterprises, Inc.)

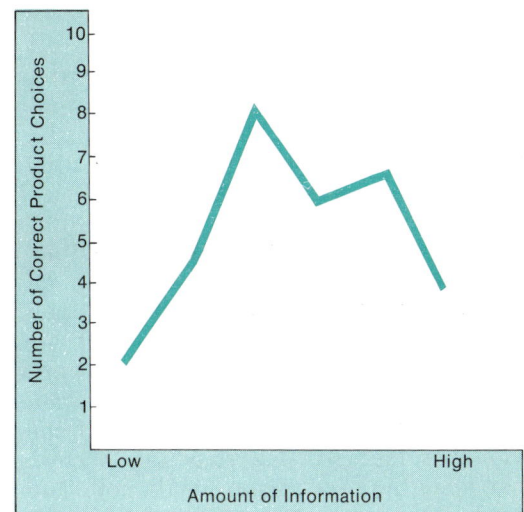

FIGURE 14-22   Recent evidence suggests that up to a point, increasing information about various products helps consumers make accurate choices among them. Beyond some level, however, added information seems to produce confusion, and may actually interfere with the ability to choose effectively. (Based on data from Jacoby, Speller, and Kohn, 1974.)

Among the more controversial of these has been the proposal that advertisements and product labels contain all the information needed by consumers to make intelligent purchase decisions—an ideal state of affairs generally known as **full and open disclosure.**

Full and Open Disclosure: How Much Information is Enough?

In general, the position of consumer groups with respect to product information has been "the more the better." Certainly, the motives behind this point of view are commendable and beyond reproach. But calls for full disclosure often overlook an important psychological fact: the capacity of human beings to perceive, process and store information has definite limits (see Chapter 6). As a result, it is quite possible that beyond some point, additional information regarding various products might prove to be too much of a good thing. Evidence pointing to such effects has been obtained in several recent experiments by Jacoby and his colleagues (Jacoby, Speller, and Kohn, 1974; Jacoby, Speller, and Berning, 1974).

In these investigations, consumers have been provided with varying amounts of information about each of several brands of common household products (e.g., laundry detergent, instant rice) and have then been asked to choose between them. Results indicate that up to a point, subjects' ability to make accurate choices—to select the brand which most closely matches their previously described notion of the "ideal" product—increases with the amount of information provided. Beyond some level, however, subjects' ability to choose in an accurate manner actually begins to decline (see Figure 14-22). These findings suggest that from the point of view of consumers, more information may *not* always be better. In fact, when it represents an "overload" of their information-processing capacity, it may actually be worse. The crucial task for consumer advocates, then, may not simply be that of increasing the amount of information presented in advertisements and package labels. Rather, it may be that of determining which types of information are most useful to consumers and then requiring that *these* be included (Jacoby, Szybillo, and Busato-Schach, 1976).

Summary

Psychologists have always attempted to apply their skills and knowledge to the solution of practical problems. As a result, they have made many important contributions to such fields as business and education. Their work in such areas, however, has often involved them in heated and long-lasting controversies.

Industrial and organizational psychologists have been primarily concerned with the solution of problems relating to work and work settings. One topic to which they have directed a great deal of attention is the development of effective methods for selecting personnel— choosing the best person for the job. Their efforts in this respect have often been quite successful, but recent attempts to eliminate all traces of racial, ethnic, and sexual discrimination have raised additional, complex problems in this area. Since performance on a job is strongly affected by **work motivation** and **job satisfaction,** these topics, too, have been the subject of much attention. Work motivation appears to be influenced not only by the rewards individuals attain from their jobs but also by the extent to which they enjoy work activities for their own sake. Job satisfaction is also affected by several different factors, but perhaps the most important is an individual's perception that he or she is being treated fairly in relation to others.

Over the years, psychologists have made many contributions to the field of education. Perhaps the most important has been the development of objective tests of intelligence. Unfortunately, such tests often suffer from **cultural bias,** which renders them inappropriate for use with the members of ethnic or racial minorities. Moreover, the scores attained on such tests by students have sometimes been misused. For example, they have frequently been employed to assign children to classes or groups in which all individuals show roughly equal intelligence. This procedure is not objectionable in and of itself, but it can produce harmful results if children learn that they have been labeled as "slow" or "dull." Existing evidence suggests that intelligence is determined both by genetic and environmental factors, with heredity playing the more important role. The fact that intelligence is strongly affected by genetic factors, however, in no way implies that it will necessarily be difficult to modify or change.

The purchasing decisions of individual consumers ultimately exert important effects upon the entire nation's economy. Thus, it is not surprising that an increasing number of psychologists recently turned their attention to the study of consumer behavior and the factors which affect it. Such **consumer psychologists** have investigated a number of different topics, and one which has been the subject of a great deal of attention is **advertising.** Many investigations—often supported by large corporations—have been conducted to determine which type of advertisements will be most likely to influence consumers. These studies have demonstrated that such factors as attention-getting properties, clever "gimmicks" of several types, and sheer repetition may all be important in this regard. Other investigations— often conducted with the support of government agencies or consumer groups—have examined the question of "full and open disclosure"—how much information must be presented in ads and product labels for consumers to make accurate product choices. The results of such research suggest that too much information may be as bad as too little, and that consumers profit more from certain types of information than from others.

Suggested Readings

Aaker, D. A., and Day, G. S.: *Consumerism: Search for the Consumer Interest.* New York: The Free Press, 1974.
    A collection of articles concerned with many of the problems faced by consumers today. Among the topics covered are deceptive advertising, consumer information, and warranties.
Dunnette, M. D.: *Work and Non-Work in the Year 2001.* Monterey, California: Brooke Cole, 1973.
    A thoughtfully chosen collection of readings dealing with changes in work, the work setting, and leisure-time activities which seem likely to take place between now and the turn of the 21st century.

Loehlin, J. C., Lindzey, G., and Spuhler, J. F.: *Race Differences in Intelligence.* San Francisco: W. H. Freeman, 1975.
    A comprehensive and clearly written discussion of evidence regarding racial differences in I.Q. One of the most thorough reviews of research on this topic currently available.
Safilios-Rothchild, C.: *Women and Social Policy.* Englewood Cliffs, N.J.: Prentice-Hall, 1974.
    A thought-provoking discussion of the social changes which may come about as a result of alterations in present sex roles for both men and women.

Changes with respect to marriage, the family, education, the economy, and child-care policy, among
others, are discussed.

Willerman, L.: *The Psychology of Individual and Group
Differences.* San Francisco: W. H. Freeman, 1977.
    The chapters on intelligence testing and the envi-
ronmental and genetic determinants of intelligence
provide an excellent introduction to recent work in
these areas.

Zajonc, R. B.: Birth order and intelligence. *Psychology
Today,* 1975, *8,* 87–43.
    A discussion of the effects of family size and birth
order upon intelligence.

Some journals which regularly publish articles on psychol-
ogy in today's society:
Journal of Applied Psychology
Journal of Applied Social Psychology
Journal of Consumer Research
Journal of Educational Psychology
Journal of Marketing Research
Journal of Social Issues
*Organizational Behavior and Human Perform-
ance*

15 Environmental Psychology: Behavior in the Physical World

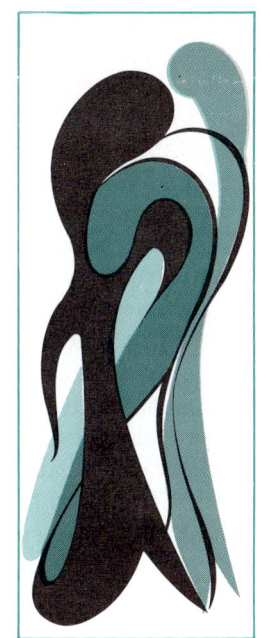

A chapter with environmental psychology as its topic is a fitting conclusion to a psychology textbook. What better way to illustrate the principles of psychology than by applying them directly to the environment around us? As we try to assess the impact of the physical world upon our daily behavior, we shall often refer back to basic findings discussed in earlier chapters.

Environmental psychology is defined as the study of man in his physical setting. It is ironic that psychologists, who have long stressed the role of the stimulus in controlling behavior, have until quite recently neglected the influence of those physical stimuli that constitute our immediate environment. But, as we shall see, this omission is quickly being rectified. Environmental psychology is one of the newest areas in psychology, and developments are occurring at a rapid pace. While it would be premature to state the direction environmental psychology may take in the future, at the moment two important components can be identified. The dominant approach appears to be derived largely from social psychology, and many prominent environmental psychologists have learned their trade by studying human interactions. A second approach is derived from engineering psychology. Here psychologists try to improve the working relationships between man and environment, just as engineering psychologists try to improve man-machine relationships. Finally, much of the work in environmental psychology has not been accomplished by psychologists but instead by a mixed bag of geographers, urban planners, architects, anthropologists, and sociologists. This interdisciplinary vigor may prove to be the greatest asset of the field.

The social psychological approach is exemplified in that portion of environmental psychology dealing with the interactions of small groups. The

535

science of **proxemics** concerns our management of the physical space immediately surrounding us, sometimes called our **personal-space bubble.** We shall examine the size and shape of this bubble, distances between bubbles, cultural factors in personal space, and ways in which each of us defends his or her own bubble from the threat of invasion.

Both social and engineering psychological approaches are represented in the study of environmental **stressors.** Our performance and ability to process information are altered by unusual environmental conditions, including loud noise, high temperature, crowding, and air pollution. Furthermore, our social interactions also can be affected by these conditions, but not always in ways we would predict on the basis of intuition or common sense.

Finally, we shall examine the city as an environment for man. How do we form a mental image of the city? What spatial features become key markers in cognitive maps of the city? How does the kind of building we live in determine behavior? In 1968, the Federal Housing Act contained guidelines forbidding location of families with children in high-rise apartments unless no other alternatives were available; why is it dangerous for children to inhabit high-rise housing projects? Architectural psychology is starting to answer such questions about construction, not only of large housing projects but also of individual rooms. What are the psychological costs and benefits of life in a big city? There is a definite psychological mechanism used by the urbanite to adapt to the stress of living in his artificially constructed environment. Environmental psychology offers suggestions and methods for improving the quality of urban life.

PROXEMICS: THE SCIENCE OF GETTING CLOSE

It is morning. You sleepily crawl out of bed, take a shower to wake yourself, and start to get dressed. But today you have something new to wear: a large, transparent, plastic dome appropriately pierced so that your arms and legs can project a comfortable distance. At the touch of a hidden switch, a magnetic force field closes a seam, keeping the dome tightly about you. Now fully dressed, you waddle out to face the world securely encased in your plastic bubble. Sounds silly, doesn't it? Who needs to wear a plastic dome, especially if it's not raining? But each and every day you carry about a *psychological* bubble designed to protect you from assorted encroachments by the people around you.

How do psychologists know that such a mysterious bubble surrounds us all? It is, after all, invisible, and cannot be touched, or heard, or smelled. How big is this bubble? What is the bubble's shape? Can anyone else fit in my bubble with me? Is my bubble flexible like a balloon or rigid like a brick wall? Questions like these can be answered by social scientists engaged in the study of personal space, or **proxemics,** a term coined by the anthropologist Edward Hall (1966) to define investigations of the use of physical space by man and animal. The concept of a portable territory or bubble that we carry with us has generated many insights into behavior which we will discuss in the following pages.

Your Own Private Bubble

Territoriality: This Land is Mine

The concept of a personal-space bubble has been derived, in part, from the ethological concept of **territoriality** (ethology is discussed in Appendix B). Territoriality is defined as the behavior used by an individual to stake out and defend a specific area against members of its own species (Hall, 1966). For example, we have all seen dogs urinating to mark their territory with their own scent. This marking behavior occurs more frequently in male dogs and can be distinguished from ordinary urination by watching the dog's posture.

When marking territory, a dog will raise its rear leg high to aim at a particular spot on its scent post. The scent post might be a fire hydrant or a rural mailbox.

There are two major ways in which a limited amount of real estate can be apportioned among animals. First, as is the case with birds returning from winter vacation, early arrivals select the areas they want, and later arrivals make do with what remains. Second, as is the case with domestic fowls, an individual's space may depend upon his status in a dominance hierarchy. It is important to realize that such spatial organization depends more upon psychological factors than upon the density of a local population. This psychological aspect of spatial organization has been demonstrated in a rather gruesome zoological study conducted by Hensley and Cope (1951). They tried to remove birds from a particular location by the simple expedient of shooting them. Nevertheless, as each feathered territorial pair bit the dust, the territories were found to be quickly reoccupied. Hence, a large population with no property rights must have been lurking in the bushes. This implies that despite a rising density with many nonterritorial birds present, the territory size did not shrink to accommodate this surplus population. Therefore, psychological factors were more important determinants of the size of a territory than was population size.

The existence of territoriality in animals should not necessarily lead us to conclude that man also is territorial in the same zoological sense as, say, certain birds, even though man does show a certain possessiveness toward parcels of real estate. Zoologist Peter Klopfer (1972) has noted that while specific property rights may have a high survival value in encouraging breeding and feeding in animals, man has no zoological need for such territories, since he is a highly mobile animal. In this regard, man is similar to marine birds and grazing animals, and a specific territory would be of as much use to him as to an antelope.

On the other hand, psychologist Robert Sommer (1971) believes that man does exhibit territoriality of the second type—that is, dependent upon status. Sommer proposes that territoriality has the function of reducing aggression (see Chapter 13) since it allows individuals to know their place and thus avoid disputes. In our society the wealthy, high-status person has both greater spatial mobility and also more space (for example, a larger home) than the person from a lower socioeconomic class.

Unfortunately, the examples used by Sommer ignore a crucial distinction between *territoriality* and *jurisdiction* (Roos, 1968). In observing life on a crowded naval warship, Roos realized that only some human spatial behavior could be explained by territoriality and personal space. Jurisdiction refers to the *temporary defense of a space with no claim of ownership*, as is required for territoriality. Man can also exhibit jurisdiction over *things*, thereby presenting the animal ethologist with a new phenomenon. Consider a quartermaster who has jurisdiction over supplies which he may or may not dispense. He can, and often will, display defensive behavior regarding these supplies, and while such behavior may at first appear similar to that of a dog barking when his territory is invaded, this similarity may exist only on the surface. Roos properly points out that we must be careful in extending ethological analogies to human behavior, and it is clear that at least in this instance, his argument is compelling. Any analogy will break down if pushed far enough, and the social scientist must be ever alert for such a fracture. It appears that a concept of fixed territoriality is of greatest value for the study of animal, rather than human, behavior, although future research may suggest that territoriality also serves a function for humans (Edney, 1974, 1976). Many people have a favorite chair that they regard as their own territory (for example, Archie Bunker in the television series "All In The Family"). But until more research on human territoriality is carried out, this concept has less value than the concept of a personal-space bubble, to which we now turn. While territory is stationary and visible, personal space is portable and defined by invisible boundaries.

Personal Space

How can social scientists measure the various properties of the bubble surrounding each of us? As long as our bubble is intact, we feel relatively secure in the privacy it affords. In the words of an unknown poet:

> It's so much fun
> In a bubble for one;
> Would you feel secure
> If your bubble held more?

It is ironic that the privacy afforded by our bubble is most often studied by encroachments which violate that privacy.

A representative attempt at measuring the dimensions of body bubbles was conducted by a psychiatrist, August Kinzel (1970), who wished to compare the bubbles of violent prisoners with those of nonviolent prisoners. Violence was defined as prior infliction of physical injury upon another person. The procedure was simple. The prisoner stood in the center of a bare 20 by 20 foot room. The experimenter then approached the prisoner until the prisoner said "Stop" to indicate that the experimenter was "too close." The experimenter then retreated and approached again from a different angle.

The results of this experiment are illustrated in Figure 15–1. It is quite clear that violent prisoners have considerably larger bubbles than do nonviolent prisoners. There is also an interesting difference in the shape of the bubbles. Nonviolent prisoners exhibited roughly the same size areas in front and back of them. However, violent prisoners had larger zones behind than in front of them. Whether or not we agree with Kinzel's interpretation that the violent prisoners had high levels of homosexual anxiety, the moral of this story is clear: Don't stand too close to a "hot-headed" person lest your invasion of his personal-space bubble trigger violence.

As Kinzel's study shows, the size of a person's bubble is not a fixed characteristic, but can vary among individuals. One excellent example is the personal-space bubble of a charismatic public figure. When John F. Kennedy entered a room, according to Theodore White in *The Making of the President*

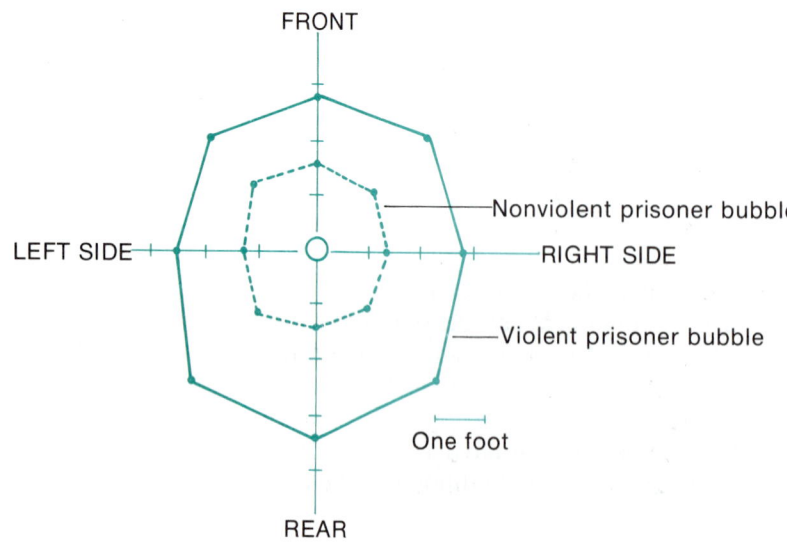

FIGURE 15–1 Looking down on average personal-space bubbles for violent prisoners (solid line) and nonviolent prisoners (dashed line). Eight different angular approaches were used to make the bubbles. Violent prisoners have larger bubbles than nonviolent prisoners, especially in the area behind the back. (Adapted from Kinzel, 1970.)

1960, he seemed to project an impassable bubble with a 30-foot radius. That is, before people would approach him, Kennedy would first have to send an emissary to physically conduct someone to his side. No one would pass the invisible barrier uninvited.

A recent review of research on personal space (Evans and Howard, 1973) noted deficiences in the methods used to collect data. They criticized the dependent variables as lacking in objectivity—e.g., a subjective statement that the experimenter was "too close," as in Kinzel's study. They recommended that several dependent measures be incorporated into an experiment in order to increase reliability. Mechanical or computer-aided scoring of eye movements, body tremors, and physiological correlates of behavior may offer more objective measures of personal space. Although we are sure that personal-space bubbles exist, we cannot yet tell the whole story. While anthropologists and sociologists have given us a good start, psychologists can try to apply more objective measures of behavior to expand our understanding of personal space.

Despite the relative paucity of the data base, some theoretical formulations concerning the function of a personal-space bubble have been advanced. Sommer (1971) and Evans and Howard (1973) have argued that the primary functions of personal space are to reduce stress and to control aggression among members of the same species. This explanation is similar to that offered by ethologists and anthropologists for the role of territoriality. An intriguing view offered by Pederson and Shears (1973) states that the personal-space bubble is used to communicate information about a person's feelings and attitudes. Nonverbal communication and the use of a person's possessions are also seen as part of this general system.

Hall (1966) has proposed that there are four *distance* zones for Americans. These zones are *intimate distance, personal distance, social-consultive distance,* and *public distance.* Each distance can be further divided into a close and a far phase.

Distances Between Bubbles

The close phase of intimate distance (less than six inches apart) is appropriate for sexual intercourse, wrestling, and protectively holding children and infants. Physical contact is great. When touching, you can feel not only the movements of the muscle and skin but also the radiant heat of your partner's body. One perceives great visual detail in combination with experiencing a strong sensation of being cross-eyed. Vocalizations are largely limited to involuntary groans and grunts and do not communicate a great deal of information.

Intimate Distance

The far phase of intimate distance, roughly six to eighteen inches, has considerably less kinesthetic contact than the close phase, but the hands can still easily make physical contact. Olfactory stimuli are strong. Vocalizations are whispered. Heat radiation may still be detected. Although college students are becoming more relaxed about using the far phase of intimate distance in public, their parents often regard public use of intimate distance as improper. When strangers are forced into intimate proximity, as in crowded subways or buses, they usually react by becoming nearly immobile and assuming rigid postures, with eyes focused upon infinity, carefully avoiding eye contact. It is considered taboo to enjoy such body contact with strangers, and references to such enjoyment may be met with hostility.

This distance corresponds to the personal-space bubble previously discussed. In the close phase (1½ feet to 2½ feet), kinesthetic contact is just barely possible. Visual distortion is virtually absent, and surface textures are easily discerned. In the far phase (2½ to 4 feet), the head is viewed with no

Personal Distance

visual distortion or exaggeration. This distance is just at arm's length, and a person beyond this distance cannot be touched. Conversation is in a moderate volume, and subjects of personal interest can be comfortably discussed. The entire face cannot be taken in in one glance, and the eyes must be focused upon some particular facial feature.

Social Distance

There is not a great difference between close (four to seven feet) and far (seven to twelve feet) phases of social distance. This distance is used for conducting impersonal business; often, people who work together use the close, rather than the far, phase. While some kind of recognition or conversation is usually mandatory within the close phase, the far phase permits ignoring another person without offending.

Public Distance

Several differences in behavior are seen when the public distance is contrasted to social and personal distances. In the close phase (12 to 25 feet), words and sentences are carefully selected along with formalized grammatical and syntactical styles. In the far phase (25 feet or more), gestures are exaggerated and vocalization is loud.

Bubbles in Foreign Lands

Hall (1966) has argued convincingly that attitudes toward space are in large part culturally determined. Thus, the psychological factors that control the personal-space bubble can and do vary from country to country. These cultural differences may be illustrated informally by one of the authors' recollections of a European camping trip taken to celebrate the granting of his doctoral degree and freedom from bondage as a graduate student.

We [the author and his wife] pitched our tent in a large campground in Oslo, Norway. It was midweek and there were many vacant campsites. Thus we could easily secure a corner site bounded on two sides by primitive access roads and on the remaining sides by vacant sites. This selection exemplified the American desire for privacy and open space. After the tent was up, we set a small folding table and chairs next to it, and dashed off to see Oslo. We were astonished and even a bit infuriated, on our return to find another tent pitched on the site directly adjoining ours, despite the great number of isolated sites available. To add insult to injury, our next door neighbor had one corner of his tent secured to a stake planted directly under our folding table! It was obvious that he had moved the table to do so. Nevertheless, not one word was exchanged between us for the duration of our stay. This episode increased our empathy for German campers, who carried portable picket fences which were immediately erected when a campsite was selected, a practice which we had originally regarded with mixed merriment and lack of understanding.

Indeed, one of the factors which lead Americans to perceive Germans as a very formal people could be their intercultural differences in personal-space bubbles. Bubble intrusions occur at precise distances for Germans, whereas Americans tend to modify the bubble size as a function of circumstance. An American will hardly notice if someone picks up a chair and moves it closer during a conversation. A German, however, would consider such behavior impolite at best. For the German, chairs and other furniture have been placed exactly where they are to define personal-space zones, and any attempt at relocating room fixtures is treated as a spatial invasion. This may explain why typical German furniture is quite heavy. Hall (1966) reports that one German working in the United States had his visitors' chair bolted to the floor to prevent its relocation!

However, before Americans congratulate themselves on not being "up tight" about spatial organization, another cross-cultural comparison is in order. The middle-class American expects his own office at work, and his children expect their own rooms at home. The middle-class Englishman, however, has been raised in a nursery and has no such expectations. Members of Parliament do not have offices. An American working in England is perceived in many ways as similar to a German working in America. The English do not understand why the American wants his own office, or at least a partition. Thus, we must realize that there is no single correct use of personal space; rather, behavior in the physical environment is, like most other kinds of behavior, learned as a result of experiences which differ across cultures.

If you have found spatial behavior in Great Britian and Germany unusual, prepare yourself for a great shock as we now discuss personal space in Japan and the Arab world. Americans consider walls as fixed barriers, and decorate a room by placing furniture adjacent to walls. In Japan, walls are movable, and the focus of interest is upon space in the center of the room. For the Japanese, American rooms are incredibly bare, because the center is invariably empty. Furniture distributed about the periphery of a room is ignored by the Japanese.

While an American carries his bubble with him in public places, an Arab's bubble dissolves in public. An American sitting in a hotel lobby would be irritated if someone stood right next to his chair when the lobby was not crowded. However, an Arab views the lobby as a public place, one in which he is entitled to the same rights as the man occupying the chair. Indeed, the Arab not only considers it entirely legitimate to stand next to the chair, but he also engages in moderate pushing and shoving to induce the present occupant to leave, so that he can then sit down. Since the chair is in a public place, it is fair game for the Arab—even if occupied!

We shall conclude our cross-culture journey by considering an imaginary conversation between a Latin American and an Englishman. The Latin American has a smaller bubble than does an American, whereas the Englishman has a larger bubble. Thus when the two try to find a reasonable distance at which normal conversation can be conducted, the Latin American feels he is too far away, while the Englishman feels too close. So the Latin American advances upon the Englishman, who backs up with alarm. After this "dance" is repeated several times, the Englishman may begin to feel the victim of an inexplicable "attack" and eventually break off the conversation, leaving the Latin American to wonder about the lack of warmth of Englishmen in general.

Invasions of Personal Space: Help, There's Someone in My Bubble!

We briefly touched upon the topic of invasion of personal space when we discussed the operational definition of a bubble. In this section, we will now focus upon defensive mechanisms and strategies used to keep the personal-space bubble intact. Although all of us have well-developed protective strategies, we do not often call them to our attention. Therefore, let us pose the following question to concentrate our awareness. Imagine that it is your duty to protect and defend some spatial location, say, a table in a library or cafeteria, against invasion by anyone. Thus, you must prevent any stranger from sitting down at your table. Furthermore, this task must be accomplished without any verbal communication from you, so that you cannot simply state "This seat is occupied." How might you defend your table?

This task was tried as a demonstration project in one of the author's classes in environmental psychology. Students entered the busy reserve book room at the Purdue library, waited until they spotted an empty table, and then tried to defend it. A student was considered a successful space defender if he or she was able to fend off intruders for half an hour. While only a few members of the class were able to meet the criterion, most students met with some success, being able to defend their tables for some period of time. Several techniques, some of which were quite ingenious, were tried out by the class. The least successful approaches involved posture, with students trying to sprawl out on the table and on adjacent chairs so as to occupy as much physical space as possible. This strategy was good for only five or ten minutes of isolation. A slightly better technique evolved by some students was the use of visual rejection. These students glared and gave "nasty looks" at potential intruders. This strategy was good for 10 to 15 minutes of isolation. Even more success was obtained by students who scattered physical objects such as books and coats over the table. This technique was good for up to 25 minutes, with items of apparel being the most successful place markers and books being the least. Finally, three students hit the jackpot and were able to defend their tables for the entire 30-minute period. One student feigned violent coughing and wheezing when approached. Another student tilted all the chairs except his up against the table so that anyone wishing to be seated would first have to straighten a chair. The third student placed a hand-lettered sign that stated "RESERVED" on the table. Of course, these efforts are but a small fraction of possible ways to defend personal space. We shall now turn to two more formal field studies conducted by Robert Sommer, a psychologist who has worked extensively both in studying personal space and in applying results to the design of better spatial arrangements.

In order to examine spatial location as an aid to defending personal space, Sommer (1966) had an observer record seating patterns in the reserve room of the library at the University of California, Davis. The observer recorded where 20 occupants sat on 61 weekday mornings. His results are illustrated in Figure 15–2. It is quite clear that people prefer to sit at the ends of a table when the table is empty or very uncrowded. A second part of Sommer's study utilized a questionnaire. Students were asked to mark on a diagram of a table the location where they could obtain the most privacy. In addition, two different kinds of privacy instructions were given. In an *avoidance* questionnaire, students were asked: "If you wanted to be as far as possible from the distraction of other people, where would you sit at the table?" In an *offensive-display* questionnaire, the table diagrams were the same but students were asked: "If you wanted to have the table to yourself, where would you sit to discourage anyone else from occupying it?" Although both sets of instructions were aimed at ensuring privacy, there were marked differences in the location selected. Students following the defensive (avoidance) instructions sat at the end of a table, while students following the other instructions selected the middle of the table. Of course, as Sommer points out, the real effectiveness of either strategy depends upon room density. If the room is relatively empty, the active defense strategy works well, but as the room becomes quite crowded the active defender runs the risk of being completely surrounded. Therefore, at high densities an end chair is a better bet.

Chairs occupied by first ten people

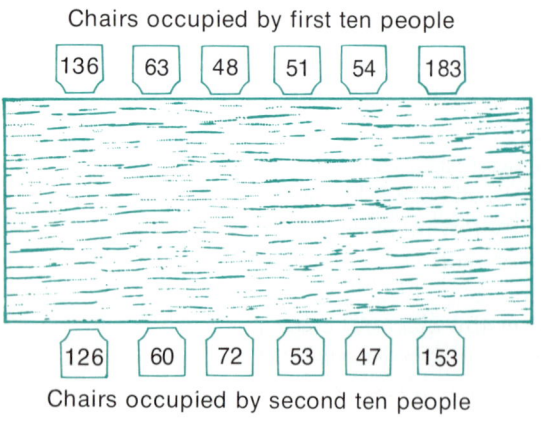

Chairs occupied by second ten people

FIGURE 15–2   The number of times that a seat at a table was chosen by one of the first or second ten people to enter the library, as shown by the number of selections indicated for each chair. Note that most people prefer to sit at the ends of the table. The two rows do not add up to multiples of ten presumably because on some days fewer than ten or twenty persons entered the reserve room during the daily 45-minute observation period. (Based on data from Sommer, 1966.)

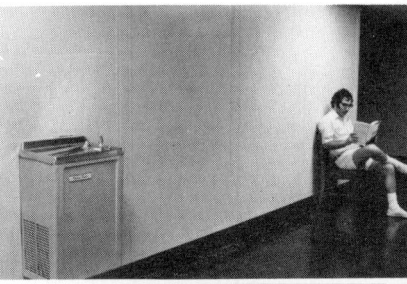

FIGURE 15-3 Which water fountain would you prefer? Most people would tend to avoid the fountain with the person close by in favor of the fountain in the right-hand photographs. (Photo by Susan Kantowitz.)

Another means of defending your personal space involves an expansion of the size of your personal-space bubble, just as countries try to expand their maritime limits beyond 20 miles when fishing density increases. A laboratory test of this defense mechanism was conducted by Dosey and Meisels (1969), who measured the size of the personal-space bubble under conditions of stress and nonstress. Subjects in the stress condition were given low ratings of their physical attractiveness, while nonstress subjects were told that they were participating in a study of the orienting reflex. The subjects walked to the experimenter and then stopped. The distance between them was recorded by an observer who used a grid of lines unobstrusively drawn on the floor. In the stress condition, subjects approached to within a mean distance of 15 inches from the experimenter, while in the nonstress condition they approached within 12 inches. Thus, the subject's perception of threatening elements resulted in a defensive expansion of the personal-space bubble.

What happens when, despite social norms and hostile nonverbal communications, a personal-space bubble is persistently violated? The usual response is escape. When Felipe and Sommer (1966) invaded the personal-space bubbles of hospital patients by sitting down six inches away, the patients simply got up and left. While such experiments do demonstrate the aversive nature of spatial invasion, it is difficult to state how much of the results depend upon the extreme novelty of having a stranger walk right up and remain within another's bubble without making any attempt at verbal communication—after all, when a stranger walks up to you, you expect him to say something, perhaps in the form of a simple request for directions or some other aid. Barefoot, Hoople, and McGlay (1972) used a "passive-experimenter" approach to avoid this methodological problem. The experimenter sat in a chair near a water fountain and pretended to read a book. Thus anyone wishing to obtain a drink of water would have to violate the experimenter's personal space. When the experimenter sat one foot away from the fountain, 10 per cent of the passersby drank from the fountain. When the experimenter sat five feet away, the figure increased to 18 per cent. Finally, when the experimenter sat ten feet away, 22 per cent drank from the fountain. Clearly, these results are in agreement with previous research which used an active invasion paradigm.

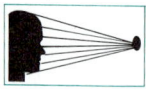

FOCUS
ON
RESEARCH: *No Place to Flee—Personal Space Invasion in a Men's Room*

As has been discussed above, persistent violation of personal space usually results in the departure of the "invaded" person. This of course makes it difficult to investigate spatial invasion in field studies. However, by cleverly choosing the location of a field study, this difficulty can be overcome. A man standing in front of a urinal has an extremely limited ability to escape invasion of his personal-space bubble, at least until he has satisfied the urge for elimination that has brought him to this spot. Furthermore, he cannot engage in other compensatory types of behaviors such as turning his back on the invader since his attention must, necessarily, be otherwise engaged. Thus a men's room is an excellent location for an environmental psychologist who wishes to study invasion in a situation in which the subject has little opportunity to immediately leave.

This reasoning, rather than a weak bladder, explains why psychologist Eric Knowles (Middlemist, Knowles, and Matter, 1976) decided to use a nearby men's room as a laboratory for the study of spatial invasion. In order to prevent possible invalidation of the study by experimenter effects, Knowles had to overcome several obstacles that blocked data acquisition. The first problem was what to do with the observer who would record the data. Subjects would become suspicious if a person washing his hands paid undue attention to activity at the urinals. This problem was solved by inventing a special periscope disguised as a stack of books (see Figure 15–4). The observer placed this periscope inside a toilet stall and closed the door. This allowed the observer to sit in comfort while obtaining data. From the outside all that was visible was a pair of feet and a stack of textbooks.

The main independent variable was the degree of spatial invasion. This was manipulated by placing an out-of-order sign in either the center or end urinal in a row of three. A confederate occupied one of the urinals so that any subject entering the men's room had only one urinal available for his use. Thus the confederate and the subject could be stationed at adjacent urinals—about 17 inches between the shoulders of the two men—or at the end urinals with an empty urinal between them—about 53 inches apart. In a control condition, no confederate was present.

The observer seated in the toilet stall recorded two dependent variables. The first was the time between the subject stepping up to the urinal and the beginning of urination. The second variable was the time required for urination. If spatial invasion produced stress, two effects would be expected. First, it would be more difficult for subjects to relax the appropriate muscles, so that onset of urination would be delayed. Second, once urination started, increased pressure should shorten the time required to complete the act.

The results of this study are shown in Figure 15–5. Men at adjacent urinals took longer to start urination but completed the task sooner than either those in the control condition or those separated from the confederate by a vacant urinal. Hence, invasion of one's personal bubble affects not only one's mental state but also biological factors related to muscle tension and urination.

FIGURE 15–4 The observation apparatus used by Middlemist et al. (1976) in their experiment on personal space invasion in a men's room. The periscope is quite unobtrusive when hidden by the stall. (Photo by Eric Knowles.)

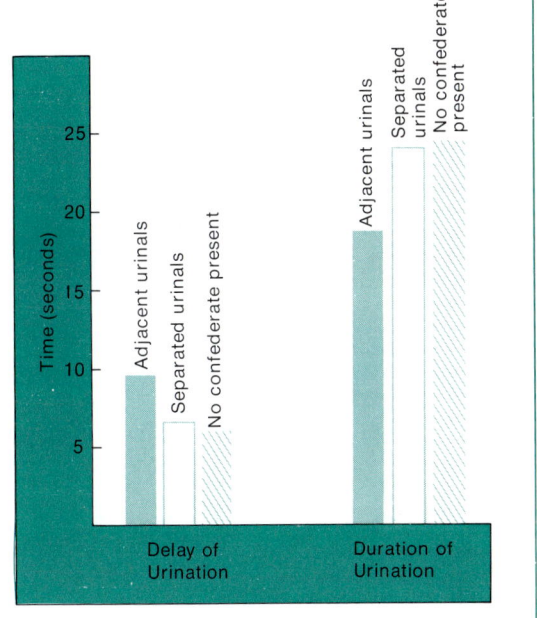

FIGURE 15–5   The results of the Middlemist et al. experiment (1976). The stress of a spatial invasion at a urinal caused male subjects to take a longer time to begin urination and a shorter time to complete the act. (Data from Middlemist, R. D., Knowles, E. S., and Matter, G. F.: Personal space invasions in the lavatory: Suggestive evidence for arousal. *Journal of Personality and Social Psychology*, 1976, *33*, 541–547.)

Sex and Your Bubble

Do men or women have bigger bubbles? While the general finding is that women have smaller bubbles (Evans and Howard, 1973), the picture becomes more complicated when we consider both mixed sex and same-sex groups. The study by Dosey and Meisels (1969) discussed earlier also looked at sex. You will recall that in this study, the subject approached a stationary experimenter, and the focus of interest was upon how close to the experimenter the subject came. Sex in this situation can be varied in two ways. First, the approaching person can be either male or female. Second, the stationary person being approached can be either the same sex as or the opposite sex of the approaching person. Both these factors must be considered for a complete picture of the relationship between sex and personal-space bubbles. The results of this study are shown in Figure 15–6. For males, the size of the personal-space bubble is independent of the sex of the person being approached. For females, however, the sex of the stationary person is very important. When females approach a male, their bubble is larger than that found when females approach another female. This was attributed to American cultural norms of females being considerably less encouraged than men to interact with strangers of the opposite sex. This suggests that measurements of personal space might be used to assess the impact of the women's liberation movement. Truly liberated women would be expected to possess personal-space bubbles equivalent in size to their male counterparts. Thus, although this problem has yet to be researched, we might speculate that Ms. Gloria Steinem would have a larger bubble than Mrs. Archie Bunker.

The experiment by Dosey and Meisels (1969) clearly showed that interpersonal distances for females depend upon the mixture of the two-person group—i.e., whether it is mixed sex or same sex. Do *feelings* about a group also depend upon group sexual composition and the degree of encroachment on the personal-space bubble? This question formed the basis of an experiment by Marshall and Heslin (1975), who looked at the joint effects of group sexual

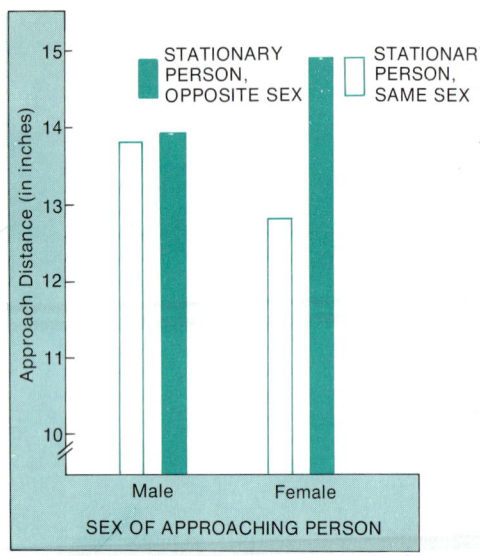

FIGURE 15–6 **How close you will approach a stationary person depends upon their sex if you are female. If you are male, you will approach either sex equally closely. (Based on data from Dosey and Meisels, 1969.)**

composition and group density. In the high density condition, the group used a 4-foot-square area; for the low density condition, the area was 18 square feet. Subjects were asked to rate their feelings about other members in the group. For mixed sex groups, both males and females liked the other group members more when the group was crowded into the high density space. However, results for same-sex groups were quite different. While men still liked each other more when crowded, the opposite outcome was obtained for women: women liked the other members of their same-sex group less when they were crowded into the high density space. Thus the Marshall and Heslin study is in general agreement with the findings of Dosey and Meisels discussed above. The effects of sex upon the personal space bubble depend upon both the sex of the person in the bubble as well as the sex of the persons close to the bubble.

ENVIRONMENTAL STRESSORS: NASTY NUISANCES

Although we have more control over our environment than any other species on this earth, we still must tolerate a wide assortment of environmental pressures in our day-to-day life. Indeed, public awareness of this fact has forced enactment of significant amounts of legislation on national, state, and local levels to control environmental hazards. While a psychology text is not the place to discuss the political and economic implications of such legislation, it does appear rather likely that the future will see more, not less, legislation designed to control environmental hazards in both the United States and throughout the world. Thus, it is of considerable importance that biological and behavioral effects of environmental factors be studied and publicized. It is essential that public decisions which will affect our lives — and the future of our country, our world, and civilization as we know it — be based upon sound data concerning the effects of various environmental hazards on human life. Without this information, rational legislation is impossible.

The following sections are devoted to a representative cross-section of findings and hypotheses about selected environmental stressors. First, we will discuss the nature of stress itself and the distinction between biological and psychological measures of stress. Our discussion will then progress to four

Try this simple exercise to map out the shape of your personal-space bubble. Have a friend stand about 15 feet away from you. Face each other and converse. Notice how loudly you both are speaking. Now have your friend walk slowly toward you. At what distance does the volume of your conversation start to diminish? Now, as your friend keeps walking toward you, pay close attention to eye contact. Finally, how close can your friend approach before you start to feel uncomfortable? Now repeat this procedure with your friend approaching from your side, and once again with your friend approaching from the rear. Are your personal distances the same? You might also want to try this exercise with a stranger and with a person of the opposite sex.

specific kinds of environmental stressors. We shall examine effects of *crowding* and *overpopulation, noise, heat,* and *pollution.* While our discussion will center about the psychological aspects of these stressors, implications for public policy should not be hard to discover.

Stress

The age-old question "Can the mind influence the body?" gains new perspective when considered in relation to stress. The example of the yogi discussed in Chapter 4 is evidence, albeit incomplete, for some control of the body by the mind. An entire branch of science, psychosomatic medicine, is devoted to the importance of psychological factors in maintaining health. Thus it is not surprising that some of the most influential conceptualizations about stress have been placed in a medical framework.

Hans Selye, a Canadian physician, has done much important work on the biological effects of stress in animals and humans. He discovered that the body has a systematic reaction to stress-inducing agents (stressors). At first there is an *alarm reaction,* in which characteristic physiological changes such as release of hormones into the bloodstream under control of the adrenal cortex occur. Since the body cannot tolerate a prolonged state of alarm without suffering severe biological damage and even death, the alarm reaction is replaced by a stage of *resistance.* This resistance stage is characterized by physiological changes directly counter to those of the alarm reaction. For example, during the alarm reaction, blood volume diminishes and body weight drops, whereas in the resistance stage body weight returns to normal and the blood is less concentrated. The last stage is *exhaustion,* in which the body is unable to resist aversive agents. This series of three stages has been termed the **general adaptation syndrome (GAS)** by Selye.

Although stress could be defined in terms of the general adaptation syndrome by stating that where there's GAS there's stress, such a definition ignores the psychological aspects of stress (McGrath, 1970). Physiological correlates of stress may be present in situations such as sexual intercourse and heavy exercise which we might not want included under a stress category; the definition is thus too broad. Moreoever, a particular response pattern such as the GAS can result from many different physical situations which would not be psychologically equivalent; for example, heart rate increases in conditions

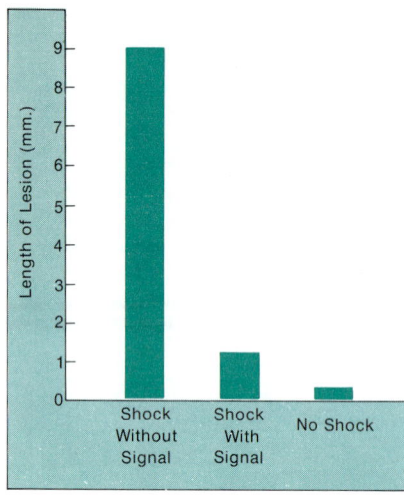

FIGURE 15–7   When rats can predict electric shocks, they have less ulceration than when the same shock occurs without warning. Control rats heard the signal but received no shock. (Adapted from Weiss, 1972.)

of fright *and* exercise. Finally, the specific physiological components of the GAS do not really occur together often enough to form an operational definition of stress (McGrath, 1970).

Difficulties also arise when definitions of stress are based upon situations or classes of physical stimuli, such as electric shock. Studies with rats (Weiss, 1972) have demonstrated that the same physical stressor will have different results depending upon the psychological environment of the animal. Weiss placed three rats matched for age and weight into three identical compartments. Two rats received electric shock through a tail electrode. One of these rats heard a tone 10 seconds before the shock. The other rat heard the tone at random intervals. Thus the first rat could predict when the shock would occur but the second rat could not. A third control rat heard the tone but never received any shock through its tail electrode. After the shocks, an autopsy was performed to detect gastric ulcers. The results of this experiment can be seen in Figure 15–7. The control rat developed little or no gastric ulceration. However, the rat which could not predict the shock developed severe ulceration, while the rat that received predictable shocks did not. Thus, although two rats received the same electric shock, it was the psychological variable of predictability, and not the shock itself, which led to formation of gastric ulcers.

These and other factors (McGrath, 1970) make it rather difficult to come up with a precise operational definition of psychological stress. In this chapter, we shall avoid this difficulty by following a suggestion made by McGrath and concentrate upon stressful situations rather than upon stress in the abstract. A stressful situation occurs when there is a substantial imbalance between demands imposed upon an organism by the environment and the organism's ability to cope with those demands. Thus stressful situations can arise both from an overload beyond the organism's capabilities and from an "underload" in which an individual's capabilities far exceed the demands imposed. It is easy to understand that an airplane pilot whose vehicle is spinning down in flames suffers from a decreased capability to handle overload imposed by the environment, and we would all agree that this situation is indeed stressful. It is more difficult to understand—although equally true, given our definition of a stressful situation—that the worker performing a boring task on an assembly line also may be in a stressful situation. Our concern for environmental overloads should not blind us to the dangers of environmental *under*loads.

All of us have endured the experience of being physically crowded at one **Population Density** time or another. Being pushed and shoved in a bus during rush hour, a depart- **and Crowding:** ment store during a sale, or in line at a rock concert is hardly a source of enjoy- **Toocloseforcomfort** ment for most people. Yet we tolerate such situations, primarily because they are of relatively short duration. What would happen if you spent your whole life immersed in such crowds? Since no ethical experimenter would attempt so drastic a study with humans, we must first turn to animal data to discover effects of long-term, severe crowding. After that, we will consider short-term experiments performed with humans.

Unlike man, most animals are able to maintain fairly stable populations *Animal Crowding* over periods of time. Ethologists have long sought to discover the precise na- *and Pathology* ture of the homeostatic mechanism that regulates population density for all animals but man. At first, population control was attributed to predators and to disease, both of which were held to limit excess populations. However, later workers (Wynne-Edwards, 1962, 1971) have argued that social mecha- nisms serve to limit reproduction and regulate population density.

What is the effect of a drastic increase in population density upon animals' social behavior? This question formed the basis for a long series of studies con- ducted by John Calhoun (1962, 1966, 1971) at the National Institute for Mental Health. The results of his experiment were astonishing.

The apparatus used by Calhoun to study crowding is shown in Figure 15–8. Notice that the environmental arrangement encourages high density in certain pens (labeled 2 and 3 in the figure) and decreased density in others (pens 1 and 4). While the "rat universe" illustrated in Figure 15–8 had space for 48 rats to live comfortably (12 in each compartment), the actual population se- lected by Calhoun was a total of 80 rats. The rats did not distribute themselves equally among the four compartments; density in pens 2 and 3 was very high, with considerably more than the normal population of 12 rats that could be comfortably accommodated. This overcrowding caused several types of ab- normal behavior to develop in the middle pens. While pregnancy rates were equivalent for all pens, the mortality rate in the pens 2 and 3 was amazingly high, with 80 to 96 per cent of the infants dying before weaning. Females in pens 2 and 3 became unable to build proper nests and would fail to trans- port all of their litter with them. The infants left behind generally died where they were dropped and were eaten by adult rats. Females in heat in pens 2 and 3 were unable to ward off the attentions of hordes of male rats, and the females developed high rates of disorders in pregnancy, leading to the death of almost half of the females by the sixteenth month. These and other pathol- ogies that developed were attributed to the formation of a **behavioral sink.** Calhoun intended the term "sink" to imply a place for collection of garbage and other noxious substances; the term "behavioral toilet" might in fact be more accurate. The behavioral sink and its accompanying pathologies result from extreme population densities.

While the higher mortality rates threatening the extinction of the popula- tion had the greatest implications for the entire rat universe, individual rats also exhibited strange behavior pathologies. The wierdest rats were those called **probers** by Calhoun. Although living in pens 2 and 3, these male rats did not join in the struggle for status. Probers were hyperactive, hypersexual, and cannibalistic. If no estrous females (females in heat) were available in their own pens, they would lurk on the ramps adjoining pens 1 and 4. Since these pens were controlled by a dominant territorial rat, the probers thus risked attack, but even if injured by the territorial rat they would soon return to peer again into the pens. Rather than waiting outside for the female to emerge, as would a

FIGURE 15–8   The pens used by Calhoun to study the effects of crowding on a rat population. The conical objects are food hoppers; the winding staircases lead to burrows (the burrow in pen 1 is shown with the top removed). The rats drank from the trays with 3 bottles. Note that it is impossible for the rats to go directly from pen 1 to pen 4. See the text for a description of the rats' behavioral pathologies. (From "Population Density and Social Pathology" by John C. Calhoun. Scientific American, February, 1962, pp. 140–141. Copyright © 1962 by Scientific American, Inc. All rights reserved.)

normal heterosexual rat engaging in a normal rat courtship ritual, the probers would dash after the female into her burrow. Since the probers often found dead infants in the burrows, they tended to become cannibalistic.

It is clear that high population density in rats leads to strange pathologies involving the complete breakdown of normal social and reproductive behavior patterns. The following section considers the implications of these amazing, and perhaps even frightening, behaviors for human crowding and over-population.

Human Crowding and Pathology

The present population of the world is four billion. Extrapolations of present demographic trends (Frejka, 1973) suggest that by the year 2100, population will level off somewhere between six and fifteen billion, with a projection of 8.4 billion being most reasonable at present. Furthermore, the bulk of this growth will be in the undeveloped countries of the world, so that while the present ratio of population between rich and poor countries is about 30:70, it will swing to 20:80 or even 10:90. Crowding will increase, especially in those nations which can least afford it. Yet we have just begun to study the psychological effects of crowding upon humans. Although a New York subway allows only 20.8 cubic feet per person, and the American Prison Association recommends a minimum of 289 cubic feet per person (Ittelson et al., 1974), it would still be a grave violation of ethics for scientists to crowd humans the way Calhoun crowded rats. Therefore, human crowding is investigated by field studies using correlation techniques. As was discussed in Chapter 1, correlation differs from causality, and extra care must be used to interpret correlational results. Such a correlational demographic study was conducted by sociologists Galle, Gove, and McPherson (1972).

Galle, Gove, and McPherson examined relationships between population density and pathology in Chicago. Two common measures of human population density are number of rooms per housing unit and number of persons per room. Human social pathologies for which data are readily available include mortality rate, fertility rate, public assistance rate, incidence of juvenile delinquency, and admissions to mental hospitals. When these sets of variables were intercorrelated, reliable statistical relationships were obtained. This finding was true even when statistical controls for ethnicity and social class were incorporated. For four of the five social pathologies (all except admissions to mental hospitals), the number of persons per room was an important determinant of behavior. Higher incidences of social pathologies were associated with greater densities. Thus, Galle et al. (1972) concluded that overcrowding has a serious impact upon human social pathology.

Later studies, however, have not always confirmed this relationship. While Freedman, Heshka, and Levy (1975) found simple correlations between density and pathology in New York, these correlations disappeared when income and other social factors were statistically controlled. However, in earlier studies of Honolulu (Schmitt, 1957, 1966), correlations between density and pathology remained even after statistical controls for other social factors were utilized. Thus, on balance, correlational studies do generally support a relationship between density and social pathology. However, the very nature of these studies, with their many unknown and uncontrolled variables, prevents one from reaching any strong conclusions about density and pathology. Therefore, it seems best to turn to laboratory studies of human crowding.

Using same-sex groups of males and females, Freedman, Levy, Buchanan, and Price (1972) found that high density served to intensify typical behavior. Thus, unpleasant situations were more unpleasant in crowded conditions, just as pleasant situations were more pleasant in the crowded state (Freedman, Heshka, and Levy, 1975). This finding also held for mixed-sex groups, which unfortunately contradicts the findings of Marshall and Heslin (1975) discussed

FIGURE 15-9 The number of rooms per housing unit and the number of persons per room can be used as indices of human population density. In an immense housing complex such as this, is there a risk of social pathology if density increases? Some studies suggest that this may, indeed, be the case.

earlier in the section on sex and your bubble. They found that the effects of crowding depend upon the sexual composition of the group.

A recent study by Fisher and Byrne (1975) may resolve this contradiction. They found that while males were more disturbed by face-to-face invasions, females responded more negatively to side-by-side invasions. Thus, although the calculated density for males and females might be mathematically the same in an experiment, the *psychological* density might very well differ for males and females, depending upon the seating arrangements used in the experiment. Females sitting side by side would feel more crowded than males sitting side by side and males sitting face to face would feel more crowded than females sitting face to face. Therefore, any conclusions relating sex and crowding must also take into account the spatial positions used in an experiment.

Until quite recently, most studies of human crowding used either a cor- relational approach or a laboratory situation. Field studies of crowding were once rare but are now becoming more frequent (Saegert, 1975). These new field studies have discovered increases in blood pressure associated with crowding (D'Atri, 1975), more complaints of illness among crowded prison inmates (McCain, Cox, and Paulus, 1977), a lesser chance of residential groups forming in crowded dormitories (Baum, Harper, and Valins, 1975), and a decrease in the number of cognitive tasks performed in a busy railroad terminal during rush hour as compared to the same terminal when not crowded (Saegert, Mackintosh, and West, 1975). Future field research on human crowding in real environments, using behavioral rather than statistical measures, will help us understand its effects without the problems in interpretation of correlational results.

One last warning must be added when correlational and laboratory studies of human crowding are compared. The correlational studies encompass data obtained over fairly long periods of time and thus are more comparable to the animal crowding studies, such as Calhoun's, where rats were enclosed in a crowded universe for several generations. The laboratory studies of human crowding typically take on the order of a few hours at most. Even field studies on living in closed underwater habitats such as TEKTITE 2 (Miller and Vander- walker, 1971) lasted only a few months. Since a laboratory study of human crowding lasting several years is at present unlikely, we may be forced to rely upon the correlational studies, despite their inherent limitations, at least until more field studies are completed.

Noise

What is noise? Some definitions take into account the listener's attitude toward the sound source. Thus while you might be offended at having the sounds of a loudly amplified heavy-metal rock group called noise, your parents might be unable to call it anything else. The limiting case of this type of defini- tion is exemplified by the age-old problem: If a tree falls in a forest and no per- son is present to hear it, does the tree make a noise? In this chapter we will avoid such philosophical issues by defining noise as any high intensity sound, say on the order of 90 dB SPL. You will recall that the unit of sound intensity, the decibel (dB), has already been discussed in Chapter 3, and that a 90 dB SPL sound is roughly as loud as a subway train.

Of course, many different kinds of sound can qualify as noise under this definition. A loud jet plane passing overhead creates noise that sounds dif- ferent from that associated with a fire alarm bell. While research has indeed used a wide variety of real-life noise, including gongs and buzzers, psycholo- gists have usually turned to a standardized noise source commonly used in laboratory studies. This is called **white noise** and contains a wide range of auditory frequencies. You can hear a sound very much like white noise by

 **PERSPECTIVE ON BEHAVIOR:** *Are There Limits to Growth? — The Tragedy of the Commons*

In England, the commons is a pasture that can be used by all herdsmen. Every day each herdsman takes his flock to graze on the commons. Although the commons is shared by all, it is owned by no single individual. Pretend for a moment that you are such a herdsman and are trying to decide whether or not to add an additional animal to your flock. Since the proceeds from the eventual sale of this animal need not be shared with others, the utility of this purchase (see Chapter 6) is definitely positive. The cost to you of an additional animal in terms of depleting the commons by overgrazing is small since you do not own the commons. Thus, any individual herdsman is acting quite rationally by deciding to add one extra animal to his flock. However, when all the herdsmen add just one extra animal, the eventual result is a depletion of the commons through overgrazing, and all the herdsmen suffer. This is the paradox: Each herdsman acts sensibly as an individual, yet the ultimate outcome of all these individual decisions is disastrous, with most of the herds dying from starvation. Is there any solution to this problem?

At first we might think that a technical solution, such as improving fertilizers to increase the capacity of the commons, could remove the difficulty. However, this only postpones the ultimate tragedy. As soon as the herds increase to the size the commons can maintain, the paradox returns. Indeed, Hardin (1968) has argued that no technical solution is possible, and that only a "fundamental extension in morality" can end the tragedy of the commons. Every individual must give up certain freedoms — the freedom to use the commons as much as desired, the freedom to have as many children as desired, the freedom to pollute the earth as desired — to protect the more basic freedoms of society. On the other hand, Crowe (1969) has replied to Hardin by stating that such an extension of morality is unlikely at best. According to this view, people usually act for their own short-term benefit and let tomorrow take care of itself. Why should I give up driving a large automobile if I can afford the high price of gasoline?

As psychologists, we have no quick or easy solution to the tragedy of the commons. For example, we don't know if it is sensible to leave future generations a legacy of tons of dangerous nuclear waste so that badly needed electric power can be generated now, in hopes that a technical solution to waste disposal lies ahead. Technology has bailed us out in the past and may do so again, and simple predictions about the nature of future technical developments often prove incorrect. A century ago one might have predicted that the major problem of urban areas today would be that of removing tons of horse manure from the streets — a problem which, of course, failed to develop. Yet our resources are limited to those we carry with us on spaceship earth. Are we, then, about to ruin the commons?

tuning your radio or television to a frequency which does not contain a station. The hissing sound that results closely approximates the sound used in laboratory studies on the effects of noise.

Until quite recently, psychologists had difficulty in finding any effects of noise upon human performance, and it would have been excusable to conclude that humans are sufficiently adaptable that noisy environments do not cause a psychological deterioration in performance. (This does not mean that

Noise and Performance

high noise levels will not eventually cause a physiological impairment of hearing.) It turns out that the kind of task being studied is more important than the kind of noise, since noise affects only certain classes of job tasks (Hockey, 1969). When a task demands considerable attention and presents high rates of information, such as in the erratically moving target in a shooting gallery or penny arcade, noise effects can be obtained. Somewhat paradoxically, however, noise does not always result in a deterioration of performance but can instead sometimes actually improve performance. This makes it difficult to simply dismiss the effects of noise as attributable to the general "distraction" of a stimulus which is irrelevant to the task at hand.

Current views instead consider noise as a motivator serving to increase the general level of arousal. This view results in some interesting predictions about the joint effects of noise and another stressor. We would all agree that after sleep deprivation, performance is poor. We have already noted that performing some information processing task under high noise levels also results in poor performance. What happens when a sleepy subject is asked to perform that task in a noisy environment? Common sense leads us to predict that performance would be even worse than when only one stressor (noise or sleep deprivation) was applied. We would expect the two adverse effects to add, resulting in terrible performance. Alas, common sense would lead us to an incorrect prediction. The real finding is that performance is *better* when the two stresses are combined (Broadbent, 1971). "Of course," you exclaim. With the clear view of hindsight, common sense now tells us that the noise serves to wake up the sleepy man so that his performance improves.

While this latter statement is indeed correct, it is only half the story. What would common sense predict about the joint effect of noise and some positive incentive, such as additional monetary payments, for good performance? Common sense suggests that performance should be outstandingly good, since the effects of noise and those of incentive will add. Once again, common sense leads to yet another incorrect prediction. The joint effects of noise and a positive incentive lead to *poorer* performance than when either factor is used by itself. By now you should be ready to give up on common sense and instead seek the theoretical explanation offered by psychologists for this seemingly odd set of results.

The current explanation relates effects of stressors to arousal level. There is a curvilinear relationship between arousal level and performance (expressed in the Yerkes-Dodson law), as we can see in Figure 15–10. It shows that at an optimum level of arousal, performance is best. When a sleepy person is exposed to noise, his arousal increases—in Figure 15–10, it moves from point A to point B. Since point B is higher, performance improves. When an awake subject is exposed to noise and some positive incentive, his arousal increases from point C in Figure 15–10 to point D. Since point D is *lower*, performance decreases. Thus, depending upon one's location on the Yerkes-Dodson function, an increase in arousal (moving to the right in Figure 15–10) can result in either an increase or a decrease in relative performance.

Noise and Control   Our previous discussion has noted that noise can affect the performance of complex tasks. But are there any aftereffects of noise? Specifically, will performance in a noise-free environment be influenced by prior exposure to noise? This question was investigated in a series of experiments conducted by psychologists David Glass and Jerome Singer (1972).

When people are exposed to noise, any change in behavior once the noise is removed in termed an "aftereffect." Glass and Singer wondered why the aftereffects of unpredictable noise were more adverse than the aftereffects of

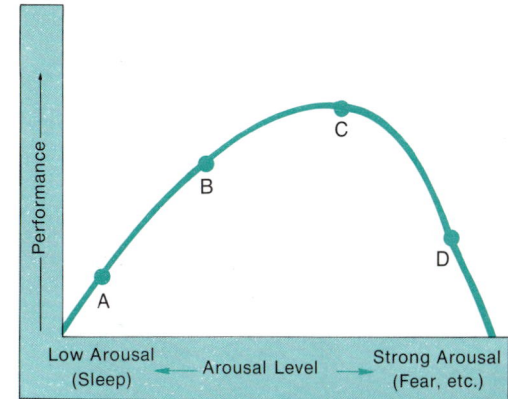

FIGURE 15–10   The Yerkes-Dodson law. Arousal level increases as we move to the right. The height of the function indicates the level of performance; performance gets better as the curve gets higher. Note that performance is best at an intermediate level of arousal and decreases when arousal is either too low or too high.

predictable noise. They hypothesized that an unpredictable stressor would lead subjects to feel more at the mercy of their environment than a predictable stressor. To test this, persons in one group were told that they could control the noise in their environment by pressing a switch, while another group was given no such control. Although the persons with access to the switch seldom used it, their post-noise performance was much better than that of persons who had no perceived control of the noise. Thus, as was the case with the rats developing ulcers (previously discussed; see Figure 15–7), psychological factors were the important determinants of reactions to stress—e.g., the production of noise aftereffects.

The interpretation suggested by Glass and Singer—that uncontrollable stress results in a feeling of helplessness—is directly related to the theory of learned helplessness discussed earlier in Chapter 4. Unpredictable noise is more aversive than predictable noise because it induces greater anxiety about one's inability to handle environmental conditions. This learned helplessness generates the greater aftereffects of unpredictable noise.

Our discussion of noise so far has been based on laboratory studies using white noise as a stressor. We now turn to a real-life field study which attempted to assess long-term effects of noise in the home upon a child's verbal skills.

Noise in the Apartment: Why Johnny Can't Read

A high-rise housing development in New York City was the scene of this study by Cohen, Glass, and Singer (1973). This development was built over a noisy expressway, and as a result the lower floors were noisier than upper floors. Tests of reading ability and auditory discrimination showed that children living on the lower floors exhibited greater impairments. These results could not be attributed to other factors such as social class, less air pollution at higher levels of the 32-story building, or physiological damage to the ear. Higher noise levels caused the greater decrements in auditory discrimination of the children living on the lowest floors. Since reading ability depends in part upon the ability to discriminate the different phonemes (sounds) of language, this impairment in auditory discrimination caused a corresponding decrement in reading ability. Despite the children's short-term psychological adaption to their noisy environment (that is, they no longer were startled when a loud truck passed beneath them), it seems quite clear that noise can have serious long-term behavioral effects in the real world.

Folk wisdom postulates a strong relationship between weather conditions and affective states and even behavior itself. Civil disorder is widely held, even by presumably authoritative sources (e.g., the U.S. Riot Commission, 1968), to

Heat

FIGURE 15-11 The high-rise housing development studied by Cohen, Glass, and Singer (1973). Traffic passes directly under the apartments. As a result of the experimenters' work, the tenants have organized to have a roof built over the expressway. (Photo by Sheldon Cohen.)

be in part attributable to the high temperatures resulting from summer heat waves. The notion that high temperatures can cause organisms to go berserk has been stressed in science fiction tales such as Alfred Bester's "Fondly Fahrenheit." High temperature and acts of violence are closely linked in the public mind. But is there really such a simple relationship between temperature and affective states, between temperature and aggression?

The effects of heat upon performance in various information processing tasks are in some ways similar to the effects of noise previously described. This similarity becomes especially great when heat is combined with other stressors. For example, when heat and noise are combined (Wilkinson, 1969), their joint effects do not simply add but are in agreement with predictions generated from the Yerkes-Dodson law.

We shall now leave performance as our dependent variable and progress to effects of stressor combinations upon feelings. How do you feel when you are hot and crowded, i.e., subjected to the joint stress induced by both high temperature and invasion of personal space? Griffitt and Veitch (1971) tested this question in a laboratory study using two temperatures (73° and 94°) and two population densities (13 square feet per person and 4 square feet per person). Groups were either all female or all male. Attraction responses such as those previously discussed in Chapter 13 were the primary measure of interpersonal affective behavior. These attraction responses were more negative in the hot condition and also more negative in the crowded condition. While the study presented data for temperature and density effects separately, it seems likely (since no interaction was reported) that combined effects of the two stressors were simply additive: the negative affect induced by heat could be added to the negative affect induced by crowding to arrive at the total attraction response for the hot and crowded situation. This supposition is, of course, contrary to results of studies of combinations of stressors with performance as the dependent variable.

However, a series of studies conducted by Baron and his associates seems to offer support for a Yerkes-Dodson type of relationship when the dependent variable is aggression induced by a heat stressor. In the latest of this series of experiments, Baron and Bell (1976) added a new wrinkle to earlier work which examined the influences of heat and negative affect upon aggression. They administered a "cooling drink" to see if this would reduce stress and aggression. Their overall procedure was similar to that described in Chapter 13: a subject heard either a positive or negative personality evaluation administered by a confederate and was then given the opportunity to aggress physically against the confederate by controlling an electric shock on an aggression machine. The results are shown in Figure 15–12. We might expect, on the basis of "common sense," that both high temperature and receiving a negative personality rating would increase aggression, and furthermore that the joint effects of these two stressors would add to produce yet greater amounts of aggression. However, a glance at the left panel of Figure 15–12 reveals that this is not the case. The effect of the combined stressors is less aggression, just as was the case when noise and incentive were combined; the results are in accord with the Yerkes-Dodson law. Indeed, this was the explanation offered by Baron and Bell, who postulated an inverted U-shaped function relating aggression and negative affect (i.e., negative affect is similar to arousal in Figure 15–10). However, a cooling drink reduced stress, moving the subject to the left on the Yerkes-Dodson function, so that as shown in the right panel of Figure 15–12, there was more aggression with negative evaluations in *both* temperature conditions.

Air Pollution

We are all aware of physiological damage created by breathing polluted air over long periods of time. Indeed, legislation to minimize harmful effects of automobile exhausts, black lung disease in miners, and cigarette smoking in public places is by now well-known. But are there any short-term effects on mental efficiency resulting from inhalation of polluted air?

Lewis, Baddeley, Bonham, and Lovett (1970) had subjects breathe either pure air from medical cylinders or air obtained 15 inches above the ground (where your car air intake is) on a road in England which "by central Londons standards" was not very busy (830 vehicles per hour). Subjects then performed a variety of information processing tasks. Of course, neither the subjects, nor the experimenter knew which air supply was used until after the tests had been completed. Subjects who had breathed polluted air showed impairment on three of the four tasks used in the study. The decrease in the mental efficiency imposed by polluted air suggests that traffic pollution itself may contribute to automobile accidents.

FIGURE 15–12 **Effects of a cooling drink on aggression. The left panel shows the amount of aggression without a drink, and the right panel shows the amount of aggression with a cooling drink. When the temperature is cool, the drink has no effect. However, when the temperature is hot, a cooling drink reverses the pattern between aggression and personality evaluation. With a cooling drink, a negative evaluation leads to more aggression, regardless of temperature. Without a drink, a negative evaluation leads to more aggression only when the temperature is cool. (From Baron and Bell, 1976.)**

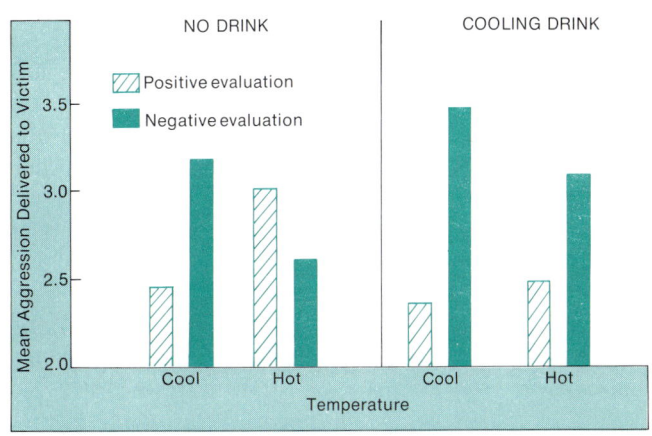

FIGURE 15–13   These drivers are breathing fumes which decrease their mental efficiency. In an emergency, they may be unable to react correctly or fast enough to save their lives.

THE CITY: ENTOPIA OR BEHAVIORAL SINK?

Utopia was an imaginary island, the best of all possible worlds, a place where every human endeavor enjoyed perfection. Typically, any ideal habitat is referred to as a utopia. We should note that the literal translation of this Greek term is "a place that does not exist." In search of a word for a desirable and realistic environment, the city planner Doxiadis (1967) has suggested the term "Entopia". This word literally means "in place," and it is intended to refer to an *attainable* substitute for Utopia. Thus, while Utopia is forever elusive, Entopia is, at least theoretically, within our grasp.

This section examines the city as an environmental setting for man. Some claim that the city represents the highest point of civilization, the peak of the human race's achievements. The joining of commerce and culture present in the great cities is said to give such cities a spirit and individual style of their own that greatly enrich the lives of their fortunate inhabitants. Therefore, if Entopia is to be found on earth, the city is the place to look. Others claim that the city is nothing but a foul aggregation of slums which, combined with the high crime rate, fosters interpersonal attitudes of indifference or worse. They claim that the cities are collapsing of their own weight, and that city bureaucracies are unable to effectively manage and plan the growth and even the continued existence of cities. In short, these critics would argue that the city is a huge, monolithic behavioral sink.

We will discuss both the psychological pros and cons of urban life. The reader must decide which term, Entopia or behavioral sink, more accurately reflects the environmental characteristics of the (fortunate or hapless) city dweller. Regardless of your choice, it remains true that the city is an intriguing laboratory for the behavioral scientist, and our following discussion of urban life should illuminate some important aspects of environmental psychology.

Cognitive Maps: Looking Out the Windows of the Mind

The concept of a mental picture of the world at large has antecedents long predating the rise of environmental psychology as an independent discipline. Psychologists of the nineteenth century debated the possibility of imageless thought—i.e., can mental activity exist without internal sensory images? In more recent times, the idea of a mental map can be traced to the work of Tolman (1948), who drew his conclusions mainly from animal data. If the lowly rat has a mental map, as Tolman believed, then surely man must have even more detailed mental pictures or images of his environment.

Cognitive mapping received its greatest impetus with the publication of a major work, *The Image of the City,* by architect Kevin Lynch. Lynch (1960) believed that principles of visual design could be applied not only to individual buildings but to whole urban regions. An effective visual image of a city would not only improve transportation by vehicle and by foot within the city but, and perhaps more importantly, would also improve the quality of life for the urban dweller. For example, residents of Seattle, Washington, are especially fortunate in being able, at least on clear days, to view the awesome and inspiring panorama surrounding Mt. Rainier. Indeed, a common question asked by Seattle residents upon awakening is "Is the mountain out today?" Lynch believed that man could build similar good environmental images in his cities, and that these images would increase emotional security and generally improve the quality of life. But before these sharp visual images could be planned, Lynch first had to establish a methodology for measuring the visual impact of the urban environment.

Lynch (1960) conducted pilot analyses of three American cities: Boston, Jersey City, and Los Angeles. He relied on two methods. First, a trained observer mapped the downtown areas based upon his own subjective judgments about visual form, interrelations among visual elements, and so on. This technique is essentially equivalent to the method of introspection used at an early period in the history of psychology. You will recall from our discussion of introspection in Chapter 1 that the method soon fell into disrepute and has long been replaced by more objective techniques. Nevertheless, this method is not an unreasonable starting point, especially for persons untrained in psychological methodology. Lynch's second method was based upon detailed interviews with small samples of city residents. During this interview, residents were asked to describe locations, draw rough sketches, and take imaginary trips through the city.

How To Make a Cognitive Map

The cognitive maps representing Jersey City and Boston are reproduced in Figure 15–14. As can be seen, Lynch formed a taxonomy based upon five elements. A **path** links various environmental features and is customarily or at least potentially available for transportation. Thus, streets, sidewalks, railroads, and canals all are paths. An **edge** is a linear element which does not qualify as a path. Riverbanks, walls, and similar barriers are edges. A **district** is a two-dimensional region within a city that has a common identity. Greenwich Village in New York and the Back Bay in Boston are districts. A **node** is a focal point within the city where transitions between different activities occur, as in a bus terminal; nodes also occur when activities are focused in some particular place as a result of either physical or functional characteristics, such as in Union Square in New York, which is a focal point for soapbox orators. Finally, **landmarks** are symbolic points viewed from the exterior, as opposed to a node, which is viewed from within. Big Ben in London is a good example of such a landmark.

How these key elements combine to form a cognitive map or image of a city is shown in Figures 15–14B and 15–14D. It is quite clear that Boston is a much more visually exciting city than is Jersey City. Nodes and landmarks are abundant and well contained within clearly defined districts. Edges and paths are strong, giving rise to a well-formed structure. In contrast, the most distinctive feature of Jersey City is the view of the distant New York City skyline. Jersey City was perceived by its inhabitants as a place on the edge of someplace else. It had no truly distinctive features of its own.

Lynch's methodology was improved by psychologist Stanley Milgram and his co-workers (Milgram et al., 1972), who drew a cognitive map of New York City. They superimposed a standard grid system on a geographic map of New York City and took photographs at grid intersections. This method is objective

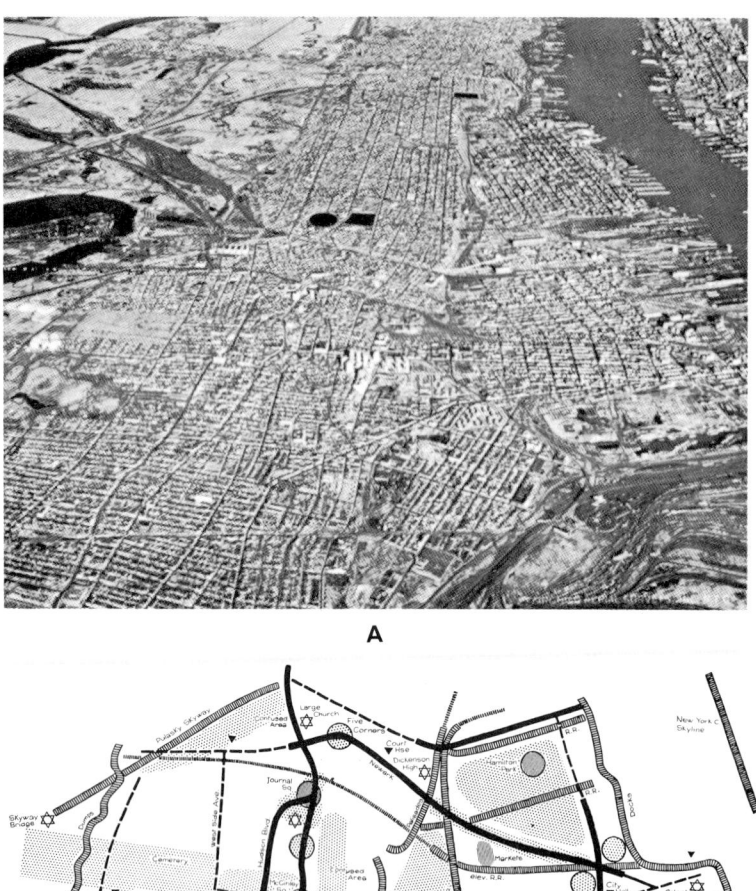

A

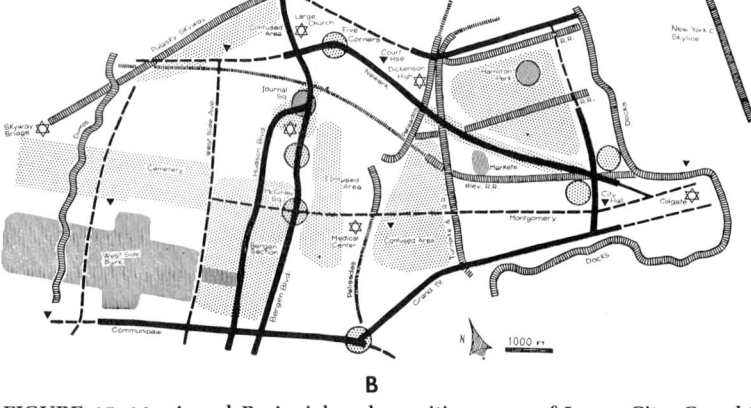

B

FIGURE 15–14   A and B: Aerial and cognitive maps of Jersey City. C and D: Aerial and cognitive maps of the Boston peninsula. Note the general lack of major cognitive elements in the Jersey City map (B), especially as compared to the highly developed Boston map (D). (From Lynch, K.: *The Image of the City*, MIT Press, 1960.)

and prevents bias due to selection of locations (e.g., Times Square in Manhattan is more readily recognized than Katz's Bakery in Brooklyn). A large number of subjects were shown the photographs and were asked to locate the borough (Manhattan, Brooklyn, the Bronx, Queens, or Staten Island) as well as the neighborhood and street, if possible. The resulting percentages of correct identifications for each location were combined in a cognitive map of New York City. Manhattan had the most distinctive image, with other boroughs, especially Queens and the Bronx, having few distinctive features. Indeed, a resident of Queens was four times more likely to correctly identify a scene from Manhattan than a scene from Queens. Two major conclusions were drawn from this result. First the recognizability of street scenes depends not only upon the architectural or social distinctiveness of a location but also upon its centrality to population flow. Non-Manhattan residents did better at recognizing

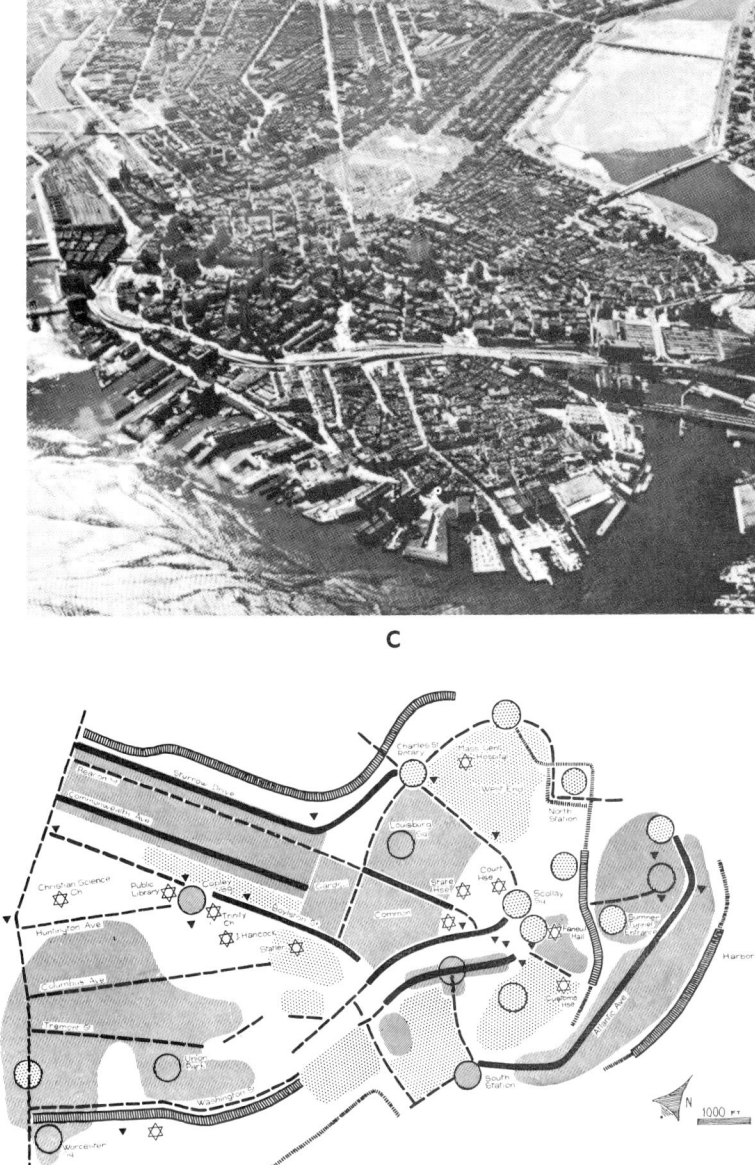

C

D

FIGURE 15-14   *Continued*

Manhattan locations because they often visited Manhattan either for business or for pleasure. Second, the dreary image of the outer boroughs, in many ways comparable to that of Jersey City, could — and should — be upgraded by building distinctive architectural works to enhance not only visual impact but also a sense of community. Of course, new buildings are only a small part of community pride, but they can serve to "prime the pump" of community spirit.

The basic tool of cognitive mapping can be put to a wide variety of uses (see Downs and Stea, 1973), whose scope greatly exceeds that of this chapter. However, we will take one last look at cognitive mapping, this time in the university. As a class exercise, students at Purdue were given sets of photographs of the campus taken along the lines of the work by Milgram et al. (1972).

Separate cognitive maps were constructed for faculty and for students. These maps showed that the faculty had hardly any image whatsoever of the university, although on the average they had been at Purdue much longer than the students. In dramatic contrast, the considerably more mobile students showed a much better image of the campus, and this image improved as they progressed from freshmen to seniors. The only locations that were well-known to both students and faculty were primarily recreational: the student union and the gymnasium. This may imply that if students and faculty are to know each other better, communication might be more effective on the playing field than in the classroom.

Architectural Psychology: Better Buildings for People

Most of us tend to take the buildings we live and work in for granted. Unless we are students of architecture, we seldom reflect on what makes a good building or a bad building, or even that there are both good and bad buildings. This distinction goes far beyond the aesthetic appeal of a handsomely designed structure or a well-appointed room. The quality of your life depends to a much greater degree than you might first suspect upon the physical features of the buildings you inhabit and use. In this section we shall examine some of the psychological characteristics that make structures easy or difficult for people to get along with. Buildings are not built for architects; they are built for you and me, and we have the right to insist that architects and urban planners place a high value on the psychological characteristics which make a building a good place to live and work. Architects have a saying: "A doctor can bury his mistakes but an architect can only advise his clients to plant ivy." This slogan, of course, represents several misplaced values, not the least of which is an undue preoccupation with the appearance of the exterior of a building relative to the importance of the interior psychological space any building surrounds.

Pruitt-Igoe: The House that Failed

Once upon a time, not so very long ago, the city of St. Louis, Missouri, built 33 eleven-story buildings not far from downtown. This public housing project contained 2,762 apartments and was called the Pruitt-Igoe Project. It seemed like a good idea at the time. To see what Pruitt-Igoe looks like today, look at Figure 15–15. How did this social disaster come about? Why was an expensive group of high-rise buildings demolished in 1972 when the project was less than twenty years old?

Pruitt-Igoe was a low-income public housing project. It was rendered completely uninhabitable through vandalism which destroyed the physical integrity of the buildings inside and out. Now, anyone who has had the misfortune to live in a typical public housing project knows that the construction is considerably sturdier than that of a typical one-family frame house. Tiles similar to those used in hospitals and prisons line the walls because they are durable and can be washed free of graffiti. The fact that such tiles are extremely ugly is, if anything, considered a plus by housing authorities (Newman, 1972): for political reasons, public housing must never appear luxurious, although it may cost as much as or more than luxury high-rise apartments. Similarly, light fixtures are protected by unattractive cases. In a study of residents in Pruitt-Igoe, the sociologist Lee Rainwater (1966) has pointed out the psychologically damaging effects of lower-class life in the institutional setting of the public housing project. The physical environment joins with the world at large to tell the resident that he is a species of inferior vermin more akin to the garbage littering the project hallways than to the more privileged members of society. Instead of providing an attractive environment in which the tenant could take pride, the housing authority provided an institutional setting which challenged the resident-inmate to destroy it. In the words of Newman (1972, p.

FIGURE 15–15 Demolition of part of the Pruitt-Igoe housing project in 1972. The buildings were no longer safe or suitable for human inhabitants and, accordingly, were destroyed. (Photo credit: United Press International.)

105): "In the long run, even the institutional wall tile and vandal-resistant radiators at Pruitt-Igoe met their match."

It is difficult for the uninitiated to comprehend the degree of destruction wrought by public-housing tenants, especially children. Teenagers have been able to anchor elevator cables so that the elevator cab is ripped off its railings and the entire elevator shaft is torn apart throughout the entire height of the building. Since middle-income tenants have been largely able to preserve the physical integrity of their high-rise dwellings, can this wanton destruction be *entirely* attributed to pathological personality defects in lower-income families? Not at all. Circumstances and physical environment conspire to bring about destruction in public housing projects throughout the United States. It is difficult to name one major city that does not share the shame of Pruitt-Igoe.

While middle-income families usually have two adults, one of whom will undertake supervision of the children, often a working female is the only head of the household in lower-income families such as resided in Pruitt-Igoe. Children therefore are largely unsupervised and in bad weather entertain themselves inside the building halls, staircases, and elevators. The typical apartment building, with a central corridor having apartments on both sides, prevents easy visual surveillance of the building interior, and vandals can inflict damage unobserved. This is but one of many serious defects in the physical environment (Newman, 1972). When lower-class residents are housed in low-rise public projects where psychological factors have been taken into consideration to provide reasonable amenities and "defensible space," to use Newman's term, destruction is not a problem. Furthermore, there is a great decrease in crime. The residents enjoy a much higher quality of life. Pruitt-Igoe and its kindred developments throughout the nation have provided a harsh lesson on the effects of the physical environment upon behavior (Yancy, 1971). Let us hope this lesson has been well learned.

The city is a magnet for most of the environmental stressors discussed earlier. Extreme crowding, intermittent and unpredictable noise, heat, and pollution are all everyday events in the modern city. One cannot help but wonder how people manage to function at all in such a stressful environment. Glass and Singer (1972b) note that the most amazing aspect of urban life is not the great amount of stress that is present but rather the ability of urban dwellers to adapt to this stressful life, despite the many "indignities" forced upon them. Visitors to New York City, especially those from non-metropolitan areas, are

The City as a Psychological Setting: Unnatural Habitat?

amazed and appalled by what they perceive as the hectic and frantic pace of the New Yorker. An attempt to obtain a taxi can embroil the visitor in seemingly mortal combat not only with hulking men but also with apparently less dangerous adversaries, including little old ladies who, armed with umbrellas, make up in ferocity what they lack in size. A trip on the subway during rush hour is even more violent, with its physical as well as psychological spatial invasions of your personal-space bubble. The New Yorker is regarded as a calloused and socially indifferent individual incapable of even the most minor social grace, such as yielding a seat to an elderly woman on a bus. How then does this adaptation to the city environment work, and what is the psychological price the city resident must pay for his adaptation?

One important psychological model of the urban dweller draws its theoretical base from the concept of information overload. You will recall our discussion of information overload, especially as it related to attention, in Chapter 6. Milgram (1970) has borrowed this concept and applied it to typical mechanisms used by the city resident to cope with the input in his or her life. First, less processing time is allocated to incoming information. Second, low-priority inputs are completely filtered out, so that no response need be made. Third, the likelihood of social interaction is intentionally decreased by such devices as perpetual scowls, burying one's head in a newspaper in public conveyances, and leaving the telephone off the hook or having an unlisted number. While it is also true that institutions such as a city adapt to information overload (Meier, 1962) — for example, by creating a welfare department so that inhabitants will not be excessively harassed by beggars, as is the case in India — our interest will center about the psychological adaptation mechanisms used by individuals to gain relief from urban stresses.

The operation of these overload-protection mechanisms usually leads to marked decreases in social responsibility. The city dweller is bombarded by such a great amount of stimulation that he lacks the psychological capacity to "give a damn" about strangers, because his capacity must be reserved for higher-priority social interactions. This indifference to the needs of others is apparent in many urban situations. Perhaps the most striking is the lack of bystander intervention discussed in Chapter 13, where the murder of Catherine Genovese was cited. You will recall that none of the many people watching from their apartments even telephoned police. But similar effects are obtained even when large numbers of bystanders are not immediately present. People living in large cities are considerably more reluctant to allow strangers into their house to use the telephone. Since this behavior may only be an accurate reflection of the statistically greater dangers of victimization upon allowing entrance of someone into your home in a metropolitan area, recent studies have had confederates telephone strangers to ask for help. An experimenter might telephone a stranger, for example, and claim to be calling from out of town. The bogus long-distance caller would apologize for getting a wrong number and then make increasingly more demanding requests of the respondent. First, the experimenter would ask for information about the weather. Then the experimenter would excuse herself and ask the other party to hold on for almost a minute. If the party did not hang up, the experimenter would then ask for the phone number of a motel. McKenna and Morgenthau (cited by Milgram, 1970) found that people in small towns were more helpful and informative in this task than were urban dwellers. Similar results have also been obtained by Latané and Darley (1970). They found that people who grew up in small communities were more likely to help a stranger in an emergency than were people from larger communities. While this research does indeed suggest that city-dwellers are more indifferent to the needs of others, the effects reported in these studies have been small. Furthermore, effects of possibly related variables, such as socioeconomic status, have not always been taken into account, so it is perhaps too early to state with complete confidence that urban life itself causes psychological indifference. As is often the case in environmental psychology, more research will be required to "nail down" this phenomenon.

Whatever the cause, the mechanisms which prove useful in limiting information overload generally tend to become part of the personality of the urbanite and are maintained even in very specific situations in which no immediate overload is likely to exist. New social norms of noninvolvement arise to govern urban behavior. Thus, as Milgram (1970) noted, a man giving up a seat on the subway to an old woman is often embarrassed because his gesture violates the norms of the city.

The psychological distinctions between small-town and big-city life can go beyond mere indifference to other people. A simple field study conducted by Fraser and Zimbardo (1969) revealed dramatic differences in the life styles of a small town (Palo Alto, California) and a big city (Bronx, New York). They parked a used automobile in each place. The license plate was removed and the hood was left up. Ten minutes after the Bronx car was "abandoned," the first vandals appeared: a young, apparently middle-class family. While the mother kept watch, the father and son cleaned out the trunk and glove compartment and then ripped off the battery and the radiator. A short time later, another adult jacked up the car and removed a tire. At the end of the first day, adults had carried off every portable part of the car. In sharp contrast, the Palo Alto car was unharmed for an entire week, after which the experiment ended. Indeed, someone even closed the hood to protect the car from rain.

This kind of vandalism cannot be explained by Milgram's information overload hypothesis. Zimbardo uses the concept of *anonymity* to explain the dramatic differences between Palo Alto and the Bronx. Being just another unknown face in the crowd releases our inhibitions about vandalism and, for that matter, about any antisocial behavior. Since the urbanite is more anonymous than a small-town resident, he is more likely to yield to the temptations of antisocial behavior when opportunity knocks. (If you think you would never do anything like this even in a big city, turn back to Chapter 9.)

The Joy of Cities

Our discussion of the city so far has been weighted towards psychological defects of the built environment. While this approach is readily justified by the importance of specifying problems in the man-made environment, this weight-

FIGURE 15-16 The result of abandoning a car in an area where passersby can commit acts of vandalism or outright theft under a cloak of anonymity.

ing may have unfairly biased you against the urban environment, especially if you have little first-hand experience with living in large cities. The present section attempts to give "equal time" to the positive aspects of city life, in order to equip us better to answer the question posed at the beginning of this section on the city.

A slum seems an unlikely place to discover the rewards of urban life. But our preconception (and a city planners' preconception, too) of life in a slum, stressing the harsh and degrading aspects of such an existence, may be naive in omitting possible sources of residential satisfaction. This other side of the coin is suggested by the remarks of a resident in an area scheduled for demolition and urban renewal. When asked if he lived in a bad neighborhood, he replied "My neighborhood is so bad that the city is tearing it down to build a slum." For him, the sterile housing project that would replace his "inferior" fourth-floor walk-up apartment was less desirable by far than his present lodging. Let us visit the West End of Boston (Gans, 1962) to see why "slum" residents might oppose urban renewal, which purportedly creates greatly improved housing.

The typical slum resident is highly committed to his dwelling and strongly resists attempts to relocate him. Contrary to public opinion, the slum is a stable residential area and not a highly transient district where people move frequently. The West End slum resident liked living where he was, and this sentiment went beyond purely practical reasons such as low rent. Almost three-quarters of those surveyed responded that the West End was their home, and half of the remaining one-quarter who did not regard the West End as home still had positive feelings about the area. Thus it was not necessary to view the West End as home in order to like it. Therefore, a sense of belonging is not the only reason for liking an area, and indeed 14 per cent of those who had this sense of belonging did not like the West End. Finally, West End residents had a strong sense of locality, as if the West End was a clearly defined spatial district or village existing within the larger urban setting. Indeed, this local physical space provided the setting for many of the important social interrelationships of the residents. It is clear that being forced out of a slum by urban renewal is a traumatic process for the lower-class slum resident. Critics of urban renewal programs (Glazer, 1965) have pointed out that merely replacing old buildings with new buildings ignores the needs of the displaced slum residents. We must help people up, while or perhaps even before we tear buildings down.

Sidewalks: More than Walkways

To the average city planner, a sidewalk has two main functions. First, it has a curb which separates vehicular and pedestrian traffic. This curb is a particularly good place along which to park vehicles. Second, the sidewalk is a place where people can walk, usually to and from cars or other forms of transportation. Whenever a conflict arises between demands of wheeled and pedestrian traffic, sidewalks are usually the loser. Since the city planner conceives of the sidewalk as merely an alternate place for transportation of people, it is easy for him to lop off a few feet from a sidewalk to provide an extra lane for cars.

In a fascinating book about city life, *Death and Life of Great American Cities*, Jane Jacobs (1961) eloquently discusses the psychological functions of a sidewalk. The old-fashioned sidewalk is the city's unique contribution to social interaction. A sidewalk, lined with shops and small businesses, teems with life and adventure. The sidewalk is one of the few places where children can learn that people without overt ties such as kinship and friendship must take at least some public responsibility for each other. When the neighborhood tailor calls out to warn a child against running into the street and later mentions the incident to the child's parents when they pass his store, the child learns more than not to run into the street. He learns about social responsibility. This lesson cannot be taught in a playground, because the playground supervisor is paid to oversee the child's behavior. The tailor, however, has no overt tie other than sharing the same street.

The sidewalk works for the adult as well. It is quite common for street residents to leave their apartment keys with a local shopkeeper when they are expecting company and cannot be present. The shopkeeper provides a multitude of small services which are unrelated to his business. In addition to holding keys, he might hold packages for nearby residents, give street directions, let children playing in the street use his toilet facilities so they don't have to run upstairs, hold merchandise for the business across the street which doesn't open for another hour, and so on. Each of these small services is by itself trivial. But the sum of these services is the cement which binds a neighborhood—and with no invasion of the privacy of the residents. Since the streets and the businesses lining them are public or semi-public territory, they provide for social interaction on neutral ground. This public accessibility allows the resident to form an extensive network of sidewalk friends who perform valuable services, such as watching children play. Despite this help, the resident need not incur extensive social obligations, such as inviting the whole neighborhood to dinner once a month. A housing project with its sterile pathways does not encourage this social system. Many parents are reluctant to send young children to play alone even in the playgrounds provided by the housing authority, because there is no one to watch them. A similar problem arises in suburbia, where housewives must truck station-wagon loads of children to play in each other's back yards. The greater economic efficiency of supermarkets and drug store chains may prove to yield inadequate compensation for the loss of social aspects of small neighborhood groceries and pharmacies. Would you rather deal with an anonymous clerk or a friendly neighborhood butcher who puts aside selected cuts for his regular customers? Would you rather receive a bill from a dispassionate computer (let alone try to get a computerized bill corrected should an error occur) or from your local pharmacist who opened his store in the middle of the night so that you could obtain an urgently needed prescription? The social structure of the sidewalk is a great benefit of city life.

While the positive functions of a sidewalk pointed out by Jacobs (1961) seem intuitively correct, we must realize that they are based solely upon the observations of one person. Jacobs did not collect any data in the formal manner required by scientific investigation, and her conclusions are essentially based upon anecdotal evidence. This certainly does not mean that her conclusions are incorrect, but psychologists, like other scientists, prefer data to speculation.

Fortunately, psychologists have become increasingly more concerned with obtaining empirical evidence to evaluate the kinds of environmental effects discussed by Jacobs. One recent field study (Holahan, 1975) looked at outdoor behavior in three urban low-income environments: an old ghetto with low-rise tenement houses, a traditional high-rise housing project similar to Pruitt-Igoe, and an innovative high-rise project in which creative architectural design had been used to encourage outdoor use. As expected, the new high-rise project showed greater amounts of socializing among neighbors than did the traditional project. But the old ghetto showed the most recreational social activity. Ninety per cent of outdoor socializing in the ghetto occurred on the sidewalks near building entrances, stoops, and curbs. In sharp contrast, the open, grassy space in the middle of the traditional project was almost never used for social interaction. These data confirm both the beneficial aspects of sidewalks observed by Jacobs and the harmful effects of traditional housing projects.

FIGURE 15–17   A home along a canyon wall near Los Angeles. Would you live in this house? (Photo credit: United States Department of Interior Geological Survey.)

Putting Environmental Psychology to Work: Design for Urban Life

Whether you think the city is an Entopia or a behavioral sink, you will agree that cities are here to stay. How can environmental psychology help us to minimize the disadvantages and to maximize the benefits of urban life? The general principle is clear. Before modifying the city environment by tearing down a slum, or building a new highway, or closing off a street to traffic, or planning for the year 2000, we must always ask, "*What are the implications of this alteration in the existing environment for the behavior of the people who will use it?*" rather than "How will this modification look in an aerial photograph or scale model?" As an educated citizen, it is your responsibility to ensure that even the most idealistic and well-intentioned of your legislative representatives apply this simple criterion when formulating the laws and codes which govern our use of the constructed environment.

Fortunately, city planners and architects are starting to place greater emphasis upon the human side of the environment (e.g., Carr, 1967; Deasy, 1970). But this concern with humanizing the city will come to nought unless we also acquire the data linking aspects of the environment to human behavior. And these data must be used. We know that personal-space bubbles have a strong bearing on social intercourse, yet airports are designed to isolate people within their own bubble (Sommer, 1974). Severe psychological disturbances can result from exposure to loud noise, yet trucks roar through our city streets. Pollution impairs mental efficiency, yet we continue to foul our air. The list is long, surpassed only by what we don't know. Why do people build homes on primary sand dunes when they know it is only a matter of time until these homes fall into the sea (McHarg, 1971)? Why after disaster do people return to build again in a flood plain? Why do we not take our meager store of knowledge, build on it and apply the results to improving our environment? Our cities can be Entopias or behavioral sinks; the choice is yours.

Summary

Territoriality is a characteristic behavior of animals and human beings. However, while animal territoriality most often centers about some fixed spatial location, man carries his territory with him in the form of a **personal-space bubble.** The size and shape of this bubble vary for different individuals. People try to maintain certain distances between bubbles according to the social requirements of their current interpersonal interaction. Private behavior is characterized by close interpersonal distances. As interpersonal distance increases, behavior becomes more public and stylized. Different cultures have different spatial norms for appropriate distances between bubbles. When people of different cultures do not realize this, strange and often amusing behavior characterizes attempts at social interaction. Various defense mechanisms are used to protect the integrity of the personal-space bubble. Many of these mechanisms are nonverbal. Sex affects the size of the bubble, but results for women are different in same- and mixed-sex groups. However, this finding may be due to uncontrolled differences in personal orientations (e.g., face-to-face or side-by-side positioning).

Biological and psychological measures of stress are not the same. Psychological factors, such as the predictability of electric shock are more important determinants of biological and psychological indices of stress than are physical measures, such as amount of shock. Stressful situations can arise from excessive environmental demands but also from insufficient environmental stimulation. When rats are crowded for long periods of time, strange behavior pathologies develop. A **behavioral sink** is thus formed. Correlational studies of human crowding tend to support a relationship between density and pathology, but such findings must be cautiously interpreted. Laboratory studies generally do not find pathological effects of crowding, but they are conducted on a short time scale relative to the correlational and animal studies of population density. The effects of **stressors** such as noise on human performance are non-additive. Combinations of stressors affect behavior according to the **Yerkes-Dodson** law. Psychological **aftereffects**

of noise are related to learned helplessness. High noise levels may impair children's reading ability. High temperatures affect behavior in ways similar to other stressors in Yerkes-Dodson law and do not simply increase aggression. Air pollution causes an immediate decrease in mental efficiency.

Cognitive maps of cities show the relations among **paths, edges, districts, nodes,** and **landmarks.** Cities differ in the crispness and vividness of their inhabitants' cognitive maps. Buildings can create good or bad psychological environments. High-rise public housing projects (e.g., Pruitt-Igoe) tend to foster destructive behaviors on the part of their residents. Psychological principles must be considered when designing any buildings, especially a large housing project. Urban residents make accommodations for the many stresses of urban life by attempting to reduce environmental information overload. These efforts reduce social responsibility and become new urban norms. The amount of time spent processing each input decreases, and people become indifferent to the needs of strangers. But cities also have sources of satisfaction for their residents. Even slum residents have many positive feelings about their homes, and they will resist relocation. Urban renewal planners must deal with the psychological needs of slum residents before tearing down buildings. Sidewalks play an important social role in city life, offering public areas for assimilation of children and other interactions without invading the privacy of city residents. Cities can be pleasant or unpleasant, depending upon the degree to which psychological requirements have been met by the built environment. Only concerned and educated citizens can ensure that our cities become more like Entopias and less like behavioral sinks.

Suggested Readings

Downs, R., and Stea, D. (eds.): *Image and Environment.* Chicago: Aldine Publishing Company, 1973.
    An interesting collection on cognitive maps. The approach is interdisciplinary, with articles representing psychology, geography, sociology, neurophysiology, sociology, anthropology, biology, and urban design and planning.
Heimstra, N. W., and McFarling, L. H.: *Environmental Psychology.* Monterey, California: Brooks/Cole Publishing Company, 1974.
    A brief undergraduate text that surveys the field. Good coverage of the constructed environment, with chapters on rooms, buildings, and cities.
Ittelson, W. H., Proshansky, H. M., Rivlin, L. G., and Winkel, G. H.: *An Introduction to Environmental*

Psychology. New York: Holt, Rinehart and Winston, 1974.
    This undergraduate text provides a more detailed treatment than that by Heimstra and McFarling but is not as well organized. It tries to provide a theoretical framework for the field.
Jacobs, J.: *Death and Life of Great American Cities.* New York: Random House, 1961.
    A fascinating and provocative discussion of the problems and potentials of the urban environment by a very astute observer. This book has become a classic but don't let that stop you from enjoying it. Researchers are still testing hypotheses proposed by Jacobs.

Overleaf: Top photo original with this edition; bottom photo, New Zealand Herald.

Appendix A

Statistics: Tool For Research

In an important sense, all scientists require two major types of tools for conducting their research. First, they require various kinds of equipment. As you can probably imagine, the specific instruments or apparatus will differ greatly from one scientific field to another. The need for *some* kind of equipment, however, seems virtually universal. For example, it is hard to imagine astronomers, biologists, or chemists performing systematic research in their respective fields in the absence of telescopes, microscopes, test tubes, and other kinds of devices. Similarly, as you already know from earlier portions of this text, psychologists also make use of many different kinds of equipment, and it would often be impossible for them to conduct their own investigations in the absence of such apparatus.

The second tool required by all scientists is some means for evaluating or interpreting the findings of their research—for making sense out of the data they so carefully collect. In most cases, this takes the form of some type of mathematical analysis. Once again, the precise techniques that are employed vary greatly from one field to another, according to the nature of the topics being studied and the type of data collected. The need for *some* form of mathematical analysis, however, is also quite universal. In the case of psychology, the most common forms of analysis involve **statistics.** We have already examined the need for statistics, as well as their crucial role in psychological research, in Chapter 1. Here, we will go a bit further and provide you with a brief introduction to some of the basic principles of these procedures. Since our main purpose is certainly *not* that of turning you into an expert statistician capable of conducting complex analyses of psychological data, we will devote relatively little time to actual methods of computation. Instead, the bulk of our attention will be focused on the manner in which psychologists employ statistics as a tool of research—that is, as an important technique for answering many complex questions about behavior.

Basically, psychologists employ statistics for four major purposes: (1) *summarizing* large amounts of information in a convenient form, (2) *comparing* the behavior of groups of individuals, (3) *relating* different traits, characteristics, or behaviors in order to determine whether they vary together in any systematic manner, and (4) *predicting* future behavior from present information. We will consider each of these major uses in turn.

"Tonight, we're going to let the statistics speak for themselves."

FIGURE A–1   Drawing by Koren; © 1974, The New Yorker Magazine, Inc.

DESCRIPTIVE STATISTICS: TELLING IT LIKE IT IS

In order to illustrate the manner in which psychologists use statistics for summarizing or describing large amounts of information, let us consider an investigation concerned with interpersonal distance—the amount of space separating individuals engaged in conversation. Assume that we start by measuring the distance between the tips of the noses of ten pairs of persons who permit us to gather such information, and that the measurements we obtain are those shown below:

5   6   6   4   4   4   4   3   5   5

Presented in this form, these data appear to have no particularly outstanding characteristics, other than that they are associated with human noses. If, however, we construct a bar graph of the measurements, grouping equal distances together, as in Figure A–2, the data begin to assume a slightly different perspective. Let us now go one step further and connect the midpoints of this bar graph with a single line, as in Figure A–3. We refer to the data in

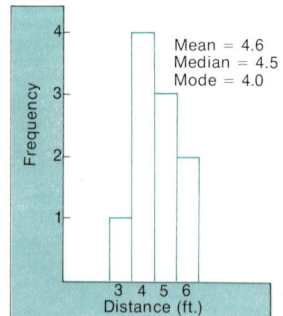

Mean = 4.6
Median = 4.5
Mode = 4.0

FIGURE A–2   A bar graph showing a hypothetical frequency distribution of interpersonal distances.

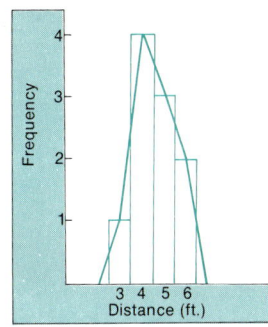

FIGURE A-3   A frequency curve drawn by connecting the midpoints of several bars.

this form as a **frequency distribution**; frequency refers to how many times each distance occurs in the sample. We can get a good idea from such diagrams of how often particular magnitudes of the variable of interest (in this case interpersonal distances) have occurred in our sample. We can note from the data presented, for example, that the most frequently occurring distances are those in the middle (i.e., 4 and 5 feet), and that the least frequently occurring distances are those toward the high and low extremes (i.e., 3 and 6 feet). We might suspect from examining this distribution that distances of 1, 2, 7, and 8 feet would be expected to occur even less frequently in other samples.

Let us now examine specific descriptive statistics for our sample. One class of such summary statistics describes **central tendency;** these measures indicate characteristics of the *center* of the distribution. A second type of statistics describes **dispersion;** such measures indicate the degree of spread *around* the center.

One of the most obvious indicators of centrality would be the most frequently occurring score (or, in our example, the most frequently occurring distance between people). We refer to this value as the **mode** of the distribution. In the data in Figure A-2, it is apparent that 4 feet is the modal distance. What happens in the case of ties, you might be wondering? Suppose in our sample we found four couples standing 4 feet apart and four couples standing 6 feet apart. In such instances, we say that our sample has two modes, and we refer to the distribution as *bimodal*.

Although the mode does identify the most frequent score, it may be somewhat deceiving as a measure of central tendency, especially if it falls far away from the center of the distribution. Suppose, for example, we had found in our sample four distances of 8 feet and two each of distances of 2, 3, and 4 feet, as in Figure A-4. Although it is true that the mode is 8, to speak only about this value ignores the fact that *most* of the distances in the sample are half that or less. In such a case, then, the mode does not give us an accurate idea of the central tendency of the distribution.

Measures of Central Tendency

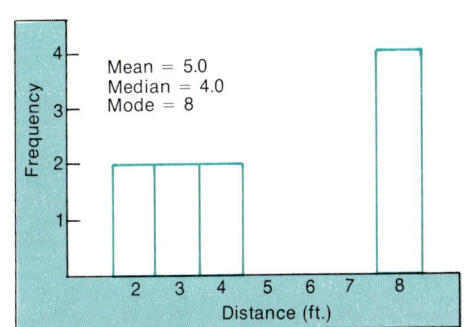

FIGURE A-4   A hypothetical frequency distribution showing a mode much larger than the mean or median.

A second measure of central tendency, and one which can be more useful than the mode in some instances, is the **median**—that point above which 50 per cent of the distribution falls and below which 50 per cent of the distribution falls. In other words, the median is the *midpoint* of the distribution. In the data presented in Figure A–2, it can be seen that half the interpersonal distances are 5 feet or greater, and half are 4 feet or less. We thus designate 4.5, or that point midway between these two categories, as the median. If our distances had been 4, 4, 5, 6, and 7, then 5.0 would have been designated as the median, since that is the point which divides the distribution in half. In the data shown in Figure A–4, in which the distances are found to be 2, 2, 3, 3, 4, 4, 8, 8, 8, 8, the median is 4.0. Note that in this case, the value of the median tells us much more about the central tendency of the distribution than does the mode of 8.0. However, in using *only* the median to describe this distribution, we lose sight of the fact that the distribution is heavily loaded toward the higher end. In such a case, we are probably wise to use both the mode *and* the median to describe our distribution.

Still another measure of central tendency is the average, or arithmetic **mean.** We calculate the mean by adding all the scores in the distribution and dividing by the total number of scores. Calculation of the means for the data shown in Figures A–2 and A–4 is presented in Table A–1. For the data in Figure A–2, the mean is found to be 4.6; for that in Figure A–4, the mean is 5.0. Note that in both cases the value of the mean is very close to the value of the median, but not necessarily close to the value of the mode. For descriptive purposes, then, the mean and median often (but not always) give us almost the same information about the central tendency of the distribution.

Look again at the distributions shown in Figure A–2 and A–4, and note that the mean, median, and mode in each distribution are distinct from each other. Now examine the distributions in Figure A–5, both of which have means and medians of 5.0. We refer to such distributions having the same value for the mean and the median as **symmetric,** since the left half is a mirror image of the right half. A distribution having a mean and median that are not the same value is referred to as **skewed.** (The distributions in Figure A–3 and A–4 are skewed.)

We have now examined three measures of central tendency, each of which tells us something slightly different about a distribution. These three descrip-

TABLE A–1   Calculation of the Mean

Data in Figure A–2	Data in Figure A–4
3	2
4	2
4	3
4	3
4	4
5	4
5	8
5	8
6	8
6	8
46	50
Mean = (46 ÷ 10) = 4.6	Mean = (50 ÷ 10) = 5.0

To find the mean of a sample, add all scores and divide by the number of scores. Graphs of these data are shown in Figures A–2 and A–4, respectively.

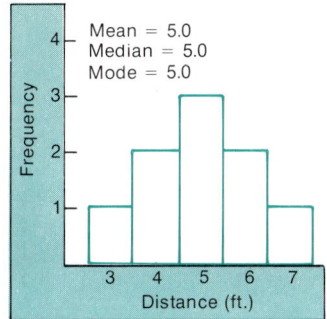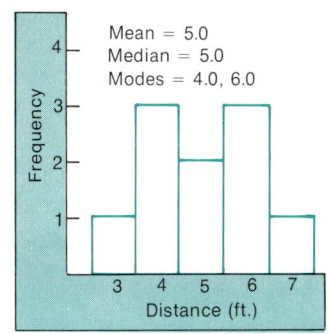

FIGURE A-5 Examples of symmetric distributions. Note that the mean and median have the same value. Also note that if divided in the middle, the left half of each distribution is a mirror image of the right half.

tive statistics, however, do not tell us much about the *shape* of the distribution. The distributions in Figures A-4 and A-5, for example, all have means of 5.0, but are quite different in shape. In order to describe the manner in which a distribution is spread out around the measures of central tendency, we employ measures of *dispersion*.

Measures of Dispersion

One useful measure of dispersion is the width of the distribution, often known as the **range.** This is simply defined as the difference (always a positive number) between the highest and lowest scores of the distribution. The ranges for the distributions shown in Figures A-2 and A-4, for example, are $6 - 3 = 3$ and $8 - 2 = 6$, respectively, while the ranges shown in Figure A-5 are both $7 - 3 = 4$. Although the range tells us the width of a distribution, it does not tell us anything about this spread relative to a measure of central tendency. If we know the range, we do not, for example, necessarily know how far the mean, median, or mode is from either end.

Two measures of dispersion which are often much more useful are the **variance** and the **standard deviation.** The variance (usually designated σ^2) is simply the average squared distance from the mean, and the standard deviation (usually designated σ) is the square root of the variance. Since that statement may have been a bit confusing, let us turn to a concrete example involving the data from Figure A-4. The specific calculations are presented in Table A-2. We begin by computing the difference between the mean of 5.0 and each of the scores (distances) in the sample. That is, we subtract 5.0 from each observed interpersonal distance. Since the variance is the average *squared* distance from the mean, we now square each of these differences. Next, we take an average of these values by adding them together and dividing by the total number of observations (in this case, 10). The reason we used squared distances is that we are interested in the average distance from the mean without regard to direction (i.e., above or below this value). If we do not square these distances and *do* take into account the direction of deviation from the mean, the sum of these signed differences must always be zero, as indicated in the second column of Table A-2 (the one labeled $X - \bar{X}$). The purpose of squaring the difference between each score and the mean, then, is to eliminate the positive or negative sign in front of each difference. When we take the square root of the variance in order to obtain the standard deviation, we "counteract" this squaring process, so to speak. Thus, the standard deviation approximates an average distance from the mean rather than an average *squared* distance. For this reason, psychologists usually prefer to use the standard deviation rather than the variance in describing or summarizing data. As you have probably already guessed, the larger the variance or the standard deviation, the greater the spread of the scores around the mean—that is, the more they tend to depart from this value.

**TABLE A-2   Calculation of the Variance and
Standard Deviation**

X	$\mathbf{X} - \overline{\mathbf{X}}$	$(\mathbf{X} - \overline{\mathbf{X}})^2$
2	$2 - 5 = -3$	$(-3)^2 = 9$
2	$2 - 5 = -3$	$(-3)^2 = 9$
3	$3 - 5 = -2$	$(-2)^2 = 4$
3	$3 - 5 = -2$	$(-2)^2 = 4$
4	$4 - 5 = -1$	$(-1)^2 = 1$
4	$4 - 5 = -1$	$(-1)^2 = 1$
8	$8 - 5 = \ \ 3$	$(3)^2 = 9$
8	$8 - 5 = \ \ 3$	$(3)^2 = 9$
8	$8 - 5 = \ \ 3$	$(3)^2 = 9$
8	$8 - 5 = \ \ 3$	$(3)^2 = 9$
50	0	64

$$\overline{X} = \frac{50}{10} = 5.0 \qquad \sigma^2 = \frac{64}{10} = 6.4$$

$$\sigma = \sqrt{\sigma^2} = \sqrt{6.4} \approx 2.5$$

The variance (σ^2) and standard deviation (σ) for the data shown in Figure A-4. The symbol $\overline{X}$ is used to designate the mean.

Together, measures of central tendency and measures of dispersion provide a great deal of information about the nature of any distribution of scores. For example, imagine that on your first psychology quiz, which contained 50 items, the mean score for the entire class was 38 correct, and the standard deviation was 1.50. These figures inform you that on the average, members of the class did quite well (they answered 76 per cent of the items correctly), and that there was not much variability around this value — most students obtained scores relatively close to the mean. In short, just two pieces of information, the mean and standard deviation, have provided you with a fairly accurate picture of an entire distribution of scores. Moreover, this would be just as true whether there were only 20 or more than 300 students in the class. It is precisely this type of efficiency to which we referred when we noted, in the introduction to this discussion, that statistics are often quite useful as a means of summarizing or describing large amounts of information.

THE NORMAL CURVE: A STATISTICIAN'S DELIGHT

We previously defined symmetric distributions as those which have the same value for the mean and median, or those in which the left half is a mirror image of the right half. A very special type of distribution, which has the same value for the mean, median, and mode, with the greatest concentration of scores toward the center of the distribution and the least concentration toward the high and low extremes, is the familiar bell-shaped **normal curve.** The normal distribution is typical of many characteristics, including height, weight, intelligence, sexual drive, and many others. Several normal curves are shown in Figure A-6. Note that all have the same mean, median, and mode. The major difference between them lies in their dispersion. The tall, thin curve (A) has a smaller variance (and thus a smaller standard deviation) than the other two, while the flat, broad curve (C) has a larger variance (and standard deviation) than the others.

One outstanding property of the normal curve which makes it very useful to psychologists is the fact that specific proportions of the distribution of scores it represents are contained within specific areas of the curve itself.

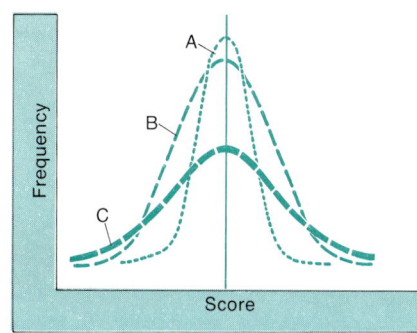

FIGURE A-6   Several normal curves. Note that curve A has the smallest variance while C has the largest.

This property is illustrated in Figure A–7, in which the distribution shown has a mean of 5.0 and a standard deviation of 1.0. The dark-shaded area in this figure corresponds to the proportion of the distribution—68 per cent, to be precise—which lies between the values 4.0 and 6.0. Note that 4.0 and 6.0 are, respectively, one standard deviation *below* and one standard deviation *above* the mean of 5.0. (Also note carefully the percentages of the distribution which fall within the other standard deviation units indicated. For example, 14 per cent of the scores fall in the interval between one and two standard deviations above the mean, 2 per cent in the interval between two and three standard deviations above the mean, and so on.) What is so valuable about this property of the normal distribution is that these same percentages hold for *all* normal distributions, regardless of their specific means or standard deviations. That is, 34 per cent of the scores fall between the mean and one standard deviation above it (and so on for the other figures indicated), regardless of the specific normal distribution we are considering.

One advantage of this property is that given an individual's score and the mean and standard deviation of the distribution, we immediately know the standing of that person's score relative to all other scores. For example, given the distribution of I.Q. scores shown in Figure A–8, with a mean of 100 and a standard deviation of 15, we know that an I.Q. of 115, which is one standard deviation unit above the mean, is equal to or greater than 84 per cent of the scores obtained by other individuals taking the test (2% + 14% + 34% + 34% = 84%). Similarly, an I.Q. of 70 (which is two standard deviation units below the mean) is equal to or greater than only 2 per cent of the scores obtained by other persons. As we noted above, similar calculations can be made for *any* normal distribution, regardless of its mean and standard deviation. For example, returning to the psychology quiz we mentioned earlier, imagine that you obtained a grade of 41. Since the mean is 38, your performance might not at first seem very impressive. Recall, however, that the standard deviation

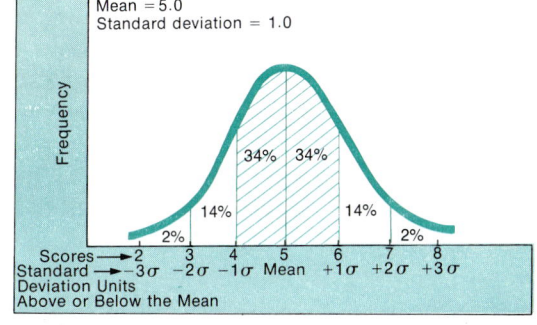

FIGURE A-7   A normal distribution showing the percentage of scores falling into the areas bounded by 1, 2, and 3 standard deviation units above (+1σ, +2σ, +3σ) and below (−1σ, −2σ, −3σ) the mean.

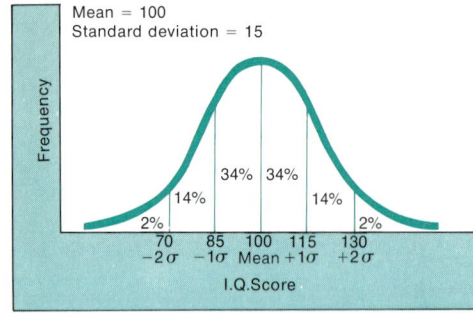

FIGURE A–8   A frequency distribution for I.Q. scores, with a mean of 100 and a standard deviation of 15. Note that the percentages shown are the same as those in Figure A–7. These figures are the same for all normal distributions.

was only 1.5. As a result, your score is fully two standard deviation units above the mean—a truly sterling performance, since it is equalled by only 2 per cent of the students in the class. In sum, the properties of the normal distribution are such that we can readily determine the relative standing of any score represented within it. And since many psychological traits and characteristics tend to be distributed in just this manner, knowledge of the properties of the normal curve often helps psychologists make comparisons between individuals along a number of different dimensions.

COMPARISONS BETWEEN GROUPS: DETERMINING WHICH DIFFERENCES ARE SIGNIFICANT

Now that we have considered the manner in which psychologists use statistics to describe or summarize large amounts of information, and the properties of the normal distribution, let us turn to what is perhaps an even more important use of such procedures—comparisons between the behavior of various groups of individuals. In order to illustrate this use, imagine that we wish to determine whether freshmen and seniors in college differ with respect to their belief in internal control—the ability to shape and influence one's own destiny. Assume that we have designed a personality inventory which measures this characteristic along a ten-point scale, with higher scores representing greater degrees of belief in internal control. Further, assume that we administer this inventory to two groups of students—65 entering freshmen and 65 graduating seniors—and that the means for the two groups are 5.5 and 4.5 respectively (that is, the freshmen have a stronger belief in their ability to control their own destinies than do the seniors). How can we determine whether this difference is significant—large enough so that it is unlikely to have occurred by chance alone? (Recall that in Chapter 1 we noted that psychologists often interpret differences as being significant only when they are likely to have occurred by chance fewer than 5 times in 100.)

In actual practice, the answer to this question is quite simple. We merely perform a few straightforward computations and then consult a special type of table which tells us the probability that a difference of the size we observed would occur by chance alone. While the actual procedures we would follow are quite simple, the logic on which they rest is considerably more complex. In greatly simplified form, the argument proceeds as follows.

Suppose that we repeated our experiment a large number of times with different samples of subjects. If we did, we would almost certainly find that the means for the two groups would vary from one occasion to the next. For example, the first time we performed the study, the means might be 5.5 and 4.5, as noted above. The next time they might be 5.2 and 4.3, while the third time they could turn out to be 5.6 and 4.9. Since each of the means would vary from occasion to occasion, the size of the difference between them would also change. In fact, mathematical procedures indicate that the size of these differences would actually be normally distributed. Assuming that there was no

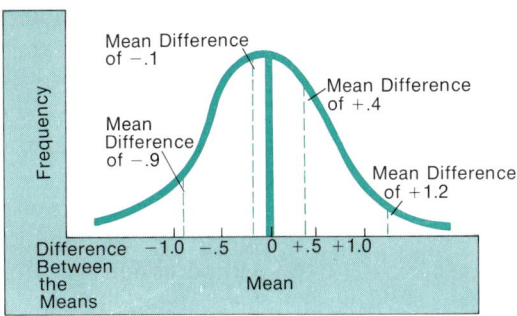

FIGURE A–9 A frequency distribution for differences between two means. Such a distribution would be produced if an experiment comparing two groups of individuals were repeated over and over again, hundreds of times, with different samples of subjects. Assuming that there was no real difference between the two groups, most of the results would be quite similar (they would cluster around the mean of 0).

real difference between the two groups, the mean of this distribution would be zero. That is, the scores would vary around this mean in such a manner that most of the differences between our two groups would be rather small, and only a relatively few would be quite large (refer to Figure A–9).

Since the differences between the two groups would be normally distributed, we could then readily determine the relative position of any given difference by procedures similar to those described in our discussion of the normal curve. For example, suppose that the standard deviation of our distribution of differences was found to be .5. Given this information, we would know that a difference as large as the one we observed between freshmen and seniors in our initial study ($5.5 - 4.5 = 1.0$) would be quite rare. In fact, it would be obtained only 2 per cent of the time. In view of this fact, we would probably conclude that this difference was large enough to be viewed as a real (i.e., significant) one, not due to chance factors alone.

At this point, you may well be wondering how we manage to obtain the mean and standard deviation of the distribution of differences we have been discussing. Must we actually repeat our study over and over again hundreds of times? Or is there a short-cut to reaching the same goal? Fortunately, the latter is true. Certain procedures known as **inferential statistics** allow us to estimate the values we seek in a highly accurate manner without repeating our research a countless number of times. By means of these techniques, it usually is possible to determine the precise likelihood that any difference we observe between various groups in an experiment arose by chance alone. Then, according to the criterion we have established in advance (for example, that the difference be large enough that it would occur by chance fewer than 5 times in 100), we can decide whether we wish to view these results as significant or nonsignificant. It should be quite obvious to you by this point that when statistics are used in this manner, they provide psychologists with a useful and powerful tool for interpreting the results of their research.

We have already described a third major use of statistics in Chapter 1, where we discussed the topic of **correlation.** Basically, correlational techniques of analysis are employed in cases in which a researcher wishes to determine whether two or more variables are related and, if so, to what extent. In order to illustrate the uses of statistics in such instances, let us consider a hypothetical study designed to determine whether there is any relationship between two simple factors—height and success. (We might suspect that there is, because of the strong bias in favor of tallness in our society, and because informal observation suggests that successful individuals do tend to be taller than average.) In order to obtain information on this topic, assume that we measure the height of several hundred persons, and also obtain information concerning their income (one index of success). If we then plot height against income and

CORRELATION
AND
PREDICTION

represent each person's scores on both by a single point, we may obtain any of the results shown in Figure A–10. The first pattern (A) seems to suggest that as height increases income also rises, the second (B) suggests that as height increases, income decreases, while the third (C) seems to indicate that there is no link between these two variables—income neither rises nor falls with height.

One way of interpreting the results of our study would then be that of simply "eyeballing" the graph we obtain. As you might suspect, this informal method is not very satisfactory. First, it tells us little about the actual strength of any relationships we observe. Second, it leaves us very much in the dark as to whether our results are real, or merely a chance occurrence. And finally, it is quite possible that while employing such procedures, we would make serious errors and either "see" relationships which do not actually exist or fail to "see" ones which are present. In this case, as in many others, statistics come to the rescue, and provides us with a mathematically sound means for interpreting our findings. Specifically, by applying an appropriate statistical formula to our data, we can obtain an index of the strength of the relationship between our two variables—an index known as the **correlation coefficient.** The formula for calculating this statistic is such that our result will always be a number between −1.00 and +1.00. Positive numbers suggest that as one of our two factors increases, so does the other, while negative numbers indicate that as one increases, the other decreases. Moreover, the greater the degree to which the value we obtain departs from 0.00 in either direction, the stronger the relationship we have uncovered. Thus, a correlation of +.80 represents a stronger relationship than one of +.60, and a correlation of −.75 represents a stronger relationship than one of −.37. (Also note that a correlation of −.43 is indicative of a stronger relationship between two variables than one of +.26; although it is negative, it still represents a greater departure from 0.00.)

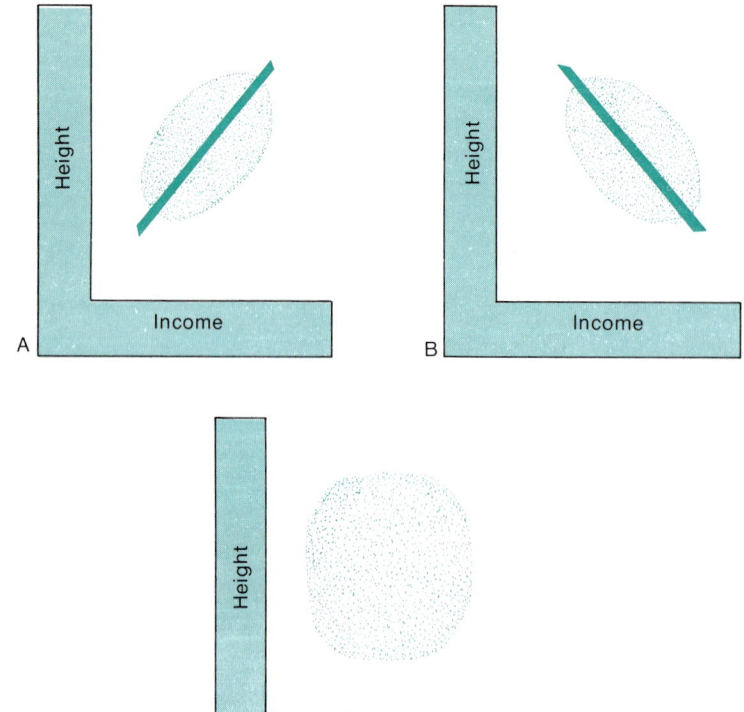

FIGURE A–10 Graphs representing the heights and incomes of several hundred persons. (Each individual's scores are represented by a single dot.) Graph A is suggestive of a positive relationship between these variables, graph B of a negative relationship, and graph C of no relationship between them.

Obtaining an appropriate correlation coefficient, of course, is only part of the story. Once we have calculated this value, it is necessary to go one step further and determine whether it is significant. That is, we must seek to determine whether it is large enough to be viewed as a real outcome rather than merely a chance occurrence. Just as in the case of comparisons between groups, we can consult a special type of table in order to determine the probability that a correlation as large as the one we have observed would occur by chance alone. And again, we would interpret the correlation we observe as being significant only when this probability is quite low (for example, fewer than 5 chances in 100).

In addition to providing us with information regarding the strength of the relationship between variables, correlation coefficients have another important property: they also tell us how accurately an individual's score on one trait or characteristic can be *predicted* from his or her score on one or more others. The larger the correlation coefficient is, the more accurately can such predictions be made. For example, if, in the study described above, the correlation between height and success was +.95, we could predict an individual's income from knowledge of his or her height (or vice versa) with great accuracy. If we found that these variables correlated only +.32, however, we could make such predictions only with a much lower degree of accuracy.

Predictions made on the basis of correlational analyses have many practical uses in psychology. For example, you may recall that in Chapter 14 we discussed the task of predicting an individual's job performance from his or her scores on various tests or questionnaires. In such cases, only persons whose scores are such that on-the-job success seems likely are hired. Similarly, many schools and universities attempt to predict the grades of all their applicants from scores on entrance tests and other information, in order to admit only those who appear to have a reasonable chance of performing adequately. In these and many other situations, the predictions yielded by statistical analyses can be of great practical benefit.

Before concluding this discussion of correlation and prediction, we should repeat a warning first issued in Chapter 1: even a very large correlation between two factors or variables tells us nothing definitive about the causal relationship between them. Since we provided many examples of this fact in Chapter 1 (do you remember our discussion of coffee drinking and heart attacks?), we will not repeat our earlier comments here. If you have forgotten the reasons why correlation does not necessarily imply causation, however, this is probably a good time to review pages 26 to 27.

LYING WITH STATISTICS: OF MOUNTAINS AND MOLEHILLS

We hope that the information presented up to this point has convinced you that in the hands of trained psychologists, statistics are a useful tool for interpreting the findings of many kinds of research. Unfortunately, they are not always used for such beneficial purposes. In many cases, statistics have been employed to mislead or deceive large numbers of persons—particularly those unfamiliar with their use. In this final section, therefore, we feel that it may be useful to point out several of these potential pitfalls. Our hope is that by familiarizing you with them, your ability to both recognize and resist their influence will be greatly increased.

The Use of Biased Samples

One television commercial aired over and over a few years ago went something as follows: "Two out of three dentists surveyed who recommend gum for their patients recommend _____." At first glance, this message seems like a reasonable one—dentists prefer that their patients chew a particular brand of gum, presumably because it is less harmful to their teeth than others.

'Ninety-nine per cent of those interviewed are in favor of the teachers' right to strike against the public.'

FIGURE A–11 By carefully selecting one's sample, it is possible to obtain almost any desired statistical result. Note the qualifying phrase "... of those interviewed." (Cartoon by LePelley in The Christian Science Monitor; © 1975, The Christian Science Publishing Society.)

The catch, however, lies in the phrase *who recommend gum for their patients.* If you consider these words carefully for a moment, you will realize that most dentists probably do *not* recommend gum to their patients. In fact, they probably caution strongly against its use. Thus, there is a very good chance that the dentists mentioned in this commercial are not a fair, representative sample of *all* dentists. Instead, they may have been selected in some special manner. For example, they might turn out to be stockholders in the gum company in question, or to be related to the advertising executives who developed this message. Yet, notice how the wording of the commercial leads you to jump to the conclusion that a majority of *all* dentists recommend chewing the sponsor's brand. The use of such biased samples is quite common, and if you watch for it carefully, you will probably notice many other examples of this technique (see Figure A–11). Regardless of the product or cause being promoted, the important point to remember remains the same: by carefully selecting one's sample, it is possible to obtain almost any desired result.

Unexpressed Comparisons

Another common form of deception with statistics lies in the failure to name the groups involved in a comparison. Consider, for example, the statement: "In a laboratory test, _____ mouthwash killed 78 per cent more germs." Left for you to imagine is the substance with which the sponsor's brand of mouthwash was compared. The commercial leads you to conclude that it was a competing brand, but was it? Perhaps it was distilled water, pickled beets, or pink champagne. In the absence of the appropriate information, there is no way for you to be quite sure. The moral in such cases, then, is clear: beware the unexpressed comparison!

"Significant" Differences Which Aren't Really There

A common theme in many advertisements is that the sponsor's brand has outperformed its competitors in a careful and impartially conducted test. For example, it may be claimed that a particular brand of gasoline yielded more miles per gallon than others, that a particular brand of toothpaste resulted in fewer cavities than its competitors, or that a particular type of antacid consumed even more irritating stomach fluids than its rivals. The implication in all such statements, of course, is that the differences obtained are important ones stemming from the superiority of the product being promoted. But is this actually the case? Often, it is impossible to tell. No information concerning the question of whether such differences were statistically significant is provided. It is quite possible that the differences reported were so small as to represent a chance or random occurrence. Indeed, a whole series of comparisons may have been performed, and only the ones which produced results favorable to the sponsor's product were reported. Because of the strong tendency of advertisers to exaggerate the benefits of their own products, we feel that the following policy is probably best: assume that all differences that are reported are *not* significant unless specific information to the contrary is presented.

Have you ever seen an advertisement in which a shopper is asked to choose the richest-looking coffee, the smoothest beer, or the softest bathroom tissue from several unlabeled brands? Generally, such ads end with the consumer making the "right" choice—that is, selecting the sponsor's brand—and the announcer stating "There's proof. Our brand is the one preferred by most." The problem with such commercials is so obvious that you may well have recognized it yourself long before reading this discussion: it is generally not reasonable to reach any firm conclusions on the basis of the reactions of a single individual. More specifically, we are left wondering what would happen if the same procedures were repeated with 10, 50, or 500 shoppers. Would the sponsor's brand actually be chosen significantly more often than its competitors? The implication in the commercial, of course, is that it would, but even a very basic knowledge of statistics suggests that jumping to such a conclusion on the basis of a sample of one person is quite risky, to say the least. In sum, from the point of view of solid, convincing evidence for the superiority of a particular brand or product, personal testimonials from one or even a few consumers are generally of little use.

Use of a Ridiculously Small Sample Size

Still another questionable maneuver which should put you firmly on your guard occurs in instances in which an advertiser quotes a set of statistics or findings regarding one aspect of a product and then jumps to the conclusion that these statistics apply to another aspect of the product as well. A particularly clear example of this type of faulty generalization can be seen in the ad for a popular pain-reliever which states: "In two studies of pain other than headache, _____ was found more effective. So the next time you suffer from a headache, take _____." The problem in such cases is that we do not know whether it is actually appropriate to generalize the evidence or findings in the manner suggested. If a product is best at relieving assorted aches and pains unrelated to headaches, is it also necessarily best in relieving that pounding in our temples? No evidence is presented either way, so we can't tell for sure. The mention of actual scientific findings lends an air of credibility to the entire message, and makes it tempting to follow along and accept the implied conclusion. Since the logic involved in such generalizations is open to serious question, however, it is usually wise to reject them, no matter how reasonable they may seem.

Faulty Generalization

"A picture is worth a thousand words" is as true in statistics as in any other field. Just as photographs can be altered so as to be misleading, however, graphs can be designed to distort the information they present. For example, examine the three graphs shown in Figure A–12, which represent the unemployment rates for two consecutive months. In all three cases, the differ-

Misleading Graphs

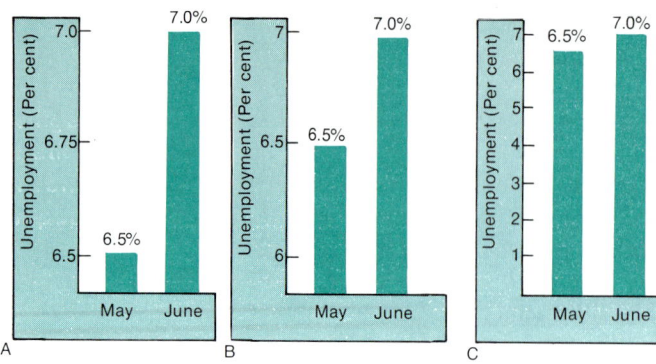

FIGURE A–12 Three bar graphs representing the same data. Note how changing the scale units of the vertical axis alters the size of the difference shown (0.5%). This difference seems huge in A, more moderate in B, and quite small in C.

ence between May and June is 0.5 per cent, but notice how the size of this difference seems to shrink in moving from (A) to (C). The reason for this apparent change lies in the size of the units along the vertical axis. By adjusting these units, it is possible to make small differences appear huge, and large ones appear small. This can often be very useful to the person preparing the graphs. Thus, suppose that as a political candidate running for office, you wished to make the point that due to your opponent's disastrous economic policies, unemployment increased dramatically in these two months. In that case, you would present graph (A) to potential voters. On the other hand, suppose you were a government official attempting to calm growing fears about a serious economic recession. Here, you would almost certainly choose to present graph (C), which seems to suggest that unemployment increased very slightly over the months in question. Such "fine-tuning" of graphs is very common, and can be found in weekly news magazines, stockholder reports, many advertisements, and political mailings. In view of this fact, it is always important to pay careful attention to the scale employed in any graph. If this important information is ignored, it is all too easy to be led into false conclusions.

Lying With Statistics: A Conclusion

The examples we have presented here should provide you with a good idea of the many ways in which statistics can be misleading. Fortunately, it is usually relatively easy to recognize most deceptive techniques, and with a little practice, the chances of your being fooled should be slight.

In concluding, we wish merely to call your attention to the fact that statistics, like almost all other tools of science, are quite neutral in and of themselves. On the one hand, they can be employed to further our understanding of human behavior, while on the other they can be used to mislead and deceive millions of unsuspecting persons. In the end, it is the character of the individuals who choose to employ them—not statistics per se—which determines whether their ultimate effects will be primarily beneficial or destructive in nature.

SAMPLE QUESTIONS AND ANSWERS

Now that you have been exposed to the concept of statistics as a research tool, we provide you with a few sample questions (and answers). By means of these brief items, you can check your understanding of the materials presented.

1. In an experiment concerned with helping, researchers were interested in the number of pennies children donated to charity. Given the following data, find the mean, median, mode, range, variance, and standard deviation: 9, 13, 10, 10, 13, 7, 11, 12, 11, 14.

X	$X - \overline{X}$	$(X - \overline{X})^2$
7	−4	16
9	−2	4
10	−1	1
10	−1	1
11	0	0
11	0	0
12	+1	1
13	+2	4
13	+2	4
14	+3	9
110	0	40

Answers:

Mean $(\overline{X}) = \dfrac{110}{10} = 11$

Median $= 11.0$

Modes $= 10, 11, 13$

Range $= 14 - 7 = 7$

$\sigma^2 = \dfrac{40}{10} = 4.0$

$\sigma = \sqrt{\sigma^2} = 2.0$

2. What are the potentially misleading aspects of the following hypothetical claim for an automobile? "In a highway comparison of our specially equipped model with our competitor's leading seller, we obtained over three more miles per gallon. So for more miles for your money, come and see our whole line of exciting new cars."

    (1) Small sample size — apparently only one competitor car was tested.
    (2) Biased sample — use of "specially equipped" version.
    (3) Faulty generalizations — (a) from highway test to all types of driving, and (b) from specially equipped model to whole line of autos.

3. If attitudes toward the equal rights amendment and authoritarianism (a personality characteristic discussed in Chapter 9) are found to correlate −.92, what do we know about the relationship between these two variables?

    We know that the more authoritarian an individual is, the less he or she favors the equal rights amendment. (We know nothing, however, about the cause-and-effect relationship between these variables.)

4. If a normal distribution of scores on a measure of anxiety has a mode of 32.0, a range of 26.2, and a standard deviation of 10.0, what is the mean?

    Since a normal distribution has the same value for the mean, median, and mode, both the mean and median must be 32.0.

5. A psychologist is interested in how well students in Sections A, B, and C of an introductory course like the teaching methods employed in each. She asks students to rate the instructional approach on a scale from 1 (dislike very much) to 20 (like very much). The mean attraction scores are found to be 13.6 for Section A, 11.2 for Section B, and 14.5 for Section C. Variances for the three groups are calculated as 6.2, 8.3, and 5.7, respectively. Which Section, on the average, probably has the most difference of opinion among its class members regarding satisfaction with the teaching methods?

    Since the variance is a measure of dispersion or how far away members are from the mean, then the larger the variance the greater the dispersion in the distribution. Thus, if the three Section distributions are normal, Section B has the greatest difference of opinion (dispersion), and Section C the least.

Overleaf: Top left photo from *The Life of Birds*, 2nd edition, by J. Welty (Philadelphia: W. B. Saunders Company, 1975). Top right photo from Annan Photo Features. Bottom left photo from *Vertebrate Biology*, 4th edition, by R. Orr (Philadelphia: W. B. Saunders Company, 1976). Bottom right photo by Herbert Eisenberg, Photo Trends.

Appendix B

The Nature-Nurture Controversy Revisited: Innate Patterns of Behavior

INNATE PATTERNS OF BEHAVIOR:
A MODERN CONTROVERSY

INNATE PATTERNS OF BEHAVIOR:
A RESOLUTION

INSTINCTS AND HUMAN BEHAVIOR:
ARE WE "PROGRAMMED" FOR
VIOLENCE?

SUMMARY

When psychology was young (in the closing decades of the nineteenth century and the early decades of the twentieth century), it was quite fashionable to explain both human and animal behavior by reference to numerous **instincts**—innate patterns of activity assumed to be universal in a species. Perhaps the most extreme example of this controversial line of thought is provided by the writings of William McDougall (1908), a psychologist who contended that virtually all forms of human behavior, including even complex types of social interaction, are based upon the operation of specific instincts. (Table B–1 contains a partial list of the instincts he proposed.)

With the advent of behaviorism (see Chapter 1), the instinct doctrine supported by McDougall and others came under very heavy attack. Led by John B. Watson, this new breed of "angry young psychologist" pointed to the fact that in reality, the technique of explaining complex patterns of behavior by attributing them to various instincts actually accomplished very little. In fact, as noted by these critics, it was quite circular in nature. First, the widespread occurrence of a given pattern of behavior was taken as evidence for the existence of a corresponding instinct. Then, in what can only be described as a

TABLE B–1

Instinct	Associated Emotional State
Flight	Fear
Repulsion	Disgust
Curiosity	Wonder
Pugnacity	Anger
Self-assertion	Elation
Parenthood	Tenderness

Some of the instincts proposed by McDougall, and the emotional states with which he believed them to be associated. (Adapted from McDougall, 1908.)

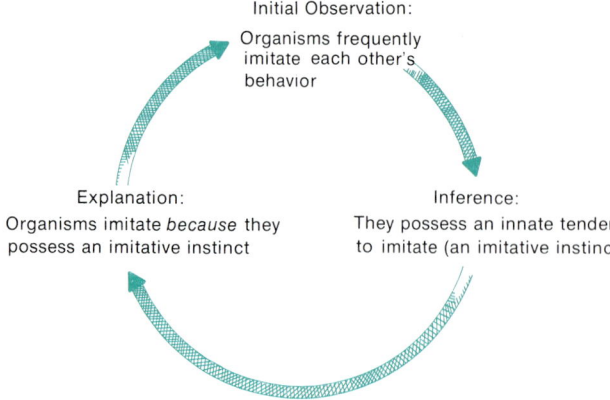

Initial Observation:
Organisms frequently
imitate each other's
behavior

Inference:
They possess an innate tendency
to imitate (an imitative instinct)

Explanation:
Organisms imitate *because* they
possess an imitative instinct

**FIGURE B-1   Partly because they often fell victim
to the type of circular reasoning shown above, attempts to "explain" various forms of behavior in
terms of instincts were soon abandoned during
psychology's early years.**

dazzling display of mental gymnastics, this hypothesized instinct was employed as an explanation for the occurrence of the behavior in question. For
example, if it were observed that organisms often imitate each other's behavior,
it was concluded that they possess an imitative instinct. The existence of this
instinct was then offered as an explanation for the widespread occurrence of
imitative actions! (See Figure B-1.) Clearly, such explanations tell us very little
about the causes and functions of important patterns of behavior and, in fact,
seem to go round and round in a particularly vicious type of closed, "logical"
circle.

Partly because of such criticisms, and partly because psychologists (especially in America) were interested in the practical task of changing or modifying
behavior, the instinct doctrine fell into severe disfavor. As early as 1924,
Watson was able to state: "The concept of instinct is no longer needed in
psychology." In fact, the whole notion of innate patterns of behavior was rejected with such force and vigor that for some time the very term *instinct* became a dirty word among psychologists—one to be avoided at all costs. As a
result, for several decades little attention was directed to the potentially important influence of genetic factors upon behavior. During the 1950's, however,
interest in the possibility of such effects increased once again, due, in large
measure, to the work of a group of European scientists known as **ethologists.**

Innate Patterns of Behavior: A Modern Controversy

In contrast to most psychologists, who generally prefer to study behavior
under carefully controlled conditions within their own laboratories, ethologists
such as Konrad Lorenz and Niko Tinbergen (see Figure B-2) have often chosen
to conduct their investigations in the open field under natural circumstances.
Typically, they go to locations inhabited by organisms whose behavior they
wish to study and, after concealing cameras, tape recorders, and microphones
in appropriate locations, make careful, long-term records of the activities of
their subjects.

During the course of such observation, ethologists have frequently noticed
the occurrence of patterns of behavior which are (1) highly *stereotyped* in
nature (i.e., performed in a similar manner by all individuals), (2) universal
in the species (or at least among one of the sexes), (3) elicited in a regular and
consistent manner by simple but specific *sign stimuli*, and (4) self-exhausting,
so that once performed, they are not soon repeated. A good example of such
behavior, and one often used for illustrative purposes by ethologists themselves, is the mating behavior of the male stickleback.

The reproductive pattern of this small fish proceeds in a rigidly ordered
and highly stereotyped manner. First, the male drives off all potential competi-

tors (other males) within a small area, thus establishing his claim to a home territory. He then builds a nest by scooping out a shallow depression in the ocean bottom or riverbed. The next step in the pattern occurs when a female bearing the appropriate sign stimulus — an abdomen distended with eggs — happens by. In response to this crucial stimulus, the male engages in a series of stereotyped courting movements in which he swims in front of the female in a wiggling pattern. Apparently, this action is highly seductive to female sticklebacks, for they generally follow the male into the nest, where they deposit their eggs. It is important to note that males respond in this manner *only* to females swollen with eggs; when exposed to females who do not exhibit this sign, or to other males who share their own bright red color, they respond with violent attempts to drive off these unwanted intruders.

Once the female has deposited her eggs in the nest, the male no longer requires her favors and chases her, too, away. He then proceeds to fertilize the eggs, and after doing so remains nearby, fanning them with his fins to ensure a steady supply of oxygen. Even when they finally hatch, he remains on the scene, caring for his offspring until they reach a large enough size to fend for themselves (see Figure B-3).

Impressed by the rigidity, orderliness, and universality of such actions, ethologists concluded that they could be regarded as instinctive in nature. Moreover, going even further, they contended that such activities are both *innate* — inherited in a direct fashion and in much the same manner as physical structures (Lorenz, 1950) — and essentially *unlearned* — uninfluenced by experience. This was a rather extreme position, and as you might guess on the basis of our earlier discussion of learning (see Chapter 4), psychologists took strong exception to it. In fact, they often adopted an equally extreme position of their own, suggesting that *all* forms of behavior are learned, and denying the existence of *any* innate patterns of behavior. Given the strong convictions of scientists on both sides, a bitter controversy soon developed, with the two opposing camps marshaling what they believed to be convincing evidence for their respective points of view.

FIGURE B-2 Two famous ethologists, Konrad Lorenz (A) and Niko Tinbergen (B). These scientists have received the Nobel prize for their research on animal behavior.

A   B

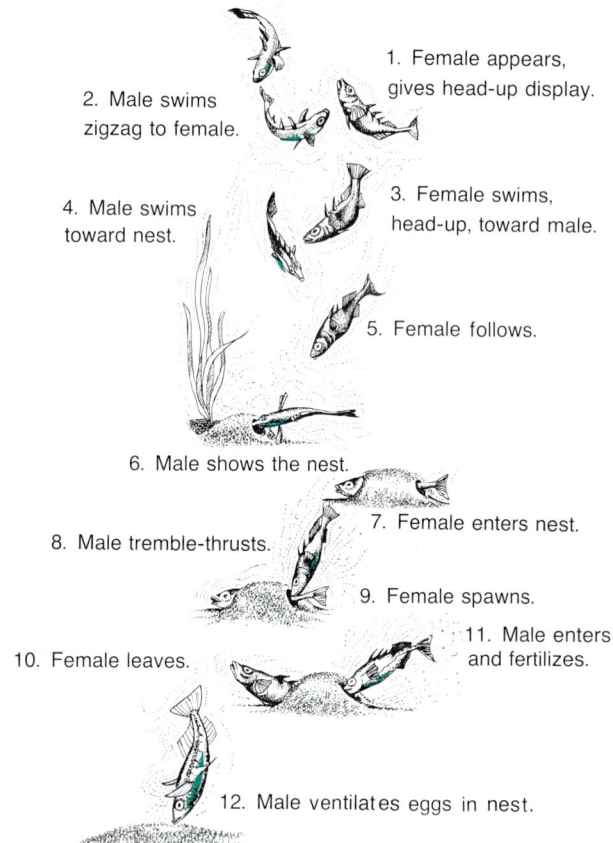

2. Male swims
zigzag to female.

1. Female appears,
gives head-up display.

4. Male swims
toward nest.

3. Female swims,
head-up, toward male.

5. Female follows.

6. Male shows the nest.

7. Female enters nest.

8. Male tremble-thrusts.

9. Female spawns.

11. Male enters
and fertilizes.

10. Female leaves.

12. Male ventilates eggs in nest.

FIGURE B-3   The mating behavior of the stickleback. Because the sequence shown here is the same for all members of the species and occurs in a highly stereotyped manner, ethologists have often viewed the stickleback's mating behavior as being largely innate. (From Clark, M.: *Contemporary Biology: Concepts and Implications.* Philadelphia: W. B. Saunders Company, 1973, p. 331.)

In support of their position, ethologists often pointed to the results of **deprivation experiments** — studies in which organisms are reared under conditions which prevent them from obtaining the kinds of experiences they would normally encounter in early life. It was argued by ethologists that if such subjects still demonstrated the patterns of behavior characteristic of their species when adults, strong evidence would be provided for the suggestion that such behavior develops in the absence of learning. Often, this seemed to be the case. For example, in one interesting but rather unsettling study, Grohmann (1939) raised pigeons in small tubes which prevented them from even opening their wings. When they were later released as adults, however, they flew as well as a control group which had not been confined soon after birth.

In response to such evidence, psychologists pointed to the fact that in many cases, the behaviors described by ethologists as innate could actually have been acquired through learning (Lehrman, 1953). Further, they cited equally convincing experiments demonstrating that many forms of species-specific behavior assumed to be unlearned by ethologists are either poorly developed or totally absent in organisms which have undergone various types of early deprivation. For example, when female rats are reared with rubber collars around their necks which prevent them from grooming and cleaning their own bodies, they are quite inadequate in cleaning and nursing their own offspring (Beach and Jaynes, 1954). Similarly, songbirds reared in isolation often fail to demonstrate the normal call of their species when they mature (Konishi, 1965; Marler, 1970). Findings such as these suggested that in many cases, species-specific behavior fails to develop in a normal manner when organisms have been deprived of experiences they would normally gain during maturation.

This debate between ethologists and psychologists continued, often with considerable bitterness, for more than a decade. The history of science is filled with such disputes, and, unfortunately, they often seem to generate far more heat than light—more angry accusations and stormy replies than actual scientific progress. In this instance, though, the opposite seems to be true. Largely as a result of the criticisms leveled against each other's views, both psychologists and ethologists have attained greatly increased sophistication concerning the nature of innate patterns of behavior. Moreover, they have recently moved toward a resolution involving a fusion or synthesis of their respective points of view (Hall, 1974; Mason and Lott, 1976). Since this resolution represents current thinking regarding the nature of innate patterns of behavior, we will examine it in some detail.

Innate Patterns of Behavior: A Resolution

Although many factors have probably contributed to the recent reconciliation of psychology and ethology, four seem to have played an especially crucial role. First, it has become increasingly clear to scientists in both fields that attempts to categorize behaviors as "innate" or "acquired" make little sense. From the very moment of conception, there is a complex interplay between genetic factors and the environment which guarantees that all forms of behavior are influenced and molded by both types of factors (Moltz, 1965; Tavolga, 1969). In the case of certain highly stereotyped species-specific actions, genetic influences clearly predominate, while in the case of many acquired reactions, interaction with the environment (i.e., experience) is of primary importance. Even in the case of these extremes, however, both classes of variables play a major role and should be given full consideration. With increasing recognition of this fact, both ethologists and psychologists have reached the conclusion that disputes over whether various behavior should be classified as innate or learned are of little value. Moreover, both groups now agree that a more useful undertaking is that of attempting to specify the relative contribution of genetic and environmental factors to the development of various forms of activity. As a result of this growing sophistication, ethologists now often describe species-specific behavior as being relatively *environment-resistant* rather than innate (Tinbergen, 1974), while psychologists have become increasingly concerned with inherited dispositions which seem to influence the course of learning itself (Seligman and Hager, 1972).

A second reason for the current reconciliation between ethology and psychology lies in the recognition by both sides that much of the past controversy regarding the "unlearned" nature of species-specific behavior stemmed from contrasting uses of the term *learning*. Ethologists often employed this term to refer to training or overt practice. As a result, they concluded—and rightly so—that many forms of species-specific behavior can arise in the absence of such experience. In contrast, as we have seen in Chapter 4, psychologists generally used this term to refer to changes in behavior induced through experience. And since even organisms reared in deprivation experiments such as we described earlier have *some* experience with the environment, they have concluded that the behaviors shown by these subjects at maturity are, at least in part, learned. A good illustration of the confusions which may arise from these contrasting definitions of learning is provided by an extensive body of research dealing with the phenomenon of **imprinting.**

This term was first introduced by Lorenz to describe the fact that young animals of many different species—especially birds—tend to follow the first moving object they see. Moreover, they seem to form a powerful attachment to this object, as indicated by these facts: they will (1) utter intense cries of distress when separated from the object, (2) choose to follow and remain near this object over all others, (3) run to it when frightened, and (4) work very hard to gain access to it if this is somehow denied (Sluckin, 1970). The adaptive value of such an instinctive tendency is readily apparent, for under natural conditions the first moving object a young organism typically sees is its mother. Thus, a strong and lasting tendency to remain near this object is likely to increase its chances of survival.

Because the young of many species tend to follow and form a strong attachment to the first moving object they see, even in the absence of any previous practice in performing such actions, ethologists once contended that imprinting represented an unlearned, instinctive form of behavior. Other evidence suggests, however, that it may actually be strongly affected by experience. For example, Hess (1962) found that the greater the effort which must be expended by subjects in reaching the imprinted object, the stronger their later tendency to follow and approach it. Similarly, it appears that once established, imprinting may sometimes be reversed or even eliminated (Moltz, 1960). In sum, imprinting does appear to be based on an innate tendency on the part of young organisms to follow the first moving object they see—indeed, they will even follow such inappropriate objects as flashing lights and human beings (see Figure B–4). However, the strength and even the direction of this tendency may be altered by experiences of various kinds. Is imprinting, then, learned or unlearned? The answer, as both psychologists and ethologists have come to realize, depends very much upon the definition of learning one adopts.

A third reason for the recent synthesis of psychology and ethology lies in the growing awareness among psychologists of the important influence of innate predispositions upon behavior. We have already examined the impact of such tendencies in Chapter 4, where we noted that organisms seem to be equipped with innate dispositions to accomplish some forms of learning more readily than others. In particular, they seem to be "prepared" by genetic factors to learn precisely those responses or stimulus-response associations they need for continued survival (do you remember the studies which indicated that rats can learn to associate certain tastes with stomach upset which

FIGURE B–4 The young of many species show a tendency to follow and form a strong attachment to the first moving object they see, even if it is as inappropriate for satisfying their needs as a human being. (Photo credit: Thomas McAvoy, Time-Life Picture Agency.)

occurs hours later?). That organisms can also be "counter-prepared" for some types of learning is suggested by additional evidence. For example, cowbirds lay their eggs in the nests of other birds. As a result, their young are raised by foster parents belonging to several different species. As adults, cowbirds recognize each other by means of a unique song (actually, an unmelodic squawk). Thus, if they learned the calls of their foster parents, they would face a very difficult task when the time for mating arrived: each individual would sing the song of its foster parents, and the males and females might never manage to get together. In view of this fact, it is essential that cowbirds *fail* to learn the songs of the species which raise them; and in fact they do not, despite months of exposure to these sounds (Greenwalt, 1969).

The increasing evidence that organisms are equipped with innate predispositions either to accomplish or to fail to accomplish certain types of learning has convinced many psychologists that genetic factors play an important role in behavior. In fact, most now believe that the kinds of learning a given species accomplishes most effectively become neatly matched, over the course of evolution, with the *ecological demands* it faces—the requirements of its particular style of life (Mason and Lott, 1976). This is not to say that specific forms of behavior are inherited in the same manner as physical traits; on the contrary, existing evidence argues against the view that specific forms of activity are directly encoded in the genes (Whalen, 1971). Rather, what *is* inherited is a complex pattern of physical characteristics which predispose organisms toward various forms of activity and specific forms of learning. The recognition of this important fact has played an important role in fostering a reconciliation between ethologists and those psychologists concerned with the study of animal behavior.

Finally, scientists in both fields have become increasingly aware of the many advantages provided by each other's methods of research. Ethologists have come to recognize the benefits of controlled experiments in laboratory settings, and have borrowed many refined techniques from psychology for use in their own studies. Similarly, psychologists have become increasingly aware of the advantages of observing organisms in the settings in which they normally function. As a result, the two fields have grown together in this respect as well.

Perhaps we can best summarize all we have said so far by returning to the basic question underlying this entire discussion: *are there any innate patterns of behavior?* In answer to this question, most psychologists as well as ethologists would currently say "yes," if by innate patterns of behavior we mean activities for which a strong predisposition is created by inherited physical characteristics, which organisms are "prepared" to acquire, and which, although affected by experience, may develop without formal training or practice. However, they would almost certainly answer "no" if by innate patterns of behavior we mean forms of activity which are directly encoded in the genes and totally independent of experience.

Before concluding, we should note that there is still one important point about which psychologists and at least some ethologists continue to disagree: the existence of innate patterns of behavior among human beings. In recent years, some ethologists—most notably Konrad Lorenz—have attempted to apply conclusions based upon the systematic observation of animals to complex forms of human behavior. For example, in his well-known book *On Aggression*, Lorenz (1966) proposes that human aggression stems, in large measure, from an *aggressive instinct*—an inborn tendency toward fighting. Further, he suggests that at one time, such instinctive behavior served an adaptive

Instincts and Human Behavior: Are We "Programmed" for Violence?

function, ensuring the dispersion of human populations over a wide geographic area. Today, however, the immense destructive power of modern weapons makes it an extremely dangerous form of activity, and threatens the survival of the entire human race.

While these and similar suggestions regarding the innate basis of various forms of behavior are both interesting and thought-provoking, most psychologists find them hard to accept. This is the case for two important reasons. First, in making such generalizations, ethologists have often tended to emphasize the similarities between various species while overlooking equally important differences between them (Mason and Lott, 1976). For example, in many of his writings, Lorenz refers to the existence of an aggressive instinct in fish, geese, and human beings. While it is certainly true that all these organisms aggress, the mechanisms underlying such behavior may well differ radically. Human beings often aggress out of a desire for vengeance, or to gain the approval of their peers, but it seems unreasonable to assume that geese or fish engage in such behavior because of similar motives. Given such underlying differences even in cases in which the behavior of several species appears to be quite similar, most psychologists are less willing to generalize from animal to human behavior than are Lorenz and other ethologists. (We hasten to add that not all ethologists have shown this tendency to extend conclusions based on observations of animal behavior to men and women. In fact, Niko Tinbergen—another noted ethologist who recently shared a Nobel prize with Lorenz—is far less willing to follow this path.)

Second, most psychologists reject the view that human behavior, with all its tremendous diversity and complexity, can be understood in terms of a relatively small number of innate dispositions. In contrast to many animal species, human beings do *not* demonstrate rigidly stereotyped, universal patterns of activity in their courting, mating, and parental behavior. In fact, quite

FIGURE B–5 Human behavior is so diverse and complex that most psychologists doubt it can be explained in terms of instincts. (Top photo from Annan Photo Features; bottom photo by Herbert Eisenberg, Photo Trends.)

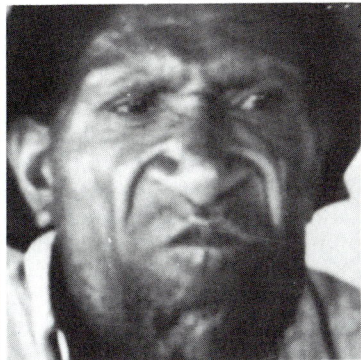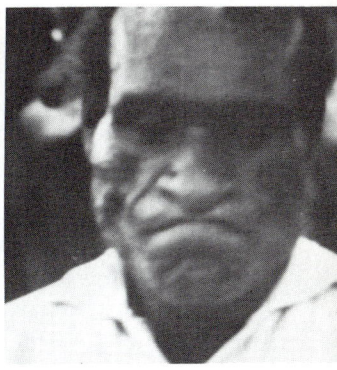

FIGURE B-6 Some forms of behavior do seem to be universal among humans. The individual shown above is a member of an isolated group living in New Guinea. Yet, his facial expressions when happy (left), sad (center), or angry (right) are probably highly similar to your own when you experience these emotions. (Photos courtesy of Dr. Paul Ekman.)

the opposite is true (see Figure B-5). Although it is possible to argue that innate tendencies toward such patterns do exist but are modified greatly through experience, such a suggestion implies that human "instincts" are far less fixed or stereotyped than those of animals—so much so that it may not be appropriate to view them as instincts at all.

Of course, this is not to imply that psychologists view human behavior as being largely uninfluenced by genetic factors. On the contrary, most are well aware of the fact that an individual's physical structure and inherited abilities may exert a profound influence upon his or her later development and behavior. For example, it is obvious that various features of a person's physical appearance (e.g., his or her height, body build, attractiveness) will influence the manner in which he or she is treated by others, and thus exert an important effect upon this individual's behavior. Similarly, as noted in Chapter 14, there is growing evidence for a major genetic contribution even to such complex human characteristics as intelligence. Finally, psychologists do not in any sense deny the possibility that at least *some* patterns of behavior may be universal among humankind. Indeed, recent findings suggest that certain facial expressions may occur in much the same manner among people in all corners of the earth and actually be part of our common human heritage (Ekman and Friesen, 1975; see Figure B-6). What *is* rejected, however, is the suggestion that relatively complex patterns of activity such as those involved in courting, child rearing, and many forms of social interaction are largely determined or programmed by genetic factors. In sum, most psychologists assume that human behavior, like that of all other organisms, ultimately rests upon a base of inherited characteristics and predispositions. They also believe, however, that the complex structure raised upon these foundations is largely a product of our continuing experience with the world around us.

Summary

At one time, psychologists attempted to explain many forms of behavior in terms of **instincts**—innate patterns of activity assumed to be universal in a given species. As it became increasingly apparent that such "explanations" were somewhat circular in nature, this concept lost popularity, and was gradually discarded by most researchers. It was revitalized during the 1950's, however, by **ethologists** such as Konrad Lorenz. On the basis of careful observation of animal behavior, these scientists concluded that some patterns of activity, at least, are both innate and unlearned. Psychologists objected strongly to these proposals, and a heated controversy developed between the two opposing camps.

Fortunately, recent years have seen a resolution of this conflict. Several factors have contributed to this growing reconciliation between psychology and ethology. First, the members of both fields now realize that all forms of behavior are jointly influenced by genetic and environmental factors. As a result, categorizing specific actions as either "learned" or "innate" makes little sense. Second, ethologists have come to realize that learning can take place without overt training or practice, simply as a function of experience with the environment, while psychologists have become increasingly aware of the important influence of innate predispositions on behavior. And finally, both groups have borrowed heavily from each others' research methods. At the present time, then, there is general agreement among psychologists and ethologists that there are indeed innate patterns of behavior. However, this phrase is now restricted to actions (1) whose performance is encouraged by inherited physical characteristics, (2) which organisms are "prepared" to acquire, and (3) which may develop without formal training or practice.

REFERENCES

Abelson, R. P.: Are attitudes necessary? *In* B. T. King and E. McGinnis (eds.), *Attitudes, Conflict, and Social Change.* New York: Academic Press, 1972.

Abramowitz, C. V., Abramowitz, S. I., Roback, H. B., and Jackson, C.: Differential effectiveness of directive and nondirective group therapies as a function of client internal-external control. *Journal of Consulting and Clinical Psychology*, 1974, *42*, 849–853.

Abramson, P. R., and Mosher, D. L.: Development of a measure of negative attitudes toward masturbation. *Journal of Consulting and Clinical Psychology*, 1975, *43*, 485–490.

Abse, D. W.: *Hysteria and Related Mental Disorders.* Baltimore: Williams & Wilkins, 1966.

Adorno, T. W., Frenkel-Brunswik, E., Levinson, D. J., and Sanford, R. N.: *The Authoritarian Personality.* New York: Harper, 1950.

Agnew, H. W., Webb, W. B., and Williams, R. L.: Comparison of stage four and 1-REM sleep deprivation. *Perceptual and Motor Skills*, 1967, *24*, 851–858.

Alexander, F., and French, T. M.: *Psychoanalytic Therapy.* New York: Ronald, 1946.

Allen, V. L., and Levine, J. M.: Social support and conformity: The role of independent assessment of reality. *Journal of Experimental Social Psychology*, 1971, *7*, 48–58.

Allport, D. A., Antonis, B. and Reynolds, P.: On the division of attention: A disproof of the single channel hypothesis. *Quarterly Journal of Experimental Psychology*, 1972, *24*, 225–235.

Allport, G. W.: Functional autonomy of motives. *American Journal of Psychology*, 1937, *50*, 141–156.

Allport, G. W., and Odbert, H. S.: Trait-names: A psycho-lexical study. *Psychological Monographs*, 1936, *47*, No. 211.

Ames, L. B., Métraux, R. W., Rodell, J. L., and Walker, R. N.: *Child Rorschach Responses.* New York: Brunner/Mazel, 1974.

Amoroso, D. M., Brown, M., Pruesse, M., Ware, E. E., and Pilkey, D. W.: An investigation of behavioral, psychological, and physiological reactions to pornographic stimuli. *In Technical Report of the Commission on Obscenity and Pornography.* Vol. VIII. Washington, D.C.: Government Printing Office, 1971, pp. 1–40.

Amsel, A.: Positive induction, behavioral contrast, and generalization of inhibition in discrimination learning. *In* H. G. Kendler and J. T. Spence (eds.), *Essays in Neobehaviorism: A Memorial Volume to Kenneth W. Spence.* New York: Appleton-Century-Crofts, 1971.

Amsel, A.: Behavioral habituation, counterconditioning, and a general theory of persistence. *In* A. Black and W. Prokasy (eds.), *Classical Conditioning II: Current Theory and Research.* New York: Appleton-Century-Crofts, 1972.

Anand, B. K., Chhina, G. S., and Singh, B.: Some aspects of electroencephalographic studies in Yogis. *EEG Clinical Neurophysiology*, 1961, *13*, 452–456. [Note: Much of the data in this study is cited in Calder, N.: *The Mind of Man.* New York: The Viking Press, 1970.]

Anderson, J. R., and Bower, G. H.: *Human Associative Memory.* Washington, D.C.: V. H. Winston, 1973.

Anderson, N. A.: Cognitive algebra: Integration theory applied to social attribution. *In* L. Berkowitz (ed.), *Advances in Experimental Social Psychology.* New York: Academic Press, 1974.

Andrews, J. D. W.: The achievement motive and advancement in two types of organizations. *Journal of Personality and Social Psychology*, 1967, *6*, 163–168.

Annett, J.: *Feedback and Human Behavior.* Baltimore: Penguin Books, 1969.

Arieti, S.: Manic-depressive psychosis. *In* S. Arieti (ed.), *American Handbook of Psychiatry.* New York: Basic Books, 1959, pp. 419–454.

Arkin, R. M., and Duval, S.: Focus of attention and causal attributions of actors and observers. *Journal of Experimental Social Psychology*, 1975, *11*, 427–438.

Arnold, C. B.: The sexual behavior of inner city adolescent condom users. *Journal of Sex Research*, 1972, *8*, 298–309.

Aronson, E., and Linder, D.: Gain and loss of esteem as determinants of interpersonal attractiveness. *Journal of Experimental Social Psychology*, 1965, *1*, 156–171.

Aronson, E., Turner, J. A., and Carlsmith, J. M.: Communicator credibility and communication discrepancy as determinants of opinion change. *Journal of Abnormal and Social Psychology*, 1963, *67*, 31–36.

Asch, S. E.: *Social Psychology.* New York: Prentice-Hall, 1952.

Austin, W., and Walster, E.: Reactions to confirmations and disconfirmations of expectancies of equity and inequity. *Journal of Personality and Social Psychology*, 1974, *30*, 208–216.

Ayllon, T., and Azrin, N. H.: *The Token Economy: A Motivational System for Therapy and Rehabilitation.* New York: Appleton, Century, Crofts, 1968.

Ayllon, T., and Haughton, E.: Control of the behavior of schizophrenic patients by food. *Journal of the Experimental Analysis of Behavior*, 1962, *5*, 343–352.

Ayllon, T., and Kelly, K.: Effects of reinforcement on standardized test performance. *Journal of Applied Behavior Analysis*, 1972, *4*, 477–484.

Bach-y-Rita, P.: *Brain Mechanisms in Sensory Substitution.* New York: Academic Press, 1972.

Bahrick, H. P.: Two-phase model for prompted recall. *Psychological Review*, 1970, *77*, 215–222.

Bandura, A.: Influence of models' reinforcement contingencies on the acquisition of imitative responses. *Journal of Personality and Social Psychology*, 1965, *1*, 589–595.

Bandura, A.: *Psychological Modeling.* Chicago: Aldine-Atherton, 1971.

Bandura, A.: *Aggression: A Social Learning Analysis.* Englewood Cliffs, New Jersey: Prentice-Hall, 1973.

Bandura, A.: *Social Learning Theory.* Englewood Cliffs, New Jersey: Prentice-Hall, 1977.

Bandura, A., Blanchard, E. B., and Ritter, B.: Relative efficacy of desensitization and modeling approaches for inducing behavioral, affective, and attitudinal changes.

Journal of Personality and Social Psychology, 1969, *13*, 173–199.

Bandura, A., and Jeffery, R. W.: Role of symbolic coding and rehearsal processes in observational learning. *Journal of Personality and Social Psychology*, 1973, *26*, 122–130.

Bandura, A., Jeffery, R. W., and Wright, C. L.: Efficacy of participant modeling as a function of response induction aids. *Journal of Abnormal Psychology*, 1974, *83*, 56–64.

Bandura, A., and McDonald, F. J.: The influence of social reinforcement and the behavior of models in shaping children's moral judgments. *Journal of Abnormal and Social Psychology*, 1963, *67*, 274–281.

Bandura, A., and Menlove, F. L.: Factors determining vicarious extinction of avoidance behavior through symbolic modeling. *Journal of Personality and Social Psychology*, 1968, *8*, 99–108.

Bandura, A., and Rosenthal, T. L.: Vicarious classical conditioning as a function of arousal level. *Journal of Personality and Social Psychology*, 1966, *3*, 54–62.

Bandura, A., Ross, D., and Ross, S. A.: Imitation of film-mediated aggressive models. *Journal of Abnormal and Social Psychology*, 1963, *66*, 3–11.

Bandura, A., and Walters, R. H.: *Adolescent Aggression*. New York: Ronald, 1959.

Barahal, H. S.: 1000 prefrontal lobotomies: Five- to ten-year follow-up study. *Psychiatric Quarterly*, 1958, *32*, 653–678.

Barbizet, J.: *Human Memory and Its Pathology*. San Francisco: W. H. Freeman, 1970.

Barefoot, J. C., Hoople, H., and McGlay, D.: Avoidance of an act which would violate personal space. *Psychonomic Science*, 1972, *28*, 205–206.

Barlow, D. H., Leitenberg, H., and Agras, W. S.: Experimental control of sexual deviation through manipulation of the noxious scene in covert sensitization. *Journal of Abnormal Psychology*, 1969, *74*, 596–601.

Barnes, C. D., and Katzung, B. G.: Stimulus polarity and conditioning in planaria. *Science*, 1963, *141*, 728–730.

Baron, R. A.: Attraction toward the model and model's competence as determinants of adult imitative behavior. *Journal of Personality and Social Psychology*, 1970, *14*, 345–351.

Baron, R. A.: Behavioral effects of interpersonal attraction: Compliance with requests from liked and disliked others. *Psychonomic Science*, 1971, *25*, 325–326.

Baron, R. A.: The "foot-in-the-door" phenomenon: Mediating effects of size of first request and sex of requester. *Bulletin of the Psychonomic Society*, 1973, *2*, 113–114.

Baron, R. A.: Threatened retaliation from the victim as an inhibitor of physical aggression. *Journal of Experimental Research in Personality*, 1973, *7*, 103–115.

Baron, R. A.: Aggression as a function of victim's pain cues, level of prior anger arousal, and exposure to an aggressive model. *Journal of Personality and Social Psychology*, 1974, *29*, 117–124 (a).

Baron, R. A.: Threatened retaliation as an inhibitor of human aggression: Mediating effects of the instrumental value of aggression. *Bulletin of the Psychonomic Society*, 1974, *29*, 117–124 (b).

Baron, R. A.: The aggression-inhibiting influence of non-hostile humor. *Journal of Experimental Social Psychology*, 1974, *10*, 23–33. (c)

Baron, R. A.: The aggression-inhibiting influence of heightened sexual arousal. *Journal of Personality and Social Psychology*, 1974, *30*, 318–322. (d)

Baron, R. A., and Bell, P. A.: Aggression and heat: Mediating effects of prior provocation and exposure to an aggressive model. *Journal of Personality and Social Psychology*, 1975, *31*, 825–832.

Baron, R. A., and Bell, P. A.: Aggression and heat: The in-fluence of ambient temperature, negative affect, and a cooling drink on physical aggression. *Journal of Personality and Social Psychology*, 1976, *33*, 245–255.

Baron, R. A., and Byrne, D.: *Social Psychology: Understanding Human Interaction*. 2nd ed. Boston: Allyn and Bacon Inc., 1977.

Baron, R. A., Byrne, D., and Griffitt, W.: *Social Psychology: Understanding Human Interaction*. Boston: Allyn and Bacon, Inc., 1974.

Barthell, C. N., and Holmes, D. S.: High school yearbooks: A nonreactive measure of social isolation in graduates who later became schizophrenic. *Journal of Abnormal Psychology*, 1968, *73*, 313–316.

Bartlett, F. C.: *Remembering: A Study in Experimental and Social Psychology*. Cambridge, England: Cambridge University Press, 1932.

Basmajian, J. V.: Electromyography comes of age. *Science*, 1972, *176*, 603–609.

Bassin, A.: Red, white, and blue poker chips: An AA behavior modification technique. *American Psychologist*, 1975, *30*, 695–696.

Bateson, G., Jackson, D. D., Haley, J., and Weakland, J.: Toward a theory of schizophrenia. *Behavioral Science*, 1956, *1*, 251–264.

Baum, A., Harper, R. E., and Valins, S.: The role of group phenomena in the experience of crowding. *Environment and Behavior*, 1975, *7*, 185–198.

Baum, A., and Valins, S.: Residential environments, group size, and crowding. *Proceedings of the 81st Annual Convention of the American Psychological Association*. Washington, D.C.: American Psychological Association, 1973.

Beach, F. A.: It's all in your mind. *Psychology Today*, 1969, *3* (2), 33–35, 60.

Beach, F. A., and Jaynes, J.: Effects of early experience upon the behavior of animals. *Psychological Bulletin*, 1954, *51*, 239–263.

Beach, F. A., and Jordan, L.: Sexual exhaustion and recovery in the male rat. *Quarterly Journal of Experimental Psychology*, 1956, *8*, 121–133.

Becker, J.: Achievement-related characteristics of manic-depressives. *Journal of Social Psychology*, 1960, *60*, 334.

Becker, W. C., and McFarland, R. L.: A lobotomy prognosis scale. *Journal of Consulting Psychology*, 1955, *19*, 157–162.

Begelman, D. A.: Ethical and legal issues of behavior modification. *In* M. Hersen, R. Eisler, and P. M. Miller (eds.), *Progress in Behavior Modification*. New York: Academic Press, 1975.

Bell, P. A., and Baron, R. A.: Aggression and heat: The mediating role of negative affect. *Journal of Applied Social Psychology*, 1976, *6*, 18–30.

Belmont, L., and Marolla, F. A.: Birth order, family size, and intelligence. *Science*, 1973, *182*, 1096–1101.

Bem, D. J.: Self-perception theory. *In* L. Berkowitz (ed.), *Advances in Experimental Social Psychology*. Vol. 6. New York: Academic Press, 1972.

Berg, K. S., and Vidmar, N.: Authoritarianism and recall of evidence about criminal behavior. *Journal of Research in Personality*, 1975, *9*, 147–157.

Berger, S. M.: Conditioning through vicarious instigation. *Psychological Review*, 1962, *69*, 450–477.

Bergmann, G.: *Philosophy of Science*. Madison, Wisconsin: University of Wisconsin Press, 1966.

Berko, J.: The child's learning of English morphology. *Word*, 1958, *14*, 150–177.

Berkowitz, L.: Some determinants of impulsive aggression: Role of mediated associations with reinforcements for aggression. *Psychological Review*, 1974, *81*, 165–176.

Berkowitz, L.: *A Survey of Social Psychology*. Hinsdale, Illinois: The Dryden Press, 1975.

Berlyne, D. E.: Novelty and curiosity as determinants of exploratory behavior. *British Journal of Psychology*, 1950, *41*, 68–80.

Berlyne, D. E.: The influence of complexity and novelty in visual figures on orienting responses. *Journal of Experimental Psychology*, 1958, *55*, 289–296.

Berlyne, D. E.: Curiosity and exploration. *Science*, 1966, *153*, 25–33.

Berlyne, D. E., and Slater, J.: Perceptual curiosity, exploratory behavior, and maze learning. *Journal of Comparative and Physiological Psychology*, 1957, *50*, 228–232.

Bernstein, B.: A sociolinguistic approach to socialization: With some reference to educability. In F. Williams (ed.), *Language and Poverty: Perspectives on a Theme*. Chicago: Markham, 1970.

Berscheid, E.: Opinion change and communicator-communicatee similarity and dissimilarity. *Journal of Personality and Social Psychology*, 1966, *4*, 670–680.

Berscheid, E., Dion, K., Walster, E., and Walster, G. W.: Physical attractiveness and dating choice: A test of the matching hypothesis. *Journal of Experimental Social Psychology*, 1971, *7*, 173–189.

Berscheid, E., and Walster, E.: A little bit about love. In T. L. Huston (ed.), *Foundations of Interpersonal Attraction*. New York: Academic Press, 1974, pp. 355–381.

Berscheid, E., and Walster, E.: Physical attractiveness. In L. Berkowitz (ed.), *Advances in Experimental Social Psychology*. Vol. 7. New York: Academic Press, 1974.

Bickman, L.: Social influence and diffusion of responsibility in an emergency. *Journal of Experimental Social Psychology*, 1972, *8*, 438–445.

Bindra, D.: *Motivation: A Systematic Reinterpretation*. New York: Ronald, 1959.

Bindrim, P.: A report on a nude marathon: The effect of physical nudity upon the practice interaction in the marathon group. *Psychotherapy: Theory, Research, and Practice*, 1968, *5*, 180–188.

Black, A. H., and Prokasy, W. F.: *Classical Conditioning II: Current Research and Theory*. New York: Appleton-Century-Crofts, 1972.

Blakemore, C. B., Thorpe, J. G., Barker, J. C., Conway, C. G., and Lavin, N. I.: The application of faradic aversion conditioning in a case of transvestism. *Behavior Research and Therapy*, 1963, *1*, 29–34.

Bledsoe, W. W., and Browning, I.: Pattern recognition and reading by machine. In L. Uhr (ed.), *Pattern Recognition*. New York: John Wiley and Sons, 1966.

Blume, S., and Sheppard, C.: The changing effects of drinking on the changing personalities of alcoholics. *Quarterly Journal of Studies on Alcohol*, 1967, *28*, 436.

Boe, E. E., and Church, R. M.: Permanent effects of punishment during extinction. *Journal of Comparative and Physiological Psychology*, 1967, *63*, 486–492.

Bolles, R. C.: Interactions with motivation. In M. H. Marx (ed.), *Learning: Interactions*. London: Macmillan, 1970, pp. 3–54.

Bolles, R. C.: What reinforces avoidance behavior? In J. M. Foley, R. A. Lockhart, and D. M. Messick (eds.), *Contemporary Readings in Psychology*. New York: Harper & Row, 1970.

Bolles, R. C.: *Theory of Motivation*. New York: Harper & Row, 1975.

Bond, N. A.: Basic strategy and expectation in casino blackjack. *Organizational Behavior and Human Performance*, 1974, *12*, 413–428.

Boneau, C. A., and Cuca, J. M.: An overview of psychology's human resources. *American Psychologist*, 1974, *29*, 821–839.

Bonner, H.: The problem of diagnosis in paranoic disorders. *American Journal of Psychiatry*, 1951, *107*, 677.

Boring, E. G.: *A History of Experimental Psychology*. New York: Appleton-Century-Crofts, 1950.

Bower, G. H.: Analysis of a mnemonic device. *American Scientist*, 1970, *58*, 496–510.

Bower, G. H.: Mental imagery and associative learning. In L. Gregg (ed.), *Cognition in Learning and Memory*. New York: John Wiley and Sons, 1972.

Bower, G. H., and Clark, M. C.: Narrative stories as mediators for serial learning. *Psychonomic Science*, 1969, *14*, 181–182.

Bower, T. G. R.: The determinants of perceptual unity in infancy. *Psychonomic Science*, 1965, *3*, 323–324.

Bower, T. G. R.: *Development in Infancy*. San Francisco: Freeman, 1974.

Bower, T. G. R., Broughton, J. M., and Moore, M. K.: Infant responses to approaching objects: An indicator of response to distal variables. *Perception & Psychophysics*, 1971, *9*, 193–196.

Bradburn, N. M.: N Achievement and father dominance in Turkey. *Journal of Abnormal and Social Psychology*, 1963, *67*, 464–468.

Brainerd, C. J.: Does prior knowledge of the compensation rule increase susceptibility to conservation training? *Developmental Psychology*, 1976, *12*, 1–5.

Bregman, E.: An attempt to modify the emotional attitude of infants by the conditioned response technique. *Journal of Genetic Psychology*, 1934, *45*, 169–198.

Brehm, J. W.: *Responses to Loss of Freedom: A Theory of Psychological Reactance*. Morristown, New Jersey: General Learning Press, 1972.

Brehm, J. W., Gatz, M., Geothals, G., McCrommon, J., and Ward, L.: Psychological arousal and interpersonal attraction. Unpublished manuscript, Duke University, 1970.

Breland, K., and Breland, M.: The misbehavior of organisms. *American Psychologist*, 1961, *16*, 681–684.

Breland, K., and Breland, M.: *Animal Behavior*. New York: Macmillan, 1966.

Brewer, V., and Hartmann, E.: Variable sleepers: When is more or less sleep required? Report to the Association for the Psychophysiological Study of Sleep, San Diego, 1973.

Bridges, K. M. B.: Emotional development in early infancy. *Child Development*, 1932, *3*, 324–334.

Briggs, G. E.: On the predictor variable for choice reaction time. *Memory & Cognition*, 1974, *2*, 575–580.

Broadbent, D. E.: *Perception and Communication*. Oxford: Pergamon, 1958.

Broadbent, D. E.: *Decision and Stress*. New York: Academic Press, 1971.

Brooks, L. R.: Spatial and verbal components of the act of recall. *Canadian Journal of Psychology*, 1968, *22*, 349–368.

Brown, B. B.: New mind, new body. *Psychology Today*, 1974, *8* (3), 45–113.

Brown, B. B.: *New Mind, New Body Biofeedback: New Directions for the Mind*. New York: Harper & Row, 1975.

Brown, D. R., Schmidt, M. J., Cosgrove, M. P., and Zuber, J. J.: Stabilized images: Further evidence for central pattern processing. *Psychonomic Science*, 1972, *29*, 106–108.

Brown, P., and Elliott, R.: Control of aggression in a nursery school class. *Journal of Experimental Child Psychology*, 1965, *2*, 103–107.

Brown, P. L., and Jenkins, H. M.: Auto-shaping of the pigeon's key-peck. *Journal of the Experimental Analysis of Behavior*, 1968, *11*, 1–8.

Brown, R.: The first sentences of child and chimpanzee. In R. Brown, *Psycholinguistics*. New York: Free Press, 1970.

Brown, R., Cazden, C., and Bellugi-Klima, U.: The child's grammar from I to III. In J. P. Hill (ed.), *Minnesota Symposia on Child Psychology*. Vol. 2. Minneapolis: University of Minnesota Press, 1969.

Bruner, J. S.: Play is serious business. *Psychology Today*, 1975, *8* (8), 81–83.

Brunswik, E.: *Perception and the Representative Design of Psychological Experiments.* Berkeley, California: University of California Press, 1956.

Brush, F. R.: *Aversive Conditioning and Learning.* New York: Academic Press, 1970.

Bryan, J. H., Redfield, J., and Mader, S.: Words and deeds about altruism and the subsequent reinforcement power of the model. *Child Development,* 1971, *42,* 1501–1508.

Bryan, J. H., and Test, M. A.: Models and helping: Naturalistic studies in aiding behavior. *Journal of Personality and Social Psychology,* 1967, *6,* 400–407.

Buck, R.: Nonverbal communication of affect in children. *Journal of Personality and Social Psychology,* 1975, *31,* 644–653.

Buck, R., Miller, R. E., and Caul, W. F.: Sex, personality, and physiological variables in the communication of affect via facial expression. *Journal of Personality and Social Psychology,* 1974, *30,* 587–596.

Buckhout, R.: Eyewitness testimony. *Scientific American,* 1974, 231.

Bugelski, B. R.: Words and things and images. *American Psychologist,* 1970, *25,* 1002–1012.

Burnam, M. A., Pennebaker, J. W., and Glass, D. C.: Time consciousness, achievement striving, and the type A coronary-prone behavior pattern. *Journal of Abnormal Psychology,* 1975, *84,* 76–79.

Burtt, E. A.: *The Metaphysical Foundations of Modern Physical Science.* Garden City, New York: Doubleday, 1955.

Buss, A. H.: Instrumentality of aggression, feedback, and frustration as determinants of physical aggression. *Journal of Personality and Social Psychology,* 1966, *3,* 153–162.

Butler, R. A.: Discrimination learning by rhesus monkeys to visual-exploration motivation. *Journal of Comparative and Physiological Psychology,* 1953, *46,* 95–98.

Butler, R. A.: Curiosity in monkeys. *Scientific American,* 1954, *190*:18, 70–75.

Byrne, D.: The effect of a subliminal food stimulus on verbal responses. *Journal of Applied Psychology,* 1959, *43,* 249–252.

Byrne, D.: Attitudes and attraction. In L. Berkowitz (ed.), *Advances in Experimental Social Psychology.* New York: Academic Press, 1969.

Byrne, D.: *The Attraction Paradigm.* New York: Academic Press, 1971.

Byrne, D.: Learning from Andy Hardy. In L. Gross (ed.), *Sexual Behavior: Current Issues.* Flushing, New York: Spectrum, 1974, pp. 121–123.

Byrne, D.: Sexual imagery. In J. Money and H. Musaph (eds.), *Handbook of Sexology.* Amsterdam: Excerpta Medica, 1976.

Byrne, D., and Byrne, L. A.: *Exploring Human Sexuality.* New York: Crowell, 1977.

Byrne, D., and Clore, G. L.: Effectance arousal and attraction. *Journal of Personality and Social Psychology Monograph Supplement,* 1967, *6,* 1–18.

Byrne, D., Fisher, J. D., Lamberth, J., and Mitchell, H. E.: Evaluations of erotica: Facts or feelings? *Journal of Personality and Social Psychology,* 1974, *29,* 111–116.

Byrne, D., Gouaux, C., Griffitt, W., Lamberth, J., Murakawa, N., Prasda, M., Prasad, A., and Ramirez, M.: The ubiquitous relationship: Attitude similarity and attraction. *Human Relations,* 1971, *24,* 201–207.

Byrne, D., and Lamberth, J.: The effect of erotic stimuli on sex arousal, evaluative responses, and subsequent behavior. In *Technical Report of the Commission on Obscenity and Pornography.* Vol. VIII. Washington, D.C.: U.S. Government Printing Office, 1971, pp. 41–67.

Byrne, D., McDonald, R. D., and Mikawa, J.: Approach and avoidance affiliation motives. *Journal of Personality,* 1963, *31,* 21–37.

Byrne, D., and Rhamey, R.: Magnitude of positive and negative reinforcements as a determinant of attraction. *Journal of Personality and Social Psychology,* 1965, *2,* 884–889.

Caggiula, A. R., and Hoebel, B. G.: "Copulation-reward site" in the posterior hypothalamus. *Science,* 1966, *153,* 1284–1285.

Calhoun, J. B.: Population density and social pathology. *Scientific American,* 1962, *206,* 139–148.

Calhoun, J. B.: The role of space in animal sociology. *Journal of Social Issues,* 1966, *22,* 46–58.

Calhoun, J. B.: Space and the strategy of life. In A. H. Esser (ed.), *Behavior and Environment.* New York: Plenum, 1971.

Cameron, N.: The functional psychoses. In J. McV. Hunt (ed.), *Personality and the Behavior Disorders.* Vol. 2. New York: Ronald, 1944, pp. 861–921.

Cameron, N.: *Personality Development and Psychopathology.* Boston: Houghton Mifflin, 1963.

Campos, J. J., Langer, A., and Krawitz, A.: Cardiac responses on the visual cliff in prelocomotor human infants. *Science,* 1970, *170,* 196–197.

Cannavale, F. J., Scarr, H. A., and Pepitone, A.: Deindividuation in the small group: Further evidence. *Journal of Personality and Social Psychology,* 1970, *16,* 141–147.

Cannon, W. B.: *Bodily Changes in Pain, Hunger, Fear, and Rage.* New York: Appleton-Century, 1929.

Capaldi, E. J.: An analysis of the role of reward and reward magnitude in instrumental learning. In J. Reynierse (ed.), *Current Issues in Animal Learning.* Lincoln, Nebraska: University of Nebraska Press, 1970.

Capaldi, E. J., and Lynch, D.: Repeated shifts in reward magnitude: Evidence in favor of an associational and absolute (noncontextual) interpretation. *Journal of Experimental Psychology,* 1967, *75,* 226–235.

Caplan, G.: *Principles of Preventive Psychiatry.* New York: Basic Books, 1964.

Carr, S.: The city of the mind. In W. R. Ewald, Jr. (ed.), *Environment for Man: The Next Fifty Years.* Bloomington, Indiana: Indiana University Press, 1967.

Carrington, P.: Dreams and schizophrenia. *Archives of General Psychiatry,* 1972, *26,* 343–350.

Cash, T., Neale, J. M., and Cromwell, R. L.: Span of apprehension in schizophrenia: Full-report technique. *Journal of Abnormal Psychology,* 1972, *79,* 322–327.

Cates, J.: Psychology's manpower: Report on the 1968 national register of scientific and technical personnel. *American Psychologist,* 1970, *25,* 254–263.

Cattell, R. B.: *Description and Measurement of Personality.* Yonkers, New York: World Book, 1946.

Cattell, R. B.: *The Scientific Analysis of Personality.* Baltimore, Maryland: Penguin Books, 1965.

Cattell, R. B., Kawash, G. F., and DeYoung, G. E.: Validation of objective measures of ergic tension: Response of the sex erg to visual stimulation. *Journal of Experimental Research in Personality,* 1972, *6,* 76–83.

Caulfield, J. B., and Martin, R. B.: Establishment of praise as a reinforcer in chronic schizophrenics. *Journal of Consulting and Clinical Psychology,* 1976, *44,* 61–67.

Chafetz, M. E.: Addiction. II. Alcoholism. In A. M. Freedman and H. I. Kaplan (eds.), *Comprehensive Textbook of Psychiatry.* Baltimore, Maryland: Williams and Wilkins, 1967.

Chaplin, J. P.: *Dictionary of Psychology.* New York: Dell, 1968.

Chomsky, N.: *Language and Mind.* New York: Harcourt Brace Jovanovich, 1968.

Chow, B. F., Simonson, M., Hanson, H. M., and Roeder, L. M.: Behavioral measurements in nutritional studies. *Conditional Reflex,* 1971, *6,* 36–40.

Church, R. M.: Response suppression. In B. A. Campbell and R. M. Church (eds.), *Punishment and Aversive*

Behavior. New York: Appleton-Century-Crofts, 1969.

Church, R. M., Wooten, C. L., and Matthews, T. J.: Contingency between a response and an aversive event in the rat. *Journal of Comparative and Physiological Psychology,* 1970, *72,* 476–485.

Clark, K. B.: The pathos of power: A psychological perspective. *American Psychologist,* 1971, *26,* 1047–1057.

Clark, R. D., and Word, L. E.: Where is the apathetic bystander? Situational characteristics of the emergency. *Journal of Personality and Social Psychology,* 1974, *29,* 279–287.

Cleary, T. A., Humphreys, L. G., Kendrick, S. A., and Wesman, A.: Educational uses of tests with disadvantaged students. *American Psychologist,* 1975, *30,* 15–41.

Clemens, L. G.: Effect of stimulus female variation on sexual performance of the male deermouse, *Peromyscus maniculatus. Proceedings, 75th Annual Convention, APA,* 1967, 119–120.

Clifford, N. M., and Walster, E.: Research note: The effect of physical attractiveness on teacher expectations. *Sociology of Education,* 1973, *46,* 248–258.

Clore, G. L., Wiggins, N. H., and Itkin, S.: Gain and loss in attraction: Attributions from nonverbal behavior. *Journal of Personality and Social Psychology,* 1975, *31,* 706–712.

Clum, G. A.: Role of stress in the prognosis of mental illness. *Journal of Consulting and Clinical Psychology,* 1976, *44,* 54–60.

Cofer, C. N.: *Motivation and Emotion.* Glenview, Illinois: Scott, Foresman, 1972.

Cohen, D. B.: Sex role orientation and dream recall. *Journal of Abnormal Psychology,* 1973, *82,* 246–252.

Cohen, D. B.: Dreaming: Experimental investigation of representational and adaptive properties. In G. E. Schwartz and D. Shapiro (eds.), *Consciousness and Self-Regulation.* Vol. II. New York: Plenum, 1976.

Cohen, D. B., and Cox, D.: Neuroticism in the sleep laboratory: Implications for representational and adaptive properties of dreaming. *Journal of Abnormal Psychology,* 1975, *84,* 91–108.

Cohen, D. B., and MacNeilage, P. F.: A test of the salience hypothesis of dream recall. *Journal of Consulting and Clinical Psychology,* 1974, *42,* 699–703.

Cohen, S., Glass, D. C., and Singer, J. E.: Apartment noise, auditory discrimination, and reading ability in children. *Journal of Experimental Social Psychology,* 1973, *9,* 407–422.

Coleman, J. C.: Facial expression of emotion. *Psychological Monographs,* 1949, 63 (1) (Whole No. 296).

Coleman, J. C.: *Abnormal Psychology and Modern Life.* 4th ed. Chicago: Scott, Foresman, 1972.

Collins, A., and Quillian, M. R.: Retrieval time from semantic memory. *Journal of Verbal Learning and Verbal Behavior,* 1969, *8,* 240–247.

Collins, A., and Quillian, M. R.: How to make a language user. In E. Tulving and W. Donaldson (eds.), *Organization of Memory.* New York: Academic Press, 1972.

Connor, J.: Olfactory control of aggressive and sexual behavior in the mouse *(Mus musclus L.). Psychonomic Science,* 1972, *27,* 1–3.

Conrad, R.: Acoustic confusions and immediate memory. *British Journal of Psychology,* 1964, *55,* 77–84.

Conrad, R., and Hull, A. J.: Information, acoustic confusion, and memory span. *British Journal of Psychology,* 1964, *55,* 429–432.

Coons, E. E., and Cruce, J. A. F.: Lateral hypothalamus: Food and current intensity in maintaining self-stimulation of hunger. *Science,* 1968, *159,* 1117–1119.

Cooper, J., Zanna, M. P., and Goethals, G. R.: Mistreatment of an esteemed other as a consequence affecting dissonance reduction. *Journal of Experimental Social Psychology,* 1974, *10,* 224–225.

Cornsweet, T. N.: *Visual Perception.* New York: Academic Press, 1970.

Corso, J. F.: Sensory processes and age effects in normal adults. *Journal of Gerontology,* 1971, *26,* 90–105.

Cosgrove, M. P., Kohl, G. A., Schmidt, M. J., and Brown, D. R.: Chromatic substitution with stabilized images: Evidence for chromatic-specific pattern processing in the human visual system. *Vision Research,* 1974, *14,* 23–30.

Cronbach, L. J.: Five decades of public controversy over mental testing. *American Psychologist,* 1975, *30,* 1–14.

Cronholm, B., and Otosson, J. O.: "Counter-shock" in electroconvulsive therapy. *Archives of General Psychiatry,* 1961, *4,* 254–258.

Crouch, J. E., and McClintic, J. R.: *Human Anatomy and Physiology.* New York: John Wiley and Sons, 1971.

Crowe, B. L.: The tragedy of the commons revisited. *Science,* November, 1969, 166.

Crowley, J. E., Levitin, T. E., and Quinn, R. P.: Seven deadly half-truths about women. *Psychology Today,* March, 1973, pp. 94–96.

Crutchfield, R. S.: Conformity and character. *American Psychologist,* 1955, *10,* 191–198.

Curran, J. P.: Examination of various interpersonal attraction principles in the dating dyad. *Journal of Experimental Research in Personality,* 1973, *6,* 347–356.

Cvetkovich, G., Grote, B., Bjorseth, A., and Sarkissian, J.: On the psychology of adolescents' use of contraceptives. *Journal of Sex Research,* 1975, *11,* 256–270.

D'Amato, M. R.: *Experimental Psychology.* New York: McGraw-Hill, 1970.

Darley, J. M., and Latané, B.: Bystander intervention in emergencies: Diffusion of responsibility. *Journal of Personality and Social Psychology,* 1968, *8,* 377–383.

Darley, J. M., Teger, A. I., and Lewis, L. D.: Do groups always inhibit individuals' responses to potential emergencies? *Journal of Personality and Social Psychology,* 1973, *26,* 395–399.

Darwin, C. A.: *The Expression of the Emotions in Man and Animals.* London: Murray, 1872.

Darwin, C. J., Turvey, M. T., and Crowder, R. G.: An auditory analogue of the Sperling partial report procedure: Evidence for brief auditory storage. *Cognitive Psychology,* 1972, *3,* 255–267.

D'Atri, D. A.: Psychophysiological responses to crowding. *Environment and Behavior,* 1975, *7,* 237–252.

Davis, K. E., and Braucht, G. N.: Reactions to viewing films of erotically realistic heterosexual behavior. In *Technical Report of the Commission on Obscenity and Pornography.* Vol. VIII. Washington, D.C.: U.S. Government Printing Office, 1971, pp. 68–96.

Davis, R. T., Settlage, P. H., and Harlow, H. F.: Performance of normal and brain-operated monkeys on mechanical puzzles with and without food incentive. *Journal of Genetic Psychology,* 1950, *77,* 305–311.

Davison, G. C.: Homosexuality: The ethical challenge. *Journal of Consulting and Clinical Psychology,* 1976, *44,* 157–162.

Davison, G. C., and Neale, J. M.: *Abnormal Psychology: An Experimental Clinical Approach.* New York: John Wiley and Sons, 1974.

Davison, G. C., and Stuart, R. B.: Behavior therapy and civil liberties. *American Psychologist,* 1975, *30,* 755–763.

Davison, M. L., and Jones, L. E.: A similarity-attraction model for predicting sociometric choice from perceived group structure. *Journal of Personality and Social Psychology,* 1976, in press.

Davitz, J. R.: *The Language of Emotion.* New York: Academic Press, 1969.

Deasy, C. M.: When architects consult people. *Psychology Today,* 1970, *3* (10), 54–79.

Deaux, K.: *The Behavior of Women and Men.* Belmont, California: Brooks/Cole, 1976.

Deaux, K., and Emswiller, T.: Explanations of successful performance on sex-linked tasks: What's skill for the male is luck for the female. *Journal of Personality and Social Psychology,* 1973, *29,* 80–85.

DeCecco, J. P., and Crawford, W. R.: *The Psychology of Learning and Instruction.* Englewood Cliffs, New Jersey: Prentice-Hall, 1974.

Deci, E. L.: *Intrinsic Motivation.* New York: Plenum, 1975.

De Lint, J., and Schmidt, W.: The epidemiology of alcoholism. *In* Y. Israel and J. Mardones (eds.), *Biological Basis of Alcoholism.* New York: John Wiley and Sons, 1971.

Dement, W. C.: *Some Must Watch While Some Must Sleep.* San Francisco: W. H. Freeman, 1975.

Dement, W. C., and Kleitman, N.: Cyclic variations in EEG during sleep and their relation to eye movements, body motility, and dreaming. *EEG Clinical Neurophysiology,* 1957, 9, 673–690.

Dengerink, H. A., and Bertilson, H. S.: The reduction of attack-instigated aggression. *Journal of Research in Personality,* 1974, 8, 254–262.

Denner, B., and Price, R. H. (eds.): *Community Mental Health: Social Action and Reaction.* New York: Holt, Rinehart, and Winston, 1973.

Deutsch, J. A.: Appetitive motivation. *In* J. L. McGaugh (ed.), *Psychobiology: Behavior from a Biological Perspective.* New York: Academic Press, 1971.

DiCaprio, N. S.: *Personality Theories: Guides to Living.* Philadelphia: W. B. Saunders Company, 1974.

DiCara, L. V., and Miller, N. E.: Instrumental learning of vasomotor responses by rats: Learning to respond differentially to the two ears. *Science,* 1968, 159, 1485–1486.

Dick, A. O.: Iconic memory and its relation to perceptual processing and other memory mechanisms. *Perception and Psychophysics,* 1975, 16, 575–596.

Diener, E., Dineen, J., Endresen, K., Beaman, A. L., and Fraser, S. C.: Effects of altered responsibility, cognitive set, and modeling on physical aggression and deindividuation. *Journal of Personality and Social Psychology,* 1975, 31, 328–337.

Diener, E., Fraser, S. C., Beaman, A. L., and Kelem, R. T.: Effects of deindividuation variables on stealing among Halloween trick-or-treaters. *Journal of Personality and Social Psychology,* 1976, 33, 178–183.

Dion, K., Berscheid, E., and Walster, E.: What is beautiful is good. *Journal of Personality and Social Psychology,* 1972, 24, 285–290.

Dishotsky, N., Loughman, W., Mogar, R., and Lipscomb, W.: LSD and genetic damage. *Science,* 1971, 172, 431–440.

Doane, B. K., Mahatoo, W., Heron, W., and Scott, T. H.: Changes in perceptual functions after isolation. *Canadian Journal of Psychology,* 1959, 13, 210–219.

Dobzhansky, T.: *Genetic Diversity and Human Equality.* New York: Basic Books, 1973.

Dollard, J., Doob, L., Miller, N., Mowrer, O. H., and Sears, R. R.: *Frustration and Aggression.* New Haven, Connecticut: Yale University Press, 1939.

Dollard, J., and Miller, N. E.: *Personality and Psychotherapy.* New York: McGraw-Hill, 1950.

Domjan, M., and Wilson, N. E.: Specificity of cue to consequence in aversion learning in the rat. *Psychonomic Science,* 1972, 26, 143–145.

Donders, F. C.: On the speed of mental processes. (Translated by W. G. Koster.) *In* W. G. Koster (ed.), *Attention and Performance II.* Amsterdam: North Holland, 1969.

Donnerstein, E., Donnerstein, M., and Evans, R.: Erotic stimuli and aggression: Facilitation or inhibition. *Journal of Personality and Social Psychology,* 1975, 21, 237–444.

Donnerstein, E., Donnerstein, M., Simons, S., and Ditrichs, R.: Variables in interracial aggression: Anonymity, expected retaliation, and a riot. *Journal of Personality and Social Psychology,* 1972, 22, 236–245.

Doob, A. N., and Wood, L.: Catharsis and aggression: The effects of annoyance and retaliation on aggressive behavior. *Journal of Personality and Social Psychology,* 1972, 22, 156–162.

Dorr, D., and Fey, S.: Relative power of symbolic adult and peer models in the modification of children's moral choice behavior. *Journal of Personality and Social Psychology,* 1974, 29, 335–341.

Dosey, M. A., and Meisels, M.: Personal space and self-protection. *Journal of Personality and Social Psychology,* 1969, 11, 93–97.

Doty, R. L., Ford, M., Preti, G., and Huggins, G. R.: Changes in the intensity and pleasantness of human vaginal odors during the menstrual cycle. *Science,* 1975, 190, 1316–1318.

Downs, R. M., and Stea, D. (eds.): *Image and Environment.* Chicago: Aldine, 1973.

Doxiadis, C. A.: The coming era of ecumenopolis. *Saturday Review,* March 18, 1967, 11–14.

Driscoll, R., Davis, K. E., and Lipetz, M. E.: Parental interference and romantic love: The Romeo and Juliet Effect. *Journal of Personality and Social Psychology,* 1972, 24, 1–10.

Duda, J. J., and Bolles, R. C.: Effects of prior deprivation, current deprivation, and weight loss on the activity of the hungry rat. *Journal of Comparative and Physiological Psychology,* 1963, 56, 569–571.

Duffy, E.: *Activation and Behavior.* New York: John Wiley and Sons, 1962.

Dustin, D. S., and Davis, H. P.: Authoritarianism and sanctioning behavior. *Journal of Personality and Social Psychology,* 1967, 6, 222–224.

Dutton, D. G., and Aron, A. P.: Some evidence for heightened sexual attraction under conditions of high anxiety. *Journal of Personality and Social Psychology,* 1974, 30, 510–517.

Dyer, F. N.: The Stroop phenomenon and its use in the study of perceptual, cognitive, and response processes. *Memory & Cognition,* 1973, 2, 106–120.

Eagly, A. H.: Comprehensibility of persuasive arguments as a determinant of opinion change. *Journal of Personality and Social Psychology,* 1974, 29, 758–773.

Eastman, W. F.: First intercourse. *Sexual Behavior,* 1972, 2(3), 22–27.

Ebbinghaus, H.: *Uber das Gedächtnis.* Leipzig: Duncker, 1885. Translation by H. A. Ruger and C. E. Bussenius in *Memory.* New York: Teachers College, Columbia University, 1913.

Eby, T.: The effect of defensive style (repression-sensitization) on the perception of nonverbal facial affect. Unpublished master's thesis, Purdue University, 1975.

Edney, J. J.: Human territoriality. *Psychological Bulletin,* 1974, 81, 959–975.

Edney, J. J.: Human territories: Comment on functional properties. *Environment and Behavior,* 1976, 8, 31–47.

Edwards, W., Lindman, H., and Phillips, L. D.: Emerging technologies for making decisions. *In* R. Brown et al. (eds.), *New Directions in Psychology II.* New York: Holt, Rinehart, & Winston, 1965.

Efran, M. C.: The effect of physical appearance on the judgment of guilt, interpersonal attraction, and severity of recommended punishment in a simulated jury task. *Journal of Research in Personality,* 1974, 8, 45–54.

Egeth, H., Blecker, D. L., and Kamlet, A. S.: Verbal interference in a perceptual comparison task. *Perception & Psychophysics,* 1969, 6, 355–356.

Eisenberger, R.: Explanation of rewards that do not reduce tissue needs. *Psychological Bulletin,* 1972, 77, 319–339.

Ekman, P.: *Darwin and Facial Expression: A Century of Research in Review.* New York: Academic Press, 1973.

Ekman, P., and Friesen, W. V.: *Unmasking the Face.* Englewood Cliffs, New Jersey: Prentice-Hall, 1975.

Eliasberg, W. G., and Stuart, I. R.: Authoritarian personality and the obscenity threshold. *Journal of Social Psychology,* 1961, 55, 143–151.

Elliot, C. H., and Denney, D. R.: Weight control through

covert sensitization and false feedback. *Journal of Consulting and Clinical Psychology*, 1975, *43*, 842–850.

Ellis, A.: *Reason and Emotion in Psychotherapy*. New York: Lyle Stuart, 1962.

Ellsworth, P., Carlsmith, J. M., and Henson, A.: Staring as a stimulus to flight in humans: A series of field studies. *Journal of Personality and Social Psychology*, 1972, *21*, 302–311.

Ellsworth, P. and Langer, E. J.: Staring and approach: An interpretation of the stare as a nonspecific activator. *Journal of Personality and Social Psychology*, 1976, *33*, 117–122.

Endler, N. S., and Hoy, E.: Conformity as related to reinforcement and social pressure. *Journal of Personality and Social Psychology*, 1967, *7*, 197–202.

Engel, J. F., Kollat, D. T., and Blackwell, R. D.: *Consumer Behavior*. New York: Holt, Rinehart, & Winston, 1973.

Ephron, H. S., and Carrington, P.: Rapid eye movement sleep and cortical homeostasis. *Psychological Review*, 1966, *75*, 500–526.

Epstein, R.: Authoritarianism, displaced aggression, and social status of the target. *Journal of Personality and Social Psychology*, 1965, *2*, 585–589.

Eriksen, C. W., and Collins, J. F.: Sensory traces versus the psychological moment in the temporal organization of form. *Journal of Experimental Psychology*, 1968, *77*, 376–382.

Erikson, E.: *Childhood and Society*. New York: W. W. Norton, 1963.

Erlenmeyer-Kimling, L., and Jarvik, L. F.: Genetics and intelligence. *Science*, 1963, *142*, 1477–1479.

Erwin, J., Maple, T., Mitchell, G., and Willott, J.: Follow-up study of isolation-reared and mother-reared rhesus monkeys paired with preadolescent conspecifics in late infancy: Cross-sex pairings. *Developmental Psychology*, 1974, *6*, 808–814.

Estes, W. K.: An experimental study of punishment. *Psychological Monographs*, 1944, *57* (Whole No. 263).

Evans, G. W., and Howard, R. B.: Personal space. *Psychological Bulletin*, 1973, *80*, 334–344.

Evans, R. I., Rozelle, R. M., Lasater, T. M., Dembroski, T. M., and Allen, B. P.: Fear arousal, persuasion, and actual versus implied behavioral change: New perspective utilizing a real-life dental hygiene program. *Journal of Personality and Social Psychology*, 1970, *16*, 220–227.

Exline, R. V.: Visual interaction. In W. J. Arnold and M. M. Page (eds.), *Nebraska Symposium on Motivation*. Lincoln, Nebraska: University of Nebraska Press, 1971.

Eyberg, S. M., and Johnson, S. M.: Multiple assessment of behavior modification with families: Effects of contingency contracting and order of treated problems. *Journal of Consulting and Clinical Psychology*, 1974, *42*, 594–606.

Eysenck, H. J.: The effects of psychotherapy. In H. J. Eysenck (ed.), *Handbook of Abnormal Psychology*. New York: Basic Books, 1961, pp. 697–725.

Eysenck, H. J.: Hysterical personality and sexual adjustment, attitudes and behavior. *Journal of Sex Research*, 1971, *7*, 274–281.

Eysenck, H. J.: Obscenity—officially speaking. *Penthouse*, 1972, *3* (11), 95–102.

Fantz, R. L.: Visual perception from birth as shown by pattern selectivity. *Annals of the New York Academy of Science*, 1965, *118*, 793–814.

Farber, I. E.: Sane and insane: Constructions and misconstructions. *Journal of Abnormal Psychology*, 1975, *84*, 589–620.

Fast, J.: *Body Language*. New York: M. Evans & Co., 1970.

Fechner, G. T.: Uber eine Scheibe zur Erzeugung subjectiver Farben. *Pogg. Ann. Physik u. Chemie*, 1838, *45*, 227–232.

Fechner, G. T.: *Elements of Psychophysics*. Leipzig: Brietkopf und Hartel, 1860.

Feldman, M. P., and MacCulloch, M. J.: *Homosexual Behavior: Therapy and Assessment*. Oxford: Pergamon, 1971.

Feleky, A.: *Feelings and Emotions*. New York: Pioneer, 1922.

Felipe, N., and Sommer, R.: Invasions of personal space. *Social Problems*, 1966, *14*, 206–214.

Feminists on Children's Literature: A feminist look at children's books. *School Library Journal*, January, 1972.

Ferrari, N. A.: Institutionalization and attitude change in an aged population: a field study of dissonance theory. Unpublished doctoral dissertation, Western Reserve University, 1962.

Ferster, C. B., and Skinner, B. F.: *Schedules of Reinforcement*. New York: Appleton-Century-Crofts, 1957.

Feshbach, S. Aggression. In P. Mussen (ed.), *Carmichael's Manual of Child Psychology*. Vol. II. New York: John Wiley and Sons, 1970.

Feshbach, S., and Singer, R. D.: *Television and Aggression: An Experimental Field Study*. San Francisco: Jossey-Bass, 1971.

Festinger, L.: *A Theory of Cognitive Dissonance*. Evanston, Illinois: Row, Peterson, 1957.

Festinger, L., and Carlsmith, J. M.: Cognitive consequences of forced compliance. *Journal of Abnormal and Social Psychology*, 1959, *58*, 203–210.

Festinger, V., Allyn, M. R., and White, C. W.: The perception of color with achromatic stimulation. *Vision Research*, 1971, *11*, 591–612.

Finch, G.: Hunger as a determinant of conditional and unconditional salivary response magnitude. *American Journal of Physiology*, 1938, *123*, 379–382.

Finger, F. W., Reid, L. S., and Weasner, M. H.: The effect of reinforcement upon activity during cyclic food deprivation. *Journal of Comparative and Physiological Psychology*, 1957, *50*, 495–498.

Fink, M., Kety, S., McGaugh, J., and Williams, T. A. (eds.): *Psychobiology of Convulsive Therapy*. New York: Halsted, 1974.

Fishbein, M., and Azjen, I.: *Belief, Attitude, Intention, and Behavior: An Introduction to Theory and Research*. Reading, Massachusetts: Addison-Wesley, 1975.

Fisher, J. D. and Byrne, D.: Too close for comfort: Sex differences in response to invasions of personal space. *Journal of Personality and Social Psychology*, 1975, *32*, 15–21.

Flavell, J. H.: The development of inferences about others. In T. Misebel (ed.), *Understanding Other Persons*. Oxford, England: Blackwell, Basil, & Mott, 1973.

Fleming, J. D.: Field report: The state of the apes. *Psychology Today*, 1974, *7*, 31–49.

Flippo, J. R., and Lewinsohn, P. M.: Effects of failure on the self-esteem of depressed and nondepressed subjects. *Journal of Consulting and Clinical Psychology*, 1971, *36*, 151.

Ford, D. H., and Urban, H. B.: *Systems of Psychotherapy: A Comparative Study*. New York: John Wiley and Sons, 1963.

Foree, D. D., and LoLordo, V. M.: Attention in the pigeon: Differential effects of food-getting versus shock-avoidance procedures. *Journal of Comparative and Physiological Psychology*, 1973, *85*, 551–558.

Fox, P. W., and Dahl, P. R.: Aided retrieval of previously unrecalled information. *Journal of Experimental Psychology*, 1971, *88*, 349–353.

Fraser, S. and Zimbardo, P. G.: [Unpublished research cited in P. G. Zimbardo] The human choice: Individuation, reason, and order versus deindividuation, impulse, and chaos. In W. J. Arnold and D. Levine (eds.), *Nebraska*

Symposium on Motivation. Lincoln, Nebraska: University of Nebraska Press, 1969.

Frazier, T. M., Davis, G. H., Goldstein, H., and Goldberg, I. D.: Cigarette smoking and prematurity: A prospective study. *American Journal of Obstetrics and Gynecology*, 1961, *81*, 988–996.

Freedman, J. L., and Fraser, S. C.: Compliance without pressure: The foot-in-the-door technique. *Journal of Personality and Social Psychology*, 1966, *4*, 195–202.

Freedman, J. L., Heshka, S., and Levy, A.: Population density and pathology: Is there a relationship? *Journal of Experimental Social Psychology*, 1975, *11*, 539–552.

Freedman, J. L., Levy, A. S., Buchanan, R. W., and Price, J.: Crowding and human aggressiveness. *Journal of Experimental Social Psychology*, 1972, *8*, 528–548.

Freedman, J. L., Wallington, S. A., and Bless, E.: Compliance without pressure: The effect of guilt. *Journal of Personality and Social Psychology*, 1967, *7*, 117–124.

Freeman, W.: Psychosurgery. *In* S. Arieti (ed.), *American Handbook of Psychiatry.* Vol. II. New York: Basic Books, 1959, pp. 1521–1541.

Freeman, W., and Watts, J. W.: The frontal lobes and consciousness of the self. *Psychosomatic Medicine*, 1941, *3*, 111–119.

Freeman, W., and Watts, J. W.: Pain mechanisms and frontal lobes: A study of prefrontal lobotomy for intractable pain. *Annals of Internal Medicine*, 1948, *28*, 747–754.

Freemon, F. R.: *Sleep Research: A Critical Review.* Springfield, Illinois: Charles C Thomas, 1972.

Frejka, T.: The prospects for a stationary world population. *Scientific American*, 1973, *228*, 15–23.

Freud, S.: *New Introductory Lectures on Psycho-Analysis.* New York: Norton, 1933.

Freud, S.: Certain neurotic mechanisms in jealousy, paranoia, and homosexuality. 1922. In *Collected Papers.* Vol. 2. London: Hogarth, 1950, pp. 232–243.

Frezza, D. A., and Holland, J. G.: Operant conditioning of the human salivary responses. *Psychophysiology*, 1971, *8*, 581–587.

Friedberg, J.: Electroshock therapy: Let's stop blasting the brain. *Psychology Today*, 1975, 9 (3), 18, 20, 22–23, 98–99.

Friedler, G., and Cochin, J.: Growth retardation in offspring of female rats treated with morphine prior to conception. *Science*, 1972, *175*, 654–656.

Frodi, A.: Sexual arousal, situational restrictiveness, and aggressive behavior. *Journal of Research in Personality*, 1976, in press.

Gael, S., Grant, D. L., and Ritchie, R. J.: Employment test validation for minority and nonminority telephone operators. *Journal of Applied Psychology*, 1975, *60*, 420–426.

Galanter, E.: Contemporary psychophysics. *In* R. Brown et al. (eds.), *New Directions in Psychology.* New York: Holt, Rinehart, and Winston, 1962.

Galizio, M., and Hendrick, C.: Effect of musical accompaniment on attitude: The guitar as a prop for persuasion. *Journal of Applied Social Psychology*, 1972, *2*, 350–359.

Galle, O. R., Gove, W. R., and McPherson, J. M.: Population density and pathology: What are the relations for man? *Science*, 1972, *176*, 23–30.

Gans, H.: *The Urban Villagers.* Glencoe, Illinois: Free Press, 1962.

Gantt, W. H.: Reminiscences of Pavlov. *Journal of the Experimental Analysis of Behavior*, 1973, *20*, 131–136.

Garbarino, J.: A preliminary study of some ecological correlates of child abuse: The impact of socioeconomic stress on mothers. *Child Development*, 1976, *47*, 178–185.

Garcia, J., and Koelling, R. A.: Relation of cue to consequence in avoidance learning. *Psychonomic Science*, 1966, *4*, 123–124.

Garcia, J., McGowan, B. K., and Green, K. F.: Biological constraints on conditioning. *In* A. H. Black and W. F. Prokasy (eds.), *Classical Conditioning II: Current Research and Theory.* New York: Appleton-Century-Crofts, 1972.

Garcia, L. T., and Griffitt, W.: Authoritarian-situation interactions in the determination of punitiveness: Engaging authoritarian ideology. Unpublished manuscript, Kansas State University, 1977.

Garrard, J., Vaitkus, A., and Chilgren, R. A.: Evaluation of a course in human sexuality. *Journal of Medical Education*, 1972, *47*, 772–778.

Garrard, J., Vaitkus, A., Held, J., and Chilgren, R. A.: One-year follow-up of effects of a medical school course in human sexuality. *Journal of Human Reproduction*, 1974.

Gatchel, R. J., and Proctor, J. D.: Physiological correlates of learned helplessness in man. *Journal of Abnormal Psychology*, 1976, *85*, 27–34.

Gazzaniga, M. S.: The split brain in man. *Scientific American*, 1967, *217*, 24–29.

Gazzaniga, M. S.: *The Bisected Brain.* New York: Appleton, 1970.

Gebhard, P. H.: Mammalian sex. Paper presented at the Institute for Sex Research, Bloomington, Indiana, June, 1974.

Geen, R. G.: Effects of frustration, attack, and prior training in aggressiveness upon aggressive behavior. *Journal of Personality and Social Psychology*, 1968, *9*, 316–321.

Geen, R. G., and Stonner, D.: Context effects in observed violence. *Journal of Personality and Social Psychology*, 1973, *25*, 145–150.

Geen, R. G., Stonner, D., and Shope, G. L.: The facilitation of aggression by agression: Evidence against the catharsis hypothesis. *Journal of Personality and Social Psychology*, 1975, *31*, 721–726.

Geer, J. H.: Direct measurement of genital responding. *American Psychologist*, 1975, *30*, 415–418.

Geer, J. H., and Fuhr, R.: cognitive factors in sexual arousal: The role of distraction. *Journal of Consulting and Clinical Psychology*, 1976, *44*, 238–243.

Geer, J. H., Morokoff, P., and Greenwood, P.: Sexual arousal in women: The development of a measurement device for vaginal blood volume. *Archives of Sexual Behavior*, 1974, *3*, 559–564.

Geldard, F. A.: *The Human Senses.* New York: John Wiley and Sons, 1972.

Gelman, R.: Conservation acquisition: A problem of learning to attend to relevant attributes. *Journal of Experimental Child Psychology*, 1969, *7*, 167–187.

Gendlin, E. T., and Rychlak, J. F.: Psychotherapeutic processes. *Annual Review of Psychology*, 1970, *21*, 155–190.

Gentry, W. D.: Effects of frustration, attack, and prior aggressive training on overt aggression and vascular processes. *Journal of Personality and Social Psychology*, 1970, *16*, 718–725.

Gerard, H. B., Conolley, E. S., and Wilhelmy, R. A.: Compliance, justification, and cognitive change. *In* L. Berkowitz (ed.), *Advances in Experimental Social Psychology.* Vol. 7. New York: Academic Press, 1974.

Gerard, H. B., Wilhelmy, R. A., and Conolley, E. S.: Conformity and group size. *Journal of Personality and Social Psychology*, 1968, *8*, 79–82.

Gerbner, G.: Violence in television drama: Trends and symbolic functions. *In* G. A. Comstock and E. A. Rubenstein (ed.), *Television and Social Behavior.* Volume 1: *Media Content and Control.* Washington D.C.: U.S. Government Printing Office, 1972.

Gergen, K. J., Ellsworth, P., Maslach, C., and Seipel, M.: Obligation, donor resources, and reactions to aid in three cultures. *Journal of Personality and Social Psychology*, 1975, *31*, 390–400.

Gibb, J. R.: The effects of human relations training. *In* A. E.

Bergin and S. L. Garfield (eds.), *Handbook of Psychotherapy and Behavior Change: An Empirical Analysis.* New York: John Wiley and Sons, 1971.

Gibson, E. J., and Walk, R. D.: The "visual cliff." *Scientific American,* 1960, *202,* 64–71.

Gibson, J. J.: Adaptation after-effect and contrast in perception of curved lines. *Journal of Experimental Psychology,* 1933, *16,* 1–31.

Gibson, J. J., Filbey, R., and Gazzaniga, M. S.: Hemispheric differences as reflected by reaction time. *Federation Proceedings, Federation of American Societies for Experimental Biology,* 1970, *29,* 658.

Gibson, R., Cohen, M., and Cohen, R.: On the dynamics of the manic-depressive personality. *American Journal of Psychiatry,* 1959, *115,* 1101.

Giesen, M., and Hendrick, C.: Effects of false positive and negative arousal feedback on persuasion. *Journal of Personality and Social Psychology,* 1974, *30,* 449–457.

Glad, D. D.: *Operational Values in Psychotherapy.* New York: Oxford University Press, 1959.

Glass, A. V., Gazzaniga, M. S., and Premack, D.: Artificial language training in global aphasics. *Neuropsychologia,* 1973, *11,* 95–103.

Glass, D. C.: Behavioral antecedents of coronary heart disease. Unpublished manuscript, University of Texas, Austin, 1974.

Glass, D. C., and Singer, J. E.: Behavioral aftereffects of unpredictable and uncontrollable aversive events. *American Scientist,* 1972, *60,* 457–465.(a)

Glass, D. C., and Singer, J. E.: *Urban Stress.* New York: Academic Press, 1972.(b)

Glazer, N.: The Renewal of Cities. *Scientific American,* 1965, *213,* 194–204.

Glueck, S., and Glueck, E.: *Physique and Delinquency.* New York: Harper, 1956.

Goldstein, J. H., Davis, R. W., and Herman, D.: Escalation of aggression: Experimental studies. *Journal of Personality and Social Psychology,* 1975, *31,* 162–170.

Goldstein, M., Kant, H., and Hartman, J. J.: *Pornography and Sexual Deviance.* Berkeley, California: University of California Press, 1974.

Goldstein, M., Kant, H., Judd, L., Rice, C., and Green, R.: Experience with pornography: Rapists, pedophiles, homosexuals, transsexuals, and controls. *Archives of Sexual Behavior,* 1971, *1,* 1–15.

Gordon, M. E., Pryor, N. M., and Harris, B. V.: An examination of scaling bias in Herzberg's theory of job satisfaction. *Organizational Behavior and Human Performance,* 1974, *11,* 106–121.

Gottesman, I., and Shields, J.: *Schizophrenia and Genetics.* New York: Academic Press, 1972.

Gough, H. G.: *Manual for the California Psychological Inventory.* Palo Alto, California: Consulting Psychologists Press, 1957.

Gough, H. G.: An attitude profile for studies of population psychology. *Journal of Research in Personality,* 1975, *9,* 122–135.

Granberg, D., and Corrigan, G.: Authoritarianism, dogmatism, and orientation toward the Vietnam war. *Sociometry,* 1972, *35,* 468–476.

Green, D.: Dissonance and self-perception analyses of "forced compliance": When two theories make competing predictions. *Journal of Personality and Social Psychology,* 1974, *29,* 819–828.

Greenspoon, J.: The reinforcing effect of two spoken sounds on the frequency of two responses. *American Journal of Psychology,* 1955, *68,* 409–416.

Greenwalt, C. H.: How birds sing. *Scientific American,* 1969, *221,* 126–139.

Greenwell, J., and Dengerink, H. A.: The role of perceived versus actual attack in human physical aggression. *Journal of Personality and Social Psychology,* 1973, *26,* 66–71.

Greer, S.: Study of parental loss in neurotics and sociopaths. *Archives of General Psychiatry,* 1964, *11,* 177–180.

Griffitt, W.: Response to erotica and the projection of response to erotica in the opposite sex. *Journal of Experimental Research in Personality,* 1973, *6,* 330–338.

Griffitt, W., May, J., and Veitch, R.: Sexual stimulation and interpersonal behavior: Heterosexual evaluative responses, visual behavior, and physical proximity. *Journal of Personality and Social Psychology,* 1974, *30,* 367–377.

Griffitt, W., and Veitch, R.: Hot and crowded: Influences of population density and temperature on interpersonal affective behavior. *Journal of Personality and Social Psychology,* 1971, *17,* 92–98.

Grinker, R. R., Miller, J., Sabshin, M., Nunn, R., and Nunnally, J. C.: *The Phenomena of Depression.* New York: Hoeber, 1961.

Grohmann, J.: Modifikation oder Functionsreifung? Ein Beitrag zur Klarung der wechselseitigen Beziehungen zwischen Instinkthandlung und Efrahrung. *Zeitschrift fur Tierpsychologie,* 1939, *2,* 132–144.

Grossman, S. P.: *A Textbook of Physiological Psychology.* New York: John Wiley and Sons, 1967, 1973.

Grossman, S. P.: Aggression, avoidance, and reaction to novel environments in female rats with ventromedial hypothalamic lesions. *Journal of Comparative and Physiological Psychology,* 1972, *78,* 274–283.

Grossman, S. P., and Rechtschaffen, A.: Variations in brain temperature in relation to food intake. *Physiology and Behavior,* 1967, *2,* 379–383.

Haaf, R. A., and Bell, R. Q.: A facial dimension in visual discrimination by human infants. *Child Development,* 1967, *38,* 893–899.

Haith, M. M.: The response of the human newborn to visual movement. *Journal of Experimental Child Psychology,* 1966, *3,* 235–243.

Hall, E.: Ethology's warning: A conversation with Niko Tinbergen. *Psychology Today,* 1974, *10*(7), 65–80.

Hall, E. T.: *The Hidden Dimension.* New York: Doubleday, 1966.

Hall, W. S., and Freedle, R. O.: A developmental investigation of standard and nonstandard English among black and white children. *Human Development,* 1973, *16,* 440–464.

Hamilton, D. L., and Fallot, R. D.: Information salience as a weighting factor in impression formation. *Journal of Personality and Social Psychology,* 1974, *30,* 444–448.

Hamilton, J., Stephens, L., and Allen, P.: Controlling aggressive and destructive behavior in severely retarded institutionalized residents. *American Journal of Mental Deficiency,* 1967, *71,* 852–856.

Hanlon, J.: Uri Geller and science. *New Scientist,* 1974, 170–185.

Hansel, C. E. M.: *ESP: A Scientific Evaluation.* New York: Scribner's, 1966.

Hardin, G.: The tragedy of the commons. *Science,* 1968, *162,* 1243–1248.

Hare, R. D.: Psychopathy and choice of immediate versus delayed punishment. *Journal of Abnormal Psychology,* 1966, *71,* 25–29.

Hare, R. D.: *Psychopathy: Theory and Research.* New York: John Wiley and Sons, 1970.

Harlow, H. F.: Mice, monkeys, men, and motives. *Psychological Review,* 1953, *60,* 23–32.

Harlow, H. F.: The heterosexual affectional system in monkeys. *American Psychologist,* 1962, *17,* 1–9.

Harlow, H. F.: Sexual behavior in the rhesus monkey. In F. Beach (ed.), *Sex and Behavior.* New York: John Wiley and Sons, 1965.

Harlow, H. F.: Lust, latency and love: Simian secrets of successful sex. *Journal of Sex Research*, 1975, *11*, 79–90.

Harlow, H. F., and Harlow, M. H.: Learning to love. *American Scientist*, 1966, *54*, 244–272.

Harlow, H. F., and Zimmermann, R. R.: Affectional responses in the infant monkey. *Science*, 1959, *130*, 421–432.

Harrell, R. F., Woodyard, E., and Gates, A. E.: *The Effects of Mothers' Diets on the Intelligence of Offspring*. New York: Teachers College, Columbia University, 1955.

Harris, V. A., and Jellison, J. M.: Fear-arousing communications, false physiological feedback, and the acceptance of recommendations. *Journal of Experimental Social Psychology*, 1971, *7*, 269–279.

Hartley, D., Roback, H. B., and Abramowitz, S. I.: Deterioration effects in encounter groups. *American Psychologist*, 1976, *31*, 247–255.

Hartmann, E. L.: *The Functions of Sleep*. New Haven, Connecticut, Yale University Press, 1973.

Hartmann, E. L. and Stern, W. C.: Desynchronized sleep deprivation: Learning deficit and its reversal by increased catecholamines. *Physiology and Behavior*, 1972, *8*, 585–587.

Hartshorne, H., and May, M. A.: *Studies in the Nature of Character. Volume I: Studies in Deceit*. New York: Macmillan, 1928.

Hartshorne, H., May, M. A., and Shuttleworth, F. K.: *Studies in the Nature of Character. Volume 3: Studies in the Organization of Character*. New York: Macmillan, 1930.

Hartsough, D. M., Zarle, T. H., and Ottinger, D. R.: Rapid response to disaster in an outlying area: The Monticello tornado. *In* H. Parad, H. L. P. Resnik, and L. Parad (eds.), *Disaster Aid and Emergency Health Services*. Bowie, Maryland: Charles Press, 1976.

Hass, R. G., and Linder, D. E.: Counterargument availability and the effects of message structure on persuasion. *Journal of Personality and Social Psychology*, 1972, *23*, 219–233.

Hastings, D.: Follow-up results in psychiatric illness. *American Journal of Psychiatry*, 1958, *114*, 1057.

Hathaway, S. R., and McKinley, J. C.: A multiphasic personality schedule (Minnesota). I. Construction of the schedule. *Journal of Psychology*, 1940, *10*, 249–254.

Hathaway, S. R., and McKinley, J. C.: *Minnesota Multiphasic Personality Inventory Manual*. New York: Psychological Corporation, 1951.

Hauri, P.: Effects of evening activity on early night sleep. *Psychophysiology*, 1968, *4*, 267–277.

Hauri, P.: Dreams in patients remitted for reactive depression. *Journal of Abnormal Psychology*, 1976, *85*, 1–10.

Hearst, E., and Jenkins, H. M.: *Sign-Trading: The Stimulus-Reinforcer Relation and Directed Action*. Austin, Texas: Psychonomic Society Monographs, 1975.

Heberlein, T. A., and Black, J. S.: Attitudinal specificity and the prediction of behavior in a field setting. *Journal of Personality and Social Psychology*, 1976, *33*, 474–479.

Heider, E. R., and Olivier, D. C.: The structure of the color space in naming and memory for two languages. *Cognitive Psychology*, 1972, *3*, 337–354.

Heilbroner, R.: The human prospect. *The New York Review of Books*, 1974, *20*, 21–34.

Heiman, N. M.: Postdoctoral training in community mental health. *Menninger Clinic Bulletin Number 17*, 1973.

Heingartner, A., and Hall, J. V.: Affective consequences in adults and children of repeated exposure to auditory stimuli. *Journal of Personality and Social Psychology*, 1974, *29*, 719–723.

Hendrick, C., and Taylor, S. P.: The effects of belief similarity and aggression on attraction and counter-aggression. *Journal of Personality and Social Psychology*, 1971, *17*, 342–349.

Hensley, M. M., and Cope, J. B.: Further data on removal and repopulation of the breeding birds in a spruce-fir forest community. *Auk*, 1951, *68*, 433–439.

Herman, L. M., and Kantowitz, B. H.: The psychological refractory period effect: Only half the double-stimulation story? *Psychological Bulletin*, 1970, *73*, 74–88.

Herndon, K., and Glass, D. C.: Learned helplessness and pattern A behavior in children. Unpublished manuscript, University of Texas, Austin, 1974.

Herzberg, F.: *Work and the Nature of Man*. New York: World, 1966.

Heslin, R., and Amo, M. F.: Detailed test of the reinforcement-dissonance controversy in the counterattitudinal advocacy situation. *Journal of Personality and Social Psychology*, 1972, *23*, 234–242.

Hess, E. H.: Imprinting and the critical period concept. *In* E. L. Bliss (ed.), *Roots of Behavior*. New York: Harper, 1962.

Hess, E. H.: Attitude and pupil size. *Scientific American*, 1965, *212*, 46–54.

Hess, E. H.: *The Tell-Tale Eye*. New York: Van Nostrand Reinhold, 1975.

Hess, E. H., and Polt, J. M.: Pupil size as related to the interest value of visual stimuli. *Science*, 1960, *132*, 349–350.

Hewitt, J.: Liking and the proportion of favorable evaluations. *Journal of Personality and Social Psychology*, 1972, *22*, 231–235.

Higbee, K. L.: Fifteen years of fear arousal: Research on threat appeals: 1953–1968. *Psychological Bulletin*, 1969, *72*, 426–444.

Hilgard, E. R., and Bower, G. H.: *Theories of Learning*. Englewood Cliffs, New Jersey: Prentice-Hall, 1975.

Hintzman, D. L., Carre, F. A., Eskridge, V. L., Owens, A. M., Shaff, S. S. and Sparks, M. E.: "Stroop" effect: Input or output phenomenon? *Journal of Experimental Psychology*, 1972, *95*, 458–459.

Hockey, G. R.: Noise and efficiency: The visual task. *New Scientist*, 1969, 244–246.

Hockey, G. R.: Changes in attention allocation in a multi-component task under loss of sleep. *British Journal of Psychology*, 1970, *61*, 473–480.

Hogan, R., DeSoto, C., and Solano, C.: Traits, tests, and personality research. Unpublished manuscript, Johns Hopkins University, 1976.

Hokanson, J. E.: Psychophysiological evaluation of the catharsis hypothesis. *In* E. I. Megargee and J. E. Hokanson (eds.), *The Dynamics of Aggression*. New York: Harper & Row, 1970.

Holahan, C. J.: Environmental effects on outdoor social behavior in a low-income urban neighborhood. *Journal of Applied Social Psychology*, 1976, *6*, 48–63.

Holden, C.: Nader on mental health centers: A movement that got bogged down. *Science*, 1972, *177*, 413–415.

Hollingshead, A. B., and Redlich, F. C.: *Social Class and Mental Illness: A Community Study*. New York: John Wiley and Sons, 1958.

Holmes, D. S., and Bennett, D. H.: Experiments to answer questions raised by the use of deception in psychological research. *Journal of Personality and Social Psychology*, 1974, *29*, 358–367.

Horner, M.: Femininity and successful achievement: A basic inconsistency. *In* J. M. Bardwick, E. Douvan, M. S. Horner, and D. Gutmann (eds.), *Feminine Personality and Conflict*. Belmont, California: Brooks/Cole, 1970.

Horner, M.: Toward an understanding of achievement-related conflicts in women. *Journal of Social Issues*, 1972, *28*, 157–176.

Horney, K.: *Our Inner Conflicts*. New York: Norton, 1945.

Houts, P. S., and Serber, M. (eds.): *After the Turn-On, What? Learning Perspectives on Humanistic Groups*. Champaign, Illinois: Research Press, 1972.

Howard, J. L., Reifler, C. B., and Liptzin, M. B.: Effects of exposure to pornography. *In Technical Report of the Commission on Obscenity and Pornography*. Vol. VIII. Washington, D.C.: U.S. Government Printing Office, 1971, pp. 97–132.

Hull, C. L.: *Principles of Behavior*. New York: Appleton-Century-Crofts, 1943.

Hull, C. L.: *A Behavior System.* New Haven, Connecticut: Yale University Press, 1952.

Hulse, S. E.: Reinforcement contrast effects in rats following experimental definition of a dimension of reinforcement magnitude. *Journal of Comparative and Physiological Psychology*, 1973, *85*, 160–170.

Hulse, S. H., Deese, J., and Egeth, H.: *The Psychology of Learning.* New York: McGraw-Hill, 1975.

Hunt, E., and Poltrock, S.: The mechanics of thought. In B. H. Kantowitz (ed.), *Human Information Processing: Tutorials in Performance and Cognition.* Hillsdale, New Jersey: Lawrence Erlbaum Associates, 1974.

Hunt, W., and Matarazzo, J.: Three years later: Recent developments in the experimental modification of smoking behavior. *Journal of Abnormal Psychology*, 1973, *81*, 107–114.

Hygge, S.: Information about the model's unconditioned stimulus and response in vicarious classical conditioning. *Journal of Personality and Social Psychology*, 1976, in press.

Ilgen, D. R., and Seely, W.: Realistic expectations as an aid in reducing voluntary resignations. *Journal of Applied Psychology*, 1974, *59*, 452–455.

Innes, J. M., and Young, R. F.: The effect of presence of an audience, evaluation apprehension, and objective self-awareness on learning. *Journal of Experimental Social Psychology*, 1975, *11*, 35–42.

Isen, A.: Success, failure, attention, and reaction to others: The warm glow of success. *Journal of Personality and Social Psychology*, 1970, *15*, 294–301.

Isen, A. M., and Levin, P. F.: Effect of feeling good on helping: Cookies and kindness. *Journal of Personality and Social Psychology*, 1972, *21*, 384–388.

Ittelson, W. H., Proshansky, H. M., Rivlin, L. G., and Winkel, G. H.: *An Introduction to Environmental Psychology.* New York: Holt, Rinehart, & Winston, 1974.

Izzett, R. R.: Authoritarianism and attitudes toward the Vietnam war as reflected in behavioral and self-report measures. *Journal of Personality and Social Psychology*, 1971, *17*, 145–148.

Jackson, D.: Family therapy in the family of schizophrenics. In M. Stein (ed.), *Contemporary Psychotherapies.* New York: Free Press, 1961.

Jacobs, J.: *Death and Life of Great American Cities.* New York: Random House, 1961.

Jacoby, J.: Consumer psychology as a social psychological sphere of action. *American Psychologist*, 1975, *30*, 977–987.

Jacoby, J.: Consumer psychology: An octennium. In M. R. Rosenzweig and L. W. Porter (eds.), *Annual Review of Psychology.* Palo Alto, California: Annual Reviews, Inc., 1976.

Jacoby, J., Speller, D. E., and Berning, C. K.: Brand choice behavior as a function of information load: replication and extension. *Journal of Consumer Research*, 1974, *1*, 33–42.

Jacoby, J., Speller, D. E., and Kohn, C. A.: Brand choice behavior as a function of information load. *Journal of Marketing Research*, 1974, *11*, 63–69.

Jacoby, J., Szybillo, G. J., and Busato-Schach, J.: Information acquisition behavior in brand choice situations. *Journal of Consumer Research*, 1976, in press.

Jaffe, Y., Malamuth, N., Feingold, J., and Feshbach, S.: Sexual arousal and behavioral aggression. *Journal of Personality and Social Psychology*, 1974, *30*, 759–764.

James, M.: Transactional analysis: The OK boss in all of us. *Psychology Today*, 1976, *9*(9), 31–36, 80.

Janis, I. L., and Field, P. B.: A behavioral assessment of persuasibility: Consistency of individual differences. *Sociometry*, 1956, *19*, 241–259.

Janis, I. L., Kaye, D., and Kirschner, P.: Facilitating effects of "eating while reading" on responsiveness to persuasive communications. *Journal of Personality and Social Psychology*, 1965, *1*, 181–186.

Janisse, M. P., and Peavler, W. S.: Pupillary research today: Emotion in the eye. *Psychology Today*, 1974, *7* (9), 60–63.

Jellinek, E. M.: *The Disease Concept of Alcoholism.* New Haven: Hillhouse Press, 1960.

Jencks, C.: *Inequality: A Reassessment of the Effect of Family and Schooling in America.* New York: Basic Books, 1972.

Jenkins, C. D., Zyzanski, S. J., and Rosenman, R. H.: Progress toward validation of a computer-scored test of the type A coronary-prone behavior pattern. *Psychosomatic Medicine*, 1971, *33*, 192–202.

Jenkins, H. M.: Effects of the stimulus-reinforcer relation on selected and unselected responses. In R. A. Hinde and J. Stevenson-Hinde (eds.), *Constraints on Learning.* London: Academic Press, 1973.

Jenkins, R. L., Holsopple, J. Q., and Lorr, M.: Effects of prefrontal lobotomy on patients with severe chronic schizophrenia. *American Journal of Psychiatry*, 1954, *111*, 84–90.

Jensen, A. R.: Scoring the Stroop test. Acta Psychologica, 1965, *24*, 398–408.

Jensen, A. R.: How much can we boost I. Q. and scholastic achievement? *Harvard Educational Review*, 1969, *39*, 1–123.

Jensen, A. R.: I.Q.'s of identical twins reared apart. *Behavior Genetics*, 1970, *1*, 133–148.

Johnson, R. N.: *Aggression in Man and Animals.* Philadelphia: W. B. Saunders Company, 1972.

Jones, C., and Aronson, E.: Attribution of fault to a rape victim as a function of respectability of the victim. *Journal of Personality and Social Psychology*, 1973, *26*, 415–419.

Jones, E. E.: *Ingratiation: A Social Psychological Analysis.* New York: Appleton-Century-Crofts, 1964.

Jones, E. E., and Davis, K. E.: From acts to dispositions: The attribution process in person perception. In L. Berkowitz (ed.), *Advances in Experimental Social Psychology.* New York: Academic Press, 1965.

Jones, M. C.: The elimination of children's fears. *Journal of Experimental Psychology*, 1924, *7*, 382–390.

Jones, M. C.: Personality correlates and antecedents of drinking patterns in males. *Journal of Consulting and Clinical Psychology*, 1968, *32*, 2–12.

Jones, M. C.: Personality antecedents and correlates of drinking patterns in women. *Journal of Consulting and Clinical Psychology*, 1971, *36*, 61–70.

Jordan, T. C.: Characteristics of visual and proprioceptive response times in the learning of a motor skill. *Quarterly Journal of Experimental Psychology*, 1972, *24*, 536–543.

Jouvet, M.: The states of sleep. *Scientific American*, 1967, 62–72.

Jouvet, M.: Biogenic amines and the states of sleep. *Science*, 1969, *163*, 32–42.

Jung, C. G.: *The Integration of the Personality.* New York: Farrar & Rinehart, 1939.

Kagan, J.: The plasticity of early intellectual development. Paper presented at the meetings of the Association for the Advancement of Science, Washington, D.C., 1972.

Kagan, J., and Klein, R. E.: Cross-cultural perspectives on early development. *American Psychologist*, 1973, *28*, 947–961.

Kagitcibasi, C.: Social norms and authoritarianism: A Turkish–American comparison. *Journal of Personality and Social Psychology*, 1970, *16*, 444–451.

Kahneman, D.: *Attention and Effort.* Englewood Cliffs, New Jersey: Prentice-Hall, 1973.

Kallmann, F. J.: *Heredity in Health and Mental Disorders.* New York: Norton, 1953.

Kallmann, F. J., Falek, A., Hurzeler, M., and Erlenmeyer-Kimling, L.: The developmental aspects of children with two schizophrenic parents. In P. Solomon and B. Glueck (eds.), Recent Research on Schizophrenia. Psychiatric Research Report No. 19. Washington, D. C.: American Psychiatric Association, 1964.

Kalven, H., Jr., and Zeisel, H.: The American Jury. Boston: Little, Brown, 1966.

Kantor, R. E., and Winder, C. L.: The process-reactive continuum: A theoretical proposal. Journal of Nervous and Mental Disease, 1959, 129, 429–434.

Kantowitz, B. H.: Double stimulation. In B. H. Kantowitz (ed.), Human Information Processing: Tutorials in Performance and Cognition. Hillsdale, N.J.: Earlbaum Associates, 1974.

Kaplan, H. B.: Self-derogation and adjustment to recent life experience. Archives of General Psychiatry, 1970, 22, 324–331.

Kaplan, M. F.: Information integration in social judgment: Interaction of judge and informational components. In M. Kaplan and S. Schwartz (eds.), Human Judgment and Decision Processes. New York: Academic Press, 1975.

Kaplan, R. M., and Singer, R. D.: Psychological effects of televised violence: A review and methodological critique. Journal of Social Issues, 1976, in press.

Kato, T., Jarvik, L. F., Roizin, L., and Maralishvili, E.: Chromosome studies in pregnant rhesus macaque given LSD-25. Diseases of the Nervous System, 1970, 31, 245–250.

Kaufman, L.: Sight and Mind: An Introduction to Visual Perception. New York: Oxford University Press, 1974.

Keating, J. P., and Brock, T. C.: Acceptance of persuasion and the inhibition of counterargumentation under various distraction tasks. Journal of Experimental Social Psychology, 1974, 10, 301–309.

Keesey, R. E., and Boyle, P. C.: Effects of quinine adulteration upon body weight of LH-lesioned and intact male rats. Journal of Comparative and Physiological Psychology, 1973, 84, 38–46.

Kelley, H. H.: Attribution in social interaction. In E. E. Jones, D. E. Kanouse, H. H. Kelley, R. E. Nisbett, S. Valins, and B. Weiner (eds.), Attribution: Perceiving the Causes of Behavior. Morristown, New Jersey: General Learning Press, 1972.

Kelley, H. H.: The processes of causal attribution. American Psychologist, 1973, 28, 107–128.

Kelsey, F. O.: Drugs and pregnancy. Mental Retardation, 1969, 7, 7–10.

Kempe, C. H., and Helfer, R. E.: Helping the Battered Child and His Family. Philadelphia: J. B. Lippincott, 1972.

Keppel, G., and Underwood, B. J.: Proactive inhibition in short-term retention of single items. Journal of Verbal Learning and Verbal Behavior, 1962, 1, 153–161.

Kessel, N., and Walton, A.: Alcoholism. Baltimore: Penguin Books, 1965.

Kety, S. S., Rosenthal, D., Wender, P. H., and Schulzinger, F.: Mental illness in the biological and adoptive families of adopted schizophrenics. American Journal of Psychiatry, 1971, 128, 302–306.

Keyfitz, N.: Population density and the style of social life. Bioscience, 1966, 16, 868–873.

Kiesler, C. A., and Munson, P. A.: Attitudes and opinions. In M. R. Rosenzweig and L. W. Porter (eds.), Annual Review of Psychology. Vol. 26. Palo Alto, California: Annual Reviews, Inc., 1975.

Kilham, W., and Mann, L.: Level of destructive obedience as a function of transmitter and executant roles in the Milgram obedience paradigm. Journal of Personality and Social Psychology, 1974, 29, 696–702.

Kimble, G. A.: Hilgard and Marquis' Conditioning and Learning. 2nd ed. New York: Appleton-Century-Crofts, 1961.

Kimbrell, D. L., and Blake, R. E.: Motivational factors in the violation of a prohibition. Journal of Abnormal and Social Psychology, 1958, 56, 132–133.

Kimmel, H. D.: Instrumental conditioning of autonomically mediated responses in human beings. American Psychologist, 1974, 29, 325–335.

Kinzel, A. F.: Body-buffer zone in violent prisoners. The American Journal of Psychiatry, 1970, 127, 59–64.

Kira, A.: The Bathroom: Criteria for Design. Ithaca, New York: Center for Housing and Environmental Studies, 1966.

Kleck, R. E., and Rubenstein, C.: Physical attractiveness, perceived attitude similarity, and interpersonal attraction in an opposite-sex encounter. Journal of Personality and Social Psychology, 1975, 31, 107–114.

Klein, D. C., Fencil-Morse, E., and Seligman, M. E. P.: Learned helplessness, depression, and the attribution of failure. Journal of Personality and Social Psychology, 1976, 33, 508–516.

Kleinke, C. L., Meeker, F. B., and La Fong, C.: Effects of gaze, touch, and use of name on evaluation of "engaged" couples. Journal of Research in Personality, 1974, 7, 368–373.

Klopfer, B., Ainsworth, M. D., Klopfer, W. G., and Holt, R. R.: Developments in the Rorschach Technique. Volume I: Technique and Theory. Yonkers-on-Hudson, New York: World Book, 1954.

Klopfer, P. H.: Behavioral Aspects of Ecology. 2nd ed. Englewood Cliffs, New Jersey: Prentice-Hall, 1972.

Kluver, H., and Bucy, P. C.: "Psychotic blindness" and other symptoms following bilateral temporal lobectomy in rhesus monkeys. American Journal of Physiology, 1937, 199, 352–353.

Knapp, M. L.: Nonverbal Communication in Human Interaction. New York: Holt, Rinehart, & Winston, 1972.

Knight, J. L., Jr., and Kantowitz, B. H.: Speed-accuracy trade-off in double stimulation: Effects on the first response. Memory & Cognition, 1974, 2, 522–531.

Kohlberg, L.: A cognitive-developmental analysis of children's sex-role concepts and attitudes. Genetic Psychology Monographs, 1966, 75, 128.

Kohlberg, L., and Gilligan, C.: The adolescent as a philosopher: The discovery of the self in a postconventional world. In J. Kagan and R. Coles (eds.), Twelve to Sixteen: Early Adolescence. New York: Norton, 1972.

Konecni, V. J., and Ebbesen, E. B.: Disinhibition vs. the cathartic effect: Artifact and substance. Journal of Personality and Social Psychology, 1976, 34, 352–365.

Konishi, M.: The role of auditory feedback in the control of vocalization in the white-crowned sparrow. Zeitschrift fur Tierpsychologie, 1965, 22, 770–783.

Koocher, G. P.: Swimming, competence, and personality change. Journal of Personality and Social Psychology, 1971, 18, 275–278.

Korman, A. K.: Industrial and Organizational Psychology. Englewood Cliffs, New Jersey: Prentice-Hall, 1971.

Krasner, L.: The therapist as a social reinforcement machine. In H. H. Strupp and L. Luborsky (eds.), Research in Psychotherapy. Vol. 2. Washington, D.C.: American Psychological Association, 1962.

Kravetz, D. F.: Heart rate as a minimal cue for the occurrence of vicarious classical conditioning. Journal of Personality and Social Psychology, 1974, 29, 125–131.

Krebs, D., and Adinolfi, A. A.: Physical attractiveness, social relations, and personality style. Journal of Personality and Social Psychology, 1975, 31, 245–253.

Laing, R. D.: Is schizophrenia a disease? International Journal of Social Psychiatry, 1964, 10, 184–193.

Lakoff, G.: Hedges: A Study in Meaning Criteria and the Logic of Fuzzy Concepts. Papers from the eighth regional meeting, Chicago Linguistics Society. Chicago: University of Chicago Linguistics Department, 1972.

Landis, C.: Studies of emotional reactions. II. General behavior and facial expression. *Journal of Comparative Psychology*, 1924, 4, 447–509.

Landy, D., and Mettee, D.: Evaluations of an aggressor as a function of exposure to cartoon humor. *Journal of Personality and Social Psychology*, 1969, 12, 66–71.

La Piere, R. T.: Attitudes vs. actions. *Social Forces*, 1934, 13, 230–237.

Larssen, K.: *Conditioning and Sexual Behavior in the Male Albino Rat*. Stockholm: Almquist & Wiksell, 1956.

Lasky, J. J.: Veterans Administration cooperative chemotherapy projects and related studies. In L. Uhr and J. G. Miller (eds.), *Drugs and Behavior*. New York: John Wiley and Sons, 1960.

Latané, B., and Darley, J. M.: *The Unresponsive Bystander: Why Doesn't He Help?* New York: Appleton-Century-Crofts, 1970.

Lazarus, A. A.: Behavior therapy in groups. In G. M. Gazda (ed.), *Basic Approaches to Group Psychotherapy and Counseling*. Springfield, Illinois: Charles C Thomas, 1968.

Leak, G. K.: Effects of hostility arousal and aggressive humor on catharsis and humor preference. *Journal of Personality and Social Psychology*, 1974, 30, 736–740.

Leavitt, F.: *Drugs and Behavior*. Philadelphia: W. B. Saunders Company, 1974.

Lehrman, D. S.: A critique of Konrad Lorenz's theory of instinctive behavior. *Quarterly Review of Biology*, 1953, 28, 337–363.

Lenneberg, E.: *Biological Foundations of Language*. New York: John Wiley and Sons, 1967.

Lepper, M. R., and Greene, D.: Turning play into work: Effects of adult surveillance and extrinsic rewards on children's intrinsic motivation. *Journal of Personality and Social Psychology*, 1975, 31, 479–486.

Leventhal, H.: Findings and theory in the study of fear communication. In L. Berkowitz (ed.), *Advances in Experimental Social Psychology*. Vol. 5. New York: Academic Press, 1970.

Leventhal, H., Jacobs, R. L., and Kudirka, N. Z.: Authoritarianism, ideology, and political candidate choice. *Journal of Abnormal and Social Psychology*, 1964, 69, 539–549.

Leventhal, H., Watts, J. C., and Pagano, F.: Effects of fear and instructions on how to cope with danger. *Journal of Personality and Social Psychology*, 1967, 6, 313–321.

Lewis, J., Baddeley, A. D., Bonham, K. G., and Lovett, D.: Traffic pollution and mental efficiency. *Nature*, 1970, 225, 96.

Leyens, J. P., Parke, R. D., Camino, L., and Berkowitz, L.: The effects of movie violence on aggression in a field setting as a function of group dominance and cohesion. *Journal of Personality and Social Psychology*, 1975, 32, 346–360.

Liddell, H. S.: *Emotional Hazards in Animals and Man*. Springfield, Illinois: Charles C Thomas, 1956.

Lieberman, M. A., Yalom, I. D., and Miles, M.: *Encounter Groups: First Facts*. New York: Basic Books, 1973.

Liebert, R. M., and Baron, R. A.: Some immediate effects of television violence on children's behavior. *Developmental Psychology*, 1972, 6, 469–475.

Liebert, R. M., Odom, R. D., Hill, J., and Huff, R.: Effects of age and rule familiarity on the production of modeled language constructions. *Developmental Psychology*, 1969, 1, 108–112.

Linder, D. E., Cooper, J., and Jones, E. E.: Decision freedom as a determinant of the role of incentive magnitude in attitude change. *Journal of Personality and Social Psychology*, 1967, 6, 245–254.

Lindsay, P. H., and Norman, D. A.: *Human Information Processing*. New York: Academic Press, 1972.

Lindsley, D. B.: Emotion. In S. S. Stevens (ed.), *Handbook of Experimental Psychology*. New York: John Wiley and Sons, 1951, pp. 473–516.

Locke, E. A.: Personnel attitudes and motivation. In M. R. Rosenzweig and L. W. Porter (eds.), *Annual Review of Psychology*. Palo Alto, California: Annual Reviews, Inc., 1975.

Loehlin, J. C., Lindzey, G., and Spuhler, J. F.: *Race Differences in Intelligence*. San Francisco: W. H. Freeman and Co., 1975.

Loehlin, J. C., Vandenberg, S. G., and Osborne, R. T.: Blood group genes and negro–white ability differences. *Behavior Genetics*, 1973, 3, 263–270.

Lorenz, K.: The comparative method in studying innate behavior patterns. *Symposium of the Society of Experimental Biology*, 1950, 4, 221–268.

Lorenz, K.: *On Aggression*. London: Methuen, 1966.

Luborsky, L., and Schimek, J.: Psychoanalytic theories of therapeutic and developmental change: Implications for assessment. In P. Worchel and D. Byrne (eds.), *Personality Change*. New York: John Wiley and Sons, 1964, pp. 73–99.

Luborsky, L., and Spence, D. P.: Quantitative research on psychoanalytic therapy. In A. E. Bergin and S. L. Garfield (eds.), *Handbook of Psychotherapy and Behavior Change: An Empirical Analysis*. New York: John Wiley and Sons, 1971.

Luria, A. R.: *The Mind of a Mnemonist*. New York: Basic Books, 1968.

Lyken, D. T.: A study of anxiety in the sociopathic personality. *Journal of Abnormal and Social Psychology*, 1957, 55, 6–10.

Lynch, K.: *The Image of the City*. Cambridge, Massachusetts: M.I.T. Press, 1960.

Macarov, D.: Work patterns and satisfactions in an Israeli kibbutz: A test of the Herzberg hypothesis. *Personnel Psychology*, 1972, 25, 483–493.

Macauley, J., and Berkowitz, L. (Eds.): *Altruism and Helping: Social Psychological Studies of Some Antecedents and Consequences*. New York: Academic Press, 1970.

Maccoby, E. E., and Jacklin, C. N.: *The Psychology of Sex Differences*. Stanford, California: Stanford University Press, 1974.

MacPhail, E. M., and Miller, N. E.: Cholinergic brain stimulation in cats: Failure to obtain sleep. *Journal of Comparative and Physiological Psychology*, 1968, 65, 499–503.

Maher, B. A.: *Principles of Psychopathology*. New York: McGraw-Hill, 1966.

Maher, B. A., Elder, S. T., and Noblin, C. D.: A differential investigation of avoidance reduction vs. hypermotility following frontal ablation. *Journal of Comparative and Physiological Psychology*, 1962, 55, 449–454.

Maher, B. A., McIntire, R. W., and House, C.: Retrograde amnesia following ECT. Paper presented at a meeting of the Southeastern Psychological Association, Miami Beach, April, 1962.

Maier, N. R. F.: Reasoning in humans: On direction. *Journal of Comparative Psychology*, 1930, 10, 115–143.

Malmo, R. B., and Amsel, A.: Anxiety-produced interference in serial rote learning with observations on rote learning after partial frontal lobectomy. *Journal of Experimental Psychology*, 1949, 38, 434–440.

Mandler, G.: Emotion. In R. Brown, E. Galanter, E. H. Hess, and G. Mandler, *New Directions in Psychology*. New York: Holt, Rinehart, and Winston, 1962, pp. 267–343.

Mann, J., Berkowitz, L., Sidman, J., Starr, S., and West, S.: Satiation of the transient stimulating effect of erotic films. *Journal of Personality and Social Psychology*, 1974, 30, 729–735.

Manning, S. A., and Taylor, D. A.: Effects of viewed violence and aggression: Stimulation and catharsis. *Journal of Personality and Social Psychology*, 1975, 31, 180–188.

Mark, J. C.: The attitudes of the mothers of male schizophrenics toward child behavior. *Journal of Abnormal and Social Psychology*, 1958, 48, 185–189.

Marks, L. E.: Synesthesia: The lucky people with mixed-up senses. *Psychology Today*, 1975, 9, 48–52.

Marks, M. W., and Vestre, N. D.: Self-perception and interpersonal behavior changes in marathon and time-extended encounter groups. *Journal of Consulting and Clinical Psychology,* 1974, *42,* 729–733.

Marlatt, G. A., Demming, B., and Reid, J. B.: Loss of control drinking in alcoholics: An experimental analogue. *Journal of Abnormal Psychology,* 1973, *81,* 233–241.

Marler, P.: A comparative approach to vocal learning: Song development in white-crowned sparrows. *Journal of Comparative and Physiological Psychology Monographs,* 1970, *71* (No. 2, Part 2), 1–25.

Marshall, J. E., and Heslin, R.: Boys and girls together: Sexual composition and the effect of density and group size on cohesiveness. *Journal of Personality and Social Psychology,* 1975, *31,* 952–961.

Martens, R.: Palmar sweating and the presence of an audience. *Journal of Experimental Social Psychology,* 1969, *5,* 371–374.

Martens, R., and Landers, D. M.: Evaluation potential as a determinant of coaction effects. *Journal of Experimental Social Psychology,* 1972, *8,* 347–359.

Marwit, S. J., and Marwit, K. L.: Black children's use of nonstandard grammar: Two years later. *Developmental Psychology,* 1976, *12,* 33–38.

Marzetta, B. R., Benson, H., and Wallace, R. K.: Combatting drug dependency in young people: A new approach. *Medical Counterpoint,* 1972, *4,* 13–37.

Mason, W. A., and Lott, D. F.: Ethology and comparative psychology. In M. R. Rosenzweig and L. W. Porter (eds.), *Annual Review of Psychology.* Vol. 26. Palo Alto, California: Annual Reviews, Inc., 1976.

Masor, H. N., Hornstein, H. A., and Tobin, T. A.: Modeling, motivational interdependence, and helping. *Journal of Personality and Social Psychology,* 1973, *28,* 236–248.

Masserman, J. H., and Yum, K. S.: An analysis of the influence of alcohol on experimental neuroses in cats. *Psychosomatic Medicine,* 1946, *8,* 36–52.

Masterton, R. B., and Berkley, M. A.: Brain functions: Changing ideas on the role of sensory, motor, and association cortex in behavior. In P. H. Mussen and M. R. Rosenzweig, (eds.), *Annual Review of Psychology.* Vol. 25. Palo Alto, California: Annual Reviews, 1974.

McCain, G., Cox, V. C., and Paulus, P. B.: The relationship between illness complaints and degree of crowding in a prison environment. *Environment and Behavior,* 1977, in press.

McCall, R. B.: Stimulus change in light-contingent bar-pressing. *Journal of Comparative and Physiological Psychology,* 1965, *59,* 258–262.

McCary, J. L.: *Human Sexuality: Physiological, Psychological, and Sociological Factors.* New York: Van Nostrand, 1973.

McClelland, D. C., Atkinson, J. W., Clark, R. A., and Lowell, E. L.: *The Achievement Motive.* New York: Appleton-Century-Crofts, 1953.

McClelland, D. C.: Methods of measuring human motivation. In J. W. Atkinson (ed.), *Motives in Fantasy, Action, and Society.* Princeton: Van Nostrand, 1958, pp. 7–42.

McClelland, D. C.: *The Achieving Society.* Princeton: Van Nostrand, 1961.

McClelland, D. C., Davis, W. N., Kalin, R., and Wanner, E.: *The Drinking Man.* New York: Free Press, 1972.

McCord, W., and McCord, J.: *The Psychopath: An Essay on the Criminal Mind.* New York: Van Nostrand, 1964.

McCord, W., McCord, J., and Gudeman, J.: *Origins of Alcoholism.* Stanford, California: Stanford University Press, 1960.

McDougall, W.: *An Introduction to Social Psychology.* London: Methuen, 1908.

McGaugh, J. L.: *Learning and Memory.* San Francisco: Albion, 1973.

McGrath, J. E. (ed.): *Social and Psychological Factors in Stress.* New York: Holt, Rinehart, & Winston, 1970.

McGuire, W. J.: The nature of attitudes and attitude change. In G. Lindzey and E. Aronson (eds.), *Handbook of Social Psychology.* Vol. 3. Reading, Massachusetts: Addison-Wesley, 1969.

McHarg, I.: *Design with Nature.* Garden City, New York: Doubleday, 1971.

McKenzie, J., and Beechey, N.: The effects of morphine and pethidine on somatic evoked responses in the midbrain of the cat, and their relevance to analgesia. *EEG,* 1962, *14,* 501–519.

Mechanic, D.: *Students Under Stress: A Study of the Social Psychology of Adaptation.* New York: Free Press, 1962.

Medelman, J.: "Does your husband know you're bisexual?" *Playboy,* 1975, *22* (1), 145–146, 152, 154, 250–252, 254–255, 258, 260–261.

Mehrabian, A.: Relationship of attitudes to seated posture, orientation, and distance. *Journal of Personality and Social Psychology,* 1968, *10,* 26–30.

Mehrabian, A.: Nonverbal communication. In W. J. Arnold and M. M. Page (eds.), *Nebraska Symposium on Motivation.* Lincoln, Nebraska: University of Nebraska Press, 1971.

Meier, R. L.: *A Communications Theory of Urban Growth.* Cambridge, Massachusetts: M. I. T. Press, 1962.

Melton, A. W.: Implications of short-term memory for a general theory of memory. *Journal of Verbal Learning and Verbal Behavior,* 1963, *2,* 1–21.

Melzack, R.: The promise of biofeedback—don't hold the party yet. *Psychology Today,* 1975, *9,* 18–22, 80–81.

Melzack, R., and Perry, C.: Self-regulation of pain: The use of alpha-feedback and hypnotic training for the control of chronic pain. *Experimental Neurology,* 1975, *46,* 452–469.

Meredith, H. V.: Body size of contemporary groups of one-year-old infants studied in different parts of the world. *Child Development,* 1970, *41,* 551–600.

Mewhort, D. J. K., Merikle, P. M., and Bryden, M. P.: On the transfer from iconic to short-term memory. *Journal of Experimental Psychology,* 1969, *81,* 89–94.

Meyer, H. H., Walker, W. B., and Litwin, G. H.: Motive patterns and risk preferences associated with entrepreneurship. *Journal of Abnormal and Social Psychology,* 1961, *63,* 570–574.

Michael, R. P., Keverne, E. B., and Bonsall, R. W.: Pheromones: Isolation of male sex attractants from a female primate. *Science,* 1971, *172,* 964–966.

Michael, V.: Experience of loss incurred in disaster. Unpublished manuscript. Weston State Hospital: Weston, West Virginia, 1972.

Miczek, K. A., and Grossman, S. P.: Effects of septal lesions on inter- and intraspecies aggression in rats. *Journal of Comparative and Physiological Psychology,* 1972, *79,* 37–45.

Miles, M.: Changes during and following laboratory training: A clinical experimental study. *Journal of Applied Behavioral Science,* 1965, *1,* 215–242.

Miles, R. C.: The relative effectiveness of secondary reinforcers throughout deprivation and habit-strength parameters. *Journal of Comparative and Physiological Psychology,* 1956, *49,* 126–130.

Miles, R. C.: Learning in kittens with manipulatory, exploratory, and food incentives. *Journal of Comparative and Physiological Psychology,* 1958, *51,* 39–42.

Milgram, S.: Behavioral study of obedience. *Journal of Abnormal and Social Psychology,* 1963, *67,* 371–378.

Milgram, S.: Liberating effects of group pressure. *Journal of Personality and Social Psychology,* 1965, *1,* 127–234. (a)

Milgram, S.: Some conditions of obedience and disobedience to authority. *Human Relations,* 1965, *18,* 57–76. (b)

Milgram, S.: The experience of living in cities. *Science,* 1970, *167,* 1461–1468.

Milgram, S.: *Obedience to Authority.* New York: Harper & Row, 1974.

Milgram, S., Bickman, L., and Berkowitz, L.: Note on the drawing power of crowds of different size. *Journal of Personality and Social Psychology,* 1969, *13,* 79–82.

Milgram, S., Greenwald, J., Kessler, S., McKenna, W., and Waters, J.: A psychological map of New York City. *American Scientist*, 1972, *60*, 194–200.

Miller, A. G.: Actor and observer perceptions of the learning of a task. *Journal of Experimental Social Psychology*, 1975, *11*, 95–111.

Miller, G. A., Galanter, E., and Pribram, K. H.: *Plans and the Structure of Behavior.* New York: Holt, Rinehart, & Winston, 1960.

Miller, J. W., and Vanderwalker, J. (eds.): *Scientist in the Sea: TEKTITE 2.* Washington, D.C.: Government Printing Office, 1971.

Miller, N. E.: Studies of fear as an acquirable drive. I. Fear as motivation and fear-reduction as reinforcement in the learning of new responses. *Journal of Experimental Psychology*, 1948, *38*, 89–101.

Miller, N. E.: Learning of visceral and glandular responses. *Science*, 1969, *163*, 434–445.

Miller, N. E., and Carmona, A.: Modification of a visceral response, salivation, in thirsty dogs, by instrumental training with water reward. *Journal of Comparative and Physiological Psychology*, 1967, *63*, 1–6.

Miller, N. E., and DiCara, L.: Instrumental learning of heart rate changes in curarized rats: Shaping and specificity to discriminative stimulus. *Journal of Comparative and Physiological Psychology*, 1967, *63*, 12–19.

Miller, N. E., and DiCara, L. V.: Experiments on psychosomatic interaction. Paper presented at the meetings of the Eastern Psychological Association, Boston, 1972.

Miller, P. H., Heldmeyer, K. H., and Miller, S. A.: Facilitation of conservation of number in young children. *Developmental Psychology*, 1975, *11*, 253.

Miller, R. L., Brickman, P., and Bolen, D.: Attribution versus persuasion as a means for modifying behavior. *Journal of Personality and Social Psychology*, 1975, *31*, 430–441.

Mills, J., and Harvey, J.: Opinion change as a function of when information about the communicator is received and whether he is attractive or expert. *Journal of Personality and Social Psychology*, 1972, *21*, 52–55.

Milner, B., Corkin, S., and Teuber, H. L.: Further analysis of the hippocampal amnesic syndrome: 14-year follow-up study of H. M. *Neuropsychologia*, 1968, *6*, 215–234.

Minge, M. R., and Ball, T. S.: Teaching of self-help skills to profoundly retarded patients. *American Journal of Mental Deficiency*, 1967, *71*, 864–868.

Minor, C. A., and Neel, R. G.: The relationship between achievement motive and occupational preference. *Journal of Counseling Psychology*, 1958, *5*, 39–43.

Mischel, W.: *Personality and Assessment.* New York: John Wiley and Sons, 1968.

Mischel, W., and Gilligan, C.: Delay of gratification, motivation for the prohibited gratification, and responses to temptation. *Journal of Abnormal and Social Psychology*, 1964, *69*, 411–417.

Mitchell, H. E.: Authoritarian punitiveness in simulated juror decision-making: The good guys don't always wear white hats. Paper presented at the meeting of the Midwestern Psychological Association, Chicago, May, 1973.

Mitchell, H. E., and Byrne, D.: The defendant's dilemma: Effects of jurors' attitudes and authoritarianism on judicial decisions. *Journal of Personality and Social Psychology*, 1973, *25*, 123–129.

Mitchell, T. R.: Expectancy models of job satisfaction, occupational preference, and effort: A theoretical, methodological, and empirical appraisal. *Psychological Bulletin*, 1974, *81*, 1053–1077.

Moltz, H.: Imprinting: Empirical basis and theoretical significance. *Psychological Bulletin*, 1960, *57*, 291–314.

Moltz, H.: Contemporary instinct theory and the fixed action pattern. *Psychological Review*, 1965, *72*, 27–47.

Money, J.: Prenatal hormones and postnatal socialization in gender identity differentiation. *In* J. K. Cole and R. Dienstbier (eds.), *Nebraska Symposium on Motivation.* Lincoln, Nebraska: University of Nebraska Press, 1974.

Moniz, E.: Psycho-chirurgie. *Nervenarzt*, 1937, *10*, 113–118.

Montgomery, K. C.: The effect of the hunger and thirst drives upon exploratory behavior. *Journal of Comparative and Physiological Psychology*, 1953, *46*, 315–319.

Montgomery, K. C.: The role of the exploratory drive in learning. *Journal of Comparative and Physiological Psychology*, 1954, *47*, 60–64.

Moore, B. R.: The role of directed Pavlovian reactions in simple instrumental learning in the pigeon. *In* R. A. Hinde and J. Stevenson-Hinde (eds.), *Constraints on Learning.* London: Academic Press, 1973.

Moreno. J. L., and Kipper, D. A.: Group psychodrama and community-centered counseling. *In* G. M. Gazda (ed.), *Basic Approaches to Group Psychotherapy and Group Counseling*, Springfield, Illinois: Charles C Thomas, 1968.

Morgan, C. D., and Murray, H. A.: Thematic apperception test. *In* H. A. Murray, *Explorations in Personality.* (1938) New York: Science Editions, 1962, pp. 530–545.

Morgan, C. T., and Morgan, J. D.: Studies in hunger. II. The relation of gastric denervation and dietary sugar to the effect of insulin upon food intake in the rat. *Journal of General Psychology*, 1940, *57*, 153–163.

Moriarty, T.: Crimes, commitment, and the responsive bystander: Two field experiments. *Journal of Personality and Social Psychology*, 1975, *31*, 370–376.

Morin, R. E. and Grant, D. A.: Learning and performance of a key-pressing task as a function of the degree of spatial stimulus-response correspondence. *Journal of Experimental Psychology*, 1955, *49*, 39–47.

Morrell, F.: Electrical signs of sensory coding. *In* G. C. Quarton, T. Melnechuk, and F. O. Schmitt (eds.), *The Neurosciences.*, New York: Rockefeller University Press, 1967.

Morris, W. N., and Miller, R. S.: The effects of consensus-breaking and consensus-preempting partners on reduction of conformity. *Journal of Experimental Social Psychology*, 1975, *11*, 215–223.

Mosher, D. L.: Sex callousness toward women. *In Technical Report of the Commission on Obscenity and Pornography.* Vol. VIII. Washington, D.C.: U.S. Government Printing Office, 1971, pp. 313–325.

Moskowitz, M. J.: Running-wheel activity in the white rat as a function of combined food and water deprivation. *Journal of Comparative and Physiological Psychology*, 1959, *52*, 621–625.

Mufson, E. J., and Wampler, R. S.: Weight regulation with palatable food and liquids in rats with lateral hypothalamic lesions. *Journal of Comparative and Physiological Psychology*, 1972, *80*, 382–392.

Munn, N. L.: The effect of knowledge of the situation upon judgment of emotion from facial expressions. *Journal of Abnormal and Social Psychology*, 1940, *35*, 324–338.

Murdock, B. B.: *Human Memory: Theory and Data.* Potomac, Maryland: Lawrence Erlbaum, 1974.

Murray, E. J.: Sociotropic-learning approach to psychotherapy. *In* P. Worchel and D. Byrne (eds.), *Personality Change.* New York: John Wiley and Sons, 1964, pp. 249–288.

Murray, H. A.: *Explorations in Personality.* (1938) New York: Science Editions, 1962.

Murstein, B. I.: Physical attractiveness and marital choice. *Journal of Personality and Social Psychology*, 1972, *22*, 8–12.

Mussen, P. H., Conger, J. J., and Kagen, J. *Child Development and Personality.* New York: Harper & Row, 1974.

Nadler, A., Fisher, J. D., and Streufert, S.: The donor's dilemma: Recipient's reactions to aid from friend or foe. *Journal of Applied Social Psychology*, 1974, *4*, 275–285.

Nel, E., Helmreich, R., and Aronson, E.: Opinion change in the advocate as a function of the persuasibility of his audience: A clarification of the meaning of dissonance. *Journal of Personality and Social Psychology*, 1969, *12*, 117–124.

Nerviano, V. J.: Common personality patterns among alcoholic males: A multivariate study. *Journal of Consulting and Clinical Psychology*, 1976, *44*, 104–110.

Newell, A. and Simon, H. A.: *Human Problem Solving.* Englewood Cliffs, New Jersey: Prentice-Hall, 1972.

Newman, O.: *Defensible Space,* New York: Macmillan, 1972.

Newtson, D.: Dispositional inference from effects of actions: Effects chosen and effects foregone. *Journal of Experimental Social Psychology*, 1974, *10*, 489–496.

Nidich, S., Seeman, W., and Seibert, M.: Influence of transcendental meditation on state anxiety. *Journal of Consulting and Clinical Psychology*, 1977, in press.

Nisbett, R. E., Caputo, C., Legant, P., and Maracek, J.: Behavior as seen by the actor and as seen by the observer. *Journal of Personality and Social Psychology*, 1973, *27*, 154–164.

Norman, D. A.: Toward a theory of memory and attention. *Psychological Review*, 1968, *75*, 522–536.

Olds, J.: Differential effects of drives and drugs on self-stimulation at different brain sites. *In* D. E. Sheer (ed.), *Electrical Stimulation of the Brain.* Austin, Texas: University of Texas Press, 1961.

Olds, J.: The central nervous system and the reinforcement of behavior. *American Psychologist*, 1969, *24*, 707–719.

Olds, J., and Milner, P.: Positive reinforcement produced by electrical stimulation of septal area and other regions of rat brain. *Journal of Comparative and Physiological Psychology*, 1954, *47*, 419–427.

Olds, J., Travis, R. P., and Schwing, R. C.: Topographic organization of hypothalamic self-stimulation. *Journal of Comparative and Physiological Psychology*, 1960, *53*, 23–28.

O'Leary, V. E.: Some attitudinal barriers to occupational aspirations in women. *Psychological Bulletin*, 1974, *81*, 809–826.

Pachella, R.: The interpretation of reaction time in information-processing research. *In* B. H. Kantowitz (ed.), *Human Information Processing.* Hillsdale, New Jersey, Lawrence J. Earlbaum Associates, 1974.

Paivio, A.: *Imagery and Verbal Processes.* New York: Holt, Rinehart, & Winston, 1971.

Partridge, N.: *Prefrontal Leucotomy.* Oxford: Blackwell, 1950.

Paul, G., and Eriksen, C. W.: Effects of test anxiety on "real life" examinations. *Journal of Personality*, 1964, *32*, 480–494.

Paulus, P. B., and Murdoch, P.: Anticipated evaluation and audience presence in the enhancement of dominant responses. *Journal of Experimental Social Psychology*, 1971, *7*, 280–291.

Pavlov, I. P.: *Conditioned Reflexes.* (Translated by G. V. Anrep.) London: Oxford, 1927.

Pearlman, C. A., and Greenberg, R.: Brief REM deprivation impairs consolidation of complex learning in rats. Paper presented to the Association for the Psychophysiological study of sleep. New York, May, 1972.

Pederson, D. M., and Shears, L. M.: A review of personal space research in the framework of general systems theory. *Psychological Bulletin*, 1973, *80*, 367–388.

Peirce, J. T., and Nuttall, R. L.: Duration of sexual contacts in the rat. *Journal of Comparative and Physiological Psychology*, 1961, *54*, 585–587.

Peterson, L. R., and Peterson, M. J.: Short-term retention of

individual verbal items. *Journal of Experimental Psychology*, 1959, *58*, 193–198.

Phillips, D.: *Statistics: A Guide to the Unknown.* New York: Holden-Day, 1972.

Piaget, J.: Piaget's theory. *In* P. H. Mussen, (ed.), *Carmichael's Manual of Child Psychology.* 3rd ed. New York: John Wiley and Sons, 1970.

Piaget, J., and Inhelder, B.: *The Psychology of the Child.* New York: Basic Books, 1969.

Pieron, H.: Le mecanisme d'apparitions des coleurs subjectives de Fechner Benham. *Ann. Psychol.*, 1923, *23*, 1–49.

Pliner, P., Hart, H., Kohl, J., and Saari, D.: Compliance without pressure: Some further data on the foot-in-the-door technique. *Journal of Experimental Social Psychology*, 1974, *10*, 17–22.

Pliskoff, S. S., Wright, J. E., and Hawkins, D. T.: Brain stimulation as a reinforcer: Intermittent schedules. *Journal of the Experimental Analysis of Behavior*, 1965, *8*, 75–88.

Polak, P. R., Emde, R. N., and Spitz, R. R.: The smiling response: II. Visual discrimination and the onset of depth perception. *Journal of Nervous and Mental Diseases*, 1964, *139*, 407–415.

Posner, M. I., and Mitchell, R. F.: Chronometric analysis of classification. *Psychological Review*, 1967, *74*, 392–409.

Postman, L., and Phillips, L. W.: Short term temporal changes in free recall. *Quarterly Journal of Experimental Psychology*, 1965, *17*, 132–138.

Powers, P. C., and Geen, R. G.: Effects of the behavior and the perceived arousal of a model on instrumental aggression. *Journal of Personality and Social Psychology*, 1972, *23*, 175–184.

Powley, T. L., and Keesey, R. E.: Relationship of body weight to the lateral hypothalamic feeding syndrome. *Journal of Comparative and Physiological Psychology*, 1970, *70*, 25–36.

Premack, A. J., and Premack, D.: Teaching language to an ape. *Scientific American*, 1972, *227*, 92–99.

Pritchard, R. M.: Stabilized images on the retina. *Scientific American*, 1961, *204*, 72–78.

Provence, S., and Lipton, R. C.: *Infants in Institutions.* New York: International Universities Press, 1962.

Pubols, B. H., Jr.: Incentive magnitude, learning, and performance in animals. *Psychological Bulletin*, 1960, *57*, 89–115.

Quay, H. C.: Psychopathic personality as pathological stimulus seeking. *American Journal of Psychiatry*, 1965, *122*, 180–183.

Quillian, M. R.: The teachable language comprehender: A simulation program and a theory of language. *Communications of the Association for Computing Machinery*, 1969, *12*, 459–476.

Rachman, S.: Sexual fetishism: An experimental analogue. *Psychological Record*, 1966, *16*, 293–296.

Rainwater, L.: Fear and the house-as-haven in the lower class. *Journal of the American Institute of Planners*, 1966, *32*, 23–31.

Rappaport, J., and Chinsky, J. M.: Models for delivery of service: An historical and conceptual perspective. *Professional Psychology*, 1976, in press.

Rappaport, J., Davidson, W. S., Wilson, M. N., and Mitchell, A.: Alternatives to blaming the victim or the environment: Our places to stand have not moved the earth. *American Psychologist*, 1975, *30*, 525–528.

Raynor, J. O.: Relationships between achievement-related motives, future orientation, and academic performance. *Journal of Personality and Social Psychology*, 1970, *15*, 28–33.

Regan, D. T.: Effects of a favor and liking on compliance.

Journal of Experimental Social Psychology, 1971, *7*, 627–639.

Regan, D. T., Williams, M., and Sparling, S.: Voluntary expiation of guilt: A field experiment. *Journal of Personality and Social Psychology*, 1972, *24*, 42–45.

Reitman, W. R.: *Cognition and Thought.* New York: John Wiley and Sons, 1965.

Rescorla, R. A.: Second-order conditioning: Implications for theories of learning. *In* F. J. McGuigan and D. B. Lumsden (eds.), *Contemporary Approaches to Conditioning and Learning.* New York: John Wiley and Sons, 1973.

Reynolds, W. F., Blau, B. I., and Hurlbut, B.: Speed in simple tasks as a function of MAS score. *Psychological Reports*, 1961, *8*, 341–344.

Rheingold, H. F., Gewirtz, J. L., and Ross, H. W.: Social conditioning of vocalizations in the infant. *Journal of Comparative and Physiological Psychology*, 1959, *51*, 68–73.

Rice, B.: Rattlesnakes, french fries, and pupillometric oversell. *Psychology Today*, 1974, *7* (9), 55–59.

Richard, W.: Crisis intervention services following natural disaster: The Pennsylvania recovery project. *Journal of Community Psychology*, 1974, *2*, 211–219.

Rips, L. J., Shoben, E. J., and Smith, E. E. Semantic distance and the verification of semantic relationships. *Journal of Verbal Learning and Verbal Behavior*, 1973, *12*, 1–20.

Roach, D. E.: Double cross validation of a weighted application blank over time. *Journal of Applied Psychology*, 1971, *55*, 157–160.

Roazen, P.: *Freud and his Followers.* New York: Knopf, 1975.

Robbins, D.: Partial reinforcement: A selective review of the alleyway literature since 1960. *Psychological Bulletin*, 1971, *76*, 415–431.

Robinson, D. N.: *The Enlightened Machine.* Encino, California: Dickenson, 1973.

Robinson, P.: The measurement of achievement motivation. Unpublished doctoral dissertation, Oxford University, 1961.

Rock, I, and Victor, J.: Vision and touch: An experimentally created conflict between the two senses. *Science*, 1964, *143*, 594–596.

Rodgers, D., and McClearn, G.: Alcohol preferences of mice. *In* E. Bliss (ed.), *Roots of Behavior.* New York: Harper, 1962.

Rodgers, J.: The great megavitamin flap. *Saturday Review*, 1976, *3* (10), 33–36.

Rodin, J., and Slochower, J.: Externality in the nonobese: Effects of environmental responsiveness on weight. *Journal of Personality and Social Psychology*, 1976, *33*, 338–344.

Roediger, H. L.: Inhibiting effects of recall. *Memory and Cognition*, 1974, *2*, 261–269.

Rogers, C. R.: *Counseling and Psychotherapy: Newer Concepts in Practice.* Boston: Houghton, 1942.

Rogers, C. R.: *Client-Centered Therapy.* Boston: Houghton-Mifflin, 1951.

Rogers, C. R.: *The Therapeutic Relationship and Its Impact: A study of Psychotherapy with Schizophrenics.* Madison, Wisconsin: University of Wisconsin Press, 1967.

Rogers, C. R.: *Carl Rogers on Encounter Groups.* New York: Harper and Row, 1970.

Rogers, C. R., and Dymond, R. F. (eds.): *Psychotherapy and Personality Change.* Chicago: University of Chicago Press, 1954.

Rokeach, M., and Kliejunas, P.: Behavior as a function of attitude-toward-object and attitude-toward-situation. *Journal of Personality and Social Psychology*, 1972, *22*, 194–201.

Roos, P. D.: Jurisdiction: An ecological concept. *Human Relations*, 1968, *21*, 75–84.

Rorschach, H.: *Psychodiagnostics.* Berne: Hans Huber, 1921.

Rosen, B. C., and D'Andrade, R.: The psychosocial origins of achievement motivation. *Sociometry*, 1959, *22*, 185–218.

Rosen, G. M.: The development and use of nonprescription behavior therapies. *American Psychologist*, 1976, *31*, 139–141.

Rosen, G. M., Glasgow, R. E., and Barrera, M., Jr.: A controlled study to assess the clinical efficacy of totally self-administered systematic desensitization. *Journal of Consulting and Clinical Psychology*, 1976, *44*, 208–217.

Rosen, M.: A dual model of obsessional neurosis. *Journal of Consulting and Clinical Psychology*, 1975, *43*, 453–459.

Rosenbaum, M. E., and Levin, I. P.: Impression formation as a function of source credibility and the polarity of information. *Journal of Personality and Social Psychology*, 1969, *12*, 24–37.

Rosenbaum, R. W.: Predictability of employee theft using weighted application blanks. *Journal of Applied Psychology*, 1976, *61*, 94–98.

Rosenhan, D. L.: On being sane in insane places. *Science*, 1973, *179*, 250–258.

Rosenhan, D. L.: The contextual nature of psychiatric diagnosis. *Journal of Abnormal Psychology*, 1975, *84*, 462–474.

Rosenhan, D. L., Underwood, B., and Moore, B.: Affect moderates self-gratification and altruism. *Journal of Personality and Social Psychology*, 1974, *30*, 546–552.

Rosenman, R. H., and Friedman, M.: Neurogenic factors in pathogenesis of coronary heart disease. *Medical Clinics of North America*, 1974, *58*, 269–279.

Rosenthal, R., Archer, D., DiMatteo, M. R., Koivumaki, J. H., and Rogert, P. L.: Body talk and tone of voice: The language without words. *Psychology Today*, 1974, *8*, 64–68.

Rosenthal, R., and Jacobson, L.: *Pygmalion in the Classroom: Teacher Expectations and Pupils' Intellectual Development.* New York: Holt, 1968.

Rosnow, L., and Aiken, L. S.: Mediation of artifacts in behavioral research. *Journal of Experimental Social Psychology*, 1973, *9*, 181–201.

Ross, M., Karniol, R., and Rothstein, M.: Reward contingency and intrinsic motivation in children: A test of the delay of gratification hypothesis. *Journal of Personality and Social Psychology*, 1976, *33*, 442–447.

Rostron, A. B.: Brief auditory storage: Some further observations. *Acta Psychologia*, 1974, *38*, 471–482.

Rosvold, H. E., Mirsky, A. F., and Pribram, K. H.: Influence of amygdalectomy on social behavior in monkeys. *Journal of Comparative and Physiological Psychology*, 1954, *47*, 173–178.

Rotter, J. B.: *Social Learning and Clinical Psychology.* Englewood Cliffs, New Jersey: Prentice-Hall, 1954.

Rotter, J. B.: Generalized expectancies for internal versus external control of reinforcement. *Psychological Monographs*, 1966, *80* (Whole No. 609).

Roueche, B. *Alcohol: Its History, Folklore, and Effects on the Human Body.* New York: Grove Press, 1962.

Routtenberg, A., and Lindy, J.: Effects of availability of rewarding septal and hypothalamic stimulation on bar-pressing for food under conditions of deprivation. *Journal of Comparative and Physiological Psychology*, 1965, *60*, 158–161.

Rozin, P., and Kalat, J. S.: Specific hungers and poison avoidance as adaptive specializations of learning. *Psychological Review*, 1971, *78*, 459–486.

Rubin, I. M.: Increased self-acceptance: A means of reducing prejudice. *Journal of Personality and Social Psychology*, 1967, *5*, 233–238.

Rubin, Z.: Measurement of romantic love. *Journal of Personality and Social Psychology*, 1970, *16*, 265–273.

Rubin, Z.: *Liking and Loving: An Invitation to Social Psychology.* New York: Holt, 1973.

Rubin, Z.: From liking to loving: Patterns of attraction in dating relationships. *In* T. L. Huston (ed.), *Foundations of Interpersonal Attraction.* New York: Academic Press, 1974, pp. 383–402.

Rubovits, P. C., and Maehr, M. L.: Pygmalion black and white. *Journal of Personality and Social Psychology,* 1973, *25,* 210–218.

Rudin, S. A.: National motives predict psychogenic death rates 25 years later. *Science,* 1968, *160,* 901–903.

Rushton, J. P.: Generosity in children: Immediate and long-term effects of modeling, preaching, and moral judgment. *Journal of Personality and Social Psychology,* 1975, *31,* 459–466.

Russell, W. R.: *The Traumatic Amnesia.* London: Oxford University Press, 1971.

Russell, W. R., and Nathan, P. W.: Traumatic amnesia. *Brain,* 1946, *69,* 280–300.

Rychlak, J. F.: *A Philosophy of Science for Personality Theory.* Boston: Houghton Mifflin, 1968.

Rychlak, J. F.: *Introduction to Personality and Psychotherapy.* Boston: Houghton Mifflin, 1973.

Sachs, B. D., and Marsan, E.: Male rats prefer sex to food after 6 days of food deprivation. *Psychonomic Science,* 1972, *28,* 47–49.

Saegert, S. (ed.): Crowding in real environments. *Environment and Behavior,* 1975, *7* (Whole No. 2).

Saegert, S., Mackintosh, E. and West, S.: Two studies of crowding in urban public spaces. *Environment and Behavior,* 1975, *7,* 159–184.

Saltzman, I. J.: Maze learning in the absence of primary reinforcement: A study of secondary reinforcement. *Journal of Comparative and Physiological Psychology,* 1949, *42,* 161–173.

Samuel, A. L.: Some studies in machine learning using the game of checkers. II. Recent progress. *IBM Journal of Research and Development,* 1967, *11,* 601–617.

Sarason, I. G., and Ganzer, V. J.: Modeling and group discussion in the rehabilitation of juvenile delinquents. *Journal of Counseling Psychology,* 1973, *20,* 442–449.

Scarr-Salapatek, S.: Race, social class, and I.Q. *Science,* 1971, *174,* 1285–1295.

Schachter, S.: The interaction of cognitive and physiological determinants of emotional state. *In* L. Berkowitz (ed.), *Advances in Experimental Social Psychology.* Vol. 1. New York: Academic Press, 1964.

Schachter, S.: Some extraordinary facts about obese humans and rats. *American Psychologist,* 1971, *26,* 129–144.

Schachter, S., and Latané, B.: Crime, cognition, and the autonomic nervous system. *In* D. Levine (ed.), *Nebraska Symposium on Motivation.* Vol. 12. Lincoln, Nebraska: University of Nebraska Press, 1964.

Schachter, S., and Rodin, J.: *Obese Humans and Rats.* Washington, D.C.: Erlbaum/Halsted, 1974.

Schachter, S., and Singer, J. F.: Cognitive, social, and physiological determinants of emotional state. *Psychological Review,* 1962, *69,* 379–399.

Schlosberg, H.: The description of facial expressions in terms of two dimensions. *Journal of Experimental Psychology,* 1952, *44,* 229–237.

Schmidt, G., and Sigusch, V.: Sex differences in responses to psychosexual stimulation by films and slides. *Journal of Sex Research,* 1970, *6,* 268–283.

Schmidt, M. J., Fulgham, D. D., and Brown, D. R.: Stabilized images: The search for pattern elements. *Perception and Psychophysics,* 1971, *10,* 295–299.

Schmitt, R. C.: Density, deliquency, and crime in Honolulu. *Sociology and Social Research,* 1957, *41,* 274–276.

Schmitt, R. C.: Density, health, and social disorganization. *Journal of American Institute of Planners,* 1966, *32,* 38–40.

Schroeder, H. E., and Rich, A. R.: The process of fear reduction through systematic desensitization. *Journal of Consulting and Clinical Psychology,* 1976, *44,* 191–199.

Schultz, D.: The human subject in psychological research. *Psychological Bulletin,* 1969, *72,* 214–228.

Schultz, T.: What science is discovering about the potential benefits of meditation. *Today's Health,* 1972, *50,* 34–37, 64–67.

Schutz, W. C.: *Joy.* New York: Grove, 1967.

Schwartz, G. E.: Biofeedback as therapy: Some theoretical and practical issues. *American Psychologist,* 1973, *23,* 666–673.

Schwartz, J., and Bellack, A. S.: A comparison of a token economy with standard in-patient treatment. *Journal of Consulting and Clinical Psychology,* 1975, *43,* 107–108.

Scott, W. A., and Petersen, C.: Adjustment, Pollyannaism, and attraction to close relationships. *Journal of Consulting and Clinical Psychology,* 1975, *43,* 872–880.

Scoville, W. B., and Milner, B.: Loss of recent memory after bilateral hippocampal lesions. *Journal of Neurology, Neurosurgery, and Psychiatry,* 1957, *20,* 11–21.

Sears, R. R., Maccoby, E. E., and Levin, H.: *Patterns of Child Rearing.* Evanston, Illinois: Row, Peterson, 1957.

Seeman, W., Nidich, S., and Banta, T.: Influence of transcendental meditation on a measure of self-actualization. *Journal of Counseling Psychology,* 1972, *19,* 184–187.

Segal, S. J. and Fusella, V.: Influence of imaged pictures and sounds on detection of visual and auditory signals. *Journal of Experimental Psychology,* 1970, *83,* 458–464.

Seiden, L. S.: Neurochemical basis of drug action: Introduction. *In* J. A. Harvey (ed.), *Behavioral Analysis of Drug Action.* Glenview, Illinois: Scott, Foresman, 1970.

Seligman, M. E. P.: On the generality of the laws of learning. *Psychological Review,* 1970, *77,* 406–418.

Seligman, M. E. P.: Phobias and preparedness. *Behavior Therapy,* 1971, *2,* 307–320.

Seligman, M. E. P.: Learned helplessness. *Annual Review of Medicine,* 1972, *23,* 207–412.

Seligman, M. E. P.: Depression and learned helplessness. *In* R. J. Friedman and M. M. Katz (eds.), *The Psychology of Depression: Contemporary Theory and Research.* Washington, D.C.: Winston-Wiley, 1973.

Seligman, M. E. P.: *Helplessness.* San Francisco: Freeman, 1974.

Seligman, M. E. P., and Hager, J. L.: *Biological Boundaries of Learning.* New York: Appleton, Century, Crofts, 1972.

Seligman, M. E. P. and Maier, S.: Failure to escape traumatic shock. *Journal of Experimental Psychology,* 1967, *74,* 1–9.

Seligman, M. E. P., Maier, S., and Solomon, R. L.: Unpredictable and uncontrollable aversive events. *In* F. R. Brush (ed.), *Aversive Conditioning and Learning.* New York: Academic Press, 1970.

Sem-Jacobsen, C. W., and Torkildsen, A.: *In* E. R. Ramey, and D. S. O'Doherty (eds.), *Electrical Studies on the Unanesthetized Brain.* New York: Hoeber, 1960.

Serber, M.: The experiential group as entertainment. *In* P. S. Houts and M. Serber (eds.), *After the Turn-on, What? Learning Perspectives on Humanistic Groups.* Champaign, Illinois, Research Press, 1972.

Shakow, D.: Psychological deficit in schizophrenia. *Behavioral Science,* 1963, *8,* 275–305.

Shapiro, D., Barber, T. X., DiCara, L. V., Kamiya, J., Miller, N. E., and Stoyva, J. (eds.), *Biofeedback and Self-Control, 1972: An Aldine Annual on the Regulation of Bodily Processes and Consciousness.* Chicago: Aldine, 1973.

Sheldon, W. H.: *The Varieties of Temperament: A Psychology of Constitutional Differences.* New York: Harper, 1942.

Sheldon, W. H., Lewis, N. D. C., and Tenney, A. M.: Psychotic patterns and physical constitution: A thirty-year follow-up of thirty-eight-hundred psychiatric patients in New York State. *In* D. V. Siva Sankar (ed.), *Schizo-*

phrenia: *Current Concepts and Research.* New York: PJD Publications, 1969.

Sheldon, W. H., Stevens, S. S., and Tucker, W. B.: *The Varieties of Human Physique: An Introduction to Constitutional Psychology.* Darien, Connecticut: Hafner, 1970.

Shepard, M.: From Freud to Yoga: Eleven different therapies. *Penthouse Forum,* 1974, *4* (2), 30–35.

Shepard, R.: Recognition memory for words, sentences, and pictures. *Journal of Verbal Learning and Verbal Behavior,* 1967, *6,* 156–163.

Sherwood, J. J.: Authoritarianism, moral realism, and President Kennedy's death. *British Journal of Social and Clinical Psychology,* 1966, *5,* 264–269.

Shettleworth, S. J.: Constraints on learning. *In* D. S. Lehrman, R. A. Hinde, and E. Shaw (eds.), *Advances in the Study of Behavior.* Vol. 4. New York: Academic Press, 1972.

Shiffrin, R. M., and Atkinson, R. C.: Storage and retrieval processes in long-term memory. Psychological Review, 1969, *76* 179–193.

Siegler, R. S., and Liebert, R. M.: Effects of presenting relevant rules and complete feedback on the conservation of liquid quantity task. *Developmental Psychology,* 1972, *7,* 133–138.

Sigall, H., Aronson, E., and Van Hoose, T.: The cooperative subject: Myth or reality? *Journal of Experimental Social Psychology,* 1970, *6,* 1–10.

Sigall, H., and Ostrove, N.: Beautiful but dangerous: Effects of offender attractiveness and nature of the crime on juridic judgment. *Journal of Personality and Social Psychology,* 1975, *31,* 410–414.

Simmons, F. B.: Monaural processing. *In* J. V. Tobias, (ed.), *Foundations of Modern Auditory Theory.* Vol. 1. New York: Academic Press, 1970.

Simon, H. A.: *The Sciences of the Artificial.* Cambridge, Massachusetts: M.I.T . Press, 1969.

Singer, D. L.: Aggression arousal, hostile humor, and catharsis. *Journal of Personality and Social Psychology Monograph Supplement,* 1968, *8,* 1–14.

Singh, D.: Role of response habits and cognitive factors in determination of behavior of obese humans. *Journal of Personality and Social Psychology,* 1973, *27,* 220–238.

Singh, D.: Psychology of obesity: Failure to inhibit responses. *Obesity/Bariatric Medicine,* 1974, *3.* (a)

Singh, D.: Role of past experience on food-motivated behavior of obese humans. *Journal of Comparative and Physiological Psychology,* 1974, *86,* 503–508. (b)

Sirota, D.: Job enrichment—another management fad? *Conference Board Record,* 1973, *10,* 40–45.

Sistrunk, F., and McDavid, J. W.: Sex variable in conforming behavior. *Journal of Personality and Social Psychology,* 1971, *17,* 200–207.

Skeels, H. M.: Adult status of children with contrasting early life experience. *Society for Research in Child Development Monographs,* 1966, *31,* No. 3, 1–65.

Skinner, B. F.: *The Behavior of Organisms.* New York: Appleton-Century-Crofts, 1938.

Skinner, B. F.: *Verbal Behavior.* New York: Appleton-Century-Crofts, 1957.

Skinner, B. F.: The steep and thorny way to a science of behavior. *American Psychologist,* 1975, *30,* 42–49.

Skinner, H. A., Reed, P. L., and Jackson, D. N.: Toward the objective diagnosis of psychopathology: Generalizability of modal personality profiles. *Journal of Consulting and Clinical Psychology,* 1976, *44,* 111–117.

Skrzypek, G. J.: The effects of perceptual isolation and arousal on anxiety, complexity preference, and novelty preference in psychopathic and neurotic delinquents. *Journal of Abnormal Psychology,* 1969, *74,* 321–329.

Slamecka, N. J.: An examination of trace storage in free recall. *Journal of Experimental Psychology,* 1968, *76,* 504–513.

Slavson, S. R.: *Analytic Group Psychotherapy with Children, Adolescents and Adults.* New York: Columbia University Press, 1950.

Slobin, D. I.: *Psycholinguistics.* Glenview, Illinois: Scott, Foresman, 1971.

Slovic, P., and Lichtenstein, S.: Relative importance of probabilities and pay-offs in risk-taking. *Journal of Experimental Psychology,* 1968, *78,* No. 3, Part 2, 1–18.

Sluckin, W.: *Early Learning in Man and Animal.* London: George Allen and Unwin, 1970.

Smilansky, B.: Paper presented at the meetings of the American Educational Research Association, Chicago, 1973.

Smith, E. E., Shoben, E. J., and Rips, L. J.: Structure and process in semantic memory: A feature model for semantic decisions. *Psychological Review,* 1974, *81,* 214–224.

Smith, G. F., and Dorfman, D.: The effect of stimulus uncertainty on the relationship between frequency of exposure and liking. *Journal of Personality and Social Psychology,* 1975, *31,* 150–155.

Smith, R. E., Ascough, J. C., Ettinger, R. F., and Nelson, D. A.: Humor, anxiety, and task performance. *Journal of Personality and Social Psychology,* 1971, *19,* 243–246.

Snyder, M., and Cunningham, M. R.: To comply or not comply: Testing the self-perception explanation of the "foot-in-the-door" phenomenon. *Journal of Personality and Social Psychology,* 1975, *31,* 64–67.

Sobell, M. B., and Sobell, L. C.: Individualized behavior therapy for alcoholics. *Behavior Therapy,* 1973, *4,* 49–72.

Solomon, R. L., and Wynne, L. C.: Traumatic avoidance learning: Acquisition in normal dogs. *Psychological Monographs,* 1953, *67* (Whole No. 354).

Sommer, R.: The ecology of privacy. *Library Quarterly,* 1966, *36,* 234–248.

Sommer, R.: Spatial parameters in naturalistic social research. *In* A. H. Esser (ed.), *Behavior and Environment,* New York, Plenum, 1971.

Sommer, R.: *Tight Spaces.* Englewood Cliffs, New Jersey: Prentice-Hall, 1974.

Speer, D. C.: An evaluation of a telephone crisis service. Paper presented at the meeting of the Midwestern Psychological Association. Cleveland, May, 1972.

Speisman, J. C.: Distribution of psychologists in universities and colleges. *American Psychologist,* 1972, *27,* 432–433.

Spence, J. T.: The thematic apperception test and attitudes toward achievement in women: A new look at the motive to avoid success and a new method of measurement. *Journal of Consulting and Clinical Psychology,* 1974, *42,* 427–437.

Spence, J. T., Helmreich, R., and Stapp, J.: Likability, sex-role congruence of interest, and competence: It all depends on how you ask. *Journal of Applied Social Psychology,* 1975, *5,* 93–109.

Spence, K. W.: *Behavior Theory and Conditioning.* New Haven, Connecticut: Yale University Press, 1956.

Spence, K. W.: *Behavior Theory and Learning.* Englewood Cliffs, New Jersey: Prentice-Hall, 1960.

Sperling, G.: The information available in brief visual presentations. *Psychological Monographs,* 1960, *74,* 11 (Whole No. 498).

Sperry, R. W.: Hemisphere deconnection and unity in conscious experience. *American Psychologist,* 1968, *23,* 723–733.

Spielberger, C. D.: The effects of anxiety on complex learning and academic achievement. *In* C. D. Spielberger (ed.), *Anxiety and Behavior.* New York: Academic Press, 1966, pp. 361–398.

Spielberger, C. D., and Smith, L. H.: Anxiety (drive), stress, and serial-position effects in serial-verbal learning. *Journal of Experimental Psychology,* 1966, *72,* 589–595.

Spies, G.: Food versus intracranial self-stimulation reinforcement in food-deprived rats. *Journal of Comparative and Physiological Psychology,* 1965, *60,* 153–157.

Spitz, R. A., and Wolff, K. M.: Anaclitic depression: An inquiry into the genesis of psychiatric conditions in early childhood. II. *In* A. Freud et al., (eds.), *The Psychoanalytic Study of the Child.* Vol. II. New York: International Universities Press, 1946.

Spitzer, R. L.: On pseudoscience in science, logic in remission, and psychiatric diagnosis: A critique of Rosenhan's "On being sane in insane places." *Journal of Abnormal Psychology*, 1975, *84*, 442–452.

Spranger, E.: *Types of Men.* (Translated by P. J. W. Pigors.) Halle: Max Niemeyer Verlag, 1928.

Squire, L. R., Slater, P. C., and Chace, P. M.: Retrograde amnesia: Temporal gradient in very long term memory following electroconvulsive therapy. *Science*, 1975, *187*, 77–79.

Standing, L., Conezio, J. and Haber, R.: Perception and memory for pictures: Single-trial learning of 2500 visual stimuli. *Psychonomic Science*, 1970, *19*, 73–74.

Stang, D. J.: Effects of "mere exposure" on learning and affect. *Journal of Personality and Social Psychology*, 1975, *31*, 7–12.

Staub, E.: Helping a distressed person: Social, personality, and stimulus determinants. *In* L. Berkowitz (ed.), *Advances in Experimental Social Psychology.* New York: Academic Press, 1974.

Stein, A. H., Friederich, L. K., and Vondracek, F.: Television content and young children's behavior. *In* G. A. Comstock and E. A. Rubenstein (eds.), *Television and Social Behavior, Volume 2: Television and Social Learning.* Washington, D.C.: U.S. Government Printing Office, 1972.

Sternberg, S.: The discovery of processing stages: Extensions of Donders' method. *Acta Psychologica*, 1969, *30*, 276–315.

Sternglanz, S. H., and Serbin, L. A.: Sex role stereotyping in children's television programs. *Developmental Psychology*, 1974, *10*, 710–715.

Stoller, F. H.: Accelerated interaction: A time-limited approach based on the brief intensive group. *International Journal of Group Psychotherapy*, 1968, *18*, 220–235.

Stroop, J. R.: Studies of interference in serial verbal reactions. *Journal of Experimental Psychology*, 1935, *18*, 643–662.

Suedfeld, P.: *Attitude Change: The Competing Views.* Chicago: Aldine-Atherton, 1971.

Suinn, R. M.: *Fundamentals of Behavior Pathology.* New York: John Wiley and Sons, 1970.

Suomi, S. J., and Harlow, H. F.: Social rehabilitation of isolate-reared monkeys. *Developmental Psychology*, 1972, *6*, 487–496.

Sutherland, E.: *Principles of Criminology.* Philadelphia: J. B. Lippincott, 1966.

Sutherland, N. S., and Mackintosh, J.: *Mechanisms of Animal Discrimination.* New York: Academic Press, 1971.

Szasz, T. S.: The myth of mental illness. *American Psychologist*, 1960, *15*, 113–118.

Szasz, T. S.: *Ideology and Insanity.* Garden City, New York: Doubleday, Anchor, 1970.

Tanner, J. M.: Physical growth. *In* P. H. Mussen (ed.), *Carmichael's Manual of Child Psychology*, Vol. 1, 3rd ed. New York: John Wiley and Sons, 1970.

Tapp, J. L., and Levine, F. J.: Compliance from kindergarten to college: A speculative research note. *Journal of Youth and Adolescence*, 1972, *1*, 233–249.

Targ, R., and Puthoff, H.: Information transmission under conditions of sensory shielding. *Nature*, 1974, *251*, 602–607.

Tarpy, R. M.: *Basic Principles of Learning.* Glenview, Illinois: Scott, Foresman, 1975.

Tarpy, R. M., and Swabini, F. L.: Reinforcement delay: A selective review of the last decade. *Psychological Bulletin*, 1974, *81*, 984–997.

Tart, C.: *On Being Stoned.* Palo Alto, California: Science and Behavior, 1971.

Tavolga, W. N.: *Principles of Animal Behavior.* New York: Harper, 1969.

Taylor, D. A.: Stage analysis of reaction time. *Psychological Bulletin*, 1976, *83*, 161–191.

Taylor, G. T.: Varied function of punishment in differential instrumental conditioning. *Journal of Experimental Psychology*, 1974, *102*, 298–307.

Taylor, J. A.: The relationship of anxiety to the conditioned eyelid response. *Journal of Experimental Psychology*, 1951, *41*, 81–92.

Taylor, J. A.: A personality scale of manifest anxiety. *Journal of Abnormal and Social Psychology*, 1953, *48*, 285–290.

Taylor, S. P., and Gammon, C. B.: Effects of type and dose of alcohol on human physical aggression. *Journal of Personality and Social Psychology*, 1975, *32*, 169–175.

Taylor, S. P., Gammon, C. B., and Capasso, D. R.: Aggression as a function of the interaction of alcohol and threat. *Journal of Personality and Social Psychology*, 1977, in press.

Taylor, S. P., Vardaris, R. M., Rawitch, A. B., Gammon, C. B., Cranston, J. W., and Lubetkin, A. K.: The effects of alcohol and delta-9-tetrahydrocannabinol on human physical aggression. *Aggressive Behavior*, 1976, *2*, 153–161.

Teeván, R. C., and McGhee, P. E.: Childhood development of fear of failure motivation. *Journal of Personality and Social Psychology*, 1972, *21*, 345–348.

Teghtsoonian, R., and Campbell, B. A.: Random activity of the rat during food deprivation as a function of environment. *Journal of Comparative and Physiological Psychology*, 1960, *53*, 242–244.

Teichner, W. H. and Krebs, M.: Laws of visual choice reaction time. *Psychological Review*, 1974, *81*, 75–98.

Teitelbaum, P.: Random and food-directed activity in hyperphagic and normal rats. *Journal of Comparative and Physiological Psychology*, 1957, *50*, 486–490.

Teitelbaum, P., Cheng, M. F., and Rozin, P.: Stages of recovery and development of lateral hypothalamic control of food and water intake. *Annals of the New York Academy of Science*, 1969, *157*, 848–860.

Temerlin, M. K.: Suggestion effects in psychiatric diagnosis. *Journal of Nervous and Mental Disease*, 1968, *147*, 349–353.

Thomas, E. A. C.: The selectivity of preparation. *Psychological Review*, 1974, *81*, 442–464.

Thorndike, E. L.: Animal intelligence. An experimental study of the associative processes in animals. *Psychological Monographs*, 1898, *2* (Whole No. 8).

Thurlow, W. R., and Small, A. M.: Pitch perception for certain auditory stimuli. *Journal of the Acoustical Society of America*, 1955, *27*, 132–137.

Tilker, H. A.: Socially responsible behavior as a function of observer responsibility and victim feedback. *Journal of Personality and Social Psychology*, 1970, *14*, 95–100.

Tinbergen, N.: *The Herring Gull's World.* New York: Harper, 1974.

Tolman, E. C.: Cognitive maps in rats and men. *Psychological Review*, 1948, *55*, 189–208.

Townsend, J. T.: Theoretical analysis of an alphabetic confusion matrix. *Perception & Psychophysics*, 1971, *9*, 40–50.

Trehub, S. E., and Rabinovitch, M. S.: Auditory-linguistic sensitivity in early infancy. *Developmental Psychology*, 1972, *6*, 74–77.

Treisman, M., and Rostron, A. B.: Brief auditory storage: A modification of Sperling's paradigm applied to audition. *Acta Psychologica*, 1972, *36*, 161–170.

Triandis, H. C.: *Interpersonal Behavior.* Monterey. California: Brooks/Cole, 1976.

Tribich, D., and Messer, S.: Psychoanalytic character type

and status of authority as determiners of suggestibility. *Journal of Consulting and Clinical Psychology*, 1974, *42*, 842–848.

Trowbridge, C. C.: On fundamental methods of orientation and "imaginary maps." *Science*, 1913, *38*, 888–897.

Truax, C. B.: Reinforcement and nonreinforcement in Rogerian psychotherapy. *Journal of Abnormal Psychology*, 1966, *71*, 1–9.

Truax, C. B., and Mitchell, K. M.: Research on certain therapist interpersonal skills in relation to process and outcome. *In* A. E. Bergin and S. L. Garfield (eds.), *Handbook of Psychotherapy and Behavior Change*. New York: John Wiley and Sons, 1971, pp. 299–344.

Tulving, E.: Theoretical issues in free recall. *In* T. R. Dixon and D. L. Horton (eds.), *Verbal Behavior and General Behavior Theory*. Englewood Cliffs, New Jersey: Prentice-Hall, 1968.

Tulving, E.: When is recall higher than recognition? *Psychonomic Science*, 1968, *10*, 53–54.

Tulving, E.: Episodic and semantic memory. *In* E. Tulving and W. Donaldson (eds.), *Organization of Memory*. New York: Academic Press, 1972.

Tulving, E., and Hastie, R.: Inhibition effects of intralist repetition in free recall. *Journal of Experimental Psychology*, 1972, *92*, 297–304.

Tulving, E. and Osler, S.: Effectiveness of retrieval cues in memory for words. *Journal of Experimental Psychology*, 1968, *77*, 593–601.

Tulving, E., and Pearlstone, Z.: Availability versus accessibility of information in memory for words. *Journal of Verbal Learning and Verbal Behavior*, 1966, *5*, 381–391.

Turner, J. H.: Entrepreneurial environments and the emergence of achievement motivation in adolescent males. *Sociometry*, 1970, *33*, 147–165.

Turner, L. H., and Solomon, R. L.: Human traumatic avoidance learning: Theory and experiments on the operant-respondent distinction. *Psychological Monographs*, 1962, *76* (Whole No. 40).

Tyhurst, J.: Individual reactions to community disaster: The natural history of psychiatric phenomena. *American Journal of Psychiatry*, 1951, *107*, 764–769.

Tyler, D. W., Wortz, E. C., and Bitterman, M. E.: The effect of random and alternating partial reinforcement on resistance to extinction in the rat. *American Journal of Psychology*, 1953, *66*, 57–65.

Udry, J. R.: *The Social Context of Marriage*. Philadelphia: Lippincott, 1971.

Ullmann, L. P., and Krasner, L. (eds.): *Case Studies in Behavior Modification*. New York: Holt, 1965.

Ullmann, L. P., and Krasner, L.: *A Psychological Approach to Abnormal Behavior*. Englewood Cliffs, New Jersey: Prentice-Hall, 1975.

United States Riot Commission: *Report of the National Advisory Commission on Civil Disorders*. New York: Bantam, 1968.

Urberg, K. A., and Labouvie-Vief, G.: Conceptualizations of sex roles: A life span developmental study. *Developmental Psychology*, 1976, *12*, 15–23.

Valenstein, E. S.: *Brain Control: A Critical Examination of Brain Stimulation and Psychosurgery*. New York: John Wiley and Sons, 1973.

Van Lawick-Goodall, J.: Mother-offspring relationships in free ranging chimpanzees. *In* D. Morris (ed.), *Primate Ethology*. London: Werdenfeld and Nicolson, 1967.

Von Bekesy, G.: Duplexity theory of taste. *Science*, 1964, *145*, 834–835.

Vroom, V. H.: *Work and Motivation*. New York: John Wiley and Sons, 1964.

Waelder, R.: *Basic Theory of Psychoanalysis.* New York: International Universities Press, 1960.

Wahba, M. A., and House, R. J.: Expectancy theory in work and motivation: Some logical and methodological issues. *Human Relations*, 1974, *27*, 121–147.

Wald, G., and Brown, P. K.: Human color vision and color blindness. *Symposia on Quantitative Biology*, 1965, XXX, 345–359. (The Cold Springs Harbour Laboratory of Quantitative Biology, Cold Springs Harbour, New York.)

Walker, E. L.: Psychological complexity as a basis for a theory of motivation and choice. In *Nebraska Symposium on Motivation*. Vol. 12. Lincoln, Nebraska: University of Nebraska Press, 1964, pp. 47–95.

Walker, R. N.: Body build and behavior in young children. Body build and nursery school teachers' ratings. *Monographs in Social Research on Child Development*, 1962, *27*, Serial No. 84.

Wallace, R. K., and Benson, H.: The physiology of meditation. *Scientific American*, 1972, *226*, 84–90.

Wallington, S. A.: Consequences of transgression: Self-punishment and depression. *Journal of Personality and Social Psychology*, 1973, *29*, 1–7.

Walster, E.: Assignment of responsibility for an accident. *Journal of Personality and Social Psychology*, 1966, *3*, 73–79.

Walster, E., Aronson, V., and Abrahams, D.: Importance of physical attractiveness in dating behavior. *Journal of Personality and Social Psychology*, 1966, *4*, 508–516.

Walster, E., Aronson, E., and Abrahams, D.: On increasing the persuasiveness of a low prestige communicator. *Journal of Experimental Social Psychology*, 1966, *2*, 325–342.

Walster, E., and Berscheid, E.: Adrenaline makes the heart grow fonder. *Psychology Today*, 1971, *5*, 47–62.

Walster, E., Berscheid, E., and Walster, G. W.: New directions in equity research. *Journal of Personality and Social Psychology*, 1973, *25*, 151–176.

Walster, E., Walster, G. W., Piliavin, J., and Schmidt, L.: "Playing hard to get": Understanding an elusive phenomenon. *Journal of Personality and Social Psychology*, 1973, *26*, 113–121.

Walters, R. H.: Implications of laboratory studies of aggression for the control and regulation of violence. *Annals of the American Academy of Political and Social Science*, 1966, *364*, 60–72.

Wanous, J. P.: Tell it like it is at realistic job previews. *Personnel*, 1975, *52*, 50–60.

Wanous, J. P.: Organizational entry: From naive expectations to realistic beliefs. *Journal of Applied Psychology*, 1976, *61*, 22–29.

Ward, A. A., Jr.: The anterior cingulate gyrus and personality. *In* J. F. Fulton, C. D. Aring, and S. B. Wortis (eds.), *The Frontal Lobes*. New York: Williams & Wilkins, 1948.

Warden, C. J.: *Animal Motivation: Experimental Studies on the Albino Rat*. New York: Columbia University Press, 1931.

Watson, J. B.: Psychology as the behaviorist views it. *Psychological Review*, 1913, *20*, 158–177.

Watson, J. B.: *Behaviorism*. New York: W. W. Norton, 1924.

Watson, J. B., and Raynor, R.: Conditioned emotional reactions. *Journal of Experimental Psychology*, 1920, *3*, 1–14.

Watson, R. I.: Investigation into deindividuation using a cross-cultural survey technique. *Journal of Personality and Social Psychology*, 1973, *25*, 342–345.

Watts, C.: *Depressive Disorders in the Community*. Bristol: John Wright and Sons, 1966.

Waugh, N. C., and Norman, D. A.: Primary memory. *Psychological Review*, 1965, *72*, 89–104.

Webb, W. B., and Friel, J.: Sleep stage and personality characteristics of "natural" long and short sleepers. *Science*, 1971, *171*, 587–588.

Wechsler, D.: Intelligence defined and undefined: A relativistic appraisal. *American Psychologist*, 1975, *30*, 135–139.

Weiner, J. W.: The effectiveness of a suicide prevention program. *Mental Hygiene*, 1969, *53*, 357–363.

Weiss, J. M.: Psychological factors in stress and disease. *Scientific American*, 1972, *226*, 104–113.

Weiss, W.: Opinion congruence with a negative source on

one issue as a factor influencing agreement on another issue. *Journal of Abnormal and Social Psychology*, 1957, *54*, 180–186.

Weitzman, L. J., Eifler, D., Hokada, E., and Ross, C.: Sex-role socialization in picture books for preschool children. *American Journal of Sociology*, 1972, *77*, 1125–1150.

Weizenbaum, J.: Contextual understanding by computers. In P. A. Kolers and M. Eden (eds.), *Recognizing Patterns*. Cambridge, Massachusetts: M.I.T. Press, 1968.

Welker, W. L.: Some determinants of play and exploration in chimpanzees. *Journal of Comparative and Physiological Psychology*, 1956, *49*, 84–89.

Wenar, C.: Reaction time as a function of manifest anxiety and stimulus intensity. *Journal of Abnormal and Social Psychology*, 1954, *49*, 335–340.

Wexler, D. A., and Butler, J. M.: Therapist modification of client expressiveness in client-centered therapy. *Journal of Consulting and Clinical Psychology*, 1976, *44*, 261–265.

Whalen, R. E.: The concept of instinct. In J. L. McGaugh (ed.), *Psychobiology: Behavior from a Biological Perspective*. New York: Academic Press, 1971.

White, R. W.: Motivation reconsidered: The concept of competence. *Psychological Review*, 1959, *66*, 297–333.

Whitehill, M., DeMyer-Gapin, S., and Scott, T. J.: Stimulation seeking in antisocial preadolescent children. *Journal of Abnormal Psychology*, 1976, *85*, 101–104.

Whorf, B. L.: *Language, Thought, and Reality*. New York: John Wiley and Sons, 1956.

Wicker, A. W.: An examination of the "other variables" explanation of the attitude-behavior inconsistence. *Journal of Personality and Social Psychology*, 1971, *19*, 18–30.

Wightman, F. L., and Green, D. M.: The perception of pitch. *American Scientist*, 1974, *62*, 208–215.

Wike, E. L., and McWilliams, J.: The effects of long-term training with delayed reward and delay-box confinement on instrumental performance. *Psychonomic Science*, 1967, *9*, 389–390.

Wilcove, W. G., and Miller, J. C.: CS–US presentations and a lever: Human autoshaping. *Journal of Experimental Psychology*, 1974, *103*, 868–877.

Wilkinson, R.: Some factors influencing the effect of environmental stressors upon performance. *Psychological Bulletin*, 1969, *72*, 260–272.

Willerman, L.: *The Psychology of Individual and Group Differences*. San Francisco: W. H. Freeman, 1977.

Willerman, L., Naylor, A. F., and Myrianthopoulos, N. C.: Intellectual development of children from interracial matings: Performance in infancy and at 4 years. *Behavior Genetics*, 1974, *4*, 83–90.

Williams, D. R., and Williams, H.: Auto-maintenance in the pigeon: Sustained pecking despite contingent nonreinforcement. *Journal of Experimental Analysis of Behavior*, 1969, *12*, 511–520.

Williams, J. E., Bennett, S. M., and Best, D. L.: Awareness and expression of sex stereotypes in young children. *Developmental Psychology*, 1975, *11*, 635–642.

Wolpe, J.: Reciprocal inhibition as the main basis of psychotherapeutic effects. *American Medical Association Archives of Neurology and Psychiatry*, 1954, *72*, 205–226.

Wolpe, J.: *Psychotherapy by Reciprocal Inhibition*. Stanford, California: Stanford University Press, 1958.

Wolpe, J.: *The Practice of Behavior Therapy*. Elmsford, New York: Pergamon, 1974.

Worchel, S.: The effect of three types of arbitrary thwarting on the instigation to aggression. *Journal of Personality*, 1974, *42*, 300–318.

Wortis, J.: *History of Insulin Shock*. New York: Philosophical Library, 1959.

Wright, L.: Psychologic aspects of the battered child syndrome. *Southern Medical Bulletin*, 1970, *58*, 14–18.

Wrightsman, L. S.: Wallace supporters and adherence to "law and order." *Journal of Personality and Social Psychology*, 1969, *13*, 17–22.

Wynne-Edwards, V. C.: *Animal Dispersion in Relation to Social Behavior*. Edinburgh: Oliver & Boyd, 1962.

Wynne-Edwards, V. C.: Space use and the social community in animals and men. In A. H. Esser (ed.), *Behavior and Environment*. New York: Plenum, 1971.

Yalom, I. D., and Lieberman, M. A.: A study of encounter group casualties. *Archives of General Psychiatry*, 1971, *25*, 16–30.

Yancy, W. L.: Architecture, interaction, and social control. *Environment and Behavior*, 1971, *3*, 3–21.

Yates, F. A.: *The Art of Memory*. Chicago: University of Chicago Press, 1966.

Zajonc, R. B.: Social facilitation. *Science*, 1965, *149*, 269–274.

Zajonc, R. B., Heingartner, A., and Herman, E. M.: Social enhancement and impairment of performance in the cockroach. *Journal of Personality and Social Psychology*, 1969, *13*, 83–92.

Zajonc, R. B., Shaver, P., Tavris, C., and Kreveld, D. V.: Exposure, satiation, and stimulus discriminability. *Journal of Personality and Social Psychology*, 1972, *21*, 270–280.

Zander, A., and Forward, J.: Position in group, achievement motivation, and group aspirations. *Journal of Personality and Social Psychology*, 1968, *8*, 282–288.

Zaretsky, H. H.: Learning and performance in the runway as a function of the shift in drive and incentive. *Journal of Comparative and Physiological Psychology*, 1966, *62*, 218–221.

Zarle, T. H., Hartsough, D. M., and Ottinger, D. R.: Tornado recovery: The development of a professional-paraprofessional response to a disaster. *Journal of Community Psychology*, 1974, *2*, 311–320.

Zax, M., and Cowen, E. L.: *Abnormal Psychology: Changing Conceptions*. New York: Holt, Rinehart and Winston, 1972.

Zeaman, D.: Response latency as a function of the amount of reinforcement. *Journal of Experimental Psychology*, 1949, *39*, 466–483.

Zelnick, M., and Kantner, J. F.: The resolution of teenage first pregnancies. *Family Planning Perspectives*, 1974, *6*, 74.

Zilboorg, G., and Henry, G. W.: *A History of Medical Psychology*. New York: Norton, 1941.

Zillmann, D.: Excitation transfer in communication-mediated aggressive behavior. *Journal of Experimental Social Psychology*, 1971, *7*, 419–434.

Zillmann, D., Bryant, J., Cantor, J. R., and Day, K. D.: Irrelevance of mitigating circumstances in retaliatory behavior at high levels of excitation. *Journal of Research in Personality*, 1975, *9*, 282–293.

Zillmann, D., Johnson, R. C., and Day, K. D.: Attribution of apparent arousal and proficiency of recovery from sympathetic activation affecting excitation transfer to aggressive behavior. *Journal of Experimental Social Psychology*, 1974, *10*, 503–515.

Zimbardo, P. G.: The human choice: Individuation, reason, and order versus deindividuation, impulse, and chaos. In W. J. Arnold and D. Levine (eds.), *Nebraska Symposium on Motivation, 1969*. Lincoln, Nebraska: University of Nebraska Press, 1970.

Zuckerman, M.: Hallucinations, reported sensations, and images. In J. P. Zuckerman (ed.), *Sensory Deprivation: Fifteen Years of Research*. New York: Appleton, Century, Crofts, 1969.

Zuckerman, M.: Physiological measures of sexual arousal in the human. *Psychological Bulletin*, 1971, *75*, 347–356.

Zuckerman, M., Lipets, M. S., Koivumaki, J. H., and Rosenthal, R.: Encoding and decoding nonverbal cues of emotion. *Journal of Personality and Social Psychology*, 1975, *32*, 1068–1076.

GLOSSARY

abnormal behavior   Behavior which is unusual or infrequent in a particular culture.

accessible information   Information in long-term memory which is actually retrieved.

accommodation   1. The tendency to acquire new responses (or alter old ones) in order to deal effectively with new events and situations.
2. The change in curvature of the lens of the eye during focusing.

achievement motivation   Motivation to excel in virtually all undertakings. The need for achievement serves as an important source of work motivation, and it may also influence occupational choice.

action potential   A rapid reversal of the tiny negative electric charge normally existing across the cell membrane of the neuron. It is through the movement of action potentials along the axon that information is communicated within neurons.

activity wheel   An apparatus that can be rotated by an animal while in its cage; the number of revolutions, the time spent in the wheel, or some other measure is recorded as an index of the animal's general activity level.

actualizing tendency   In Rogerian theory, the primary motive to maintain and enhance the self.

addiction   A physical or psychological dependence upon one or more drugs. Once *addicted* to a particular drug, individuals cannot function normally in its absence.

advertising   Persuasive appeals designed to influence consumer purchasing decisions.

affective schizophrenia   A type of schizophrenic disorder involving unrealistic elation or depression.

alcoholism   A type of conduct disorder involving heavy drinking that interferes with the individual's ability to function at home and at work.

algorithm   A set of rules that will eventually guarantee the successful solution of a problem.

all-or-none principle   A concept in neurology which holds that a neuron either conducts a nerve impulse at full strength or it fails to conduct one at all.

alpha waves   Relatively fast, low-magnitude pulses which are characteristic of the electrical activity of the brain during waking restfulness.

amnesia   A failure of memory often due to some traumatic injury.

amphetamines   A group of drugs which exert strong activating effects upon behavior. Individuals taking amphetamines can often sustain high levels of activity far beyond the normal point of exhaustion.

amplitude   The maximum height of a sine wave.

amygdala   One of the structures of the limbic system. Removal or destruction of the amygdala reduces emotionality.

analgesics   Drugs such as aspirin or morphine which have the ability to provide relief from pain.

anal personality   In psychoanalytic theory, a psychosexual type involving obsession with saving and collecting various objects and with the traits of orderliness, neatness, and obstinacy.

anal stage   In psychoanalytic theory, the developmental stage involving learning to control bowel functions.

androgens   The male sex hormones.

anxiety reaction   A type of neurotic behavior in which the defenses fail, and the individual becomes acutely anxious.

aphasia   Impairment in language abilities. Aphasias may be *sensory* in nature, involving losses in the ability to read or understand speech, or *motor*, involving losses in the ability to write or to speak.

archetypes   In Jung's theory, the universal symbols that are contained in the collective unconscious.

arousal   A neurophysiological concept related to the degree of alertness of an organism. Arousal is measured by physiological indicators such as the cortical EEG and pupillary dilation of the eye.

assimilation   The tendency to apply old ideas and responses to new objects or problems.

attachment   The strong affective bond on the part of young infants toward their mother. Signs of attachment include infants' recognition of their mother, their tendency to smile more at her than at others, and attempts on their part to seek her out.

authoritarian   An individual who characteristically shows (1) obedience and respect for authority, (2) suppression of some sexual impulses, and (3) expression of hostility toward those who deviate from conventional values. An authoritarian individual receives a high score on the F scale. *Authoritarianism* is the name given the personality trait encompassing all these elements.

autism   The tendency to be more concerned with one's own personal thoughts and wishes than with objective reality.

automaton   A machine exhibiting purposive behavior.

autonomic nervous system   That portion of the peripheral nervous system which regulates the non-voluntary muscles and glands. Basically, it is concerned with the regulation of internal bodily processes.

autoshaping   A process in which organisms come to direct operant behavior (e.g., key-pecking, lever-pressing) toward stimuli which are regularly associated with the presentation of reinforcement.

available information   Information in long-term memory which can potentially be retrieved.

aversive conditioning   A type of counterconditioning in which punishment is used in order to associate negative feelings with an undesirable response.

avoidance conditioning   The process through which organisms learn to avoid unpleasant consequences by engaging in preventative actions. Often, external stimuli signal the necessity for such responses, but in some cases such warning signals are internally generated by the passage of time.

axon   That portion of the neuron which conducts nerve impulses away from the cell body.

bait-shyness   The ability of many organisms (including human beings) to learn to avoid foods which make them sick, despite the fact that the interval between eating and illness may be as long as several hours.

barbiturates   Drugs which produce sharp reductions in levels of activity. Because they exert such effects, barbiturates are used in sleeping pills and similar medications.

bar grating   A pattern of parallel black and white lines.

basilar membrane   The site of the organ of Corti, the actual organ of hearing, found within the cochlea.

Bedlam   Nickname for the St. Mary of Bethlehem asylum for mental patients, which was founded in London in 1547. "Bedlam" has long had a connotative meaning as a place of chaotic disorder.

behavioral sink   A sociopathological condition resulting from extreme crowding.

behaviorism   The view, first expressed by John B. Watson, that psychology should focus upon the study of behavior—overt actions capable of direct observation and measurement.

behavior modification   The altering of overt behavior in accordance with the principles of learning and by means of manipulating the conditions under which learning takes place (for example, by having an individual learn unpleasant associations—say, an electric shock—with undesirable acts—smoking, perhaps).

biofeedback   A technique in which minute changes occurring in the body or brain are amplified and displayed to individuals experiencing them. By means of such feedback, many persons can learn to exert voluntary control over their internal bodily processes.

biotherapy   Procedures designed to alter psychopathological behavior by treating the body.

bit   The information or uncertainty present in the toss of a (fair) coin. Before the coin is tossed, there is one bit of uncertainty. After the coin has been tossed, one bit of information is gained.

blind spot   That area of the eye, specifically the retina, which is optically insensitive, located at the junction of the retina and the optic nerve.

branching flow chart   A flow chart in which events or operations need not occur in a fixed order.

bubble   See *Personal space.*

castration fear   In psychoanalytic theory, the male fear during the phallic stage that the father will castrate him because of his sexual longings for his mother.

catatonic schizophrenia   A type of schizophrenic disorder involving bodily immobility.

categorized list   A list of memory items consisting of related words, such as the names of various four-legged animals.

central nervous system   A complex structure consisting of the brain and spinal cord which (1) regulates overt behavior, (2) controls internal bodily states, and (3) is responsible for all mental processes.

central tendency   A statistical measure applied to the center of a distribution of scores. The mean, median, and mode are all measures of central tendency.

cerebellum   A structure of the brain that serves to regulate motor activities, particularly their coordination.

cerebral cortex   The outer covering of the cerebral hemispheres. Areas controlling bodily movement, sensory experiences, and higher mental processes are located in this structure.

cerebrotonia   In Sheldon's theory, the temperament type that includes love of privacy, emotional restraint, and intellectual intensity.

chlorpromazine   A tranquilizing drug.

choice reaction time   The time between the onset of one of a set of possible stimuli and the completion of one of the set of responses associated with the stimulus.

chronometric analysis   Analysis based upon the *duration* of mental operations.

ciliary muscle   The muscle that changes the curvature of the lens of the eye during focusing.

cingulate gyrus   One of the structures of the limbic system. Removal or destruction of this region may markedly reduce all emotional reactions.

clairvoyance   A form of ESP in which hidden objects can be perceived.

classical conditioning   A basic form of learning in which stimuli initially incapable of evoking certain responses acquire the ability to do so through repeated pairing with other stimuli that are able to elicit such responses.

client-centered therapy   The type of psychotherapy developed by Carl Rogers based on acceptance and unconditional respect for the client.

cochlea   An organ of the inner ear which transduces fluid vibrations into nerve impulses.

cognitive map   A mental picture which organizes some spatial arrangement of topographic features.

collective unconscious   In Jung's theory, the shared memories of mankind, consisting of the repeated experiences of our common ancestors.

Columbia obstruction box   An apparatus in which a rat is separated from a goal object by an electric grid, used to measure strength of motivation.

community psychology   The application of psychological principles to the study (and support) of the mental health of individuals in their social sphere—i.e., as inhabitants of a locale, members of groups with mutual interests, and so on. Community psychology involves the active participation of professionals, paraprofessionals, and volunteers in dealing with environmentally caused problems.

comparator   That part of a feedback control system that matches input and feedback signals. If these signals do not agree, a corrective signal is generated by the comparator.

competence   The ability to deal effectively with one's environment.

compound schedules of reinforcement   Schedules in which the delivery of various rewards is determined by two or more rules.

computer assisted instruction   An educational technique in which computers serve as "teachers." This procedure seems to be very effective, perhaps because it provides students with immediate knowledge of results and with individualized instruction as well.

concrete operational stage   A stage of cognitive development in which children demonstrate understanding of relational terms, serialization, and mastery of the principle of conservation, but are still generally incapable of logical thought.

conditioned response   A response evoked by a conditioned stimulus.

conditioned stimulus   A stimulus which acquires the capacity to evoke particular responses through repeated pairing with another stimulus capable of eliciting such reactions.

conduct disorder   A pattern of maladjusted behavior which primarily causes distress to society.

cones   The cells on the retina responsible for color vision.

conscious   In psychoanalytic theory, mental functioning of which an individual is aware or about which he or she is able to verbalize.

conservation   The principle that various substances or objects do not change in quantity when they change in shape. According to Piaget, mastery of this principle represents an important step in cognitive development.

constraints upon learning   Literally, factors which make it difficult for the members of various species to accomplish particular types of learning. The term has a general application to those factors which make for *different* degrees of learning in species *expected* to show acquisition uniformly.

consumer psychology   That branch of psychology which focuses on factors influencing both the purchase and use of various products and services.

contact-comfort   A built-in need for physical contact with soft objects. Monkeys deprived of such contact fail to demonstrate normal social development.

continuous reinforcement   Conditions under which a particular form of behavior is followed by reinforcement on every occasion when it is emitted.

control group   A group in an experiment which is not exposed to the independent variable under investigation. The behavior of subjects in this condition is used as a base-line against which to evaluate the effects of experimental treatments.

controller   That part of a feedback control system accepting a signal from the comparator and modifying the process being controlled.

conventional stage   A stage of moral development during which the ''goodness'' or ''badness'' of various actions is judged in terms of the approval of others and respect for established authority.

cornea   The transparent cover of the eye.

corpus callosum   A broad band of nerve fibers connecting the right and left cerebral hemispheres.

correlational method of research   A method of research in which variables of interest are observed in a careful and systematic manner in order to determine whether changes in one are associated with changes in the other.

correlation coefficient   A statistic which indicates the degree of relationship between two or more variables. The larger the correlation (the more it departs from 0.00), the stronger the observed relationship.

counterconditioning   A behavior modification technique in which a desired response is substituted for an undesirable one by means of conditioning procedures.

covert sensitization   A type of aversive conditioning in which the patient's own imagination is used to create negative feelings.

c-reaction time   The time between the onset of a stimulus and the occurrence of a response to it when not all stimuli have associated responses. In a c-reaction task, the observer must respond to certain stimuli only and ignore other stimuli.

crisis intervention   In community psychology, the procedures involved in responding to an emergency.

criterion   With respect to psychological tests, some measure of behavior used to determine whether a test is actually measuring what it is supposed to measure. For example, a common criterion for tests of intelligence is school performance.

critical band   A narrow range of frequencies near the signal frequency.

culture-fair test   An intelligence test designed to minimize the effects of special types of prior experience or language skills on performance. Such tests are often employed to measure the intelligence of children belonging to ethnic or racial minorities.

decibel   A ratio of two sound intensities. The numerator in the ratio is the intensity of the sound source being measured; the denominator is an agreed-on standard of intensity.

decision criterion   The determinant of how likely an observer is to report detecting a signal. The higher the criterion, the less likely a signal will be reported, regardless of the intensity of the stimulus.

deep structure   In linguistics, the inferred structure which underlies the meaning of a sentence.

defense mechanisms   Common behavior patterns which are utilized to reduce anxiety in everyday life.

delirium tremens   The reaction of alcoholics to withdrawal of alcohol, characterized by bodily trembling, disorientation, and hallucinations.

delusion   An unrealistic belief which is strongly held and defended.
   Delusions of *grandeur* are characterized by the belief that one is a person of very special importance.
   Delusions of *persecution* are characterized by the belief that plots and actions are being directed against oneself.
   Delusions of *reference* are characterized by the belief that others are constantly referring to oneself.

demand characteristics   Any cues which serve to reveal an experimenter's hypothesis to subjects. Once they are aware of such expectations, subjects may (1) attempt to ensure that they are confirmed, (2) do everything in their power to ensure that they are *not* confirmed, or (3) simply try to "look good" (present themselves in the most favorable light possible).

dementia praecox   "Youthful mental deterioration," a term used in the past to refer to schizophrenia.

dendrite   That portion of the neuron which conducts nerve impulses toward the cell body.

dependent variable   The variable (usually some measure of behavior) which is expected to change in a psychological experiment as one or more additional factors (the independent variables) are changed or varied.

depressants   Drugs which lower the overall level of activity in the nervous system. Among commonly used depressants are alcohol and various barbiturates.

dichotic listening task   A test of attention in which separate messages are sent to each ear.

discriminative cue   Any stimulus which serves as a signal for the performance of a specific form of behavior. Responses in the presence of the discriminative stimulus yield reinforcement, while responses in its absence fail to produce such consequences.

discriminative stimulus   A stimulus which indicates that some particular form of behavior will or will not be reinforced.

dispersion   The spreading out of the scores of a distribution around the center. The variance and standard deviation are two common measures of dispersion.

displacement   A defense mechanism in which responsibility is shifted from oneself to another person. Also, the substitution of one fear for another.

dissociative reaction   A type of neurotic behavior in which major aspects of one's identity are repressed, as in amnesia, fugue states, excessive somnambulism, and multiple personality.

double bind   A set of conflicting demands in which it is impossible to meet one without failing to meet the other.

drive   An aroused condition of an organism resulting from deprivation of the means of fulfilling a physiological need.

drugs   Chemical substances which influence the functioning of living organisms in some manner.

drug therapy   A form of biotherapy in which pharmaceutical agents are used to alter behavior.

eardrum   The membrane (called the tympanic membrane) separating the middle ear from the external ear.

echoic memory   The sensory storage system for auditory information.

echolalia   A distorted pattern of speech involving the meaningless repetition of the last word one has heard.

ectomorph   In Sheldon's theory, a dimension of body type characterized by a thin, flat-chested, delicate build.

educational psychology   That branch of psychology concerned with various aspects of the educational process. Among the topics studied by educational psychologists are the role of teacher expectancies on pupil performance, various techniques of instruction, and school-related behavior problems.

effectance (motive)   The need to explore and manipulate one's environment.

effectors   Cells which permit organisms to respond to changing environmental conditions or alterations in the internal states of their bodies.

ego   In psychoanalytic theory, the reality-oriented region of the mind; it involves perception, reasoning, learning, and all other activities necessary to interact effectively with the world.

electroconvulsive therapy   A form of biotherapy in which electric current is passed through the patient's head to induce a seizure and unconsciousness.

electroencephalograph   A device for recording the electrical activity of the brain, usually by means of electrodes attached to the scalp. The electroencephalograph has frequently been used to study the changes in brain function which take place as organisms fall asleep and awake.

embryo The term applied to the developing child between the second and eighth weeks of life.

emotion See *Emotional reactions*.

emotional insight Insight involving understanding of one's behavior at the "gut level," rather than at a purely intellectual level.

emotional reactions Complex changes in feelings and physiological states of the body which occur in response to a wide variety of external and internal stimuli. Generally, we attach specific labels to such reactions (e.g., fear, anger, joy, sorrow, etc.).

empathy The sharing of another's feelings and concerns as personally comprehensible emotions. In counseling, the therapist seeks to *empathize* with the client—i.e., to understand and appreciate his or her emotional state.

empirical determinism Broadly, the assumption that the relationships and occurrences of all natural phenomena are governed by discoverable laws. In the study of behavior, this philosophy dictates that it is the goal of psychological research to determine those conditions under which a particular behavior occurs.

encounter group A psychotherapeutic group in which the expression of interpersonal feelings in the group situation is emphasized.

endomorphy In Sheldon's theory, a dimension of body type characterized by a soft, rounded build.

energizing drug A drug which reduces depression and apathy and leads to an increase in activity level.

entering behavior The behavior demonstrated by an organism at the start of operant conditioning.

entopia The best habitat that can be attained in the real world.

equalitarian (egalitarian). An individual who characteristically shows (1) a negative response to authority figures, (2) freedom of sexual impulses, and (3) a tolerance of those who deviate from conventional values. An equalitarian receives a low score on the F Scale.

ethology The study of animal behavior, emphasizing the interplay of environmental and genetic factors, particularly in the period of initial development.

euphorics Drugs such as marijuana which produce positive shifts in mood.

expectancy theory (of work motivation) The idea that an individual's degree of effort on the job depends upon the strength of his or her expectancies that such effort will lead to various desired outcomes.

experimental method of research A technique of scientific inquiry in which one or more factors (independent variables) are varied in a systematic manner in order to determine the effects of such alterations on another factor (the dependent variable).

experimental neurosis Disturbances in behavior produced in the laboratory by requiring organisms to make discriminations of which they are incapable.

extinction The process through which conditioned responses are weakened and eventually eliminated.

extraversion In Jung's theory, an inborn aspect of personality involving an easy, confident orientation toward the outside world.

facial deceit Misrepresentation, in terms of facial expressiveness, of one's true emotional state. See also *falsifying, modulating,* and *qualifying*.

false alarm In information-processing theory, the incorrect reporting of a signal when only noise is present.

falsifying A form of facial deceit in which an individual (1) pretends to be experiencing some feeling he or she doesn't actually have, (2) shows no emotion when he or she is actually aroused, or (3) substitutes signs of one emotional reaction for those of another.

fear of success A motive to avoid achievement or success supposedly possessed by many women in our society. This motive stems from the fact that women are often taught, during socialization, that success and achievement are incompatible with femininity.

feature testing A type of pattern recognition based upon a list of distinctive elements in a figure.

feedback The return flow of information in a system, especially as it pertains to maintaining output within set limits.

fetus The term applied to the developing child between the ninth week of life and birth.

fixation   1. Remaining at a particular stage of development rather than progressing to the next stage.

2. A strong attachment to or focusing on a person or thing.

fixed interval schedule of reinforcement   A schedule in which the first response following the passage of a fixed interval of time yields reinforcement.

fixed ratio schedule of reinforcement   A schedule in which the first response following the emission of a specific number of responses yields reinforcement.

flow chart   A schematic rendering of a series of events or operations occurring sequentially.

formal operations stage   The final stage of cognitive development, during which the abilities to think logically and reason deductively appear.

Fourier analysis   A mathematical method of decomposing a complex wave into its sine wave components.

fovea   A small region on the retina containing only cones.

free association   A psychoanalytic procedure in which patients are instructed to say whatever comes to mind.

frequency   The reciprocal of the *period* of a sine wave.

frequency distribution   A set of scores arranged according to size, and grouped into specific intervals. A frequency distribution indicates how many times each score is obtained.

frontal lobe   A region of the cerebral cortex containing areas essential to the regulation of bodily movement, as well as to higher mental processes.

F scale   The personality test constructed to measure the trait of authoritarianism.

fugue state   A type of dissociative reaction in which amnesia is combined with travel away from one's usual surroundings.

full and open disclosure   The presentation, in advertisements and on product labels, of all the information needed by consumers to make accurate and rational purchase decisions.

functional fixedness   An inability to recognize a solution to a problem due to prior experience with the solution in a different context.

functionalism   An early school of psychology devoted to the study of the uses or functions of "mind."

fundamental   The lowest frequency in a complex wave.

ganglia   Clumps of neurons lying outside the central nervous system either (1) along the spinal cord or (2) near various internal organs.

general adaptation syndrome   A three-stage biological reaction to stressors. The stages are (1) alarm reaction, (2) resistance, and finally (3) exhaustion.

genital stage   In psychoanalytic theory, the developmental stage in which sexual desire is blended with affection, and adult roles are assumed.

glands   Structures which, through the secretion of complex substances, regulate the internal state of the body.

goal   An object or activity which satisfies a motive.

GPS   The General Problem Solver, a computer program that simulates human problem solving.

group psychotherapy   Therapy in which more than one patient is treated at the same time.

habit strength   A Hullian learning construct. Habit strength increases whenever a stimulus-response combination is followed by reinforcement.

hair cell   A cell on the *basilar membrane* which transduces vibratory energy into electrical impulses.

hallucination   An experience which has no external stimulus correlate.

hallucinogens   Drugs which induce vivid hallucinations and other major changes in perception. Many hallucinogens are found in nature, but the most controversial, LSD, is an artificial substance.

harmonics   Higher frequencies which are integer multiples of the *fundamental*.

hebephrenic schizophrenia   A type of schizophrenic disorder involving grotesque silliness and childish behavior.

heritability   That proportion of variability in a given characteristic among the members of a large population which stems from genetic factors. The greater the heritability of any characteristic, the greater the extent to which individual variations in it are determined by heredity.

hertz   A unit of sound frequency equal to one cycle per second.

heuristic   A guessing approach that may rapidly solve a problem or fail to solve it at all.

Hick's law   The linear relation between reaction time and information.

hierarchical structure. An arrangement of the elements of a system (e.g., governmental, social, theoretical) in a ranking based on increasing attainment of greater complexity, sophistication, or importance (e.g., greater authority in power, higher status in society, special applicability in a theory). The arrangement forms a pyramid with the lowest measures of attainment as the base and the highest as the top point (few elements in a system meet the highest measures).

higher-order conditioning A process in which previously established conditioned stimuli serve as the basis for further conditioning.

hit The correct detection of a signal.

holophrastic speech Children's earliest form of speech, in which single words are used to express complex intentions and meanings.

hormones Complex substances secreted by ductless glands (endocrine glands) into the blood stream in order to maintain or in response to the regulation of many internal bodily processes.

hyperphagia A conditioning of gross overeating produced by damage to the ventromedial hypothalamus.

hypochondriasis A type of neurotic behavior involving an exaggerated concern with one's health or one's own body.

hypothalamus A deep-lying cerebral structure which plays a major role in the regulation of eating, drinking, and emotional reactions.

hypothesis A proposition that seeks to place certain facts (or variables) within a construct that will explain or predict relationships between these facts. A prediction regarding the relationship between two variables is tested by conducting research: if the findings offer support for the hypothesis, confidence in its accuracy may be increased, while if findings fail to offer such support, confidence in its accuracy may be reduced.

iconic memory The sensory storage system for visual information.

id In psychoanalytic theory, the totally unconscious, primitive region of the mind which strives for immediate personal pleasure and satisfaction.

ideal concept (of self) In Rogerian theory, the self-concept an individual would like to have.

illusion An incorrect perception usually resulting from misleading stimulus cues.

imprinting The process through which young organisms of many different species form a strong attachment to the first moving object they see.

incentive An external stimulus which activates a motive.

independent variable The factor in an experiment which is varied by the researcher in a systematic manner in order to determine its effect(s) on the dependent variable.

industrial sabotage Intentional destruction of products or equipment by a company's employees. Often, the workers act out of feelings that they are being treated unfairly by their employers.

inequity Literally, unfairness; can be taken as an individual's subjective judgment of unfairness in how he or she is treated relative to others.

inferential statistics Mathematical procedures through which psychologists can generalize findings obtained with relatively small samples of subjects to much larger groups.

information In decision-making theory, a mathematical value equal to the logarithm of the number of equiprobable alternatives (base 2 is used for this logarithm). Information is gained *after* an event occurs.

insight In psychoanalysis, the therapeutic goal of increased understanding of the meaning of one's behavior.

insight psychotherapy A term applied to various types of therapy designed to help the patient gain greater self-understanding.

instinct(s) Innate urges or patterns of behavior. (See also *Species-specific behavior*.)

instinctive drift The tendency for the behavior of many organisms to "drift" away from conditioned responses and toward innate reactions.

instrumental conditioning A basic form of learning in which responses that yield positive (i.e., desirable) consequences or lead to escape from or avoidance of negative (i.e., undesirable) outcomes are strengthened.

intellectual insight Insight based on verbal understanding rather than on emotion. That is, the person "knows" the explanation but doesn't "feel" it.

intelligence In conventional terms, the ability to adapt to new circumstances, deal with complex or abstract materials, or solve intellectual problems.

interaction Refers to instances in which the effects of one independent variable are determined or influenced by another.

interference hypothesis The idea that memory information is lost due to confusion and competition among several memory traces.

interpolated task A task used to fill the retention interval in order to prevent or minimize rehearsal.

interpretation In psychoanalysis, the statements of the analyst designed to help the patient gain understanding of his or her unconscious processes.

intrinsic motivation Motivation to engage in some activity because it is attractive or enjoyable in its own right. Motivation of this type may be sharply reduced when individuals are provided with external rewards for engaging in some inherently satisfying tasks.

introspection A method of research employed by early psychologists in which trained observers attempted, in standardized laboratory situations, to report upon their conscious experience.

introversion In Jung's theory, an inborn aspect of personality involving a hesitant, cautious orientation focusing on one's inner self.

iris A ring-like device in the eye similar to the diaphragm of a camera lens which controls the size of the *pupil opening*.

James-Lange theory of emotion A theory which suggests that emotional reactions stem primarily from our perception of various changes in bodily states. For example, according to this theory, when we feel our heart pounding and notice that we have broken out in a "cold sweat," we conclude that we must be afraid.

job analysis A preliminary step in personnel selection in which the behavioral requirements of a given job are carefully specified.

job enrichment Attempts to improve worker morale through the provision of favorable work conditions (e.g., increased responsibility and autonomy, greater recognition of good performance, more varied and interesting work activities).

language acquisition device A hypothetical innate neural system which permits children to understand basic rules of grammar at an early age.

lateral hypothalamus A portion of the hypothalamus which seems to function in an excitatory manner with respect to eating. Destruction of this region often leads to sharp reductions in both eating and drinking.

law of effect Thorndike's conclusion that responses which produce positive consequences are strengthened, while responses which yield unpleasant consequences are weakened.

learned helplessness In learning experiments, a subject's passive response to stress after being placed in situations in which there is no way to avoid an electric shock.

learning The process in which relatively permanent changes in behavior are produced through experience.

limbic system A system of several structures in the brain which play an important role in the regulation of emotional reactions. Included in the limbic system are the amygdala, hippocampus, cingulate gyrus, and septal area.

limited-capacity channel model An analogy in attention theory in which human information processing abilities are considered bounded—just as the amount of material able to be passed through a pipeline (channel) of fixed size is limited. The model basically suggests that humans can transmit only a small amount of information each second.

linguistic relativity The hypothesis that language shapes thought.

long-term memory A memory storage system in which items do not decay and are maintained without rehearsal.

loop A continuous pathway for information flow.

maladjustment A socially inappropriate pattern of behavior which results in unhappiness for the individual and/or for others.

manic-depressive reaction A type of psychotic behavior involving periodic emotional swings to unrealistic elation and/or unrealistic depression.

Manifest Anxiety Scale A test which measures individual differences in anxiety (which affects drive level).

mantra The syllable (or syllables) repeated over and over again by individuals engaging in transcendental meditation.

mean The arithmetic average of a set of scores. The mean is computed by adding all of the scores together and then dividing by the number of scores in the set.

means-end analysis The framework used by the General Problem Solver to reach a solution.

mechanism In philosophy, the notion that behavior is caused entirely by mechanical physical forces.

median   The midpoint of a set of scores. Fifty per cent of the scores fall above the median, fifty per cent below.

medical model of maladjustment   The belief that psychopathology represents a disease.

medulla   A region of the brain lying immediately above the spinal cord. Major sensory and motor pathways to and from the brain are found in this area.

mental age   A measure of intellectual ability obtained on early experimenters' tests of intelligence. An individual's mental age was assumed to reflect his or her level of intellectual maturity.

meprobamate   A tranquilizing drug.

mesomorphy   In Sheldon's theory, a dimension of body type characterized by a strong, muscular build.

method of loci   A mnemonic based upon associating information with a list of known places.

midbrain   A portion of the brain lying above the pons and containing primitive centers for both hearing and vision.

missing fundamental   A complex wave whose fundamental frequency has been filtered out.

MMPI   Minnesota Multiphasic Personality Inventory. An objective test in questionnaire form which compares a particular subject's responses to those of individuals in various diagnostic categories.

mnemonic   A formal scheme to improve memory.

mode   The most frequently occurring score(s) in a set of scores.

modeling   A technique sometimes used in behavior modification in which the desired behavior is acted out by a live or filmed model. Modeling also occurs in real-life situations whenever one individual imitates—models—the behavior of another.

modulating   A form of facial deceit in which individuals adjust their facial expressions so as to show more or less of an emotion than they are actually experiencing.

morpheme   In linguistics, the smallest meaningful unit of language.

motivation   A hypothetical internal process that provides the energy for behavior and directs it toward a specific goal.

motive   An acquired motivational system.

multiple personality   A type of dissociative reaction in which two or more complete personalities are alternately expressed by one individual.

myelin sheath   A fatty covering which appears on some axons and plays a role in the conduction of action potentials.

need   A physiological requirement of an organism.

negative reinforcer   Any event which serves to strengthen responses which lead to the removal or termination of that event.

neologism   A new word which has meaning only to the person who has created it.

nerve(s)   The bundles (collections) of axons or dendrites which pass through various portions of the body and convey impulses between the CNS and some other region of the body.

neurons   Cells which have become specialized for the task of communication—moving information from one part of the body to another.

neurosis   A pattern of maladjusted behavior characterized by anxieties, worries, and fears, sometimes involving bodily concerns, repression, or unhappiness.

nodes of Ranvier   Small gaps or spaces in the myelin sheath. Action potentials jump from node to node rather than traveling down the entire axon.

noise   A random disturbance to some ongoing process.

nondirective therapy   That aspect of client-centered therapy based on the belief that the therapist should not direct or control the interaction with the client.

normal distribution   A symmetrical, bell-shaped frequency distribution. Many psychological traits or characteristics are distributed in accordance with this function.

NREM sleep   One of the two major states of sleep. During NREM sleep, physiological processes slow, the organism is relaxed and quiet, and the electrical activity of the brain assumes a pattern of slow, high-magnitude waves.

nuclei   Clumps of cell bodies lying within the central nervous system. The neurons within any given nucleus are assumed to be concerned with the same general function.

nuclei of raphe   Structures located within the medulla which seem to play an important role in the regulation of sleep. Destruction of the neurons in these regions produces insomnia.

numeric pegword   A mnemonic related to the method of loci, with the memory key consisting of an ordered list of concepts rather than place names.

nystagmus   Tiny involuntary eye movements which prevent constant stimulation of a particular point on the retina.

object constancy   The tendency for an object to be perceived as having the same size regardless of its distance from the observer.

object permanence   Literally, the fact that objects which pass from view continue to exist. According to Piaget, comprehension of this fact is absent during the earliest stages of cognitive development.

objective moral orientation   An early stage of moral development during which children judge the "goodness" or "badness" of acts in terms of the consequences they produce.

objective test   A personality test involving structured items and a limited set of responses (such as TRUE–FALSE).

observational learning   The process through which organisms acquire new forms of behavior merely by observing the actions of others.

obsessive-compulsive neurosis   A type of neurotic behavior involving uncontrolled and repetitive thoughts (obsessions) or physical acts (compulsions).

occipital lobe   An area of the cerebral cortex containing important visual centers.

Oedipal conflict   In psychoanalytic theory, the conflict in males (during the phallic stage) between sexual desire for the mother and fear of retaliation from the father.

operant conditioning   Often synonymous with instrumental conditioning (see separate entry). A form of learning in which the presentation of positive or negative reinforcers alters the rate at which responses are emitted.

operants   Responses freely emitted by organisms. The frequency with which such responses appear may be strongly affected by the application of various schedules of reinforcement.

optic nerve   The nerve that transmits electrical signals from the eye to the brain.

oral personality   In psychoanalytic theory, a psychosexual type involving dependency, conformity, trust, optimism, and a concern with food.

oral stage   In psychoanalytic theory, the developmental stage involving the mouth and eating.

osmoreceptors   Cells within the hypothalamus which respond to the movement of water through their membranes and consequently play an important role in the regulation of drinking.

paranoid disorder   A type of psychotic behavior involving highly organized conceptual systems which are characterized by delusions of persecution and of reference.

paranoid schizophrenia   A type of schizophrenic disorder involving delusions of persecution and reference.

parasympathetic system   A subdivision of the autonomic nervous system. The parasympathetic system seems to play an important role in readying the body for vigorous physical activity and for facing various stressful situations.

parietal lobe   A region of the cerebral cortex containing centers which mediate sensations from the skin (e.g., touch, warmth, pressure).

partial reinforcement   Conditions under which a particular form of behavior is followed by reinforcement only on some occasions on which it is emitted.

partial reinforcement effect   The resistance of responses acquired under conditions of partial reinforcement to extinction, often greater than that of responses acquired under conditions of continuous reinforcement.

partial report   One of two kinds of reports required of subjects in Sperling's memory tests. For the partial report, observers were asked, after seeing a brief presentation of a letter array, to cite the letters in one *row* of the array. For the *whole report*, observers were asked to cite *all* the letters in the array after a brief look at it.

pay-off   The costs and benefits associated with *hits* and *false alarms*.

penile plethysmograph   A device attached to the penis to indicate changes in volume or circumference, used to measure sexual arousal.

penis envy   In psychoanalytic theory, the female's reaction during the phallic stage to the discovery that the female genitals are "inferior" to male genitals.

perception   A psychological process that transforms external stimuli into meaningful organized patterns. Also, the psychological process of knowing the external world by forming an internal mental representation.

period   The distance between two successive peaks of a sine wave.

peripheral nervous system   That portion of the nervous system outside the brain and spinal cord. The peripheral system consists primarily of a number of nerves connecting various portions of the body to the central system, and includes the autonomic nervous system.

personality   An individual's characteristic patterns of behavior.

personality type   One of a small number of categories into which behavior is classified. (The classification is known as a *typology*.)

personal space   The physical area immediately surrounding an individual.

personnel selection   The process used by employers to choose the best person for a given job. Modern techniques which permit the prediction of future work performance from psychological tests and other measures have greatly increased the accuracy of this process.

phallic stage   In psychoanalytic theory, the developmental stage involving sexual urges of the male child toward the parent and the resolution of the resulting Oedipal conflict.

phenomenology   The study of human interactions with the world, *as experienced by the individual*. The phenomenologist takes care to view the world as it appears to the particular perceiver or reporter. This philosophy accordingly takes into account life as it is lived by the observer, with its possible inherent distinctions from the world view of the researcher or investigator.

pheromones   Substances secreted in the vagina which produce an odor that excites males.

phobia   See *Phobic reaction*.

phobic reaction   A type of neurotic behavior involving an unrealistic fear of some aspect of the environment.

phoneme   The smallest unit of speech (cf. *morpheme*).

pitch   The psychological correlate of *frequency*.

placebo effect   Changes in behavior stemming from conditions or procedures which accompany, but are not directly related to, independent variables in an experiment. For example, changes in behavior following injections of a specific drug may result from the act of being injected, rather than from the drug itself.

pons   A region of the brain lying immediately above the medulla, and through which major sensory and motor pathways pass.

population density   A statistical measure which tells how crowded or uncrowded an area is (e.g., in terms of number of people per acre).

positive reinforcer   Any event which serves to strengthen those responses which precede the event.

postconventional stage   A stage of moral development during which the "goodness" or "badness" of various actions is judged in terms of self-chosen moral principles.

preconscious   In psychoanalytic theory, the stored memories which are not currently conscious but which can be made so with effort.

preconventional stage   A stage of moral development during which the "goodness" or "badness" of various actions is judged in terms of the consequences they produce. Actions which produce favorable outcomes are "good," while those which produce unfavorable outcomes are "bad."

prefrontal lobotomy   A specific type of psychosurgery in which the nerve pathways between the brain's prefrontal lobes and the thalamus are severed.

preoperational stage   The stage of cognitive development during which children first begin to use mental symbols (e.g., words) to represent external objects and events.

primacy effect   In memory, the better performance for items occurring early in a list.

proactive interference   Forgetting due to the influence of earlier learning upon present learning.

probers   Calhoun's term for the most pathologic of the rat subjects in his study of the "behavioral sink."

problem solving   In information theory, a search process aimed at getting from an initial state to a final state.

process schizophrenia   A type of schizophrenia believed to result from hereditary factors.

program   A series of instructions carried out by a computer.

projection   A defense mechanism involving denying the existence of an impulse in oneself while attributing it to another person.

projective test   A personality test involving ambiguous stimuli. A subject's responses are supposed to reveal aspects of the unconscious.

proxemics   A branch of social science which studies the use of physical space by man and animals.

proximity   A principle of Gestalt psychology which states that elements of an array that are physically close together tend to be perceived as related units.

psychoanalysis   The type of psychotherapy developed by Sigmund Freud, involving techniques designed to help the patient gain insight (as through the interpretation of free associations).

psychodrama   The type of group therapy developed by J. L. Moreno, in which patients act out their interpersonal problems on a stage before an audience.

psychokinesis   A form of ESP in which physical objects can be mentally manipulated.

psychological model of maladjustment   The belief that psychopathology represents learned behavior which functions to reduce anxiety.

psychological refractory period   A delay in responding to the second of two closely spaced stimuli.

psychopathic personality   A type of conduct disorder involving lack of conscience development, absence of anxiety and guilt, inability to delay gratification, and superficial interpersonal relationships.

psychopathology   Literally, the science that deals with mental illness. It is commonly used as a synonym for mental illness.

psychosis   The most severe type of psychopathology, characterized by distortions in perception, thinking, emotions, and speech.

psychosurgery   A form of biotherapy in which a brain operation is performed in order to attempt to alter behavior.

psychotherapy   The application of psychological techniques by professionally trained individuals to change a socially inappropriate pattern of behavior into a more appropriate one.

punishment   Any aversive (painful or unpleasant) stimulus which is contingent upon the performance of a particular response.

pupil opening   The opening inside the *iris* through which light enters the eye.

Purkinje shift   The change in the most sensitive wavelength after dark adaptation.

purposive behavior   Behavior directed toward reaching some goal.

qualifying   A mild form of facial deceit in which individuals add a further expression to one they have just shown as a comment upon it. For example, an individual who has just shown signs of anger may smile as a sign that he or she is not as angry as may have seemed to be the case.

quota systems   Arrangements whereby a specific proportion of the available openings in colleges, professional schools, or other institutions are reserved for the members of racial or ethnic minorities.

range   The difference between the highest and lowest scores in a distribution.

rationalization   A socially acceptable reason to explain one's behavior. This is considered a defensive process which helps us deceive ourselves about our true, possibly unacceptable feelings.

reaction formation   A defense mechanism in which an individual expresses an impulse contrary to the one he or she actually harbors.

reaction time   See *Choice reaction time, c-reaction time,* and *Simple reaction time.*

reactive depression   A type of neurotic behavior in which unhappiness over a sad event continues beyond the appropriate period of time and interferes with the individual's life.

reactive schizophrenia   A type of schizophrenia believed to result from environmental stress.

recall   A measure of memory in which previously learned items must be reproduced (as by listing them or repeating them).

recency effect   In memory, the improved performance for items occurring at the end of a list.

receptors   Cells of the body specialized for the task of transforming physical energy (e.g., light, heat) into a form usable by the nervous system.

recognition   A test of memory in which items are judged for familiarity.

regression   Moving from one's present stage of development to a previous, less mature stage.

reliability   The extent to which scores on a test are stable or dependable. A high degree of reliability indicates that individuals taking the test on several different occasions are likely to obtain the same score each time.

REM sleep   One of the two major states of sleep. Such sleep is characterized by profound muscle relaxation, rapid and sudden changes in physiological processes, and an EEG pattern closely resembling that of resting wakefulness. Dreaming often occurs during REM sleep.

representative sample   A group of subjects who are similar in certain important respects to other members of the larger group from which they have been selected. If the subjects in an experiment are not representative of the larger group, generalizations from experimental findings to this group are not justified.

repression   In psychoanalytic theory, the act of forcing into the unconscious any anxiety-evoking mental image.

reserpine   A tranquilizing drug.

resistance   In psychoanalysis, a blocking by the patient which interferes with free association.

resting potential   A small difference in electrical potential (i.e., voltage) between the inside and outside of the neuron during periods when it is not actively conducting nerve impulses.

retention interval   The time between the initial presentation of an item and the subsequent calling up of that item from memory (as in response to a memory test).

reticular activating system   A dense network of interconnected neurons which runs through the center of the brain and plays an important role both in producing and maintaining a state of wakefulness.

retina   The membrane at the back of the eye where light rays are focused.

retrieval   The process of obtaining memory information from wherever it has been stored.

retroactive interference   Forgetting due to the influence of present learning upon earlier learning.

rods   Cells on the retina responsible for black-white vision (rods cannot detect color).

Rorschach test   A projective measure of personality in which subjects indicate what they perceive in each of ten ink blots. This test was developed by a Swiss psychiatrist, Hermann Rorschach.

schedules of reinforcement   Rules governing the delivery of reinforcement. When a given schedule is in effect, reinforcement can be obtained only by meeting its requirements.

schizophrenic disorder   A severe type of psychotic behavior involving withdrawal into one's own thoughts and fantasies.

schizophrenogenic parent   A parent whose behavior brings about schizophrenia in an offspring.

secondary reinforcer   A stimulus which acquires reinforcing properties through association with a primary reinforcer such as food or water.

second-order conditioning   Classical conditioning established on the basis of earlier conditioning. That is, previously established conditioned stimuli are employed as the basis for further conditioning.

self-actualization   The process of fulfilling one's potential.

self-addressable memory   Memory in which the same plan that is used to store information is also used to retrieve it.

self-concept   In Rogerian theory, the attitudes and beliefs an individual has about himself.

semantics   The study of the relationship between meaning and surface structure in language.

sensitivity training group   A therapeutic group first assembled at the National Training Laboratories, focusing on feelings and interpersonal interactions. Sometimes called a T-group.

sensorimotor stage   The first stage of cognitive development. During this stage, infants are unable to use mental symbols to represent external objects and events. As a result, they do not realize that objects which pass out of their sight continue to exist.

sensory deprivation   A situation which greatly reduces the amount of normal sensory stimulation.

sensory storage   A system which holds information for less than one second and maintains it in the same modality as that in which it has been presented.

septal area   One of the structures of the limbic system. Removal or destruction of this structure leads to increased emotionality.

serialization   The ability to order a number of objects along some dimension (e.g., in terms of size or weight). According to Piaget, serialization is not attained until the stage of concrete operations.

serial position   The order in which items appear on a list, specifically a list to be reproduced in a test of memory. Successful recall for each item depends on its order in the list.

serial position curve   A graph showing memory performance for items presented in a series. The curve obtained shows that items presented early on are retained fairly well, and that those presented last are remembered quite well. Items in the middle are less well remembered. (The graph thus represents the function of the *serial position effect*.)

serial recall   A test of memory in which items are considered correct only if they are recalled in their correct order.

sexism   Discrimination on the basis of sex. The term refers almost exclusively to bias against women, in the form of either overt discriminatory practices or a complex of negative attitudes. Sexism has prevented women from obtaining equal rights and fair treatment in many areas of life.

sex-typing   The process through which children acquire a firm sexual identity and knowledge of the roles and behavior of both sexes.

shaping   A technique based on principles of operant conditioning in which an organism's behavior is gradually molded into specific desired patterns through the careful administration of positive reinforcement.

short-term memory   A memory system subject to decay and in which information must be maintained by rehearsal.

shuttle box   An apparatus employed in the investigation of escape or avoidance conditioning. Usually, organisms are placed in one side of the apparatus and must jump to the other in order to escape or avoid painful electric shocks.

signal detection theory   A two-stage model of perception combining sensory transduction and decision processes.

significant difference   A statistical concept of probability—specifically, that the likelihood of a large difference occurring in the behavior of subjects in various groups of an experiment *by chance alone* is quite low. When such a difference *does* occur, it is assumed to reflect some aspect of the experimental manipulation of conditions and therefore (since chance is ruled out) can be used as a reliable basis for further work.

sign stimulus   A stimulus which serves to activate instinctive patterns of behavior.

simple reaction time   The time between the onset of a stimulus and the completion of a response to it. Only one stimulus and one response are possible.

simple schizophrenia   A type of schizophrenic disorder characterized by apathy, indifference, and passive withdrawal from society.

situational determinants   Those factors in an individual's physical or social surroundings which influence his or her behavior.

size constancy   The tendency for an observer to perceive objects as having the same size regardless of their distance from him.

skewed distribution   A distribution of scores which is not symmetrical (i.e., scores are not distributed evenly or symmetrically around the mean).

somatotonia   In Sheldon's theory, the temperament type which includes love of physical adventure, boundless energy, boldness, aggressiveness, and the need for exercise and activity.

somatotype   Sheldon's term for body type, classified along the three dimensions of endomorphy, mesomorphy, and ectomorphy.

somnambulism   A type of dissociative reaction in which the individual engages in excessive sleepwalking.

source traits   In Cattell's system, the 16 basic clusters of personality traits.

span of apprehension   In memory testing, the maximum number of items that can be perceived and remembered in a single glance.

species-specific behavior   Behavior which is universal within a species, highly stereotyped in nature, and elicited by specific sign stimuli. Generally, species-specific behavior has been viewed as instinctive in nature.

spinal cord   A portion of the central nervous system which extends from the base of the brain down to the lower portion of the back and is encased within the spinal column. The spinal cord serves mainly a communicative function, but it is also concerned with the regulation of various reflexes.

spinal reflexes   Seemingly "automatic" reactions to various stimuli. In their simplest form, reflexes involve the operation of only a single sensory neuron and a single motor neuron. In most cases, however, input from many other neurons and even higher centers of the brain is involved.

S-R compatibility   The degree to which relationships between sets of stimuli and responses agree with one's expectations or experience, as determined by one's culturally stereotyped patterns of association (what "ordinarily" goes with what).

stabilized image   An image which remains in a constant location on the eye.

standard deviation   Essentially, the average distance from the mean of each score in a distribution. (Standard deviation is the square root of the variance.)

Stanford-Binet test   One of the first successful individual tests of intelligence. The test has gone through a number of revisions, and is still in use, in modified form, today.

statistics   A form of mathematics by which psychologists evaluate the findings of their research. When employed appropriately, statistics permit investigators to determine whether the findings of their research are reliable or trustworthy (i.e., whether they would be likely to occur again if the research were repeated).

stimulants   Drugs such as caffeine, nicotine, and amphetamines which increase the functioning of the nervous system and thereby facilitate physical and mental activity.

stimulus   Anything that elicits a physiological or psychological activity (i.e., a response).

stimulus discrimination   The ability to tell the difference between two or more stimuli.

stimulus generalization   The tendency for a response conditioned to a particular stimulus to be elicited by similar stimuli as well.

stress   See *Stressful situation.*

stressful situation   A situation resulting from an imbalance between demands imposed upon an organism by its environment and the organism's ability to handle such demands.

stressor   Any variable which induces stress.

Stroop effect   An impairment in an observer's ability to process relevant information only, demonstrated in the following task: A subject is asked to identify the *color* of an ink (say, green) when the ink is used to spell out a color *name* different from that of the ink (the word RED, for example). The subject perceives the name of the color—which is unnecessary to the task—and this causes a delay in identifying the color of the ink.

structuralism   An early school of psychology devoted to the task of analyzing the structure of the mind's conscious processes.

subjective moral orientation   A stage of moral development during which children judge the "goodness" or "badness" of actions in terms of the intentions behind their performance.

subliminal perception   The "unconscious" registering of impressions of stimuli presented too briefly for overt recognition. At one time, subliminal perception was played on by advertisers, who presented their commercial messages as extremely brief stimuli thought to be capable of persuading the viewer without directly addressing him. (It was found that "subliminal advertising" has little effect upon consumers.)

successive approximations   Small changes in behavior in the direction desired by a trainer. Such changes are reinforced during the process of shaping.

superego   In psychoanalytic theory, that region of the mind which includes a view of ideal behavior (ego-ideal) and a view of right and wrong (conscience).

superior colliculi   Structures located in the midbrain which, in human beings, serve as primitive centers for vision.

supernatural model of maladjustment   The belief that psychopathology is caused by either good or evil supernatural forces.

surface structure   In linguistics, the framework of language considered apart from meaning. The tree diagram of a sentence after parsing represents the surface structure of the sentence—how it works, or what rules it follows. The surface structures of the world's languages vary, because different elements serve different functions in these tongues. *Deep structure,* on the other hand, is thought by many to be consistent throughout all languages.

surface traits   In Cattell's system, personality traits which are openly expressed in behavior and which are based on the 16 underlying source traits.

surveys   A method of research in which the opinions of a large number of individuals are measured. Provided the sampling is genuinely representative, the results of surveys can often be employed to predict product sales, public reactions to various events, or the results of political elections.

sympathetic system   A subdivision of the autonomic nervous system. The sympathetic system seems to play a role in regulating those internal bodily processes (e.g., digestion) which serve to restore or regenerate the body's resources.

synapse   A region of close approach between neurons. Although the space separating adjoining cells at the synapse is very small, it is large enough to prevent direct physical communication between them.

synaptic terminals   Round structures found at the ends of telodendria. It is from these structures that the transmitter substance is released to cross the synapse.

synaptic vesicles   Structures found within the synaptic terminals which appear to be involved in the production of transmitter substance.

synesthesia A blending of the senses in which sounds are seen as glowing colors, words are smelled or tasted, and colors are heard as well as seen. Synesthesia is often induced by hallucinogenic drugs, but it also seems to occur normally among some persons.

systematic desensitization A form of counterconditioning in which positive feelings are substituted for fears and anxieties.

TAT (thematic apperception test) A projective test consisting of a series of pictures for which the subject makes up stories.

teacher expectancies Expectations on the part of teachers that certain children will do well while others will fail. Because a teacher's behavior toward individual students is often strongly (but unconsciously) influenced by such expectancies, they frequently have a disturbing self-fulfilling quality.

telepathy A form of ESP in which other people's thoughts can be read.

telodendria Small branch-like structures found at the end of axons.

temperament A characteristic mood which is considered one aspect of personality.

template matching A type of pattern recognition based upon comparison of standard and test figures.

temporal lobe A region of the cerebral cortex containing important centers for hearing.

terminal responses The final pattern of behavior that organisms are expected to demonstrate after the completion of shaping procedures.

territoriality The behavior used by an individual to stake out and defend a specific area against members of its own species.

tests Standardized procedures, often involving questionnaires, used to measure many different abilities, interests, or traits.

t-group See *Sensitivity training group*.

thalamus A structure located close to the center of the brain which receives a great deal of sensory input from lower areas and transmits this information to the cerebral hemispheres in a highly diffuse manner. As a result, it is often termed the "great relay station" of the brain.

theory A systematic set of assumptions about the nature or causes of some phenomenon. Theories usually explain existing findings or evidence, and predict new events or results.

threshold A hypothetical barrier which stimuli must pass to enter the mind.

tilt cage A delicately balanced cage which records activity level by means of electrical contacts at each corner.

timbre The quality of a complex sound.

time sharing A paradigm requiring simultaneous performance of two separate tasks.

token economy A system of "payments" governed by principles of operant conditioning, under which some type of token is given as a positive reinforcement for desired behavior; the tokens can later be exchanged for some rewarding object or activity.

TOTE unit A form of feedback loop with Test, Operate, Test, and Exit components.

trace The (hypothetical) neurological correlate of memory.

trace decay hypothesis The idea that memory information fades away without rehearsal to maintain it.

traditional rationalism The philosophical idea that human beings act because they have a reason to do so.

trait In personality theory, one of numerous dimensions along which individuals vary in their behavior.

tranquilizing drug A drug which reduces anxiety and induces a feeling of calmness.

transcendental meditation A form of meditation in which individuals silently repeat special Hindu syllables for short periods of time. Meditation of this type has been found to induce substantial changes in physiological processes, and it often leads to a reduction in frequency of drug use among individuals who adopt it.

transducer A device which changes energy from one form to another.

transference In psychoanalysis, the positive and negative feelings directed toward the analyst.

transmitter substances Complex substances that are thought to be manufactured by synaptic vesicles and that cross the synapse, thereby allowing communication between adjacent neurons.

traumatic neurosis An anxiety reaction brought about by frightening events, such as war or a natural disaster.

trial and error An approach to problem solving that is based upon continuous attempts at a solution (*trials*), with each attempt pursued until it ends in failure (*error*) or success. This common heuristic technique is methodical rather than intuitive.

two-factor theory (of avoidance conditioning)   A theory holding that avoidance reactions are learned through a process in which (1) neutral stimuli acquire the ability to elicit strong fear reactions (by classical conditioning), and (2) the performance of avoidance responses is then reinforced by the reductions in fear they produce.

type A personality   A behavior classification applied to individuals who are competitive, hard-driving, and aggressive, and who feel an urgency about time; they are susceptible to developing coronary heart disease.

type B personality   A behavior classification applied to individuals who are easy-going, relaxed, and unconcerned about time pressures; they are not likely to develop coronary heart disease.

typology   A theoretical system which classifies elements into a small number of categories (or types).

uncertainty   The amount of information present *before* one event is selected from some set of events. Uncertainty is reduced only after information is obtained.

unconditional positive regard   In client-centered therapy, the therapist's positive feelings toward the client, which are expressed without any conditions being attached.

unconditioned response   A response elicited by an unconditioned stimulus.

unconditioned stimulus   Any stimulus possessing the capacity to elicit reactions from organisms in the absence of prior conditioning.

unconscious   In psychoanalytic theory, all the memories and desires of which we are unaware.

urethral personality   In psychoanalytic theory, a psychosexual type involving ambition, feelings of inferiority, and the tendency to give up in the face of difficulty.

urethral stage   In psychoanalytic theory, the developmental stage involving learning to control urinary functions.

utility   The psychological correlate of value.

Utopia   A term used by Sir Thomas More in 1516 to refer to an imaginary island where all was perfect. Typically used as a name for any ideal community or visionary scheme for perfection.

vaginal plethysmograph   A device inserted in the vagina to detect changes in the flow of blood in the vaginal walls, taken as an index of sexual arousal.

validity   The extent to which a psychological test actually measures what it is designed to measure. Usually, validity is assessed by observing the degree of relationship between test scores and appropriate aspects of behavior. For example, the validity of intelligence tests is often measured by relating scores on such tests to school performance.

variable interval schedule of reinforcement   A schedule in which the first response performed after the passage of a variable interval of time yields reinforcement. The interval which must elapse varies around some average value.

variable ratio schedule of reinforcement   A schedule in which reinforcement is delivered only after the completion of a variable number of responses. The number which must be completed varies around some average value.

variance   The average squared distance of the scores of a distribution from the mean of that distribution.

ventromedial hypothalamus   A portion of the hypothalamus which seems to function in an inhibitory fashion with respect to eating. Destruction of this area often leads to tremendous amounts of overeating.

viscerotonia   In Sheldon's theory, the temperament type which includes love of physical comfort, sociability, tolerance for others, and extraversion.

visual capture   The dominance of vision over other sense modalities.

visual cliff   An optical illusion employed to study depth perception in infants. Created by means of equipment deployed in such a manner that the floor seems to drop sharply away at a given point, the illusion is studied in terms of the willingness of children to venture out onto the "deep" side.

wavelength   The distance traveled by a wave in one cycle.

white noise   An artificial hissing sound containing a wide range of auditory frequencies.

whole report   See *Partial report.*

work motivation   The desire to work in a competent and effective manner. Differences in work motivation are often reflected in contrasting levels of job performance.

Yerkes-Dodson law   An inverted U-shaped function relating performance to arousal level.

AUTHOR INDEX

SUBJECT INDEX

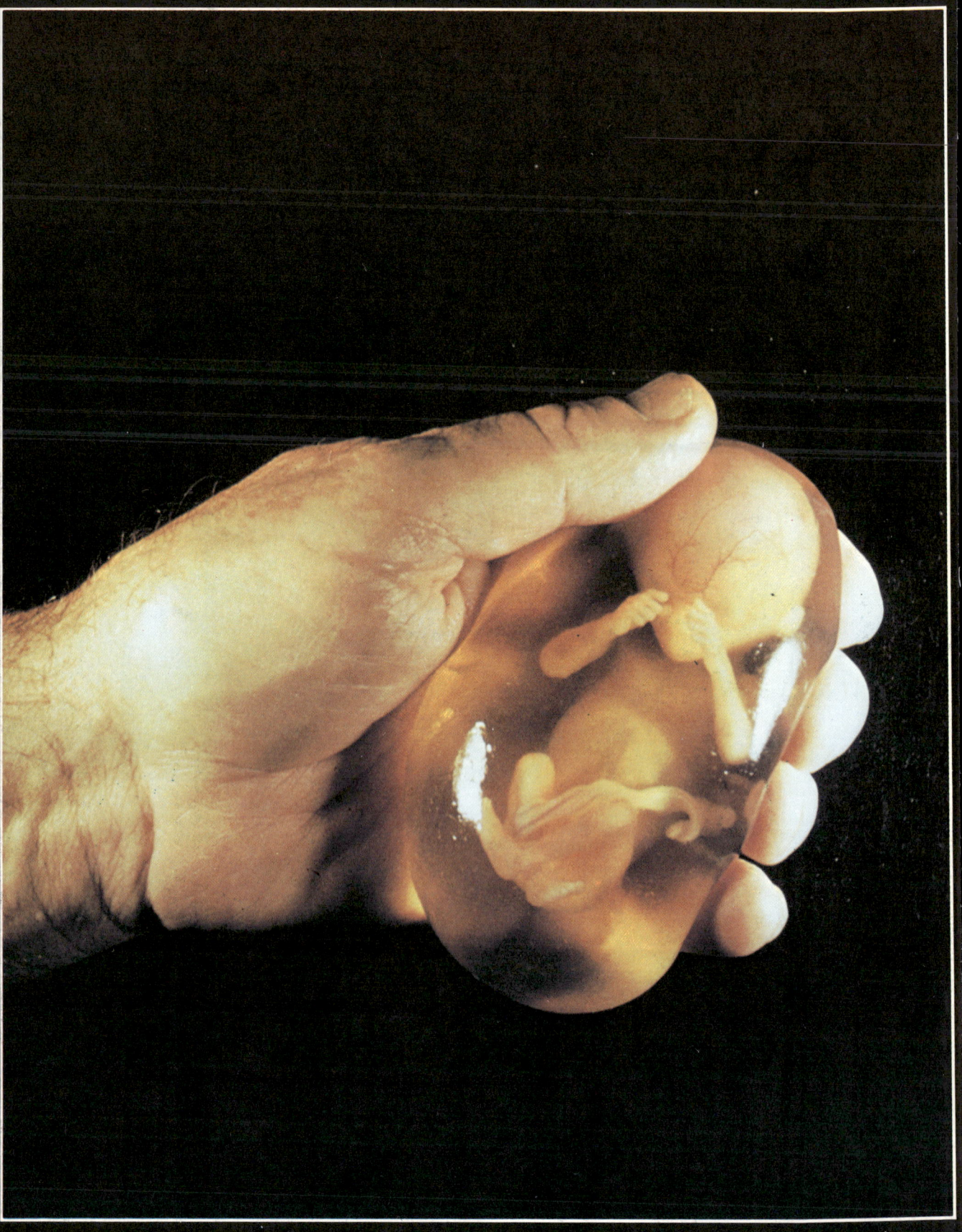

PLATE 12   A 12-week-old human fetus in amniotic sac showing size relative to adult human hand. (Courtesy of Drs. R. Rugh and L. D. Shettles, authors of *From Conception to Birth: The Drama of Life's Beginnings,* New York, Harper and Row, 1971.)